the Writer's Handbook 2003

Preface by
Elizabeth Berg

Edited by Elfrieda Abbe

the **Writer** books

The Writer Books is an imprint of Kalmbach Trade Press, a division of Kalmbach Publishing Co. These books are distributed to the book trade by Watson-Guptill.

For all other inquiries, including individual orders or details on special quantity discounts for groups or conferences, contact:

Kalmbach Publishing Co.
21027 Crossroads Circle
Waukesha, WI 53187
(800) 533-6644

Visit our website at http://www.writermag.com
to learn more about *The Writer* magazine, view current articles,
or order copies of *The Writer's Handbook.*
Secure online ordering available.

Printed in the United States of America

02 03 04 05 06 07 08 09 10 11   10 9 8 7 6 5 4 3 2 1

Publisher's Cataloging-in-Publication
(Provided by Quality Books, Inc.)

The writer's handbook 2003 / edited by Elfrieda Abbe ;
    preface by Elizabeth Berg. — 1st ed.
        p. cm.
        ISBN: 0-87116-196-6

        1. Authorship—Handbooks, manuals, etc.
    2. Publishers and publishing. I. Abbe, Elfrieda.

PN137.W73 2002   808'.02
                        QBI02-200417

Project Editor: Philip Martin
Assistant Editor: Amy Glander

Art Director: Kristi Ludwig
Cover Design: Lisa Zehner

Permissions

Most of the articles included here first appeared in the pages of *The Writer* magazine, with a few selections drawn from other sources, and are used by permission of the authors or their agents and publishers. In particular, we would like to acknowledge the following permissions:

The preface is © Elizabeth Berg, 2002.

The article "About That Novel" is © Hui Corporation, 1978. Reprinted by arrangement with Gelfman Schneider Literary Agents, Inc.

The article "A Discussion of Story" is excerpted from *Steering the Craft: Exercises and Discussions on Story Writing for the Lone Navigator or the Mutinous Crew* by Ursula K. Le Guin, ©1998 by Ursula K. Le Guin, published by the Eighth Mountain Press, Portland, Oregon 1998. Reprinted by permission of the author and publisher.

The article "10 Rules for Success and Happiness Writing Fiction" is © 2001 by Elmore Leonard. Originally published in *The New York Times*. Reprinted with the permission of the Wylie Agency, Inc.

The excerpt "On Walking & Ideas" from *If·You Want to Write* is copyright 1987 by the Estate of Brenda Ueland. Reprinted from *If You Want to Write* with the permission of Graywolf Press, Saint Paul, Minnesota.

Acknowledgments

Thanks to Philip Martin, project editor, for his assistance in assembling this volume. Thanks also to many others at Kalmbach Publishing Co. who helped with the preparation of this 67th edition, especially to those who helped to verify information in the market listings section, in particular Amy Glander, as well as Jeff Reich and Sally Laturi of *The Writer* magazine staff, Lisa Wolter, and Mary Graf and her wonderful staff. Thanks also to Mary Algozin for her tireless copy-editing of this thousand-page tome.

We all know that the publishing world is in a constant state of flux, and some information in the market listings may have changed since last updated. We would greatly appreciate any feedback from readers, with corrections or comments on how better to improve the usefulness of the information presented. Kalmbach Publishing Co. has a tradition of outstanding customer service, and we look forward to continuing to improve and refine this long-standing resource to writers in coming years by incorporating your feedback.

If you know of new or overlooked markets of significance to aspiring writers that you wish to recommend for future volumes, please forward those ideas to Philip Martin, The Writer Books, 21027 Crossroads Circle, P.O. Box 1612, Waukesha, WI 53187-1612, or send an e-mail directly to the attention of books@kalmbach.com.

CONTENTS

THE ARTICLES

CONTENTS

THE MARKETS

Nonfiction Magazines

CONTENTS

PREFACE

If you want to be a writer, be yourself

by Elizabeth Berg

I began my writing career under a bed, at about age five. Truly. Because more than anything else, writing is about accessing the imagination, and that is exactly what I was doing there, lying on the floor behind the fabric walls of bedspread. This dusty retreat was my sacred space, the place where it was safe for everything inside of me to come out. I did not have pencil and paper, but I had an open mind and an open heart and I was learning the value of keeping still and being aware. That way, the information I wanted could find me, giving me answers to questions I couldn't even formulate—at least not in my mind. They were questions of the heart.

I had a sister who died at eight months of age, from meningitis. I never knew her; I was born a couple of years after she died. But I felt a profound attachment to her. I knew she was not in the everyday world around me—we did not share the bathtub or the breakfast table or tinker toys, but she loomed large in other ways. I believed I could feel her spirit. And I felt close to her when I isolated myself under my bed, when I made my world small and free of distraction. I would stare up at the underside of the mattress and I would "talk" to her. And I will swear until my dying day that I could hear her listening.

Thus I learned my first and most important lessons as a writer: writing isn't just about putting words on a page. It's having a certain sensibility, and it's honoring the message to do what calls most strongly to you. It's understanding that the most important part of writing isn't writing at all. Rather it is observing—a very careful kind of observing that requires using all of your senses and all of your might. A true writer's essence of self is always on reconnaissance missions—that is what makes us such dismal lunch partners—we're always staring into space, listening to that other story.

If the practice of isolation and concentration was good training for the kind of writer I became, so too was my annoying habit of over-dramatizing and over-reacting. (Not for nothing did my parents call me "Sarah Bernhardt" after the tragic French film actress.) This intensity stayed with me as I grew up, and eventually served me by making its way into the novels I write. I'm interested in intimate emotions, and in exploring personal relationships in the fullest and most honest way I can. What can be a liability in "real life" became a distinct advantage in the writing world. I use my oversensitivity to write novels full of feelings to which readers respond in the most wonderful of ways. "You say what I feel, but can't put into words," they tell me. "You make me cry," they say, but they are smiling when they tell me that. "I made my husband read one of your books," one woman told me. "Now he understands."

Trust me when I tell you that I am not always an easy person to live with: to say that I am thin-skinned is a vast understatement. But trust me also when I tell you that it is this depth of feeling that makes me able to do the kind of work I want to do; and getting the kind of response from readers that I just described fills me with great satisfaction. Next to the act of writing itself, it's what I love most about being a writer. The connection: that's the thing. (That, and room service, when you go on book tour. Those cowboy breakfasts of eggs, bacon, and hashbrowns, with the baby bottles of catsup.)

I don't work under a bed any longer. But I might as well. What I do when I write is essentially the same thing I did as a child: make my world small, and quiet, and, in a way, unearthly. I sit in an office full of things that hold great meaning for me: fetish stones, small gifts from people I love, photos that have a particular significance, books that I admire, flowers and rocks and feathers. My computer is stationed so that I look at a wall, but a window is to my right so that if a good-looking dog walks by, I can take full advantage.

When I am in "the zone," though, when I am really into what I'm writing, I don't see the objects in the room, I don't see the window, and I barely see the computer. I see my characters. Maybe one is sitting at the side of his bed and putting his socks on. Maybe one is out in the garden weeding, a pony tail at the top of her head, the summer sun coming through the tops of her ears, making them glow red. I hear characters talking: one might be arguing, one might be praying, one might be fabricating an outrageous lie, one might be telling a difficult truth. In this "zone," my job is simply to be the typist: the story passes through me and I catch what I can. I once said, in a speech I gave about writing, "I am not here when I write. I am there. I like it there very much. It feels like heaven to me."

If you're reading this book, it's probably because you want to write. And you're going to read the information contained here because you are looking for inspiration, impetus, validation, tools, and techniques. That's great. But what I want to tell you is that when you read any "how to" piece about writing, factor in your own individuality. Respect it. If a piece of advice feels right to you, use it. If it feels wrong for any reason, ignore it. Use what's unique about you to write uniquely. That is, don't try to write "like" anyone; rather, try always to write in your own voice. Tell your own stories in your own ways, for your own reasons.

Maybe you want to write only for yourself. That's the best reason to write, in my opinion; and that's where you have to start, no matter what kind of writing you want to do. I have enjoyed considerable success as a writer, but for me the best moments are always those that hearken back to those days of wonder, those days of the self addressing the self.

Maybe you want to write to be read by others. That's good too, although you must prepare yourself for the cuckoo world of publishing, which is as full of perils as it is pleasures. If you do want to publish, here's some advice: Don't be one of those writers who solicits editors because "they have this idea. . . ." Usually, the ideas of would-be writers like that have to do more with royalty checks than with crafting sentences. Rather than being a writer focused on the imagined glories of literary fame, be instead a writer who does what she does to satisfy a soulful yearning. Do the work. Then think about where to send it.

A famous writer I know once told me she was on book tour in Seattle, and she went to Elliot's Bay, a huge bookstore. She said she looked at all those rows of books and thought, Oh God, we don't need any more writers. I couldn't disagree more. I think we do need more writers, but of a certain kind: writers who keep their process clean, who are true to themselves and to what inspires them.

We need especially writers who aren't afraid to take chances and try something new, and writers who help us to see things in a new way, because they themselves see things that way and aren't afraid to say so.

Whatever your reasons for writing, whatever your goals, I wish you well. If you subscribe to the belief, as I do, that the greatest happiness in writing comes in the work itself, you will find great satisfaction, under the bed or anywhere else.

Elizabeth Berg is the author of many acclaimed works of fiction, including the novels *Durable Goods* and *Joy School*, both of which were selected as ALA Best Books of the Year. Her other novels, including *Talk Before Sleep*, *Pull of the Moon*, and *What We Keep*, have all been national bestsellers; her novel *Open House* was a selection of the Oprah Book Club. She is also the author of a highly recommended book on the writing process, *Escaping into the Open* (HarperCollins, 1999). Her most recent novel (2002) is called *True to Form*. She lives in Chicago.

INTRODUCTION

by Elfrieda Abbe

For more than a century, *The Writer* magazine has provided a place for writers to share writing tips, experiences, and ideas. The magazine's archives are rich in writing wisdom. Looking through back issues, I wonder how the process of writing has changed, or if it has changed, over the years. It seems that writers, no matter what their level of achievement, continually look for ways to improve their art. Again and again, the magazine addresses some of the same questions writers are asking today: How do I get ideas? How do I start writing? How do I finish my story? How do I know if the story is any good?

How do I get published? How much should I be paid?

How do I keep going when I get discouraged? How do I get beyond the fear of writing, of rejection?

Informed by each generation's specific and accumulated perspectives, the answers to these questions are varied, reflecting different experiences, values, and histories. One constant, however, is the conviction that writing—telling our stories—is an important and necessary part of being human. Writing, and reading, help us find meaning in a world that may at times seem out of our control but has a profound effect on our lives. Whether you write privately or for publication, whether you write journal entries, stories, books, or articles, your writing documents not only the times in which you live but also your understanding of them.

Writing also helps us look beyond ourselves and connect with broader intellectual and cultural communities. It enriches our lives. It makes a difference. As author Arthur Plotnik writes, "words chronicle, interpret, comfort, and heal.

They make the inexpressible expressible and sometimes—because language is our best medium of understanding—understood."

The Writer and *The Writer's Handbook 2003* are essential tools to help writers communicate well. Part of that process is talking with other writers to get ideas, honest feedback, and suggestions. If there is one thing I've learned in my writing career, it's that there is more than one approach to each writing concern. In the magazine and the handbook, our goal is to provide you with intelligent, practical options based on the experiences of successful writers, so you can choose the approach that is right for you. We view both publications as places where writers meet and exchange ideas.

The importance of this sustained community dialogue cannot be overstated. Writing is a process, not a destination. The only way to be a writer is to write. But writing is a messy endeavor; the path is strewn with the detritus of words, sentences, and paragraphs, which seldom, if ever, emerge in a tidy pattern. You write, you cross out, you write again.

If, like me, you've more than once looked at your first draft and hated it, you may find it heartening to know you're not alone. At the very moment you are ready to abandon the whole thing, it helps to hear (or read) someone saying, "Wait! There's some good stuff here. Give it another look. See what needs to be fixed." Reading what other writers say about the process helps us work through roadblocks and continue writing.

As with the previous editions, the 67th *Writer's Handbook* is a sampling of some of the best articles from recent issues of *The Writer*. Both are filled with encouragement, support, and advice from some of the best authors of our time: Jonathan Franzen, John Irving, Joyce Carol Oates, James Ellroy, Evan Hunter, Anita Shreve, Sue Miller, Studs Terkel, Elmore Leonard, Marge Piercy, Susan Vreeland, and many more. Sharing what they've learned about writing in today's publishing climate, they are role models and mentors guiding us on our paths.

I hope you will find on these pages the instruction and inspiration you need to sustain you on your writing journey.

Elfrieda Abbe is Editor of *The Writer*.

SECTION ONE

Professional Basics

PROTECT YOUR RIGHTS

A basic guide to copyrighting your work

by Kelly James-Enger

Perhaps no concept is as confusing to beginning writers as copyright—what it is, how it's created, and how to protect your own. What exactly is copyright, anyway? Must you use the © symbol to protect your work? Is it necessary to register the copyright in your work for it to be effective?

I'll answer some of the most common copyright questions and explain how to protect your work—and why you need to. (Note: While the United States is party to several international treaties regarding copyright, this article will focus solely on U.S. law.)

Myths and misconceptions

According to the U.S. Copyright Office, "copyright" refers to a form of protection provided by U.S. law to the authors of "original works of authorship" including literary, dramatic, musical, artistic, and other intellectual rights. The owner of copyrighted material generally has the exclusive right to authorize such things as reproducing, distributing, and displaying the work.

Copyright protection exists from the time the work is created "in fixed form." This means that as soon as you finish a poem, novel, or article, you automatically own the copyright and it's yours until you sell or license it to someone else, or until the period of protection ends. However, many writers have misconceptions about how copyright is created, says Portland-based attorney Leonard DuBoff, author of *The Law (in Plain English) for Writers* (John Wiley & Sons) and *The Book Publisher's Legal Guide* (Fred B. Rothman & Co.). One of the most common is that you must mail a copy of your work to yourself to acquire copyright protection.

"People tell me all the time, 'I mailed a copy of that to myself so I have a form of protection,' " says DuBoff. "Mailing something to yourself generates revenue for the postal service but serves no practical purpose." Many writers have also been advised that they do not need the copyright notice on their work. While this is accurate, it is misleading. The symbol doesn't create copyright, but it does give notice of ownership to those who might steal it and defend their actions under the so-called "innocent infringement" doctrine.

Let's say you write a poem and give it to several friends. If you don't put a copyright notice on your poem, and someone relies in good faith on the fact that there's no copyright notice—and makes 100 copies of your poem to distribute—that person may not be liable for damages, and may even be permitted to continue copying the work! (For this example, we'll assume that the person who copied your work doesn't fall under the "fair-use doctrine," which permits limited use of copyrighted material under certain conditions.)

"The copyright has rubber teeth," says DuBoff. "So my recommendation is

WHOSE RIGHTS ARE THESE?

When you create a written work, you own a "bundle of rights," including the right to reproduce and sell the work. A brief rundown on types of rights a publisher may ask for:

• **First North American serial rights.** The right to publish the story for the first time in a North American magazine.

• **Electronic rights.** The right to publish, disseminate, and store your article electronically (such as on a Web site or an online database).

• **All rights.** What it sounds like. The publisher buys all rights to the piece; bad news for writers, because it prevents you from reselling the story later.

• **Work for hire.** Technically, it means the publisher owns the copyright to the piece, which by definition includes all rights. Again, this is bad news for writers, because you're giving up all rights to the story.

• **Reprint rights.** (Also called second rights.) The right to publish an article after it has already been published elsewhere.

• **Exclusive rights.** Many publishers will ask for exclusive rights to the story for a period of time like 90 days or six months.

that even though we in the United States do not require notice, one is silly not to have copyright notice on the work even before it's published. Then, if it's inadvertently published or published at all with notice, you defeat the defense of innocent infringement." The notice required is the © symbol, or the word "copyright" or its abbreviation, the date the work was first published, and the author's name—for example, © 2001, Kelly James-Enger.

So why register?

You may be thinking, "Well, if I automatically own the copyright and put a notice on my work, what's the point of registering my copyrights?" The answer is simple—to be able to effectively protect your copyrights in the future. "The only time you must register is when the copyright office says you must, or when you want to enforce it," says DuBoff. The problem with not registering the work "in a timely fashion" is that any infringement that occurs prior to registration will not give rise to attorneys' fees or statutory damages.

That may not seem like a big deal, but attorneys' fees and statutory damages are two of your best remedies in a copyright infringement suit. Registering your copyright is evidence that can be used at trial that you are the legal copyright owner and that the copyright is valid. If you've registered the work within three months of publication or before any infringement occurs and you win an infringement suit, you're entitled to attorneys' fees and statutory damages—a specified amount of money set out by law. If you haven't registered your work within three months or before the infringement, you may still have a cause of action for the wrong, but you'll be limited to injunctive relief (meaning that the violator can be prohibited from using your copyrighted work) and/or actual damages—i.e., the amount of money you have lost because of the violator's actions or the amount the infringer earned. But proving actual damages can be difficult, especially in the relatively new area of electronic rights.

Once your work is published, you have three months in which to register it. That time period is retroactive, meaning that if you register within those three months, you're protected back to the date of publication. Currently, it costs $30 to register work with the U.S. Copyright Office, but you can include more than one piece of writing on the same application. All unpublished work can be bunched and registered together and all work published at the same time can similarly be included in a single application. (For more information about copyright registration procedures, visit www.loc.gov/copyright; forms are available at www.loc.gov/copyright/forms.)

Don't give it away

Another important aspect of protecting your copyrights is being aware of exactly what you're selling to a publisher. The copyright statute refers to a "bundle of rights"—the right to reproduce the work, to sell the work, to publicly display the work, and the like. As a writer, you want to sell as few rights as possible—one-time-only rights would be ideal. Then, if the publisher wants additional rights—say, to reprint the piece or post it on the magazine's Web site—it has to offer you additional money for those rights. Of course, publishers take the opposite approach—they want to obtain as many rights as possible (often, all rights), so that they're free to use and reuse the work in print publications, on Web sites, in books, in electronic databases, and as one of my contracts reads, "all media whether now existing and hereafter devised, created and invented."

Read every contract and make sure you understand what rights you're selling before you sign. "When I'm representing a writer, photographer, or artist, I want the contract to be specific and include exactly what is being sold or licensed," says DuBoff. And I want a reservation of rights clause, i.e., all rights not specifically conveyed are reserved to the creator."

As a writer, you're probably much more concerned with creating work than protecting it. But by giving notice of your copyright—and registering your work on a regular basis—you'll help prevent it from being stolen or misappropriated in the future. Better yet, it will give you an effective weapon to use against violators if you need to.

Kelly James-Enger of Downers Grove, Ill., writes about health, fitness, nutrition, and other subjects for more than 30 publications, including *Woman's Day*, *Shape*, and *Fit*. James-Enger, a former attorney, leads writing programs and workshops throughout Illinois. Her new book for freelance writers, tentatively titled *How to Create Your Own Writing Niche* (The Writer Books) will be available early in 2003.

IT'S ABOUT TIME

Use a timely angle to get an editor's attention

by Roberta Sandler

Suppose I pitched a roundup article about Thomas Jefferson's Virginia homes? "Discover the private side of Thomas Jefferson by visiting his three Virginia homes—Tuckahoe Plantation, Monticello, and Poplar Forest."

The editor of a general interest, travel, history, or gardening magazine might accept my article, but he or she wouldn't be in a hurry to schedule it. It could, in fact, languish in the editor's "evergreen" pile. Suppose, however, that I wrote the following:

"In 1801, Thomas Jefferson became our nation's third president. Since 2001 is the bicentennial of his presidency, it's an ideal time to discover the private Thomas Jefferson by visiting his three Virginia homes—Tuckahoe Plantation, Monticello, and Poplar Forest."

Now, my evergreen has advanced to timely!

Why write "timely" articles?

I discovered the advantage of a timely tie-in when the travel editor of the *Indianapolis News* requested my article and photos about Morristown, N.J., which is especially historic because it was George Washington's winter head-quarters during the American Revolution.

After the editor sat with my article and photos for four months, I asked him if he had scheduled a publication date. He nonchalantly informed me that since the article was an evergreen, he would wait until he found space for it. Three months later, he still hadn't scheduled it. I contacted the Morristown Chamber of Commerce in hopes the city was planning some commemorative event that could speed up my article's publication. Nothing exceptional was on the chamber's events calendar. My article could sit in a pile on the editor's desk for another seven months. I withdrew it.

By connecting your article to a time frame, you compel an interested editor to publish your article sooner rather than later. If the magazine pays on publication, you'll get paid sooner, and you'll sooner be able to submit the article to reprint markets. Finally, the immediacy of your subject will quickly hook the reader. For many years, I've sought ways to either inject a note of timeliness into my evergreen articles or write articles because they are timely. I try to link these articles to a specific date, event, time of year, or milestone. I submit the article or query with enough lead time for the editor to run the article so that it coincides with whatever date my article mentions.

Find a peg

Think about articles you have written or intend to write. Can you take your previously published pieces, attach a timely spin to them, and recycle them? Among the articles you plan to write, how can you inject a simple note of timeliness into them? Here are suggestions: You want to re-sell your previously published article "How to Select the Right Pet for Your Family." Add a simple opening sentence before you recycle it, such as "February is Responsible Pet Owner Month." Other pet-related dates include National Pet Memorial Day (in September), Pet I.D. Week (April), and National Pet Week (May). I am going to try to recycle my human interest story about a couple whose family dog suffered from heart failure, and which could be saved only by having a tiny pacemaker connected to her heart muscle. I'll probably use National Pet Week or National Heart Month as my peg.

Say your article on treatments for breast cancer has previously been published. You could recycle it with a timely spin such as "October is Breast Cancer Awareness Month," or "In 112 U.S. cities during the next two months, men, women, and children will be gearing up for the annual 'Race for the Cure.' "

Or you're writing a profile of a local businesswoman. Instead of generalizing, "Mary Jones, president of XYZ Company, strives to satisfy her customers," put your article into a time frame.

"During National Business Women's Week (Oct. 18 to 24), Mary Jones, the president of XYZ Co., will be doing what she does throughout the year: striving to satisfy her customers."

Or, "Next week, Mary Jones, president of XYZ Co., will celebrate her 15th year in business, and she continues to satisfy her customers."

I wanted to write an article about how hotel guests can remain safe during a hotel fire. This is a topic that, while useful to vacationers and travelers, can sit on the editor's back burner until there's space for it. But coat it with timeliness and it will quickly move from the back burner to the pages of an upcoming issue.

When I proposed "Local Hotels Pay Extra Attention to Fire Safety," the editor of my local newspaper wasn't interested. I reminded him that Fire

Prevention Week was coming up in four weeks. That gave my article immediacy and relevance. The editor gave me a go-ahead, and planned the publication date to tie in with Fire Prevention Week.

GET TIMELY

If you're thinking about a timely article, here are some holidays to keep in mind:

January: Human Resources Month, National Soup Month, National Oatmeal Month, National Hot Tea Month.

February: National Grapefruit Month, National Embroidery Month, National Children's Dental Health Month.

March: National Women's History Month, Red Cross Month, National Procrastination Week, National Nutrition Month.

April: Keep America Beautiful Month, Prevention of Animal Cruelty Month.

May: Older Americans Month, National Arthritis Awareness Month, Historic Preservation Week.

June: Dairy Month, Turkey-Lovers Month, National Pest Control Month, National Rose Month.

July: National Baked Bean Month, National Recreation and Parks Month.

August: National Eye Exam Month, International Clowns Week.

September: National Chicken Month, National Piano Month.

October: Polish American Heritage Month, Vegetarian Awareness Month, Spinal Health Month.

November: Child Safety and Protection Month, National Alzheimer's Disease Awareness Month, National Diabetes Month.

December: Colorectal Cancer Education and Awareness Month, Wright Brothers First Powered Flight Anniversary.

Planning ahead

If you're going to add a timely slant to your article or query, you need to send it to the publication far enough in advance for the editor to slot it for the event or time of year mentioned in that article. Generally, that means submitting it to a magazine six months in advance, or to a daily newspaper about six weeks in advance.

Whatever you write, think about corresponding holidays or annual events. You can build a roundup article around a timely question: "What's your idea of a romantic Valentine's Day?" "What's the most memorable Christmas gift you ever received?" "What are your New Year resolutions?" Think about seasons. Every year, snowbirds (part-time residents) leave the Sunbelt states to return to their Northern homes. I wrote a service article, "Closing Your Snowbird Home for the Summer," that appeared in my local newspaper and in maturity publications in Florida and Canada.

Emily Rosen, a prolific writer friend of mine, once wrote an essay for *The New York Times* suggesting that each New Year begins not on Jan. 1, but around Labor Day, when summer patio furniture gets hauled into the garage, when children need back-to-school clothes, and when summer heat will soon make way for autumn leaves.

In anticipation of the 60th anniversary of Pearl Harbor Day in December [2001], can you interview a local war veteran? Perhaps your neighborhood VFW Post is planning commemorative activities you could write about for your local paper. On a national scope, you could pitch an article about safety rules for children when they go trick-or-treating. Send the query with enough lead time so that it can be published in October, before Halloween. When I wrote my *Prime Times* profile of Judith Levy, bestselling author of *Grandmother Remembers* and *Grandfather Remembers*, I suggested that the editor publish it soon—in September—to coincide with National Grandparents Day.

Whether you write a personal essay or a consumer article, you can usually find some way to make it timely. For example, write an essay about a Father's Day or Mother's Day that had special meaning to you. Write a food article about clever ways to decorate Easter eggs (did you know that there is a National Egg Salad Day?) or that gives tips for storing, preparing, cooking, and serving a Thanksgiving turkey.

> By connecting your article to a time frame, you compel an interested editor to publish your article sooner rather than later.

Biding your time

At some point, you may write an article that has little chance of being published at any time other than the far-off date to which the article is connected. If that happens, wait patiently for the payoff. Here's what I mean:

I visited Rochester, N.Y., in April during its annual

Lilac Festival, which attracts about 250,000 people. For all of its attractions, Rochester is sweetest when its lilacs bloom, and there seemed no more enticing slant than the Lilac Festival.

I waited until the following January and then pitched my travel article, with an opening hook describing the explosive rainbow of colors and perfumed scents that permeate the Lilac Festival. Thanks to that timely event, my article appeared in two newspaper travel sections in April.

One autumn day, while cleaning out a drawer, I came across a Valentine's Day card I had kept for decades and forgotten about. Reading the card again reminded me of my college days in the early 1960s, and the male classmate who gave me the card. In it, he admitted that his feelings for me were more than platonic. I hadn't known. I wrote a nostalgic personal essay, then put it away until December. I sent my essay to *The New York Times*, which published it on Valentine's Day weekend. I patiently waited another year, and found a reprint market in the *Worcester* (Mass.) *Telegram*. Years later, I re-sold my essay to two Florida newspapers, which ran it on Valentine's Day.

Somewhere in time

Would you wait four or five years before having your article re-published? I would. I did.

As youngsters, my friend Janie and I were crazy about James Dean. Knowing that the 40th anniversary of his death was approaching, I wrote "James Dean, Janie and Me," a personal essay that pondered Dean's ascent to cult status. In September 1995, the Fort Lauderdale, Fla., *Sun Sentinel* ran my essay. I'm planning to change "40th" to "50th" when I look for more markets in 2005!

In October 1995, I visited the ancient ruins of Olympia, which inspired me to write a travel article about this historic site. I suspected that the easiest way for me to sell it was by connecting it to the forthcoming 1996 Summer Olympics in Atlanta. I waited until February before I submitted it. "Crowds will soon stampede Atlanta to witness the 1996 Summer Olympics, but if you decide instead to visit the place where the Olympics were born, you must travel to Olympia, Greece, a hilly vista that was once the sanctuary of the gods."

That was my timely tie-in to "Visitors Lured to Games' Cradle," which appeared in *The Miami Herald* in late April. In July, my article, with only minor variation, appeared in the New Orleans *Times Picayune*. I put my article to bed for the next four years. In early 2000, out it came. To update the article's sidebar information, I contacted the Greek Tourist Office and the director of a company that conducts tours of Greece. The body of my article needed no updates, no changes. That's the beauty of writing about historic destinations. History doesn't change.

"In September, spectators can witness the 2000 Olympics in Sydney, but the origins, legends, and history of the games echo from across the Mediterranean, within a hilly vista that was once the home of the gods." There again was my timely tie-in! My revived Olympia article appeared in August 2000 in the

Easton, Pa., *Express Times* and in *50 Plus Lifestyles*. As the 2004 Summer Olympics in Athens approaches, you can bet I'll again be recycling it.

This doesn't mean that I write only timely articles, or that I'm sitting around until I can pitch the articles. I'm busy writing many articles that don't need a timely reference. I do, however, keep an eye on dates that I can tie into articles. I believe that a timely reference gives my articles an edge, and that it speeds up their publication date. That's why I often refer to sources such as *The Big Book of Dates* by Laurie E. Rozakis (McGraw-Hill), *Chase's Annual Events* (Contemporary Books), or an almanac.

I recently wrote a travel article entitled "Pensacola: History Under Five Flags," but I didn't want it to suffer the same fate as my Morristown, N.J., article. By checking information in my encyclopedia, I made my evergreen article timely. It appeared in the summer 2001 issue of a Florida lifestyle magazine. My opening sentence read: "Florida is celebrating its 180th birthday as a U.S. territory. In 1821, Andrew Jackson stood in Pensacola's public square, and officially accepted Florida from Spain. Visitors to Pensacola can see the site of Jackson's residence after he became the first territorial governor."

Your articles will sell more quickly once you add a timely connection. It's merely a matter of time!

Roberta Sandler of Wellington, Fla., is a freelance writer and travel editor of *Upbeat Senior*. Her latest book is *Guide to Florida Historical Walking Tours* (Pineapple Press).

THE NEWS ANGLE

Major news stories can be springboards for your writing career

by Jodee Blanco

We've all seen it happen. A major news story breaks and suddenly, seemingly out of nowhere, formerly obscure writers start popping up on radio and television talk shows being interviewed as "leading experts," and their books begin hitting bestseller lists all across the country.

Have you ever wondered how these writers achieve such an enviable feat and whether you could do the same thing? As a veteran publicist, I'm here to tell you that you can.

We live in a "media-centric" culture. Consider for a moment some of the news stories that have dominated the press in recent years—the O.J. Simpson case, the Bush-Gore election controversy, terrorism. Each of these long-term stories not only consumed enormous airtime and print space, but also gave birth to numerous bestsellers, as well as creating fresh publicity platforms for previously published books.

During the O.J. Simpson case, books about racism, domestic violence, and the legal system flourished. Reporters and producers sought authors who had written on these subjects for interviews; literary agents and publishers looked for writers who had written or could write books on these topics.

If you've written a biography of a film director who has just been nominated for an Academy Award, media producers may seek you out for print and radio interviews.

The bottom line? If it's in the news, it's on people's minds. Where there's curiosity, there's opportunity. If you're a writer, that opportunity falls into two primary categories: fresh possibilities for promoting and publicizing a book of yours that's already been published; and piggy-backing current topics or trends with book proposal and magazine article ideas that tie into major news stories.

Whether you're in a position to take advantage of one or both of the above, here are a few steps to turn news stories into publishing success:

Watch television and read newspapers from a marketing perspective and look for media trends. Every day for at least a month, watch as much television news and talk show programming as you possibly can, and read at least one national newspaper and your local daily paper. Pay close attention to which news stories are making the most headlines, and the names of the reporters and producers covering those stories. If you've authored a book, ask yourself if there's anything in your book that relates to these current hot topics, and pitch yourself as an expert to the press on that subject.

For example, I was publicizing a book on divorce and getting little response from the news media until the Donald Trump divorce broke in the press. I immediately started calling every television and radio show in the country, telling producers that I had an expert who could make sense of New York's most scandalous breakup. The author got so many bookings that the book hit best-seller lists coast-to-coast. The same goes for getting a book deal.

Publishers are always looking for book proposals that capitalize on current media trends. If you can cleverly tie a book idea to a hot media topic, your chances of getting a publishing deal are increased exponentially.

While I was getting my divorce-expert author on television, literary agents were getting book deals for writers who had manuscripts on the subjects of relationships and divorce law, among many other related topics.

Think creatively about how you can position yourself and your subject to tie in with current events. Think beyond the obvious. When a front door is closed, you can usually find a side door that's open. Look at the big stories the press is covering, and develop an unusual approach or an intriguing take on a hot topic.

For example, let's say you've written a cookbook called *Comfort Foods,* featuring recipes for higher-calorie dishes such as macaroni and cheese or chocolate cake. If you wanted a publicity placement in your local paper, the obvious reporter to pitch would be the food writer. If the food writer says no, how could "working the headlines" help you snag the coverage you want? Suppose you're doing your media research as described in Step 1 and you come across a huge feature article about stress written by the psychology writer at your local paper. You could custom-design a pitch for him that focuses on the emotional importance of comfort foods.

Perhaps the article could be entitled "Food for the Soul." Taking this idea one step further, that article could even become the genesis for another book that you write with a psychologist or that very same psychology writer on the value of comfort foods, why we love them, and their place in culinary history. The point here is not just to be creative, but also to be creative in a whole new kind of way.

I remember once doing publicity for a novel written by a former U.S. Drug Enforcement Administration agent. The publisher was struggling to obtain coverage because the media kept insisting that if the book were nonfiction they would do something, but a novel wasn't news from their perspective.

So what did I do? I turned to a beat reporter, who rarely gets any attention from publicists, whose work—covering high school sports—often has been taken for granted.

To me, the tie-in was obvious. The author was an expert on drugs. Where else is the threat of drug abuse more disturbing than in America's high schools, particularly among young athletes who want to improve their athletic performance? I pitched the high school sports reporter at the *Chicago Sun-Times* about interviewing the author on this topic: "10 warning signs a student may be using illegal drugs to enhance his/her game, and what to do about it."

The reporter was thrilled, because his readers were parents and coaches. I agreed to give him a great interview and he did a boxed review of the former DEA agent's novel.

When the piece ran, it was a two-page spread that not only went out on the wire and ran in over 500 papers nationwide, but generated so much buzz that the author was then sought after by all the country's top talk shows.

Look for opportunities in your hometown news. Following media trends and headline stories not only generates book publicity and book proposal ideas, it can also lead to exciting and lucrative collaborative projects. It's all about looking at the world from a new vista.

As you're reading newspapers and watching TV news shows, keep a creative eye on big, unfolding local stories with national potential. They could lead to book deals and commissioned articles. Here's how. Often, a story will emerge in the press that has tremendous human-interest appeal. These are small-town dramas that over time capture the attention of the entire country. They can range from bizarre murder cases, dramatic legal battles, and major corporate debacles to medical stories, unusual personal tragedies and triumphs, and intriguing local mysteries. Frequently, these stories can be fodder for successful books and major magazine articles. Stay alert when it comes to big news stories in your hometown.

Several years ago, a college football star made local headlines because "boosters" (college football fans who give star players money, girls, cars—you name it) were lavishing such riches on this particular player that it drew the attention and ire of the FBI. It also landed this kid in prison. The debacle became an unprecedented scandal. A local journalist who followed the story decided it had enough juice to make a good book. He approached an agent who agreed, and within weeks he had secured a generous publishing deal. The book, which I then publicized, made headlines, too.

If there's a particular story that's dominating local press and it's something you're genuinely interested in, seize the reins. You could approach individuals directly involved in the story and ask if they'd like to explore the possibility of doing a book with you. Or, pay attention to the name of the reporter who's covering the story in the paper and contact him about the possibility of co-authoring a book with you. Many journalists who cover these prominent stories would love to author a book but don't have the time to do it on their own, and would be happy to have a collaborator.

Watch what's happening around you. Use the local news as your guide and barometer. If you see a story that could be told in a book or magazine article, jump on it. You have a gift. Offer it, use it, and feed it.

Jodee Blanco of Bethlehem, Pa., is a top publishing and publicity expert. A founding member of the PR firm Blanco & Peace, she has put 15 books onto the *New York Times* bestseller lists, five of which hit the number one slot. She is a faculty member at the University of Chicago and New York University, and is author of three books, including *The Complete Guide to Book Publicity* (Allworth Press).

HOOKS FROM THE HEADLINES

Mayflower Madam Sidney Biddle Barrows given jail sentence for running bordello
Possible book spin-offs: a novel featuring a debutante who turns into a criminal; a nonfiction book on good girls who go bad and why; the history of famous American madams.

New England Journal of Medicine study says eating chocolate can lower cholesterol by 80 percent
Possible publicity angles for books already published: If you've written a cookbook, pitch food writers on succulent chocolate recipes; if you've written a history book that touches on the history of certain foods, pitch the cultural reporter on the history of chocolate; if you're a romance writer, pitch the relationship reporter on how to use chocolate to sweeten up your love life, or write a romance novel featuring chocolate in the plot.

HOW TO WRITE
A SUCCESSFUL QUERY

by Moira Allen

As editors become increasingly swamped with inappropriate manuscripts, more and more publications are closing their doors to unsolicited submissions. This means that the query letter is fast becoming the only way to break into some of the best markets.

The Value of a Query

Queries benefit both editors and writers. Editors much prefer to review a one-page letter than a 10-page manuscript, so queries spend less time in the slush pile. They also enable an editor to determine, quickly, whether you:

- Can write effectively
- Have a coherent, well-thought-out idea that fits the publication's content
- Have a basic grasp of grammar and spelling
- Have read the publication
- Have the credentials or expertise to write the article
- Are professional in your approach to writing

Queries save *you* time by ensuring that you don't invest time and energy into writing an article that won't be accepted. Keep in mind that articles are often rejected for reasons that have nothing to do with quality. An editor may already have a similar piece on file, or assigned, or have covered something similar in a recent issue. It's much easier to find this out through a query, than to tailor an article for a publication and then have to rewrite it and send it somewhere else. It's also easier to obtain interviews when you can say you have a solid assignment.

By querying first, you also give the editor a chance to provide feedback on your idea. The editor may want to suggest a particular length, or approach, or recommend experts to interview. S/he may want you to cover other aspects of your subject in sidebars. By finding out what the editor wants before you start writing, you'll avoid having to revise the piece later.

A well-written query can also result in assignments you didn't expect. If the editor is impressed by your style and credentials, s/he may offer you some other assignment, even if your original idea isn't usable. This can often be the beginning of a long, rewarding relationship!

Query Letter Essentials

But how do you "sell" an editor on your article when you have no more than a page to explain your concept and display your writing skill? The answer is: By including everything the editor needs to know about your article—and about you. A successful query letter generally includes these five basic components:

- The hook
- The pitch
- The body
- The credentials
- The close

The Hook

Your very first line should grab an editor's attention. It must demonstrate that you can write effectively, and that you understand your market.

There are several ways to approach the "hook," including:

The problem/solution hook. This defines a problem or situation common to the publication's audience, then proposes an article that can help solve that problem. Here's an example:

> The pet magazine market is an ideal place for newer writers to "break in." However, it is constantly flooded with inappropriate submissions. To break in, one must understand what these magazines want, and what they won't accept. ("Writing for Pet Magazines," sold to *Byline*.)

The informative hook. This usually presents two or three lines of useful information (e.g., facts, statistics), followed by an explanation of how this applies to the target audience. For example:

> Thanks to a translation glitch, Microsoft was forced to pull its entire Chinese edition of Windows 95 from the marketplace. Microsoft recovered—but that's the sort of mistake few small businesses can afford! ("How to Localize Your Website," sold to *Entrepreneur's Home Office*.)

The Question. Often, this is a problem/solution or informative hook posed as a question, such as:

> Did you know . . . ?
> What would you do if . . . ?
> Have you ever wondered . . . ?

The personal experience/anecdote. Many writers like to take a personal approach, as it immediately establishes the credential of "experience." Be sure, however, that your market uses more personal articles, or first-person accounts, before attempting a hook like this:

> Forget-me-nots. I love their wistful name. I love their tiny blue flowers. And yes, I love that growing them is as simple as pie. ("Forget-me-nots: Simply Unforgettable Spring Flowers," by Mary R., sold to *Fine Gardening*.)

The attention-grabber. The goal of this type of hook is to make the reader sit up and take notice—hopefully long enough to read the rest of the story. This might be a good "hook" for a query about parachuting in Yosemite:

> As I fell from the top of Yosemite's El Capitan, I wondered if my life would truly flash before my eyes—or if I would stop screaming long enough to notice.

Hooks to Avoid

Certain hooks scream "amateur" and are guaranteed to speed a query to the rejection pile, including:

The personal introduction. Never start with a line like "Hi, my name is John, and I'd like to send you an article about . . ." Don't offer irrelevant information, such as "I'm a housewife and mother of three lovely children. Recently I decided to pursue my lifelong dream of writing . . ."

The "suck-up" hook. Yes, editors want to know that you've read their publication, but they also want you to prove it by offering an appropriate query—*not* by saying, "I've been a subscriber for 20 years and just *love* your magazine . . ."

The "bid for sympathy." Don't tell an editor that you've never been published before, or that you need to sell this piece or your children will starve.

The "I'm perfect for you" hook. Never sing your own praises: "I am a highly experienced professional and will be an asset to your magazine." Don't inform the editor that your article is "perfect" for his readers. Never declare that your article is "wonderful" or "fascinating." Prove it—with a good query.

The "I'm an amateur" hook. Never announce that you have never been published before, or that you've tried to sell the same article to 20 other magazines, or that your writing teacher (or mother or spouse) suggested that you send this to a magazine. Even if you haven't sold anything before, you can still *act* like a professional.

The Pitch

Once you have an editor's attention, move on to the pitch. Usually, this is your second paragraph, and its purpose is to explain exactly what you're offering. For example, the pitch that followed the "localization" hook, above, went like this:

> I'd like to offer you a 1,500-word article titled "Internationalizing Your Online Market." The article would discuss how small businesses can take advantage of "localizing" agents to tailor their products and market strategies to the international marketplace. ("How to Localize Your Website.")

If possible, your pitch should include a working title for your article (titles help editors "visualize" what you're proposing), a word-count (make sure you've checked the publication's guidelines!), and a brief summary of what the article will cover.

The Body

This is where you really start to "sell." The body of your query will usually be from two to four paragraphs, and presents the details of your article. Remember that an editor wants to know exactly what the article will cover, so by this time you should have a working outline of the piece in your own mind.

A good way to present an overview of your topic is to break it into logical subtopics—e.g., the sections that would be likely to appear under subheads in the finished piece. The longer the article, the more subtopics you can include (though it's usually not advisable to have more than four or five). For example, a 700-word article on cancer in pets might only cover "the ten warning signs of cancer," while a 2,000-word article on the same topic might cover "common types of cancer, warning signs, and current treatment options." A good way to determine whether you have the right number of subtopics is to divide your word-count by the number of topics—e.g., a 2,000-word article with five subtopics gives you a budget of 400 words per topic.

Here's how I described the content of an article on quilt care:

> The article covers techniques of hand-cleaning delicate quilts to avoid damaging fragile fabrics and prevent fading and staining. It discusses ways to remove spot stains (including blood spots and rust stains from needles and other metal contact). It also discusses ways to mend damaged quilts without destroying the integrity of an heirloom piece. Finally, it discusses the best ways to store or display quilts in order to preserve and protect them. ("Caring for Heirloom Quilts," sold to *DownUnder Quilts.*)

Some writers like to use block paragraphs; others like to use bullets. There's no rule on the best style; choose a style that makes your query visually appealing and easy to read.

The Credentials

Editors want to know why you are the best person to write the article you've proposed. This is where your credentials come in. Don't assume, however, that these must include writing credits. While a list of previous articles on relevant topics is nice, you may also be able to prove your qualifications with credentials such as:

• Professional experience (some publications accept material *only* from qualified experts)
• Academic degrees or training
• Teaching experience in the subject area
• Personal experience (especially if the article relates to personal issues/problems)
• Writing experience
• Interviews with experts (a way to demonstrate that even if you don't have the credentials, you'll be able to get information from those who *do*)

Credentials are usually listed in the last or next-to-last paragraph. Here's an example:

> As webmaster of www.musicphotographer.com, it has been my job to connect music writers and photographers with the markets that need their work. This is the only site devoted to music journalism on the Web. I'm also writing the first guide on the topic. Reviews for my last book, *The Van Halen Encyclopedia,* are available at Amazon.com. (C. Chilver's successful pitch to *Inkspot* for "How to Write for the Music Market.")

The Close

Use the final paragraph of your article to thank the editor for reviewing your proposal—and to offer one last "nudge" to encourage the editor to respond. I usually include a time-estimate in this paragraph—e.g., "If you are interested in this article, I can have it on your desk within XX days." Here's a typical closing paragraph:

> I hope this topic interests you, and look forward to your response. If you would like to see the article, I can have it on your desk within two weeks of receiving your go-ahead. Thank you for your time!

Format

The presentation of your letter can be as important as your content. A traditional (paper) query should include the following elements:

A decent letterhead. At the very least, your name and address and other contact information should be printed at the top of your letter (*not* at the bottom or under your signature) in an attractive font. You can have an inexpensive letterhead designed and typeset at your local printing shop, or online through iPrint.com. Or, design your own on your computer.

A business-style body. Always include a blank line between paragraphs, and don't indent more than five spaces (if at all).

A formal salutation. Don't address the editor by first name unless you know him/her personally.

Clean, proofread copy. Don't rely on your spellchecker; review your query yourself before mailing it out.

Quality paper. Use at least 20-lb. bond paper for queries. Some writers like to use fancier papers—parchment, linen, etc.—on the theory that a nicer paper with a professional tint will stand out amidst all the white paper on an editor's desk. Don't go to "colors" however—pink paper and blue type scream for rejection.

An SASE (self-addressed stamped envelope). Don't use "insert" envelopes; fold a full-size business envelope (#10) in thirds and use that. Be sure it has adequate postage. If you are submitting a query from another country, be sure that your SASE has the correct postage for the target country—or else include an appropriate number if IRCs (international reply coupons).

These guidelines are for traditional "paper" queries. Needless to say, not all of these "rules" are possible when sending an e-mail query.

Clips

Many editors ask for clips so that they can review a sample of your writing style. Clips are simply copies of previously published materials. Never send copies of unpublished works! Don't send clips of work you've self-published or posted on your own website. And remember, bad clips are worse than no clips at all.

It's best to send clips that are relevant to the proposal, if you have them. If you don't, send samples from your most prestigious publications. If most of your published works are electronic, print out copies from your website; don't just ask the editor to "visit" unless you are sending an e-mail query.

If you have no clips, don't despair. Most editors consider the merits of a query first and the clips second. (To be honest, many editors don't even have time to read clips, even though they request them.) If your query is strong enough, the absence of clips shouldn't be enough to trigger a rejection, unless the publication works *only* with published writers.

Following Up

How long should you wait for a response? Usually, you should wait at least as long as the publication's guidelines suggest (e.g., 4 to 6 weeks)—and then add another two weeks "grace period." Then, send a polite follow-up. Attach a copy of your original query, so that the editor won't have to search the files for it. If you still hear nothing after another 3-4 weeks, consider a polite phone call. (No, it won't cause your article to be rejected.) If you *still* can't get an answer, and you would like to withdraw the query, send a final letter informing the editor that, as you have received no response, you are officially withdrawing the query from consideration. This protects you from charges of "simultaneous submissions" if the first editor finally decides to reply after you've already sent the query on to someone else.

The ability to write a good query is one of the most important skills in a writer's toolbox. A good query shows an editor that you can write and that you are a professional—qualities that may result in an assignment even if the editor can't use your original proposal. Think of your query as a letter of introduction, your first and only opportunity to get your foot through that particular door. If you make a good impression, you're likely to be invited back (even if your original pitch is rejected). If you make a bad impression, you may find that door forever closed.

Moira Allen of Chesapeake, Va., is a freelance writer and the editor of Writing-World.com. This article, from her website, www.writing-world.com, is excerpted from her book *The Writer's Guide to Queries, Pitches & Proposals* (Allworth Press). Copyright © 2001 Moira Allen.

FIND YOUR OWN NICHE

With a specialty, work less and earn more

by Kelly James-Enger

When I started freelancing five years ago, I wrote about a variety of subjects. I wrote real estate advertorials for the local paper, brochure copy for small businesses, and magazine articles on topics that ranged from new developments in treating urinary tract infections to "10 reasons to date a shy guy." I had plenty of work, but I was not very efficient.

About two years ago, I changed my approach. I decided to focus my writing in several areas—primarily health, fitness, nutrition, and bridal writing—and that decision has paid off. I spend less time researching queries and articles, I know where to find experts and relevant data, and, knowing of my specialty, editors often call me with health, fitness, and nutrition assignments. Even better, I make twice as much money while working fewer hours than before.

Want to set yourself apart from other freelancers, nab better-paying assignments, and spend less time at your computer? Develop a writing specialty and you can do all of the above. Contrary to what you might think, you needn't be an M.D. or other recognized "expert" to focus your writing on a particular area. Your educational background, life experience, and interest in certain subjects can all be translated into a writing-related specialty.

What makes you special?

When I teach magazine writing, I have students write down at least five things they have specialized knowledge of or interest in. Make a list of your own unique qualifications to help you start thinking about what you're bringing to the table when you pitch a story.

For example, have you traveled the world? Lived in different parts of the country? Raised children? Dealt with a chronic medical condition? Are you an avid gardener? Can you whip up fantastic dinners in 30 minutes' time? Have you run your own business? Do you have firsthand knowledge of a particular industry, trade, or profession? Who are your friends, family members, co-workers, and colleagues? What sorts of specialized knowledge do they have?

Creating a list of these subjects will often trigger story ideas and will give you an idea of the areas in which you have a background that other writers may not. For example, when I created a list of my own in a recent writing workshop, I came up with the following:

- My dad is a dentist.
- I've been a runner 16 years.
- My sister is a police officer.
- I'm a vegetarian.
- I'm a lawyer.

Even a quick look at this list reveals that I have some unique knowledge I can use when pitching and writing articles. Granted, there's probably not a huge demand for articles about vegetarian attorneys, but I do know more about teeth than the average person does. Not only is my dad a dentist, I once worked for him as a dental receptionist. This doesn't mean I'm a dental expert, but when I was writing about canker sores and had a quick question, I knew whom to ask.

If I have questions about law enforcement or how the criminal justice system works, I can ask my sister. Maybe I'll pitch an article on how to avoid speeding tickets, or ways to reduce the risk of becoming a crime victim. Stephie can answer these questions and lead me to other sources of information I might not otherwise know about.

And my years of running have given me an endless supply of story ideas. I've written about using heart-rate monitors, stretching for flexibility, and how to get more out of your workouts. The fact that I pay attention to what I eat has led to stories about easy ways to eat better, overcoming diet pitfalls, the negative emotional consequences of constant dieting, and a slew of weight-loss stories. Again, I'm not a fitness or nutrition expert per se, but my longstanding interest in both subjects gives me a depth of knowledge the average writer simply doesn't have. Can I call it a specialty? Sure thing.

Get ready, get set, specialize!

Ready to create your own writing niche? There are basically three ways to do it. You can specialize from the outset; you can wind up specializing without really intending to; or you can consciously decide to specialize after you've already been writing for a while.

Some writers consciously choose a niche at the beginning of their careers to set themselves apart from other writers in the field. If you're a new writer, this can be an effective way of getting your foot in the door. Melba Newsome, a freelancer in Matthews, N.C., was working full time as a paralegal when she decided to start writing. She found the process frustrating at first. "I got absolutely nowhere sending out service or health ideas," Newsome says. "Then I pitched true-life stories and got a response. I got my first assignment for a national magazine—*Family Circle*—with a true-life story. I continued writing everything but realized that I had a much better batting average with these types of stories."

Newsome decided to focus on finding and writing stories that editors wouldn't come up with on their own. "It was clear that so many of the lifestyle or general-interest ideas were generated in-house. But there was no one at the editorial meetings saying, 'I have a great story about a woman who was in a harem for six months,' " she explains. "They needed writers on the ground and outside of New York for that. That was me!" In the years since then, she's written more than 50 true-life stories for magazines including *Cosmopolitan, Marie Claire, Essence, Good Housekeeping,* and *Family Circle.* Her unique niche and the fact that she's willing to dig to find stories have made her invaluable to editors—and ensure a constant stream of work.

Other writers, like Kathy Sena of Manhattan Beach, Calif., simply fall into niches that complement their backgrounds and skills. Sena, a former technical writer and editor, started freelancing full time in 1994 with sales to *Weight Watchers* magazine and *Cosmopolitan.* Since then, she's written hundreds of articles about health, lifestyle, and parenting. She says her specialties have helped open new markets to her and boosted her income as well.

"I write two syndicated health columns for United Parenting Publications. . . . That helped me break into markets such as the *L.A. Times* health section and *Shape* magazine," Sena says. "In addition to getting more assignments, I'm able to get higher rates for my work because of specializing. Also, when you specialize, you tend to more quickly build up a Rolodex full of great contacts—which leads to more article ideas and more work."

Finally, many writers start out as generalists before deciding to concentrate in one or more areas. Freelancer Sam Greengard of Burbank, Calif., wrote for a variety of consumer magazines, writing about "pretty much anything and everything" until about 10 years ago. "At that point, I recognized there was a pretty huge opportunity in business and technology writing, so I made a conscious effort to focus on business and tech," says Greengard, who had a business background as well as an interest in technological issues. "I never told anyone that I wouldn't work for them. I simply stopped pitching

> When you specialize, you tend to more quickly build up a Rolodex full of great contacts—which leads to more article ideas and more work.
>
> —Kathy Sena, freelance writer

editors in the general-interest arena and began focusing on business and tech-nology. It probably took about three to four years to really take off."

Greengard's choice of specialties has allowed him to develop a lucrative niche and a stable of regular clients who come to him for business and technology assignments for consumer, trade, custom, and corporate publications. He's also improved his productivity, because stories take him less time to report and write. "By specializing," he says, "I've developed a body of knowledge, so I don't have to reinvent the wheel every time or research a topic I know nothing about—chances are I know something about it and I know enough to ask the right questions."

No matter what type of writing you do, you only have a limited number of hours in the day to create your work. Specializing can help you make the most of that time, set you apart from the thousands of other writers out there, and improve your bank balance. Consider how you can mine your own life experi-ence and background to create a lucrative niche of your own.

Kelly James-Enger of Downers Grove, Ill., writes about health, fitness, nutrition, and other subjects for more than 30 publications, including *Woman's Day*, *Shape*, and *Fit*. James-Enger, a former attorney, leads writing programs and workshops throughout Illinois. Her new book for freelance writers, tentatively titled *How to Create Your Own Writing Niche* (The Writer Books) will be available early in 2003.

LEARN FROM CRITICISM

Tips for sorting through what others say about your work

by Catherine Ryan Hyde

When my first short story was accepted, the editor praised the way I "depicted the characters with brief brush strokes." The same story had just been rejected by another magazine because of the "hollowness" of the characters.

Another of my stories was accepted with such enthusiasm that the editor thanked me for sending it to his magazine, citing such work as his reason for being an editor. He went on to nominate it for *Best American Short Stories*, the O. Henry Award, and the Pushcart Prize. Another editor who had read the same story rejected it, saying it did not hold the reader's interest and that it told rather than showed.

When my novel *Pay It Forward* came out, *Time* called my dialogue tinny and my characters stunted, while the *Chicago Tribune* called my dialogue believable and my characters well drawn.

It starts the day you join a critique group; it intensifies when you get an agent. Every time your agent sends out the work, the comments get more confusing. One editor says it's too this, the other says it's too that. In the face of such conflicting opinions, what do you keep and what do you throw away?

I often say that you must never, ever, under any circumstances, change your work just because someone tells you to—unless, of course, they're right.

The writers in the group usually laugh. Because, of course, knowing who is right is the problem to begin with. I can't sum up this thorny situation in a handful of words and make it all come clear. But I can offer a few ideas for consideration:

1. There is no "right" and "wrong" concerning art or creativity. Everyone's opinion is just that—an opinion. For example, I dislike the work of Ernest

Hemingway. If I had been a contemporary, I might have told Papa not to quit his day job. Would he have been wise to accept my opinion?

2. Author Georg Christoph Lichtenberg said, "A book is a mirror; if an ass peers into it, don't expect an apostle to peer out." This is not cited to characterize those who disagree with you, only to make the point that people bring their own experiences and perceptions along when they read your work.

3. Our egos tend to dictate that all the advice given us regarding our work is wrong. This is what I like to call the "you just don't get it" syndrome. Sometimes that same advice sounds a lot saner and more workable a few days later. In a critique situation, it helps to write down everything that's said and sleep on it.

4. Try saying nothing when faced with advice. When you begin to argue, you stop listening. Even if the person really is saying stupid things, arguing will only make him or her say more stupid things. Right or wrong, just listen.

5. Your reader is important. If your reader doesn't get it, you're not done. Then again, there will always be someone who doesn't get it. If it's one in 10, you can't please everybody. If it's nine in 10, it's time to listen.

6. Important as your readers are, their names do not go on the finished product. It's your own sensibility that you ultimately have to please. No matter how strongly someone disagrees with the direction of your work, it must remain your work, or you've lost everything worth having.

7. One of the biggest breakthroughs I ever had was when I learned to stop saying, "Is it good or is it bad?" and switched to, "What is the market for this? Who would like this kind of work?"

Dealing with the opinions of others is, in my estimation, the hardest part of being a writer. I don't know that anything I've said makes it all that much easier. But there's a question you can ask yourself at times such as these, and the answer will tell you everything you need to know. The catch is that you have to ask it on a deep level and answer honestly.

The question is, "Do I agree?"

When you can answer that question honestly, a great deal of initial confusion will fall away. When you base changes—or the refusal to make changes—on that answer, you will be honoring your reader, your work, and yourself.

Catherine Ryan Hyde of Cambria, Calif., is the award-winning author of *Pay It Forward* and *Walter's Purple Heart* (Simon & Schuster). This article is reprinted with permission from the author and *The SouthWest Sage* (July 2001), the newsletter of SouthWest Writers (www.southwestwriters.org).

10 TIPS FOR TOP-NOTCH INTERVIEWS

by Lynn Alfino

A national newspaper had given me the go-ahead for a profile, so armed with advice from fellow writers and some tidbits garnered from a shelf full of writing books, I set out for my first interview. During the first minutes of introductions and small talk, I feigned confidence and an old-pro attitude, but my voice raised an octave. Both the interviewee and I were nervous, but once we realized we were in this soup together, we relaxed and had a wonderful interview. Over time, I have come to love interviewing, and you can, too. Being prepared can help bolster your ability to ask relevant questions, develop camaraderie with your subjects, and coax out quotes with aplomb. The following 10 tips, compiled from my experiences and those of my writer colleagues, will help you conduct interviews that will make your articles shine.

1. Remember the reason for the interview. I once interviewed a Catholic nun who was running a busy literary center. Apart from getting information on the business endeavor, I wanted to know how she had adjusted to an enterprise so different from her vocation of working in a community of handicapped people. Your story will be much better if you can find out what makes your subject tick. Remember when you frame your questions to focus not only on the facts but also on the subject's motivations and inspirations. The interview may take longer but the result will be worth it.

Never presume that you are taking up your subject's valuable time. Positive publicity is usually welcome, so think of the interview as being mutually beneficial. Amy D. Shojai, author of numerous books on pet care, including *The First Aid Companion for Dogs and Cats*, often interviews authors, veterinarians, researchers, and animal behaviorists, all of whom welcome the publicity. Joyce Berridge, nonfiction writer and co-owner of *The Writer's BBS* (see Web site at www.writersbbs.com), frequently interviews home-based rural business owners who are eager to be considered unique and included in her articles and books.

2. Research your subject and use that knowledge. Author Bill Warner, whose articles on model aviation have appeared in publications in the United States, England, and France, does extensive research before interviews. He refers to related newspaper and magazine articles, press kits, and the person's Web site, if any. He also talks to people who may know the potential interviewee.

All of this can help in formulating a list of questions you want to ask. The person may be an expert from whom you need facts, statistics, or an authoritative opinion. Knowing something about the subjects—their work, talent, or whatever makes them special in your eyes—can open doors to a great interview. People love talking about themselves, and your subject will share more if you show you care enough to do advance research.

3. Don't be afraid to send a few questions in advance. I once interviewed a famous author who was media-shy. He had been burned by being misquoted in another interview and felt he had been depicted unfairly. By faxing him a short list of three to five questions, showing him the general direction I was heading with my article, I eased his fears and got my interview. Doing this can give your subjects a chance to consider a few responses in advance and reduce some of their own nervousness. Shojai, who interviews almost exclusively by phone, says that she doesn't mind the subject knowing questions in advance, because the answers are usually more usable when the subject is "calm, collected, and prepared."

Choose open-ended questions that require some thought in answering. A question that can be answered with a simple "yes" or "no" is going to make for a very short and dull interview.

E-mailed interviews are gaining in popularity. Yasmine Galenorn, author of numerous metaphysical books, including *Embracing the Moon*, finds that e-mailed answers allow for more detail, rather than just a few short quips. She feels e-mail allows the person "to think about what the questions mean to them and to elaborate on things they otherwise might gloss over when they are fumbling for quick answers." If time is an issue and you are having difficulties reaching the person for a phone interview, e-mail may be the answer for you.

4. Interview with your readers in mind. Having been trained in religious history, I began my own writing career in the Christian press, doing mainly historical and travel pieces and interviewing leading religious figures. When I decided to expand my markets to include secular publications, the learning curve was steep. My audience changed, and it was important to find out who my readers were so I could interview with questions of interest to them. Are you writing for a popular women's magazine? A science bimonthly? A children's newsletter? Vocabulary, slant, and tone will differ in each case, and the best way to prepare is to read past issues of the magazines you intend to write for.

Consider the publication's demographics when formulating and asking questions. To whom are the advertisements geared? A trade or specialty periodical may be more technical, while a consumer magazine may be a lighter read and more service-oriented. Knowing your market will help you ask the kinds of questions your readers want answered. And don't be afraid to ask your subjects for clarification if their answers are too technical, vague, or jargon-filled.

5. Develop an easy rapport with your subject. Dress comfortably and professionally, so you feel at ease. If you're tense because you just noticed a button missing, it can throw off the entire interview. If you are well-groomed, the interviewee will take you more seriously. Also, an unkempt appearance can be distracting. The attention should be on the interviewee, not on you.

Remember, you are both human and likely to be somewhat nervous. A warm greeting and some light conversation the first few minutes allows everyone to take a few deep breaths before getting down to business. Giving your undivided attention and positive feedback to their responses will go a long way toward getting the person to loosen up. Your goal is to get them to talk, so don't hog center stage. If you help them feel comfortable enough to be themselves in your presence, your problem won't be getting them to open up, but rather, getting them to stop!

6. Be ready to wing it and deviate from your initial questions. There is a poetry to interviewing that can only be learned by doing it. Sometimes, an interview will change direction as a result of something your subject says. I once interviewed a woman who had recently lost her close friend and had taken over that friend's business. She shared heartfelt emotions about the extensive process of learning how to run a business in the face of grief. This was unexpected, but turned out to be the highlight of my article. Gems like these could have been missed if I had ignored her wistful sighs or allusions to sorrow. If you clue in to what is being said, you will learn to pick up on body language that bespeaks powerful stories untold.

Balancing spontaneity with the necessary questions you simply must ask can be a gamble. You will need to trust yourself to wander into uncharted territory. Leaving room for spontaneity can mean the difference between lifeless facts and information borne out of human experience.

Spontaneity can, however, also lead to an interview spinning out of control, where the interviewee's own agenda snakes its way into the interview. The person may insist on getting colleagues' names in print, expect to tell you how and what to write, or insist on discussing topics outside your scope. While you want to be courteous and not cut the person off, it is important that you swing the discussion back to the subject at hand. Remember, you are the writer.

THE KLUTZ'S GUIDE TO TAPE RECORDING INTERVIEWS

by John Brady

Maybe it's one of those left brain/right brain things, but most writers and editors of my acquaintance are a bit klutzy when handling a tape recorder. The scary "dog ate my tape recorder" stories that surround this checklist are all too familiar; in fact, they barely scratch the surface of the topic. After conducting hundreds of interviews, I've concluded that there's an inverse relationship between reporting/writing skills and mechanical know-how. Brady's Theorem: The greater the writer, the less likely that person can reset the time on a VCR, never mind handle the intricacies of a tape recorder.

Here are some tips to ease the way as you make your own forays into the reporting wars, tape recorder in hand.

Get permission. Never assume the subject is going to agree to being recorded. Ask in advance. This is important for several reasons. One, it is unethical (and illegal in many states) to make secret recordings—easily done on the phone, for instance. Two, a tape recording gives an editor peace of mind about the accuracy of quotes used in the story, making it unlikely a source will holler, "I was misquoted!" If a subject balks at the idea of recording an interview, point out that you are doing so in order to be 100 percent accurate. Also point out that taping the interview will save time for the subject, as you won't be slowing her or him down to take notes. And finally, reassure the subject that you are using the tape recorder as a notebook, and no one is going to hear the recording except yourself. If necessary, offer to make a copy of the tape for the subject's file.

Have a backup plan. Always bring note-taking equipment on the job. Sometimes, even after a subject has agreed to the use of a tape recorder, he or she will change field. "Please turn that thing off," a source—who knew I would be taping—once told me after an interview was under way. "I'm just too self-conscious talking into a machine." Of course, I had no choice but to turn off the recorder and take notes as best I could. Later, driving away from the interview, I turned the recorder on in my car and "acted out" the interview verbally, reconstructing as much as I could while memory was fresh. This gave me enough to write my story.

Bring a spare everything. Create an "interviewer's kit" in a camera bag or small piece of luggage (gym bags are excellent). In it, include all of the things you need to record an interview, plus spare parts—extra tapes, batteries (with battery tester), note-taking materials and, yes, a second tape recorder. This way, you always have a safety net when something fails.

Test before you talk. At the start of the interview, always test your equipment. Include the source in this process so that you have a vocal sound check. "This is Joe Bulldog, talking with Mister Hot Source on May 15 in Boston," you might say into the microphone. Then ask Mr. Source to say something, and then play it back for review before pushing on with the interview.

Choose the right extras. Recorders come in all sizes and price ranges. Choose one that is affordable and manageable for you, but try to include two extras that are interviewer-friendly—automatic reverse, so that the tape doesn't have to be turned manually when it reaches the end of side one; and an external microphone that can be used to override the condenser mike built into most recorders today. Condenser microphones work nicely in 75 percent of interviews; but when there is background noise, you need to plug in a "hand-held" mike (actually they are tiny and usually snaked across, say, the table of a crowded restaurant) to capture the source's voice without the intrusion of crowd or workplace noise.

Don't forget to write. Take notes, even though the tape recorder is getting all the quotes. Start each side of each cassette at zero on your tabulator, and keep a running index to the content as the interview moves along. This will take a lot of the chore work out of reporting, and allow you to revisit good quotes or complicated stories. Your notes should also include gestures, mannerisms, and details that enable you to create a scene for readers.

Copy your copy. It's a good idea to make a duplicate copy of your tapes before you start replaying them to take notes. Rewinding and replaying a tape can create wear, and even breakage. If a tape has sensitive information, it's even more important to make a duplicate for safekeeping.

Don't spindle or reuse. Taped interviews should be kept on file for as long as necessary to support a story. Magazine editors often ask that they be submitted with a story for fact-checking and accuracy. Someone may claim they have been misquoted years after a story has run, and when this occurs the editor will want to revisit the taped archives. In short, don't toss or record over the evidence.

Telephone tactics. Most interviews are conducted by phone today, and most of the previous tips apply, but there are a few extra considerations. Foremost, turn off call-waiting before you dial a source. Be sure to advise the subject that you are recording the interview, and I recommend taking notes on a keyboard for speed of delivery. A wise investment for the frequent caller is a headset (consisting of earphones and a microphone) to clear the hands for this task.

Leave the door open. At the end of the interview, be sure to get complete information on your source—e-mail address, cell phone, home phone (to be used in emergency only), travel plans, and anything else that will allow you to get in touch on short notice. Ask the subject if it's OK to get back for some follow-up, just in case something is missing—and that may include a listenable recording. Thus, if you have an afterthought, or—horrors—the dog has chewed up your tape or something has gone wrong mechanically, you can return for another round and stay on deadline with your story.

John Brady of Newburyport, Mass., teaches journalism at Boston University. He is the author of several books, including *The Craft of Interviewing* (Vintage Books).

ARE YOU READY TO TAKE THE PLUNGE?

The pleasures and perils of freelancing full time

by Moira Allen

Rare is the writer who hasn't dreamed of turning a love of writing into a full-time career. At the same time, we've all heard how difficult it is to "make it" as a self-employed writer. But does freelancing have to mean living in a garret on a diet of canned beans? The truth is that many writers have become success-ful—but the freelancing life certainly isn't for everyone. Before you decide to "take the plunge," take a look at some of the benefits and drawbacks of this coveted career.

I interviewed 20 full-time freelance writers whose writing brings in at least 50 percent of their total household income. While several were earning barely enough to live on, the majority reported annual incomes of $50,000 or more, and two earned more than $100,000. All had much to share about the advantages and disadvantages of a freelancing career, along with strategies for success.

You're the boss

Benefit: As a freelance writer, you can choose to write about what interests you. No boss is standing over your shoulder, assigning boring projects, or interfering with your creativity. Karen Briggs enjoys "the luxury of choosing the projects that most interest me," while Marc Tyler Nobleman relishes "the free-dom to do what I want, when I want it, creatively and otherwise." Being your own boss also means having the freedom to set your own schedule and to choose your clients.

Drawback: Financial insecurity. Being your own boss also means that you're responsible for your own paycheck—and a host of expenses you did not have to think about as an employee. Freelancing income is notoriously irregular. "Some months are fat, others are lean," says Carol Turk, who has freelanced for more than 13 years as a medical writer and is the author of more than 40 nonfiction books. Unfortunately, bills are due on a much more regular basis; mortgage companies don't want to hear that you're still waiting for your next royalty check. To freelance effectively, therefore, you need to be able to budget and to put aside income from the "fat" periods to cover the leaner times.

Solution: To ensure a relatively steady flow of income, it's important to continually market yourself. Don't stop sending out queries just because you have a number of assignments. You could find yourself with no work (or income) coming in. Most respondents spent nearly 20 percent of their time on marketing—looking for new markets, sending out queries, staying in touch with clients. Most respondents also recommend accepting any reasonable assignment, particularly if it might lead to more profitable work.

Drawback: Lack of benefits. Another disadvantage to self-employment is the lack of benefits: Freelancers have no employer-paid health plans, vacation or sick days, paid holidays, or retirement plans. The lack of health benefits was a particular concern to most of the writers interviewed; most paid for their health policies out-of-pocket and "up the snout," as editor and proofreader A.J. Sobczak puts it. Briggs, a Canadian, is covered by that nation's health benefits but has no dental insurance, and reports that she hasn't seen a dentist in more than three years. Most of the respondents report having little or no retirement savings. "It's pathetic, I know," says magazine writer Paula Hendrickson, "but when every penny goes to pay bills, it's not like I have an extra $2,000 sitting around every year."

Solution: Some writers obtain health insurance through professional organizations such as the National Writers Union or the Society of Children's Book Writers and Illustrators. One obtained group coverage through her local chamber of commerce. For retirement, respondents recommend regularly setting aside a percentage of your income to establish IRAs or Keoghs, noting that these also provide tax benefits.

Freelancing can offer an opportunity to do what most people only dream of— the chance to earn a living by doing what you love!

Working at home

Benefit: Most writers consider the ability to work at home to be one of the most positive aspects of freelancing. You can get up when you want, work wherever you're comfortable and wear what you like.

Working at home also means having more time to spend with your family. "I love being with my children every day," says Shirley Kawa-Jump, who divides her time between writing freelance articles and marketing materials. "I see them off to school, go on the field trips, bake the cookies, read them stories at night." Briggs has been able to save money by keeping her four horses on her property instead of at a boarding stable. "This is a wonderful luxury, even if it means a lot of time spent with a pitchfork in my hand," says Briggs.

Drawback: Isolation. Working at home, however, can also mean working alone. If you're used to lunches with coworkers, chatting around the water cooler, or regular face-to-face meetings with clients and customers, you may find the writing life rather lonely. "When the FedEx guy shows up, it's an event!" says Briggs. Peter Vogt, who writes primarily for electronic markets, agrees: "You know you're lonely when you walk to the gas station just to talk to someone."

Solution: Writers have found many ways to overcome this isolation. Some keep up "virtual" connections and stay in touch with friends and other writers by e-mail. Or they join online critique and discussion groups. "I rely heavily on e-mail for human contact and work-related discussions and gossip," says Briggs. Other writers make a special effort to get out of the house and meet colleagues for breakfast or lunch, or they keep in touch by phone. "I don't have any rules about not chatting with friends during working hours," says magazine writer Barbara Stahura. "When I get a little twitchy from lack of face time, I go out to lunch or for an evening with friends." Several writers recommend taking a class at a community college, signing up for exercise classes at a gym, or taking one's writing to a local coffeehouse.

Patricia Fry, author of 11 books and articles for more than 160 magazines, has solved the isolation problem by incorporating human interaction into her work. "I do a lot of interviews, for example, and I work with an occasional client. I speak publicly to promote my book. I belong to writers/publishers groups and attend book fairs and other events. I also get out and do some volunteering locally. And I have the company of four lovely cats."

Variety, flexibility, and self-esteem

Benefit: "It simply would not be possible to write for such a wide variety of audiences in a salaried job," notes Suzan St. Maur, who divides her time between business and corporate clients and writing nonfiction books. "It is this variety that keeps me interested, perky, and inspired." Stahura reports that her magazine topics range from spirituality to technology, including personal essays, radio essays, and poetry. "I get to talk with interesting people I'd never otherwise have the opportunity to meet . . . [and] to indulge my curiosity about a wide variety of subjects and get paid for it." Sobczak's writing ranges from speculative fiction to nonfiction coverage of a variety of social topics (including minority relations, ethics, business law, and history), as well as "nongenre works centered on relationships and modern means of communication." Lawrence Schimel, who left New York City to pursue his writing career in Spain, publishes fiction and poetry and edits a variety of fiction anthologies.

A writing career is psychologically rewarding as well. "Any success is sweeter because it is based solely on me expressing myself," says Nobleman, who divides his time between magazine articles, nonfiction books, and cartoons.

Briggs feels that writing puts her in "control of her destiny." Another magazine writer, Amanda Vogel, enjoys "the sense of accomplishment I feel when I complete an article or score a plum assignment—and the opportunity to constantly set and achieve new goals."

Drawback: Your job is now "9-to-forever." That sense of accomplishment often comes with a price: When one's home is one's office, it can be very difficult to "leave" the office. "There is almost no line at all between my business and home life," says Turk. "I take a weekend day off very reluctantly. I constantly check e-mail after hours and on weekends and work on projects until late in the evening, on weekends and vacations."

While some writers (notably those who were single) don't consider this a problem, those with families note that work often interferes with family time. Kawa-Jump notes that in her case, family was actually the cause of her erratic work hours: "With a 3-year-old, I work around his schedule, which means lots of early mornings, late nights, and working weekends. Clients and interviews happen during the day, so there really is no time when I am not working."

The temptation to take on more work than you can handle (or handle on a "normal" work schedule) can be hard to resist, especially when income is tight and every new assignment can mean a much-needed check.

Solution: Experienced freelancers advise that you choose your assignments carefully. A $500 article offers a much better payoff for your time than five $100 articles. Another suggestion is to learn to say no, especially when editors make unreasonable demands. One writer, for example, was asked to proof her book-manuscript galleys over the Christmas break. Yet another is to learn to recognize, and turn down, "bad" clients—clients who don't know what they want, or keep changing their minds, or ask for endless revisions.

Another solution is to take physical steps to "close the office door" at the end of the day. One way to do this is to set an alarm clock for a particular time—for example, 5 p.m. When the alarm rings, your workday is over. Granted, there will always be times when an important assignment requires "overtime," but this should be the exception rather than the rule. Another approach is to change into "work clothes" during the day, and back into "casual clothes" at night. A simple change of wardrobe can mean a change of attitude as well. Finally, if you find it hard to resist the temptation to check e-mail, actually turn your computer off at the end of your workday.

What it takes to succeed

If you want to be a successful freelancer, forget the 40-hour work week. Most respondents work at least 45 to 55 hours per week, and nearly a third work more than 60 hours. In addition, the majority of those hours (generally as much as 80 percent) were spent *writing*, rather than in other tasks such as marketing or bookkeeping. Respondents offer these additional tips for success:

Don't quit your day job right away. Rather than plunging directly into full-time freelancing, start by freelancing in your spare time, while keeping your regular job. "It may initially mean late nights, weekend work, and missing some social engagements," says Nobleman. It also means, however, building up a client list, building skills and work habits, and determining whether this really is viable and something you want to do full time. In addition, keeping your day job will help you build a financial reserve. Medical writer Turk recommends having at least six months'—but preferably a year's—income stashed away before you "make the break."

Diversify. Several writers recommend finding more than one type of market area. "I've found diversification instrumental in growing my business—I've written for Web sites, corporations, hospitals, magazines, newspapers," says Amy Sutton, who has been freelancing for just under a year. "Don't limit yourself by saying 'I only write for magazines.'" Schimel agrees. "Some years I make scads of money from writing poems, and other years it's the anthologies, and other years it's my own story collections. I think it's exactly that versatility that lets me be a full-time freelancer, because whenever one of the genres bottoms out or if my muse in a particular area dries up (last year it was fiction), I can still make a living writing in other arenas."

DO YOU HAVE WHAT IT TAKES?

Strong writing skills aren't enough to ensure a successful career as a full-time freelancer. Here are some of the qualities other freelancers consider vital to success:

- Persistence and perseverance
- Willingness to work incredibly long hours
- Tenacity to keep going in the face of difficulties
- Commitment
- Willingness to take risks
- Ability to work alone
- Networking skills
- Self-discipline
- Patience
- Faith in oneself
- Resourcefulness
- Flexibility
- Self-motivation
- Determination
- Organizational ability
- Strong work ethic
- Focus
- Long-term view

Specialize. Even as you diversify into different market areas, it may be a good idea to pick a subject specialty. Pick an area in which you have particular expertise, so that you can sell editors on your credentials as well as your writing ability. "You're more appealing to editors if you know what you're writing about," says Vogt, a career counselor who writes about career development issues. "Figure out what you'd like to write about, and then find markets for it."

Work hard. "Be prepared to work harder at this than any other job," says Kawa-Jump. Again, most respondents report working far more than 40 hours a week. Keep in mind that as a freelance writer, you also have to handle all the administrative tasks that would normally be handled by "other departments" in a corporate office, including marketing, bookkeeping, and billing. In the office, you get paid "even when you're having a nonproductive day," Sobczak points out; as a freelancer, if you're not working, you're not earning.

Learn to market. In the corporate office, work lands on your desk whether you want it or not (and often, you don't!). The freelance life is just the opposite; work doesn't come to you unless you go out and find it. This means learning how to write effective queries, how to conduct good market research and find opportunities, how to negotiate contracts and payments, and how to follow up.

Some writers make a commitment to send out a specific number of queries per week—five, 10, even 20. "I think many freelancers underestimate the time and effort involved with marketing themselves," says Briggs. "They don't feel comfortable *selling* their work, but they need to come to grips with the fact that editors aren't going to come swarming to their door, begging them to write for them for large sums of money!"

Be professional. "Your reputation is everything," says W. Thomas Smith Jr., who specializes in everything from military science to Southern culture and history, and also teaches a senior-level course in magazine writing at the University of South Carolina's College of Journalism and Mass Communications. "Never lie or misrepresent anything to an editor. Never make excuses about anything. Meet your deadlines. Don't be afraid to send flowers and thoughtful notes to an editor, but very sparingly, and never in a fawning, kiss-up manner. It's all about commitment." Good writing may bring in your first assignment; qualities like reliability and responsiveness are what keep editors coming back.

Accept rejection. Rejection is an inevitable part of the writing life. "Don't get discouraged by rejections; learn from them," says magazine writer Vogel. "Let the negatives roll off," Smith agrees. Keep in mind that rejection often has nothing to do with the quality of your work; editors can accept only a limited number of articles, which means even very good work must often be turned away.

Have faith in yourself. If you don't believe in your writing ability, you'll have a tough time trying to "sell" yourself to others. It's important to keep a realistic perspective: Success in the writing business rarely happens overnight. "Work diligently; be patient," says Stahura. "If you're following your heart, success will come." Smith agrees: "Be persistent. Never quit, because that's when you lose." Successful freelancers are those who stay with it in spite of the rejections and the setbacks.

Success can also take time. Though half the respondents became self-supporting in less than one year, nearly a third found that it took two to five years to become fully independent.

Follow your heart! "Don't become a full-time freelancer unless it is a compulsion," says Fred Bortz, who left a 25-year career as a physicist in 1996 to pursue a career in writing. He notes that freelancing is a perilous venture; it isn't for the easily discouraged. But if writing is your joy and your passion, freelancing can offer an opportunity to do what most people only dream of—the chance to earn a living by doing what you love!

Moira Allen of Chesapeake, Va., is a freelance writer and editor of Writing-World.com. Her latest book is *The Writer's Guide to Queries, Pitches & Proposals* (Allworth Press).

TEST YOUR FREELANCE POTENTIAL

The following checklist can help you determine whether you're ready to freelance full time:

I write more than five hours per week, every week.
• Yes. You have discipline. It's tough to find five hours a week for writing when working a day job. You've already passed one of the biggest hurdles writers face.
• No. If you're not spending a significant amount of time writing now, you can't be sure you'll be happy doing this full time. Build up a solid writing habit, so that you'll have the discipline and practice you need for a career.

I submit at least one new query or article per week.
• Yes. You have a high output. Clearly, you don't spend those five hours a week (or whatever) repolishing old material, or stuffing it in a drawer. You're already in the marketplace.
• No. Every two weeks? Every month? Even if you're not querying or producing an article a week, be sure that you're doing so on a regular basis.

[cont.]

[sidebar cont.]

More than 50 percent of my queries and/or articles are accepted.
• Yes. You know how to target markets effectively, and you obviously write well enough to impress the majority of the editors to whom you submit.
• No. You may need to focus either on better marketing techniques (matching the right ideas to the right markets) or on the content of your queries themselves. If you're getting consistently rejected, consider taking an online writing course to help you focus your queries.

More than 50 percent of my markets pay more than $100 per article.
• Yes. You've found the guts to break out of the low-paying "ghetto." You have confidence that your work is worth more.
• No. Sticking with low-paying markets can be an indication of low self-esteem: You may fear that "better" markets won't consider your work. Keep in mind that as a full-time freelancer, your time is precious: Do you want to spend five hours writing an article that pays $100 or $500?

My work has been accepted regularly by at least one market.
• Yes. You have a steady source of income.
• No. You may not be following up on your successes. Whenever an editor accepts something of yours, be sure to go back with new ideas. Soon, the editor will consider you a "regular" contributor, which can mean regular assignments and better pay.

I have at least one "regular" market that contacts me with assignments.
• Yes. You must be reliable and dependable. You meet deadlines and produce quality work. Otherwise, editors wouldn't come to you with ideas.
• No. See previous question.

I am familiar with the practices and terminology of the publishing marketplace (e.g., I know what FNASR and SASE mean and I know how to format a manuscript).
• Yes. You know the basics, and won't have to waste precious time "gearing up."
• No. If you don't know the basics, you won't be able to compete. Spend some time learning the terminology and practices of a professional.

I know how to cope with rejection.
• Yes. You won't be daunted by the inevitable disappointments of this type of career.

[cont.]

[sidebar cont.]

• No. This probably means that you aren't sending out much material yet. Start submitting more work—and learn to accept rejection as "part of the business" rather than taking it as a personal failure.

I earned more than $5,000 from writing activities last year.
• Yes. It won't keep a roof over your head, but it's more than many free-lancers ever make in a year. It's one of those invisible lines: If you know how to earn this much, you know how to earn more. Probably the only thing holding you back is lack of time.
• No. Don't be discouraged; instead, consider setting this as a goal for your next year's writing income—and make a plan for meeting that goal.

I currently report freelance writing income and expenses for tax purposes and know how to maintain proper business and tax records.
• Yes. You know that "writing" isn't just putting words on a page. It's also a matter of records, accounting, and good business practices.
• No. Even if you're not earning sufficient writing income to report on your taxes, it's a good idea to learn how to keep the proper records; you'll need this skill later.

I keep a household budget.
• Yes. You already have an idea of what it will take to support your household—which means you know how close you are to being able to go full time.
• No. If you don't know how much you spend now, you won't know how much you'll need to earn as a writer—or how you might be able to econo-mize while getting started. Start tracking your expenses—even the small-est, like parking and cups of coffee. The results may surprise you!

If you answered yes to only a few of these questions, it's a pretty good indication that you need to build up more of a foundation for your writing career before attempting to rely on it as your only source of income.

—*Moira Allen*

THE DREADED SYNOPSIS

Do it right and help sell your book

by Moira Allen

Sooner or later, you will need to provide a synopsis of your novel to an editor or agent. In some cases, you'll be expected to send it with your initial query; in others, you'll be asked to send it only on request. Few things terrify the first-time novelist (or even experienced novelists) so much as the demand for "the dreaded synopsis." Condensing the salient points of a 100,000-word novel into a five- to 10-page summary is no easy task. But it can be done. The first step is to understand the purpose of the synopsis. While it is a selling tool for your novel, it is not a sales pitch (like the overview in your query letter).

The primary goal of your synopsis is to demonstrate that your story is coherent, logical, well thought out, and well organized. It should show that your characters act and interact in a realistic, consistent fashion; that the plot unfolds logically and at an appropriate pace; that plot twists don't seem contrived or coincidental; that the story will hold the reader's attention from beginning to end; and that the ending (the "resolution") is believable and satisfying.

While some publishers still ask for a chapter-by-chapter synopsis, most now prefer a "narrative" synopsis that follows the flow of the story as a whole. This format lets you focus on the key points of the story, without having to "say something" about each individual chapter. It also lets you focus on the primary plot and major characters, without confusing the issue with subplots and secondary characters.

Synopsis format

A synopsis should generally be formatted like a regular manuscript. Some writers double-space; some single-space. Some use a cover page that includes the book title, author's name (or pen name), author's contact information, and the word count of the book as a whole. Others include this information on the first page of the synopsis itself, as with an article or story.

How long should it be? If the agent or publisher offers no guidelines on maximum length, a good rule is to allow one page of synopsis per 10,000 words of novel—up to a maximum of 10 pages. Shorter is better; if you can say it in five pages, don't stretch it to 10.

A synopsis is written in the present tense: "Andrea returns to her home town for the holidays, to find . . ." Try to avoid long blocks of text; break it up into shorter paragraphs.

Put character names in caps or boldface the first time they appear. Try to limit the number of characters you actually name in your synopsis; too many names become confusing. (Thus, instead of saying, "Andrea shares her concerns with her best friend, Ginny," it would be better to leave the friend unnamed unless she plays a major role in the action.)

Content

What should your synopsis cover? What should you leave out? If you ask 10 different writers this question, you're likely to get 10 different answers. See the next article for what one novelist has to say about "the basics" of a synopsis.

Response times for publishers and agents are notoriously slow, especially if your work is unsolicited. Agents may take from two to four months to respond; publishers may take between six months and a year.

The proposal package

Once you've written a synopsis for your novel, you've accomplished the most difficult—and most important—part of the proposal process. You may have to edit that synopsis for different publishers, but you have the basics.

The final thing that most publishers and agents will request from you is "three sample chapters." These must be *the first three chapters of your book*—not three chapters that you choose at random. Need I say, therefore, that it is in your best interest to polish those three chapters to the best of your ability? Review them. Edit them. Run them by a critique group. Ask someone to help you proofread them. Make sure they're the best example of your work you could possibly send. Format them according to basic manuscript format principles—indented paragraphs, ample margins, double-spaced, no extra spaces between paragraphs, numbered pages, etc. (If you have any doubts about proper format, see my article "A Quick Guide to Manuscript Format" by accessing www.writing-world.com/basics/manuscript.html.)

Do not send any of the following items with your proposal:

- A personal (or publicity) photo
- An expanded bio, resume, or curriculum vitae (in some cases, it might be appropriate to include a list of relevant publications)
- Samples of other published (or unpublished) writings
- Letters of reference or recommendation

Now it's time to assemble your package. Be sure that you include a self-addressed, stamped envelope (SASE). If you would like confirmation that an editor or agent received your query or proposal, include a self-addressed, stamped postcard for an immediate response. Just type a line on the back that reads something like:

> Dear Author,
> We received your manuscript, (title), on (date).
> We hope to be able to respond to your manuscript query by (date).
> (Signed)

The second line is optional, but useful if you'd like an estimate of when you can expect to hear from the editor or agent.

If you have a professional business card, add one of those as well, as it will make it easier for the recipient to keep track of your contact information.

If your total proposal is more than 20 pages, sandwich it between two 8½-by-11-inch pieces of cardboard (e.g., cardboard from the back of a notepad), and secure it with a rubber band. This will prevent the pages from being damaged during shipping. Choose a sturdy manila or Tyvek envelope that will hold your proposal snugly. (Too large an envelope will allow your proposal to slide around and become battered; too small an envelope will cause it to bend and crimp the pages.) If your proposal is too large for an envelope, use a thin stationery box instead.

After you've assembled your package (but before you seal it), weigh it. If it weighs less than a pound, you might wish to include a SASE of sufficient size and postage to allow the return of your entire proposal. If, however, the proposal weighs more than a pound, it's better to include a letter-size SASE for a response only, and allow the editor or agent to discard the proposal itself (assuming, of course, that it isn't wanted!).

Now that your proposal is out the door, there is one more thing for you to do: *wait*. Response times for publishers and agents are notoriously slow, especially if your work is unsolicited. Agents may take from two to four months to respond; publishers may take between six months and a year. (Electronic publishers tend to respond more quickly—usually within less than two months.) Check the response times listed in the publisher's (or agent's) guidelines, and assume that in many cases, these may be underestimates.

If the specified response time has elapsed and you've heard nothing, follow up with a polite letter or e-mail inquiring about the status of your proposal. Wait two weeks, then follow up again. If you still receive no reply, you may wish to send a final letter withdrawing your proposal from consideration (it's important to do this to avoid confusion or accusations of "simultaneous submission"), and send it to the next agent or editor on your list. Don't be surprised if you have to repeat this several times.

The key at this point is persistence. Your goal is to find an editor or agent who will believe in your book as much as you do. That person may not be the first on your list, or even the 15th or the 20th. But if you're willing to persevere in the belief that such an editor or agent is out there, you're a thousand times more likely to achieve publication than the writer who despairs after the first or second rejection.

Moira Allen of Chesapeake, Va., is a freelance writer and editor of Writing-World.com. Her latest book is *The Writer's Guide to Queries, Pitches & Proposals* (Allworth Press). This article is excerpted from that book, with permission of the author and Allworth Press.

THE BASIC ELEMENTS OF A SYNOPSIS

by Rebecca Vinyard

1. The setup. This is the starting point of your story: premise, location, time frame, and main characters' backgrounds. Just as you want to hook your readers with the first page of your book, you also want to hook the editor on the first page of your synopsis. The sooner you can establish your setup, the better. Choose your words with care to present the background information in a concise and entertaining way.

2. Why? I'm listing this second, but this is something you should consider throughout your synopsis: If you pose a question, answer it. A synopsis is not the time to tease a reader. Suppose your story begins with the heroine quitting her job. You should explain why she quit it. Reactions, decisions . . . whatever your character does within the framework of your synopsis, the reasons behind the actions must be clear.

For example, you can't just say, "Something happens to make the heroine change her mind." Instead, you need to explain what that something is and why it made her change her mind. Clarity, clarity—make that your synopsis mantra.

3. Characterization. This includes background, personality, occupation—everything that makes up your character. It is not, however, a physical description of your hero and heroine. Usually, the less said about that the better, unless the character's physique affects her/him emotionally. Example: She's extremely short and feels self-conscious about it.

Bear in mind that you want the reader of your synopsis to feel a connection with your characters. Focus on the emotional elements: "a deeply religious woman," "a savvy businesswoman," "an introverted professor," "an agitated accountant." Phrases like these can be your friends because they give emotional and background information in just a few words.

You should name only characters that play major roles in your story. Often, writers feel the need to mention secondary characters (maybe because they fall in love with them). Unless those characters' actions affect the main plot throughout the story, you shouldn't include them, because then you'll need to provide characterization and background for them as well (and in the process, inflate your synopsis!). If a necessary reference pops up once or twice, you can simply say something like "her best friend," "his sister," etc.

4. Plot points. These occur whenever your story departs from all that has gone before. Your character is forced to make a decision, or something unexpected and outside the experience of the character occurs. You should include *all* the major plot points in your synopsis. Do not, however, include plot points for subplots. If it has nothing to do with the main plot, forget it. Always concentrate on theme.

5. Conflict. Yes, I know. This one is another workshop. Quick conflict lesson: Internal conflict comes from within the character; e.g., she has poor self-esteem. External conflict comes from without the character; e.g., a villain is blackmailing the hero.

For the purpose of synopsis writing, you need to present your conflict clearly. Which brings us back to the why element again: Why is your heroine afraid of dogs? This is important if she refuses to go to the hero's house because he has a Doberman named Rex lurking about. Or perhaps your heroine refuses to go because she fears involvement, and she uses the dog as an excuse. Why does she fear involvement? By the same token, how does your hero feel about being rejected like this? Is she rejecting Rex or him? Perhaps rejection makes him defensive because he seeks to be accepted. He resolves never to have anything to do with her again.

In other words, conflicts are the obstacles the main characters must overcome to achieve their goals. In a romance, the main goal is for the hero and heroine to fall in love and stay together. In a science-fiction story, maybe the goal is to overthrow an evil corporation dominating the planet. Whatever the goal, it can't be easy to achieve, or else you have no story. We need to know there's a problem and why this is a problem.

6. Emotion. This element is of utmost concern for romance writers, because for romance the magic is in the emotion, although I feel any synopsis should include it. Actions cause reactions. He kisses her . . . how does she feel about it? How does he feel? Whenever you have the chance to put emotion into your synopsis, do it. It makes the difference between a dull summary and a lively recounting of your story.

7. Action. Action drives most stories and is probably the story element used the most. In your synopsis, however, you should only include those actions that have consequences. If your heroine takes a trip to the store for some eggs, don't include that unless something happens to her along the way. This is fairly obvious, I know. But as a contest judge, I've read many synopses that included unnecessary action descriptions. If in doubt, leave it out.

8. Dialogue. Two schools of thought here. Some folks say you should never include dialogue in a synopsis. Some feel a sprinkling of it here and there helps. My personal preference is the latter. If a specific line has more impact than a description of the same conversation, why not use it? I wouldn't advise, however, more than a few lines of dialogue. Don't go crazy and start quoting all over the place.

9. Black moment. This is the moment when your characters realize that all is lost, when it appears they will never reach their goals and when the odds seem to be on the opposing forces' side. In a romance, perhaps it's a conflict so overwhelming that it would appear the hero and heroine will never be together. Whatever the genre, this moment of reckoning should not only be in your story but also in your synopsis.

10. Climax. Your story has been thundering along to this point. Everything that has gone before should lead up to it. Whether it's the bad guy getting what's coming to him, the hero finally getting over his lack of self-esteem, or the heroine riding to the rescue, this is the moment when it all happens. Naturally, this element must also be included in your synopsis.

11. Resolution. All your loose ends get tied up here. Any questions posed in your synopsis should be answered by the time you reach this point. And yes, as we all know, the goal is for the hero and heroine to live happily ever after. Or not, depending on your genre. Whatever the case, include the resolution to your story. This is not the time to play "guess the ending"!

12. The essential basics. The number-one essential is to write your synopsis in present tense. Think of it as telling a friend about your book. Avoid passive voice. You want those words to flow evenly and keep the reader involved. Perhaps you've heard the saying that a writer's best work should be the query letter and synopsis. That puts the pressure on, doesn't it? Well, I'm not sure it's true; a better saying might be that a writer's *clearest* work should be the query and synopsis. Focus on the main story and avoid extraneous information.

13. Formatting. From my experience, most houses prefer a double-spaced format. There are exceptions, however, so *check the publisher's submission guidelines.* Or contest guidelines, whichever is the case. The majority of publishers prefer that you give your contact information and word count on the upper left corner of the first page. On subsequent pages, include the title, your last name, and the page number in your headers.

14. Submissions. Check the guidelines. Am I making this point clearly enough? And for heaven's sake, make sure you have the editor's name spelled right. Always include a SASE with every submission. If you want to make sure your submission is received, include a stamped, self-addressed postcard that can be sent back to you.

Rebecca Vinyard of Allen, Texas, is the author of two romance novels, *Diva* and *Deadly Light* (Petals of Light), and is the Webmaster of http://romance-central.com.

10 RULES FOR SUCCESS & HAPPINESS WRITING FICTION

by Elmore Leonard

These are rules I've picked up along the way to help me remain invisible when I'm writing a book, to help me show rather than tell what's taking place in the story. If you have a facility for language and imagery and the sound of your voice pleases you, invisibility is not what you are after, and you can skip the rules. Still, you might look them over.

1. Never open a book with weather. If it's only to create atmosphere, and not a character's reaction to the weather, you don't want to go on too long. The reader is apt to leaf ahead looking for people. There are exceptions. If you happen to be Barry Lopez, who has more ways to describe ice and snow than an Eskimo, you can do all the weather reporting you want.

2. Avoid prologues. They can be annoying, especially a prologue following an introduction that comes after a forward. But these are ordinarily found in nonfiction. A prologue in a novel is backstory, and you can drop it in anywhere you want.

There is a prologue in John Steinbeck's *Sweet Thursday*, but it's OK because a character in the book makes the point of what my rules are all about. He says: "I like a lot of talk in a book and I don't like to have nobody tell me what the guy that's talking looks like. I want to figure out what he looks like from the way he talks . . . figure out what the guy's thinking from what he says. I like some description but not too much of that . . . Sometimes I want a book to break loose with a bunch of hooptedoodle . . . Spin up some pretty words maybe or sing a little song with language. That's nice. But I wish it was set aside so I don't have to read it. I don't want hooptedoodle to get mixed up with the story."

3. Never use a verb other than "said" to carry dialogue. The line of dialogue belongs to the character; the verb is the writer sticking his nose in. But *said* is far less intrusive than *grumbled, gasped, cautioned, lied.* I once noticed Mary McCarthy ending a line with "she asseverated," and had to stop reading to get the dictionary.

4. Never use an adverb to modify the verb "said" . . . he admonished gravely. To use an adverb this way (or almost any way) is a mortal sin. The writer is now exposing himself in earnest, using a word that distracts and can interrupt the rhythm of the exchange. I have a character in one of my books tell how she used to write historical romances "full of rape and adverbs."

5. Keep your exclamation points under control. You are allowed no more than two or three per 100,000 words of prose. If you have the knack of playing with exclaimers the way Tom Wolfe does, you can throw them in by the handful.

6. Never use the words "suddenly" or "all hell broke loose." This rule doesn't require an explanation. I have noticed that writers who use "suddenly" tend to exercise less control in the application of exclamation points.

7. Use regional dialect, patois, sparingly. Once you start spelling words in dialogue phonetically and loading the page with apostrophes, you won't be able to stop. Notice the way Annie Proulx captures the flavor of Wyoming voices in her book of short stories *Close Range*.

8. Avoid detailed descriptions of characters. Which Steinbeck covered. In Ernest Hemingway's "Hills Like White Elephants," what do the "American and the girl with him" look like? "She had taken off her hat and put it on the table." That's the only reference to a physical description in the story, and yet we see the couple and know them by their tone of voice, with not one adverb in sight.

9. Don't go into great detail describing places and things. Unless you're Margaret Atwood and can paint scenes with language or write landscapes in the style of Jim Harrison. But even if you're good at it, you don't want descriptions that bring the action, the flow of the story, to a standstill.
And finally:

10. Try to leave out the part that readers tend to skip. A rule that came to mind in 1983. Think of what you skip reading a novel: thick paragraphs of prose you can see have too many words in them. What the writer is doing, he's writing, perpetrating hooptedoodle, perhaps taking another shot at the weather, or has gone into the character's head, and the reader either knows what the guy's thinking or doesn't care. I'll bet you don't skip dialogue.

My most important rule is one that sums up the 10.

If it sounds like writing, I rewrite it. Or, if proper usage gets in the way, it may have to go. I can't allow what we learned in English composition to disrupt the sound and rhythm of the narrative. It's my attempt to remain invisible, not distract the reader from the story with obvious writing. (Joseph Conrad said something about words getting in the way of what you want to say.)

If I write in scenes and always from the point of view of a particular character—the one whose view best brings the scene to life—I'm able to concentrate on the voices of the characters telling you who they are and how they feel about what's going on, and I'm nowhere in sight.

What Steinbeck did in *Sweet Thursday* was title his chapters as an indication, though obscure, of what they cover. "Whom the Gods Love They Drive Nuts" is one, "Lousy Wednesday" another. The third chapter is titled "Hooptedoodle 1" and the 38th chapter "Hooptedoodle 2" as warnings to the reader, as if Steinbeck is saying: "Here's where you'll see me taking flights of fancy with my writing, and it won't get in the way of the story. Skip them if you want."

Sweet Thursday came out in 1954, when I was just beginning to be published, and I've never forgotten the prologue.

Did I read the hooptedoodle chapters? Every word.

Elmore Leonard is the author of more than 35 novels, including *Get Shorty* (Delta) and *Freaky Deaky* (William Morrow & Co.), and recipient of the Grand Master Award from the Mystery Writers of America. He lives near Detroit. This article appeared previously in *The New York Times*. Reprinted with author's permission.

MEASURE YOUR WORDS

How to keep your writing lean

by Katherine Hauswirth

The need to slice and dice one's own creation is one of the more painful aspects of writing, especially for a breed that lives to generate words. But alas, editors and publishers are absolutely hung up on word counts. The format and layout of their publications determine these necessary limits. And while editors may sometimes help out with word surgery, publications expect you to acknowledge their guidelines by submitting the word count they require.

Besides making a good impression, there are other advantages to putting your article under the knife. Our English teachers were on to something when they penciled "clear and concise" in our margins. Hemingway was admired for simple words spoken with power. Thomas Wolfe had the opposite approach—reams of beautiful descriptions that were cut by the stackful before publication. On the other hand, Wolfe had a unique relationship with an especially indulgent editor. Today's fast-paced publishing world no longer allows for these singularly devoted writer-editor relationships. We are faced with the need to trim the fat before a prospective publisher sees our submission. What to do—in 930 words:

> A great side-effect of word reduction is that it forces you to look at your piece with fresh eyes.

Walk away from your piece. The title of Betsy Lerner's book on writing, *The Forest for the Trees*, captures the perfect metaphor for rewrites. While no writer can claim complete objectivity, distancing yourself for a while will allow some measure of perspective. When you return to your piece, print it out.

Reread your story and make notes. This seems to work better on hard copy, hence the printout. Misguided writers treat word reduction like a contagious disease. They hold their paper at arm's length, cease to breathe, and wincing, randomly strike out sentences. But they lose the structure of their stories with this technique.

Instead, read aloud and mark anything that sounds awkward or unusual. Look for overkill, where you over-explain a particular element of the story. Hunt for dead ends—prose that wanders off on loosely related tangents, as in the following perplexing passage:

> That autumn, Sylvia met Steve. She had recently become a Joan Baez fan, and wore her hair long with dangling earrings like her idol. She was wearing her Baez earrings when she met Steve. Her first impression of Steve was decidedly negative. He greeted her with a scowl when she stumbled in late to sociology class.

Sylvia's earrings keep dangling as we read on without finding a connection—what does her taste in music and jewelry have to do with this new relationship?

Also, look for clichés during your rereading ("clandestine love affair," "carefree as a summer's day," "the city never slept"). These worn-out phrases should land face down on the cutting-room floor. A further example: Let's say you have reduced your beginning sentence, "It was a dark and stormy night, and I feared for my life," to "On that dark, stormy night, I was deathly afraid." You may have cut four words, but a great side effect of word reduction is that it forces you to look at your piece with fresh eyes. Either version of that first sentence is a lackluster cliché. Get rid of it.

Read with your audience in mind. You need a good sense of your key message. Starting with the passages you have marked, ask yourself, "Why do my readers need to know this?" Will your words help them toward that goal? Sometimes, writing is part psychotherapy. If you realize that some words were written more for your ego than for your reader, slice away.

Don't be afraid to restructure. Many writers start off slowly and introduce their key idea well into the piece. Consider pulling that third paragraph up and reworking it for your introduction.

Walk away again. Take another break after you tackle your initial round of rewrites. When you return, review and count. How much closer are you to the limit? Has your message been lost? If you are on the right track, your message will ring with new clarity.

Cut the fat. Your piece has already been helped by your careful review. You are *still* above the sacred count. What to do? Dissect your specimen and think about each of its components. Do redundant or empty words lurk between the good ones?

> Even on the dullest, most soporific days of drudgery, a conversation with lively Tina always seemed to lift the cobwebs and liven things up in the most heartening way.

Phrases like "even on," "always," and "in the most" do not add meaning but certainly add bulk. The repetition of meaning in "dullest," "soporific," and "drudgery" speaks for itself, and the description of Tina's liveliness is equally overpeppered with redundant adjectives.

Are your descriptions too general to lend real color and meaning? Is your sentence heavy with commas or semicolons? Stephen King asserts in *On Writing* that the road to hell is paved with unnecessary adverbs, arguing that closing the door firmly is no better than closing the door. If you describe your characters well, you won't need to describe every action in painstaking detail. Note how overused parts of speech and punctuation can weigh you down:

> We were one very big, happy family, and whenever the mood struck us, we always cooked a large, Italian pasta dish together.

> ~~We were one very big,~~ Our large, happy family~~, and whenever the mood struck us, we always~~ often reunited spontaneously ~~cooked a~~ to cook an ~~large, Italian pasta dish together~~ oversized vat of eggplant parmesan.

> I often tried to impress the boys when I was young by wearing tight, revealing jeans and short crop-tops that screamed loudly, "I am available," to all who would listen.

> I ~~often~~ tried to impress the boys ~~when I was young~~ at school by wearing ~~tight,~~ revealing jeans and ~~short~~ crop-tops that screamed ~~loudly,~~ "I am available." ~~to all who would listen.~~

What did we lose in these last two examples? Eighteen unnecessary words were laid to peaceful rest. Good riddance to redundancy, vague wording, superfluous adverbs, and too many clauses separated by commas. Multiply that sort of revision by the 14 paragraphs in your story and you have retired an impressive 252 words.

Get help. Ask friends and allies to read your piece and comment. Besides their general impression, ask them to point out confusing words or transitions and irrelevant details. Your first readers may confirm a doubt you've been harboring all along. Remember, your reader has something you do not: objectivity. Renew your slashes—with vigor.

Compressing your words is often a dreaded chore, but a hidden benefit of word reduction is its culmination in a more refined and effective piece. So take heart, your delicate surgery will have a rewarding outcome. You can count on it.

Katherine Hauswirth of Deep River, Conn., a freelancer and medical writer, is the author of the self-published *Things My Mother Told Me: Reflections on Parenthood.*

HOW TO BUILD A CLIP FILE

by Shelle Castles

You can't get published without clippings of your work, and you can't get clips without being published. This is the unpublished writer's lament. But don't despair, there are several ways to get around this obstacle.

I decided to go straight to the source for advice. I asked editors and publishers for suggestions on ways writers can build a clip file. Here are their tips:

• Check out your local newsletters, newspapers, and business publications. You can write a letter to an editor or pitch an idea to the local small-business association for its next newsletter. Offer to write a brochure, flier, or newsletter for a new business.

• Submit an article to your favorite Web site. Perhaps you frequently visit certain Web sites because it's your hobby or passion. Got a great idea for an article? Query them. Chances are they'll use it. You may not get paid, but it adds a clip to your portfolio that can lead to a paid assignment.

• Get technical. If you have a background in engineering, marketing, computers, business, customer service, communications, or even designing, look into writing for technical publications. Local companies may need to hire someone to write out a step-by-step process on how to handle customer complaints, or to compile a handbook on the policies and procedures of their workplace.

• Contact church and nonprofit organizations. Offer to write a piece for your church newsletter. Do you have a soft heart for animals? Contact your local

Humane Society chapter and ask if you can put together a brochure. Volunteer to do a newsletter for a nonprofit you support. This not only will get you some clips, but also will give you an opportunity to network with others in the community, which can lead to future assignments.

• Enter contests. You gain a clip if you win or receive an honorable mention, plus you learn how to follow guidelines and meet deadlines. One proviso: Don't enter contests in which the entry fee is disproportionate to the prize, such as a $40 fee for a $100 prize.

• Make your opinion heard. Most local newspapers have an op-ed column. Editors often are looking for essays that bring a different perspective or new information to a timely issue.

• Start a community newsletter. Write about the issues of concern in your neighborhood, city services or ordinances that affect your area, and neighborhood events.

• Pen fillers and quips. Magazines, newspapers, and newsletters often use 100- to 200-word fillers. These can be obscure quotes, quips, humorous anecdotes, historical facts, epigrams, jokes, puzzles, or tongue-twisters.

• Write for city tourist publications. Most communities offer visitors a brochure or magazine highlighting places of interest in the area. Contact your local convention bureau or chamber of commerce to see if they need copy. Perhaps you can write about a historic building, or maybe there's an offbeat museum you could profile.

• Profile local people and places. Do you personally know the traffic guard who dances while directing traffic? Does your Aunt Sally have the oldest collection of paper dolls in the world? Does your best friend hold the title of most broken bones in the history of your local hospital? Perhaps you can write about a coffee shop that features poetry readings or musical performances once a week.
Be on the lookout for colorful characters and unique places in your city. Most newspaper feature editors welcome fresh stories with local angles.

Remember that building a clip file will help you get assignments. So get out there and start writing!

Shelle Castles of Saltillo, Miss., is a freelancer and novelist who has been published extensively in Internet and print markets.

PREPARE BEFORE YOU GO

Get the most out of writers' conferences

by Ann Dee Allen

Attending your first writers' conference is like engaging in a free-write. It's an exercise in openness. Put pen to paper—a conference registration form—and see what happens.

As poet and fiction writer Anya Achtenberg instructed participants at a 2001 SouthWest Writers Conference free-write session: "You enter, in a way, a new world or new knowledge or new condition or a new consciousness. As you enter this new knowledge, it's a kind of 'first-ness,' a place you have never been before or a situation you've never been in before."

In a free-write, you don't restrict yourself to a particular character, setting, plot or other limitation. You might start with a general idea or an object or person in view, take a blank page and write your thoughts as they come to you.

Just as when you are doing a free-write, your experiences, ideas, creativity and skills prepare you for a conference. At the same time, you are taking a fresh approach and opening yourself to unlimited results.

What you experience at a conference can range from the academic to the visceral. Here is what you can expect to glean from the experience:

- Learn practical skills for direct application to your writing.
- Become more motivated to write.
- Share your experiences with other writers.
- Network with writers and publishing professionals.
- Hear leading writers speak about their work.
- Gain an understanding of the publishing business.
- Learn about writing markets.

- Meet editors, agents and authors.
- Obtain critiques of your work.
- Enter your writing in contests.
- Join a writers' organization.
- Discover effective new writing tools and resources.

To get the most from a conference, however, you should prepare for it in advance. Fate usually smiles on those who put themselves in its sights. After researching and selecting the right conference for you, spend time planning for your success once you arrive. Use these tips to prepare:

- Plan for and meet deadlines for contests, manuscript evaluations and consultations.
- Prepare contest and manuscript materials as professionally as you would for publication.
- Learn more about the writing and publishing professionals who will be there, their interests and preferences, by researching the Internet and other resources.
- Select conference sessions based on your goals.
- Budget for books, tapes, and other resources that will be available at the conference.

Finally, enjoy yourself once you get there. A conference is also intended to be a break from your regular schedule. Take time to introduce yourself to other writers and publishing professionals, just for the pleasure of meeting them. But don't forget to bring your business cards!

Ann Dee Allen of Waukesha, Wis., is director of communications at a statewide business association. She has 25 years of experience as a nonfiction writer and editor.

SECTION TWO

The Craft
of Writing

E. B. WHITEWASHED?

Elements of Style author knew writing
rules were meant to be bent

by Arthur Plotnik

No American writing guide is more revered than the 5-ounce Strunk & White, a.k.a. *The Elements of Style* (Allyn & Bacon). "Timeless," "the best book of its kind we have," gush its idolaters. Yet, for all its glory, the tiny-shouldered book is also a magnet for bashers.

It is geriatric. First appearing in 1918, it underwent its fourth resuscitation in 2000. It is small and vulnerable—as pokable as the Pillsbury Doughboy for determined critics. And the coddling it enjoys from the writing establishment makes rebel blood boil. In a 1989 bashing, one alternative-press writer dubbed White "a cranky old man."

Who is correct? For every basher who attacks *Elements* as a meager, authoritarian fossil, a corps of literati hails its grace, concision, and moral sense. In a review of the fourth edition, conservative columnist Andrew Ferguson called it "a book about life—about the value of custom, the necessity of rules, the corruptions of vanity, the primacy of good taste."

The controversy, however, erupted long before the latest edition.

War baby

In the late 1950s, a war flared between liberal and conservative language authorities. The liberals took a stand against "elitist" notions of "correctness." They argued that actual widespread usage, not prescribed forms, determined the validity of language. This "descriptive" approach to standard English raised the hackles of "prescriptivists," who believed in established rules and a hierarchy of expression.

One such prescriptivist was *New Yorker* writer and master essayist E. B.

White. He condemned the descriptivist view of language as an "Anything Goes" school. Encouraged by a publisher, he entered the fray by updating the stern little handbook of William Strunk Jr., his 1919 English professor at Cornell. Strunk had called his privately printed book *The Elements of Style.*

White began the new *Elements* with a paean to Strunk and to the professor's belief in "right and wrong." He added his touch to mundane points of grammar and form, then concluded with "An Approach to Style," a classic of writing advice. Here he showcased his own skills as he warned against excesses that tempt new and youthful writers.

Aside from this essay, the book treats only the most commonly violated fundamentals as the authors saw them: a few dozen issues in grammar and composition and a sampling of usage problems. Some entries support such fading niceties as the distinctions between "shall" and "will." Others simply reflect White's antiquated bugaboos—for example, the sin of using "fix" to mean "mend" in formal English.

Selective and quirky as it may be, Strunk & White has succored confused students and forgetful communicators for more than 40 years. As a guide to the "plain English style," the book may yet save America from choking on its jargon and obfuscations. And all writers must take seriously the perceptions of "correctness" in English. Readers sense "correct" and disciplined patterns, whether or not they favor or even understand them. Jarring this sense of order can do two things: It can lose readers by sidetracking them into concerns about wrongness. Or—as *Elements* fails to make clear—it can wake readers up and set them dancing.

Breaking the rules

Both Strunk and White knew well that bending the rules—judiciously breaking them—can give writing its distinction, its edge, its very style. Bending them can spring writers from ruts, get them out of themselves, out of the ordinary, and into prose that comes alive, gets noticed, gets published.

"I felt uneasy at posing as an expert on rhetoric," White wrote in 1957, "when the truth is I write by ear, always with difficulty and seldom with any exact notion of what is taking place under the hood."

And Strunk himself affirmed that "the best writers sometimes disregard the rules of rhetoric. When they do so, however, the readers will usually find in the sentence some compensating merit, attained at the cost of the violation."

Writing is risk-taking. We bungee-jump from a sentence and pray the cord stops short of catastrophe. We day-trade in language, gambling that a hot image will hold up.

White described expression as "a living stream, shifting, changing, receiving new strength from a thousand tributaries," but advised "there is simply a better chance of doing well if the writer holds a steady course, enters the stream of English quietly, and does not thrash about."

Who, then, draws strength from those tributaries? Whose prose comes alive in the churning waters? Some writers who "thrash about" go under—but others make waves!

White's admonitions may apply in Composition 101, or for those with a riveting story that best tells itself. But what happens when quieted-down expression meets today's rock concert-like din of overloaded and understimulated brains?

White wrote in an era when the well-tempered essay found receptive minds, when readers willingly entered into quiet dialogue with an author. But the last few decades have brought New Journalism and rude, in-your-face communications media into the mainstream.

In this sometimes disparaging, sometimes liberating environment, expressiveness calls for break-a-leg performance; it wants aggressiveness, surprise, exuberance, responsiveness, intensity, *rebelliousness*—most of which White seems to disdain, except in his own prose.

In his essays and three unconventional children's classics, White went his own way as a writer. But in *Elements of Style*, he offered little encouragement for others to do so. Instead, he warned them against the "disinclination to submit to discipline." But how inclined to submission was White?

As a youth, he skimped through Cornell University with "anemic" interests in everything but writing. Shunning his native East Coast, he peddled roach powder in Minneapolis, reported for the *Seattle Times,* and served as messboy aboard a ship cruising the Aleutian Islands before returning East as an advertising copywriter. He called himself disciplined, but he took risks in life and in writing, including the death-defying risk of telling others how to write.

White probably never meant to advise against taking chances, against drawing on all levels of language, against demolishing any rule to get attention.

It just comes out that way.

Arthur Plotnik of Chicago is a contributing editor to *Editorial Eye* and has written several books, including *The Elements of Editing* and *The Elements of Expression.* His latest work is *The Urban Tree Book: An Uncommon Field Guide for City and Town* (Three Rivers Press).

RULE BREAKERS & BENDERS

It's easy to find violations of Strunk & White in good journalism, literature, and even the prose of E. B. White. In this sampling, some violations achieve the "compensating merit" or worthwhile effect that William Strunk Jr. mentions. Others are harmless.

Place yourself in the background.
"I sat there wondering what would happen to me if I were to jump up and say in a loud voice, 'If you folks like liberty and justice so much, why do you keep Negroes from this theater?' " —E. B. White, "On a Florida Key"

Do not affect a breezy manner.
"Descend with me to the seventh circle of buzz, the ground zero of zing, the hub of hip, the Sodom of synergy. Beneath the Statue of Liberty, the masses, the tired and unhumble, yearning to be chic, huddled at Tina Brown's *Talk* party." —Maureen Dowd, *The New York Times*

Use orthodox spellings.
I ast Shug Avery what she want for breakfast. —Alice Walker, *The Color Purple*

Use figures of speech sparingly.
"Will felt that the reader was . . . floundering in a swamp, and that it was the duty of anyone attempting to write English to drain this swamp quickly and get the reader up on dry ground, or at least throw him a rope."
—E. B. White, *The Elements of Style*

Avoid foreign languages.
"It was Will Strunk's *parvum opus,* his attempt to cut the vast tangle of English rhetoric down to size." —E. B. White, *The Elements of Style*

Do not break sentences in two (do not use periods for commas).
"He had thrown a book. Hers. From across the room. A hot welt across the cheek." —Sandra Cisneros, *Woman Hollering Creek*

Avoid fancy words.
Algolagniac, cicatrices, deracinate, pelagic, and piliginious. —Some words used by T. C. Boyle in *Water Music*

—*Arthur Plotnik*

THE ART OF BEGINNINGS

Seduce the reader with an irresistible,
well-crafted opening

by Marge Piercy and Ira Wood

A novel or memoir takes time to read, and the art of writing in either of these forms involves seduction. On the first page and every page thereafter, you have to engage the reader and persuade him or her to keep going. That's why the beginning is the most important and often the most challenging section of your book to write. You don't have the luxury of starting your narrative slowly, for you are competing with other books and magazines, as well as the Internet, movies and television, for the readers' attention. Whoever doesn't read the beginning of your book will never read the rest of it.

And, you'll never get published to begin with if you don't get the attention of one person—an editor. Basically, you can count on an editor reading the first page in a short story, maybe the first two pages; and in a novel, the first 10 pages. If you haven't grabbed him or her by then, you're sunk.

We hope the following excerpt from *So You Want to Write: How to Master the Craft of Writing Fiction and the Personal Narrative*, which I co-wrote with my partner, Ira Wood, will help you begin your story effectively. We teach classes in writing personal narrative or fiction, and the book is a product of our workshops. Though the following excerpt is written in first person, we both contributed to the contents. It includes guidelines and tips that we've developed over the years to help writers get their novels or memoirs off to a good start.

Writing a good beginning is a demanding process. There is no one right or wrong approach. The main thing is to begin.

Time is your master

To craft a good beginning, you have to understand why people read fiction or memoirs. The most primitive answer is the most real: to get to the next page. To find out what happens next and then what happens after that, to find out how it all comes out.

We want stories that help us make sense out of our lives. We want to see that all this mess means something, even if what we discover is a shape that is perhaps beautiful but not necessarily comforting. Similarly, we don't want to read something that sounds like a diary: "I went to the store, and on the way back I met my old friend George, and we talked about the Red Sox, and then I ate a banana." Shapelessness loses readers.

Again, the novel is about time and patterns in time. It is not a simultaneous art but one of transition and sequence. You can do a lot with juxtaposition, cutting, transitions or the lack of them. Using these techniques, you can create the illusion of things happening simultaneously. Your beginning sets up the book's time patterns; everything follows from that, so it has to be right.

You can spend 600 pages on one night or pass over 100 years in a sentence. You can start at the beginning: Josephine was born on a wild wintry night just as the old cow died. You can begin at the end: Josephine was buried on a wild wintry day just as a calf was born to the old brown cow. You can start at the end and go back to the beginning. You can open in the classic epic manner, in *medias res* (in the middle), as Homer did with *The Iliad*. You can start anywhere on the continuum of days and years and proceed in either direction. You can go in one large or several smaller circles. You can overlap blocks of time from different viewpoints. You can move into parallel or alternate universes. But time is always your servant and master and substance.

The more things are happening—that the reader can follow, at least mostly—the more likely he will read on. Your exposition needs to be there, but you have to learn to do it on the wing, subtly, without stopping the story and laying out everything while the characters shuffle their feet, the suspense dies, and the story is stuck out in the middle of nowhere like a becalmed sailboat.

You have to pass along the exposition with the story and the characters as you go. The trick, of course, is not to confuse the readers. They have to be able to follow it all. (We got a submission recently in which the novelist begins at an intriguing wedding, a very good place to introduce families and their conflicts. But there were too many people not sufficiently differentiated and ultimately it was confusing. It felt very much like being at a wedding and not knowing the bride's family from the groom's or whose friends were whose. Focusing more deeply on fewer characters and their conflicts might have been a better strategy.)

For example, if you are writing science fiction or speculative fiction, you must indicate some unusual things in the beginning, but not by getting lost in the hardware. You want to let the reader know right away that this is perhaps another time, another place, another planet, an alternate reality, but it is more important to introduce your characters and get your plot under way. It is more essential for the reader to be engaged and interested in what is going on and the people to whom it is happening, than it is for the reader to grasp every detail of the situation you have created. That you have to do on the fly, in bits and pieces as the story moves on.

Here's an example from my novel *He, She & It*:

> Josh, Shira's ex-husband, sat immediately in front of her in the Hall of Domestic Justice as they faced the view screen, awaiting the verdict on the custody of Ari, their son. A bead of sweat slid down the furrow of his spine—he wore a backless business suit, white for the formality of the occasion, very like her own—and it was hard even now to keep from delicately brushing his back with her scarf to dry it. The Yakamura-Stichen dome in the Nebraska desert was conditioned, of course, or they would all be dead, but it was winter now and the temperature was allowed to rise naturally to thirty Celsius in the afternoon as the sun heated the immense dome enclosing the corporate enclave. Her hands were sweating too, but from nervousness. She had grown up in a natural place and retained the ability to endure more heat than most Y-S gruds. She kept telling herself she had nothing to fear, but her stomach was clenched hard and she caught herself licking her lips again and again. Every time she called up time on her internal clock and read it in the corner of her cornea, it was at most a minute later than when last she had evoked it.

There is certainly a lot to be explained in the above excerpt. Backless business suits? A clock on the corner of her cornea? The Yakamura-Stichen dome? But it's the familiar situation in the midst of all this weirdness—the custody battle—that grounds the reader and compels attention, that causes the reader to be engaged and interested in what is going on and to identify with the people to whom it is happening.

If, for example, your story is about a doctor, you could use the first page to tell us how old she is, whether she went to an Ivy League med school or a state school, what she chose to specialize in, whether she's a risk-taker or plays it safe. Or you could begin in the middle of open heart surgery and allow the reader to discover her background while seeing her in action. You could begin the story of this doctor at her birth and move forward through medical school to the daring new type of heart implant that won her world fame.

You could start with a description, but it had better be a rather unusual description. Here's an example from our book *Storm Tide*:

> When the winter was over and my nightmares had passed, when someone else's mistakes had become the subject of local gossip, I set out for the island. I made my way in increments, although the town was all of 18 miles square. To the bluff overlooking the tidal flats. Down the broken black road to the water's edge. To the bridge where her car was found, overturned like a turtle and buried in mud.

What you are trying to do is to start with something lively, intriguing, mysterious, or fascinating—and fast-moving. Then you can go back and insert your necessary background and context. No one needs to know the name of the dead woman who was in the car or why she died, or what kinds of weird things happened on the island. At this point, you're competing for the readers' attention. You're hoping that those questions will occur to them and they'll want to read on.

Write and the beginning will come

Writing a good beginning is a demanding process. This does not mean that you should stare at your computer and freeze up and write nothing until you discover the perfect place to start. Never be afraid to get going on something. You can rework your beginning endless times. All writers do. You don't have to have the perfect beginning to get to the middle—not at all.

Here are three rules that, if not golden, are certainly useful in getting started:

• Do not confuse the beginning of the story with the beginning of the events in the story. There is infinite regression in all stories, or they would all begin with the Big Bang when the universe started. The particular events you are shaping may start with the birth of your character, but that is not where the story starts.

• Never confuse the beginning of the story with how you begin to write it. In hindsight, there is usually a correct place to begin in the plot, but in your own work, begin writing where you can. If you are having trouble entering a character, sometimes you can find a scene that you can imagine yourself in, a point of commonalty, of empathy, where you can make a doorway into that character. That might be the first scene you write, even if it turns out to be in the middle or even at the end of the finished product.

Both of Ira's novels, *The Kitchen Man* and *Going Public*, have as a second chapter what was, in early drafts, the first chapter.

• No matter how cute or compelling or chic or gripping your beginning may be, if it does not lead to your story, be prepared to scrap it rather than distorting the entire book in the service of a good start.

I knew a writer who won two awards on the strength of the first chapter to a novel, from which the novel not only did not but could not follow. But she could never abandon that chapter, because it was the strongest part of the book. It was arresting, but all the fireworks were burned out by the end of it, and she could not develop it into the material she really had for a novel. Therefore, while the material paid off financially, for a while, she never got a novel, never got more than a couple of excerpts published, and never got on with her writing.

Even more to the point, if the rest of the book does not follow from the beginning, you will disappoint your readers. They thought it was blood and guts, but it's a tender psychological study of a boy who loves a pigeon; they thought it was going to be a humorous trip through contemporary adolescence, but it's a psychopath's revenge. The beginning must be powerful and it must begin with what you are actually going to continue.

The beginning is that important: It is all-important. Without a good beginning, no one, with the possible exception of your mother or partner, will ever bother to continue reading what you have written.

Marge Piercy has written poetry, fiction, and nonfiction. Her latest book is the memoir *Sleeping with Cats* (Morrow). **Ira Wood** is the author of The *Kitchen Man* and co-author, with Piercy, of the novel *Storm Tide.* The two live on Cape Cod, Mass. This excerpt from "Beginnings," in *So You Want to Write: How to Master the Craft of Writing Fiction and the Personal Narrative* by Marge Piercy and Ira Wood, is reprinted here with permission of Leapfrog Press (www.leapfrogpress.com) and the authors. For more information about Marge Piercy, Ira Wood, and their fiction and memoir workshops, visit: www.margepiercy.com.

GOOD STARTS

There are a number of books on writing that emphasize the necessity of starting with a snappy first sentence. We are more concerned with the situation you choose to begin with, and the way various writers have solved the problem of attempting to hook the reader.

Mary Flanagan begins her story "Cream Sauce" with Lydia, the world's slowest cook. Lydia likes to drink Bordeaux as she prepares dinner, while her suffering family is enticed by "tantalizing aromas accompanied by interminable waits," likely to be followed by "not infrequent failures, which must, out of sheer physical necessity, be consumed." Anybody who cooks, or lives with a cook like Lydia, would read on.

Dorothy Allison begins her novel *Bastard Out of Carolina* inside a speeding car with all the important characters, based on the women in her family. The implication is that something important is about to happen, and she creates a strong sense of social class and regional characters.

[cont.]

[sidebar cont.]

Gore Vidal begins his memoir *Palimpsest* with the wedding of two members of high society in "the church of the presidents" across the avenue from the White House, where he was one of the ushers, JFK was another, and Jackie Kennedy went off to the bathroom with the bride and showed her how to douche, post-sex. Name-dropping, the hint of scandal, the promise of gossip, and the insider's view of the lives of the rich and famous are Vidal's hooks.

William Gibson begins his cyber-punk novel *Count Zero* with his hero, Turner, being chased through the ghettos of India by an intelligent bomb called a Slamhound filled with "a kilogram of recrystallized hexogene and flaked TNT." What's a Slamhound? Why is it chasing him? Is there such a thing as recrystallized hexogene? Who cares? Turner is blown to bits and it takes three months to put him together again, with eyes and genitals bought on the open market. It's the speed, the violence, the absurd details of the author's future world, that keep the reader wondering: What the hell is going on?

A DISCUSSION OF STORY

by Ursula K. Le Guin

I define story as a narrative of events (external or psychological) which moves through time or implies the passage of time, and which involves change.

I define plot as a form of story which uses action as its mode, usually in the form of conflict, and which closely and intricately connects one act to another, usually through a causal chain, ending in a climax.

Climax is one kind of pleasure; plot is one kind of story. A strong, shapely plot is a pleasure in itself. It can be reused generation after generation. It provides an armature for narrative that beginning writers may find invaluable.

But most serious fictions can't be reduced to a plot, or retold without fatal loss except in their own words. The story is not in the plot but in the telling. It is the telling that moves.

Modernist manuals of writing often conflate story with conflict. This reductionism reflects a culture that inflates aggression and competition while cultivating ignorance of other behavioral options. No narrative of any complexity can be built on or reduced to a single element. Conflict is one kind of behavior. There are others, equally important in any human life, such as relating, finding, losing, bearing, discovering, parting, changing.

Change is the universal aspect of all these sources of story. Story is something moving, something happening, something or somebody changing.

We don't have to have the rigid structure of a plot to tell a story, but we do need *a focus*. What is it about? Who is it about? This focus, explicit or implicit, is the center to which all the events, characters, sayings, doings of the story originally or finally refer. It may be or may not be a simple or a single thing or person or idea. We may not be able to define it. If it's a complex subject it probably can't be expressed in any words at all except all the words of the story. But it is there.

And a story equally needs what Jill Paton Walsh calls *a trajectory*—not necessarily an outline or synopsis to follow, but a movement to follow: the shape of a movement, whether it be straight ahead or roundabout or recurrent or eccentric, a movement which never ceases, from which no passage departs entirely or for long, and to which all passages contribute in some way. This trajectory is the shape of the story as a whole. It moves always to its end, and its end is implied in its beginning.

Ursula K. Le Guin is the acclaimed author of nearly twenty novels and numerous collections of short stories, poetry, and essays. This passage is taken from her book on the craft of writing, with many exercises for individual and group use, titled *Steering the Craft: Exercises and Discussions on Story Writing for the Lone Navigator or the Mutinous Crew,* published 1998 by Eighth Mountain Press of Portland, Ore.

GOLDEN NOTEBOOKS

Turn your journal pages into creative riches

by Alexandra Johnson

In 1976, novelist Ron Carlson rescued a shopping bag his wife had mistakenly put on the curb as trash. It was his journal. He'd just finished the first draft of his first novel, *Betrayed by F. Scott Fitzgerald*, and he dumped the bag onto his recently cleaned desk.

"My journal those years had been a large . . . shopping bag, which by that August was full of half a bushel of little papers on which I had scribbled: envelopes, folded memos, torn slips, wedding announcements, rodeo programs, and such."

After spending the better part of that day typing up the journal's contents, he says, "I went through this freshly typed miscellany and penciled where I thought each entry might fit into the novel." He found spots for three-quarters of his "observations" and gradually wove them into the novel's second draft.

Today, Carlson uses a folder instead of a shopping bag, and once or twice a year, when he needs an activity that requires no thinking, he pulls it out and types the contents into a computer file titled "notes." But, he adds, even the first chaotic jottings he used to stuff into the bag as scraps were "the physical manifestation of the way my mind works, sparks flying off the wheel."

It would take me time to learn this same trick. But I was making a similar discovery as I first began to move into larger creative work, moving from journalism into publishing two books, *The Hidden Writer* and *Leaving a Trace*. What sped up the process?

When I was 21, I was living in London, a great city for a writer to find the books she needs to read. I was hungry for information, not only about how one became a writer, but also how one stayed a writer. So much of what I wanted to know about creative lives I found in published writers' diaries. I loved eavesdropping on writers, such as Franz Kafka and Virginia Woolf, who in deep internal conversations discussed the writing process.

One morning, I came across a long-published journal that changed my writing life. It was a journal strangely like my own. It was a mess. Composed of several mismatched notebooks, its pages were often half filled or crosshatched with corrections. Weeks, often months, were skipped between entries. Grocery lists appeared next to ideas for future writing projects; travel notes were jotted beside comments on marriage; unsent letters stuck randomly among the pages.

I was fascinated since the journal keeper, New Zealand short story writer Katherine Mansfield, changed her creative fate with her odd assortment of notebooks. Mansfield, who had burned the "huge complaining diaries" of childhood, kept journals "to practice craft as much as to clarify thoughts."

"I am 33," she wrote, "yet I am only just beginning to see now what it is I want to do. It will take years of work to really bring it off. How unbearable it would be to die—leave 'scraps,' 'bits,' nothing really finished." Mansfield died of tuberculosis a year later, but not before mining her journals, producing a quarter of her final work. Notes jotted in doctors' waiting rooms ("My sciatica! Remember to give that to someone in a story one day"), the unsent letters, the grocery lists next to characters' names—all had been waiting to be used.

No matter how messy or incomplete, journals are the missing links in creative life. For centuries, they've helped beginning and seasoned writers alike trigger new work and sustain inspiration. Anne Frank used hers for the basis of a book she wanted to write after the war. She mined it for details and later rewrote entries and compressed scenes.

Novelist Woolf invented herself as a writer in her journal. From age 17 until four days before her death at 60, she used journals to move from family sketches to memoir to novels. A journal was a "deep old desk," helping her store "this loose, drifting material of life; finding another use for it."

The secret of keeping—and transforming—journals is seeing them as a savings account. Novelist and poet Phillip Lopate, for example, uses his journals "like a squirrel hiding away nuts for the older me who would raid the stash." In *Leaving a Trace*—about how to transform half-filled journals into longer creative work—I encourage writers to trust whatever form a journal takes. Carlson used his shopping-bag journal to transform the first of four novels. Novelist Jill McCorkle wrote *Carolina Moon* from notes that she tossed in a suitcase she stored under her bed.

What sort of diary would I like mine to be? Something loose knit and yet not slovenly, so elastic that it will embrace anything, solemn, slight, or beautiful that comes into my mind.

—Virginia Woolf, *A Writer's Diary*

While a computer disk or a shoebox filled with scraps is a journal, writers quickly learn the invaluable secret of giving journals a specific purpose. Keep one journal for story ideas, another for passages copied out from favorite writers. The biggest shift for any writer is moving from self-reflection to creative expression. It turns a journal from a mirror into a window. That journey is summed up by novelist Gail Godwin, (referring to her journal as "he"): "In adolescence, I weight him down with feelings of gloom and doom . . . in my 20s, I drove him to near death-from-boredom with . . . abortive plans for 'the future.' In my 30s, as my craft of fiction was consolidated . . . I shared ideas for future work . . . As a rule, I complain less and describe more. I try to lace even my complaints with memorable description."

Inspiration isn't something "to sit and wait for," writes poet David Lehman. For two years he invited it daily. Inspired by items in the newspaper or by movies, he wrote a poem a day, many while waiting in restaurants or even while driving. By keeping himself open to the observed world, he practiced keeping a poem "honest by rubbing its nose in the details of daily life." His notebook was the basis for his praised collection, *The Daily Mirror: A Journal in Poetry.*

As Lehman discovered, it's often good to start fresh. Before mining old journals for stories or poems, you might try the following approach. Start by sketching a series of narrative snapshots. They can range from one paragraph to two pages. Often they can be sparked by a single remembered detail. An apartment that I'd described in a travel journal, for example, triggered a long sketch I wrote about a summer in Italy.

Like many writers, I use prompts to help me get started. They are narrative building blocks, working as memory itself works—sparked by concrete or strong sensory details. The following exercises work well for me.

Describe an object

Objects are encoded with life stories. We surround ourselves with objects to remind us who we or others are. Anything kept permanently on a desk, taken to college, or packed with every move teems with unexplored stories. Such objects can be quick inspiration triggers. Begin with a single item, something you've had at least six months. It may be as simple as a photo or cheap souvenir, or something that has no obvious value to another's eye—a movie stub, an odd-shaped rock. It may be an object stashed in a cupboard, or the first thing you would rescue in a fire.

How would you describe it to a stranger? Jot down precise details. That makes it concrete, countering the worst tendency in journals—their cloudy, complaining abstractions. Select four or five significant details and jot down why you chose this object. Let your hand begin to tell the story it has long stored. Images and stories will release in a rush. Look for the incongruous, slightly off-center details.

A writer I know described a violin and how it had been stolen. In her journal she jotted:

"The violin smelled of old wood, sweat, and rosin. A brown thick-waisted figure eight with baroque curves. Holes shaped like an 'S' in old script. Ebony fixtures linked by metal strings in tension over a miniature suspension bridge."

Four sentences unfurled these stories: how a burglar in Philadelphia had stolen the violin she'd owned since childhood. How her father took her shopping to replace the lost violin.

Those entries triggered the opening of a memoir that describes her father and her entering her mother's hospital room. Standing on the cold linoleum floor, she played Schubert with the new violin. Her mother, in the final stages of illness, was soothed, listening to her favorite composer. Once a gifted pianist, "her breathing through a valve in her neck grew harsh with excitement." The writer realized that it was time, not the violin, that was really being stolen. The imagination had encoded the story in the object, and the narrative snapshot released it.

Recall a place

Our earliest memories are rooted in place: a lifetime of kitchens we've sat in, or a grandparent's attic smelling of newspapers and mothballs. To recall a place vividly is to trace the route memory first took—through the senses.

Do this simple sensory prompt. Think of a place where, after a long day, you yearn to return, if only in memory. (The most resonant memories are often from childhood—but not always.) On a sheet of paper, list the five senses. Quickly free-associate on each. What smells do you recall (roses and mildew; the itchy, dry smell of stored canvas); sounds (an owl on a wintry night); touch (starched white linen); taste (winter oranges); sights (V-shaped rust spots under old faucets.

In "Goodbye to All That," a dark valentine to her years in New York before marriage, Joan Didion used such details long stored in notebooks: standing eating a peach, feeling warm subway air on her legs; noticing the lights above Rockefeller Center blink "Time Life" as her 20s lapsed "with the deceptive ease of a film dissolve."

Mining old journals

In 1975, writer Annie Dillard was living in a small cabin near Puget Sound, Wash. She'd just won the Pulitzer Prize for *Pilgrim at Tinker Creek* (written partly in the form of a nature journal). Yet now she was having a hard time writing except in journals. An old one, though, contained two entries that would spark her now famous essay "Transfiguration," about claiming her vocation as a writer.

Embedded in her journal was an incident she'd witnessed one night: a moth burning steadily in a candle. It was a persistent memory. "I went back to my piles of journals, hoping I'd taken some specific notes." What she found disappointed her—long descriptions of owl sounds. The next night's entry, though, "after pages of self-indulgent drivel," held a fuller description. "The journal had some details I could use (bristleworms on the ground, burnt moths' wings sticking to pans), some phrases (her body acted like a wick, the candle had two flames, the moth burned until I blew it out) and, especially, some verbs (hiss, recoil, stick, spatter, jerked, crackled)."

She slowly started to uncover what the emerging piece was really about. She began remembering how at 16 she'd read a biography of the self-destructive French poet Rimbaud.

How did the moth, the poet, the memory fit into the emerging essay? She realized that her experience with the moth and discovery of Rimbaud were linked to her love of writing. "With my old journals beside me, I took up my current journal and scribbled and doodled my way through an account." Writing about that memory broke the dry spell in her creative life.

"We only store in memory images of value," observes memoirist and journal-keeper Patricia Hampl. "To write about one's life is to live it twice, and the second time is both spiritual and historical." For many writers, journals are the first stage in that creative process.

Alexandra Johnson of Medford, Mass., is the author of *The Hidden Writer* and *Leaving a Trace: The Art of Transforming a Life into Stories.*

AUTHORS AND THEIR DIARIES

"I never travel without my diary. One should always have something sensational to read in the train." —Oscar Wilde

Journals have long been catalysts in creative lives, not all of them literary. Leonardo da Vinci invented the modern helicopter and submarine in his notebooks. Even while sailing, Einstein scribbled notes and fragments of formulas into his pocket travel diary. Aboard the *Beagle,* Darwin filled five journals that shaped his theories of evolution. Elias Howe dreamed of the sewing machine before he invented it and recorded the dream the next morning.

Like Da Vinci, novelist Virginia Woolf used her journals to generate creative work. With a notebook propped on her knee at tea, she wrote without letting her pen lift from the page. It helped outwit her internal censor. "The advantage," she noted, "is that it sweeps up accidentally . . . diamonds." Hers were pages filled with fiction ideas, characters' names, and ways to revise novels. Woolf's five published journals comprise the

[cont.]

[sidebar cont.]

most complete record of a creative mind at work. A single volume, *A Writer's Diary,* excerpts entries just on writing and creativity. It shows the many ways she returned to a journal to find material used later in novels such as *The Years.*

Poet and novelist May Sarton began journals late in life. At 60, she published *Journal of a Solitude,* which is still a bestseller. It was the first of eight published journals, all of which chronicle a single year. Sarton had begun *Journal of a Solitude* as a private record. Deciding to publish it changed her relation to journal-keeping. All subsequent journals were kept with readers in mind. Sarton wanted others to be part of a larger journey in which she explored creativity as well as its obstacles—illness, love affairs gone wrong, depression, loneliness. *Recovering: A Journal* and *After the Stroke* chart how a creative life slowly re-emerges after serious illness. At 80, unable to write in her journal, Sarton used a tape recorder instead to keep her journal and dictate poems.

Many writers have used other people's journals to spark their own creativity. Poet William Wordsworth routinely read his sister Dorothy Wordsworth's nature journal. In its pages he found material for his famous daffodil poem and others, such as "The Leech Gatherer." Dorothy Wordsworth's is a model nature journal that has never been out of print.

Tolstoy and his wife, Sonya, read each other's diaries for 42 years. Right after he proposed, he gave her his bachelor diary in exchange for her most current one. Hers contained part of a short story. Years later Tolstoy used the heroine's name, Natasha, and many of the story's details for *War and Peace.*

Writers are often careful to keep their own journals secret. Da Vinci wrote in handwriting only decipherable when held up to a mirror. Samuel Pepys, who wrote about the Great Plague in London, wrote in code.

No one, though, surpassed novelist Anaïs Nin. Terrified that her hundreds of journals would be read, she erected a false wall in her closet, later removing the journals to a Brooklyn bank vault. She even kept a "decoy" diary for her husband. Nin, it turned out, had a lot to hide, including husbands on both coasts.

—*Alexandra Johnson*

ARTFUL RESEARCH

Valuable resources for fiction writers
in search of authentic details

by Susan Vreeland

> Is it possible for an ordinary person to climb over the area railings of #7 Eccles Street, either from the path or the steps, lower himself down from the lowest part of the railings till his feet are within two feet or three of the ground and drop unhurt? I saw it done myself but by a man of rather athletic build. I require this information in detail in order to determine the wording of a paragraph.

James Joyce wrote this to his aunt when he was away from Dublin. Can't you just imagine her muttering, "That boy! What will he think of next?" as she gets her umbrella to go out in the rain and take the trolley to Eccles Street?

Excessive? Unnecessary? Stalling from the act of writing? Joyce's letter is instructive and revealing.

Similarly, I must admit that I sent my French translator on a mission to find out if the carvings of heads on the facade of the Ministère de la Défense on Boulevard Saint-Germain in Paris are repeats of the same face or different faces. Among other things, she told me I had the wrong street! While some writers may be more cavalier, claiming that it's fiction, after all, I hold with the meticulous Joyce, not wholly out of allegiance to a recognized master, but for the sake of the richness of story that results. For me, research gives direction, depth, and authority to the writing; it doesn't just decorate a preconceived story with timely trivia.

Early research tends to be scattered, while one searches for the story, but later, usually during or after a first draft when one discovers in the work some needed information, it becomes pinpoint precise. At either time, an array of interesting material, some of it crucial, some merely usable, will emerge—and sometimes leap off the page. The results can be exciting. A single unexpected line can prompt a whole story. For example, the line in Jacob Presser's grim history, *Ashes in the Wind: The Destruction of Dutch Jewry*, indicating that in 1941 Jews were not allowed to keep pigeons, provided the genesis of my story "A Night Different From All Other Nights."

That story is one of eight linked narratives comprising my composite novel, *Girl in Hyacinth Blue*, which traces an alleged Vermeer painting in reverse chronology through the centuries, showing how defining moments in people's lives are lived under its influence. Besides the present, six time periods and numerous locales in the Netherlands are evoked: 1942 in Amsterdam; 1896 in Vreeland (yes, a real village located between Amsterdam and Utrecht); 1798 in The Hague during French rule; 1717 in Oling, Delfzijl, Westerbork, and Groningen (which I learned had been a university town since 1614, prompting my focal character to be a student); 1665 in Delft; and 1685 in Amsterdam. Naive in understanding what such a project entailed, I found that by the end I had consulted 76 books.

I'd been to the Netherlands only once, 25 years ago for three days, and I had never seen a Vermeer painting face to face. Blithely, I went ahead. I read books on Vermeer, Dutch art and social and cultural history, the Holocaust as experienced in the Netherlands, the changing geography of the Netherlands, Erasmus' adages, the history of costume, Passover and the practice of Jewish customs, Amsterdam's diamond trade, Dutch superstitions and treatment of witches, the French occupation, and the engineering of windmills and dikes.

Twenty printout pages from the Internet on the engineering of windmills (they vary regionally), on gears, wallowers, Archimedean screws, and drive shafts yielded one paragraph establishing the authority of the windmill engineer. The research also suggested a metaphor appropriate for the character who says, "I had fancied love a casual adjunct and not the central turning shaft making all parts move. I had not stood astonished at the power of its turning." I would not have arrived at his critical self-assessment and the epiphany of the story without meandering through gears and drive shafts.

> I climbed the 400 steps of Giotto's bell tower in Florence not only to see what my characters would have seen, but to be able to describe the steps.

Where to find factual details

Here are 10 research sources and approaches, beginning with the most obvious and ending with the ultimate—travel—that I used for either *Girl in Hyacinth Blue* or my latest novel, *The Passion of Artemisia*, which takes place in 17th-century Italy.

Social conditions, history, and politics. A smattering of titles might serve to show how I approached possible narratives from different angles: *Daily Life in Rembrandt's Holland* by Paul Zumthor and Simon Watson Taylor; *The Embarrassment of Riches: An Interpretation of Dutch Culture in the Golden Age* by Simon Schama; *Persecution, Extermination, Literature* by Sem Dresden and Henry G. Schogt; *Vermeer and His Milieu—A Web of Social History* by John Michael Montias. Some I used as browser books; others for specific information. Their bibliographies proved to be good sources for characters' names.

For fiction of more recent times, newspaper archives in university or large city libraries provide details, a tone of immediacy, and accounts of personal involvement in events, movements, and trends that history books seldom record. Advertisements in newspapers reveal values—the larger cultural values as well as monetary values—by comparison of product prices, property values and wages. Historical societies archive material, often catalogued in files about local events and individuals whose lives intersected with history. You also will find useful information in diaries, recorded oral histories, period maps, and photographs.

Biography, autobiography, personal narrative, and oral history. The mere memory of Anne Frank's *Diary of a Young Girl* suggested that I create a young character the antithesis of Anne in terms of self-expression, yet suffering similar revelations. *Memorbook: History of Dutch Jewry* gave me personal accounts, photos, and reproductions of public notices such as an auction of art held to support German Jewish refugees, which I developed into a scene.

A search for personal narratives might start at Columbia University's library Web site, www.columbia. edu/cu/lweb. Click on "Electronic Resources/Databases," then "Archival Resources" to locate manuscripts, archives, and oral history collections—not only at Columbia but throughout the United States and abroad. Similar finding aids are available at the Library of Congress site, www.loc.gov, under "American Memory."

Geography books. These tomes provide information about weather, topography, crops, industry, indigenous plants, birds, and other animals. In my case, *The Making of the Dutch Landscape* and *Brave Little Holland and What She Taught Us* were the sources of story ideas as well as the details to make them work. I also consulted field guides to birds and plants, and a history of Dutch agriculture.

Maps. Besides those available in travel bookstores, universities often have historical map collections. This was essential for *Girl* because I had to know if certain villages and canals existed at the time of each of the stories. What a horrible mistake that would have been if I had set a story in a village that was still under the sea when the story took place. From works by authors from Guy de Maupassant to Hemingway, place names give authenticity, which helps to put the reader right there. The Library of Congress has a wealth of zoom-in maps at www.loc.gov. Click "American Memory: American History in Words, Sounds and Pictures," then click "Collection Finder" and go to "Maps."

Travel books. Look for the descriptive sort, the older the better. They provide visual and cultural detail. Early English narratives of the Grand Tour, such as Henry James' *Italian Hours* and *James Boswell in Holland*, are apt to convey attitudes toward places and people that might suggest how your characters think. For a series of stories on artists, I found the Michelin guide to Paris enormously helpful, giving me street names, maps, and line drawings of significant buildings, together with historical data on how the buildings and districts changed. This helped me avoid the mistake of assuming that what is present now was present then. Don't neglect contemporary narratives of place, such as *Under the Tuscan Sun* by Frances Mayes, to get a flavor of the food and landscapes.

Other novels written at the time, about the time or set in the same place. Fiction can reveal helpful details, such as attitudes, concerns, expressions, syntax, and diction. Dava Sobel's *Galileo's Daughter* illustrated the prose style of letter-writing in 17th-century Italy. The stories of Colette suggested the voice for Claudine in the chapter "Hyacinth Blues," which takes place during the French rule. *A Sampling of Dutch Literature* gave me the suggestion to play my characters against Holland's greatest enemy—storm floods—and gave me characteristics of Dutch people. Rainer Maria Rilke's *Letters on Cezanne* provided insights into the artistic temperament.

Artwork. Paintings that were done in the same time and place as one's fiction are excellent sources of information about costume, hairstyles, jewelry, household furnishings, landscape, available foods, flowers typical of the region, even the quality of light in a region, Vermeer's "trademark."

Photography books and the online photo archives of the Library of Congress provide similar visual references. Go to www.loc.gov, click on "American Memory: American History in Words, Sounds and Pictures," then go to "Collection Finder."

Children's and juvenile fiction and nonfiction. These books often offer valuable information that is sufficient in some cases, and have the advantages of providing evocative illustrations and simplifying complicated political histories. Books for young readers tend to give personalities to historical persons. One book about a medieval illuminator of manuscripts explained in a clear, nonacademic way the grinding of pigments for the making of paint, which I used in both books.

Interviews. People are intrigued by novelists and are usually delighted to be consulted. For *Girl*, I consulted a pigeon breeder to learn why the owning of pigeons was prohibited to Jews under the German occupation, and how homing pigeons "worked." I called the Dutch embassy to find out about coinage in the 17th century. A teacher of Jewish culture explained the traditions of Passover and gave me a Haggadah. Open-ended questions can be surprisingly helpful. I asked a friend who had been a child in London during the blitzkrieg what she remembered, and she mentioned that she and her friends played parachutes by jumping off porches with open umbrellas whenever they heard planes above—a detail that I transferred to Amsterdam in *Girl*.

For *Artemisia*, I called an aquarium to learn the color of the edible sea urchins in the Bay of Genoa. Two characters of that novel are nuns at the convent of Santa Trinità above the Spanish Steps in Rome (though the steps weren't there when Artemisia climbed the Pincian Hill, a fact I luckily learned while browsing in a travel book). To find out how a nun might respond in a particular situation, I asked a friend who knew a former nun who called another nun who e-mailed the present mother superior of the Order of the Sacred Heart at Santa Trinità, who invited me to stay at that very convent when I came to Rome!

Travel. While travel is not always practical (I wrote *Girl in Hyacinth Blue* entirely while undergoing cancer treatment and could not travel), it will yield unexpected insights. On just a two-week trip to Italy, I learned much that corrected mistakes in an early draft of *The Passion of Artemisia*, and it gave me visual material, tastes, sounds, distances, relative sizes, and positions of things. There's nothing like walking where your character walked to discover uneven pavements, mosquitoes, river stench, the smell of plaster frescoes, and old wood in a convent. For *Artemisia*, I climbed the 400 steps of Giotto's bell tower in Florence not only to see what my characters would have seen (which I had imagined incorrectly), but to be able to describe the steps.

If you are fortunate enough to travel for research, take a lightweight audio recorder for snippets of reaction and description, a small, simple camera, and an easy-to-carry notebook. Record your impressions. Ask waiters what herbs and spices are in the entrees, bus drivers what crops are growing alongside the road. You might not get what you asked for, but you might get something else equally usable.

Don't go on such a trip too early in the writing. Have a draft first. Before leaving, prepare prioritized lists of what you'll need to find out. Go online to find the hours and locations of museums, libraries, and cemeteries, so you won't be in the right place on the wrong day. Remember, too, that it might take longer to do things in foreign countries than it does at home.

Now it's time to write

So when does one stop researching and start writing? You write when the story comes to life and assumes some structure, when you can't help but start, not when you know everything you'll need to know. That's impossible to anticipate before you get into the heart of the writing. You might need to push yourself away from the safer act of research and leap into a first draft.

Some commonsense advice: Keep phone numbers and e-mail addresses. Use your bookmark function online to go back easily to a site. Take notes just as you did for high school term papers, giving title, author, call number, pages consulted for each reference. You never know if you'll need to go back. During the writing of *Girl*, I checked out the National Gallery catalog of the 1995-'96 Vermeer exhibit nine times. I've had to spend countless hours letting my fingers do the re-walking when a quick page number noted would have saved me frustration. When your story is in the formative stages, take down more than you think you'll need. Keep a list of possible names for characters.

Don't get bogged down with fears of historical inaccuracy when writing a first draft. In one of the flood stories in *Girl*, the student needs to write a note. He's in a rowboat. He can't dip a pen in an inkwell. Did they have pencils in 1717? Look it up later. Keep writing. Keep the momentum going. If you don't know what they ate, leave it blank and get down the more important elements of the scene.

One caveat: Even if you put into your manuscript some fact delectable to you, recalling your delight in discovering it, if the story does not justify it, take it out. Type it up. Pin it on your wall. Use it elsewhere, but don't include it. The book is about characters, not about research.

Susan Vreeland of San Diego is the author of *The Passion of Artemisia* (Viking), *Girl in Hyacinth Blue* (Penguin), and *What Love Sees* (Macmillan). Her short fiction has appeared in *The Missouri Review*, *New England Review*, and *Confrontation*.

A WISH LIST FOR HISTORICAL-FICTION WRITERS

Crowning every historical-fiction writer's wish list is the mother of all dictionaries, *The Oxford English Dictionary*, which indicates when individual words came into use, and how and when their meanings changed. There are three versions that won't break the bank: *The New Shorter OED*, two volumes; *The Compact OED*, small print with magnifying glass; and *The Oxford English Dictionary CD-ROM*.

Here are some other reference books on my shelves that I turn to often:

Timetables of History: A Horizontal Linkage of People and Events by Bernard Grun is an indexed grid, with years beginning at 5000 B.C. down the left column, and categories across the top: history and politics; literature and theater; religion and philosophy; visual arts; music; science and technology; daily life. If I'm looking for whether I can have a character turn on a water faucet in a Paris flat in 1883, (indexed under "plumbing"), or more general, timely references that I could have my character mention, this is the first book I turn to.

Timelines: Day by Day and Trend by Trend from the Dawn of the Atomic Age to the Close of the Gulf War by Paul Dickson offers news items by date as well as innovations, hot topics, additions to the national lexicon, and words or phrases typical of the time, such as beatnik, hot tubs, gridlock, test-tube babies, or "may the force be with you."

English Through the Ages by William Brohaugh gives approximate dates of the first recorded use of words, by category.

Roget's International Thesaurus with an index (not a thesaurus in dictionary form) has lists of items of apparel, fabrics, furniture, hairstyles, tools and machinery, vehicles and carriages, vessels, musical instruments, animals, husbandry breeds, plants, stones, minerals, woods, colors, types of glass, manners of cooking, and foods, which can be checked against *English Through the Ages* and *Timetables of History*.

Other valuable resources are:
Everyday Life in the 1800s by Marc McCutcheon, *The Writer's Guide to Everyday Life in Renaissance England* by Kathy Lynn Emerson, and *The Writer's Guide to Everyday Life in the Middle Ages* by Sherrilyn Kenyon.

Other resources include:
Histories of art by time period and country
Histories of music and costume
Histories of transportation, manufacturing, household devices
Books of names of things, including tools and architecture
Atlases with street maps of cities
Foreign-language dictionaries
Time-sequence histories
Field guides to birds, flowers, and trees

—*Susan Vreeland*

CREATIVE NONFICTION

Literary journalists use fictional techniques
to tell a good story

by Pegi Taylor

What happens when writers have experiences that leave them lost for words? What can a writer do to convey, say, the grim ramifications of some foster care or even the inexplicable fads of teenagers? Fiction writers have always relied on devices like dialogue, point of view, or metaphor. In the 20th century, many leading nonfiction writers looked to fiction for the resources to describe the indescribable.

A group of journalists in the late 1950s and early 1960s started to experiment, more than any writers had before them, with just how many techniques they could snitch from fiction and still stick to the facts. Tom Wolfe's stylistically flamboyant pieces for the *New York Herald Tribune* justified his immediate inclusion in this club that came to be labeled "New Journalism." Calling himself "the Hectoring Narrator," Wolfe often would start his stories by insulting his subjects. "The Peppermint Lounge Revisited," a portrait of some New Jersey teenagers, begins:

> All right, girls, into your stretch nylon denims! You know the ones—the ones that look like they were designed by some leering, knuckle-rubbing old tailor with a case of workbench back. . . . Next, hoist up those bras, up to the angle of a Nike missile launcher. Then get into the cable-knit mohair sweaters, the ones that fluff out like a cat by a project heating duct. And then unroll the rollers and explode the hair a couple of feet up in the air into bouffants, bee-hives, and Passaic pompadours.

The high-energy Wolfe became a spokesperson for New Journalism. In 1973, he wrote three essays that formed a manifesto at the beginning of *The New*

Journalism, followed by his annotated anthology of what he considered the best of what New Journalism had produced. (The collection, for which Wolfe was co-editor, is out of print.)

Wolfe defined New Journalism as appropriating four specific fictional devices: "scene-by-scene construction"; recording the dialogue "in full"; and taking advantage of the third-person point of view, "presenting every scene to the reader through the eyes of a particular character."

Although Wolfe never refers to New Journalists as anthropologists or sociologists, he describes the fourth element as "Recording the everyday gestures, habits, manners, customs, styles of furniture, clothing, decoration, styles of traveling, eating, keeping house, modes of behaving toward children . . . and other symbolic details that might exist within a scene."

As an example of a writer carefully amassing details to construct dramatic scenes as any novelist might, Wolfe included a selection from Truman Capote's *In Cold Blood*. Primarily a fiction writer prior to that book, Capote studied novelists like Gustave Flaubert, Jane Austen, Marcel Proust, and Willa Cather in 1958 as he trained himself to produce "a narrative form that employed all the techniques of fictional art but was nevertheless immaculately factual." The following year he read about the murder of four members of the Clutter family in a small town in Kansas, with no apparent motives and almost no clues. He devoted the next six years to researching the crime, compiling 6,000 pages of interviews, and then wrote his stunning "nonfiction novel" that became an instant bestseller when it was published in 1965.

> There is little in this book, even when it falls under the category of nonfiction or argument, that has not derived . . .
>
> —Norman Mailer, in *The Time of Our Time*

James Agee also influenced Capote's writing. In 1936, a magazine asked Agee and photographer Walker Evans to collaborate on an article about tenant farming in the U.S. by looking at a few families' daily lives. The project resulted in the 1939 landmark book *Let Us Now Praise Famous Men*. To bring readers into the tenants' homes, Agee commands readers in the second person to see what he sees: "Leave this room and go very quietly down the open hall that divides the house, past the bedroom door, and the dog that sleeps outside it."

Wolfe excerpts part of Norman Mailer's Pulitzer Prize-winning *The Armies of the Night: History as a Novel/The Novel as History* to show how New Journalists were manipulating point of view. Mailer chronicles his own participation in the 1967 March on the Pentagon using the third person. "Sin was his favorite fellow, his tonic, his jailer, his horse, his sword," writes Mailer about his own behavior at a party before the march, matching all the vividness of fiction. In the introduction to *The Time of Our Time*, a literary retrospective of his fiction and nonfiction, Mailer asserts, "There is little in this book, even when it falls under the category of nonfiction or argument, that has not derived . . . from my understanding of how one writes fiction."

Hunter S. Thompson, who became touted as the "Gonzo Journalist" after he abandoned any reportorial distance to describe riding with the Hell's Angels in 1965, copied pages from the novels of William Faulkner and F. Scott Fitzgerald earlier in his writing career. Reading Jack Kerouac taught Thompson "that you wrote about what you did." Wolfe characterizes Thompson's frenzied accounts of his experiences as featuring "a manic, highly adrenal first-person style in which Thompson's own emotions continually dominate the story."

It takes tremendous craft for a nonfiction writer to dominate his subject. Wolfe, Capote, Mailer, and Thompson could pull this off, but once they became celebrities in their own right, it became harder and harder for them to act as reporters. The instant they arrived to cover a story, their presence altered it. Other less-gifted writers who tried to copy them often failed when technique overwhelmed or even changed substance.

Sticking strictly to the facts and finding the most vibrant ways to convey those facts to readers continues to challenge nonfiction writers. "Most journalists experience a professional tug-of-war between the desire to tell a good story, and the desire to report thoroughly, analyze, and explain," Christopher Hanson wrote in a 1999 article in the *Columbia Journalism Review*.

New York Times reporter Nina Bernstein was initially hesitant to let go of "conventional journalism" when she started to expand into a book her series of articles about foster care in New York. Published in 2001, her critically acclaimed *The Lost Children of Wilder: The Epic Struggle to Change Foster Care* chronicles both a '70s lawsuit meant to dismantle discrimination in New York's system and the lives of children, like Lamont Wilder, caught up in the foster care bureaucracy. During the drafting process, an editor persuaded Bernstein to engage in a tug-of-war and draw on fictional devices. Bernstein insists, similarly to Wolfe's defense of New Journalism, that composing a scene "takes enormous amounts of information to glean the telling detail."

"As I became more comfortable applying literary techniques to my store of notes," Bernstein recalls, "I think an unconscious but real influence was George Eliot's *Middlemarch*." Eliot brings to the reader an "empathic irony" through changing points of view. In following the fractured childhood of Lamont Wilder, who rarely lived in the same place for more than a year, Bernstein recounts the young

> Most journalists experience a professional tug-of-war between the desire to tell a good story, and the desire to report thoroughly, analyze, and explain.
>
> —Christopher Hanson, in *Columbia Journalism Review*

boy killing a gerbil. To tell this story, Bernstein needed "to understand and identify with Lamont's actions, to feel what he felt and make readers feel it, or else this would be the point at which they distanced themselves emotionally from him." Based on information from many interviews, she draws readers in:

> It was dark in the latchkey room at school. The other children were watching a movie, but Lamont tiptoed to the back, where the gerbil lived in a metal cage. It twitched its whiskers at him, brown eyes appealing for release. Carefully, Lamont slid the cage door open and took the gerbil out. It lay warm and soft between his hands, the pulse of its heart like undemanding love. It was content to have its fur stroked, and Lamont felt each caress as though he, not the gerbil, were being gentled. He cuddled the creature, seeking the comfort that had eluded him all these months. . . . And the gerbil bit him, hard.
>
> The unexpected pain was like the opening of a sluicegate on the boy's rage. In an instant, he dropped the gerbil to the floor and stamped it. If the animal cried out, no one heard it. Its small, broken body lay still on the linoleum floor beside Lamont's foot, its life extinguished by his overpowering anger. He ran from the room and hid in the boys' bathroom. Like the gerbil in its cage, he crouched in a corner and defecated on the floor.

Bernstein slowly describes the dim light and Lamont edging away from the group to pet the gerbil. She uses a simile, "the pulse of its heart like undemanding love," to establish the psychological weight of the moment for Lamont. The pace suddenly quickens, as the gerbil's teeth sink into Lamont's flesh, and the reader empathizes with his violent reaction.

For inspiration, Bernstein looked to some of the same fiction writers as New Journalists, including F. Scott Fitzgerald and especially Charles Dickens. The latter's satirical *Bleak House*, published in 1853, follows the legal delays, lasting for generations, of the suit of Jarndyce vs. Jarndyce, which uncannily parallels the multiple generations involved in the class-action Wilder suit that Bernstein analyzed. From the beginning, Bernstein says, "I knew that I was attempting a kind of modern-day nonfiction Dickens in scope and incident. I knew the narrative drive had to be strong enough to carry the weight of the history, law, and politics that I wanted to include."

Adopting fictional devices opens up seemingly limitless possibilities for nonfiction writers, as well as making them more conscious of their craft. This consciousness has led to increased interest in literary nonfiction. In 1984, Robert Atwan sought a trade publisher to start an annual collection of essays for general readers. He could point to the success of Annie Dillard's Pulitzer Prize-winning *Pilgrim at Tinker Creek*. "Like the bear who went over the mountain," Dillard spent a year observing and describing the natural world, using more metaphors and similes than bees swarming around a hive thick with honey.

Houghton Mifflin published the first volume of *The Best American Essays* in 1986. From 1991 to 2000, *BAE* published 219 essays by 170 authors. Cynthia

Ozick is represented six times, more than any other writer. Like most of the multiple contributors, including William H. Gass, Edward Hoagland, Jamaica Kincaid, and John Updike, Ozick writes fiction as well as nonfiction. In the introduction to the 1998 *BAE*, for which she was guest editor, Ozick distinguishes what she calls "the marrow of the essay from the marrow of fiction" and maintains, "Essays, unlike novels, emerge from the sensations of the self." Speaking of the essay like "a character in a novel or a play," she concludes, "Above all, she is not a hidden principle or a thesis or a construct: she is there, a living voice. She takes us in." Joyce Carol Oates, who collaborated with Atwan to edit *The Best American Essays of the Century*, lists some of the ways the essay takes us in, "employing dialogue, dramatic scenes, withheld information, suspense."

These editors applaud authors employing the tools of fiction in nonfiction. The tactic, however, is not without risk. A clear case in point was Edmund Morris' broadly criticized 1999 *Dutch: A Memoir of Ronald Reagan*. In order to narrate particular scenes, Morris wrote himself into the book as a fictional friend of Reagan's. Critics found this Doppelganger device confusing and distracting. An original member of the New Journalism club for her 1968 essay collection *Slouching Towards Bethlehem*, Joan Didion reviewed *Dutch* for *The New York Review of Books*. Unrelenting in her diatribe against Morris for shoddy research, Didion also assesses his insertion of fictional characters. "Literary conceits are tricky, hard work," she concludes. "When this kind of thing works, it works unnoticed. When it does not work, it swamps the narrative, and leaves the reader toting up errors or misapprehensions."

Fictional devices work in nonfiction when they enhance the narrative's realism. At 21, Dave Eggers started raising his 8-year-old brother after their parents died of cancer within two months of each other. In *The New York Times Book Review*, Sara Mosle calls Eggers' account of parenting under these conditions, titled *A Heartbreaking Work of Staggering Genius*, "a furious whirlwind of energy and invention." The book became a bestseller in hardcover and paperback partly for mimicking the antics of fiction writer David Foster Wallace. Eggers' memoir includes "Rules and Suggestions for Enjoyment of This Book" along with an "Incomplete Guide to Symbols and Metaphors." Under the surface of this play, Eggers engages in nonstop stream-of-consciousness—whether in the middle of lovemaking or after he summons the police to help calm a suicidal friend:

The other cop is writing things down in his pad. The pad is so small. His pen is really small, too. They seem too small, the pen and pad. Personally, I would want a bigger pad. Then again, with a bigger pad, where would I put it? You'd need a pad-holster, which might look cool but would make it even harder to run, especially if you have the flashlight attachment . . . I guess you need a small pad so it'll fit on your utility belt—Oh, it would be so great if they called it a utility belt. Maybe I could ask. Not now, of course, but later.

This narrative verve and focus on the oh-so-particular slices through his humor and lets the reader see Eggers' full force. For a young man to witness both his parents die of cancer, every act of living becomes imbued with meaning. Eggers never writes directly about the impact of his parents' deaths. It is in his endless meditation on the minute that Eggers reveals his own indescribable pain and fear and longing.

Pegi Taylor of Milwaukee is a freelance writer and educator. She has written for Salon. com, the-cake.com, *Milwaukee Magazine*, and other publications.

CHOICE EXAMPLES OF CREATIVE NONFICTION

If you wish to study how nonfiction writers adopted the techniques of fiction, here is some suggested reading:

Essay collections
The Best American Essays of the Century, Joyce Carol Oates and Robert Atwan, editors (2000). Not only do the 55 essays provide readers a survey of style, but the book includes an invaluable appendix of "Notable Twentieth-Century American Literary Nonfiction."

Every fall Houghton Mifflin publishes its *The Best American Essays* collection. Robert Atwan has served as series editor since its inception in 1986.

The Book of Twentieth-Century Essays, selected and with a foreword and notes by Ian Hamilton (2000). This broader survey covers a century of nonfiction writing in the English language.

Graywolf Press started publishing thematic essay collections in the '80s, often in response to conservative cultural forces. In 1988, its *Multicultural Literacy* countered the return-to-the-classics movement activated by Allan Bloom's book *The Closing of the American Mind*. Last year, Molly Peacock edited *Private Eye: Privacy in a Public World* for the Graywolf Forum series.

Last year, Issue 16 of *Creative Nonfiction* was devoted to "The Line Between Fact and Fiction." Founder and editor Lee Gutkind featured contributors who "employ the diligence of a reporter, the shifting voices and viewpoints of a novelist, the refined wordplay of a poet, and the analytical modes of the essayist." See Web site at www.creativenonfiction.org.

[cont.]

[sidebar cont.]

Some heavy hitters, pre-New Journalism

Let Us Now Praise Famous Men by James Agee (1939). Agee describes his collaboration with photographer Walker Evans to examine the daily lives of three tenant families as "an independent inquiry into certain normal predicaments of human divinity."

Hiroshima by John Hersey (1946). Hersey used extensive interviews to reconstruct the lives of a group of survivors after the nuclear devastation of Hiroshima during World War II.

Notes of a Native Son by James Baldwin (1955). Baldwin found reading William Faulkner, Charles Dickens, and Ralph Ellison instrumental in the development of his writing.

Some heavy hitters of New Journalism

Slouching Towards Bethlehem by Joan Didion (1961). These essays about California are shot full of irony. "This is California where it is easy to Dial-A-Devotion, but hard to buy a book," writes the caustic Didion.

The Kandy-Kolored Tangerine-Flake Streamline Baby by Tom Wolfe (1965). A collection of 22 pieces Wolfe pumped out in 15 months. Wolfe captures Americans of a "new age": "The new world, submerged so long, invisible, and now arising, slippery, shiny, electric—Super Scuba-man?—out of the vinyl deeps."

In Cold Blood by Truman Capote (1965). Capote's in-depth account of the murder of the small-town Clutter family, culminating in the hanging of Eugene Hickock and Perry Smith for the crime. Foreshadowing fills the first section of the book, with a "liver-colored carpet" in the Clutter home and the ominous arrival of some pheasant hunters.

The Armies of the Night by Norman Mailer (1968). Robert Scholes categorizes Mailer as a "hystorian," who "asserts the importance of his impressions and his vision of the world."

Fear and Loathing in Las Vegas by Hunter S. Thompson (1971). Thompson drives with his lawyer from Los Angeles to Las Vegas to cover a motorcycle race. Considered by many the best of Thompson's Gonzo journalism. Thompson currently writes weekly for the *San Francisco Examiner.*

Other books mentioned in this story

The Lost Children of Wilder by Nina Bernstein (2001).
A Heartbreaking Work of Staggering Genius by Dave Eggers (2000).

POTENT PROSE: SCIENCE REPORTING

Turning dry data into compelling human stories

by Douglas Starr

So few people believed Dr. Barry J. Marshall when he said that peptic ulcers were an infectious disease caused by bacteria that hid out in the stomach, that he decided to make his point in the most vivid way possible. One July day in 1984, he awoke early, skipped breakfast, drove to the hospital, went to his lab, donned his white coat and fixed himself a drink containing about a billion of the suspect bacteria. "Ulcer bugs," he called them.

As Marshall stood by a high lab bench, thoughtfully swirling his turbid cocktail, a guy who worked in the lab said to him, "You're crazy."

Marshall said, "Here goes," and downed it. He cringed. "Tastes like swamp water," he observed.

So begins "Marshall's Hunch," Terence Monmaney's memorable *New Yorker* piece about the surprising discovery that a bacterium, not aggravation, causes ulcers. Like any good science journalist, Monmaney spent months poring over scientific papers and interviewing experts—in this case, in bacteriology and gastroenterology. Given the technical nature of the story, he could easily have produced a 10,000-word trudge. Instead, he wrote a compelling, humorous, and informative adventure.

No journalism subjects are more important than science, medicine, and the global environment. Developments in these areas affect our lives more than any others. Yet people often see science as dull, dry, or divorced from daily life. We can blame many factors, including an educational system that sets science apart from the arts, and Hollywood portrayals of scientists as oddballs—

Einsteins or Frankensteins. But as Monmaney and other skilled practitioners demonstrate, science can provide the basis for a gripping narrative.

What makes the difference between a story people want to read and one they merely feel they should? We could say all the usual things about narrative arc and the art of writing and rewriting, but most of the work should actually occur before you sit down at your computer. It's all about the choices you make and the context you put them in. Here, then, are a few steps to writing compelling stories about science, medicine, and the environment.

Do the research

The currency of science is the scientific paper—that dry, often impenetrable article in journals such as *Science, Nature,* or *The New England Journal of Medicine*. As a nonfiction science writer, you should inhabit these magazines, much as a travel writer visits the country he or she is writing about. (Many -journals are going online as well, which effectively brings the world to your desk.) Browse through the articles, get a feel for the issues people are talking about, and become familiar with the language and culture. Read the front sections describing the latest developments, then flip through the rest for scientific papers.

Of course, you won't limit yourself to the journals. As an observer of the science scene, you'll attend conferences, make contacts, and spend hours on the phone. But when you dig into a subject, you'll inevitably find yourself consulting the journal articles.

Here's where any courses or training you've had in science will help. Read the study, understand it, and prepare some thought-provoking questions. Don't worry if you don't work for *The New Yorker* or *The New York Times*—scientists are curious people by nature, and you can draw them into a rewarding conversation if the questions you pose are informed and provocative. Be sure to go beyond the particular study at hand. Flesh out the issue. Remember: The scientist you're talking to is a person, with all the normal motivations and feelings. How did he or she get involved in the project? What are its implications? What hopes or doubts does the scientist harbor?

Like other forms of nonfiction research, you should never base a story on a single source, so your work does not end with the first interview. Ask who else you might talk to in reference to the work. You might be surprised. Many scientists consider themselves so academically fair-minded that they will not only provide a list of colleagues who can evaluate their papers, but also those who disagree with them, as well.

Establish the context

"Location, location, location," the real-estate people say, and we can make an analogous assertion about context in science writing. It's all about context: scientific context, social context, and dramatic context.

Scientific studies have origins and implications. Every research piece has roots in something that came before, and in exploring that history you'll uncover a narrative line. If your interview does not reveal this information, look at the "references" section of the study—it may provide a road map to the work on which the study was based and to other researchers who will offer perspective.

Sometimes this perspective comes from the researchers themselves, if you know enough to ask. Medical writer Patricia Thomas tells of a press conference she attended at Harvard Medical School, in which scientists announced their latest discovery. They touted it as an important advance—conceivably the answer to the common cold. As reporters prepared to file their stories, one inquired, "Is anyone else working on this problem?"

"Well, yes," came the reply. "They've actually made the same discovery at Yale."

Instantly the story changed, from a dramatic breakthrough at a single university to a promising new avenue of general research—all because a reporter asked about the scientific context.

Few areas show the need for context-building as much as writing about medical research. Every day we're bombarded by stories about diseases of the week or cures of the moment. But much of this information is speculative. We've all read about dramatic cures that yielded amazing results in mice. What writers often fail to explain is that those same drugs must go through years of clinical trials in humans, and that more than 99 out of 100 drugs never succeed. Thus, a drug that shows great promise in mice has less than a 1 percent chance of succeeding in humans. As a disgruntled researcher once told me, "Mouse studies don't mean [anything]." That is not to say you should never write a story about drug testing in mice. Just be sure to put the story in perspective.

Once you've established the story's scientific context, try to understand its larger social meaning. Explore the implications of the issue you're reporting, for they add depth, importance, and drama.

Consider technology stories, for example. Any new invention creates haves and have-nots—those who profit from sales, employment, or convenience, and those who might lose business or jobs. Ask about those effects when you do your research on stories about technical innovations or cyberspace. Environmental issues have obvious social consequences. There's a growing awareness that the poor and working class suffer most from pollution. Stories about nutrition can change mass behavior, as seen in the dietary craze of a few years ago that resulted from reports on the benefits of oat bran. Explore implications like these, for they add meaning and resonance to the science story you're telling.

Next you'll want to think about the dramatic context of your story and what it means to the setting and character. Years ago, I researched the story of botanist Robert Betz, who was trying to restore the Illinois tallgrass prairie. I knew about Aldo Leopold and the great tradition of prairie conservation in the Midwest, and saw Betz as part of that scientific and social context. Still, I needed a deeper context relating the character to his work. I considered the logistical problem he faced—finding a very large area for his prairie that would remain forever undeveloped and undisturbed. His solution was to scout out an unusual location. He went to the Fermilab National Accelerator Laboratory near Chicago. There, scientists perform experiments in high-energy particle physics in an enormous underground accelerator tunnel. The tunnel creates a donut-shaped hump above ground about a mile in diameter, where no one is admitted. Betz spoke to the directors and got permission to build his prairie there.

The story had the makings of an interesting context—restoring an old prairie inside a high-tech nuclear ring. But it got better when Betz filled me in on his background. He was a city kid, an ex-jock whose idea of a prairie had been the outfield at Chicago's old Comiskey Park. This project, and the years of work leading up to it, had made him an unlikely champion of the rural American botanical heritage.

Finally, I had the scientific, social and dramatic context, all in a fun and significant story. Indeed, the story was so quirky, yet quintessentially American, that it was published in, of all places, *Sports Illustrated*.

Embrace complexity

When science writer Ellen Ruppel Shell undertook one of her many assignments for *The Atlantic Monthly*, she found herself embroiled in a story that became more complex as she went along. The story involved the high rates of asthma among inner-city children. To research the story, she went to "asthma central"—a poor neighborhood in the Bronx, where children are exposed to high levels of dust, grime, and allergy-causing cockroaches. The story seemed straightforward: Asthma was a disease of poverty. But then it got complicated. For while asthma proliferates in America's poor neighborhoods, she learned, it does not occur frequently in poor countries. Nor does it express itself in America's farms, where children grow up amid dust and dirt. There were other confounding connections: Asthma rates also seemed correlated to time spent indoors, passive entertainment, processed foods, and to early exposure to antibiotics.

It was clear that no single cause accounted for high asthma rates, but rather an accumulation of factors related to a strange combination of disadvantage and modern life. Asthma seemed a disease of both poverty and affluence. Another writer might have been discouraged by the conflicting variables, but Shell was intrigued. She included them all in an article called "Does civilization cause asthma?"—a compelling piece of journalism that earned respect from readers and public health officials alike.

Complexity can work for you if you embrace it.

Questions reporters should ask scientists about their predictions: What's going to happen? What are the odds that it will happen? How do you know?

Chaos: Making a New Science, James Gleick's bestseller, describes the birth of a new science that appreciates the complexity found in every level of nature. *The Coming Plague: Newly Emerging Diseases in a World Out of Balance* by Laurie Garrett tells how an accumulation of factors, including global travel, climate change, shifting populations, and the collapse of public health systems, is causing a re-emergence of infectious disease. *Guns, Germs, and Steel: The Fates of Human Societies*, the Pulitzer Prize-winning epic by Jared Diamond, describes how a combination of factors, some of which were mere accidents of nature, led to the primacy of the West in world civilization.

What these and other authors share is an appreciation that few things are simple, and you can tell a better story if you don't expect them to be. Events have multiple causes, and numerous and unrelated effects. So don't oversimplify. Acknowledge the complexity and give the scientific information a thematic framework that will help your readers understand it.

Appreciate uncertainty

People expect scientists to be authoritative and cocksure, but nothing could be further from the truth. Science is not certainty, nor is it a point of arrival. It's a process.

Few areas of science involve process and uncertainty as much as the environment. Environmental stories defy conventional storytelling rules. Conventional narratives recount past events. Environmental stories, in contrast, often deal with vague and future events such as global warming or the depletion of the ozone layer. They necessarily involve much uncertainty, since the future is not predictable.

As with complexity, uncertainty is not something to avoid. In fact, it's often the central point of the story. For example, scientists may never be completely certain about global warming—surely not in the next decade, when we as a society must make crucial decisions. But the story does not depend on whether the scientists will be sure. Indeed, the whole tension of the narrative involves what we as a society should do given the uncertainty. Should we ignore the issue, or hedge our bets by beginning to take action?

This isn't to say that your stories about the environment should promote an agenda. The point is that in cases where scientists (and the public) are faced with many doubts, don't ignore the issue of uncertainty—appreciate it as the core of your story.

Even when you acknowledge uncertainty, you'll find varying degrees of accuracy and truth. As an authoritative writer, you cannot let fly with every unsubstantiated prediction you hear. Qualify the predictions in ways that give faithful guidance to your readers.

Some years ago, prominent atmospheric scientist Stephen H. Schneider proposed three questions reporters should ask any scientist predicting an uncertain future:

1. What's going to happen? Identify the threat clearly to your readers. Be specific and don't exaggerate. Use worst-case scenarios only if you also include the most-likely scenarios.

2. What are the odds that it will happen? Give a sense of the relative risk. Is this event highly likely, or just a remote possibility?

3. How do you know? This key point will help readers evaluate the risk. How solid is this prediction? Is it based on a hunch or a substantial body of data?

Now, write your story

You've got your information, nested it in a context, and explored it for all its complexity and uncertainty. You've done the groundwork in setting up your story. At this point, all the usual rules of nonfiction apply. Think through your themes. Develop your characters. Establish the story premise clearly and write in the active voice. Create a satisfying story with a clear beginning, middle, and end. If you've done your homework, you'll have all the elements.

Don't be intimidated when you write about science. Consider it a human activity much like any other, whether politics, sports, film, or dance. It's OK to admire the people who perform it, but you also must remain critical of what they do.

Think of the scientist as someone prospecting for gold in a dark cave with a flashlight. Every once in a while, something glitters in the beam. "Maybe this is gold!" the scientist exclaims, picking it up and writing a journal article about it. But when viewed in the sunlight, it turns out to be iron pyrite, not gold.

Of course, it would be easier to floodlight the cave and immediately see the difference between gold nuggets and iron pyrite. But strong-enough floodlights haven't been invented yet. And so he and his colleagues go back to their prospecting, continuing the search with the best lights they have.

This is the way we as nonfiction writers should view science—advancing, hobbling, and sometimes going backward. But it is always fascinating and almost never standing still.

Douglas Starr lives near Boston and is co-director of the Center for Science and Medical Journalism at Boston University. His book *Blood: An Epic History of Medicine and Commerce* (Knopf) won the 1998 Los Angeles Times Book Prize.

TO LEARN MORE

Several books will help inform you about science-writing, providing guidance and examples.

A few of the more useful ones include:
A Field Guide to Science Writing (Oxford University Press)
Best Science Writing (Oryx Press)
The New Science Journalists (Ballantine Books)

Houghton Mifflin also publishes annually:
The Best American Science
Nature Writing

You can also consult Web sites:
National Association of Science Writers (www.nasw.org)
Society of Environmental Journalists (www.sej.org)

WRITING FICTION FOR CHILDREN

Good writing is essential
for readers of all ages

by Sam McCarver

Successful children's books are not a world apart from adult books, as some writers might think—they reflect the same principles of good writing. For this reason, adults and children can often enjoy the same books, and writers, by understanding the similarities, can gain a much clearer understanding of how to write fiction for children.

A good example of such a mutually enjoyable "crossover" book is the middle-grade children's book *Angel on the Square* by Gloria Whelan, a fascinating historical story that is told in the first person and set in Russia during World War I. It opens with an air of expectation: "I could feel the crowd holding its breath, awaiting the moment when Tsar Nikolai II and Empress Alexandria would arrive."

And no matter what your age, the following opening from Eva Ibbotson's *Dial-A-Ghost* ("for ages 8 to 88") is bound to engage you: "The Wilkinson family became ghosts quite suddenly during the Second World War when a bomb fell on their house." Imagine the fun of a story about the Dial-A-Ghost Agency, which "finds good homes for ghosts." And a pair of spooks called The Shriekers, and Fulton Snodde-Brittle, "who wants the wickedest ghosts he can get for his grand home."

While intended for children, adults can well appreciate the stories in these two middle-grade books. Naturally, there are similarities and differences in style and content. *Angel on the Square* is a historical novel in the first person, while *Dial-A-Ghost* is in third person. Each is around 50,000 words. What makes both of them a good read is that each opens with characters who are involved in something intriguing and unexpected.

Turning to a "crossover" example from adult fiction, my novel *The Case of Cabin 13*, about adventure and suspense aboard the *Titanic*, was enjoyed not only by adults but also many children and teenagers. Notice the similarity in concept as the book opens: "Professor John Darnell smiled as he poked his way along through the clammy opaqueness of the thick moist fog, using his black umbrella as a walking stick. Predictably, his work as a paranormal investigator always increased with 'pea-soupers.' " The main character is involved in something interesting. A 13-year-old boy who read it e-mailed me, "I'm going to buy every book you write!" So the line between adult and children's fiction can be thin—and sometimes erased.

Why is this so? To apply to writing Gertrude Stein's famous quote on roses, "A good book is a good book is a good book"—because it is written following effective fiction principles that apply equally to adult fiction and children's fiction. Glancing at an adult novel and a middle-grade book for children 8 to 12 years old, you might conclude that such books are totally unalike. After all, books for adults may be larger, and the words in children's books are pitched to the younger reader. But it is the similarities that actually are more compelling, especially in the basic concepts, the structure, and the manner of writing. A potential writer of children's fiction can learn much by studying the craft in adult fiction.

Learning from adult fiction

The goal in writing popular books for both adults and children is identical: Fiction is *entertainment*. Your children's book should not be designed to teach a lesson, send a message, or expound upon a moral theme. A theme, such as *honesty is the best policy* or *perseverance pays,* may be implicit in the storyline, but the point should be made subtly by the outcome of the plot. A theme not flatly stated will have more impact and be more personal and valuable when a reader sees and understands the cause-and-effect relationship of forces at work in the story and its results, and learns from the progress of the story. *Don't preach or teach. Entertain!*

Let's look at some other common story elements:

The main character. In adult fiction, you must begin by creating an interesting, empathetic main character and giving that person an important desire and challenge. "The secret of a story, to me," said Marion Zimmer Bradley, "is a likeable character going through almost overwhelming odds to win a worthwhile goal." Ernest Hemingway went beyond this, advising writers to create *"living people,"* not merely characters. Your story should be built around your main character, who then drives the story. Therefore, something important to your main character should be at stake in your story. Something must be investigated, achieved, understood, overcome. And your story for children, just as for adults, must be a strong one. Besides being appropriate for the target age-level, it should include action, excitement, and perhaps mystery, consistent with the overall tone and plot.

The "magic" plot. Fiction for both adults and children must show the reader, through the character's actions and thoughts, an empathetic main actor who has something important at stake, and who also has a personal problem, is facing obstacles, resolving conflicts, and achieving goals in a climax that is leading to a satisfying conclusion. Fiction readers, irrespective of their age, have much the same needs: a close, vicarious identification with a main character, and a desire to see that person succeed. Referring to his own technique for mystery fiction, Elmore Leonard says, "I let the story come through the eyes and feelings of my characters." This intimate approach improves reader identification with characters.

Subplot. Both adult fiction and books for children need subplots. A subplot is a separate storyline, usually dealing with the main character's personal challenges, which may or may not be related to the main plot but which must be resolved in the book. The subplot's resolution may be integrated with that of the primary plot line.

For example, in my novel *The Case of Cabin 13*, John Darnell's primary goal is to solve the White Star Line's deadly Cabin 13 jinx. But on the *Titanic*, John meets Penny, a young American woman, and they fall in love. He soon finds he must save her from a shipboard serial killer. Thus, the main plot and subplot intersect.

Similarly, as an example in children's fiction, a child character, Danny, might be investigating a mysterious light in an abandoned house while also trying to deal with a bully in his school. How does he solve both situations? Perhaps by asking the bully to help in his investigation of the "haunted house"—after which they go on to become close friends.

Humor. Don't overlook putting in humorous touches, which children love, and which can lighten up any storyline. In *Dial-A-Ghost*, Mother Margaret, who wants ghosts for her convent, says, "I know you will understand that we need ghosts who are not too noisy," and "Someone headless would be all right, too, as long as they didn't frighten the goats." Imagine negotiating the hiring of ghosts and setting forth the specifications!

Visuality and introspection. Any story you write should be visual, since we live in a visual age of movies, television, video games, and the Internet. That means the story is shown largely in scenes rather than told in narration—shown through the eyes and from the points of view of characters who are interacting, moving the plot forward, revealing their personalities, and working toward their goals through their actions and dialogue. In adult fiction, you "go into the main character's head"—that is, into thoughts and feelings that reveal the nature and depth of motivations propelling the character. Do the same in your children's fiction—especially for the main character. We want to know how that character feels, inside.

Conflict. Your story, as in all popular adult fiction, must involve conflict among characters, which often occurs when an antagonist tries to prevent the main character's achievement of goals. For adult examples, think no further than the latest John Grisham or Patricia Cornwell mystery. For a children's example, consider this scenario: A rival student, Mary, holds back a homework assignment from the main character, Trisha, who is struggling with math. Trisha resolves the conflict by offering to help Mary with her spelling, in return for Mary helping Trisha with math.

How kids books are different

Now, while we have focused on the striking similarities between children's and adult popular fiction, there are some differences the children's writer must take into account.

The right zone. First, be aware that children are not "small adults." They do not have the life experiences, schooling, or more fully developed vocabularies adults can draw upon in their reading. It's important not to lose your child reader by writing at a level too lofty or with a structure too complex for their reading comfort zone. On the other hand, don't try to be too cute. It doesn't take long for a child to spot that sort of affectation.

Words and word counts. Children like simpler sentences and shorter paragraphs. Words used in middle-grade books should be those that children under 12 would know, and sentences to a large extent should be simple and declarative. As British children's author Beatrix Potter, who wrote *The Tale of Peter Rabbit*, said, "The shorter and the plainer the better." Avoid long opening clauses and phrases and complex sentences. And keep chapters on the shorter side. All of this will keep the child reading.

Paperback books for children 8 to 12 may have 30,000 to 50,000 words, six to 10 pages per chapter, and a total of 130 to 200 pages, depending upon font size and lines per page. Hardcovers sometimes may be no longer than that but, as a group, they tend to range a bit higher, from 40,000 to 60,000 words.

The reader's connection with the main character. To promote a vicarious connection, the main character of a middle-grade novel must always be a child or young teenager—never an adult. Parents may be present or referred to in the story, but should not be critical to the plot, and children should provide their own solutions to their problems. Mild conflict with a parent or other adult might be in the plot, just as in life. Generally, the main-character child is as old as the oldest potential reader's age, or one or two years older. Eight-year-old readers may want a main character to be 9 or 10, while those closer to 12 may like a main character who is 12 to 14.

Children want to feel the story, as it proceeds, through a close, vicarious connection with the main character and an appreciation of his or her goal—which should be a challenge a young reader could face, or imagine facing.

For example: Danny's desire might be to blend well into a new school, to conceal a secret, to be accepted on a sports team, to attempt to solve a mystery, or, in fantasy, to deal with special powers or the supernatural. Through suspension of disbelief, children can imagine themselves in such circumstances. A key difference from adult fiction is that in children's books, children should think and speak in language and with vocabulary consistent with their age level, not the author's, and scenes should be described whenever possible by them, in their own words.

Another example: When Danny, walks into a dark room, it's better that he says, "It's dark as a cave in here," than it is for the author to narrate, "The room was so dark Danny couldn't see a thing."

Emotional appeal. Feelings, attitudes, and emotions at a child's level are important for a good connection between the reader and main character. Fear may be a prominent feeling—or courage, or pleasure. But to evoke a reader's

HOW TO BEGIN A CHILDREN'S BOOK

• Open the book with your empathetic, main-character child involved with an event, with something happening.

• Give the child an important goal—something to achieve, something at stake, something to overcome.

• Get your main character quickly into a scene, with dialogue and interaction with another character.

• Bring a sidekick into the story early in the book to share events with the main character.

• Include a sprinkling of humor wherever possible.

• Use age-appropriate words, mostly short, simple declarative sentences, as well as lots of dialogue.

• Know your writing goals: the average number of pages in a chapter, the number of chapters, and the total words in the book.

emotions, the writing should trigger such feelings. As Robert Frost said, "No tears in the writer, no tears in the reader." If the story is a mystery, thriller or fantasy, include plenty of excitement, suspense, and hooks.

Just as in adult fiction, children's mystery stories, for example, may include strange events, secrets, and even dangerous elements. And as with adult-level mysteries, such stories will have suspects, clues, red herrings, and other mystery elements, only with less graphic content and less emotional impact.

Other writing issues

In all popular fiction, but especially in children's fiction, authors should grip readers from Page 1 with an event that captures the reader's attention. For example, in my book *The Case of Compartment 7*, the first chapter begins with the following paragraph, which establishes the main characters and the direction for the entire novel:

> John and Penny Darnell left their cab at the Gare de Lyon train station in Paris and hurried forward to the massive building. Porters followed them with their bags. A drizzle of fine rain greeted them, and the streets were dark and wet on this cool spring night.

An ideal standard to aim for is that each scene and chapter should begin with an intriguing paragraph, and that each chapter should end with a hook.

Here are other key factors of style and technique:

• Your story must be compelling, clear, organized, and well-written. The main character should be focused on a specific, primary goal, which is achieved in the book. And your book should simply be many visually presented scenes, linked by the storyline.

• Your word choices and the length and nature of dialogue should be appropriate to the readers' age. Use lots of dialogue that moves the plot forward and reveals character, accordingly leaving much "white space" on the pages.

Check the naturalness of your dialogue by reading it aloud, along with other passages of your book, to children in your target age group. Use concrete sensory details of clothing, food, and surroundings for a greater feeling of real life.

In language and tone, the author should respect the reader's intelligence, and not "write down" to an adult or a child.

• And lastly, adopt as your own the writer's creed, incorporating the following points:

Character endures longer than plot in your stories.
Action intrigues the reader more than passive language.
Scenes excite the reader more than narration.

Dialogue interests the reader more than exposition.
Nouns and verbs trump adjectives and adverbs.

Don't skimp on preparation

To prepare yourself for writing a children's book, study recent children's fiction in the category in which you'll be writing—such as fantasy, adventure, or mystery—just as you would to prepare for writing an adult novel. The object here is to make certain your book falls into the same general range of experience formed by the current, published books you study.

Don't read the books passively. Note how they begin, study the characters and names, the challenges, and the climax. Note word choices, lengths of scenes and chapters, and book length. Evaluate the proportions of narration, description, scenes, and dialogue. Seeing what good authors have done in polished, published books and learning from them will help you position your children's book within appropriate parameters.

Read textbooks and magazine articles on how to write children's stories. Find a way to get your work critiqued, perhaps by joining writing clubs or groups that involve writing for children. Locate a library or other venue where you can read portions of your manuscript to children of the age level you're writing for, to learn from their reactions.

And finally, put yourself into the minds and hearts of your character-children as you write, by introspection. Reveal your main character as one who is empathetic, good and strong in character, but yet may have small failings. Make your characters "real people," drawing upon your own childhood experiences, reflecting upon knowledge and understandings you've gained in your interaction with both adults and children, and observing children you're close to, such as your own children, nieces, nephews, grandchildren, or students.

Then readers will connect not only with your characters but, indirectly, with you, who breathed life into their new friends. And they'll want to read more about these characters, who seem like real people to them—in your next book.

Sam McCarver of Dana Point, Calif., writes and teaches novel writing. Penguin Putnam has published four novels in his John Darnell Mystery Series; his fifth, *The Case of The Uninvited Guest*, will be released in Fall 2002.

DECISIONS, DECISIONS

As an author of any book of fiction, whether it's an adult novel or a children's book, you'll need to make some key decisions:

Point of view?
Should you use first person or third person? Using first person—showing the thoughts and feelings of only the single main character—may give a reader a greater vicarious connection. But to reveal the thoughts and feelings of more than one character for the sake of variety and possibly greater interest, third person will be more effective.

In my first book, *The Case of Cabin 13*, John Darnell is the main character, but we are able to see into other characters' minds and feelings by way of a third-person, multiple point of view, such as in these thoughts of Captain Smith of the *Titanic:* "He wasn't sure he wanted to learn much more of the new technology. Part of him longed for the older, simpler days; part yearned for his retirement; part of him wanted the glory of captaining the largest ship in the world. He sighed, confused with his contradictory feelings."

Series or stand-alone?
In a series, the main character will star in all the books, and often will be accompanied by other key characters. Therefore, that main character must be a complete, well-rounded one, with continuing interest, and other characters in the series should also be solidly established. Children's series are extremely popular and very prominent.

A children's book series that is quirky and fascinating is *A Series of Unfortunate Events* by Lemony Snicket (a name to be envied), featuring The Baudelaire Orphans. On the back cover of *The Wide Window* in the series is this typical comment: "You should know this: Violet, Klaus, and Sunny are kindhearted and quick-witted, but their lives, I am going to say, are filled with bad luck and misery." And a further comment by the author: "Their adventure would be exciting and memorable, like being chased by a werewolf through a field of bushes at midnight with no one to help you."

Stand-alone books introduce different main characters with different storylines but often in the same genre. Gloria Whelan's *Angel on the Square* is an example of a good stand-alone.

[cont.]

[sidebar cont.]

Your target age?
For children's books, deciding upon the target age of your reader and
determining your reading audience are critical. A target age range of 8 to
10 will suggest shorter books, while youngsters 10 to 12 will prefer longer
ones. The age range also will affect your writing style, the vocabulary level
you use, and even the genre.

For example, the younger group loves the *Goosebumps* series. Older
middle-grades enjoy imaginative works such as the *Dinotopia* series,
which features humans living alongside intelligent dinosaurs, and
T°Witches, with twin witches Cam and Alex.

—*Sam McCarver*

SIX WEEKS TO WRITE A CHILDREN'S BOOK

How to plan & write a marketable children's book
in just six weeks

by Shirley Raye Redmond

Did you love curling up with a stack of library books when you were a child? If so, you've probably dreamed—off and on—of writing for kids. But life keeps getting in the way. There's been no time, and besides, you're not even sure where or how to begin.

Have you got six weeks? If you're working full time, can you set aside six weeks of evenings and weekends? If so, you can start and finish a marketable book for youngsters. I've used this method six times and each completed manuscript, including all those mentioned in this article, sold to a major New York publisher. Use the following blueprint and make the project your top priority for the given time period.

Week 1

This week of planning is every bit as important as the actual weeks of writing and revision. Don't take it lightly. You need an idea and a plan. Had you elected to undertake a six-week home improvement project, you would first decide if you were going to build a deck or a garage. Then you would need a building plan before you actually purchased supplies or invited friends to a Saturday afternoon construction party.

I had been reading Richard Ellis' *The Search for the Giant Squid: The Biology and Mythology of the World's Most Elusive Sea Creature*. Recalling my own childhood interests, I knew that inquisitive youngsters would relish a book about this fascinating subject. That was my idea—to write my own book about the giant squid.

But my plan was more specific than that: I wanted to write a nonfiction book for readers in grades 2-4. I spent my planning week in bookstores and the children's section of my local library. I read dozens of books aimed at youngsters in this age category. I studied the diction and sentence structure. I counted words, paragraphs and pages. This intensive market analysis provided me with a suitable blueprint, or pattern for construction. I figured the book should have 48 pages, with about 1,000 words of text.

I also compiled a list of suitable publishers that had already published books similar in style to the one I intended to write. With that, I had a premise, a pattern, and a list of possible publishers.

Week 2

Now you can start drafting a rough outline of your manuscript. If you're writing fiction, you'll need to plot your story, develop character dossiers, and establish a believable setting. Nonfiction writers will use this week to do research and take notes. If your topic is one that has been written about many times before—such as the 1804 Lewis and Clark expedition—consider a creative new slant to make your manuscript more marketable.

On a trip to Yellowstone National Park, I picked up materials about the expedition and learned how the explorers attempted to capture a prairie dog for Thomas Jefferson as a souvenir of their westward journey.

The image of 40 grown men peering and reaching down into prairie-dog burrows (while the prairie dogs watched curiously in the background) tickled my "inner child."

It was that episode I chose to focus on while writing my 48-page reader *Lewis and Clark: A Prairie Dog for the President* (due from Random House in January 2003). I spent my research time discovering how the explorers' Corps of Discovery actually shipped the little creature back to Washington, D.C.

Persistence, patience, professionalism, and perseverance are more often the keys to writing success than talent or creative originality.

Week 3

Using the rough outline you drafted last week, you're now ready to start scribbling a story. Do it quickly. Don't worry about grammar, punctuation, spelling, paragraph structure, or anything else. Simply write. Give in to the temptation to ramble on and on. Want to write your ending first? Go ahead! If a particular scene comes to mind and you're eager to put it on paper, do so. You can stitch everything together later.

To help you stay on course, however, keep your working title in sight at all times—at the top of each page, if you're writing longhand, or on a sticky note attached to your computer. This "word map" will help you maintain focus and keep you on the road you wish to travel, without accidentally veering off a side street. I used "Prairie Dog" instead of "Lewis and Clark" at the top of my page so that everything I scribbled would relate directly or indirectly to the capture of that rodent.

Week 4

If you're prone to procrastinate, this will be your most dangerous week. Don't let your will power wane. Take your craft—and yourself—seriously. Persistence, patience, professionalism, and perseverance are more often the keys to writing success than talent or creative originality, so don't quit now. If you're working on a long manuscript, keep those creative juices flowing. If necessary, set a word or page quota for yourself. Be your own merciless drill instructor—don't slack off.

If you've been working on a shorter manuscript, you may already be done with your second draft. What now? Yet another draft—this time separating the wheat from the chaff. Don't edit or tackle grammatical errors at this time. You'll do that during Week 6. Now you want to focus on quality control. Get rid of anecdotes or scenes that do not move your story forward. Concentrate on the "why" of it all. Why are you writing this story? To inform? Inspire? Entertain? Does each page or chapter reflect your purpose? Does the dialogue enhance the plot or pace of your story? If not, get rid of it.

Week 5

How does your story measure up? Check for consistency. Does your protagonist still have blue eyes, or have they suddenly become brown? Have you been consistent with your spelling of Sacagawea (the preferred spelling of the U.S. Mint)? Is your story still being told from the same character's viewpoint?

While stitching together any out-of-order scenes or chapters, consider the emotion in your story. Like mortar between bricks, emotion and humor will stabilize your narrative. Children are emotional creatures. Let them giggle, worry, and even weep. But if your story must have a sad ending—such as two friends parting—at least make it hopeful so that young readers can imagine the two friends will meet again one day.

Week 6

Now's the time to tackle the good, the bad, and the ugly. You can be sure your final draft will still need polishing and revision. Clean up that sloppy copy. Perfect your punctuation. A professional presentation is essential for attracting the attention of a discerning editor. Don't skimp on hard work this week. Rigorous revision is often what separates the published writers from the unpublished ones.

Consider your paragraphs one by one. Are they all tightly focused? Are the transitions smooth? Is your sentence structure too complex? Are your word choices age-appropriate and accurate? In polishing my Lewis and Clark manuscript, I realized I had misused the words "marmot" and "woodchuck" to describe two very different rodents. Actually, these two words refer to the same animal.

And your young readers will notice those lapses in logic. In my 96-page chapter book *Grampa and the Ghost*, the Gaffney youngsters rebel against the very idea of ghosts, while their grandfather readily accepts Tallulah's spooky presence. I knew savvy young readers would wonder why. So I addressed the problem head-on by having one of my characters declare: "You don't believe in ghosts, do you? There are no such things as ghosts and goblins anyway!" His grandfather replies with a sigh: "Mark, when I was a boy, there were no supersonic jets—I went to Africa on a ship. Man only dreamed of going to the moon, and we couldn't even imagine such things as heart transplants. Microwave ovens, high-tech computers, and even televisions weren't even dreamed of. So you see, an old-fashioned ghost isn't such a hard thing for me to believe in at all."

So that's the basic blueprint. Take it and custom-build your very own marketable children's book!

Shirley Raye Redmond of Los Alamos, N.M., is a fulltime freelance writer. Three of her nonfiction children's books will be published next year.

CHOOSING YOUR SCREEN STORY

A screenwriter's checklist

by Cynthia Whitcomb

What are the basic ingredients that make a great script, and thence a great film? Before you invest weeks in structuring and writing a script, it's wise to step back and run through this basic list of criteria to see if the story holds up. Will it play? Will it hook an audience and keep it on the line until the final fade? They are questions that need to be addressed before you begin writing your screenplay.

They are a screenwriter's checklist, not too far afield from the journalist's "Who, What, When, Where, How, and Why."

Is my central character active?

Someone an audience can relate to and identify with? Is he (or she) sympathetic? Driven? What does he want and how badly? A passive protagonist can be a big problem. In fact, he can sink an otherwise good script. Find ways to make your main character an integral part of the story, not merely an observer. An active protagonist makes things happen, he doesn't just have things happen to him.

The Big Lebowski by the Coen brothers is one example of a passive protagonist killing a film's energy. He's one of those laid-back surfer/stoner/slacker dudes (pick your era) whose primary response to any event is "Far out." Even a strong actor like Jeff Bridges can't help him out of the pit of passivity. This guy could be a great, funny secondary character, like a best friend or sidekick, but if he has to carry the film, it's going to end up lying there on the chaise lounge next to him, with the audience nodding off.

For god's sake, make your protagonist grab the wheel and drive the movie! If you're stuck here, ask yourself, what does he want? How badly? And what's he willing to do to make it happen?

What's the problem?

Is there a central conflict strong enough to drive the engine of the film all the way through without losing momentum? What is at stake? Will people care? If the stakes are high (life and death, world threat, lost child) this will take care of itself. If the stakes are more subtle—for example, if the central question is "Will Murray sell out, give up being the eccentric lovable fool he is and become just another pencil pusher?"—it will be harder to get the audience emotionally invested. If you can get the audience to care about the character and the character to care about the problem, you'll get there.

The problem (or central question) must be in place by page 15 at the latest. Page 10 is better. And page 1 is great. And it must not be solved until the climax of the movie.

Can this story be told visually?

Is it all "talking heads"? Or can the story be shown rather than told? As you begin to plan the story, think about ways to avoid people talking in cars, over meals, or on telephones (these are "talking heads scenes"). Find more visual ways to stage these interactions.

What large set-pieces could it include? A carnival, planetary collision, car chase, scaling Mount Everest? Try to see cinematic possibilities now. Imagine what clips they could choose for the Coming Attractions trailer.

What are the locations?

Where does the story take place? Does it need to be broken out onto a broader canvas? If it is a prison story, can you find ways to get us out of the cells so the audience can breathe? If it all takes place in a submarine, the close quarters and limited visual stimulus may work to help create the claustrophobic feel you want. Even so, an occasional enemy ship or storm on the surface will open it up and give the audience more to see.

> Can this story be told visually? Is it all "talking heads"? Or can the story be shown rather than told?

Is it basically an internal story or can it be externalized?

Novels and plays can be difficult to translate into screenplays because they are often basically internal stories. Movies need to play out visually. If the central problem is purely emotional, for example, and not physical, how will you take the audience on a mental, emotional ride? You can't tell us that Joe is having trouble with relationships. You have to show Joe dating, blowing it, and so on. Movie audiences don't have a lot of patience for long, philosophical discussions. But they'll go anywhere, from Alcatraz to Auschwitz, and deal with any issues you choose, if those issues are translated into visual movie terms. In other words: show them, don't tell them.

What is the time frame?

How much time does this story cover? Is it compact or does it ramble over years? Is there any way to compress it to add energy to the movie? Almost always, the more tightly you can compress time, the better the script (and film) will move. Having to stop the story and wait while characters sleep for the night, for instance, is tedious.

When does it take place?

Is it contemporary? Historical? Most movies bought and made today are set in the present day. On the other hand, most of the Best Picture Oscars over the last two decades have gone to period pictures. Either way is fine to go, but if you are going historical, be sure to do your homework and research the period carefully.

Does it involve another reality?

Science fiction, fantasy, futuristic, or horror? If so, you need to be clear on the reality base and the rules before you begin. For example, in a vampire movie, the rules may be that the vampire:

- casts no reflection in mirrors
- needs to drink human blood to survive
- can only be killed by sunlight or a stake in the heart

You can make your own rules, but then you must follow them.

Is there an antagonist?

Is he a worthy opponent—strong enough to be a real challenge to your protagonist? Who is he and what is motivating him? For the conflict between the antagonist and protagonist to work well, they should be equally matched in terms of power, intellect, presence/charisma, and resources at the disposal of each. A weak or stupid opponent saps the game of its energy and fun. A football game won by 50 points is boring. One that is won by one point in the last three seconds is not. Make both sides strong and equally matched for a good game. If one is an underdog, it needs to be the hero. The villain should never be the underdog.

Is there a love story?

If so, think it through. Make those two people unique individuals, not just standard cardboard figures plugged into the plot. And why do they fall in love? It can't be just because they are played by gorgeous movie stars. It is your job to script their meeting and the development of their relationship with enough freshness and detail that we are hooked by it and become invested in its outcome. Avoid slow-motion montages of strolling on beaches at sunset, flower markets, kissing in rain, and so on. Show us scenes of two real people making a real connection.

Who are the other characters you need to tell this story?

The protagonist usually needs someone to play off of. Even the strongest, most silent heroes have relationships—whether with a mother, drinking buddy, best friend, or psychologist. Make sure you people your movie with vivid secondary characters.

What's it all about?

What are you saying? "Love prevails"? "Justice can be won, even if it's a tough fight"? "Life sucks"? You need to be clear before you begin, so your story can be clear as you write it. You may not plan to send a message with your movie, but it will send one anyway. All stories do. Be clear what it is, and make sure it's one that you want to send.

Cynthia Whitcomb of Lake Oswego, Ore., has taught screenwriting for nearly 20 years, including seven at the UCLA Film School. In her career, she has sold over 70 feature-length scripts to Hollywood for film and television, including *Buffalo Girls* starring Anjelica Huston, Melanie Griffith, and Reba McEntire. She is author of *The Writer's Guide to Writing Your Screenplay* (Spring 2002), from which this excerpt is taken, and *The Writer's Guide to Selling Your Screenplay* (Fall 2002), both published by The Writer Books.

THE "IS IT COMMERCIAL?" CHECKLIST

I know that you are only in this for two basic reasons: to see your own words and story made into a movie—and to sell your script for a lot of money. So let's look at a checklist that will help us sweeten the odds.

Do you love it?
Good. Now ask yourself, which movies you have loved in the last five years that were commercially successful? There is a wide spectrum of material that could be commercially successful. Find the niche that fits you and look for some examples of movies in that niche that have been successful. If you don't remember, walk the aisles of your video store and look around.

Is it castable?
Can you imagine well-known actors playing the leading roles? This doesn't mean every character has to be gorgeous and 30 years old. We have movie stars of all ages, from tots to tottering. But if your lead is an amoeba from the Galaxy Andromeda, a robot that looks like a garbage disposal with crab legs, a talking armadillo, or whatever least castable idea you can come up with—well, it's going to be harder to sell that script.

   Don't blame Hollywood. It's our fault. Do we rush out and see the new Julia/Mel/Brad/Harrison/Tom movie the first weekend? Yes, we do. And as long as those stars open movies, Hollywood will keep buying scripts with parts for those people to play.

Is it high concept?
Is it a story that can be told in a few sentences so that people understand what it's about? This doesn't mean that it has to be "Three guys make a bet they can get laid on prom night." No. It can be "Young Will Shakespeare falls in love for the first time and it helps him write *Romeo and Juliet.*" Write the *TV Guide* blurb. Write what people will tell their friends about this great movie they saw last weekend. Word of mouth is powerful.

   If you can tell it in a strong, abbreviated version now, it will be easier for you to get it right as you write. (And then to pitch it, too.)

Can you imagine the billboard?
Magazine ads? Posters? Imagine opening your newspaper to the movie section and seeing the ad for your movie. Imagine the title. The stars. The ad line. If you can visualize it, someone else can, too.

—*Cynthia Whitcomb*

POINT OF VIEW

Why mystery writers give their sleuths a say

by William G. Tapply

Among the many decisions you must make when planning your novel, none is more important than point of view. POV determines how your readers will experience the story. It gives them eyes, ears, noses, tongues, and fingers, as well as a brain for processing and interpreting the signals their senses send. POV tells readers where to sit, stand, walk, and run as your novel's events unfold. It determines what they will know and what will be withheld from them.

POV options are myriad. Single or multiple? First or third person? Intimate or omniscient?

For no literary form is the POV decision more critical than for the mystery novel. In most cases, successful mystery novelists choose to narrate their tales from a single point of view, usually first person.

Mystery-novel conventions

Mysteries, by definition, turn on the central plot question: "Whodunit?" This definition produces the six universal requirements (call them "conventions") of the mystery novel:

The puzzle. A crime (generally a murder, often more than one) has been committed. At the beginning, the reader doesn't know who did it or why or how it was done.

Detection. The plot revolves around the efforts of the sleuth to solve the puzzle. When he succeeds, the story ends.

The sleuth as hero. The protagonist of the mystery is the character who attempts to solve the puzzle.

The worthy villain. The murderer, like the sleuth, is clever and highly motivated. He wants to get away with it. He tests the limits of the detective's powers, making the puzzle a supreme challenge for the sleuth.

The reader as participant. Mystery readers will not settle for the role of spectator. They want to think along with the sleuth to see if they can deduce the solution to the puzzle.

Fair play. Readers want to match wits with the sleuth. They demand that all of the evidence known to the sleuth be presented to them. They want to know what the sleuth knows and what he's thinking. If the solution to the puzzle hinges on some fact that the writer withholds from them, readers feel cheated. If they know more than the sleuth, the puzzle-solving challenge is diminished and unsatisfying.

The preferred choice

Given these conventions, it's easy to understand why most mystery novelists write from the single, intimate POV—that of their sleuth. Experiencing the story as the sleuth does—seeing, hearing, smelling, tasting, and feeling what he does, and sharing his thoughts and speculations, his hopes and fears and worries along the way—gives readers exactly the same information. No more, no less. It allows readers to play along with the sleuth in a fair game, to become detectives themselves.

Mystery fiction is famous for its sleuths, both professional and amateur. Its enduring popularity, in fact, can be attributed to the power of reader identification with heroes and heroines as diverse as Sherlock Holmes, Hercule Poirot, Nero Wolfe, Sam Spade, Travis McGee, Kinsey Millhone, Kay Scarpetta, and Stephanie Plum. The roster of indelible mystery protagonists goes on and on. Readers feel they know these characters with whom they've shared puzzle-solving challenges. Readers care about them, think of them as friends, worry about them. They like them and root for them to succeed, and they look forward to spending more time with them.

Create a highly motivated sleuth, give him plenty of personal as well as professional problems, and put your readers into his head, and you're well on your way to a long-running series of novels and a successful career as a mystery writer.

Here, for example, is how I wrote a key scene early in *Past Tense*, my recent Brady Coyne whodunit:

> I scrambled out of bed, pulled on my pants, and ran barefoot out of the house.
>
> Evie was still screaming. "Help! Brady, help! Oh, please, somebody help me."
>
> I followed the sound of her voice up the driveway, and around the bend about a hundred yards from the cottage I saw her kneeling at the side of the dirt road.

I ran up to her. A man was lying in the weeds. He was sprawled on his back.
It was Larry Scott. . . . He looked thoroughly dead.

The problem with multiple POVs

The storytelling advantages of the single, intimate point of view are lost in
stories told from multiple POV. Experiencing the story from the points of view
of more than one character dilutes the strong reader identification with a single protagonist that is the hallmark of mystery fiction.

There are also tactical problems with multiple POV. In mysteries, virtually
every character except the sleuth is a possible suspect. The more suspects, the
more complicated—and compelling—the puzzle. But when readers are allowed
into the mind of a character, the rule of fair play requires that they instantly
know if that character is the villain. If he's not, that's one less suspect. If he is,
the puzzle is solved prematurely. Entering into the POV of several characters
gives readers an advantage over the sleuth, who can only observe suspects from
the outside. Even when the writer avoids the POV of the villain, smart readers
(unlike the sleuth) are able to narrow the field by the process of elimination.
When readers know more than the sleuth, the game is no longer fair.

If that scene from my novel were told from both Brady's and Evie's POVs,
readers would instantly know that Evie should not be considered a suspect,
even though Brady's not so sure:

> The first thing Evie saw was a sneaker in the weeds beside the driveway.
> She stopped, hesitated, moved closer. Then she saw that the sneaker was
> attached to a foot, and the foot was attached to a man's body.
>
> She knelt beside him. It was Larry. He was lying on his back, staring up at
> the sky. Half-dried blood drenched his shirt. She touched his face. His skin felt
> waxy. "Who did this to you?" she thought.
>
> Then she started screaming.
>
> When Brady heard Evie's screams, his first thought was that she'd seen a
> snake. Evie was petrified of snakes. He ran out the door and up the driveway.
> Then he saw Scott's body, and he thought: Evie has finally done it. She's killed
> the bastard.

POV tells
readers where
to sit, stand,
walk, and run
as your novel's
events unfold.

The all-knowing narrator

A variation of the multiple point of view is the
omniscient. When the all-knowing writer moves
freely over the landscape, dipping into and out of
the heads of characters, observing and commenting
on events, divulging and withholding information at
will, readers feel manipulated. They know they're
not being told everything, and what they are allowed
to know feels arbitrary and whimsical. The dominant
mind at work belongs not to the sleuth but to the

writer, who speaks directly to readers and blatantly controls the puzzle-solving game. Readers don't have a fair and equal chance to play. The writer knows the solution from the first page:

> The killer arranged Scott's body in the weeds beside the road where the girl was bound to see it. Then he got the hell out of there. He felt good. No way anybody could connect him to it. If he'd known Brady Coyne better, he wouldn't have felt so good.
>
> Two hours later Evie Banyon came jogging down the driveway, her long slim legs pumping, her auburn ponytail bouncing on her back. She was sweating from her morning run, feeling good, looking forward to a shower and a big glass of OJ, and she nearly tripped on the dead man's foot, sticking out of the weeds.
>
> When she saw it, she knew instantly he was dead. She thought she had a pretty good idea who had done it, and it took her only a moment to figure out how she had to handle it. Brady wouldn't like it. That made her feel bad, but she had no choice.
>
> Then she began to scream. She thought her screams sounded quite convincing. In a couple of weeks, she'd find herself screaming again. This time they wouldn't be phony.
>
> Coyne came running. She's probably just seen a snake, but still, he'd never heard Evie scream like that. When he saw her kneeling beside Larry Scott's dead body, rocking back and forth on her heels, screaming and screaming, he got the picture. It was hard to think of Evie Banyon as a killer. But she had the means, the motive, and the opportunity, and he couldn't help believing she'd done it. He was wrong, of course, but you couldn't blame him.

Bonding with the reader

It's no coincidence that most series mystery novels are told in the conversational first-person voices of the sleuths. Readers readily identify with the "I" who narrates these stories, who moves through his world, observing, speculating, feeling, and confiding in them. Everyone else is an outsider. When it's done well, readers quickly lose any sense of the writer at work. The sleuth and the reader form an intimate relationship.

For it to work, readers must respect the intelligence of the single-POV sleuth. She must be at least as clever and observant as they are if the puzzle-solving quest is to challenge both reader and narrator equally. Mystery readers do not want to solve the problem while the sleuth is still muddling around gathering clues and acting confused.

The bond between reader and sleuth depends on trust. The sleuth should never withhold information from readers—even if it means "giving away" a vital clue. She should never, for example, read a letter, or look out the window or have a telephone conversation without sharing with readers what she has read, seen or heard. Doing so might seem like a good way to build suspense; in fact, it's a violation of the rule of fair play and a cheap trick that irritates readers and causes them to mistrust—and even dislike—their friend.

Single-POV novels work best when the sleuth/narrator is actively engaged in the story's quest. Give her reasons to go places, witness events, encounter danger. She should be doing things—not just passively asking questions and sitting around thinking. No matter how probing the questions or clever the deductions, a stay-at-home sleuth makes a poor narrator. Getting the sleuth out of the house to where things are happening is the plotting challenge of the single-POV novel.

Suspense—the most important quality of any novel—becomes intense in mysteries as the stakes grow for the narrator. She sometimes takes risks, miscalculates, underestimates the danger, confronts a desperate adversary, is surprised. Readers, identifying with the POV character, accept her danger as their own.

Suppose your sleuth is restricted by a wheelchair or confined to a prison cell. Maybe he's a wealthy, sedentary orchid grower who refuses to leave his Manhattan apartment. A passive sleuth such as Rex Stout's Nero Wolfe makes a brilliant detective—but a poor POV character. Stout solved this dilemma by giving Archie, Wolfe's caustic sidekick, the job of doing the legwork—and narrating his novels, much the same way as Conan Doyle made Dr. Watson, not Sherlock Holmes, his narrator.

In some mysteries, the "sleuth" is a collective entity, not a single character. In many of Tony Hillerman's Navajo novels, for example, the detecting job is shared more or less equally by Jim Chee and Lt. Joe Leaphorn. This requires Hillerman to divide the point of view between the two—a risky undertaking for many writers. Hillerman carries it off by alternating between two strong, intimate, and distinct third-person POVs. Readers identify with both.

Police procedurals, a subgenre of mysteries, sometimes use the entire police force as a collective sleuth. Ed McBain has made his 87th Precinct into a single, memorable "character" by spreading the POV job among as many as a dozen detectives, forensic experts, prosecutors, and cops.

If you violate any one of the six mystery-novel conventions mentioned at the beginning of this article, you are either writing a poor mystery, or you're writing something else. Your choice of point of view follows from those six rules. For most mysteries, it's usually a no-brainer: Understand that the sleuth is the novel's hero, and let him tell his story.

William G. Tapply is the author of *The Elements of Mystery Fiction: Writing a Modern Whodunit* (The Writer, Inc., 1995), and the author of many mystery novels featuring attorney Brady Coyne, with the 19th book in the series to be released by St. Martin's Press in 2002. Tapply also writes nonfiction articles and books on his other avocation, fly-fishing.

WHEN IS A MYSTERY NOT A MYSTERY?

Nowadays, the "mystery" shelves of libraries and bookstores are stuffed with novels that are not, technically, mysteries—books by such perennial bestselling authors as Mary Higgins Clark, John Grisham, Tom Clancy, Clive Cussler, Ken Follett, Frederick Forsyth, and Thomas Harris. Superficially, these books appear to be mysteries. The plot involves crime-busting. The hero finds himself matched up against an evil and highly motivated criminal. The story's energy comes from the efforts of the protagonist to identify, track down, and nail the villain. When he succeeds, as he inevitably does, the story ends.

Such books are called "thrillers" or "novels of suspense." The term "high concept" is often associated with these novels, because the stakes are typically higher than mere murder.

Thrillers do not invite readers to solve puzzles. They differ from mysteries in this crucial way: The key plot question is not "Whodunit?" but rather, "What's going to happen next?" Thrillers often begin like mysteries, with a crime, a corpse, and many puzzling questions for the hero. But sooner or later, the villain and his deadly intentions are revealed to the reader, and from that point the plot-driving issue becomes: Will this evil-doer succeed? Will he kidnap more children, murder more innocent women, assassinate the president, blow up the House of Commons? Will he kill our hero?

Mystery conventions don't apply to the thriller, simply because it's not a puzzle. Readers are typically invited to follow the moves of both hero and villain, and turn the pages because they are worried about what might happen.

Authors of thrillers almost always tell their stories from multiple third-person points of view. Perhaps an introductory scene from the POV of a victim, a tense grabber, the narrative hook, terminates with her murder. Then comes a scene from the POV of the hero going about his everyday business, unaware, at this point, of the challenges and dangers he will soon face. This might be followed by a scene from the POV of a future victim, who is blithely innocent of the evil that awaits her.

[cont.]

[sidebar cont.]

The game is afoot. The reader, from the beginning, knows more than the hero/sleuth.

Soon comes a scene from the POV of the villain, who may or may not be identified. At this point, readers might be given a hint about the villain's grand plan. Or maybe not. The author has no obligation to play fair with his readers. The multiple third-person narration allows the thriller writer to reveal and withhold information at will, consistent with his singular purpose of building unbearable suspense.

Thrillers can be "stand-alone" novels or entries in a series. Many suspense writers introduce a new protagonist with each book; others relate the exploits of the same hero through a series of adventures.

Suspense writers, like mystery writers, select the POV that best serves their storytelling purposes. Just as the single, intimate POV works best for whodunit mysteries, so do multiple POVs maximize the effects that the writers—and readers—of thrillers want.

—*William G. Tapply*

SECRETS OF ROMANTIC CONFLICT

by Vanessa Grant

Romance is a massive market, with thousands of developing writers struggling to crack it. Those who succeed know how to create and resolve romantic conflict to sustain suspense.

Romance literature tells us that love is the most powerful force in our lives. A story that does not convey this message is not a romance, although it may contain a romantic subplot.

Even romances that end unhappily, like *Casablanca* and *Bridges of Madison County*, show readers how love can help one achieve personal growth. In the best romances, this powerful love-message is inseparable from story conflict and suspense.

What is romantic conflict?

In a romance, falling in love creates problems for both hero and heroine, but ultimately love's power provides the solution. During their romantic journey, characters must experience both internal and external conflict as they struggle to achieve their goals.

Internal conflict is the result of a character's wanting two incompatible things. A hero wants love, yet fears being vulnerable. A heroine must keep a secret, although her moral code demands honesty.

In my novel *Hidden Memories* my heroine Abby has a secret. Her daughter Trish was conceived with Ryan, a stranger she met when she was in shock after her husband's death. Abby knows she should be honest about her daughter's real father, but fears the consequences of telling the truth. She wants to be an honest person, but she wants to hide the truth. Because she can't have both, she struggles inwardly.

If your characters don't experience internal conflict, you're telling the reader that the issues in this story aren't important enough to worry about. Internal conflict is essential, but external conflict generates excitement. If your hero and heroine don't experience *external* threats to their goals, they'll spend the book agonizing about the internal struggle and your reader will become impatient. External conflict occurs when characters struggle with each other over opposing goals. When characters with opposing goals have transactions with each other, conflict moves out in the open, becoming visible to readers and other characters.

Whenever a character experiencing internal conflict acts in response to that struggle, it becomes externalized and may create conflict with other characters. Abby's internal conflict, when she acts on it, has the potential to affect Ryan, her daughter, her daughter's grandfather, and her parents.

In Chapter One, Abby tries to hide when she recognizes Ryan across a crowded room. He could expose her secret and throw her life into turmoil. Even before Abby makes the first move in her struggle with this hero, she's fighting with her conscience, Ryan's right to know his child, and her desire to avoid exposure. When Ryan recognizes Abby, his attempt to learn all he can about her threatens to expose her secret even more. She fears he'll learn she has a daughter and realize he's the father. Abby's frightened response to the external conflict generates intensifying internal conflict.

In your novel, external conflict should always intensify the internal conflict.

Ryan wants to know why Abby disappeared after their brief affair. Once he learns she's had his child, he wants to form a strong relationship with his daughter. Because Abby wants to maintain the fiction that Trish is her dead husband's daughter, she can't let him have what he wants. Their opposing goals create both internal and external conflict.

Every step in the external struggle between Ryan and Abby makes Abby's internal conflict worse. Because of her internal conflict, when the external conflict begins, her reactions are instinctive, not logical. Characters experiencing heightened internal conflict often behave irrationally.

Abby is under stress, attacked from outside by Ryan, from inside by her own conscience. She tries to hide, to pretend, to evade. Ryan becomes suspicious. Abby's mother, who likes Ryan, makes things worse when she tries some matchmaking. As Abby and Ryan fall in love, both internal and external conflict skyrocket.

With strong internal conflict and strong interlinking external conflict, the stakes rise. The reader fears it won't work out for these characters. Will Abby drive Ryan away with her inability to live openly with the truth? Will Ryan become angry and leave? The more uncertainty readers feel over the outcome, the more satisfied they will be when hero and heroine come together in the end.

As your story progresses, the conflict must change and develop. Your hero and heroine must have trouble getting what they want, they must worry about it, doubting whether their relationship can work. For good reasons, they must offend one another. We all commit offenses against people we love because we're tired, worried, or afraid we're not loved as much as we love. Those are valid emotional reasons arising from our internal conflicts. They generate transactions that are part of external conflict.

In a love story, the conflict eventually develops to make the reader ask: "Do hero and heroine care enough about each other to make the necessary compromises? Can they trust each other enough to reveal their inner selves and commit to a believable, lasting relationship?

How to create conflict

Conflict is created when goals meet obstacles. To create conflict, first give your character an important goal, then have someone oppose that goal.

Every strong desire has its corresponding fear. If you combine your character's goal to a fear, you'll achieve a high level of internal conflict when things begin to go wrong. Abby's goal of keeping her secret is attached to her fear of what will happen if the truth becomes known. Her late husband was a famous artist, and although he destroyed Abby's sense of self, the world believed their marriage was idyllic. Now, however, if the truth is exposed, both Abby and her daughter will suffer.

Strong goals conceal strong fears.

By the time Ryan discovers Abby's lie, they are struggling with their own new relationship. The external conflict issues have grown. They are in conflict over Ryan's desire to be acknowledged as Trish's father, Abby's fear of committing to another disastrous relationship, and his insistence that they marry and become a family.

To create conflict in your story, give your character a goal, then ask yourself what fear hides behind that goal. The more powerful the fear, the higher the level of conflict. If your hero's goal is financial power, why is money so important to him? What does he fear? Did he live in severe poverty as a child? Perhaps he vowed never to be poor again. If he fears poverty, intensify the fear by making it personal. Perhaps his baby brother had a disease requiring expensive medical care. The hero worked a paper route, mowed lawns, and dug ditches for extra money, but it wasn't enough. The brother died.

This hero has a deep emotional fear that someone he loves will suffer again, and he won't be able to provide enough. With this fear behind his drive to achieve wealth, any threat to his financial security will create strong internal conflict. If this hero must choose between money and the woman he loves, all his fears about poverty will be aroused, and he'll be thrown into severe conflict. If he chooses money, he'll lose his love and the joy in life. If he chooses love, he'll lose the money and may be unable to keep his love safe. Unless your story is a tragedy, the hero will have to win the battle against his demons and choose love. His struggle will involve pain, suffering, and sacrifice.

From conflict to resolution

A good story begins by putting forth a story question in the reader's mind. In a romance novel, the story question is usually, "Will heroine and hero overcome the obstacles to love—their conflict issues—and find happiness?"

In *Hidden Memories,* Abby's opening conflict arises from her internal struggle between honesty and fear. As the story progresses, the conflict changes and develops. When Ryan discovers Trish is his daughter, he wants Abby to marry him so that they can be a family, but she believes their marriage would be a disaster. Abby and Ryan still struggle over their daughter's identity, but a new element has been added: Abby's fear of the pain she risks if she surrenders to her growing love for Ryan and agrees to marry him.

As your story progresses, new problems should continue to emerge as the romantic conflict moves through several stages: beginning, middle, black moment, and ending. Ideally, the beginning of your story will create suspense and curiosity in your reader by showing or hinting at internal or external conflict. If you didn't put conflict in the first page of your manuscript, try beginning the story at a different point.

Here are a few examples from the opening paragraphs of my own stories:

> It couldn't be him!
> Abby had dreamed him in nightmares, dreams suppressed and almost forgotten. A man's head and shoulders glimpsed across a room . . .
> —from *Hidden Memories*

> Eight hours was too long. She should have walked right up to Connar and faced him this morning at the exhibition. "Let's talk," she should have said.
> —from *Yesterday's Vows*

> "We may have to turn back!" the pilot shouted over the engine noise.
> "Can't you give it a try?" Sarah squinted to see through the windscreen and wished herself back in her Vancouver office.
> —from *Nothing Less Than Love*

If you begin your story by tossing your characters into strong conflict—with themselves, each other, or circumstances—you'll be off to a good start. As your story progresses, your characters should face a series of problems that create increasing conflict, thus forcing them to wrestle with the real issue. A satisfying novel pits characters against overwhelming odds, then leaves them to struggle through disaster after disaster until victory is won.

Heroine and hero may have a wonderful time on a date. They may laugh, make love, even get married, but despite their ultimate victories, the problems keep coming until happiness seems impossible. The harder you make life for your characters, the better your readers will like the book. Until you reach the final scene, every transaction must present new problems, or new developments to old problems. Forget everything you ever learned about being nice to people. To be a good storyteller, you must treat your characters terribly, throwing their worst fears in their faces

In a satisfying romance, the suspense between hero and heroine culminates in a black moment when all seems lost. To be powerful, the black moment must emerge from the personality and fears of your characters, and it must be deeply related to the conflict issue. The more powerful your moment, the more satisfying the resolution.

It is only after the black moment, when hero and heroine realize that they've lost each other, that they can experience the full strength of their love. In the aftermath of the black moment, hero and heroine each realize that their relationship matters more than the convictions they held so rigidly. After this realization, they are willing to make the necessary sacrifice to achieve their happy ending.

Panicked by Ryan's demands for marriage and her own fears, Abby finally succeeds in driving Ryan away, only to realize how bleak life will be without the man she loves. If the conflict is based on your characters' fears and personal history, the sacrifice must be related. The hero who fears poverty must sacrifice the illusion that money can prevent personal loss. Abby, who fears exposure, must embrace truth and risk herself.

To achieve a happy ending, lovers must always sacrifice their need to protect themselves against abandonment. They must allow themselves to become vulnerable, to risk broken hearts and grief, before they can win the prize of true intimacy.

It is only at the end of the romance novel, when hero and heroine make their sacrifices and emerge victorious over the conflicts that threaten their future, that the reader's suspense is ended with the satisfying answer to the story question.

Can this couple overcome the obstacles to love and find a happy ending?

Yes, they can, but it isn't easy.

Vanessa Grant has successfully published 27 romance novels and *Writing Romance,* a critically acclaimed guide for romance writers. She has more than 10 million books in print in 15 languages. Living on the West Coast of Canada, she now divides her time between writing, traveling, lecturing, and her family.

HIDDEN TREASURES

Techniques to help you find
the essence of your poem

by Rachel Hadas

To talk about revising poems raises the question of when or whether a poem is ever finished. That crucial but insoluble issue in turn suggests other poetic debates, such as whether it's best to wait for inspiration to strike, to toil daily, or something in between. Is genius, or even talent, really 1 percent inspiration and 99 percent perspiration?

To such vexed and venerable questions, I have no authoritative answers. But having written poems for more than 30 years, I do have a sense of how poetic revision works. Of course, every poet's practice is unique. Still, revision is a widespread and important part of the process. Most of the examples in what follows are taken from my own work, but the principles can apply to other poets.

There are four major ways of revising a poem. First, one can make relatively small changes, sometimes involving less than a line—changes that nevertheless turn out to make a tremendous difference.

The seventh line of Keats' sonnet "On First Looking into Chapman's Homer"—"But never did I breathe its pure serene"—was originally the much less memorable and transcendent "But never could I tell what men did mean." More extensive changes transformed Robert Frost's sonnet "Design" from a good poem to a great one. The sonnet's final line was originally "Design, design! Do I read the word aright?" Contrast this with the delicately deadly line with which the revised poem ends: "If design govern in a thing so small."

The other three kinds of revision I have in mind are more thoroughgoing, if not always radical. They are cutting, expanding, or transforming your poem.

Cutting or expanding

Poems that say more than the poet means, often using fancy language to needlessly embellish their essential gesture, benefit from small trims or deep cuts. When I revised my poem "Bays," taking out superfluous associations and images—basically, unnecessary information—the result was the much leaner "Lentil soup."

> Bays [title]
> I reach into the fridge
> for oranges. Greek winter:
> blood oranges! Or sitting
> in the half-moon harbor
> waiting to catch the boat
> away that final summer,
> watching some gypsies washing
> their blankets in the bay.
> Into the lentil soup I toss a bay
> leaf. A laurel tree—
> bushy, fragrant, glowing
> with classical patina
> grew in the gorge between
> the village and the sea.
> Stirring the soup, turning
> to squeeze the oranges
> clean of their vitamin C,
> remembering the sickly satiation,
> waiting to go, and waiting,
> washing dirty linen
> in the basin of the sea,
> smelling the herbs and steam,
> the orange rind, the onions,
> spoon in hand, I stop
> and rise above the island and look
>   down
> from hunger's other shore.

After simmering my poem, I realized the central images I was after—the two "bays"—were lost in the first version. The opening eight lines essentially were my trying to get to the connection between the fragrant soup and the gypsies washing their laundry in the bay—the beauty of the ordinary. By beginning instead with "Into the bubbling soup I toss a bay," I hoped to appeal immediately to the senses. I loved the references to the blood oranges in the first version, but they competed with the "bushy, glossy, fragrant" laurel tree and the "blue basin of the bay" for the reader's attention, thus diffusing the overall sensuous impact. By cutting the orange references and reducing the remaining images to their essence, I came up with a more succinct and focused version, which also rhymes more consistently and avoids the abstract, open-ended close of "Bays." It's as if I was learning to keep my eye on the object, or at most on two things (now and then), without indulging confusing associations. The result:

> Lentil soup [title]
> Into the bubbling soup I toss a bay
> leaf. The laurel tree—
> bushy, glossy, fragrant—
> grew in the gorge between
> the village and the sea.
> We sat near the half-moon
> harbor at Vathy
> one August afternoon.
> Not very far away,
> some gypsies washed their laundry,
> then rinsed it in the blue
> basin of the bay.
> Onions, garlic, oil,
> vinegar—salt of summer
> seasoning the winter.

   Some poems, instead of being too long, are incomplete. They have failed to develop an idea or an anecdote. (The Imagists, in my view, are responsible for swarms of tiny, unsatisfying poems.) A visit to the Greek galleries at The Metropolitan Museum of Art a few years ago yielded a short poem about a vase depicting Achilles arming himself. But just describing, which was all this poem had done, wasn't enough. I gradually realized that I needed to include my entire gallery stroll in the extended version of the poem, which became "Greek Gold" (from *Halfway Down the Hall*, 1998). Instead of a cameo, Achilles becomes one (midway through the poem) of a series of things seen and recorded in Sapphics.
   When it comes to expansion, perhaps my experience as an English teacher helps. Just as I often point out that a student's essay has more to say, so I've learned to see when a poem should unpack its ideas. Does a point arrive, though, at which poems turn talky, prosaic, dull? Yes, of course. That moment will vary from poet to poet and reader to reader, but the poem certainly needs to be vigilant. Too much expansion and one may end up with an essay.

Transformation

   This type of revision involves turning a poem from one thing into something quite different. Perhaps a line or a single image turns out to be crucial.

Recently, revising and expanding a rather drab old poem called "The New Word," I stumbled, in the middle of working on a simile, upon a memory of the precise and scrupulous way my late mother used to answer my childish questions. Not only did this memory merit several new lines in the new, longer, and more ambitious version, but remembering the whole matter of questions and answers launched me into an essay still in progress, tentatively entitled "Q and A." Had I not been somehow moved to revisit the poem, I doubt if I'd ever have started to write the essay.

Revising poems takes patience and judgment. It can be disconcerting and humbling. You wonder "Did I really write as badly as that?" or "How could I have not noticed that the poem ended there?"

On the other hand, revision can be surprisingly rewarding. A buried treasure may come to light—your own treasure, which you yourself first created and then proceeded to bury by surrounding it with inferior material. Or maybe the treasure is brand new, freshly crafted in the process of rooting around old drafts. In either case, it is up to you to polish what you've found. You never know what new facet you'll discover.

Rachel Hadas of New York City is the author of 15 books of poetry, essays, translations, and criticism. Her latest book of poetry is *Indelible* (Wesleyan University Press). She teaches English at Rutgers University.

FIND A FRESH VOICE

Techniques to shake you out of a comfortable rut

by Lisa Verigin

The first poetry workshop in which I participated had some unusual rules, such as: Avoid comment on the faults of a poem. Having entered this group with a massive chip on my shoulder—I had, after all, been collecting rejection slips for a few years and felt ready for anything—I thought this rule to be patently ridiculous. After all, how could I grow as a poet by getting only smiles and pats on the back? How would I know what was failing to move an audience, what made no sense to them or simply showed messy technique?

Yet, I did grow. What I discovered was that when others neglected certain aspects of a poem, it was usually a sign that something was amiss, that I had not, as Katherine Mansfield once phrased it, "hit the note." On the other hand, if I received praise, I took it as a sign to do more of what I was already doing, for it's only human to repeat what has brought us into favor with others.

However, I didn't see the risk involved in doing this: the risk of writing the same poem over and over again, falling victim to a kind of self-parody.

Any number of other forces may push us toward self-parody. We may fear change. Perhaps the little traumas of daily life are impinging on our creative processes. Or we may be in that awkward time of development or experimentation during which we occasionally want a safety net. Yet the fact remains that most of us go through periods of self-repetition. And this is to the detriment of poetry. For poetry is, in part, about showing our experience of the world in fresh ways.

Interestingly, how the rut of repetition is realized in poetry has little to do with pure matters of mechanics or technique. Nor does it deal much with fundamental matters of content. What drops us into the rut is not the recycling of cadences, phrasing, words, or images. Rather, it is stagnancy of voice.

But what do we really mean when we talk about voice? Broadly, we may conceive of it as the collective term for every technical quirk that identifies our writing as our own. It is our tendencies toward certain rhythmic and metrical patterns, tempos, sonic effects, tone, and so on—tendencies that may develop unconsciously and thus feel wholly natural to us. Collectively, these form what we each may call our dominant voice.

For example, consider the closing stanza from "Disposal" (*Selected Poems, 1957-1987*, Soho Press), a typical, early W. D. Snodgrass poem in which he describes taking care of his sister's belongings after her death.

> Like a pair of party shoes
> That seemed to never find a taker;
> We send back to its maker
> A life somehow gone out of fashion
> But still too good to use.

The voice here may be defined in part by its gentle, reflective tone paradoxically tinged with anger, its simple phrasing and unexceptional vocabulary, and the slight tendency to juxtapose falling and rising metrical feet. Compare this with the closing stanza from his "Fourth of July," another poem on his sister's death, written during the same time period.

> It is an evil, stupid joke:
> My wife is pregnant; my sister's in her grave.
> We live in the home of the free and
>   the brave.
> No one would hear me, even if I spoke.

Looking at these two stanzas in isolation, we can readily see the persistence of a single, identifiable voice. And if we look at the full text of the poems, we may also notice repetitions of imagery and even some similarity in feeling (a sense of pity toward the sister, inability to grasp the mystery of death, resentment toward the family's response to the sister's death). Yet the poems remain differentiated, chiefly by what we may call the modulation of voice. His voice takes on a slightly different attitude in each poem.

Though both poems are written in the first person, the first example shows a distance between the poet and the events, while the second puts him in the center. This shift in perspective is realized through the modulation in voice: he end-stops lines much more frequently in this poem, suggesting a greater difficulty in speaking. This slightest of changes makes the poems distinct.

The following stanzas from my work show how vocal modulation works. The first example is the closing stanza of "As Seen on TV," a poem in which the speaker describes watching the neighbors engage in a brutal fight.

> With a dirty white towel, I wipe the window
> so I can see better. I pry apart another Oreo
> and pour a fresh cup of Joe.
> There is so much to interest me here.

Compare this with the closing passage from "Matinee," a poem in which the speaker describes her flights of fancy when attending a musical for the first time since she was a child.

> Posed like a Miss Beadle—
> marmy, smug and mum—
> I sip my club soda and watch them file
> through the loge entrance, through which
>   I hear
> a familiar riff overlaying the warming chaos
> of the pit. That, not bodies, is what rustles
> the curtain when the houselights blink,
> I think, fanning myself with my program
> and dreaming the first pearlish note
> from the ingenue's throat could joy my body
> into such numbness,
> I might find it over the balcony rail,
> breaking upon the head of some child.

Both passages are written in my dominant voice, which involves, among other things, heavily enjambed lines, occasionally thick sound-play, neologisms, and old-style slang, and a tendency toward falling rhythms.

Both wrangle with ideas of violence, innocence, and theater. In fact, their closing lines are nearly identical in that both speak of violence as a rather beautiful or compelling thing. And it is here where we can see the poems bleeding together. In both cases, my voice maintains an unchanging point of view. The ideas informing the poems are different, but my voice refuses to acknowledge it.

In essence, I let the voice write the poems instead of using it to articulate my ideas through image. The danger of the unmodulated voice is that we will become used by it, instead of using it to express our visions.

One may describe how the sky looks on a clear day and then describe how it looks on an overcast day, but if voice is not modulated, both descriptions will rely on and show an identical conception of sky. Some may argue it's not a matter of voice at all, but point of view. Yet point of view is only realized through voice.

We must look carefully at a selection of our poems and ask what habits they show in terms of image, rhythm, sound, syntax, word choice. Once we have a sense of that, it becomes much easier to locate instances of self-parody. Then, there are any number of tricks to kick ourselves out of the rut and still keep a dominant voice fresh while expanding its capabilities.

One of the easiest techniques is to adopt and speak through a persona, be it a historical figure, celebrity, icon, or fictional character. Writing through a deliberately alternate perspective can initiate shifts in language and syntax that may refresh one's dominant voice.

Another trick—one I've found especially useful—is to write in one of the more difficult fixed forms, letting its constraints push one's voice toward more clever expressions that may reveal new possibilities, as well as deepen and widen the perspective of the poems.

Yet another favorite trick for revivifying voice is to write in a location in which I don't normally write—a park, a coffee shop, or even someone else's house. Disrupting even the slightest aspect of one's usual writing habits is often enough to allow fresh ways of speaking "spontaneously" arise. And these may, in turn, grow "natural" to us, even as they push us toward new forms of expression.

Lisa Verigin is a poet and teaches at the University of Nebraska at Lincoln. Her poetry has been published in the *American Literary Review*, *Comstock Review*, *Nebraska Review*, and other publications.

EXERCISE

Change directions and see what happens

Nine times of 10, disruption of one's "natural" writing process is the key to getting out of a rut, whether it be general writer's block or repeating the same voice over and over. Shaking up the process disorients one enough so that simply getting something down on paper or disk may be a sufficient task on its own, the inner critic be damned. We may always go back and revise.

The following exercise, adapted from a writing exploration I commonly do with college writing students, is intended to create disruptions while one is writing in a familiar environment and help one use those disruptions to freshen one's voice—or at least reveal possibilities for doing so. You will need a timer of some sort, scissors, a relatively large, clear working space, and, of course, paper and a writing instrument. I recommend doing this exercise in longhand, as it personalizes the exercise (voice is, after all, a deeply personal thing) and forces one to proceed a bit more slowly than when composing on a computer.

[cont.]

[sidebar cont.]

1. Choose a subject on which to write, ideally a subject of no great personal consequence but one about which you think you could write a lot. Set your timer for 10 minutes and begin composing a poem on this subject. Write for the full 10 minutes, continuing with your poem, even if you think you've said everything there is to say about your subject or digress from it. Important: Use only one side of each sheet of paper.

2. When the timer sounds, immediately shift from poetry to informal prose, continuing from the last sentence or line of the poetry. Again, write for 10 minutes.

3. When the timer sounds, choose a persona through which to continue your prose, writing from where you left off. Write for 10 minutes.

4. When the timer sounds, revert to your own poetic voice and write for 10 more minutes, continuing from where you left off with the prose.

5. Read what you've written, starring, highlighting, or otherwise marking the passages you like best. Then, physically cut out those passages and arrange them into a poem on a tabletop or other large, flat surface. Play with different arrangements, letting your imagination run free with the possibilities. At this point, forget about keeping to your original subject. Let this "cut-and-paste" poem be whatever it wants to be.

6. Once you've arranged the fragments in a way that pleases you, hand-copy your poem on paper and see what you've got. Now, choose a subject similar to that of your cut-and-paste poem and write an imitation of that poem.

When done, compare and evaluate your poems.

Does the imitation sound too much like the first poem?
If so, what seems to be creating this effect?
What might you need to change to make these poems distinct?
If the poems sound different, try to pinpoint what's creating the difference.
How has your voice changed?

—*Lisa Verigin*

SECTION THREE

Professional Development

"ON" AND "OFF" THE RECORD

by John Brady

Let's assume you are working on a story about unethical publishing practices and I am one of your key sources. During one of our interviews I tell you—off the record—that I once knew a well-known literary agent who used his well-known clients, including a bestselling novelist, as a front to collect "reading fees" from unsuspecting beginning writers who were invited to submit their manuscripts to this agency for an "evaluation." Would you be able to use the information?

If, in another interview, I tell you—off the record—that a well-known first novel competition, with modest cash prizes, is making a very nice profit from thousands of "entry fees," would you be able to use the information?

It all depends on how you define "off the record." If it means the information given is for your knowledge only and is not to be printed or made public in any way, and that the information cannot be taken to another source with the aim of getting official confirmation, then, as a writer, you're all dressed up with nowhere to go.

We are being hypothetical here, of course, but a real-life version of this dilemma turned up in a notorious case recently, when a private investigator named Len Jenoff tearfully told Nancy Phillips, a reporter for the *Philadelphia Inquirer*, that he had arranged the murder of Carol Neulander at the request of her husband, Rabbi Fred Neulander. Phillips had cultivated Jenoff as a source, meeting him over meals, talking on the phone, pushing him to talk about his secrets while allowing him to speak off the record. There's the rub. "He would not give me permission to tell the story and because I had agreed to keep his confidence, I had to honor that and could not tell the authorities,"

Phillips wrote. "I wanted Jenoff to keep talking to me, with the hope that I could persuade him to go on the record."

Eventually, Phillips arranged for Jenoff to confess to authorities, and the case is scheduled for court this month. Until there was a confession for the arresting officers, however, the information that Phillips had gained "off the record" was like handcuffs on the reporter.

Does "off the record" always have to be so restrictive? Again, it all depends on how you define the term. There is so much confusion over what "off the record" means that when *Folio: The Magazine for Magazine Management* asked an array of magazine editors in 1991 what "off the record" meant, there was no consensus. Here is a sampling of replies, which demonstrates how ambiguous the term is:

> "It means you can't quote the person directly. If it's an important bit of information, we'd probably suggest it in the piece."
> —*Zone Magazine*

> "It means the person shouldn't be quoted. File away the information and try to get more on it from other sources."
> —*Seafood Business*

> "The information is to be used only to enhance your understanding of where to go reportorially."
> —*Mother Jones*

> "If somebody tells me something is off the record, I do not run it—but I will ask to run it without attribution."
> —*Travel Agent*

Perhaps the most helpful response to *Folio's* question was expressed by Kenneth T. Walsh, a senior writer at *U.S. News & World Report*. "I'd always clarify with the source what he means by off the record," he said. "It can mean just his name, or the information itself."

When *Folio* asked an array of magazine editors what "off the record" meant, there was no consensus.

The importance of a full and complete understanding of the term by both parties has not been lost in the courts, where a confidentiality pledge is viewed as a legally enforceable promise. In 1991, Dan Cohen was awarded $200,000 when the U.S. Supreme Court ruled against the St. Paul (Minn.) *Pioneer Press* and Minneapolis *Star Tribune* for revealing his name as a source in a political story after he had been promised anonymity.

Writers should tread carefully when using off-the-record reporting techniques, which is usually how we obtain the best information in an interview. This is especially true if the topic is even mildly investigative. When I was working on a biography of Republican operative Lee Atwater, at least half of the 400 interviews I conducted were off the record. Before conducting each interview, however, I made it clear that I defined "off the record" as not for attribution to the source, but I would remain free to verify the information elsewhere and try to bring the information into the story from other sources.

Information gathered this way is also called "for background only," meaning anything that is said in the interview is usable, but not in direct quotation and not for attribution. The writer writes it on his own. Just make very, very certain that you get the story right, and be prepared to defend yourself in court, if necessary. For the Atwater book, I often heard the same story from several sources—all off the record. Then I had to decide whether or not to use the material from my own perspective as consensus reportage. In some cases, I did; in others, I backed off. As you get deeper and deeper into reporting a story, you develop a sense of situational ethics, and you will know when it is right to write.

Just be certain to verify "off the record" information before you use it to vilify someone in print. In May, *Boston Herald* columnist Margery Eagan was highly critical of WHDH-TV (Channel 7) owner Ed Ansin's role in the decision not to renew the contract of anchor Kim Carrigan, who was seven months pregnant at the time. Egan wrote that Ansin had been "described by employees as a despicable, ruthless, egomaniacal, power-mad narcissistic troll in need of psychoanalytic intervention."

Ansin's attorney called the column "nothing short of an unfounded personal attack," adding that Eagan had launched "highly charged, personal invectives at Mr. Ansin" based in part on "unidentified 'sources' at Channel 7." "The only thing you can do in this circumstance is file a lawsuit," Ansin told *Boston Globe* media columnist Mark Jurkowitz. "It's something I feel I have to do." Shortly afterward, Ansin and the *Herald* reached an out-of-court settlement.

By now you may be thinking, hmmm, maybe I should just explain at the beginning of each interview that nothing is off the record. That way, if a source doesn't want to say something, he should refrain from commenting. But if he calls the boss "a power-mad narcissistic troll in need of psychoanalytic intervention," then I've got a lively quote on the record and a source for attribution.

While this is certainly a safer approach, it is also rigid and may affect the rapport you are trying to establish at the outset of an interview. Moreover, because so many good stories are heard, initially, off the record, you may never know about the big ones that got away.

For those of you who want to hear the good, the bad, even the ugly, here are five tips and tactics for using "off the record" to your advantage:

• Agree on what "off the record" means at the beginning of the interview. Don't wait until it comes up midway through your conversation or—worse—right after you have heard a juicy story.

• Define "off the record" so that you are not handcuffed by the information. Put the source at ease with your methodology: "If you want to go off the record, tell me in advance and I will not attribute the information to you, but I may find it elsewhere, or I may even have the information from another source as we speak. In any case, there will be no fingerprints linking the information to you."

• Verify all off-the-record information before using it in your story. Some sources will hide behind "off the record" to slam others or to promote their own personal agendas. Don't be fooled.

• When in doubt, do without. If off-the-record information cannot be confirmed, remember the old newsroom axiom, "Sometimes it's better to kill a story than to be killed by a story."

• Protect your sources. If a confidential source gives you helpful information that makes the story, mum's the word when lawyers call. According to the *American Journalism Review*, your promise is backed in varying degrees by "shield laws" in 30 states and the District of Columbia, but, regardless, do the right thing and be prepared to go directly to jail, if the situation comes to that.

John Brady is a Boston-area magazine consultant and former editor-in-chief at *Writer's Digest*. Brady is the author of several books, including *The Craft of Interviewing* (Vintage) and *Bad Boy: The Life and Politics of Lee Atwater* (Addison-Wesley).

COMING CLEAN ON QUOTES

How much can you tidy up what someone tells you?

by Mark Fitzgerald

You can quote me, freelance writer Jim Edwards says over the phone from Jersey City, N.J. He has only one request: Please don't use the name of the nationally recognized business magazine where he learned that some writers and editors regard quotation marks around spoken words as malleable starting points, and not as "No Trespassing" signs.

Edwards had both writing and editing responsibilities at the magazine. One day, an article he wrote was edited by another department—and came back with verbatim quotes reworded to the point that their meanings were altered. "That's when it became clear there were two different systems in the same magazine," says Edwards, who also was senior writer at the media watchdog magazine *Brill's Content* until it folded last year. "My policy was not to change quotes at all, so my stories, and the stories that came through me, had lots of ellipses and brackets and paraphrasing. On the other side of the magazine, their style was to neaten it up, to do anything to keep the narrative flow."

While it surely is rare that a magazine would tolerate two policies on cleaning up quotes, the publication's schizophrenia neatly illustrates the confusion and division this subject engenders among writers of all types of nonfiction. Writers seek quotes that soar and sing, that punctuate their prose like a fat piano chord landing in perfect sync with the rhythm of a jazz combo's bass and drum. And what do their interview subjects offer instead? Stuttered, stumbling sentences that wander around in search of a verb and skitter off in a dozen directions.

By nature, we humans are maddeningly discursive. We ruin even our best quotes. Everyone of a certain age, for instance, recalls former White House counsel John Dean's stirring warning about Watergate to President Nixon in the Oval Office on March 21, 1973: "There's a cancer on the presidency." But Dean's actual comment was caught on tape and transcribed, and here is what he really said: "We have a cancer within, close to the presidency, that is growing. It is growing daily. It's compounded, growing geometrically now, because it compounds itself. That will be clear if I, you know, explain some of the details of why it is." Somehow the real quotation doesn't have the ring of, you know, history about it.

Faced with inconveniently rambling remarks, many writers routinely preserve the quotation marks but change some of the words they attribute to speakers. As Edwards discovered, some publications encourage writers to "clean up" quotes with a power hose. Pick any page in a supermarket tabloid and the person quoted inevitably sounds like, well, a supermarket tabloid writer. *The National Enquirer* quotes "a friend" as saying about actress Gwyneth Paltrow: "Gwyneth has truly hit on Mr. Right with Mr. Wilson. . . . She's confided her altar ambitions with Luke to former lover and close friend Ben Affleck." Does anyone talk like that? And how is it that so many people quoted in *The New Yorker* appear to speak with an impeccable syntax straight out of the pages of H. W. Fowler's *Dictionary of Modern English Usage*?

How ethical is all of this? Interestingly, most news organizations strictly forbid "cleaning up" quotes, yet journalists are the most frequent offenders—and defenders—of the practice. *The Associated Press Stylebook*, followed by most American newspapers and many magazines, is unforgiving on the subject: "Never alter quotations even to correct minor grammatical errors or word usage." At the same time, the *AP Stylebook* also advises against using fragmentary quotes or ellipses. So what's a writer gonna do? (AP, incidentally, specifically abjures the routine use of "abnormal spellings such as gonna.")

Many journalists draw their own line. Steve Doig was an investigative reporter at *The Miami Herald* for 20 years before he became a professor at the Walter Cronkite School of Journalism at Arizona State University. "I tell my students: Quote a person as you hear them. What you learn to do as a reporter is filter out all those false starts and the oh's and um's and all the other things, and write what people are saying with all the noise filtered out," Doig says. "The point of journalism, of nonfiction in general, is to communicate ideas to readers. If they have to plow their way through the circumlocutions and rhetorical figures and asides . . . it would be very hard, stultifying, and boring reading."

Last winter, M. L. "Mike" Stein taught a course at the University of California, Irvine with the same title as his latest book, co-authored by Susan F. Paterno: *Talk Straight, Listen Carefully: The Art of Interviewing* (Iowa State University Press). "You don't change the meaning of what an individual says. That is taboo," says Stein, the author of 17 books and a frequent travel writer. "But in my writing, I have no hesitation about straightening out syntax, as long as I do not change the essence of the quote, or alter the image or character of the person you are interviewing."

Other writers do have hesitations, sometimes paralyzing ones. While he was working on a book that re-examines the Columbine High School shootings, Dave Cullen, a regular contributor to Salon.com, agonized over how to handle the quotations from the many explosive interviews he conducted. "At first, I was afraid to take out even the um's," he says. "And then I wouldn't take anything out of order, or take out a stray thinking-out-loud phrase in the middle of a sentence."

Like a surprising number of writers, Cullen confesses to the fear that one day, something will happen that will subject all his nonfiction work to a merciless public scrutiny. It's not an entirely irrational apprehension. Consider what happened to well-known—and now former—*Boston Globe* columnists Mike Barnicle and Patricia Smith. In each case, an initial question about a particular column ended up revealing multiple instances of apparent fabrication and plagiarism. Then, too, there was the celebrated and costly libel suit that psychologist Jeffrey Masson launched against author Janet Malcolm and *The New Yorker* over allegedly fabricated quotes. (A federal jury ultimately found in Malcolm's favor.)

These authorial versions of the death penalty keep him on the straight and narrow, freelance writer Edwards says. This is his nightmare scenario: "Imagine a story of yours becomes the subject of a libel suit that goes to a jury trial. The plaintiff's lawyer demands to hear your tape-recorded interviews and reveals that the quotes in the allegedly libelous story are actually different to [sic] the ones that appeared in print because you were tidying things up. A jury of ordinary people would rightly regard this practice as suspicious and bizarre, and might consider it evidence of your malice or recklessness toward the reputation of the plaintiff. They certainly wouldn't see it as part of your commitment to accuracy."

Cloud Over Columbine author Cullen eventually got over his fear of cleaning up quotes. It was his editor that put him straight, he says: "My editor made the point that books are typically different." More important than a quote that is as accurate as a court transcript is the larger truth of the story or style of the person quoted, Cullen concluded. "And the requirement for a narrative flow is much stronger," he says. "So now I think you want to get to the gist of [a rambling quote], and discard the useless parts. The main concern is that you are being 100 percent ethical about not distorting what they are saying. You are clarifying rather than changing."

Mark Fitzgerald of Chicago is editor-at-large for *Editor & Publisher* magazine. He won the 2001 Jesse H. Neal National Business Journalism Award for editorial writing.

SNEAK PEEKS

When is it okay to show sources
a story before publication?

by Mark Fitzgerald

When Mark Bowden arrived at *The Philadelphia Inquirer* 21 years ago, the newspaper had a reputation for aggressive investigative journalism, and a rule that remains in effect to this day: Reporters do not give story subjects an advance look at what they are writing. Yet in his new bestselling book, *Killing Pablo*, the story of the hunt for Colombian cocaine kingpin Pablo Escobar, Bowden thanks former U.S. Ambassador Morris D. Busby for having "kindly reviewed an early draft of the story prior to its being published as a newspaper series in *The Philadelphia Inquirer*."

Busby wasn't the only one who got a sneak peek at *Killing Pablo*, Bowden cheerfully acknowledges in an interview. "I'm now very much inclined to share [material] with sources. I have no problem with showing almost anyone a story before it runs, with the proviso that I am giving it to them without giving them any veto power over the story," says Bowden, who also let U.S. Army Rangers and intelligence operatives pore over drafts of *Black Hawk Down*, his detailed 1999 bestseller about a firefight in Somalia. If his editors objected, Bowden says, they never let him know.

For Bowden, it's a simple matter of being fair to his sources, some of whom, in the case of *Killing Pablo*, took big personal risks talking to a writer. "I wanted to make sure I didn't put anyone in jeopardy," he says. Occasionally, Bowden rewrote passages when confidential sources pointed out details that could put them in jeopardy. "I suppose the hard-assed way to approach that is to publish and let them deal with the consequences, but I just didn't think that was the right thing to do," he says.

At the opposite extreme is New York City freelance writer Robert Neuwirth, whose work has appeared in such alternative magazines as *Metropolis, City Limits,* and *Dwell.* "I won't read quotes back to sources," he says flatly. Neuwirth has even convinced fact-checkers at some publications not to vet his quotes with sources. "I always tell people they've got to trust me to be fair. If someone objects, I like to tell them, if I were covering the mayor, you wouldn't want me to read the quotes back to him and let him edit them. That generally quiets people down," Neuwirth says.

It's an ethical dilemma nearly every nonfiction writer has faced at one time or another: When should you show sources what you are writing about them? Never before publication? Only if they ask? Or only if you're confused about a quote or fact? And what should you show or read back: Only the isolated quote or fact itself? Or just enough so the source knows the context of the quote? Or, like Bowden, the entire manuscript?

"There is no one rule. With journalists, you can never get a consensus on anything," says Brant Houston, executive director of Investigative Reporters and Editors. But Houston guesses most IRE members draw the line where he does: "Personally, I never had a problem reading back passages or discussing data with people to be sure I had it right. But I did not feel it was wise to give somebody a complete draft. If you do that and in the end you're still convinced you're right and that person—say, the target of your investigation—decides to go to court after the story comes out, they can tear you apart in court. If they have the previous drafts, they can say, why did you leave this out, and that out?"

Alan Wolper, who writes the monthly Ethics Corner for *Editor & Publisher* magazine, says writers of investigative pieces should let their targets know what's being said about them. "That's where the ethical issues come in. You want them to be able to respond to the whole body of work," he says. But Wolper quickly adds that there's no ethical obligation to show an entire manuscript. In fact, Wolper, a journalism professor at Rutgers University in Newark, N.J., advises students and professionals against it: "When you do that, you put yourself in a position where (the source) becomes your editor. The danger is that they will call up your real editor and the story will stay on hold forever, or a piece of it won't ever run."

What happens if a source asks to see the story before it runs? "My jaw drops open and I'll say that's something we just don't do," says John Crewsden, who has written award-winning science articles for the *Chicago Tribune.* "The worst is when they say, well, so-and-so always lets me see a story before it runs, or so-and-so always lets me change my quotes. That always surprises me. Maybe science journalists are different." Crewsden

> The ethical obligation to be fair to the people they are writing about is the chief reason many authors will check quotes, even if they don't believe in showing an entire manuscript.

says he simply sticks to his guns on those occasions, which happen perhaps two or three times a year.

But Crewsden will read material back to a source to ensure its accuracy: "Cancer, for instance. You really want to get that right, and if it's technical—and most of it is—I show it to Dr. So-and-So. That's just helping the reader in my opinion. The whole point is not to mislead the reader. I can't imagine a reporter not doing that," he says.

The ethical obligation to be fair to the people they are writing about is the chief reason many authors will check quotes, even if they don't believe in showing an entire manuscript. "It's always a good idea to read back quotes that are the least bit incendiary," Crewsden says. "You really don't want to blindside people. The point is to quote them saying what they want to say. If you got it wrong the first time, or if they want to modify their language, it's in everybody's interest to get it right—including the reader's."

Some writers say they feel a special obligation to read quotes back if the speaker is very young or naive about the media. "When I'm talking to a less savvy person, I can see better than they can the consequences of what they're saying," says *Killing Pablo* author Bowden. "I think in kindness you can say to someone, 'You should think hard about whether you want to say that in that way.' I'm personally disinclined to engage in ambush-style interviewing."

While many writers say there's nothing wrong with letting sources make minor changes in their quotes, no one advises letting them change the meaning of a quote. "What you have to do then is say something like, 'He said this on June 1 and this on June 5,'" Wolper says. But the ethics columnist says the best advice of all is to get a tape recorder: "Every writer should tape every interview as long as they're not breaking the law."

There are few clear rules about pre-publication review, but one experience is guaranteed to help writers sort out its ethical issues, says the IRE's Houston: "The best thing that can happen to any writer is to be written about. You find out what it's like to be on the other side. I think empathy does make people better writers."

Mark Fitzgerald of Chicago is editor-at-large for *Editor & Publisher* magazine. He won the 2001 Jesse H. Neal National Business Journalism Award for editorial writing.

A SITE OF ONE'S OWN

How to create a writer's Web site and promote yourself

by Roxyanne Young

Once upon a time, a writer's business letterhead listed his or her address, phone number, and maybe a fax number. These days, writers are finding that they also need to list their Web site address. Professional Web sites have become much more than just a trendy calling card, however; they also serve as many writers' primary form of self-promotion.

On a Web site, you can post all of the information you would normally put on book jackets, brochures, and fliers—but much more of it, and with better-quality graphics. In addition, you have the option of changing this information at will, ensuring that it is always current—without incurring printing costs. You can create your own unique work in this digital domain, just as you can on the blank page that faces you at the start of each writing project.

While you may want to enlist the help of a talented Web designer, many Internet Service Providers (ISPs) now offer template tools to create your own Web site. While these tools may limit the complexity of the layout and graphics you can use, they allow you to create a wide variety of looks for your site—from a spiral-bound notebook page for freelance journalists to a shadowy "film noir" feel for mystery writers, to a storybook forest suitable for creators of children's books. The site's look is only the beginning, though. It is content that will draw visitors back time and again.

Besides the usual autobiographical or "meet the author" information, there are many ways to include literary content on professional sites, according to the interests and needs of the individual writer. Here are some suggestions:

• Sample chapters and book-jacket art can promote your upcoming releases or backlist titles. Fans will put their favorite writer's next release date on their calendars months ahead of time. Be sure to get permission before posting any copyrighted content, such as cover art or photographs, online.

• A calendar of book signings, convention dates, and workshop appearances will let readers, teachers, librarians, and booksellers know when you will be in their area, boosting attendance and perhaps book sales at these functions. The organizers are happy. Your fans are happy. And you're happy. It's all good—and all possible through your Web site.

• Writers who make school visits should post their policies, the subjects they cover, and fee schedules, along with glowing teacher reviews and thank-you notes from students.

• Freelancers take note: Editors actually do visit a site when you include a Web address with your query letter, so make sure you have a current list of writing credits posted, complete with links to any newspapers, literary journals, magazines, e-zines, or other online publications where your work appears. If your list is rich and varied, all the better.

• Novelists or nonfiction writers with favorable reviews by online publications should include a link to that review prominently placed near the book title with the tagline, "Read a review by . . ."

• Be sure to add links to online booksellers where visitors can purchase your books. As with the review links, make these links prominent, maybe even including a "Buy This Book!" tag in bold letters.

• You may want to include information about other interests in your life that inform your writing, such as scuba diving, hiking, or raising horses. By including links to sites of relevant interest (Civil War sites if your new book is a biography of Robert E. Lee, or an African savanna if you're an adventure travel writer, for example), readers who enjoy your books and articles will learn that your site is a great resource for their continued reading. You might even request that those linked sites reciprocate with a link to your own.

The site's design is only the beginning. It is content that will draw visitors back time and again.

• If your work could be used in the classroom, offer teacher supplements, lesson plans, or interactive games that educators can use.

• Link to sites of writing colleagues and ask that they do the same for you.

• Link to your favorite writing-related sites that offer market information, legal resources, editorial needs, or research. Such links will make your site a directory of sorts for visitors who may come back when they need, say, a recipe

[cont.]

GREAT AUTHOR SITES

www.sidneysheldon.com. Sidney Sheldon's site is professionally designed, and it shows. Polished, clean navigation easily carries visitors between his bibliography, biography, awards, current projects, and more. The site is packed with information.

www.kingsolver.com. Developed by her publisher, Barbara Kingsolver's site contains the standard biography and bibliography in an easy-to-navigate format. She also has a page where she answers frequently asked questions from readers about *The Poisonwood Bible.*

www.joanholub.com. Holub's whimsical style comes through in her Web site where, besides her biography, books, and information on school visits and book-signings, she also has practical classroom tools, activities for teachers, and writing tips for for kids. "I have heard thanks for the Web site activities from many teachers and other educators," Holub says. No doubt, those folks come back again and again to see what new teacher resources she has posted.

www.chucklebait.com. John Scieszka and Lane Smith, creators of *The Stinky Cheese Man, Squids Will Be Squids,* and *The True Story of the Three Little Pigs,* among other wacky children's books, have also created a dynamic site that offers detailed biographies, a list of books complete with sample illustrations, a form to ask questions, and an interactive Rock-Scissors-Paper game. But the great promotional tool here is their e-mail mailing list—visitors sign up to receive updates on this dynamic duo's upcoming releases and special appearances.

www.peggyrathmann.com. Peggy Rathmann's lively illustrations come through bright and clear on her home page, which is a departure from the usual layout. Check out her HamsterTours.com, an interactive tie-in with her book *10 Minutes Till Bedtime.*

www.peaksandvalleys.com. Humorist Cathy Morelli brings Web visitors into her kitchen for a virtual cup of tea and a bit of this and that about being a wife and mother. The site is funny, personable, and easy to navigate; she's got her book of personal essays for sale right there.

for 18th-century mead and know you've got a link to the Society for Creative Anachronism.

• A Frequently Asked Questions (FAQ) page should include answers to the questions you often hear about your work or writing life. Professional tips for aspiring writers are always well received, and if you've got the time to post these questions and answers on a regular basis, it will guarantee repeat traffic to your site.

• You can offer a newsletter to site visitors who sign up. Send regular e-mail updates to this willing and receptive audience, which will be hungry for news of your release dates and local appearances. More and more ISPs are offering this sort of automated e-mail service, but if yours doesn't, you can still do your own. It will just be a bit more work. Make sure that those who opt in have a way to opt out, too.

Sadly, you can't just build www.yourname.com and expect the world to beat a path to your Web site. It's a great misconception that people (especially people as busy as editors) will be casually surfing the Net and happen across your site. You need to market your Web site just as actively as you do your latest release. Include your Web address on your letterhead, business cards, brochures, and fliers. Notify your publishers so they can include links to your site from theirs. Have your Web address printed in the jacket copy of your newest book or in the bio of your newest article or short story. Every time your name appears professionally, and even personally, in the public eye, make sure your Web address is attached to it.

When constructing the site itself, use META tags (the description of your site's content) and keywords that your readers will likely use when searching for you. Submit your site address to search engines and be sure to follow their rules—you'd be surprised how many folks get banned from search engines because they submit their site every month or use inappropriate search words in their META tags.

While professionally designed Web sites can be cost-prohibitive, with careful planning they don't have to be. And new Web tools are being developed every day to help you take advantage of this medium. In spite of the great opportunities for networking and self-promotion it offers, however, many people are still timid about the Internet. It is definitely worth exploring. Remember that your Web site can become an extension of yourself, a window into your professional and/or personal life, and a great marketing tool.

Roxyanne Young is owner and Editorial Director of SmartWriters.com, which combines her interests in building Web sites and writing for kids. She is also a freelance writer, photographer, graphics designer, and co-founder of 2-Tier Software, Inc., where she helped create a template-based program to create Web sites especially for writers and illustrators.

SEVEN ROOKIE ERRORS TO AVOID

1. Text that runs into the margins. This is a glaring error that is easily fixed by setting the table width.

2. Graphics that have absolutely nothing to do with the site content. Sure, that flaming pyramid in the background looks cool, but does it have anything to do with the books you write? If not, leave it for the gaming sites and find something more appropriate to your subject matter.

3. The same thing goes for music and other sound files. It's fairly easy to add sound to your site, but make sure it's relevant and that your visitors have the option to turn it off.

4. Teeny-tiny text on a busy, textured background. No one can read this. If you find a great background graphic you like, use it as a border, but leave the space behind the text a solid color. And make your text reasonably large—at least 10 points—so folks can read it easily.

5. Fonts that belong on an engraved envelope. Script fonts are beautiful and expressive, especially if you write romance novels, but when you factor in grainy onscreen resolution, they can be very difficult to read. Plus, many browsers don't support these fonts, so they come out as plain text anyway. Make a nameplate graphic with your name in a large script font if you like, but keep the body text in Arial, Helvetica, or Times. All browsers support these.

6. Navigation that is hard to follow. I once visited a store site that had all of the navigation at the very bottom of an extremely long home page. I had to scroll down, down, down past several over-large photos and product descriptions to find the navigation buttons. Notice I said that I visited this page only once. Put your site navigation where it is easily accessible—at the top or side—and make sure there is a link back to your home page on all subpages.

7. Broken links. It's great to offer site visitors more information by linking out to sites that might be of interest to them, but check these periodically to make sure they're still up and running. Sites do go down, and if your links don't work, it makes you look bad.

—*Roxyanne Young*

WRITING A SERIES

12 tips from
an experienced pro

by David Poyer

Once your first novel is published, what's next? One answer is to follow that debut effort with more books using the same characters and settings. Writers as disparate as J. K. Rowling, Patrick O'Brian, James Lee Burke, Philip Roth, and P. D. James have made more trips back to the well. I've done three series myself, and am starting a fourth. But it pays to do your thinking before you jump out of the airplane, rather than on your way down!

Writing any form of fiction involves a succession of unsatisfactory compromises among irreconcilable ends. Writing follow-on books involves the same problems involved in writing one book, plus fresh quandaries. For example, the protagonist must persist in a recognizable form, yet somehow change in each work. Here's another: If the character's in danger at any point and the reader knows there'll be more books, how can you create suspense?

Another sticky requirement: Each work must stand alone, for readers who haven't followed previous books. Yet you can't bore those who have with repetitive details of earlier events.

Writing a series has its advantages, though. They're easier to sell. Commercial publishers are more willing to underwrite a follow-on to a book that made money than to finance an entirely new project. In fact, sometimes it's hard to get them to stop, as the careers of V. C. Andrews and other long-deceased authors illustrate. The reason? Subsequent properties begin with the guarantee of a pre-existing audience. Why throw away such a marketing advantage, to start all over?

From the writer's point of view, series work can be easier in some ways. He or she already knows the characters, has done much of the research, and has established tone, point of view, motivation, and other matters of technique.

And some writers simply discover more possibilities in the character and milieu than they can exhaust at one pass. I never set out to write more than one book about Hemlock County, Pa., or about a black-sheep diver from Hatteras. I simply found, when I'd published one, that it was only the beginning of a larger story.

On the other hand, series work imposes unique strains on the writer in forcing him or her to be creative, budgetary, and chronological. It puts you on the line for many years, perhaps even for a working lifetime.

These are the challenges and realities I've had to cope with over the last 25 years. Some of my early solutions worked; others proved wrong. All had to be fine-tuned as I learned the business and craft. Here are some tips based on what I've learned.

1. Plan your series front to back, not from the middle (or worse, backward!). I did neither my Dan Lenson books nor the Hemlock County novels in chronological order. Instead, I wrote what I thought at the time was a stand-alone (also called a one-off). Then, I belatedly discovered that I had stories to tell predating the one I had written. This led me into the jungle of the dreaded prequel.

Prequels, the opposite of sequels, are stories that happened before the current action. For instance, in my first three Hemlock County novels, the central character is a prickly recluse in his 70s. But as I wrote them, his codger cronies kept talking about events in 1936. Gradually, I realized they were pointing me toward a story from their youth, one that went far toward explaining what they and Hemlock County, Pa., had become.

In the same way, I began my Navy books with Lenson as a lieutenant (jg) in *The Med*. In the second volume, *The Gulf*, he was a lieutenant-commander. To clarify the progression of events, both in my own and the readers' minds, I then had to go back and write books dealing with him as an ensign and as a lieutenant.

After considerable sweat and argument with my publishers, I was able to correct these chronological issues. They agreed to do *Thunder on the Mountain: A Novel of 1936* because I'd established the Halvorsen character in the previous books. And I finally straightened Dan out by going backward for several years before I could go forward again. But how much simpler everything would have been if I'd designed it front to back! So that's what I made sure to do with the Civil War at Sea series I started last year, opening in April 1861 with *Fire on the Waters*.

2. Give your protagonist not just a problem, but a tragic flaw. A problem can carry reader interest through a short story or short novel, but to sustain interest longer than that, say, for four to 10 novels, your character must have more depth, and continuing depth. That means a personal, internal problem in addition to the other challenges a book presents; a flaw or continuing dilemma that, at least in the short term, looks insoluble.

3. Never repeat your plot or formula. To some extent, series books are looked down on because they can be formulaic. The antidote? Consciously struggle *against* the formula.

Actually, if your character is growing, he or she will not encounter the same challenges again, or at least will not respond in the same way. This can be a formula-breaker: Present the same challenge, but have the character respond in a different way, either more maturely, or less morally defined, depending on his arc at that point in the series.

Another way is to shift focus from the original central character, either by adding a co-protagonist, or replacing him or her (at least for one book) with a supporting actor.

4. Develop supporting characters. Don Quixote had Sancho Panza. Shreck had Donkey. Supporting characters provide alternate takes on events. They can be played for comedy. They allow you to appeal to different audiences; in the Harry Potter books, Hermione Granger gives girls someone to relate to.

If you have a continuing antagonist, a formula-breaker would be to write from the point of view of that antagonist. I wonder what Professor Moriarty would have had to say about Sherlock Holmes!

Finally, over time, subordinate characters may spin off individual books or even a series of their own.

5. Let continuing characters leave the stage from time to time. This is something to consider both within each book, especially if they run over 60,000 words or so, and for the series as well. Confining your work too tightly can lead to burnout, repetition, and formulaic writing.

Shift your locales. Shift focus to a son, a daughter, a parent, a sidekick. Give yourself freedom within the book. The Civil War series I just started has not one but five point-of-view characters: male, female, black, white, Southerner, and Yankee. I'll be following them around all the theaters of the war from 1861 to 1865.

Realize, though, that if you have a central character established over a number of books, shifting focus will confuse and turn off some readers. You'll likely want to give him at least a walk-on in every book.

6. Never let the reader assume a character survives. In fiction slanted to an undemanding public, the hero's survival is accepted as a convention. We know that as the comic book ends, Batman will emerge unscathed. In more ambitious work, we have to modify this convention. This applies most directly to situations in which the character faces physical danger, but it has some application to every type of fiction. The physical death of a protagonist may be nothing compared to the emotional, spiritual, intellectual, or other defeat that might face him or her.

In my diving series, Tiller Galloway is no invulnerable hero. He suffers wounds, losses, and defeats, usually due to his own greed and poor judgment. When we last saw him in *Down to a Sunless Sea,* he had serious decompression sickness with obvious after-effects. Now that his son is working and diving with him, his mortality is even more in evidence. That's not to say he'll die in the next book, but clearly, it's not impossible. The reader senses that, and hey, presto, suspense has returned.

7. Take control of the book. It's a sad reality that over any book deal taking more than a year, you'll have to live with personnel changes. The art director, editor, publisher (the editor's boss), publicist, or all four may "move on," as they say in New York. The only person who really owns your work is you. It behooves you to take an interest in every aspect of its presentation.

If you suspect there'll be more volumes down the road, take extra thought over the jacket art, design, title, and internal layout of your first book. That packaging should be distinctive enough to establish a series look. (Realize, though, that it may evolve over time, depending on the marketplace. Also, publishers like different looks for different formats and price points; that is, for hardcover, trade, and mass market editions.)

I never succeeded in doing this with the Hemlock County books. Each package was different. This crippled series identification and lost repeat sales. We never gathered enough momentum to launch them into enduring print status, though each volume got excellent reviews and sold well in hardcover.

On the other hand, the Lensons and Galloways have evolved a consistent look. Readers who liked one can easily locate the rest, and they're consistent earners long after their initial publication.

8. Aim your work at an existing audience. I've always reckoned that if I'm having fun, readers will, too. Their letters, and my sales figures, warn me when they aren't. But I don't think waiting for this belated feedback is the smart way to work. Really dedicated commercial writers should have a much sharper sense of who their audience is and what they want than I do.

In general, screening out ideas that won't elicit a mass audience is the publisher's job. And they do it all too well, in that they tend to avoid concepts that don't pigeonhole into an existing category. But you need to be aware of the market, too. If you write a book no one will buy, you've just wasted a year or more.

From a cold, hard sales perspective, then, you should probably aim your first series at a niche already inhabited by other successful authors—what I call a "me too" book. That doesn't mean to slavishly copy someone, but to reinterpret a preexisting genre with your own individual style and themes. Once you've got a toehold, you can reorient later work toward where you really want to go.

9. Match your publisher to your intended audience. Most beginners don't understand this. To them, all publishers are alike; they print books, don't they? Here's an analogy. If you confected a tastier pork sausage, it would be futile to market it through a New Age vegetarian store. Gay fiction will not sell well through a conservative publisher. Work with a right-wing slant will not sell at a house that prides itself on "liberal" ideas. Literary fiction will not do well with a genre publisher, and vice versa.

Note that I don't say the publisher won't *buy* it. They sometimes do, to present the appearance of a balanced list, or because one of the editors has an individual agenda, or just to dip a toe into a new market. What I'm saying is that over time, if your series is at the wrong publisher, it won't flourish, no matter how good it is, how much you like your editor, or how hard you work to promote it.

Ask retailers and agents about your house's reputation, read its lists, note who else publishes with them. If the match isn't right, move on. You'll do better in the long run.

10. Set a sensible delivery schedule. Once your first book makes a reasonable showing, you'll be asked when you can deliver the next one. Think hard before you answer this question.

Today, most brand-name commercial authors publish a book a year, with new hardcovers tied to the release date of the previous book in mass market. If you want to ascend to bestseller status, you might need to work at that pace.

But each writer's life is different. You may have a job or a family. You may write poetry and like to travel. Don't base your delivery schedule on how long it takes you to write a book. Base it on how much of a complete slice of your life writing that book will take.

In other words, if you have six months' work in a book, but due to everything else it took you two years to put in that six months on the keyboard, don't give way to euphoria and commit to delivering your next book in six months. Build in a cushion for alternate approaches, research, false starts, and overcoming blocks. Include time for your family, too. Writing's great, but it isn't everything.

11. Build in some stress-releasers. Just knowing you have extra time is the biggest de-stresser I know of, but there are other ways to stay happy over the long haul of series work.

One is crop rotation. That's what I call running two or three series simultaneously, alternating types of books. Since each of mine is different in tone, setting and their demands in terms of craft, I find swapping out quite refreshing.

(Again, you'll have to clear this with your editor, or perhaps do different books with different houses. Many mystery writers juggle multiple series, as do some thriller writers. But your publisher may want you to reserve your name for one particular series, especially if it's selling well, and use a pseudonym for the others.)

Vacations and sabbaticals are good. Occasionally doing a part-time gig at something entirely unrelated to writing is a great stress-reliever, and can give you new material. It also reminds you, usually in short order, of why you became a writer in the first place.

12. Keep in mind you need a graceful exit strategy. Just as every creature dies and every piece of fiction has a natural end, so does every series. If sales are good, the publisher may pressure you to keep on after you've said all you have to say. We've all read the result: tired, half-hearted, regurgitated work.

The solution? Plan for the end from the beginning.

The simplest ending to a series is the death of the protagonist (though Conan Doyle couldn't make it stick, it landed him in such hot water with his fans). Artistically, the final work should mark the resolution of the central conflict that has propelled the character throughout the chain of books. A driven character may find rest; a doubter, faith; a drifter, home at last.

Formal ceremonies can mark a transition or ending. A funeral, a retirement ceremony, a wedding, a decommissioning, mark consummations in our lives. The last installment in your epic should also come full circle, if only in internal monologue or some symbolic reminder of how it all began.

Once you've finished, don't look back. Look ahead to the next book, the next series, if you will, and use what you've learned to make it better than the last.

Good luck!

David Poyer of Franktown, Va., has written more than 20 books, including *The Med* and *China Sea* (St. Martin's). His latest book is *Fire on the Waters* (Simon & Schuster).

SEVEN HABITS OF HIGHLY EFFECTIVE BOOK MARKETERS

by David Poyer

Is there a magic key to getting published? After 25 years in the business, I'd have found it—if it existed. But it doesn't. Even when pitching sequels to books that made money, I've been turned down.

But the last few months have been exceptional. First, with the help of a first-rate agent, I placed the seventh novel in an ongoing series. Then we signed a three-book contract with another publisher. After that, I managed a bidding situation for a friend's literary novel. Working with a partner, I then helped a new writer secure an agent and a two-book contract, and, last but not least, placed a children's book by two poets I know.

Thus, I've been involved in selling a total of eight books in a few months. The sales occurred in various ways, but never in the way they're "supposed" to—by writing a manuscript and sending it off to an agent. My conclusions: A writer needs to understand how the market works today, how to use proposals and make contacts—in short, how to *act* rather than wait passively to be noticed.

In that spirit, then, here are four case studies of how books today move from concept to a contract, and the seven "habits" beginning writers can learn from them.

1. Follow one banjo act with another banjo act. This is the simplest case I'll present. I've been with St. Martin's Press since 1983, in a long and rewarding association with George Witte, who is now the editor-in-chief there. My Dan Lenson novels (*The Med*, *The Gulf*, *The Circle*, *The Passage*, *Tomahawk*,

China Sea) are works of modern naval fiction. I run the stories about 10 years behind current events, so it was time to do a Desert Storm book.

Black Storm focuses on a team of Marines sent into Iraq to locate a biological weapon. My primary selling tool was an 11-page proposal. It consisted of a color cover, which I did with a scanner, word processor, and a color printer; a title page; a six-page, double-spaced chapter outline; and a paragraph each on narrative structure, research requirements, author bio, and literary and film agent contact data.

I sent the fourth draft of the proposal to my agent, Sloan Harris of ICM. He suggested minor changes, which I made, and then sent the proposal to George. We had a contract within a month.

2. Diversify. With *Black Storm* contracted, my long-term plan said it was time to start a new series. That's how I've worked for years: Keep two or more series going, quite different in terms of milieu and style, and alternate writing the books. It's literary crop rotation, but it also keeps me from being totally dependent on the fortunes of one genre.

What people seem to want from me these days are sea stories, but I've done two historical novels and they got good reviews. So it seemed natural to try a historical sea novel. I'd never read any fiction about the Civil War at sea, and I've always been fascinated by the era.

I began by envisioning seven books that would cover the principal phases and theaters—for example, the opening of hostilities, the blockade-runners, the war on the Mississippi. Then I tried to create some fictional characters who would fascinate me (and the reader) enough to keep us all going through that many books. When I thought I had them, I wrote a series outline, one paragraph per book.

I did a proposal for the first volume. But since this was a new concept, not a sequel, this proposal was much longer than that for *Black Storm*. This time I included a two-page series introduction, complete texts of Chapter 1 and the pivotal burning-of-Norfolk Chapter 15 (a total of 16,500 words), a 15-page single-spaced outline, and a marketing plan. The proposal took three months to write, between previous commitments and book tours.

After the usual—his critique, my polishing—Sloan circulated the Civil War-at-sea proposal to five carefully selected houses. We got several indications of interest, but good offers eventually came from St. Martin's and Simon & Schuster. Interestingly, the offers were identical per book, but St. Martin's offered a two-book contract, while S&S wanted three.

All other things being equal, I prefer to deal with more than one publisher. Paranoid? Maybe, but I learned this lesson back when my total income came from freelancing for magazines. I learned from experience that editors move on, and new editors bring their own favorites with them. Publishers change direction, and companies go broke. Depending on one person or company for your entire paycheck is just asking for trouble.

But I still postponed my decision until I could meet personally with editor Marysue Rucci, who had made the offer for S&S. We got along, and since I had the other books going at St. Martin's, I decided to try my luck with Simon & Schuster. Sloan and ICM wrapped up the contract, I wrote the other 29 chapters, and *Fire on the Waters* was published in July.

Diversify—different series, different genres, different publishers. It's not a guarantee against sudden storms, but it gives you the reserve buoyancy to ride them out.

3. Be aware of trends in the marketplace. It's worth noting that this was the second time I'd gone through this whole process. The year before, I developed and marketed an idea for a female Naval Criminal Investigative Service agent investigating modern-day crimes in the U.S. Navy. Not one publisher made an offer. They said the flop of Demi Moore's movie *G.I. Jane* proved that the combination of "women" and "military" did not spell commercial success. If I'd been reading the trade papers more closely, I could have saved myself three months of work. Well, someday its time will come, and the outline and opening chapter are still on my hard drive.

4. Make and keep up good contacts throughout your career. Lenore Hart is a novelist, poet, and short story writer who completed her MFA at Old Dominion University last year. (Lenore and I are the two main judges for the First Coast Novel Contest discussed later in this article.) Her thesis was a literary novel, set in the early 20th century, about a young Virginia woman who takes over her waterman father's boat after his death. Defying the mores of the time, she becomes a waterwoman. One of Hart's thesis advisors, novelist Sheri Reynolds (*Bitteroot Landing, The Rapture of Canaan, A Gracious Plenty*), was so taken with *Waterwoman* that she offered introductions to her editors at Putnam and Crown.

> To succeed, a writer needs to understand how the market works, how to use proposals and make contacts—in short, how to act rather than wait passively to be noticed.

First, Hart drafted a one-page query letter. She sent this not only to the editors Reynolds named, but to others she'd culled from the usual references. She mailed complete manuscripts to those who responded positively. She quickly received offers back from Susan Allison at Putnam and Shaye Ayreheart at Crown.

Suddenly, she had a problem—the kind we should all have, but a problem nonetheless. She didn't feel confident as a horse-trader, but she was looking at a dickering situation with two of the biggest houses in New York. Who could she get to negotiate for her? She'd fired a previous agent whose work she'd been unhappy with, had been turned down by the two agents she'd really wanted to represent this book, and didn't feel like going back to any of them now that she'd sold the book.

At this point in the process, it would have taken too long to contact a new agent, get him or her smart on the property, and orient him or her to the playing field to start gaining yardage. She could have gotten *an* agent, but she wanted the *right* agent—one who had personal contacts with publishers, one with a national reputation, one with good film-industry contacts, and one who understood and felt committed to the book—or none at all. So she asked me to step in as a "business manager" and handle the bidding.

The process was stressful for both of us. The opening bid had been from Signature/Putnam. Then Crown said they'd see it and raise it. Over the next week, while I tried to elicit a better offer from one party and stall the other, Lenore spoke at length on the phone to both Ayreheart and Allison. Midway through the week, Houghton Mifflin expressed interest, too, making the chili even spicier. Lenore was impressed by both editors, and both represented solid publishers, but Allison's plan was to feature *Waterwoman* as the first hardcover in a new line. This augured a more solid commitment, since everyone at a house works extra hard to launch a new line successfully. Based on this, Lenore decided Putnam had the edge.

By now we were discussing considerably larger figures than they'd first offered, but I knew we had to nail down other terms than just the advance. In some ways, the amount of the advance can be less important than other aspects of the contract. I worked with Allison to define the publisher's offer in terms of world rights; hardcover, trade, and mass-market royalty rates; payout schedule; and all subsidiary-rights splits.

Once we had their offer well defined, I made counteroffers for an increased advance and better terms on trade-paper royalties. I also asked for cover consultation, more author's copies, and better subsidiary-rights splits. Since Hart didn't have a regular agent, we signed over foreign-language rights and audio-book rights to Putnam to market, but reserved lyric, dramatic, film, radio, TV, and commercial rights. When I was sure we had gotten the best deal possible, only then did we close.

Hart wrote a good novel, but she did more: She used the contacts she had to get it to market.

5. Once you have a breakthrough, push quickly on other fronts. With the book end settled, we immediately turned to Hollywood. Lenore had been corresponding with a well-known producer for some years. Their original project hadn't panned out, but the producer wanted to see her new book when it was done. Based on that and the Putnam sale, we persuaded Amy Asbury at ICM Los Angeles to represent Hart's work for films. The manuscript is now with two well-known screenwriters and packaging is starting to roll.

6. Be receptive to informed advice. I'm one of the judges for the annual Novel Contest at the First Coast Writers' Festival, held each spring in

Jacksonville, Fla. (www.fccj.org/wf). Winners get cash, but the real prize is our recommendation to agents and editors we know—many of whom have attended the festival in years past.

The 1998 winner was *Private Heat*, a detective novel told with humor and insider knowledge—author Bob Bailey had been a private investigator for 25 years. But it needed work. Bailey puts it this way:

"In 1998 I won the Bancroft Award at the [Florida] First Coast [Writers'] Festival, which came with a plaque and a small cash prize. The real award was a five-page single-spaced (oh my God—why did I win?) critique from two professional novelists, David Poyer and Lenore Hart. The critique motivated the most extensive rewrite of the novel to date—but for the first time I had a compass, a heading, and a map.

"I sent the resulting draft to Poyer and Hart and they sent it to an acquaintance of theirs—Andy Zack, of the Zack Company, Inc. (Web site at www.zackcompany.com). Andy felt the novel had merit and signed me as a client. Then he beat me senseless with a *Chicago Manual of Style* and pointed out redundant metaphors and passages that would prove cryptic to readers who had not spent 25 years as a street detective." The next draft was 100 pages shorter and a lot more accessible.

He used it to land me a two-book hardcover contract with M. Evans and Co. to launch my Art Hardin detective series.

"It takes a monumental ego to sit down, waste a ream of paper, and think anyone will care. . . . Creating a well-crafted novel requires not only native skill but input from readers, critics, and occasional browbeating from benevolent mentors."

I could not have put it better myself.

7. Be willing to work hard . . . and not just at writing. The message is clear. No longer can a writer wall himself off and simply write. To place your fiction in the coming years, you'll have to work harder and know more than writers did in years past. You'll need to study the market, the selling process, contract law, and the impact of technology on publishing. What I call the "downhill flow" continues. Agents do what editors used to; things agents once did are now your responsibility. Contacts, knowledge, and negotiating skills are increasingly necessary as the market changes ever more rapidly.

That said, the essential element remains. You've still got to produce good writing, the kind that brings something new and exciting to the reader. Do that, climb into the ring, and success will be yours.

David Poyer of Franktown, Va., has written more than 20 books, including *The Med* and *China Sea* (St. Martin's). His latest book is *Fire on the Waters* (Simon & Schuster).

THE SIDEBAR SOLUTION

Article add-ons can boost your freelance fees

by Bill Nelson

Wouldn't it be grand if freelance writers could find a magic potion that would make their work:

- Look more professional
- Sell more readily
- Command higher fees
- And, in a time of shrinking editorial holes in many newspapers and magazines, give writers a license to go on for greater lengths?

Well, such an elixir does exist, although many writers remain only dimly aware of its profitable possibilities. We're talking about the miracle of sidebars.

Are you using them at all, or with any degree of regularity, in the articles you submit to magazines and newspapers?

The word sidebar has been floating around journalistic circles a long time, but still hasn't made it into Webster's (side*cars,* yes, but side*bars,* no). Nevertheless, they represent a golden opportunity for enterprising—and sometimes wordy—freelance writers.

That insight hit me a decade ago, when I wrote a travel story on the Canary Islands, Spain's "land of eternal spring." A volcanic cluster of islands off northwest Africa, the Canaries are a favorite vacation destination for Europeans—the Hawaii of Europe. There, you find spring-like temperatures all year, as well as mountains, deserts, lush tropical growth, and volcanic terrain that often resembles a moonscape.

My article came to a whopping 50 inches and brought a horrified look from the travel editor of the newspaper for which I was writing. "It's good reading," she said, "but the front office has issued a decree that 30 inches should be the maximum length."

"Is there any way around that?" I asked.

"Tell you what," she said, smiling, "Trim your piece to 30 inches, then use your cuts to give me two sidebars to go along with it. That way, we'll keep management happy, and I'll be able to pay you more, besides."

So that's what happened. The main text focused on Tenerife Island, and the two sidebars covered the other tourist-oriented islands and the dearth of English-speaking tourists (in our resort hotel, we heard Spanish, German, Italian, and French spoken, but only rarely, English). A third sidebar told about the topless surprises we found on the beaches where, for many European women, going *au naturel* is the norm.

Thanks to the magic of sidebars, the Canary Islands package earned $500 instead of the usual $300 payment, and was given a dazzling four-story spread far more impressive than I had imagined.

USA Today underscored the sidebar strategy soon afterward, when it gave me an assignment to profile the late master motivator Leo Buscaglia.

"Do a 500-word story on Leo, then give us two or three short sidebars to go with it," an editor said. "Today's readers love sidebars. One might be on how he got started as America's 'love doctor.' Another could be on his penchant for hugs. And the third, well, we'll leave that up to you."

As it turned out, the newspaper used only one sidebar, but the other two helped make the sale.

THIS IS A SIDEBAR

By definition, a sidebar is a companion story that appears adjacent to a longer feature story, often in a box or toned in a different typeface to set it apart. The text touches briefly on a subject related to the feature.

Today's readers find these small bites of information irresistible. Sometimes they'll read them before tackling the main feature (caught you skimming this first!).

Some examples of sidebars: I recently read an article on "Rehearsing before a person retires." A sidebar listed five key steps in financial planning to ensure solvency after saying goodbye to the daily rat race.

Another piece on Wisconsin's many bicycle routes carried a sidebar on a relatively new offering, the Gandy Dancer Trail—how could one not be intrigued by the name?

Look for sidebar possibilities each time you write an article.

What type of sidebars might you consider?

The useful list is one. (Americans are hooked on lists.) *McCall's*, for instance, did a story on how wives could get their husbands more involved in child-rearing. A sidebar listed five jobs fathers might do that mothers usually handled, like packing a child's lunch.

The glossary is another sidebar. For example, *Martha Stewart Living* did a story on apple growing, and a sidebar identified three dozen varieties of the fruit. I wrote about Wisconsin's scenic Kettle Moraine area, and a sidebar listed definitions of 10 key terms of glacial handiwork, including drumlins, kettles, kames, and eskers.

You-can-do-it-too suggestions are a third type of sidebar. *Country Journal,* for instance, focused on a booming food co-op in New England, and a sidebar gave suggestions on how readers might form their own cooperatives.

Another popular sidebar provides readers with a resource list—where to go for more information. A New York story on child abuse, for example, ran a sidebar listing treatment centers, self-help groups, and useful books for both children and adults.

Gone are the days when a writer tried to cram everything into one seemingly never-ending article. That no longer works in the era of the One Minute Manager and television's 20-second sound bite. Today's time-pressed readers generally appreciate sidebars. These article add-ons—and the organizing of information they require—are something to think about each time you begin to write a story.

As an editor friend confided: "When I get a sidebar along with a manuscript, I know I'm dealing with a professional who's hip to what's going on today."

Bill Nelson is a copy chief and special projects writer for a Wisconsin-based public relations agency and teaches college writing workshops.

OTHER ARTICLE ADD-ONS:

- Listings of related articles or books of interest
- Web site URLs
- Summaries or expansions of key points
- Charts and graphs
- Background information
- Timelines of important events
- Brief articles relevant to primary story
- Professional organizations related to topic

BARGAIN FOR BETTER RATES

Tips for negotiating with editors

by Kelly James-Enger

Your phone rings. Good news—it's a magazine editor who's intrigued by your recent query and wants to assign the story. The two of you discuss word count, deadline, angle and possible sources. Then she offers you $1 per word—for all rights to the piece.

What do you do? You can accept the assignment, turn it down because she's asking for all rights, or try to negotiate a better deal. While the last option is often the wisest one, I've found that many writers are either afraid to negotiate with editors or would like to, but don't know how to broach the subject.

When I started freelancing full time four years ago, I accepted whatever editors offered me and signed work-for-hire and all-rights contracts without complaint. (With a work-for-hire agreement, the publisher owns the copyright to the story; with an all-rights agreement, you own the copyright to the story but transfer all rights to the publisher.) I soon realized, though, that every time I did so, I was also giving up any chance of making more money from that particular story by reprinting it.

I started asking for better rates and more writer-friendly contracts instead of automatically agreeing to the editor's offer, and my strategy has paid off. I've made more money on individual stories, and today reprints comprise nearly 10 percent of my income.

Still, negotiating can be stressful, especially when you don't know where to begin. Read on for some strategies that can help to boost your bottom line—without turning off editors.

Set your standards.

You can't effectively negotiate until you know what you want, what you're willing to concede on and what your absolute bottom line or "walk-away" position is. When I started freelancing, I took on every assignment regardless of pay. I focused on developing relationships with editors, building my portfolio and improving my writing abilities.

Today, however, I don't write for less than $1 per word, and I usually get more than that. Then, if an editor offers me a story for a lower rate, I say something like, "You know, I'd like to work for you, but I get $1 per word or more for most articles. Can you match that?" Your rate will depend on your experience, whether you've worked with the editor before, and the amount of work that a specific story might require.

Prove your worth.

If the offer is decent, I usually don't ask for more money the first time I work with an editor. I figure that even if you have hundreds of clips to your name, the editor is taking a chance on you—there are plenty of talented writers who are lazy about deadlines or turn in sloppy copy. After you've done a great job on your first piece, you're in a better position to ask for a higher per-word rate for the next story the publication assigns to you.

I'll often ask for a "raise" on my second or third assignment, using language like, "You've worked with me before, so you know I'll do a good job, meet my deadline, and that the story will fact-check out OK. Considering that, can we bump my rate up?" I used this approach on my third story for a fitness magazine, and the editor raised my rate by 25 cents per word—not bad for a five-minute phone call.

Make your case.

Being assigned a straightforward story that will require minimal research is one thing. If, however, you're asked to write a piece with a tight deadline or one that will entail significant legwork and time, use these factors as bargaining points.

I've found that many writers would like to negotiate their rates, but don't know how to broach the subject.

Last year, an editor I'd worked with before called to assign a 2,000-word piece on oral contraceptives with five sidebars—and then offered $1 per word. I said something like, "I really want to write this piece, but obviously this story is going to take me weeks of research and interviews, especially with all the sidebars. I don't think $1/word is really fair for this particular story. Can you do better than that?" She agreed that the story would require extensive research and bumped the rate to $1.50 per word.

Back it up.

Rather than just turning down an all-rights contract, explain why you don't want to sign it. In one case, an editor and I had agreed on the basics of a story— a rate of $1 per word, sources, and format. Then came the killer—the magazine's all-rights contract. I said, "I'm really excited about this story and I want to work with you, but I usually don't sign all-rights contracts because I make a significant amount of income from reprint rights. How about if we agree that you can have all rights to the piece for a certain period of time, after which they will revert back to me?" She agreed to this compromise, and we used the same contract language for future stories, as well.

Offer an alternative.

If the contract asks for more rights than you want to sell, suggest a compromise. Three years ago, a fitness magazine assigned me a story on how to determine your "exercise personality." The editor sent a work-for-hire contract, but I knew the story had definite reprint possibilities. I called the editor and suggested that I sell first North American serial rights, with the provision that I wouldn't write about the same subject for a competing magazine for six months after the piece was published. The editor accepted that language, and I've reprinted that story twice since it first ran.

Ask for more money.

On rare occasions, I will sign a work-for-hire contract—if certain circumstances are met. I consider how much time the piece will take, whether it's unlikely to be reprinted, and how much money the editor is offering me to write it.

For example, I recently wrote a short piece on new birth-control developments for a magazine that requires writers to sign work-for-hire agreements. However, the story would only take a few hours to research and write because it was a subject I was familiar with. Because of the nature of the piece, it would immediately become outdated, so reprints weren't likely. And the editor was offering $1.50 per word, certainly a decent rate. Even then, I explained why I usually don't do work-for-hire stories, and asked the editor if she could boost her usual rate. She offered an additional 50 cents per word for the story, and I took it.

If you're asked to write a piece that requires fast turnaround or significant time, use these factors as bargaining points.

Know when to walk away.

Of course, not every negotiation will go the way you want it to. In some instances, an editor may refuse to offer better terms and/or the money you were hoping for. At that point, you must decide whether the money and clip are worth it to you. An editor once offered me $800 for a 1,500-word story that would require a lot of research—and then insisted on an all-rights contract. In that case, I had no qualms about turning down the work. However, If he had offered $3,000 for the same piece, my decision would have been more difficult.

Sure, it's easier to say simply "yes" or "no" to an offer than to negotiate with an editor—but that's not a good reason not to try. Take a deep breath, summon your courage and ask if the editor can do better.

You can usually find a compromise that will make both of you happy—and pay off in the long run, as well.

Kelly James-Enger of Downers Grove, Ill., writes about health, fitness, nutrition, and other subjects for more than 30 publications, including *Woman's Day*, *Shape*, and *Fit*. James-Enger, a former attorney, leads writing programs and workshops throughout Illinois. Her new book for freelance writers, tentatively titled *How to Create Your Own Writing Niche* (The Writer Books) will be available early in 2003.

THE ROAD LESS TRAVELED

A nontraditional "travel writer" discovers butterflies and much more off the beaten track

by Robert Bittner

Too many travel writers are settling for second-best when it comes to selling their stories and earning good money. These are folks who love to travel and have the skills to write about it. But their concept of travel writing is limited to traditional travel articles that describe where to stay and what to see. And their target markets are limited to traditional travel magazines and newspaper travel sections. As a result, they're missing out on a lot of potential sales.

Instead, I take a two-pronged approach to travel writing. Sure, I write the occasional typical travel story. But I also use travel as a springboard for a wide variety of other kinds of articles—selling travel-based stories to magazines ranging from *American Profile* and *Preservation* to *Working Mother*.

Most travel writers focus on finding those hotels and hot spots that lure readers to a particular locale. The resulting articles, what I call "traditional" travel pieces, describe "10 Great Things to Do in Cleveland" or "San Antonio—On $20 a Day!" complete with a sidebar of driving directions and local prices. Don't get me wrong: Such articles are still the meat-and-potatoes of travel writing. But should you stop there?

Instead of seeing the world only as a travel writer, I try to experience new places and new people as a writer who travels. Hundreds of publications are looking for business profiles, human-interest stories, real-life dramas, basic service pieces. As writers who travel, we are in a great position to find these kinds of stories. We just have to look.

During a driving trip to explore downtown Detroit, for example, I realized that green spaces in the city seemed to be increasing. Previously, I equated

Detroit's central city with glass-strewn vacant lots and boarded-up buildings; the presence of so many trees and parks surprised me. I got curious.

Back home, I did some research and learned that Detroit had once been known as "The City of Elms," until Dutch elm disease and urban expansion took their toll. I also learned that the green spaces I had noticed were there thanks to a volunteer organization called The Greening of Detroit, a group working to fill the city with new trees and parks. That sounded like a good story to me, and I found an editor who agreed. My story about The Greening's efforts to revitalize central-city neighborhoods and encourage community involvement in tree planting and upkeep was my first sale to *Preservation*.

But is it really travel writing?

Some people might say such stories aren't really "travel" stories at all. I disagree. Like the best travel writing, they focus on a unique story of interest that is set in a specific locale. In addition, travel plays a key role in finding and researching these stories. Because we have been there, we can fill our queries and stories with a rich sense of place.

Consider this passage from a travel-based query of mine that sold to *Working Mother*:

> Deborah Payne smiles as she mentions the comments that greeted her four children after the family opened their new ranch in the Texas Hill Country. "The first couple of weeks, they heard a lot of jokes like, 'Bet those herds are pretty hard to lasso!' and 'Isn't it kind of hard to keep them in the corral?' It didn't take too long for that to get old," she says, laughing. Of course, she should have expected it. After all, this part of the country is known for its cattle and horses and the occasional llama. The last thing you'd expect to find is a rancher whose herds flock and flutter. But then, the Fredericksburg Butterfly Ranch and Habitat isn't a typical Texas ranch.
>
> Owner Deborah Payne . . . urges guests to spend time relaxing in the landscaped butterfly habitat of water fountains and plant varieties that provide nectar and food for her colorful herds. She leads the curious on tours of her new 1,500-square-foot walk-through butterfly house, a temperature-controlled environment where orange-black clouds of adult Monarchs and Painted Ladies flutter past. Armed with a wealth of knowledge and a passion for her work, Deborah is like an enthusiastic park ranger who can hold the wonders of her natural world—eggs, chrysalises, caterpillars—in the palm of her hand.
>
> I think your readers would enjoy Deborah's story. In less than two years, she has turned a fascination with butterflies into a thriving business with a growing national reputation. I'll take readers on a tour of the Fredericksburg Butterfly Ranch and Habitat and describe the curious business of butterfly ranching. But most importantly, I'll focus on the way Deborah has fully integrated her family life with her business, creating a nurturing and stimulating world for her butterflies as well as for her husband and young children.

Imagine trying to manufacture these quotes, these scenes, from a telephone conversation. It just wouldn't happen. Travel was an essential part of the process.

Whether you're traveling on your own or as part of an organized group, you can usually take the time to step back, look where other people aren't looking, ask questions that probe a little deeper, and nail down the details that will give your article or query the individuality and freshness it needs to succeed. That means going after the traditional story while also keeping an eye out for the hidden angle.

Finding the hidden stories

In Nashville, Tenn., I met a tour guide at the Country Music Hall of Fame (getting the traditional story) who also works as a Patsy Cline impersonator at local clubs (discovering a hidden story). I didn't pursue that angle, but I can imagine other writers spinning off stories about non-Elvis celebrity impersonators, how to take the backdoor route to a music career, and Nashville's diverse nightclub scene.

In Berkeley, Calif., I was visiting the Judah L. Magnes Museum (traditional story) when some older folks began arriving for a writing group that met upstairs. The group consisted of Jewish Holocaust survivors who were writing about their life experiences (hidden story). An inventive writer could probably come up with a dozen story angles based on this discovery—from how the arts have enabled this community to deal with great pain and loss to how to turn personal experiences into publishable memoir.

In Johnstown, Pa., I stepped into a nondescript restaurant called The Back Door and discovered a menu that included corn rings with ginger butter and Belgian chocolate mint tortelets. Finding inventive food in such an unexpected place would add an interesting element to a traditional travel story about the area. But I also discovered that the menu changes daily as the owners raid their garden for the freshest ingredients and forage for more than a dozen varieties of local mushrooms. Someday I might write about restaurants that grow their own ingredients, how to forage for tasty mushrooms yourself, or even a story on the emotional satisfaction of finding a hidden treasure (like an out-of-the-way gourmet restaurant).

It isn't hard to find stories like these and get assignments. Wherever you go, you just have to be willing to look beneath the surface, ask a lot of questions, and let curiosity be your guide.

Robert Bittner of Charlotte, Mich., is a fulltime freelance writer. His fourth book, *So What Are You Going to Do Now?*, a lifelong career guide, will be published in 2003 by Waterbrook Press.

SECTION FOUR

Ideas & Inspiration

ABOUT THAT NOVEL

by Evan Hunter

Starting

If you haven't got an idea for one, forget it. If you haven't got an idea you want to express on paper, in words, forget it. If you prefer putting paint on canvas, or rolls on your pianola or in your oven, forget it. You're going to be with this novel for a long, long time, so you'd better have *thought* about it before you start writing. When it's ready to be written, you'll know. You'll know because you can't get it out of your mind. It'll be with you literally day and night. You'll even dream about it—but don't get up and rush to your typewriter. Go back to sleep. Only in movies do writers get up in the middle of the night with an inspiration. The time to go to the typewriter is when you're fresh and ready to do battle. There *will* be a battle, no question, a siege that will seemingly go on forever. So sit down, make yourself comfortable, and begin.

No outline at first, except the loose one in your head, draped casually around the idea. The thing you are trying to find is the voice. This is the single most important thing in any novel. The voice. How it will *sound*. Who is telling the story? Why is he telling it? If you're 60 years old and writing in the first person singular about a 16-year-old high school student, beware of the voice. It may be your own, and that is wrong. If you're writing in the third person, you can change the tone of the voice each time you switch to another character, but the *voice* itself must remain consistent throughout. The voice is your style. Except in my mystery series, I try to change my style to suit the subject matter of any novel I'm writing. I've come a hundred pages into a novel using the wrong voice, and I've thrown those pages away and started a new search for the right voice.

Don't worry about spending days or weeks trying to find a voice. It will be time well spent. You'll know when you hit upon it. Things will suddenly *feel* right.

Once you've found the voice, write your first chapter or your first scene. Test the water. Does it still feel right? Good. *Now* make your outline. First of all, determine how long the book will be. The average mystery novel runs about 200 pages in manuscript, but a straight novel can be something as slim as *Love Story* or as thick as *Gone With the Wind*. You are the only person who knows in advance what your story is about. You are the only one who can figure how many pages you will need to tell this story. Take out your calculator. Are you writing a 300-page novel? OK, how many chapters will you need? The length of each chapter will be determined by how much you have to *say* in that chapter. If you're depicting the Battle of Waterloo, it might be a trifle difficult to compress it into 10 pages. If you're writing about a man putting out the garbage, you probably have only a scene, and you'll need additional scenes to make a full chapter.

Outline the novel in your own way—never mind freshman high school English courses. I've outlined a 40-page chapter with just the words "Father-son confrontation." The outline is you, talking to yourself on paper. Get friendly with yourself. Tell yourself what you, as the writer, want to accomplish in any given chapter. "OK, now we want a big explosion in the garage, and we want to see all these goddamn flames, and smell the smoke, and we want neighbors running over with garden hoses. Bring the little girl in at the end of the scene, shocked by what she's done." Got it? *Talk* to yourself. You don't have to outline the whole book. Just take the outline as far as your invention will carry it. Later, when you've written all the chapters you've already outlined, you can make another outline of the *next* several chapters. If a chapter is needed between something that has happened before and something that will happen later, and you don't know what to put between those two slices of bread, just type in the words "scene missing." You'll come back to it later. You're going to be here awhile.

Moving

Set yourself a definite goal each day. Tack it on the wall. Ten pages? Five pages? Two pages? Two paragraphs? It doesn't matter. Set the goal, make it realistic, and meet it. If you're writing a planned 400-page novel, it will seem impossible ever to get it finished. Four hundred pages may be a year away. But your daily goal is here and now, and it's important to set that goal and meet it so that you'll have a sense of immediate reward. At the end of each week, on your calendar, jot down the number of pages you've already written. Store your kernels. Watch the cache grow. Keep the thing moving. If it bogs down, if you're supposed to write a tender love scene and you've just had a fight with your accountant, put the anger to good use. Jump ahead and write the Battle of Waterloo chapter. Don't stop writing! It's easier to go fishing or skiing—but sit at that damn typewriter, and look at the four walls all day long if you have to. There is nothing more boring than looking at the walls. Eventually, if only to relieve the boredom, and because you've made a deal with yourself not to get out of that chair, you'll start writing again. At the end of the day, read over what you've written. If you think it's lousy, don't throw it away. Read it again in the morning. If it still looks lousy, do it over again. Or if it's still bothering you, and you don't know why, move on. Keep it moving. The nice thing about writing, unlike public speaking, is that you can correct all your mistakes later.

Changing

The only true creative aspect of writing is the first draft. That's when it's coming straight from your head and your heart, a direct tapping of the unconscious. The rest is donkey work. It is, however, donkey work that must be done. Whether you rewrite as you go along—taking that bad chapter from the night before and putting it through the machine again from the top—or whether you rewrite everything only after you've completed the book, you *must* rewrite. But be careful. You can hone and polish something until it glows like a diamond, but you may end up with something hard and glittering and totally without the interior spark that was the result of your first commitment to paper. Try to bring to each rereading of your own material the same innocence you brought to it the first time around. You will be rereading it *20* times before you're finished. Each time, ask yourself what you intended. Do you want me to cry when I read this scene? Well, are *you* crying? If you're not, why aren't you? Find out why you aren't. Did someone say something that broke the mood of the scene? Is the field of daffodils too cheerful for the tone of the scene? Has your heroine stamped her foot when she should be tearing out her hair? Work it, rework it. When you yourself begin crying, you've got it.

Ending

How do you know when you're finished? You're finished when you're satisfied. If a scene is right the first time around, leave it alone. Tell yourself, "Terrific, pal," and leave it alone. You'll know you're getting to the end because you'll suddenly slow down. When that happens, set smaller goals for yourself. Instead of those five pages today, make it three. Your pace is slower because you don't want to let go of this thing. You've been living together for a long, long time, you've let this smelly beast into your tent, and you've grown to love it, and now you're reluctant to have it gallop out over the sands and out of your life forever. The temptation is to keep it with you forever, to constantly bathe it and scent it, groom it and curry it, tweeze its lashes and tie a bow on its tail. *Recognize* the temptation and recognize, too, that everything eventually grows up and leaves home. When you've done the best you can possibly do at this time (there *will* be other books, you know), put the manuscript in a box, give it a farewell kiss, and send it out into that great big hostile world.

Sending

Where do you send it? Be exceedingly careful in choosing your agent or your publisher. Don't send the book to anyone who charges a fee for reading it or publishing it. In the real world of publishing, people pay *you* for your work. The Association of Authors' Representatives, Inc. (if you decide to go the agent route) will send you on request a list of reputable agents in the United States. The address is P.O. Box 237201, Ansonia Sta., New York, N.Y., 10003. Just write and ask, enclosing a self-addressed, stamped envelope. If you decide to submit your manuscript directly to a publisher instead, a long list of publishers looking for various kinds of novels appears in *The Writer* every year. Although some publishers today have given up reading unsolicited manuscripts, many others still maintain reading staffs, and their sole purpose is to search for publishing possibilities. Send the novel manuscript out. One publisher at a time. Multiple submissions are frowned upon except when an agent is conducting a huge auction, and then the publishers are made aware beforehand that the book is being submitted simultaneously all over the field. Choose a publisher who has previously published your sort of book. Don't shotgun it around blindly. If your novel espouses atheism, don't send it to a religious publisher.

Waiting

So now your monster is out roaming the countryside, trying to earn a living. No, there it is in the mailbox. Damn thing. Wish you hadn't given it life at all. Tear open the package. Nice little noncommittal note. Thanks a lot, but no. . . . Despair. Chin up, kiddo, send it out again. But here it is *back* again. And *again*. And *yet* again. Plenty of publishers in the world, just keep trying. Pack it, send it, wait again. Why? Why wait? Why set up a vigil at the mailbox? Why hang around the post office looking like someone on the Wanted posters? You should be *thinking* instead. You should be mulling a new idea. *Don't* wait. What you *should* be doing is—

Starting

If you haven't got an idea for one, forget it. If you haven't got an idea you want to express on paper, in words, forget it. If you prefer putting paint on canvas, or rolls on your pianola or in your oven, forget it. You're going to be with the novel for a long, long time, so you'd better have thought about it before you start writing. When it's ready to be written, you'll know.

Write it.

Evan Hunter (aka Ed McBain) is the author of more than 90 novels, including his breakout novel, *The Blackboard Jungle* (1954). Over 60 of his books have been released under his popular pseudonym, Ed McBain, including over 50 crime novels featuring the police of the 87th Precinct. He is the winner of the Mystery Writers of America Grand Master Award.

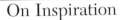

ON WALKING & IDEAS

by Brenda Ueland

I will tell you what I have learned myself. For me, a long five or six-mile walk helps. And one must go alone and every day. I have done this for many years. It is at these times I seem to get re-charged. If I do not walk one day, I seem to have on the next what Van Gogh calls "the meagerness." "The meagerness," he said, "or what is called depression." After a day or two of not walking, when I try to write I feel a little dull and irresolute. For a long time I thought that the dullness was just due to the asphyxiation of an indoor, sedentary life (which all people who do not move around a great deal in the open air suffer from, though they do not know it).

But I have come to learn otherwise. For when I walk grimly and calisthenically, just to get exercise and get it over with, to get my walk out of the way, then I find I have not been re-charged with imagination. For the following day when I try to write there is more of the meagerness than if I had not walked at all.

But if when I walk I look at the sky or the lake or the tiny, infinitesimally delicate, bare, young trees, or wherever I want to look, and my neck and jaw are loose and I feel happy and say to myself with my imagination, "I am free," and "There is nothing to hurry about," I find then that thoughts begin to come to me in their quiet way.

My explanation of it is that when I walk in a carefree way, without straining to get to my destination, then I am living *in the present*. And it is only then that the creative power flourishes.

Of course all through your day, however busy you are, these little times come. But they are very short in most lives. We are always doing something—talking, reading, listening to the radio, planning what next. The mind is kept naggingly busy on some easy, unimportant, external thing all day.

That is why most people are so afraid of being alone. For after a few minutes of unpleasant mental vacancy, the creative thoughts begin to come. And these thoughts at first are bound to be depressing, because the first thing they say is: what a senseless thing life is with nothing but talk, meals, reading, uninteresting work, and listening to the radio. But that is the beginning. It is just where your imagination is leading you to see how life can be better.

But if you would only persist. If you would continue to be alone for a long time, amblingly swinging your legs for many miles and living in the present, then you will be rewarded: thoughts, good ideas, plots for novels, longings, decisions, revelations will come to you. I can absolutely prove that.

And I found this. In the days when I thought a walk was just exercise, the ideas did not come until the end. "It is only in walks that are a little too long, that one has any new ideas," I find that I wrote in my diary. I now understand this. It was because I was nearly home and so gave up the willing, the striving to get this calisthenic chore, the walk, out of the way.

At once I felt released, lazy and free. I suddenly lived in the present and not in my destination where I would be (dully enough) reading the newspaper or eating dinner. Suddenly I was seeing how pretty the winter evening was, how black the trees in the phosphorescent moonlight, how the stars are different colors, how egotism is fear and self-preservation, but how there is an egotism that is great and divine. In other words ideas came and even poetic feelings.

Brenda Ueland (1891-1985) was a writer, editor, and teacher of writing. This passage is excerpted from her book on the creative process, *If You Want to Write: A Book About Art, Independence, and Spirit*, first published in 1938. Carl Sandburg called it, "The best book ever written about how to write." This classic bestseller is available in paperback from Graywolf Press of St. Paul, Minn.

JONATHAN FRANZEN: HOW I WRITE

With his third novel, *The Corrections*, Jonathan Franzen revitalizes the notion of The Great American Novel. (He lamented its demise in a 1996 *Harper's* essay.) His rambunctious, darkly humorous, and ultimately moving portrayal of the dysfunctional Lambert family in the throes of chaos touches readers with personal and social themes befitting a "big book." The novel's reach extends from the family home in the Midwest to Greenwich Village to Philadelphia to Lithuania, but never loses the thread of family angst that holds it all together. Franzen won the 2001 National Book Award for *The Corrections*. A frequent contributor to the *New Yorker*, he lives in New York.

His credits include: *The Corrections* (2001), *Strong Motion* (1992), *The Twenty-Seventh City* (1988).

Why. I got the bug bad when I was in high school. I wrote a couple of plays with a friend of mine; one of them was properly published. We actually got paid $50 each. That really set the hook. It was an amazing thing to happen to a 17-year-old. I've had a novel of some sort cooking ever since then. I write fiction because it's what I'm best at. I wouldn't be better at any other profession. Writing is hard, and I love all of it in its hardness. I'm never bored.

When and where. Keep in mind I'm speaking in broad generalities. I write Monday through Friday. If I don't go straight to the desk after breakfast, I'm in trouble and the day is usually shot. The process of sinking into that state of anxious isolation from which the writing comes has to begin in the morning.

It's really hard to concentrate, and I like a dimly lit, cool, quiet room. For the last four years, I've had a small office in East Harlem. I've soundproofed the walls and double-glazed the windows to keep it quiet. I keep it very dark. Sometimes I turn all the lights off. I have two sets of blinds. I hate looking out. The window is a distraction. Two things writers do are unfathomable to me: Some listen to music while they work; some like to look out the window at nature. If I go to an artists' colony and I'm looking out at nature, the first thing I do is pull the curtains, and if there aren't curtains, I tape up newsprint to cover the windows, at least up to the point there is only sky. I don't mind sky.

How. Once I have some clear idea of what the book is about, I get a very rough structure. Then, the work for weeks or months is to come up with a topic sentence—something that captures the plight of the characters. For Chip [in *The Corrections*], it was: "He's no good at making money, and he thought it was OK to live the life of the mind." For Gary, it was: "He's struggling to persuade himself that he's not mentally ill."

I think the most important thing—it may sound strange—is to get inside the character to the point that there is a lot of anxiety and shame. The real struggle is to find a dramatic setup and a corresponding tone that make it possible to dwell in that anxiety and shame without feeling icky as a reader. That's a big challenge. My approach to that—pretty much with all the characters—was that when it started seeming funny to me, I knew I was there. If it seemed anguished or earnest, I knew I wasn't there.

I have a thick binder with about a year-and-a-half's worth of notes. It's a record of the struggle to figure out what the book was supposed to look like and how it was supposed to be built. If writing could be reduced to a formula or algorithm, everyone would do it.

Challenges. The hardest part of the life is that you have to be in this raw emotional state in order to dare to do the things that need to be done and be fully alive to your sensations and your emotions. That makes it difficult to be in the world. Difficult to sleep. You have to spend a lot of time alone. Generally, it creates a sensation of weirdness.

Advice. I constantly remind myself that there is no hurry. If I work hard and get nowhere, it's still a day well spent. It doesn't have to be done this year or even next. When you live in fast-paced times, that's a hard thing to know. Remember there is plenty of time, and don't accept something if you think you can do better. That's something that took me a long time to figure out.

How I Write is a staff-written monthly feature of *The Writer* magazine.

CONVERSATION WITH ANITA SHREVE

Taking risk is an essential part of writing

by Robert Allen Papinchak

Anita Shreve followed a roundabout path to novel-writing, but once she arrived, success quickly followed. Her first novel, *Eden Close*, published in 1989, was a Book of the Month Club selection. Her second novel, *Strange Fits of Passion* (1991), continued to explore her interests in themes that were only hinted at in *Eden Close*. Passion, obsession, and betrayal—all grounded by the sense that love is "something extraordinary that happens to ordinary people"—dominate her books.

After *Where or When* (1993), *Resistance* (1995), and *The Weight of Water* (1997), she hit another high-water mark by being chosen as an Oprah author for *The Pilot's Wife* (1998). Not one to rest on her laurels, she experimented with language and subject (a relationship between a young Lolita-like protagonist and an older married man) to test the bounds of the historical novel in the spellbinder *Fortune's Rocks* (1999).

Shreve continues to climb bestseller lists with her most recent risk-taking experiment in technique, *The Last Time They Met* (2001), both a prequel and a sequel to *The Weight of Water* (which was tentatively scheduled for a fall release as a film starring Sean Penn and Elizabeth Hurley).

Before her novel-writing career soared, she was a high school teacher and short story writer, and taught two semesters of creative writing at Amherst College. She published a number of short stories in small literary magazines. One of those stories, "Silence at Smuttynose," was later developed into the novel *The Weight of Water*, and another, "Past the Island, Drifting," won an O. Henry Award in 1976.

Believing she couldn't make a living as a fiction writer, Shreve became a journalist, traveled to Africa, and wrote articles for *Quest, US,* and *Newsweek.* Freelance essays originally published in *The New York Times Magazine* turned into well-received nonfiction titles: *Remaking Motherhood* and *Women Together, Women Alone.*

Soon after the publication of *Eden Close,* she gave up journalism and turned to novel-writing full time.

The author lives in western Massachusetts with her husband and son. An eclectic reader and impassioned writer, she freely shares invigorating ideas on her writing process, enduring themes, important influences, and goals.

You began your professional life as a teacher, a short-story writer and a journalist. How did you make the move from one area to another? How does your background and training affect your writing?

I couldn't make a living writing short stories, so I turned to journalism. I worked as an editor in Nairobi, Kenya, for three years.

When I came back to the U.S., I worked in the magazine business, first as an editor for *US* magazine, then briefly as a writer for *Newsweek* special issues. Then I started a family.

I spent a decade freelancing, writing for everything from *Seventeen* to *The New York Times.* During 1987 to 1988, I used the advance from a nonfiction book to help subsidize the writing of my first novel. I wrote the novel in the morning, the nonfiction book in the afternoon. As it happened, both books were published within three days of each other in August 1989 by two different publishers.

Fiction is, and has always been, my first love. I consider myself a better writer as a fiction writer, even though I have used a number of journalistic techniques in my fiction: shaping a story, trying to have a captivating first page, not being afraid of research.

What is an average writing day?

I start in the morning as soon as I can after waking. Although I don't remember my dreams, there is something about that unconscious state that fuels my writing. I work until about noon. I've found that what gets written after that time probably isn't worth saving.

How do you come upon what I'll call "true details," those small, concrete, specific images that ring true, that tell the reader that you've been there and the reader can instantly recall a similar, very individualized detail? For instance, the "linen runner" that Andrew sees on his mother's dresser in Eden Close *or the slush under the cafeteria table in* The Last Time They Met—*do these details come naturally as you write?*

Those little details come from imagining myself in the scene, in the room, and noticing everything around me. Probably the biggest mistake beginning fiction writers make is impatience. They want to "get to" the story, not realizing that the "story" is in the details, the patient layering of reality.

Do you keep a journal for those "little details"?
I don't keep a journal. Believe it or not, I used to be an advocate of *not* keeping a journal. My feeling is that words should not be squandered. When writing, one should be in the habit of making sentences as perfect as one can. Journal-writing steals a certain energy away from that process. I think it contributes to sloppy writing. That said, I did keep journals once—when I was in Africa. Recently, I unearthed them and they became an invaluable source of impressionistic material for the Nairobi section in *The Last Time They Met.*

Houses seem to have a special place in your fiction. In Eden Close, *Andrew wonders who will live in a house after "a family is finally dismantled . . . a couple looking for an affordable starter home, a couple who will imagine this house to have more charm than it does, a couple who will furnish it with inauthentic country antiques."* The Pilot's Wife *and* Fortune's Rocks *share the same site. What is there about certain houses that draws you to them as plot elements?*
Stories unfold in houses. A house with any kind of age has dozens of stories to tell. I live in an old house. It has cracked ceilings, no closets, no bathroom big enough in which to take an actual bath. Sometimes, when I'm sitting by the hearth in the kitchen, I think about the people who have gone before me—the baby who was born in the room adjacent to the kitchen, the woman who cried at the inattentions of her husband in the upstairs bedroom, the girl who died of diphtheria croup in what is now my son's room. The house is full of stories.

Do you plot carefully? How do you usually begin a novel?
When I begin a novel, I have what I would call a "broad strokes" outline. I often know my endings. That is, I have an image or even a sentence that I see as the end. But even though I sometimes know my ending, I often have no idea of how I am going to get there. It's the slow unfolding of the characters and the story and the different journeys on which the characters take you that are unpredictable and exciting.

Then which do you find harder, endings or beginnings?
Beginnings are harder by far. I think it's accurate to say that I spend half the time of writing a novel on the first 50 pages, the second half on the second 250 pages. I write and rewrite those first 50 pages exhaustively. One would think that after half a dozen novels it would get easier, but I find that each book

> When writing, one should be in the habit of making sentences as perfect as one can. Journal-writing steals a certain energy away from that process.

is like reinventing the wheel. Most of the really difficult decisions have to be made in those first 50 pages. Who is going to tell the story? Will there be multiple points of view? What is the tone, the language of the story? By comparison, endings are a breeze.

When do you make the conscious choice about point of view? Do you ever imagine your novels from a different point of view or have you ever written one of your novels in one point of view and then had to abandon it and rewrite it from another? Do you think the choice of point of view affects the nature of characterization?

I have often written whole beginnings to novels only to discover that the point of view has to be changed. The most startling example was *Eden Close*. I originally planned to write it from Eden's point of view. In probably the smartest decision of my writing career, I changed it to a man's point of view, Andrew's. That allowed me some distance from my main character. That was essential to completing the novel, which was my first. I'm not sure I'd be a novelist today if I hadn't done that.

Do you have any special approach to creating a minor character? For instance, even in a fleeting first impression of Muriel, the motel owner in Strange Fits of Passion, *you manage to convey an exact sense of that type of character.*

I have such fond feelings for Muriel. I've actually thought of doing an entire novel in her voice. It was her voice that allowed me to know her. Once I heard her speak, I knew her character.

In some of your novels, a community often functions as a character of its own. This is true in Eden Close, Strange Fits of Passion, Resistance, Fortune's Rocks. *How important is the closed unit of a community—a town, a neighborhood—to you? What does such a social structure offer a writer as a theme for exploration?*

A closed community makes a novel easier, pure and simple. It's probably a cheat to limit a book to a closed community, because no community can be truly closed. But in a novel, the writer creates a universe. Sometimes this conceit is fragile. By creating a closed community, one can more easily persuade the reader of this fictional universe.

In The Last Time They Met, *you write that love is "the central drama of our lives . . . something extraordinary that happens to ordinary people." Your novels focus on themes of passion, obsession, deception, betrayal, love triangles, adultery. What do you think draws you to these themes? Why are they so all-pervasive in your work?*

I suppose I could go to a shrink to find out why I am so drawn to the theme of love, with all of its attendant emotions. I don't examine this too closely, for fear of defusing the very thing that makes me want to write. I can tell you, however, that the arena of love is a wonderful place in which to place characters. It's something extraordinary that happens to ordinary people. It's often, as well, a terrific testing ground for moral character.

What is more likely to trigger an idea for a book—setting? character? story?
Ideas come from all directions. A novel is often a collision of ideas, some of them completely unrelated. For example, take *Fortune's Rocks*. I was looking for a vehicle to revisit 19th-century language. At the same time, I had recently had a daughter pass through that delicate age of 14 to 15 and found it most intriguing. It was a fortunate collision of ideas.

You pay homage to Edith Wharton's Ethan Frome *in a number of places, beginning in* Eden Close. *And you mention that title more often than any other when asked about your favorite books or ones that have influenced you. Why does* Ethan Frome *have such a large place in your life?*
Each writer has a particular book that unlocked the desire to write. For me, I think *Ethan Frome* was that book. I read it when I was a junior in high school. I consider it a nearly perfect novel. It's a framed story and contains within it the delicate thread of literary suspense.

There is a "paperback shelf of doomed love" novels in Strange Fits of Passion. *The titles include* Ethan Frome, Anna Karenina, The French Lieutenant's Woman. *What attracts you, as a writer, to those titles?*
Many of my favorite novels are about doomed love. I love *A Student of Weather* by Elizabeth Hay. It's about doomed love, but I'm loving it not entirely because of the subject matter. I also love the novels of Elinor Lipman and Mameve Medwed. They might be called romantic comedies, but I see them as wry, astringent, and wonderfully funny.

My advice to the new writer with thin skin is to write and forget about everyone else. You can't have thin skin if you want to be published.

Without naming names, when you haven't liked a book, why haven't you liked it? Or why haven't you finished reading a book?
As they say in Massachusetts, I'm "wicked tough" on novels. Like most readers, I give a book the first-page test. If the writing isn't arresting, I'll put it down. I'm a very impatient browser. I'm not talking about the story, because I don't know at that point what the story is. I'm talking about the quality of the writing, the ability of the writer to seize my attention.

Do you have an ideal reader in mind?
I made the decision very early on in my career to put everyone out of my mind when I write.

Relatives, editors, Hollywood, critics. I have no reader in mind. I think it's death to a writer to consider how anyone else will view the work. One writes for oneself in much the same way one daydreams for oneself.

Readers and writers are always curious about The Oprah Factor. Could you give some brief details about how she contacted you, your immediate reaction, the aftermath?

Oprah called me one night, unexpectedly, about having chosen *The Pilot's Wife*. I was shocked. Shocked speechless. It was clear she had read the book and had made the decision because she had all sorts of urgent questions. I think she must love calling authors. I hope she's kept tapes. It would make for amusing listening some day—reducing the articulate to the babbling.

I am thrilled that Oprah called and I wouldn't change a second of all that has happened to me and to my books as a result of having been selected for her reading club. Some reviewers, however, have come to the table with an agenda that I can only call "Oprah bashing." A recent review in *The New York Times* about *The Last Time They Met* (a novel that has nothing to do with Oprah and is two removed from *The Pilot's Wife*) mentioned Oprah seven times. The reviewer spent so much time bashing Oprah, it was impossible to get a sense of what the book was about. It wasn't apparent from the review that the reviewer had even finished the book.

How do you deal with reviews? Any advice for the new writer?

I read some of the reviews I get. Sometimes there are so many that I don't see them until months afterwards. I think it's probably a bad idea to read reviews. Just as I think it's a bad idea to write with anyone in mind. My advice to the new writer with thin skin is to write and forget about everyone else. You can't have thin skin if you want to be published.

Some writers say they work on planes or in hotel rooms or coffee shops during book tours. Do you?

As a matter of fact, I write very well in planes. It's almost a perfect environment. No one can get to you. You really can't do anything else. And you're surrounded by white noise. What could be better?

Because of its structure, The Last Time They Met *was a risk-taking novel. Are there other novels of yours in which you took risks? What is the greatest risk you think you've taken as a writer?*

Taking risks is part of the pleasure. *The Weight of Water* felt extremely risky to write. I couldn't know until the end, until the very last puzzle piece was in place, whether or not the structure worked. It was either going to work very well or not at all. I didn't see any middle ground. I think the most audacious thing I've done as a writer is in *Resistance*, when I put myself inside the head of a pilot behind the controls of a B-17 in combat during World War II.

How do you decide on titles? Has a title ever come first? Or helped to define the structure of a book?

Titles are tricky. The original title for *Eden Close* was *Silence at Smuttynose*. My agent, Ginger Barber, and my editor, Michael Pietsch, were more or less horrified by that title and sent me back to the drawing board. The title for *The Last Time They Met* was supposed to be *The Magdalene Poems*. That's a title that makes a great deal of sense once you've read the book. The difficulty, however, was that it might not attract a reader. It was felt that the double whammy of religion and poetry would put readers off. My editor and I spent months trying to come up with the new title.

What is your greatest fear as a writer?

That I'll wake up one day and it will all be gone. I'll have nothing to say.

What is your constant goal as a writer?

To be inventive with the language and structure of a novel; to write arrestingly.

Robert Allen Papinchak of Edmonds, Wash., is a freelance writer, literary critic, and former college professor. He reviews books regularly for newspapers and magazines.

OLIVER SACKS: HOW I WRITE

An alchemist who turns scientific explorations into literary gold, Oliver Sacks, one of the nation's foremost neurologists, is, above all, a facile storyteller. Whether exploring mysterious neurological puzzles or recalling his early fascination with chemistry, he weaves a compelling human drama in each of his eight books.

Born in London into a family of doctors, metallurgists, chemists, physicists, and teachers, Sacks developed early a passion for the natural world and learned quickly to value curiosity, experimentation, and reading. He obtained a medical degree from Oxford and studied neurology at UCLA. Since 1965, he has lived in New York City, where he has a practice, writes, and teaches.

His credits include: *Oaxaca Journal* (2002); *Uncle Tungsten* (2001); *The Island of the Colorblind* (1996); *An Anthropologist on Mars* (1995); *Seeing Voices* (1989); *The Man Who Mistook His Wife for a Hat* (1985); *A Leg to Stand On* (1984); *Awakenings* (1973); and *Migraine* (1970).

Why. It comes out of a necessity to articulate what's in my head. To come to terms with it, fix it, transform it imaginatively, and communicate it. I really don't know what I think and what I feel until I write. It's not planned out beforehand; that realization comes with the act of writing. At the same time, the desire to tell a story may come from a sort of desire to bear witness.

When and where. I try to be consistent and to put aside the morning for writing, but often it doesn't work because I'm distracted. I have a room that, when I was writing [*Uncle Tungsten*], was lined with books on chemistry and physics. I have a manual typewriter in the car and electric typewriters in my apartment and office. I'm a hunt-and-peck typist but a quick one. I don't know how I do it, but I can keep up 60 or 70 words a minute. Apparently, it looks rather bizarre.

I do a certain amount of my writing underwater. I'm a passionate swimmer and sometimes as I swim, sentences start swimming through my mind. This was particularly strong when I wrote *A Leg to Stand On*. I would swim for half an hour, come out dripping, and scribble. I remember sending my editor a water-stained manuscript. He said, "No one has sent me a handwritten manuscript for 30 years, let alone a water-stained one!"

How. I do much of my writing with pen and paper. I've had notebooks of all shapes and sizes. I've written endless journals since I was 14—tens of millions of words.

I sort of start a sculpture, not knowing either the form or the content. It begins to emerge, then I start to see what I'm doing, and what I need to do.

When I'm working on a particular theme and an issue is in my mind, I will go over it again and again and try to find ways of saying it. It's sort of obsessive and keeps me awake at night. I will write it out, then be unhappy and redo it. I don't find it easy to go over what I write. I tend to produce another draft from a different angle. For better or worse, I write multiple versions.

Occasionally I get on a roll, and then I work nonstop. I don't want to go to bed in case it's all gone in the morning. It's partly systematic work and partly a series of rushes. There is no joy like those rushes when they come and no frustration like having them interrupted.

Writer's block. For me, writer's block is a state of not knowing what to do, not knowing what comes next. Although it may seem like a block, it's sort of a testing internally. Then a solution may come and I can move ahead.

Advice. Be oneself. When I was in my early 20s, I submitted a piece to an editor, and he said it was very nice but he found my sentences too elaborate. He said, "Why don't you be snappier, write like Hemingway?" I didn't submit anything for 15 years after that. I think the advice to be like Hemingway or emulate anyone is dangerous advice. One should only write about what genuinely moves and interests one. If you don't, the falsity will show.

How I Write is a staff-written monthly feature of *The Writer* magazine.

CONVERSATION WITH DAVID MCCULLOUGH

The Pulitzer Prize-winning author
discusses the art of biography

by Ronald Kovach

For 30 years, some of the biggest and best works of popular history in America have emerged from a little shed in David McCullough's back yard on Martha's Vineyard, Mass. There, working on a manual typewriter and surrounded by up to 1,000 books, McCullough has established himself, in the words of recent reviewers, as America's "most celebrated popular historian" and "most beloved biographer."

Working loyally in the nonacademic tradition of Bruce Catton and Barbara Tuchman, McCullough has masterfully brought grand historical subjects to life for the general reader, devoting many years of research and writing to understanding and elucidating the context and human drama of great events. He is a historian of deep feeling with a journalist's eye for telling detail. "There's no great mystery about how to make history interesting," he once told an interviewer; "that is simply to tell stories." The smooth, clean prose style he has used to tell those stories is a model for nonfiction writers.

His narrative histories have won a host of prestigious prizes, including the Pulitzer Prize for his 1,117-page biography *Truman;* a National Book Award for *The Path Between the Seas*, his epic study of the creation of the Panama Canal; and a second National Book Award for *Mornings on Horseback*, his absorbing look at Teddy Roosevelt's formative years. An emblem of quality is the fact that all of his books, which also include *The Great Bridge*, a superb narrative of the building of the Brooklyn Bridge, and *The Johnstown Flood*, his 1968 debut, remain in print.

McCullough, 68, has also become a familiar voice as the narrator of Ken Burns' hit PBS documentary on the Civil War and the host of the PBS series

The American Experience and *Smithsonian World*. His voice, like his writing, is crisp and clear.

A few naysayers, including Princeton historian Sean Wilentz in a major piece on McCullough in *The New Republic* last summer, have faulted him for being too easy on his subjects, or for sacrificing critical analysis for narrative flow and uplifting storytelling. But with his new biography, *John Adams* (Simon and Schuster, 2001), McCullough is enjoying another chorus of praise in most reviews. Gordon S. Woods, a leading academic historian of the American revolutionary era, wrote in *The New York Review of Books*, "This big but extremely readable book is by far the best biography of Adams ever written." Woods said McCullough has the respect of academic historians, and that "his special gift as an artist is his ability to recreate past human beings in all their fullness and all their humanity."

Long overshadowed by George Washington and Thomas Jefferson, John Adams gets his due in McCullough's biography—and indeed, clearly gets the better of Jefferson, at least in the character and courage department. Adams' service as the nation's first vice president and second president is comparatively well known; what's overlooked is his brilliant role as one of the great movers of independence, and his perilous journeys and persistence in obtaining crucial foreign money for the American rebels.

McCullough also mines two compelling subplots in the story: the marriage of Adams and his exceptional wife, Abigail, which he calls "one of the great love stories in American history," and the troubled friendship of John Adams and Thomas Jefferson—two remarkably different men who also had much in common and who "helped make the country happen."

In fact, McCullough originally considered doing his book strictly on the intertwining lives of the two men. "Adams and Jefferson are friends and fellow patriots and then even closer friends when they go to Europe," he says, tracing the checkered history of their relationship. "And then they come back and get back in the political swing at a time when the party system is on the rise, find themselves on opposite sides, and become rivals, then, really, enemies. There's a long spell, almost 11 years, when they don't speak to each other. And then they become friends again. There's a reconciliation. And they carry on what is one of the greatest exchanges of letters in American history—one of the greatest exchanges of letters in the English language. And then they die on the same day [amazingly, on July 4, 1826, the 50th anniversary of independence]. I mean, it's unbelievable. If you suggested that as the plot of a novel, your editor would say, well, that doesn't happen in real life."

As McCullough got farther into his material, something clicked. "I realized that something inside me was saying: Adams is your subject—I had to do a book about John Adams. And I've been on it for more than six years. And I've never—never—had such material to work with."

In an interview with *The Writer* in Chicago during his book tour for *John Adams*, McCullough talked about the challenges he faced in writing the book, and had much to say about developing as a writer, his work habits, and the joy of research.

By and large, you've written about pretty admirable people. Is there a danger in that while immersing yourself in the research, you grow to admire them in many ways? Is there a danger of becoming a booster or a cheerleader, versus writing about a scoundrel—a Stalin, a Hitler, a Pol Pot?

Oh, people ask me that. Sure, there's a danger, but not if you're professional about it. You can also say, is there danger in never doing anyone admirable that you get a very jaundiced view of life? People are admirable. People can be admirable. There's a Seamus Heaney poem that was just in *The [New York] Times* yesterday: "There comes a time when each of us needs to celebrate miracles when we see them." And I think that's true.

What draws me to the subject is not whether the characters are admirable or not. Though I'm sure I would not want to do a Hitler. You've got to keep company with these people every day, for six or seven years or more.

People like monsters. Little kids like monsters. It's in us. We're fascinated by monsters. And some people like to write about monsters. I don't. I like to tell a good story. And while it may be true that the people I write about may be seen, in the last analysis, as admirable people, I don't think there's been anything derogatory said about them or anything that's known to be a failing in them that's not in the story I tell. In fact, you need the unpleasant; you can't see the light if you don't have the shadow.

I think one of the themes of my [Adams] book is that [the founding fathers] all had their failings and frailties, which is part of the point, that they weren't gods, they weren't perfect, they weren't superhuman. If they had been, then we really needn't give them credit for what they did because gods can do anything. The fact is that they, as failed, flawed, inconsistent, contradictory, sometimes unpleasant, sometimes devious human beings, accomplished what they did. That's what makes it such an emblem to take heart from.

You said that with Adams, *you've never had such good material to work with. This despite the fact that you obviously didn't have interviews to supplement your research?*

That's right. That's a very good point—I didn't have interviews, I didn't have photographs, I didn't have film, I didn't have television tape. Because other things make up for those deficiencies: the diaries, the letters, the quality of the thinking—and it's not just the quantity of what John and Abigail and others have left us, but the quality of it. To have over a thousand letters between John Adams and his wife, Abigail, is like opening up a cave and there are the treasures.

And you went through all of them?

Oh yes, of course. And I don't think Abigail was capable of writing a dull letter, and neither was capable of writing a short letter [laughs]. And the candid quality of them, the trust they have in one another—they're just pouring it out: everything they feel, everything wonderful that's happening in their life. And his diaries are no less revealing and in many ways the most revealing of all, particularly his early diaries.

Did you have to decipher all that tiny handwriting?
No, because of the published Adams papers, which have been coming out steadily for 50 years. Now I didn't go through all the family papers—that's 608 reels of microfilm. But I read all the books.

For important letters, I always went and read the real letter. You can tell a lot from a letter, the actual letter, that doesn't come through when it's reproduced. With Adams you can often tell what kind of mood he's in, unlike Jefferson, whose writing is always the same no matter what. Adams is very expressive in his writing. If he's angry, you can sort of tell its angry feeling. If he's up, it runs uphill; if he's down, it runs downhill. If he's trying to save paper, it's minute.

Those diaries that he kept when he was a schoolteacher in Worcester [Mass.], I actually had to use a magnifying glass to read. And yet he's writing by candlelight with a quill pen. And they're tiny—they're only about the size of your hand.

And there's some sort of physical contact, kind of a tactile connection with those people [the Adamses], when you hold those same pieces of paper in your hand, and you see when she [Abigail] had to stick her quill in to get more ink because it was running out.

All of your books have been, to varying degrees, pretty massive research projects. What would you say to writers who are interested in doing historical articles, maybe a book, but feel intimidated by a daunting research task?
Lucky you. Because you have to have 10 times what you're going to use or more. Maybe it's because I grew up in Pittsburgh that I sometimes think of it as processing ore. You have to have *carloads* of that ore to make the steel you want to produce. So the more you have to choose from, the more fortunate you are, the less you have to resort to conjecture.

And don't pick a subject for which there's not much to work with. Far better to take a subject that may be relatively unknown which provides a great abundance of material to work with.

Let's take an example. Let's suppose you decide Martha Washington would make a wonderful book (and I don't know that this is true). You find out that Martha Washington left relatively little to work with. Far better to pick the wife of an army surgeon in a remote army post in the West in the 1870s if that woman kept a wonderful diary and wrote marvelous letters, and was involved in a court trial for which there are transcriptions of all that was said, and there are pictures and maybe she was also a painter who did little drawings and sketches. She'd make a terrific subject, whereas I'd stay away from Martha Washington.

But isn't it human nature for writers reading about the kinds of projects you take on to sort of hold their head in despair—like, oh my God, how do you get through all that?

Well, you do get through it because you're motivated by the material. You get your energy from the material. The better the material, the more energy you have. Your excitement builds. It's human nature that the more you know, the more you want to know. It's accelerative.

There are several mistakes people make in undertaking the kind of book I do. One is that they think that the way you do it is that you do all the research and then you write the book. That's not the way it happens. That's the way I *thought* it worked, and when I did my first book that's what I did.

I was an English major in college; I didn't know how to do historic research. But I had worked as a writer and a journalist, and I knew something about how you find things out. And I knew you kept asking not where and when and what, but *why* do things happen?

The first mistake I made was that I should conceal what I was up to because somebody might steal my wonderful idea. In fact, the reverse is true: Tell everyone you can possibly tell what you're working on, because you never know from whence is going to come a good lead, a wonderful entree to a whole collection of material you didn't know about, or an interview with someone you didn't realize was still alive.

The second mistake is, don't try to do all the research and then start writing. Start writing when you feel you have a good grasp of the overall content of the subject, of the story, if you will, and enough primary-source research and reading, in the early part of the book, to at least get you going.

And then start writing, because it's when you start writing that you find out what you don't know. You find out what you need to know. You see what you're missing and what you need to concentrate on. The tendency, if you do all the research, is you often spend an immense amount of time on individual characters or issues that really aren't as important as you think they are, until you get into it.

You're on a journey, and a journey includes both the reading and research, and the writing. And they should go forward together. I'm still researching right up until the last page, and I'm still researching things that I've already written about. You can always go back and change it.

Does this mean you're writing a rough draft as you go?

No. Never. I'm writing and rewriting all the time as I proceed. Now if I find something that either changes my point of view about something I've already written, or which ought to be included in what I've written earlier, I go back and change it.

I try to write four double-spaced, typewritten pages a day that I'm happy with *that* day, until I've gotten the whole first draft. Then I rewrite the whole chapter. And people say, "If you had a computer, you wouldn't have to retype that way." Well, that's perfectly true; I understand that. Look, I'm not just retyping it; I'm going through hearing it again. And the most important writing I do is often when I'm retyping that first draft.

I then turn it over to an assistant, who does it up on a computer. And that then becomes the manuscript. And we can change the manuscript at any point along the way, up to and including the last final days of working on it, by various miracles of the computer.

I would also say to every writer: Don't try to do it all yourself. Get help. Talk to people. Get people to look at what you've written; get people to give you an opinion on what you've written. But I think the most important thing to do is, once you've gotten to the point where you think, "This is very good," put it aside. Don't look at it for a month, two months. Then come back to look at it. You'll be amazed at what flaws and needs for further work are then seen. You've been too close to it.

Each of your rewritings is a rethinking, the way you explain it.
Writing is thinking. That's what it is. And that's why it's so damn hard [laughs].

Writing forces you to think, to bear down on the subject, makes you think as nothing else does. It's why writing ought to be stressed far more in schools. It's a way of working out problems, working out your thoughts, and arriving at

THE LITTLE SHED THAT COULD

David McCullough wrote *John Adams*, as well as his other books, on a Royal manual typewriter in an 8-by-12-foot shed, 100 yards from his home on Martha's Vineyard, the island off Cape Cod in southeastern Massachusetts.

He speaks fondly of his book-lined writing space, which is heated and contains several filing cabinets. "It's wonderful," he says. "First of all, there's no telephone, and second of all, my need for some quiet and lack of distractions doesn't impinge on the life of my family."

He adds, "I tell you, I'm inclined to judge people by how they react to where I work. If they come out there and say, as some have, 'This is where you *work*?' their stock goes way down. Others say, 'Oh, isn't this wonderful?'

"Everybody should have one, I really mean that. It's a place where you can go and be by yourself and think and take stock."

insights, conclusions, revelations, that you never could have obtained otherwise. That's really the reward of it. And you can do so much more on a printed
page than any other medium. You know, these other mediums—television,
movies—they're very limited. It's almost impossible to deal with an abstract
thought on television.

Trust your feelings. Trust your instinct in choosing a subject, in choosing
where you begin. I think where you begin is one of the most crucial decisions
in the whole process. Page 1. Chapter 1. How do you begin?

You have a beautiful, scene-setting opening in Adams, *where the two horsemen are on the road in the winter of 1776. [Adams and a servant are headed
toward a meeting in Cambridge, Mass., with George Washington, commander
of the American revolutionary forces, and then on to Philadelphia.] It's almost
a cinematic opening. Now did that come to you real easily?*

Yes. I had a picture in my mind. And I've had that with most of my books. It's
sort of the way I think. I had a picture of these two men on those horses coming through that snow. That bleak, anonymous landscape. They're anonymous—you can't tell who they are. There's nothing to tip you off. Just two men
on horses riding through the snow. Who are they and where are they going?
And when you realize they're setting off to ride by horseback nearly 400 miles
to go to Congress, you have to *care* to do that. And how much they care is so
important.

*In the whole area of academic versus so-called popular history, is there a nec-
essary conflict between doing technically precise, complete work and writing a
book that's "a good read"?*

No, there is not a necessary conflict there at all.

Academic writers who do pioneering work in the field are sometimes spec-
tacular writers, wonderful writers. Just as so-called popular historians can do
pioneering historical work of the first rank. No, there's no conflict. The conflict
is between facts and truth. Facts aren't necessarily the truth.

One of my favorite writers of all is [historian] Francis Parkman. As Parkman
points out, you can have all of the facts right, and get what happened wrong.
That's why you have to understand the atmosphere in which things happened,
the context in which they happened—how tired was that man that next morning when he had to make those decisions, what else was on his mind, how
healthy was he, what was the chemistry of these two different personalities that
when they came together was going to inevitably lead to an explosion? That has
nothing to do with facts.

*Didn't you say once that the problem with most academic historians is that
they don't care enough about people?*

Well, if I said that, it's probably an oversimplification. What has to be understood is that academic historians are of necessity writing principally for other academic historians. They're not writing for you and me. I don't put them down, because that's the nature of their profession. That's not what I do.

The simplest thing I can tell you is that I try to write the kind of book I like to read. I'm writing for me. Just as if I was writing a novel, I'd try as hard as I could to write the kind of novel I would like to read.

I think of myself as a writer, not a historian. I'm a writer who's chosen history and biography as my field, but to me, the writing problems, the writing opportunities, the writing adventure, are what runs the engine, not being a historian or biographer.

In his review of your book, Gordon Woods used the word "sensuous" in reference to Adams. I think most people before they read this book would say, "John Adams, sensuous?" And yet how can you read the chandelier passage and not see that?

Passionate. He's the antithesis in many ways of the stereotypical New Englander, the cliché Yankee. He's not taciturn at all. He's not cool about his emotions. He's not calculating. He has extraordinary common sense. He often has an amazingly clear-eyed vision of what it's all leading to.

And that's true of writing a book. If you know where it begins and you know where it ends, you have accomplished an enormous amount.

People ask me when I start one of these projects, what is your theme? I haven't the faintest idea. That's why you're writing the book, it seems to me, to find out. To me, it's a journey. It's an adventure. It's traveling in a country you've never been in and everything is going to be new, and because of that, vivid. And don't make up your mind too soon. Let it be an experience.

What would you say to writers about achieving the kind of crisp, clean prose style that you have, which services the material beautifully and yet stays a little out of the way?

Well, the old writer's adage, which I believe absolutely: Don't tell me, show me. Don't tell me he was a miser; show him being a miser.

Be careful what you read. Willa Cather used to read from the Bible every morning before she started writing. There's some possibility, of course, that it was an act of piety, but it was also, I'm sure, a way of getting those rhythms, that music, that poetry.

And disdain—with all your might!—the cheap, easy jargon of today, the cliche words, the "viable alternatives" and "a very special moment," "a personal friend"—is that to be distinguished from an impersonal friend?

I'm hearing a little E. B. White coming out here.

Well, absolutely. Here's what I believe. Don't strive for literary effect. Don't write what you think of as writing. Say it so it's clear. Say it so it's to the point.

Don't give away everything up-front. Be very careful about those lines you think are such ringing moments of high artistic achievement on your part [chuckles]. You know Faulkner's old line: "Kill all your darlings."

Remember, your reader is as intelligent as you are, and is probably a step or two ahead of you. They're getting it.

Go back when you're finished and cut out all the lumber; cut out all the extraneous things. Obviously, look carefully at all those adverbs and see if you really need them. I cut and cut and condense again and again. The hardest thing about writing this book was what I had to leave out—by far. It would have been far easier for me had I written this in two volumes.

I think also, it's very important to read what you've written aloud, or have it read to you aloud. In the process, you hear these little verbal tics we all fall into, whereas you might not see them.

You're quite well known for going to the scene of things—for literally trying to walk in the footsteps of your subjects, when possible.

Always. I really try to go to every setting where anything of importance took place. I may be overly concerned. I think we're shaped by the buildings we live in and work in. The rooms in which things happen shape what happens in those rooms—the size of the room, the way the light falls through the windows, the prospect outside the windows. All of that bears on how people feel and how they act.

So I wanted to go to every house that John and Abigail ever lived in. And there are a lot of them still standing in Europe. And particularly the house in Amsterdam where he nearly died, and where he was about as down, as blue, as he ever was in his whole life. I knew he walked all around Amsterdam for exercise or to clear his head. So I wanted to walk around those streets, in the night, the day.

With my wife I went on the same tour of the English gardens that he and Jefferson made. I wanted to go the same time of year. What did it look like? What was in bloom?

Your works have now ranged pretty much over three centuries of American history. You've written about great people, great events, great engineering feats. How do you master so much different material?

Because I want to. I want to. I don't consider myself an intellectual. But I am very curious. I really love to find things out. And I'm interested in people and I'm interested in why people do what they do. How did that come to be? Why did it turn out like this?

And maybe the most important single conception I hope to convey is that nothing ever had to turn out the way it did. You know, we're taught history like "This fellow, that fellow, you'd better remember that, you'd better get it straight, because it's going to be on the test next Thursday." But none of it had to happen the way it happened. It could have gone off in any number of directions.

What would you say to young writers thinking about doing historical articles or books?

Well, it's very common to say to young, aspiring writers: Write what you know. I would turn that around: Know what you write.

Really study something. Learn something. Know about it. And if it moves you, if it interests you, if you think it's interesting and if you take pleasure from it, others will, too, if you convey that to them. I can tell you absolutely that there are *hundreds* of subjects that either haven't been done or haven't been done for a very long time or, if they were done, were done inadequately. There are probably 35 subjects that I would just really like to do.

Never, never, ever be afraid or timid about revealing to other people what you don't know in the process of the work. Never try to convey to a librarian, for example, that you know all the ways in which to find something out [chuckles]. Throw yourself at their mercy. Tell them how limited is your knowledge, how much you don't know, and tell them *what* you're trying to find out. Enlist the support of others to help you achieve this objective.

Read good writers! [See sidebar, page 229] You know, the old idea "we are what we eat." You are what you read. So read the best. Read *really good writers*. And don't just read in your own time. Go back and read the 18th-century writers, go back and read the Greeks, and of course, read Shakespeare, of course, read the Bible, read some of the great works in other languages— Goethe and La Fontaine, Voltaire, the French and Italian novelists, and see what a lot you have to learn, and how much higher others have climbed than you have. Take inspiration from it, and study what they do.

I think there's a further point to be made for young writers who might be drawn to the kind of work I do. Many writers lament how lonely the life is. In this kind of work, it is not lonely, because you have to, of necessity, be in contact with all kinds of people: librarians, archivists, specialists in your subject. If you're doing someone who can be reached through living people, the interviews are of the utmost importance. You just can't hole up in your secluded writing room with this work; you've got to get out there and look around. You've got to contact hundreds of people if it's a large project. And you make some of the best friends you've ever made in your life. That's as appealing as any aspect of the work.

When you're trying to break in, to get that first book done, chances are pretty good you're going to have a full-time job while trying to moonlight. Do you have any advice along these lines—trying to get that first book out?

I can only tell you from my own experience that I wrote my first book at night and on weekends. I was at a very demanding, full-time job. I did the research during my lunch hour at the 42nd Street Library in New York. I had a wife and four children. I don't mean to ever suggest that it was an ordeal; it never was.

I would come home, we'd have dinner, we'd put the children to bed, and I'd go to work at 9 o'clock. And I'd try to write two pages that I was satisfied with each night, at least for five nights a week. And I would be less tired at 11 o'clock than I was at 9 o'clock. And my wife would have to come in and turn off the light and tell me, you've gotta stop and come to bed.

You have to set yourself a production schedule. I'm easily distracted; there's a lot of things I love to do that can put off doing what I have to do. It's habit. A lot of life is habit. Have a habit of work. And enjoy it—*enjoy* it. If you're enjoying it, chances are the reader will. If you're not, chances are the reader won't.

I'm doing four pages a day when I'm writing. Two pages in the morning; lunch; two in the afternoon. People say, "Well, what's your writing schedule?" I work every day. They say, "Well, not all day." Yes, all day. Every day. Now, I'm not always writing; sometimes I'm doing what they call thinking. Or I'm reading my notes or I'm looking over what I wrote the day before. But I'm out there every day, and I find that if you do it every day it's easier.

Ronald Kovach is senior editor of *The Writer*.

MCCULLOUGH'S PICKS

Want to become a better writer? One of the important ways is to watch what you read, says biographer David McCullough. Here are some of the authors and books he mentions as personal favorites, and from which any writer can profit:

A Summing Up by W. Somerset Maugham, which, McCullough says, "I've underlined so heavily for so many years that there's scarcely anything left that hasn't been underlined. It's a wonderful, wonderful guide. He says to look for your material in the commonplace."

Reveille in Washington 1860-1865 by Margaret Leech, "if you want to see how to really begin a book."

The Expedition of Humphrey Clinker by Tobias Smollett. An 18th-century novel which, he says, is "a fabulous book that has spirit and charm and wonderful descriptive passages" and shows "how character is conveyed by what people say."

Wind, Sail, and Stars by Antoine de Saint-Exupery. "One of my favorite books: a man writing about flying and telling you a great deal about life in a poetic way that is not self-consciously poetic. It's the opposite of purple prose, but it's very poetic. It's honed down to the essences of what he's trying to say."

Ruth Rendell: "For pure storytelling, I would say read almost anything by the English mystery writer."

Tolstoy by Henri Troyat: "A delightful biography. I love that book."

Bernard Bailyn: "If you want to read really good history, read almost anything by Bernard Bailyn."

Elmore Leonard: His early novels "are fabulous, stripped down, clean. I love these writers who can do so much on one page. It's like watching a great figure skater or something—they just know how to do it."

JOYCE CAROL OATES: HOW I WRITE

Acclaimed author Joyce Carol Oates' passion for writing and delight in the process has produced a wonderfully diverse body of work, including 28 novels; dozens of poetry, short story, and essay collections; screenplays; and a libretto. She also has edited several essay and short story anthologies and literary journals.

Oates has received the Rea Award for the Short Story for her significant contribution to the art form, the PEN/Malamud Award for a lifetime of achievement in the short story form, and a National Book Award for her novel *them*.

She is the Roger S. Berlind Distinguished Professor in the Humanities at Princeton University and a member of the American Academy and Institute of Arts and Letters. Oates lives in Princeton, N.J.

Her credits for novels include: *Blonde: A Novel* (2001), *We Were the Mulvaneys* (1996), *Zombie* (1995), *What I Lived For* (1994), *Because It Is Bitter*, and *Because It Is My Heart* (1991) and *them* (1969). Her credits for short-story collections include: *Faithless: Tales of Transgression* (2001) and *Will You Always Love Me?* (1996).

Why. Writing to me is very instinctive and natural. It has something to do with my desire to memorialize what I know of the world. The act of writing is a kind of description of an inward or spiritual reality that is otherwise inaccessible. I love transcribing this; there's a kind of passion to it.

When and where. I write every day. I have a desk with numerous pieces of paper arranged on it in a way that's important to me. When I'm on a trip, I write on the airplane or in my hotel room. It's easy because I'm alone, and instead of getting lonely and miserable, I turn to my characters.

How. I write in longhand. I don't have a word processor. I sometimes write on little notepads and have 60 pages of notes that I spread out and organize [by characters or scenes]. If I had a word processor, I couldn't do that sort of thing. It wouldn't be so physical or visual. I take the strongest parts and build slowly, doing a lot of rewriting as I go along.

I lose myself in the physical world. I describe it very assiduously. When I'm writing fiction, I populate the [narrative] with people who are expressions of a specific place.

Writer's block. I have many ideas. They come easily to me. The hardest part of writing is getting the voice and the structure. The only thing I can do is keep trying. I can write a scene over and over 17 times, and I'm very unhappy if it's not working, but I never give up.

Influences. *Alice in Wonderland*, which I read when I was 9 or 10, has had the most profound influence in my life. Alice has bizarre adventures but she never gets frightened. She's thoughtful, she's skeptical, she has a sense of humor, and she's rational. She is coherent and calm when confronted by nightmarish situations. Her calmness made a strong impression. That's the way I am. I can write about nightmares and bizarre things in a coherent, calm way.

Advice. My advice springs from my own experience when I was quite young. Read what you want to read, not what you are told to read. Read what makes you happy.

Remember that writing is a craft; it's not an experience like an emotion. It's not like going to a psychiatrist and delivering yourself of emotions. It's made up of text, the text has paragraphs, the paragraphs have sentences, and all of this has to be coherent and as beautifully composed as you can make it.

How I Write is a staff-written monthly feature of *The Writer* magazine.

CONVERSATION WITH JOHN IRVING

by Dorman T. Shindler

Before his bestselling 1978 novel *The World According to Garp* made him a literary superstar, John Irving could barely squeeze two hours of writing time into his schedule each day. His days were filled with teaching, grading papers, coaching wrestling, and caring for his children. Twenty-three years later, Irving, who last summer published his 10th novel, *The Fourth Hand* (about a person's inability to change), is working on several screenplays as well as a novel—"writing all the time," as he puts it. "I love being this busy."

In fact, Irving is so excited about his new novel-in-progress that he proceeds to recount nearly the entire plot to me. Tentatively titled *Until I Find You*, he calls this tale of love and vengeance his "tattoo and organ music story." It is, he says, "about the relationship between a tattoo artist's daughter and a church organist." His research for the book took him all over Northern Europe, where he learned about organ music and the art of making tattoos.

Irving has won his fair share of awards—including an O. Henry Award, a Pushcart Prize, and a National Book Award—and has been elected to the American Academy of Arts and Letters (not to mention being an inductee into the National Wrestling Hall of Fame). But his greatest exposure so far came during the telecast of the 2000 Academy Awards, when he accepted the award for best adapted screenplay for *The Cider House Rules*. The award was especially sweet for Irving, who had gained unprecedented control for a screenwriter (he had approval of the script, director, and cast) and spent nearly 14 years shepherding his script to the silver screen. (He wrote about it all in *My Movie Business*.)

I interviewed Irving in Toronto, where he keeps an apartment in addition to his home in Vermont. Our conversations ran the gamut from fatherhood

(Irving, 59, has three sons—Colin and Brendan, from his first marriage, and 10-year-old Everett with his second wife, Janet Turnbull) to screenwriting (Irving was contracted last summer to write the screenplay of *The Fourth Hand*) to what he laughingly calls his "day job"—writing novels.

You spent 14 years trying to get your screenplay of The Cider House Rules *produced. Once the project took off in earnest, did that change your attitude about Hollywood?*

It's been an exciting two or three years—especially since we were so long in getting *The Cider House Rules* made. I give [producer] Richard Gladstein credit. Because about the time I was getting worn down by the thought that we're never gonna get this thing made, Richard came in with a kind of new enthusiasm. He came in after the death of the first director, and despite the fact that the next two didn't work out, his energy was really good. I loved working with Lasse Hallstrom [the film's director]. We seemed to talk on the same page about the qualities of the story. I like Lasse because he cuts straight to the ending.

As a novelist, one of the things that makes writing screenplays easier is that I not only write a very plot-oriented novel, I write outlines. I know before I write the first sentence where the end of the book is, and what all the important details of the book are. These aren't things which are common in literary practice in modern or postmodern times. I spend a year or 18 months making a street map of a novel before I ever begin to write. So I'm familiar with that aspect of writing a screenplay. I really like the craft of it.

You've said that a discussion with your wife about a donor for a hand transplant—and the possibility of the donor's wife wanting visitation rights—was the creative and darkly comedic impetus behind The Fourth Hand. *Did any other concepts spark your creativity?*

One of the most impressive things about some people is that they stay the same, that they will never change. But there is another impressive thing about people: They *can* change. Or they *do* change. When you're telling a story, you have to know what kind of people you're dealing with; you have to know, is that a character who can or is going to or will change?

> I spend a year or 18 months making a street map of a novel before I ever begin to write.

In *A Widow for One Year*, that Eddie O'Hare will never change is a likeable aspect of his character. That Ted Cole will never change is an also likeable quality. But the reason Ruth Cole is a character with more dimension than any of them is that she's a character who's going to change. Having a child and losing a husband is going to have that effect on her. Because when you first meet her, she's a bitch. She's really nasty.

Whereas Patrick Wallingford [in *The Fourth Hand*] is always kind of likeable. Morally and intellectually, you don't take him seriously until, when the hand is gone, he has achieved the kind of success in his career that has heretofore eluded him. You don't hit that melancholy until he is handless, in New York. And you've got this sense of this truly lost soul who is this pretty, empty face.

The switch from comedy to drama in The Fourth Hand *is more pointed than any of your other novels. The first few chapters are hilarious, and then things suddenly turn around and become more somber, more serious. Was this deliberate?*

I think the first six chapters are my most strictly comedic writing since *The Water-Method Man*, which was a comedy, and is the only novel of mine that I would say is unequivocally a comedy. [*The Fourth Hand*] has movement like the acts of a play. The structure is, in that sense, very similar to *A Widow for One Year*, in which there are these dramatic shifts. In *A Widow*, they happen because of time; in Wallingford's case, they are literally related to losing the hand, getting the hand, and losing the hand.

And the second [act] is the problem. Because that's really the dark side of the moon. It's not just I've lost this damn hand again—it's what else have I lost? So there's this thing that happens in *The Fourth Hand*—and it certainly happens in all my books—but the degree to which it happens in *The Fourth Hand* is heightened, because the novel is half the length of the others and because the moment of this happening is so sudden. It's very deliberate and I'm pleased with how it's set up.

I always try to disarm the reader into thinking that this is a comedy, this is a farce. You're gonna have fun here. Nothing too bad is gonna happen. In other words, the opening chapters of my books are not only shorter than the latter chapters, but they're more comic in tone.

Then I want that to turn. You suddenly realize that this is more serious than you thought. And that when somebody's been hurt or is about to get hurt, that your care for someone has developed to the point where you like him or her better than you thought you would.

Mrs. Clausen [*The Fourth Hand*] is that character. For all of Wallingford's sensational encounters—the sex, the speed of his life, the drama of his life—that woman in her jeans and running shoes and old parka is not only the first pretty thing he's ever seen, she's the first pretty thing you come to in the novel. She's the first person who makes you take her seriously. And I wanted to keep it a little dark and unclear . . . the degree to which she was a participant in what happened to her husband. It's like the light and dark side of a planet. You want a story to sort of revolve and show its other side.

When dissecting your novels, critics often underscore the fact that most of your characters have an absentee, or dead, father or mother. Or that wrestling was mentioned so much in the first few books. Are they on the money or missing the boat?

First of all, that autobiographical idea of where the missing father or parents in John Irving's novels come from—one reason Dickens wrote about orphans was not because he was an orphan, but because orphans make good stories! I make use of such characters for the same reasons. People always write about the wrestling, and its discipline being somehow reflected in my discipline as a writer. That's a common thing.

I think that my view of the world was intrinsically informed by having children and my fear for what happens to them. I think that's something that . . . I could not have imagined. The fear for your children. I'm the last person to say, "You have to experience it to imagine it." In most cases I would say, "Bullshit!" But I think you've gotta have a child to know what it's like to be really afraid. Because being afraid for someone else is not the same as being afraid for yourself. It's different. There's a kind of edge of helplessness.

The characters in my novels, from the very first one, are always on some quixotic effort of attempting to control something that is uncontrollable. Some element of the world that is essentially random and out of control. And they're not gonna do it. It's not gonna happen.

I had a doctor's appointment today with my youngest child [Everett], and the doctor made an analogy that was just chilling to me—as I think it would be to any parent. Not because the diagnosis was at all serious, but because it speaks to that issue of control. I was looking for a course of medication that we hadn't found. And the doctor said, "The problem with you is that you think you're driving a car. And what you don't understand is that you're driving a boat." The hairs stood up on the back of my neck. I don't like driving a boat. I don't like turning the wheel and then waiting to see what happens.

That's very much like the situation I try to imagine in every novel. I want the principal character—and then the reader—to feel it's OK, I'm in a car. Then, whoops, they're not in a car. That level of unpredictability is something that doesn't come from not knowing who my biological father is or from being competitive as a wrestler from the age of 13 until I was 34. It comes from having children.

I think that my view of the world was intrinsically informed by having children and my fear for what happens to them.

In terms of difficulty, which novel gave you the most trouble?

A Son of the Circus, because the novel was first written as a screenplay, there were times when I thought I had bitten off more than I could chew. In [the screenplay], the main characters are children. Dr. Daruwalla is sort of a secondary character. But then I said, "This is the guy I'm interested in," and that became the basis for the novel. [The heavily symbolic tale explores the nature of religion and nationalism.]

If storytelling and especially a complex and narrative novel—the novel as a linear exercise—can be likened to juggling or some sort of a circus act, I don't believe I will ever do anything as complicated, as intricate, and as satisfying as *A Son of the Circus* again. But it almost killed me to get there. There were so many balls in the air that I think it's page 200 before Daruwalla gets to the end of the messages on his answering machine—then the story begins!

So that novel was certainly a watershed. I finished that novel and said to Janet, "Stop me if I start *anything* this complicated again. Don't let me do this!" I felt my health was compromised. I wasn't sleeping for the last six or eight months when I was trying to pull those final chapters together. I wasn't just writing eight hours a day; I was writing eight hours, then I'd have supper, then I'd go back to my office again at night and go to bed at two or three in the morning, then I'd be up again at 6:30 or 7 a.m. I was like somebody who was drinking 12 cups of espresso. Only I *wasn't!* I just couldn't stop thinking. The synapses were firing, saying, "and then, and then, and then . . . ."

You mentioned finding the right voice in "Getting Started" [an essay in the 1992 edition of The Writer's Handbook]*—first person vs. third person. Do you have a preference?*

I only reluctantly use a first-person narrative; I much prefer third person. And those novels where I have felt that there's no other way to tell the story but to have a narrator, I have always come to rather reluctantly. I like *The Hotel New Hampshire*. I like *A Prayer for Owen Meany* better. In both cases I knew that . . . you can't tell a story about a so-called religious miracle if you don't have a believer. You can't tell that from an omniscient point of view, unless you're claiming that you, the author, and everyone else should believe in religious miracles. You gotta have a witness. Somebody who's a little crazy. Who says no matter what you think it is, this is what I saw.

So there had to be a John Wheelwright or you couldn't have an Owen Meany. And you can't tell—in straight, third-person—the story of some kid who is sexually obsessed with his sister. You can't tell an incest story without getting in the mind of that boy. It's only in his eyes that his sister is the most beautiful thing in the world, and it's perfectly normal for him to be in love with her.

In general, it is not just the omniscience of that third-person voice that I prefer, but it is the speed with which you can go from one moment in time to another. In the first person, it becomes so cumbersome; you have to account for what the witness saw. The progression of those first-person novels is so much slower. So I'm generally not a fan of first person.

You've said your writing schedule is generally from 9 a.m. until 3 or 4 p.m., six or seven days a week. Has it always been so structured?

When Colin, who is now 36, was younger, I used to write the first couple of hours every morning. I used to get up before he did—around 5 a.m. I think I got into those habits and could do that because I was still competing as a wrestler until I was 34. I was training hard and going to bed early. And for many years, when I was teaching and coaching and trying to write at the same time, I always said to everyone that if I ever was self-supporting as a writer, I would work seven days a week, eight, nine hours a day.

And I'd go into the whole thing about, "Ask a doctor to be a good doctor when his practice is two hours a day; do you want a lawyer who works only two hours a day?" I always would say that, but *The World According to Garp* was my fourth novel. By the time it was published, I had said this so many times that when I realized I didn't have to teach anymore, that I could write all day long, I was so disappointed in myself! Because, like a physical thing, like being in shape, I hadn't trained myself to write eight hours a day. I had just projected that—wouldn't it be nice to write eight hours a day? I didn't know how. So suddenly there was an income I felt I could rely on—I didn't have to go back to teaching—and I couldn't work more hours a day on *The Hotel New Hampshire* than I'd been able to work on the first four novels. And I felt almost ashamed that I could not make good on my promise to myself that I would fill this time. And it wasn't until the next novel, *The Cider House Rules*, that I did. Like running or lifting, you don't get there overnight; you get there incrementally. I suddenly realized with *Cider House* that I had stretched that capacity and I had to make myself stop writing—I had to say, "If I don't stop writing now, I'm not gonna get to the gym today." And it's been that way ever since.

Do you have a favorite among all your novels?
The common sort of stereotypical answer is, "Oh, they're like children, and I don't like one any better than the other." I've heard countless writers say that. Well, that's not true either. You do like some better than the others. I can say with absolute authority that any one of the last five novels—beginning with *The Cider House Rules*, and including *A Prayer for Owen Meany*, *A Son of the Circus*, *A Widow for One Year*, and *The Fourth Hand*—any one of the last five is better made than any one of the first five—including *The World According to Garp*.

The whole screenwriting thing has been another progression for me. It has given me another way to concentrate, another way to simply be writing all the time. I can finish a draft of *The Fourth Hand* and go to the screenplay of *A Son of the Circus*, which I haven't looked at for six months, talk to that director, and 48 hours later I'm writing again. I'm writing all the time—but I'm not complaining about it!

Dorman T. Schindler of Kansas City is a freelance writer who regularly contributes to *The Dallas Morning News*, *The Denver Post*, *Bloomsbury Review*, and other publications.

JOHN IRVING IN PRINT

Here's a list of John Irving's published books in chronological order:

Setting Free the Bears (Random House, 1968)

The Water-Method Man (Random House, 1972)

The 158-Pound Marriage (Random House, 1974)

The World According to Garp (Dutton, 1978)

The Hotel New Hampshire (Dutton, 1981)

The Cider House Rules (Morrow, 1985)

A Prayer for Owen Meany (Morrow, 1989)

A Son of the Circus (Random House, 1994)

Trying to Save Piggy Sneed (Arcade, 1996)—short stories, essays, memoir

A Widow for One Year (Random House, 1998)

My Movie Business (Random House, 1999)—memoir

The Cider House Rules: A Screenplay (Talk Miramax/Hyperion, 1999)

The Fourth Hand (Random House, 2001)

Writer's Perspective

TERRY MCMILLAN: HOW I WRITE

The author of five novels, Terry McMillan combines a keen sense of family dynamics, an ear for dialogue, and astute social observation to create a cast of characters that one critic calls "sassy, resilient, and full of life." Two of her books made *The New York Times* bestseller list: *Waiting to Exhale*, for 38 weeks, and *How Stella Got Her Groove Back* for 21 weeks; she also co-wrote the screenplays for both, which were made into successful movies.

McMillan received an Endowment for the Arts Fellowship in 1988 and the Barnes and Noble Writers Award in 1999. She was a Yaddo Colony Fellow in 1982, 1983, and 1985, and a MacDowell Fellow in 1983. McMillan has taught English at Stanford University, the University of Wyoming, and the University of Arizona at Tucson. She lives in Northern California.

Her credits include: *A Day Late and a Dollar Short* (2001), *How Stella Got Her Groove Back* (1996), *Waiting to Exhale* (1992), *Disappearing Acts* (1989), *Mama* (1987). Editor: *Breaking Ice: An Anthology of Contemporary African-American Fiction* (1990).

Why. I write because the world is an imperfect place, and we behave in an imperfect manner. I want to understand why it's so hard to be good, honest, loving, caring, thoughtful, and generous. Writing is about the only way (besides praying) that allows me to be compassionate toward folks who, in real life, I'm probably not that sympathetic toward. I want to understand myself and others better, so what better way than to pretend to be them?

When and where. I like getting up at 5 a.m., when the house is quiet, and I don't have to worry about anybody calling. Even the dogs and birds are

239

asleep. It's quiet, and I can think. I write in my office or at a cabin at Lake Tahoe. Four to five hours is normal. If all goes well, I'm pretty wiped out emotionally by that time.

How? When I'm working on a novel, I usually do a chapter a day. Once I finish the entire draft, I go back and rewrite the story in general (filling in holes, things that don't make any sense, things I forgot or want to remember, character development, story movement, time, etc.). The next draft is when I edit for the particular (tone, language). I nitpick big time.

Ideas. I'm nosy. I'm a good listener. Airplanes are good. Newspaper articles, especially "Dear Abby!" The news. Most often, I just think about people in situations that I don't know if I could handle or tolerate. I worry about them and wonder how they manage. This is usually how a story comes about.

Writer's block. I think that most writers suffer from writer's block because they're trying too hard to make it perfect out of the gate when, in fact, they should be writing it for themselves, as if no one is ever going to read it at all. I find it makes for more honest writing—less pretentious or cautious—and it's fluid. I write from my heart without thinking about it too much. And it's been working so far.

Advice. Write in your own voice in your own style and don't worry about it. There's room out here for all kinds of stories and voices, and the world is waiting for them.

How I Write is a staff-written monthly feature of *The Writer* magazine.

CONVERSATION WITH JAMES ELLROY

A hard-hitting crime writer
looks to broaden his scope

by Dorman T. Shindler

The rugged odyssey that has taken James Ellroy from a life on the streets to increasing prominence as a bestselling writer is, in part, the story of persistence and powerful concentration. The novelist-memoirist praised by some critics as the best living crime writer in America turns his skills loose in his latest novel, *The Cold Six Thousand*, a rollicking ride through the tumultuous 1960s in America.

Ellroy, according to Nat Soble, his best friend and agent of 16 years, is dogged and determined, the kind of writer who spends an inordinate amount of time and energy polishing his work. Ellroy sets no particular hours for his workdays, working until he is physically or mentally exhausted. His outlines are meticulous, and the note-taking process that precedes his actual writing can go on for months.

"I've always had that amount of mental discipline and control," Ellroy says. "It's a by-product of having grown up living in my head. I was a career fantasist as a youth. I am maybe the most disciplined, diligent, meticulous novelist you'll ever meet. And I am certainly, of all those I've met, the one most capable of sustaining concentration."

His efforts have produced an impressive body of work, including the novels *L.A. Confidential*, *The Black Dahlia*, *American Tabloid*, and *White Jazz* and the memoir *My Dark Places*.

Ellroy's Tudor-style house in the upscale Kansas City suburb of Shawnee Mission, Kan., which he shares with his wife, Helen Knode, and dog, Dudley, is a far cry from the jail cells he once occupied on a regular basis in Los Angeles.

Ellroy was then living the life of a petty criminal, stealing drugs from pharmacies and breaking into unoccupied homes to spend the night.

According to Ellroy's own testimony, recorded in *My Dark Places* (1996), his troubled life as a youth included a ne'er-do-well father and a mother who was murdered when he was 10 years old. This sort of dysfunction led to Ellroy's self-destructive bent as a teenager and young adult. During that time, he got hooked on alcohol and Benzedrex, a sinus inhaler. Instead of inhaling it, he would swallow it to get a speed high.

After the Benzedrex nearly drove him into schizophrenia and the alcohol caused what a doctor called "post-alcohol brain syndrome," Ellroy cleaned himself up. He took a job caddying at posh L.A. country clubs and, at the age of 27, wrote the crime novel *Brown's Requiem* (1981).

Stretching out his 6-foot-plus frame as we chat in his sparsely furnished office, Ellroy recalls, "The smartest and boldest and bravest thing I ever did was write a novel first thing out." He speaks machine-gun style, in rhythmic fits and starts. "I didn't start with short stories or anything like that. What I found, early on, was that the form I understood instinctively was the form of the novel."

Ellroy writes in longhand, block-printed in capital letters. "I like the way it looks on the page, and I've never really learned to write cursive," says the writer. Furthermore, "I don't know how to type—and I'm not interested in learning!"

Drawing much critical praise for his hard-hitting, take-no-prisoners style, Ellroy soon found himself on bestseller lists across the country, and it wasn't long before Hollywood came knocking at his door. *Brown's Requiem, Blood on the Moon* (1983), and *L.A. Confidential* (1990) all were turned into movies.

While the money and fame were fine with Ellroy, what he saw as the phoniness of Los Angeles soon began to wear on him. Meeting his soon-to-be wife helped ease him out of the fast lane. When she brought him along to visit relatives in Kansas City, Ellroy fell in love with the place. It was quiet, the sort of place where a writer could get some work done in peace, and where he could reflect upon his past. So in 1995 the couple moved to Kansas City.

> Ellroy, whose early work was crime fiction, now avoids the strictures of the genre. He describes himself as a historical novelist on a grand scale.

A year later, Ellroy published *My Dark Places*, a tell-all memoir that recounted his troubled adolescence and young adulthood, and recounted his attempt to solve his mother's murder. The book marked a turning point in his life, standing as a link, and a point of evolution, between Ellroy's past and present. It marks the time when Ellroy finally came to terms with his tortuous past, and denotes a period when he changed gears and broadened his literary scope. Instead of focusing on the history of Los Angeles, Ellroy had begun taking on the history of America and its politics.

Once known strictly for crime-fiction novels like

Because the Night (1984), Ellroy drew the attention of "serious" critics at publications such as *Time and The New York Times Book Review* for his epic *American Tabloid* (1995), a novel that embraces political history as well as America's seamy underbelly. His economic style, which reflects the ugliness of his characters, was praised by the Associated Press as a "hard, cutting tool." Ellroy says, "I tried to revise my style to suit the content of the book, the violence of the era."

That experiment is continued in *The Cold Six Thousand*, which features Ellroy's starkest prose styling yet. "The language is attuned to the era," he says. "It's very much an amalgam of racist invective, Yiddish, good old American slang and hep-cat talk. To me, it's suited to the events I'm describing."

For a time, Ellroy actually cultivated his former image as a crime-fiction writer, calling himself the "Demon Dog of Crime Fiction" (later changing it to the "Demon Dog of American Literature"). He even adopted a persona during readings to promote his books, sometimes howling out loud or simulating sex acts. Worries about offending potential readers were dismissed with off-handed, profane remarks.

But lately, it seems he has been purposefully separating himself from the constraints of genre fiction. In recent interviews, Ellroy has said he is trying to destroy the strictures of genre and that he'll never write another book that can be categorized as crime fiction.

"If you have to subdivide me as novelist," he says, "I would say I'm a historical novelist. I think the 'L.A. Quartet' books [*The Black Dahlia* (1987), *The Big Nowhere* (1988), *L.A. Confidential*, and *White Jazz* (1992)] are so dense in period detail and historical subtext, that you can call me a historical novelist going back to *The Black Dahlia* and then, most especially, with *American Tabloid* and *The Cold Six Thousand*. Those are historical novels on a grand scale."

Like *American Tabloid* before it, *The Cold Six Thousand*, the second novel in what Ellroy calls "The Underworld USA trilogy," recounts the lives and misdeeds of seamy characters like Wayne Tedrow Jr. and Pete Bondurant as they mix it up with big-time politicos and criminals, getting involved in everything from the assassination of President Kennedy to Cuban exiles and drugs in Vietnam.

The first volume spans the '50s and early '60s. The second takes on the '60s. The as-yet unwritten final volume will cover the '70s.

"When I came up with the title 'The Underworld USA trilogy,' I was thinking of two things: Don DeLillo's novel *Underworld*, a great, great work of art, and Sam Fuller's snappy 1961 movie, *Underworld USA*. I actually wrote *American Tabloid* as a stand-alone, and saw, as I neared completion of the book, and discussed it with my agent, Nat Soble, that the plot threads were certainly there for a sequel."

Tabloid and its sequel delve into some dark places in American history, including conspiracies surrounding the assassination of JFK. Does Ellroy actually buy into such theories? "I think it's humanistically and morally valid," he says, recalling how Gerald Posner's *Killing the Dream*, which deals with the assassination of Martin Luther King Jr. and the use of James Earl Ray as both assassin and patsy, laid out the groundwork for him.

To keep all the dates and facts straight in his new book, Ellroy, who seems to have a photographic memory, called on some help. "I hired researchers, two colleagues of mine, to compile chronologies from a fact list. I had the salient points of the book worked out in advance. I had the basic sense of chronology. I needed the fill-in, and that's what I hired the researchers for."

Asked if he is the sort of writer who hangs out with cops and hoodlums to research his characters, Ellroy shakes his head. The characters, he says, pointing to his head, "come from up here," meaning his imagination. The rest is a matter of research. And though *American Tabloid* began as a stand-alone, Ellroy had no trouble turning it into a trilogy. "I saw that all of the plot threads [I needed] to continue into the next book were there.

"*The Cold Six Thousand*," he continues, "is a story about violent men in a violent time doing terrible, violent things. This is the epic of bad white men doing bad things in the name of authority. This is the humanity of bad white men.

"Every book mandates a certain level of language and of style. I've developed a style over many years and many books. This is a much grander story than I've ever told before, and it mandated a strictly formalized, plain, ugly, direct sentence style." Here, for example, Ellroy describes Pete Bondurant conspiring with a crooked cop to commit murder:

> The smartest and boldest and bravest thing I ever did was write a novel first thing out. I didn't start with short stories or anything like that. What I found, early on, was that the form I understood instinctively was the novel.

A prowl car pulled up. A cop got out. He fed Peter three guns. Three calibers: .38/.45/.357 mag.

Throwdown guns. Taped and initialed: L.W./O. S./C. S.

The cop knew the plan. They had two crime scenes. They had viable blood—good Red Cross stock.

—from *The Cold Six Thousand*

That tough, no-frills style of writing, an Ellroy trademark, has an interesting origin dating to 1989, when Ellroy and Soble were huddled over the manuscript of *L.A. Confidential*. An editor at Warner Books told them that the manuscript—sight unseen—had to be cut by 30 percent because its size would eliminate any profits. Since the book featured a complicated plot and had already been pared down, the two were at creative loggerheads with the editor.

Then Soble jokingly suggested cutting out all the small words like "and" or "but." Ellroy was struck by lightning. "I can do better than that," Ellroy told his agent. Taking the manuscript back home, he cut out every extraneous word.

Suddenly, Ellroy had arrived at what Soble describes as "this incredible style that matched the violence of the book. And James has never looked back since. That editor, unbeknownst to her, really helped crystallize the style that started with *L.A. Confidential.*"

Soble believes very few writers have the ability to shape their prose to the needs of the story and the character. "I think that he wants to be treated as a serious stylist, a trailblazer of the English language," Soble says, citing Ellroy's ability to match his style to the content. "That is so rarely seen in writing. He is constantly honing his style."

Ellroy's evolution in writing style is all the more apparent when a passage from his earlier work is compared with one from his latest book. Here are two examples:

> He rented a room at the Holiday Inn on the edge of Chinatown and a late-model Ford, and watched from a distance as his wife made her rounds of the city as an antique broker and met her lovers for drinks, dinner and overnight visits at her Pacific Heights apartment; from a further distance he followed his daughters to school, on errands and out on dates.
> —from *Suicide Hill* (1986)

> He wrote tithe checks. Five grand per. He wrote them under pseudonyms. He print-wiped the envelopes.
> Drac and the Boys meet Dr. King—We Shall Overcome.
> —from *The Cold Six Thousand*

That staccato, in-your-face, tough-as-nails style lets the reader know right away that *The Cold Six Thousand* isn't your average historical novel. As the sometimes flamboyant Ellroy puts it, "You don't like it? You want PC? Get yourself another book, 'cause you ain't gonna find it here."

Though he adopted the noir style of fiction when starting out, Ellroy blended it with the social history of Los Angeles, lending his novels a much grander scale than the fiction of, say, Raymond Chandler. Early influences on his style range from Dashiell Hammett to Joseph Wambaugh. But it was James Jones' *From Here to Eternity* that really knocked him for a loop.

"It made a huge impression on me," Ellroy says. "It's a large, dense book. A world that I didn't know existed, wholly encapsulated. Everything is imbued with great insight. The U.S. Army in 1941 prior to Pearl Harbor; the corruption of institutions; the man apart, told with great verve; the horrible complexity of male/female adult relationships. *From Here to Eternity* got me to the point of being able to write *The Cold Six Thousand.*"

Ellroy's fascination with history seems to have taken root as a child. Seeking escape from his dysfunctional family, the young Ellroy often read crime-fiction novels. But while his nose was usually buried in a book, his eyes and ears remained open. "Generally, as a youngster in the '60s, I took note of great public events," says Ellroy.

"And I sensed, inchoately, that there was a human infrastructure there. It wasn't until I began to write history much later that I realized just how much that sense of human infrastructure was already existing in me. Hence the great human stories of the characters real and imagined that inhabit *The Cold Six Thousand*."

The latest volume of Ellroy's Underworld Trilogy covers a lot of ground: Howard Hughes' Las Vegas occupation, the early days of the Vietnam War, and the CIA moving heroin; the FBI's war on the civil rights movement; the assassinations of Dr. Martin Luther King Jr. and Robert F. Kennedy; the mob in the 1960s; Cuban exiles.

A *Library Journal* critic called the novel "complex in its character development and critical examination of U.S. public policy."

The number of American writers currently exploring such grandiose and dark fictional territory can be counted on two hands—perhaps even one. Other than Ellroy, one might name Robert Stone and Don DeLillo. At the mention of the latter's name, Ellroy waxes rhapsodic.

"DeLillo is the greatest living American writer. Impact-wise, he's huge. He bodes huge for me, and I've only read two of his books. I read *Libra* in the fall of '88 and it burned my world down. I had never been interested in the Kennedy assassination. I realized that *Libra* precluded me from ever writing about Lee Harvey Oswald or the Kennedy assassination. I saw the utter, classic simplicity of DeLillo's design, the bas-relief, which is that he took this ultimate American loser, this stupid S.O.B., and made him a profoundly sympathetic, moving, and complex character. I also saw for the first time the anti-Communist mindset, the Red Scare mentality illuminated.

"I saw that the logic of the conspirators, their motives for killing John Kennedy, were both wholly sympathetic, historically precise, and brilliantly offset. [DeLillo] captured the mindset of the white, right-leaning American male in that era brilliantly. And I saw that I could never write a book about the Kennedy assassination. But now I wanted to. And I saw that his thesis—that John Kennedy died as result of messing with organized crime, crazy Cuban exiles, and a renegade CIA man—was valid. And if it didn't happen that way in real life, it sure as hell should have.

"I began to read up on the assassination. And that's when I got the whole idea of *American Tabloid*. The progenitors of the assassination start to kick in about 1958, when Bobby is still chief counsel for the Senate Rackets Committee and Jack is only thinking about the White House. I wrote DeLillo a letter, and sent him a copy of *American Tabloid* when it was published, crediting him with inspiring the book. He sent me a nice note back. He read the book, praised the book. We've exchanged a few notes over the years, and we ran into each other in Amsterdam and had breakfast."

Such rhapsodizing for a fellow writer doesn't mean Ellroy has given up his evolutionary process. Far from it. In Ellroy's mind, there is always the possibility of improvement, and change. Although he wants to continue to write "big historical novels," he plans to pen something with a bit more levity.

"I will write a book somewhat less harsh, three books down the line," he says. "I want to write about Warren Harding's presidency in America in the 1920s. He was a gentleman, he was a buffoon, and he was way out of his depth; because the evil and the corruption in his administration was administered by those around him."

For now, though, Ellroy will keep himself busy by plotting out the final volume of his Underworld USA trilogy and dabbling in things like electronic publishing.

"I did it because it was a couple of bucks and it was a way to get books into the homes of shut-ins," says the author. "They could download it and read it on their computer screen."

Asked if he worries about the future of the old-fashioned book, Ellroy scoffs. "Beautifully designed books—like the Knopf books with the beautiful rough-cut edges, the wonderful bindings, and the great cover art—they are here to stay.

The novel is here to stay, too, he adds. It's "the great organic art form. All a person needs to write a novel is an imagination, a pen, and some paper."

Dorman T. Shindler of Kansas City is a freelance writer who regularly contributes to *The Dallas Morning News*, *The Denver Post*, *Bloomsbury Review*, and other publications.

ANN RULE: HOW I WRITE

In the course of writing 20 books, Ann Rule has established herself as a dean of true-crime writing, but a novelist couldn't have created a better twist for her debut title, *The Stranger Beside Me* (1980). It was to be a book about an unknown serial killer then murdering women in the Seattle area. At the time, Rule was working nights alone at a suicide hotline with a handsome young student. The two had become close friends. The serial killer and her colleague turned out to be the same man: Ted Bundy.

Since then, Rule has developed a loyal following. A former Seattle policewoman and a mother of five, she earned a degree in creative writing and extensively studied criminology, police, and forensic procedures. Her expertise qualifies her to teach seminars to law enforcement groups. She lives near Seattle.

Her credits include: 1,400 articles; other books (20 million in print) include *Every Breath You Take*, due out this month, and *And Never Let Her Go*, *A Rage to Kill*, *Empty Promises*, *Bitter Harvest,* and *Small Sacrifices*.

Why. I can remember when I was 9 thinking, one thing I never want to do is be a writer, because it would be too hard. And yet I found myself in junior high involved in school newspapers and writing at home. It was such a wonderful way of expressing how I see life, and the things that interest me that I want to share with others.

When and where. I live on the beach in Puget Sound and I bought the little cottage next door. So I go about 50 feet from my front door to my little cottage and I write there. I sit down at the computer about 10 and go until 8 at night. I can write through everything but an earthquake, because I started writing when the kids were little and kept going unless they were fighting on top of the typewriter. Then I'd stop and scrape them off and start over.

First draft. I pretty much go for it [a polished first draft], and I will usually write 10 to 30 pages a day. I usually start the next morning by going over what I've done the day before in order to prime the pump.

Ideas. I look for an anti-hero or -heroine who seems to have everything in the world the rest of us would be happy with—good looks, money, power, love, charisma. And yet they're not who they seem at all. Once I pick the right subject (I go through 500 cases), I then can count on these people to continue to be outrageous. And all I do is describe how they're acting out behind the perfect mask.

Writer's block. I don't have the luxury. I have a book due every nine months—it's sort of like being pregnant all the time. I have two contracts, with Simon & Schuster/Free Press and for original paperbacks with Pocket Books. When one's done, the other pops up.

Attitude. I don't believe in the devil with horns, but I do believe there's a spirit of evil. We have our own free will and people can tap into evil and become lost. The hardest thing for me to understand emotionally is the lack of concern for other creatures' pain. People I write about see themselves as the very center of the world and the rest of us are like paper dolls.

Every single book [of mine] has someone who's really horrific, but for that one person there must be three or four dozen brave and good people who I meet—the prosecutors, the detectives, the witnesses who will come forward whether frightened or not, certainly the families of the victims. So in the end, the good so far outnumber the one sociopath that I really feel the world is basically good.

Advice. The thing I learned that probably helped the most is that there will be days when you write wonderfully and days when it's like pulling teeth. But it's a job and you go to your desk and you write whatever you've ordained is your output. If you write one page a day, at the end of a year you'll have a 365-page book.

How I Write is a staff-written monthly feature of *The Writer* magazine.

CONVERSATION WITH EVAN HUNTER

After 90-plus novels, Hunter—aka Ed McBain—is still going strong

by Ronald Kovach

It is just the sort of voice you might expect from Evan Hunter/aka Ed McBain: a little bit of gravel, a lot of savvy, and a very urban, street-smart quality that's right out of the 87th Precinct in Isola, his fictional rough equivalent of New York City. His engaging vocal manner aside, Hunter also comes across in an interview as highly focused in his work and alert to material that can be turned into stories.

In his 50-year writing career, he has spun his tightly written tales into more than 90 novels, including 51 87th Precinct novels and 13 Matthew Hope novels by his pseudonymous sidekick, Ed McBain, and another 17 or so under his own name, including his breakthrough novel *The Blackboard Jungle* (1954), which later became a popular movie.

Hunter is considered a master of the "police procedural" (a label he shuns as too narrow), and is credited with influencing the modern police drama in both books and on screen. His peers in the mystery-writing community hold him in the highest esteem: He is the only American recipient of the Diamond Dagger from the British Crime Writers Association, and Mystery Writers of America gave him its top honor, the Grand Master Award. About 100 million of his books are in print, according to his publisher. His screenplay credits include Alfred Hitchcock's film *The Birds*.

Fans of the 87th Precinct series get to know McBain's main characters and bit players like old friends who seem to age hardly at all. There is Steve Carella, the decent, steady detective with the slightly Chinese cast to his eyes; his deaf-mute wife, the beautiful, dark-haired Teddy; the diabolical Deaf Man; Artie Brown, the only black man on the detective squad; Meyer Meyer, the bald Jewish cop with the funny name; Fat Ollie Weeks, a slob and bigot who, when he's not eating, manages to effectively cover Carella's back.

Readers enjoy the squad's banter, routine and black humor, which offers some levity amid the mayhem. (When lions at the city zoo have at a victim's body, McBain writes, "By Carella's rough estimate, four-fifths of the vic's body was in the Eight-Seven. The remaining fifth, the vic's leg, was over there in the Eight-Eight, where Fat Ollie—watching a young lion claw and gnaw at the leg—was beginning to get hungry himself.") Just as much a fixture in the 87th Precinct novels is the author's prefaced note: "The city in these pages is imaginary. The people, the places are all fictitious. Only the police routine is based on established investigatory technique."

But perhaps the leading character is *the city*, a dazzling but ominous presence composed of one part romance and three parts menace. It is a metropolis of stark contrasts, a theme sounded on the opening page of Hunter's first 87th Precinct novel, *Cop Hater* (1956):

> The city lay like a sparkling nest of rare gems, shimmering in layer upon layer of pulsating intensity.
> The buildings were a stage set.
> They faced the river, and they glowed with man-made brilliance, and you stared up at them in awe, and you caught your breath.
> Behind the buildings, behind the lights, were the streets.
> There was garbage in the streets.

Surprisingly, Hunter says his story lines often originate with the search for a good title—and then for a plot to hang it on. That wasn't the case, though, with his latest 87th Precinct novel, *Money, Money, Money*. Hunter found the counterfeiting origin of the book on the streets of New York. "I kept wandering into stores in New York and seeing signs saying, 'We will not accept bills larger than $50,' " Hunter recalls. "And I begin asking how come, and they said, 'We've been getting burned a lot, we're getting a lot of phony hundred-dollar bills.' And I thought, humphff, that's interesting—are there more phony $100 bills around now than before? And I began investigating it." Eerily, Hunter happened to tie the bogus bills into a massive fictional conspiracy involving foreign-sponsored terrorism and an American city landmark. The novel, which included a reference to Osama Bin Laden, was officially published only two days after the Sept. 11 attacks.

The Writer caught up with Hunter by phone at his writing studio in Connecticut. He speaks proudly of his third wife, drama coach Dragica Dimitrijevic-Hunter, his three sons and stepdaughter. At 75, Hunter has had three heart attacks, and survived a life-threatening encounter with an aortic aneurysm last year. But he talks with the grit and energy of a much younger man.

With Money, Money, Money, *I found myself thinking that maybe this fellow is entitled to coast a little after writing 90 novels. But the fact is, this is one of the best 87th Precinct novels of all those I've read, and other readers have said*

*the same thing. One reviewer said the Precinct novels had become "more tex-
tured, more thoughtful—and more thought-provoking." Has your novel-
writing gotten any easier with experience?*

It gets harder, I think. Actually, my wife mentioned something last night. We
were talking about the terrorist bombing and the similarity to *Money, Money,
Money*, and it occurred to me from something she said that that particular book
had been germinating for years before I put a word on paper. I think I began
researching terrorism and counterfeit money and all that two, three years ago.
And it's a very convoluted plot—you know, I almost lost track of it myself
[chuckles]. It was a more difficult book to write than most of the 87th Precinct
novels. It took longer to research and longer to do the actual writing to make it
all come together, and also to give it a comic flair that I think took away from
some of the weightiness of the subject matter.

*Can you take your average 87th Precinct novel from start to finish and gen-
eralize about the process?*

When I say I usually start with a title, there was a time when I was doing a
title for every letter of the alphabet—*Ax, Bread, Calypso, Doll*. And as an example—this is a very good example because it shows how a novel did evolve from
a title—when I was looking for a title for "i," I came up with ice, and the first
association this had for me was diamonds—diamonds are ice in the underworld
lingo. And then I began thinking, OK, ice, what else is ice? And the association
was snow, which is cocaine. So I already had in the mix diamonds and cocaine.
And then because of the very literal meaning of ice, it had to be wintertime, so
I knew it was going to be set in wintertime. And then I discovered that ice was
a show biz scam, a way of robbing the box office—selling tickets to a hit show
at exorbitant prices, what's called ice. So I knew then that it had to be a background of show business somehow in there. So I had diamonds, cocaine and
show business and I had wintertime and then to ice somebody is to kill somebody. So there was murder. I had virtually the whole plot simply from the associations of the title.

And I went from there. It opens with a show girl coming out of the theater at
the end of a performance and it's snowing, and instead of getting on the bus, she
decides to walk home, which we *all* know in an Ed McBain novel is a bad idea.

It sounds like your mind forms itself around a concept and you then fill in.

I think so. I hate to keep saying titles because maybe it's not the title itself. . . .
We said something the other day to someone—"No good deed goes unpun-
ished." I thought, gee, "No Good Deed" is a good title for a mystery. And it
would be about guys who are doing good deeds—they're benefactors of
mankind, they give huge monies to charity—and they're being killed and you
can't figure out why. Why are these good guys being killed? And that's the way
my mind works.

Your books are often full of specialized information. I recently read one of your Matthew Hope novels, Jack and the Beanstalk, *that's full of snapbean farming and cattle-raising. Do you just head to the library, or how do you go about getting all this specialized information into your books?*

Well, nobody goes to the library anymore; we go to the Internet. But I also have a guy who does a lot of research for me. Specific things. For example in *Money, Money, Money,* a lot of the research on counterfeit money was done by this guy [Daniel Starer]. He does research for Nelson DeMille and Ken Follett, a lot of guys; he's a good researcher.

In the early days, you spent a lot of time riding around with police in a number of cities. But investigative techniques are always evolving. How have you kept up?

Anything that ever appears about scientific techniques or DNA or what have you I will immediately clip out of the paper. I have a whole file on stuff like that.

I also have a friend who's a criminal lawyer and used to be a district attorney, so I will call him and I'll say, "I've got this guy found with 20 pounds of heroin and he claims so and so, blah, blah, blah. What's the deal I can offer him?" And he'll say, "Well, why don't you offer him blah, blah, blah?" And I'll say, "He won't accept that deal; what can I counter with?" And he'll say, "Why don't you counter with blah, blah, and blah?" And we get a whole dialogue going for 20 minutes, plea-bargaining a guy. I think those are some of the best scenes in the 87th Precinct novels.

If someone had known Evan Hunter as a youngster, would they have said, "Man, does that kid have an imagination"?

I think so. I was very fortunate. My father was an uneducated man who was a letter carrier. He had his own band. He was the kind of guy where I went to him and said, "Hey Dad, let's start a newspaper." He'd say, "Wow! Great idea!" And the next thing I know, he'd bought a little hectograph [duplicating] machine and he was hand-lettering all the stories I wrote for the paper because, you know, I had a childish hand and he had a beautiful penmanship. We were selling ads around the neighborhood to the butcher and the baker. We got all the neighborhood kids to dig up stories and write about them. It was an enterprise.

Another time I said to him, "Dad, why don't we put on a puppet show?" He said, "Yeah! Wow, great idea!" Next thing I know, he's building a stage. And I remember we had a war scene in it where soldiers were on the battlefield and one of them yells out, "*Gas! Gas!*" And my father was crouched offstage with his cigar blowing smoke across the stage to simulate a gas attack. So he was great in that respect. He encouraged every creative urge I ever had, and joined in.

When you're doing a series, how do you avoid becoming formulaic? A series has its conveniences, but you are stuck with the same cast of characters to a certain extent, right?

Yeah, you are. Carella is almost always at the forefront. Not always—sometimes he's a sidekick. And I try to bring one of the minor players into focus, so that we learn something about him or her, and get a different slant.

The next 87th Precinct novel, for example, is called *Fat Ollie's Book* [to be published in October]. It's partially about him solving a murder mystery but it's also about his book—in *Money, Money, Money* he's writing a book. He's a hard character to write about and a hard character to use to carry a book because he's so obnoxious. So you have to concentrate on the humor of him, but you must never forget he's an outrageous bigot. So that's the challenge in this one.

It has always seemed to me that Carella and Teddy have acted as the moral center of gravity in the 87th Precinct series, and I always got the impression that you admired them. Where did you get the inspiration for these two characters?

I don't know where Carella came from. I just figured I could have a decent cop who is happily married to a woman who needs a lot of help. In the beginning of the series she needed a lot of help—she's a deaf-mute; now she's developed into a very strong and resourceful character on her own.

But I thought [this would make] Carella a man first and a cop second—you know, it happened that he went to work every morning and his job was being a cop, but he didn't have to particularly enjoy pistol-whipping guys or anything like that. Just a decent man in a job that required extreme patience and a strong stomach.

How many hours and pages are you writing a day?

I usually start sometime about 9:30, 10 o'clock, I would say, and break for lunch, and I continue through to 6. Occasionally I'll take my wife for a cappuccino in the afternoon and come back and continue till about 6 o'clock.

I'm working on two novels simultaneously now and this is something I started doing about six months ago, I guess. I'll work on one book in the morning and then I'll put it aside, and then in the afternoon I'll go to a different book. I like the way it works. Instead of coming back after lunch and feeling tired and "gee, I have to continue with this," instead I switch over to the second book and it's like a pick-me-up, you know. And I can look at it and say, "Ah, here we are, something fresh."

I try to do five pages in the morning on the Evan Hunter novel and five in the afternoon on the Ed McBain. So I try to do 10 pages a day, and I figure four days a week is a fair amount of time without, you know, doctor visits or going to the city for some reason or another.

How much are you outlining?

[I'm working now on] an Evan Hunter novel with a rather complicated family in it and my outline consists, of course, of their ages and their dates of birth and when they married whom and how many children they have and all that stuff, but it also highlights important events in the lives of the guy and his sister, who are the two lead characters. And it'll be just a headline outline—"1987: She goes to India following the drug trail, whatever."

In *Fat Ollie's Book*, it's again, as they tend to become these days, complicated. In fact, there's one character in it who says, "Oh shit, it's about to get complicated again."

So there are sort of three plots that I haven't fully outlined in my head yet and I know I must do it and it's staring me in the face and it's saying, "OK, kid, you've done enough winging it. So let's get down to brass tacks and see what this is *about*!"

You know, I will often write myself a sort of letter on paper, saying, "OK, now what have we got? Here's where we are, here's what we don't have, and here's what we have to learn. And here's what we have to look at and examine and see where it's going." It's like a heart-to-heart talk with myself.

Traditionally, there's such an entertainment component in writing mysteries. Is that your first obligation versus things like social commentary, cultural insight, literary achievement?

Well, with whatever I write I feel I have to keep the reader engaged, I have to keep the reader reading. And that's the contract I make. You may not have a good time but you're going to be engrossed.

With anything I write, I have the reader firmly in mind. And if I find that I'm getting too erudite, if I find that I'm examining my own navel, I'll back away and say hey, there's somebody out there who is going to read this.

I once got a letter from a guy saying, "If you have a speech to make, get a soapbox." And I remembered that. I thought, hmm, he's right, I shouldn't make speeches; I'm just writing.

Since you're a champion of productivity, what advice do you have for writers about being productive?

I always tell anyone who wants to be a writer: You had better love it more than anything in the world. You had better want to write more than you want to do anything else in this universe. And if you don't love it, forget it, forget about being a writer—just develop a strong backhand and a good serve.

But I think aside from loving the act of writing itself, I know what keeps me productive is that I still feel I have a lot of things to say. I have books ahead of me that I just want to write and I want to get them published before I'm dead.

What words of advice do you have for people who are trying to get a novel together, to develop a regimen of writing?

I've always felt this and I think it's very important: Even when I was in college and writing stories and sending them out to the magazines—I papered an entire small bathroom with rejection slips and it filled every inch of space on the wall—even then I had a supreme sense of confidence that what I was writing was good and that one day it would sell. I would ask every beginning writer, if he believes in what he's doing, to keep that belief in himself, that sense of confidence. And keep writing—the more you write, the more you learn.

The other thing I learned in those years [was about editors]: I used to feel, "These guys, they don't know what they're talking about, I'm too good for them. I'm too good for the pulps, I'm too good for the slicks, I'm too good for the quality mags—*they don't understand me.*" Right? And that's wrong. That is dead wrong. These people do know what they want for their particular market. If they're an editor at *Ladies' Home Journal*, they know what their *Ladies' Home Journal* readers want to read. And so just don't dismiss them. Try to learn from what editors tell you, if they tell you anything at all.

You wrote many years ago in our magazine the line: "If you want to win either the Pulitzer or a National Book Award, stay far away from corpses among the petunias." Does that get into the issue of mystery writers not getting the respect they deserve?

Oh yeah. I see so many times still, reviewers—even though we [mystery writers] have all hit upon that [goal of] "transcending the genre"—saying the writing is incredibly good *"for a mystery."* That's what you see all the time in reviews, in literary journals. It's not right.

Has the writing life been a good life? Any regrets?

I can't imagine anything I'd rather be. . . . I still enjoy it, and I'm paid well for what I do, there's some measure of respect in the community for me, I'm very happily married now with a wife who loves my work and is creative herself.

A creative life is a good one. You know, I think a lot of people have jobs they don't like to do, and that's really sad. I can't imagine getting up in the morning and going to some place where you don't want to go.

Ronald Kovach is senior editor of *The Writer*. For more about Evan Hunter/Ed McBain, visit www.edmcbain.com.

THE EVAN HUNTER FILE

• Evan Hunter actually began life as Salvatore Lombino, the name his American-born parents gave him at birth. He legally changed his name to Evan Hunter in 1952, and has since used that name on his more complex, mainstream novels, reserving "Ed McBain" for most of his crime fiction.

• Growing up in East Harlem and the Bronx, Hunter loved art and studied at the Art Students League of New York and Cooper Union Art School. After serving on a destroyer in the Navy (1944-'46), where he began reading and writing in earnest, he changed his career plans to writing and earned a degree at Hunter College.

• Using a variety of pseudonyms to disguise his multiple appearances in the same pulp magazines, Hunter began turning out tales of adventure, crime, and sports as well as westerns and fantasy stories.

• A stint as an agent at the Scott Meredith Literary Agency in the 1950s taught Hunter much about writing. He remembers the first time he showed Meredith some of his short stories: "He called me into his office Monday morning and he said: "This—*burn;* this—*burn;* this—I think I can show you how to make it work; this—I think I can sell; this—blah, blah, blah."

• Hunter has done a number of screenwriting projects, but he was never smitten with the Hollywood scene. "I always felt as if I was a killer getting off the airplane and putting on the black gloves, you know, and doing the murder and then taking the money and going home. I never felt comfortable in that community, truly. Swimming pools, swapping ideas at the Bel-Air [Hotel]—I never felt comfortable."

• His memories of Alfred Hitchcock: "We had a lot of fun together. We worked a lot, we joked a lot—he was a marvelous raconteur. He knew everyone there was to know, and all the best restaurants, and all the best wines. It was like having a very erudite uncle."

• Last fall, Hunter finished writing a two-hour pilot movie for a new 87th Precinct series being developed for television.

• TV and movie directors have adapted a number of Hunter/McBain novels over the years, including *Strangers When We Meet* and *Last Summer.* Hunter reserves special praise for Akira Kurosawa's transformation of *King's Ransom,* an 87th Precinct novel, into the film *High and Low.*

CONVERSATION WITH SUE MILLER

Diving deep to explore submerged emotional worlds

by Elfrieda Abbe

Sue Miller was a struggling single mother, working as a day care provider in the early '80s, when her first short story was published in *Ploughshares*. The emerging writer received a modest $50 and copies of the magazine. More important, her story caught the eye of a literary agent who offered to represent her. Miller, who had been writing most of her life, began to think, "Maybe this is rather good stuff." As it turned out, that was an understatement. Her first novel, *The Good Mother* (1986), about a single mother caught up in a custody battle, became an immediate bestseller.

Early on, Miller displayed a remarkable talent for casting a revealing light on the shadowy corners of intimacy.

In *The Good Mother*, Miller explores the tensions created by a woman's need for self-fulfillment and her responsibilities as a mother. As one critic wrote, she takes readers to "the intersection of motherhood and desire."

While she never faced a custody fight, the author drew from her own experiences as a single parent. She clearly understands the vulnerabilities that go with the territory. "You have this sense of people being ready to step forward and judge the job you are doing as a parent, to say nothing of how you are integrating falling in love with that job."

With each subsequent novel, Miller continues to examine the idea of self-knowledge—in the context of marriage, family, and society.

"To what degree is the self something we will? To what extent is it shaped by circumstances? These questions make for fascinating exploration," she said in a *BookPage* interview.

An astute and honest observer of domestic life, she dives deep into the emotional waters of broken marriages, alienated child-parent relationships, and hidden, often disturbing, parts of her characters' inner lives.

Family Pictures (1990), which was nominated for a National Book Critics Circle Award, explores the heartbreak and anger of a husband and wife who respond differently to their autistic son. In *While I Was Gone* (2000), Miller introduces Jo, a middle-aged woman who is confronted by a turbulent, secret past life that infringes on the seemingly tranquil present.

Her latest novel, *The World Below*, perhaps her most richly layered work, intertwines the stories of a granddaughter and grandmother, contrasting the way each deals with disappointments and compromises in their lives.

Catherine moves into the home of her grandmother, Georgia, and discovers the deceased woman's diaries, which reveal a love affair she had when she was a patient in a tuberculosis sanatorium in 1919.

This bittersweet story causes the reader to reflect on parts of oneself that have been lost or buried over time, or what might have been.

Miller's other novels include *For Love* (1993) and *The Distinguished Guest* (1995). She also published a book of short stories, *Inventing the Abbotts* and *Other Stories* (1987).

While in Milwaukee on a book tour for *The World Below*, Miller talked with *The Writer* about her work and her writing process.

How did you come up with the idea of using the lives of these two women from different eras?

I have these diaries from my family that I inherited. The two that are central to this work were one of my [great-great-]grandmother's, written from 1869 to 1870, and my mother's diary from high school.

My great-great-grandmother was a farmer's wife and a seamstress in Maine. They had a hard life in some ways, but the diary is similar to Georgia's, maybe even more on the surface than Georgia's. "March 13: was a lovely day. The wind blew 'til noon then it calmed down. John did this in the orchard. I cut out a dress." It's fascinating in some ways, and in some ways it's pretty boring. Then suddenly, on June 13 (I don't have the exact words): ". . . was a beautiful day. I'm a person destined to disappointment in everything she takes pride in in life. Sometimes I wish I were . . . sleeping the sleep that knows no waking." The next entry refers to [that passage] slightly: "It's been a clear day unlike the turbulence in my soul" and "I sewed a dress." Then the day after that, the waters have folded over—to [use] my metaphor from the book, and it's never mentioned again. There is not a clue to what it refers. It's this *cri de coeur* with no connection anywhere else in the diary to what is going on in her life. No other protests, no other complaints.

Then I have my mother's diaries written in the '30s. She was a person in love with herself, and she was utterly self-preoccupied. I mean these are adolescent diaries to be sure, but my mother sort of stayed that way.

That was the impetus: my thinking about the way one would have lived such a life, where she couldn't indulge that cry. It was something she expressed once and felt no right to. And then to think about a person like my mother, who was keenly aware of herself and every nuance of her emotional life, sexuality, and religious beliefs—very excessive and extreme. Some of that is simply two personalities, but some of it is history. I was interested in doing something that made use of that.

[Another theme in the book came from] an argument I had with a friend one night at a dinner party. His parents had emigrated from the Ukraine. He was speaking of his parents' sense of exile and alienation from where they ended up living and the way their children grew up. My argument was that I thought everyone thought they had raised their children in a different universe than the one in which they had been raised. Everyone is kind of appalled at the distance they have come from their own past—the past was like a country they were in exile from.

My own parents were these radical-pacifist Christians—deep believers, who raised four of us kids who are really not involved in the religious life in any way. We must have seemed like savages to them—as though we were being raised in a country that was taking us over and taking us away from everything they held dear and had grown up cherishing.

How did you pin that idea of alienation down to the structure of the novel?

I began to think about Georgia earlier on and decided to have something like an illness that severed her life, that cut her off. The tuberculosis sanatorium seemed to be a good solution to that. She would be sent away, and all life would change for her, and then she would have to come back and go on living in a world where she no longer felt at home. Then I got very interested in the TB phenomenon.

This feeling of alienation from the past and parts of oneself runs through much of your work. For example, in While I Was Gone, *Jo keeps her past life hidden from her family and then she is forced to confront it. What interests you about this theme?*

To me, that's a very common thread in 20th-century American literature in particular—that sense of our having invented ourselves. We are a country of people who are cut off from the past. Even if we do a good job of inventing ourselves, we experience a sense of dislocation. That's one of the things I'm interested in exploring.

In The World Below, *Catherine's life runs parallel to her grandmother's. Both have mothers who die*

> We are a country of people who are cut off from the past. Even if we do a good job of inventing ourselves, we experience a sense of dislocation.

when they are young. Both have a sense of dislocation. Was it always your intention to build the novel this way?

That was part of the picture from the start. I set up things that made their lives seem, in terms of some details, quite parallel, so I could play around with what in a deeper way was and wasn't parallel. I wanted the reader to speculate on what it means to be uprooted and whether uprootedness is something that everyone has always felt, or whether it's a modern phenomenon.

Were you interested in the idea that there are parts of our parents' or grandparents' lives that are hidden from us?

It wasn't so much the sense of our not knowing about our ancestors as the difference in the way we are conscious of life. I wanted to be looking at a post-Freudian character who is very self-analytical and self-aware, who has spoken very openly to her children about her inner life, and at a person whose practice of life was very different, pre-Freudian. I wanted to look at these two ways of being conscious of difficulty and pain and of expressing that in life. I was looking at what time has done to the way we comport ourselves and think of ourselves.

Your title, The World Below, *refers to the novel's central metaphorical image (a village that is submerged after a reservoir is built). Could you talk about how you use metaphor in your work?*

I did think of it working metaphorically in lots of ways in the book. The most direct way is when Cath sees the village [underwater] and says it's like memories, it's like looking at your past and looking at what is lost to you, what you can see and can't touch, what you can recall but you can't relive. But I also thought of it, obviously, as being true for Georgia's whole life, that there was this submerged world of feelings and passions and unexpressed emotions.

I don't think I use metaphor in language very much. But I think of it often as an overarching element in my work. It's there for me, and it's exciting for me in thinking about the work. For instance, in *The Good Mother*, I thought about the process of the legal system. The changes in language that forced the narrator into a place where she couldn't speak of her experience in words that were familiar to her. I thought of it as this narrow dark tunnel. For me, what happened in that book was that Anna was forced into this kind of alternate shape of her experience, which was very foreign to her, very alien to what she had understood was going on as she had lived through it.

How did you deal structurally with telling two stories at once in The World Below?

I had written big chunks of Georgia's life and Cath's life separately, so one of my big tasks on revision was weaving them into each other more than I had. I didn't want to have alternating chapters. I didn't want it to be as patterned as that is and as boring, to me, as that. On the other hand, I wasn't exactly sure

how to do it. So some of the work I did on revision was restructuring everything, moving chunks of one person's narrative into the other person's story,
then writing connective tissue between the two.

You begin The World Below *with Georgia's grandparents riding into town in
a buggy, in hopes of getting Georgia and her siblings after their mother dies, but
the father refuses. It's very dramatic and cinematic. How do you decide where
to begin a novel?*

The first chapter is really important, no matter what. It's a decision that is
intrinsic to whatever book you are working on. There are no real answers for
what needs to happen in the first chapter, except that it needs to draw the
reader in to make the story seem compelling and of great interest. The most
remarkable thing is how different beginnings are from one another.

It was very clear to me that I wanted to begin with the grandparents and the
possibility of their rescuing Georgia. For some reason, as I wrote it, I knew that
this grandmother was not going to appear later in the book. This would be her
scene, then we would move into Georgia's life. It was less visually focused the
first go around, but it was very clear to me that I wanted to begin with the
grandmother's offer and her sense that unless she took Georgia, Georgia
wouldn't have a childhood.

With my second novel, *Family Pictures*, I made a really prolonged false
start—several hundred pages and a couple of years of work. It really didn't
work, but I had made a commitment to those characters and what I wanted to
do with them. Even though I had to discard a lot of it, it wasn't ever a question
of not doing it.

How did you change it?

It was about this huge family, and they have an autistic kid. I had started it
before the parents met and moved with them through their meeting and the
early part of their marriage. I just cut an enormous amount, began in a very different place and ended up occasionally using little bits of [what had been cut] as
memory or referring to some experience. It just needed to enter more directly
and more quickly into the dilemma, into the issue of the book, which was the
child and the different answers each of the parents had for the meaning of his
presence in their lives—what they were, therefore, meant to be doing about it.

Could you describe your writing process?

I make a lot of notes before I get going. I know what I want to do pretty
much. I don't necessarily know everything that is going to happen in the book;
there is some serendipity, but I have a sense of what the ideas are that I'm
working with and how I want to embody them. I've made a lot of notes about
specific scenes, not complete themes but kind of . . . she'll do this, he'll do this,
he'll say this. . . . Then when I get to that [scene], I know why I'm there, and
what I want to do around it.

I write in longhand in a bound notebook. When I near the end of the book, I often go through those notes and look at things I haven't used. I think about whether they belong any longer. If they might or they do, I take a Post-it note and make this row of small themes and bits of dialogue. I'm looking at them everyday, thinking: Would they fit here or work there? It's all a big, fat mess.

I do feel a sense of eagerness and commitment to the enterprise with each book. I was very perplexed by the weaving of the two stories [in *The World Below*] and really worried about how it was going to go.

How and when do you decide the novel's point of view?

This one was a funny one because I knew Cath [*The World Below*] would be narrated in first person, and I wanted her to tell her grandmother's story, but also tell it in a way that she simply wouldn't have been able to know. I was thinking of someone like Marlow in Joseph Conrad's *Heart of Darkness*, where he tells this story that seems preposterous for him to tell and to have privileged information. In that sense, it's maybe a bit of a stretch in some ways, but it was something I wanted to be fooling around with to interest myself.

With the third person, you virtually can write a first-person kind of thing. You can descend very much down on the character's shoulder, but then you also can float around and be very godlike, and comment on the character and what the character doesn't understand about herself. I like that very much.

There was only one book—*For Love*—where I really wasn't sure whether I'd write it in the first person or third. The others all seemed to me to need to be a certain way.

Family Pictures was a little confused, too—some of it was in the first person, some in the third. It moved around among a lot of different characters.

I like the third person best of all because of its flexibility. The first person is so enclosed. I felt that particularly in *While I Was Gone.* [Jo] was in some ways an unreliable narrator; she's trying for reliability, but it's not in her nature to be reliable. By the end of the book, I felt very confined by her perspective and by inhabiting her personality as a whole.

What is your writing routine? When you are really into the writing, is it difficult to break away and participate in other areas of your life?

I try to make myself work three hours a day. If things are going really well and I'm excited about what I'm doing, I work longer than that. During revisions, I'm working on it all at once. It's more complicated at that point—it's not just writing a scene, but making sure the whole book is doing something. And I'm moving things around within the whole book. That's when I often put in long days. I get very lost in it. I get a little dreamy, particularly toward the very end, when the whole book is existing for me in this simultaneity of thought. It is hard to attend to the dailiness of human interaction. But earlier on [in the process], writing is more workmanlike.

What do you enjoy the most about writing?

Making the notes and thinking about [the story] before you have to confront the reality of what you are able to get on the page—when it seems you will be able to get everything you want on the page and you're not holding yourself accountable word by word. You're not working on it yet; you're just conjuring it and it feels you might do anything.

Could you describe how you work with editors?

My first editor, Ted Solotaroff, was a well-known editor at *New American Review* (later called the *American Review*). He was terrific as an editor. He would ask these open-ended questions: "One wonders. . . ." He would leave it up to you whether you cared or didn't care. I remember in *Family Pictures*, which he edited, I had a certain tendency to sort of announce what was going to happen in the chapter and then to have it happen.

He talked about the fact that the book itself wasn't very dramatic, and it didn't have much of a plot. It was basically an account of this family's history. He thought that each chapter needed to be as compellingly dramatic as it could, and that tendency on my part undercut any sense of suspense in the book.

I went back and looked at the chapters. In some cases, I eliminated parts of the chapters or moved them around.

My present editor, Jordan Pavlon, is my son's age, I would guess. She's a wonderful reader. What she tends to do is write me a dense three-or four-page single-spaced letter about the book, responding to it, saying what she thinks is strong and what she would like to think more about. Occasionally she'll say, as Ted did, "This word choice seems off to me. I don't think she should say this here." It comes down to line-editing kinds of things. But those things are always up to me. If I think she *should* say that, I leave it in, but I'm always interested, because they're both good readers and such generous readers of my work that I think about why they might have those thoughts, if there is something else I ought to do. That's basically the process. It's comfortable for me. I've trusted both of them. It's important that editors understand your impulses in your work. Both have been very respectful of my saying, "That's not something I want to change."

Does your agent also give you feedback?

That has changed a lot over time. Initially, she [Maxine Groffsky] was very important to me as a first editor. She worked with me on *The Good Mother*. There was a chunk of family history floating around loose in the book, and she helped me find the right home for it and tighten it up a bit. She had been an editor. I think that's changed. She's done less editing as time has gone on, and I've developed more of a relationship with my editors and gotten better at editing myself. I've learned from the editors about what my tendencies are, what my weaknesses are.

At this point, her role is very different. She's much more a friend. I've been with her a long time. I rely on her enthusiasm and an emotional connection with her, using her as someone to talk about business or my career.

Is there anything you fear about writing?
A lot. I think every writer is anxious about putting a book out there, fearing judgment of the book, fearing it's being profoundly misunderstood somehow. There's that, but I think the deeper fears are of not being able to do what you want to do, of not getting the central thing down on paper somehow, of not being able to embody the notion that you're entertaining, or to think of the right fictional reality for it, of going off, of being wrong.

Elfrieda Abbe is Editor of *The Writer.*

THE SUE MILLER FILE

• Born in Chicago, the second of four children. She grew up in Hyde Park, on the city's South Side, and went to college at Harvard. She married at 20, shortly after she graduated. Her son, Ben, was born in 1968.

• She has taught at Boston University, Tufts, Emerson, Harvard Summer School, and MIT.

• *While I Was Gone* was an Oprah Book Club selection. On Oprah.com, Miller wrote of her background: "My family was ecclesiastical to its roots— my father was an ordained minister (though he never had a church), and both grandfathers and various great-grandfathers and so on back through the ages were preachers. More important, my parents struggled to make their lives meaningful in terms of witness to conscience, to pacifism, to racial equality; and though I don't see the direct embrace of religion among my siblings and the cousins in my generation, I'm aware, in myself anyway, of a tendency toward self-examination and examination of others—intention, meanings, scruples, ethics—that seems to connect directly to that tradition, and has served me well as a writer."

• Movies have been made of *The Good Mother* (1988), with Diane Keaton and Liam Neeson) and *Inventing the Abbotts* (1997).

[cont.]

[sidebar cont.]

• Writers who have influenced her: "Australian writer Helen Garner wrote one book, *The Children's Bach*, that I think is brilliant. It's out of print. Penelope Fitzgerald and Garner are very compressed, very elliptical in a way that I'm not. I look to them as a corrective, a medicine that I don't mind taking at all. Alice Munro, Ian McEwan, and Carol Shields are more like me in some ways, but each does something I admire very much, and I think that I'm partly doing something they do, so they are inspiring to me."

• When Miller gets stuck writing, she does "something else for a week or 10 days. I don't think of it as being blocked. I think of it as problems I need to solve. Usually, when I'm stopped, I'll make notes in that period. I feel as though the underpinnings aren't firmly enough there for me or I haven't thought it through enough, so I go back to that part of the process for awhile, and that usually launches me again. But I do stop often in a course of a book, in a way I don't hear about other writers doing. I stop for however long it takes me to get going again."

• Miller lives in Cambridge, Mass. She currently is writing a memoir about her father's death from Alzheimer's disease.

SUE GRAFTON: HOW I WRITE

Before Sue Grafton became an international bestselling author with her Kinsey Millhone mystery series, she made the best, literarily speaking, of two bad situations: She hated her screenwriting job, but learned a lot from it about how to put together a story. And she channeled malevolent impulses over her dissolving second marriage into plotting her first Millhone book, starring a feisty, twice-divorced, highly independent PI who's considerably better at solving cases than picking men.

Today, 20 years and 16 mysteries later, Grafton lives in a multimillion-dollar home near Santa Barbara, Calif., and a residence in her hometown of Louisville, Ky. Her file full of readers who have named their children Kinsey is testament to the chord her private detective has struck with readers.

Her credits include: *P Is for Peril* (2001), *O Is for Outlaw* (1999), *N Is for Noose* (1998), and 13 other books in the Kinsey Millhone mystery series; two early nonmysteries, *Keziah Dane* and *The Lolly-Madonna War*.

Why. I've been writing for so long (nearly 45 years now) that I can no longer remember the "why" of it. This is simply what I do. I love a well-structured story. I'm interested in what motivates an individual to do good or ill and I'm fascinated by the dark side of human nature. Basically, any mystery writer is both magician and moralist . . . two species of artist in short supply. Sometimes I claim I write because I put in an application at Sears and they've never called back.

How. I confess I'm a prissy little thing. Like Goldilocks, I want every sentence, every scene, and every move in a book to be "just right" before I move on. I revise constantly and only leave a chapter behind when I'm able to read it 10 times in a row without changing a word. Even then, I go back, of course, if I realize that I've left something out or need to modify the early sections for consistency. I'm a slow writer but persistent, and that counts for everything.

When and where. I have two homes—one in California, the other in Kentucky—and I write in both, taking my disk with me when I travel from place to place. I write from 8 in the morning until midafternoon, using a word processor, the telephone, and mounds of research materials.

Ideas. My goal with this series is never to tell the same story twice, which means I keep elaborate charts tracking the setup for each book, the killer, the victim, the motive for the crime, and the nature of the climax. I start with the title and the overall game plan, and I proceed from there. Every book represents a separate challenge. For instance, with *K Is for Killer*, I decided to see if I could write a book set entirely at night. *M Is for Malice* was my ghost story, *N Is for Noose*, a western, and so it goes. I read everything because you never know when a good idea is going to pop into view. The real trick is recognizing one when it comes along.

Writer's block. I only get writer's block about once a day. I used to view it with abhorrence, like a dragon in my path, to be fought with every means at my disposal; slashing, bashing, torment and self-flagellation . . . whatever it took. Now I see writer's block as a whispered message from my Shadow [unconscious] side, who wants me to realize that I have moved off-grid. Instead of doing battle, I become as still as a mouse, going back over my work until I see where I've strayed. Once I spot the error and repent my sins, Shadow's perfectly content to let the work proceed.

Advice. Writing is a craft that takes many years to develop. I'm most peevish with unpublished writers who manage to complete one book and then imagine they're ready to compete in the open marketplace. The publishing world is full of talented, hardworking writers who've struggled for years to learn the necessary skills. I counsel any writer to focus on the job at hand—learning to write well—trusting that when the time comes, the Universe will step in and make the rest possible. Writing isn't about the destination—writing is the journey that transforms the soul and gives meaning to all else.

How I Write is a staff-written monthly feature of *The Writer* magazine.

CONVERSATION WITH STUDS TERKEL

On the art of interviewing

by Ronald Kovach

For 50 years, Studs Terkel has created in books and on radio his rough draft of our times by talking mostly to ordinary people—at least 9,000 of them, to be exact. In 10 books of oral history, the voices he has recorded and condensed have told a tale of struggle in 20th-century America—of the things that divide and unite us, of war and peace and Depression, of the way the races get along and don't get along, of growing old, of the kinds of things we do all day at work.

The latest book from Terkel, age 90, is a compelling book about death and dying called *Will the Circle Be Unbroken? Reflections on Death, Rebirth, and Hunger for a New Faith* (New Press). The book is not as forbidding as it sounds, and, in fact, is every bit as absorbing as his strongest work, which includes the Pulitzer Prize-winner *"The Good War": An Oral History of World War Two* (1984) and *Working: People Talk About What They Do All Day and How They Feel About What They Do* (1974). As Terkel put it during an interview in Milwaukee, "Who wants to talk about death? Everybody. It's the most alive book I've ever done."

It is not hard to see why people might open up to Terkel. He comes across as the type of engaging, grandfatherly figure who is feisty and full of opinion, yet unthreatening and always ready to lend an ear. Before they know it, they find themselves having a genuine conversation with this diminutive man in the red socks and red-and-white-checked shirt, and sharing, in the case of the latest book, some of their most painful memories and privately held religious—or irreligious—thoughts.

Being interviewed by Studs "is like having the intimacy of a therapist's office," says Sydney Lewis, who has transcribed the interviews for a number of Terkel's books and is herself the author of three oral histories. "You feel like you're cocooned by his interest. He listens really hard. He makes you feel wanted.

"I have typed so many interviews of his and part of me is studying the process while I'm doing it," she adds. "I'll be typing along and all of a sudden there will be a moment when you can feel that the person has completely opened to him, and it's nothing Studs said. It's this gift he has. I think it comes from his immense respect for all human beings, and his incredible deep and genuine curiosity—a real hunger to know, a certain nonjudgmentalness. And there's just something gleeful about him that makes you give him what he's asking for."

Studs, a man who loves to talk, draws plenty of revealing talk out of his 60 subjects in *Will the Circle Be Unbroken?* Among the voices are police officers and firefighters, paramedics, doctors and nurses, a former gang member, a woman who was in a coma for two years, a parent who lost his son to violence, people remembering their combat or near-death experiences, a few famous figures like bluegrass musician Doc Watson, who lost a son, and Kurt Vonnegut. While full of sad or harrowing tales, the book also offers life-affirming stories of healing and hope, and a variety of candid reflections on the afterlife and even reincarnation.

Studs clearly knows how to put his subjects at ease. A physicist at the Los Alamos National Laboratory tells him, "I believe that there are things beyond science. . . . My conclusion is, there are layers and layers and layers and layers of articulation and organization in this world that go far beyond anything that you and I can either perceive or understand."

A retired Brooklyn firefighter remembers trapped colleagues in the basement of a burning grocery store crying for their mothers. A social worker describes living through the atomic bomb blast in Hiroshima that killed her mother.

A Chicago paramedic recalls: "About 48 hours before [my father] died we were at the hospital . . . and something happened where emotionally I knew this was it: my dad was going to be dead in a day or two, and I'll never see him again. It just ate me up inside and I broke down and cried and cried for about a half-hour. It was a terror inside of me. It dawned on me that this is it, and the daddy I had when I was a little boy, the smells, the feel of his clothes—the smell of the T-shirt he wore, even with the nicotine on it—that's what I identified with him. All the memories."

One of the most powerful interviews is with

"Part of how Studs creates the atmosphere is it's not a one-way conversation. It really is a conversation. He contributes and you contribute, and out of that comes a real dialogue."

—Ed Townley

Mamie Mobley, mother of Emmett Till, the black Chicago youth who was murdered in 1955 while visiting relatives in Mississippi, because he supposedly whistled at a white woman. His death helped catalyze the civil rights movement. Mobley's description of examining her 14-year-old son's battered body when it arrived back in Chicago is not soon forgotten. ("That was incredible, of course," Terkel says of the interview. "All you could do is listen and sit there.")

A poignant footnote to the book is that shortly after Terkel began working on it, his wife, Ida, his companion of 60 years, died after heart surgery. She was 87. (Her cardiologist is one of Terkel's interview subjects in the book.)

In our talk with this master interviewer, Terkel had some simple but important things to say about an essential task many readers of *The Writer* face in developing their own articles and books: talking to people.

An interview so often involves two strangers talking to each other. How do you get past that strangeness?

Well, first of all, you appear as yourself, not as someone from Mount Olympus, or it might be Mike Wallace from *60 Minutes* or Dan Rather. No, you appear as yourself, as someone who's going to listen to them. This is not a celebrity, not a celebrity—this is an "average person." (I hate that phrase—"ordinary people" are capable of extraordinary things; I know that. Throughout all the books I've celebrated the ordinary person.)

And so I'm a guy, a stranger, but I want to know about this person—his experiences during the Great Depression, or the Great War, or how this black guy feels in the white society and the other way around. Or growing old—what it's about.

And so I sit down, and sometimes I have a tape recorder but I have trouble with the tape recorder. You see, I'm not good mechanically. I'm very inept, and sometimes I goof up on the tape recorder. And that person sees me as a flawed person, as someone who's no different than he is or she is, and the person [says]—"Look, your reel's not right [when it was reel-to-reel], it's not working." I say, "I pressed the wrong thing, I'm sorry."

Immediately, that person feels pretty good to feel needed. Suddenly, he feels, "This guy needs me as much as I need him. He needs me." And so that helps a lot.

People think I deliberately do it, you know. Mike Royko, the [late Chicago] columnist, said, "You bastard, you deliberately do that, don't you?" I said, "No, I'm inept, you know I am—I can't drive a car." So that's one thing.

The other is listening—listening is key. The person may suddenly do something strange—suddenly stop or go off the subject. Why'd that person stop? Come back to it.

Every now and then you hear a black guy laugh when recounting a moment of humiliation to himself. I had a friend named Big Bill Broonzy [a famous country-blues singer]. Big Bill, many older black guys, were grandsons of slaves, skilled craftsmen, jacks of all trades—could be a mason, an electrician, a carpenter. Could do all these things. Big Bill knew welding. He says, "I taught this white boy how to weld, and as soon as I did, they fired me." And he chuckles. Now why'd he chuckle? And you realize it's a safety valve.

There's a blues line, "laughing to keep from crying." (Or you could say, "laughing to keep from raging.") It's a safety valve. I once asked Dr. [Martin Luther] King [Jr.] about that. And I said, why is it, the laughter? He says, "It's essential. Without humor through adversity, we'd never make it."

But mostly, it's listening. And that's pretty much the key.

When you first sit down at an interview, how do you start out?

There's no one way. What is it I want to find out? Let's say it's a book about the Depression, right? Well, I gather that this person doesn't like bananas. Why don't you like bananas? "Because during the Depression my poor family, we'd get the rotten bananas tossed off the trucks. Ate rotten bananas—I can't stand them."

There's no one rule. There's no one way to open it.

With all your experience interviewing, do you run into people where it's hard to get them to open up?

Some people you have to give up on. People are not all the same . . . I see this woman, she says, "You know who you should see, you should see Florence, the woman three houses away from me. See Florence." I say, "Why do you want me to see Florence?" "Well, you see Florence, you'll find out why. See Florence."

Now Florence is like she is. Both are working class. Both have little education. Both are the same religion. But Florence happens to have a certain kind of insight. A certain kind of articulateness. And she said what that woman feels but can't say.

There's no one way. I'm what I am—you know, this guy who goofs up. And they feel good about that.

I have no written questions. I know [them] in my head. That then makes the conversation easier. And also, I've got to listen more, see?

What are you? A writer? Someone who knows how to pick good storytellers? What do you think is your main talent?

You know what a whatnot is? Look it up. I'm a whatnot. A whatnot's a piece of furniture—you put everything in it. Checks, bills, love letters. I'm a whatnot. I was a disc jockey—it's true. Journalist? I never went to journalism school; I went to law school. But I write now and then, a thing here and there, an op-ed piece. I was an actor, a pioneer, you might say, in television. I don't have any talent; I'm a whatnot.

The other thing is listening—listening is key. The person may suddenly do something strange—suddenly stop or go off the subject. Why'd that person stop? Come back to it.

How do you go about condensing your interviews?

I compare myself to a gold prospector—1849, gold discovered in California, here come the covered wagons, "Oh My Darling Clementine." The guy finds a piece of soil, he puts his spike in it. That's my gold. Now comes the digging, and he digs up a ton of ore. Now comes the effort to transcribe—40 pages. He filters; I edit. He has a handful of gold dust; and I edit it down to about 10 pages.

Now, the editing is the key. How do you edit? Well, there you have to know, what does this person want to say? You make it almost like a soliloquy; you cut yourself out of it as much as you can. Now you're like a brain surgeon—you take pieces out and there it is. And so it's not simply the truth; it's highlighting the truth, almost like a playwright would do.

How do you cut people out? That's the worst part. You're like the director of a play—you've got two guys, and they're both good.

You try to make your interviews like a conversation.

That's it. Absolutely. Oh, conversation is what it's about. Now and then I say a few things—"Yeah, I know that." If I know it'll help the other person, I might say, "You know what happened to me?" It's conversation.

Ronald Kovach is senior editor of *The Writer.*

A CONVERSATION, NOT AN INTERVIEW

What is it like to be interviewed by Studs Terkel?

It is a memorable experience, according to Ed Townley, one of the voices in Terkel's latest book, *Will the Circle Be Unbroken?* Townley, 56, senior pastor at the Unity in Chicago church, offered Terkel a vivid description of his near-death experience and his rugged journey from alcohol and drug abuse to the ministry.

Here's how Townley described the interview:

"Well, the first thing is, Studs manages to make you feel like you're the only interview he's ever had. He is so committed to the matter at hand that there's no sense of this as part of a larger project. He is just genuinely interested in what you have to say—that probably is the key to any great interviewer. You don't get the sense that he's mentally writing the book as he's talking to you.

[cont.]

[sidebar cont.]

"Studs is very disarming. When you're being interviewed, you find yourself saying things you wouldn't imagine yourself saying were he less genuinely focused on the interview. He's so interested and he's so concerned
about what you're saying and excited about what you're saying that it just
pulls you in, gently massaging you into really revealing things you might
not have done otherwise. Studs is like relaxing with a very close friend."

Did Studs talk much during the interview?

"Oh yes. Something you say will remind him of a story or something
somebody else said. Part of how he creates the atmosphere is it's not a
one-way conversation. It really is a conversation.

"He contributes and you contribute, and out of that comes a real dialogue. It's not like he has a list of questions and he runs through them
and you answer. It went places neither of us thought it would go, and
that's very exciting."

NONFICTION MAGAZINES

NONFICTION MAGAZINES

The magazines in the following list are in the market for freelance articles in many categories. Unless listings state otherwise, a writer should submit a query first, including a brief description of the proposed article and any relevant qualifications or credits. A few editors want to see samples of published work, if available.

Submit photos or slides only if the editor has specifically requested them. A self-addressed envelope with postage sufficient to cover the return of the manuscript or the answer to a query should accompany all submissions.

All information in these lists comes from query responses from the editors, publishers, and directors and from their published guidelines, but personnel and addresses change, as do requirements. No published listing can give as clear a picture of editorial needs and tastes as a careful study of several issues of a magazine, and writers should never submit material without first thoroughly researching the prospective market. If a magazine is not available in the local library or on the newsstand, write directly to the editor for the price of a sample copy. Many companies also offer a formal set of writer's guidelines, available for an SASE (self-addressed, stamped envelope) upon request, or posted on its Web site.

While some of the more established markets may seem difficult to break into, especially for the beginner, there are thousands of lesser-known publications where editors will consider submissions from first-time freelancers.

All manuscripts must be typed double-space and submitted with self-addressed envelopes bearing postage sufficient for the return of the material. If a manuscript need not be returned, note this with the submission, and enclose an SASE or a self-addressed, stamped postcard for editorial reply. Use good white paper. Always keep a copy, since occasionally material is lost in the mail. Magazines may take several weeks, or longer, to read and report on submissions. If an editor has not reported on a manuscript after a reasonable length of time, write a brief, courteous letter of inquiry.

Some publishers will accept, and may in fact prefer, work submitted on computer disk, usually noting the procedure and type of disk in their guidelines.

ABILITIES

ABILITIES MAGAZINE
Canadian Abilities Foundation
489 College St., Suite 501, Toronto, Ontario M6G 1A5 Canada. 416-923-1885.
E-mail: lisa@abilities.ca. Web site: www.abilities.ca. Quarterly. Lisa Bendall, Managing Editor. **Description:** For people with disabilities, their families, and professionals engaged in disabilities issues. Covers travel, health, sport, recreation, employment, education, housing, social policy, sexuality, movie/book reviews, profiles. **Nonfiction:** Articles, 500-2,000 words, $50-$400. **Columns, Departments:** News and updates (FYI); humor (The Lighter Side). **Art:** Photos. **Queries:** Preferred. **Unsolicited mss:** Accepts. **Rights:** 1st.

ABLE

P.O. Box 395, Old Bethpage, NY 11804-0395. 516-939-2253.
E-mail: ablenews@aol.com. Web site: www.ablenews.com. Monthly. Circ.: 35,000.
Angela Miele Melledy. **Description:** "Positively for, by, and about the disabled."
Features news, events, and informative articles that are of interest to people with disabilities, family and friends, and involved professionals. **Nonfiction:** to 500 words;
pays $40. **Art:** Color and B&W photos. **Queries:** Required. **E-Queries:** No.
Unsolicited mss: Accepts. **Freelance Content:** 40%. **Payment:** On publication.

ACCENT ON LIVING

P.O. Box 700, Bloomington, IL 61702-0700. 309-378-2961.
E-mail: acntlvng@aol.com. Web site: www.accentonliving.com. Quarterly. $12/yr.
Circ.: 21,000. Betty Garee, Editor. **Description:** Provides information about new
devices and approaches so people with physical disabilities can enjoy a better lifestyle.
Nonfiction: Product information helpful to individuals with limited physical mobility. Intelligent articles about physically disabled persons in "normal" living situations.
How-to articles on everyday living; up-to-date news; profiles of disabled personalities;
800-1,000 words; $.10/word. **Fillers:** Cartoons (humorous incidents encountered by
physically disabled individuals in everyday living; a person in a wheelchair is typical,
should be depicted in humorous but normal situations); $20. **Art:** B&W, color (provide captions); prints, disk, electronic (TIF, 300 dpi); $5-$50 (color cover). **Tips:**
Don't write for able-bodied audience about being disabled. Use informal, not academic, style. Show individuals with disabilities involved in all aspects of life. Good
photos or illustrations helpful. **Queries:** Preferred. **E-Queries:** Accepts.
Unsolicited mss: Accepts. **Response:** Queries 2 weeks, submissions 3 weeks, SASE
required. **Freelance Content:** 75%. **Rights:** One-time. **Payment:** On publication.

CLOSING THE GAP

See page 328 for full listing.
Description: Articles on microcomputer products for persons with disabilities.

DIALOGUE

Blindskills, Inc.
P.O. Box 5181, Salem, OR 97304-0181. 503-581-4224; 800-860-4224.
E-mail: blindskl@teleport.com. Web site: www.blindskills.com. Quarterly. Carol
McCarl, Editor. **Description:** Seeks to give readers an opportunity to learn about
interesting and successful people who are visually impaired. Subject matter covers a
variety of topics including independence, mobility, employment, technology, and
health. Also spotlights short pieces of fiction in each issue. **Nonfiction:** Articles for
youth and adults who are visually impaired. Career opportunities, educational skills,
and recreational activities; 800-1,200 words; pay varies. **Queries:** Preferred.
Response: SASE. **Payment:** On publication.

KALEIDOSCOPE

See page 676 for full listing.

Description: Explores the experience of disability through literature and fine arts.

MINDPRINTS

See page 683 for full listing.

Description: Literary journal of short fiction, memoirs, poetry, and art for writers and artists with disabilities and those with an interest in this field.

WEMEDIA

130 William St., New York, NY 10038. 212-931-6700.

E-mail: editorial@wemedia.com. Web site: www.wemedia.com. Bimonthly. Cary Fields, Publisher. **Description:** For people with disabilities, their families and friends, focusing on news, sports, accessible and assistive technologies, politics and advocacy, shopping, employment, education, finance, and real estate from a disability perspective. **Fiction:** 1,500-2,000 words. **Nonfiction:** Varying lengths; pay varies. **Art:** Photos. **Tips:** Include a JPEG photo of the author and a JPEG logo of the organization the author represents, plus a one to two line description that states the author's role and organization. **Queries:** Preferred. **Payment:** On publication.

AGRICULTURE & RURAL LIFE

ACRES USA

P.O. Box 91299, Austin, TX 78709. 512-892-4400.

E-mail: editor@acresusa.com. Web site: www.acresusa.com. Fred C. Walters, Editor. **Description:** Articles offer ecological and economical advice for farmers who practice sustainable agriculture. Features hands-on techniques and natural methods for growing crops and raising livestock. **Nonfiction:** Emphasis on commercial production of quality food without use of toxic chemicals; pays $.05/word. **Unsolicited mss:** Accepts. **Payment:** On publication.

AG JOURNAL

122 San Juan, P.O. Box 500, La Junta, CO 81050. 719-384-8121.

E-mail: ag-edit@centurytel.net. Web site: www.agjournalonline.com. Weekly. $32. Circ.: 12,000. Jeanette Larson, Managing Editor. **Description:** Publication covering agriculture news in the Western and Southwestern states. **Nonfiction:** Features articles on prominent people in agriculture. Also covers ag market and pricing trends, latest industry news, grain and forage production, equestrian happenings, and equipment for-sale listings; 250-2000 words; $.04/word. **Art:** Color slides and negatives accepted; TIF or JPG at 200 dpi+; $8/photo, $25 cover shot. **Queries:** Required. **E-Queries:** Yes. **Unsolicited mss:** Accepts. **Response:** 2 weeks. **Rights:** All, no reprints. **Payment:** On publication.

AMERICAN BEE JOURNAL

51 S 2nd St., Hamilton, IL 62341. 217-847-3324.
E-mail: abj@dadant.com. Web site: www.dadant.com. Joe M. Graham, Editor.
Description: Articles on beekeeping for professionals. **Nonfiction:** Articles, pays
$.75/column inch. **Art:** Photos. **Queries:** Preferred. **Payment:** On publication.

BACKHOME

Wordsworth Communications, Inc.
P.O. Box 70, Hendersonville, NC 28793. 828-696-3838.
E-mail: backhome@ioa.com. Web site: www.backhomemagazine.com. Bimonthly.
$4.95/$21.97. Circ.: 30,000. Lorna K. Loveless, Editor. **Description:** Do-it-yourself
information on sustainable, self-reliant living. Offers information and resources on
rural land, mortgage-free building, solar/renewable energy, chemical-free gardening,
wholesome cooking, home business, home schooling, small livestock, vehicle and
workshop projects, family activities. **Nonfiction:** On self-sufficient, sustainable-living
practices, preferably first-person experiences; buying a used tractor, installing a door,
maintaining a pasture, etc.; 800-3,000 words; $35/printed page. **Art:** To accompany
articles; prints, slides; $20/image. **Tips:** Focus not on "dropping out," but on becom-
ing better citizens and caretakers of the planet. Avoid essays. **Queries:** Not necessary.
E-Queries: Accepts. **Unsolicited mss:** Accepts. **Response:** 2-4 weeks, SASE.
Freelance Content: 80%. **Payment:** On publication; kill fee offered.

BEE CULTURE

623 W Liberty St., Medina, OH 44256. 330-725-5624 x3214.
E-mail: kim@beeculture.com. Web site: www.beeculture.com. Monthly. $3.95/issue,
$21.50/year. Circ.: 11,500. Mr. Kim Flottum, Editor. **Description:** Beekeeping, pol-
lination, gardening with bees, nature. **Nonfiction:** Basic how-to, some profiles of
commercial operations; 1,000-2,000 words; $100-$250. **Art:** Slides, B&W prints,
color, or electronic. **Tips:** Must know bee and commercial beekeeping. Avoid "How
I got started in beekeeping." **Queries:** Preferred. **E-Queries:** Yes. **Unsolicited mss:**
Accepts. **Response:** Queries 1 month, submissions 1-3 months; SASE required.
Freelance Content: 25%. **Rights:** 1st NA. **Payment:** On publication or negotiated.

BEEF

PRIMEDIA Business Magazines & Media
7900 International Dr., Suite 300, Minneapolis, MN 55425. 952-851-9329.
E-mail: beef@primediabusiness.com. Web site: www.beef-mag.com. 12 issues/year.
Circ.: 101,000. Joe Roybal, Editor. **Description:** Informational articles for cattlemen
and cattle industry; covers production, animal health, nutrition, finance and marketing issues. **Nonfiction:** Articles on feeding, cowherds, stock operations, cattle industry; up to $300. **Art:** To accompany articles. **Queries:** Required. **E-Queries:** Yes.
Unsolicited mss: Does not accept. **Payment:** On acceptance.

BRAHMAN JOURNAL

P.O. Box 220, Eddy, TX 76524-5507. 254-859-5507.
E-mail: jebrockett@aol.com. Web site: www.brahman.org/journ.html. Monthly. Circ.: 3,900. Joe Brockett, Editor. **Description:** Covers Brahman breed of beef cattle. **Nonfiction:** About the Brahman breed or people who work with them; 1,500 words; up to $250. **Queries:** Preferred. **E-Queries:** No. **Unsolicited mss:** Accepts. **Freelance Content:** 5%. **Rights:** All. **Payment:** On acceptance.

THE CATTLEMAN

Texas and Southwestern Cattle Raisers Association
1301 W Seventh St., Fort Worth, TX 76102-2660. 817-332-7064.
E-mail: lionel@thecattlemanmagazine.com. Web site: www.cattlemanmagazine.com. Lionel Chambers, Editor. **Description:** For ranchers who raise beef cattle. **Queries:** Preferred.

COUNTRY

Reiman Publications
5400 S 60th St., P.O. Box 991, Greendale, WI 53129-091. 414-423-0100.
E-mail: editors@country-magazine.com. Web site: www.country-magazine.com. Bimonthly. $14.98/year. Circ.: 1,400,000. Jerry Wiebel, Editor. **Description:** Articles and photographs describing the allure of country life today. Mostly reader-written. **Nonfiction:** First-person articles; 500-700 words; $75-$200. **Art:** Good candid color photos. **Tips:** No articles on farm production techniques. **Queries:** Not necessary. **Unsolicited mss:** Accepts. **Response:** 2 months. **Freelance Content:** 90%. **Payment:** On publication.

COUNTRY FOLK

HC 77 Box 608, Pittsburg, MO 65724-9717.
E-mail: salaki@countryfolkmag.com. Web site: www.countryfolkmag.com. Bimonthly. $2.75/$16.50. Circ.: 6,500. Susan Salaki, Editor. **Description:** True Ozark history stories, old rare recipes, historical photos, and interesting fillers. **Nonfiction:** Ozark history; 800-1,000 words; $5-$25. **Poetry:** Standard rhyming; 3 verses max.; complimentary copy. **Freelance Content:** 99%.

COUNTRY WOMAN

Reiman Publications
5400 S 60th St., Greendale, WI 53129. 414-423-8463.
E-mail: editors@countrywomanmagazine.com. Web site: www.countrywoman-magazine.com. Bimonthly. $3.99/issue. Circ.: 1,700,000. Kathy Pohl, Executive Editor. **Description:** For women living in the country or interested in country life. Recipes, craft projects, fiction and nostalgia stories, decorating, profiles of country woman, and poetry. **Fiction:** Wholesome fiction with country perspective or rural theme; 1,000 words; $90-$125. **Nonfiction:** Nostalgia pieces, essays on farm/country life, humorous stories, decorating features, inspirational articles; 750-1,000 words; $50-$75. **Poetry:** Good rhythm and rhyme, seasonal in nature; 12-24 lines; $10-$25.

Art: Good candid color photos. **Queries:** Not necessary. **Unsolicited mss:** Accepts. **Response:** 2-3 months, SASE required. **Freelance Content:** 90%. **Payment:** On acceptance. **Contact:** Kathleen Anderson, Managing Editor.

DAIRY GOAT JOURNAL
P.O. Box 10, Lake Mills, WI 53551. 920-648-8285.
Web site: www.dairygoatjournal.com. 6x/year. $2.50/$21. Circ.: 7,000. Dave Thompson, Editor. **Description:** Magazine for successful dairy-goat owners. Features interesting people and practical husbandry ideas. **Nonfiction:** 1,000-1,500 words; $75-$150. **Fillers:** $25-$75. **Art:** B&W prints, $25-$75. **Tips:** Needs practical stories about goats and their owners; about marketing goat cheese and dairy products. Readership in U.S. and over 70 foreign countries. **Queries:** Preferred. **E-Queries:** No. **Unsolicited mss:** Accepts. **Response:** 2 weeks, SASE. **Freelance Content:** 50%. **Rights:** All. **Payment:** On acceptance.

FARM AND RANCH LIVING
Reiman Publications
5400 S 60th St., Greendale, WI 53129. 414-423-0100.
E-mail: editors@farmandranchliving.com. Web site: www.farmandranchliving.com. Bimonthly. $3.99/issue, $17.98/year. Circ.: 350,000. Nick Pabst, Editor. **Description:** For U.S. and Canadian families that farm or ranch full-time. Focuses on people; includes diaries, humor, rural nostalgia, tractor talk, 4-H, events calendar. **Nonfiction:** Photo-illustrated stories about today's farmers and ranchers; 1,200 words; $75-$150. **Fillers:** Farm-related humor; 100 words; $25-$50. **Tips:** Submit upbeat, positive stories. **Queries:** Not necessary. **E-Queries:** Yes. **Unsolicited mss:** Accepts. **Response:** 4 weeks, SASE required. **Freelance Content:** 30%. **Rights:** 1st NA, one-time. **Payment:** On publication.

FARM INDUSTRY NEWS
7900 International Dr., Suite 300, Minneapolis, MN 55425. 612-851-4609.
Web site: www.farmindustrynews.com. Karen McMahon, Editor. **Description:** For farmers, on new products, machinery, equipment, chemicals, and seeds. **Nonfiction:** Articles; pays $350-$500. **Queries:** Required. **Payment:** On acceptance.

FARM JOURNAL
610 Freedom Business Center, Suite 114, King of Prussia, PA 19406. 610-491-9800.
E-mail: feedback@agweb.com. Web site: www.agweb.com. Sonja Hillgren, Editor. **Description:** On the business of farming. **Nonfiction:** Articles, 500-1,500 words, with photos; pays $.20-$.50/word. **Queries:** Preferred. **Payment:** On acceptance.

FLORIDA GROWER
1555 Howell Branch Rd., Suite C-204, Winter Park, FL 32789. 407-539-6552.
E-mail: flg_edit@meisternet.com. Monthly. Circ.: 15,000. Michael Allen, Editor. **Description:** The voice of Florida agriculture. Covers all aspects of commercial fruit and vegetable industries. **Nonfiction:** On production or marketing Florida's agricul-

tural products; 1,400 words; $300. **Queries:** Not necessary. **E-Queries:** Yes. **Unsolicited mss:** Accepts. **Freelance Content:** 20%. **Rights:** All. **Payment:** On publication.

THE LAND
The Free Press Co.
P.O. Box 3169, Mankato, MN 56002-3169. 800-657-4665.
E-mail: kschulz@the-land.com. Web site: www.the-land.com. Weekly zoned. $20/year. Circ.: 40,000. Kevin Schulz, Editor. **Description:** Agricultural and rural-life magazine for Minnesota farm families. **Nonfiction:** On Minnesota agriculture and rural issues, production, how-tos; 500 words; $35-$60. **Queries:** Preferred. **E-Queries:** Yes. **Unsolicited mss:** Does not accept. **Response:** Queries 3-4 weeks, submissions 1-2 weeks, SASE. **Freelance Content:** 50%. **Rights:** 1st NA. **Payment:** On acceptance.

THE MAINE ORGANIC FARMER & GARDENER
662 Slab City Rd., Lincolnville, ME 04849. 207-763-3043.
E-mail: jenglish@midcoast.com. Web site: www.mofga.org. Quarterly. $12/yr. Circ.: 5,000. Jean English. **Description:** Published by the Maine Organic Farmers and Gardeners Association. **Nonfiction:** Organic farming and gardening, environmental issues relating to food/health, consumer issues, book reviews; 250-2,000 words; $.08/word. **Fillers:** Gardening and farming tips; $.08/word. **Art:** Photos with articles. **Tips:** Avoid rehashing old material. No chemical fertilizers and no potato-flake recipes. Readers know organic methods, and they seek new ideas, new crops, and new cultivation techniques. **Queries:** Preferred. **E-Queries:** Yes. **Unsolicited mss:** Accepts. **Response:** Queries in 2 weeks, submissions in 1 month, SASE. **Freelance Content:** 50%. **Rights:** 1st, reprint. **Payment:** On publication.

NATIONAL CATTLEMEN
5420 S Quebec St., Englewood, CO 80111-1905. 303-694-0305.
Web site: www.beef.org. Curt Olson. **Description:** Publication for the cattle industry. **Nonfiction:** Articles, 400-1,200 words; pay varies. **Tips:** Does not accept unsolicited material. **Payment:** On publication.

NEW HOLLAND NEWS
New Holland, N.A., Inc.
P.O. Box 1895, New Holland, PA 17557-0903. 717-393-3821.
Web site: www.newholland.com/na. 8x/year. Gary Martin, Editor. **Description:** Farm management, rural features for modern farm families. **Nonfiction:** People stories about farm struggles; ways to improve farm income; 800-1,500 words; $600-$800. **Art:** Transparencies, prints; $500/cover. **Tips:** No farmer profiles. **Queries:** Preferred. **E-Queries:** No. **Unsolicited mss:** Accepts. **Response:** 2 months, SASE. **Freelance Content:** 60%. **Rights:** 1st NA. **Payment:** On acceptance.

OHIO FARMER

Farm Progress Companies

117 W Main St. 202, Lancaster, OH 43130. 740-654-6500.

E-mail: twhite@farmprogress.com. Web site: www.farmprogress.com. Tim White, Editor. **Description:** On farming and rural living in Ohio. **Nonfiction:** Technical articles; pays $50/column. **Payment:** On publication.

ONION WORLD

Columbia Publishing

P.O. Box 9036, Yakima, WA 98909-9036. 509-248-2452.

E-mail: brent@freshcut.com. Web site: www.onionworld.net. 8x/year. Circ.: 6,000. D. Brent Clement, Editor. **Description:** On marketing and production, for U.S. and Canadian onion industries (growers, packers, shippers). **Nonfiction:** On onion production, packing, and shipping businesses; varieties grown, challenges, solutions, etc.; to 1,500 words; $5/column inch. **Art:** Include photos with article. **Tips:** No meaningless drivel. No gardening articles. **Queries:** Preferred. **E-Queries:** Yes. **Unsolicited mss:** Accepts. **Response:** Queries 7 days, submissions 2 weeks, SASE. **Freelance Content:** 25%. **Rights:** 1st. **Payment:** On publication.

PEANUT FARMER

5808 Faringdon Pl., Raleigh, NC 27609. 919-872-5040.

E-mail: publisher@peanutfarmer.com. Web site: www.peanutfarmer.com. Monthly. $15. Circ.: 19,000. Mary Ann Rood, Editor. **Description:** Magazine for commercial peanut farmers. **Nonfiction:** Production practices; 500-2,000 words; **Queries:** Preferred. **E-Queries:** Yes. **Unsolicited mss:** Accepts. **Response:** 2 weeks, SASE. **Freelance Content:** 10%. **Rights:** 1st NA. **Payment:** On publication.

PROGRESSIVE FARMER

Southern Progress Corp.

2100 Lakeshore Dr., Birmingham, AL 35209-6721. 205-877-6415.

E-mail: letters@progressivefarmer.com. Web site: www.progressivefarmer.com. Monthly. Circ.: 600,000. Jack Odle, Editor. **Description:** For farmers. Covers new developments in agriculture; rural communities; personal business issues for farmstead and home office; relationships; worker safety; finances, taxes, and regulations. **Nonfiction:** Articles; to 5 double-spaced pages (3 pages preferred); pays $50-$400. **Queries:** Preferred. **Payment:** On publication.

RURAL HERITAGE

281 Dean Ridge Ln., Gainesboro, TN 38562-5039. 931-268-0655.

E-mail: editor@ruralheritage.com. Web site: www.ruralheritage.com. Bimonthly. $8/$26. Circ.: 4,500. Gail Damerow, Editor. **Description:** Covers modern farming and logging with horses, mules, and oxen. **Nonfiction:** draft animal use, training, implements, etc.; 1,200 words; $.05/word. **Poetry:** Humorous, twist of fate, action-oriented. **Queries:** Preferred. **E-Queries:** Yes. **Unsolicited mss:** Accepts.

Response: Queries 1 week, submissions to 3 months. **Freelance Content:** 90%. **Rights:** 1st serial. **Payment:** On publication.

RURALITE
P.O. Box 558, Forest Grove, OR 97116. 503-357-2105.
E-mail: curtis@ruralite.org. Web site: www.ruralite.org. Monthly. $10/yr. Circ.: 287,600. Curtis Condon, Editor. **Description:** For rural electric cooperatives and public power districts in 7 western states. General interest and energy-related. **Nonfiction:** For rural/small-town audiences (OR, WA, ID, WY, NV, northern CA, AK), on rural/urban interests, regional history and celebrations, self-help, profiles; 400-2,000 words; $50-$400. **Art:** 35mm, 2¼; $25-$300. **Tips:** Readership 60% women, 50 years and older. **Queries:** Required. **E-Queries:** Yes. **Unsolicited mss:** Does not accept. **Response:** 1-2 months, SASE. **Freelance Content:** 80%. **Payment:** On acceptance.

SHEEP! MAGAZINE
P.O. Box 10, Lake Mills, WI 53551. 920-648-8285.
Web site: www.sheepmagazine.com. 6x/yr. $21/yr. Circ.: 12,000. Dave Thompson, Editor. **Description:** For sheep and wool farmers across the U.S. and Canada. How-tos, flock owner stories, and industry news. **Nonfiction:** Articles, to 1,500 words, on successful shepherds, woolcrafts, sheep raising, sheep dogs; 800-1,500 words; $80-$125. **Art:** Yes. **Tips:** Especially interested in people who raise sheep successfully as a sideline enterprise. **Queries:** Preferred. **E-Queries:** No. **Unsolicited mss:** Accepts. **Response:** 1 month, SASE. **Freelance Content:** 50%. **Payment:** On acceptance.

SMALL FARM TODAY
3903 W Ridge Trail Rd., Clark, MO 65243-9525. 573-687-3525.
E-mail: smallfarm@socket.net. Web site: www.smallfarmtoday.com. Bimonthly. $4.95/$23.95. Circ.: 12,000. Ron Macher, Editor. **Description:** A "how-to" magazine of alternative and traditional crops, livestock, and direct marketing, to help farmers make their operations profitable and sustainable. **Nonfiction:** Stories about a specific crop, livestock, or marketing method, with how-to and budget information.; 1,000-1,800 words; $.35/word. **Tips:** Readers prefer alternative sustainable methods over traditional chemical farming. **Queries:** Preferred. **E-Queries:** Yes. **Unsolicited mss:** Accepts. **Response:** Queries 2 months, submissions 4 months, SASE. **Freelance Content:** 40%. **Rights:** 1st. **Payment:** On publication.

SMALL FARMER'S JOURNAL
P.O. Box 1627, Sisters, OR 97759-1627. 541-549-2064.
E-mail: agrarian@smallfarmersjournal.com. Web site: www.smallfarmersjournal.com. Quarterly. $8.50/$30 yr. Circ.: 18,000. Mr. Lynn R. Miller, Editor. **Description:** Covers practical farming for families who own small farms. Subject matter includes natural farming, stock raising, alternative farm research, and research on horses and horsedrawn equipment sales. **Nonfiction:** How-tos, humor, practical work-horse information, livestock and produce marketing, gardening, and articles for the inde-

pendent family farm. Pay varies. **Tips:** Write of your own farm experiences. Avoid use of chemicals. **Queries:** Not necessary. **E-Queries:** Yes. **Unsolicited mss:** Accepts. **Response:** 3 months, SASE. **Freelance Content:** 50%. **Rights:** 1st. **Payment:** On publication.

SUCCESSFUL FARMING
Meredith Corp.
1716 Locust St., Des Moines, IA 50309-3023. 515-284-2853.
Web site: www.agriculture.com. Monthly. $15/yr. Circ.: 475,000. Loren Kruse, Editor. **Description:** For farmers and ranchers, all sizes and types. **Nonfiction:** About successful family farms/businesses, big and small, that illustrate positive aspects. **Art:** Color transparencies preferred; pay varies. **Tips:** Provide ideas families can take right to the barn, shop, office, home, and heart to add value to their lives. Measure new practices and trends with dollar signs; use examples; use multiple sources. **Queries:** Preferred. **E-Queries:** No. **Unsolicited mss:** Accepts. **Response:** Queries 2 days, submissions 1 week, SASE. **Freelance Content:** 20%. **Rights:** All. **Payment:** On acceptance. **Contact:** Gene Johnston, Managing Editor.

WALLACES FARMER
Farm Progress Companies
6200 Aurora Ave., Suite 609E, Urbandale, IA 50322. 515-278-7782.
E-mail: fholdmeyer@farmprogress.com. Web site: www.wallacesfarmer.com. 15x/year. Circ.: 60,000. Frank Holdmeyer, Editor. **Description:** Provides Iowa farmers with useful information that helps them profitably manage their farming operations. **Nonfiction:** Interviews and articles on methods and equipment; 600-700 words. **Queries:** Required. **E-Queries:** Yes. **Unsolicited mss:** Accepts. **Freelance Content:** 1%. **Payment:** On acceptance.

THE WESTERN PRODUCER
P.O. Box 2500, 2310 Miller Ave.
Saskatoon, Saskatchewan S7K 2C4 Canada. 306-665-3544.
E-mail: bwashburn@producer.com. Web site: www.producer.com. Brenda Washburn. **Description:** On agricultural and rural subjects, preferably with Canadian slant. **Nonfiction:** Articles, to 800 words (prefer under 600 words); pays from $.23/word. **Art:** Color photos ($50-$100). **Payment:** On publication.

ANIMALS & PETS

AKC GAZETTE
American Kennel Club, Inc.
260 Madison Ave., New York, NY 10016. 212-696-8321.
E-mail: gazette@akc.org. Web site: www.akc.org. Monthly. Circ.: 60,000. Erika Mansourian, Features Editor. **Description:** Official journal for the sport of purebred dogs. **Nonfiction:** Articles, 1,000-2,500 words, for serious breeders,

exhibitors, and judges of purebred dogs; pays $250-$600. **Queries:** Preferred. **Payment:** On acceptance.

AMERICAN FIELD

American Field Publishing Co.
542 S Dearborn St., Suite 1350, Chicago, IL 60605. 312-663-9797.
E-mail: amfieldedit@att.net. Web site: www.americanfield.com. B.J. Matthys, Managing Editor. **Description:** Short items and anecdotes on hunting dogs and field trials for bird dogs. Yarns on hunting trips, bird-shooting; articles, to 1,500 words, on dogs and field trials, emphasizing conservation of game resources. Pay varies. **Payment:** On acceptance.

ANIMAL PEOPLE

P.O. Box 960, Clinton, WA 98236. 360-579-2505.
E-mail: anmlpepl@whidbey.com. Web site: www.animalpeoplenews.org. 10x/year. Circ.: 30,000. Merritt Clifton, Editor. **Description:** Leading independent newspaper providing original investigative coverage of animal protection worldwide. **Nonfiction:** Articles and profiles, of individuals of positive accomplishment, in any capacity that benefits animals or illustrates the intrinsic value of other species. **Tips:** No fiction or poetry. No stories about atrocities, essays on why animals have rights, or material that promotes animal abuse (hunting, fishing, trapping, and slaughter). **Queries:** Preferred. **Payment:** On acceptance.

ANIMALS

Massachusetts Society for the Prevention of Cruelty to Animals
350 S Huntington Ave., Boston, MA 02130. 617-522-7400.
Web site: www.mspca.org/animals. Quarterly. $15/year. Circ.: 50,000. Paula Abend, Editor. **Description:** Full-color publication with timely, reliable, provocative coverage of wildlife issues, pet-care topics, and animal protection concerns. **Nonfiction:** Informative, well-researched articles, to 2,500 words. **Columns, Departments:** Profiles, 800 words, on individuals who work to make life better for animals, wild or domestic, or to save habitat. Reviews, 300-500 words. **Art:** Do not send originals. **Tips:** No personal accounts or favorite pet stories. **Queries:** Required. **E-Queries:** No. **Unsolicited mss:** Accepts. **Response:** 6 weeks, SASE required. **Freelance Content:** 90%. **Rights:** 1st NA. **Payment:** On acceptance.

AQUARIUM FISH

Fancy Publications, Inc.
P.O. Box 6050, Mission Viejo, CA 92690. 949-855-8822.
E-mail: aquariumfish@fancypubs.com. Web site: www.animalnetwork.com/fish. Russ Case, Editor. **Description:** On all types of freshwater, saltwater, and pond fish. **Nonfiction:** Articles (with or without color transparencies); 2,500 words; pay varies. **Tips:** No "pet fish" stories. Send SASE for photo or writer guidelines. **Payment:** On publication.

THE BACKSTRETCH
United Throroughbred Trainers of America
P.O. Box 7065, Louisville, KY 40257-0065. 502-893-0025.
Web site: www.thebackstretch.com. Bimonthly. $25/yr. Circ.: 10,000. Kevin Baker, Editor. **Description:** Publication for the thoroughbred industry. **Nonfiction:** Feature articles, with photos, on subjects related to thoroughbred horse racing. **Payment:** On publication.

BIRD TALK
Fancy Publications, Inc.
P.O. Box 6050, Mission Viejo, CA 92690. 949-855-8822.
E-mail: birdtalk@fancypubs.com. Web site: www.animalnetwork.com/birds. Monthly. Circ.: 160,000. Melissa Kauffman, Editor. **Description:** Articles for pet bird owners (care and feeding, training, safety, outstanding personal adventures, exotic birds in their native countries, profiles of celebrities' pet birds, travel to bird parks or shows). **Nonfiction:** Good transparencies a plus; pays to $.10/word. **Queries:** Required. **Payment:** On publication.

BIRDS AND BLOOMS
Reiman Publications
5400 S 60th St., P.O. Box 991, Greendale, WI 53129-091. 414-423-0100.
E-mail: editors@birdsandblooms.com. Web site: www.birdsandblooms.com. Bimonthly. Jeff Nowak, Editor. **Description:** For people who love the beauty of their own backyard. Focuses on backyard birding and gardening. **Nonfiction:** First-person experiences from your own backyard; 200-900 words; $100-$200. **Fillers:** 50-300 words; $50-$75. **Art:** Slides or prints; $75-$300. **Tips:** Write conversationally, include tips to benefit readers, keep stories short and to the point. Submit photos. No bird rescue stories. **Queries:** Not necessary. **E-Queries:** Yes. **Unsolicited mss:** Accepts. **Response:** Queries 1-2 months, submissions 2-3 months, SASE. **Freelance Content:** 25%. **Rights:** 1st NA. **Payment:** On publication. **Contact:** Jeff Nowak.

CAT FANCY
Fancy Publications, Inc.
P.O. Box 6050, Mission Viejo, CA 92690. 949-855-8822.
E-mail: aluke@fancypubs.com. Web site: www.animalnetwork.com/cats. Monthly. Circ.: 303,000. Ellyce Rothrock, Editor. **Description:** Covers cat care, health, and grooming. **Nonfiction:** to 2,500 words; $.20/word. **Queries:** Required. **Response:** SASE required. **Payment:** On publication.

CITY & COUNTRY PETS
City & Country Publications
P.O. Box 7423, Dallas, TX 75209-0423. 214-368-3658.
E-mail: ndegan@aol.com. Web site: www.ccpets.com. Monthly. Circ.: 35,000. Nancy Egan, Editor. **Description:** Features articles on dogs, cats, birds, horses, and fish, and their owners. **Nonfiction:** Articles with universal appeal or local focus. Especially

seeks pieces about pet birds and how to train them; 600-1,000 words; $50. **Tips:** Submit query with complete manuscript by mail. Welcomes new writers. **Queries:** Preferred. **Unsolicited mss:** Accepts. **Response:** SASE required. **Rights:** Nonexclusive.

DOG FANCY

Fancy Publications, Inc.

P.O. Box 6050, Mission Viejo, CA 92690-6050. 949-855-8822.

E-mail: sbiller@fancypubs.com. Web site: www.animalnetwork.com/dogs. Monthly. Circ.: 286,000. Steven Biller, Editor. **Description:** On the care and enjoyment of all dogs, purebreds and mixed breeds. Readers are college-educated, middle-class adults interested in dog training, health, behavior, activities, and general care. **Nonfiction:** Well-written, well-researched articles on dog care, health, grooming, breeds, activities, and events; 850-1,200 words; pay varies. **Art:** Quality color slides or photos. **Tips:** No poetry, fiction, or articles in which the dog speaks as if human. Avoid tributes to dogs that have died or to beloved family pets. **Queries:** Preferred. **Freelance Content:** 80%. **Payment:** On publication.

DOG WORLD

PRIMEDIA Enthusiast Group

260 Madison Ave., Fl. 8, New York, NY 10016-2401. 917-256-2200.

E-mail: dogworld3@aol.com. Web site: www.dogworldmag.com. Monthly. $3.99/$23.70. Circ.: 60,000. Donna Marcel, Editor. **Description:** For breeders, exhibitors, hobbyists, and professionals in kennel operations, veterinary medical research, grooming, legislation, show awards, training and dog sports. **Nonfiction:** 1,500-5,000 words; pay varies. **Columns, Departments:** 1,000 words. **Tips:** Written for the serious enthusiast. Seeking in-depth science, training, and health stories. Only one human-interest piece per issue; no poetry or fiction. **Queries:** Preferred. **E-Queries:** Yes. **Unsolicited mss:** Accepts. **Response:** 4-6 months, SASE. **Freelance Content:** 25%. **Rights:** 1st. **Payment:** On publication.

EQUUS

PRIMEDIA Enthusiast Group

656 Quince Orchard Rd., Suite 600, Gaithersburg, MD 20878-1409. 301-977-3900.

E-mail: equuslts@aol.com. Web site: www.equusmagazine.com. Circ.: 148,000. Laurie Prinz, Editor. **Description:** On all breeds of horses, covering their health and care as well as the latest advances in equine medicine and research. **Nonfiction:** Articles, 1,000-3,000 words; pays $100-$400. **Tips:** Speak as one horseperson to another. **Payment:** On publication.

FERRETS

Fancy Publications, Inc.

P.O. Box 6050, Mission Viejo, CA 92690. 949-855-8822.

E-mail: ferrets@fancypubs.com. Web site: www.animalnetwork.com/critters. Bimonthly. **Description:** For all ferret lovers.

THE FLORIDA HORSE
Florida Thoroughbred Breeders' and Owners' Association
801 SW 60th Ave., Ocala, FL 34474. 352-732-8858.
Web site: www.thefloridahorse.com. Michael Compton, Editor-in-Chief. **Description:** On Florida thoroughbred breeding and racing. Also veterinary articles, financial articles, topics of general interest to horse owners and breeders. **Nonfiction:** Articles, 1,500 words; pays $200-$300. **Queries:** Preferred. **Payment:** On publication.

FRESHWATER AND MARINE AQUARIUM
The Magazine Channel, Inc.
144 West Sierra Madre, P.O. Box 487, Sierra Madre, CA 91025-0487. 626-355-6415.
E-mail: dondewey@msn.com. Web site: www.mag-web.com. Monthly. $22.00/yr.
Circ.: 53,000. Don Dewey, Publisher/Editor. **Description:** For tropical-fish enthusiasts. **Nonfiction:** How-to articles, varying lengths, on basic, semi-technical, and technical aspects of freshwater and marine aquariology; pays $50-$350. **Fillers:** $25-$75.

GOOD DOG!
Good Communications, Inc.
2900 Silverleaf Dr., P.O. Box 10069, Austin, TX 78766-1069. 512-454-6090.
E-mail: judi@gooddogmagazine.com. Web site: www.gooddogmagazine.com.
Bimonthly. Circ.: 40,000. Judi Becker, Editor. **Description:** Dog news and information, advice on food and nutrition, flea and tick products, behavior problems, training, puppies, breeds, and animal health. **Nonfiction:** Informative, fun to read. No material "written" by the dog; pay varies. **Tips:** Be informative, friendly, expert, fun. Write in third person, unless first person is more appropriate for a humor or opinion piece. **Queries:** Preferred. **Rights:** 1st electronic. **Payment:** On publication.

GREYHOUND REVIEW
National Greyhound Association
P.O. Box 543, Abilene, KS 67410-0543. 785-263-4660.
E-mail: nga@jc.net. Web site: http://nga.jc.net. Monthly. $30. Circ.: 4,000. Gary Guccione, Editor. **Description:** Covers the greyhound racing industry; trade news, special events at tracks, medical news, etc. Intended for greyhound owners, breeders, trainers, and racetrack officials. **Nonfiction:** Articles are generally how-to pieces, historical/nostalgia, or interviews. 1,000-10,000 words; $85-$150. **Art:** Photos, $85-150. **Tips:** Does not accept general interest pieces about dogs or pet ownership. Does not accept pieces about racetrack gambling. **Queries:** Preferred. **E-Queries:** Yes. **Unsolicited mss:** Accepts. **Response:** Queries 2 weeks, SASE required. **Freelance Content:** 80%. **Rights:** 1st. **Payment:** On acceptance. **Contact:** Tim Horan, Managing Editor.

GUN DOG
PRIMEDIA Enthusiast Group
6420 Wilshire Blvd., Suite 14, Los Angeles, CA 90048-5502. 323-782-2316.

Bimonthly. Circ.: 49,000. Roger Sparks, Editor-in-Chief. **Description:** On bird hunting (how-tos, where-tos, dog training, canine medicine, breeding strategy). Some fiction, humor. **Nonfiction:** Features, 1,000-2,500 words, with photos; $150-$450. **Fillers:** $150-$450 for features. **Payment:** On acceptance.

HORSE ILLUSTRATED
Fancy Publications, Inc.
P.O. Box 6050, Mission Viejo, CA 92690. 949-855-8822.
E-mail: horseillustrated@fancypubs.com. Web site: www.animalnetwork.com/horses.
Monthly. $3.50. Circ.: 200,000. Moira C. Harris, Editor. **Description:** For horse owners, covers all breeds, all disciplines. Also, medical care, training, grooming, how-to, and human interest. **Nonfiction:** How-to (horse care/owning horses), training (English and Western), profiles (industry celebrities); 2,000 words or less; $300-$400. **Fillers:** humor. **Art:** Color transparencies, prints; $60-$90; cover, $200. **Tips:** Readers are mostly women, ages 18-40, who ride and show for pleasure and are concerned about well-being of their horses. **Queries:** Preferred. **E-Queries:** Yes. **Unsolicited mss:** Accepts. **Response:** Queries 3 weeks, submissions 6 weeks, SASE required. **Freelance Content:** 15-20%. **Rights:** 1st NA. **Payment:** On publication.

HORSE & RIDER
See page 575 for full listing.
Description: Covers all aspects of competitive and recreational Western riding.

THE HORSEMEN'S YANKEE PEDLAR
83 Leicester St., North Oxford, MA 01537. 508-987-5886.
E-mail: info@pedlar.com. Web site: www.pedlar.com. Molly Johns, Editor. **Description:** About horses and horsemen in the Northeast. **Nonfiction:** News and feature-length articles, with photos; pays $2/published inch. **Payment:** On publication.

I LOVE CATS
16 Meadow Hill Ln., Armonk, NY 10123. 908-222-0990.
E-mail: yankee@izzy.net. Web site: www.iluvcats.com. Bimonthly. Circ.: 100,000. Lisa Allmendinger, Editor. **Description:** All about cats. **Fiction:** 500-700 words. **Nonfiction:** Features, to 1,000 words; pays $40-$150. **Fillers:** $25. **Art:** Photos. **Tips:** Send us your cat's picture and interesting story and we'll publish it on our site. **Queries:** Preferred. **Payment:** On publication.

MODERN FERRET
Crunchy Concepts, Inc.
P.O. Box 1007, Smithtown, NY 11787. 631-981-3574.
E-mail: mary@modernferret.com. Web site: www.modernferret.com. Bimonthly. $27.95/yr. Mary R. Shefferman, Editor. **Description:** For ferret owners, by ferret owners. **Columns, Departments:** Special People; stories about how ferrets helped you through a difficult time (injury, illness, disability, rehabilitation, addiction recovery, etc.).

MUSHING
See page 577 for full listing.
Description: Dog-driving how-tos, innovations, history, profiles, interviews, and features related to sled dogs. International audience.

PERFORMANCE HORSE
2895 Chad Dr., P.O. Box 7426, Eugene, OR 97401. 541-341-6508.
E-mail: betsylynch@performancehorse.com. Web site: www.performancehorse.com. Monthly. $24.95/yr. Circ.: 15,000. Betsy Lynch, Editor. **Description:** Seeks to help high-level western performance horse breeders, owners, trainers, and competitors to excel in the sports of cutting, reining, and working cow-horses. **Nonfiction:** Training, breeding, management, competitive strategies, how-to; for reining, cutting, and working cow-horse competition; 500-3,000 words; to $500. **Art:** Photos to accompany feature stories and articles; 35mm or larger prints or slides; to $50. **Queries:** Preferred. **E-Queries:** Yes. **Unsolicited mss:** Accepts. **Response:** 4-6 weeks, SASE. **Freelance Content:** 80%. **Rights:** FNASR. **Payment:** On publication.

PET BUSINESS
See page 318 for full listing.
Description: Covers animals and products found in pet stores.

PETLIFE
Magnolia Media Group
3451 Boston Ave., Fort Worth, TX 76116-6330. 817-560-6100.
E-mail: awilson@mmgweb.com. Web site: www.petlifeweb.com. Bimonthly. $3.95/$19.99. Circ.: 120,000. Alexis Wilson, Editor. **Description:** For pet owners and enthusiasts. **Nonfiction:** On pet health-care and nutrition, training, interviews, products, humor and general interest; 100-1,500 words; payment varies. **Columns, Departments:** Pet Health, Vet Perspective, Odd Pets, Celebrity Interviews; 100-1,000 words; payment varies. **Tips:** Most readers are women. Seeking ways to better care for animal companions; heartwarming stories about human/animal bond. **Queries:** Required. **E-Queries:** Yes. **Unsolicited mss:** Does not accept. **Response:** 3-4 weeks. **Freelance Content:** 80%. **Rights:** Worldwide. **Payment:** On publication.

PRACTICAL HORSEMAN
See page 581 for full listing.
Description: How-to articles with advice on English riding, training, and horse care.

THE RETRIEVER JOURNAL
Village Press, Inc
2779 Aero Park Dr., P.O. Box 968, Traverse City, MI 49685. 231-946-3712.
E-mail: editor@villagepress.com. Web site: www.retrieverjournal.com. $25.95/yr. Steve Smith. **Description:** On topics of interest to hunting retriever owners and breeders. **Nonfiction:** Articles, 1,500-2,200 words; pays $250 and up. **Queries:** Preferred.

TROPICAL FISH HOBBYIST
T.F.H. Publications, Inc.
211 W Sylvania Ave., Neptune, NJ 07753. 732-988-8400.
E-mail: editor@tfh.com. Web site: www.tfh.com. Monthly. $3.95/issue. Circ.: 65,000. Mary Sweeney, Editor. **Description:** Covers tropical fish and aquariums. **Nonfiction:** For beginning and experienced tropical and marine fish enthusiasts; 2,500 words; $100-$250. **Fillers:** cartoons (1/4 page vertical); $25. **Queries:** Not necessary. **E-Queries:** Yes. **Unsolicited mss:** Accepts. **Response:** 60 days, SASE. **Freelance Content:** 50%. **Rights:** All. **Payment:** On acceptance.

THE WESTERN HORSEMAN
P.O. Box 7980, Colorado Springs, CO 80933-7980. 719-633-5524.
E-mail: edit@westernhorseman.com. Web site: www.westernhorseman.com. Pat Close, Editor. **Description:** on care and training of horses; farm, ranch, and stable management; health care and veterinary medicine. **Nonfiction:** Articles, about 1,500 words, with photos; pays to $800. **Payment:** On acceptance.

YOUNG RIDER
See page 475 for full listing.
Description: About horses and children.

ARTS & ARCHITECTURE
(For music, dance, etc., see Performing Arts)

AIRBRUSH ACTION
See page 431 for full listing.
Description: Showcases innovative airbrush art.

AMERICAN ART JOURNAL
Kennedy Galleries, Inc.
730 Fifth Ave., New York, NY 10019-4105. 212-541-9600.
E-mail: aaj@kgny.com. Web site: www.kgny.com/journal. Annual. $35.00/issue. Circ.: 2,000. Jayne A. Kuchna, Editor-in-Chief. **Description:** American art of 17th through mid-20th centuries. **Nonfiction:** Scholarly articles; 2,000-10,000 words; $200-$500. **Art:** Photos. **Payment:** On acceptance.

AMERICAN INDIAN ART
7314 E Osborn Dr., Scottsdale, AZ 85251-6401. 602-994-5445.
Quarterly. Circ.: 30,000. Roanne P. Goldfein, Editorial Director. **Description:** Detailed articles on the American Indian arts: painting, carving, beadwork, basketry, textiles, ceramics, jewelry, etc. **Nonfiction:** Art by American Indian artists; 6,000-7,000 words; pay varies. **Queries:** Preferred. **Response:** 6 weeks. **Rights:** One-time. **Payment:** On publication.

ARCHITECTURE

BPI Communications, Inc.

770 Broadway, New York, NY 10003-9522. 646-654-5766.

E-mail: info@architecturemag.com. Web site: www.architecturemag.com. Monthly. $42/yr. Circ.: 67,000. Reed Kroloff, Editor-in-Chief. **Description:** Architectural design and culture. **Nonfiction:** Articles on architecture, building technology, professional practice; up to 2,000 words; $.50/word. **Queries:** Preferred.

ART & ANTIQUES

Trans World Publishing, Inc.

2100 Powers Ferry Rd., Atlanta, GA 30339. 770-955-5656.

E-mail: editor@artantiquesmag.com. Web site: www.artantiquesmag.com. 11x/year. $5/$39.95. Circ.: 190,000. Barbara S. Tapp, Editor. **Description:** For lovers of fine art and antiques. **Nonfiction:** Research articles, art and antiques in context (interiors), overviews, personal narratives; 150-1,200 words; $1/word. **Tips:** Query with resume and clips. **Queries:** Preferred. **E-Queries:** Yes. **Unsolicited mss:** Accepts. **Response:** Queries 1 month, submissions 2 months. **Freelance Content:** 90%. **Payment:** On acceptance. **Contact:** Patti Verbanas, Managing Editor.

ART-TALK

Dandick Company

P.O. Box 8508, Scottdale, AZ 85252-8508. 480-948-1799.

E-mail: arttalked@hotmail.com. 9x/yr. $18. Circ.: 40,000. John Jarvis, Editor. **Description:** A fine-art publication, for the collector. **Nonfiction:** Articles, fillers; pay varies. **Payment:** On acceptance.

THE ARTIST'S MAGAZINE

F&W Publications, Inc.

1507 Dana Ave., Cincinnati, OH 45207. 513-531-2690.

E-mail: tamedit@fwpubs.com. Web site: www.artistsmagazine.com. Monthly. $3.99/issue, $19.96/year. Circ.: 250,000. Sandra Carpenter, Editor. **Description:** Written by artists for artists. Offers instruction for professional success, on painting techniques, media and materials, design and composition, problem solving, special effects, marketing, and other business topics. **Nonfiction:** Specific art instruction (e.g., "Behind the Scenes," from start to finish: master the elements to improve your watercolor landscapes); 1,200-1,500 words; $300-$500. **Columns, Departments:** Color Corner (e.g., "Paint it Black," get those tubes of black paint out of the closet and use them to improve your paintings); 900-1,200 words; $200-$300. **Art:** Art-related cartoons; $65. **Tips:** Best opportunities include: Artist's Life and Business columns. Must be able to write from the artist's viewpoint, using the language of art. **Queries:** Preferred. **E-Queries:** No. **Unsolicited mss:** Accepts. **Response:** 90 days, SASE required. **Freelance Content:** 80%. **Rights:** FNASR. **Payment:** On publication. **Contact:** Tom Zeit, Senior Editor.

ARTS ATLANTIC

Arts Atlantic, Inc., 145 Richmond St., Charlottetown, Prince Edward Island C1A 1J1 Canada. 902-628-6138.
E-mail: artsatlantic@isn.net. Web site: www.isn.net/artsatlantic. 3x/yr. Circ.: 2,700. Joseph Sherman, Editor. **Description:** Articles and reviews, 600-3,000 words, on visual, performing, and literary arts primarily in Atlantic Canada. Also, "idea and concept" articles of universal appeal. **Queries:** Preferred.

BLACKLINES

Blacklines of Architecture, Inc.
2011 Newkirk Ave., Suite 7D, Brooklyn, NY 11226. 718-703-8000.
E-mail: kathleen@blacklines.net. Web site: www.blacklines.net. Quarterly. Scott Louis, Managing Editor. **Description:** Features black designers in architecture, interior design, construction, development, and the arts. Challenges traditional ideas and perceptions, offers a context for design and a means to exchange ideas and information. **Tips:** Send cover letter and resume for consideration, with 2-5 clips that show your ability to interview diverse subjects. **Queries:** Preferred. **E-Queries:** Yes. **Unsolicited mss:** Accepts.

BOMB

See page 386 for full listing.
Description: Interviews on artists, musicians, writers, actors, and directors.

CAMERA ARTS

P.O. Box 2328, Corrales, NM 87048. 505-899-8054.
E-mail: camartsmag@aol.com. Web site: www.cameraarts.com. Bimonthly. $22/yr. Circ.: 18,000. Steve Simmons, Editor. **Description:** The art and craft of photography in the 21st century. **Nonfiction:** Articles on photography. New writers need to send samples of previous work; 1,000-2,000 words; $.25/word. **Art:** Photographs need to be very good; pay varies. **Tips:** Before you write about a photographer, send query with samples of his/her artwork first. **Queries:** Required. **E-Queries:** Yes. **Unsolicited mss:** Accepts. **Response:** 2-8 weeks, SASE required. **Freelance Content:** 80%. **Rights:** 1st NA. **Payment:** On publication.

THE COMICS JOURNAL

Fantagraphics Books, Inc.
7563 Lake City Way NE, Seattle, WA 98115-4218. 206-524-1967.
E-mail: tcjnews@tcj.com. Web site: www.tcj.com. Monthly. $20/5 issues. Circ.: 9,000. Gary Groth, Editor. **Description:** Covers the comics medium as an art form. An eclectic mix of industry news, interviews, and reviews, for readers worldwide. **Nonfiction:** Comics news, journalism, and criticism; 200-2,000 words; $.07/word. **Queries:** Preferred. **E-Queries:** Yes. **Unsolicited mss:** Accepts. **Response:** 1-2 months, SASE. **Freelance Content:** 95%. **Payment:** On publication.

CONTEMPORARY STONE & TILE DESIGN
Business News Publishing
210 Route 4 East, Suite 311, Paramus, NJ 07652. 201-291-9001.
E-mail: michael@stoneworld.com. Web site: www.stoneworld.com. Quarterly. Michael Reis, Editor Director/Associate Publisher. **Description:** On using stone in architecture and interior design. **Nonfiction:** Articles, 1,500 words; $6/column inch. **Art:** Photos, drawings. **Payment:** On publication.

DECORATIVE ARTIST'S WORKBOOK
See page 436 for full listing.
Description: How-to articles on decorative painting.

DOUBLETAKE
55 Davis Square, Somerville, MA 02144. 617-591-9389.
E-mail: dtmag@doubletakemagazine.org. Web site: www.doubletakemagazine.org. Quarterly. $19/yr. Circ.: 40,000. Robert Coles, Editor. **Description:** Fiction, poetry, and photography devoted to revealing "extraordinary events and qualities found in everyday lives of Americans and others." **Fiction:** Realistic fiction in all its variety. **Nonfiction:** Narrative reporting or personal essays distinguished by documentary, literary, aesthetic, or reportorial excellence. **Poetry:** Yes. **Art:** Photos. **Queries:** Not necessary. **E-Queries:** No. **Unsolicited mss:** Accepts. **Response:** 3 months, SASE. **Freelance Content:** 90%. **Rights:** 1st worldwide English-language serial. **Payment:** On publication.

FASHION-FLASHBACKS MAGAZINE
Platform Publishing
P.O. Box 138, San Mateo, CA 94401. 650-344-6977.
E-mail: lanajean@groovyjuice.com. Web site: www.groovyjuice.com. Lanajean Vecchione, Editor/Publisher. **Description:** Online and in print. Focuses on fashion design and history from 1960-1979. **Nonfiction:** Articles, photos, and press releases about notable events accepted. **Columns, Departments:** Favorite Finds; Home Sewing Showcase. **Tips:** Include both your e-mail and mailing addresses. **Payment:** In copies.

FIBERARTS
See page 437 for full listing.
Description: Publication covering all types of fiber arts.

LOG HOME DESIGN IDEAS
See page 453 for full listing.
Description: For people interested in log homes.

POPULAR PHOTOGRAPHY
Hachette Filipacchi Magazines
1633 Broadway, New York, NY 10019. 212-767-6000.

E-mail: popphoto@hfnm.com. Web site: www.popphoto.com. Monthly. Circ.: 450,000. Jason Schneider, Editor. **Description:** For serious amateur photographers. **Nonfiction:** Illustrated how-to articles, 500-2,000 words. **Art:** With all photos, submit technical data (camera used, lens, film, shutter speed, aperture, lighting, etc.) to show how picture was made; pay varies. **Tips:** Interested in new, unusual phases of photography not covered previously. No general articles. **Queries:** Required. **Payment:** On acceptance.

PROFESSIONAL PHOTOGRAPHER
Professional Photographers of America, Inc.
229 Peachtree St. NE, Suite 2200 International Tower
Atlanta, GA 30303. 404-522-8600.
E-mail: cbishopp@ppa.com. Web site: www.ppmag.com. Monthly. $27/yr. Circ.: 24,000. **Description:** Since 1907, for professional photographers engaged in all types of photography.

SCULPTURE
International Sculpture Center
1529 18th St. NW, Washington, DC 20036. 202-234-0555.
E-mail: sculpt@dgsys.com. Web site: www.sculpture.org. Glenn Harper. **Description:** Articles on sculpture, sculptors, collections, books, criticism, technical processes, etc. **Nonfiction:** Pay varies. **Queries:** Preferred. **Unsolicited mss:** Accepts.

SOUTHWEST ART
Sabot Publishing, Inc.
5444 Westheimer, Suite 1440, Houston, TX 77056. 713-296-7900.
E-mail: southwestart@southwestart.com. Web site: www.southwestart.com. Monthly. $5.99/$32.00. Circ.: 65,000. Margaret L. Brown, Editor. **Description:** For collectors of Western art (about the West or created, exhibited, or sold in the West). Provides artist profiles and gallery/museum events. **Nonfiction:** On artists, collectors, exhibitions, events, dealers, history, trends in Western American art. Most interested in representational or figurative arts; 1,400 words; $600. **Art:** Slides, transparencies. **Queries:** Preferred. **E-Queries:** Yes. **Unsolicited mss:** Accepts. **Response:** Queries/submissions 4 months, SASE. **Freelance Content:** 70%. **Rights:** Exclusive worldwide. **Payment:** On acceptance.

SUNSHINE ARTIST MAGAZINE
Palm House Publishing Co.
3210 Dade Ave., Orlando, FL 32804. 407-228-9772.
E-mail: editor@sunshineartist.com. Web site: www.sunshineartist.com. Monthly. $29.95/yr. Circ.: 18,000. Leigh Duncan, Editor. **Description:** Covers national outdoor art shows, fairs, festivals. Business focus.

U.S. ART

220 S Sixth St., Suite 500, Minneapolis, MN 55402. 612-339-7571. E-mail: tmccormick@mspmag.com. 6x/yr. $32.95/yr. Circ.: 50,000. Tracy McCormick, Editor. **Description:** For collectors of reproductions, original prints and paintings. **Nonfiction:** Features and artist profiles; 1,200 words; $300-$600. **Queries:** Required. **Payment:** On acceptance.

WATERCOLOR

BPI Communications
770 Broadway, New York, NY 10003. 646-654-5220.
Quarterly. M. Stephen Doherty, Editor-in-Chief. **Description:** Features and articles on watercolor and other water media (gouache, casein, acrylic, etc.). **Nonfiction:** How-to articles, varying lengths; pay varies. **Queries:** Preferred. **Payment:** On publication.

WESTART

198 Hillmont Ave., P.O. Box 6868, Auburn, CA 95604-6868. 530-885-0969. Semimonthly. $16/yr. Circ.: 4,000. Martha Garcia, Editor-in-Chief. **Description:** Tabloid magazine featuring fine arts and crafts. **Nonfiction:** Features, 700-800 words. No hobbies; $.50/column inch. **Art:** Photos. **Queries:** Preferred. **Rights:** All. **Payment:** On publication.

ASSOCIATIONS

AOPA PILOT

Aircraft Owners and Pilots Association
421 Aviation Way, Frederick, MD 21701. 301-695-2350.
E-mail: pilot@aopa.org. Web site: www.aopa.org. Monthly. $5/issue. Circ.: 341,339. Thomas B. Haines, Editor. **Description:** Nation's leading general aviation magazine. **Fiction:** Detailed, concise, to convey message without overloading (or boring) the reader; length varies, usually 1,000-1,500 words. **Art:** 35mm color slides. **Tips:** Accepts articles relating to personal flight stories in which a lesson was learned, personal profiles of pilots, and pieces that depict an adventurous destination. Emphasis on aeronautical themes is preferred. Avoid subject matter relating to aviation history. **Queries:** Preferred. **E-Queries:** No. **Unsolicited mss:** Accepts. **Payment:** On publication.

CATHOLIC FORESTER

355 Shuman Blvd., P.O. Box 3012, Naperville, IL 60566-7012. 630-983-4900. E-mail: cofpr@aol.com. Web site: www.catholicforester.com. Bimonthly. Circ.: 97,000. Mary Anne File, Editor. **Description:** Full-color, with organizational news, general interest, fiction, and some nonfiction articles for members. Pays $.20/word. **Fiction:** Humor, children, inspirational; 500-1,500 words. **Nonfiction:** Health, fitness, parenting, financial; 500-1,500 words. **Poetry:** Inspirational, religious; 25-50

words. **Queries:** Not necessary. **E-Queries:** Yes. **Unsolicited mss:** Accepts. **Response:** Submissions 8 weeks, SASE required. **Freelance Content:** 20%. **Rights:** 1st NA. **Payment:** On acceptance. **Contact:** Patricia Baron.

ELKS
BPO Elks of the USA
425 West Diversity Parkway, Chicago, IL 60614. 773-755-4900. E-mail: elksmag@elks.org. Web site: www.elks.org/elksmag/. 10x/year. Circ.: 1,100,000. Fred D. Oakes, Editor. **Description:** General interest magazine published by the Elks fraternal organization. Typical reader is over 40 with an above-average income and living in a town of 500,000 or less. **Nonfiction:** Authoritative articles (please include sources) for lay person, varied topics: technology, science, sports, history, seasonal. Accepts material related to membership or lodge events; 1,500-2,500 words; $.20/word. **Art:** Cover art; slides, transparencies; $25 per photo. **Tips:** No fiction, travel, business, health, political or religious material, humor, filler, or poetry. Avoid queries or clips. **Queries:** Not necessary. **E-Queries:** No. **Unsolicited mss:** Accepts. **Response:** Queries 1 week, submissions 1-6 weeks, SASE required. **Freelance Content:** 30%. **Rights:** 1st NA serial. **Payment:** On acceptance.

HARVARD MAGAZINE
7 Ware St., Cambridge, MA 02138-4037. 617-495-5746. Web site: www.harvardmagazine.com. Bimonthly. $4.95/$30. Circ.: 225,000. John Rosenberg, Editor. **Description:** Articles and profiles on Harvard faculty, staff, students, and alumni. Also, features on research and teaching being conducted in this educational community. **Nonfiction:** Profiles and examples of work and research; 800-10,000 words; $300-$2,000. **Queries:** Required. **E-Queries:** Yes. **Unsolicited mss:** Accepts. **Response:** 1-2 weeks, SASE. **Freelance Content:** 50%. **Rights:** One-time. **Payment:** On publication.

KIWANIS
KIWANIS International
3636 Woodview Trace, Indianapolis, IN 46268-3196. 317-875-8755. E-mail: cjonak@kiwanis.org. Web site: www.kiwanis.org. 10x/year. $2/issue. Circ.: 240,000. Chuck Jonak, Managing Editor. **Description:** Service organization that supports children and young adults around the world. **Nonfiction:** Articles focus on a variety of topics including, family life, small business, international issues, community concerns, health/fitness, and the needs of children (especially under age 6). Also feature pieces relating to personal finance, technology, religion, education, and consumer trends. No travel pieces, interviews or profiles; 1,500-2,000 words; $400-$1,000. **Tips:** Articles are considered based on two criteria. They should have an overall subject or scope, versus relating to a specific individual, place, or event. They should be applicable to the lives of Kiwanis members and readers. **Queries:** Preferred. **E-Queries:** Yes. **Unsolicited mss:** Accepts. **Response:** Queries 3-4 weeks, submissions 2-4 weeks, SASE required. **Freelance Content:** 40%. **Rights:** First. **Payment:** On acceptance.

THE LION

300 W 22nd St., Oak Brook, IL 60523. 630-571-5466.
E-mail: rkleinfe@lionsclub.org. Web site: www.lionsclubs.org. 10x/year. Circ.: 510,000. Robert Kleinfelder, Senior Editor. **Description:** Published by Lion's Clubs International, reflecting service activities for men and women interested in voluntary community service. **Nonfiction:** Primarily photo stories of Lion's service activities; 50-2,000 words; $300-$600. **Fillers:** Family-oriented humor; 500-1,000 words; $300-$500. **Art:** Photos. **Tips:** No political, religious, or autobiographical topics. **Queries:** Preferred. **E-Queries:** Yes. **Unsolicited mss:** Accepts. **Response:** Queries 1-2 weeks, submissions 2-3 weeks, SASE required for articles. **Freelance Content:** 20%. **Rights:** All. **Payment:** On acceptance.

MANAGERS REPORT

Advantage Publishing Co., Inc.
4600 W Markam St., Little Rock, AR 72205.
E-mail: info@managersreport.com. Web site: www.managersreport.com. Monthly. $18. Circ.: 10,000. Lisa Pinder, Executive Editor. **Description:** For managers and board members of condominiums, homeowners associations, coops, and community associations. Motto is "Helping Community Associations Help Each Other." **Nonfiction:** Prefers how-to format, featuring readers and how they resolved problems in their communities; length varies; $25-$150. **Art:** Prefers photos to accompany all stories; $10. **Tips:** Welcomes new writers. **Queries:** Preferred. **E-Queries:** Yes. **Unsolicited mss:** Accepts. **Response:** SASE required. **Freelance Content:** 40%. **Rights:** 1st. **Payment:** On acceptance.

MODERN WOODMEN

Modern Woodmen of America
1701 First Ave., P.O. Box 2005, Rock Island, IL 61204-2005. 309-786-6481.
E-mail: jweaver@modern-woodmen.org. Web site: www.modern-woodmen.org. Quarterly. Circ.: 400,000. Gloria Bergh, Editor. **Description:** For members of Modern Woodmen of America, a fraternal life-insurance society. **Fiction:** Stories that promote family, patriotism, and volunteerism; 1,000 words; $100-$500. **Nonfiction:** On positive family and community life, community service, patriotism, and financial well-being; 1,000 words; $100-$500. **Tips:** Readers mostly middle-class, with children in the home. **Queries:** Not necessary. **E-Queries:** No. **Response:** Queries/submissions 4 weeks. **Freelance Content:** 20%. **Rights:** One-time. **Payment:** On acceptance.

OPTIMIST

Optimist International
4494 Lindell Blvd., St. Louis, MO 63108. 314-371-6000.
E-mail: magazine@optimist.org. Web site: www.optimist.org. Dena Hull, Editor. **Description:** On activities of local Optimist Clubs, and techniques for personal and club success. **Nonfiction:** Articles, to 1,000 words; pays from $100. **Queries:** Preferred. **Payment:** On acceptance.

RETIREMENT LIFE
See page 562 for full listing.
Description: Focuses on issues of interest to retired federal employees.

ROTARIAN
Rotary International, One Rotary Center
1560 Sherman Ave., Evanston, IL 60201-3698. 847-866-3000.
E-mail: aversanv@rotaryintl.org. Web site: www.rotary.org. Monthly. $12. Circ.:
500,000. Vince Aversano, Editor. **Description:** Personal and business interests for
Rotary members (international understanding, goodwill and peace, vocational relationships, community life, human relationships). **Nonfiction:** Business, travel,
health, education, environment, management and ethics, sciences, sports, and adventure. **Columns, Departments:** Executive Health, Book Review, Trends, Manager's
Memo, Earth Diary. **Queries:** Preferred. **Unsolicited mss:** Accepts. **Contact:**
Janice Chambers, Managing Editor.

THE TOASTMASTER
Toastmasters International
P.O. Box 9052, Mission Viejo, CA 92690-9052. 949-858-8255.
E-mail: pubs@toastmasters.org. Web site: www.toastmasters.org. Monthly. for members. Circ.: 180,000. Suzanne Frey, Editor. **Description:** On public speaking, leadership, and communication skills. **Nonfiction:** Articles on decision making, leadership, language, interpersonal and professional communication, humor, logical thinking, rhetorical devices, public speaking, profiles of great orators, etc. Payment negotiable upon acceptance; 700-2,200 words. **Queries:** Preferred. **E-Queries:** Yes.
Unsolicited mss: Accepts. **Response:** 3-4 months. **Rights:** All. **Payment:** On
acceptance.

VFW
406 W 34th St., Kansas City, MO 64111. 816-756-3390.
E-mail: pbrown@vfw.org. Web site: www.vfw.org. Monthly. $15/yr. Circ.: 1,800,000.
Richard K. Kolb, Editor. **Description:** Focuses on military history and issues relating to veterans and the military. **Nonfiction:** Articles on current foreign policy and
defense, along with all veterans' issues; 1,000 words. **Tips:** Write with clarity and simplicity, concrete detail and short paragraphs. Use active voice, and avoid flowery prose
and military jargon. **Queries:** Preferred. **Unsolicited mss:** Accepts. **Rights:**
FNASR. **Payment:** On publication.

WOODMEN
1700 Farnam St., Omaha, NE 68102. 402-342-1890.
E-mail: wow@woodmen.com. Web site: www.woodmen.com. Scott J. Darling,
Editor. **Description:** On history, insurance, family, health, science, fraternal lodge
activities, etc. **Nonfiction:** Articles; pay is negotiable. **Art:** Photos. **Queries:**
Preferred. **Payment:** On acceptance.

AUTOMOTIVE

AMERICAN MOTORCYCLIST
The American Motorcyclist Association
13515 Yarmouth Dr., Pickerington, OH 43147. 614-856-1900.
Web site: www.amadirectlink.com. Bill Wood, Editor. **Description:** Articles and fiction, to 3,000 words, on motorcycling: news coverage, personalities, tours. **Nonfiction:** Pay varies. **Art:** Photos. **Queries:** Preferred. **Response:** SASE required. **Payment:** On publication.

AUTO REVISTA
14330 Midway Rd., Suite 202, Dallas, TX 75244-3514. 972-386-0120.
E-mail: info@autorevista.com. Web site: www.autorevista.com. Weekly. Circ.: 40,000. Aaron Esslinger, Editor. **Description:** Bilingual, automotive newspaper.

AUTOMUNDO
Automundo Productions, Inc.
2960 SW 8th St., Fl. 2, Miami, FL 33135. 305-541-4198.
E-mail: editor@automundo.com. Web site: www.automundo.com. Monthly. $19.95. Circ.: 50,000. Ernesto Lanata, Editor. **Description:** Spanish-language publication for auto fans. Articles on makes, models, scenic drives, the latest technology and more.

CAR AND DRIVER
Hachette Filipacchi Magazines
2002 Hogback Rd., Ann Arbor, MI 48105-9795. 734-971-3600.
E-mail: spence1cd@aol.com. Web site: www.caranddriver.com. Monthly. Circ.: 1,300,000. Steve Spence, Managing Editor. **Description:** Profiles unusual people or manufacturers involved in cars or racing. **Nonfiction:** To 2,500 words. **Tips:** Mostly staff-written; query with clips. **Queries:** Required. **E-Queries:** Yes. **Unsolicited mss:** Does not accept. **Freelance Content:** 5%. **Payment:** On acceptance.

CAR CRAFT
PRIMEDIA Enthusiast Group
6420 Wilshire Blvd. 9th Fl., Los Angeles, CA 90048-5502. 323-782-2000.
E-mail: carcraft@primediacmmg.com. Web site: www.carcraft.com. Monthly. Circ.: 375,186. Matt King, Editor-in-Chief. **Description:** Covers high-performance street machines, drag cars, and racing events. Also includes technical pieces and action photos. **Nonfiction:** Articles and photo-features; pays from $150/page. **Payment:** On publication.

CC MOTORCYCLE NEWS
P.O. Box 808, Nyack, NY 10960-0808. 845-353-6686.
E-mail: info@motorcyclenews.cc. Web site: www.motorcyclenews.cc. Monthly. $20/yr. Circ.: 60,000. Mark Kalan, Editor. **Description:** Motorcycles news, travel, technology, and entertainment. **Fiction:** About motorcycles or on sport of motorcy-

cling, in a positive manner; 1,200 words; $10. **Nonfiction:** Motorcycle themes; up to 2,500 words; $50-$150. **Poetry:** Poems with a positive theme and tone; $10. **Fillers:** Humorous stories; $10. **Columns, Departments:** Technical on the sport of motorcycling; 800 words; $75-$100. **Tips:** Don't submit "I used to ride but . . . " stories. **E-Queries:** Yes. **Unsolicited mss:** Accepts. **Response:** 60 days, SASE. **Freelance Content:** 10%. **Rights:** All. **Payment:** On publication.

CYCLE NEWS

Cycle News, Inc.
3505 Cadillac Ave. #M, P.O. Box 5084, Costa Mesa, CA 92628-5084. 715-751-7433. E-mail: editor@cyclenews.com. Web site: www.cyclenews.com. Weekly. $38. Circ.: 37,718. Paul Carruthers, Editor. **Description:** For motorcycle enthusiasts. **Columns, Departments:** Technical articles on motorcycling; profiles and interviews with newsmakers. Pays $2/column inch. **Queries:** Preferred.

CYCLE WORLD

Hachette Filipacchi Magazines
1499 Monrovia Ave., P.O. Box 1757, Newport Beach, CA 92658-1757. 949-720-5300. E-mail: dedwards@hfmag.com. Web site: www.cycleworld.com. David Edwards, Editor-in-Chief. **Description:** News items on the motorcycle industry, legislation, and trends. **Nonfiction:** Technical and feature articles for motorcycle enthusiasts; 1,500-2,500 words; $100-$200/page. **Art:** Photos. **Queries:** Preferred. **Payment:** On publication.

EASYRIDERS

Paisano Publications, Inc.
28210 Dorothy Dr., P.O. Box 3000, Agoura Hills, CA 91376-3000. 818-889-8740. E-mail: dnichols@easyriders.net. Web site: www.easyriders.com. Monthly. $39.95. Dave Nichols, Editor. **Description:** Hard-hitting, rugged fiction, 1,200-2,000 words, that depicts bikers in a favorable light; humorous bent preferred. Pays $.10-$.25/word. **Payment:** On acceptance.

HOT BIKE

PRIMEDIA Enthusiast Group
2400 E Katella Ave. Suite 1100, Anaheim, CA 92806. 714-939-2400. E-mail: howardk@mcmullenargus.com. Web site: www.hotbikeweb.com. Monthly. $20.95. Circ.: 49,732. Howard Kelly, Editor. **Description:** On Harley-Davidson motorcycles (contemporary and antique). Event coverage on high-performance street and track and sport touring motorcycles, with emphasis on Harley-Davidsons. Geographical motorcycle features. **Nonfiction:** Articles, 250-2,500 words, with photos; pays $50-$100/printed page. **Payment:** On publication.

HOT ROD

PRIMEDIA Enthusiast Group
6420 Wilshire Blvd., Los Angeles, CA 90048-5502. 323-782-2280.

E-mail: hotrod@primediacmmg.com. Web site: www.hotrod.com. Monthly. $3.99/issue, $12/yr. Circ.: 805,035. David Freiburger, Editor. **Description:** Publication for automotive enthusiasts. Articles on street machines, rods, customs, engine buildups, nostalgia, and recent trends. **Nonfiction:** How-tos and articles on auto mechanics, hot rods, track and drag racing. Photo-features on custom or performance-modified cars. $300-$500/page. **Tips:** Freelance content is limited. Writers need either a deep sense of automotive history or hands-on technical know-how. **Queries:** Required. **E-Queries:** Yes. **Unsolicited mss:** Accepts. **Response:** SASE required. **Freelance Content:** 10%. **Rights:** All.

MOTOR TREND

PRIMEDIA Enthusiast Group
6420 Wilshire Blvd., Los Angeles, CA 90048-5515. 323-782-2220.
Web site: www.motortrend.com. Kevin Smith, Editor. **Description:** On autos, auto history, racing, events, and profiles. **Nonfiction:** Articles, 250-2,000 words, photos required; pay varies. **Queries:** Preferred. **Payment:** On acceptance.

MOTORCYCLIST

PRIMEDIA Enthusiast Group
6420 Wilshire Blvd., Los Angeles, CA 90048. 323-782-2230.
E-mail: mcmail@primediacmmg.com. Monthly. $11.97. Circ.: 500,000. Mitch Boehm, Editor-in-Chief. **Description:** Features in-depth information for motorcycle enthusiasts. Includes technical how-to stories, riding tips, gear information, motorcycle tests, and useful bike-buying advice. Purpose is for readers to maximize their riding experience. **Nonfiction:** Articles with photos; 1,000-3,000 words; $150-$300/published page. **Payment:** On publication.

OLD CARS WEEKLY

Krause Publications, Inc.
700 E State St., Iola, WI 54990. 715-445-4612.
E-mail: vanbogarta@krause.com. Web site: www.oldcarsweekly.com. Weekly. $39.98/yr. Angelo Van Bogart. **Description:** On the hobby of collectible cars and trucks (restoration, researching, company histories, collector profiles, toys, etc.). **Nonfiction:** Features, to 2,000 words; pays $.03/word. **Art:** Photos to accompany articles; $5/photo. **Queries:** Preferred.

OPEN WHEEL

3816 Industry Blvd., P.O. Box 7157, Lakeland, FL 33807-7157. 863-644-0449. Monthly. $31. Circ.: 165,000. Doug Auld, Editor. **Description:** On open-wheel drivers, races, and vehicles. **Nonfiction:** Articles, to 6,000 words; pays to $400. **Art:** Photos. **Payment:** On publication.

RIDER

2575 Vista Del Mar Dr., Ventura, CA 93001. 805-667-4100.
Monthly. Circ.: 140,000. Mark Tuttle Jr., Editor. **Description:** Covers travel, touring,

commuting, and camping motorcyclists. **Nonfiction:** to 2,000 words. $100-$750. **Art:** Color slides. **Tips:** Editorial guidelines available upon request. **Queries:** Required. **Response:** SASE. **Payment:** On publication.

ROAD KING
Hammock Publishing
3322 W End Ave., Suite 700, Nashville, TN 37203. 615-385-9745.
E-mail: editor@roadking.com. Web site: www.roadking.com. Bimonthly. $15/yr. Circ.: 250,000. Bill Hudgins, Editor-in-Chief. **Description:** An advocate for the trucking industry and its people. **Nonfiction:** New products, trends, services, technical and how-to issues, profiles, human interest articles; 1,500+ words; $100-$400. **Fillers:** cartoons; pays $50. **Art:** Color (slide, print, digital). **Tips:** Include samples of previously published work. If submitting electronically, send a hard copy for backup. No articles previously published by competitors or articles about competitors will be accepted. **Queries:** Required. **E-Queries:** Yes. **Unsolicited mss:** Accepts. **Response:** Queries 6 weeks, submissions 4 weeks, SASE. **Freelance Content:** 60%. **Rights:** 1st NA and electronic. **Payment:** On acceptance. **Contact:** Bill Hudgins.

ROAD & TRACK
Hachette Filipacchi Magazines
P.O. Box 1757, 1499 Monrovia Ave., Newport Beach, CA 92663. 949-720-5300.
E-mail: tbryant@hfmmag.com. Web site: www.roadandtrack.com. Monthly. $11.97/yr. Circ.: 740,000. Thomas L. Bryant, Editor. **Description:** For knowledgeable car enthusiasts. **Nonfiction:** Short automotive articles of a ""timeless nature"; to 450 words. **Queries:** Required. **Payment:** On publication. **Contact:** Ellida Maki.

STOCK CAR RACING MAGAZINE
PRIMEDIA Enthusiast Group
3816 Industry Blvd., Lakeland, FL 33811-1340. 863-644-0449.
E-mail: bourned@emapusa.com. Web site: www.stockcarracing.com. Monthly. $12. Circ.: 257,296. David Bourne, Editor. **Description:** For oval-track enthusiasts. **Nonfiction:** Technical automotive pieces, and profiles of interesting racing personalities. Articles on stock car drivers, races, and vehicles; up to 6,000 words; pay varies. **Payment:** On publication.

WOMAN RIDER
6420 Sycamore Ln., Maple Grove, MN 55369. 513-932-5461.
E-mail: womanrider1@aol.com. Web site: www.riderreport.com. Quarterly. Circ.: 40,000. Genevieve Schmitt, Editor. **Description:** National motorcycle magazine aimed at women. Focus is on the lifestyle side of motorcycling from a female point of view. **Tips:** Seeks people who are motorcyclist journalists who can write a mostly third person point of view. First person stories are rarely used. Submit query with bio. **Queries:** Required.

BUSINESS

ACCESSORIES
Business Journals, Inc.
185 Madison Avenue, Fl. 5, New York, NY 10016. 212-686-4412.
E-mail: irenka@busjour.com. Web site: www.busjour.com. Monthly. $35. Circ.: 20,229. Irenka Jakubiak, Editor-in-Chief. **Description:** Illustrated articles, for women's fashion-accessories buyers and manufacturers. **Nonfiction:** Profiles of retailers, designers, manufacturers; articles on merchandising and marketing. Pays $75-$200 (short articles), $200-$500 (features). **Queries:** Preferred. **Payment:** On publication.

ACROSS THE BOARD
The Conference Board, Inc.
845 Third Ave., New York, NY 10022-6679. 212-339-0214.
E-mail: atb@conference-board.org. Web site: www.acrosstheboardmagazine.com. 6x/yr. $59/yr. Circ.: 35,000. Vadim Liberman, Assistant Editor. **Description:** Features in-depth articles on business-management and social-policy issues for senior managers of global companies. Presents fresh business ideas and sharp opinions from business management experts. **Nonfiction:** Articles are thought-provoking and cover the most recent topics in business and management. 1,000-3,500 words; pay varies. **Tips:** Do not send highly technical pieces nor simple "how-to" pieces on business or market strategy. Prefers pieces that present new ideas that are applicable to real business. **Queries:** Preferred. **E-Queries:** Yes. **Unsolicited mss:** Accepts. **Response:** Queries 2-3 weeks. **Freelance Content:** 70%. **Rights:** 1st NA. **Payment:** On acceptance.

ALASKA BUSINESS MONTHLY
Alaska Business Publishing Company, Inc.
501 Northern Lights Blvd. Suite 100
P.O. Box 241288, Anchorage, AK 99524-1288. 907-276-4373.
E-mail: info@akbizmag.com. Web site: www.akbizmag.com. Monthly. $3.95/$21.95. Circ.: 10,000. Debbie Cutler, Editor. **Description:** For Alaskans and other audiences interested in the business affairs of the 49th State. Thorough, objective analysis of issues and trends affecting Alaskan businesses. **Art:** 35mm photos; pay varies. **Tips:** Query first, Alaska business topics only. Avoid generalities, need to be specific for this market. **Queries:** Preferred. **E-Queries:** Yes. **Unsolicited mss:** Accepts. **Response:** 1 month. **Freelance Content:** 80%. **Rights:** All. **Payment:** On publication.

ALTERNATIVE ENERGY RETAILER
Zackin Publications, Inc.
70 Edwin Ave., P.O. Box 2180, Waterbury, CT 06722. 800-325-6745.
E-mail: griffin@aer-online.com. Web site: www.aer-online.com. Michael Griffin, Editor. **Description:** For retailers of hearth products (appliances that burn wood, coal, pellets, and gas, also accessories and services). **Nonfiction:** Articles address top-

ics related to the hearth manufacturing and retail industry. 1,500 words. **Art:** Accepts charts, tables, and photographs to illustrate articles. **Tips:** Articles should focus on the hearth industry, but should not mention the author's company. **Queries:** Preferred. **Payment:** On publication.

AMERICAN BANKER
American Banker Group
One State Street Plaza, Fl. 26, New York, NY 10004. 212-803-8200.
E-mail: david.longobardi@tfn.com. Web site: www.americanbanker.com. David Longobardi, Editor-in-Chief. **Description:** Articles, 1,000-3,000 words, on banking and financial services, technology in banking, consumer financial services, investment products. Pay varies. **Queries:** Preferred. **Payment:** On publication.

AMERICAN SALESMAN
National Research Bureau
320 Valley St., Burlington, IA 52601. 319-752-5415.
Monthly. $48.60. Circ.: 1,500. Teresa Levinson, Editor. **Description:** For company sales reps. Articles on techniques to increase sales (case histories or public-relations articles). **Nonfiction:** Sales seminars, customer service, closing sales, competition, phone usage, managing territory, new sales concepts; 900-1,200 words. **Tips:** Freelance content limited. **Queries:** Preferred. **Unsolicited mss:** Does not accept.

ART BUSINESS NEWS
Advanstar Communications
One Park Avenue, New York, NY 10016-5802. 212-951-6646.
E-mail: jmacdonald@advanstar.com. Web site: www.artbusinessnews.com. 12x/yr. Circ.: 32,000. Julie Macdonald, Editor. **Description:** For art dealers and framers, on trends and events of national importance to the art and framing industry, and relevant business subjects. **Nonfiction:** Articles; 1,000 words; pay varies. **Queries:** Preferred. **Payment:** On publication.

BARRON'S
Dow Jones & Company, Inc
200 Liberty St., New York, NY 10281-0099. 212-416-2700.
E-mail: editors@barrons.com. Web site: www.barrons.com. Weekly. Circ.: 300,000. Edwin Finn, Publisher. **Description:** Provides information on such topics as investing, financial portfolios, industrial developments, market analysis, and electronic investing. **Tips:** Send queries to Richard Rescigno, Managing Ed. **Queries:** Preferred.

BARTENDER
Foley Publishing Corporation
P.O. Box 158, Liberty Corner, NJ 07938. 908-766-6006.
E-mail: foley@bartender.com. Web site: www.bartender.com. Quarterly. $25. Circ.: 147,000. Jaclyn W. Foley. **Description:** On liquor and bartending for bartenders, tav-

ern owners, and owners of restaurants with full-service liquor licenses. **Nonfiction:** General interest, how-to pieces, new products or bartending techniques, interviews, descriptions of unique or interesting bars. 100-1,000 words; $50-$200. **Fillers:** Humor, news, anecdotes; 25-100 words; $5-$25. **Art:** 8x10 color or B&W glossy prints. **Unsolicited mss:** Accepts. **Response:** 2 months. **Freelance Content:** 100%. **Rights:** 1st NA. **Payment:** On publication.

BICYCLE RETAILER AND INDUSTRY NEWS
Bill Communications, Inc.
310 Broadway St., Laguna Beach, CA 92651-1809. 949-376-8161.
E-mail: mgamstetter@bicycleretailer.com. Web site: www.bicycleretailer.com. 18x/yr. $45. Circ.: 13,000. Michael Gamstetter, Editor-in-Chief. **Description:** On employee management, employment strategies, and general business subjects for bicycle manufacturers, distributors, and retailers. **Nonfiction:** Articles, to 1,200 words; pays $.20/word (higher rates by assignment). **Queries:** Preferred. **Payment:** On publication.

BLACK ENTERPRISE
Earl G. Graves, Ltd.
130 Fifth Ave., Fl. 10, New York, NY 10011. 212-242-8000.
E-mail: edmonda@blackenterprise.com. Web site: www.blackenterprise.com. Monthly. $17.95/yr. Alfred Edmond, Editor-in-Chief. **Description:** Articles on money management, careers, political issues, entrepreneurship, high technology, and lifestyles for black professionals. Also profiles and interviews with successful black professionals. **Queries:** Preferred. **Payment:** On acceptance.

BOATING INDUSTRY
National Trade Publications, Inc.
13 Century Hill Dr., Latham, NY 12110-2197. 518-783-1281.
Web site: www.boating-industry.com. John Kettlewell, Senior Editor. **Description:** On recreational marine products, management, merchandising and selling, for boat dealers and marina owners/operators. **Nonfiction:** Articles; 1,000-2,500 words; pay varies. **Art:** Photos. **Queries:** Preferred. **Payment:** On publication.

BOXOFFICE
RLD Communications, Inc.
155 South El Molino Ave., Suite 100, Pasadena, CA 91101. 626-396-0250.
E-mail: editorial@boxoffice.com. Web site: www.boxoffice.com. Monthly. Circ.: 8,000. Kim Williamson, Editor-in-Chief. **Description:** Business magazine for the movie theatre industry. **Nonfiction:** Interviews, profiles, new products, technical information, and other topics in the movie theatre industry; 800-2,500 words; $.10/word. **Columns, Departments:** Insights on business of movie theaters; 600 words. **Art:** Captions required; 8x10 B&W prints; $10 maximum. **Tips:** Do not submit pieces that cover gossip or celebrity news. Content must cover the real issues and trends facing this industry. Submit proposal with resume and clip samples. **Queries:**

Preferred. **E-Queries:** Yes. **Unsolicited mss:** Accepts. **Response:** 1 month, SASE. **Freelance Content:** 15%. **Rights:** All, including electronic. **Payment:** On publication. **Contact:** Christine James.

BUSINESS START-UPS
2445 McCabe Way, Suite 400, Irvine, CA 92614.
E-mail: bsumag@entrepreneur.com. Web site: www.bizstartups.com. Karen E. Spaeder, Editor. **Description:** Entrepreneur's BizStartUps.com is an online magazine for Gen-X entrepreneurs who have started a business recently or plan to soon. **Nonfiction:** How-to, motivational/psychological, trend pieces, sales/marketing, technology, start-up money issues, management; 1,000 words; $400 and up. **Tips:** Send well-written queries with relevant clips. **Queries:** Required. **E-Queries:** Yes. **Unsolicited mss:** Does not accept. **Response:** 8-12 weeks, SASE or by e-mail. **Freelance Content:** 10%. **Rights:** FNASR. **Payment:** On acceptance.

CHIEF EXECUTIVE
The Chief Executive Group
733 Third Ave., Fl. 24, New York, NY 10017-3204. 212-687-8288.
E-mail: editorial@chiefexecutive.net. Web site: www.chiefexecutive.net. Monthly. Circ.: 42,000. C. J. Prince, Executive Editor. **Description:** Features articles for CEOs on management, financial, and global business issues. Also provides strategies and ideas for creating an effective organization. Also covers issues related to the personal side of this profession—the hopes, fears, and frustrations that are part of the job. **Nonfiction:** Articles, by CEOs; 2,000-2,500 words; pay varies. **Columns, Departments:** 750 words, on investments, corporate finance, technology, Internet, emerging markets. **Queries:** Preferred. **Payment:** On acceptance.

CHRISTIAN RETAILING
Strang Communications
600 Rinehart Rd., Lake Mary, FL 32746. 407-333-0600.
E-mail: leech@strang.com. Web site: www.christianretailing.com. Larry J. Leech II, Editor. **Description:** Covers new products, trends pertaining to books, music, video, children, and Spanish, and topics related to running a profitable Christian retail store. **Nonfiction:** Features, 1,500-2,300 words; pays $150-$400. **Payment:** On publication.

CLUB MANAGEMENT
Finan Publishing Co., Inc.
107 W Pacific Ave., St. Louis, MO 63119-3776. 314-961-6644.
E-mail: avincent@finan.com. Web site: www.club-mgmt.com. Bimonthly. $21.95/yr. Circ.: 16,702. Anne Marie Vincent, Editor. **Description:** For managers of private clubs in U.S. and abroad. Provides executives with information and resources for successful operations. **Nonfiction:** Construction/renovation profiles, insurance, technology, staffing issues, golf-course design and maintenance, special events, maintenance, food/beverage trends, guest-room amenities, spa facilities, outsourcing; 1,500-2,000 words. **Columns, Departments:** Sports, tax, law, management, membership mar-

keting, manager career perspectives, service, beverage/food trends, pools, entertainment; 1,200-1,600 words. **Queries:** Preferred. **E-Queries:** Yes. **Unsolicited mss:** Accepts. **Response:** 2-3 weeks, SASE required. **Freelance Content:** 40%. **Rights:** 1st NA, Electronic. **Payment:** On publication.

COLORADOBIZ
Wiesner Publishing, LLC
7009 S Potomac St., Suite 200, Englewood, CO 80112. 303-662-5283.
E-mail: rschwab@cobizmag.com. Web site: www.cobizmag.com. Monthly. $3.95/issue, $22.97/yr. Circ.: 17,000. Robert Schwab, Editor. **Description:** Features articles on business in Colorado. Readers are business owners and managers who work and reside in Colorado. **Nonfiction:** Articles cover market analysis, economic trends, forecasts, profiles, and individuals involved in business activities in Colorado; 650-1,200 words; $50-$400. **Art:** Accepts original color transparencies, slides, and digital art. Digital work should be scanned to 8x10, 300 dpi, CMYK in TIF format; pay varies. **Tips:** Articles must target business in Colorado. Do not send general business articles, book reviews, commentaries, syndicated work, humor, or poetry. **Queries:** Required. **E-Queries:** Yes. **Payment:** On publication.

CONVENIENCE STORE NEWS
Bill Communications
770 Broadway, Fl. 4, New York, NY 10003-9522. 646-654-4500.
E-mail: jlofstock@csnews.com. Web site: www.csnews.com. 15x/yr. Circ.: 101,095. Claire Pumplin, Editor-in-Chief. **Description:** Articles cover the convenience store and petroleum marketing industry. Provides news, research, trends, and best-practice information to convenience store and petroleum chain executives, store owners and managers, suppliers, and distributors. **Nonfiction:** Features, news items. Pay negotiated; 750-1,200 words. **Art:** Photos; pay varies. **Queries:** Preferred.

CORPORATE GIFT REVIEW
Festivities Publications, Inc.
815 Haines St., Jacksonville, FL 32206.
Quarterly. $19.95. Circ.: 5,000. Debra Paulk, Editor; Tonya Ringgold, Writer/ Researcher, Editor. **Description:** Innovative tips and how-tos on sales, marketing, management, and operations. Focuses on business gifting. Hard data, stats and research requested. Readers are college-educated, successful business owners. **Tips:** Avoid generalizations, basic content, and outdated theories. **Queries:** Not necessary. **E-Queries:** No. **Unsolicited mss:** Accepts. **Response:** 30 days, SASE required. **Freelance Content:** 50%. **Rights:** One-time. **Payment:** On publication.

THE COSTCO CONNECTION
Costco Wholesale Corporation
P.O. Box 34088, Seattle, WA 98124-1088. 425-313-6442.
E-mail: athompson@costco.com. Web site: www.costco.com. Monthly. Free. Anita Thompson, Managing Editor. **Description:** About small business and Costco mem-

bers. **Nonfiction:** Articles, 100-1,200 words; pays to $400 and up. **Queries:** Preferred. **Payment:** On acceptance.

COUNTRY BUSINESS
Emmis Publishing LP
707 Kautz Rd., St. Charles, IL 60174. 630-377-8000.
E-mail: cbiz@sampler.emmis.com. Web site: www.country-business.com. Bimonthly. Circ.: 32,000. Susan Wagner, Editor. **Description:** For retailers of country gifts and accessories. Articles feature new products and trends in giftware markets and provide business and marketing advice. **Nonfiction:** Seeking business articles on small business management and retail (e.g. finance, legal, technology, marketing, management, etc); 800-1,800 words; pay varies. **Queries:** Preferred. **E-Queries:** Yes. **Unsolicited mss:** Accepts. **Response:** SASE required. **Freelance Content:** 60%. **Payment:** On acceptance.

DOTCEO
733 Third Ave., Fl. 24, New York, NY 10017. 212-687-8288.
E-mail: editorial@chiefexecutive.net. Web site: www.dotceo.com. Christine Larson, Editor-in-Chief. **Description:** For chief executive officers of dot.com companies. Online and print versions.

EMPLOYEE SERVICES MANAGEMENT
Employee Services Management Association
2211 York Rd., Suite 207, Oak Brook, IL 60523-2371. 630-368-1280.
E-mail: reneemula@esmassn.org. Web site: www.esmassn.org. 10x/yr. Renee Mula, Editor. **Description:** For human resource professionals, employee services professionals, and ESM members. Articles cover topics in relation to recruitment and retention, becoming an employer of choice, work/life issues, employee services, wellness, management and more. **Nonfiction:** Articles, 1,200-2,500 words. **Payment:** In copies.

ENTREPRENEUR
Entrepreneur Media, Inc.
2445 McCabe Way, Suite 400, Irvine, CA 92614. 949-261-2325.
E-mail: kspaeder@entrepreneur.com. Web site: www.entrepreneur.com. Monthly. $15.97/yr. Karen Spaeder, Editor. **Description:** Features accurate, unbiased business information and innovative strategies for entrepreneurs. Covers all aspects of running and growing a successful business. **Nonfiction:** Articles and features should convey the voice of experience. Style should be informative, yet have an interesting flair. Primary purpose is to educate readers and include them in the business community; 1,000 words. **Tips:** Read sample articles by this publication before submitting work. Do not send complete manuscript. **Queries:** Required. **Response:** 8 weeks. **Payment:** On acceptance.

FLORIDA TREND
Trend Magazines, Inc.
490 First Ave. S, St. Petersburg, FL 33701. 727-821-5800.
E-mail: mhoward@floridatrend.com. Web site: www.floridatrend.com. Monthly.
Mark R. Howard, Executive Editor. **Description:** Features articles and profiles on
business, technology, the economy, etc. in the state of Florida. Targets businessmen
and other professionals who work and reside in this region. **Queries:** Required.
Response: SASE.

FLOWERS &
Teleflora
11444 W Olympic Blvd., Los Angeles, CA 90064-1549. 310-966-3590.
E-mail: flowersand@teleflora.com. Monthly. $42. Circ.: 40,000. Bruce Wright,
Editor. **Description:** How-to information for retail florists. **Nonfiction:** Articles,
500-1,500 words; pays $.50/word. **Tips:** Send clips. **Queries:** Preferred. **Payment:**
On acceptance.

GIFT BASKET REVIEW
Festivities Publications, Inc.
815 Haines St., Jacksonville, FL 32206-6050. 904-634-1902.
Web site: www.festivities-pub.com. Monthly. $39.95/yr. Circ.: 15,000. Debra Paulk,
Editor; Tonya Ringgold, Writer/Researcher. **Description:** Covers products, cutting-
edge ideas, and up-to-date industry news. **Nonfiction:** Inspiring ideas, professional
tips, industry news. **Tips:** Avoid generalizations and basic content. Submit specific
tips and how-tos on sales, marketing, management, and operations. Hard data, stats,
and research appreciated. Readers are college-educated, successful business owners.
Queries: Not necessary. **E-Queries:** No. **Response:** Submissions 30 days, SASE
required. **Freelance Content:** 50%. **Rights:** One-time. **Payment:** On publication.

GREENHOUSE MANAGEMENT & PRODUCTION
P.O. Box 1868, Fort Worth, TX 76101-1868.
David Kuack, Editor. **Description:** For professional greenhouse growers.
Nonfiction: How-tos, innovative production or marketing techniques; 500-1,800
words. **Art:** Color slides; $50-$300. **Queries:** Preferred. **Unsolicited mss:** Accepts.
Payment: On acceptance.

GREYHOUND REVIEW
See page 290 for full listing.
Description: Covers the greyhound racing industry.

GROWERTALKS
Ball Publishing
335 N River St., P.O. Box 9, Batavia, IL 60510-0009. 630-208-9080.
E-mail: beytes@growertalks.com. Web site: www.growertalks.com. Monthly. $25/yr.
Circ.: 9,500. Chris Beytes, Editor. **Description:** Seeks to help commercial green-

house growers (not florist/retailers or home gardeners) perform their jobs better. Covers trends, successes in new types of production, marketing, business management, new crops, and issues facing the industry. **Queries:** Preferred. **Payment:** On publication.

HARDWARE TRADE

Screened Porch Publishing Company

10617 France Ave. S, Suite 225, Bloomington, MN 55431. 952-944-3172.

E-mail: hrdwrtrade@aol.com. Web site: www.hardwaretrade.com. Bimonthly. Russ Goold, Editor. **Description:** Magazine for hardware manufacturers, wholesalers, and dealers. The majority of readers are owners, but some are employed. Appreciates stories on unusual hardware and home center stores or promotions throughout the nation. Also features stories about people in the hardware business and general interest stories on how readers might improve their businesses. **Nonfiction:** 800-1,000 words; no payment offered. **Queries:** Preferred.

HARVARD BUSINESS REVIEW

Harvard Business School Publishing Corp.

60 Harvard Way, Boston, MA 02163. 617-783-7410.

E-mail: hbr_editorial@hbsp.harvard.edu. Web site: www.hbsp.harvard.edu. Suzy Wetlaufer, Senior Executive Editor. **Description:** Articles cover a wide range of business related topics such as leadership, strategy, manufacturing, and teamwork. Objective is to target senior-level managers or CEOs by offering innovative, strategic ideas for managing a large organization. **Nonfiction:** Articles are written by experts whose ideas and theories for business practice and management have been tested in the real world. **Tips:** Query should be a 3-4 page summary of proposed topic. Include your objective, intended audience, and credentials in proposal. Also describe the real-world application of your proposed idea. **Queries:** Required. **Response:** 6-8 weeks, SASE.

HEARTH & HOME

Village West Publishing

P.O. Box 2008, Laconia, NH 03247-2008. 603-528-4285.

E-mail: mailbox@villagewest.com. Monthly. Richard Wright, Editor. **Description:** Profiles and interviews, with specialty retailers selling both casual furniture and hearth products (fireplaces, woodstoves, accessories, etc.). **Nonfiction:** 1,000-1,800 words; pays $150-$250. **Payment:** On acceptance.

HISPANIC BUSINESS

Hispanic Business, Inc.

425 Pine Ave., Santa Barbara, CA 93117-3709.

E-mail: jim.medina@hbinc.com. Web site: www.hispanicbusiness.com. Jim Medina, Managing Editor. **Description:** Features a variety of personalities, political agendas, and fascinating stories. **Nonfiction:** Articles; especially on technology and finance issues; $350 (negotiable). **Tips:** Has an ongoing need for experienced freelance writers.

HISPANIC MARKET NEWS

13014 N Dale Mabry Hwy. #663, Tampa, FL 33618-2808. 813-264-0560.
Monthly. Circ.: 25,000. **Description:** Newspaper for people involved with merchandising to Hispanic markets. Printed in both English and Spanish.

HOBBY MERCHANDISER

See page 439 for full listing.
Description: For the professional craft business; also general small-business advice.

HOMEBUSINESS JOURNAL

Steffen Publishing
9584 Main St., Holland Patent, NY 13354. 800-756-8484.
E-mail: kim@homebusinessjournal.net. Web site: www.homebusinessjournal.net.
Bimonthly. $18.96 (U.S.), $34 (Canada). Circ.: 50,000. Kim Lisi, Managing Editor.
Description: National publication offering quality information and advice for readers in a home business (or those seriously interested in such work) to help them thrive and enjoy working at home. **Nonfiction:** Editorials pertaining to home-based business issues: financial, family, health, etc.; 1,000 words; $75. **Tips:** Common mistake is to fail to note the difference in needs between small businesses and home businesses. Welcomes new writers. **Queries:** Required. **E-Queries:** Yes. **Unsolicited mss:** Accepts. **Response:** 3-4 weeks. **Rights:** FNASR. **Payment:** On publication.

HUMAN RESOURCE EXECUTIVE

LRP Publications Co.
747 Dresher Rd. Suite 500, P.O. Box 980, Horsham, PA 19044-0980. 215-784-0910.
E-mail: dshadovitz@lrp.com. Web site: www.hrexecutive.com. 16x/yr. David Shadovitz, Editor-in-Chief. **Description:** Profiles and case stories for executives in the HR profession. **Nonfiction:** 1,800-2,000 words; pay varies. **Queries:** Required. **Payment:** On acceptance.

INC. MAGAZINE

38 Commercial Wharf, Boston, MA 02110. 617-248-8000.
E-mail: editors@inc.com. Web site: www.inc.com. 14x/yr. $5/issue, $20/year. Circ.: 660,000. George Gendron, Editor-in-Chief. **Description:** Business magazine focusing on small, rapidly growing, privately held companies. **Nonfiction:** Helpful how-to tips on how readers can grow and manage their companies; payment varies. **Tips:** Looks for stories not specific to only one industry. Don't write about products; write about managing the company. **Queries:** Preferred. **E-Queries:** No. **Unsolicited mss:** Accepts. **Response:** 30 days; SASE required. **Freelance Content:** 3%. **Rights:** First serial. **Payment:** On publication.

INDUSTRYWEEK

Penton Media, Inc.
The Penton Media Building, 1300 E 9th St.,
Cleveland, OH 44114-2543. 216-696-7000.

E-mail: tvinas@industryweek.com. Web site: www.industryweek.com. Monthly. Circ.: 233,000. Patricia Panchak, Editor-in-Chief. **Description:** Written for a senior-level management audience, IndustryWeek delivers powerful editorial on the challenges facing today's companies. **Nonfiction:** Articles on business, management, and executive leadership; 1,800-3,000 words; pay varies. **Columns, Departments:** Executive Briefing, Emerging Technologies, Finance, Economic Trends. **Queries:** Required. **Rights:** All. **Payment:** On acceptance. **Contact:** Tonya Vinas, Managing Editor.

INSTANT & SMALL COMMERCIAL PRINTER
The Innes Publishing Co.
28100 North Ashley Circle, P.O. Box 7280, Libertyville, IL 60048. 847-816-7900.
E-mail: iscpmag@innespub.com. Web site: www.innespub.com. Monthly. Circ.: 47,787. Denise Lontz, Editor. **Description:** Covers small commercial and instant printing market. **Nonfiction:** Case histories, how-tos, technical pieces, small-business management; 1,000-5,000 words; pay negotiable. **Queries:** Preferred. **E-Queries:** Yes. **Unsolicited mss:** Accepts. **Response:** 1-6 months, SASE required. **Freelance Content:** 20%. **Payment:** On publication.

IQ
Hachette Filipacchi Magazines
460 W 34th St., Fl. 20, New York, NY 10001. 212-560-2100.
E-mail: iq-editorial@cisco.com. Web site: www.cisco.com/go/iqmagazine. Bimonthly. Circ.: 70,000. Heather Alter, Editor-in-Chief. **Description:** All about the Internet economy: news, analysis, cutting edge technology reviews, trends, resources, and more.

LATIN TRADE
95 Merrick Way, Suite 600, Coral Gables, FL 33134. 305-358-8373.
E-mail: mzellner@latintrade-inc.com. Web site: www.latintrade.com. Monthly. Circ.: 110,000. Mike Zellner, Editor-in-Chief. **Description:** For business persons in Latin America. Covers a wide variety of topics relating to trade, markets, research, technology, and investments. **Queries:** Required. **E-Queries:** Yes. **Unsolicited mss:** Does not accept. **Response:** Queries 2 weeks. **Freelance Content:** 55%. **Rights:** All. **Payment:** On publication.

LONG ISLAND BUSINESS NEWS
Dolan Media Company
2150 Smithtown Ave., Ronkonkoma, NY 11779. 631-737-1700.
E-mail: carl.corry@libn.com. Web site: www.libn.com. Weekly. Circ.: 11,000. John Kominicki, Publisher. **Description:** Covers regional economic and business news. Targeted towards the business and financial community of Nassau and Suffolk counties in New York. **Nonfiction:** Articles should cover topics such as finance, technology, health, travel, and the environment and should be aimed at business professionals in this region. $.20-$.30/word. **Queries:** Preferred. **E-Queries:** Yes. **Response:**

2 weeks, SASE required. **Rights:** One-time. **Payment:** On publication. **Contact:** Peter Mantius, Editor.

MANAGE
The National Management Association (NMA)
2210 Arbor Blvd., Dayton, OH 45439-1580. 937-294-0421.
E-mail: nma@nma1.org. Web site: www.nma1.org. Quarterly. Circ.: 30,000. Doug Shaw, Editor-in-Chief. **Description:** Covers human resource development, team building, leadership skills, ethics in the workplace, law, compensation, and technology. **Nonfiction:** On management and supervision for first-line and middle managers. 600-1,000 words; $.05/word. **Fillers:** Business management/leadership related; 500-600 words. **Queries:** Not necessary. **E-Queries:** Yes. **Unsolicited mss:** Accepts. **Response:** Queries 3 months, SASE. **Freelance Content:** 60%. **Rights:** 1st NA. **Payment:** On acceptance.

MARKETING NEWS
The American Marketing Association
311 S Wacker Dr., Suite 5800, Chicago, IL 60606-6629. 312-542-9000.
E-mail: news@ama.org. Web site: www.marketingpower.com. Biweekly. $100/yr. Circ.: 30,000. Lisa M. Keefe, Editor. **Description:** Authoritative analysis of news, current trends, and application of developments in marketing profession; also, information on American Marketing Association. **Nonfiction:** Timely articles on advertising, sales promotion, direct marketing, telecommunications, consumer and business-to-business marketing, and market research; 800-1,200 words; $.75/word. **Tips:** Due to potential conflict of interest, no news stories written by marketing professionals. **Queries:** Preferred. **E-Queries:** Yes. **Unsolicited mss:** Does not accept. **Response:** Queries 6-8 weeks, submissions 2-4 months. **Freelance Content:** 30%. **Rights:** 1st, all media. **Payment:** On acceptance.

THE MEETING PROFESSIONAL
Meeting Professionals International (MPI)
4455 LBJ Freeway, Suite 1200, Dallas, TX 75244-5903. 972-702-3000.
E-mail: publications@mpiweb.org. Web site: www.mpiweb.org. Monthly. $50 U.S., $69 outside U.S. Circ.: 30,000. **Description:** For meeting professionals. **Tips:** Only works with published writers. Submit query by e-mail; send resume and clips by mail (with SASE). **Queries:** Preferred. **E-Queries:** Yes. **Unsolicited mss:** Accepts. **Response:** 2 weeks, SASE required. **Freelance Content:** 50%. **Rights:** All. **Payment:** On acceptance.

MODERN PHYSICIAN
Crain Communications, Inc.
360 N Michigan Ave., Fl. 5, Chicago, IL 60601. 312-649-5350.
E-mail: moddoc@crain.com. Web site: www.modernphysician.com. Monthly. $45. Circ.: 31,500. Joseph Conn, Editor. **Description:** Covers business and management news for physician executives. **Nonfiction:** Business stories about how medical prac-

tices are changing; 1,000-1,500 words; $.50/word. **Tips:** No product or clinical stories. **Queries:** Required. **E-Queries:** Yes. **Unsolicited mss:** Accepts. **Response:** Varies, SASE required. **Freelance Content:** 30%. **Rights:** All. **Payment:** On acceptance.

MUTUAL FUNDS MAGAZINE

Time, Inc.
Time Life Building, Rockefeller Center, New York, NY 10020. 212-552-1212.
E-mail: letters@mfmag.com. Web site: www.mfmag.com. Monthly. $14.95. Circ.: 830,000. Norman Pearlstine, Editor-in-Chief. **Description:** Seeking writers experienced in covering mutual funds for the print media. Send resume and clips. **Queries:** Preferred.

NEEDLEWORK RETAILER

See page 441 for full listing.
Description: Trade magazine for needlework industry.

NETWORK JOURNAL

The Network Journal Communications, Inc.
139 Fulton St., Suite 407, New York, NY 10038. 212-962-5414.
E-mail: editors@tnj.com. Web site: www.tnj.com. Monthly. Circ.: 15,000. Njeru Waithaka, Editor. **Description:** Small-business, personal finance, and career management for African-American small-business owners and professionals. **Nonfiction:** Profiles of entrepreneurs; how-to pieces; articles on sales and marketing, managing a small business, and personal finance; 1,200-1,500 words; $150. **E-Queries:** Yes. **Freelance Content:** 25%. **Rights:** All. **Payment:** On publication.

NSGA RETAIL FOCUS

National Sporting Goods Association
1601 Feehanville Dr., Suite 300, Mt. Prospect, IL 60056-6035. 847-296-6742.
E-mail: info@nsga.org. Web site: www.nsga.org. Bimonthly. members only. Circ.: 3,000. Larry Weindruch, Editor. **Description:** Official publication of NSGA. Covers industry news, consumer trends, management and store operations, and new product development for retailers, wholesalers, manufacturers, and members of NSGA. **Queries:** Required. **E-Queries:** Yes. **Unsolicited mss:** Does not accept. **Response:** Queries 1 week, SASE. **Freelance Content:** 15%. **Rights:** 1st NA and electronic. **Payment:** On publication.

PARTY & PAPER RETAILER

107 Mill Plain Rd., Suite 204, Danbury, CT 06811. 203-730-4090.
E-mail: editor@partypaper.com. Web site: www.partypaper.com. Monthly. $39. Circ.: 20,000. Jacqueline Shanley, Editor-in-Chief. **Description:** Features retail success stories, gives tips on creative display designs, and offers practical retail advice to party and stationery store owners. Articles cover employee management, marketing, advertising, promotion, finance, and legal matters. **Nonfiction:** Articles, factual anecdotes appreciated; 800-1,800 words; pay varies. **Tips:** Send query with published clips.

Queries: Preferred. **Response:** Queries 2 months. **Freelance Content:** 90%. **Rights:** 1st NA. **Payment:** On publication.

PET BUSINESS
Macfadden Communications Group,
333 Seventh Ave., Fl. 11, New York, NY 10001. 212-979-4800.
Web site: www.petbusiness.com. 14x/yr. $49.97/yr. David Litwak, Editor-in-Chief.
Description: Covers animals and products found in pet stores. Offers research findings, legislative/regulatory actions, and business and marketing tips/trends. **Nonfiction:** Brief, well-documented articles; pays $.10/word, $20/photo. **Payment:** On publication.

PET PRODUCT NEWS
Fancy Publications, Inc.
P.O. Box 6050, Mission Viejo, CA 92690. 949-855-8822.
E-mail: miturri@fancypubs.com. Web site: www.petproductnews.com. Monthly. Circ.: 30,000. Marilyn Iturri, Editor. **Description:** Audience is pet-store retailers and managers of such operations, large and small. Includes pet and pet-product merchandising, retailer tips, industry news and opinion. **Nonfiction:** Articles with photos; 1,200-1,500 words; $250 and up. **Tips:** Do not send fiction or pet stories. Articles should target pet store owners, product suppliers/distributors, and product manufacturers. **Queries:** Required. **E-Queries:** Yes. **Unsolicited mss:** Does not accept. **Response:** Queries 2 weeks. **Freelance Content:** 70%. **Rights:** FNASR. **Payment:** On publication.

PHOTO MARKETING
Photo Marketing Association International
3000 Picture Place, Jackson, MI 49201. 517-788-8100.
Web site: www.photomarketing.com. Bonnie Gretzne, Editor. **Description:** For owners and managers of camera/video stores or photo processing labs. **Nonfiction:** Business articles; 1,000-3,500 words; pays $150-$500, extra for photos. **Queries:** Preferred. **Unsolicited mss:** Does not accept. **Payment:** On acceptance.

POOL & SPA NEWS
Hanley-Wood, LLC
4160 Wilshire Blvd., Los Angeles, CA 90010. 323-801-4900.
E-mail: plakdawalla@hanley-wood.com. Web site: www.poolspanews.com. 2x/month. Circ.: 16,012. Pervin Lakdawalla, Editor-in-Chief. **Description:** Provides industry news and feature articles to builders, retailers, technicians, and other pool and spa professionals. Articles cover design, construction, renovation, equipment repair, merchandising, etc. Also provides annual directory, product listings, and technical manuals. **Queries:** Preferred. **Payment:** On publication.

PRO
Cygnus Business Media
P.O. Box 803, Fort Atkinson, WI 53538. 920-563-6388.
E-mail: noel.brown@cygnuspub.com. Web site: www.promagazine.com. Noel Brown, Editor-in-Chief. **Description:** On business management for owners of lawn-maintenance firms. **Nonfiction:** Articles, 1,000-1,500 words; pays $150-$250. **Queries:** Preferred. **Payment:** On publication.

QUICK PRINTING
Cygnus Business Media
445 Broad Hollow Rd., Melville, NY 11747. 631-845-2700.
E-mail: editor@quickprinting.com. Web site: www.quickprinting.com. Gerald Walsh, Editor. **Description:** For owners and operators of quick print shops, copy shops, and small commercial printers. How to make their businesses more profitable (including photos and figures). Also, articles on using computers and peripherals in graphic arts applications. **Nonfiction:** Articles, 1,500-2,500 words; pays from $150. **Tips:** No generic business articles. Will not be buying much unsolicited material in 2002. **Payment:** On publication.

RETAIL SYSTEMS RESELLER
Edgell Communications
4 Middlebury Blvd., Randolph, NJ 07869. 973-252-0100.
E-mail: dbreeman@edgellmail.com. Web site: www.retailsystemsreseller.com. Monthly. Circ.: 20,000. Daniel Breeman, Managing Editor. **Description:** Covers news, products, technology and services for value-added resellers and system integrators selling into the retail channel. Focuses retail point-of-sale and payment processing, extending into backend systems and retail supply chain. **Nonfiction:** 600-1,500 words; $400-$800. **Tips:** Seeking writers who can write for this specific market and know how to dig as a reporter. No syndicated articles or general business ideas. **E-Queries:** Yes. **Unsolicited mss:** Accepts. **Response:** 60-90 days, SASE required. **Freelance Content:** 80%. **Rights:** 1st NA. **Payment:** On publication.

REVOLUTION
Haymarket Group
220 Fifth Ave., Fl. 14, New York, NY 10001. 212-471-8700.
E-mail: stovin.hayter@revolutionmagazine.com.
Web site: www.revolutionmagazine.com. Stovin Hayter, Editor. **Description:** Articles feature information that provides marketers and senior business people with an understanding of digital media. Also evaluates what products and services they can best use in their companies.

SALES & MARKETING MANAGEMENT
Bill Communications, Inc.
770 Broadway, New York, NY 10003. 646-654-7606.
E-mail: cgalea@salesandmarketing.com. Web site: www.salesandmarketing.com.

Christine Galea, Managing Editor. **Description:** Provides useful information for sales and marketing executives. Articles focus on techniques for better job performance, networking with colleagues, the value of continued education, and the most recent research and marketing tools. **Nonfiction:** Features and short articles; pay varies. **Tips:** Seeks practical "news you can use." **Queries:** Preferred. **Payment:** On acceptance.

SAN FRANCISCO BUSINESS TIMES
American City Business Journals
275 Battery St., Suite 940, San Francisco, CA 94111. 415-989-2522.
E-mail: ssymanovich@bizjournals.com. Web site: www.bizjournals.com/sanfrancisco. Steve Symanovich, Editor. **Description:** Features articles that focus on business, commerce, and technology in the San Francisco Bay area. **Nonfiction:** Limited freelance market; pays $250-$350. **Queries:** Preferred. **Payment:** On publication.

SIGN BUILDER ILLUSTRATED
Simmons-Boardman Publishing Corporation
323 Clifton St. Suite #7, Greenville, NC 27858. 252-355-5806.
E-mail: jeff@signshop.com. Web site: www.signshop.com. Bimonthly. Jeff Wooten, Editor. **Description:** On the sign industry. **Nonfiction:** How-to articles and editorials, 1,500-2,500 words; pays $300-$500. **Payment:** On acceptance.

SIGN BUSINESS
National Business Media, Inc.
P.O. Box 1416, Broomfield, CO 80038-1416. 303-469-0424.
E-mail: sbeditor@nbm.com. Web site: www.nbm.com/signbusiness. Monthly. Circ.: 18,400. Regan Dickinson, Executive Editor. **Description:** For the sign business. **Nonfiction:** Prefers step-by-step, how-to features; pays $150-$300. **Payment:** On publication.

SOFTWARE
See page 611 for full listing.
Description: For corporate systems managers and MIS personnel.

SOUVENIRS, GIFTS, AND NOVELTIES
Kane Publications
7000 Terminal Sq., Suite 210, Upper Darby, PA 19082. 610-734-2420.
E-mail: souvnovmag@aol.com. Tony De Masi, Editor. **Description:** On retailing and merchandising gifts, collectibles, and souvenirs for managers at zoos, museums, hotels, airports, and souvenir stores. **Nonfiction:** Articles, 1,500 words; pays $.12/word. **Payment:** On publication.

T & D MAGAZINE
See page 327 for full listing.
Description: On workplace learning, career development, and job performance.

TANNING TRENDS
3101 Page Ave., P.O. Box 1630, Jackson, MI 49204-1630. 517-784-1772.
E-mail: joe@smarttan.com. Web site: www.smarttan.com. Monthly. Joseph Levy.
Description: On small businesses and skin care for tanning salon owners. Seeks to help salon owners move to the "next level" of small business ownership. Focuses on business principles, emphasis on public relations and marketing. **Nonfiction:** Scientific pro-tanning articles, "smart tanning" pieces. Query for profiles. Pay varies. **Payment:** On publication.

TEA & COFFEE TRADE JOURNAL
Lockwood Publications, Inc.
26 Broadway Fl. 9M, New York, NY 10004. 212-391-2060.
E-mail: editor@teaandcoffee.net. Web site: www.teaandcoffee.net. Monthly. $42/year. Jane P. McCabe, Editor. **Description:** On issues of importance to the tea and coffee industry. **Nonfiction:** Articles, 3-5 pages; pays $.20/word. **Queries:** Preferred. **Payment:** On publication.

TEENPRENEUR
Earl G. Graves, Ltd.
130 5th Ave., Fl. 10, New York, NY 10011. 212-242-8000.
6x/year. Circ.: 4,000. **Description:** For African-American teens interested in business.

TEXAS TECHNOLOGY
Power Media Group
13490 TI Boulevard, Suite 100, Dallas, TX 75243. 972-690-6222.
E-mail: lkline@ttechnology.com. Web site: www.thetechmag.com. Monthly. $30. Circ.: 700,000. Laurie Kline, Editor. **Description:** Articles address the latest innovations in technology and the ways it affects our lives. Also covers news in technology, consumer trends, new products, and more. Targets general consumers as well as technology and computer professionals. **Nonfiction:** Technology trends, new products information, features on obtaining and retaining employees in high-tech sector; 1,200-3,500 words; $200-$400. **Tips:** Not interested in company or product-specific stories. Seeking stories on trends and general topics to appeal to both business and mainstream audience. Welcomes new writers! **Queries:** Required. **E-Queries:** Yes. **Unsolicited mss:** Accepts. **Response:** Queries 3 weeks, submissions 2 months. **Freelance Content:** 95%. **Rights:** 1st print and electronic. **Payment:** On publication.

TEXTILE INDUSTRIES
Billian Publishing, Inc.
2100 Powers Ferry Rd., Atlanta, GA 30339. 770-955-5656.
E-mail: editor@textileindustries.com. Web site: www.textileworld.com. Monthly. $57/yr. Circ.: 33,000. **Description:** Serves textile executives in their dual roles as technologists and managers. **Nonfiction:** Technical textile articles; 1,500 words; pay negotiable. **Art:** Slides, prints, electronic. **Queries:** Required. **E-Queries:** Yes. **Response:** 4 weeks. **Freelance Content:** 5%. **Rights:** All. **Payment:** On publication.

TOURIST ATTRACTIONS AND PARKS

Kane Publications

7000 Terminal Sq., Suite 210, Upper Darby, PA 19082. 610-734-2420.
E-mail: tapmag@aol.com. Scott C. Borowsky, Editor-in-Chief. **Description:** On successful management of parks, entertainment centers, zoos, museums, arcades, fairs, arenas, and leisure attractions. **Nonfiction:** Articles, 1,500 words; pays $.12/word. **Queries:** Preferred. **Payment:** On publication.

TREASURY & RISK MANAGEMENT

Wicks Business Information

52 Vanderbilt Ave., Suite 514, New York, NY 10017. 212-557-7480.
E-mail: pwechsler@treasuryandrisk.com. Web site: www.treasuryandrisk.com. 9x/year. Patricia Wechsler, Editor. **Description:** On management for corporate treasurers, CFOs, and vice-presidents of finance. **Nonfiction:** Articles, 200-3,000 words; pays $.50-$1.00/word. **Tips:** Seeking freelance writers. **Queries:** Preferred. **Payment:** On acceptance.

UPSIDE

731 Market St., Fl. 2, San Francisco, CA 94103-2005. 415-489-5600.
E-mail: eperkins@upside.com. Web site: www.upside.com. Monthly. Circ.: 300,000. Emily Perkins, Managing Editor. **Description:** On business and technology. **Nonfiction:** Short articles about computer and technology businesses, profiles of successful business people. **Queries:** Required. **Unsolicited mss:** Does not accept.

VENDING TIMES

Vending Times, Inc.

1375 Broadway Fl. 6, New York, NY 10018-7001. 212-302-4700.
E-mail: editor@vendingtimes.net. Web site: www.vendingtimes.com. 14x/yr. $35/yr. Circ.: 17,400. Timothy Sanford, Editor. **Description:** Features articles on the business issues of companies providing vending, refreshment, hospitality, and catering services. Target audience includes independent and chain vending operators, caterers, suppliers, distributors, and other individuals involved in the food service industry. **Nonfiction:** Articles address the latest industry news and events. They also cover financial issues and list trade association events. **Queries:** Preferred. **Payment:** On acceptance.

VIRGINIA BUSINESS

See page 527 for full listing.
Description: Covers the business scene in Virginia.

WALL STREET JOURNAL SUNDAY

Dow Jones & Co., Inc.

200 Liberty St., Fl. 9, New York, NY 10281-1003. 212-416-2000.
Weekly. Circ.: 5,000,000. **Description:** Sunday insert to more than 15 major-market newspapers.

WOMEN IN BUSINESS

American Business Women's Association
9100 Ward Parkway, P.O. Box 8728, Kansas City, MO 64114-0728. 816-361-6621.
E-mail: kisaacson@abwa.org. Web site: www.abwa.org. Bimonthly. $12/yr (members), $20/yr (others). Kathleen Isaacson, Editor. **Description:** Focuses on leadership, education, networking support, and national recognition. Helps business women of diverse occupations to grow personally and professionally. **Nonfiction:** How-to business features for working women, ages 35-55 (trends, small-business ownership, self-improvement, retirement issues). Profiles of ABWA members only; 500-1,000 words; $.20/word. **E-Queries:** Yes. **Unsolicited mss:** Accepts. **Freelance Content:** 2%. **Payment:** On publication.

WORKING WOMAN

Working Mother Media
135 W 50th St., Fl. 16, New York, NY 10020-1201. 212-445-6100.
E-mail: editors@workingwoman.com. Web site: www.workingwoman.com. **Description:** On business, finance, and technology. Readers are high-level executives and entrepreneurs looking for newsworthy information about the changing marketplace and its effects on their businesses and careers. **Nonfiction:** Articles, 200-1,500 words; pays from $250. **Tips:** No profiles of executives or entrepreneurs. Seeking trend pieces targeting a specific industry, showing how it is affected by new technology, business practices, market situations. **Queries:** Preferred. **Unsolicited mss:** Does not accept. **Payment:** On acceptance.

CAREER & PROFESSIONAL DEVELOPMENT

AMERICAN CAREERS

Career Communications, Inc.
6701 W 64th St., Overland Park, KS 66202. 913-362-7788.
Web site: www.carcom.com. 2x/yr. Circ.: 500,000. Mary Pitchford, Editor. **Description:** Classroom career-development magazine for elementary, middle, and high school students. Introduces varied careers in different industries that offer realistic opportunities. **Nonfiction:** Articles on resumes, interviews, developing marketable work skills, and making career decisions. Also provides information on a variety of occupations, salaries, and the education/training needed to obtain employment; 300-1,000 words; $100-$450. **Tips:** Send query letter with resume and writing samples. Seeking stories that reflect racial and gender equality. **Queries:** Required. **E-Queries:** No. **Unsolicited mss:** Does not accept. **Response:** Queries 1 month, SASE not needed. **Freelance Content:** 50%. **Rights:** All, work for hire. **Payment:** On acceptance.

BLACK COLLEGIAN

iMinorites, Inc.
909 Poydras St., Fl. 36, New Orleans, LA 70130. 504-523-0154.

E-mail: robert@black-collegiate.com. Web site: www.black-collegian.com. Semi-annually (Oct. & Feb.). Circ.: 112,000. Robert G. Miller, Editor. **Description:** Articles focus on the opportunities and experiences of African-American college students and recent graduates in relation to careers and self-development. Provides entry-level career opportunities and methods on preparing to enter the work force. Also read by faculty, career counselors, and placement directors. **Nonfiction:** Most pieces focus on professional life, but the culture and experiences of African-American collegians is also explored by offering information on sports, personalities, history, interviews/profiles, opinions, and current events; 900-1,900 words; $100-$500. **Tips:** Personalize your article; use "you" rather than the impersonal "college students." Most articles are assigned; will consider ideas with a brief, detailed query letter to the editor. **Queries:** Required. **E-Queries:** Yes. **Unsolicited mss:** Does not accept. **Response:** Queries 60 days. **Freelance Content:** 90%. **Rights:** 1st. **Payment:** On publication.

CAMPUS.CA

5397 Eglinton Ave. W, Suite 101, Toronto, Ontario M9C 5K6 Canada. 416-928-2909. E-mail: turnbull@campus.ca. Web site: www.campus.ca. Quarterly. Lesley Turnbull, Editor. **Description:** Articles to inform, entertain, and educate the student community in Canada. **Nonfiction:** Pay varies. **Queries:** Preferred.

CAREER WORLD

General Learning Communications
900 Skokie Blvd., Suite 200, Northbrook, IL 60062-4028. 847-205-3000.
E-mail: crubenstein@glcomm.com. Web site: www.glcomm.com. 6x/school yr. Carole Rubenstein, Senior Editor. **Description:** Educational magazine aimed at junior and senior high school students to help prepare them for college and making career choices. **Nonfiction:** Gender-neutral articles about specific occupations, career awareness, and development. Topics: evaluating interests, setting goals, career planning, college and tech choices, getting hired, hot jobs, etc. **Tips:** Send query, with resume and clips. **Queries:** Required. **E-Queries:** Yes. **Unsolicited mss:** Does not accept. **Response:** Queries 1-6 months. **Freelance Content:** 80%. **Rights:** All. **Payment:** On publication.

CAREERS AND THE COLLEGE GRAD

Brass Ring Diversity
170 High St., Waltham, MA 02454. 888-222-3678.
E-mail: diversity@brassring.com. Web site: www.brassringdiversity.com. Annual. Kathleen Grimes, Publisher. **Description:** Career-related articles, for junior and senior liberal arts students. No payment. Publishes a number of other specialty magazines for the college market. **Nonfiction:** 1,500-2,000 words. **Fillers:** Career-related fillers; 500 words. **Art:** Line art, color prints. **Queries:** Preferred.

CAREERS & COLLEGES

E.M. Guild, Inc.
989 Avenue of the Americas, Fl. 6, New York, NY 10018. 800-964-0763.

E-mail: staff@careersandcolleges.com. Web site: www.careersandcolleges.com. Quarterly. $5.95. Circ.: 500,000. Don Rauf, Editor-in-Chief. **Description:** Guides high-school juniors and seniors through college admissions process, financial aid, life skills, and career opportunities. **Nonfiction:** Interesting, new takes on college admission, scholarships, financial aid, work skills, and careers; 800-2,500 words; pay varies. **Queries:** Required. **E-Queries:** No. **Unsolicited mss:** Does not accept. **Response:** 1 month, SASE. **Freelance Content:** 80%. **Rights:** 1st NA (for one year). **Payment:** On publication. **Contact:** Traci Mosser, Senior Editor.

CIRCLE K MAGAZINE
Circle K International
3636 Woodview Trace, Indianapolis, IN 46268-3196. 317-875-8755.
E-mail: ckimagazine@kiwanis.org. Web site: www.circlek.org/magazine. 5x/year. $6/year. Circ.: 15,000. Amy Wiser, Executive Editor. **Description:** Official publication of Circle K International (world's largest collegiate service organization). Articles are targeted to college students who are committed to community service and leadership development. **Nonfiction:** Articles are both serious and light nonfiction and focus on community leadership and service. Articles that center on college lifestyle, such as trends, music, health, travel, and technology, are also accepted; 1500-2,000 words; $150-$400. **Tips:** Focus on interviews and research, not personal insights. Use illustrative examples and expert quotes. **Queries:** Preferred. **E-Queries:** Yes. **Unsolicited mss:** Accepts. **Response:** Queries 2 months. **Freelance Content:** 60%. **Rights:** FNASR. **Payment:** On acceptance.

COLLEGE RECRUITER.COM NEWSLETTER
3722 W 50th St., Suite 121, Minneapolis, MN 55410-2016. 952-848-2211.
E-mail: steven@collegerecruiter.com. Web site: www.collegerecruiter.com. Semi-weekly. Steven Rothberg, Publisher. **Description:** Online newsletter offering techniques on seeking employment for students and college graduates. Topics include work skills, professional roles and expectations, and resume/interviewing tips. **Tips:** No payment for articles, but will include byline and link to website of author's choice.

DIRECT AIM
Communications Publishing Group
3100 Broadway, 660 Pen Tower, Kansas City, MO 64111. 816-960-1988.
Quarterly. Michelle Paige, Editor. **Description:** Articles provide college and career information to Black and Hispanic students who attend colleges, universities, or technical/vocational institutions. **Fiction:** Accepts fictional stories that are historical, cultural, humorous, etc.; 500-2,000 words; pay varies. **Nonfiction:** Topics include career preparation, college profiles, financial-aid sources, and interviews with college students from across the U.S. Also accepts pieces on general interest, personal experience, travel, humor, or new products/trends for college students; 750-2,000 words; pay varies. **Fillers:** Humor, anecdotes, newsbreaks; 25-250 words; $25-$100. **Queries:** Required. **Response:** Queries 1 month. **Freelance Content:** 80%. **Rights:** Reprint, work-for-hire.

FLORIDA LEADER

Oxendine Publishing, Inc.
412 NW 16th Ave., P.O. Box 14081, Gainesville, FL 32604-2081. 352-373-6907.
E-mail: vince@studentleader.com. Web site: www.floridaleader.com. 3x/year.
Vincent Alex Brown, Editor. **Description:** Articles focus on leadership, college success, and career growth in Florida and the Southeast. Targets Florida high school
and college students who participate in student government, academic societies,
honor societies, community-service organizations, and other student activities.
Payment: On publication.

HISPANIC TIMES

P.O. Box 579, Winchester, CA 92596. 909-926-2119.
Web site: www.hispanictimescareers.com. Circ.: 35,000. **Description:** Magazine for
Hispanic professionals and college students. Focus is on careers, businesses, and
employment opportunities.

HTC: CANADA'S HI-TECH CAREER JOURNAL

BrassRing Canada, Inc.
4-355 Harry Walker Parkway, Newmarket, Ontario L3Y 7B3 Canada. 905-773-7405.
E-mail: htcjinfo@brassring.com. Web site: www.brassring.ca. 6x/year. Free (Canada),
$19.95 (US). Circ.: 80,000. Lynn Lievonen, Editor-in-Chief. **Description:** For
Canadian IT and engineering professionals; covers industry trends and issues affecting work environment and employment opportunities in the industry. **Nonfiction:**
Hi-tech employment issues in Canada; 750 words. **Tips:** Welcomes new writers. Send
brief outline of proposed article; must be written exclusively for hi-tech with
Canadian content, except for annual supplement, "Uncle Sam Wants You" (employment opportunities and issues in U.S.). **Queries:** Required. **E-Queries:** Yes.
Unsolicited mss: Accepts. **Response:** 24 hours by e-mail, SASE (for mailed
queries). **Freelance Content:** 50%. **Rights:** 1st. **Payment:** On publication.

MINORITY ENGINEER

Equal Opportunity Publications, Inc.
445 Broad Hollow Rd., Suite 425, Melville, NY 11747. 631-421-9421.
E-mail: jschneider@eop.com. Web site: www.eop.com. 3 issues/year. Circ.: 17,000.
James Schneider, Editor. **Description:** Targets engineering, computer-science, and
information technology students and professionals who are Black, Hispanic, Native
American, and Asian American. **Nonfiction:** Career opportunities, job-hunting tech-
niques, new technologies, role-model profiles and interviews; 1,000-2,000 words;
$.10/word. **Queries:** Preferred. **E-Queries:** Yes. **Unsolicited mss:** Accepts.
Response: 2 weeks; SASE required. **Freelance Content:** 60%. **Rights:** First.
Payment: On publication.

STUDENT LEADER

Oxendine Publishing, Inc.
412 NW 16th Ave., P.O. Box 14081, Gainesville, FL 32604-2081. 352-373-6907.

E-mail: john@studentleader.com. Web site: www.studentleader.com. Semiannual. John Lamothe, Associate Editor. **Description:** Articles discuss leadership issues and career and college success for outstanding students who are involved in campus leadership activities. **Nonfiction:** Articles should cover leadership issues and should demonstrate useful methods for running an organization effectively and ethically. Sample topics include promotion, raising money, recruiting volunteers, communicating with administration and the media, etc.; 800-1,000 words; $50-$100. **Tips:** Include quotes from faculty, corporate recruiters, current students, and recent alumni. **Queries:** Required. **Unsolicited mss:** Accepts. **Payment:** On publication.

SUCCEED

Ramholtz Publishing, Inc.
1200 South Ave., Suite 202, Staten Island, NY 10314. 718-761-4800.
E-mail: editorial@collegebound.net. Web site: www.classesusa.com/succeedonline. Quarterly. $15/yr. Circ.: 155,000. Gina LaGuardia, Editor-in-Chief. **Description:** Articles appeal to readers interested in lifelong learning, recommitment to education, and career transition. Includes database of graduate programs and continuing education classes. **Columns, Departments:** On financial advice, career-related profiles, news, book and software reviews, continuing education resources; 400-600 words; $75-$100. **Tips:** Query with 3 writing clips. Manuscripts must be accompanied by a source list. Use attributable expert advice and real-life scenarios. **Queries:** Preferred. **E-Queries:** Yes. **Unsolicited mss:** Accepts. **Response:** Queries 6-8 weeks, SASE. **Freelance Content:** 70%. **Rights:** 1st, 2nd. **Payment:** 30 days upon publication.

T & D MAGAZINE

American Society for Training & Development
1640 King St., Alexandria, VA 22313. 703-683-7250.
E-mail: submissions@astd.org. Web site: www.astd.org. Monthly. $85/yr. Circ.: 70,000. Haidee E. Allerton, Editor. **Description:** The official publication of ASTD. Articles cover workplace learning, career development, and job performance. Targets ASTD members and other training and development professionals. **Nonfiction:** Articles should cover topics relating to career development, fun in the workplace, e-learning, workplace training, etc.; 2,000-5,000 words; $.80/word. **Tips:** Submit query with one-page outline before sending completed manuscript. Do not send speeches, theory, opinions, dissertations, internal reports, or articles that promote a product or service. **Queries:** Required. **E-Queries:** Yes. **Unsolicited mss:** Accepts. **Response:** 4-6 weeks. **Freelance Content:** 10%. **Rights:** All.

UNIQUE OPPORTUNITIES

455 S Fourth Ave., Suite 1236, Louisville, KY 40202. 502-589-8250.
E-mail: tellus@uoworks.com. Web site: www.uoworks.com. Bimonthly. $5/$25. Circ.: 80,000. Mollie V. Hudson, Editor. **Description:** Articles offers guidance to physicians on career development by providing the economic, business, legal, and career-related issues involved in finding and running a practice. **Nonfiction:** Articles should be geared toward helping physicians navigate their careers. Sample topics include

securing a position, making decisions, financial/legal matters, practice management, etc.; 1,500-3,500 words; $.50-$.75/word. **Queries:** Required. **E-Queries:** Yes. **Unsolicited mss:** Accepts. **Response:** Queries 2 months, SASE. **Freelance Content:** 45%. **Rights:** FNASR. **Payment:** On acceptance.

COMPUTERS

C/C++ (USERS JOURNAL)
CMP United Business Media
1601 W 23rd St., Suite 200, Lawrence, KS 66046-2700. 785-841-1631.
E-mail: apettle@cmp.com. Web site: www.cuj.com. Amy Pettle, Managing Editor. **Description:** Features articles and source code on C/C++ and Java programming for professional programmers. **Nonfiction:** Articles should be practical, "how-to" guides that provide sample source code. Algorithms, libraries, frameworks, class designs, book reviews, tutorials, and other special techniques that solve programming problems are also accepted; 800-2,500 words (80-300 lines of code). **Tips:** Send proposal with 1-2 paragraph abstract, 1-page outline, and brief bio. Prefers to receive proposals and mss via e-mail. Check Call For Papers for immediate story needs. **Queries:** Preferred. **E-Queries:** Yes. **Unsolicited mss:** Does not accept. **Response:** 2-4 weeks. **Payment:** On publication.

CLOSING THE GAP
526 Main St., P.O. Box 68, Henderson, MN 56044. 507-248-3294.
E-mail: info@closingthegap.com. Web site: www.closingthegap.com. Bimonthly. Megan Turek, Managing Editor. **Description:** Newspaper that focuses on micro-computer products that serve the needs of persons with disabilities. Features articles that cover how technology enhances the education, vocation, recreation, mobility, communication, etc., of these individuals. **Nonfiction:** Articles should cover all aspects of assistive technology and new products in this industry. Non-product related articles also used; 800-1,000 words. **Tips:** Keep the language level the same as for a daily newspaper (third-grade level). Use "person first" wording. Refer to the person first followed by disability, e.g., the boy with a disability. **E-Queries:** Yes. **Rights:** All.

COMPUTER GRAPHICS WORLD
PennWell Corporation
98 Spit Brook Rd., Nashua, NH 03062-5737.
E-mail: phill@pennwell.com. Web site: www.cgw.com. Monthly. Circ.: 67,000. Phil LoPiccolo, Editor-in-Chief. **Description:** On computer graphics technology and its use in science, engineering, architecture, film and broadcast, and interactive entertainment. Computer-generated images. **Nonfiction:** Articles, 800-3,000 words; pays $600-$1,200. **Queries:** Preferred. **Payment:** On acceptance.

COMPUTOR EDGE MAGAZINE

3655 Ruffin Rd., Suite 100, P.O. Box 83026, San Diego, CA 92123. 858-573-0315. E-mail: editor@computoredge.com. Weekly. $35. Circ.: 525,000. Patricia Smith, Editor. **Description:** Features non-technical, entertaining articles on computer hardware and software for both average users and experts. **Nonfiction:** Feature articles and columns cover a variety of topics including online systems, the Internet, Macintosh systems, common computer problems, etc.; 1,000 words; pay varies. **Columns, Departments:** Beyond Personal Computing, Mac Madness, I Don't Do Windows; 750-900 words. **Queries:** Required. **E-Queries:** Yes. **Unsolicited mss:** Does not accept. **Response:** 1-3 months. **Freelance Content:** 80%. **Rights:** 1st NA.

HTC: CANADA'S HI-TECH CAREER JOURNAL

See page 326 for full listing.

Description: Covers industry trends, work environment and employment opportunities for Canadian IT and engineering professionals.

IEEE COMPUTER GRAPHICS AND APPLICATIONS

IEEE Computer Society

10662 Los Vaqueros Circle, Los Alamitos, CA 90720.

E-mail: cga@computer.org. Web site: www.computer.org/cga. Bimonthly. Circ.: 7,000. Robin Baldwin, Group Managing Editor. **Description:** Peer-reviewed publication that covers the field of computer graphics and applications. **Nonfiction:** Articles should show how computer graphics solve real world problems; 3200-5500 words; $400 per page. **Tips:** New writers should submit resume and writing samples. **Response:** 1 week. **Rights:** All.

MACWORLD COMMUNICATIONS

Mac Publishing LLC

301 Howard St., Fl. 15, San Francisco, CA 94105. 415-243-0505.

E-mail: rlepage@macworld.com. Web site: www.macworld.com. Rick LePage, Editor-in-Chief. **Description:** Covers all aspects of Macintosh computers. **Nonfiction:** Reviews, news, consumer, how-to articles, varying lengths, related to Macintosh computers. Query with clips only. Pays $150-$3,500. **Queries:** Preferred. **Unsolicited mss:** Does not accept. **Payment:** On acceptance.

NETWORK WORLD

118 Turnpike Rd., Southborough, MA 01772-9108. 508-460-3333.

E-mail: jdix@nww.com. Web site: www.nwfusion.com. John Dix, Editor-in-Chief. **Description:** About applications of communications technology for management level users of data, voice, and video communications systems. **Nonfiction:** Articles, to 2,500 words; pay varies. **Payment:** On acceptance.

PEI (PHOTO ELECTRONIC IMAGING)
Professional Photographers of America, Inc.
229 Peachtree St. NE, Suite 2200 International Tower
Atlanta, GA 30303. 404-522-8600.
Web site: www.peimag.com. Cameron Bishopp, Executive Editor. **Description:** On electronic imaging, computer graphics, desktop publishing, pre-press and commercial printing, and multimedia. **Nonfiction:** Articles on professional imaging trends and techniques, hardware/software reviews, and the latest advances in electronic imaging technology; 1,000-3,000 words; pay varies. **Tips:** By assignment only. **Queries:** Required. **Payment:** On publication.

TECHNOLOGY & LEARNING
See page 352 for full listing.
Description: For K-12 teachers on uses of computers/technology in the classroom.

TECHNOLOGY REVIEW
Massachusetts Institute of Technology
One Main St., Fl. 7, Cambridge, MA 02142. 617-475-8000.
E-mail: john.benditt@technologyreview.com. Web site: www.techreview.com. John Benditt, Editor-in-Chief. **Description:** General-interest articles on technology and innovation. **Nonfiction:** Pay varies. **Queries:** Preferred. **Payment:** On acceptance.

WIRED
See page 482 for full listing.
Description: Lifestyle magazine for the "digital generation."

YAHOO! INTERNET LIFE
See page 335 for full listing.
Description: Consumer magazine on Internet, lifestyle, and cultural topics.

CONSUMER & PERSONAL FINANCE

THE AMERICAN SPECTATOR
Gilder Publications, LLC
291A Main St., Great Barrington, MA 01230.
E-mail: spectatoreditorial@gilder.com. Web site: www.spectator.org. Monthly. Circ.: 130,000. Richard Vigilante, Editor. **Description:** Technical, political, and cultural guide for the investor in the new economy. **Nonfiction:** Pay varies. **Tips:** Query with article clips. Sample copy, $5.95. **Queries:** Required. **E-Queries:** No. **Unsolicited mss:** Does not accept. **Response:** 30 days. **Freelance Content:** 50%. **Rights:** All.

CONSUMER REPORTS
101 Truman Ave., Yonkers, NY 10703. 914-378-2000.
Web site: www.consumerreports.org. Monthly. $26. Circ.: 4,100,000. David Heim,

Managing Editor. **Description:** Award-winning journalistic research on health, personal finance, and matters of public policy. Also, independent product-testing reports. **Tips:** Mostly staff-written, except for occasional back-of-book columns on health or personal finance. **Queries:** Required. **E-Queries:** Yes. **Unsolicited mss:** Accepts. **Response:** 1-3 weeks, SASE required. **Freelance Content:** 1%. **Rights:** All. **Payment:** On acceptance.

CONSUMERS DIGEST

8001 N Lincoln Ave., 6th Fl., Skokie, IL 60077. 847-763-9200.
E-mail: busdev@consumersdigest.com. Web site: www.consumersdigest.com.
Bimonthly. $2.99/issue, $15/year. Circ.: 1,200,000. John Manos, Editor. **Description:** Helps readers make lifestyle, purchasing, investment, and personal financial decisions to benefit their daily lives. Thoroughly and objectively evaluates a wide range of brand-name products and services. **Nonfiction:** Consumer issues. **Tips:** Also covers how to get the best value for key services: doctors, lawyers, hospitals, financial advisers, etc. No "how-to" articles. **Queries:** Required. **E-Queries:** No. **Unsolicited mss:** Does not accept. **Rights:** All. **Payment:** On publication. **Contact:** Jim A. Gorzelany.

CONSUMER REPORTS FOR KIDS ONLINE

101 Truman Ave., Yonkers, NY 10703-1057. 914-378-2985.
Web site: www.zillions.org. **Description:** An online version of *Consumer Reports* for kids, ages 8-14.

KIPLINGER'S PERSONAL FINANCE

Kiplinger Washington Editors, Inc.
1729 H Street NW, Washington, DC 20006-3904. 202-887-6400.
Web site: www.kiplinger.com. Monthly. Ted Miller, Editor. **Description:** Covers personal finance issues. **Nonfiction:** Articles on personal finance (i.e., buying insurance, mutual funds). **Queries:** Required. **Payment:** On acceptance.

THE MONEYPAPER

1010 Mamaroneck Ave., Mamaroneck, NY 10543. 914-381-5400.
E-mail: moneypaper@moneypaper.com. Web site: www.moneypaper.com. Monthly. $90/yr. Vita Nelson, Publisher/Editor. **Description:** Financial news and money-saving ideas. Brief, well-researched articles on personal finance, money management, saving, earning, investing, taxes, insurance, and related subjects. **Nonfiction:** Pays $75 for articles. **Tips:** Include resume and writing sample. Seeking information about companies with dividend reinvestment plans. **Queries:** Preferred. **Payment:** On publication.

PRIME TIMES

See page 562 for full listing.
Description: For credit union members 50 years and older.

YOUR MONEY
8001 N Lincoln Ave., Fl. 6, Skokie, IL 60077-2403. 847-763-9200.
Web site: www.consumersdigest.com. Bimonthly. Circ.: 500,000. Dennis Fertig, Editor. **Description:** For the general reader on investment opportunities and personal finance. **Nonfiction:** Informative, jargon-free personal finance articles; to 2,000 words; $.60/word. **Tips:** Send clips for possible assignments. **Queries:** Required. **Payment:** On acceptance. **Contact:** Brooke Hessel, Assistant Editor.

CONTEMPORARY CULTURE

AMERICAN DEMOGRAPHICS
PRIMEDIA Business Magazines & Media
470 Park Ave. S, New York, NY 10020. 212-332-6300.
E-mail: editors@demographics.com. Web site: www.demographics.com. Monthly. Circ.: 22,400. Seema Nayyar, Editor. **Description:** Articles, 500-2,000 words, on four key elements of a consumer market (size, needs and wants, ability to pay, and how it can be reached). With specific examples of how companies market to consumers. Readers include marketers, advertisers, and planners. **Queries:** Preferred.

AMERICAN SCHOLAR
1606 New Hampshire Ave., NW, Washington, DC 20009. 202-265-3808.
E-mail: scholar@pbk.org. Web site: www.pbk.org. Quarterly. $6.95/issue. Circ.: 25,000. Anne Fadiman, Editor. **Description:** For intelligent people who love the English language. **Nonfiction:** By experts, for general audience; 3,000-5,000 words; $500. **Poetry:** Highly original; up to 33 lines; $50. **Queries:** Preferred. **E-Queries:** Yes. **Unsolicited mss:** Accepts. **Response:** 2-4 months, SASE required. **Freelance Content:** 100%. **Rights:** First. **Payment:** On acceptance.

AMERICAN VISIONS
1101 Pennsylvania Ave NW, Suite 820, Washington, DC 20004. 202-347-3820.
E-mail: editor@avs.americanvisions.com. Web site: www.americanvisions.com. Bimonthly. Circ.: 125,000. Joanne Harris, Editor. **Description:** Focuses on African-American culture with special emphasis on the arts. **Nonfiction:** Articles 500-2,500 words; pays $100-$600. **Columns, Departments:** Columns; 1,000 words; pay varies. **Queries:** Required. **Freelance Content:** 75%. **Payment:** On publication.

AMERICAS
See page 362 for full listing.
Description: Features on Latin America and the Caribbean.

BRICK
Box 537, Stn Q, Toronto, Ontario M4T 2M5 Canada.
E-mail: info@brickmag.com. **Description:** Literary journal for creative nonfiction. **Queries:** Not necessary. **Response:** up to 3 months.

CHRONICLES
The Rockford Institute
928 N Main St., Rockford, IL 61103. 815-964-5054.
E-mail: tri@rockfordinstitute.org. Web site: www.chroniclesmagazine.org. Scott Richert. **Description:** "A Magazine of American Culture." Articles and poetry that display craftsmanship and a sense of form.

COMMONWEAL
See page 535 for full listing.
Description: Catholic publication covering public affairs, religion, and the arts.

GEIST
1014 Homer St., Suite 103, Vancouver
British Columbia V6B 2W9 Canada. 604-681-9161.
E-mail: geist@geist.com. Web site: www.geist.com. Quarterly. **Description:** "Canadian Magazine of Ideas and Culture." **Nonfiction:** Creative nonfiction, 200-1,000 words; excerpts, 300-1,500 words, from works in progress; long essays and short stories; 2,000-5,000 words; pay varies. **Tips:** Strongly prefers Canadian content. **Queries:** Preferred. **Payment:** On publication.

HISPANIC
See page 366 for full listing.
Description: General-interest magazine on issues affecting Hispanic communities.

JUXTAPOZ
High Speed Productions, Inc.
1303 Underwood Ave., San Francisco, CA 94124-3308. 415-822-3083.
E-mail: editor@juxtapoz.com. Web site: www.juxtapoz.com. Jamie O'Shea, Editor.
Description: About modern arts and culture.

LOLLIPOP
P.O. Box 441493, Boston, MA 02144-0034. 617-623-5319.
E-mail: scott@lollipop.com. Web site: www.lollipop.com. Quarterly. Circ.: 20,000. Scott Hefflon, Editor. **Description:** On music and youth culture. Fiction, essays, and "edgy" commentary. Reviews and interviews related to underground culture. **Nonfiction:** To 2,000 words; pays $25 (for anything over 1,000 words). **Art:** Photos, drawings; $25. **Queries:** Preferred.

NATIVE PEOPLES
See page 370 for full listing.
Description: Portrays the arts and lifeways of the native peoples of the Americas.

PARABOLA
See page 490 for full listing.
Description: Features essays and retellings of traditional myths and fairy tales.

ROLLING STONE
See page 496 for full listing.
Description: Magazine of American music, culture, and politics.

SOUTHWEST REVIEW
Southern Methodist University
P.O. Box 750374, Dallas, TX 75275-0374. 214-768-1037.
E-mail: swr@mail.smu.edu. Web site: www.southwestreview.org. Quarterly. $6/issue.
Elizabeth Mills, Editor. **Description:** Varied, wide-ranging content of adult interest:
contemporary affairs, history, folklore, fiction, poetry, literary criticism, art, music,
and theater. **Fiction:** 3,500-7,000 words; $100-$300. **Nonfiction:** 3,500-7,000 words;
$100-$300. **Poetry:** 1 page (generally); $50-$150. **Queries:** Not necessary.
E-Queries: No. **Unsolicited mss:** Accepts. **Response:** Submissions 3 months,
SASE required. **Rights:** 1st NA. **Payment:** On publication.

THIRSTY EAR MAGAZINE
Thirsty Ear Productions
P.O. Box 29600, Santa Fe, NM 87592-9600. 505-473-5723.
E-mail: thirstyearmag@yahoo.com. Web site: www.thirstyearmagazine.com. 5x/year.
$15. Circ.: 50,000. Michael Koster, Editor. **Description:** Covers music, art, and cul-
ture. **Fiction:** Short stories with music, arts, or American culture themes; up to 2,500
words; $75-$100. **Nonfiction:** Articles on "non-tuxedo" music; also reviews; 300-500
words. **Columns, Departments:** Opinion; 800-1,000 words; $100. **Queries:**
Required. **E-Queries:** Yes. **Unsolicited mss:** Does not accept. **Response:** Varies.
Freelance Content: 80%. **Rights:** 1st NA. **Payment:** On publication.

TROIKAMAGAZINE.COM
P.O. Box 1006, Weston, CT 06883. 203-319-0873.
E-mail: eric@troikamagazine.com. Web site: www.troikamagazine.com. Daily. Circ.:
400,000. Jonathan P. Atwood, Senior Editor. **Description:** Cutting-edge, online contemporary culture forum. Informs, entertains, and enlightens; a global voice in a rapidly globalizing world. **Fiction:** All types; varied length; $200 and up. **Nonfiction:**
Features on arts, health, science, human interest, international interests, business,
leisure, ethics. For educated, affluent baby-boomers, seeking to balance personal
achievements, family commitments, and community involvement; varied length;
$200 and up. **Poetry:** All types; varied length;. **Queries:** Not necessary. **E-Queries:**
Preferred. **Unsolicited mss:** Accepts; "Please send—we respond to all!" **Response:**
Queries 10 days, submissions to 3 months, SASE. **Freelance Content:** 100%.
Rights: Worldwide, 1st NA. **Payment:** 90 days from publication. **Contact:**
submit@troikamagazine.com.

UTNE READER
Lens Publishing Co.
1624 Harmon Pl., Fawkes Bldg., Minneapolis, MN 55403-1906. 612-338-5040.
E-mail: editor@utne.com. Web site: www.utne.com. Bimonthly. $4.99/issue

$19.97/year. Circ.: 232,000. Jay Waljasper, Editor. **Description:** Offers alternative ideas and culture, reprinting articles selected from over 2,000 alternative media sources. **Nonfiction:** Short pieces and reviews; 300-1,000 words. Provocative perspectives, analysis of art and media, down-to-earth news and resources; compelling people and issues. **Queries:** Preferred. **E-Queries:** Yes. **Unsolicited mss:** Accepts. **Response:** 4-6 weeks, SASE. **Freelance Content:** 20%. **Rights:** Nonexclusive worldwide. **Payment:** On publication.

YAHOO! INTERNET LIFE
Ziff Davis Media, Inc.
28 E 28th St., Fl. 13, New York, NY 10016. 212-503-4790.
E-mail: marshall_vickness@ziffdavis.com. Web site: www.yil.com. 13 issues/year. $3.99/issue, $14.97/year. Circ.: 1.1 million. Barry Golson, Editor. **Description:** Consumer magazine on Internet, lifestyle, cultural topics. **Queries:** Not necessary. **Unsolicited mss:** Accepts. **Freelance Content:** 30%. **Payment:** On publication. **Contact:** lisa_ronis@ziffdavis.com.

CURRENT EVENTS & POLITICS

AMERICAN EDUCATOR
See page 342 for full listing.
Description: Articles and essays on trends and news in education.

AMERICAN LEGION
P.O. Box 1055, Indianapolis, IN 46206-1055. 317-630-1200.
E-mail: magazine@legion.org. Web site: www.legion.org. John B. Raughter, Editor. **Description:** Covers current world affairs, public policy, and subjects of contemporary interest. **Nonfiction:** 750 to 2,000 words; pay negotiable. **Queries:** Preferred. **Payment:** On acceptance.

BRIARPATCH
2138 McIntyre St., Regina, Saskatchewan S4P 2R7 Canada. 306-525-2949.
E-mail: briarpatch.mag@sk.sympatico.ca. Web site: www.briarpatchmagazine.com. 10x/year. $3/$24.61. Debra Brin, Editor. **Description:** Progressive Canadian newsmagazine with a left-wing political slant. **Nonfiction:** Articles on politics, women's issues, environment, labor, international affairs for Canadian activists involved in social-change issues. Also, short reviews of recent books, CDs. **Tips:** Use journalistic style, with quotes from involved people. Looking for hard-hitting, thought-provoking stories. **Queries:** Preferred. **E-Queries:** Yes. **Unsolicited mss:** Accepts. **Response:** Immediately. **Freelance Content:** 100%. **Rights:** None. **Payment:** In copies.

CALIFORNIA JOURNAL
2101 K St., Sacramento, CA 95816. 916-444-2840.
E-mail: edit@statenet.com. Web site: www.californiajournal.com. Monthly. $39.95.

Circ.: 11,000. David Lesher, Editor. **Description:** Features nonpartisan reports on California government and politics. **Nonfiction:** 1,000-2,500 words; $400-$1,200. **Queries:** Required. **E-Queries:** Yes. **Unsolicited mss:** Does not accept. **Response:** 1-2 weeks, SASE. **Freelance Content:** 30%. **Rights:** All. **Payment:** On publication.

CAMPAIGNS & ELECTIONS

1414 22nd St., NW, Washington, DC 20037. 202-887-8530.
E-mail: rfaucheux@campaignline.com. Web site: www.campaignline.com. Ron Faucheux, Editor-in-Chief. **Description:** On strategies, techniques, trends, and personalities of political campaigning. **Nonfiction:** Features, 700-4,000 words; campaign case studies, 1,500-3,000 words; how-tos, 700-2,000 words, on aspects of campaigning; in-depth studies, 700-3,000 words, on public opinion, election results, and political trends. **Columns, Departments:** 100-800 words, for Inside Politics. **Payment:** In copies.

CHRISTIAN SOCIAL ACTION

See page 533 for full listing.
Description: Features on the role and involvement of the church in social issues.

COLUMBIA JOURNALISM REVIEW

Columbia University
2950 Broadway #207 Journalism Bldg., New York, NY 10027-7004. 212-854-1881.
E-mail: cjr@columbia.edu. Web site: www.cjr.org. Bimonthly. $25.95/yr. Circ.: 28,000. Gloria Cooper, Deputy Executive Editor. **Description:** Amusing mistakes in news stories, headlines, photos, etc. (original clippings required), for "Lower Case." Pays $25. **Payment:** On publication.

COMMENTARY

See page 534 for full listing.
Description: On contemporary issues, Jewish affairs, religious thought, and culture.

THE CRISIS

See page 364 for full listing.
Description: A journal of civil rights, politics, African-American history and culture.

FOREIGN SERVICE JOURNAL

2101 E St. NW, Washington, DC 20037. 202-338-4045.
E-mail: journal@afsa.org. Web site: www.afsa.org/fsj/index.html. Monthly. $3.50/issue. Circ.: 12,000. Bob Guldin, Editor. **Description:** Covers foreign affairs and the U.S. Foreign Service. **Fiction:** Stories with overseas settings, for fiction issue (summer), submit in April; 3,000 words; $250. **Nonfiction:** On foreign policy and international issues, for Foreign Service and diplomatic community. **Columns, Departments:** Short travel pieces about foreign scene, person, place, incident; 600-700 words; $100. **Tips:** Knowledge of foreign service concerns essential. **Queries:**

Not necessary. **Unsolicited mss:** Accepts. **Response:** Queries 1 month. **Freelance Content:** 25%. **Payment:** On publication.

FREE INQUIRY
P.O. Box 664, Amherst, NY 14226-0664. 716-636-7571.
E-mail: tflynn@centerforinquiry.com. Web site: www.secularhumanism.com. $6.95/issue. Circ.: 30,000. Thomas Flynn, Editor. **Description:** Edited from the secular humanist viewpoint, which holds that life should be guided by science and reason. **Fiction:** 1,500-3,000 words. **Nonfiction:** 1,500-3,000 words. **Poetry:** ½ to 1 page. **Fillers:** 100-300 words. **Columns, Departments:** 800-1,200 words. **Art:** PDF; $50-$100. **Tips:** Write for sophisticated, well-educated audience interested in academic research, politics, religion, current events in U.S. and abroad. **Queries:** Not necessary. **E-Queries:** Yes. **Unsolicited mss:** Accepts. **Response:** Queries 1 week, submissions 6 weeks, SASE required. **Freelance Content:** 10%. **Rights:** 1st NA.

HARPER'S
Harper's Magazine Foundation
666 Broadway, Fl. 11, New York, NY 10012-2317. 212-420-5720.
E-mail: editorial@harpers.org. Web site: www.harpers.org. Monthly. $18/yr. Circ.: 213,000. Lewis H. Lapham, Editor. **Description:** On politics, literary, cultural, scientific issues. **Fiction:** Will consider unsolicited manuscripts; SASE required. **Nonfiction:** Very limited market; 2,000-5,000 words. **Queries:** Required. **Response:** SASE required.

THE HOMELESS REPORTER NEWS-SHEET
P.O. Box 1053, Dallas, TX 75221-1053.
Bill Mason, Editor. **Description:** An insider's view and dialogue on solving homelessness. Seeks articles and essays on ways to solve the socioeconomic problems of homelessness and poverty. Also publishes human-interest love stories set in that context. **Nonfiction:** Articles, essays; 300-1,500 words. **Queries:** Preferred. **E-Queries:** No. **Unsolicited mss:** Accepts. **Payment:** In copies.

IDEAS ON LIBERTY
The Foundation for Economic Education
30 S Broadway, Irvington, NY 10533. 914-591-7230.
E-mail: fee@fee.org. Web site: www.fee.org. Sheldon Richman, Editor. **Description:** On economic, political, and moral implications of private property, voluntary exchange, and individual choice. **Nonfiction:** Articles, to 3,500 words; pays $.10/word. **Payment:** On publication.

IN THESE TIMES
2040 N Milwaukee Ave., Fl. 2, Chicago, IL 60647. 773-772-0100.
E-mail: itt@inthesetimes.com. Web site: www.inthesetimes.com. Biweekly. $2.50/issue, $36.95/year. Circ.: 20,000. Joel Bleifuss, Editor. **Description:** Seeks to inform and analyze popular movements for social, environmental, and economic jus-

tice in the U.S. and abroad. **Nonfiction:** News reporting, op-eds, and book reviews on left politics, the environment, human rights, labor, etc; 500-3,000 words; $.12/word. **Tips:** Avoid excessive editorializing; strong news reporting and writing skills more valued. **Queries:** Preferred. **E-Queries:** Yes. **Unsolicited mss:** Accepts. **Response:** 6-8 weeks. **Freelance Content:** 90%. **Rights:** Reprint. **Payment:** On publication. **Contact:** Craig Aaron.

JUNIOR SCHOLASTIC
See page 468 for full listing.
Description: On-the-spot reports from countries in the news.

LATINO LEADERS
See page 369 for full listing.
Description: Profiles the lives of successful Hispanic-American leaders.

MIDSTREAM
633 Third Ave., Fl. 21, New York, NY 10017.
E-mail: info@midstream.org. Web site: www.midstream.org. 8x/year. $3/$21/year. Circ.: 8,000. Leo Haber, Editor. **Description:** Zionist publication with content on political U.S. and Israel culture, literature, book reviews, religion, and poetry. Varied points of view presented. **Fiction:** Stories on Jewish themes; 1,500-4,000 words; $.05/word. **Nonfiction:** Jewish (Zionist) political, cultural, literary, religious themes; 1,500-6,000 words; $.05/word. **Poetry:** Jewish themes; 20 lines; $25/poem. **Tips:** Readers mostly scholarly, Israel-oriented professionals. **Queries:** Not necessary. **E-Queries:** No. **Unsolicited mss:** Accepts. **Response:** up to 3 months, SASE. **Freelance Content:** 20%. **Rights:** 1st. **Payment:** On publication.

MIDWEST QUARTERLY
Pittsburgh State University
Pittsburgh, KS 66762. 316-235-4369.
E-mail: midwestq@pittstate.edu. Web site: www.pittstate.edu/engl/midwest.htm. Quarterly. $15. Circ.: 550. James B. M. Schick, Editor. **Description:** Scholarly articles on varied subjects of current interest. **Nonfiction:** Scholarly articles on contemporary academic and public issues; 18-20 pages. **Poetry:** up to 70 lines. **Queries:** Preferred. **E-Queries:** Yes. **Unsolicited mss:** Accepts. **Response:** Queries 1 week, submissions 4-6 months, SASE required. **Payment:** none.

MONTHLY REVIEW
122 W 27th St., New York, NY 10001. 212-691-2555.
E-mail: mrmag@monthlyreview.org. Web site: www.monthlyreview.org. 11x/year. $4/issue, $29/year. Circ.: 7,000. John Bellamy Foster, Editor. **Description:** Covers political, economic, international affairs, current events, from an independent socialist perspective. **Nonfiction:** Analytical articles on politics and economics; articles, 3,000-4,000 words, $50; reviews, 1,500-2,000 words, $25. **Tips:** Avoid pieces that date quickly, as it takes 6 months to publish. Looking for solid Marxist analysis. **Queries:**

Not necessary. **E-Queries:** Yes. **Unsolicited mss:** Accepts. **Response:** Submissions, 8 weeks. **Freelance Content:** 95%. **Payment:** On publication.

MOTHER JONES

731 Market St., Suite 600, San Francisco, CA 94103. 415-665-6637. E-mail: query@motherjones.com. Web site: www.motherjones.com. Bimonthly. $4.95/issue $20/year. Circ.: 170,000. Roger Cohn, Editor. **Description:** Independent journalism publication focusing on issues of social justice. **Nonfiction:** Features, 1,500-4,000 words, $1,500-$4,000. Short pieces, 100-800 words, $100-$500. Book, film, and music reviews. **Art:** photos, illustrations. **Tips:** Looking for investigative reports exposing government cover-ups, corporate malfeasance, scientific myopia, institutional fraud or hypocrisy. **Queries:** Required. **E-Queries:** Yes. **Unsolicited mss:** Does not accept. **Response:** 2-3 months, SASE. **Freelance Content:** 95%. **Payment:** On acceptance.

MS.

Liberty Media for Women, LLC
20 Exchange Pl., Fl. 22, New York, NY 10005-3201. 212-509-2092. E-mail: info@msmagazine.com. Web site: www.msmagazine.com. Bimonthly. $45/yr. Circ.: 200,000. Marcia Gillespie, Editor-in-Chief. **Description:** Articles relating to feminism, women's roles, and social change. **Nonfiction:** National and international news reporting, profiles, essays, theory, and analysis. **Tips:** Query with resume, published clips, and SASE. No fiction or poetry. **Queries:** Required.

THE NATION

33 Irving Place, Fl. 8, New York, NY 10003-2332. 212-209-5400. E-mail: info@thenation.com. Web site: www.thenation.com. Weekly. $48/yr. Circ.: 100,000. Katrina vanden Heuvel, Editor. **Description:** Politics and culture from a liberal, left perspective, on national and international affairs. **Nonfiction:** Editorials and full-length pieces; 1,500-2,500 words; $75/printed page ($300 max.). **Poetry:** Quality poems. **Columns, Departments:** Editorials; 750-1,000 words. **Tips:** Looking for reporting, with fresh analysis and national significance, on U.S. civil liberties, civil rights, labor, economics, environmental, feminist issues, and role and future of Democratic Party. **Queries:** Required. **Unsolicited mss:** Accepts. **Response:** SASE. **Payment:** On publication.

NETWORK

See page 561 for full listing.
Description: National advocacy magazine for older adults.

NEW JERSEY REPORTER

See page 515 for full listing.
Description: New Jersey politics and public affairs.

THE NEW YORKER

The New Yorker, Inc., 4 Times Square, New York, NY 10036. 212-286-5900.
E-mail: themail@newyorker.com. Web site: www.newyorker.com. Weekly.
$3.50/issue. Circ.: 851,000. **Description:** Covers the vital stories of our time with
intelligence, wit, stylish prose, and a keen eye. **Fiction:** Short stories, humor, and
satire. **Nonfiction:** Amusing mistakes in newspapers, books, magazines, etc. Factual
and biographical articles for Profiles, Reporter at Large, etc. Political/social essays,
1,000 words. **Poetry:** Quality poetry. **Queries:** Not necessary. **E-Queries:** No.
Unsolicited mss: Accepts. **Payment:** On publication. **Contact:** Perri Dorset.

NEWSDAY

235 Pinelawn Rd., Melville, NY 11747-4250. 516-843-2900.
E-mail: oped@newsday.com. Web site: www.newsday.com. Daily. Circ.: 555,203.
Noel Rubinton, Viewpoints Editor. **Description:** Opinion section of newspaper cov-
ering issues of national or local importance, lifestyle, government, current events and
trends. **Nonfiction:** Op-ed pieces, on varied topics; 700-800 words; $150. **Queries:**
Preferred. **Payment:** On publication.

THE OLDER AMERICAN

See page 561 for full listing.
Description: Local, state, and national advocacy magazine for older adults.

ON EARTH

See page 359 for full listing.
Description: Journal for the general public on environmental affairs.

POLICY REVIEW

818 Connecticut Ave. NW, Suite 601, Washington, DC 20006. 202-466-6730.
E-mail: polrev@hoover.stanford.edu. Web site: www.policyreview.org. Bimonthly.
$6/issue. Circ.: 8,000. Tod Lindberg, Editor. **Description:** Book reviews and full-
length articles on public policy; 1,000-5,000 words. **Tips:** Freelance content limited.
Queries: Preferred. **E-Queries:** Yes. **Unsolicited mss:** Accepts. **Response:** 2-4
weeks, SASE. **Freelance Content:** 5%. **Payment:** On publication. **Contact:** Kelly
Sullivan.

THE PROGRESSIVE

409 E Main St., Madison, WI 53703. 608-257-4626.
E-mail: editorial@progressive.org. Web site: www.progressive.org. Monthly.
$3.50/issue, $32/yr. Circ.: 35,000. Matthew Rothschild, Editor. **Description:** A leading voice for peace and social justice, with fresh and lively commentary on major
issues. **Nonfiction:** Investigative reporting; coverage of elections, social movements,
foreign policy; interviews, activism, book reviews; $50-$1,300. **Poetry:** On political
concerns; $150/poem. **Columns, Departments:** On the Line; $50-100. **Queries:**
Preferred. **Unsolicited mss:** Accepts. **Freelance Content:** 30%. **Payment:** On
publication.

REASON

3415 S Sepulveda Blvd., Suite 400, Los Angeles, CA 90034. 310-391-2245.
E-mail: malissi@reason.com. Web site: www.reason.com. Mike Alissi, Publisher. **Description:** "Free Minds and Free Markets." Looks at politics, economics, and culture from libertarian perspective. **Nonfiction:** Articles, 850-5,000 words; pay varies. **Queries:** Preferred. **Payment:** On acceptance.

ROLL CALL

50 F Street NW, Suite 700, Washington, DC 20001. 202-824-6800.
E-mail: letters@rollcall.com. Web site: www.rollcall.com. Susan Glasser, Editor. **Description:** Covers Capitol Hill. Factual, breezy articles, political or Congressional angle (history, human-interest, political lore, opinion, commentary). **Queries:** Preferred. **Payment:** On publication.

SOCIAL JUSTICE REVIEW

3835 Westminster Pl., St. Louis, MO 63108-3409. 314-371-1653.
E-mail: centbur@juno.com. Web site: www.socialjusticereview.org. Bimonthly. $20. Circ.: 5,500. Rev. John H. Miller, C.S.C., Editor. **Description:** Focuses on social justice and related issues. **Nonfiction:** under 3,000 words; $.02/word. **Tips:** Submissions must be faithful to doctrine of the Catholic Church. **Queries:** Preferred. **E-Queries:** No. **Unsolicited mss:** Accepts. **Response:** Queries 2 weeks, SASE. **Freelance Content:** 80%. **Rights:** 1st. **Payment:** On publication.

TIKKUN

2107 Van Ness Ave., Suite 302, San Francisco, CA 94109. 415-575-1200.
E-mail: magazine@tikkun.org. Web site: www.tikkun.org. Bimonthly. $5.95/$29. Circ.: 20,000. Michael Lerner, Editor. **Description:** Progressive Jewish commentary on politics, culture, and society. Based on the Jewish principle of Tikkun Olam (healing the world), encourages writers to join spirituality to politics, for politics infused with compassion and meaning. **Fiction:** 3,000 words. **Nonfiction:** 1,600 words. **Poetry:** 20 lines. **Art:** Electronic (JPG, TIF); $50/photo. **Tips:** Avoid "My trip to Israel (or Eastern Europe/Auschwitz)," "My adult bar mitzvah," "How I became religious." **Queries:** Not necessary. **E-Queries:** No. **Unsolicited mss:** Accepts. **Response:** 3-4 months, SASE. **Freelance Content:** 20%. **Rights:** 1st NA, web reprint. **Payment:** In copies.

UTNE READER

See page 334 for full listing.
Description: Offers alternative ideas and culture.

THE WASHINGTON MONTHLY

733 15th St. NW, Suite 1000, Washington, DC 20005. 202-393-5155.
Web site: www.washingtonmonthly.com. Paul Glastris, Editor. **Description:** Helpful, informative articles, 1,000-4,000 words, on DC-related topics, including politics, and government and popular culture. Pays $.10/word, on publication.

YES!

P.O. Box 10818, Bainbridge Island, WA 98110. 206-842-0216.
E-mail: editors@futurenet.org. Web site: www.futurenet.org. Quarterly. Circ.: 14,000.
Description: "Journal of Positive Futures." Focuses on ways people are working to create a more just, sustainable, and compassionate world. **Tips:** Don't simply expose problems; highlight a practical solution. Honorarium. **Queries:** Required.

EDUCATION

AMERICAN EDUCATOR

American Federation of Teachers
555 New Jersey Ave. NW, Washington, DC 20001. 202-879-4400.
E-mail: amered@aft.org. Web site: www.aft.org. Quarterly. Ruth Wattenberg, Editor.
Description: On trends in education; also well-researched news features on current problems in education, education law, professional ethics; "think" pieces and essays that explore current social issues relevant to American society. **Nonfiction:** Articles, 500-2,500 words; pays from $300. **Queries:** Preferred. **Payment:** On publication.

AMERICAN SCHOOL BOARD JOURNAL

National School Boards Association
1680 Duke St., Alexandria, VA 22314-3455. 703-838-6722.
E-mail: asbj@nsba.org. Web site: www.asbj.com. Monthly. Circ.: 36,000. Sally Zakariya, Editor. **Description:** Publishes informative articles in a practical format regarding educational trends for school board members and administrators.

AMERICAN SCHOOL & UNIVERSITY

9800 Metcalf, P.O. Box 12901, Overland Park, KS 66212. 913-967-1960.
Web site: www.asumag.com. Joe Agron, Editor. **Description:** Articles and case studies, 1,200-1,500 words, on the design, construction, operation, and management of school and university facilities. **Queries:** Preferred.

AMERICAN STRING TEACHER

See page 492 for full listing.
Description: Features research-based articles with national appeal.

BLACK ISSUES IN HIGHER EDUCATION

10520 Warwick Ave., Suite B-8, Fairfax, VA 22030-3136. 703-385-2981.
E-mail: hilary@cmabiccw.com. Web site: www.blackissues.com. Biweekly. $3.50/$26. Circ.: 12,000. Hilary L. Hurd, Editor. **Description:** News and features on blacks in post-secondary education and public policy. **Nonfiction:** On issues affecting minorities in higher education. **Fillers:** On education and public policy. **Columns,**

Departments: Opinion pieces. **Queries:** Preferred. **E-Queries:** Yes. **Unsolicited mss:** Accepts. **Freelance Content:** 40%. **Payment:** On publication.

BOOK LINKS

American Library Association
50 E Huron St., Chicago, IL 60611. 312-280-5718.
E-mail: ltillotson@ala.org. Web site: www.ala.org/booklinks. Bimonthly. $25.95. Circ.: 25,000. Laura Tillotson, Editor. **Description:** Professional journal for K-12 teachers, librarians, parents, and other educators who wish to connect children's and young adult literature into the curriculum. **Nonfiction:** Articles should demonstrate ways in which thematic literature can be integrated into curriculum for preschool-high school students; 2,000 words; $100. **Tips:** Query first or send draft as an attachment if it is written using Book Links style. **Queries:** Required. **E-Queries:** Yes. **Response:** 6-8 weeks. **Freelance Content:** 90%. **Rights:** All. **Payment:** On publication.

CABLE IN THE CLASSROOM

CCI/Crosby Publishing
214 Lincoln St., Suite 112, Boston, MA 02134. 617-254-9481.
E-mail: edhazell@ccicrosby.com. Web site: www.ciconline.org. Monthly. $21.95/yr. Circ.: 120,000. Al Race, Editor. **Description:** Lists commercial free, educational cable programming, plus online resources. Profiles educators who use programming and resources; offers tips for finding and using resources effectively. **Nonfiction:** Articles by or about K-12 teachers, librarians, and media specialists who use educational cable technology and programming to benefit students. By assignment, no unsolicited manuscripts; 500-1,000 words; $250-$500. **Columns, Departments:** Teacher-authored tips for using Cable in the Classroom resources to meet curriculum requirements. Query first; 100-150 words; $50. **Tips:** By assignment only. Don't pitch a story without identifying educators and the classroom cable connection. **Queries:** Required. **E-Queries:** Yes. **Unsolicited mss:** Does not accept. **Response:** Queries 1-3 months, SASE. **Freelance Content:** 50%. **Payment:** On acceptance.

CHURCH EDUCATOR

Educational Ministries, Inc.
165 Plaza Dr., Prescott, AZ 86303. 800-221-0910.
E-mail: edmin2@aol.com. Web site: www.educational ministries.com. Monthly. $28/year. Circ.: 3,000. Robert G. Davidson, Editor. **Description:** Resource for mainline Protestant Christian educators. **Nonfiction:** Programs used in mainline churches; 200-1,500 words; $.03/word. **Queries:** Not necessary. **E-Queries:** Yes. **Unsolicited mss:** Accepts. **Response:** Queries 1 week, submissions 3 months, SASE required. **Freelance Content:** 80%. **Rights:** One-time. **Payment:** On publication. **Contact:** Linda Davidson.

CLASS ACT

P.O. Box 802, Henderson, KY 42419.

E-mail: classact@lightpower.net. 9x/yr. $25/yr. Circ.: 300. Susan Thurman, Editor. **Description:** Newsletter for English and language arts teachers. Provides fun, ready-to-use lessons and units that help teachers make learning language, writing, and literature interesting to students. **Nonfiction:** Seeks articles with ideas that teachers can use immediately. "What a Character" (developing characterization); "Writing Similes, Metaphors and Extended Metaphors"; 300-1,000 words; $10-$40. **Fillers:** English education related only. "One Plus One Equals One"(portmanteaux words; "Horsin' Around (idioms involving horses); 1-2 pages; $10-$20. **Tips:** Know how to write for teenagers. Humor helps. Avoid telling part of your life as a writer. **Queries:** Not necessary. **E-Queries:** Yes. **Unsolicited mss:** Accepts. **Response:** 1 month, SASE. **Freelance Content:** 70%. **Rights:** All. **Payment:** On acceptance.

CLASSROOM NOTES PLUS

National Council of Teachers of English (NCTE)

1111 W Kenyon Rd., Urbana, IL 61801-1096. 217-278-3870.

E-mail: notesplus@ncte.org. Web site: www.ncte.org/notesplus. 4x/yr. $60/yr. (includes membership). Circ.: 17,000. Editor: Felice A. Kaufmann, NCTE. **Description:** Newsletter offering practical teaching ideas for the secondary classroom. Includes in-depth articles on literature, poetry, and writing. Also provides classroom management tips, recommended websites and resources, and advice for new teachers. Nonfiction: Articles must be orginal, previously unpublished, and identify any necessary sources. **Tips:** See website for specific submission guidelines.

THE CLEARING HOUSE

Heldref Publications

1319 18th St. NW, Washington, DC 20036. 202-296-6267.

E-mail: tch@heldref.org. Web site: www.heldref.org. Bimonthly. $12.50/$41. Circ.: 2,000. Rachel Petrowsky, Editor. **Description:** Scholarly journal, covers topics for middle-level and high-school teachers and administrators. **Nonfiction:** Scholarly articles on educational trends and philosophy, learning styles, curriculum, effective schools, testing and measurement, instructional leadership; up to 2,500 words;. **Columns, Departments:** Short articles, new trends; 100-900 words. **Tips:** Writers are generally university professors in education. **Queries:** Not necessary. **E-Queries:** No. **Unsolicited mss:** Accepts. **Response:** Submissions 3-4 months, SASE. **Freelance Content:** 100%. **Payment:** In copies.

COLLEGE COMPOSITION AND COMMUNICATION

National Council of Teachers of English (NCTE)

1111 W Kenyon Rd., Urbana, IL 61801-1096. 217-278-3870.

E-mail: mmcooper@mtu.edu. Web site: www.ncte.org/ccc. 4x/yr.. $58/yr.. Circ.: 9,000. Editor: Marilyn M. Cooper, Michigan Technological University, Houghton. **Description:** Seeks submission of research and scholarship in composition studies that supports college teachers in reflecting on and improving their practices in teaching writing. **Nonfiction:** The field of composition studies draws on research and theories from many humanistic disciplines (e.g. English, linguistics, cultural/racial studies, communication, sociology, etc.), therefore submitted articles may present discussions within any of these fields provided the argument presented is clearly relevant to the work of college writing teachers and composition studies. **Tips:** See website for specific submission guidelines.

COLLEGE ENGLISH

National Council of Teachers of English (NCTE)
1111 W Kenyon Rd., Urbana, IL 61801-1096. 217-278-3870.
E-mail: coleng@scu.edu. Web site: www.ncte.org/ce. 6x/yr.. $65/yr. (includes membership). Circ.: 10,000. Editor: Jean Gunner, Santa Clara University, California. **Description:** Provides a forum in which scholars working within any of the various subspecialties of the discipline can address a broad cross-section of the profession. Covers a wide spectrum of topics relevant to the discipline of English at the level of higher education. **Nonfiction:** Publishes articles on literature, composition, and other disciplinary concerns; open to all theoretical approaches and schools of thought. Does not accept practical articles on classroom practice. Readership is broad-based therefore seeks to insure that articles appeal to nonspecialists as well as specialists in particular areas. **Tips:** See website for specific guidelines.

COMMUNITY COLLEGE WEEK

10520 Warwick Ave., #B-8, Fairfax, VA 22030. 703-385-2981.
E-mail: scottc@cmabiccw.com. Web site: www.ccweek.com. Bi-weekly. $2.75/issue. Circ.: 10,000. Scott Cech, Editor. **Description:** A national newspaper covering community, technical, and junior-college issues. **Nonfiction:** Articles of interest to 2-year academia; 500-700 words; $.35/word. **Tips:** Use AP style. "Always query by e-mail. Check our website for current issue, and make sure your idea fits within the rubric of one of our sections." **Queries:** Required. **E-Queries:** Yes. **Unsolicited mss:** Accepts. **Response:** 1-14 days, SASE. **Freelance Content:** 95%. **Rights:** 1st NA and electronic. **Payment:** On publication.

CREATIVE CLASSROOM

149 Fifth Ave., Fl. 12, New York, NY 10010. 212-353-3639.
E-mail: ccmedit@inch.com. Web site: www.creativeclassroom.com. **Description:** Hands-on magazine for elementary-school teachers. Articles on all curriculum areas, child developmental issues, technology and the Internet in the classroom, professional development, and issues facing elementary teachers. **Tips:** Send SASE for guidelines. Send query letters or mss to attention of Susan Evento, Editorial Director.

CURRENT HEALTH

General Learning Communications
900 Skokie Blvd., Suite 200, Northbrook, IL 60062-4028. 847-205-3000.
E-mail: crubenstein@glcomm.com. Web site: www.glcomm.com. 8x/school year. $9.65 each (quantities of 15). Carole Rubenstein, Editor. **Description:** Magazine for

classrooms covering physical and psychological health. Printed in two editions (for grades 4-7, and grades 7-12). **Nonfiction:** Articles on drug education, nutrition, diseases, fitness and exercise, first aid and safety, psychology, and relationships. By assignment only, no unsolicited manuscripts. Pay varies. **Tips:** Must write well for appropriate age level. Send query with resume and clips. **Queries:** Required. **E-Queries:** Yes. **Unsolicited mss:** Does not accept. **Response:** Queries 1-6 months. **Freelance Content:** 80%. **Rights:** All. **Payment:** On publication.

EARLY CHILDHOOD NEWS

2 Lower Ragsdale, Suite 125, Monterey, CA 93940. 831-333-2000.
E-mail: mshaw@excelligencencemail.com. Web site: www.earlychildhoodnews.com. Bimonthly. Circ.: 50,000. Megan Shaw, Editor. **Description:** For teachers and parents of young children, infants to age 8, on developmentally appropriate activities, behavior, health, safety, and more. **Fiction:** Personal-experience stories from teacher's perspective; up to 500 words. **Nonfiction:** Research-based articles on child development, behavior, curriculum, health and safety; 500-2,000 words. **Poetry:** Related to young children (birth-age 6), teaching, educating, or family; 100 words. **Columns, Departments:** Ask the Expert, Problem-Solving Parent, newsletters for child care staff; 500-600 words. **Queries:** Preferred. **E-Queries:** Yes. **Unsolicited mss:** Accepts. **Response:** 6 weeks for queries, 2-3 months for submissions. **Freelance Content:** 75%. **Rights:** All. **Payment:** On publication.

EARLY CHILDHOOD TODAY

Scholastic, Inc.
555 Broadway, Fl. 5, New York, NY 10012-3919. 212-343-6100.
E-mail: ect@scholastic.com. Web site: www.earlychildhoodtoday.com. 8x/yr. Circ.: 55,000. Judsen Culbreth, Editor-in-Chief. **Description:** For teachers. Offers practical information, strategies, and tips on child development and education. Also personal stories and program spotlights. **Nonfiction:** Articles, 500-900 words; pay varies. **Queries:** Preferred. **Payment:** On publication. **Contact:** Article Submissions.

ENGLISH EDUCATION

National Council of Teachers of English (NCTE)
1111 W Kenyon Rd., Urbana, IL 61801-1096. 217-278-3870.
E-mail: engedu@gsu.edu. Web site: www.ncte.org/ee. 4x/yr.. $55/yr. (includes memberships). Circ.: 3,000. Editors: Dana L. Fox, Georgia State University, Atlanta, and Cathy Fleischer, Eastern Michigan University, Ypsilanti. **Description:** Features articles that focus on issues related to the nature of the discipline and the education and development of teachers of English at all levels. **Tips:** See website for specific submission guidelines. Response: 3 months.

THE ENGLISH JOURNAL

National Council of Teachers of English (NCTE)
1111 W Kenyon Rd., Urbana, IL 61801-1096. 217-328-3870.
E-mail: english.journal@as.ysu.edu. Web site: www.cc.ysu.edu/tej. 6x/yr. Circ.:

31,000. Editor: Virginia Monseau, Youngstown State University, Ohio. **Description:** Professional journal for middle, junior high, and high-school teachers, supervisors, and teacher educators. **Tips:** See website for specific submission guidelines.

ENGLISH LEADERSHIP QUARTERLY

National Council for Teachers of English
1111 W Kenyon Rd., Urbana, IL 61801-1096. 217-278-3870.
E-mail: jwilcox@toolcity.net. Web site: www.ncte.org/elq. 4x/yr.. $58/yr. (includes memberships). Circ.: 2,000. Editor: Bonita L. Wilcox, Duquesne University. **Description:** Seeks to help department chairs, K-12 supervisors, and other leaders in their role of improving the quality of English instruction. Nonfiction: Short articles on a variety of important issues. **Tips:** See website for specific submission guidelines.

GIFTED EDUCATION PRESS QUARTERLY

10201 Yuma Ct., Manassas, VA 20109. 703-369-5017.
E-mail: mfisher345@comcast.net. Web site: www.giftededpress.com. Quarterly. Circ.: 1,000. Maurice Fisher, Editor. **Description:** Covers problems and issues of identifying and educating gifted students. GEPQ is now issued through password codes on website. **Nonfiction:** Issues related to educating gifted students, including teaching science and humanities, home education, and more; 3,500-4,000 words. **Tips:** Looking for highly imaginative, knowledgeable authors to write about this field. **Queries:** Required. **E-Queries:** Yes. **Unsolicited mss:** Does not accept. **Response:** 1 month; SASE required. **Freelance Content:** 50%. **Payment:** In copies.

THE HISPANIC OUTLOOK IN HIGHER EDUCATION

210 Rt. 4 E., Suite 310, Paramus, NJ 07652. 201-587-8800.
E-mail: sloutlook@aol.com. Web site: www.Hispanicoutlook@com. Adalyn Hixson, Editor. **Description:** On issues, concerns, and potential models for furthering academic results of Hispanics in higher education. **Nonfiction:** Articles, 1,700-2,000 words; pay varies. **Tips:** Queries should be sent 3 months in advance of tentative submission. **Queries:** Required. **Payment:** On publication.

HOME EDUCATION

P.O. Box 1083, Tonasket, WA 98855-1083. 509-486-1351.
E-mail: hem@home-ed-magazine.com. Web site: www.home-ed-magazine.com. Bimonthly. $6.50/issue,$32.50/yr. Circ.: 12,000. Helen Hegener, Managing Editor. **Description:** For families who homeschool their children. Seeking submissions from writers who are familiar with homeschooling and who can share the humorous side without being negative about the alternatives. **Nonfiction:** Articles on homeschooling; 1,000-2,000 words; $50-$150. **Tips:** Encourages submissions from homeschooling parents who love to write. Focus on practical experience, not textbook theories. **Queries:** Not necessary. **E-Queries:** Yes. **Unsolicited mss:** Accepts. **Response:** 1-2 months, SASE required. **Freelance Content:** 60%. **Rights:** FNASR. **Payment:** On acceptance.

INSTRUCTOR

Scholastic, Inc.

524 Broadway, New York, NY 10012. 212-343-6100.

Web site: www.scholastic.com/instructor. 8x/year. $14/yr. Circ.: 218,000. Jennifer Prescott, Managing Editor. **Description:** Prominent national magazine for K-8 teachers. **Nonfiction:** Topics for teachers (timely issues, classroom ideas, activities, ways to improve, etc); 800-2,000 words; $500-$1,200. **Fillers:** E-Activities (tech-based activities); also, short, ready-to-use activities by teachers, for teachers; 100-200 words; $50. **Columns, Departments:** End of the Day (revelatory or humorous pieces about your experience as a teacher); 400-500 words; $250. **Tips:** Keep in mind: Can a teacher take these ideas into the classroom immediately? **Queries:** Not necessary. **E-Queries:** Yes. **Unsolicited mss:** Accepts. **Response:** Queries 1 month, submissions 2 months, SASE. **Freelance Content:** 80%. **Rights:** All. **Payment:** On publication.

JOURNAL OF HEALTH EDUCATION

1900 Association Dr., Reston, VA 20191. 703-476-3400.

Web site: www.aahperd.org/aahe.html. **Description:** For health educators, sponsored by American Alliance for Health, Physical Education, Recreation, and Dance. For those who work with students (elementary to college grades), to encourage professional growth. **Queries:** Preferred.

LANGUAGE ARTS

National Council of Teachers of English (NCTE)

1111 W Kenyon Rd., Urbana, IL 61801-1096. 217-278-3870.

E-mail: langarts@u.arizona.edu. Web site: www.ncte.org/la. 6x/yr.. $65/yr. (includes membership). Circ.: 13,000. Coeditors: Kathy G. Short, University of Arizona, Tucson; Jean Schroeder, Gloria Kauffman, Sander Kaser, Tucson Unified School District, Arizona.. **Description:** Professional journal for elementary and middle school teachers and teacher educators. Provides a forum for discussion on all aspects of language arts learning and teaching, primarily as they relate to children in pre-kindergarten through the eighth grade. Issues discuss both theory and classroom practice, highlight current research, and review children's and young adolescent literature, as well as classroom and professional materials of interest to language arts educators. **Nonfiction:** Original articles on all facets of language arts education. **Tips:** See website for specific guidelines.

MOMENTUM

National Catholic Educational Association

1077 30th St. NW, Suite 100, Washington, DC 20007-3852. 202-337-6232.

Web site: www.ncea.org. Brian Gray, Editor. **Description:** Publication covering outstanding programs, issues, and research in education. **Nonfiction:** Articles, 500-1,500 words; pays $25-$75. **Columns, Departments:** Book reviews. **Tips:** No simultaneous submissions. **Queries:** Preferred. **Payment:** On publication.

RESEARCH IN THE TEACHING OF ENGLISH
National Council of Teachers of English (NCTE)
1111 W Kenyon Rd., Urbana, IL 61801-1096. 217-278-3870.
E-mail: smago@coe.uga.edu. Web site: www.ncte.org/rte. 4x/yr.. $60/yr. (includes membership). Circ.: 5,000. Editors: Peter Smagorinsky, University of Georgia, Athens, and Michael W. Smith, The State University of New Jersey. **Description:** Multidisciplinary journal publishing original research and scholarly essays on the relationships between language teaching and learning at all levels, preschool through adult. **Tips:** See website for specific submission guidelines.

SCHOLASTIC DYNAMATH
Scholastic, Inc.
555 Broadway, New York, NY 10012-3999. 212-343-6100.
E-mail: dynamath@scholastic.com. Web site: www.scholastic.com. 8x/year. Circ.: 200,000. David Goody, Editor-in-Chief. **Description:** Offers an engaging mix of humor, news, popular-culture references, and original activities to help readers enjoy learning, while reinforcing and applying key math curriculum concepts. Content must be acceptable for classroom use. **Nonfiction:** Fun math content, tied to current events, popular culture, cool real-life kids, or national holidays (i.e., Martin Luther King Day, President's Day, Thanksgiving); to 600 words; $350-$450/article. **Fillers:** $25-$50 puzzles, to 75 words. **Art:** $50-$400. **Tips:** Has dual goals of being entertaining and educational. Need to get style and mathematical grade level just right. Request a sample copy to familiarize yourself with unique approach. **Queries:** Preferred. **E-Queries:** Yes. **Unsolicited mss:** Accepts. **Response:** 2 months, SASE required. **Freelance Content:** 25%. **Rights:** All. **Payment:** On acceptance.

THE SCHOOL ADMINISTRATOR
American Association of School Administrators
1801 N Moore St., Arlington, VA 22209-1813.
E-mail: magazine@aasa.org. Web site: www.aasa.org. 11x/year. Members only. Circ.: 23,000. Jay P. Goldman, Editor. **Description:** For school administrators (K-12), on school system practices, policies, and programs with wide appeal. **Nonfiction:** 1,500-3,000 words; pay varies. **Fillers:** To 400 words. **Columns, Departments:** To 750 words. **Art:** See guidelines on web. **Queries:** Preferred. **E-Queries:** Yes. **Unsolicited mss:** Accepts. **Response:** Queries 2 weeks, submissions 8-10 weeks. **Freelance Content:** 10%. **Rights:** All. **Payment:** On publication.

SCHOOL ARTS
Davis Publications, Inc.
50 Portland St., Worcester, MA 01608. 508-754-7201.
E-mail: contactus@davis-art.com. Web site: www.davis-art.com. 9x/year. $4/issue. Circ.: 25,000. Dr. Eldon Katter, Editor. **Description:** Covers the field of art education. **Nonfiction:** Articles, 600-1,400 words, on art education in the classroom: successful, meaningful approaches to teaching, innovative projects, uncommon applications of techniques or equipment, etc. Pays $30-$150. **Art:** professional-quality

photos showing lessons in art; pay varies. **Queries:** Preferred. **E-Queries:** Yes. **Unsolicited mss:** Accepts. **Response:** 3 months, SASE. **Freelance Content:** 85%. **Rights:** All. **Payment:** On publication.

SCIENCE & CHILDREN

National Science Teachers Association
1840 Wilson Blvd., Arlington, VA 22201-3000. 703-243-7100.
E-mail: s&c@nsta.org. Web site: www.nsta.org. Joan McShane, Editor. **Description:** Articles and activities, based on current approaches to instruction and issues in science education. For Pre-K to 8th-grade science teachers. **Queries:** Preferred.

TALKING POINTS

National Council of Teachers of English (NCTE)
1111 W Kenyon Rd., Urbana, IL 61801-1096. 217-278-3870.
E-mail: pma8@mindspring.com; koshewa@lclark.edu. Web site: www.ncte.org/tp. 2x/yr.. Circ.: 2,000. Editors: Peggy Albers, Georgia State University, Atlanta, and Allen Koshewa, Lewis and Clark College, Portland, Oregon. **Description:** Helps promote literacy research and the use of whole language instruction in classrooms. Provides a forum for parents, classroom teachers, and researchers to reflect about literacy and learning. **Tips:** See website for specific submission guidelines.

TEACHING ELEMENTARY PHYSICAL EDUCATION

Human Kinetics Publishers, Inc.
P.O. Box 5076, Champaign, IL 61825-5076. 217-351-5076.
E-mail: marjorier@hkusa.com. Web site: www.humankinetics.com. Bimonthly. Circ.: 3,500. Marjorie Robinson, Managing Editor. **Description:** Resources and ideas on instructional and fun physical education programs for K-8 physical education teachers. **Queries:** Preferred.

TEACHING ENGLISH IN THE TWO-YEAR COLLEGE

National Council of Teachers of English (NCTE)
1111 W Kenyon Rd., Urbana, IL 61801-1096. 217-278-3870.
E-mail: htinberg@bristol.mass.edu. 4x/yr.. $60/yr. (includes membership). Circ.: 5,000. Editor: Howard Tinberg, Bristol Community College, Fall River, Massachusetts. **Description:** Publishes articles for two-year college teachers those teaching the first two years of English in four-year institutions. Seeks articles in all areas of composition (basic, first-year, and advanced); business, technical, and creative writing; and the teaching of literature in the first two college years. Also publishes articles on topics such as staffing, assessment, technology, writing program administration, speech, journalism, reading, ESL, and other areas of professional concern. Columns, Departments: Instructional Notes (short articles describing successful classroom practices); Readers Write (50-200 word comments on published articles or professional issues); What Works for Me (brief descriptions on successful classroom activities, 50-200 words); also reviews of books, software, and other nonprint materials. **Tips:** See website for specific submission guidelines.

TEACHING K-8

40 Richards Ave., Norwalk, CT 06854. 203-855-2650.
E-mail: pat@teachingk-8@aol.com. Web site: www.teachingk-8. 8x/year. $23.97/yr.
Circ.: 100,000. Patricia Broderick, Editor. **Description:** A classroom service maga-
zine. Provides useful teaching ideas for teachers who work with grades K-8.
Nonfiction: Articles, 1,000 words, on classroom-tested ideas, techniques, strategies
for teaching students (K-8). **Queries:** Not necessary. **E-Queries:** No. **Unsolicited
mss:** Accepts. **Response:** Submissions 1 month, SASE. **Freelance Content:** 0%.
Rights: All. **Payment:** On publication.

TEACHING THEATRE

Educational Theatre Association
2343 Auburn Ave., Cincinnati, OH 45219. 513-421-3900.
Web site: www.edta.org. Quarterly. **Description:** Journal for middle and high school
drama educators. Offers play suggestions, curriculum ideas, classroom exercises, and
technical production. **Queries:** Preferred.

TEACHING TOLERANCE

Southern Poverty Law Center
400 Washington Ave., Montgomery, AL 36104.
Web site: www.teachingtolerance.org. Semi-annual. Free to educators. Circ.:
600,000. Jim Carnes. **Description:** Helps teachers promote interracial and intercultural understanding in the classroom and beyond. **Nonfiction:** E.g., role of white
teachers in multicultural education; teaching respect for dialects; creating safe space
for refugee students to tell their stories; how assistive devices allow more inclusion for
disabled; gay student comes out at school, etc.; 500-3,500 words; $1/word. **Art:** Rarely
uses stock images. Seeking photographer to travel on assignment, work well with
school children and teachers/administrators, in varied locations; B&W, color, hand-
tinted; $100-$800. **Tips:** Submit clear focused query. No rhetoric, scholarly analysis,
articles that reinvent the wheel on multicultural education. **Queries:** Preferred.
E-Queries: No. **Unsolicited mss:** Accepts. **Response:** up to 3 months, SASE.
Freelance Content: 75%. **Rights:** All. **Payment:** On acceptance.

TECH DIRECTIONS

Prakken Publications
3970 Varsity Dr., Box 8623, Ann Arbor, MI 48107-8623. 734-975-2800.
E-mail: tom@techdirections.com. Web site: www.techdirections.com. Tom Bowden,
Editor. **Description:** For teachers in science, technology, and vocational educational fields. Seeking classroom projects for students from upper elementary
through community college levels. **Nonfiction:** Articles, 9-12 double-spaced typed
pages; $50-$150. **Fillers:** Cartoons (pays $20); puzzles, brainteasers, humorous
anecdotes, short classroom activities (pays $25); humorous anecdotes (pays $5).
Payment: On publication.

TECHNOLOGY & LEARNING

CMP Media, LLC

600 Harrison St., San Francisco, CA 94107-1370. 415-947-6000.
E-mail: smclester@cmp.com. Web site: www.techlearning.com. Circ.: 80,000. Susan McLester, Editor-in-Chief. **Description:** For K-12 teachers on uses of computers and related technology in the classroom: human-interest and philosophical articles, how-to pieces, software reviews, and hands-on ideas. **Nonfiction:** Articles should be of general interest to K-12 educators and should encourage them to try new approaches to teaching by using the latest technology in computers, peripherals, integrated learning systems, etc; 1,200-2,500 words; $400. **Tips:** Do not send electronic submissions. **Response:** 8 weeks, SASE. **Payment:** On publication.

TODAY'S CATHOLIC TEACHER

2621 Dryden Rd., Dayton, OH 45439. 800-523-4625.
E-mail: mnoschang@peterli.com. Web site: www.catholicteacher.com. Bimonthly. $14.95/year. Circ.: 50,000. Mary Noschang, Editor. **Description:** For K-12 educators concerned with private education and particularly Catholic education. **Nonfiction:** Curriculum, classroom management, other articles (religious and non-religious) for classroom teachers in Catholic K-12 schools; 700-3,000 words; $150-$300. **Queries:** Not necessary. **E-Queries:** Yes. **Unsolicited mss:** Accepts. **Response:** 2 months, SASE. **Freelance Content:** 80%. **Rights:** 1st NA. **Payment:** On publication.

UNIVERSITY BUSINESS

Professional Media Group

488 Main St., Norwalk, CT 06851. 203-847-7200.
E-mail: kgrayson@universitybusiness.com. Web site: www.matrix-magazine.com. Katherine Grayson, Editorial Director. **Description:** For managers in the field of higher education. Online and print versions.

VOICES FROM THE MIDDLE

National Council of Teachers of English (NCTE)

1111 W Kenyon Rd., Urbana, IL 61801-1096. 217-278-3870.
E-mail: cschanche@ncte.org. Web site: www.ncte.org/vm. 4x/yr.. $60/yr. (includes membership). Circ.: 10,000. Editor: Kylene Beers, University of Houston, Texas. **Description:** Journal for teachers at the middle school level. Based on the premise that middle school teachers face a unique set of circumstances and challenges, this journal presents a variety of voices. Each issue is devoted to one topic or concept related to literacy and learning at the middle school level. Nonfiction: Each issue includes teachers' descriptions of authentic classroom practices, middle school students' reviews of adolescent literature, a technology column, adn reviews of professional resources for teachers. Also explores the connections between the theory and practice of each issue's topic. **Tips:** See website for specific submission guidelines.

YOUTH AND CHRISTIAN EDUCATION LEADERSHIP

1080 Montgomery Ave. NE, P.O. Box 2250
Cleveland, TN 37320-2250. 423-478-7649.
E-mail: ycessse@extremegen.org. Web site: www.pathwaypress.org. Quarterly. $8.
Circ.: 10,000. Tony P. Lane, Editor. **Description:** For Christian education workers
who teach God's word to kids, teens, and adults. **Nonfiction:** To encourage, inform,
and inspire those who teach the Bible in local churches; 500-1,000 words; $25-$45.
Queries: Not necessary. **E-Queries:** No. **Unsolicited mss:** Accepts. **Response:**
Submissions 6-9 months, SASE. **Payment:** On publication.

ENVIRONMENT, CONSERVATION, NATURE

(See also Sports, Recreation, Outdoors)

ADIRONDACK LIFE

P.O. Box 410, Jay, NY 12941. 518-946-2191.
E-mail: gcrane@adirondacklife.com. Web site: www.adirondacklife.com. 8 issues/
year. Circ.: 50,000. Elizabeth Folwell, Editor. **Description:** Covers outdoor and environmental activities, issues, arts, wilderness, and wildlife of the Adirondack Park
region of New York State. **Fiction:** Excerpts of upcoming Adirondack and related
books; up to 4,000 words; $.25/word. **Nonfiction:** Contemporary and historical arti-
cles on employment, poverty, prison system, water quality, timber industry, etc; up to
5,000 words; $.25/word. **Columns, Departments:** Profiles of people and places,
first-person travel/outdoor historical vignettes; up to 2,200 words; $.25/word. **Art:**
Photographs; color transparencies, B&W prints; $125/full page photo, $300/cover.
Queries: Preferred. **E-Queries:** Yes. **Unsolicited mss:** Accepts. **Response:** 1
month; SASE required. **Freelance Content:** 80%. **Rights:** FNAR. **Payment:** On
publication.

ALTERNATIVES JOURNAL

Faculty of Environmental Studies
University of Waterloo, Waterloo, Ontario N2L 3G1 Canada. 519-888-4442.
E-mail: alternat@fes.uwaterloo.ca. Web site: www.alternativesjournal.ca. Quarterly.
Ray Tomalty. **Description:** Environmental thought, policy, and action. Canadian
focus. **Nonfiction:** Feature articles, 4,000 words; notes, 200-500 words; and reports,
750-1,000 words; no payment.

AMERICAN FORESTS

910 17th St., Suite 600, Washington, DC 20006. 202-955-4500.
E-mail: mrobbins@amfor.org. Web site: www.americanforests.org. Quarterly. $3/$25.
Circ.: 25,000. Michelle Robbins, Editor. **Description:** For people, rural and urban,
who share a love for trees and forests. **Nonfiction:** Articles on trees, forests, issues
(worldwide); inspirational, educational; 150-2,000 words; $100-$1,200. **Columns,**
Departments: Communities (working together on problems); Woodswise (for
small-forest owners); Perspectives (current events); Earthkeepers (1-page profiles);

Clippings (news briefs). **Art:** 35mm or larger; B&W or color; $75-$400. **Tips:** Write for general audience but on a slightly more informed level. Tell specifics: issues, what's being done, how it has affected forests. Looking for skilled science writers for assignments documenting forest use, enjoyment, and management. **Queries:** Required. **E-Queries:** Yes. **Unsolicited mss:** Accepts. **Response:** Queries 2-3 months, submissions 2-3 months, SASE required. **Freelance Content:** 75%. **Rights:** One-time. **Payment:** On acceptance.

ANIMALS
See page 287 for full listing.
Description: Covers wildlife issues, pet-care topics, and animal protection concerns.

ATLANTIC SALMON JOURNAL
Atlantic Salmon Federation
P.O. Box 5200, Saint Andrews, New Brunswick E5B 3S8 Canada. 506-529-4581.
E-mail: asfpub@nbnet.nb.ca. Web site: www.asf.ca. Quarterly. Circ.: 11,000. Jim Gourlay, Editor. **Description:** Covers fishing, conservation, ecology, travel, politics, biology, how-tos, and anecdotes. **Nonfiction:** Articles related to Atlantic salmon; 1,500-3,000 words; $100-$400. **Fillers:** Salmon politics, conservation, and nature; 50-100 words; $25. **Queries:** Preferred. **Payment:** On publication.

AUDUBON
National Audubon Society
700 Broadway, New York, NY 10003-9501.
E-mail: editor@audubon.org. Web site: www.audubon.org. Bimonthly. Circ.: 460,000. David Seideman, Editor-in-Chief. **Description:** Conservation and environmental issues, natural history, ecology, and related subjects. **Nonfiction:** Articles; 150-4,000 words; pay varies. **Tips:** Submit queries, with clips and SASE, to Editorial Asst. **Queries:** Required. **Payment:** On acceptance.

BIRD WATCHER'S DIGEST
See page 567 for full listing.
Description: Bird-watching experiences/expeditions, backyard topics and how-tos.

BIRDER'S WORLD
See page 567 for full listing.
Description: On all aspects of birds and birding.

BLUELINE
See page 656 for full listing.
Description: Poems, stories, and essays on the Adirondack and regions similar in geography and spirit, or on the shaping influence of nature.

BUGLE

Rocky Mountain Elk Foundation
2291 W Broadway, Missoula, MT 59808. 406-523-4570.
E-mail: bugle@rmef.org. Web site: www.rmef.org. Bimonthly. $30/yr. Circ.: 132,000.
Dan Crockett, Editor. **Description:** Journal of the Rocky Mountain Elk Foundation.
Original, critical thinking about wildlife conservation, elk ecology, and hunting.
Fiction: Thoughtful elk-hunting stories; human-interest stories; 1,500-4,500 words;
$.20/word. **Nonfiction:** About conservation, elk ecology and natural history, elk hunt-
ing; 1,500-3,000 words; $.20/word. **Poetry:** 1 page; $100/poem. **Fillers:** Humor.
Columns, Departments: Essays on hunting or conservation issues; 1,000-3,000
woods; $.20/word. **Art:** See photo wish-list on website. **Tips:** Do not submit how-to
pieces. All articles must have a connection to elk. **Queries:** Preferred. **E-Queries:**
Yes. **Unsolicited mss:** Accepts. **Response:** 3 months, SASE. **Freelance Content:**
80%. **Rights:** 1st NA. **Payment:** On acceptance. **Contact:** Lee Cromrich, Assistant
Editor.

CALIFORNIA WILD

California Academy of Sciences
Golden Gate Park, San Francisco, CA 94118-4599. 415-750-7116.
E-mail: calwild@calacademy.org. Web site: www.calacademy.org. Quarterly.
$4.00/$12.95. Circ.: 30,000. Kathleen Wong, Senior Editor. **Description:** Based at
the research facility, natural-history museum, and aquarium in San Francisco's
Golden Gate Park. **Nonfiction:** Well-researched articles on natural history and
preservation of the environment; 1,000-2,500 words; $.30/word. **Columns,
Departments:** Skywatcher; A Closer Look; Wild Lives; In Pursuit of Science. **Art:**
Color, transparencies. **Tips:** Prefers queries with clips. **Unsolicited mss:** Accepts.
Rights: 1st NA. **Payment:** On publication.

CANADIAN GEOGRAPHIC

39 McArthur Ave., Ottawa, Ontario K1L 8L7 Canada. 613-745-4629.
E-mail: editorial@canadiangeographic.ca. Web site: www.canadiangeographic.ca.
Bimonthly. $5.95/$29.95. Circ.: 240,000. Rick Boychuk, Editor. **Description:** Covers
Canadian landscape, nature, and people. **Nonfiction:** On interesting places, nature,
and wildlife in Canada. Pay varies. **Art:** Yes. **Queries:** Required. **E-Queries:** Yes.
Unsolicited mss: Does not accept. **Response:** 3 months, SASE. **Rights:** 1st.
Payment: On publication.

CANADIAN WILDLIFE/BIOSPHERE

Tribute Publishing Co.
71 Barber Green Rd., Don Mills, Ontario M3C 2A2 Canada. 416-445-0544.
E-mail: wild@tribute.ca. $25 (Canada), $37 (outside Canada). Circ.: 35,000. Kendra
Toby, Editor. **Description:** On national and international wildlife issues.
Nonfiction: On wild areas, nature-related research, endangered species, wildlife
management, land-use issues, character profiles, and science and politics of conservation. **Queries:** Preferred. **Payment:** On publication.

THE COUNTRY CONNECTION

Pinecone Publishing

691 Pinecrest Rd., Boulter, Ontario K0L 1G0 Canada. 613-332-3651.
E-mail: magazine@pinecone.on.ca. Web site: www.pinecone.on.ca. 3x/yr. $3.95. Circ.: 10,000. Gus Zylstra, Editor. **Description:** Eco-friendly publication for Ontario. Focuses on nature, heritage, "green" travel, and the arts. **Tips:** Canadian material only. **Queries:** Not necessary. **E-Queries:** Yes. **Unsolicited mss:** Accepts. **Response:** Queries 1 week, submissions to 6 months, SASE (Canadian postage). **Freelance Content:** 75%. **Rights:** 1st. **Payment:** On publication.

THE DOLPHIN LOG

Cousteau Society, Inc.

3612 E Tremont Ave., Bronx, NY 10465-2022. 718-409-3370.
E-mail: cousteauny@aol.com. Bimonthly. Circ.: 80,000. Lisa Rao, Editor. **Description:** On a variety of topics related to our global water system (marine biology, ecology, natural history, and water-related subjects), for 7-13-year-olds. **Nonfiction:** Articles, 400-600 words; pays $50-$200. **Queries:** Preferred. **Payment:** On publication.

E MAGAZINE

Earth Action Network

28 Knight Street, Norwalk, CT 06851. 203-854-5559.
E-mail: info@emagazine.com. Web site: www.emagazine.com. Semi-annual. $3.95/issue, $20/year. Circ.: 50,000. Jim Motavalli, Editor. **Description:** "The environmental magazine." Focuses on environmental concerns. **Nonfiction:** Features and short pieces, on environmental issues (community gardens, mass transit, global warming, activism, trends, etc.); 400-4,200 words. **Columns, Departments:** Your Health, Money Matters, Eating Right, Going Green, House and Home, Consumer News; 750-1,200 words. **Art:** Color. Send stock list only, or upon request. **Tips:** Must be objective reporting, include quoted sources and end-of-article contact information. Sample copy, $5. **Queries:** Preferred. **E-Queries:** Yes. **Unsolicited mss:** Accepts. **Freelance Content:** 60%. **Rights:** 1st. **Payment:** On publication.

ENVIRONMENT

Helen Dwight Reid Educational Foundation

1319 18th St. NW, Washington, DC 20036-1826. 202-296-6267.
E-mail: env@heldref.org. Web site: www.heldref.org. Monthly. $4.95/issue. Barbara T. Richman, Managing Editor. **Description:** Solid analysis of environmental science and policy issues. **Nonfiction:** On major scientific and policy issues of a significant topic; concise, objective, accurate, jargon-free; use graphics and sidebars for key points; 2,500-4,000 words. **Fillers:** Cartoons; $50. **Columns, Departments:** Education, energy, economics, public opinion; 1,000-1,700 words; $100. **Tips:** Avoid news and feature formats. **Queries:** Required. **E-Queries:** Yes. **Unsolicited mss:** Accepts. **Response:** 6-8 weeks, SASE not required. **Freelance Content:** 98%. **Rights:** 1st. **Payment:** On publication.

FLORIDA WILDLIFE

620 S Meridian St., Tallahassee, FL 32399-1600. 850-488-5563.
Web site: www.floridawildlifemagazine.com. Bimonthly. Dick Sublette, Editor.
Description: Published by Florida Fish and Wildlife Conservation Commission.
Nonfiction: Articles, 800-1,200 words, that promote native flora and fauna, hunting, fishing in Florida's waters, outdoor ethics, and conservation of natural resources. Pays $55/page. **Payment:** On publication.

HIGH COUNTRY NEWS

P.O. Box 1090, Paonia, CO 81428. 970-527-4898.
E-mail: editor@hcn.org. Web site: www.hcn.org. Biweekly. $32/year. Circ.: 23,000.
Paul Larmer, Editor. **Description:** Environmental and cultural newspaper covering the American West from the West Coast to the Great Plains. Covers Western environmental and public lands issues, management, rural community, and natural resource issues, profiles of innovators, and Western politics. **Nonfiction:** Well-researched stories on any natural resource (including people, culture, and aesthetic values) or environmental topic; 4,000 words; $.25/word and up. **Columns, Departments:** Bulletin boards (book reviews, activist profiles, event announcements); 200 words. Hotlines (news briefs); 250 words. Roundups (topical stories); 800 words. Essays; up to 1,000 words; $.25/word and up. **Art:** Color or B&W prints (8x10 preferred); 35mm negatives and slides; JPG files, 300 dpi or higher; $35-$100. **Queries:** Preferred. **E-Queries:** Yes. **Unsolicited mss:** Accepts. **Freelance Content:** 90%. **Payment:** On publication.

THE ILLINOIS STEWARD

See page 427 for full listing.
Description: Illinois history and heritage, with natural-resource stewardship theme.

INTERNATIONAL WILDLIFE

National Wildlife Federation
11100 Wildlife Center Dr., Reston, VA 20190-5362. 703-438-6510.
E-mail: pubs@nwf.org. Web site: www.nwf.org. Bimonthly. $26 (members). Circ.: 130,000. Jonathan Fisher, Editor. **Description:** Covers wildlife, conservation, and environmental issues outside the U.S. **Nonfiction:** Articles on nature, and human use and stewardship of it; buys species profiles and status reports, on-scene issue pieces, personality profiles, science stories; 1,200-2,000 words; $800-$2,200. **Art:** 35mm; $300 up. **Tips:** Visually oriented; consider photo potential of story ideas. **Queries:** Required. **E-Queries:** Yes. **Unsolicited mss:** Does not accept. **Response:** 4 weeks, SASE required. **Freelance Content:** 85%. **Rights:** Exclusive 1st-time worldwide rights; non-exclusive worldwide thereafter. **Payment:** On acceptance.

MOTHER EARTH NEWS
See page 479 for full listing.
Description: Publication that emphasizes resourceful living and country skills for rural residents and urbanites who aspire to a more independent lifestyle.

NATIONAL GEOGRAPHIC
National Geographic Society
1145 17th St. NW, Washington, DC 20036-4688. 202-857-7000.
E-mail: opayne@ngs.org. Web site: www.nationalgeographic.com. Monthly. $3.95/$29 year. Circ.: 7,800,000. William Allen, Editor. **Description:** On geography, world cultures, and environmental conservation. **Nonfiction:** First-person, general-interest, heavily illustrated articles on science, natural history, exploration, and geographical regions. **Tips:** 40% staff-written; balance by published authors. **Queries:** Required. **E-Queries:** No. **Unsolicited mss:** Does not accept. **Response:** 4 weeks, SASE. **Freelance Content:** 70%. **Rights:** One-time worldwide serial, plus secondary NGS rights. **Payment:** On publication. **Contact:** Oliver Payne, Senior Editor, Manuscripts.

NATIONAL GEOGRAPHIC WORLD
See page 469 for full listing.
Description: Increases geographic awareness for kids ages 8-14.

NATIONAL PARKS
National Parks Conservation Association
1300 19th St., NW, Suite 300, Washington, DC 20036. 202-223-6722.
E-mail: npmag@npca.org. Web site: www.npca.org. Bimonthly. $2.50. Circ.: 380,000. Linda M. Rancourt, Editor-in-Chief. **Description:** Covers areas within the National Park System. **Nonfiction:** Articles, 1,500-2,000 words, on National Park areas, proposed new areas, threats to parks or wildlife, new trends in use, legislative issues, endangered species. **Tips:** Write for non-scientific but well-educated audience. Be specific, with descriptive details and quotes. No "My Trip to . . . " stories. **Queries:** Required. **E-Queries:** Yes. **Unsolicited mss:** Does not accept. **Response:** 2 months, SASE. **Freelance Content:** 60%. **Rights:** FNASR. **Payment:** On acceptance.

NATURE FRIEND
See page 470 for full listing.
Description: Stories, puzzles, activities, and experiments about nature for children.

THE NEW YORK STATE CONSERVATIONIST
625 Broadway Fl. 2, Albany, NY 12233-4502. 518-402-8047.
E-mail: dhnleson@gw.dec.state.ny.us. Web site: www.dec.state.ny.us. Bimonthly. $12. Circ.: 110,000. David H. Nelson, Editor. **Description:** Published by New York State Dept. of Environmental Conservation. **Nonfiction:** Articles on environmental/conservation programs and policies of New York; pays $50-$100. **Columns,**

Departments: Books, letters. **Art:** Transparencies, photos, slides; $50. **Queries:** Preferred. **Payment:** On publication.

ON EARTH

Natural Resources Defense Council
40 W 20th St., New York, NY 10011. 212-727-4412.
E-mail: onearth@nrdc.org. Web site: www.nrdc.org/onearth. Quarterly. $2.95/issue. Circ.: 140,000. Kathrin Day Lassila, Editor. **Description:** Journal of thought and opinion for the general public on environmental affairs, especially on policies of national and international significance. Strives to be a flagship of environmental thinking and covers critical emerging events and new ideas. **Nonfiction:** Investigative articles, profiles, book reviews, and essays; pay varies. **Poetry:** Conveying emotional and spiritual sources of environmental commitment; $50. **Art:** By request only. **Tips:** Submit strong, well-conceived ideas. Indicate who you will interview and why your topic or idea is of great importance. Must send clips. **Queries:** Required. **E-Queries:** No. **Unsolicited mss:** Accepts. **Response:** 6-8 weeks, SASE required. **Freelance Content:** 40%. **Payment:** On publication.

ORION

Orion Society
187 Main St., Great Barrington, MA 01230. 413-528-4422.
E-mail: orion@orionsociety.org. Quarterly. $7.50/issue. Circ.: 25,000. H. Emerson Blake, Managing Editor. **Description:** Explores the relationship between people and nature. Looks for compelling, reflective writing that connects readers to important issues by heightening awareness of the interconnections between humans and nature. **Nonfiction:** 750-4,000 words; manuscripts longer than 4,000 words may not be considered; $.10/word. **Columns, Departments:** Natural history, arts, poetry, book reviews; 750 words; $.10/word. **Tips:** Orion is meant as a lively, personal, informative, and provocative dialogue. Review copies of submission guidelines and magazine before submitting. Contact for upcoming themes. **E-Queries:** No. **Unsolicited mss:** Accepts. **Response:** 10-12 weeks, SASE. **Freelance Content:** 20%. **Rights:** FNASR. **Payment:** On publication. **Contact:** H. Emerson Blake.

ORION AFIELD

Orion Society
187 Main St., Great Barrington, MA 01230. 413-528-4422.
E-mail: orionafield@orionsociety.org. Web site: www.oriononline.org. Quarterly. $5.50/issue. Circ.: 13,000. Jennifer Sahn, Managing Editor. **Description:** Stories and profiles of organizations and individuals exploring new models for effecting change through grassroots and community-building work. **Nonfiction:** Portraits of extraordinary individuals; conservation, restoration, education, and environmental success stories; 750-2,400 words; manuscripts longer than 4,000 words may not be considered; $0.10/word. **Columns, Departments:** Opinion pieces; book reviews (including manuals, field guides, curriculum); 750 words; $0.10/word. **Tips:** Review copies of submission guidelines and magazine before submitting. Contact for upcoming

themes. **Queries:** Not necessary. **E-Queries:** No. **Unsolicited mss:** Accepts. **Response:** 10-12 weeks, SASE. **Freelance Content:** 20%. **Rights:** FNASR. **Payment:** On publication. **Contact:** Dianna Downing.

OUTDOOR AMERICA
Izaak Walton League of America
707 Conservation Ln., Gaithersburg, MD 20878-2983. 301-548-0150.
E-mail: oa@iwla.org. Web site: www.iwla.org. Quarterly. Circ.: 40,000. Jason McGarvey, Editor. **Description:** Publication of the Izaak Walton League of America. Covers national conservation issues that are top priorities of the league. **Nonfiction:** On endangered species, public lands management, and the protection of air quality, water quality, and water resources. Also, farm-related issues, wildlife and fisheries management controversies of national interest; 1,500-3,000 words; $.25-$.30/word. **Tips:** Send clips. **Queries:** Preferred. **Response:** SASE required.

RANGE
106 E Adams, Suite 201, Carson City, NV 89706. 775-884-2200.
E-mail: cj@range.carson-city.nv.us. Web site: www.rangemagazine.com. Quarterly. $3.95/$19.95. Circ.: 21,000. Caroline Joy Hadley, Editor. **Description:** No stranger to controversy, Range is a forum for opposing viewpoints, seeking solutions to halt the depletion of a national resource: the American cowboy. Devoted to issues that threaten the West, its people, lifestyles, rangelands, and wildlife. **Nonfiction:** Feature articles; 1,500-1,800 words;. **Poetry:** Short; $40-$75. **Columns, Departments:** Red Meat Survivors (500 words, interviews with oldtimers, including historic/current photos); $100-$150. **Art:** Original illustrations, slides, high-quality prints; $40-$150. **Tips:** Submit concise, colorful pieces that address issues affecting those who live on and work the land. Avoid academic, overly technical material. **Queries:** Preferred. **E-Queries:** Yes. **Unsolicited mss:** Accepts. **Response:** Queries 6-8 weeks, submissions 8-10 weeks, SASE. **Freelance Content:** 90%. **Rights:** 1st NA. **Payment:** On publication.

SIERRA
85 2nd St., Fl. 2, San Francisco, CA 94105-3441.
E-mail: sierra.letters@sierraclub.org. Web site: www.sierraclub.org. Bimonthly. $2.95/issue. Circ.: 670,000. Joan Hamilton, Editor. **Description:** Publication of the Sierra Club with a strong environmental emphasis. Provides outstanding nature photography and outdoor recreation and travel information. **Nonfiction:** Stories on nature and environmental issues; 100-4,000 words; $1/word. **Columns, Departments:** what you can do in your home to make the environment safer; visiting a wild place; environmental problems, policy, etc; 750-1,500 words; $1/word. **Queries:** Required. **E-Queries:** Accepts. **Unsolicited mss:** Accepts. **Response:** 6 weeks. **Freelance Content:** 70%. **Rights:** FNASR and electronic. **Payment:** On acceptance.

TEXAS PARKS & WILDLIFE

Fountain Park Plaza, 3000 S Interstate Hwy. 35
Suite 120, Austin, TX 78704. 512-912-7000.
E-mail: magazine@tpwd.state.tx.us. Web site: www.tpwmagazine.com. Monthly.
$15.95. Circ.: 153,000. Susan Ebert, Publisher/Editor. **Description:** Promotes con-
servation and enjoyment of Texas wildlife, parks, waters, and all outdoors.
Nonfiction: Features on hunting, fishing, birding, camping, and the environment.
Photos a plus; 400-1,500 words; $.30-$.50/word. **Payment:** On acceptance.

VIRGINIA WILDLIFE

4010 W Broad St., Richmond, VA 23230. 804-367-1000.
E-mail: lwalker@dgif.state.va.us. Web site: www.dgif.state.va.us. **Description:** On
fishing, hunting, wildlife management, outdoor safety and ethics; with Virginia tie-in.
Nonfiction: Articles, 500-1,200 words, may be accompanied by color photos; pays
from $.18/word, extra for photos. **Queries:** Preferred. **Payment:** On publication.

WHOLE EARTH

1408 Mission Ave., San Rafael, CA 94901. 415-256-2800.
E-mail: editor@wholeearthmag.com. Web site: www.wholeearthmag.com. Quarterly.
Circ.: 30,000. Peter Warshall, Editor. **Description:** Covers issues related to the environment and conservation, culture, social change, education, media, technology,
medical self-care, and all aspects of creating a more interesting life in a sustainable
society. **Nonfiction:** Articles, pay varies. Reviews of books and other tools, $50. **Tips:**
Good article material can be found in passionate personal statements or descriptions
of the writer's activities in this area. **Queries:** Preferred. **Payment:** On publication.

WILD OUTDOOR WORLD

See page 474 for full listing.
Description: On North American wildlife, for readers ages 8-12.

WILDLIFE CONSERVATION

Wildlife Conservation Society
2300 Southern Blvd., Bronx, NY 10460-1090. 718-220-5121.
E-mail: jdowns@wcs.org. Web site: www.wcs.org. Bimonthly. $19.95. Circ.: 154,000.
Joan Downs, Editor. **Description:** Popular natural history. First-person articles,
based on authors' research and experience. **Nonfiction:** Include personal observa-
tions; weave in atmosphere, sights, sounds, smells, colors, weather; if pertinent,
include your own feelings; 1,500-2,000 words; $1,500-$2,000. **Columns,
Departments:** Wild places; 1,200 words; $750-$1,200. **Art:** 35mm color slides. **Tips:**
Contribute short news items for Conservation Hotline. **Queries:** Required.
E-Queries: Yes. **Unsolicited mss:** Accepts. **Response:** 1 month, SASE. **Freelance
Content:** 75%. **Rights:** 1st NA. **Payment:** On acceptance.

ETHNIC & MULTICULTURAL

AFRICAN VOICES
See page 648 for full listing.
Description: Literary magazine of fiction, nonfiction, poetry and visual arts created by people of color.

AIM
1704 Alder, Milton, WA 98354. 253-952-3930.
E-mail: apiladoone@aol.com. Web site: www.aimmagazine.org. Quarterly. $5/issue. Circ.: 7,000. Dr. Myron Apilado, Editor. **Description:** America's Intercultural magazine. Committed to fighting racism. **Fiction:** Short stories reflecting that people from different backgrounds are more alike than different; 3,500 words; $25-$100. **Nonfiction:** 1,000-1,500 words; $15-$25. **Poetry:** 20 lines; $3. **Fillers:** 30 words; $5. **Columns, Departments:** 1,500 words; $15. **Art:** Images promoting racial equality; $10. **Tips:** Write about your experiences. **Queries:** Not necessary. **E-Queries:** No. **Unsolicited mss:** Accepts. **Response:** 1 month; SASE required. **Freelance Content:** 75%. **Rights:** First. **Payment:** On publication. **Contact:** Ruth Apilado, P.O. Box 1174, Maywood, IL 60153.

ALBERTA SWEETGRASS
Aboriginal Multi-Media Society of Alberta
15001 112th Ave., NW, Edmonton, Alberta T5M 2V6 Canada. 780-455-2945.
E-mail: edsweet@ammsa.com. Web site: www.ammsa.com. Monthly. Circ.: 7,500. Rob Mckinley, Editor. **Description:** Newspaper covering Aboriginal issues for communities in Alberta. **Nonfiction:** Articles, 300-900 words (prefers 500-800 words; briefs, 100-150 words): features, profiles, and community-based topics.

AMERICAN INDIAN ART
See page 293 for full listing.
Description: Detailed articles on the American Indian arts.

AMERICAN LEGACY
See page 423 for full listing.
Description: Covers all aspects of Black history and culture.

AMERICAN VISIONS
See page 332 for full listing.
Description: Focuses on African-American culture with emphasis on the arts.

AMERICAS
1889 F Street NW, Washington, DC 20006. 202-458-3510.
E-mail: americas@oas.org. Web site: www.oas.org. James Patrick Kiernan, Director. **Description:** Features on Latin America and the Caribbean. Wide focus: anthropology, the arts, travel, science, and development. **Nonfiction:** 2,500-4,000 words;

pays from $400. **Tips:** Prefers stories that can be well-illustrated. No political material. **Payment:** On publication. **Contact:** Rebecca Read Medrano, Managing Editor.

ASIAN PACIFIC AMERICAN JOURNAL
See page 653 for full listing.
Description: Short stories, also excerpts from longer fiction works by emerging or established Asian American writers.

AUTO REVISTA
See page 302 for full listing.
Description: Bilingual, automotive newspaper.

AUTOMUNDO
See page 302 for full listing.
Description: Spanish-language publication for auto fans.

AVANCE HISPANO
See page 501 for full listing.
Description: Spanish-language publication for people in the San Francisco Bay area.

BLACK COLLEGIAN
See page 323 for full listing.
Description: Career opportunities for African-American students and graduates.

BLACK ENTERPRISE
See page 308 for full listing.
Description: Articles on business, politics and technology for black professionals.

BLACK ISSUES IN HIGHER EDUCATION
See page 342 for full listing.
Description: Features on blacks in post-secondary education and public policy.

BLACK ROMANCE/BRONZE THRILLS
See page 716 for full listing.
Description: Short romantic fiction for African-American women.

BLACK SECRETS
Sterling/MacFadden Partnership
333 7th Ave., Fl. 11, New York, NY 10001-5004. 212-780-4800.
E-mail: tpowell@sterlingmacfadden.com. Web site: www.sterlingmacfadden.com.
Monthly. $11/yr. Circ.: 70,000. Takesha Powell, Editor. **Description:** For African-American women. **Fiction:** Erotic, short, romantic fiction; $100. **Columns, Departments:** $125. **Queries:** Required. **E-Queries:** Yes. **Unsolicited mss:** Accepts. **Response:** SASE required. **Freelance Content:** 100%. **Rights:** All. **Payment:** On publication.

BLACKLINES

See page 295 for full listing.
Description: Black designers in architecture, design, construction, and the arts.

BRAZZIL

2039 N Ave. 52, Los Angeles, CA 90042. 323-255-8062.
E-mail: brazzil@brazzil.com. Web site: www.brazzil.com. Monthly. $2/issue. Circ.: 12,000. Rodney Mello, Editor. **Description:** Publication printed in English that centers on the politics, way of life, economy, ecology, tourism, music, literature, and arts of Brazil. Some short stories printed in Portuguese. **Fiction:** 1,000-5,000 words. **Nonfiction:** 1,000-5,000 words. **Tips:** Liberal viewpoint; controversial material preferred. **Queries:** Not necessary. **E-Queries:** Yes. **Unsolicited mss:** Accepts. **Response:** Queries 2 days, submission 2 days, SASE. **Freelance Content:** 60%. **Rights:** One-time. **Payment:** On publication.

CALLALOO

See page 658 for full listing.
Description: African Diaspora literary journal, with original work by and critical studies of Black writers worldwide.

CATHOLIC NEAR EAST

Catholic Near East Welfare Association
1011 First Ave., New York, NY 10022-4195. 212-826-1480.
E-mail: cnewa@cnewa.org. Web site: www.cnewa.org. Bimonthly. $2.50/$12.00. Circ.: 90,000. Michael La Civita, Executive Editor. **Description:** Offers educational profiles of cultures, histories, religions, and social issues of the peoples of Eastern Europe, India, the Middle East, and Northeast Africa. **Nonfiction:** 1,500 words; $.20/word. **Art:** Slides, prints; $50 and up. **Tips:** Writers and photographers in each Pontifical Mission city and in other CNEWA countries offer the most objective, accurate, sensitive portraits of their subjects. **Queries:** Preferred. **Unsolicited mss:** Accepts. **Response:** SASE required. **Payment:** On publication.

THE CRISIS

NAACP
7600 Georgia Ave. NW, Suite 405, Washington, DC 21207. 202-829-5700.
Web site: www.thecrisismagazine.com. Victoria Valentine, Editor-in-Chief. **Description:** A journal of civil rights, politics, African-American history and culture. **Nonfiction:** Articles range from short briefs to 3,000 word features. **Payment:** On acceptance.

DIRECT AIM

See page 325 for full listing.
Description: Provides college/career information to Black and Hispanic students.

ESSENCE
See page 624 for full listing.
Description: The first national magazine for African-American women.

FACES
See page 465 for full listing.
Description: Diversity magazine for young readers ages 8-14.

FILIPINAS
363 El Camino Real, Suite 100, S. San Francisco, CA 94080. 650-872-8660.
E-mail: myuchengco@filipinasmag.com. Web site: www.filipinasmag.com. Monthly.
$2.95/i$18. Circ.: 30,000. Mona Lisa Yuchengco, Editor. **Description:** For and about Filipinas and their communities in North America. **Nonfiction:** Profiles on successful Filipino Americans, human-interest stories, issues affecting the Filipino American community; 750-3,000 words; $50-$100. **Art:** color photo, $25; B&W, $15. **Queries:** Required. **E-Queries:** Yes. **Unsolicited mss:** Accepts. **Response:** SASE. **Freelance Content:** 70%. **Rights:** All. **Payment:** On publication.

FOOTSTEPS
See page 466 for full listing.
Description: African and African-American history and culture for kids 8-14.

GERMAN LIFE
Zeitgeist Publishing
P.O. Box 3000, Denville, NJ 07834. 800-875-2997.
E-mail: editor@GermanLife.com. Web site: www.GermanLife.com. Bimonthly.
Circ.: 40,000. Carolyn Cook, Editor. **Description:** German culture, its past and present, and how America has been influenced by its German immigrants: history, travel, people, the arts, and social and political issues. **Nonfiction:** Up to 2,000 words; $300-$500. **Fillers:** Up to $80. **Columns, Departments:** Book reviews and short articles; 250-800 words; $100-$130. **Art:** Photos and illustrations that capture and/or detail the diversity of German(-American) life and culture; everyday life, landscapes, people, architecture, art, festivals. **Queries:** Preferred. **Response:** 4-6 weeks. **Rights:** First English/German language serial rights. **Payment:** On publication.

GLOBAL CITY REVIEW
See page 671 for full listing.
Description: Intellectual literary forum for women, lesbian, and gay, and other culturally diverse writers; writers of color, international writers, activist writers.

GOSPEL TODAY
See page 539 for full listing.
Description: Gospel lifestyle magazine for African-American Christians.

HEALTH QUEST
See page 416 for full listing.
Description: Health magazine on body, mind, and spirit for African-Americans.

HEART & SOUL
See page 417 for full listing.
Description: Health magazine for African-American women.

HIGHLANDER
See page 426 for full listing.
Description: Scottish heritage (history, clans, families) in the period 1300-1900 A.D.

HISPANIC
Hispanic Publishing Corp.
999 Ponce de Leon Blvd., Suite 600, Coral Gables, FL 33134-3037. 305-442-2462.
E-mail: editor@hispaniconline.com. Web site: www.hispaniconline.com. Monthly.
Circ.: 250,000. Carlos Verdecia, Editor. **Description:** General-interest (career, business, politics, and culture). Confronts issues affecting the Hispanic community, emphasis on solutions rather than problems. English-language. **Nonfiction:** Features, 1,400-2,500 words; $450. **Columns, Departments:** Hispanic Journal, Portfolio; $75-$150. **Queries:** Preferred.

HISPANIC BUSINESS
See page 313 for full listing.
Description: Features a variety of personalities, political agendas, and stories.

HISPANIC MARKET NEWS
See page 314 for full listing.
Description: Newspaper for those involved in merchandising to Hispanic markets.

THE HISPANIC OUTLOOK IN HIGHER EDUCATION
See page 347 for full listing.
Description: Provides information on Hispanics in higher education.

HISPANIC TIMES
See page 326 for full listing.
Description: Business and career magazine for Hispanic professionals and students.

HURRICANE ALICE
Rhode Island College, Dept. of English, Providence, RI 02908. 401-456-8377.
E-mail: mreddy@ric.edu. Quarterly. $2.50/$12. Circ.: 1,000. Maureen Reddy, Editor.

Description: Feminist exploration, from diverse perspectives, of all aspects of culture. Especially committed to work by women of color, lesbians, working-class women, and young women. **Fiction:** Fictional critiques of culture; 3,500 words max. **Nonfiction:** Articles, essays, interviews, and reviews; 3,500 words max. **Poetry:** Yes. **Art:** B&W (5x7 or 8x10). **Queries:** Not necessary. **E-Queries:** Yes. **Unsolicited mss:** Accepts. **Response:** Queries 30 days, submissions 6 months, SASE required. **Freelance Content:** 100%. **Rights:** FNASR. **Payment:** In copies.

IMAGEN: REFLECTIONS OF TODAY'S LATINO
See page 509 for full listing.
Description: News and profiles of people in the Latino community in New Mexico.

INDIA CURRENTS
P.O. Box 21285, San Jose, CA 95151. 408-274-6966.
E-mail: editor@indiacurrents.com. Web site: www.indiacurrents.com. 11x/year. $19.95/yr. Circ.: 25,800. Vandana Kumar, Editor. **Description:** Explores the heritage and culture of India. **Fiction:** Max. 3,000 words; $50-$150. **Nonfiction:** Articles on India culture, arts, and entertainment in the U.S. and Canada. Also, music/book reviews, commentary on events affecting the lives of Indians. Travel articles (first-person stories of trips to India or the subcontinent); Max. 3,000 words; $50-$150. **Queries:** Preferred. **E-Queries:** Yes. **Unsolicited mss:** Accepts. **Response:** 4 weeks, SASE. **Freelance Content:** 99%. **Rights:** One-time. **Payment:** On publication.

INDIAN LIFE
Box 3765, Redwood Post Office
Winnipeg, Manitoba R2W 3R6 Canada. 204-661-9333.
E-mail: jim.editor@indianlife.org. Web site: www.indianlife.org. Bimonthly. $10. Circ.: 32,000. Jim Uttley, Editor. **Description:** Presents news from across Native North America. **Fiction:** Stories which accurately portray Native Americans; 500-2,000 words; $20-$150. **Nonfiction:** News, first-person views, special features, interviews; 500-1,200 words; $20-$75. **Poetry:** Up to 100 words; $20-$40. **Fillers:** 50-200 words; $10-$25. **Art:** Photos and illustrations; JPG, 200 dpi; $25-$75. **Tips:** Need to know Native Americans (historical and contemporary). No Native spirituality, politics, land claims. **Queries:** Preferred. **E-Queries:** Yes. **Unsolicited mss:** Accepts. **Response:** 4 weeks queries, 8 weeks submissions, SASE required. U.S. contributors please send check for $2.00 with return envelope. **Freelance Content:** 20%. **Rights:** First or all. **Payment:** On publication.

IRISH AMERICA
432 Park Ave. S, Suite 1503, New York, NY 10016-8013. 212-725-2993.
E-mail: irishamag@aol.com. Web site: www.irishamerica.com. Bimonthly. $19.95. Circ.: 85,000. Patricia Harty, Editor-in-Chief. **Description:** For Irish-American audience; prefers history, sports, the arts, and politics. **Nonfiction:** Articles, 1,500-2,000 words; pays $.10/word. **Queries:** Preferred. **Payment:** On publication.

IRISH AMERICAN POST

301 N. Water St., Milwaukee, WI 53202. 414-273-8132.
E-mail: irishampost@execpc.com. Martin Hinz, Publisher. **Description:** For Irish and Irish Americans. **Fiction:** Considers short pieces. **Nonfiction:** Features, 800-1200 words, $100. Profiles, business stories, sports, travel, politics. **Poetry:** Yes. **Art:** Photos, $25. **Tips:** No quaint photos or stories, no "going back home" stories. **Queries:** Preferred.

THE IRISH EDITION

903 E Willow Grove Ave., Wyndmoor, PA 19038-7909. 215-836-4900.
Jane M. Duffin, Editor. **Description:** Short fiction, nonfiction, fillers, humor, and puzzles, for Irish-American and Irish-born readers. Pay negotiable **Queries:** Preferred. **Payment:** On acceptance.

ITALIAN AMERICA

219 E Street NE, Washington, DC 20002-4922. 202-547-2900.
E-mail: italianamerica@osia.org. Web site: www.osia.org. Quarterly. $12/yr. Circ.: 65,000. Dr. Dona De Sanctis, Editor. **Description:** Published by the Order Sons of Italy in America. Covers Italian-American news, history, personalities, culture, etc. **Nonfiction:** Articles on people, institutions, and events of interest to the Italian-American community. Also book reviews; 1,000-2,500 words; $500-$1,000. **Fillers:** 500-750 words. **Columns, Departments:** Postcard from Italy (on one aspect of travel to Italy), Community Notebook (events, personalities with local Italian-American theme); 500-750 words; $150-$350. **Art:** JPG, TIF, BMP, etc. **Tips:** Avoid "My grandmother used to spend hours making her spaghetti sauce . . . " Focus on unique, interesting cultural facets. **Queries:** Preferred. **E-Queries:** Yes. **Unsolicited mss:** Does not accept. **Response:** 2-3 months. **Freelance Content:** 65%. **Rights:** FNASR. **Payment:** On publication.

JAPANOPHILE

P.O. Box 7977, 415 N Main St., Ann Arbor, MI 48107. 734-930-1553.
E-mail: japanophile@aol.com. Web site: www.japanophile.com. Semi-annual. $7/issue. Circ.: 3,000. Susan Aitken, Editor. **Description:** Journal of Japanese culture as it relates to Americans and other non-Japanese persons. **Fiction:** Must involve at least one Japanese and one non-Japanese; 5,000 words max; $20. **Nonfiction:** Articles about Americans or other non-Japanese and their relation to Japanese culture. **Poetry:** Either poems whose subjects deal with Japanese culture in some way or poems that employ haiku, tanka, or other Japanese forms. **Fillers:** Must relate to Japanese culture. **Art:** Yes. **Queries:** Not necessary. **E-Queries:** Yes. **Unsolicited mss:** Accepts. **Response:** 2 months, SASE required. **Freelance Content:** 85%. **Rights:** 1st NA. **Payment:** On publication.

JIVE

See page 716 for full listing.
Description: Romantic fiction for African-American women.

JOURNAL OF ASIAN MARTIAL ARTS

Via Media Publishing Co.

821 W 24th St., Erie, PA 16502. 814-455-9517.

E-mail: info@goviamedia.com. Web site: www.goviamedia.com. Quarterly. Michael A. DeMarco, Editor. **Description:** On martial arts and Asian culture: interviews (with scholars, master practitioners, etc.) and scholarly articles based on primary research in key disciplines (cultural anthropology, comparative religion, etc.). **Nonfiction:** Articles, 2,000-10,000 words; pays $150-$500. **Columns, Departments:** Reviews, 1,000 words, of books and audiovisual material; pays in copies. **Response:** 2-4 weeks for queries; 1-2 months for ms. **Rights:** 1st world and reprint. **Payment:** On publication.

LA FACTORIA DE SONIDO

See page 495 for full listing.

Description: Hispanic music and art publication.

LATIN STYLE MAGAZINE

P.O. Box 2969, Venice, CA 90294-2969. 323-462-4409.

E-mail: info@latinstylemag.com. Web site: www.latinstylemag.com. Monthly. Circ.: 120,000. **Description:** Latin arts and entertainment magazine targeting English-speaking Hispanic markets. Covers entertainment, music, fashion, art, and leisure.

LATIN TRADE

See page 315 for full listing.

Description: For business persons in Latin America. Covers a wide variety of topics relating to trade, markets, research, technology and investments.

LATINA

See page 626 for full listing.

Description: For Hispanic women living in the U.S.

LATINO LEADERS

4229 Hunt Dr., Suite 3910, Carrollton, TX 75010. 888-528-4532.

E-mail: editor@latinoleaders.com. Web site: www.latinoleaders.com. Bimonthly. $2.95. Circ.: 100,000. Patrizia Rossi, Editor. **Description:** Profiles the lives of successful Hispanic-American leaders through inspirational stories that reveal who they really are and how they got to be where they are today. **Columns, Departments:** Mundo Latino (news and events); Up and Coming (Hispanic event guide); Leader of the Past; Leader of the Future; Gallery (photos); Shelf Life (book, movie, music reviews). **Tips:** Does not accept unsolicited material. **E-Queries:** Yes. **Response:** Varies. **Contact:** Patrizia Rossi.

LILITH

250 W 57th St., #2432, New York, NY 10107. 212-757-0818.

E-mail: lilithmag@aol.com. Web site: www.lilithmag.com. Quarterly. $6/issue,

$18/year. Circ.: 10,000. Susan Weidman Schneider, Editor-in-Chief. **Description:** Showcases Jewish women writers, educators, and artists; illuminates Jewish women's lives in their religious, ethnic, sexual, and social-class diversity. **Fiction:** On the lives of Jewish women; 1,000-2,000 words. **Nonfiction:** Autobiographies, interviews, social analysis, sociological research, oral history, new rituals, reviews, investigative reporting, opinion pieces; also news briefs (500 words); Letters to the Editor; lists of resources, projects, events; 1,000-2,000 words. **Poetry:** Yes. **Art:** Yes. **Tips:** Welcomes new writers. **Queries:** Not necessary. **E-Queries:** Yes. **Unsolicited mss:** Accepts. **Response:** 12-16 weeks, SASE. **Rights:** 1st NA, electronic. **Payment:** On publication.

LIVING BLUES
See page 495 for full listing.
Description: About living African-American blues artists.

MOMENT
4710 41st St NW, Washington, DC 20016. 202-364-3300.
E-mail: editor@momentmag.com. Web site: www.momentmag.com. Bimonthly. $4.50/issue. Circ.: 50,000. Hershel Shanks, Editor. **Description:** On Jewish culture, politics, and religion. **Fiction:** 8,000 max. **Nonfiction:** Sophisticated articles on Jewish culture, politics, religion, personalities. Pay negotiated; 100-3,500 words;. **Poetry:** 150-300 words. **Columns, Departments:** Shorts (250 words, on events, people, and living); Olam/The Jewish World (colorful, first-person reports); Book Reviews (to 400 words). **Tips:** Seeking fresh angles on Jewish themes. **Queries:** Preferred. **E-Queries:** Yes. **Unsolicited mss:** Accepts. **Response:** 3-4 months, SASE. **Freelance Content:** 90%. **Rights:** FNASR. **Payment:** On publication.

NA'AMAT WOMAN
350 Fifth Ave., Suite 4700, New York, NY 10118. 212-563-5222.
E-mail: judith@naamat.org. Web site: www.naamat.org. Quarterly. $25 members, $10 non-members. Circ.: 20,000. Judith A. Sokoloff, Editor. **Description:** For Jewish communities, covering varied topics: aspects of life in Israel, Jewish women's issues, social issues, Jewish art and literature. **Fiction:** 2,000-3,000 words; $.10/word. **Nonfiction:** 2,000-3,000 words; $.10-$.12/word. **Columns, Departments:** Book reviews (ca. 800 words); personal essays (ca. 1,200-1,500 words); $.10/word. **Art:** B&W (hard copy or electronic); $25-$100. **Tips:** Avoid trite Jewish humor, maudlin fiction, war stories. **Queries:** Preferred. **Unsolicited mss:** Accepts. **Response:** Queries 1-2 months, submissions 2-3 months, SASE. **Freelance Content:** 75%. **Rights:** 1st NA. **Payment:** On publication.

NATIVE PEOPLES
5333 N Seventh St., Suite C-224, Phoenix, AZ 85014-2804. 602-265-4855.
E-mail: gavey@nativepeoples.com. Web site: www.nativepeoples.com. Bimonthly. $4.95/issue. Circ.: 60,000. Gary Avey, Publisher. **Description:** Dedicated to the sensitive portrayal of arts and lifeways of the native peoples of the Americas. **Nonfiction:**

Artist profiles (traditional and contemporary); issue-oriented pieces with Native American angle; program/people profiles in education, health, politics; economic development; 1,000-3,000 words; $.25/word. **Columns, Departments:** Pathways (travels with Native site/culture/history focus; Viewpoint (open subject matter); 400-1,200 words; $.25/word. **Art:** Color, B&W. **Tips:** Readership is both Native American and those interested in Native culture. Our stories need to appeal to both, serving as a bridge between cultures. **Queries:** Preferred. **E-Queries:** Yes. **Unsolicited mss:** Accepts. **Response:** 4 weeks, SASE required. **Freelance Content:** 80%. **Rights:** First time rights. **Payment:** On publication. **Contact:** Dan Gibson, Editor.

NETWORK JOURNAL
See page 317 for full listing.
Description: Small-business, personal finance, and career management for African-American small-business owners and professionals.

NEW YORK TREND
TTW Associates, Inc.
14 Bond St., Suite 176, Great Neck, NY 11021. 516-466-0028.
E-mail: nytrend@aol.com. Web site: www.nytrend.com. Biweekly. $1/$15. Circ.: 50,000. Felicia Persand, Editor. **Description:** Articles focus on the issues affecting Black and other minority communities in New York City and other regions across the United States. Topics include politics, business, entertainment, and other special features. **Columns, Departments:** Seeks material on politics, human rights, and hard news; 800 words; $30. **Art:** JPGs; $10/picture. **Tips:** "Avoid fluff writing." Strong interest in hard news and business features. **E-Queries:** Yes. **Unsolicited mss:** Accepts. **Response:** 1 week. **Freelance Content:** 50%. **Rights:** 1st print.

PAPYRUS
See page 637 for full listing.
Description: "The writer's craftletter featuring the black experience."

RAISING BLACK AND BIRACIAL CHILDREN
See page 383 for full listing.
Description: For black, interracial, and transracial families who have children with African-American heritage. Readers include parents, professionals and educators.

RUSSIAN LIFE
P.O. Box 567, Montpelier, VT 05601-0567. 802-223-4955.
E-mail: ruslife@rspubs.com. Web site: www.russian-life.com. Bimonthly. $29/yr. Circ.: 15,000. Mikhail Ivanov, Editor. **Description:** Russian culture, travel, history, politics, art, business, and society. Very visual; most stories include professional-quality photos. **Nonfiction:** 1,000-3,000 words; $.07-$.10/word. **Art:** Slides, prints, color, B&W; $20-$50. **Tips:** Submit solid, third-person American journalism (AP stylebook); frank, terse, and incisive. No stories about personal trips to Russia, editorials on developments in Russia, or articles promoting a specific company, organiza-

tion, or government agency. **Queries:** Required. **E-Queries:** Yes. **Unsolicited mss:** Accepts. **Response:** 1 month, SASE. **Freelance Content:** 40%. **Rights:** All. **Payment:** On publication.

SCANDINAVIAN REVIEW

American-Scandinavian Foundation
58 Park Ave., New York, NY 10016. 212-879-9779.
E-mail: rjlitell@amscan.org. Web site: www.amscan.org. 3x/year. Circ.: 6,000. Richard J. Litell, Editor. **Description:** Presents the arts, sciences, business, politics, and culture of contemporary Denmark, Finland, Iceland, Norway, Sweden to lay audience with interest in Nordic countries. Illustrated articles, essays, and poetry; pays $300 honorarium. **Nonfiction:** 1,500-2,000 words. **Tips:** No original English-language poetry, only Nordic poetry in translation. **Queries:** Preferred. **E-Queries:** Yes. **Response:** 1 month, SASE. **Freelance Content:** 50%. **Rights:** one-time. **Payment:** On publication.

SELECCIONES DEL READER'S DIGEST

See page 411 for full listing.
Description: Spanish-language version of Reader's Digest.

SELECTA

1717 N Bayshore Dr., Suite 113, Miami, FL 33132-1195. 305-579-0979.
E-mail: selectamag@aol.com. Web site: www.revistaselecta.com. Monthly. $36. Circ.: 30,000. Eva Hughes, Editor. **Description:** For upscale Hispanics in the U.S. and Latin America.

SISTERS IN STYLE

See page 597 for full listing.
Description: Articles on beauty and fashion for African-American teens.

SOUTH AMERICAN EXPLORERS

South American Explorers Club
126 Indian Creek Rd., Ithaca, NY 14850-1310. 607-277-0488.
E-mail: don@saexplorers.org. Web site: www.saexplorers.org. Quarterly. $22/yr. Circ.: 8,600. Don Montague, Editor. **Description:** Publishes feature articles on scientific studies, travel, historical personalities, archeology, exploration, social sciences, peoples and culture, etc. **Nonfiction:** Length varies from 1,200-10,000 words. **Art:** Photos, sketches, maps. Rates: $50-$250, vary with number of contributions. **Tips:** Write or e-mail for guidelines or sample issue. **Queries:** Preferred. **E-Queries:** Yes. **Unsolicited mss:** Accepts. **Payment:** On publication.

TEACHING TOLERANCE

See page 351 for full listing.
Description: Helps teachers promote interracial and intercultural understanding.

TEENPRENEUR
Earl G. Graves, Ltd.
130 5th Ave., Fl. 10, New York, NY 10011. 212-242-8000.
6x/year. Circ.: 4,000. **Description:** For African-American teens interested in business.

TEMAS
300 W 55th St., Apt. 14P, New York, NY 10019-5172. 212-582-4750.
E-mail: temas582@aol.com. Web site: www.cdiusa.com/revistatemas. Monthly. Circ.: 119,000. Lolita de la Vega, Editor-in-Chief. **Description:** Topics of interest to Spanish-speaking people in the United States.

VISTA
999 Ponce de Leon Blvd., Suite 600, Coral Gables, FL 33134. 305-442-2462.
E-mail: jlobaco@hisp.com. Web site: www.vistamagazine.com. Monthly. Circ.: 1 million. Julia Bencomo Lobaco, Editor. **Description:** Covers news, events, and issues of interest to the Hispanic community throughout the United States. **Nonfiction:** On job advancement, bilingualism, immigration, the media, fashion, education, medicine, sports, and food; up to 1,500 words. **Columns, Departments:** Book reviews, and profiles of interesting, community-oriented Hispanics; 100 words. **Art:** Photos to accompany stories. **Queries:** Required. **Payment:** On publication.

FAMILY & PARENTING

ADOPTIVE FAMILIES MAGAZINE
42 W 38th St., Ste. 901, New York, NY 10018. 646-366-0830.
E-mail: beth@adoptivefam.com. Web site: www.adoptivefam.com. Bimonthly. Beth Kracklauer, Editor. **Description:** On parenting adoptive children and other adoption issues. **Nonfiction:** Middle-school and teen years, relatives and community, adoptive parent support groups, school, foster adoption, transracial adoption, domestic adoption, adoptive parents of color; 1,000-1,500 words; payment negotiable. **Columns, Departments:** The Waiting Game, Parenting the Child Who Waited, About Birthparents, Been There, Adoption & School, In My Opinion, At Home, Single Parent, Living with Diversity, Parent Exchange. **Tips:** Prefers queries by fax (646-366-0842) or e-mail. **Queries:** Preferred. **E-Queries:** Yes. **Response:** 6-8 weeks.

AMERICAN BABY
PRIMEDIA Consumer Media & Magazine Group
110 Fifth Ave., Fl. 4, New York, NY 10011-5300. 212-886-3600.
Web site: www.americanbaby.com. Monthly. Circ.: 2,000,000. Judith Nolte, Editor-in-Chief. **Description:** For new or expectant parents on prenatal and infant care. **Fiction:** No fantasy pieces or dreamy musings. **Nonfiction:** Features, 1,000-2,000 words; personal experience pieces (do not submit in diary format), 900-1,200 words; $800-$2,000. **Columns, Departments:** Crib Notes (news and feature topics); 50-350 words; $500. **Payment:** On acceptance.

ATLANTA PARENT

2346 Perimeter Park Dr., Suite 101, Atlanta, GA 30341. 770-454-7599. E-mail: atlantaparent@atlantaparent.com. Web site: www.atlantaparent.com. Monthly. $15. Circ.: 85,000. Liz White, Editor. **Description:** For parents with children, birth to 18 years. **Nonfiction:** On family, child, and parent topics; 300-1,500 words; $15-$35. **Fillers:** Humor; 800-1,200 words. **Queries:** Preferred. **E-Queries:** Yes. **Unsolicited mss:** Accepts. **Response:** 3-6 months, SASE. **Freelance Content:** 50%. **Rights:** One-time. **Payment:** On publication. **Contact:** Amy Dusek.

BABY TALK

The Parenting Group
530 5th Ave., Fl. 4, New York, NY 10036. 212-522-8989.
E-mail: letters@babytalk.com. Web site: www.parenting.com. 10x/yr. Circ.: 1,725,000. Susan Kane, Editor-in-Chief. **Description:** Pregnancy, babies, baby care, women's health, child development, work and family. **Nonfiction:** Articles, by professional writers with expertise and experience; 1,000-3,000 words; pay varies. **Queries:** Required. **Response:** SASE required. **Payment:** On acceptance. **Contact:** Brittani Boyd, Editorial Assistant.

BAY AREA PARENT

United Parents Publications
987 University Ave., Suite 4, Los Gatos, CA 95032-7640. 408-399-4842.
E-mail: jbordow@unitedad.com. Web site: www.parenthood.com. Monthly. Free. Circ.: 77,000. Joan Bordow, Editor. **Description:** Parenting issues for California's Santa Clara County and South Bay area. **Nonfiction:** For parents of children from birth to early teens; 500-1200 words; $.10/word. **Queries:** Required. **E-Queries:** Yes. **Unsolicited mss:** Accepts. **Response:** Queries and submissions 2 months, SASE required. **Freelance Content:** 50%.

BEST WISHES

Family Communications, Inc.
37 Hanna Ave., Unit 1, Toronto, Ontario M6K 1W9 Canada. 416-537-2604.
Web site: www.parentscanada.com. Semi-annual. Circ.: 155,000. Bettie Bradley, Editor. **Description:** For new moms and dads. Staff written.

BIG APPLE PARENT

Family Communications, Inc.
9 E 38th St., Fl. 4, New York, NY 10016. 212-889-6400.
E-mail: edit@parentsknow.com. Web site: www.parentsknow.com. Monthly. Free. Circ.: 70,000. Helen Rosengren Freedman, Managing Editor. **Description:** Newspaper for New York City parents, with separate editions for Queens and Westchester County. **Nonfiction:** For parents, on parenting, humor features, op-ed; best chances are "newsy" features with New York slant; 750 words; $50. **Art:** Hard copy, JPG; $25. **Tips:** Cover more than your personal experience. Stories should be

about New York City or have information that can be localized. **Queries:** Not necessary. **E-Queries:** Yes. **Unsolicited mss:** Accepts. **Response:** within 1 week, SASE
required. **Freelance Content:** 90%. **Rights:** 1st. **Payment:** On publication.

BRAIN CHILD

P.O. Box 1161, Harrisonburg, VA 22801-1161. 540-574-2379.
E-mail: editor@brainchildmag.com. Web site: www.brainchildmag.com. Quarterly.
$5/$18. Circ.: 10,000. Jennifer Niesslein and Stephanie Wilkinson, Co-Editors.
Description: Explores the personal transformation that motherhood brings.
Spotlights women's own view of motherhood. **Fiction:** Literary short stories on an
aspect of motherhood; e.g., "The Life Of the Body," by Jane Smiley; 1,500-4,500
words; pay varies. **Nonfiction:** Personal essays, features, book reviews, parodies,
debate essays. **Columns, Departments:** Nutshell (stories you won't find in the
mainstream media; e.g., "Mom Brain Explained," by Libby Gruner; 200-800 words.
Tips: Seeking smart, down-to-earth work that's sometimes funny, sometimes
poignant. Send query for features, reviews, and Nutshell stories. Send full manuscript
for all other categories. **Queries:** Preferred. **E-Queries:** Yes. **Unsolicited mss:**
Accepts. **Response:** 1-3 months, SASE. **Freelance Content:** 90%. **Rights:** 1st NA,
electronic. **Payment:** On publication. **Contact:** Jennifer Niesslein.

CATHOLIC PARENT

Our Sunday Visitor, Inc.
200 Noll Plaza, Huntington, IN 46750. 219-356-8400.
E-mail: cparent@osv.com. Web site: www.osv.com. Woodeene Koenig-Bricker,
Editor. **Description:** For Catholic parents. Anecdotal and practical, with an emphasis on values and family life. **Nonfiction:** Features, how-tos, and general-interest articles, 800-1,000 words; pay varies. **Tips:** Don't preach. **Payment:** On acceptance.

CENTRAL CALIFORNIA PARENT

7638 N Ingram Ave., Suite 101, Fresno, CA 93711-6201. 559-435-1409.
Monthly. $15. Circ.: 35,000. Sally Cook. **Description:** For parents. **Nonfiction:**
Articles, 500-1,500 words; pay varies. **Queries:** Preferred. **Payment:** On publication.

CENTRAL PENN PARENT

Journal Publications, Inc.
101 N Second St., Harrisburg, PA 17101-1402. 717-236-4300.
E-mail: karrenm@journalpub.com. Web site: www.journalpub.com. Monthly. $16.95.
Circ.: 35,000. Karren Miller, Editor. **Description:** On family and parenting issues
Nonfiction: 1,400 words; $125. **Columns, Departments:** 700 words; $50. **Art:**
Submit photos with article. **Tips:** Welcomes new writers. **Queries:** Required.
E-Queries: Yes. **Unsolicited mss:** Accepts. **Response:** 3 weeks, SASE required.
Freelance Content: 50%. **Rights:** 1st. **Payment:** On publication.

CHICAGO PARENT
141 S Oak Park Ave., Oak Park, IL 60302-2972. 708-386-5555.
Web site: chicagoparent.com. Monthly. Circ.: 125,000. **Description:** Magazine for parents in the Chicago metro area.

CHILD
Gruner + Jahr USA Publishing
375 Lexington Ave., New York, NY 10017. 212-499-2000.
E-mail: mailcenter@child.com. Web site: www.child.com. 10x/yr. Circ.: 1.2 million. Miriam Arond, Editor-in-Chief. **Description:** A sophisticated lifestyle magazine for today's young parents. **Columns, Departments:** Kids' Fashion, Mom's Beauty, Fashion and Home, Pregnancy column, Baby Bytes column, and "What I Wish Every Parent Knew" back-page essay. Also features lifestyle section which includes travel and home design. Fees vary depending upon length and positioning. **Tips:** Offer news that parents need to know, options for products/services, and ways to preserve precious parenthood time, in a lively, stylish fashion, current issues facing parents. Accepts requests for guidelines via e-mail, but prefers that queries and manuscripts be sent by regular mail. **Queries:** Preferred. **E-Queries:** Yes. **Unsolicited mss:** Accepts. **Response:** 2 months, SASE required. **Freelance Content:** 95%. **Rights:** 1st NA. **Payment:** On acceptance.

CHILDBIRTH
PRIMEDIA Enthusiast Group
1440 Broadway, Fl. 14, New York, NY 10018-2306. 212-204-4200.
E-mail: judith_nolte@primediamags.com. Web site: www.americanbaby.com. Semi-annual. Circ.: 2,014,815. Judith Nolte, Editor-in-Chief. **Description:** For expectant parents.

CHRISTIAN PARENTING TODAY
Christianity Today
465 Gundersen Dr., Carol Stream, IL 60188-2489. 630-260-6200.
E-mail: cptmag@aol.com. Bimonthly. Circ.: 90,000. Carla Barnhill, Editor. **Description:** Serves the needs of today's families in a positive and practical format. **Nonfiction:** Articles on real-life experiences and the truths of the Bible. **Queries:** Required.

CITY PARENT
467 Speers Rd., Oakville, Ontario L6K 3S4 Canada. 905-815-0017.
E-mail: cityparent@metroland.com. Web site: www.cityparent.com. Monthly. Circ.: 250,000. Jane Muller, Editor. **Description:** Offers stories, new-product information, computer news, parenting advice, places to go and things to do with kids. **Nonfiction:** Pays $75-$150. **Queries:** Required. **E-Queries:** Yes. **Unsolicited mss:** Accepts. **Freelance Content:** 50%. **Rights:** All.

CLEVELAND/AKRON FAMILY
Hearth Marketing and Media
3050 Prospect Ave., Cleveland, OH 44115. 216-426-8300.
E-mail: editor@hearthmarketingandmedia.com. Monthly. Circ.: 50,000. Jackie Elfvin, Editor. **Description:** For parents in the Cleveland/Akron region. Seeks to encourage positive family interaction. Provides articles on general topics, area events, trends, and services for area families. **Nonfiction:** Pays $30/article or column. **Queries:** Required. **E-Queries:** Yes. **Unsolicited mss:** Accepts. **Payment:** On publication.

THE COMPLEAT MOTHER
5703 Hillcrest, Richmond, VA 60071. 815-678-7531.
E-mail: greg@rsg.org. Web site: www.compleatmother.com. Quarterly. Circ.: 12,000. **Description:** For new moms and mom-to-be.

DALLAS FAMILY
United Parent Publications
1321 Valwood Parkway, Suite 530, Carrollton, TX 75006-8412. 972-488-3555.
E-mail: phwcomments@unitedad.com. Web site: www.parenthood.com. Monthly. $19.95. Circ.: 80,000. Bill Lindsay, Editor-in-Chief. **Description:** For parents in the Dallas metro area.

DOVETAIL
775 Simon Greenwell Lane, Boston, KY 40107. 502-549-5499.
E-mail: di-ifr@boardstown.com. Web site: www.dovetailinstitute.org. Bimonthly. $29.95/year. Circ.: 1,000. Mary Helène Rosenbaum, Editor. **Description:** Resources for dual-faith couples, and their families, friends, and professionals who serve them, from a non-denominational perspective. Readers cover the intermarriage spectrum, including single-faith and dual-faith households. **Nonfiction:** Advice, anecdotes, and research on aspects of interfaith marriage; e.g., "Challah Baking: Thoughts of a Christian Cook," or "Intermarriage in Australia"; 800-1,000; $25. **Fillers:** Related cartoons, humor, and photos also used. **Tips:** Have experience or knowledge in the field of intermarriage. Avoid broad generalizations, or strongly partisan religious creeds. **Queries:** Not necessary. **E-Queries:** Yes. **Unsolicited mss:** Accepts. **Response:** Queries 2-4 weeks, submissions 4-6 weeks, SASE required. **Freelance Content:** 80%. **Rights:** All. **Payment:** On publication.

EASTSIDE PARENT
United Parenting Publications
1530 Westlake Ave. N, Suite 600, Seattle, WA 98109. 206-441-0191.
E-mail: epnwpp@aol.com. Web site: www.parenthoodweb.com. Bill Lindsay, Editor-in-Chief. **Description:** For parents of children under 14. Readers tend to be professional, two-career families. Also publishes *Portland Parent, Seattle's Child*, etc. **Nonfiction:** Articles, 300-2,500 words; pays $50-$600. **Queries:** Preferred. **Payment:** On publication.

EP NEWS
National Association of Entrepreneurial Parents
P.O. Box 320722, Fairfield, CT 06432. 203-371-6212.
E-mail: epideas@en-parent.com. Web site: www.en-parent.com. Monthly. Lisa Roberts, Cofounder. **Description:** E-zine for entrepreneurial parents. Serves as a resource for parents who balance family and professional careers. Offers advice, serves as a support network, and addresses the needs of these parents from both the business and parenting perspectives.

EXPECTING
Family Communications, Inc.
37 Hanna Ave., Unit 1, Toronto, Ontario M6K 1W9 Canada. 416-537-2604.
E-mail: info@pregnancycanada.com. Web site: www.parentscanada.com. Semi-annual. Circ.: 292,000. Tracy Hitchcock, Editor. **Description:** For pregnant Canadian women.

FAITH & FAMILY
432 Washington Ave., North Haven, CT 06473. 203-230-3800.
E-mail: editor@faithandfamilymag.com. Web site: editor@faithandfamilymag.com. Bimonthly. Circ.: 30,000. Duncan Maxwell Anderson, Editorial Director. **Description:** How-to articles and interviews of interest to Catholic families, with photos. **Nonfiction:** 1,000-2,000 words; pays $75-$300. **Columns, Departments:** Opinion or inspirational columns, 600-800 words, with strict attention to Catholic doctrine. **Queries:** Preferred. **Unsolicited mss:** Accepts. **Freelance Content:** 70%. **Rights:** 1st. **Payment:** On publication.

FAMILY
Military Force Features, Inc.
51 Atlantic Ave., Suite 200, Floral Park, NY 11001. 516-616-1930.
E-mail: hq1@familymedia.com. Web site: www.familymedia.com. Monthly. Stacy P. Brassington, Editor. **Description:** For military families. Covers topics of interest to women with children (military lifestyle, home decorating, travel, moving, food, personal finances, career, relationships, family, parenting, health and fitness). **Nonfiction:** Articles, 1,000-2,000 words; pays to $200. **Payment:** On publication.

FAMILY
Kids Monthly Publications
1122 U.S. Highway 22 W, Mountainside, NJ 07092-2812. 908-232-2913.
E-mail: ucfamily@aol.com. Monthly. Circ.: 121,000. Farn Dupre, Editor. **Description:** New Jersey information for families.

FAMILY LIFE
Time, Inc.
530 5th Ave., Fl. 3, New York, NY 10036-5101. 212-522-6240.
E-mail: familylife_letters@timeinc.com. Web site: www.familylife.com. Monthly.

$19.94. Circ.: 565,300. Janet Siroto, Editor-in-Chief. **Description:** For parents of children, ages 5-12. Most readers are women. **Nonfiction:** Essays on parenting issues, short departments, and features; 2,000-3,500 words. **Columns, Departments:** Mom's health, children's health, crafts, news briefs; 50-400 words. **Queries:** Required. **E-Queries:** Yes. **Unsolicited mss:** Does not accept. **Response:** Queries 6-8 weeks, SASE. **Freelance Content:** 50%. **Rights:** All. **Payment:** On acceptance. **Contact:** Jacqueline Ross.

FAMILYFUN
Disney Magazine Publishing, Inc.
244 Main St., Northampton, MA 01060-3107. 413-585-0444.
Web site: www.familyfun.com. Jonathan Adolph, Executive Editor. **Description:** For parents of children ages 3-12. Offers fun ideas and activities. **Columns, Departments:** My Great Idea; Family Ties (essays on family life); also recipes, crafts and games; $.50 - $1/word. **Tips:** New writers should consider contributing to departments first. **Contact:** Ann Hallock, Editor.

FLORIDA FAMILY MAGAZINE
1840 Glengary St., Sarasota, FL 34231-3604. 941-922-5437.
E-mail: emily@floridafamilymagazine.com.
Web site: www.floridafamilymagazine.com. Bimonthly. Circ.: 60,000. Emily Leinfuss, Executive Editor. **Description:** For families in and around Sarasota, central Florida, and Tampa.

FOCUS ON THE FAMILY
8605 Explorer Dr., Colorado Springs, CO 80920-1051. 719-531-3400.
E-mail: janzenkw@fotf.org. Web site: www.family.org. Monthly. Circ.: 2,600,000. Ken Janzen, Senior Director. **Description:** Provides information for Christian families.

HEALTHY KIDS
PRIMEDIA Consumer Media & Magazine Group
1440 Broadway, New York, NY 10018-2301. 212-462-3300.
E-mail: hkletters@primediamags.com. Web site: www.healthykids.com. Bimonthly. Circ.: 1,554,000. Phyllis Steinberg, Editor. **Description:** Focuses on raising a healthy, happy child. Two editions: Birth-3 (quarterly) and 4-10 Years (3 times a year). All articles written by experts or based on interviews with pediatricians and health-care professionals. **Nonfiction:** On basic care, analysis of growing mind, behavior patterns, nutrition, emergencies, etc. 1,500-2,000 words, pays $500-$1,000. **Tips:** Freelance content limited. **Queries:** Preferred. **Payment:** On acceptance.

HOMELIFE
LifeWay Christian Resources
One Life Plaza, Nashville, TN 37234-0175. 615-251-2860.
Monthly. Circ.: 400,000. **Description:** Information for Christian families about honoring God in their daily lives. **Nonfiction:** Articles must be consistent with the vision

and doctrinal statements of LifeWay Christian Resources. **Tips:** All articles are by assignment. Accepts queries, but no freelance submissions. No simultaneous submissions. Purchases all rights; no reprints or first rights. Photographers and illustrators must also sign an all-rights contract. **Unsolicited mss:** Does not accept. **Response:** 8 weeks, SASE.

HOUSTON FAMILY
United Parent Publications
2620 Fountain View Dr., Suite 200, Houston, TX 77057-7627. 713-266-1885.
E-mail: houstonparenting@unitedad.com. Web site: www.parenthood.com. Monthly. $15. Circ.: 80,000. Wendy Slaton, Editor. **Description:** For parents in the Houston area.

L.A. PARENT
United Parenting Publications
443 E Irving Dr., Suite D, Burbank, CA 91504-2447. 818-846-0400.
Web site: www.parenthoodweb.com. Monthly. Circ.: 110,000. Karen Lindey, Regional Editor. **Description:** Articles on child development, health, nutrition, education, and local travel/activities for parents of children up to age 12. Also publishes *San Diego Parent, Parenting* (Orange Co.), and *Arizona Parenting*. **Nonfiction:** Articles, 1,000 words; pays $100-$350. **Queries:** Preferred. **Payment:** On acceptance.

LIVING WITH TEENAGERS
Lifeway Christian Resources
1 Lifeway Plaza, Nashville, TN 37234-0174. 615-251-2226.
E-mail: lwt@lifeway.com. Web site: www.lifeway.com. Monthly. $18.95/yr. Circ.: 48,000. Sherrie Thomas, Editor. **Description:** Informs and educates parents of teenagers on how to best deal with typical issues and problems faced by teens. Provides strong Christian emphasis and biblical solutions.

METROKIDS
Kidstuff Publications, Inc.
1080 N Delaware Ave., Suite 702, Philadelphia, PA 19125. 215-291-5560 x102.
E-mail: editor@metrokids.com. Web site: www.metrokids.com. Monthly. Circ.: 125,000. Nancy Lisagor, Editor-in-Chief. **Description:** For Delaware Valley area, on parenting kids, ages 0-16. **Nonfiction:** Parenting subjects, products reviews, and travel in the Philadelphia metro region; 800-1500 words; $30-$100. **Columns, Departments:** Product reviews, books, music, video, software, health, women's subjects, family finance; 800; $30-$50. **Queries:** Preferred. **E-Queries:** Yes. **Unsolicited mss:** Accepts. **Response:** Queries 2 months, submissions 2 months. **Freelance Content:** 60%. **Rights:** one-time only, Web site. **Payment:** On publication.

NEW BEGINNINGS
La Leche League International
P.O. Box 4079, Schaumburg, IL 60168-4079. 847-519-7730.

E-mail: editornb@llli.org. Web site: www.lalecheleague.org. Bimonthly. Circ.: 25,000. Kathleen Whitfield, Managing Editor. **Description:** Member publication of a non-profit organization. Provides articles and information for women who breast-feed. **Tips:** Does not pay for submissions.

NEW PARENT

Impact Media Communications, Inc.
10 New King St., White Plains, NY 10604-1205. 914-949-4726.
E-mail: astudabaker@newparent.com. Web site: www.newparent.com. Semi-annual. Circ.: 900,000. Anne Studabaker, Editor. **Description:** For new parents and parents-to-be.

NEW YORK FAMILY

United Parenting Publications
141 Halstead Ave., Mamaroneck, NY 10543-2607. 914-381-7474.
E-mail: hhart@unitedad.com. Web site: www.parenthoodweb.com. Monthly. Circ.: 58,000. Heather Hart, Editor-in-Chief. **Description:** Articles related to family life in New York City and general parenting topics. **Nonfiction:** Pays $50-$200. **Payment:** On publication.

NICK, JR.

See page 470 for full listing.
Description: Fun activities, games, and stories for kids ages 2-7 and their parents.

NORTHWEST BABY & CHILD

15417 204th Ave. SE, Renton, WA 98059-9021. 425-235-6826.
E-mail: editor@nwbaby.com. Web site: www.nwbaby.com. Monthly. Circ.: 45,000. Betty Freeman, Editor. **Description:** For parents in Western Washington. **Tips:** Writer's guidelines and editorial calendar available on website. **E-Queries:** Yes.

NORTHWEST FAMILY

2275 Lake Whatcom Blvd., Ste B-1, Bellingham, WA 98226-2777. 360-734-3025.
E-mail: nwfamily@earthlink.net. Web site: www.nwfamily.com. Monthly. Circ.: 50,000. **Description:** Regional parenting and family publication for Western Washington. **Nonfiction:** Pays $25-$40. **Fillers:** Humor; pays $25-$40. **Art:** Photos; pays $5-$20. **Tips:** Send articles in e-mail (no attachments); include word count. **Queries:** Required. **E-Queries:** Yes. **Unsolicited mss:** Accepts. **Freelance Content:** 65%. **Rights:** One-time (print & electronic).

PARENT CONNECTION

Times Beacon Record Newspapers
P.O. Box 707, Setauket, NY 11733-0769. 631-751-0356.
E-mail: parent@tbrnewspapers.com. Web site: www.tbrnewspapers.com. Monthly. Circ.: 125,000. Leah Dunaief, Editor. **Description:** For parents in the New York City and surrounding area.

THE PARENT PAPER

Bergen Record Corp.

1 Garret Mountain Plaza, West Paterson, NJ 07424-3320. 973-569-7720.

E-mail: info@parentpaper.com. Web site: www.parentpaper.com. Monthly. $25/yr. Circ.: 50,000. Mary Vallo, Editor. **Description:** For parents in New Jersey.

PARENTGUIDE NEWS

419 Park Ave. S., Fl. 13, New York, NY 10016. 212-213-8840.

E-mail: annmarie@parentguidenews.com. Web site: www.parentguidenews.com. Monthly. $19.95/year. Circ.: 210,000. Annmarie Evola, Editor. **Description:** For parents with children under 12 years old. **Fiction:** 1,000 words. **Nonfiction:** Articles on families and parenting: health, education, child-rearing; 1,000 words. **Queries:** Preferred. **E-Queries:** Yes. **Unsolicited mss:** Accepts. **Response:** 1-2 weeks; SASE required. **Freelance Content:** 80%.

PARENTING

Time, Inc.

530 Fifth Ave., Fl. 4, New York, NY 10019. 212-522-8989.

E-mail: letters@parenting.com. Web site: www.parenting.com. 10x/year. Circ.: 1,560,000. Janet Chan, Editor-in-Chief. **Description:** Seeks to make pregnancy and parenthood easier and less stressful by educating parents. Offers resources, tools, real-life wisdom, and solutions/strategies for effective parenting to moms and dads. **Nonfiction:** On education, health, fitness, nutrition, child development, psychology, and social issues for parents of young children; 500-3,000 words. **Tips:** Focuses on the early years, when parents have many questions and concerns. **Queries:** Preferred. **E-Queries:** No. **Unsolicited mss:** Accepts. **Response:** 2 months, SASE.

PARENTING TODAY'S TEEN

P.O. Box 11864, Olympia, WA 98508.

E-mail: editor@parentingteens.com. Web site: www.parentingteens.com. Bimonthly. Diana Kathrein, Publisher/Editor. **Description:** E-zine, written by parents and professionals, about the issues of parenting teenagers, including tough issues like drug/alcohol abuse, sex, AIDS, violence, and running away. **Nonfiction:** Pays $10-$25. **Queries:** Required. **E-Queries:** Yes. **Response:** 2-3 weeks. **Rights:** 1st NA, reverts to author after 90 days. **Contact:** Diana Kathrein.

PARENTLIFE

LifeWay Christian Resources

1 Lifeway Plaza, Nashville, TN 37234-0001. 615-251-2000.

E-mail: parentlife@lifeway.com. Web site: www.lifeway.com. Monthly. Circ.: 105,000. Mary Ann Bradberry, Editor-in-Chief. **Description:** Publication focusing on Christian parenting.

PARENTS
Gruner + Jahr USA Publishing
375 Lexington Ave., New York, NY 10017-5514. 212-499-2000.
E-mail: mailbag@parentsmagazine.com. Web site: www.parents.com. Monthly.
$12.97/yr. Circ.: 2,153,000. Sally Lee, Editor-in-Chief. **Description:** Features articles on parenting and raising healthy, well-adjusted children. Topics include children's health/safety, behavior, new technology, family life, and travel.

PARENTS EXPRESS
290 Commerce Dr., Fort Washington, PA 19034. 215-629-1774.
Web site: www.parents-express.net. Laura Winchester. **Description:** For parents in southeastern Pennsylvania and southern New Jersey. **Nonfiction:** Articles; pays $35-$150. **Payment:** On publication.

PITTSBURGH PARENT
P.O. Box 374, Bakerstown, PA 15007-0374. 724-443-1891.
E-mail: pgparent@nauticom.net. Monthly. Circ.: 55,000. **Description:** For parents in the Pittsburgh metro area.

PORTLAND PARENT
United Parenting Publications
1530 Westlake Ave. N, Suite 600, Seattle, WA 98109-3096. 206-441-0191.
Web site: www.parenthoodweb.com. Monthly. $15. Circ.: 42,000. Bill Lindsay, Editor-in-Chief. **Description:** For parents in the Portland, Ore., metro area.

QUEENS PARENT
Family Communications, Inc.
9 E 38th St., Fl. 4, New York, NY 10016-0003. 212-889-6400.
E-mail: edit@parentsknow.com. Web site: www.parentsknow.com. Helen Rosengren Freedman, Managing Editor. **Description:** For parents in the borough of Queens, NYC.

RAINY DAY CORNER
See page 638 for full listing.
Description: On-line and print publication that provides information and tips to kids and parents who enjoy writing.

RAISING BLACK AND BIRACIAL CHILDREN
RBC Magazine, 1336 Meadow View Lane #1, Lancaster, CA 93534. 310-562-5538.
E-mail: intrace@aol.com. 5x/year. $19.95/yr. Circ.: 16,000. Billee Mills, Editor.
Description: For black, interracial, and transracial families who have children with African-American heritage. Readers include parents, professionals and educators.
Nonfiction: Building character in African American children; articles on parenting, family values, interracial friendship among children, self-esteem, African American culture and heritage; 500-1,000 words; $.04/word. **Columns, Departments:** 400-

600 words. **Art:** Images of African American or biracial babies, toddlers, and children up to teens; also, black and interracial families. Prints (to 8x10), B&W or color; pay negotiable. **Tips:** Seeking unique, and standard pieces on parenting, with emphasis on African American perspective. **Queries:** Not necessary. **Unsolicited mss:** Accepts. **Response:** 4 weeks, SASE. **Freelance Content:** 50%. **Rights:** One-time. **Payment:** On publication.

SACRAMENTO SIERRA PARENT
457 Grass Valley Hwy, Suite 5, Auburn, CA 95603-3725. 530-888-0573.
Monthly. Circ.: 55,000. **Description:** Provides articles and information to families with children and grandchildren of all ages in California. **Nonfiction:** Interested in articles that promote a developmentally appropriate, healthy, and peaceful environment for children. 300-500 words for short pieces; 700-1,000 words for feature articles.

SAN DIEGO FAMILY MAGAZINE
1475 6th Ave., Fl. 5, P.O. Box 23960, San Diego, CA 92193-3960. 619-685-6970.
E-mail: editor@sandiegofamily.com. Web site: www.sandiegofamily.com. Monthly. Circ.: 65,000. Sharon Bay, Publisher/Editor-in-Chief. **Description:** Family magazine for residents in the San Diego area. Provides informative, educational articles on parenting with a distinct San Diego focus. **Tips:** Does not accept phone or e-queries. Submit query by mail with outline and clips. See Web site for submission guidelines. **Queries:** Required. **E-Queries:** No. **Freelance Content:** 50%. **Rights:** 1st & 2nd.

SEATTLE'S CHILD
Northwest Parent Publishing
123 NW 36th St., Suite 215, Seattle, WA 98107. 206-441-0191.
Web site: www.parenthood.com. Karen Matthee, Editor. **Description:** For parents, educators, and childcare providers in the Puget Sound region with children 14 and under. Investigative reports and consumer tips on issues affecting families. **Nonfiction:** Articles, 400-2,500 words; pays $75-$600. **Queries:** Preferred. **Payment:** On publication.

SINGLE PARENT FAMILY
Focus on the Family
8655 Explorer Dr., Colorado Springs, CO 80920-1049. 719-531-3400.
E-mail: singleparent@family.org. Web site: www.singleparentfamily.org. Monthly. $15. Circ.: 75,000. Susan Goodwin Graham, Editor. **Description:** Information for the Christian single-parent. Addresses issues of divorce, grief, finances, and more. **Nonfiction:** Pay varies. **Queries:** Preferred. **E-Queries:** Yes. **Unsolicited mss:** Accepts. **Response:** SASE required. **Rights:** 1st. **Payment:** On acceptance.

SINGLEPARENTS
BenMar Multimedia, Inc.
2118 Wilshire Blvd., Suite 318, Santa Monica, CA 90403-5784. 323-298-3020.

E-mail: Info@singleparents.com. Web site: www.singleparentsmag.com. Quarterly. $12. Circ.: 50,000. Benell Grant, Publisher/Editor. **Description:** Practical information for single heads of households. Pay varies. **Columns, Departments:** Family News, Tips & Tidbits, Sanity Savers, Never a Dull Moment, Spiritual Abundance, other columns. **Tips:** Check website for detailed submission information. **Queries:** Required. **E-Queries:** Yes. **Response:** 6 weeks. **Rights:** All.

SOUTH FLORIDA PARENTING

5555 Nob Hill Rd., Sunrise, FL 33351-4707. 954-747-3050. E-mail: vmccash@sfparenting.com. Web site: www.sfparenting.com. Monthly. Circ.: 100,000. **Description:** For parents in south Florida.

TODAY'S FAMILY

280 N Main St., East Longmeadow, MA 01108. 413-525-6661. E-mail: news@thereminder.com. Web site: www.thereminder.com. Bimonthly. $9.99. Circ.: 20,000. Carla Valentine, Editor. **Description:** Parenting magazine for Western Massachusetts. Focuses on local news, events, and activities for families. Columns on family issues, health, day trips, etc., by local writers. **Tips:** Writers must have expertise on the subject and be from the region (Western Mass., Pioneer Valley). **Queries:** Required. **E-Queries:** Yes. **Unsolicited mss:** Does not accept. **Response:** Queries 2 weeks; SASE required. **Freelance Content:** 10%.

TODAY'S GRANDPARENT

See page 564 for full listing.
Description: For grandparents of all ages.

TOLEDO AREA PARENT NEWS

1120 Adams St., Toledo, OH 43624. 419-244-9859. Web site: www.toledoparent.com. Monthly. Circ.: 50,000. Marcia Chambers, Editor. **Description:** For parents in Northwest Ohio and Southern Michigan. **Nonfiction:** On parenting, child and family health, and other family topics. Writers must be from the region; 750-1,200 words; $75-$200. **Queries:** Preferred. **Unsolicited mss:** Accepts.

TWINS

5350 S Roslyn St., Suite 400, Englewood, CO 80111-2125. 303-290-8500. E-mail: twins.editor@businessword.com. Web site: www.twinsmagazine.com. Bimonthly. Circ.: 55,000. Sharon Withers, Editor. **Description:** Expert advice from professionals and parents, about the needs of multiple-birth parents. **Nonfiction:** Parenting issues specific to multiples; 1,200 words; $200-$250. **Fillers:** Practical tips (for specific ages: birth-2, 3-4, 5-6); 125-150 words; $20. **Columns, Departments:** Special Miracles (personal experiences); 500-600 words; $40. **Art:** Yes. **Queries:** Preferred. **E-Queries:** Accepts. **Unsolicited mss:** Accepts. **Response:** 3 months. **Freelance Content:** 60%. **Payment:** On publication.

WASHINGTON PARENT

4701 Sangamore Rd., #N270, Bethesda, MD 20816-2508. 301-320-2321.
Web site: www.washingtonparent.com. Monthly. Circ.: 90,000. **Description:** For
parents in and around Washington, D.C.

ZELLERS FAMILY

Today's Parent Group
269 Richmond St. W, Toronto, Ontario M5V 1X1 Canada. 416-596-8675.
4x/year. Circ.: 1,200,000. Beth Thompson, Editor. **Description:** Magazine for Zellers
store customers. Focuses on fashion, decorating, cooking, etc.

FILM, TV, ENTERTAINMENT

BACK STAGE WEST/DRAMA-LOGUE

BPI Communications, Inc.
5055 Wilshire Blvd., Fl. 5, Los Angeles, CA 90036-6100. 323-525-2356.
E-mail: bsweditorial@backstage.com. Web site: www.backstage.com. Weekly. $79/yr.
Circ.: 12,000. Robert Kendt, Editor-in-Chief. **Description:** Actor's trade paper, West
Coast. **Nonfiction:** Articles and reviews; pays $.10-$.15/word. **Queries:** Required.
Payment: On publication.

BOMB

594 Broadway, Suite 905, New York, NY 10012. 212-431-3943.
E-mail: info@bombsite.com. Web site: www.bombsite.com. Quarterly. $4.96/$18.
Circ.: 25,000. Betsy Sussler, Editor. **Description:** Interviews, varying lengths, on
artists, musicians, writers, actors, and directors. Special section in each issue featur-
ing new fiction and poetry. **Fiction:** 20 pages max.; $100. **Poetry:** 10 pages; $100.
Queries: Preferred. **E-Queries:** Yes. **Unsolicited mss:** Accepts. **Response:**
Queries 4 months, submissions 4 months, SASE. **Freelance Content:** 5%. **Rights:**
1st serial. **Payment:** On publication. **Contact:** Susan Sherman, Associate Editor.

CINEASTE

304 Hudson St., Fl. 6, New York, NY 10013-1015. 212-366-5720.
E-mail: cineaste@cineaste.com. Web site: www.cineaste.com. Quarterly. $6/$20.
Circ.: 11,000. Gary Crowdus, Editor-in-Chief. **Description:** Covers the art and politics of the cinema. Views, analyzes, and interprets films. **Nonfiction:** Articles should
discuss a film, film genre, a career, a theory, a movement, or related topic, in depth.
Interviews with people in filmmaking; 2,000-3,000 words; $75-$100. **Columns,
Departments:** 1,000-1,500 words. **Tips:** Readers are intelligent general public,
sophisticated about art and politics. No matter how complex the ideas or arguments,
style must be readable. **Queries:** Preferred. **E-Queries:** Yes. **Unsolicited mss:**
Accepts. **Response:** 2-3 months, SASE. **Freelance Content:** 50%. **Rights:** 1st NA.
Payment: On publication.

COUNTRY WEEKLY
See page 493 for full listing.
Description: Provides features on the country music and entertainment industry.

EMMY
5220 Lankershim Blvd., North Hollywood, CA 91601-2800. 818-754-2800.
E-mail: polevoi@emmys.org. Web site: www.emmys.org. Bimonthly. $4.95/$28. Circ.: 15,000. Gail Polevoi, Editor. **Description:** Publication covering people who work in the television industry; for industry professionals. **Nonfiction:** Profiles and trend stories; 1,500-2,000 words; $800-$1,200. **Columns, Departments:** New writers, could break in with Labors of Love or Viewpoint; 500-1,000 words; $350-$750. **Tips:** Should have TV business background. No academic, fan-magazine, or highly technical articles. **Queries:** Required. **E-Queries:** Yes. **Unsolicited mss:** Accepts. **Response:** 4-6 weeks, SASE required (unless by e-mail). **Freelance Content:** 80%. **Rights:** 1st NA. **Payment:** On publication.

ENTERTAINMENT DESIGN
See page 604 for full listing.
Description: Trade publication on the art and technology of entertainment.

FANGORIA
475 Park Ave. S., 8th Fl., New York, NY 10016. 212-689-2830.
Web site: www.fangoria.com. 10x/year. $7.99/$39.97. Circ.: 260,000. Anthony Timpone, Editor. **Description:** Nonfiction articles and interviews on horror films, TV series, books, and the artists who create this genre. Emphasizes personalities and behind-the-scenes angles of horror film making. **Nonfiction:** Movie, TV, and book previews; reviews; and interviews connected to upcoming horror films; 2,000-3,000 words; $150-$250. **Tips:** A strong love of the genre is essential. Readers are experts on horror who want to read about the latest films and film makers. **Queries:** Required. **E-Queries:** No. **Unsolicited mss:** Does not accept. **Response:** 6-8 weeks, SASE. **Freelance Content:** 92%. **Rights:** All. **Payment:** On publication.

FILM COMMENT
Film Society of Lincoln Center
70 Lincoln Center Plaza, New York, NY 10023-6595. 212-875-5610.
E-mail: filmcomment@filmlinc.com. Web site: www.filmlinc.com. Bimonthly. $24.95. Circ.: 45,000. Gavin Smith, Editor. **Description:** On films (new and old, foreign and domestic), also performers, writers, cinematographers, studios, national cinemas, genres. Opinion and historical pieces also used. **Nonfiction:** Articles, 1,000-5,000 words; pays $.33/word. **Payment:** On publication.

FILM QUARTERLY
University of California Press
2000 Center St., Suite 303, Berkeley, CA 94704-1233. 510-643-7154.
Web site: www.ucpress.edu/journals/fq. Quarterly. Circ.: 7,600. Ann Martin, Editor.

Description: Historical, analytical, and critical articles, to 6,000 words. Also, film reviews, book reviews. **Queries:** Preferred.

HADLEY MEDIA
21 Melrose Ave., Norwalk, CT 06855.
Web site: www.univercity.com. 10x/year. D. Patrick Hadley, Editor. **Description:** Publisher of *Univercity Magazine* and Univercity.com. Provides entertainment news, fashion trends, celebrity interviews, and reviews of music, movies, and books for New York City and Boston college students. **Queries:** Preferred.

HEROES FROM HACKLAND
1225 Evans, Arkadelphia, AR 71923. 870-246-6223.
3x/year. $5/$20. Circ.: 150. Mike Grogan, Editor. **Description:** Takes a nostalgic, popular-culture approach to the review of B-movies, cartoons, series books, radio, TV, comic books, and newspaper comic strips. **Nonfiction:** Any fresh article casting light on the popular culture of yesterday and its relation to today; 220-1500 words; $5 and copies. **Poetry:** Nostalgic with a bite, coherent imagery, no impenetrable college quarterly stuff; up to 40 lines; $5 and copies. **Fillers:** Vignettes about customs, little-known facts about pop culture icons. **Art:** B&W only; $5/photo. **Queries:** Not necessary. **Unsolicited mss:** Accepts. **Response:** 10 days, SASE. **Freelance Content:** 35%. **Rights:** 1st. **Payment:** On publication.

HOT
See page 595 for full listing.
Description: Covers fashion, beauty, celebrities, and music for girls ages 8-14.

ILLINOIS ENTERTAINER
Roberts Publishing Co.
124 W Polk, Suite 103, Chicago, IL 60605-1770. 312-922-9333.
E-mail: ieeditors@aol.com. Web site: www.illinoisentertainer.com. Monthly. Circ.: 73,000. Michael C. Harris, Editor. **Description:** Covers entertainment and media, especially music. Open to non-music/band features, especially of odd, quixotic kind. **Nonfiction:** On local and national entertainment (especially alternative music) in greater Chicago area. Personality profiles; interviews; reviews. 500-1,500 words; $75. **Art:** by assignment; $30-200. **Tips:** Send clips (via snail mail) and be patient. **Queries:** Not necessary. **E-Queries:** Yes. **Unsolicited mss:** Accepts. **Response:** Queries 30 days, submissions 30-90 days, SASE not required. **Freelance Content:** 70%. **Rights:** FNASR. **Payment:** On publication.

INDEPENDENT FILM AND VIDEO MONTHLY
304 Hudson St., Fl. 6, New York, NY 10013. 212-807-1400.
E-mail: editor@aivf.org. Web site: www.aivf.org. 10x/year. $4.95/issue. Circ.: 15,000.
Description: For active mediamakers, covers all aspects of independently-produced film and video. Topics included scripting, funding, production, technology, editing, film festivals, and distribution. **Nonfiction:** 700-1,300 words; production techniques;

interviews with directors, producers, writers; book reviews; technology news, legal issues; media advocacy. Pay varies. **Queries:** Required. **E-Queries:** Yes. **Unsolicited mss:** Accepts. **Response:** to 4 months, SASE. **Freelance Content:** 80%. **Rights:** 1st NA, Web rights for extra fee. **Payment:** On publication.

KIDS TRIBUTE
See page 468 for full listing.
Description: Articles on movies and entertainment for young readers ages 8-13.

NEW ENGLAND ENTERTAINMENT DIGEST
P.O. Box 88, Burlington, MA 01803. 781-272-2066.
E-mail: jacneed@aol.com. Web site: www.jacneed.com. Monthly. $2/issue, $20/year. Circ.: 5,000. JulieAnn Charest, Editor. **Description:** Newspaper covering theater and entertainment news for residents in New England and New York. **Nonfiction:** Articles covering professional, regional, college, community, and children's theatre, all types of dance, music, film, and video; length varies; payment varies. **Columns, Departments:** Length varies; payment varies. **Art:** Photographs, illustrations; electronic format; $5/print. **Queries:** Preferred. **E-Queries:** Yes. **Unsolicited mss:** Accepts. **Freelance Content:** 25%. **Payment:** On publication.

PERFORMING ARTS AND ENTERTAINMENT IN CANADA
104 Glenrose Ave., Toronto, Ontario M4T 1K8. 416-484-4534.
E-mail: kbell@interlog.ca. Quarterly. $8.56/issue. Circ.: 44,000. Karen Bell, Editor. **Description:** Canadian performing arts and entertainment, including theater, music (especially classical, new, jazz, world, and folk), dance, film, TV and related fields. Also profiles, opinion, issues, etc. **Nonfiction:** Should be of national interest, but values submissions from smaller, out-of-the-way locations (not just downtown Montreal and Toronto). Especially interested in stories that reflect some aspect of Canadian diversity. Publishes very few reviews; 600-1,500 words; $95-$170. **Art:** Prints (B&W or color); no payment. **Tips:** Welcomes new writers. Prefers stories with original ideas and opinions, or addressing issues of some complexity or sophistication—not just simple profiles of people or companies. **Queries:** Required. **E-Queries:** Yes. **Unsolicited mss:** Accepts. **Response:** Slow to respond, be patient, SASE required. **Rights:** 1st print and electronic. **Payment:** On publication.

PLAYBILL
52 Vanderbilt Ave., New York, NY 10017. 212-557-5757.
E-mail: rsimonson@playbill.com. Web site: www.playbill.com. Robert Simonson, Editor. **Description:** Increases the understanding and enjoyment of each Broadway production, certain Lincoln Center and Off-Broadway productions, and regional attractions. Also, features about theatre personalities, fashion, entertainment, dining, etc. **Unsolicited mss:** Does not accept.

SOAP OPERA DIGEST

PRIMEDIA Consumer Media & Magazine Group

261 Madison Ave., Fl. 10, New York, NY 10016-2303. 212-716-2700.

E-mail: sodeditor@aol.com. Web site: www.soapdigest.com. Weekly. $69.95. Circ.: 1,111,621. Carolyn Hinsey, Executive Editor. **Description:** Investigative reports and profiles about New York and Los Angeles-based soaps. **Nonfiction:** to 1,500 words; pays from $250. **Payment:** On acceptance.

SOAP OPERA UPDATE

Bauer Publishing Co.

270 Sylvan Ave., Englewood Cliffs, NJ 07632-2521. 201-569-6699.

E-mail: soapupdate@aol.com. Biweekly. Circ.: 279,000. Sue Weiner, Editor-in-Chief. **Description:** Soap-opera oriented. **Nonfiction:** Articles, 750-1,250 words; pays $200. **Fillers:** to 500 words. **Queries:** Preferred. **Payment:** On publication.

STAR

American Media, Inc.

5401 Broken Sound Blvd. NW, Boca Raton, FL 33487-3512. 561-997-7733.

E-mail: letters@starmagazine.com. Web site: www.starmagazine.com. Weekly. Circ.: 1,630,000. Tony Frost, Editor-in-Chief. **Description:** On show business and celebrities, health, fitness, parenting, and diet and food. **Nonfiction:** Topical articles, 50-800 words; pay varies.

TIGER BEAT

See page 598 for full listing.

Description: On young people in show business and the music industry.

TV GUIDE

Gemstar-TV Guide International, Inc.

1211 Avenue of the Americas, New York, NY 10036-8701. 212-852-7500.

Web site: www.tvguide.com. Weekly. $39.88. Circ.: 10,000,000. Steven Reddicliffe, Editor-in-Chief. **Description:** Short, light, brightly written pieces about humorous or offbeat angles of television and industry trends. Most personality pieces are staff-written. **Queries:** Required. **Payment:** On acceptance.

UNIVERCITY

Hadley Media

21 Melrose Ave., Norwalk, CT 06855. 203-838-5303.

E-mail: katie@univercity.com. Web site: www.univercity.com. Patrick Hadley, Publisher. **Description:** An entertainment magazine for college students. Has east-coast and west-coast editions. **Tips:** To submit, visit UniverCity's website for details. Also interested in screenplays for their production company. **Queries:** Preferred. **E-Queries:** Yes. **Unsolicited mss:** Accepts.

VIDEOMAKER

P.O. Box 4591, Chico, CA 95927. 530-891-8410.
E-mail: editor@videomaker.com. Web site: www.videomaker.com. Monthly. Circ.: 80,000. Stephen Muratore, Editor. **Description:** Covers consumer video production: camcorders, computers, tools and techniques. For hobbyists and professional users. **Nonfiction:** Authoritative how-to articles, instructionals, editing, desktop video, audio/video production, innovative applications, tools and tips, industry developments, new products; up to 1,500 words; $.10/word. **Queries:** Preferred. **E-Queries:** Yes. **Unsolicited mss:** Accepts. **Response:** 6-8 weeks, SASE. **Freelance Content:** 60%. **Rights:** All. **Payment:** On acceptance.

WRITTEN BY

7000 W Third St., Los Angeles, CA 90048-4329. 213-782-4522.
9x/yr. Circ.: 12,500. **Description:** Official publication of the Writers Guild of America. Written by and for America's screen and television writers. **Nonfiction:** Feature articles (2,500 words), special reports (1,500-2,000 words), interviews, technical articles, and product reviews. **Tips:** Review previous issues before submitting queries or manuscripts. **Unsolicited mss:** Accepts. **Response:** 8 weeks. **Rights:** 1st world-wide and electronic. **Payment:** On acceptance.

FITNESS

(see also Health)

AMERICAN FITNESS

15250 Ventura Blvd., Suite 200, Sherman Oaks, CA 91403. 818-905-0040.
Web site: www.afaa.com. Bimonthly. $48/year. Circ.: 42,000. Meg Jordan, Editor. **Description:** Trade journal for fitness instructors. **Nonfiction:** Articles on exercise, health, trends, research, nutrition, class instruction, alternative paths. No first-person stories; 1,200 words; $200/article. **Art:** Slides; $35/slide. **Tips:** Needs research-oriented articles. **Queries:** Required. **E-Queries:** Yes. **Unsolicited mss:** Accepts. **Response:** 2 months, SASE required. **Freelance Content:** 90%. **Rights:** All. **Payment:** On publication.

FITNESS

Gruner + Jahr USA Publishing
15 E 26th St., New York, NY 10010. 646-758-0430.
Monthly. $3/issue. Circ.: 1,000,000. Emily Listfield, Editor-in-Chief. **Description:** Features on health, exercise, nutrition, and general well-being. Targets women in their twenties and thirties. **Nonfiction:** Articles on exercise, nutrition, beauty, sex and relationships, stress, etc. Also includes features on new products, how-to pieces on exercise, and first-person profiles of individuals with healthy lifestyles; 1,500-2,500 words; $1,500-$2,500. **Queries:** Required. **Response:** Queries 2 months. **Rights:** 1st NA. **Payment:** On acceptance.

FITNESS PLUS
3402 E Kleindale Rd., Tucson, AZ 85716. 520-881-6696.
Monthly. Kari Redfield, Editor. **Description:** On serious health and fitness training. **Nonfiction:** Articles, 600 words; pay varies. **Queries:** Required. **Payment:** On publication.

FITNESS RX
Advanced Research Press
690 Rt. 25A, Setauket, NY 11733.
Description: For women featuring well-researched articles on diet, fitness, health, cosmetic enhancement, and sexual fulfillment. **Queries:** Preferred. **Payment:** On publication.

IDEA HEALTH & FITNESS SOURCE
IDEA, Inc.
6190 Cornerstone Ct. E, Suite 204, San Diego, CA 92121-4701. 858-535-8979.
E-mail: lofshultd@ideafit.com. Web site: www.ideafit.com. Monthly. $40. Circ.: 19,000. Diane Lofshult, Executive Editor. **Description:** Leading publication for all levels of fitness professionals. **Nonfiction:** Practical articles on new exercise programs, business management, nutrition, health, motivation, sports medicine, group exercise, one-to-one training techniques. Length, pay varies. **Tips:** Must be geared toward exercise studio owner or manager, personal trainer, and fitness instructor. No consumer or general health pieces. **Queries:** Preferred. **E-Queries:** Yes. **Unsolicited mss:** Accepts. **Response:** Queries 2-3 months. **Freelance Content:** 75%. **Rights:** All NA (print and electronic). **Payment:** On acceptance.

IDEA PERSONAL TRAINER
IDEA, Inc.
6190 Cornerstone Ct. E, Suite 204, San Diego, CA 92121-4701. 858-535-8979.
Web site: www.ideafit.com. Monthly. $36.70. Circ.: 10,000. Gayle Bennett, Managing Editor. **Description:** For the professional personal trainer. **Nonfiction:** On exercise science; program design; profiles of successful trainers; business, legal, and marketing topics; tips for networking with other trainers and with allied medical professionals; client counseling; and training tips. Pay varies. **Columns, Departments:** What's New (industry news, products, research). **Queries:** Preferred. **E-Queries:** Yes. **Unsolicited mss:** Accepts. **Response:** 1 month, SASE for mailed materials. **Payment:** On publication.

MEN'S FITNESS
Weider Publications,Inc.
21100 Erwin St., Woodland Hills, CA 91367-3712. 818-884-6800.
E-mail: mensfitness@weiderpub.com. Web site: www.mensfitness.com. Monthly. $21.97/yr. Circ.: 607,000. Jerry Kindela, Editor-in-Chief. **Description:** On sports, fitness, health, nutrition, and men's issues. **Nonfiction:** Authoritative, practical articles,

1,500-1,800 words; pays $500-$1,000. **Columns, Departments:** 1,200-1,500 words. **Tips:** Send clips. **Queries:** Preferred. **Payment:** On acceptance.

MUSCULAR DEVELOPMENT

Advanced Research Press
690 Rt. 25A, Setauket, NY 11733.
Steve Blechman, Editor-in-Chief. **Description:** For serious weight-training athletes, on any aspect of competitive body building, powerlifting, sports, and nutrition. **Nonfiction:** Articles, 1,000-2,500 words, photos; pays $50-$400. **Queries:** Preferred. **Payment:** On publication.

THE PHYSICIAN AND SPORTS MEDICINE MAGAZINE

4530 W 77th St., Minneapolis, MN 55435. 952-835-3222.
E-mail: jim_wappes@mcgrawhill.com. Web site: www.physsportmed.com. Susan Hawthorne, Editor. **Description:** News articles, with sports-medicine angle. **Nonfiction:** Pays $300-$500. **Queries:** Preferred. **Payment:** On acceptance.

SHAPE

Weider Publications, Inc.
21100 Erwin St., Woodland Hills, CA 91367-3772. 818-595-0593.
Web site: www.shape.com. Monthly. $3.99. Circ.: 1,600,000. Barbara Harris, Editor-in-Chief. **Description:** Provides women with tools to create better lives and a deeper understanding of fitness. **Nonfiction:** New and interesting ideas on physical and mental aspects of getting and staying in shape; 1,200-1,500 words; pay varies. **Tips:** Uses only solid, well-respected experts in fields of exercise, health, nutrition, sport, beauty, and psychology. **Queries:** Preferred. **Unsolicited mss:** Does not accept. **Payment:** On acceptance. **Contact:** Anne M. Russell.

SWEAT

736 E Loyola Dr., Tempe, AZ 85282. 480-947-3900.
E-mail: Westwoman@aol.com. Web site: www.sweatmagazine.com. Joan Westlake, Editor. **Description:** Covers amateur sports, outdoor activities, wellness, and fitness, with an Arizona angle. **Nonfiction:** Articles, 500-1,200 words. No self-indulgent or personal tales. Prefers investigative pieces, must relate to Arizona or Arizonans. Pays $25-$60. **Art:** Photos, $15-$70. **Queries:** Required. **Unsolicited mss:** Does not accept. **Payment:** On publication.

TEACHING ELEMENTARY PHYSICAL EDUCATION

See page 350 for full listing.
Description: Resources and ideas for K-8 physical education teachers.

VIM & VIGOR

1010 E Missouri Ave., Phoenix, AZ 85014. 602-395-5850.
E-mail: careyj@mcmurry.com. Web site: vigormagazine.com. Quarterly. $2.95. Circ.:

1,500,000. Carey E. Jones, Editor. **Description:** A national health and fitness publication with 20 regional editions. **Nonfiction:** Positive articles, with medical facts, healthcare news, medical breakthroughs, exercise/fitness, health trends, wellness, general physical and emotional health, disease updates; written for a general reader; 900-1,500 words; up to $750. **Tips:** No healthcare product promotion, book reviews, personal accounts (unless to illustrate a topic), or unfounded medical claims for disease prevention and treatment. Style is serious, poignant, informative; with a slant that speaks to the reader as "you." Write for an educated reader, but remember to explain scientific terms and complex procedures. **Queries:** Preferred. **E-Queries:** Yes. **Unsolicited mss:** Does not accept. **Rights:** 1st NA, international and electronic. **Payment:** On acceptance.

WEIGHT WATCHERS
See page 421 for full listing.
Description: Health, nutrition, fitness, and weight-loss motivation and success.

FOOD & WINE

BON APPETIT
Condé Nast Publications, Inc.
6300 Wilshire Blvd., Fl. 10, Los Angeles, CA 90048-5204. 323-965-3600.
Web site: www.bonappetit.com. Monthly. $3.50/$20. Circ.: 1,283,375. Victoria von Biel, Executive Editor. **Description:** Covers food, entertainment, and travel. **Art:** Photos, illustrations. **Queries:** Preferred. **E-Queries:** No. **Unsolicited mss:** Does not accept. **Response:** 4-6 weeks, SASE required. **Rights:** All. **Payment:** On acceptance.

BREW YOUR OWN
Battenkill Communications
5053 Main St., Suite A, Manchester Center, VT 05255. 802-362-3981.
E-mail: edit@byo.com. Web site: www.byo.com. Monthly. Circ.: 40,000. Kathleen James Ring, Editor. **Description:** Practical information for homebrewers. **Queries:** Required. **Payment:** On publication.

CHEF
Talcott Communications Corp.
20 N Wacker Dr., Suite 1865, Chicago, IL 60606. 312-849-2220.
Web site: www.chefmagazine.com. Brent T. Frei. **Description:** "The Food Magazine for Professionals." Offers professionals in the foodservice business ideas for food marketing, preparation, and presentation. **Nonfiction:** Articles, 800-1,200 words; pays $250 to first-time writers, others $400. **Payment:** On publication.

CHOCOLATIER
Haymarket Group Ltd.
45 W 34th St., Suite 600, New York, NY 10001-3073. 212-239-0855.
E-mail: chocmag@aol.com. Web site: www.godiva.com. Bimonthly. $21.95/yr. Circ.: 150,000. Michael Schneider, Publisher/Editor-in-Chief. **Description:** Articles related to chocolate and desserts, cooking and baking techniques, lifestyle and travel. **Nonfiction:** Pay varies. **Queries:** Required. **Payment:** On acceptance.

COOK'S ILLUSTRATED
17 Station St., Brookline, MA 02445. 617-232-1000.
Web site: cooksillustrated.com. Bimonthly. Christopher Kimball, Editor. **Description:** Articles on techniques of home cooking. Features master recipes based on careful testing, trial and error. **Nonfiction:** Pay varies. **Art:** Hand-drawn illustrations. Send portfolio. **Queries:** Required. **Payment:** On acceptance.

COOKING FOR PROFIT
See page 603 for full listing.
Description: Publication for foodservice professionals.

FANCY FOOD & CULINARY PRODUCTS

Talcott Communications Corp.

20 N Wacker Dr., Suite 1865, Chicago, IL 60606-2905. 312-849-2220, ext. 34.
E-mail: fancyfood@talcott.com. Web site: www.talcott.com. monthly. $3.95/issue.
Circ.: 28,000. Daniel von Rabenau, Editor-in-Chief. **Description:** Covers the busi-
ness of specialty foods, coffee and tea, natural foods, confections, and upscale house-
wares. **Nonfiction:** 1,200-1,500 words; $300. **Art:** prints, transparencies, digital; $50.
Tips: Readers are retailers, not customers. **Queries:** Required. **E-Queries:** Yes.
Unsolicited mss: Accepts. **Response:** 1 month. **Freelance Content:** 35%.
Rights: FNASR. **Payment:** On publication. **Contact:** Brent Frei, Managing Editor.

GOURMET

Condé Nast Publications, Inc.

4 Times Square, New York, NY 10036. 212-286-2860.
Web site: www.epicurious.com. **Description:** "The magazine of good living."
Queries: Preferred. **Unsolicited mss:** Does not accept.

HOMETOWN COOKING

Meredith Corp.

1716 Locust St., Des Moines, IA 50309. 515-284-3000.
Web site: www.hometowncook.com. Bimonthly. Joy Taylor, Executive Editor.
Description: Great-tasting, tried-and-true recipes from America's most popular
hometown cookbooks. **Nonfiction:** Features include dinnertime survival recipes,
prizewinning recipes, family-approved recipes, interesting stories about hometown
cooks and their recipes, and beautiful full-color photos of recipes. Pay varies.

VEGGIE LIFE

EGW Publishing

1041 Shary Circle, Concord, CA 94518. 925-671-9852.
Web site: www.veggielife.com. Quarterly. Shanna Masters. **Description:** For people
interested in lowfat, meatless cuisine and nutrition. **Nonfiction:** Food features
(include 7-8 recipes); 1,500-2,000 words. **Columns, Departments:** 1,000-1,500
words. **Queries:** Preferred. **Payment:** On publication.

WINE SPECTATOR

387 Park Ave. S, New York, NY 10016. 212-684-4224.
Web site: www.winespectator.com. Thomas Matthews, Executive Editor.
Description: On news and people in the wine world, travel, food, and other lifestyle
topics. **Nonfiction:** Features, 600-2,000 words, preferably with photos; pays from
$400, extra for photos. **Queries:** Required. **Payment:** On publication.

WINE TIDINGS

Kylix Media, Inc.

5165 Sherbrooke St. W, Suite 414, Montreal
Quebec H4A 1T6 Canada. 514-481-5892.

E-mail: winetidings@netcom.ca. 8x/year. Circ.: 13,000. Tony Aspler, Editor. **Description:** Accurate wine information, written for Canadian audience. **Nonfiction:** Articles (1,000-1,500 words, $100-$300), and shorts (400-1,000 words, $30-$150). **Art:** B&W photos, $20-$50; color, $200-$400 (covers). **Queries:** Preferred. **Payment:** On publication.

WINEMAKER
Battenkill Communications
5053 Main St., Suite A, Manchester Center, VT 05255. 802-362-3981.
E-mail: edit@winemakermag.com. Web site: www.winemakermag.com. Monthly. Circ.: 35,000. Kathleen James Ring, Editor. **Description:** Practical information for home winemakers. **Queries:** Required. **Payment:** On publication.

WINES & VINES
1800 Lincoln Ave., San Rafael, CA 94901. 415-453-9700.
E-mail: edit@winesandvines.com. Web site: www.winesandvines.com. Monthly. Philip E. Hiaring, Editor. **Description:** On grape and wine industry, emphasizing marketing, management, vineyard techniques, and production. Emphasizes technology with valuable, scientific winemaking articles. **Nonfiction:** Articles, 2,000 words; pays $.15/word. **Queries:** Required. **E-Queries:** Yes. **Unsolicited mss:** Accepts. **Payment:** On acceptance.

ZYMURGY
See page 447 for full listing.
Description: Articles appealing to beer lovers and homebrewers.

GAMES & PASTIMES
(See also Hobbies, Crafts, Collecting)

BINGO BUGLE
Frontier Publications, Inc.
P.O. Box 527, Vashon, WA 98070-0527. 206-463-5656.
E-mail: tara@bingobugle.com. Web site: www.bingobugle.com. Monthly. Circ.: 1,061,000. Tara Snowden, Managing Editor. **Description:** For bingo players.

CARDPLAYER
3140 S Polaris Ave., Suite 8, Las Vegas, NV 89102. 702-871-1720.
E-mail: info@cardplayer.com. Web site: www.cardplayer.com. Biweekly. $59/year. Circ.: 50,000. Steve Radulovich, Editor. **Description:** For competitive players, on poker events, personalities, legal issues, new casinos, tournaments, strategies, and psychology to improve poker play. **Nonfiction:** Any length; payment negotiable. **Fillers:** Humor. **Queries:** Preferred. **E-Queries:** No. **Unsolicited mss:** Accepts. **Response:** 1 month. **Freelance Content:** 1%. **Payment:** On publication.

CASINO PLAYER
Ace Marketing, Inc.

8025 Black Horse Pike, Suite 470, West Atlantic City, NJ 08232-2950. 609-484-8866. E-mail: afine@casinocenter.com. Web site: www.casinocenter.com. Monthly. $24. Circ.: 200,000. Adam Fine, Editor-in-Chief. **Description:** For beginning to intermediate gamblers, on slots, video poker, and table games. **Nonfiction:** Articles, 1,000-2,000 words, with photos; pays from $250. **Tips:** No first-person or real-life gambling stories. **Payment:** On publication.

CHANCE: THE BEST OF GAMING
ARC Publishing, Inc.

16 E 41st St., Fl. 2, New York, NY 10017-7213. 212-889-3467. E-mail: letters@chancemag.com. Web site: www.chancemag.com. Bimonthly. $25. Circ.: 190,000. Anthony C. Reilly, Editor-in-Chief. **Description:** "The Best of Gaming." For casino and betting individuals.

CHESS LIFE
3054 U.S. Rte. 9W, New Windsor, NY 12553-7698. 716-676-2402. E-mail: magazines@uschess.org. Web site: www.uschess.org. Monthly. $3.75/issue, $30/year. Circ.: 70,000. Peter Kurzdorfer, Editor. **Description:** Published by United States Chess Federation. Covers news of major chess events (U.S. and abroad), with emphasis on the triumphs and exploits of American players. **Nonfiction:** Articles on news, profiles, technical aspects. Features on history, humor, puzzles, etc; 500-3,000 words; $105/page. **Art:** B&W glossies, color slides; $25-$25. **Tips:** Does not accept fiction. **Queries:** Preferred. **Unsolicited mss:** Accepts. **Payment:** On publication.

COMPUTER GAMES MAGAZINE
The Globe.com

63 Millet St., Richmond, VT 05477-9492. 802-434-3060. E-mail: editor@cdmag.com. Web site: www.cgonline.com. Monthly. $9.99. Circ.: 374,500. **Description:** Computer gaming information.

COMPUTER GAMING WORLD
Ziff-Davis Publishing Co.

50 Beale St., Suite 12, San Francisco, CA 94105-1813. 415-357-4900. E-mail: cgwletter@zd.com. Web site: www.computergaming.com. Monthly. Circ.: 345,200. Jeff Green, Editor-in-Chief. **Description:** All aspects of computer gaming.

ELECTRONIC GAMING MONTHLY
Ziff-Davis Publishing Co.

P.O. Box 3338, Hinsdale, IL 60522-3338. 630-382-9000. E-mail: egm@zd.com. Web site: www.videogames.com. Monthly. Circ.: 426,794. Dan Hsu, Editor-in-Chief. **Description:** Reports on home video console games.

GAMEPRO

Games Media Group

501 2nd St., Suite 114, San Francisco, CA 94107-4133. 415-979-9845.
E-mail: letters@gamepro.com. Web site: www.gamepro.com. Monthly. Circ.: 500,000. Wes Nihei, Editor-in-Chief. **Description:** For computer and video gamers.

GAMES

7002 W Butler Pike, Suite 210, Ambler, PA 19002. 215-643-6385.
E-mail: gamespub@voicenet.com. 9x/year. Circ.: 100,000. R. Wayne Schmittberger, Editor-in-Chief. **Description:** "For creative minds at play." **Nonfiction:** Features and short articles on games and playful, offbeat subjects. Visual and verbal puzzles, pop culture quizzes, brainteasers, contests, game reviews. **Tips:** Send SASE for guidelines (specify writer's, crosswords, variety puzzles, or brainteasers). **Payment:** On publication.

JACKPOT!

Morris Specialty Publications, LLC

6064 Apple Tree Dr., Suite 9, Memphis, TN 38115-0307. 901-360-0777.
E-mail: jackpot@memphisonline.com. Web site: www.jackpotmagazine.com. Semimonthly. Circ.: 40,000. Lori Beth Sunderman, Executive Editor. **Description:** Covers all aspects of casino entertainment, gaming, and food.

POOL & BILLIARD

810 Travelers Blvd. Bldg. D, Summerville, SC 29485. 843-875-5115.
E-mail: poolmag@poolmag.com. Web site: www.poolmag.com. Monthly. $34.95. Circ.: 20,000. Shari J. Staunch, Executive Editor. **Description:** Consumer and trade magazine for players and others interested in the pool industry. **Nonfiction:** Articles relevant to the game of pool. Particular interest in instruction and tourney coverage; 600-2,500 words; $130/page. **Tips:** No fiction or poetry. **Response:** 5 days. **Freelance Content:** 10%.

REALMS OF FANTASY

See page 721 for full listing.
Description: Topics and reviews of interest to readers of science fiction.

RENAISSANCE

See page 429 for full listing.
Description: Renaissance and Medieval history, costuming, heraldry, reenactments, role-playing, and Renaissance faires.

WINNING!

NatCom, Inc.

15115 S 76th E Ave., Bixby, OK 74008-4114. 918-366-6191.
E-mail: editor@newslinc.com. Web site: www.winningnews.com. Monthly. Circ.: 125,000. Jason Sowards, Managing Editor. **Description:** Articles on how to win.

GAY & LESBIAN

EMPIRE
Two Queens, Inc.
230 W 17th St., Fl. 8, New York, NY 10011. 212-352-3535.
E-mail: akrach@hx.com. Web site: www.empiremag.com. Aaron Krach, Editor.
Description: For gay men who want the most out of life.

GENRE
7080 Hollywood Blvd., Suite 818, Hollywood, CA 90028. 323-467-8300.
E-mail: lfreeman@genremagazine.com. Web site: www.genremagazine.com.
Monthly. $4.95/issue, $24.95/year. Circ.: 60,000. Andy Towle, Editor. **Description:**
Fashion, entertainment, travel, fiction, and reviews for gay men. **Fiction:** Gay
themes. Pay varies; 2,000 words. **Nonfiction:** Travel, celebrity interviews, etc; 300-
1,500 words. **Art:** Slides, JPGs. **Queries:** Preferred. **E-Queries:** Yes. **Unsolicited
mss:** Accepts. **Response:** SASE required. **Freelance Content:** 60%. **Rights:** Print,
electronic. **Payment:** On publication.

GLOBAL CITY REVIEW
See page 671 for full listing.
Description: Intellectual literary forum for women, lesbian, gay, and other culturally
diverse writers, writers of color, international writers, and activist writers.

HURRICANE ALICE
See page 366 for full listing.
Description: Articles that explore feminist issues on all aspects of culture.

JAMES WHITE REVIEW
Lambda Literary Foundation
P.O. Box 73910, Washington, DC 20056-3910. 202-682-0952.
E-mail: jwr@lambdalit.org. Web site: www.lambdalit.org. Quarterly. $4.95/$17.50.
Circ.: 3,000. Patrick Merla, Editor. **Description:** Gay men's literary magazine, with
fiction, poetry, photography, art, essays, and reviews. Welcomes both unpublished and
established writers. **Fiction:** Seeking well-crafted literary fiction with strongly-devel-
oped characters; gay themes; to 10,000 words; pay varies. **Poetry:** Submit up to 3
poems at a time. **Tips:** Be patient, small staff with a lot of submissions. **Queries:**
Preferred. **E-Queries:** No. **Unsolicited mss:** Accepts. **Response:** Queries 3 weeks,
submissions 3-6 months, SASE. **Rights:** 1st. **Payment:** On publication. **Contact:**
Greg Harren, Assistant Editor.

LAMBDA BOOK REPORT
See page 636 for full listing.
Description: Reviews and features on gay and lesbian books.

OUT MAGAZINE
80 Eighth Ave., Suite 315, New York, NY 10011. 212-242-8100.
Web site: www.out.com. Brendan Lemon, Editor-in-Chief. **Description:** Articles on arts, politics, fashion, finance, and other subjects for gay and lesbian readers. No fiction or poetry. Pay varies. **Queries:** Preferred. **Payment:** On publication.

GENERAL INTEREST

AMERICAN HERITAGE
See page 422 for full listing.
Description: Features pieces that shed light on the American experience.

THE ARIZONA REPUBLIC
Gannett Newspapers
200 E Van Buren St., Phoenix, AZ 85004-2238. 602-444-8000.
E-mail: feedback@arizonarepublic.com. Web site: www.arizonarepublic.com. Daily. Tom Callinan, Editor. **Description:** Newspaper, with diverse articles, 800-1,000 words, on lifestyles, environment, religion, politics, law, etc. **Queries:** Preferred. **Rights:** Exclusive (AZ).

THE ATLANTA JOURNAL-CONSTITUTION
See page 501 for full listing.
Description: Articles related to the Southeast, Georgia, and the Atlanta metro area.

THE ATLANTIC MONTHLY
77 N Washington St., Boston, MA 02114. 617-854-7700.
E-mail: letters@theatlantic.com. Web site: www.theatlantic.com. Monthly. $3.95/issue. Circ.: 500,000. Michael Kelly, Editor. **Description:** At the leading edge of contemporary issues, plus offers the best in fiction, travel, food, and humor. **Fiction:** 2,000-6,000 words; up to $3,000. **Nonfiction:** 1,000-7,500 words; payment varies. **Poetry:** Accepts. **Queries:** Preferred. **E-Queries:** No. **Unsolicited mss:** Accepts. **Response:** 2-4 weeks, SASE required. **Freelance Content:** 50%. **Rights:** FNAR. **Payment:** On acceptance.

BALTIMORE SUN
P.O. Box 1377, Baltimore, MD 21278-0001. 410-332-6051.
E-mail: richard.gross@baltsun.com. Web site: www.sunspot.net. Daily. 50¢/issue. Circ.: 337,000. Richard C. Gross, Editor. **Description:** Op-Ed section of the newspaper serving the Baltimore metropolitan region. **Nonfiction:** Domestic/foreign affairs, lifestyles, science, education, humor, politics, environment, and regional interest; 300-700 words; $50-$150. **Queries:** Not necessary. **E-Queries:** No. **Unsolicited mss:** Accepts. **Response:** 1 week, SASE required. **Freelance Content:** 75%. **Rights:** Exclusive. **Payment:** On publication.

BLACK BOOK
116 Prince St., Fl. 2, New York, NY 10012-3178. 212-334-1800.
Web site: www.blackbookmag.com. Bimonthly. Anuj Desai, Editor-in-Chief.
Description: General interest lifestyles magazine covering trends, entertainment, arts, beauty and fashion, news, and cutting-edge journalism. Also features some fiction. **Queries:** Preferred.

BOSTON HERALD
One Herald Square, P.O. Box 2096, Boston, MA 02106-2096. 617-426-3000.
E-mail: feedback@bostonherald.com. Web site: www.bostonherald.com. Daily.
Andrew Costello, Executive Editor. **Description:** On economics, foreign affairs, politics, regional interest, seasonal topics. **Nonfiction:** Short articles; 600-700 words; pay varies. **Tips:** Prefers submissions from regional writers. **Rights:** Exclusive for MA, RI, and NH. **Payment:** On publication.

BUTTON
P.O. Box 26, Lunenburg, MA 01462.
E-mail: buttonx26@aol.com. Web site: www.moonsigns.net. Annual. $2/issue. Circ.:
1,500. Sally Cragin, Editor. **Description:** "New England's Tiniest Magazine of Poetry, Fiction, and Gracious Living." **Fiction:** Short stories. **Nonfiction:** Wit, brevity, well-conceived essay, recipes, sheet music, how-to, celebrity gossip, book and album reviews; pay varies. **Poetry:** No sentimental or song lyrics. **Queries:** Not necessary. **E-Queries:** No. **Unsolicited mss:** Accepts. **Response:** Submissions 2-3 months, SASE. **Freelance Content:** 60%. **Payment:** On publication.

THE CAPITAL TIMES
P.O. Box 8060, Madison, WI 53708. 608-252-6400.
E-mail: jnichols@madison.com. Web site: www.captimes.com. Daily. John Nichols, Associate Editor. **Description:** On education, environment, regional interest, and religion. **Nonfiction:** Short articles; 600-700 words; pays $25. **Payment:** On publication.

CHARLOTTE OBSERVER
Knight Ridder, P.O. Box 30308, Charlotte, NC 28230-0308. 704-358-5000.
E-mail: feedback@charlotteobserver.com. Web site: www.charlotteobserver.com.
Daily. Jennie Buckner, Editor. **Description:** On local (Carolinas) issues or that use local examples to illustrate larger issues. **Nonfiction:** Well-written, thought-provoking articles; to 700 words; pays $50. **Tips:** No simultaneous submissions in NC or SC. **Payment:** On publication.

CHICAGO READER
See page 505 for full listing.
Description: Free weekly publication for residents in the Chicago area.

CHICAGO TRIBUNE
Tribune Company
435 N Michigan Ave., Chicago, IL 60611-4066. 312-222-3232.
E-mail: ctc-editor@tribune.com. Web site: www.chicagotribune.com. Daily. Ann
Marie Lipinski, Editor-in-Chief. **Description:** On domestic and international affairs,
environment, regional interest, and personal essays. **Nonfiction:** Short articles (to
800 words); profiles and features, to 6,000 words, on public, social, and cultural issues
in the Midwest/Chicago area; pays $250-$1,500. **Queries:** Preferred. **Response:**
SASE required. **Payment:** On publication.

CHICAGO TRIBUNE MAGAZINE
Chicago Tribune
435 N Michigan Ave., Chicago, IL 60611. 312-222-3232.
Web site: www.chicagotribune.com. **Description:** Sunday magazine of the *Chicago
Tribune.*

CHRISTIAN SCIENCE MONITOR
One Norway St., Boston, MA 02115. 617-450-2372.
E-mail: oped@csps.com. Web site: www.csmonitor.com. Daily. Circ.: 95,000.
Description: Lifestyle trends, women's rights, family, community, and how-to.
Nonfiction: Pieces on domestic and foreign affairs, economics, education, environment, law, media, politics, and cultural commentary. Retains all rights for 90 days
after publication; 400-900 words; up to $400. **Poetry:** Finely crafted poems that
explore and celebrate daily life. Short preferred; submit no more than 5 poems at a
time. Seasonal material always needed. (No violence or sensuality; death or disease;
helplessness or hopelessness.) **Columns, Departments:** Arts and Leisure,
Learning, Ideas, Home Front, National, International, Work & Money; 800 words;
pay varies.

THE CLEVELAND PLAIN DEALER
1801 Superior Ave., Cleveland, OH 44114. 216-999-4800 or 216-999-4145.
E-mail: forum@plaind.com. Web site: www.cleveland.com. Daily. **Description:** On
variety of subjects: domestic affairs, economics, education, environment, foreign
affairs, humor, politics, and regional interest. **Nonfiction:** Op-ed pieces, to 700
words; pays $75. **Tips:** No room for historical pieces not tied to a recent event.
E-Queries: Yes. **Response:** 2-5 days. **Freelance Content:** 10-15%. **Rights:** non-
exclusive worldwide. **Payment:** On publication.

COLUMBIA
See page 534 for full listing.
Description: Magazine published by the Knights of Columbus.

CONVERSELY
PMB #121, 3053 Fillmore St., San Francisco, CA 94123.
E-mail: writers@conversely.com. Web site: www.conversely.com. Quarterly.

Description: Online publication exploring all aspects of relationships between men and women. **Fiction:** Literary stories on male-female relationships; to 3,000 words; $50-$150. **Nonfiction:** Essays and personal stories (memoirs); 750-3,000 words; $50-$150. **Tips:** Value personal opinion highly, witty, intelligent, entertaining. Avoid how-to, didactic material, or over-used romantic themes. **Queries:** Not necessary. **E-Queries:** Yes. **Unsolicited mss:** Accepts. **Response:** 2-3 weeks queries, 8-10 weeks submissions, SASE (for submissions via mail). **Freelance Content:** 70%. **Rights:** 90-day exclusive electronic, non-exclusive thereafter; one-time, non-exclusive print anthology rights. **Payment:** On publication.

DALLAS MORNING NEWS
A.H. Belo Corporation
P.O. Box 655237, Dallas, TX 75265-5237. 214-977-8222.
E-mail: rpederson@dallasnews.com. Web site: www.dallasnews.com. Daily. Rena Pederson, Editor. **Description:** Op-Ed pieces, 750 words, on politics, education, foreign and domestic affairs, cultural trends, seasonal and regional issues. Pays $75. **Response:** SASE required. **Payment:** On publication.

DENVER POST
MediaNews Group
P.O. Box 1709, Denver, CO 80201-1709. 303-820-1010.
E-mail: newsroom@denverpost.com. Web site: www.denverpost.com. Daily. Glenn Guzzo, Editor. **Description:** Newspaper. Articles, 400-700 words, with local or regional angle. No payment for freelance submissions. **Queries:** Preferred.

DES MOINES REGISTER
Gannett Newspapers
P.O. Box 957, Des Moines, IA 50304-0957. 515-284-8000.
E-mail: metroiowa@news.dmreg.com. Web site: www.desmoinesregister.com. Daily. Rick Tapscott, Managing Editor. **Description:** National and Iowa focus.

DETROIT FREE PRESS
600 W Fort St., Detroit, MI 48226. 313-222-6400.
E-mail: oped@freepress.com. Web site: www.freep.com. Daily. **Description:** Magazine covering a wide range of topics. **Tips:** Priority given to local writers. **Queries:** Preferred. **Payment:** On publication.

THE DETROIT NEWS
Gannett Newspapers
615 W Lafayette Blvd., Detroit, MI 48226-3197. 313-222-6400.
E-mail: metro@detnews.com. Web site: www.detnews.com. Daily. Mark Silverman, Editor. **Description:** Wide variety of subjects. **Queries:** Preferred. **Payment:** On publication.

ELKS
See page 299 for full listing.
Description: General-interest magazine published by the Elks organization.

FLORIDA
See page 507 for full listing.
Description: Online service of *Orlando Sentinel* newspaper.

FRESNO BEE
1626 E St., Fresno, CA 93786-0001. 559-441-6111.
Web site: www.fresnobee.com. Daily. **Description:** Newspaper with articles, 750 words, written by authors in Central California.

FRIENDLY EXCHANGE
C-E Publishers
P.O. Box 2120, Warren, MI 48090-2120. 586-753-8326.
Web site: www.friendlyexchange.com. Quarterly. Circ.: 5,500,000. Dan Grantham, Editor. **Description:** For policyholders of Farmers Insurance Group of Companies. **Nonfiction:** Articles with "news you can use," on home, health, personal finance, travel; 700-1,500 words; $400-$1,000. **Art:** Photos. **Queries:** Required.

GLOBE
American Media, Inc.
5401 Broken Sound Blvd. NW, Boca Raton, FL 33487-3589. 561-997-7733.
E-mail: newstips@globefl.com. Weekly. $29.97. Circ.: 775,600. Joe Mullins, Managing Editor. **Description:** Exposés, celebrity interviews, consumer and human-interest pieces. **Nonfiction:** Articles, 500-1,000 words, with photos; pays $50-$1,500.

GRIT
Ogden Publications
1503 SW 42nd St., Topeka, KS 66609-1265. 785-274-4300.
E-mail: grit@cjnetworks.com. Web site: www.grit.com. Biweekly. $1.95/issue, $27.98/year. Circ.: 120,000. Donna Doyle, Editor-in-Chief. **Description:** On American life and traditions with stories about ordinary people doing extraordinary things. **Fiction:** Heartwarming stories with a message, upbeat storyline and ending; 1,000-10,000 words; $.10-.$15/word. **Nonfiction:** Features on places or events, unsung heroes, nostalgic remembrances of rural communities and small towns; 500-1,800 words. **Poetry:** Romance; relationships; nature; family interaction; up to 30 lines; $2/line. **Fillers:** Sayings, humor, funny sayings from children; up to 25 words; $5-$15. **Art:** Photos must accompany features; $35-$50 ($100-$250 cover). **Tips:** Prefers full manuscript with photos. **Queries:** Not necessary. **E-Queries:** No. **Unsolicited mss:** Accepts. **Freelance Content:** 90%. **Rights:** 1st. **Payment:** On publication.

HAPPY

240 E 35th St., Suite 11A, New York, NY 10016.
E-mail: bayardx@aol.com. Bi-annual. $15/issue, $40/4 issues. Circ.: 350. Bayard, Editor. **Description:** General-interest publication. **Fiction:** Original work only. No racist, sexist, pornographic; 500-6,000 words; $.01-$.03/word. **Tips:** Avoid being dull, dim witted, boring. **Queries:** Not necessary. **E-Queries:** No. **Unsolicited mss:** Accepts. **Response:** 1 week, SASE. **Freelance Content:** 100%. **Rights:** One-time. **Payment:** On publication.

HOPE

P.O. Box 160, Brooklin, ME 04616. 207-359-4651.
E-mail: info@hopemag.com. Web site: www.hopemag.com. Quarterly. Circ.: 22,000. Kimberly Ridley, Editor. **Description:** About people making a difference. **Nonfiction:** No nostalgia, sentimental, political, opinion, or religious pieces; 150-3,000 words; $75-$1,500. **Queries:** Required. **Payment:** On publication.

IDEALS

535 Metroplex Dr., Suite 250, Nashville, TN 37211. 615-333-0478.
Web site: www.idealsbooks.com. Bimonthly. $5.95 issue, $19.95/year. Circ.: 200,000. Michelle Prater Burke, Editor. **Description:** Inspirational, seasonal poetry and prose, with artwork and photography, in turn on Easter, Mother's Day, Country, Friendship, Thanksgiving, and Christmas. **Fiction:** Holiday themes; 800-1,000 words; $.10/word. **Nonfiction:** On issue's theme; 800-1,000 words; $.10/word. **Poetry:** Light, nostalgic pieces; $10/poem. **Queries:** Not necessary. **E-Queries:** No. **Unsolicited mss:** Accepts. **Response:** Submissions 4-6 weeks, SASE required. **Rights:** One-time. **Payment:** On publication.

INDIANAPOLIS STAR

Gannett Newspapers
P.O. Box 145, Indianapolis, IN 46206-0145. 317-444-4000.
E-mail: info@indystar.com. Web site: www.indystar.com. Daily. Terry Eberle, Editor. **Description:** Newspaper. **Nonfiction:** Short articles, 700-800 words; pays $40. **Rights:** Exclusive (IN). **Payment:** On publication.

INQUIRER

400 N Broad St., P.O. Box 8263, Philadelphia, PA 19101. 215-854-4580.
E-mail: inquirer.magazine@phillynews.com. Web site: www.phillynews.com. Weekly. Circ.: 800,000. Ms. Avery Rome, Editor. **Description:** Sunday newspaper magazine, with strong journalism and storytelling, focusing on Philadelphia area. **Nonfiction:** Varied topics for family audiences, and local-interest features; 3,000 words; $500-$2,500. **Queries:** Required. **E-Queries:** Yes. **Unsolicited mss:** Accepts. **Response:** SASE required. **Freelance Content:** 20%. **Rights:** One-time. **Payment:** On publication.

JOURNAL AMERICA
2019 Greenwood Lake Tpke, Hewitt, NJ 07421-3027. 973-728-8355.
E-mail: journal@warick.net. Web site: www.ajournal.com. Monthly. $19.95/yr. Circ.:
75,000. Glen Malmgren, Editor. **Description:** Covers varied subjects of interest to
the American family. **Nonfiction:** On science, nature, or "true but strange stories."
Also, articles on all aspects of today's demanding lifestyle, with a touch of humor; 200-
1,000 words; pay varies.**Queries:** Preferred.

KIWANIS
See page 299 for full listing.
Description: Official publication for the Kiwanis service organization.

LATIN STYLE MAGAZINE
See page 369 for full listing.
Description: Latin arts and entertainment magazine.

LOS ANGELES TIMES
Tribune Company
202 W First St., Los Angeles, CA 90012-4105. 213-237-5000.
Web site: www.latimes.com. Weekly. Circ.: 1,300,000. John Carroll, Editor.
Description: Major urban newspaper, with weekly magazine. **Nonfiction:** Articles
on issues, general interest, profiles, crime, first persons, photo spreads, narratives on
current events; 400-4,000 words; $1/word. **Queries:** Preferred. **E-Queries:** Yes.
Unsolicited mss: Accepts. **Response:** 4 weeks, SASE. **Freelance Content:** 60%.
Payment: On publication.

LOUISVILLE COURIER-JOURNAL
Gannett Newspapers
525 W Broadway, Louisville, KY 40202-2137. 502-582-4011.
Web site: www.courier-journal.com. Daily. Edward Bennett, Editor. **Description:**
Newspaper. Very limited market. **Nonfiction:** Op-Ed pieces, 750 words, on regional
topics. Local writers preferred. Pays $25-$50. **Payment:** On publication.

NATIONAL ENQUIRER
American Media, Inc.
5401 Broken Sound Blvd. NW, Boca Raton, FL 33487-3512. 561-997-7733.
E-mail: letters@nationalenquirer.com. Web site: www.nationalenquirer.com. Weekly.
Circ.: 2,075,000. Steve Plamann, Executive Editor. **Description:** Short, humorous,
or philosophical fillers, witticisms, anecdotes, jokes, tart comments. Original items
only. Mass audience: topical news, celebrities, how-to, scientific discoveries, human
drama, adventure, medical news, personalities. **Poetry:** Short, 8 lines or less, traditional rhyming verse (amusing, philosophical, or inspirational in nature). No obscure
or artsy poetry. **Tips:** Submit seasonal/holiday material at least 3 months in advance.
Queries: Preferred. **Response:** SASE. **Payment:** On publication.

NATIONAL GEOGRAPHIC
See page 358 for full listing.
Description: On geography, world cultures, and environmental conservation.

NEW YORK SPIRIT
See page 516 for full listing.
Description: General interest publication for readers in Manhattan.

THE NEW YORK TIMES
The New York Times Company
229 W 43rd St., New York, NY 10036. 212-556-1234.
E-mail: oped@nytimes.com. Web site: www.nytimes.com. Daily. **Description:** Newspaper. **Nonfiction:** Travel articles; query with writer's background, description of proposed article. Opinion pieces: 650-800 words, any topic (public policy, science, lifestyles, and ideas). **Tips:** Include your daytime phone number and e-mail address with submission. "If you haven't heard from us in 2 weeks, assume we are not using your piece." **Rights:** 1st NA. **Payment:** On publication.

THE NEW YORK TIMES MAGAZINE
The New York Times Company
229 W 43rd St., New York, NY 10036. 212-556-1234.
Web site: www.nytimes.com. **Description:** On news items, trends, and culture. **Nonfiction:** Timely articles, up to 4,000 words; pays $1,000-$2,500. **Tips:** Send clips. **Queries:** Preferred. **Payment:** On acceptance.

NEWSWEEK
Newsweek, Inc.
251 W 57th St., Fl. 17, New York, NY 10019-1802. 212-778-4000.
E-mail: letters@newsweek.com. Web site: www.newsweek.com. Weekly. $41.87/yr. Circ.: 3,144,000. Richard M. Smith, Editor-in-Chief. **Description:** Covers news throughout the world. Mostly staff-written. **Columns, Departments:** My Turn (original first-person opinion essays, must contain verifiable facts. Submit manuscript with SASE); 850-900 words; $1,000. **Queries:** Preferred. **Response:** 2 months, SASE. **Rights:** Non-exclusive worldwide. **Payment:** On publication. **Contact:** Pam Hamer.

THE ORANGE COUNTY REGISTER
625 N Grand Ave., Santa Ana, CA 92701. 714-796-7951.
E-mail: tkatz@ocregister.com. Web site: www.ocregister.com. Daily. Tonnie Katz, Editor. **Description:** Newspaper. Op-Ed articles on a wide range of local and national issues and topics. **Nonfiction:** Pays $50-$100. **Payment:** On publication.

PARADE
711 Third Ave., New York, NY 10017. 212-450-7000.
Web site: www.parade.com. Weekly. Circ.: 76,000,000. Lee Kravitz, Editor.

Description: National Sunday newspaper magazine. Subjects of national interest. **Fiction:** No fiction. **Nonfiction:** Factual and authoritative articles on social issues, common health concerns, sports, community problem-solving, and extraordinary achievements of ordinary people; 1,200 to 1,500 words; from $1,000. **Poetry:** No poetry. **Fillers:** No games, nostalgia, quotes, or puzzles. **Art:** No cartoons. **Tips:** "We seek unique angles on all topics." **Queries:** Required. **Contact:** Steven J. Florio.

PEOPLE
Time, Inc.
1271 Avenue of the Americas, New York, NY 10020-1300. 212-522-1212.
E-mail: editor@people.com. Web site: www.people.com. Weekly. $93/yr. Circ.: 3,550,000. Carol Wallace, Managing Editor. **Description:** Mostly staff-written. Will consider article proposals, 3-4 paragraphs, on timely, entertaining, and topical personalities. **Payment:** On acceptance.

PORTLAND PRESS HERALD
Blethen Maine Newspapers
P.O. Box 1460, Portland, ME 04104-5009. 207-791-6650.
E-mail: info@mainetoday.com. Web site: www.portland.com. Daily. David Langzettel, Editor. **Description:** Newspaper. Op-Ed articles, 750 words, on any topic with state tie-in. **Rights:** exclusive (ME).

PRESS-TELEGRAM
MediaNews Group
604 Pine Ave., Long Beach, CA 90844-0001. 562-435-1161.
E-mail: ptnews@presstelegram.com. Web site: www.presstelegram.com. Daily. Rich Archbold, Executive Editor. **Description:** Newspaper. **Nonfiction:** Op-Ed articles, 750-900 words, on regional topics. Pays $75. **Rights:** exclusive (regional). **Payment:** On publication.

READER'S DIGEST
Readers Digest Association, Inc.
Readers Digest Rd., Pleasantville, NY 10572-7000. 914-238-1000.
E-mail: jacqueline_leo@readersdigest.com. Web site: www.readersdigest.com. Monthly. $24.76. Circ.: 13,000,000. Jacqueline Leo, Editor-in-Chief. **Description:** Offers stories of broad interest. **Nonfiction:** Only general-interest articles already in print and well-developed story proposals will be considered. Send reprint or query to any editor on the masthead. **Fillers:** Short humor, check "Wanted: Your Laugh Lines" page in guidelines, or Web site. **Tips:** Submissions are not acknowledged or returned. **Queries:** Preferred.

THE SACRAMENTO BEE
McClatchy Newspapers
2100 Q St., P.O. Box 15779, Sacramento, CA 95852-0779. 916-321-1000.
E-mail: ombud@sacbee.com. Web site: www.sacbee.com. Daily. Rick Rodriguez,

Executive Editor. **Description:** Newspaper covering North Central California. Op-Ed pieces, to 750 words; state and regional topics preferred.

ST. LOUIS POST-DISPATCH

900 N Tucker, St. Louis, MO 63101. 314-340-8391.
E-mail: oped@post-dispatch. Web site: www.stltoday.com. Daily. Donna Korando. **Description:** Newspaper. Op-Ed articles, 700 words, on economics, education, science, politics, foreign and domestic affairs, and the environment. Pays $60. **Tips:** Seeks local writers. Do not send attachments. **Payment:** On publication.

ST. PAUL PIONEER PRESS

Knight Ridder
345 Cedar St., St. Paul, MN 55101-1057. 651-222-5011.
E-mail: feedback@pioneerplanet.com. Web site: www.pioneerplanet.com. Daily. **Description:** Newspaper. Op-Ed articles, to 750 words, on a variety of topics. Pays $75. **Tips:** Strongly prefers authors or topics with a local connection. **Payment:** On publication.

ST. PETERSBURG TIMES

Poynter Institute for Media Studies
490 First Ave. S, St. Petersburg, FL 33701-4223. 727-893-8111.
E-mail: local@sptimes.com. Web site: www.sptimes.com. Daily. Circ.: 350,000. Paul Tash, Editor. **Description:** Newspaper. Authoritative articles, to 2,000 words, on current political, economic, and social issues. Pay varies. **Queries:** Preferred. **Payment:** On publication.

THE SAN FRANCISCO CHRONICLE

Hearst Newspapers
901 Mission St., San Francisco, CA 94103-2934. 415-777-1111.
E-mail: chronfeedback@sfgate.com. Web site: www.sfgate.com. Daily. Phil Bronstein, Executive Editor. **Description:** Newspaper. Articles, 400-650 words, with lively writing, pertinent to public policy debates, moving the debate forward. Pays to $150 ($75-$100 for unsolicited pieces). **Payment:** On publication.

SAN FRANCISCO EXAMINER

988 Market St., San Francisco, CA 94102-4002. 415-359-2600.
E-mail: letters@sfexaminer.com. Web site: www.examiner.com. Daily. Circ.: 90,000. Ted Fang, Editor. **Description:** Newspaper. Well-written articles, 500-650 words; prefers local/state issues and subjects bypassed by other news media. Pay varies. **Tips:** No sports. **Payment:** On publication.

SAN FRANCISCO EXAMINER MAGAZINE

988 Market St., San Francisco, CA 94102-4002. 415-777-2424.
Web site: www.examiner.com. **Description:** Sunday magazine of the *San Francisco Examiner.*

SATURDAY EVENING POST

Saturday Evening Post Society

1100 Waterway Blvd., Indianapolis, IN 46202-2174. 317-634-1100.

E-mail: satevepst@aol.com. Web site: www.satevepst.org. Bimonthly. $13.97. Circ.: 385,000. Ted Kreiter, Executive Editor. **Description:** Family-oriented, with humor, preventive medicine, health and fitness, destination-oriented travel pieces (not personal experience), celebrity profiles, arts, and sciences. **Nonfiction:** 1,500-3,000 words; pay varies. **Fillers:** Humor/satire, to 100 words, upbeat and positive. Light verse, cartoons, jokes, humorous, clean limericks, short narratives. No conventional poetry, original material only. Pays $15 for verse; $125 for cartoons. **Queries:** Preferred. **Response:** SASE. **Payment:** On publication.

SEATTLE POST-INTELLIGENCER

P.O. Box 1909, Seattle, WA 98111-1909. 206-448-8000.

Web site: www.seattle-pi.com. Daily. Ken Bunting, Executive Editor. **Description:** Seattle-based newspaper. Features articles, 750-800 words, on foreign and domestic affairs, the environment, education, politics, regional issues, religion, and science. Also features seasonal material. Prefer writers who live in the Pacific Northwest. Pays $75-$100. **Response:** SASE required. **Payment:** On publication.

SELECCIONES DEL READER'S DIGEST

Readers Digest Association, Inc.

1 Reader's Digest Rd., Pleasantville, NY 10570-7000. 914-238-1000.

E-mail: jacqueline_leo@readersdigest.com. Web site: www.readersdigest.com. Monthly. Circ.: 138,700. Jacqueline Leo, Editor-in-Chief. **Description:** Spanish-language version of Reader's Digest.

SELECTA

See page 372 for full listing.

Description: For upscale Hispanics in the U.S. and Latin America.

SMITHSONIAN

Smithsonian Institution

750 9th St. NW, Suite 7100MRC, Washington, DC 20560-0001. 202-275-2000.

Web site: www.smithsonianmag.com. Monthly. $28. Circ.: 2,000,000. Carey Winfrey, Editor-in-Chief. **Description:** Wide-ranging coverage of history, art, natural history, physical science, profiles, etc. **Nonfiction:** History, art, natural history, physical science, profiles; 2,000-5,000 words; pay varies. **Queries:** Required. **E-Queries:** Yes. **Unsolicited mss:** Accepts. **Response:** 6-8 weeks, SASE. **Contact:** Marlan A. Liddell, Articles Editor.

STAR

See page 390 for full listing.

Description: On show business, celebrities, health, fitness, parenting, and food.

STORYHOUSE.COM

4019 SE Hawthorne Blvd., Portland, OR 97214. 503-233-1144.
E-mail: submissions@storyhouse.com. Web site: www.storyhouse.com. Ongoing.
Todd and Esther Cowing, Editors. **Description:** Story House is an online retailer of
fresh roasted coffee in the Pacific Northwest. Coffee is shipped within 24 hours of
roasting. Every week they publish original art, stories, and essays on their coffee can
labels. **Fiction** and **Nonfiction:** Art, stories, letters, articles, and poetry. Current
need is for short-short/flash fiction, mysteries, and romances. Stories can be run over
several weeks, so if a piece will run over 1,000 words, chapter or section breaks should
be provided at points of suspense every 1,000 words. Also, seeking debate and academic pieces; 1,000 words. 1,000 words; $25/1,000 words. **Tips:** See guidelines on
Web site for details on editorial process involved. E-queries only; does not accept submissions by mail. **Queries:** Preferred. **E-Queries:** Yes. **Unsolicited mss:** Accepts.
Response: SASE required for regular mail. **Rights:** Author retains copyright.
Payment: On acceptance.

THE SUN

Sun Publishing Co.
107 N Roberson St., Chapel Hill, NC 27516. 919-942-5282.
E-mail: sy@thesunmagazine.org. Web site: www.thesunmagazine.org. Monthly.
$3.95/issue, $34 yr. Circ.: 50,000. Sy Safransky, Editor. **Description:** Essays, stories,
interviews, and poetry in which people write of their struggles to understand their
lives, often with surprising intimacy. Looking for writers willing to take risks and
describe life honestly. **Fiction:** Fiction that feels like a lived experience; to 7,000
words; $300-$500. **Nonfiction:** Personal essays and interviews; to 7,000 words; $300-
$1,000. **Poetry:** 1-2 pages; $50-$200. **Art:** B&W photographs only; $50-$200. **Tips:**
No journalistic, academic, opinion pieces. **Queries:** Not necessary. **E-Queries:** No.
Unsolicited mss: Accepts. **Response:** 3 months, SASE. **Freelance Content:** 80%.
Rights: One-time. **Payment:** On publication.

TEMAS

See page 373 for full listing.
Description: Topics of interest to Spanish-speaking people in the United States.

TEXAS MAGAZINE

801 Texas Ave., Houston, TX 77002. 713-220-7501.
E-mail: ken.hammond@chron.com. Web site: www.houstonchronicle.com. Kenneth
Hammond, Editor. **Description:** Sunday magazine of the *Houston Chronicle.*

TULSA WORLD

P.O. Box 1770, Tulsa, OK 74102-1770. 918-581-8300.
E-mail: alex.adwan@tulsaworld.com. Web site: www.tulsaworld.com. Daily. Alex
Adwan, Senior Editor. **Description:** Newspaper. Articles, about 600 words, on subjects of local or regional interest. No payment offered. **Tips:** Prefers local or regional
writers. **Rights:** Exclusive (Tulsa area).

USA TODAY
Gannett Newspapers
1000 Wilson Blvd., Arlington, VA 22229-0001. 703-276-3400.
E-mail: news@usatoday.com. Web site: www.usatoday.com. Daily. Karen Jurgensen, Editor. **Description:** Newspaper. Op-Ed articles, 700-1,000 words, on American culture, politics, economics, and "the real lives people live." No unnamed sources or composite anecdotes. Pays $300. **Payment:** On publication.

USA WEEKEND
Gannett Newspapers
1000 Wilson Blvd., Arlington, VA 22229-0001. 703-276-3400.
Web site: www.usaweekend.com. Weekly. Circ.: 20,000,000. **Description:** Sunday supplement to more than 500 newspapers.

THE WASHINGTON POST
Washington Post Co.
1150 15th St. NW, Washington, DC 20071-0002. 202-334-6000.
E-mail: pgextra@washpost.com. Web site: www.washingtonpost.com. Daily. Leonard Downie, Executive Editor. **Description:** Sunday Post edition offers groundbreaking journalism, lifestyle features, and political and popular-culture commentary. **Nonfiction:** Length, pay varies. **Queries:** Preferred. **E-Queries:** Prefer hard copy. **Unsolicited mss:** Accepts. **Response:** 3 weeks. **Freelance Content:** 2%.

WASHINGTON TIMES
The Washington Times, Inc.
3600 New York Ave. NE, Washington, DC 20002-1996. 202-636-3000.
E-mail: general@washingtontimes.com. Web site: www.washtimes.com. Daily. **Description:** Newspaper. Op-Ed articles, 800-1,000 words, on a variety of subjects. No first-person. Pays $150. **Tips:** Find a topic that is off the beaten path. **Rights:** Exclusive (Washington, DC, and Baltimore). **Payment:** On publication.

THE WORLD & I
The Washington Times Corp.
3600 New York Ave. NE, Washington, DC 20002. 202-635-4000.
E-mail: editor@worldandimag.com. Web site: www.worldandi.com. Monthly. $60. Circ.: 16,400. Michael Marshall, Executive Editor. **Description:** Current issues, arts, natural science, life, and culture. **Nonfiction:** Scholarly articles; 2,500 words; pay varies. **Payment:** On publication.

HEALTH
(See also Fitness)

AMERICAN JOURNAL OF NURSING
345 Hudson St., Fl. 16, New York, NY 10014. 212-886-1200.

E-mail: ajn@lww.com. Web site: www.nursingcenter.com. Circ.: 342,000. Diana Mason, Editor-in-Chief. **Description:** Practical, hands-on articles, 1,500-2,000 words, with photos or illustrations, on nursing or disease processes. **Tips:** Send query with outline. **Queries:** Preferred. **Response:** 2 weeks to queries; 10 weeks to ms.

AMERICAN MEDICAL NEWS
515 N State St., Chicago, IL 60610. 312-464-5000.
E-mail: kathryn_trombatore@ama-assn.org. Web site: www.amednews.com. Kathryn Trombatore, Editor. **Description:** Articles, on socioeconomic developments in health care, of interest to physicians across the country. Guidelines available. **Nonfiction:** Seeks well-researched, innovative pieces about health and science from physician's perspective; 900-1,500 words; pays $500-$1,500. **Queries:** Required. **Payment:** On acceptance.

ARTHRITIS TODAY
Arthritis Foundation
1330 W Peachtree St., Atlanta, GA 30309. 404-872-7100.
E-mail: writers@arthritis.org. Web site: www.arthritis.org. Bimonthly. $4.95/issue $20/year. Circ.: 650,000. Marcy O'Koon Moss, Editor. **Description:** Comprehensive information about arthritis research, care, and treatment, offering help and hope to over 40 million Americans with an arthritis-related condition. **Nonfiction:** Features on research, care, treatment of arthritis; self-help, how-to, general interest, general health, lifestyle topics (very few inspirational articles); 200-1,000 words; $75-$1,000. **Tips:** Readers are well-informed; desire fresh, in-depth information. Looking for talented writers/reporters to execute staff-generated ideas; send published clips. **Queries:** Preferred. **E-Queries:** Yes. **Unsolicited mss:** Accepts. **Response:** 4 weeks. **Freelance Content:** 50%. **Rights:** FNASR. **Payment:** On acceptance. **Contact:** Michele Taylor, Associate Editor.

ASTHMA
Mosby, Inc.
11830 Westline Industrial Dr., St. Louis, MO 63146. 800-325-4177.
E-mail: rebutler@atti.com. Web site: www.mosby.com/asthma. Bimonthly. $21/yr. Circ.: 65,000. Rachel Butler, Editor. **Description:** Focuses on ways to manage asthma. **Nonfiction:** Articles on health and medical news, also human-interest stories about children, adults, and the elderly; to 1,200 words. **Queries:** Required. **Payment:** On acceptance.

BABY TALK
See page 374 for full listing.
Description: Articles on pregnancy, health, child development, work and family.

BETTER HEALTH
Saint Raphael Healthcare System
1450 Chapel St., New Haven, CT 06511-4440. 203-789-3972.

Web site: www.srhs.org/betterhealth.asp. Bimonthly. Cynthia Wolfe Boynton, Editor. **Description:** Wellness and prevention magazine, published by Hospital of Saint Raphael. **Nonfiction:** Upbeat articles to encourage healthier lifestyle, with quotes and narrative from healthcare professionals at Saint Raphael's and other local services. No first-person or personal-experience articles; 2,000-2,500 words; $500. **Queries:** Required. **Response:** SASE. **Payment:** On acceptance.

CONSCIOUS CHOICE
920 N Franklin, Suite 202, Chicago, IL 60610-3179.
E-mail: editor@consciouschoice.com. Web site: www.consciouschoice.com. Monthly. $36/yr. Circ.: 50,000. James Faber, Senior Editor. **Description:** Covers issues and information on natural health, natural foods, and the environment. **Nonfiction:** 1,200-2,200 words; $75-$150. **Tips:** Readers are mostly well-educated women, average age 35, with substantial income level. **Queries:** Preferred. **E-Queries:** Yes. **Unsolicited mss:** Accepts. **Response:** 1-8 weeks. **Freelance Content:** 90%. **Rights:** 1st NA (print and web). **Payment:** On publication.

COPING WITH ALLERGIES & ASTHMA
Media America, Inc.
P.O. Box 682268, Franklin, TN 37068-2268. 615-790-2400.
E-mail: copingmag@aol.com. Web site: www.copingmag.com. 5x/yr. $13.95/year. **Description:** Provides "knowledge, hope, and inspiration to help readers learn to live with their conditions in the best ways possible." Seeks original manuscripts and photography. No payment. **Queries:** Not necessary.

COPING WITH CANCER
Media America, Inc.
P.O. Box 682268, Franklin, TN 37068. 615-790-2400.
E-mail: copingmag@aol.com. Web site: www.copingmag.com. 6x/yr. $19/year. Kay Thomas, Editor. **Description:** Uplifting and practical articles for people living with cancer: medical news, lifestyle issues, and inspiring personal essays. No payment.

CURRENT HEALTH
See page 345 for full listing.
Description: Magazine for classrooms covering physical and psychological health.

DIABETES SELF-MANAGEMENT
150 W 22nd St., Ste. 800, New York, NY 10011. 212-989-0200.
E-mail: editor@diabetes-self-mgmt.com. Web site: www.diabetes-self-mgmt.com. Bimonthly. $18/year. Circ.: 465,000. James Hazlett, editor. **Description:** Publication for people with diabetes who want to know more about controlling and managing their diabetes. **Nonfiction:** How-to articles on nutrition, pharmacology, exercise, medical advances, and self-help; 2,000-2,500 words; payment varies. **Tips:** Use plain English; avoid medical jargon, but explain technical terms in simple language. Writing style: upbeat, and leavened with tasteful humor where possible. Information should

be accurate, up-to-date, and from reliable sources; references from lay publications not acceptable. No celebrity profiles or personal experiences. **Queries:** Required. **E-Queries:** Yes. **Unsolicited mss:** Accepts. **Response:** 3-4 weeks; SASE required. **Rights:** All. **Payment:** On publication. **Contact:** Ingrid Strauch, Managing Editor.

FIT PREGNANCY
21100 Erwin St., Woodland Hills, CA 91367-3712. 800-423-5590.
Web site: www.fitpregnancy.com. Peg Moline, Editor. **Description:** Healthy Mom, Healthy Baby. Expert advice for the pregnant or postpartum woman and her newborn. Provides safe workouts, nutrition guidance, meal plans, medical news, baby gear, and more. **Nonfiction:** Articles, 500-2,000 words, on women's health (pregnant and postpartum), nutrition, and physical fitness. **Queries:** Preferred. **Unsolicited mss:** Accepts. **Payment:** On publication.

HEALTH PRODUCTS BUSINESS
Cygnus Business Media
445 Broad Hollow Rd., Suite 21, Melville, NY 11747. 631-845-2700 x214.
E-mail: susanne.alberto@cygnuspub.com.
Web site: www.healthproductsbusiness.com. Monthly. Circ.: 16,100. Susan Alberto, Editor. **Description:** Helps retailers and manufacturers navigate the challenges of the health and nutrition industry. **Nonfiction:** Stories on health products (supplements, skin/body care, organic food and medicine, sports nutrition, etc.); 1,000-2,000 words; pay varies. **Tips:** Seeking writers in the industry with credentials and expert knowledge on health/nutrition products. **Queries:** Required. **E-Queries:** Yes. **Unsolicited mss:** Does not accept. **Response:** SASE. **Freelance Content:** 25%. **Rights:** All. **Payment:** On publication.

HEALTH PROGRESS
Catholic Health Association
4455 Woodson Rd., St. Louis, MO 63134-3701. 314-427-2500.
E-mail: hpeditor@chausa.org. Web site: www.chausa.org. Bimonthly. $50. Circ.: 13,000. Carrie Stetz, Managing Editor. **Description:** On hospital/nursing-home management and administration, medical-moral questions, health care, public policy, technological developments and their effects, nursing, financial and human resource management for administrators, and innovative programs in hospitals and long-term care facilities. **Nonfiction:** Features, 2,000-4,000 words; pay negotiable. **Queries:** Preferred.

HEALTH QUEST
200 Highpoint Dr., Suite 215, Chalfont, PA 18914. 215-822-7935.
E-mail: editor@healthquestmag.com. Web site: www.healthquestmag.com. Bimonthly. Circ.: 500,000. Gerda Gallop-Goodman, Editor. **Description:** Health and wellness magazine on body, mind, and spirit for African-Americans. Covers traditional and alternative medicine. **Nonfiction:** Health articles. **Queries:** Preferred. **E-Queries:** No. **Unsolicited mss:** Accepts. **Freelance Content:** 20%. **Payment:** On publication.

HEART & SOUL
Vanguarde Media, Inc.
315 Park Ave. S, Fl. 11, New York, NY 10010-3607. 646-654-4200.
E-mail: heartandsoul@vanguarde.com. Web site: www.heartandsoul.com. Bimonthly.
$16.97. Circ.: 308,000. Corynne Corbett, Editor-in-Chief. **Description:** The African-American woman's ultimate guide to total well-being—body, mind, and spirit.
Nonfiction: Health, beauty, fitness, nutrition, and relationships for African-American women; 800-1,500 words; pay varies. **Queries:** Preferred. **Payment:** On acceptance.

HERBALGRAM
American Botanical Council
P.O. Box 144345, Austin, TX 78714-4345. 512-926-4900.
E-mail: herbcowboy@aol.com. Web site: www.herbalgram.org. Quarterly. Circ.: 50,000. Mark Blumenthal, Editor. **Description:** On herb and medicinal plant research, regulatory issues, market conditions, native plant conservation, and other aspects of herbal use. **Nonfiction:** Articles, 1,500-3,000 words. **Payment:** In copies.

HERBS FOR HEALTH
Real Health Media
243 E Fourth St., Loveland, CO 80537. 970-663-0831.
E-mail: herbsforhealth@realhealthmedia.com. Web site: www.discoverherbs.com.
Bimonthly. $4.99/issue. Circ.: 255,000. Amy Mayfield, Editor. **Description:** Offers sound information for general public on the wide range of benefits of herbs, including their role in various healing arts. **Fiction:** 500-2000 words; pays $.33/word.
Columns, Departments: 200-500 words. **Art:** 300 dpi (CMYK), slides. **Tips:** List your sources, keep it short, focus on reader benefit. **Queries:** Preferred. **E-Queries:** Yes. **Unsolicited mss:** Accepts. **Response:** 3 months, SASE required. **Freelance Content:** 90%. **Rights:** 1st NA. **Payment:** On publication.

HOMECARE
PRIMEDIA Business Magazines & Media, Inc.
6151 Powers Ferry Rd., Atlanta, GA 30339. 770-618-0121.
E-mail: jpieratt@primediabusiness.com. Web site: www.homecaremag.com.
Monthly. J.P. Pieratt, Managing Editor. **Description:** Leading resource for the home health industry. Covers the business of renting and selling home care products and services; industry news, trend analysis, product segment features, stories with management and operational ideas. **Nonfiction:** Seeking writers with health industry experience; $.50/word. **Queries:** Required. **E-Queries:** Yes. **Unsolicited mss:** Accepts. **Response:** 2-8 weeks, SASE required. **Freelance Content:** 20%. **Payment:** On acceptance.

JOURNAL OF HEALTH EDUCATION
See page 348 for full listing.
Description: Publicaton for health educators.

LET'S LIVE

P.O. Box 74908, 11050 Santa Monica Blvd., Los Angeles, CA 90025. 310-445-7500. E-mail: info@letslivemag.com. Web site: www.letsliveonline.com. Monthly. Circ.: 1,700,000. Beth Salmon, Editor-in-Chief. **Description:** Preventive medicine and nutrition, alternative medicine, diet, vitamins, herbs, exercise. **Nonfiction:** 1,500-1,800 words; up to $800. **Queries:** Required. **Payment:** On publication. **Contact:** Nicole Brechka, Associate Editor.

LISTEN

See page 596 for full listing.
Description: Educates teens with the problems that arise from the use of tobacco, alcohol, and other drugs.

LIVING IN BALANCE

See page 478 for full listing.
Description: A "health, wealth, and happiness" magazine.

MAMM

54 W 22nd St., Fl. 4, New York, NY 10010. 646-365-1350.
E-mail: elsieh@mamm.com. Web site: www.mamm.com. Monthly. **Description:** On cancer prevention, treatment, and survival, for women. **Nonfiction:** Articles on conventional and alternative treatment and medical news; survivor profiles; investigative features; essays; pay varies.**Queries:** Preferred. **Payment:** On acceptance.

MANAGED CARE

275 Phillips Blvd., Trenton, NJ 08618. 609-671-2100.
E-mail: editors@managedcaremag.com. Web site: www.managedcaremag.com. Monthly. $93/yr., $120 (internationally). Circ.: 60,000. John Marcille, Editor. **Description:** Publishes feature articles about managed health care, healthcare financing, and cost-effectiveness. Also, peer-reviewed scientific manuscripts about models of health care delivery and costs associated with them. **Nonfiction:** 1,000-3,000 words; $.60-$.80/word. **Columns, Departments:** News and Commentary, 300 words, $100. **Art:** Provide contact info for prominent people interviewed in your articles; they will assign a photographer to take photos. **Tips:** Current needs: Writers who cover the business side of health care with an ear to the ground for trends or who can relate interesting case-studies involving cost-effective care. Also, looking for academic-style writers willing to contribute scientific or medical review articles for peer review. **Queries:** Preferred. **E-Queries:** Yes. **Unsolicited mss:** Accepts. **Response:** 1 month, SASE required. **Freelance Content:** 60%. **Rights:** All. **Payment:** On publication.

MEN'S HEALTH

See page 484 for full listing.
Description: On fitness, health, sex, nutrition, relationships, sports, and travel.

THE NEW PHYSICIAN
American Medical Student Association
1902 Association Dr., Reston, VA 20191-1502. 703-620-6600.
E-mail: tnp@www.amsa.org. Web site: www.amsa.org. Monthly. $25/yr. Circ.: 30,000.
Rebecca Sernett, Editor. **Description:** On medical issues of interest to medical students. **Nonfiction:** On social, ethical, and political issues in medical education.
Recent articles: space medicine, dating in med school, history of surgeon general, etc;
up to 3,500 words; pay varies. **Tips:** Readers are highly educated, generally in their
20s. **Queries:** Preferred. **Unsolicited mss:** Accepts. **Freelance Content:** 40%.
Rights: 1st. **Payment:** On publication.

NURSING 2001
1111 Bethlehem Pike, P.O. Box 908, Springhouse, PA 19477-0908. 215-646-8700.
Web site: www.springnet.com. Cheryl L. Mee, RN.C, MSN, Editor. **Description:**
Magazine covering legal, ethical, and career aspects of nursing for direct caregivers.
Also features narratives about personal nursing experiences. **Nonfiction:** All articles
written by nurses; $25-$300. **Queries:** Preferred. **Payment:** On publication.

NUTRITION HEALTH REVIEW
P.O. Box 406, Haverford, PA 19041. 610-896-1853.
Quarterly. $3.00/issue, $24/year. Andrew Rifkin, Editor. **Description:** Vegetarian-oriented publication. **Nonfiction:** Articles on medical progress, nutritional therapy,
genetics, psychiatry, behavior therapy, surgery, pharmacology, animal health;
vignettes on health and nutrition. **Fillers:** Humor, cartoons, illustrations. **Tips:** No
material involving subjects that favor animal testing, animal foods, cruelty to animals,
recipes with animal products. **Queries:** Required. **Unsolicited mss:** Accepts.
Response: SASE required. **Payment:** On publication.

PATIENT CARE
Medical Economics
5 Paragon Dr., Montvale, NJ 07645-1725. 201-358-7421.
E-mail: patientcare@medec.com. Web site: www.patientcareonline.com. 24x/yr.
$99/yr. Circ.: 135,000. Deborah Kaplan, Editor. **Description:** On medical care, for
primary-care physicians. **Nonfiction:** Articles; pay varies. **Tips:** All articles by assignment only. **Queries:** Required. **Payment:** On acceptance.

THE PHOENIX
7152 Unity Ave. N., Brooklyn Ctr., MN 55429. 651-291-2691.
E-mail: psamples@inti.net. Web site: www.phoenixrecovery.org. Monthly. Free at
newsstands; $18 by mail. Circ.: 40,000. Pat Samples, Editor. **Description:** For people working on their physical, mental, emotional and spiritual well-being, seeking
peace and serenity. Covers a broad spectrum of recovery, renewal, and growth information. **Nonfiction:** Articles, 800-1,500 words. **Columns, Departments:** Getting
a Life; Basic Steps; Bodywise. **Tips:** Contact for upcoming themes. **Queries:** Not
necessary. **E-Queries:** Yes. **Unsolicited mss:** Accepts. **Response:** Queries 2

months, submission 3 months, SASE. **Freelance Content:** 90%. **Rights:** 1st. **Payment:** On publication.

PREVENTION
Rodale, Inc.
33 E Minor St., Emmaus, PA 18098. 610-967-5171.
E-mail: prevention@rodale.com. Web site: www.prevention.com. Monthly. $21.97/yr. Circ.: 3,008,000. Catherine Cassidy, Editor-in-Chief. **Description:** Leading magazine for preventative health research and practices. **Tips:** Freelance content limited. **Queries:** Required.

PSYCHOLOGY TODAY
Sussex Publications, Inc.
49 E 21st St., Fl. 11, New York, NY 10010-6213. 212-260-7210.
E-mail: psychtoday@aol.com. Web site: www.psychologytoday.com. Bimonthly. $16. Circ.: 323,000. Michael Seeber, Deputy Editor. **Description:** On general-interest psychological research. Timely subjects and news. **Nonfiction:** Articles, 800-2,000 words; pays varies. **Tips:** No personal "memoir-style" stories. **Payment:** On publication.

T'AI CHI
See page 588 for full listing.
Description: For those interested in T'ai Chi Ch'uan, Qigong, and other martial arts.

TOTAL HEALTH FOR LONGEVITY
Total Health Communications, Inc.
165 N 100 E, Suite 2, St. George, UT 84770-2502. 435-673-1789.
E-mail: thm@infowest.com. Web site: www.totalhealthmagazine.com. Bimonthly. Circ.: 60,000. Lyle Hurd, Editor/Publisher. **Description:** On preventative health care, fitness, diet, and mental health. **Nonfiction:** Articles, 1,200-1,400 words; pays $50-$75. **Art:** Color or B&W photos.**Queries:** Preferred. **Payment:** On publication.

TURTLE MAGAZINE
Children's Better Health Institute
1100 Waterway Blvd., P.O. Box 567, Indianapolis, IN 46206-0567. 317-636-8881.
E-mail: t.harshman@cbhi.org. Web site: www.turtlemag.org. Bimonthly. Circ.: 300,000. Ms. Terry Harshman, Editor. **Description:** Emphasis on health and nutrition for 2- to 5-year-olds. The only new material that is being accepted at this time is short rebus stories (100-200 words), and short simple poems (4-8 lines). **Payment:** $.22/word. **Poetry:** from $25. **Rights:** All. **Payment:** On publication.

VEGETARIAN TIMES
301 Concourse Blvd., Suite 350, Glen Allen, VA 23059. 203-328-7040.
Web site: www.vegetariantimes.com. Carla Davis, Managing Editor. **Description:** Articles on vegetarian cooking, nutrition, health and fitness, travel, and entertaining.

Pay negotiable. **Columns, Departments:** Wellness, First Person, Lifestyle. **Queries:** Required. **Payment:** On acceptance.

VEGETARIAN VOICE
P.O. Box 72, Dolgeville, NY 13329. 518-568-7970.
E-mail: navs@telenet.net. Web site: www.navs-online.org. Quarterly. Maribeth Abrams-McHenry, Managing Editor. **Description:** Consumer concerns, health, nutrition, animal rights, the environment, world hunger, etc. Offers vegetarian philosophy; all recipes are vegan and does not support the use of leather, wool, silk, etc. **Payment:** In copies.

VIBRANT LIFE
Review and Herald Publishing Association
55 W Oak Ridge Dr., Hagerstown, MD 21740-7301. 301-393-3000.
E-mail: vibrantlife@rhpa.org. Web site: www.vibrantlife.com. Bimonthly. $13.97. Circ.: 31,000. Larry Becker, Editor. **Description:** Total health: physical, mental, and spiritual. **Nonfiction:** Upbeat articles on the family and how to live happier and healthier lives, emphasizing practical tips; Christian slant; 600-2,000 words; $80-$250. **Payment:** On acceptance.

WEIGHT WATCHERS
W/W TwentyFirst Corp.
360 Lexington Ave., New York, NY 10017-6547. 212-370-0644.
E-mail: wwm@wwpublishinggroup.com. Web site: www.weightwatchers.com. 6x/year. $24.95. Circ.: 350,000. Nancy Gagliardi, Editor-in-Chief. **Description:** Health, nutrition, fitness, and weight-loss motivation and success. **Nonfiction:** Articles on fashion, beauty, food, health, nutrition, fitness, and weight-loss motivation and success; from $1/word. **Queries:** Required. **Payment:** On acceptance.

YOGA JOURNAL
See page 482 for full listing.
Description: On holistic health, meditation, conscious living, spirituality, and yoga.

HISTORY

AIR COMBAT
See page 485 for full listing.
Description: Articles on air battles, warplanes, and the men who fly them.

ALABAMA HERITAGE
University of Alabama, P.O. Box 870342, Tuscaloosa, AL 35487-0342. 205-348-7467. Web site: bama.va.edu/heritage/. Quarterly. $6/$18.95. Circ.: 6,500. T. J. Beitelman, Editor. **Description:** Focuses on the events that have shaped Alabama and the South. **Nonfiction:** Interested in stories ignored, forgotten, or given short-shrift by

historians. Also, Civil War articles if the story has an Alabama connection; 4,000-5,000 words; up to $400. **Columns, Departments:** Recollections (a specific remembrance of an Alabamian, often sent in by readers), up to 1,000 words; Alabama Album (the story behind an old photograph), up to 250 words; no payment. **Queries:** Not necessary. **E-Queries:** No. **Unsolicited mss:** Accepts. **Response:** Queries 1-2 weeks, submissions 3-4 weeks. **Freelance Content:** 40%. **Payment:** On publication.

AMERICA'S CIVIL WAR
PRIMEDIA History Group
741 Miller Dr. SE, Suite D2, Leesburg, VA 20175. 703-771-9400.
E-mail: americascivilwar@thehistorynet.com. Web site: www.historynet.com. Bimonthly. $4.99/issue. Circ.: 75,000. Dana B. Shoaf, Managing Editor. **Description:** Popular history for general readers and Civil War buffs, on strategy, tactics, history, narrative. **Nonfiction:** Strategy, tactics, personalities, arms and equipment; 3,500-4,000 words, plus 500-word sidebar; $200-$400. **Columns, Departments:** Up to 2,000 words; $100-$200. **Art:** Cite known color or B&W illustrations, and sources (museums, historical societies, private collections, etc.). **Tips:** Readable style and historical accuracy imperative. Use action and quotes where possible. Attribute quotes, cite major sources. **Queries:** Required. **E-Queries:** Yes. **Unsolicited mss:** Accepts. **Response:** 6 months; SASE required. **Freelance Content:** 98%. **Payment:** Both on acceptance and on publication; kill fee offered.

AMERICAN HERITAGE
90 Fifth Ave., New York, NY 10011. 212-367-3100.
E-mail: mail@americanheritage.com. Web site: www.americanheritage.com. 8x/year. $4.95/issue. Circ.: 310,000. Richard F. Snow, Editor. **Description:** Covers the American experience, from serious concerns to colorful sidelights, from powerful institutions to ordinary men and women, using the past to illuminate the present. **Nonfiction:** On the American experience. Annotate all quotations and factual statements; include brief biographical note about yourself; 1,500-6,000 words; pay varies. **Art:** B&W prints, color slides. **Tips:** Welcomes freelancers, but needs detailed queries in advance. Also, consult indexes first. No fiction or poetry. **Queries:** Preferred. **E-Queries:** No. **Unsolicited mss:** Accepts. **Response:** 8-10 weeks, SASE required. **Freelance Content:** 70%. **Payment:** On acceptance.

AMERICAN HERITAGE OF INVENTION & TECHNOLOGY
Forbes, Inc.
28 W 23rd St., New York, NY 10010. 212-367-3100.
E-mail: mail@americanheritage.com. Web site: www.americanheritage.com. Quarterly. Circ.: 200,000. Frederick Allen, Editor. **Description:** Lively, authoritative prose and illustrations (archival photos, rare paintings), on the history of technology in America, for the sophisticated general reader. **Nonfiction:** Articles, 2,000-5,000 words, on our nation's technological history. **Queries:** Not necessary. **E-Queries:** Yes. **Payment:** On acceptance.

AMERICAN HISTORY

6405 Flank Dr., Harrisburg, PA 17112. 717-657-9555.
E-mail: christine@cowles.com. Web site: www.thehistorynet.com. Bimonthly.
$3.99/$23.95. Circ.: 95,000. Tom Huntington, Editor. **Description:** Features the cultural, military, social, and political history of the United States for a general audience.
Nonfiction: Well-researched articles. General interest, not scholarly, with a good focus and strong anecdotal material. No travelogues, fiction, or puzzles; 2,000-4,000 words; $500-$600. **Tips:** Seeking tightly focused stories that show an incident or short period of time in history. **Queries:** Preferred. **E-Queries:** No. **Unsolicited mss:** Does not accept. **Response:** 10 weeks, SASE required. **Freelance Content:** 60%. **Rights:** 1st NA. **Payment:** On acceptance. **Contact:** Christine E. Teehlay.

AMERICAN LEGACY

28 W 23rd St., New York, NY 10010. 212-620-2200.
E-mail: amlegacy@americanheritage.com.
Web site: www.americanlegacymagazine.com. Quarterly. $2.95/$9.95. Circ.: 500,000.
Audrey Peterson, Editor. **Description:** Covers all aspects of Black history and culture. **Nonfiction:** Articles on people and events that have shaped history for African-Americans; up to 4,000 words; pay negotiable. **Tips:** No lifestyle articles or features on contemporary figures in the Black community unless they have a strong connection with history. Proposals should be 1 page only plus a 1 page cover letter. **Queries:** Required. **E-Queries:** Yes. **Unsolicited mss:** Accepts. **Response:** 2-4 months, SASE. **Freelance Content:** 95%. **Payment:** On acceptance.

AMERICAN OUTBACK JOURNAL

See page 499 for full listing.
Description: Print and e-zine publication on the American West.

ANCESTRY

360 W 4800N, Provo, UT 84604. 801-705-7000.
E-mail: ameditor@ancestry.com. Web site: www.ancestry.com. Bimonthly. $24.95/yr.
Circ.: 60,000. Jennifer Utley, Managing Editor. **Description:** Family history/genealogy magazine for professional family historians and hobbyists interested in getting the most out of their research. **Nonfiction:** Family articles, especially stories where novel approaches are used to find information on the lives of ancestors; 2,000-2,500 words; $500. **Fillers:** Humorous pieces about pursuit of the author's family history; 600 words; $200. **Art:** Interesting old photographs of ancestors. **Tips:** No typical family histories, only interesting angles on family history, research methods, and specific case studies. **Queries:** Preferred. **E-Queries:** Yes. **Unsolicited mss:** Accepts. **Response:** Queries 3 months, submissions 3 months, SASE. **Freelance Content:** 20%. **Rights:** All. **Payment:** On publication. **Contact:** Jennifer Utley.

ANCIENT AMERICAN

P.O. Box 370, Colfax, WI 54730. 715-962-3299.
E-mail: articles@ancientamerican.com. Web site: www.ancientamerican.com.

Bimonthly. $4.95/issue, $24.95/year. Circ.: 12,000. Frank Joseph, Editor. **Description:** Describes the prehistory of the American continent, regardless of presently fashionable beliefs. A public forum for experts and nonprofessionals alike to freely express their views. **Nonfiction:** Articles on prehistory in clear, nontechnical language, with original color photographs and artwork; 2,000-3,000 words; $75-$150. **Art:** Adobe PhotoShop, TIF. **Tips:** Translate complex research into accessible, attractive language with visually appealing format for ordinary readers. **Queries:** Not necessary. **E-Queries:** Yes. **Unsolicited mss:** Accepts. **Response:** SASE required. **Freelance Content:** 50%. **Payment:** On publication. **Contact:** Wayne May.

ARMOR
See page 485 for full listing.
Description: Professional magazine of the Armor Branch for military units and agencies responsible for direct-fire ground combat.

AVIATION HISTORY
PRIMEDIA Enthusiast Group
741 Miller Dr. SE, Suite D-2, Leesburg, VA 20175-8994. 703-771-9400.
E-mail: aviationhistory@thehistorynet.com. Web site: www.thehistorynet.com/aviationhistory. Bimonthly. Circ.: 62,500. Arthur H. Sanfelici, Editor. **Description:** On aeronautical history. **Nonfiction:** Articles, 3,500-4,000 words, with 500-word sidebars and excellent illustrations. **Columns, Departments:** 2,000 words; pays $150-$300. **Queries:** Preferred. **Payment:** On publication.

THE BEAVER
167 Lombard Ave., #478, Winnipeg, Manitoba R3B 0T6 Canada. 204-988-9300.
E-mail: beaver@historysociety.ca. Web site: www.historysociety.ca. Bimonthly. $4.95/$27.50. Circ.: 45,000. Annalee Greenberg, Editor. **Description:** Canadian history for a general audience. **Nonfiction:** Canadian history subjects; max. 3,500 words; $.30/word. **Tips:** Combine impeccable research with good nonfiction story-writing skills. **Queries:** Required. **E-Queries:** No. **Unsolicited mss:** Accepts. **Response:** 6 weeks, SASE. **Freelance Content:** 50%. **Rights:** FNASR, electronic. **Payment:** On acceptance.

CALLIOPE
See page 461 for full listing.
Description: Covers world history for children ages 8-14.

CAROLOGUE
See page 504 for full listing.
Description: On South Carolina history.

CIVIL WAR TIMES ILLUSTRATED
PRIMEDIA History Group
6405 Flank Dr., Harrisburg, PA 17112. 717-657-9555.

E-mail: cwt@cowles.com. Web site: www.thehistorynet.com. 7x/year. Circ.: 111,000. James Kushlan, Editor. **Description:** Accurate, annotated stories of the Civil War. Relies heavily on primary sources and words of eyewitnesses. **Nonfiction:** Articles; 2,500-3,000 words; $400-$650. **Tips:** Prefers gripping, quote-rich, well-documented accounts of battles, unusual events, eyewitness accounts (memoirs, diaries, letters), and common soldier photos. **Payment:** On acceptance.

COBBLESTONE
See page 463 for full listing.
Description: American history for kids ages 8-14.

COLUMBIA: THE MAGAZINE OF NORTHWEST HISTORY
Washington State Historical Society (WSHS) Research Center, 315 N Stadium Way, Tacoma, WA 98403. 253-798-5918.
E-mail: cdubois@wshs.wa.gov. Web site: www.wshs.org. Quarterly. $7.50/issue. Circ.: 4,000. Christina Dubois, Editor. **Description:** History publication for the Pacific Northwest. **Nonfiction:** Articles and commentary edited for the general reader. Submissions average 4,000 words. **Queries:** Preferred. **E-Queries:** Yes. **Unsolicited mss:** Accepts. **Response:** 2-4 weeks, SASE. **Freelance Content:** 80%. **Rights:** 1st.

COMMAND
See page 486 for full listing.
Description: On military history and current military affairs.

COUNTRY FOLK
See page 281 for full listing.
Description: Features true Ozark history, old rare recipes, and historical photos.

EARLY AMERICAN LIFE
207 House Ave., Suite 103, Camp Hill, PA 17011. 717-730-6263.
E-mail: ginnys@celticmooninc.com. Web site: www.earlyamericanlife.com. 8x/year. $3.99/$19.97. Virginia P. Stimmel, Editor. **Description:** On early American past (traditions, antiques, architecture, history, period style). For people who are passionate about tangible aspects of the American past and aspire to incorporate them into their lifestyles and homes. **Nonfiction:** Detailed articles about American domestic past (1600-1850); travel, historic places, preservation, restoration, antiques, houses, textiles, furniture, decorative objects; 1,500-2,000 words; $500-$600. **Columns, Departments:** Eye on Antiques, Worth Seeing, Life in Early America, Side by Side; 800-1,500 words; $250-$600. **Queries:** Preferred. **E-Queries:** Yes. **Unsolicited mss:** Accepts. **Response:** 30 days, SASE required. **Freelance Content:** 10-20%. **Rights:** One-time worldwide. **Payment:** On acceptance.

FAMILY TREE
F&W Publications, Inc.
1507 Dana Ave., Cincinnati, OH 45207. 513-531-2690.
Web site: www.familytreemagazine.com. Bimonthly. Circ.: 73,000. David Fryxell, Editorial Director. **Description:** Features articles on how to discover, preserve, and celebrate family history and traditions. **Queries:** Preferred.

FASHION-FLASHBACKS MAGAZINE
See page 296 for full listing.
Description: Covers fashion design and its history from 1960-1979.

GOLDENSEAL
WV Division of Culture & History
The Cultural Center, 1900 Kanawha Blvd. E, Charleston, WV 25305. 304-558-0220. E-mail: goldenseal@wvculture.org. Web site: www.wvculture.org/goldenseal. John Lilly, Editor. **Description:** On traditional West Virginia culture and history. Oral histories, old and new b/w photos, research articles. **Nonfiction:** Features, 3,000 words, and shorter articles, 1,000 words; pays $.10/word. **Payment:** On publication.

GOOD OLD DAYS
306 E Parr Rd., Berne, IN 46711. 260-589-4000.
E-mail: editor@goodolddaysonline.com. Web site: www.goodolddaysonline.com. Monthly. $2.50/issue. Circ.: 200,000. Ken Tate, Editor. **Description:** First-person nostalgia from the "Good Old Days" era (defined as 1900-1955), with particular attention to the period from the Great Depression to the end of World War II. **Nonfiction:** First-person nostalgia within this timeframe; 500-1,500 words; $.03-$.05/word. **Poetry:** Metered and rhymed; 8-24 lines; payment varies. **Columns, Departments:** Good Old Days in the Kitchen, Good Old Days on Wheels; 500-1,500 words; $.03-$.05/word. **Art:** Photos to accompany articles; prints; $5/photo. **Tips:** Good photos are a key to acceptance of your story. Readers are generally older, rather conservative. Keep a positive, pleasant tone. **Queries:** Not necessary. **E-Queries:** Yes. **Unsolicited mss:** Accepts. **Response:** 2 months; SASE required. **Freelance Content:** 85%. **Rights:** All. **Payment:** On acceptance.

HERITAGE QUEST
See page 439 for full listing.
Description: Publication offering help with genealogical research.

HIGHLANDER
560 Green Bay Rd., Suite 204, Winnetka, IL 60093. 847-784-9660.
E-mail: sray5617@aol.com. 7x/year. $17.50/year. Circ.: 35,000. Sharon Kennedy Ray, Editor. **Description:** Covers Scottish heritage (history, clans, families), related to Scotland in the period 1300-1900 A.D. **Nonfiction:** 1,500-2,000 words; $185-$250. **Art:** Photos must accompany manuscripts; B&W, color transparencies, maps, line drawings. **Tips:** Not concerned with modern Scotland. **Queries:** Preferred.

E-Queries: No. **Unsolicited mss:** Accepts. **Response:** Queries 1-2 weeks, submissions 1-2 months, SASE required. **Payment:** On acceptance.

THE ILLINOIS STEWARD
1102 S Goodwin Ave., W503 Turner Hall, Urbana, IL 61801. 217-333-3650. E-mail: preston1@uiuc.edu. Web site: http://ilsteward.nres.uiuc.edu. Phyllis Picklesimer, Editor. **Description:** On Illinois history and heritage, with natural-resource stewardship theme. No payment. **Nonfiction:** Articles, 1,700-1,800 words. **Queries:** Preferred.

MHQ: QUARTERLY JOURNAL OF MILITARY HISTORY
PRIMEDIA History Group
741 Miller Dr. SE, Suite D-2, Leesburg, VA 20175-8994. 703-771-9400. E-mail: militaryhistory@thehistorynet.com. Web site: www.historynet.com. Quarterly. $69.95/yr. Circ.: 54,000. Mike Haskew, Editor. **Description:** Offers an undistorted view of history, encourages understanding of events, personalities, and artifacts of the past. **Nonfiction:** Well-written military history; 3,500-4,000 words, with 500-word sidebar; $200-$400. **Columns, Departments:** 2,500 words. **Art:** Color, B&W illustrations. **Queries:** Preferred. **E-Queries:** Yes. **Unsolicited mss:** Accepts. **Response:** Queries 2-4 weeks, submissions 6-8 weeks, SASE. **Freelance Content:** 50%. **Payment:** On publication.

MILITARY
See page 487 for full listing.
Description: Military history (WWII, Korea, Vietnam, and today).

MONTANA
Montana Historical Society
225 N Roberts St., P.O. Box 201201, Helena, MT 59601. 406-444-4741. E-mail: cwhitehorn@state.mt.us. Web site: www.montanahistoricalsociety.org. Quarterly. $8.50/$29 yr. Circ.: 10,000. W. Clark Whitehorn, Editor. **Description:** For members of state historical society and Western History Assn., covering history of Montana and the American and Canadian west. **Nonfiction:** Authentic articles on history of the region; new interpretative approaches to major developments in western history. Must use footnotes or bibliography; 3,500-5,500 words. **Queries:** Preferred. **E-Queries:** Yes. **Unsolicited mss:** Accepts. **Response:** Queries 3 months, submissions 1 month, SASE. **Freelance Content:** 95%. **Rights:** All. **Payment:** N/A.

NAVAL HISTORY
291 Wood Rd., Annapolis, MD 21402. 410-295-1079. E-mail: fschultz@usni.org. Web site: www.usni.org/navalhistory/nh.html. Bimonthly. Circ.: 40,000. Fred L. Schultz, Editor-in-Chief. **Description:** On international naval and maritime history, published by U.S. Naval Institute. **Nonfiction:** Essays, book excerpts, interviews, profiles, personal experience, technical, photo feature; 1,000-

3,000 words; pays $300-$500 (assigned articles); $75-$400 (unsolicited). **Fillers:** Humor, inspirational; 50-100 words; pays $10-$50. **Tips:** Write a good, concise story; support it with primary sources and good illustrations. Historian David McCullough called this "one of the best magazines in the country." **Queries:** Preferred. **E-Queries:** Yes. **Unsolicited mss:** Accepts. **Response:** Queries 1 month, submissions 2 months, SASE required. **Freelance Content:** 90%. **Rights:** FNASR. **Payment:** On acceptance.

NEBRASKA HISTORY

P.O. Box 82554, Lincoln, NE 68501. 402-471-4748.
E-mail: dcunning@mail.state.ne.us. Web site: www.nebraskahistory.org. Quarterly. $30/yr. Circ.: 3,800. David B. Cunningham, Editor. **Description:** Publishes well-researched articles, edited documents, and other annotated primary materials on the history of Nebraska and the Great Plains. **Nonfiction:** 3,000-7,000 words. **Art:** 8x10 B&W, 600 dpi scans. **Tips:** Rarely publishes family histories or reminiscence. **Queries:** Preferred. **E-Queries:** Yes. **Unsolicited mss:** Accepts. **Response:** Queries 1 week, submissions in 2 months, SASE. **Payment:** In copies.

NOW & THEN

See page 517 for full listing.
Description: Each issue focuses on one aspect of life in the Appalachian region.

OLD CALIFORNIA GAZETTE

2454 Heritage Park Row, San Diego, CA 92110. 619-491-0099.
E-mail: gazettes@cts.com. Monthly. Circ.: 1,000,000. Karen Spring, Editor. **Description:** California history, 1800-1920s. **Fiction:** 500-1,000 words; $.10/word. **Nonfiction:** 500-1,000 words; $.10/word. **Tips:** $50 bonus for front cover piece. $50 bonus if humorous. **Queries:** Preferred. **E-Queries:** Yes. **Unsolicited mss:** Accepts. **Response:** 1 month, SASE not needed. **Freelance Content:** 50%. **Rights:** 1st. **Payment:** On publication.

PENNSYLVANIA HERITAGE

Pennsylvania Heritage Society
300 N St., Harrisburg, PA 17120-0024. 717-787-2407.
E-mail: momalley@phmc.state.pa.us. Web site: www.paheritage.org. Quarterly. $20/yr. Circ.: 13,000. Michael J. O'Malley III, Editor. **Description:** Published by Pennsylvania Historical and Museum Commission and the Pennsylvania Heritage Society, to introduce readers to the state's rich culture and historic legacy. **Nonfiction:** Articles on Pennsylvania fine and decorative arts, architecture, archaeology, history, industry and technology, travel, and folklore, with suggestions for possible illustration; 2,500-3,500 words; to $500. **Art:** Photos, drawings; photo essays; up to $100. **Tips:** Seeks unusual, fresh angle to make history come to life, including pictorial or photo essays, interviews, travel/destination pieces. Submit complete manuscript. **Queries:** Preferred. **Payment:** On acceptance.

PERSIMMON HILL

1700 NE 63rd St., Oklahoma City, OK 73111. 405-478-6404.
E-mail: editor@nationalcowboymuseum.org. Web site: www/nationalcowboymuseum.org. Quarterly. $30/yr. Circ.: 15,000. M. J. Van Deventer, Editor. **Description:** Historical and contemporary themes related to the American West, from Hollywood to cowboys. Honors those who have made positive contributions to the West, past or present. **Nonfiction:** On Western history and art, cowboys, ranching, rodeo, and nature; 1,000-1,500 words; $150-$350. **Columns, Departments:** Great hotels and lodgings; entrepreneurs; events, interesting places to visit, personalities; 750-1,000 words; $75-$150. **Art:** Slides, transparencies; up to $50/image. **Tips:** No stories on western outlaws or "bad guys" (Billy the Kid) stories. **Queries:** Required. **E-Queries:** Yes. **Unsolicited mss:** Accepts. **Response:** Queries 6 weeks, submissions 2 months, SASE. **Freelance Content:** 95%. **Rights:** One-time NA. **Payment:** On publication.

PRESERVATION

1785 Massachusetts Ave. NW, Washington, DC 20036. 202-588-6388.
E-mail: preservation@nthp.org. Web site: www.preservationonline.org. Bimonthly. $5/issue, $20/year. Circ.: 200,000. Robert Wilson, Editor. **Description:** Encourages a sense of place and passion for historic preservation. **Nonfiction:** Articles on the built environment, place, architecture, preservation issues, and people involved. Mostly freelance; 150-6,000 words; $.50-$1.00/word. **Queries:** Preferred. **E-Queries:** Yes. **Unsolicited mss:** Accepts. **Response:** Queries 2-3 weeks, submissions 6-8 weeks, SASE required. **Freelance Content:** 80%. **Rights:** 1st NA, archival. **Payment:** On acceptance.

REMINISCE

Reiman Publications
5400 S 60th St., P.O. Box 991, Greendale, WI 53129. 414-423-0100.
E-mail: editors@reminisce.com. Web site: www.reminisce.com. Bimonthly. $17.98/yr. Circ.: 1,000,000. **Description:** "A stroll down memory lane." Vintage photographs and real-life, first-person stories recall the "good old days" (1960s and back). **Nonfiction:** Needs an "I remember" element; 750 words. **Art:** Good, candid photos. **Tips:** Send SASE or request via e-mail for full submission guidelines. **Queries:** Not necessary. **Unsolicited mss:** Accepts. **Response:** 2 months. **Freelance Content:** 90%. **Payment:** On publication.

RENAISSANCE

Queue, Inc.
338 Commerce Dr., Fairfield, CT 06432.
E-mail: renaissance@queueinc.com. Web site: www.renaissancemagazine.com. Quarterly. Circ.: 30,000. Kim Guarnaccia, Managing Editor. **Description:** Renaissance and Medieval history, costuming, heraldry, reenactments, role-playing, and Renaissance faires. **Nonfiction:** Interviews and reviews of books, music, movies and games; $.07/word. **Queries:** Preferred. **Payment:** On publication.

SOUTH CAROLINA HISTORICAL MAGAZINE

South Carolina Historical Society
100 Meeting St., Charleston, SC 29401-2299. 843-723-3225.
E-mail: info@schistory.org. Web site: www.schistory.org. Eric Emerson, Editor.
Description: Scholarly articles, to 25 pages including footnotes, on South Carolina history. Look at previous issues to be aware of scholarship. **Payment:** In copies.

SOUTHERN OREGON HERITAGE TODAY

106 N Central Ave., Medford, OR 97501-5926. 541-773-6536.
Web site: www.sohs.org. Monthly. Cynthia Wicklund. **Description:** On the history of the southern Oregon region (people, places, buildings, and events). **Nonfiction:** Well-written articles; 700-3,500 words; $50-$250. **Tips:** "Make sure there is a storyline, not just a reiteration of facts." **Payment:** On publication.

TIMELINE

1982 Velma Ave., Columbus, OH 43211-2497. 614-297-2360.
E-mail: timeline@ohiohistory.org. Bimonthly. $6/$30. Circ.: 15,000. Christopher S. Duckworth, Editor. **Description:** Covers fields of history, prehistory, and natural sciences, directed towards readers in the Midwest. **Nonfiction:** History, politics, economics, social, and natural history for lay readers in Ohio and the Midwest; 1,000-5,000 words. **Tips:** Writing style should be simple and direct; avoid jargon. **Queries:** Preferred. **E-Queries:** Yes. **Unsolicited mss:** Accepts. **Response:** 2 weeks, SASE. **Freelance Content:** 90%. **Rights:** 1st NA. **Payment:** On acceptance.

TRUE WEST

P.O. Box 8008, Cave Creek, AZ 85327. 888-587-1881.
E-mail: editor@truewestmagazine.com. Web site: www.truewestmagazine.com. 8x/yr. Circ.: 50,000. Marc Rosenbaum, Editor. **Description:** Since 1953, *True West* Magazine has been celebrating the history of the American West. "From classic gunfights to Native Americans, it's all red, white, and true." **Payment:** On publication.

VIETNAM

PRIMEDIA History Group
741 Miller Dr. SE, Suite D2, Leesburg, VA 20175-8994. 703-771-9400.
E-mail: davidz@cowles.com. Web site: www.thehistorynet.com. Bimonthly. $3.99/$19.95. Circ.: 60,000. David T. Zabecki, Editor. **Description:** Popular military-history magazine. Seeks to record and document "the many truths about Vietnam." **Nonfiction:** First-person and third-person accounts of all aspects of Vietnam War; strategy, tactics, personalities, arms and equipment; 3,500-4,000 words; $200. **Columns, Departments:** Arsenal, Fighting Forces, Personality, Perspectives; 1,500-2,000 words; $100-$150. **Tips:** Readers are Vietnam veterans, current military personnel, military historians and enthusiasts. Does not publish "war stories." **Queries:** Preferred. **E-Queries:** Accepts. **Unsolicited mss:** Accepts. **Rights:** All worldwide, reprint. **Payment:** On publication.

THE WESTERN HISTORICAL QUARTERLY

Utah State University, Logan, UT 84322-0740. 435-797-1301. E-mail: whq@hass.usu.edu. Web site: www.usu.edu/history/whq. Quarterly. Circ.: 2,200. Anne M. Butler, Editor. **Description:** Covers the American West—the United States, Canada, and Mexico. Subject matter centers on occupation, settlement, and political, economic, social, cultural, and intellectual history. **Nonfiction:** Original articles about the American West, the Westward movement, 20th-century regional studies, Spanish borderlands, Canada, northern Mexico, Alaska, and Hawaii; to 10,000 words; no payment. **Tips:** Prefers descriptive, interpretive, and analytical essays on broad themes; use of primary sources and monographic literature. **Queries:** Not necessary. **E-Queries:** Yes. **Unsolicited mss:** Accepts. **Response:** 1 week, SASE required.

WILD WEST

PRIMEDIA History Group
741 Miller Dr. SE, Suite D-2, Leesburg, VA 20175-8920. 703-779-8302.
Web site: www.thehistorynet.com./wildwest. Bimonthly. Gregory Lalire, Editor. **Description:** History of people, places, battles, and events that led to the taming of the great American frontier. **Nonfiction:** Articles, artwork, and picture essays on life and times of settlers, cowboys, Indians, gunmen, lawmen, all the fascinating characters and aspects of Western lore and culture; 3,500-4,000 words; $200-$400. **Columns, Departments:** up to 2,000 words. **Art:** Put your full name on each photo. **Queries:** Preferred. **E-Queries:** Yes. **Unsolicited mss:** Accepts. **Response:** 6 months, SASE. **Payment:** On publication.

WORLD WAR II

PRIMEDIA History Group
741 Miller Dr. SE, Suite D-2, Leesburg, VA 20175-8994. 703-779-8302.
E-mail: mhaskew@cowles.com. Web site: www.thehistorynet.com. Bimonthly. $27.95. Circ.: 152,300. Chris Anderson, Editor. **Description:** Strategy, tactics, personalities, arms and equipment. **Nonfiction:** Features, 3,500-4,000 words, plus 500-word sidebar; up to $200. **Art:** Cite any color or B&W illustrations, and sources. **Tips:** Readable style and historical accuracy imperative. **Queries:** Preferred. **Unsolicited mss:** Accepts. **Response:** 6 months, SASE. **Rights:** Exclusive worldwide. **Payment:** On publication.

HOBBIES, CRAFTS, COLLECTING

(See also Games & Pastimes)

AIRBRUSH ACTION

P.O. Box 438, 3209 Atlantic Ave., Allenwood, NJ 08720. 732-223-7878.
E-mail: kpriest@idt.net. Web site: www.airbrushaction.com. Bimonthly. $5.99/issue, $26.95/year. Circ.: 60,000. Kathryn Priest, Editor. **Description:** Showcases innovative airbrush art. Profiles on notable artists, step-by-step "how-to"; columns on T-shirt

painting, automotive airbrushing, fingernail design. Also, regular Buyer's Guides with comparisons of airbrush art supplies. **Nonfiction:** Profiles of artists by request only; 1,000-2,000 words; $.15/word. **Queries:** Required. **E-Queries:** Yes. **Unsolicited mss:** Accepts. **Response:** 2 weeks, SASE required. **Freelance Content:** 50%. **Rights:** All. **Payment:** On publication.

ANCESTRY
See page 423 for full listing.
Description: Family history/genealogy magazine for family historians and hobbyists.

ANTIQUE SHOPPE
P.O. Box 2175, Keystone Heights, FL 32656. 352-475-1679.
E-mail: antshoppe@aol.com. Web site: www.antiqnet.com/antiqueshoppe. Monthly. $17. Circ.: 20,000. Bruce G. Causey, editor. **Description:** Serves the antique and collection industry. **Nonfiction:** On antiques, collectibles, communities with antique districts, historical locations, local auctions or shows; 1,000 words; $50. **Art:** Photographs to accompany articles. **Queries:** Preferred. **E-Queries:** Yes. **Unsolicited mss:** Accepts. **Freelance Content:** 60%. **Payment:** On publication.

ANTIQUE TRADER PUBLICATIONS
Krause Publications, Inc.
700 E State St., Iola, WI 54990. 319-588-2073.
Web site: www.collect.com. Sharon Korbeck, Managing Editor. **Description:** Covers all types of antiques and collectors' items. **Nonfiction:** Articles; 500-1,200 words; $50-$250. **Art:** Photos. **Rights:** Exclusive. **Payment:** On publication.

ANTIQUES & AUCTION NEWS
P.O. Box 500, Mount Joy, PA 17552. 717-653-1833.
Weekly. Denise Sater, Editor. **Description:** Factual articles, 600-1,500 words, on antiques, collectors, collections, and places of historic interest. **Nonfiction:** Pays $18-$40. **Art:** Photos. **Queries:** Required. **Payment:** On publication.

ANTIQUEWEEK
DMG World Media
27 N Jefferson St., P.O. Box 90, Knightstown, IN 46148-0090. 765-345-5133.
E-mail: antiquewk@aol.com. Web site: www.antiqueweek.com. Weekly. $28.45/yr. Circ.: 64,000. Tom Hoepf, Connie Swaim, Editors. **Description:** Weekly antique, auction, and collectors' newspaper. Guidelines available. **Nonfiction:** Articles, 500-2,000 words, on antiques, collectibles, genealogy, auction and antique show reports; pays $40-$200 for in-depth articles. **Art:** Photos. **Queries:** Preferred. **Payment:** On publication.

ARTS & CRAFTS
Krause Publications, Inc.
700 E State St., Iola, WI 54990-0001. 715-445-2214.

Web site: www.krause.com. Monthly. Circ.: 76,000. **Description:** Patterns and projects for sewing, needlework, and crafts.

AUCTION EXCHANGE

929 Industrial Parkway, P.O. Box 57, Plainwell, MI 49080-0057. 616-685-1343. E-mail: auctionexchange@wmis.net. Web site: www.eauctionexchange.com. Weekly. $24.50/yr. Circ.: 13,000. Lars Svendsen, Editor. **Description:** Serves Michigan, Indiana, Ohio. For dealers and collectors, on auctions, antiques, and collectibles. **Nonfiction:** 500 words; $1.50/column, $3/photo. **Art:** $3/photo. **Queries:** Not necessary. **E-Queries:** Yes. **Unsolicited mss:** Accepts. **Freelance Content:** 70%. **Rights:** One-time. **Payment:** On publication. **Contact:** Lars Svendsen.

AUTOGRAPH COLLECTOR

Odyssey Publications
510-A S. Corona Mall, Corona, CA 91719-1420. 909-371-7137.
E-mail: ev@collectors.com. Web site: www.autographcollector.com. Ev Phillips, Editor. **Description:** Covers all areas of autograph collecting (preservation, framing, and storage, specialty collections, documents and letters, collectors and dealers). **Nonfiction:** Articles; 1,000-2,000 words; pay varies. **Queries:** Preferred.

BEAD & BUTTON

Kalmbach Publishing Co.
21027 Crossroads Circle, P.O. Box 1612, Waukesha, WI 53187-1612. 262-796-8776. Web site: www.kalmbach.com. 6x/year. Circ.: 91,000. Alice Korach, Editor. **Description:** Illustrated bead projects for enthusiasts: jewelry, home decor, clothing, and more. **Nonfiction:** Pay varies. **Art:** Art is by authors; photo and illustration guidance is by authors; final photos and illustrations are done in-house. **Tips:** Articles are written by artisans in this hobby. **Queries:** Required. **E-Queries:** Yes. **Unsolicited mss:** Does not accept. **Response:** 3 months. **Rights:** All. **Payment:** On acceptance.

BECKETT BASKETBALL CARD MONTHLY

Beckett Publications, Inc.
15850 Dallas Pkwy., Dallas, TX 75248-3308. 972-91-6657.
E-mail: jkelley@beckett.com. Web site: www.beckett.com. Monthly. $4.99/$27.99. Circ.: 245,200. John Kelley, Managing Editor. **Description:** For hobbyists who collect cards and memorabilia. (Also publishes *Beckett Sports Collectibles & Autographs, Football Card Monthly, Hockey Collector*, and *Racing and Motorsports*.) **Nonfiction:** Sports collectibles stories, with a trading card/basketball angle; 800-2,000 words. **Tips:** Promote the hobby in a positive, fun-loving way. **Queries:** Preferred. **E-Queries:** Yes. **Unsolicited mss:** Accepts. **Response:** 10 days, SASE not needed. **Freelance Content:** 30%. **Rights:** All. **Payment:** On publication.

THE BLADE

Krause Publications, Inc.
700 E State St., Iola, WI 54945-5010. 715-445-2214.

E-mail: blade@krause.com. Web site: www.blademag.com. Monthly. $4.95/issue, $25.98/year. Circ.: 72,000. Steve Shackleford, Editor. **Description:** Information for knife makers, collectors, daily knife users, and enthusiasts. **Nonfiction:** Anything new and unusual about handmade and factory knives, historical pieces, interviews, celebrities, values on collectible knives and accessories, tips on use; 1,000-1,500 words. **Art:** Varied formats. **Queries:** Preferred. **E-Queries:** Yes. **Unsolicited mss:** Accepts. **Response:** Queries 1 month, submissions 2 months, SASE required. **Freelance Content:** 5%. **Rights:** All. **Payment:** On publication.

BREW YOUR OWN
See page 395 for full listing.
Description: Practical information for homebrewers.

CANADIAN STAMP NEWS
Trajan Publishing Corporation
103 Lakeshore Rd., Suite 202, St. Catharines
Ontario L2N 2T6 Canada. 905-646-7744.
E-mail: stamps@trajan.com. Web site: www.canadianstampnews.ca. Biweekly. Virginia St-Denis, Editor. **Description:** Hobby magazine of worldwide philatelic news with a focus on Canadian stamps. Special issues throughout the year. **Nonfiction:** Articles, 800-1,200 words; pays from $50-$85. **Art:** Photos, stamps, and covers. **Payment:** up to 2 months after publication.

CAROUSEL NEWS & TRADER
87 Park Ave. W, Suite 206, Mansfield, OH 44902-1612. 419-529-4999.
E-mail: cnsam@aol.com. 10x/year. $3.95/issue $35/year. Circ.: 3,500. Walter L. Loucks, Editor. **Description:** Covers all aspects of carousels (merry-go-rounds), including complete machines, individual animals, restoration, history, carving, buy-sell-trade. **Nonfiction:** On carousel history, profiles of operators and carvers, collectors, preservationists, restorationists; 500-1,000 words plus photos; $50/printed page. **Art:** Photos. **Queries:** Preferred. **E-Queries:** Yes. **Unsolicited mss:** Accepts. **Response:** 4 weeks, SASE. **Payment:** On publication.

CLASSIC TOY TRAINS
Kalmbach Publishing Co.
21027 Crossroads Circle, P.O. Box 1612, Waukesha, WI 53187-1612. 262-796-8776.
E-mail: editor@classtrain.com. Web site: www.classtrain.com. 9x/year. $4.95/issue, $36.95/year. Circ.: 65,000. Neil Besougloff, Editor. **Description:** For enthusiasts of old and new toy trains produced by Lionel, American Flyer, and their competitors. **Nonfiction:** Articles, with photos, on toy train layouts and collections. Also toy train manufacturing history and repair/maintenance. Pays $75/printed page. **Queries:** Preferred. **E-Queries:** Yes. **Unsolicited mss:** Accepts. **Response:** Queries 15 days, submissions 30 days. **Freelance Content:** 60%. **Rights:** All. **Payment:** On acceptance.

COLLECTOR EDITIONS

P.O. Box 1219, Old Chelsea Station, New York, NY 10113-1219. 212-989-8700. Web site: www.collectoreditions.com. Bimonthly. $4.99/issue, $29.90/year. Circ.: 50,000. Joan M. Pursley, Editor. **Description:** Covers limited and open-edition collectibles, figurines, plates, prints, crystal glass, porcelain, and other related items for individual collectors. **Nonfiction:** 250-1,000 words; pays $100-$300. **Queries:** Required. **Unsolicited mss:** Does not accept. **Response:** Queries 30 days. **Freelance Content:** 10-15%. **Rights:** 1st NA. **Payment:** 6 weeks after acceptance.

COLLECTOR GLASS NEWS

P.O. Box 308, Slippery Rock, PA 16057. 724-946-2838. E-mail: mark@glassnews.com. Web site: www.glassnews.com. Bimonthly. $3/issue. Circ.: 850. Dr. Mark E. Chase, Managing Editor. **Description:** For collectors of cartoon, promotional, sports, and fast-food glassware produced in past 70 years. **Nonfiction:** Well-researched pieces on specific promotions, glass sets, glass producers, or personalities; 100-500 words; $30-$50. **Tips:** No general articles; readers are advanced collectors looking for information on obscure sets or producers. **Queries:** Preferred. **E-Queries:** Yes. **Unsolicited mss:** Accepts. **Response:** 1-2 weeks, SASE required. **Freelance Content:** 30%. **Rights:** 1st NA. **Payment:** On publication.

COLLECTORS NEWS

P.O. Box 306, 502 2nd St., Grundy Ctr., IA 50638. 319-824-6981. E-mail: collectors@collectors-news.com. Web site: www.collectors-news.com. Monthly. $4/issue, $28/year. Circ.: 10,000. Linda Kruger, Editor. **Description:** Antiques and collectibles magazine for casual collectors and experienced dealers. Accurate information on wide variety of types, market trends, events, and collector interaction. **Nonfiction:** Background of collectibles; how to identify, care for, value items. 20th-century nostalgia, Americana, glass and china, music, furniture, transportation, timepieces, jewelry, farm-related items, and lamps; 900-1,200 words; $1.10/column inch. **Art:** Quality color or B&W photos. **Queries:** Preferred. **E-Queries:** Yes. **Response:** Queries 2 weeks, submissions 6 weeks, SASE required. **Freelance Content:** 30%. **Rights:** 1st serial, one-time. **Payment:** On publication.

CRAFTING TRADITIONS

Reiman Publications
5400 S 60th St., P.O. Box 991, Greendale, WI 53129-091. 414-423-0100. E-mail: editors@craftingtraditions.com. Web site: www.reimanpub.com. Kathleen Anderson, Editor. **Description:** All types of craft designs (needlepoint, quilting, woodworking, etc.) with complete instructions and full-size patterns. **Nonfiction:** Pays $25-$250. **Rights:** all. **Payment:** On acceptance.

CRAFTS

PRIMEDIA Enthusiast Group
14901 Heritagecrest Way, Bluffdale, UT 84065-4818. 801-984-2070. E-mail: editor@craftsmag.com. Web site: www.craftsmag.com. Monthly. Circ.:

350,000. Valerie Pingree, Editor. **Description:** Project-based publication seeking writers who are professional craft designers and who can write detailed instructions for the creation of their crafts. **Nonfiction:** Interested in projects that include traditional and contemporary crafts: crochet, knitting, sewing, embroidery and needlework, decorative painting, beads, papercrafts, seasonal, kitchen crafts, etc. Seeks unique gifts and creative techniques for re-using second hand items (but not household trash such as empty food containers). **Art:** Photos must illustrate steps in making the project/craft. **Tips:** Do not send projects. Submit written query or e-query with photos. Queries for seasonal projects must be submitted 7 months prior to publication. **Queries:** Required. **E-Queries:** Yes.

CRAFTS 'N THINGS

Clapper Communications
2400 Devon, Suite 375, Des Plaines, IL 60018-4618. 847-635-5800.
E-mail: bsunderlage@clapper.com. Web site: www.craftideas.com. 8x/year. $4.99/issue. Circ.: 250,000. Barbara Sunderlage, Editor. **Description:** How-to articles on varied craft projects, with instructions. **Nonfiction:** Instructions, with photo of finished item. Pays $50-$250. **Tips:** Limited freelance content. **Queries:** Required. **Payment:** On acceptance.

THE CRAFTS REPORT

300 Water St., P.O. Box 1992, Wilmington, DE 19899-1992. 302-656-2209.
E-mail: nbacker@craftsreport.com. Web site: www.craftsreport.com. Monthly. Circ.: 18,000. Noelle Backer, Editor. **Description:** Focuses on the business side of the crafts industry; marketing, growing your craft business, time management, studio safety, retail relationships, features on other crafts professionals at all levels of the field, industry news, and more.

DECORATIVE ARTIST'S WORKBOOK

F&W Publications, Inc.
4700 E Galbraith, Cincinnati, OH 45236. 513-531-2690.
E-mail: dawedit@fwpubs.com. Web site: www.decorativeartist.com. Bimonthly. Circ.: 90,000. Anne Hevener, Editor. **Description:** How-to articles on decorative painting. **Nonfiction:** Step-by-step instructions on decorative painting subjects, including folk art, stroke work, stenciling, fabric painting and faux finishing methods; 1,000-2,000 words; $200-$300. **Queries:** Required. **Unsolicited mss:** Does not accept. **Response:** 2 weeks to queries, SASE required. **Freelance Content:** 75%. **Rights:** FNASR. **Payment:** On acceptance.

DOLL WORLD

306 E Parr Rd., Berne, IN 46711. 219-724-0499.
E-mail: doll_world@whitebirches.com. Web site: www.dollworldmagazine.com. Bimonthly. $4.50/issue, $19.97/year. Circ.: 65,000. Vicki Steensma, Editor. **Description:** For readers of all ages, about antique, contemporary, and collectible dolls of all kinds. **Nonfiction:** On doll history, preservation, restoration, events, muse-

ums, costumes, artists; 1,000-1,200 words; pay varies. **Fillers:** Nostalgia and humor are welcome touches. **Art:** Prefers that doll makers/collectors send us the doll(s) whenever possible to get photos shot in our studio. If not possible, send high-quality slides and disk images; TIF, high resolution, 266 dpi, CMYK color, Mac format. **Tips:** Be professional, neat and respectful. Know your subject and be familiar with the magazine you are submitting to. **Queries:** Not necessary. **E-Queries:** Yes. **Unsolicited mss:** Accepts. **Response:** 1 month, SASE required. **Freelance Content:** 50%. **Rights:** All. **Payment:** On acceptance.

DOLLHOUSE MINIATURES
Kalmbach Publishing Co.
21027 Crossroads Circle, P.O. Box 1612, Waukesha, WI 53187-1612. 262-796-8776. E-mail: cstjacques@dhminiatures.com. Web site: www.dhminiatures.com. Monthly. $4.95/$39.95 year. Circ.: 35,000. Candice St. Jacques, Editor. **Description:** America's leading miniatures magazine, for artisans, collectors, and hobbyists. Stories on artisans, exhibits, and collections from around the world to inspire readers to try colorful, creative, and fun projects. **Nonfiction:** How-to articles with easy-to-follow instructions, photos, and illustrations. Also features, profiles, and articles on collections, museums, and industry news. **Art:** Color slides essential. Pay varies. **Tips:** Focus on an artisan or collector, with careful, specific story and professional visuals. Don't condescend; this is art form for high-end artisans. **Queries:** Preferred. **E-Queries:** Yes. **Unsolicited mss:** Accepts. **Response:** Queries 2-4 months, submissions 3-6 months, SASE. **Freelance Content:** 50%. **Rights:** All. **Payment:** On acceptance.

DOLLS
Jones Publishing Co., Inc.
N7450 Aanstad Rd., P.O. Box 5000, Iola, WI 54945. 715-445-5000. E-mail: jonespub@jonespublishing.com. Web site: www.jonespublishing.com. 10x/year. $26.95/yr. Circ.: 100,000. **Description:** For knowledgeable doll collectors. **Nonfiction:** Sharply focused, with strong collecting angle and concrete information (value, identification, restoration, etc.). Include quality slides or transparencies; 500-1,500 words; $100-$350. **Queries:** Required. **Payment:** On acceptance.

FIBERARTS
50 College St., Asheville, NC 28801. 828-253-0467. E-mail: editor@fiberartsmagazine.com. Web site: www.fiberartsmagazine.com. 5x/year. $5.50/issue, $22/year. Circ.: 24,000. Sunita Patterson, Editor. **Description:** Covers all fiber-arts: weaving, quilting, embroidery, wearable art, 3-D work, basketry, and more. Readers include professional artists, craftspeople, hobbyists, collectors, and curators. **Nonfiction:** Articles and interviews (outstanding artists and craftspeople, trends and issues, exhibitions, business concerns, historic and ethnic textiles); 250-2,000 words; $65-$500. **Columns, Departments:** Profile (1 artist); Reviews (exhibits/books). Commentary; Notable Events (conferences, exhibitions); Art & Technology; 250-500 words; $65-$125. **Art:** 35mm slides, transparencies; B&W

glossies; electronic images (if 300 dpi or greater resolution). No color prints. **Tips:** Good visuals key to acceptance. Submit with synopsis, outline, writing samples. Use accessible, not scholarly, writing tone. **Queries:** Preferred. **E-Queries:** No. **Unsolicited mss:** Accepts. **Response:** 1-2 months, SASE required. **Freelance Content:** 90%. **Rights:** 1st NA. **Payment:** On publication.

FINE WOODWORKING
Taunton Press
63 S Main St., P.O. Box 5506, Newtown, CT 06470-5506. 203-426-8171.
E-mail: fw@taunton.com. Web site: www.taunton.com. Bimonthly. Circ.: 270,000. Timothy Schreiner, Publisher. **Description:** Covers high-quality workmanship, thoughtful designs, and safe and proper procedures for outstanding results. **Nonfiction:** Articles on basics of tool use, stock preparation and joinery; specialized techniques and finishing; shop-built tools, jigs, and fixtures; or any stage of design, construction, finishing, and installation of cabinetry and furniture; $150/page. **Columns, Departments:** Methods of Work, Q&A, Master Class, Finish Line, Tools & Materials, and Notes & Comment; from $10. **Queries:** Required. **Payment:** On publication. **Contact:** Anatole Burkin, Executive Editor.

FINELINES
P.O. Box 8928, New Castle, PA 16107. 724-652-6259.
E-mail: hngoffice@aol.com. Web site: www.historicneedlework.com. Quarterly. $6/issue. Circ.: 3,800. Deborah Novak Crain, Editor. **Description:** All about needlework. **Nonfiction:** Travel to historic places with significant needlework; museums; stitching (samplers, needlework tools, etc.); pay varies; 500-1,500 words. **Queries:** Not necessary. **E-Queries:** Yes. **Unsolicited mss:** Accepts. **Response:** SASE. **Freelance Content:** 35%. **Rights:** 1st NA. **Payment:** On publication.

FINESCALE MODELER
Kalmbach Publishing Co.
21027 Crossroads Circle, P.O. Box 1612, Waukesha, WI 53187-1612. 262-796-8776.
E-mail: editor@finescale.com. Web site: www.finescale.com. 10x/year. $4.50/issue, $37.95/year. Circ.: 60,000. Mark Thompson, Editor. **Description:** Largest-circulation magazine for scale modelers, especially builders of model aircraft, armor, ships, autos, and military figures. **Nonfiction:** How-to articles for people who make non-operating models of aircraft, automobiles, boats, and figures. Photos and drawings should accompany articles. Also, 1-page model-building hints and tips. Length, pay varies. **Art:** Prefers slides or medium-format transparencies. **Tips:** Stories on scale-modeling hobby only. Prefers how-to stories. **Queries:** Preferred. **E-Queries:** Yes. **Unsolicited mss:** Accepts. **Response:** Queries 4 weeks, SASE required. **Freelance Content:** 80%. **Rights:** All. **Payment:** On acceptance.

GARDEN RAILWAYS
Kalmbach Publishing Co.
P.O. Box 460222, Denver, CO 80246. 303-377-7785.

E-mail: mhorovitz@gardenrailways.com. Web site: www.gardenrailways.com. Bimonthly. Circ.: 36,000. Marc Horovitz, Editor. **Description:** Covers all aspects of the garden-railroading hobby, including building, operating, and landscaping of garden railway trains. **Nonfiction:** Articles; 500-2,500 words; pays $45/page (including photos). **Queries:** Required. **E-Queries:** Yes. **Unsolicited mss:** Accepts. **Response:** 30 days. **Freelance Content:** 75%. **Rights:** All, one-time. **Payment:** On acceptance.

GOOD OLD BOAT

7340 Niagara Lane N, Maple Grove, MN 55311-2655. 763-420-8923.
E-mail: karen@goodoldboat.com. Web site: www.goodoldboat.com. Bimonthly. $39.95 in U.S./Canada, $63.95 other. Karen Larson, Editor. **Description:** Provides articles and information on upgrading, maintaining, and restoring sailboats 10 years old and older. Also provides information and news on products and services in the sailing industry and profiles influential people and companies who have helped shape this hobby. **Nonfiction:** Technical material relevant to most older sailboats: in-depth, how-to articles on blister repair, deck delamination repair, tank repair, and so on. Also short refit articles with "quick and easy" tips; 1,500-5,000 words. **Columns, Departments:** Articles or stories on boatowners and their boats, reflections, book reviews, and other features. **Art:** Prefers slides, but also accepts color prints, B&W photos, and drawings/sketches. Will accept electronic files if resolution is at least 300 dpi; covers $100, special photo spreads $200. **Tips:** Review products and services honestly for the benefit of fellow readers. **E-Queries:** Yes. **Response:** 2-6 weeks, SASE required. **Rights:** 1st NA. **Payment:** 60 days in advance of publication.

HERITAGE QUEST

669 W 900 N, North Salt Lake, UT 84054. 801-298-5358.
E-mail: leland@heritagequest.com. Web site: www.heritagequest.com. Bimonthly. $6.95/issue, $28/year. Circ.: 21,000. Leland Meitzler, Editor. **Description:** Offers help with genealogical research. **Nonfiction:** Genealogical how-to articles; 1,800-4,000 words; $75/printed page. **Art:** To accompany articles; TIF. **Tips:** Readers range from beginners to professionals. **Queries:** Preferred. **E-Queries:** Yes. **Unsolicited mss:** Accepts. **Response:** 90 days. **Freelance Content:** 90%. **Rights:** All. **Payment:** On publication.

HOBBY MERCHANDISER

225 Gordons Corner Rd., P.O. Box 420, Manalapan, NJ 07726-0420. 800-969-7176.
E-mail: editor@hobbymerchandiser.com. Web site: www.hobbymerchandiser.com. Monthly. $20/yr. Jeff Troy, Editor-in-Chief. **Description:** For the professional craft business; also general small-business advice. **Nonfiction:** Articles, 800-1,500 words; pays $75-$200. **Payment:** On publication.

INTERWEAVE KNITS

Interweave Press
201 E Fourth St., Loveland, CO 80537-5655. 970-669-7672.

E-mail: knits@interweave.com. Web site: www.interweave.com. Quarterly. Melanie Falick. **Description:** For those who love to knit. Presents beautifully finished projects, with clear step-by-step instruction. **Nonfiction:** Related to knitting; profiles of people who knit; pays $100/published page. **Queries:** Preferred. **Payment:** On publication.

KITPLANES
8745 Aero Dr., Suite 105, San Diego, CA 92123. 858-694-0491.
E-mail: dave@kitplanes.com. Web site: www.kitplanes.com. Monthly. $4.99/issue, $29.95/year. Circ.: 72,000. Dave Martin, Editor. **Description:** For designers, builders, and pilots of home-built experimental aircraft. **Nonfiction:** On all aspects of design, construction, and performance for aircraft built from kits and plans by home craftsmen; 1,500-2,500 words; $70/page. **Queries:** Preferred. **E-Queries:** Yes. **Unsolicited mss:** Accepts. **Response:** Queries 2 days, submissions 2 weeks, SASE not required. **Freelance Content:** 80%. **Payment:** On publication.

LAPIDARY JOURNAL
PRIMEDIA Enthusiast Group
60 Chestnut Ave., Ste 201, Devon, PA 19333-1312. 610-964-6300.
Web site: www.lapidaryjournal.com. Monthly. Circ.: 55,000. **Description:** All about amateur and professional jewelry making.

LOST TREASURE
P.O. Box 451589, Grove, OK 74345. 918-786-2182.
E-mail: managingeditor@losttreasure.com. Web site: www.losttreasure.com. Monthly. $4.50/issue, $27.95/year. Circ.: 50,000. Patsy Beyerl, Managing Editor. **Description:** The treasure hunter's "magazine of choice." **Nonfiction:** How-tos, legends, folklore, stories of lost treasures; 500-1500 words; $.04/word. **Art:** JPG, color, B&W photos; $5. **Queries:** Not necessary. **E-Queries:** Yes. **Unsolicited mss:** Accepts. **Response:** Queries/submissions 1-2 weeks. **Freelance Content:** 35%. **Rights:** All. **Payment:** On publication.

MINIATURE COLLECTOR
801 W. Norton Ave., Suite 200, Muskegon, MI 49441-4155. 231-733-9382.
Barbara Aardema, Editor. **Description:** Showcases outstanding 1/12-scale and other scale (dollhouse) miniatures and the people who make and collect them. Features original, illustrated how-to projects for making miniatures. **Nonfiction:** Articles, 800-1,000 words, with photos; pay varies. **Tips:** Submit photos with queries. **Queries:** Preferred. **Payment:** On publication.

MODEL AIRPLANE NEWS
Air Age Publishing, Inc.
100 E Ridge Rd., Ridgefield, CT 06877-4623. 203-431-9000.
E-mail: man@airage.com. Web site: www.modernairplanenews.com. Monthly. $34.95/yr. Circ.: 100,000. Debra D. Sharp, Executive Editor. **Description:** For

enthusiasts of radio-controlled model airplanes. **Nonfiction:** Articles include advice from experts in the radio-controlled aviation field; also pieces on design and construction of model airplanes, reviews of new products. Pay varies. **Queries:** Preferred.

MODEL RAILROADER
Kalmbach Publishing Co.
21027 Crossroads Circle, P.O. Box 1612, Waukesha, WI 53187-1612. 262-796-8776. E-mail: mrmag@mrmag.com. Web site: www.modelrailroader.com. Monthly. $4.95/issue, $39.95/year. Circ.: 190,000. Terry Thompson, Editor. **Description:** Everything related to the hobby of model railroading. Covers hobby topics with expanded reporting. **Nonfiction:** How-to stories on model railroading; any length; $90/printed page. **Tips:** Authors must be model railroad hobbyists. **Queries:** Preferred. **E-Queries:** Yes. **Unsolicited mss:** Accepts. **Rights:** All. **Payment:** On acceptance.

MODELER'S RESOURCE
4120 Douglas Blvd., #306-372, Granite Bay, CA 95746-5936. 916-784-9517. E-mail: modres@quiknet.com. Web site: www.modelersresource.com. Bimonthly. $34. Fred DeRuvo, Executive Publisher. **Description:** Caters to builders of models, especially sci-fi, fantasy, vehicular, and figures. Each issue includes previews, photos, reviews, and features on the latest genre kits. **Nonfiction:** Quality articles that delve into building and painting models, product reviews, interviews with the names behind the product, show coverage; 2,000-2,500 words; pays fee per published page. **Art:** Quality color photos or slides. Digital photos accepted if resolution is 300 dpi; No payment. **Tips:** Occasionally works with new writers. Seeking articles that go beyond the norm. Be clear and concise, yet allow your personal style to flow. "Often, new writers tend to not be instructive enough, or conversely, tend to go off on tangents." **E-Queries:** Yes. **Response:** 2-4 weeks, SASE required. **Freelance Content:** 10-15%. **Rights:** All. **Contact:** Managing Editor.

NEEDLEWORK RETAILER
Yarn Tree Designs
P.O. Box 724, Ames, IA 50010. 515-232-3121. E-mail: info@yarntree.com. Web site: yarntree.com/nr.htm. Bimonthly. $12/yr. Megan Chriswisser, Editor. **Description:** Trade magazine that features the latest products, trends, and designs in the counted cross stich and needlework industry. Also includes updated information on trade associations and trade shows. For owners and managers of independent needlework retail stores. **Nonfiction:** Profiles of shop owners; articles about a successful store event or promotion, 500-1,000 words; pay varies. **Tips:** No generic business articles. **Payment:** On acceptance.

NEW ENGLAND ANTIQUES JOURNAL
4 Church St., Ware, MA 01082. 800-432-3505. E-mail: neajtpub@aol.com. Web site: www.antiquesjournal.com. Monthly. $3/$22.95.

Circ.: 25,000. Jamie Mercier, Editor. **Description:** For antiques trade, with informative features for antiques professionals and casual collectors. Includes event calendars, auction coverage, and more. Also publishes a glossy supplement magazine insert, *Living with Antiques*, with features on preserving, restoring, and repairing antiques and historic properties. **Nonfiction:** On antiques, fine arts, and collectibles; 2,000 words; $200-$295. **Tips:** Submit well-researched articles with at least 12 high-quality images. **Queries:** Preferred. **E-Queries:** Yes. **Unsolicited mss:** Accepts. **Response:** Queries 1 month, submissions 2 months. **Freelance Content:** 50%. **Rights:** 1 year. **Payment:** On publication.

PETERSEN'S PHOTOGRAPHIC MAGAZINE
PRIMEDIA Enthusiast Group
6420 Wilshire Blvd., Los Angeles, CA 90048-5502. 323-782-2200.
E-mail: photographic@primediacmmg.com. Web site: www.photographic.com.
Monthly. $11.97. Circ.: 204,500. Ron Leach, Editor-in-Chief. **Description:** On all phases of still photography, for the amateur and advanced photographer. **Nonfiction:** How-tos; pays $125/printed page for articles, with photos. **Payment:** On publication.

PIECEWORK
Interweave Press
201 E 4th St., Loveland, CO 80537. 970-669-7672.
E-mail: piecework@interweave.com. Web site: www.interweave.com. Bimonthly. $5.95/$24. Circ.: 47,000. Jeanne Hutchins, Editor. **Description:** Features needlework and textile history. Presents stories and projects based on makers and techniques from needlework's rich past. **Nonfiction:** Well-researched articles on history of needlework techniques, motifs, and artists; 1,500-2,000 words; $100-$300. **Tips:** Prefers stories with needlework projects to demonstrate techniques covered in the article. Contact for upcoming editorial themes. **Queries:** Preferred. **E-Queries:** Yes. **Unsolicited mss:** Accepts. **Response:** Queries 1-2 weeks, submissions 1-4 months, SASE. **Freelance Content:** 80%. **Rights:** 1st NA. **Payment:** On publication.

POPTRONICS
275-G Marcus Blvd., Hauppauge, NY 11788. 631-592-6720.
E-mail: popeditor@gernsback.com. Web site: www.gernsback.com. Monthly. Circ.: 81,932. Chris La Morte, Editor. **Description:** For electronics hobbyists and experimenters. **Nonfiction:** Readers are science and electronics oriented, understand computer theory and operation, and like to build electronics projects; 2,000-3,500 words; $150-$500. **Payment:** On publication.

POPULAR MECHANICS
The Hearst Corp.
810 7th Ave., Fl. 6, New York, NY 10019-5818. 212-649-2000.
E-mail: popularmechanics@hearst.com. Web site: www.popularmechanics.com.
Monthly. $19.97. Circ.: 1,200,000. Joe Oldham, Editor-in-Chief. **Description:** Latest developments in mechanics, industry, science, telecommunications. **Nonfiction:**

Features on hobbies with a mechanical slant; how-tos on home and shop projects; features on outdoor adventures, boating, and electronics. Photos and sketches a plus; 300-1,500 words; to $1,500 (to $500 for short pieces). **Rights:** All. **Payment:** On acceptance. **Contact:** Sarah Deem, Managing Editor.

POPULAR WOODWORKING
F&W Publications, Inc.
1507 Dana Ave., Cincinnati, OH 45207. 513-531-2690.
E-mail: popwood@fwpubs.com. Web site: www.popularwoodworking.com. Circ.: 200,000. Steve Shanesy, Editor. **Description:** Technique articles, tool reviews, and projects for the home woodworker. Emphasis on practical techniques that have stood the test of time. **Nonfiction:** On woodworking (600 words); woodworking tips and tricks; techniques; 1-6 pages; $150/page and up. **Tips:** Tool reviews written in-house. No profiles of woodworkers. Seeking well-written essays on the craft, good techniques, and the occasional project. **Queries:** Preferred. **E-Queries:** Yes. **Unsolicited mss:** Accepts. **Response:** 3-4 months, SASE. **Freelance Content:** 30%. **Rights:** 1st worldwide, 2nd. **Payment:** On acceptance.

QUICK & EASY CRAFTS
House of White Birches, Inc.
306 E Parr Rd., Berne, IN 46711-1138. 219-589-8741.
E-mail: beth_wheeler@whitebirches.com. Web site: www.qandecrafts.com. Bimonthly. Circ.: 250,000. Beth Schwartz Wheeler, Editor. **Description:** How-to and instructional needlecrafts and other arts and crafts, book reviews, and tips. **Nonfiction:** Pay varies. **Art:** Photos. **Payment:** On acceptance.

QUILTING TODAY
Chitra Publications
2 Public Ave., Montrose, PA 18801. 570-278-1984.
E-mail: chritra@epix.net. Web site: www.quilttownusa.com. Bimonthly. $4.99/$19.95. Joyce Libal, Editor. **Description:** Features colorful pictures, quilting-world news, and projects for traditional and original designs from teachers and talented quilters. **Nonfiction:** Features on quilt history, techniques, and tools. Quilt patterns (following magazine's established format). Book and product reviews; 750-1,500 words; $75 (800 words). **Art:** Professional-quality photos of quilts; 35mm glossy; pay varies. **Queries:** Not necessary. **E-Queries:** Accepts. **Unsolicited mss:** Accepts. **Response:** 4 weeks, SASE. **Payment:** On publication.

R/C MODELER
P.O. Box 487, Sierra Madre, CA 91025. 626-355-1476.
E-mail: info@rcmmagazine.com. Web site: www.rcmmagazine.com. Monthly. $3.99/$25 yr. Circ.: 165,000. Patricia E. Crews, Editor. **Description:** For the radio-control model aircraft enthusiast. **Nonfiction:** How-to, related to radio-control model aircraft, helicopters, boats, cars. Pays $50-$350 for features; $50-$250 for other articles. **Fillers:** $25-$75. **Queries:** Not necessary. **E-Queries:** Yes. **Response:**

Queries 1 week, submissions 1-3 weeks, SASE. **Freelance Content:** 60%. **Rights:** 1st worldwide. **Payment:** On publication.

RAILROAD MODEL CRAFTSMAN

Carstens Publications, Inc.

P.O. Box 700, Newton, NJ 07860-0700. 973-383-3355.

E-mail: bills@rrmodelcraftsman.com. Web site: www.rrmodelcraftsman.com. Monthly. $23.75. Circ.: 75,000. William C. Schaumburg, Editor. **Description:** How-to articles on scale model railroading; cars, operation, scenery, etc. **Payment:** On publication.

RUG HOOKING

Stackpole Magazines

1300 Market St., Suite 202, Lemoyne, PA 17043. 717-234-5091.

E-mail: rughoo@paonline.com. Web site: www.rughookingonline.com. 5x/year. $6.95/$27.95. Patrice Crowley, Editor. **Description:** How-to features on rug hooking for beginners and advanced artists. **Nonfiction:** Instructional articles; also, profiles of fiber artists; 500-3,000 words; pay varies. **Queries:** Preferred. **E-Queries:** Yes. **Unsolicited mss:** Accepts. **Response:** 3 months, SASE. **Freelance Content:** 90%. **Payment:** On publication.

SCALE AUTO

Kalmbach Publishing Co.

21027 Crossroads Circle, P.O. Box 1612, Waukesha, WI 53187-1612. 262-796-8776.

E-mail: editor@scaleautomag.com. Web site: www.scaleautomag.com. Patrick Mulligan, Managing Editor. **Description:** For the adult model builder. Features "how-to" articles, modeling history, contest coverage, and kit and product news. **Nonfiction:** To 3,000 words, with photos; pays $60/page. **Tips:** For "how-to" articles, the key is including many clean, crisp, step-by-step photos. **Queries:** Required. **E-Queries:** Yes. **Unsolicited mss:** Accepts. **Response:** 90 days. **Freelance Content:** 50%. **Rights:** All. **Payment:** On acceptance.

SCHOOL MATES

U.S. Chess Federation

3054 U.S. Rt. 9W, New Windsor, NY 12553-7646.

E-mail: magazines@uschess.org. Web site: www.uschess.org. Quarterly. $2.50/issue, $12/year. Circ.: 35,000. Peter Kurzdorfer, Editor. **Description:** Published by United States Chess Federation. Covers major chess events, U.S. and abroad, with emphasis on triumphs and exploits of American players. **Fiction:** Chess related. **Nonfiction:** Instructive, and short fillers, for beginning chess players (primarily children, ages 6-15); 800-1,000 words; $50/page. **Fillers:** Puzzles, cartoons, anecdotes. **Art:** B&W, or color slides (preferred), glossies accepted; $25 1st use, $15 subsequent use. **Queries:** Preferred. **Unsolicited mss:** Accepts. **Payment:** On acceptance.

SEW NEWS

741 Corporate Circle, Suite A, Golden, CO 80401. 800-289-6397.
Web site: www.sewnews.com. Linda Turner Griepentrog, Editor. **Description:** Seeks articles that teach a specific technique, inspire a reader to try new sewing projects, or inform about an interesting person, company, or project related to sewing, textiles, or fashion. Emphasis on fashion (not craft) sewing. **Nonfiction:** Articles, to 3,000 words; pays $25-$400.**Queries:** Preferred. **Unsolicited mss:** Does not accept. **Payment:** On acceptance.

SPORTS COLLECTORS DIGEST

Krause Publications, Inc.
700 E State St., Iola, WI 54990. 715-445-2214.
E-mail: kpsports@aol.com. Web site: www.krause.com. Weekly. Circ.: 52,000. T.S. O'Connell, Editor. **Description:** Sports memorabilia and collectibles. **Nonfiction:** Articles on old baseball card sets and other sports memorabilia; 750-2,000 words; $50-$100. **Columns, Departments:** Query; 600-3,000 words; $90-$150. **Art:** Unusual collectibles; B&W photos; $25-$150. **Response:** Queries 5 weeks, submissions 2 months. **Rights:** FNASR. **Payment:** On publication.

TEDDY BEAR AND FRIENDS

PRIMEDIA Enthusiast Group
6405 Flank Dr., Harrisburg, PA 17112. 717-657-9555.
Web site: www.teddybearandfriends.com. Marianne Clay, Managing Editor. **Description:** For adult collectors of teddy bears; profiles of artists and manufacturers. **Nonfiction:** Articles, 1,000-1,500 words; pays $.30-$.35/word. **Tips:** Now accepting some fiction or personal-experience stories. **Queries:** Preferred. **Payment:** On acceptance.

TEDDY BEAR REVIEW

Jones Publishing Co., Inc.
N7450 Aanstad Rd., P.O. Box 5000, Iola, WI 54945-5000. 715-445-5000.
E-mail: editor@teddybearreview.com. Web site: www.teddybearreview.com. Bimonthly. $4.99/$19.95. Circ.: 50,000. Trina Laube, Editor. **Description:** Bimonthly publication for collectors, bearmakers, and teddy bear enthusiasts. **Nonfiction:** On antique and contemporary teddy bears for makers, collectors, enthusiasts; 800-1,000 words; $300. **Art:** Yes. **Tips:** Looking for articles on artists and manufacturers; prefers specialized topics. Submit photos of bears with queries. Readers treat teddy bears as art. No stories from the bear's point of view. **Queries:** Preferred. **E-Queries:** Yes. **Unsolicited mss:** Accepts. **Response:** 8-12 weeks, SASE. **Freelance Content:** 70%. **Rights:** All. **Payment:** On acceptance.

THREADS

Taunton Press
63 S Main St., P.O. Box 5506, Newtown, CT 06470. 203-426-8171.
Web site: www.taunton.com. Bimonthly. Circ.: 176,000. Carol Spier, Executive

Editor. **Description:** Garment construction and embellishment. **Nonfiction:** Technical pieces on garment construction and embellishment by writers who are expert sewers, quilters, embellishers, and other needle workers. Also covers sewing soft furnishings for home decor; $150/published page. **Payment:** On publication.

TRADITIONAL QUILTWORKS
Chitra Publications
2 Public Ave., Montrose, PA 18801. 570-278-1984.
E-mail: chitraed@epix.net. Web site: www.quilttownusa.com. Bimonthly. $4.99/$19.95. Joyce Libal, Senior Editor. **Description:** Pattern magazine with articles on quilt history, techniques, and tools. **Nonfiction:** Articles with 1-2 pages of text and quilts that illustrate the content; 750 words; pay varies. **Art:** 35mm color slides. **Queries:** Not necessary. **E-Queries:** No. **Unsolicited mss:** Accepts. **Response:** Queries 2 weeks, submissions 4 weeks, SASE. **Rights:** 1st. **Payment:** On publication.

TRAINS
Kalmbach Publishing Co.
21027 Crossroads Circle, P.O. Box 1612, Waukesha, WI 53187-1612. 262-796-8776.
E-mail: editor@trainsmag.com. Web site: www.trainsmag.com. Monthly. $4.95. Circ.: 120,000. Mark W. Hemphill, Editor. **Description:** Railroad news, features, and stories. **Nonfiction:** History, business analysis, economics, technology, and operations studies of railroads in North America and elsewhere. Occasional first-person recollections; 600-8,000 words; $.10-$.15/word. **Art:** 35mm or medium-format slides; quality 8x10 or larger. Color and B&W prints; $30-$300. **Tips:** Avoid first-person travelogues or trip reports, unless historical. Requires a good knowledge of industry and its technology. **Queries:** Preferred. **E-Queries:** Yes. **Unsolicited mss:** Accepts. **Response:** Queries 60 days, submissions 90 days, SASE. **Freelance Content:** 90%. **Rights:** All (manuscripts), one-time (art). **Payment:** On acceptance.

WATERCOLOR
See page 298 for full listing.
Description: On watercolor and other water media (gouache, casein, acrylic, etc.).

WESTERN & EASTERN TREASURES
P.O. Box 219, San Anselmo, CA 94979. 415-454-3936.
E-mail: treasurenet@prodigy.net. Web site: www.treasurenet.com. Monthly. $4.50/$27.95. Circ.: 100,000. Rosemary Anderson, Editor. **Description:** For metal detectorists, covers all aspects of the hobby. Field-proven advice and instruction; entertaining presentation. **Nonfiction:** Articles new, true and treasure-oriented, from all fields of responsible recreational metal detecting; 1,500 words; $.02-$.04/word. **Art:** Photo prints/35mm; $5-$7.50, $50-$100 (cover). **Queries:** Not necessary. **E-Queries:** No. **Unsolicited mss:** Accepts. **Response:** 1 month, SASE required. **Freelance Content:** 100%. **Rights:** All rights reserved. **Payment:** On publication.

WILDFOWL CARVING
Stackpole Magazines
1300 Market St. Suite 202, Lemoyne, PA 17043-1420. 717-234-5091.
Web site: wildfowl-carving.com. Candice Tennant, Editor-in-Chief. **Description:** Articles on bird carving and collecting antique and contemporary carvings. **Nonfiction:** How-to and reference articles, of varying lengths; pay varies. **Queries:** Preferred. **Payment:** On acceptance.

WINEMAKER
See page 397 for full listing.
Description: Practical information for home winemakers.

WOODWORK
42 Digital Dr., Suite 5, Novato, CA 94949. 415-382-0580.
E-mail: woodwork@rossperiodicals.com. Bimonthly. $4.99/$17.95. John Lavine, Editor. **Description:** Covers all aspects of woodworking. Assumes medium to advanced understanding in technical articles. Also, artist profiles, reviews. **Nonfiction:** Profiles, technical articles, projects, how-to; also shows, exhibition reviews, etc; 1,000-4,000 words; $150-$200/printed page. **Art:** Slides preferred. **Queries:** Preferred. **E-Queries:** Yes. **Unsolicited mss:** Accepts. **Freelance Content:** 90%. **Rights:** 1st. **Payment:** On publication.

YELLOWBACK LIBRARY
P.O. Box 36172, Des Moines, IA 50315. 515-287-0404.
Monthly. $30/yr. Circ.: 500. Gil O'Gara, Editor. **Description:** For collectors, dealers, enthusiasts and researchers of children's series books such as Hardy Boys, Nancy Drew, Tom Swift. Dime novels and related juvenile literature also included. **Nonfiction:** Especially interested in interviews with, or articles by, past and present writers of juvenile series fiction; 300-3,000 words. **Tips:** No articles that ridicule the literature or try to fit it into a political, sexual, psychological, or religious context. Nostalgic reflections okay if interesting. **Queries:** Preferred. **E-Queries:** No. **Unsolicited mss:** Accepts. **Response:** Queries 2 days, submissions 1 week. **Freelance Content:** 100%. **Payment:** In copies.

YESTERYEAR
P.O. Box 2, Princeton, WI 54968.
E-mail: yesteryear@vbe.com. Michael Jacobi, Editor. **Description:** Publishes articles on antiques and collectibles for readers in WI, IL, IA, MN, and surrounding states. **Nonfiction:** Articles; pays from $20. **Art:** Photos. **Tips:** Will consider regular columns on collecting or antiques. **Payment:** On publication.

ZYMURGY
American Homebrewers Association, Inc.
736 Pearl St., Boulder, CO 80302-5006. 303-447-0816.
E-mail: ray@aob.org. Web site: www.beertown.org. Ray Daniels, Editor-in-Chief.

Description: Articles appealing to beer lovers and homebrewers. **Queries:** Preferred. **Payment:** On publication.

HOME & GARDEN
(See also Lifestyles)

AFRICAN VIOLET
2375 North St., Beaumont, TX 77702. 409-839-4725.
Web site: www.avsa.org. Ruth Rumsey. **Description:** Offers techniques and methods for growing African violets. No payment. **Nonfiction:** Articles, 700-1,400 words; history and personal experience with African violets.

AMERICAN GARDENER
7931 E Boulevard Dr., Alexandria, VA 22308-1300. 703-768-5700.
Web site: www.ahs.org. Bimonthly. $4.95. Circ.: 20,000. David J. Ellis, Editor. **Description:** Published by American Horticultural Society (AHS), national organization for gardeners. **Nonfiction:** Feature-length articles sought include in-depth profiles of individual plant groups, descriptions of innovative landscape design projects (especially relating to use of regionally native plants or naturalistic gardening), profiles of prominent American horticulturists and gardeners, descriptions of historical developments in American gardening, profiles of unusual public or private gardens, and descriptions of important plant breeding and research programs tailored to a lay audience. Runs relatively few how-to articles; these should address relatively complex or unusual topics that most other gardening magazines won't tackle. Photography needs to be provided; 1,500-2,500 words; $300-$500. **Columns, Departments:** Natural Connections, Conservationist's Notebook, Regional Happenings; 250-1,200 words; $50-$200. **Tips:** Queries should describe topic and explain relevance to a national audience of knowledgeable gardeners; outline the major points to be covered. First-time authors should send relevant writing samples and qualifications. **Queries:** Preferred. **E-Queries:** No. **Unsolicited mss:** Accepts. **Response:** 90 days, SASE. **Freelance Content:** 75%. **Rights:** 1st NA, electronic for members-only Web site. **Payment:** On publication.

AMERICAN ROSE
P.O. Box 30000, Shreveport, LA 71130-0030. 318-938-5402.
E-mail: ars@ars-hq.org. Web site: www.ars.org. **Description:** Articles on home rose gardens (varieties, products, helpful advice, rose care, etc.). **Queries:** Preferred.

ATLANTA HOMES AND LIFESTYLES
Weisner Publishing, LLC
1100 Johnson Ferry Rd., Suite 595, Atlanta, GA 30342-1743. 404-252-6670.
E-mail: oblaise@atlantahomesmag.com. Web site: www.atlantahomesmag.com. 8x/yr.
$3.95/$24. Circ.: 33,000. Oma Blaise Ford, Editor-in-Chief. **Description:** On upscale home and gardens. **Nonfiction:** Original stories with local angle (mostly by

assignment), on homes, gardening, food, wine, entertaining, and remodeling; 300-1,200 words; $75-$500. **Columns, Departments:** Remodeling, shopping, profiles (on assignment; 200-700 words; $75-$200). **Queries:** Required. **Unsolicited mss:** Does not accept. **Response:** 3 months, SASE. **Freelance Content:** 50%. **Payment:** On acceptance.

BETTER HOMES AND GARDENS

Meredith Corp.
1716 Locust St., Des Moines, IA 50309-3038. 515-284-3000.
E-mail: jshao@mdp.com. Web site: www.bhg.com. Monthly. $2.99/issue, $19/year. Circ.: 7,600,000. Jeannine Shao Collins, Publisher. **Description:** Home and family magazine. Covers entertainment, building, decorating, food, money management, health, travel, pets, environment, and cars. **Tips:** A freelancer's best chances are in travel, health, parenting, and education. No political subjects, poetry, beauty, or fiction. **Queries:** Preferred. **E-Queries:** No. **Unsolicited mss:** Does not accept. **Response:** 2-3 weeks, SASE required. **Freelance Content:** 15%. **Rights:** All. **Payment:** On acceptance.

BIRDS AND BLOOMS

Reiman Publications
5400 S 60th St., P.O. Box 991, Greendale, WI 53129-091. 414-423-0100.
E-mail: editors@birdsandblooms.com. Web site: www.birdsandblooms.com. Bimonthly. Jeff Nowak, Editor. **Description:** For people who love the beauty of their own backyard. Focuses on backyard birding and gardening. **Nonfiction:** First-person experiences from your own backyard; 200-900 words; $100-$200. **Fillers:** 50-300 words; $50-$75. **Art:** Slides or prints; $75-$300. **Tips:** Write conversationally, include tips to benefit readers, keep stories short and to the point. Submit photos. No bird rescue stories. **Queries:** Not necessary. **E-Queries:** Yes. **Unsolicited mss:** Accepts. **Response:** Queries 1-2 months, submissions 2-3 months, SASE. **Freelance Content:** 25%. **Rights:** 1st NA. **Payment:** On publication. **Contact:** Jeff Nowak.

CANADIAN GARDENING

340 Ferrier St., Suite 210, Markham, Ontario L3R 2Z5 Canada. 905-475-8440.
E-mail: letters@canadiangardening.com. Web site: www.canadiangardening.com. Aldona Satterthwaite, Editor. **Description:** Canadian publication that features articles on gardening in Canada. Presents practical home gardening solutions and seeks to inspire readers with new ideas. Canadian angle imperative. **Nonfiction:** How-to pieces (to 1,000 words) on garden projects, include introduction and step-by-step instructions. Profiles of gardens (to 2,000 words). Pays $125 and up. **Columns, Departments:** 200-400 words. **Queries:** Preferred. **Payment:** On acceptance.

CAROLINA GARDENER

P.O. Box 4504, Greensboro, NC 27404-4504. 336-574-0087.
Web site: www.carolinagardener.com. Bimonthly. Circ.: 27,000. L.A. Jackson, Editor. **Description:** Specific to Southeast gardening (profiles of gardens in the region, new

cultivars, "good ol' southern heirlooms"). **Nonfiction:** Articles, 750-1,000 words; slides and illustrations essential to accompany articles; pays $175. **Queries:** Required. **Payment:** On publication.

COUNTRY GARDENS
Meredith Corp.
1716 Locust St., Des Moines, IA 50309-3023. 515-284-3515.
Quarterly. LuAnn Brandsen. **Description:** Features gardens that are informal, lush, and old-fashioned. Stories emphasize both inspiration and information. **Nonfiction:** Garden-related how-tos and profiles of gardeners, 750-1,500 words; pays $500-1,500. **Columns, Departments:** 500-700 words, on garden-related travel, food, projects, decorating, entertaining; pays $450 and up. **Queries:** Required. **Payment:** On acceptance.

COUNTRY KITCHENS
1115 Broadway, Fl. 8, New York, NY 10010-2803. 212-462-9652.
Annual. Barbara Jacksier. **Description:** Articles offering bright, inviting, and affordable decorating ideas. **Queries:** Preferred.

COUNTRY LIVING
224 W 57th St., New York, NY 10019. 212-649-3500.
Web site: www.countryliving.com. Monthly. $3.50. Circ.: 1,700,000. Nancy Soriano, Editor-in-Chief. **Description:** Covers lifestyle, decorating, antiques, cooking, travel, home building, crafts, and gardens. **Nonfiction:** 500 words and up; pay varies. **Tips:** Avoid grandmother stories. **Queries:** Preferred. **E-Queries:** No. **Unsolicited mss:** Does not accept. **Response:** 8 weeks, SASE. **Freelance Content:** 30%. **Rights:** All, 1st serial. **Payment:** On acceptance. **Contact:** Marjorie E. Gage.

ELLE DECOR
Hachette Filipacchi Magazines
1633 Broadway, Fl. 41, New York, NY 10019-6708. 212-767-5800.
E-mail: elledecor@hfmmag.com. 8x/yr. $29. Circ.: 465,000. Mitchell Owens, Interior Design Director. **Description:** On designers and craftspeople, and on houses and apartments with notable interior design and/or architecture. **Nonfiction:** Articles, 300-800 words; pays $2.00/word. **Tips:** Query with photos of designers and their work. **Queries:** Preferred. **Payment:** On publication.

FINE GARDENING
Taunton Press
P.O. Box 5506, 63 S Main St, Newtown, CT 06470-5506. 203-426-8171.
E-mail: fg@taunton.com. Web site: www.finegardening.com. Bimonthly. Circ.: 200,000. Elizabeth Conklin, Editor-in-Chief. **Description:** For readers with a serious interest in gardening. Focuses on ornamental gardening and landscaping. **Nonfiction:** How-tos, garden design, as well as pieces on specific plants or garden

tools. Picture possibilities are essential; 800-2,000 words; $300-$1,200. **Art:** Photos; $75-$500. **Queries:** Required. **Payment:** On acceptance.

FLOWER & GARDEN
51 Kings Hwy. West, Haddenfield, NJ 08033. 856-354-5034.
E-mail: kcpublishing@earthlink.net. Web site: www.flowerandgardenmag.com. Bimonthly. $3.99/issue, $19.95/year. Circ.: 300,000. Jonathan Prebich, Editor. **Description:** Offers ideas for outdoor environments, for home gardens. **Nonfiction:** Practical how-to articles. Historical and background articles, if related to home gardening; 1,000 words max. **Art:** Yes. **Tips:** Provide well-researched material. **Queries:** Not necessary. **E-Queries:** Yes. **Unsolicited mss:** Accepts. **Response:** Queries 3 months, SASE required. **Freelance Content:** 75%. **Rights:** One-time (print and electronic).

GARDEN COMPASS
1450 Front St., San Diego, CA 92101. 619-239-2202.
E-mail: siri@gardencompass.com. Web site: www.gardencompass.com. Bimonthly. Circ.: 112,000. Siri Kay Jostad, Editor. **Description:** For California gardening enthusiasts. **Nonfiction:** Features, to 2,000 words. **Fillers:** Crossword puzzles. **Art:** Photos. **E-Queries:** Yes. **Response:** several months. **Freelance Content:** 20%.

GARDEN DESIGN
World Publications, LLC
460 N Orlando Ave., Winter Park, FL 32789. 407-628-4802.
E-mail: editor@gardendesignmag.com. Web site: www.gardendesignmag.com. Bill Marken, Editor-in-Chief. **Description:** On private, public, and community gardens; articles on art and history as they relate to gardens. **Nonfiction:** Features, 500-1,000 words, pays from $1.00/word. **Payment:** Within 30 days of contract.

GARDEN RAILWAYS
Kalmbach Publishing Co.
P.O. Box 460222, Denver, CO 80246. 303-377-7785.
E-mail: mhorovitz@gardenrailways.com. Web site: www.gardenrailways.com. Bimonthly. Circ.: 36,000. Marc Horovitz, Editor. **Description:** Covers all aspects of the garden-railroading hobby, including building, operating, and landscaping of garden railway trains. **Nonfiction:** Articles; 500-2,500 words; pays $45/page (including photos). **Queries:** Required. **E-Queries:** Yes. **Unsolicited mss:** Accepts. **Response:** 30 days. **Freelance Content:** 75%. **Rights:** All, one-time. **Payment:** On acceptance.

GARDEN SHOWCASE
P.O. Box 23669, Portland, OR 97281-3669. 503-684-0153.
E-mail: gseditor@gardenshowcase.com. Web site: www.gardenshowcase.com. Monthly except Dec. and Jan. $2.95/issue, $19.95/year. Circ.: 30,000. Lynn Lustberg, Editor. **Description:** Distributed in Oregon and Washington. Features regional

plants, gardens, and nurseries, with gardening ideas and examples. Also, home decorating and design articles to connect the garden and the home. **Nonfiction:** Articles on outstanding gardens, etc; 800-1,000 words; $160. **Columns, Departments:** Q&A, Planting by Design, Gardening 101, Through the Grapevine; 380-400; $100. **Queries:** Preferred. **E-Queries:** Yes. **Unsolicited mss:** Accepts. **Response:** Queries 1-2 mos. Submissions 2-3 months, SASE required. **Freelance Content:** 100%. **Rights:** 1st. **Payment:** On publication.

THE HERB COMPANION

Herb Companion Press, LLC
243 E Fourth St., Loveland, CO 80537. 970-663-0831.
E-mail: herbcompanion@hcpress.com. Web site: www.discoverherbs.com. Bimonthly. $4.99/issue. Circ.: 160,000. Susan Clotfeller, Editor-in-Chief. **Description:** For herb gardeners, cooks, crafters, and general enthusiasts. **Nonfiction:** Practical horticultural information, original recipes using herbs, well-researched historical insights, step-by-step instructions for herbal craft projects, book reviews; 500-2,000 words; $.33/word, negotiable. **Columns, Departments:** 200-500 words. **Art:** 300 dpi, slides; pay varies. **Tips:** Technical accuracy essential. Strive for conciseness, clear organization; include subheads where appropriate, lists of similar information in chart form. **Queries:** Preferred. **E-Queries:** Yes. **Unsolicited mss:** Accepts. **Response:** 1-3 months, SASE. **Freelance Content:** 90%. **Payment:** On acceptance.

THE HERB QUARTERLY

EGW Publishing
1041 Shary Circle, Concord, CA 94518. 925-671-9852.
E-mail: jenniferbarrett@earthlink.net. Web site: www.herbquarterly.com. Quarterly. Circ.: 36,753. Jennifer Barrett, Editor. **Description:** Covers practical and professional aspects of herbs. **Nonfiction:** Practical uses, cultivation, gourmet cooking, landscaping, herb tradition, medicinal herbs, crafts ideas, unique garden designs, profiles of experts, and how-tos for the herb businessperson; 1,500-3,000 words. **Tips:** Include garden design when possible. **Payment:** On publication.

HOME POOL & BAR-B-QUE

Hawks Media Group, Inc.
P.O. Box 272, Cranford, NJ 07016-0272. 908-755-6138.
E-mail: jeanette@hawksmedia.com. Annual. $10. Circ.: 2,500. Jeanette Hawks, Editor. **Description:** For upscale owners of pools, hot tubs, and spas. **Nonfiction:** Pool experiences and recipes; 1,500 words; $40. **Art:** Photos of pools. spas, and barbecue grills (built-in especially); B&W, color, or digital photos; $10. **Queries:** Preferred. **E-Queries:** Yes. **Unsolicited mss:** Accepts. **Response:** 1 month, SASE. **Freelance Content:** 40%. **Rights:** All, may reassign. **Payment:** On publication.

HORTICULTURE
PRIMEDIA Enthusiast Group
98 N Washington St., Boston, MA 02114-1922. 617-742-5600.
E-mail: horteditorial@primediasi.com. Web site: www.hortmag.com. 6x/year. $28.
Circ.: 205,000. Trish Wesley Umbrell, Editor. **Description:** Covers all aspects of gardening. **Nonfiction:** Authoritative, well-written articles on gardening; 500-2,500 words; pay varies. **Queries:** Required. **Payment:** On publication.

HOUSE BEAUTIFUL
The Hearst Corp.
1700 Broadway, Fl. 29, New York, NY 10019-5905. 212-903-5084.
E-mail: mmcevoy@hearst.com. Web site: www.housebeautiful.com. Monthly.
$19.97/yr. Circ.: 853,000. Marian McEvoy, Editor-in-Chief. **Description:** Pieces on design, travel, and gardening. **Nonfiction:** A literary, personal memoir, each month, 3,000 words, "Thoughts of Home." Pays $1/word. **Tips:** Send detailed outline and SASE. **Queries:** Preferred. **Payment:** On acceptance.

L.A. HOUSE & HOME
3742 Sepulveda Blvd., #193, Torrance, CA 90505. 310-323-3094.
E-mail: lahh@lamediainc.com. Monthly. $30/yr. Circ.: 35,000. E. Hirata, Editor.
Description: A resource magazine for home decorating, renovations, and landscaping. **Nonfiction:** All articles must focus on Los Angeles homes, activities showcasing homes or decorating, or shopping for unique home items; starting at $75. **Tips:** Articles are mostly staff-written; however, occasionally seeks shorter articles for columns relating to Los Angeles' unique shopping areas or activities showcasing architecture, home tours, or decorating ideas. **Queries:** Preferred. **E-Queries:** Yes. **Unsolicited mss:** Accepts. **Response:** Queries 3-5 days, submissions 5-7 days. **Payment:** On publication.

LANDSCAPE TRADES
See page 608 for full listing.
Description: Canadian trade publication with articles on landscape design, construction, and maintenance.

LOG HOME DESIGN IDEAS
Sabot Publishing, Inc.
1620 Lawe St., Suite 2, Appleton, WI 54915-2411. 920-830-1701.
E-mail: editor@athenet.net. Web site: www.loghomedesignideas.com. Monthly.
$23.95. Circ.: 92,000. Teresa Hilgenberg, Editor. **Description:** For people interested in log homes. **Queries:** Preferred.

LOG HOME LIVING
4200-T Lafayette Center Dr., Chantilly, VA 20151-1208. 703-222-9411.
E-mail: plobred@homebuyerpubs.com. Web site: www.loghomeliving.com. Monthly.
Circ.: 110,000. Peter Lobred, Editor. **Description:** For people who own or are plan-

ning to build contemporary log homes. Readers are mostly married couples, 30-45 years old, well-educated, do-it-yourselfers. **Nonfiction:** About people who have built modern log homes from manufactured or handcrafted kits. Conversational; describe home, tell how it came to be. Emphasize special elements: intent, design, solutions to problems, features, furnishings, interior design, landscaping; 1,000-2,000 words; $350-$550/article. **Art:** If possible, please include color (professional quality) photos; floor plans, construction costs, schedules a plus. **Tips:** Seeks long-term relationships with contributors who deliver quality work. **Queries:** Preferred. **E-Queries:** Yes. **Response:** SASE. **Freelance Content:** 50%. **Rights:** FNASR. **Payment:** On acceptance.

METROPOLITAN HOME

Hachette Filipacchi Magazines
1633 Broadway, Fl. 41, New York, NY 10019-6708. 212-767-6041.
E-mail: dwarner@hfmmag.com. Web site: www.hfnm.com. Bimonthly. $15.94/yr. Circ.: 604,000. Donna Warner, Editor-in-Chief. **Description:** Service and informational articles for residents of houses, co-ops, lofts, and condominiums, on real estate, equity, wine and spirits, collecting, trends, etc. Interior design and home furnishing articles with emphasis on lifestyle. **Nonfiction:** Pay varies. **Tips:** Send clips. **Queries:** Preferred.

NATURAL HOME

Natural Home LLC/Interweave
201 E 4th St., Loveland, CO 80537-5601. 970-669-7672.
E-mail: robynl@naturalhomemagazine.com.
Web site: www.naturalhomemagazine.com. Bimonthly. $24.95/yr. Circ.: 54,000. Robyn Griggs Lawrence, Editor-in-Chief. **Description:** Promotes earth-inspired living. Features "green," sustainable homes and lifestyles. **Nonfiction:** Pays $.33-$1.00/word; 300-2,000 words. **Tips:** Needs fresh, cutting-edge ideas on green living; also small, newsy items for front-of-the-book Journal section. Submit query or complete manuscript. Guidelines available for SASE or by e-mail. **Queries:** Preferred. **E-Queries:** Yes. **Unsolicited mss:** Accepts. **Rights:** 1st NA.

OG MAGAZINE

33 E Minor St., Emmaus, PA 18098. 610-967-8926.
E-mail: organicgardening.com. Web site: www.organicgardening.com. 6x/year. $3.99/$24.96. Circ.: 300,000. John Grogan, Editor. **Description:** North America's only gardening magazine dedicated wholly to organic practices. **Nonfiction:** Gardening how-to, solid organic advice; profiles of organic gardens and gardeners; profiles of a vegetable, fruit, or flower; 1,000-1,800 words; $.60-$1.00/word. **Columns, Departments:** My Journal; 500 words; $400. **Queries:** Preferred. **E-Queries:** Yes. **Unsolicited mss:** Accepts. **Response:** Queries 4 weeks, submissions 6 weeks, SASE. **Freelance Content:** 40%. **Rights:** All. **Payment:** On acceptance.

OLD HOUSE INTERIORS
108 East Main St., Gloucester, MA 01930. 978-283-3200.
E-mail: editorial@oldhouseinteriors.com. Web site: www.oldhouseinteriors.com.
Bimonthly. Circ.: 125,000. Regina Cole, Senior Editor. **Description:** On architecture, decorative arts, and history. **Nonfiction:** Articles, 300-1,500 words; pays $1/word, or $200 page min. **Tips:** Most important thing is the art; when proposing an article, know how it should be illustrated. Professional photos not necessary. Query, with clips. **Payment:** On acceptance.

SOUTHERN ACCENTS
See page 481 for full listing.
Description: Celebrates southern style in interiors, gardens, art, and entertaining.

STYLE AT HOME
25 Sheppard Ave. W, Suite 100, Toronto, Ontario M2N 6S7 Canada. 416-733-7600.
E-mail: letters@styleathome.com. 9x/year. Circ.: 195,000. Gail Johnston Habs, Editor.
Description: Profiles of Canadian homes, renovation, decoration, and gardening. Canadian content and locations only. **Nonfiction:** Articles; 300-800 words; $300-$800 (Canadian). **Queries:** Preferred. **Payment:** On acceptance.

SUNSET
See page 481 for full listing.
Description: Regional magazine for Western America, covering travel and recreation; garden and outdoor living; food and entertaining; building, design, and crafts.

VICTORIAN HOMES
Y-Visionary Publishing
LP, 265 S Anita Dr., Suite 120, Orange, CA 92868. 714-939-9991.
E-mail: erika.kotite@prodigy.net. Web site: www.victorianhomesmag.com.
Bimonthly. $3.99/$19.95. Circ.: 80,000. Erika Kotite, Editor. **Description:** Covers the lifestyle of Victorian Revival. Articles explore decoration and architecture of 19th- and early 20th-century homes restored, decorated, and lived-in by real people, also period museum houses. **Nonfiction:** On interior design, furnishings, gardens, florals, table settings, and decorative accessories. Also, kitchen or bathroom makeovers, whole-house restorations, renovation tips, paint colors/wall coverings, etc; 1,000-1,500 words; $400-$500. **Columns, Departments:** Victorian furnishings, antiques, collectibles, lighting, flowers and food, for today's home. **Queries:** Preferred. **E-Queries:** Accepts. **Unsolicited mss:** Accepts. **Response:** 6-8 weeks. **Freelance Content:** 80%. **Rights:** All or 1st (1 year). **Payment:** On acceptance.

IN-FLIGHT MAGAZINES

ABOARD PUBLISHING
100 Almeria Ave., Suite 220, Coral Gables, FL 33134. 305-441-9738.
E-mail: editorial@aboardpublishing.com. Web site: www.aboardpublishing.com.
Sarah Munoz, Editor. **Description:** Publishes seven bilingual (English and Spanish)
in-flight magazines for travelers going to and from Central and South America.
Fiction: Travel, legends, tourism; 750 words; $.20/word. **Nonfiction:** Travel,
tourism; 750 words; $.20/word. **Fillers:** Accepts. **Art:** By request; transparencies,
slides. **Queries:** Not necessary. **E-Queries:** Yes. **Unsolicited mss:** Accepts.
Response: SASE required. **Freelance Content:** 60%. **Rights:** First Western
Hemisphere. **Payment:** On publication. **Contact:** Angel Martinez.

ABOVE & BEYOND
First Air
P.O. Box 13142, Kanata, Ontario K2K 1X3 Canada. 613-599-4190.
E-mail: info@above-n-beyond.com. Web site: www.above-n-beyond.com. Bimonthly.
$15.50. Circ.: 25,000. Season Osborne, Editor. **Description:** In-flight magazine for
First Air Airlines (in the Canadian arctic).

ALASKA AIRLINES
Paradigm Communications Group
2701 First Ave., Suite 250, Seattle, WA 98121-1125. 206-441-5871.
E-mail: editorialaska@paradigmcg.com. Monthly. $50. Circ.: 45,700. Paul Frichtl,
Editor. **Description:** On business, travel, and profiles of regional personalities for
West Coast business travelers. **Nonfiction:** Articles, 250-2,500 words; pay varies.
Queries: Preferred. **Payment:** On publication.

AMERICA WEST AIRLINES
Skyword Marketing, Inc.
4636 E Elwood St., Suite 5, Phoenix, AZ 85040-1963. 602-997-7200.
Web site: www.skyword.com. Monthly. Circ.: 135,000. Michael Derr, Editor.
Description: Offers articles on business trends, first-person profiles, destination
pieces, fiction, arts and culture, thoughtful essays. **Tips:** Does not accept unsolicited
queries or manuscripts. **Queries:** Not necessary.

AMERICAN WAY
14770 Trinity Blvd., Fort Worth, TX 76155-2642. 817-967-1804.
E-mail: editor@americanway.com. Web site: www.americanway.com. Biweekly. Jill
Becker, Executive Editor. **Description:** Travel, business, food and wine, health, and
technology. **Nonfiction:** Features; 1,500-2,000 words. **Columns, Departments:**
Sojourns; Travel Stories. **Queries:** Required. **Response:** SASE.

ATMOSPHERE

Melaine Communications Group, Inc.

703 Evans Ave., #106, Toronto, Ontario M9C 2E9 Canada. 416-622-1680.

E-mail: atmosphere@melainecommunications.com. 3x/year. Circ.: 75,188. Susan Melnyk, Editor. **Description:** For airline passengers of Canada 3000.

BOSTON AIRPORT JOURNAL

Travel Publications

256 Marginal St., East Boston, MA 02128-2800. 617-561-4000.

E-mail: travelnews@att.net. Monthly. $55. Circ.: 30,000. Robert H. Weiss, Publisher/Editor. **Description:** Logan International Airport publication.

ENROUTE

Spafax Canada, Inc.

355 Sainte Catherine W #400, Montreal, Quebec H3B 1A5 Canada. 514-844-2001.

E-mail: info@enroutemag.net. Monthly. $45. Circ.: 200,000. Arjun Basu, Editor-in-Chief. **Description:** Air Canada in-flight magazine.

FRONTIER

Adventure Media

3983 S McCarran Blvd., Suite 434, Reno, NV 89502. 775-856-3532.

E-mail: laurah@adventuremedia.com. Web site: www.frontiermag.com. Monthly. Circ.: 20,000. Laura Hengstler, Editor-in-Chief. **Description:** In-flight magazine for Frontier Air Lines, serving the northwest U.S. **Nonfiction:** 50-2000 words; $.25-$.50/word. **Queries:** Required. **E-Queries:** Yes. **Unsolicited mss:** Accepts. **Response:** 6 weeks. **Freelance Content:** 70%. **Rights:** 1st NA serial, exclusive Web (90 days). **Payment:** On publication.

HEMISPHERES

Pace Communications

1301 Carolina St., Greensboro, NC 27401. 336-378-6065.

Web site: www.hemispheresmagazine.com. Monthly. $50/yr. Circ.: 500,000. Randy Johnson, Editor. **Description:** Offers global perspective in a fresh, artful publication. **Fiction:** 1,500-3,000 words; Pay varies. **Nonfiction:** Articles on universal issues; 2,000-3,000 words; $.75/word and up. **Columns, Departments:** See writer guidelines; 1,500-1,800 words; $.50/word. **Tips:** Prefers writers who live in the places whereof they write. **Queries:** Preferred. **E-Queries:** Yes. **Unsolicited mss:** Accepts. **Response:** 2 months, SASE. **Freelance Content:** 95%. **Rights:** 1st worldwide. **Payment:** On acceptance. **Contact:** Selby Bateman.

HORIZON AIR

2701 First Ave., #250, Seattle, WA 98121-1123. 206-441-5871.

Monthly. $45/yr. Circ.: 416,000. Michele Andrus Dill, Editor. **Description:** For travelers in the Northwest, Silicon Valley, California, Arizona, Southern British Columbia, and Southern Alberta. **Nonfiction:** Business, travel, lifestyle, sports, and leisure;

500-2,500 words; pay varies. **Columns, Departments:** Personal essay on business, travel, life in Northwest; 500-1,500 words. **Art:** Transparencies, slides. **Tips:** Query with samples (photocopies preferred, not originals). **Queries:** Required. **E-Queries:** No. **Unsolicited mss:** Accepts. **Response:** 1-6 months, SASE. **Freelance Content:** 80%. **Rights:** FNASR. **Payment:** On publication.

MIDWEST EXPRESS
Paradigm Communications Group
2701 First Ave., Suite 250, Seattle, WA 98121. 206-441-5871.
E-mail: editormidwest@paradigmcg.com. Bimonthly. Steve Hansen, Managing Editor. **Description:** Inflight magazine for Midwest Express Airlines. **Nonfiction:** Travel stories, business trends, and general features; 300-1,600 words. **Tips:** Keep queries concise. **Queries:** Required. **E-Queries:** No. **Unsolicited mss:** Accepts. **Response:** 2 months, SASE. **Freelance Content:** 60%. **Rights:** 1st NA. **Payment:** On publication.

NORTHWEST AIRLINES WORLD TRAVELER
Skies America Publishing Co.
P.O. Box 4005, Beaverton, OR 97076-4005. 503-520-1955.
E-mail: editors@skies.com. Monthly. $50. Circ.: 350,000. Beverly Dirks, Editor. **Description:** For passengers of Northwest Airlines.

SKY
Pace Communications, Inc.
1301 Carolina St., Greensboro, NC 27401-1090. 336-378-6065.
E-mail: editorial@delta-sky.com. Web site: www.delta-sky.com. Monthly. $50. Circ.: 500,000. David Bailey, Editor. **Description:** Delta Air Lines inflight magazine. **Nonfiction:** Articles on business, lifestyle, high tech, sports, arts; pay varies. **Art:** Color slides. **Queries:** Preferred. **Response:** SASE required. **Payment:** On acceptance.

SOUTHWEST AIRLINES SPIRIT
American Airlines Publishing
14770 Trinity Blvd., Fort Worth, TX 76155. 817-967-1804.
Web site: www.spiritmag.com. Monthly. Circ.: 360,000. **Description:** For passengers of Southwest Airlines.

SPIRIT OF ALOHA

Honolulu Publishing Company Ltd.
707 Richards St., Suite 525, Honolulu, HI 96813. 808-524-7400.
E-mail: jotaguro@honpub.com. Web site: www.spiritofaloha.com. Janice Otaguro, Editor. **Description:** Magazine for Aloha Airlines with Hawaiian Island focus. **Queries:** Preferred.

US AIRWAYS ATTACHÉ

1301 Carolina St., Greensboro, NC 27401. 336-378-6065.
E-mail: attacheair@aol.com. Web site: www.attachemag.com. Monthly. $50/yr. Circ.: 375,000. Lance Elko, Editor. **Description:** Entertaining articles for travelers. Ongoing departments, some features. **Nonfiction:** 350-2,000 words; $1/word. **Columns, Departments:** Homefront; Sports; Things that Grow; Things that Go; Golf; Insider's Guide to . . . (destination piece). **Art:** Photos from professional photographers or stock houses only. Writers should not submit photos. **Tips:** Include clips or list of past clients. **Queries:** Required. **E-Queries:** Yes. **Unsolicited mss:** Accepts. **Response:** 1 month, SASE. **Freelance Content:** 60%. **Rights:** exclusive worldwide for 90 days. **Payment:** On acceptance.

JUVENILE

AMERICAN GIRL

Pleasant Company Publications
8400 Fairway Pl., Middleton, WI 53562. 608-836-4848.
E-mail: im_agmag_editor@pleasantco.com. Web site: www.americangirl.com. Bimonthly. $3.95/$19.95. Circ.: 650,000. Kristi Thom, Editor. **Description:** For girls ages 8 and up. **Fiction:** Protagonist should be a girl between 8 and 12. No science fiction, fantasy, or first romance stories. Good children's literature, with thoughtful plots and characters; 2,500 words; payment varies. **Nonfiction:** By assignment only; 150-1,000 words; $1/word. **Fillers:** Visual puzzles, mazes, math puzzles, word games, simple crosswords, cartoons; $50/puzzle. **Columns, Departments:** Girls Express; short profiles of girls doing great, interesting things; 150 words; $1/word. **Tips:** The girl must be the story's "star," told from her point of view. "Girls Express" offers best chance to break in. **Queries:** Preferred. **E-Queries:** No. **Unsolicited mss:** Accepts. **Response:** 3 months; SASE required. **Freelance Content:** 5%. **Payment:** On acceptance.

APPLESEEDS

140 E 83rd St., New York, NY 10028. 603-924-7209.
E-mail: swbuc@aol.com. Web site: www.cobblestonepub.com. 9 issues/year. Barbara Burt and Susan Buckley, editors. **Description:** For children ages 7-10; covers multi-disciplinary social studies. **Fiction:** Short fiction, to 300 words. **Nonfiction:** Feature articles, profiles, how-to; 100-600 words; $50/page. **Fillers:** Games and activities; 100-300 words; $50/page. **Columns, Departments:** Reading Corner, Your Turn, Experts in Action, The Artist's Eye; 100-600 words; $50/page. **Tips:** All material must be theme-related; check Web site for coming themes. **Queries:** Required. **E-Queries:** No. **Rights:** All.

BABYBUG

Carus Publishing Co.
315 Fifth St., P.O. Box 300, Peru, IL 61354-0300. 815-224-6656.
Web site: www.babybug.com. Monthly. $5/issue, $35.97/year. Circ.: 45,000. Paula Morrow, Editor. **Description:** Offers simple rhymes and stories that parents will delight in reading to their babies. **Fiction:** Very simple and concrete; read-aloud and picture stories for infants and toddlers; 4-6 short sentences; $25. **Nonfiction:** Very basic words and concepts; up to 10 words; $25. **Poetry:** Rhythmic, rhyming. Humor or ending with mild surprise a plus; up to 8 lines; $25. **Fillers:** Parent/child interactive activities; up to 8 lines; $25. **Art:** Art by assignment only; no photos. Submit samples (tear sheets, photocopies) for consideration. Pays $250/page, $500/spread. **Queries:** Not necessary. **E-Queries:** No. **Unsolicited mss:** Accepts. **Response:** 6-8 weeks; SASE required. **Rights:** All. **Payment:** On publication.

BOYS' LIFE

Boy Scouts of America
1325 W Walnut Hill Ln., Irving, TX 75038. 972-580-2366.
Web site: www.bsa.scouting.org. Monthly. $18/year. Circ.: 1,300,000. W. E. Butterworth IV, Managing Editor. **Description:** Magazine for boys ages 8-14. Covers broad range of interests (sports, hobbies, careers, crafts, and special interests of scouting). **Fiction:** 1-2 short stories per issue; featuring 1 or more boys; humor, mystery, science fiction, adventure; 1,000-1,500 words; $750 and up. **Nonfiction:** From professional sports to American history to how to pack a canoe; 500-1,500 words; $400-$1,500. **Columns, Departments:** Science, nature, earth, health, sports, space and aviation, cars, computers, entertainment, pets, history, music; 300-750 words; $150-$400. Also, last page how-to features ($250-$300). **Art:** Quality photos only; most work by assignment. **Tips:** Write for a boy you know who is 12. Use crisp, punchy writing; short, straightforward sentences. **Queries:** Required for nonfiction. **E-Queries:** Prefer mail. **Unsolicited mss:** Accepts fiction only. **Response:** 6-8 weeks, SASE required. **Freelance Content:** 75%. **Rights:** FNASR. **Payment:** On acceptance.

BOYS' QUEST

P.O. Box 227, Bluffton, OH 45817-0227. 419-358-4610.
Web site: www.boysquest.com. Bimonthly. $4.95/$17.95. Circ.: 8,500. Marilyn
Edwards, Editor. **Description:** Captures interests of all boys with exciting, unique
activities and fascinating articles. Each issue focuses on a theme. **Fiction:** Stories on
childhood interests, featuring young boys in wholesome childhood activities and pursuits; 350-600 words; $.05/word min. **Nonfiction:** About boys in activities both
unusual and worthwhile. Photos with story essential; 500 words; $.05/word min.
Poetry: Yes; $10/poem min. **Fillers:** Puzzles, jokes, riddles, games; $10/puzzle min.,
varies for other fillers. **Art:** B&W photos, color slides, pen-and-ink illustrations; $5-
$35. **Tips:** Readers are boys, ages 8-10. Avoid Halloween, horror, etc. Prefers tradi-
tional childhood themes. Buys 3 nonfiction articles for each 1 fiction story. **Queries:**
Not necessary. **E-Queries:** No. **Unsolicited mss:** Accepts. **Response:** 4-6 weeks,
SASE. **Rights:** 1st NA. **Payment:** On publication.

CALLIOPE

Cobblestone Publishing
30 Grove St., Suite C, Peterborough, NH 03458. 603-924-7209.
E-mail: custsvc@cobblestone.mu.com. Web site: www.cobblestonepub.com. 9x/year.
$29.95/yr. Circ.: 11,000. Rosalie F. Baker, Editor. **Description:** Covers world history
for ages 8-14. Issues are thematic, exciting, colorful, with maps, timelines, illustrations, and art from major museums. **Fiction:** Authentic historical and biographical
fiction, adventure, retold legends, plays; up to 800 words; $.20-$.25/word.
Nonfiction: In-depth nonfiction, biographies; 700-800 words; $.20-$.25/word.
Poetry: Up to 100 lines. **Fillers:** Puzzles and games; activities including crafts,
recipes, and woodworking; up to 700 words. **Columns, Departments:**
Supplemental nonfiction; 300-600 words; $.20-$.25/word. **Art:** Photographs to
accompany articles; $25-$100. **Tips:** Contact for upcoming themes. **Queries:**
Required. **E-Queries:** No. **Unsolicited mss:** Prefers not to accept. **Response:** 2-4
months; SASE required. **Freelance Content:** 80%. **Rights:** All. **Payment:** On
publication.

CHICKADEE

Bayard Canada, The Owl Group
49 Front St. E, Fl. 2, Toronto, Ontario M5E 1B3 Canada. 416-340-2700.
E-mail: bayard@owl.on.ca. Web site: www.owlkids.com. 10x/year. $3.50/issue,
$24/year. Circ.: 70,000. Hilary Bain, Editor. **Description:** For children, ages 6-9.
Well-written animal features, also fiction, games, simple science experiments that
help children look more closely at their surroundings. **Fiction:** Stories to encourage
children to read and learn at the world around them; 600-800 words; $100-$300.
Nonfiction: Encouraging, inspiring articles for children; $100-$300. **Poetry:**
Humorous; $100-$300. **Fillers:** Puzzles, activities, observation games. **Art:** Slide
(max. 20); electronic (max. 10); $125-$450. **Tips:** Lively writing and strong visual
component are needed in any piece for Chickadee. **Queries:** Not necessary.
E-Queries: No. **Unsolicited mss:** Accepts. **Response:** 12 weeks, SASE required.

Freelance Content: 1%. **Rights:** Worldwide. **Payment:** On publication. **Contact:** Klara Pachner.

CHILDREN'S DIGEST

Children's Better Health Institute
1100 Waterway Blvd., P.O. Box 567, Indianapolis, IN 46206-0567. 317-636-8881.
E-mail: cbhiseif@tcon.net. Web site: www.childrensdigestmag.org. 8x/year. $21.95.
Circ.: 106,000. Penny Rasdall, Editor. **Description:** Health and fitness for ages 10-12. **Fiction:** Stories with a message about health: exercise, sports, safety, nutrition, hygiene, drug education; 500-1,500 words; up to $.12/word. **Nonfiction:** Profiles of famous amateur and professional athletes, "average" athletes (especially children) who have overcome obstacles to excel in their areas, new or unusual sports, exercise, safety, nutrition, hygiene, drug education; 500-1,000 words; up to $.12/word. **Poetry:** $25 and up. **Fillers:** Healthy recipes that children can make, puzzles, games. **Queries:** Not necessary. **Unsolicited mss:** Accepts. **Response:** 3 months; SASE required. **Rights:** All.

CHILDREN'S PLAYMATE

Children's Better Health Institute
1100 Waterway Blvd., P.O. Box 567, Indianapolis, IN 46206-0567. 317-636-8881.
E-mail: customercare@cbhi.org. Web site: www.childrensplaymatemag.org. 8x/year.
Circ.: 114,000. Terry Harshman, Editor. **Description:** For 6-8 year-olds, emphasizing health, fitness, sports, safety, and nutrition. **Fiction:** Plays. **Nonfiction:** Articles, crafts, recipes, general-interest, and health-related short stories. Easy recipes and how-to crafts pieces with simple instructions; 500-600 words; to $.17/word. **Poetry:** Yes; from $30. **Fillers:** Puzzles, games, mazes. **Queries:** Preferred. **Rights:** All. **Payment:** On publication.

CHIRP

Bayard Canada, The Owl Group
49 Front St. E, Fl. 2, Toronto, Ontario M5E 1B3 Canada. 416-340-2700.
E-mail: bayard@owl.on.ca. Web site: www.owlkids.com. 9x/year. **Description:** Offers puzzles, games, rhymes, stories, and songs for children, ages 2-6. Goal is to introduce preschool children to the relationship between words and pictures. **Fiction:** 300-400 words; pay varies. **Nonfiction:** 300-400 words; pay varies. **Queries:** Preferred. **E-Queries:** Yes. **Unsolicited mss:** Accepts. **Payment:** On publication.

CLICK

332 S Michigan Ave., Suite 1100, Chicago, IL 60604. 312-939-1500.
Web site: www.caruspub.com. 10 issues/year. $4.95/issue, $32.97/year. Circ.: 42,000.
James L. Plecha, Editor. **Description:** For children ages 3-7. Themes introduce ideas and concepts in natural, physical, or social sciences, the arts, technology, math and history. **Fiction:** Stories that explain nonfiction concepts; 600-1,000 words; payment varies. **Nonfiction:** Articles that explain the how and why of something; 200-400 words; payment varies. **Poetry:** Up to 20 lines; payment varies. **Fillers:** 1 page;

payment varies. **Art:** By commission. **Queries:** No. **E-Queries:** No. **Unsolicited mss:** Accepts. **Response:** 3-4 months; SASE required. **Rights:** 1st. **Payment:** On publication.

CLUB CONNECTION

1445 N Boonville Ave., Springfield, MO 65802. 417-862-2781 ext. 4067. E-mail: clubconnection@ag.org. Web site: www.missionettes.ag.org. Quarterly. $6.50/yr. Circ.: 13,000. Debby Seler, Editor. **Description:** Full-color publication for Missionettes ages 6-12. Brings girls together with common interests. The message of salvation is presented in each issue. **Fiction:** Fictional short stories; up to 700 words; $25-$40. **Nonfiction:** Articles on subjects of friends, school, God, family, music, nature, and fun activities; up to 700 words; $25-$40. **Poetry:** Pertaining to leadership/devotional; up to 700 words; $25-$40. **Fillers:** Crafts, games, puzzles, snack recipes, etc; pays $10. **Tips:** For leaders of Missionettes clubs; Leader's Connection provides ideas and resources, discipleship materials, etc. **Queries:** Preferred. **E-Queries:** Yes. **Unsolicited mss:** Accepts. **Freelance Content:** 35%. **Rights:** 1st. **Payment:** On acceptance. **Contact:** Ranee Carter.

CLUBHOUSE

Box 15, Berrien Springs, MI 49103. 616-471-3701. E-mail: etrumbo@hotmail.com. Web site: www.yourstoryhour.org. Monthly. $5/year. Circ.: 1,000. Elaine Trumbo, Editor. **Description:** Offers B&W photography, stories, poems, puzzles, recipes, and cartoons (for kids ages 9-12), with Christian background. **Nonfiction:** Action-oriented Christian stories, 800-1,200 words, with children in stories who are wise, brave, funny, kind. Pays $25-$35. **Queries:** Preferred.

CLUBHOUSE JR.

8605 Explorer Dr., Colorado Springs, CO 80920. 719-531-3400. Monthly. $1.50/$15. Circ.: 96,000. Annette Bourland, Editor. **Description:** Inspires, entertains, and teaches Christian values to children ages 4-8. **Fiction:** Fresh, inviting, well-developed characters; fast-paced, interesting story. Stories not explicitly Christian but built on foundations of belief and family values; 250-750 words (for young readers); $125-$300. **Nonfiction:** Articles about real children with interesting experiences. Science and nature told from unique perspective. Use short-caption styled format; 500 max.; $125-$200. **Poetry:** Real-life experience of young children; humorous, descriptive; 250 max.; $50-$100. **Fillers:** Puzzles (no crosswords); fun crafts, parent/child together; repetition of images, concise wording, humorous or insightful ending; 1 page; $25-$45. **Art:** Send samples to Carol Brown, Designer. **Tips:** No queries. **E-Queries:** No. **Unsolicited mss:** Accepts. **Response:** Submissions 4-6 weeks, SASE. **Freelance Content:** 25%. **Rights:** 1st. **Payment:** On acceptance.

COBBLESTONE

30 Grove St., Suite C, Peterborough, NH 03458. 603-924-7209. Web site: www.cobblestonepub.com. 9 issues/year. $4.95/issue. Circ.: 33,000. Meg

Chorlian, editor. **Description:** American history for 8- to 14-year-olds; themed issues. **Fiction:** Authentic historical and biographical fiction, adventure, retold legends; up to 800 words; $.20-$.25/word. **Nonfiction:** In-depth nonfiction, plays, first-person accounts, and biographies; 300-800 words; $.20-$.25/word. **Poetry:** Serious or light verse with clear, objective imagery; 30 lines; payment varies. **Fillers:** Crosswords, mazes, picture puzzles; payment varies. **Columns, Departments:** Activities such as crafts, recipes, and woodworking projects; payment varies. **Art:** Photographs related to theme; color or B&W, transparencies or slides; $15-$100. **Queries:** Required. **E-Queries:** Yes. **Unsolicited mss:** Does not accept. **Response:** 6 months queries, 2 months submissions, SASE required. **Freelance Content:** 85%. **Rights:** All. **Payment:** On publication.

CONSUMER REPORTS FOR KIDS ONLINE

101 Truman Ave., Yonkers, NY 10703-1057. 914-378-2985.
Web site: www.zillions.org. **Description:** An online version of *Consumer Reports* for kids, ages 8-14.

CRICKET

Carus Publishing Co.
315 Fifth St., P.O. Box 300, Peru, IL 61354-0300. 815-224-6656.
Web site: www.cricketmag.com. $5/issue, $35.97/year. Circ.: 71,000. Marianne Carus, Editor-in-Chief. **Description:** Folk tales, fantasy, science fiction, history, poems, science, sports, and crafts, for young readers. **Fiction:** Any topic of interest to children; up to 2,000 words; $.25/word. **Nonfiction:** Science, biography, history, nature; up to 1,500 words; $.25/word. **Poetry:** Brief lyric poems; up to 25 lines; $3/line. **Fillers:** Word or math puzzles, recipes, crafts, experiments; 150-200 words; $100. **Tips:** Include bibliography with nonfiction. **Queries:** Not necessary. **E-Queries:** No. **Unsolicited mss:** Accepts. **Response:** Submissions 8-12 weeks. **Freelance Content:** 90%. **Rights:** All. **Payment:** On publication.

DISCOVERIES

WordAction Publishing Co.
6401 The Paseo, Kansas City, MO 64131.
E-mail: hendrixson@nazarene.org. weekly. Circ.: 22,000. Virginia Folsom, Editor. **Description:** Full-color story paper for 3rd and 4th graders connecting Evangelical Sunday School learning with daily growth. **Fiction:** Contemporary, true-to-life portrayals of 8-10 year olds; 500 words; $.05/word. **Fillers:** Trivia, puzzles, miscellaneous areas of interest. **Tips:** Illustrate character building and scriptural application. Send for guidelines and coming themes. **Queries:** Preferred. **E-Queries:** Yes. **Unsolicited mss:** Accepts. **Response:** 6-8 weeks, SASE required. **Freelance Content:** 80%. **Rights:** Multi-use. **Payment:** On publication. **Contact:** Kathy Hendrixson.

DISCOVERY TRAILS

1445 N Boonville Ave., Springfield, MO 65802-1894. 417-862-2781.
E-mail: rl-discoverytrails@gph.org. Web site: www.radiantlife.org. Quarterly. Circ.: 20,000. Sinda Zinn, Editor. **Description:** Take-home paper for children 10-11 years old, with fiction stories, activities, poems, articles, and puzzles to reinforce daily Christian living. **Fiction:** Stories that promote Christian living through application of biblical principles by the characters; 1000 words; $.07-$.10/word. **Nonfiction:** Articles about topics that show God's power, wisdom in creation, or correlation to a relationship with God; 300-500 words; $.07-$.10/word. **Tips:** No Santa, Easter Bunny, Halloween stories. **Queries:** Not necessary. **E-Queries:** No. **Unsolicited mss:** Accepts. **Response:** Submission 2-4weeks, SASE required. **Freelance Content:** 90%. **Payment:** On acceptance.

EXPLORE!

Pinatubo Press
P.O. Box 2539, Asheville, NC 28802-2539. 828-254-9400.
E-mail: info@exploremagazine.com. Web site: www.exploremagazine.com. 10x/year. $3.95. Circ.: 50,000. Nat Belz, Publisher/Editor. **Description:** To foster curiosity, honor vocations, and challenge kids to think critically about how the world works. Articles from ancient history to modern technology. **Tips:** SASE for author guidelines.

FACES

Cobblestone Publishing
30 Grove St., Suite C, Peterborough, NH 03458-1454. 603-924-7209.
E-mail: facesmag@yahoo.com. Web site: www.cobblestonepub.com. 9x/year. $29.95/year. Circ.: 11,000. Elizabeth Crooker Carpentiere, Editor. **Description:** Introduces young readers (ages 8-14) to different world cultures, religion, geography, government, and art. **Fiction:** Retold folktales, legends, plays; must relate to theme; up to 800 words; $.20-$.25/word. **Nonfiction:** In-depth articles on aspect of featured culture; interviews and personal accounts; 600-800 words; $.20-$.25/word. **Fillers:** Activities (crafts, recipes, word puzzles); 100-600 words. **Art:** 35mm; $25-$100. **Tips:** Avoid judgmental tone; give readers a clear image of life in other cultures. Check Web site for coming themes. **Queries:** Required. **E-Queries:** Yes. **Unsolicited mss:** Accepts. **Response:** Queries 4 weeks, submissions 4 months, SASE required. **Freelance Content:** 80%. **Rights:** All. **Payment:** On publication.

FOOTSTEPS

30 Grove St., Suite C, Peterborough, NH 03458. 603-924-7209.
E-mail: cfbaker@meganet.com. Web site: www.footstepsmagazine.com. 5x/year. $23.95/yr. Circ.: 4,000. Charles F. Baker, Editor. **Description:** African-American history and heritage for students in grades 4-9. **Fiction:** Authentic retellings of historical and biographical events, adventure, and legends; 200-1,000 words; $.20-$.25/word. **Nonfiction:** On issue's theme; 200-1,000 words; $.20-$.25/word. **Art:** Slides, transparencies, digital, prints; pay varies. **Fillers:** Activities, short articles, to 600 words. **Tips:** Cultural sensitivity and historical accuracy required. Contact for upcoming themes. **Queries:** Required. **Unsolicited mss:** Accepts. **Response:** Queries 2-4 months, submissions 2-6 months, SASE. **Freelance Content:** 90%. **Rights:** All. **Payment:** On publication. **Contact:** Charles F. Baker.

THE FRIEND

See page 645 for full listing.
Description: Nonfiction literary journal for children up to 12 years of age.

GIRLS' LIFE

Monarch Publishing
4517 Harford Rd., Baltimore, MD 21214. 410-426-9600.
E-mail: kellygirl@girlslife.com. Web site: www.girlslife.com. Bimonthly. $2.95/issue, $14.99/year. Circ.: 2,000,000. Kelly White, Senior Editor. **Description:** For girls, ages 10-15, on friends, parents, school, siblings, beauty, and fashion. Offers honest advice, fun quizzes, and real-life solutions to growing-up problems. **Nonfiction:** Fun features and quizzes on school, friendships, crushes, pop culture; 750-2,000 words; $75-$800. **Columns, Departments:** Sports, Celebrity Interviews, New Trends; 750-1,000 words. **Art:** Color slides. **Tips:** Include resume and samples. Use teen language, and don't condescend. **Queries:** Preferred. **E-Queries:** No. **Unsolicited mss:** Accepts. **Response:** 90 days, SASE required. **Freelance Content:** 25%. **Rights:** 1st, all. **Payment:** On publication.

GUIDEPOSTS FOR KIDS ON THE WEB

1050 Broadway, Suite 6, Chesterton, IN 46304. 219-929-4429.
E-mail: gp4k@guideposts.org. Web site: www.gp4k.com. Rosanne Tolin, Editor. **Description:** E-zine for children, ages 7-12. Offers inspiring stories that focus on traditional values. Also has fun puzzles, trivia, animal stories, and interactive features such as a club, discussion boards, and monitored chats. **Fiction:** Stories by noted authors; 500-1,000 words; $100-$250. **Nonfiction:** Profiles of athletes and celebrities (150-500 words) and features that encourage kids to think (250-1,000 words); $75-$300. **Poetry:** 50-150 words; $25-$100. **Fillers:** $25-$150. **Tips:** "We do not consider ourselves a religious e-zine. No Bible-toting kids or preachy stories, please." Include bullets, links, sidebars, etc. **Queries:** Preferred. **E-Queries:** Yes. **Unsolicited mss:** Accepts. **Response:** 6 weeks, SASE. **Freelance Content:** 80%. **Rights:** All. **Payment:** On acceptance. **Contact:** Rosanne Tolin, Managing Editor.

HIGHLIGHTS FOR CHILDREN
803 Church St., Honesdale, PA 18431-1824. 570-253-1080.
E-mail: eds@highlights-corp.com. Web site: www.highlights.com. Monthly.
$29.64/year. Circ.: 2,500,000. Christine French Clark, Editor. **Description:** "Fun
with a purpose." The stories, Hidden Pictures, jokes, and activities bring engaging
entertainment to children ages 2-12, while developing learning skills. **Fiction:**
Humor, mystery, sports, adventure, folktales, world cultures, urban stories. Engaging
plot, strong characterization, lively language; up to 800 words; $150 and up.
Nonfiction: Biography, autobiography, arts, science, history, sports, world cultures,
up to 800 words. If for younger readers (ages 3-7 years), 400 words or less; $150 and
up. **Poetry:** 16 lines, $25 and up. **Fillers:** Crafts (3-7 numbered steps), $30 and up;
include a sample; use common household items or inexpensive, easy-to-obtain materials. Holiday/religious/world cultures crafts welcome. **Tips:** Prefers stories in which
protagonist solves a dilemma through his/her own resources. Avoid stories that
preach. **Queries:** Preferred. **E-Queries:** No. **Unsolicited mss:** Accepts.
Response: 6-8 weeks, SASE required. **Rights:** All. **Payment:** On acceptance.

HOPSCOTCH
P.O. Box 164, Bluffton, OH 45817-0164. 419-358-4610.
Web site: www.hopscotchmagazine.com. Bimonthly. $4.95/issue, $17.95/year. Circ.:
15,000. Marilyn Edwards, Editor. **Description:** Written for girls, without the emphasis on fads/fashion, boyfriends, and shopping. Focuses on educational activities and
stories. Makes reading an adventure and problem-solving fun. **Fiction:** Feature girls
in wholesome childhood activities and pursuits; 500 words; $.05/word and up.
Nonfiction: Features girls directly involved in an unusual and worthwhile activity.
Nonfiction is 75% of magazine's contents. Photos essential; 500 words; $.05/word and
up. **Poetry:** $10/poem. **Fillers:** Puzzles, games, crafts, cartoons, recipes; $10/puzzle
min. **Art:** B&W photos, color slides, and illustrations; $5-$35. **Tips:** Contact for
upcoming themes. **Queries:** Not necessary. **E-Queries:** No. **Unsolicited mss:**
Accepts. **Response:** 4-6 weeks, SASE required. **Rights:** 1st NA. **Payment:** On
publication.

THE HORN BOOK MAGAZINE
See page 635 for full listing.
Description: A critical review of introductory children's and young adult books.

HUMPTY DUMPTY'S
Children's Better Health Institute
1100 Waterway Blvd., P.O. Box 567, Indianapolis, IN 46206-0567. 317-636-8881.
Web site: www.humptydumptymag.org. 8x/year. $25.95/year. Circ.: 200,000. Nancy S.
Axelrad, Editor. **Description:** Encourages children, ages 4-6, to strive for excellence,
with focus on academics, health, personal fitness, medicine, and science. **Fiction:** up
to 350 words; to $.22/word. **Nonfiction:** up to 350 words; to $.22/word. **Poetry:**
Short verse, narrative; $25 min. **Fillers:** Games, puzzles, crafts, simple science exper-
iments, healthy and "no-cook" recipes (with minimum adult guidance). Clear brief

instructions. **Tips:** Should have good "read-aloud" quality. **Unsolicited mss:** Accepts. **Response:** Submissions 3 months, SASE required. **Freelance Content:** 25-30%. **Rights:** All. **Payment:** On publication.

JACK AND JILL
Children's Better Health Institute
1100 Waterway Blvd., P.O. Box 567, Indianapolis, IN 46206-0567. 317-634-1100.
Web site: www.jackandjillmag.org. 8x/year. $21.95/year. Circ.: 200,000. Daniel Lee, Editor. **Description:** For children, ages 7-10, offers health, fitness, science, and general-interest material. Encourages active, challenging lifestyles, and accomplishment and learning with a hearty helping of fun! **Fiction:** 700 words; $.17/word. **Nonfiction:** On history, biography, life in other countries, etc; 500 words; $.17/word. **Poetry:** $15-$50. **Fillers:** Games, puzzles, projects, recipes. **Art:** Photos. **Tips:** Avoid usual topics of divorce, moving, new kid in school, etc. **Queries:** Not necessary. **E-Queries:** No. **Unsolicited mss:** Accepts. **Response:** Submissions 12 weeks, SASE required. **Freelance Content:** 50%. **Rights:** All. **Payment:** On publication.

JUNIOR SCHOLASTIC
Scholastic, Inc.
555 Broadway, New York, NY 10012. 212-343-6295.
E-mail: junior@scholastic.com. Web site: www.juniorscholastic.com. Lee Baier. **Description:** On-the-spot reports from countries in the news. **Nonfiction:** Pay varies. **Queries:** Required. **Payment:** On acceptance.

KIDS TRIBUTE
71 Barber Greene Rd., Don Mills, Ontario M3C 2A2 Canada. 416-445-0544.
Web site: www.tribute.ca. Quarterly. Sandra Stewart, Editor-in-Chief. **Description:** Features articles on movies and entertainment for young readers, ages 8-13. **Nonfiction:** 350 words; pays $150-$200 (Canadian). **Queries:** Required. **Payment:** On acceptance.

LADYBUG
Carus Publishing Co.
315 Fifth St., P.O. Box 300, Peru, IL 61354-0300. 815-224-6656.
Web site: www.ladybugmag.com. Monthly. $5/issue, $35.97/year. Circ.: 130,000. Paula Morrow, Editor. **Description:** Stories, poems, songs, games, and adventures for young children, ages 1-2. Each page illustrated to delight parents and children alike. **Fiction:** Picture, read-aloud, and early reader stories with lively characters. Genres: adventure, humor, mild suspense, fairy tales, folktales, contemporary fiction; up to 850 words; $.25/word, $25 min. **Nonfiction:** How-to, informational and humorous pieces, on age-appropriate topics; up to 300 words; $.25/word, $25 min. **Poetry:** Rhythmic, rhyming, serious, humorous, active; up to 20 lines; up to $3/line, $25 min. **Fillers:** Rebus, learning activities, games, crafts, songs, finger games. **Art:** see guidelines. **Tips:** Always looking for more activities. Does not accept query letters. **Queries:** Not necessary. **E-Queries:** No. **Unsolicited mss:** Accepts.

Response: 12 weeks, SASE required. **Freelance Content:** 70%. **Rights:** 1st serial. **Payment:** On publication.

MAD
1700 Broadway, Fl. 5, New York, NY 10019. 212-506-4850.
Web site: www.madmag.com. Monthly. **Description:** Humorous pieces on a wide variety of topics. **Art:** cartoons, 2-8 panels (not necessary to include sketches with submission); pays top rates. **Response:** SASE. **Freelance Content:** 100%. **Payment:** On acceptance. **Contact:** Editorial Department.

MUSE
The Cricket Magazine Group
332 S Michigan Ave., Suite 1100, Chicago, IL 60604. 312-939-1500.
E-mail: muse@caruspub.com. Web site: www.musemag.com. 10x/year. Diana Lutz, Editor. **Description:** Focuses on problems connected with a discipline or area of practical knowledge, for children, ages 8-14. **Nonfiction:** 1,000-2,500 words; $.50/word. **Tips:** No longer accepts unsolicited manuscripts or queries. **Queries:** Not necessary. **Response:** SASE.

MY FRIEND
Pauline Books & Media, Daughters of St. Paul
50 St. Paul's Ave., Boston, MA 02130. 617-522-8911.
E-mail: myfriend@pauline.org. Web site: www.myfriendmagazine.com. Monthly. $2/issue. Circ.: 11,500. Maria Grace Dateno, Editor. **Description:** Provides kids and their families with a wealth of information and contacts on every aspect of the Catholic Faith. **Fiction:** Stories with good dialogue, realistic character development and current lingo; 800-1,100 words; $75-$150. **Nonfiction:** Fresh perspectives into a child's world: imaginative, unique, challenging, informative, fun; 800-1,100 words; $75-$150. **Tips:** Also accepts craft ideas. First send idea and if accepted, provide well-made sample. Send SASE for upcoming themes. Send $2.95 for sample copy. **Queries:** Not necessary. **E-Queries:** No. **Unsolicited mss:** Accepts. **Response:** 3 months; SASE required. **Freelance Content:** 30% mostly fiction. **Rights:** FNAR. **Payment:** On acceptance.

NATIONAL GEOGRAPHIC WORLD
National Geographic Society
1145 17th St. NW, Washington, DC 20036-4688. 202-857-7000.
E-mail: jajnone@ngs.org. Web site: www.national geographic.com/world. Monthly. $17.95/year. Circ.: 900,000. Melina Bellows, Editor-in-Chief. **Description:** For kids, ages 8-14, who dare to explore. Seeks to increase geographic awareness by inspiring young readers' curiosity, with big, bold photos and fun, fact-filled stories. **Nonfiction:** Adventure, outdoors, sports, geography, history, archaeology, paleontology, human interest, natural history, science, technology, "My World" (stories on lives of remarkable kids; "Friends USA" (on groups of kids doing things together); 400-1,200 words; $.80-$1/word. **Fillers:** Just Joking, Fun Stuff (games, laughs, things to do); $.80-

$1/word. **Columns, Departments:** World News (short, fun news items with kid appeal), Kids Did It! (achievements), Amazing Animals; 50-150 words; $.80-$1/word. **Art:** Yes. **Tips:** Send relevant clips with cover letter; research magazine first. **Queries:** Required. **E-Queries:** No. **Unsolicited mss:** Does not accept. **Response:** 2 months, SASE. **Freelance Content:** 90%. **Rights:** All. **Payment:** On publication. **Contact:** Julie Agnone, Executive Editor.

NATURE FRIEND

Carlisle Press

2673 Township Rd. 421, Sugarcreek, OH 44681. 330-852-1900.

Monthly. Circ.: 10,000. Marvin Wengerd, Editor. **Description:** Stories, puzzles, activities, and experiments about nature for children. **Nonfiction:** Articles for children that teach them to be kind to animals, plants, and nature, increase their awareness of God, and illustrate spiritual lessons; 250-1,200 words; $.05/word. **Fillers:** Games, puzzles, and activities concerning nature; 150-250 words; $15. **Art:** Photos to accompany mss; transparencies, prints; $35-$50. **Tips:** Sample issues, $5. **Response:** 1 month queries, 4 months submissions. **Freelance Content:** 80%. **Rights:** First or one-time. **Payment:** On publication.

NEW MOON

P.O. Box 3620, Duluth, MN 55803-3620. 218-728-5507.

E-mail: girl@newmoon.org. Web site: www.newmoon.org. Bimonthly. $5.50/$29. Circ.: 30,000. Deb Mylin, Managing Editor. **Description:** Celebrates girls—their accomplishments and efforts to hold onto their voices, strengths, and dreams as they move from being girls to becoming women. **Fiction:** Stories by female authors, with girls as main characters. Fiction should fit theme (contact for upcoming list), for girls ages 8-14; 900 words; $.06-$.10/word. **Nonfiction:** Women's work (profiles a woman and her job, relates to theme); Herstory (profiles a woman from history); Body Language (about puberty, body image, depression, menstruation, etc.); Girls on the Go (by girl or woman adventurers); 600 words; $.06-$.10/word. **Art:** By assignment; send samples; pay varies. **Queries:** Not necessary. **E-Queries:** Accepts. **Unsolicited mss:** Accepts. **Response:** 2 months, SASE. **Freelance Content:** 10%. **Rights:** All. **Payment:** On publication.

NICK, JR.

1633 Broadway, New York, NY 10019-6708. 212-654-6388.

E-mail: nickjr.editors@nick.com. Web site: www.nickjr.com. Bimonthly. Circ.: 800,000. Freddi Greenberg, Editor-in-Chief. **Description:** For children ages 2-7 and their parents. Features fun activities, games, and stories.

ON THE LINE

616 Walnut Ave., Scottdale, PA 15683. 724-887-8500.

E-mail: otl@mph.org. Web site: www.mph.org/otl. Monthly. $2.25/$27.25. Circ.: 5,000. Mary Clemens Meyer, Editor. **Description:** For youth, ages 9-14, to reinforce Christian values. Seeks to help upper elementary and junior high school kids understand God, the created world, themselves, and others. **Fiction:** Solving everyday problems, humor, holidays, Christian values; 1,000-1,800 words; $.03-$.05/word. **Nonfiction:** Nature, history, health, how-to; 300-500 words; $.03-$.05/word. **Poetry:** Light verse, humor, nature, holidays; 3-24 lines; $10-$25. **Fillers:** Cartoons, crosswords, word finds, scrambled letters, mazes, codes, jokes, riddles, and recipes; $10-$20. **Tips:** Let the story give the moral subtly; keep it fun. **Queries:** Not necessary. **E-Queries:** No. **Unsolicited mss:** Accepts. **Response:** 1 month; SASE required. **Freelance Content:** 85%. **Rights:** One-time. **Payment:** On acceptance.

OWL

Bayard Canada, The Owl Group
49 Front St. E, Fl. 2, Toronto, Ontario M5E 1B3 Canada. 416-340-2700. E-mail: bayard@owl.on.ca. Web site: www.owlkids.com. 9x/year. Circ.: 75,000. Elizabeth Siegel, editor. **Description:** For children ages 9-12, about animals, science, people, technology, new discoveries, activities. **Nonfiction:** Science, nature and environmental articles; 500-1,000 words; payment varies. **Art:** Photos to accompany articles. **Tips:** No fiction. **E-Queries:** Yes. **Response:** 3 months. **Freelance Content:** 25%. **Rights:** All. **Payment:** On acceptance.

PASSPORT

6401 The Paseo, Kansas City, MO 64131.
E-mail: hendrixson@nazarene.org. Quarterly printing, weekly distribution. Circ.: 18,000. Emily Freeburg, Editor. **Description:** Full-color newspaper for preteens with resources for spiritual transformation and holy living. Corresponds with WordAction Sunday School materials (for 11-12 year olds). **Nonfiction:** Articles for grades 5-6 on hot topics and relevant issues; 400-600 words; $30 for main feature for original work. **Fillers:** Pays $15 for cartoons and puzzles. **Queries:** Preferred. **E-Queries:** Yes. **Unsolicited mss:** Accepts. **Response:** 6-8 weeks, SASE required. **Freelance Content:** 30%. **Rights:** Multi-use. **Payment:** On publication. **Contact:** Kathy Hendrixson.

POCKETS

P.O. Box 340004, 1908 Grand Ave., Nashville, TN 37203-0004. 615-340-7333. E-mail: pockets@upperroom.org. Web site: www.upperroom.org. 11x/year. $19.95/yr. Circ.: 90,000. Janet Knight, Editor. **Description:** Non-denominational publication seeking to promote the Gospel of Jesus Christ to children and help them grow in their relationship with God. Readers include children of many ethnic and cultural backgrounds. **Fiction:** Stories to help children deal with everyday life. Prefers real-life settings; 600-1400 words; $.14/word. **Nonfiction:** Theme for each issue. Profiles of persons whose lives reflect Christian communities; value articles about children involved in environmental, community, peace/justice issues; 400-1000 words; $.14/word. **Fillers:** Puzzles, games (on theme); $25 and up. **Columns, Departments:** Pocketsful of Love and Pocketsful of Prayer; $.14/word. **Tips:** Looking for puzzles and activities with colorful illustrations and graphics. Publishes one story in each issue for kids 5-7 years. No more than 600 words. For sample copy send 9x10 SASE (4 first-class stamps). **E-Queries:** No. **Unsolicited mss:** Accepts. **Response:** SASE. **Freelance Content:** 90%. **Payment:** On acceptance.

RANGER RICK
National Wildlife Federation
11100 Wildlife Center Dr., Reston, VA 20190. 703-438-6000.
Web site: www.nwf.org. Monthly. $17/year. Circ.: 550,000. Gerald Bishop, Editor. **Description:** Write for photo and art guidelines. No unsolicited queries or manuscripts.

SHINE BRIGHTLY
P.O. Box 7259, Grand Rapids, MI 49510.
E-mail: sara@gemsgc.org. Web site: www.gospelcom.net/gems. Sara Lynne Hilton, Editor. **Description:** Upbeat fiction and features, 500-1,000 words, for Christian girls ages 8-14. Topics include personal life, nature, crafts, etc. **Nonfiction:** Pays $.03/word, extra for photos. Send full ms. **Fillers:** Puzzles, pays $10-$15. **Tips:** Send SASE for upcoming themes and writer's guidelines. **Queries:** Not necessary. **Payment:** On publication.

SKIPPING STONES
P.O. Box 3939, Eugene, OR 97403. 541-342-4956.
E-mail: skipping@efn.org. Web site: http://www.efn.org/~skipping//. 5x/year. $25/yr. Circ.: 2,500. Arun N. Toké, Executive Editor. **Description:** Publishes original writing, art, and photography. Encourages cooperation, creativity, celebration of cultural diversity, and nature awareness. **Fiction:** Social awareness, interpersonal relationships; 750 words max. **Nonfiction:** Nature awareness, multicultural education, social responsibility, travelogues, journal entries; up to 750 words. **Poetry:** by authors under age 19 only; on nature, social issues, reflections; up to 30 lines. **Fillers:** Multicultural, nature; 150 words. **Art:** Original B&W or color prints with captions or photo essays. **Tips:** Include personal information in cover letter (i.e., cultural background, languages you speak, source of inspiration for submission). **Queries:** Not necessary. **E-Queries:** Accepts. **Unsolicited mss:** Accepts. **Response:** Queries to 1 month, submissions to 3 months, SASE. **Freelance Content:** 80%. **Rights:** 1st serial, nonexclusive reprint. **Payment:** In copies.

SOCCER JR.
Scholastic, Inc.
555 Broadway, New York, NY 10012-3919. 212-343-6830.
E-mail: soccerjrol@aol.com. Web site: www.soccerjr.com. 6x/yr. $16.97. Circ.: 150,000. Mark Wright, Editor. **Description:** Fiction and fillers about soccer for readers ages 8-14. Pays $450 for a feature or story; $250 for shorter pieces. **Queries:** Preferred. **Payment:** On acceptance.

SPIDER

Carus Publishing Co.

315 Fifth St., P.O. Box 300, Peru, IL 61354-0300. 815-224-6656.

Web site: www.spidermag.com. Monthly. $4.95/issue. Circ.: 78,000. Heather Delabre, Associate Editor. **Description:** Stories, poems, science, fantasy, and activities for children. Original artwork fills each issue. **Fiction:** Easy-to-read realistic stories (fantasy, myths, fairy tales, fables, and science fiction). **Nonfiction:** Interviews, profiles, and how-to articles; on science, animals, nature, technology, and multicultural topics. **Poetry:** Yes. **Fillers:** Yes. **Art:** Art (especially children, animals, action, scenes from a story); photography (photo essays or article illustrations), color preferred, B&W considered. **Tips:** Does not accept query letters. Looking for more nonfiction submissions, also activity ideas, puzzles, and jokes. **Queries:** Preferred. **E-Queries:** No. **Unsolicited mss:** Accepts. **Response:** 12 weeks, SASE. **Freelance Content:** 95%. **Rights:** All. **Payment:** On publication.

SPORTS ILLUSTRATED FOR KIDS

Time, Inc.

135 W 50th St., New York, NY 10020-1201. 212-522-1212.

E-mail: kidletters@sikids.com. Web site: www.sikids.com. Monthly. $2.99/$29.95. Circ.: 1,002,000. Neil Cohen, Managing Editor. **Description:** Focuses on the excitement, joy, and challenge of sports, for boys and girls, ages 8-14. Provides action photos, interactive stories, profiles, puzzles, playing tips. Also, drawings and writing by kids. **Nonfiction:** Current, biographical, sports-related articles for kids age 8-14; 500-700 words; $500-1,250. **Columns, Departments:** 300-500 words. **Art:** Photos, illustrations (submit non-returnable portfolio). **Queries:** Required. **E-Queries:** Yes. **Unsolicited mss:** Accepts. **Response:** 4-6 weeks, SASE. **Rights:** Exclusive. **Payment:** 40% on acceptance, 60% on publication. **Contact:** Kim Fusco.

STONE SOUP

P.O. Box 83, Santa Cruz, CA 95063-0083. 831-426-5557.

E-mail: editor@stonesoup.com. Web site: www.stonesoup.com. Bimonthly. $5.50/$33. Circ.: 20,000. Gerry Mandel, Editor. **Description:** Stories, poems, book reviews, and art by young writers and artists, ages 8-13. **Fiction:** Personal narratives, arrival stories, family histories, sport stories, science fiction; 2,500 words; $35. **Nonfiction:** Book reviews by children under 14. Prefers writing based on real-life experiences. **Poetry:** Free-verse only; $35. **Art:** For ages 8-13 only; please send 2-3 samples of your work. **Tips:** No adults! **Queries:** Not necessary. **E-Queries:** No. **Unsolicited mss:** Accepts. **Response:** Queries 2 weeks, submissions 4 weeks, SASE. **Freelance Content:** 100%. **Rights:** All. **Payment:** On publication.

STORY FRIENDS

Faith and Life Press/A Division of the Mennonite Publishing House

616 Walnut Ave, Scottdale, PA 15683. 724-887-8500.

Monthly. Circ.: 6,000. Susan Reith Swan, Editor. **Description:** For ages 4-9, a general interest magazine that promotes and reinforces traditional values taught by

Christian families. **Fiction:** Realistic stories that empower children to face fears, resolve conflicts, creatively solve problems, and help them enjoy and care for things in nature; 300-800 words; $.03/word. **Nonfiction:** About animals, unusual nature facts, children in action, crosscultural experiences; 100-300 words; $.03/word. **Poetry:** Seasonal, humorous, active poems about ordinary things and events in children's lives; 6-12 lines; $10/poem. **Fillers:** Short and simple crafts and activities, age-appropriate puzzles. **Tips:** Humor and unique treatment of problem helps to break in to this market. Avoid talking animals, "naughty children" stories, and preachiness. Avoid stories where adults provide the solution or explanation, respect younger characters' strength and ingenuity. Also, many parents of these readers have lived in third-world countries and value cross-cultural understanding. **Queries:** Not necessary. **E-Queries:** No. **Unsolicited mss:** Accepts. **Response:** SASE. **Freelance Content:** 70%. **Rights:** 1st, one-time. **Payment:** On acceptance.

TURTLE MAGAZINE
See page 420 for full listing.
Description: Emphasis on health and nutrition for kids ages 2-5.

U.S. KIDS
Children's Better Health Institute
1100 Waterway Blvd., P.O. Box 567, Indianapolis, IN 46206-0567. 317-634-1100.
E-mail: danny885@aol.com. Web site: www.uskids.com. 8x/year. $21.95/yr. Circ.: 250,000. Daniel Lee, Editor. **Description:** For kids, ages 6-10. True-life stories, science/nature features, health/fitness, kids in the news, color photos, and lots of fun games, activities, and contests. **Fiction:** Science fiction, nature, etc; 700 words; $.17/word. **Nonfiction:** Looking for profiles on interesting, regular kids (no celebrities), ages 5-10, involved in unusual pursuits (sports, adventures, science); 500-600 words; pay varies. **Fillers:** Humor; 75 words; $35-$50. **Tips:** Avoid counter culture, irony/sarcasm, depressing topics. Stay upbeat and wholesome. **Queries:** Preferred. **E-Queries:** Yes. **Unsolicited mss:** Accepts. **Response:** 12 weeks, SASE. **Freelance Content:** 20%. **Rights:** All. **Payment:** On publication.

WILD OUTDOOR WORLD
Rocky Mountain Elk Foundation
P.O. Box 1329, Helena, MT 59624-1329. 406-449-1335.
E-mail: wowmagazine@qwest.net. Web site: www.wildoutdoorworld.org. 5x/yr. $14.93. Circ.: 290,000. Carolyn Cunningham, Editorial Director. **Description:** On North American wildlife, for readers ages 8-12. **Nonfiction:** Articles, 600-800 words; pays $100-$300. **Tips:** Seeks stories that encourage outdoor activity and appreciation for North American wildlife and habitats. **Queries:** Preferred. **E-Queries:** Yes. **Rights:** 1st NA and electronic. **Payment:** On acceptance.

YES MAG
3968 Long Gun Place, Victoria, British Columbia V8N 3A9 Canada. 250-477-5543.
E-mail: editor@yesmag.ca. Web site: www.yesmag.ca. Bimonthly. $3.50/$19.95

(Canadian). Circ.: 18,000. Shannon Hunt, Editor. **Description:** Canadian children's science magazine. Makes science accessible, interesting, and exciting for children ages 8-14. Covers science and technology news, do-at-home projects, science-related book and software reviews, profiles of Canadian students and scientists. **Nonfiction:** Science, technology, engineering, and math articles for kids, ages 8-14; 250-1,250 words; $.15/word. **Tips:** Seeking imaginative, fun, well-researched pieces. Be specific in query; ideally send an outline of the article, indicating how you will approach the topic. **Queries:** Preferred. **E-Queries:** Yes. **Unsolicited mss:** Accepts. **Response:** 2 weeks, SASE. **Freelance Content:** 60%. **Rights:** One-time. **Payment:** On publication.

YOUNG BUCKS OUTDOORS

10350 Highway 80 E, P.O. Box 244022, Montgomery, AL 36124-4022. 800-240-3337. E-mail: gsmith@buckmasters.com. Web site: www.youngbucksoutdoors.com. Quarterly. Free for 1st year, $11.95 per year thereafter. Circ.: 55,000. Gita M. Smith, Editor. **Description:** For readers ages 7-13. Encourages children of all races, genders, and abilities to step outside and enjoy themselves. **Fiction:** Buys four fiction pieces per year. Stories with child at the center of the plot. No "I recall when I was a child" stories. Pays $350 for original fiction with outdoors theme or setting; up to 1,000 words. **Nonfiction:** Stories about nature and outdoors pursuits (camping, hiking, fishing, hunting, ecology, nature, outdoor pastimes) written at a level a bright 10-year old would enjoy. Query first and include photo ideas to support the story. Pays $150-400 depending on story length (200-900 words) with color photos. Query by e-mail is okay, will take unsolicited mss with photos or slides enclosed. We don't use JPG images as those are not high resolution enough. **Tips:** No anti-hunting/fishing sentiments. We like good science content in stories and specific how-to tips so that kids will learn skills. **Queries:** Required. **E-Queries:** Yes. **Unsolicited mss:** Accepts. **Response:** Queries 1-2 weeks, submissions 3 months, SASE. **Freelance Content:** 90%. **Rights:** 1st print, electronic. **Payment:** On publication.

YOUNG RIDER

Fancy Publications, Inc.
496 Southland Dr., Lexington, KY 40503. 859-260-9800.
Web site: www.youngrider.com. Bimonthly. Lesley Ward. **Description:** About horses and children. **Nonfiction:** Horse health, grooming tips, interesting breeds and famous horses, show-ring secrets, how to improve their riding skills, celebrity rider interviews; 1,200 words; $140. **Art:** Photos. **Tips:** Query or send manuscript. **Queries:** Not necessary. **Unsolicited mss:** Accepts. **Payment:** On publication.

YOUTHLINE USA WEEKLY

Bartash Printing
300 Knickerbocker Rd., Cresskill, NJ 07626-1343. 201-568-1333.
E-mail: susan@youthline-usa.com. Web site: www.youthline-usa.com. Weekly. $7. Circ.: 618,000. Susan Gertler, Editor-in-Chief. **Description:** Educational magazine for children and young teens.

LIFESTYLES

ACTIVE LIVING

2276 Rosendene Rd., St. Ann's, Ontario L0R 1Y0 Canada. 905-957-6016.
E-mail: lfleming@softhome.net. Web site: www.activelivingmagazine.com. Bimonthly.
Liz Fleming, Managing Editor. **Description:** Health, fitness, and recreation magazine for people with disabilities. **Nonfiction:** Articles, 750-1,000 words, on improving fitness and mobility, accessible travel and leisure, and new therapeutic and sporting activities; pays $.18/word. **Tips:** Avoid labeling or condescending language. **Queries:** Preferred. **Payment:** On publication.

AMERICAN SURVIVAL GUIDE

Y-Visionary Publishing
262 S Anita Dr., Suite 120, Orange, CA 92868. 714-939-9991, ext.204.
Jim Benson. **Description:** On human and natural forces that pose threats to everyday life, all forms of preparedness, food production and storage, self defense and weapons, etc. **Nonfiction:** Articles, 1,500-2,000 words, with photos; pays $80/published page. **Art:** Photos essential for all articles. **Queries:** Preferred. **Payment:** On publication.

BLUE

Blue Media Ventures, Inc.
611 Broadway, Suite 405, New York, NY 10012-2608. 212-777-0024.
E-mail: info@blueadventure.com. Web site: www.blueadventures.com. Bimonthly.
$19.95. Circ.: 175,000. Claire Horchacka, Executive Editor. **Description:** Seeks material that is wonderfully hip, personal, and alive, and also delivers information. Described by one reviewer as "National Geographic with a rock-and-roll soundtrack." **Nonfiction:** Features in 3 categories: Blue Planet, Blue Nation, and Blue Asphalt. Exploration is key, whether a profile of coal miners of Bolivia, or inline skating through Central Park. **Tips:** A well-written query is a good start. Convey your idea in a 500-word pitch; include any appropriate writing samples. Relies on freelance contributions; is seeking new writers stationed in exotic locales with great stories to tell— who feel that life is, well, an adventure. **Queries:** Preferred. **E-Queries:** Yes. **Unsolicited mss:** Accepts.

CAPPER'S

Ogden Publications
1503 SW 42nd St., Topeka, KS 66609-1265. 785-274-4345.
E-mail: cappers@cjnetworks.com. Web site: www.cappers.com. Biweekly. $27.98/year.
Circ.: 210,000. Ann Crahan, Editor. **Description:** Focuses on home and family, for readers in the rural Midwest. **Fiction:** Query first, with brief description; $75-$300. **Nonfiction:** Inspirational, nostalgic, family-oriented, travel, human-interest; 700 words max; $2.50/inch. **Poetry:** Easy to read, down-to-earth themes; 4-16 lines; $10-$15. **Fillers:** Jokes (limit submissions to batches of 5-6; no jokes returned); $2 gift certificate. **Art:** 35mm color slides, transparencies, or sharp color prints; include captions;

$10-$40. **Tips:** Query for novel-length manuscripts only; submit all others complete. Does not accept simultaneous submissions. **Queries:** Not necessary. **E-Queries:** No. **Unsolicited mss:** Accepts. **Response:** Submissions 2-6 months. SASE required. **Freelance Content:** 25%. **Rights:** FNASR. **Payment:** On publication.

CHRISTIAN SINGLE
One Lifeway Plaza, Nashville, TN 37234-0175.
Description: For single adults on leisure activities, issues related to single parenting, and life from a Christian perspective. Also offers inspiring personal experiences and humor. **Nonfiction:** Articles, 600-1,200 words; pay varies.**Queries:** Preferred. **Payment:** On acceptance.

COLORADO HOMES AND LIFESTYLES
7009 S Potomac St., Englewood, CO 80112. 303-662-5204.
E-mail: emcgraw@coloradohomesmag.com. Web site: www.coloradohomesmag.com. 9x/year. $3.95/$19.97. Circ.: 35,000. Evalyn K. McGraw, Editor. **Description:** Affluent, upscale homes and lifestyles. **Nonfiction:** Articles, 1,300-1,500 words, on Colorado homes and interiors. Features on upscale homes, unusual lifestyles. **Columns, Departments:** Architecture, artists, food and wine, design trends, profiles, gardening, and travel; 1,100-1,300 words. **Queries:** Preferred. **Payment:** On acceptance.

DATING LIFE
9903 Santa Monica Blvd., Beverly Hills, CA 90212.
E-mail: editor@datinglifemag.com. Web site: www.datingmag.com. Monthly. Circ.: 100,000. Mary A. Spio, Editor. **Description:** Articles cover dating trends, relationships, communication, and other issues that are relevant to the dating scene in modern culture. Includes profiles of single men and women. **Nonfiction:** General articles on dating, movie and music reviews, photos, jokes, first-person profiles, etc; 3000 words; negotiable. **Tips:** Submit query with complete ms and bio. **Queries:** Required. **Response:** 1-4 weeks, SASE. **Freelance Content:** 50%. **Rights:** Negotiable. **Payment:** On acceptance.

DIVERSION
1790 Broadway, New York, NY 10019. 212-969-7517.
E-mail: ewetshcler@hearst.com. Web site: www.diversion.com. Monthly. Circ.: 185,000. Ed Wetschler, Editor-in-Chief. **Description:** Lifestyle magazine for physicians. Does not accept articles on health-related subjects, but does accept features and profiles of doctors who excel at nonmedical pursuits and who do volunteer medical work. **Nonfiction:** Sports, books, electronic gear, gardening, photography, art, music, film, television, travel, food, and humor; 2,000 words; $500. **Columns, Departments:** 1,200 words, $650. **Art:** Do not send originals or slides. **Tips:** Query first with brief proposal explaining story focus and include credentials/clips of published work. **Queries:** Required. **E-Queries:** No. **Unsolicited mss:** Accepts. **Response:** SASE required. **Payment:** On acceptance.

FIFTY PLUS
Richmond Publishing
1510 Willow Lawn Dr., Suite 203, Richmond, VA 23230-3429. 804-673-5203.
E-mail: rpmag@aol.com. Web site: www.fiftyplusrichmond.com. Monthly. $15/yr.
Circ.: 30,000. George Cruger, Editor. **Description:** 50-plus lifestyles in Virginia
region, with reader dialogue and input. **Queries:** Required. **E-Queries:** Yes.
Response: 2-4 weeks, SASE. **Rights:** 1st (regional). **Payment:** On publication.

HOME EDUCATION
See page 347 for full listing.
Description: Publication for families who homeschool their children.

INMOTION
Amputee Coalition of America
900 E Hill Ave., Suite 285, Knoxville, TN 37915. 865-524-8772.
Web site: www.amputee-coalition.org. Bimonthly. Nancy Carroll, Editor.
Description: Covers topics of interest to amputees such as new technology, inspira-
tional profiles, etc. **Nonfiction:** Articles, to 3,000 words; pays $.25/word. **Art:** Photos.
Payment: On publication.

INSIDE MAGAZINE
2100 Arch St., Philadelphia, PA 19102-3392. 215-832-0797.
E-mail: mledger@insidemagazine.com. Quarterly. $3.50/issue, $10.95/year. Circ.:
60,000. Robert Leiter, Editor. **Description:** Focuses on Jewish lifestyle. Covers ethnic interest, as well as lifestyle subjects (fashion, home, health, finance, travel, dining).
Fiction: 2,000 words; $350. **Nonfiction:** On Jewish issues, health, finance, and the
arts; 2,000-3,000 words; $500. **Art:** $250, illustrations. **Tips:** Write gracefully for
upscale readers. Teach something useful. **Queries:** Preferred. **E-Queries:** Yes.
Unsolicited mss: Accepts. **Freelance Content:** 80%. **Rights:** 1st only. **Payment:**
On publication.

LIVING ABOARD
P.O. Box 91299, Austin, TX 78709-1299. 512-892-4446.
E-mail: editor@livingaboard.com. Web site: www.livingaboard.com. Linda Ridihalgh,
Editor. **Description:** Lifestyle magazine for those who live or dream of living on
their boats. **Nonfiction:** Articles, 1,000-2,000, on personal experience or practical
information about living aboard; pays $.05/word. **Art:** Photos welcomed. **Tips:** Send
complete manuscript with bio and credits; e-mail or disk submissions preferred.
Payment: On publication.

LIVING IN BALANCE
Beach House Publishing, Inc.
P.O. Box 8608, Ft. Lauderdale, FL 33310. 954-382-4325.
E-mail: publisher@livinginbalancemagazine.com.
Web site: www.livinginbalancemagazine.com. **Description:** A "health, wealth, and

happiness" magazine. Strives to provide straightforward, expert and motivational solutions to pressing issues facing baby boomers. **Nonfiction:** Short articles on self-development and personal growth; 250-500 words. **Tips:** Send submissions in an e-mail attachment. Send 15 word bio. **Queries:** Preferred. **E-Queries:** Yes. **Unsolicited mss:** Accepts.

MAGICAL BLEND
133-1/2 Broadway St., Chico, CA 95928-5317. 888-296-2442.
E-mail: editor@magicalblend.com. Web site: www.magicalblend.com. Bimonthly. Circ.: 105,000. Michael Richman, Editor. **Description:** Offers an entertaining and unique look at modern spiritual lifestyles. **Nonfiction:** Positive, uplifting articles on spiritual exploration, alternative health, social change, self improvement, stimulating creativity, lifestyles, and interviews; 2000 words max. **Art:** Hard or digital copies (233-3000 dpi). **Tips:** No preaching. **Queries:** Not necessary. **E-Queries:** Yes. **Unsolicited mss:** Accepts. **Response:** Queries 1-3 months, submissions 1-6 months. **Freelance Content:** 90%. **Payment:** On publication.

MEN'S JOURNAL
See page 484 for full listing.
Description: Lifestyle magazine for active men, ages 25-49.

MOTHER EARTH NEWS
Ogden Publications, Inc.
1503 SW 42nd St., Topeka, KS 66609-1265. 785-274-4300.
E-mail: letters@motherearthnews.com. Web site: www.motherearthnews.com. Bimonthly. Circ.: 320,000. Cheryl Long, Managing Editor. **Description:** Publication that emphasizes resourceful living and country skills for rural residents and urbanites who aspire to a more independent lifestyle. **Nonfiction:** Articles on do-it-yourself living, gardening, home building and repair, natural health, cooking, hobbies, and outdoor living; 300-3,000 words; $.30/word. **Tips:** Mostly staff-written. Submit seasonal material 5 months in advance. Review magazine before submitting material. **Queries:** Required. **Response:** 6 months. **Payment:** On acceptance.

MOTORHOME
See page 617 for full listing.
Description: Covers destinations for RV travelers.

MOUNTAIN LIVING
Wiesner Publishing
7009 S Potomac St., Englewood, CO 80112-4037. 303-662-5211.
E-mail: irawlings@mountainliving.com. Web site: www.mountainliving.com. 6x/year. $3.95/issue. Circ.: 38,000. Irene Rawlings, Editor. **Description:** Features lifestyle pieces for people who live in the mountains or who dream of living there. Articles on home, garden, travel, architecture, art, cuisine, sports, and people. **Nonfiction:** Book reviews, essays, interviews, and personal experience; 100-1,200 words; $35-$500.

Columns, Departments: Destinations, Trail's End. **Tips:** Make sure your query reflects the content of the magazine. Preview magazine or visit Web site to see the kind of material that is published. **Queries:** Required. **E-Queries:** Yes. **Unsolicited mss:** Accepts. **Response:** 4 weeks. **Freelance Content:** 50%. **Rights:** FNASR. **Payment:** On acceptance.

NATURAL HOME
See page 454 for full listing.
Description: Features "green," sustainable homes and lifestyles.

NATURAL LIVING TODAY
See page 627 for full listing.
Description: On all aspects of a natural lifestyle for women.

PENTHOUSE VARIATIONS
11 Penn Plaza, Fl. 12, New York, NY 10001. 212-702-6000.
E-mail: variations@generalmedia.com. Monthly. $4.99/issue, $30/year. Circ.: 400,000. Barbara Pizio, Executive Editor. **Description:** Couples-oriented erotica. **Nonfiction:** First-person narrative accounts of highly explicit sex scenes; 3,000; $400. **Tips:** Original work only. **Queries:** Not necessary. **E-Queries:** No. **Unsolicited mss:** Accepts. **Response:** Queries 1 month, submissions 2 months, SASE required. **Freelance Content:** 100%. **Rights:** All. **Payment:** On acceptance.

POSITIVE THINKING
66 E Main St., Pawling, NY 12564. 845-855-5000.
10x/year. Circ.: 400,000. Patricia M. Planeta, Editor. **Description:** Magazine with inspirational messages. **Nonfiction:** First-person stories, an emphasis on faith or positive thinking. Practical how-to pieces; to 2,300 words; pay varies. **Queries:** Preferred. **E-Queries:** Yes. **Unsolicited mss:** Accepts. **Response:** SASE. **Rights:** One-time. **Payment:** On publication. **Contact:** Ann Zaengle.

REUNIONS MAGAZINE
P.O. Box 11727, Milwaukee, WI 53211-0727. 414-263-4567.
E-mail: reunions@execpc.com. Web site: www.reunionsmag.com. Quarterly. $6/$24. Circ.: 12,000. Edith Wagner, Editor. **Description:** For persons who are organizing a family, class, military, or other reunion. **Nonfiction:** Reunion tips and techniques (e.g. how to make a memory book sparkle, how to cook for 150 people, etc.). **Fillers:** Brief tips/hints; Clippings (about reunions for us to summarize); funny material; puzzles (appropriate for reunions). Examples: photo preservation, should you invite teachers?, time capsules, hot ideas, etc; 500 words or less; $5-$10. **Art:** With articles. **Tips:** Avoid class-reunion catharsis. **Queries:** Not necessary. **E-Queries:** Yes. **Response:** over 2 years at present, SASE. **Freelance Content:** 70%. **Rights:** 1st NA, occasionally electronic. **Payment:** On publication.

ROBB REPORT
1 Acton Pl., Acton, MA 01720. 978-795-3000.
Web site: www.theluxurysource.com. Monthly. Circ.: 100, 000. Larry Bean, Editor.
Description: Consumer magazine for high-end luxury market. Lifestyles, home interiors, boats, travel, investment opportunities, exotic automobiles, business, technology, etc. **Nonfiction:** Geared to affluent lifestyles (travel, fashion, automobiles, etc.); 500-5,000 words. **Queries:** Required. **E-Queries:** No. **Unsolicited mss:** Accepts. **Response:** 1-3 months, SASE. **Freelance Content:** 75%. **Rights:** All. **Payment:** On publication.

SELF HELP FOR HER.COM
See page 629 for full listing.
Description: Online publication with inspiration and advice for women.

SMOKE AFFAIR
See page 485 for full listing.
Description: Publication focusing on the lifestyle of the cigar smoker.

SOUTHERN ACCENTS
2100 Lakeshore Dr., Birmingham, AL 35209. 205-877-6000.
Web site: www.southernaccents.com. Bimonthly. $28. Circ.: 350,000. Frances MacDougall, Managing Editor. **Description:** Celebrates southern style in interiors, gardens, art, antiques, and entertaining. Focuses on affluent homes and gardens in a 16-state region. Also features the homes of southerners living abroad and the travel destinations visited by upscale readership. **Nonfiction:** Query first with appropriate story ideas; 800-1,200 words; pay negotiable. **Queries:** Preferred. **Payment:** On acceptance.

SUNSET
80 Willow Rd., Menlo Park, CA 94025. 650-321-3600.
E-mail: openhouse@sunset.com. Web site: www.sunset.com. Monthly. $4.50. Circ.: 1,500,000. Katie Tamony, Editor. **Description:** Regional magazine for Western America, covering travel and recreation; garden and outdoor living; food and entertaining; building, design, and crafts. **Nonfiction:** Looking for well-written stories and Travel Guide items offering satisfying travel experiences accomplished in a day or weekend, or as part of a vacation, in American West, also parts of Canada and Mexico. 4 month lead-time; 300-1,000 words; $1/word. **Queries:** Preferred. **E-Queries:** No. **Unsolicited mss:** Does not accept. **Response:** 1-3 months, SASE. **Freelance Content:** 5%. **Payment:** On acceptance.

TOWN & COUNTRY
The Hearst Corp.
1700 Broadway, New York, NY 10019-5905. 212-903-5000.
E-mail: tnc@hearst.com. Web site: www.tncweddings.com. Monthly. Pamela Fiori, Editor. **Description:** For upscale market, covers travel, beauty, fashion, individuals,

and the arts. **Nonfiction:** Considers 1-page proposals; include clips, resume. **Queries:** Required. **Unsolicited mss:** Does not accept. **Freelance Content:** 40%. **Payment:** On acceptance.

TRAILER LIFE

2575 Vista Del Mar, Ventura, CA 93001. 805-667-4100.
E-mail: bleonard@affinity.com. Web site: www.trailerlife.com. Monthly. $3.99. Circ.: 280,000. Barbara Leonard, Editor. **Description:** New product information and vehicle tests, do-it-yourself articles, plus exciting travel and lifestyle features for RVers. **Nonfiction:** Features on trailers, motorhomes, truck campers used by active adventurous travelers, interesting destinations and on-the-road hobbies; 200-2,000 words; $100-$600. **Fillers:** 50-1,000 words; $75-$400. **Art:** 35mm, 2¼; $75-$250; $500-$700 (cover). **Tips:** Supply good 35mm slides and submit a complete package. **Queries:** Required. **E-Queries:** No. **Response:** 2-3 weeks, SASE. **Freelance Content:** 45%. **Rights:** 1st NA and electronic. **Payment:** On acceptance.

VEGGIE LIFE

See page 396 for full listing.
Description: For people interested in lowfat, meatless cuisine and nutrition.

WHOLE LIFE TIMES

21225 Pacific Coast Hwy., Suite B, P.O. Box 1187, Malibu, CA 90265. 310-317-4200.
E-mail: swholelifex@aol.com. Web site: www.wholelifetimes.com. Monthly. Free. Circ.: 58,000. Abigail Lewis, Editor. **Description:** Covers holistic lifestyles by offering information on health, healing, food and nutrition, environment, spirituality, personal growth, travel, science and metaphysics, and longevity. **Nonfiction:** Up to 2,000 words; $.05/word for features only. **Tips:** Understand the holistic mindset. Readers are fairly sophisticated; avoid "Yoga 101." Contact for upcoming themes. **Queries:** Not necessary. **E-Queries:** Yes. **Unsolicited mss:** Accepts. **Response:** 1 month-1 year, SASE. **Freelance Content:** 75%. **Rights:** 1st NA. **Payment:** 30 days after publication. **Contact:** Kerri Hikida, Associate Editor

WIRED

Lycos, Inc.
660 3rd St. 1st Fl., San Francisco, CA 94107. 800-769-4733.
E-mail: george@wired.com. Web site: www.wired.com. Monthly. Circ.: 500,000. George Shirk, Editor-in-Chief. **Description:** Lifestyle magazine for the "digital generation." Discusses the meaning and context of digital technology in today's world. **Fiction:** Yes. **Nonfiction:** Articles, essays, profiles, etc; pay varies. **Payment:** On acceptance.

YOGA JOURNAL

2054 University Ave., Berkeley, CA 94704-1082. 510-841-9200.
E-mail: nisaacs@yogajournal.com. Web site: www.yogajournal.com. Monthly. Circ.: 215,000. Kathryn Arnold, Editor-in-Chief. **Description:** Serves the hatha yoga com-

munity. Holistic health, meditation, conscious living, spirituality, and yoga. **Queries:** Preferred. **E-Queries:** Yes. **Unsolicited mss:** Accepts. **Response:** 8 weeks, SASE. **Freelance Content:** 10%. **Rights:** non-exclusive worldwide, print and non-print. **Payment:** On acceptance. **Contact:** Nora Isaacs.

MEN'S

ADAM
4517 Harford Rd., Baltimore, MD 21214. 410-254-9200.
E-mail: adameditor@aol.com. Web site: adam-mag.com. Bimonthly. $9.97/yr. Tom Dworetzky, Editor. **Description:** For men, ages 21-35. Offers creative nonfiction, opinion, personal experience, informational and self-help articles, profiles, and interviews. **Nonfiction:** Articles on history, video, audio, music, relationships, electronics, computers, sports and entertainment; 1,500-2,000 words; $350-$400. **Columns, Departments:** 500-800 words; $300. **Tips:** Avoid first-person, and use quotes from experts. **Queries:** Preferred. **E-Queries:** Yes. **Response:** 2-4 weeks, SASE required. **Freelance Content:** 50%. **Rights:** 1st. **Payment:** On publication.

ESQUIRE
The Hearst Corp.
250 W 55th St., New York, NY 10019-5201. 212-649-4020.
E-mail: esquire@hearst.com. Web site: www.esquire.com. Monthly. Circ.: 679,000. David Granger, Editor-in-Chief. **Description:** For intelligent adult male readers. **Fiction:** Short stories; submit only 1 at a time. No pornography, science fiction, poetry, or "true romance"; pay varies. **Nonfiction:** 2,500-6,500 words; pay varies. **Tips:** Query with clips; unpublished writers, send complete manuscripts. **Queries:** Required. **Payment:** On publication.

GALLERY
Montcalm Publishing Corp.
401 Park Ave. S, New York, NY 10016-8802. 212-779-8900.
E-mail: csobrien@gallerymagazine.com. Web site: www.gallerymagazine.com. Circ.: 500,000. C. S. O'Brien, Editor. **Description:** Articles, investigative pieces, interviews, profiles. Also, erotic and general fiction, short humor, satire, service pieces, to 2,500 words, for men's market. We encourage quality work from unpublished writers. Pay varies, send SASE for guidelines. **Freelance Content:** 50%. **Payment:** On publication.

GENTLEMEN'S QUARTERLY
Condé Nast Publications, Inc.
4 Times Square, New York, NY 10036-6518. 212-286-2860.
E-mail: gqmag@aol.com. Web site: www.gq.com. Monthly. $19.97. Circ.: 898,508. Arthur Cooper, Editor-in-Chief. **Description:** For male readers. Covers politics, personalities, lifestyles, trends, grooming, sports, travel, business. **Nonfiction:**

Articles, 1,500-4,000 words. **Columns, Departments:** Private Lives (essays by men on life); All about Adam (nonfiction by women about men); Games (sports); Health; Humor; also on fitness, nutrition, investments, music, wine and food. 1,000-2,500 words. **Tips:** Send clips. **Queries:** Required. **Unsolicited mss:** Does not accept.

MEN'S FITNESS
See page 392 for full listing.
Description: On sports, fitness, health, nutrition, and men's issues.

MEN'S HEALTH
Rodale Press
33 E Minor St., Emmaus, PA 18098. 610-967-5171.
Web site: www.menshealth.com. 10x/year. $3.79. Circ.: 1,600,000. David Zinczenko, Editor-in-Chief. **Description:** Covers fitness, health, sex, nutrition, relationships, lifestyle, sports, and travel. **Nonfiction:** Useful articles, for men ages 25-55; 1,000-2,000 words; $.50/word. **Queries:** Required. **E-Queries:** Yes. **Payment:** On acceptance.

MEN'S JOURNAL
1290 Avenue of the Americas, New York, NY 10104-0298. 212-484-1616.
E-mail: letters@mensjournal.com. Web site: www.mensjournal.com. 12 x/year. Circ.: 635,000. Sid Evans, Editor. **Description:** Lifestyle magazine for active men, ages 25-49. **Nonfiction:** Articles and profiles on travel, fitness, health, adventure, and participatory sports; 2,000-7,000 words; good rates. **Columns, Departments:** Equipment, Fitness; 400-1,800 words. **Queries:** Required. **Payment:** On acceptance.

PENTHOUSE
General Media Communications
11 Penn Plaza, Fl. 12, New York, NY 10001. 212-702-6000.
Web site: www.penthousemag.com. Monthly. $46. Circ.: 980,000. Peter Bloch, Editor. **Description:** Essays, sociological studies, travel, humor, food, and fashion, for the sophisticated male. **Fiction:** No unsolicited fiction. **Nonfiction:** General-interest profiles, interviews (with introduction), and investigative or controversial pieces; to 5,000 words; to $1/word. **Queries:** Preferred.

PLAYBOY
680 North Shore Dr., Chicago, IL 60611. 312-751-8000.
E-mail: articles@playboy.com. Monthly. Circ.: 3,125,000. Stephen Randall, Executive Editor. **Description:** Magazine for urban men. **Fiction:** Sophisticated fiction, 1,000-10,000 words (5,000 preferred). Pays $2,000 for short-shorts. Barbara Wellis, Fiction Editor. **Nonfiction:** Articles; 3,500-6,000 words; pays to $5,000. **Queries:** Required. **E-Queries:** No. **Unsolicited mss:** Does not accept. **Response:** 1 month, SASE. **Rights:** FNASR. **Payment:** On acceptance.

SMOKE AFFAIR
6685 Via Regina, Boca Raton, FL 33433. 561-347-7669.
E-mail: micky@smokeaffair.com. 3x/year. $11.50. Circ.: 50,000. Micky Handler, Editor. **Description:** Upscale, full-color, glossy publication focusing on the lifestyle of the cigar smoker. **Nonfiction:** Articles featuring travel and leisure, financial, real estate investment, the arts, and cigar personalities; 1,000-4,000 words; negotiable fee. **Art:** Photo/art discussed on assignment. **Tips:** Welcome new writers; seeking writers for assignments. **Queries:** Preferred. **E-Queries:** Yes. **Unsolicited mss:** Accepts. **Response:** 30 days, SASE required. **Rights:** negotiable. **Payment:** On publication.

MILITARY

AIR COMBAT
230 Dale Place, Fullerton, CA 92833. 714-522-7590.
Web site: www.aircombatusa.com. Bimonthly. Michael O'Leary. **Description:** Articles on latest warplanes and the men who fly them, recent air battles, and America's aerial involvement in Vietnam. **Tips:** Send for guidelines. **Queries:** Preferred.

AMERICA'S CIVIL WAR
PRIMEDIA History Group
741 Miller Dr. SE, Suite D2, Leesburg, VA 20175. 703-771-9400.
E-mail: americascivilwar@thehistorynet.com. Web site: www.historynet.com. Bimonthly. $4.99/issue. Circ.: 75,000. Dana B. Shoaf, Managing Editor. **Description:** Popular history for general readers and Civil War buffs, on strategy, tactics, history, narrative. **Nonfiction:** Strategy, tactics, personalities, arms and equipment; 3,500- 4,000 words, plus 500-word sidebar; $200-$400. **Columns, Departments:** Up to 2,000 words; $100-$200. **Art:** Cite known color or B&W illustrations, and sources (museums, historical societies, private collections, etc.). **Tips:** Readable style and historical accuracy imperative. Use action and quotes where possible. Attribute quotes, cite major sources. **Queries:** Required. **E-Queries:** Yes. **Unsolicited mss:** Accepts. **Response:** 6 months; SASE required. **Freelance Content:** 98%. **Payment:** Both on acceptance and on publication; kill fee offered.

ARMOR
Bldg. 1109 A Sixth Ave., Room 371, Fort Knox, KY 40121-2103. 502-624-2249.
Bimonthly. $20/yr., $37 (foreign). Circ.: 12,500. Jon Clemens, Managing Editor. **Description:** Professional magazine of the Armor Branch for military units and agencies responsible for direct-fire ground combat. **Nonfiction:** Military history; research and development of armaments; tactical benefits and strategies, logistics, and related topics. **Art:** Write captions on paper and tape to the back of the photos (don't write on photo backs). Indicate if you want the photos returned. **Tips:** Does not pay contributors. **Response:** Submissions, 2 weeks.

ARMY MAGAZINE

2425 Wilson Blvd., Arlington, VA 22201-3385. 703-841-4300 x204.
E-mail: armymag@ausa.org. Web site: www.ausa.org. Monthly. Circ.: 85,000. Mary Blake French, Editor-in-Chief. **Description:** Military subjects, essays, humor, history (especially Korea and World War II), news reports, first-person anecdotes. **Nonfiction:** 1,500 words; $.12-$.18/word. **Fillers:** Cartoons, strong military slant; $35-$50. **Columns, Departments:** Military news, books, commentary. **Art:** 35mm slides, 8x10 B&W; 8x10 color glossy prints; pay varies. **Queries:** Not necessary. **E-Queries:** No. **Unsolicited mss:** Accepts. **Freelance Content:** 70%. **Rights:** All. **Payment:** On publication. **Contact:** Mary Blake French.

ARMY RESERVE

2400 Army Pentagon, Washington, DC 20310-2400. 703-601-0854.
E-mail: usarmag@ocar.army.pentagon.mil. Quarterly. Circ.: 450,000. **Description:** Publication emphasizing the training and employment of Army Reservists. **Art:** Uses 80-120 photos/issue. Seeks photos related to the mission or function of the U.S. Army Reserve; 5x7 color prints; 35mm transparencies; high resolution digital photos. **Tips:** Seeks well-written articles accompanied by high-quality photos.

COAST GUARD

Commandant (G-IPA-1), 2100 2nd St. SW
Room 3403, Washington, D.C. 20593-0001.
E-mail: vroth@comdt.uscg.mil. Web site: www.uscg.mil/hq/g-cp/cb/magazine.html. Monthly. $44/yr. Circ.: 14,000. PAC Veronica Roth, Editor. **Description:** Mainly for active-duty members of the Coast Guard. No payment offered. **Fiction:** Coast Guard or general military-related items only. **Nonfiction:** Same as fiction. **Art:** Photos, illustrations. **Queries:** Preferred. **E-Queries:** Yes. **Unsolicited mss:** Does not accept. **Response:** Queries, 5-10 days. **Freelance Content:** 0%. **Rights:** Associated Press only.

COMMAND

XTR Corp.
P.O. Box 4017, San Luis Obispo, CA 93403-4017. 805-546-9596.
E-mail: ty@commandmagazine.com. Web site: www.commandmagazine.com. Bimonthly. $24.95. Circ.: 50,000. Ty Bomba, Editor. **Description:** On military history or current military affairs. **Nonfiction:** Articles; popular, not scholarly, analytical military history, 800-10,000 words; pays $.05/word. **Queries:** Preferred. **Payment:** On publication.

FAMILY

See page 378 for full listing.
Description: Publication for military families.

LEATHERNECK

P.O. Box 1775, Quantico, VA 22134-0776. 703-640-6161.
Web site: www.mca-marines.org. Walter G. Ford, Editor. **Description:** On U.S. Marines. **Nonfiction:** Articles, to 2,500 words, with photos; pays $75/printed page. **Queries:** Preferred. **Payment:** On publication.

MARINE CORPS GAZETTE

P.O. Box 1775, Quantico, VA 22134. 703-640-6161.
E-mail: gazette@mca-marines.org. Web site: http://mca-marines.org/Gazette/ gaz.html. Monthly. $3.50/$29. Circ.: 29,000. Jack Glasgow, Editor. **Description:** Professional journal of U.S. Marines, oriented toward officers and senior enlisted personnel; provides a forum for open discussion and a free exchange of ideas relating to the U.S. Marine Corps and military capabilities. **Nonfiction:** On the U.S. Marine Corps of today, tomorrow, and yesterday; 750-1,500 words; payment varies. **Art:** To accompany articles. **Tips:** Serves primarily as a forum for active duty officers to exchange views on professional topics. **Queries:** Preferred. **E-Queries:** Yes. **Unsolicited mss:** Accepts. **Response:** 2-4 weeks. **Freelance Content:** 80%. **Rights:** All. **Payment:** On publication.

MHQ: QUARTERLY JOURNAL OF MILITARY HISTORY

PRIMEDIA History Group
741 Miller Dr. SE, Suite D-2, Leesburg, VA 20175-8994. 703-771-9400.
E-mail: militaryhistory@thehistorynet.com. Web site: www.historynet.com. Quarterly. $69.95/yr. Circ.: 54,000. Mike Haskew, Editor. **Description:** Offers an undistorted view of history, encourages understanding of events, personalities, and artifacts of the past. **Nonfiction:** Well-written military history; 3,500-4,000 words, with 500-word sidebar; $200-$400. **Columns, Departments:** 2,500 words. **Art:** Color, B&W illustrations. **Queries:** Preferred. **E-Queries:** Yes. **Unsolicited mss:** Accepts. **Response:** Queries 2-4 weeks, submissions 6-8 weeks, SASE. **Freelance Content:** 50%. **Payment:** On publication.

MILITARY

2122 28th St., Sacramento, CA 95818. 916-457-8990.
E-mail: generalinfo@milmag.com. Web site: www.milmag.com. Monthly. $14.79/yr. Circ.: 20,000. Rick McCusker, Editor. **Description:** Military history (WWII, Korea, Vietnam, and today). A conservative publication prided in printing the truth, dedicated to all who served in the armed forces. **Nonfiction:** Personal war experiences; 4,000 words or less. **Fillers:** Humor in uniform, military humor; 1,000 words or less. **Art:** 200 dpi or better. **Queries:** Preferred. **E-Queries:** Yes. **Unsolicited mss:** Accepts. **Payment:** No payment.

NATIONAL GUARD

National Guard Association of the United States,
One Massachusetts Ave. NW, Washington, DC 20001-1402. 202-789-0031.
E-mail: magazine@ngaus.org. Web site: www.ngaus.org. Monthly. $20. Circ.: 45,000.

Richard Alexander, Publisher. **Description:** Articles on national defense. **Nonfiction:** Pay varies. **Queries:** Preferred. **Payment:** On publication.

NAVAL AVIATION NEWS
1242 10th St. SE Navy Yard, Washington, DC 20374-0001. 202-433-4407. E-mail: nanews@nhc.navy.mil. Web site: www.history.navy.mil. Bimonthly. $16. Circ.: 30,000. Sandy Russell, Managing Editor. **Description:** For the U.S. Naval Aviation community, with history, technology, and personnel issues. Limited freelance content. **Nonfiction:** Naval Aviation history, operations. **Art:** High-rez JPG or TIF; color, B&W, slide. **Queries:** Preferred. **E-Queries:** Yes. **Unsolicited mss:** Accepts. **Response:** 3 weeks, SASE not needed. **Freelance Content:** 2%.

RETIRED OFFICER
See page 562 for full listing.
Description: For retired and soon-to-be-retired members. Readers (commissioned/warrant officers, families, and surviving spouses) represent one of the youngest, most active groups in the senior market.

SIGNAL
4400 Fair Lakes Court, Fairfax, VA 22033-3899. 703-631-6100. E-mail: signal@afcea.org. Web site: www.afcea.org/signal. Monthly. $56. Circ.: 30,000. Maryann Lawlor, Senior Editor. **Description:** Focuses on communications, electronics in the information systems arena. Readers include military, industry, and government leadership. **Nonfiction:** Communications/electronics issues within military, industry, and government; 1,400-2,500 words; $650 for 1,800 words. **Art:** Must include art with submission. **Tips:** Only works with published writers. **Queries:** Required. **E-Queries:** Yes. **Unsolicited mss:** Accepts. **Response:** 1-4 months, SASE required. **Freelance Content:** 10%. **Rights:** 1st. **Payment:** On publication.

TIMES NEWS SERVICE
Army Times Publishing Co.
Springfield, VA 22159. 703-750-7479.
E-mail: gwillis@atpco.com. Web site: www.militarycity.com. Weekly. $2.25/$52. Circ.: 300,000. G.E. Willis, Features Editor. **Description:** Publishes *Air Force Times, Army Times, Navy Times* (Gannett weeklies serving the military community, covering breaking developments that affect the careers of readers). **Nonfiction:** Features on contemporary home and family life in the military. Recreation, finances, parenting, etc; up to 1,500 words; up to $500. **Columns, Departments:** Fitness for young and athletic people; personal finance for moderate incomes; 500 words; $200. **Art:** Color slides, electronic (high-rez JPG); $75/image. **Tips:** Pitch an original story, interesting and entertaining, with a military connection, preferably with military people in the story. **Queries:** Required. **E-Queries:** Yes. **Unsolicited mss:** Does not accept. **Response:** Queries 2-8 weeks, submissions 1-3 weeks, SASE. **Freelance Content:** 75%. **Payment:** On acceptance.

VFW
406 W 34th St., Kansas City, MO 64111. 816-756-3390.
E-mail: pbrown@vfw.org. Web site: www.vfw.org. Monthly. $15/yr. Circ.: 1,800,000.
Richard K. Kolb, Editor. **Description:** Focuses on military history and issues relating to veterans and the military. **Nonfiction:** Articles on current foreign policy and defense, along with all veterans' issues; 1,000 words. **Tips:** Write with clarity and simplicity, concrete detail, and short paragraphs. Use active voice, and avoid flowery prose and military jargon. **Queries:** Preferred. **Unsolicited mss:** Accepts. **Rights:** FNASR. **Payment:** On publication.

VIETNAM
See page 430 for full listing.
Description: Seeks to record and document "the many truths about Vietnam."

WORLD WAR II
See page 431 for full listing.
Description: Strategy, tactics, personalities, arms and equipment.

NEW AGE & SPIRITUAL

ALIVE NOW
P.O. Box 340004, Nashville, TN 37203-0004. 615-340-7218.
E-mail: alivenow@upperroom.org. Web site: www.upperroom.org/alivenow.
Bimonthly. $3.50/issue, $14.95/year. Circ.: 70,000. Melissa Tidwell, Editor.
Description: Seeks to nourish people who are hungry for a sacred way of living. Each issue focuses on contemporary topic, explored through prayers, personal experiences, poetry, photographs, and art. **Nonfiction:** Personal experiences of how contemporary issues affect spiritual life, meditations on scripture, prayers, and litanies; 350-600 words; $40-$150. **Poetry:** On the issue's theme; 40 lines or less; $25-$100. **Tips:** See Web site for coming themes. Material unrelated to themes is not considered. Use inclusive language, and personal approach. Readership is clergy and lay, across denominations and theological spectrum. SASE required. **Queries:** Not necessary. **E-Queries:** Yes. **Unsolicited mss:** Accepts. **Freelance Content:** 30%. **Rights:** serial (print and electronic). **Payment:** On acceptance.

AQUARIUS
1035 Green St., Roswell, GA 30075. 770-641-9055.
E-mail: aquarius-editor@mindspring.com. Web site: www.aquarius-atlanta.com.
Monthly. Free at newsstands; $30/year. Circ.: 50,000. Kathryn Sargent, Editor.
Description: Seeks to expand awareness and support all those seeking spiritual growth. **Nonfiction:** On astrology, divination, alternative spirituality, energy healing, genetically engineered foods, intentional communities, meditation, yoga, herbs, aromatherapy, etc.; 850 words. **Poetry:** Up to 850 words. **Fillers:** Cartoons, puzzles. **Art:** Cover art, full color, light tones; JPGs, transparencies. **Tips:** Avoid spaceships,

aliens, channeled communications, lots of biblical quotations. **Queries:** Preferred. **E-Queries:** Yes. **Unsolicited mss:** Accepts. **Response:** 1 month for queries, varies for submissions; SASE required. **Freelance Content:** 90%.

FATE

P.O. Box 460, Lakeville, MN 55044. 800-728-2730.
E-mail: fate@fatemag.com. Web site: www.fatemag.com. Monthly. $4.95/$29.95. Circ.: 35,000. Phyllis Galde, Editor. **Description:** Covers the strange and unknown, for people willing to believe that unexplainable things happen. **Nonfiction:** True reports of the strange and unknown; 1,500-5,000 words; $.10/word. **Fillers:** Briefs on unusual events, odd folklore; Up to 1,500 words; $.10/word. **Columns, Departments:** My Proof of Survival (true personal accounts of survival after death); True Mystic Experiences (personal accounts of unexplained happenings); up to 1,000 words; $25. **Tips:** Much of the content contributed by readers. **Queries:** Preferred. **E-Queries:** Yes. **Response:** Queries 6 weeks, submissions 3 months, SASE required. **Freelance Content:** 80%. **Rights:** All. **Payment:** On publication.

NEW AGE: THE JOURNAL FOR HOLISTIC LIVING

42 Pleasant St., Watertown, MA 02472. 617-926-0200.
E-mail: editor@newage.com. Web site: www.newage.com. Bimonthly. $4.95/issue, $14.95/year. Circ.: 225,000. **Description:** Serves as a guide for all those who want to live healthier, more balanced lives **Nonfiction:** Alternative medicine, natural foods, self-help psychology, spirituality, mind/body connection, right livelihood, and green politics; 1,500-3,500 words; up to $1,500. **Fillers:** Short news items; 50-250 words; $50. **Columns, Departments:** Holistic Health, Food/Nutrition, Spirit, Home, Community, Travel, Life Lessons; 600-1,300 words. Book and music reviews; 200-750 words. **Art:** Photographs to accompany articles. **Tips:** Include recent clips and resume. **Queries:** Preferred. **E-Queries:** No. **Unsolicited mss:** Accepts. **Response:** 8 weeks; SASE required. **Freelance Content:** 90%. **Rights:** FNASR and electronic. **Payment:** On acceptance. **Contact:** Christine Richmond, Editorial Assistant.

PANGAIA

P.O. Box 641, Point Arena, CA 95468-0641. 707-882-2052.
E-mail: editor@pangaia.com. Web site: www.pangaia.com. Quarterly. Circ.: 7,000. Anne Newkirk Niven, Editor. **Description:** Publishes articles and features that explore the Pagan world. **Nonfiction:** 1,500-3,000 words; $.01/word. **Tips:** Query for guidelines.

PARABOLA

Society for Study of Myth & Tradition
656 Broadway, New York, NY 10012-2317. 212-505-9037.
E-mail: parabola@panix.com. Web site: www.parabola.org. Quarterly. Circ.: 40,000. Natalie Baan, Managing Editor. **Description:** "The magazine of myth and tradition." Thematic issues present essays and retellings of traditional myths and fairy tales.

Nonfiction: Articles on myth, symbol, and spiritual teachings; to 3,000 words. Retellings of traditional stories; to 1,500 words; pay varies. **Tips:** Contact for upcoming themes and guidelines. Looking for a balance between scholarly and accessible writing, on the ideas of myth and tradition. **Queries:** Preferred.

SAGEWOMAN
P.O. Box 469, Point Arena, CA 95468. 707-882-2052.
E-mail: editor@sagewoman.com. Web site: www.sagewoman.com. Quarterly. $6.95/issue, $21/year. Circ.: 25,000. Anne Newkirk Niven, editor. **Description:** Publishes articles that help women explore spiritual, emotional, and mundane lives and respect all people, creatures, and Earth. Celebrates the Goddess in every woman. **Nonfiction:** On women's spiritual experience; focuses on issues of concern to pagan and other spiritually-minded women; 1,000-5,000 words; $.01-.025/word. **Poetry:** 10-50 lines; $10. **Art:** Photographs, drawings, paintings, prints; $15-$200. **Tips:** Write in the first person. **Queries:** Not necessary. **E-Queries:** Yes. **Unsolicited mss:** Accepts. **Response:** 1 month queries, 3 months submissions, SASE required. **Freelance Content:** 80%. **Rights:** First worldwide serial. **Payment:** On publication.

SCIENCE OF MIND
Science of Mind Publishing
3251 W 6th St., P.O. Box 75127, Los Angeles, CA 90075-0127. 213-388-2181.
E-mail: sdelgado@scienceofmind.com. Web site: www.scienceofmind.com. Monthly. Circ.: 68,000. Randall Friesen, Editor/Publisher. **Description:** Thoughtful perspective on how to experience greater self-acceptance, empowerment, and a meaningful life. **Nonfiction:** Inspiring first-person pieces; 1,000-2,000 words. Interviews with notable spiritual leaders; 3,500 words; $25/page.

VENTURE INWARD
215 67th Ave., Virginia Beach, VA 23451. 757-428-3588.
E-mail: are@edgarcayce.org. Web site: www.edgarcayce.org. Bimonthly. Circ.: 25,000. A. Robert Smith, Editor. **Description:** Membership magazine for Edgar Cayce organizations (A.R.E., Edgar Cayce Fdn., Atlantic Univ.), on holistic health, spiritual development, mystical experiences, and Cayce philosophy (reincarnation, etc.). **Nonfiction:** Personal mystical or holistic health experiences; up to 3,000 words; $300-$400. **Columns, Departments:** Guest Column (opinion, to 800 words); Turning Point (a personal turning-point experience, to 800 words); The Mystical Way (a personal paranormal experience, to 1,500 words); Holistic Health (brief accounts of success using Edgar Cayce remedies); book reviews, to 500 words. Pays $50-$400. **Queries:** Required. **E-Queries:** Yes. **Unsolicited mss:** Does not accept. **Response:** Queries 2 weeks, submissions 1 month, SASE. **Freelance Content:** 75%. **Payment:** On publication.

WHOLE LIFE TIMES
See page 482 for full listing.
Description: Offers information on living a holistic lifestyle.

PERFORMING ARTS

ACOUSTIC GUITAR
P.O. Box 767, San Anselmo, CA 94979. 415-485-6946.
Web site: www.acousticguitar.com. Simone Solondz, Editor. **Description:** For players and makers of acoustic guitars. **Tips:** Prefers to receive material from musicians. **Queries:** Preferred.

AMERICAN SQUAREDANCE
E & PJ Enterprises
P.O. Box 777, North Scituate, RI 02857-0751. 401-647-9688.
E-mail: asdmag@loa.com. Web site: www.squaredance.ws. $25. Circ.: 12,000. Ed & Pat Juaire, Editors. **Description:** Articles and fiction, 1,000-1,500 words, related to square dancing. Pays $1.50/column inch. **Poetry:** Yes. **Fillers:** To 100 words.

AMERICAN STRING TEACHER
4153 Chain Bridge Rd., Fairfax, VA 22030-4102. 703-279-2113.
E-mail: editorast@aol.com. Web site: www.astaweb.com. Quarterly. Circ.: 11,500. AshLee Gahagan, Editor. **Description:** Published by American String Teachers Association and National School Orchestra Association. Seeking research-based articles with national appeal. **Tips:** Avoid opinion or personal-experience stories. **Queries:** Preferred.

BACK STAGE
770 Broadway, New York, NY 10003. 646-654-5500.
E-mail: seaker@backstage.com. Web site: www.backstage.com. Sherry Eaker, Editor-in-Chief. **Description:** "The Performing Arts Weekly." Service features on learning one's craft, dealing with succeeding in the business, interviews with actors, directors, and playwrights, and industry news/trends. **Nonfiction:** Pay varies. **Queries:** Preferred. **Payment:** On publication.

BLUEGRASS UNLIMITED
P.O. Box 771, Warrenton, VA 20186. 540-349-8181.
E-mail: editor@bluegrassmusic.com. Web site: www.bluegrassmusic.com. Monthly. Circ.: 27,000. Peter V. Kuykendall, Editor. **Description:** Covers bluegrass and traditional country music. **Nonfiction:** Articles; to 3,000 words; pays $.08-$.10/word. **Art:** Photos. **Queries:** Preferred.

CHART
Chart Communications, Inc.
200-41 Britain St., Toronto, Ontario M5A 1R7 Canada. 416-363-3101.
E-mail: chart@chartattack.com. Web site: www.chartattack.com. Monthly. $3.95/$19.95. Circ.: 40,000. Nada Laskovski, Editor. **Description:** Covers Canada's music and pop culture, with slant to the cutting edge. **Queries:** Preferred.

CLAVIER

200 Northfield Rd., Northfield, IL 60093. 847-446-5000.
10x/year. Circ.: 16,000. Judy Nelson, Editor. **Description:** Professional journal for piano teachers at all levels. **Nonfiction:** Interview/profiles on artists, teachers, composers; teaching articles, music discussion, master classes, and humor pieces for performers and teachers; 8-10 page mss; $80-$100/printed page. **Art:** Color prints, $100/full page. **Tips:** Writers should have music degrees. **Queries:** Preferred. **E-Queries:** No. **Unsolicited mss:** Accepts. **Response:** 4-6 weeks, SASE required. **Freelance Content:** 75%. **Rights:** All. **Payment:** On publication.

COUNTRY WEEKLY

118 16th Ave. S, Nashville, TN 37203. 615-259-1111.
E-mail: lholden@countryweekly.com. Web site: www.countryweekly.com. 26x/yr. $29.95. Larry Holden, Associate Editor. **Description:** Provides features on the country music and entertainment industry. Includes latest industry news and profiles of musicians and other country music personalities. **Art:** Clear, sharp, color transparencies; varies. **Queries:** Required. **E-Queries:** Yes. **Rights:** All. **Payment:** On publication.

DANCE

111 Myrtle St., Suite 203, Oakland, CA 94607. 510-839-6060.
E-mail: dancemag@dancemagazine.com. Web site: www.dancemagazine.com. K. C. Patrick, Editor-in-Chief. **Description:** Covers all aspects of the world of dance. **Nonfiction:** On dancers, companies, history, professional concerns, health, news events. **Tips:** Freelance content limited. **Queries:** Preferred.

DANCE SPIRIT

Lifestyle Ventures, LLC
250 W 57th St., Suite 420, New York, NY 10107. 212-265-8890.
E-mail: editor@dancespirit.com;sjarrett@lifestyleventures.com.
Web site: www.dancespirit.com. Monthly. Circ.: 100,000. Kimberly Gdula, Editorial Director. **Description:** For dancers of all disciplines. **Nonfiction:** Articles on training, instruction and technique, choreography, dance styles, and profiles of dancers; pay varies. **Art:** Photos. **Payment:** On publication. **Contact:** Sara Jarrett.

DANCE TEACHER

Lifestyle Ventures, LLC
250 W 57th St., Suite 420, New York, NY 10107. 212-265-8890.
E-mail: csims@lifestyleventures.com. Web site: www.dance_teacher.com. Monthly. Circ.: 20,000. Caitlin Sims, Editor. **Description:** For dance professionals. **Nonfiction:** For educators, students, and professionals; practical information on economic/business issues. Profiles of schools, methods, and people; 500-1,500 words. Pays $100-$300. Photos helpful. **Tips:** Must be thoroughly researched. **Queries:** Preferred. **E-Queries:** Yes. **Unsolicited mss:** Accepts. **Freelance Content:** 70%.

ELECTRONIC MUSICIAN
See page 604 for full listing.
Description: Technical publication on audio recording and live sound engineering.

FLUTE TALK
Instrumentalist Publishing Co.
200 Northfield Rd., Northfield, IL 60093. 847-446-5000.
Monthly. $2. Circ.: 13,000. Victoria Jicha, Editor. **Description:** For flute teachers or performers. **Nonfiction:** Interviews with players, teachers, composers; other articles on flute playing; 3-5 pages; $90-$100/printed page. **Art:** Slides, color prints. **Queries:** Preferred. **E-Queries:** No. **Unsolicited mss:** Accepts. **Response:** Queries 1 week, submissions 1 month, SASE required. **Payment:** On publication.

GLORY SONGS
One Life Way Plaza, Nashville, TN 37234. 800-458-2772.
E-mail: don.schlosser@lifeway.com. Don Schlosser, Editor. **Description:** Choral music, for volunteer and part-time music directors and members of church choirs. Very easy music and accompaniments designed specifically for the small church (4-6 songs per issue). **Queries:** Preferred. **Payment:** On acceptance.

GUITAR ONE
Cherry Lane Music
6 E 32nd St., Fl. 6, New York, NY 10016.
E-mail: editors@guitaronemag.com. Web site: www.guitaronemag.com. Chris O'Byrne, Associate Editor. **Description:** For serious guitarists. **Queries:** Preferred.

GUITAR PLAYER
2800 Campus Dr., San Mateo, CA 94403. 650-513-4300.
Web site: www.guitarplayer.com. Emily Fasten, Managing Editor. **Description:** On guitars and related subjects. **Nonfiction:** Articles; from 200 words; $100-$600. **Rights:** All. **Payment:** On acceptance.

INTERNATIONAL MUSICIAN
American Federation of Musicians
1501 Broadway, Suite 600, New York, NY 10036-5599. 212-869-1330.
E-mail: afollett@afm.org. Web site: www.afm.org. Monthly. $25. Circ.: 120,000. Antoinette Follett, Managing Editor. **Description:** Official publication of AFM. Targets professional musicians. **Queries:** Required. **Payment:** On acceptance.

JAZZIZ
Jazziz Magazines, Inc.
2650 N Military Trail, Suite 140, Boca Raton, FL 33431-6339. 561-893-6868.
E-mail: mail@jazziz.com. Web site: www.jazziz.com. Monthly. $69.95. Circ.: 159,000. David Pulizzi, Editor. **Description:** Jazz musician publication. **Nonfiction:** On all aspects of adult contemporary music: interviews, profiles, concept pieces; pay varies.

Columns, Departments: Reviews of varied music genres, radio, and video; mostly new releases; pay varies. **Tips:** Send resume with manuscript. **E-Queries:** Yes. **Freelance Content:** 80%. **Payment:** On acceptance.

KEYBOARD MAGAZINE
United Entertainment Media, Inc.
2800 Campus Dr., San Mateo, CA 94403-2506. 650-513-4300.
E-mail: keyboard@musicplayer.com. Web site: www.keyboardonline.com. Monthly. Circ.: 72,000. Marvin Sanders, Editor. **Description:** On keyboard instruments, MIDI and computer technology, and players. **Nonfiction:** Articles, 300-5,000 words, photos; pays $200-$600. **Queries:** Preferred. **Payment:** On acceptance.

LA FACTORIA DE SONIDO
Barrera Publishing
43 W 38th St., Fl. 5, New York, NY 10018-5515. 212-840-0227.
E-mail: sonidocd@aol.com. Web site: www.lafactoriadesonido.com. Bimonthly. Circ.: 120,000. Jennifer Barrera, Executive Editor. **Description:** Hispanic music and art publication. Music events, reviews, interviews, fashion, and clubs focusing on Hispanic music of all kinds.

LIVING BLUES
University of Mississippi
Hill Hall, Room 301, University, MS 38677. 662-915-5742.
Web site: www.livingbluesonline.com. Bimonthly. David Nelson, Editor.
Description: About living African-American blues artists. **Nonfiction:** Interviews, some retrospective, historical articles or investigative pieces; 1,500-10,000 words; pays $75-$200. **Art:** Photos, $25-$50. **Queries:** Preferred. **Payment:** On publication.

LOLLIPOP
See page 333 for full listing.
Description: Fiction, essays, and "edgy" commentary on music and youth culture.

MIX
PRIMEDIA Business Magazines & Media
6400 Hollis St., Suite 12, Emeryville, CA 94608. 510-653-3307.
E-mail: gpeterson@primediabusiness.com. Web site: www.mixmag.com. Monthly. $46/yr. Circ.: 53,000. George Peterson, Editorial Director. **Description:** For professionals, on audio, audio post-production, sound production, live sound, and music entertainment technology. **Nonfiction:** Articles, varying lengths; pay varies. **Queries:** Preferred. **Payment:** On publication.

MODERN DRUMMER
12 Old Bridge Rd., Cedar Grove, NJ 07009. 209-239-4140.
E-mail: mdinfo@moderndrummer.com. Web site: www.moderndrummer.com.

Monthly. Circ.: 102,000. Ronald L. Spagnardi, Editor-in-Chief. **Description:** Features drumming how-tos, interviews, and more. **Nonfiction:** 500-2,000 words; $50-$500. **Payment:** On publication.

OPERA NEWS
The Metropolitan Opera Guild, Inc.
70 Lincoln Ctr. Plaza, New York, NY 10023-6548. 212-769-7080.
E-mail: info@operanews.com. Web site: www.operanews.com. Monthly. Circ.: 100,000. Rudolph S. Rauch, Publisher/Editor. **Description:** On all aspects of opera. **Nonfiction:** Articles, 600-2,500 words; pay varies. **Queries:** Preferred. **Payment:** On publication.

PERFORMING ARTS AND ENTERTAINMENT IN CANADA
104 Glenrose Ave., Toronto, Ontario M4T 1K8. 416-484-4534.
E-mail: kbell@interlog.ca. Quarterly. $8.56/issue. Circ.: 44,000. Karen Bell, Editor. **Description:** Canadian performing arts and entertainment, including theater, music (especially classical, new, jazz, world, and folk), dance, film, TV, and related fields. Also profiles, opinion, issues, etc. **Nonfiction:** Should be of national interest, but values submissions from smaller, out-of-the-way locations (not just downtown Montreal and Toronto). Especially interested in stories that reflect some aspect of Canadian diversity. Publishes very few reviews; 600-1,500 words; $95-$170. **Art:** Prints (B&W or color); no payment. **Tips:** Welcomes new writers. Prefers stories with original ideas and opinions, or addressing issues of some complexity or sophistication—not just simple profiles of people or companies. **Queries:** Required. **E-Queries:** Yes. **Unsolicited mss:** Accepts. **Response:** Slow to respond, be patient, SASE required. **Rights:** 1st print and electronic. **Payment:** On publication.

ROLLING STONE
1290 Avenue of the Americas, Fl. 2, New York, NY 10104. 212-484-1616.
Web site: www.rollingstone.com. **Description:** Magazine of American music, culture, and politics. **Tips:** Rarely accepts freelance material. No fiction. **Queries:** Required. **Unsolicited mss:** Does not accept.

SHEET MUSIC MAGAZINE
Shacor, Inc.
333 Adams St., Bedford Hills, NY 10507-2001. 914-244-8500.
E-mail: editor@sheetmusicmagazine.com. Web site: www.sheetmusicmagazine.com. Bimonthly. $3.95/$18.97. Circ.: 75,000. Kirk Miller, Editor. **Description:** For amateur and professional musicians. Most content is the actual reproduction of popular songs (words and music). **Fiction:** On golden era of popular music, 1900-1950; 2,000 words; pay varies. **Nonfiction:** Pieces for pianists, organists, and singers; on musicians, composers, music education, pedagogy; also reviews (to 500 words); no hard rock or heavy metal; 2,000 words; pay varies. **Fillers:** Cartoons on golden era, 1900-1950; $10-$50. **Columns, Departments:** On golden era; keyboard and guitar; how-to; 1,000 words max. **Art:** hard copy, digital. **Queries:** Preferred. **E-Queries:** Yes.

Unsolicited mss: Accepts. **Response:** 2 months, SASE. **Freelance Content:** 50%. **Rights:** Reprint.

STAGE DIRECTIONS

SMW Communications, Inc.

250 W 57th St., Suite 420, New York, NY 10107. 212-265-8890.

E-mail: idorbian@lifestyleventures.com. Web site: www.stage-directions.com. Iris Dorbian. **Description:** On acting, directing, costuming, makeup, lighting, set design and decoration, props, special effects, fundraising, and audience development, for readers active in all aspects of community, regional, academic, or youth theater. **Nonfiction:** How-to articles, to 2,000 words; pays $.10/word. **Tips:** Short pieces, 400-500 words, "are a good way to approach us first." **Payment:** On publication.

STORYTELLING

101 Courthouse Sq., Jonesborough, TN 37659. 423-913-8201.

E-mail: nsn@naxs.net. Web site: www.storynet.org. Bimonthly. $4.95, member benefit. Circ.: 5,000. Grace Hawthorne, Editor. **Description:** For the professional storyteller; focuses on the oral tradition. **Nonfiction:** On the oral tradition; 1,000-2,000 words. **Columns, Departments:** Unusual events or applications; 200-400 words. **Queries:** Required. **E-Queries:** Yes. **Unsolicited mss:** Accepts. **Response:** 2 weeks. **Payment:** In copies.

SYMPHONY

33 W 60th St., Fl. 5, New York, NY 10023. 212-262-5161.

E-mail: editor@symphony.org. Web site: www.symphony.org. Bimonthly. $35. Circ.: 20,000. Melinda Whiting, Editor-in-Chief. **Description:** Discusses issues critical to the orchestra community. Communicates to the public the value and importance of orchestras and their music. **Columns, Departments:** Book and CD reviews; profiles of musicians, orchestras, and conductors; 1,000-3,000 words; $250-$500. **Art:** Photos. **Tips:** Welcomes new writers. Prefers queries with ideas that can be shaped to match readers' interests. Serves the orchestral industry; while general-interest classical-music subjects may be of interest, look first for specific orchestral connection before querying. **Queries:** Preferred. **E-Queries:** Yes. **Unsolicited mss:** Accepts. **Response:** 1 day to 3 months, SASE required. **Freelance Content:** 30-50%. **Rights:** 1st. **Payment:** On acceptance. **Contact:** Rebecca Winzenried, Managing Editor.

TDR

721 Broadway, 6th Fl., New York, NY 10003. 212-998-1626.

E-mail: tdr@nyu.edu. Quarterly. $10/$38, $22 (students). Circ.: 3,000. Richard Schechner, Editor. **Description:** "The drama review." A journal of performance studies; with intercultural, intergeneric, interdisciplinary focus. About performance in its broadest sense: dance, music, media; sports, rituals, daily life; anthropology, psychology, and politics. **Nonfiction:** Eclectic articles on experimental performance and performance theory; cross-cultural, examining social, political, historical, and theatrical contexts in which performance happens; to 30 pages (mss.). **Queries:** Required. **E-Queries:** No. **Unsolicited mss:** Accepts. **Response:** 3 months, SASE. **Freelance Content:** 50%. **Payment:** On publication.

TEACHING THEATRE
See page 351 for full listing.
Description: Journal for middle and high school drama educators.

THIRSTY EAR MAGAZINE
See page 334 for full listing.
Description: Covers music, art and culture.

URB
2410 Hyperion Ave., Los Angeles, CA 90027. 323-315-1700.
E-mail: word2urb@urb.com. Web site: www.urb.com. 10x/year. $3.95/$12. Circ.: 75,000. Stacy Osbaum, Editor. **Description:** Focuses on future music culture: electronic dance music, independent hip-hop and DJ culture. **Nonfiction:** Features, on dance and underground hip-hop music (profiles of emerging musicians, singers, and groups); pays $.10/word. **Tips:** Send published clips. **Queries:** Required. **E-Queries:** Yes. **Response:** Queries 1 month. **Freelance Content:** 80%. **Payment:** On publication.

REGIONAL & CITY

ALABAMA HERITAGE
See page 421 for full listing.
Description: Focuses on the events that have shaped Alabama and the South.

ALASKA
619 E Ship Creek Ave., Suite 329, Anchorage, AK 99501. 907-272-6070.
E-mail: bwwoods@alaskamagazine.com. Web site: www.alaskamagazine.com.
Monthly. Circ.: 205,000. Bruce Woods, Editor. **Description:** Covers all aspects of life
in Alaska. **Nonfiction:** Articles on well-researched, interesting topics. Travel, historical, interview/profile, personal experience, destination pieces, etc; 100-2,500 words;
$100-$2,500. **Tips:** Send SASE for guidelines. **Queries:** Preferred. **Freelance
Content:** 70%. **Payment:** On publication. **Contact:** Donna Rae Thompson,
Editorial Assistant.

ALASKA BUSINESS MONTHLY
See page 306 for full listing.
Description: For those interested in the business affairs of the 49th State.

ALBEMARLE
375 Greenbrier Dr., Suite 100, Charlottesville, VA 22901. 804-817-2000.
E-mail: rhart@cjp.com. Web site: www.cjp.com. Bimonthly. Circ.: 10,000. Ruth Hart,
Editor. **Description:** Lifestyle magazine highlighting the news and events of
Virginia. **Nonfiction:** Topics include health and medicine, the arts, home architec-
ture, interior design, and gardening; pay varies.

ALBERTA SWEETGRASS
See page 362 for full listing.
Description: Newspaper covering Aboriginal issues for communities in Alberta.

AMERICAN OUTBACK JOURNAL
New Media Group, LLC
111 W Telegraph St., Suite 202, Carson City, NV 89703. 775-888-9330.
E-mail: curt@americanoutback.com. Web site: www.americanoutback.com. Curtis
Pendergraft, Editor. **Description:** Print and e-zine on the American West. Publishes
articles on lore, history, culture, ecology, politics, humor, and travel to off-beat western destinations. **Queries:** Preferred.

ARIZONA HIGHWAYS
2039 W Lewis Ave., Phoenix, AZ 85009. 602-712-2024.
E-mail: arizonahighways.com. Web site: www.arizonahighways.com. Monthly.
$3.99/$21 (US), $31 (Canada). Circ.: 365,000. Robert J. Early, Editor. **Description:**
Covers travel in Arizona. Pieces on adventure, humor, lifestyles, nostalgia, history,
archaeology, Indian culture/crafts, nature, etc. Some Arizona-based fiction on occa-

sion. **Fiction:** Preferably frontier-oriented, must be upbeat and wholesome (for December and April issues); 1,800-2,500 words; $.55-$1.00/word. **Nonfiction:** Travel-adventure, travel-history, travel-destination; personal-experience pieces. Insightful and third-person; 800-1,800 words; $.55-$1.00/word. **Fillers:** Jokes (humor page); 200 words or less; $75. **Columns, Departments:** Focus on Nature, Along the Way, Back Road Adventures, Hiking, Destination Humor. Insightful or nostalgic viewpoint; 800 words; $440-$450. **Art:** 4x5 preferred; landscapes, also images to illustrate a story; pay varies. **Tips:** To break in, submit short items to Off-ramp department. Use active verbs. No stories on religion, government, or politics. **E-Queries:** Yes. **Unsolicited mss:** Does not accept. **Response:** 30 days or less, SASE required. **Freelance Content:** 100%. **Rights:** print (online for extra fee). **Payment:** On acceptance. **Contact:** Query Editor.

ARIZONA TRENDS OF THE SOUTHWEST

Dandick Company
P.O. Box 8508, Scottsdale, AZ 85252-8508. 480-948-1799.
10x/year. Circ.: 32,000. Randi Barocas, Editor. **Description:** Features on fashion, health and beauty, special events, dining, the performing arts, and book reviews. **Queries:** Preferred.

ARKANSAS TIMES

201 E Markham, Suite 200, P.O. Box 34010, Little Rock, AR 72203. 501-375-2985.
E-mail: arktimes@arktimes.com. Web site: www.arktimes.com. John Brummett, Editor. **Description:** On Arkansas history, people, travel, politics. **Nonfiction:** Articles, strong Arkansas orientation; to 6,000 words; pays to $500. **Payment:** On acceptance.

ASPEN MAGAZINE

720 E Durant Ave., #E-8, Aspen, CO 81611-2071. 970-920-4040.
E-mail: edit@aspenmagazine.com. Web site: www.aspenmagazine.com. Bimonthly. $4.95. Circ.: 20,000. Janet O'Grady, Editor-in-Chief. **Description:** City and regional news about Aspen, Colorado. **Nonfiction:** Lifestyle articles on Aspen, Snowmass, and the Roaring Fork Valley; outdoor sports, arts, profiles, food and wine, environment news, and photos essays related to Aspen and surrounding area. **Queries:** Required. **E-Queries:** Yes. **Unsolicited mss:** Does not accept. **Response:** 4 weeks, SASE required. **Freelance Content:** 30%. **Payment:** On publication. **Contact:** Dana R. Butler, Managing Editor.

ATLANTA

Emmis Communications Co.
1330 W Peachtree St., Suite 450, Atlanta, GA 30309-3214. 404-872-3100.
E-mail: walburn@atlantamag.emmis.com. Web site: www.atlantamagazine.com. Monthly. Circ.: 65,000. Lee Walburn, Editor-in-Chief. **Description:** Atlanta subjects or personalities. **Nonfiction:** Articles; 1,500-5,000 words; pays $300-$2,000. **Queries:** Required. **Payment:** On acceptance.

ATLANTA HOMES AND LIFESTYLES
See page 448 for full listing.
Description: On upscale home and gardens in Atlanta.

THE ATLANTA JOURNAL-CONSTITUTION
P.O. Box 4689, Atlanta, GA 30302. 404-526-5151.
E-mail: hpost@ajc.com. Web site: www.ajc.com. Daily. Hyde Post, Editorial Director.
Description: Articles related to the Southeast, Georgia, and the Atlanta metro area.
Nonfiction: Submit complete manuscript. Varied topics: law, economics, politics, science, environment, performing arts, humor, education; religious, seasonal; 200-600 words; pays $75-$125. **Payment:** On publication.

AVANCE HISPANO
4230 Mission St., San Francisco, CA 94112-1520. 415-585-1080.
Monthly. Circ.: 30,000. **Description:** Spanish-language publication for people in the San Francisco Bay area.

BACK HOME IN KENTUCKY
295 Old Forge Mill Rd., P.O. Box 710, Clay City, KY 40312-0710. 606-663-1011.
10x/yr. $3/$20. Circ.: 8,000. Jerlene Rose, Editor/Publisher. **Description:** Focuses on Kentucky destinations, profiles, personal memories, county spotlights, natural history, and nostalgia. **Nonfiction:** 400-1000 words; $25 and up. **Columns, Departments:** Chronicles (Kentucky history, 400-1,000 words); $25- $100. **Art:** Slides, photos; $25 and up. **Queries:** Not necessary. **E-Queries:** Yes. **Unsolicited mss:** Accepts. **Response:** 60 days. **Freelance Content:** 75%. **Payment:** On publication.

BALTIMORE
Rosebud Entertainment, LLC
1000 Lancaster St., Suite 400, Baltimore, MD 21202-4382. 410-752-4200.
E-mail: iken@baltimoremag.com. Web site: www.baltimoremagazine.net. Monthly.
$3.50/$15. Circ.: 52,000. Ken Iglehart, Managing Editor. **Description:** Covers Baltimore metro area: local people, events, trends, and ideas. **Nonfiction:** Consumer advice, investigative, lifestyle, profiles, humor, personal experience; 250-4,000 words; $125 and up. **Columns, Departments:** News You Can Use; 800-2,000 words; $200 and up. **Tips:** Consider short articles for departments; send query letter and clips. **Queries:** Required. **E-Queries:** Yes. **Unsolicited mss:** Accepts. **Response:** 1 month queries, 2 months submissons, SASE required. **Freelance Content:** 60%. **Rights:** First serial; reprint. **Payment:** On publication.

BAY AREA PARENT
See page 374 for full listing.
Description: Parenting issues for California's Santa Clara County/South Bay area.

BIG APPLE PARENT

See page 374 for full listing.
Description: Newspaper for New York City parents.

BIG SKY JOURNAL

P.O. Box 1069, Bozeman, MT 59771. 406-586-2712.
Web site: www.bigskyjournal.com. 6x/year. Michelle A. Steven-Orton. **Description:** On Montana art and architecture, hunting and fishing, ranching and recreation. **Fiction:** To 4,000 words. **Nonfiction:** Articles, to 2,500 words; pay varies. **Queries:** Preferred. **Payment:** On publication.

BIRMINGHAM

Birmingham Area Chamber of Commerce
P.O. Box 10127, Birmingham, AL 35202-0127. 205-250-7653.
E-mail: jodonnell@bhammag.com. Web site: www.bhammag.com. Monthly. Circ.: 12,000. Joe O'Donnell, Editor. **Description:** Spotlights events, people, and activities in and around Birmingham. **Nonfiction:** Profiles, business articles, and nostalgia pieces, with local focus. Also, business features, dining, fashion, and general-interest. To 2,500 words; pays $50-$175. **Response:** SASE. **Payment:** On publication.

BLUE RIDGE COUNTRY

P.O. Box 21535, Roanoke, VA 24018. 540-989-6138.
E-mail: krheinheimer@leisurepublishing.com. Web site: www.blueridgecounty.com. Bimonthly. $3.95/$17.95. Circ.: 80,000. Kurt Rheinheimer, Editor. **Description:** Regional magazine. **Nonfiction:** Articles that explore and extol the beauty, history, and travel opportunities in the mountain regions of VA, NC, WV, TN, KY, MD, SC, and GA; 250-1,800 words; $25-$250. **Art:** Color slides; B&W prints considered; $25-$100 for photo features. **Queries:** Preferred. **Response:** 1-2 months, SASE. **Freelance Content:** 70%. **Payment:** On publication.

BOCA RATON

JES Publishing
Amtec Ctr., Suite 100, 6413 Congress Ave., Boca Raton, FL 33487. 561-997-8683.
E-mail: bocamag@aol.com. Web site: www.bocamag.com. Bimonthly. Circ.: 20,000. Lisa Ocker, Editor. **Description:** Focuses on southern Florida. Regional issues, lifestyle trends, relationships, cuisine, travel, fashion, and profiles of local residents and celebrities. **Nonfiction:** Articles on Florida topics, personalities, and travel; 800-3,000 words; $350-$1,000. **Tips:** Query first, clips required. **Queries:** Required. **Payment:** On acceptance.

THE BOSTON GLOBE

P.O. Box 2378, 135 Morrissey Blvd., Boston, MA 02107-2378. 617-929-2000.
E-mail: letter@globe.com. Web site: www.boston.com/globe/magazine. Weekly. Nick King, Editor. **Description:** Covers arts, entertainment, shopping, and news in the Boston area. **Nonfiction:** 2,500-5,000 words. **Tips:** Send query first. **Queries:**

Preferred. **Unsolicited mss:** Accepts. **Response:** 3 weeks, SASE required. **Freelance Content:** Varies. **Rights:** 1st NA. **Payment:** On publication.

BOSTON MAGAZINE
300 Massachusetts Ave., Boston, MA 02115. 617-262-9700.
Web site: www.bostonmagazine.com. Monthly. Circ.: 125,000. Jon Marcus, Editor.
Description: Offers expository features, narratives, and articles on Boston-area personalities, institutions, and phenomena. No fiction. 500-700 words, pays $1/word. **Queries:** Required. **Payment:** On publication.

BOSTONIA
Boston University, 10 Lenox St., Brookline, MA 02446-4042. 617-353-3081.
E-mail: bostonia@bu.edu. Web site: www.bu.edu/alumni/bostonia/index.html.
Quarterly. Circ.: 200,000. Michael B. Shavelson, Editor. **Description:** "The magazine of culture and ideas." Covers politics, literature, music, art, science, and education, especially from a Boston angle. **Nonfiction:** Articles; to 3,000 words; pays $150-$2,500. **Queries:** Required.

BROOKLYN BRIDGE
388 Atlantic Ave., Brooklyn, NY 11217-1703. 718-596-7400.
E-mail: bbridge@mennen.tiac.net. Web site: www.w-rabbit.com/b_bridge/. Bimonthly. Circ.: 40,000. Joe Fodor, Sr. Editor. **Description:** Topics of regional and national interest, including arts and cultural activities, investigative reports, and the "politics" of Brooklyn.

BUFFALO SPREE
5678 Main St., Williamsville, NY 14221. 716-634-0820.
E-mail: elicata@buffalospree.com. Web site: www.buffalospree.com. Bimonthly. Circ.: 25,000. Elizabeth Licata, Editor. **Description:** City/regional magazine for western New York. **Nonfiction:** Articles of local interest; to 1,800 words; $125-$150. **Tips:** Unsolicited articles discouraged. **Queries:** Preferred. **Unsolicited mss:** Does not accept. **Payment:** On publication.

CAPE COD LIFE
4 Barlow Landings Rd., Unit 14, P.O. Box 1385
Pocasset, MA 02559-1385. 508-564-4466.
E-mail: jrohlf@capecodlife.com. Web site: www.capecodlife.com. 7x/year. Circ.: 40,000. Janice Randall Rohlf, Managing Editor. **Description:** About life on Cape Cod, Martha's Vineyard, and Nantucket (past, present, and future). **Nonfiction:** On events, business, art, history, gardening, lifestyle of region; 800-2,500 words; $.20-$.25/word. **Art:** Transparencies. **Queries:** Preferred. **E-Queries:** Yes. **Unsolicited mss:** Accepts. **Response:** 1-2 months, SASE required. **Freelance Content:** 90%. **Rights:** All. **Payment:** On publication.

CAROLINA GARDENER
See page 449 for full listing.
Description: Articles and features specific to Southeast gardening.

CAROLOGUE
South Carolina Historical Society
100 Meeting St., Charleston, SC 29401-2299. 843-723-3225.
E-mail: info@schistory.org. Web site: www.schistory.org. Eric Emerson, Editor.
Description: On South Carolina history. **Nonfiction:** General-interest articles, to 10 pages. **Queries:** Preferred. **Payment:** In copies.

CASCADES EAST
See page 569 for full listing.
Description: Outdoor activities and scenic tours in the central Oregon Cascades.

CENTRAL CALIFORNIA PARENT
See page 375 for full listing.
Description: Parenting issues for families in California.

CENTRAL PA
WITF, Inc.
P.O. Box 2954, Harrisburg, PA 17105-2954. 717-221-2800.
E-mail: cenpa@centralpa.org. Web site: www.centralpa.org. Monthly. $45. Circ.: 40,000. Stephanie Anderson, Managing Editor. **Description:** Topics of interest to central Pennsylvania, including profiles of notable central Pennsylvanians, and broadly based articles of social interest that "enlighten and inform." **Nonfiction:** Articles, 1,500-3,500 words; pays $.10/word. **Payment:** On publication.

CENTRAL PENN PARENT
See page 375 for full listing.
Description: Parenting issues for families in Pennsylvania.

CHARLESTON
P.O. Box 1794, Mt. Pleasant, SC 29465-1794. 843-971-9811.
E-mail: dshankland@charlestonmag.com. Web site: www.charlestonmag.com. Bimonthly. Circ.: 22,000. Darcy Shankland, Editor. **Description:** Nonfiction articles on local topics. **Nonfiction:** Past articles have ranged from winter getaways and holiday gift ideas to social issues like homeless shelters. **Columns, Departments:** In Good Taste, Top of the Shelf, Cityscape, Insight, Doing Business, Native Talent, Chef at Home, On the Road. **Tips:** Send SASE for guidelines. **Queries:** Preferred. **Payment:** 30 days from publication.

CHARLOTTE
Abarta Media Group
127 W Worthington Ave., Suite 208, Charlotte, NC 28203-4474. 704-335-7181.

E-mail: editor@charlottemag.com. Web site: www.charlottemag.com. Monthly. Circ.: 30,000. Richard Thurmond, Editorial Director. **Description:** Covers social, economic, and cultural life of Charlotte and surrounding area. **Nonfiction:** Politics, business, art and entertainment, education, sports, travel, society; pay varies.

CHESAPEAKE BAY MAGAZINE

1819 Bay Ridge Ave., Annapolis, MD 21403. 410-263-2662.
E-mail: editor@cbmmag.net. Web site: www.cbmmag.net. Monthly. $3.95/issue. Circ.: 46,000. T. F. Sayles, Editor. **Description:** For recreational boaters on the Chesapeake Bay. **Nonfiction:** Boating, fishing, destinations, people, history, and traditions of the Chesapeake Bay; up to 4,000 words; $75-$1,200. **Art:** Photos; $100-$700. **Tips:** Need to be familiar with Chesapeake Bay region and boating. Readers are well educated, well traveled. **Queries:** Preferred. **E-Queries:** Yes. **Unsolicited mss:** Accepts. **Response:** 1 week queries, 1 month submissions, SASE required. **Freelance Content:** 30%. **Rights:** FNASR. **Payment:** On acceptance. **Contact:** Jane Meneely, Managing Editor.

CHICAGO MAGAZINE

PRIMEDIA Consumer Media & Magazine Group
500 N Dearborn, Suite 1200, Chicago, IL 60610-4901.
E-mail: shane_tritsch@primediamags.com. Web site: www.chicagomag.com. Monthly. Circ.: 175,000. Shane Tritsch, Managing Editor. **Description:** Publication covering topics related to Chicago. **Nonfiction:** 1,000-5,000 words; pay varies. **Queries:** Required. **Payment:** On acceptance.

CHICAGO READER

11 E Illinois St., Chicago, IL 60611. 312-828-0350.
Web site: www.chicagoreader.com. **Description:** Free weekly publication for residents in the Chicago area. **Queries:** Preferred.

CINCINNATI MAGAZINE

Emmis Publishing Corp.
One Centennial Plaza, 705 Central Ave., Suite 175
Cincinnati, OH 45202-1900. 513-421-4300.
E-mail: editors@cintimag.emmis.com. Monthly. Kitty Morgan, Editor. **Description:** Cincinnati people and issues. **Nonfiction:** 500-3,500 words; $50-$500. **Tips:** Query with writing sample.

CITY AZ DESERT LIVING

342 E Thomas Rd., Phoenix, AZ 85012. 602-667-9798.
E-mail: info@cityaz.com. Web site: www.cityaz.com. Bimonthly. Circ.: 40,000. Leigh Flayton, Executive Editor. **Description:** For Phoenix area professionals, artists, and architechture/design aficionados. Covers food, fashion, travel, etc; local and national profiles. **Queries:** Required.

CITY & SHORE

The Sun-Sentinel

200 E Las Olas Blvd., Fort Lauderdale, FL 33301-2293. 954-356-4685.
Web site: www.cityandshore.com. Bimonthly. Mark Gauert, Editor. **Description:**
Lifestyle magazine of the *Sun-Sentinel.* **Nonfiction:** Articles on topics of interest to
south Floridians; 1,000-3,000 words; $400-$1,500. **Queries:** Preferred. **Payment:**
On acceptance.

COLORADO HOMES AND LIFESTYLES

See page 477 for full listing.
Description: Affluent, upscale homes and lifestyles.

COMMON GROUND

P.O. Box 99, 6 W John St., McVeytown, PA 17051-0099. 717-899-6133.
E-mail: commonground@acsworld.net. Quarterly. $3.50/$12.95. Circ.: 9,000. Ruth
Dunmire, Pam Brumbaugh, Editors. **Description:** Focuses on Pennsylvania's
Juniata River Valley. **Nonfiction:** Hiking destinations, local history, personality pro-
files; $40/printed page. **Poetry:** Short; $5-$25. **Art:** Prints; $15-$25. **Tips:** Do not
send queries; prefers complete manuscript with illustrations on spec. Read magazine
for upcoming themes. **Queries:** Not necessary. **E-Queries:** No. **Unsolicited mss:**
Accepts. **Response:** 1 month, SASE. **Freelance Content:** 90%. **Rights:** 1st.
Payment: On publication.

COMMONWEALTH

18 Tremont St., Suite 1120, Boston, MA 02111. 617-742-6800.
E-mail: rkeough@massinc.org. Web site: www.massinc.org. Quarterly. $5. Circ.:
8,000. Robert Keough, Editor. **Description:** Politics, ideas, and civic life in
Massachusetts. Pays $.35-$.50/word **Nonfiction:** On politics, public policy; 3,000
words and up. **Columns, Departments:** Reflective essays on civic life; 800-1,500
words. **Queries:** Preferred. **E-Queries:** Yes. **Unsolicited mss:** Accepts. **Response:**
Varies, SASE. **Rights:** FNASR. **Payment:** On acceptance.

CONNECTICUT MAGAZINE

Journal Register Company

35 Nutmeg Dr., Trumbull, CT 06611. 203-380-6600.
E-mail: cmonagan@connecticutmag.com. Web site: www.connecticutmag.com.
Monthly. Circ.: 86,675. Charles Monagan, Editor. **Description:** Connecticut topics,
issues, people, and lifestyles. **Nonfiction:** 1,500-3,500 words; $500-$1,200.
Payment: On acceptance.

THE COUNTRY CONNECTION

See page 356 for full listing.
Description: Eco-friendly publication for Ontario.

CRAIN'S CHICAGO BUSINESS
Crain Communications, Inc.
360 N Michigan Ave., Chicago, IL 60601. 312-649-5411.
E-mail: editor@chicagobusiness.com. Web site: www.chicagobusiness.com. Weekly.
Circ.: 50,500. Robert Reed, Editor. **Description:** Provides business owners, executives, professionals, and other consumers with articles covering the current news and analysis of the business community in the Chicago metro area.

CRAIN'S DETROIT BUSINESS
1400 Woodbridge Ave., Detroit, MI 48207. 313-446-0419.
E-mail: jmelton@crain.com. Web site: www.crainsdetroit.com. Weekly. $1.50/issue.
Circ.: 38,000. Cindy Goodaker, Executive Editor. **Description:** Local business publication. **Columns, Departments:** Business articles about Detroit; 800 words; $10/column inch. **Queries:** Required. **E-Queries:** Yes. **Payment:** On publication. **Contact:** James Melton, Assistant Editor.

DELAWARE TODAY
Division of Today Media, Inc.
P.O. Box 2800, Wilmington, DE 19805-0800. 302-656-1809.
E-mail: editors@delawaretoday.com. Web site: www.delawaretoday.com. Marsha Mah, Editor. **Description:** On topics of local interest. **Nonfiction:** Service articles, profiles, news, etc. Pays $150 for department pieces, $200-$500 for features. **Tips:** Queries with clips required. **Payment:** On publication.

EMERALD COAST
Rowland Publishing, Inc.
1932 Miccosokee Rd., P.O. Box 1837, Tallahassee, FL 32302-1837. 850-878-0554.
E-mail: jbettinger@rowlandinc.com. Web site: www.rowlandinc.com. Quarterly. $2.95/$16.95. Circ.: 17,300. Julie Strauss Bettinger, Editor. **Description:** Lifestyle magazine celebrating life on Florida's Emerald Coast. **Columns, Departments:** Travel, People Profile, What's New (business section), Dining Guide, Sporting Life. **Queries:** Not necessary. **E-Queries:** Yes. **Unsolicited mss:** Accepts. **Response:** 1 week, SASE. **Freelance Content:** 15%. **Payment:** On publication.

FLORIDA
Orlando Sentinel, 633 N Orange Ave., Orlando, FL 32801. 407-420-5000.
E-mail: mdame@tribune.com. Web site: www.orlandosentinel.com. Mike Dame, Executive Producer. **Description:** Online service of *Orlando Sentinel* newspaper.

FLORIDA MONTHLY
Florida Media, Inc.
102 Drennen Road, Suite C-5, Orlando, FL 32806. 407-816-9596.
E-mail: dpacuch@floridamagazine.com. Web site: www.floridamagazine.com. Monthly. $2.99/$21.95. Circ.: 225,000. Debbie Pacuch, Editor. **Description:** Statewide lifestyle. **Nonfiction:** Articles and columns; 700-2,000 words; pays

$.25/word. **Art:** Transparencies; $50 and up. **Queries:** Preferred. **E-Queries:** Yes. **Unsolicited mss:** Accepts. **Response:** 4 weeks, SASE. **Freelance Content:** 50%. **Rights:** 1st. **Payment:** On publication.

FLORIDA WILDLIFE

See page 357 for full listing.
Description: Published by Florida Fish and Wildlife Conservation Commission.

FREDERICK

6 East St., Suite 301, Frederick, MD 21701.
E-mail: dpatrell@fredmag.com. Web site: www.fredmag.com. Monthly. $2.95/issue, $19.95/year. Circ.: 18,000. Dan Patrell, Editor. **Description:** Covers lifestyles and issues in and around Frederick County, Maryland. **Nonfiction:** Articles with a direct link to Frederick County; 800-3,000 words; $100-$300. **Art:** Electronic, transparencies, slides; $25-$300. **Queries:** Required. **E-Queries:** Yes. **Unsolicited mss:** Does not accept. **Response:** 1-3 months. **Freelance Content:** 90%. **Rights:** FNASR. **Payment:** On publication.

GARDEN SHOWCASE

See page 451 for full listing.
Description: Gardening magazine distributed in Oregon and Washington.

GO MAGAZINE

6600 AAA Dr., Charlotte, NC 28212-8250. 704-569-7733.
E-mail: trcrosby@aaaqa.com. Web site: www.aaa.com. 7x/year. for members. Circ.: 750,000. Tom Crosby. **Description:** For AAA members in North and South Carolina. Features on automotive, finance, insurance, and travel. **Columns, Departments:** Travel, auto safety; 750-1,000 words; $.15 /word. **Queries:** Preferred. **E-Queries:** No. **Unsolicited mss:** Accepts. **Response:** 1-3 weeks, SASE. **Freelance Content:** 15%. **Payment:** On publication. **Contact:** Jacquie Hughett, Associate Editor.

GOLDENSEAL

See page 426 for full listing.
Description: On traditional West Virginia culture and history.

GRAND RAPIDS

Gemini Publications
549 Ottawa NW, Grand Rapids, MI 49503-1444. 616-459-4545.
Web site: www.geminipub.com. Monthly. Circ.: 20,000. Carole R. Valade, Editor. **Description:** Covers local area. **Nonfiction:** Service articles (dining guide, travel, personal finance, humor) and issue-oriented pieces. Pays $35-$200. **Queries:** Preferred. **Unsolicited mss:** Accepts. **Payment:** On publication.

GULFSHORE LIFE
Gulfshore Media, Inc.
9051 Tamiami Trail N, Suite 202, Naples, FL 34108-2520. 941-594-9980.
E-mail: bmorris@gulfshorelifemag.com. Web site: www.gulfshorelifemag.com.
Monthly. $25. Circ.: 30,000. Bob Morris, Editor. **Description:** On southwest Florida
personalities, travel, sports, business, interior design, arts, history, and nature.
Nonfiction: Articles, 800-3,000 words; pays from $200. **Queries:** Preferred.

HAWAII
Fancy Publications, Inc.
P.O. Box 6050, Mission Viejo, CA 92690-6050. 949-855-8822.
E-mail: hawaii@fancypubs.com. Web site: www.hawaiimagazine.com. Bimonthly.
$27.97/yr. Circ.: 75,000. June Kikuchi, Editor. **Description:** On topics related to
Hawaii. **Nonfiction:** Articles, 1,000-2,500 words; pays $.10/word. **Queries:**
Preferred. **Payment:** On publication.

HONOLULU
PacificBasin Communications, Inc.
1000 Bishop St., Suite 405, Honolulu, HI 96813. 808-537-9500.
E-mail: johnh@pacificbasin.net. Web site: www.honolulumagazine.com.
John Heckathorn, Editor. **Description:** Features highlighting contemporary life in
the Hawaiian islands: politics, sports, history, people, arts, and events. **Nonfiction:**
Pays $300-$700. **Queries:** Required. **Payment:** On acceptance.

ILLINOIS ENTERTAINER
See page 388 for full listing.
Description: Covers entertainment, media, and music in Illinois.

IMAGEN: REFLECTIONS OF TODAY'S LATINO
P.O. Box 7487, Albuquerque, NM 87194-7487. 505-889-4088.
Web site: www.imagenmag.com. Monthly. **Description:** Magazine featuring news
and profiles of interesting people in the Latino community in New Mexico.

INDIANAPOLIS MONTHLY
Emmis Publishing Corp.
1 Emmis Plaza, 40 Monument Circle, Suite 100 NE, Indianapolis, IN 46204-3019.
317-237-9288.
E-mail: lou@indymonthly.emmis.com. Web site: www.indianapolismonthly.com.
Monthly. $19.95. Circ.: 45,000. Lou Harry, Executive Editor. **Description:** All mate-
rial must have an Indianapolis/Indiana focus. **Nonfiction:** Profiles, sports, business,
travel, crime, controversy, service, first-person essays, book excerpts; 2,500-4,000
words, $400-$500. **Columns, Departments:** IndyScene (trendy "quick hits"), to 200
words, $50; departments, 1,500-2,500 words, $250-$350. **Payment:** On publication.

INSIDE CHICAGO
4710 N Lincoln Ave., Chicago, IL 60625. 773-878-7333.
E-mail: inside@suba.com. Web site: www.insideonline.com. Weekly. Free. Circ.: 49,500. David Harrell, Editor. **Description:** Community newspaper for Chicago's north side. **Nonfiction:** News/features on Chicagoans, nightlife, arts, and lifestyle. **Art:** $25/photo. **Queries:** Preferred. **E-Queries:** Yes. **Unsolicited mss:** Accepts. **Response:** 1 week, SASE required. **Freelance Content:** 20%. **Rights:** One-time (print and electronic). **Payment:** On publication.

THE IOWAN
218 Sixth Ave., Suite 610, Des Moines, IA 50309. 515-282-8220.
E-mail: kroberson@iowan.com. Web site: iowan@iowan.com. Bimonthly. $24.50 year. Circ.: 25,000. Kelly Roberson, Editor. **Description:** Covers history, culture, people, places, and events of Iowa. **Fiction:** Short stories; up to 5,000 words; $.30/word. **Nonfiction:** Life in Iowa; up to 5,000 words; $.30/word. **Art:** All formats. **Queries:** Not necessary. **E-Queries:** Yes. **Unsolicited mss:** Accepts. **Response:** 12 weeks, SASE required. **Freelance Content:** 80%. **Rights:** One-time NA. **Payment:** On acceptance.

JACKSONVILLE
White Publishing Co.
1032 Hendricks Ave., Jacksonville, FL 32207. 904-396-8666.
Monthly. Circ.: 25,000. Joseph White, Editor. **Description:** Issues and personalities of interest to readers in the greater Jacksonville area. **Nonfiction:** Service pieces and articles. Home and garden articles on local homeowners, interior designers, remodelers, gardeners, craftsmen, etc. **Columns, Departments:** Business, health, travel, personal finance, real estate, arts and entertainment, sports, dining out, food; 1,200-1,500 words. **Queries:** Required. **Payment:** On publication.

KANSAS!
Kansas Dept. of Commerce and Housing
1000 SW Jackson St., Suite 100, Topeka, KS 66612. 785-296-3479.
E-mail: ksmagazine@kdoch.state.ks.us. Web site: www.travelks.com. Quarterly. $4/issue, $15/year. Circ.: 48,000. **Description:** Aim is to encourage people to travel through Kansas to experience its rich history, scenic landscape, exciting attractions, and Midwestern hospitality. **Nonfiction:** Length, pay varies. **Tips:** Avoid politics, religion, sex, and other topics unrelated to travel. **Queries:** Preferred. **E-Queries:** Yes. **Unsolicited mss:** Does not accept. **Freelance Content:** 100%. **Payment:** On acceptance. **Contact:** Carole Frederick.

KANSAS CITY
118 Southwest Blvd., Kansas City, MO 64108. 816-421-4111.
E-mail: lelmore@abartapub.com. Web site: www.kcmag.com. 12x/year. $3.50/$9.98. Circ.: 27,000. Leigh Elmore, Editor. **Description:** Celebrates life in Kansas City. **Nonfiction:** Serious piece on local issues, personality profiles, and fun features

(Weekend Getaways, etc.); 1,000-3,000 words; $700-$1,000/features. **Columns, Departments:** Excursions (regional travel); Arts (local scene); 1,200 words; $200-$400. **Art:** Prints, transparencies, B&W, JPG. **Tips:** Avoid generic "fit any market" features. **Queries:** Preferred. **E-Queries:** Yes. **Unsolicited mss:** Accepts. **Response:** Queries 2 weeks, submissions 4 weeks. **Freelance Content:** 90%. **Rights:** 1st. **Payment:** On acceptance.

KENTUCKY LIVING
P.O. Box 32170, Louisville, KY 40232. 502-451-2430.
E-mail: e-mail@kentuckyliving.com. Web site: www.kentuckyliving.com. Monthly. $15/year. Circ.: 480,000. Paul Wesslund, Editor. **Description:** On the character and culture of Kentucky. **Nonfiction:** On personalities, history, biography, recreation, travel, and leisure; 1,000 words; $450. **Queries:** Preferred. **E-Queries:** Yes. **Unsolicited mss:** Accepts. **Response:** Queries and submissions 4-6 weeks, SASE required. **Freelance Content:** 75%. **Payment:** On acceptance.

L.A. HOUSE & HOME
See page 453 for full listing.
Description: Magazine for home decorating, renovations, and landscaping.

L.A. PARENT
See page 380 for full listing.
Description: Child development, health, nutrition, education, and local activities

LAKE SUPERIOR
P.O. Box 16417, Duluth, MN 55816-0417. 218-727-2765.
E-mail: edit@lakesuperior.com. Web site: www.lakesuperior.com. Bimonthly. Konnie LeMay, Editor. **Description:** Focuses on Lake Superior region (U.S. and Canada) and its peoples. **Nonfiction:** People, events, and places; 1,000-2,000 words; $100-$600. **Fillers:** Short pieces on Lake life; 600 words or less; $50-$125. **Columns, Departments:** Science, history, humor, reminiscences; 600-1,500 words; $50-$225. **Art:** Varied formats; $25 b/w, $40 color, $125 cover. **Tips:** Lake Superior regional topics only. **Queries:** Preferred. **E-Queries:** No. **Unsolicited mss:** Accepts. **Response:** 3-6 months, SASE required. **Freelance Content:** 80%. **Rights:** FNASR. **Payment:** On publication. **Contact:** Konnie LeMay, Editor.

LONG ISLAND WOMAN
P.O. Box 309, Island Park, NY 11558. 516-897-8900.
E-mail: editor@liwomanonline.com. Web site: www.liwomanonline.com. Monthly. Circ.: 35,000. Jane F. Lane, Editor. **Description:** For educated, active women of the Long Island, NY region. **Nonfiction:** Seeking service-oriented pieces. Preferably not first-person; 525-1,000 words; $10-$150. **Tips:** Does not accept mss over 1,500 words. No phone calls. **Queries:** Required. **E-Queries:** Yes. **Unsolicited mss:** Accepts. **Freelance Content:** 80%. **Rights:** 1st. **Payment:** On publication. **Contact:** Lauralyn Avallone, Associate Editor.

THE LOOK
Hawks Media Group, Inc.
P.O. Box 272, Cranford, NJ 07016-0272. 908-755-6138.
E-mail: jrhawks@thelookmag.com. Web site: www.thelookmag.com. Monthly. Free. Circ.: 3,500. John R. Hawks, Editor. **Description:** New Jersey entertainment magazine. **Nonfiction:** Articles and profiles on fashion, student life, employment, and relationships for readers ages 16-26. Also, beach stories about the New Jersey shore; 1,500-3,000 words; $30-$200. **Fillers:** Puzzles, trivia, and quizzes about area people, places, and events. **Queries:** Preferred. **E-Queries:** Yes. **Unsolicited mss:** Accepts. **Response:** Queries 30-60 days. **Freelance Content:** 50%. **Rights:** All, may reassign. **Payment:** On publication.

LOS ANGELES
5900 Wilshire Blvd., Fl. 10, Los Angeles, CA 90025. 323-801-0100.
Web site: www.lamag.com. Monthly. $3.50. Circ.: 184,000. Kit Rachlis, Editor. **Description:** The diary of a great city for those enthralled by what the city has to offer and those overwhelmed by it. An essential guide. **Nonfiction:** Articles, 400-5,000 words; pay varies. **Queries:** Required. **E-Queries:** Yes. **Unsolicited mss:** Accepts. **Response:** 3-4 weeks, SASE. **Freelance Content:** 50%. **Rights:** 1st NA. **Payment:** On acceptance.

LOUISVILLE
137 W Muhammad Ali Blvd., Suite 101, Louisville, KY 40202. 502-625-0100.
Web site: www.louisville.com/loumag.html. Monthly. $3.75. Circ.: 20,000. Bruce Allar, Editor. **Description:** City magazine. **Nonfiction:** Articles on community issues, personalities, and entertainment in the Louisville area; 500-2,500 words; $150-$600. **Queries:** Required. **E-Queries:** Yes. **Unsolicited mss:** Accepts. **Response:** 60 days, SASE. **Freelance Content:** 60%. **Rights:** FNASR. **Payment:** On acceptance.

MATURE LIFESTYLES
See page 560 for full listing.
Description: For readers over 50, in Florida.

MATURE LIVING
See page 560 for full listing.
Description: For older adults in and around Palm Springs, CA.

MEMPHIS
Contemporary Media, Inc.
P.O. Box 1738, Memphis, TN 38101-1738. 901-521-9000.
E-mail: memmag@memphismagazine.com. Web site: www.memphismagazine.com. Monthly. Circ.: 21,000. James Roper, Editor. **Description:** Topics related to Memphis and the Mid-South region: politics, education, sports, business, history, etc. **Nonfiction:** Articles on a variety of subjects. Profiles; investigative pieces; 1,500-4,000 words; $50-$500. **Queries:** Required. **Payment:** On publication.

Get writing tips and inspiration every month!

3 FREE TRIAL ISSUES!

The Writer Magazine has something to offer both novice and experienced writers of all genres! Each issue includes:

Writer's Wanted Up-to-date market news, special markets, and market listings

Bottom Line A look at the business of writing

Ethics The issues that face writers today

Poet to Poet Strictly poetry

@ Deadline Industry and people news of interest to writers

WriteStuff Current book, tape, and product reviews

Dear Writer Answers to readers' questions

Your satisfaction is guaranteed!

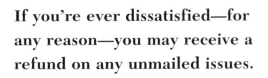

If you're ever dissatisfied—for any reason—you may receive a refund on any unmailed issues.

Since 1887, this highly respected magazine has helped writers at all levels improve their writing, get published, launch careers, and stay inspired.

The Writer covers every genre of writing including fiction, poetry, freelance articles, scripts, children's books, profiles, memoirs and more!

Mail this card today!

METROKIDS
See page 380 for full listing.
Description: For the Delaware Valley area, on parenting kids, ages 0-16.

MIAMI METRO
Micro Media Affiliates
2800 Biscayne Blvd., Suite 1100, Miami, FL 33137-4544. 305-755-9920.
E-mail: miamimetro@bellsouth.net. Web site: www.miamimetro.com. Monthly.
$14.97. Circ.: 40,000. Nancy Moore, Editor-in-Chief. **Description:** News and hot
topics on South Florida. **Nonfiction:** Features; 1,100-2,000 words. **Columns,
Departments:** 200-1,300 words, on news, profiles, and hot topics related to south
Florida. Short, bright items, 200-400 words. **Queries:** Preferred. **Payment:** On
acceptance. **Contact:** Felicia Levine, Executive Editor.

MICHIGAN LIVING
Automobile Club of Michigan
1 Auto Club Dr., Dearborn, MI 48126-4213. 248-816-9265.
E-mail: michliving@aol.com. Web site: www.aaamich.com. Ron Garbinski, Editor.
Description: Michigan topics, also area and Canadian tourist attractions and
recreational opportunities **Nonfiction:** Informative travel articles, 300-2,000
words; pays $55-$500. **Art:** Photos; pay varies. **Queries:** Preferred. **Payment:** On
publication.

MIDWEST LIVING
Meredith Corp.
1716 Locust St., Des Moines, IA 50309-3038. 515-284-2662.
E-mail: mwl@mdp.com. Web site: www.midwestliving.com. Bimonthly. $19.97/yr.
Circ.: 822,000. Dan Kaercher, Editor-in-Chief. **Description:** Lifestyle articles relat-
ing to any or all of the 12 midwest states. **Nonfiction:** Town, neighborhood, and per-
sonality profiles. Humorous essays occasionally used. Pay varies. **Rights:** All.
Payment: On acceptance.

MILESTONES
See page 561 for full listing.
Description: For seniors in the greater Philadelphia area.

MILWAUKEE MAGAZINE
417 E Chicago St., Milwaukee, WI 53202. 414-273-1101.
E-mail: john.fennell@qg.com. Web site: www.milwaukeemagazine.com. Monthly.
$3.00/$18.00. Circ.: 40,000. John Fennell, Editor. **Description:** Offers in-depth
reporting and analysis of issues affecting the Milwaukee metro area by providing service features, stories, and essays. **Nonfiction:** Must be specific to Milwaukee area,
solid research and reporting; 2,000-5,000 words; $500-$1,000. **Columns,
Departments:** Issue-oriented commentary; 900-1200 words; $300-$600. **Queries:**
Required. **E-Queries:** Yes. **Unsolicited mss:** Accepts. **Response:** Queries 6 weeks,

submission 6 weeks if unsolicited, SASE. **Freelance Content:** 50%. **Rights:** 1st. **Payment:** On publication.

MINNESOTA MONTHLY

10 S Fifth St., Suite 1000, Minneapolis, MN 55402. 612-371-5800. E-mail: phnettleton@mnmo.com. Web site: www.mnmo.com. Monthly. Circ.: 80,000. Pamela Hill Nettleton, Editor. **Description:** People, places, events, and issues in or about Minnesota. **Nonfiction:** To 2,000 words; $150-$2,000. **Queries:** Required. **Payment:** On acceptance.

MISSOURI LIFE

P.O. Box 421, Fayette, MO 65248. 660-248-3489. E-mail: info@missourilife.com. Web site: www.missourilife.com. Bimonthly. $4.50/$19.99. Circ.: 50,000. Danita Allen, Editor. **Description:** Explores Missouri and its diverse people and places, past and present. History, weekend getaways and day-trips, interesting people and events. **Nonfiction:** Regular features: Our Town, History, Roundups, People; 1,000-2,000 words; $.30/word. **Fillers:** Best of Missouri; to 300 words; $50. **Columns, Departments:** Missouri Artist, Made in Missouri, Historic Homes, Missouri Memory; 500 words. **Art:** Color slides, photos; $50-$150. **Queries:** Required. **E-Queries:** No. **Unsolicited mss:** Accepts. **Response:** 1 week queries, 6 months submissions, SASE. **Freelance Content:** 40%. **Payment:** On acceptance. **Contact:** Danita Allen.

MONTANA MAGAZINE

P.O. Box 5630, Helena, MT 59604. 406-443-2842. Web site: www.montanamagazine.com. Bimonthly. $4.95. Circ.: 40,000. Beverly R. Magley, Editor. **Description:** Full-color photography and articles reflecting the grandeur and personality of Montana. **Nonfiction:** Articles on Montana's culture, history, outdoor recreation, communities, and people. Contemporary issues, places and events, ecology and conservation; 1,500-2,000 words; $.15/word. **Art:** Slides, transparencies, no digital. **Queries:** Required. **E-Queries:** Yes. **Unsolicited mss:** Accepts. **Response:** 4 months, SASE. **Freelance Content:** 100%. **Rights:** One-time. **Payment:** On publication.

MPLS.ST. PAUL

220 S Sixth St., Suite 500, Minneapolis, MN 55402-4507. 612-339-7571. E-mail: edit@mspcommunications.com. Web site: www.mspmag.com. Monthly. $3.50. Circ.: 72,000. Brian E. Anderson, Editor. **Description:** Covers what is new, exciting, newsworthy in the Twin Cities. **Nonfiction:** Timely local issues; dining, arts, and entertainment; home decorating; profiles. **Columns, Departments:** City Limits (news/gossip); About Town (arts and entertainment sidebars). **Queries:** Preferred. **E-Queries:** Yes. **Unsolicited mss:** Accepts. **Response:** 6-8 weeks, SASE. **Payment:** On acceptance.

NEBRASKA HISTORY
See page 428 for full listing.
Description: Articles on the history of Nebraska and the Great Plains.

NEVADA
401 N Carson St., Suite 100, Carson City, NV 89701-4291. 775-687-5416.
E-mail: editor@nevadamagazine.com. Web site: www.nevadamagazine.com.
Bimonthly. Circ.: 80,000. David Moore, Editor. **Description:** Covers topics related
to Nevada such as travel, history, recreation, profiles, humor, and attractions.
Nonfiction: 500-1,800 words; pay varies. **Art:** Photos. **Payment:** On publication.

NEW HAMPSHIRE EDITIONS
150 Dow St., Manchester, NH 03101. 603-624-1442.
E-mail: editor@nh.com. Web site: www.nhmagazine.com. Monthly. $2/$20. Circ.:
21,000. Rick Broussard, Editor. **Description:** Covers people, places, issues, and
lifestyles of New Hampshire as revealed by the state's best writers, photographers,
and artists. **Nonfiction:** Lifestyle, business, and history articles with New Hampshire
angle, sources from all regions of the state; 400-2,000 words; $50-$200. **Art:** Prints,
slides, negatives, or digital; $25-$300. **Queries:** Preferred. **E-Queries:** Yes.
Unsolicited mss: Accepts. **Response:** 1 month, SASE. **Freelance Content:** 30%.
Rights: 1st serial and online reprint. **Payment:** On publication.

NEW JERSEY MONTHLY
55 Park Place, P.O. Box 920, Morristown, NJ 07963-0920. 973-539-8230.
E-mail: editor@njmonthly.com. Web site: www.njmonthly.com. Nancy Nusser,
Editor. **Description:** Publication covering events and news in New Jersey.
Nonfiction: Well-organized, well-written, thoughtful articles, profiles, and service
pieces on a topic that is well-grounded in New Jersey; 1,500-3,000 words; $750-
$2,500. **Columns, Departments:** Health, business, education, travel, sports, local
politics, arts, humor; $400-$700. **Tips:** Send query with clips to Christopher Hann,
Senior Editor. **Queries:** Preferred. **Payment:** On satisfactory completion of fact-
checking.

NEW JERSEY REPORTER
The Public Policy Center of New Jersey
36 W Lafayette St., Trenton, NJ 08608. 609-392-2003.
E-mail: njreporter@rcn.com. Web site: www.njreporter.org. Bimonthly. Circ.: 3,200.
Mark Magyar, Editor. **Description:** New Jersey politics and public affairs.
Nonfiction: In-depth articles; 1,000-4,000 words; $175-$800. **Queries:** Required.
Payment: On publication.

NEW MEXICO
Lew Wallace Bldg., 495 Old Santa Fe Trail, Santa Fe, NM 87501. 505-827-7447.
E-mail: enchantment@newmexico.org. Web site: www.hmmagazine.com. Monthly.
$3.95/$23.95. Circ.: 115,000. Emily Drabanski, Editor. **Description:** About

everything New Mexican (products, places, style, history, books, fashion, food, sports, recreation, photos). **Nonfiction:** Regional interest only; 2,000 words max.; $.30/word. **Fillers:** On museum exhibits, outdoor activities, and interesting people. **Art:** Slides, transparencies; pay varies. **Tips:** Avoid fiction, first-person accounts, political statements, cemeteries, subjects outside region. **Queries:** Required. **E-Queries:** No. **Unsolicited mss:** Accepts. **Response:** Queries 1-3 months, submissions 3-6 months, SASE. **Freelance Content:** 20%. **Rights:** 1st NA, all NA. **Payment:** On acceptance.

NEW MEXICO JOURNEY

3333 Fairview Rd., A-327, Costa Mesa, CA 92626. 714-885-2380.
Web site: www.aaa-newmexico.com. Bimonthly. Circ.: 80,000. Annette Winter, Editor. **Description:** For AAA members. Covers travel and people of New Mexico and surrounding states. **Nonfiction:** 1,000-2,000 words; $1/word. **Columns, Departments:** AutoNews, TravelNews; 75-200 words; $1/word. **Art:** 35mm. **Tips:** Seeks stories about off-beat and established destinations. **Queries:** Required. **E-Queries:** No. **Unsolicited mss:** Does not accept. **Response:** 6 weeks. **Freelance Content:** 80%. **Rights:** 1st NA. **Payment:** On acceptance.

NEW ORLEANS MAGAZINE

MC Media, 111 Veterans Blvd., Metairie, LA 70005. 504-832-3555.
E-mail: nom@nogp.com. Web site: www.neworleansmagazine.com. Monthly. $19.95/yr. Circ.: 37,700. Errol Laborde, Editor. **Description:** On New Orleans area people and issues. **Nonfiction:** Articles, 3-15 triple-spaced pages; pays $15-$500, extra for photos. **Art:** Photos. **Queries:** Preferred. **Payment:** On publication.

NEW YORK FAMILY

See page 381 for full listing.
Description: Articles on family life in New York City and general parenting topics.

NEW YORK SPIRIT

107 Sterling Place, Brooklyn, NY 11217. 718-638-3733.
E-mail: office@nyspirit.com. Web site: www.nyspirit.com. Bimonthly. Circ.: 50,000. Paul English, Editor. **Description:** On environmental issues, holistic health, political issues, culture/art, and general interest for readers in Manhattan. Interviews welcomed. **Nonfiction:** Articles, 4,000 words; pays $.10/word. **Queries:** Preferred. **Payment:** On acceptance.

NEWPORT LIFE

55 Memorial Blvd., Newport, RI 02840. 401-841-0200.
E-mail: info@newportlifemagazine.com. Web site: www.newportlifemagazine.com. Bimonthly. Circ.: 10,000. Lynne Tungett, Publisher/Editor. **Description:** On people, places, attractions of Newport County. **Nonfiction:** Articles, 500-2,500 words, general-interest, historical, profiles, international celebrities, and social and political issues. **Columns, Departments:** 200-750 words; sailing, dining, food and wine,

home and garden, arts, in Newport County. **Art:** Photos needed for all articles. **Queries:** Preferred. **Response:** SASE required.

NORTH DAKOTA HORIZONS

P.O. Box 2639, Bismarck, ND 58502. 701-222-0929.
E-mail: lyle_halvorson@gnda.com. Web site: www.ndhorizons.com. Quarterly. $5/$15. Circ.: 12,000. Lyle Halvorson, Editor. **Description:** Showcases North Dakota people, places, and events. **Nonfiction:** 1,000-3,000 words; $100-$300. **Art:** All formats; $10-$150/image. **Queries:** Preferred. **E-Queries:** Yes. **Unsolicited mss:** Accepts. **Response:** Queries/submissions up to 1 month, SASE. **Freelance Content:** 90%. **Rights:** One-time. **Payment:** On publication.

NORTH GEORGIA JOURNAL

P.O. Box 127, Roswell, GA 30077. 770-642-5569.
E-mail: info@georgiahistory.ws. Web site: www.georgiahistory.ws. Quarterly. $4.50/issue, $24/year. Circ.: 18,000. Olin Jackson, editor. **Description:** For travelers in northern Georgia, offering travel destinations, leisure lifestyles, and history. **Nonfiction:** Travel; lifestyles, history, and historic real estate; 1,500-3,000 words; $.08-$.15/word. **Columns, Departments:** 1,200 words; $.08-$.15/word. **Art:** Photographs; 35mm slides; $10/inside use, $150/cover. **Queries:** Required. **E-Queries:** Yes. **Unsolicited mss:** Accepts. **Response:** Queries 2 weeks, submissions 3-4 weeks, SASE required. **Freelance Content:** 65%. **Rights:** All. **Payment:** On publication.

NORTHEAST

Hartford Courant
285 Broad St., Hartford, CT 06115. 860-241-3700.
E-mail: northeast@courant.com. Weekly (Sunday only). Circ.: 316,000. Larry Bloom, Editor. **Description:** Sunday magazine for the major daily newspaper for Connecticut. **Nonfiction:** Articles spun off the news and compelling personal stories, 750-3,000 words, for Connecticut residents. Pays $250-$1,000. **Queries:** Preferred. **E-Queries:** No. **Unsolicited mss:** Accepts. **Response:** Queries/submissions 2-3 months, SASE. **Freelance Content:** 2%. **Rights:** One-time. **Payment:** On acceptance. **Contact:** Jane Bronfonan, Editorial Assistant.

NORTHEAST OUTDOORS

See page 578 for full listing.
Description: On camping and recreational vehicle (RV) touring in northeast U.S.

NOT BORN YESTERDAY

See page 561 for full listing.
Description: For Southern California seniors.

NOW & THEN

CASS/ETSU
P.O. Box 70556, Johnson City, TN 37614-1707. 423-439-5348.

E-mail: woodsidj@etsu.edu. Web site: www.cass.etsu.edu/n&t. 3x/year. $25. Circ.: 1,500. Jane Harris Woodside, Editor. **Description:** Each issue focuses on one aspect of life in Appalachian region (from Northern Mississippi to Southern New York). Previous themes: natural resources, fiction, rivers, museums, and language. **Fiction:** 1,500-3,000 words: must relate to theme of issue and Appalachian region. **Nonfiction:** Articles, interviews, essays, memoirs, book reviews; 1,000-2,500 words. **Poetry:** up to 5 poems. **Tips:** Topics can be contemporary or historical. **Queries:** Preferred.

OHIO
62 E Broad St., Columbus, OH 43215. 800-426-4624.
E-mail: editorial@ohiomagazine.com. Web site: Ohiomagazine.com. Monthly. Circ.: 90,000. Richard Osborne, Editorial Director. **Description:** On everything in Ohio—from people and places to food and entertainment. **Nonfiction:** On travel around Ohio with profiles of people, cities, towns, historic sites, tourist attractions, and little-known spots; 1,000-1,200 words. **Tips:** Seeking fresh stories with a decisively different Ohio angle. **Queries:** Preferred. **E-Queries:** Yes. **Unsolicited mss:** Accepts. **Response:** 6 weeks, SASE. **Freelance Content:** 25%. **Payment:** On acceptance.

OKLAHOMA TODAY
P.O. Box 53384, Oklahoma City, OK 73102. 405-521-2496.
E-mail: editorial@oklahomatoday.com. Web site: www.oklahomatoday.com. 7 issues/year. $3.95/issue, $16.95/year. Circ.: 43,000. Louisa McCune, Editor. **Description:** Explores the people, places, history, and culture of Oklahoma. **Nonfiction:** Travel, history, nature, personality profiles; 250-3,000 words; $25-$750. **Fillers:** $25-$50. **Columns, Departments:** $75 and up. **Art:** Must evoke a sense of place; color transparencies, slides, B&W prints; $50-$100/B&W, $50-$750/color. **Tips:** Query with biography and published clips. **Queries:** Preferred. **E-Queries:** Yes. **Unsolicited mss:** Accepts. **Response:** Queries 4 months, submissions 6 months, SASE. **Freelance Content:** 80%. **Rights:** First serial worldwide. **Payment:** On publication.

ORANGE COAST
3701 Birch St., #100, Newport Beach, CA 92660-2618. 949-862-1133.
E-mail: agrenda@orangecoastmagazine.com.
Web site: www.orangecoastmagazine.com. Monthly. $3.50/$9.98. Circ.: 50,000. Nancy Cheever, Editor. **Description:** Covers Orange County, California, for educated, sophisticated readers. **Nonfiction:** Local trends, people, and news stories; workplace and family issues; 1,500-3,000 words; $250-$700. **Columns, Departments:** Escape (weekend travel), $250; Short Cuts (local items, 200 words), $50-$100. **Queries:** Required. **E-Queries:** No. **Unsolicited mss:** Accepts. **Response:** 1-2 months. **Freelance Content:** 85%. **Rights:** FNASR; non-exclusive Web. **Payment:** On publication. **Contact:** Anastacia Grenda, Managing Editor.

OREGON COAST

4969 Highway 101, #2, Florence, OR 97439. 541-997-8401.
E-mail: judy@ohwy.com. Web site: www.ohwy.com. Circ.: 65,000. Stefani Blair, Stefanie Griesi, and Judy Fleagle, Editors. **Description:** Covers communities, businesses, people, events, activities, and the natural wonders that make up the Oregon coast. **Nonfiction:** First-person experiences, 500-1,500 words, with details in sidebars, with slides preferred. On travel, history, town/city profiles, outdoor activities, events, and nature. News releases, 200-500 words; $65-$250/features. **Art:** Some stand-alone photos (verticals); also 2 calendars/yr; slides and transparencies; $25-75, $325 (cover). **Queries:** Preferred. **E-Queries:** Yes. **Unsolicited mss:** Accepts. **Response:** Queries 3 months, submissions 2-3 months, SASE. **Freelance Content:** 60%. **Rights:** 1st NA, one-time photos. **Payment:** On publication.

THE OREGONIAN

1320 SW Broadway, Portland, OR 97201.
E-mail: op-ed@news.oregonian.com. Web site: www.oregonlive.com. Daily. Circ.: 360,000. **Description:** Newspaper featuring diverse articles and op-ed pieces on regional topics; to 650 words, pays $75-$100. **Queries:** Not necessary. **Unsolicited mss:** Accepts. **Rights:** All. **Payment:** On publication.

ORLANDO

ABARTA Media Group
225 South Westmonte D., #1100, Altamonte Springs, FL 32714. 407-767-8338.
Web site: www.orlandomag.com. James C. Clark, Editor. **Description:** Locally-based articles for residents of Central Florida. Covers news, personalities, health, fashion, and technology. **Tips:** Send clips. **Queries:** Preferred.

OUR STATE: DOWN HOME IN NORTH CAROLINA

P.O. Box 4552, Greensboro, NC 27404. 336-286-0600.
E-mail: editorial@ourstate.com. Monthly. $3.95/$21.95. Circ.: 80,000. Mary Ellis, Editor. **Description:** About North Carolina culture, travel, and folklore. **Fiction:** About North Carolina; 1,500 words; $125-$300. **Nonfiction:** Features on people, events, food, history, travel in North Carolina; 1,500 words; $125-$300. **Columns, Departments:** North Carolina memories (holidays, summer, family). **Art:** 35mm slides; call for editorial calendar; $75-$300. **Tips:** Most readers are over 50. **Queries:** Preferred. **E-Queries:** Yes. **Unsolicited mss:** Accepts. **Response:** Queries 4 weeks, submissions 12 weeks, SASE. **Freelance Content:** 30%. **Rights:** 1st NA. **Payment:** On publication.

PALM SPRINGS LIFE

Desert Publications, Inc.
303 N Indian Canyon Dr., Palm Springs, CA 92262. 760-325-2333.
E-mail: stewart@palmspringslife.com. Web site: www.palmspringslife.com. Monthly. $3.95/$38. Circ.: 20,000. Stewart Weiner, Editor. **Description:** Looks at upscale lifestyle of desert residents. Features celebrity profiles and articles on architecture,

fashion, desert ecology, art, interior design, and history. **Nonfiction:** 1,500-2,500 words; $250-$500. **Columns, Departments:** On ecology, people, humor, desert sports, politics; 750; $250-$300. **Queries:** Required. **E-Queries:** Yes. **Unsolicited mss:** Accepts. **Response:** Queries 1 month, submissions 2 months, SASE. **Freelance Content:** 80%. **Rights:** 1st NA, all. **Payment:** On publication.

PARENTS EXPRESS
See page 383 for full listing.
Description: For parents in southeastern Pennsylvania and southern New Jersey.

PENNSYLVANIA MAGAZINE
P.O. Box 755, Camp Hill, PA 17001. 717-697-4660.
E-mail: pamag@aol.com. Bimonthly. $3.50/issue, $19.97/year. Circ.: 30,000. Matthew Holliday, editor. **Description:** Profiles events, people, and history of Pennsylvania. **Nonfiction:** General-interest features; 1,000-2,500 words; $.10-$.12/word. **Columns, Departments:** 400-600 words; $.10-$.12/word. **Art:** To accompany articles; $20-$25/photo. **Tips:** No sports, poetry, hunting, or political. **Queries:** Preferred. **E-Queries:** Yes. **Unsolicited mss:** Accepts. **Response:** 4-6 weeks; SASE required. **Freelance Content:** 95%. **Rights:** One-time. **Payment:** On acceptance.

PHILADELPHIA
1818 Market St., Fl. 36, Philadelphia, PA 19103. 215-564-7700.
E-mail: duane@phillymag.com. Web site: www.phillymag.com. Monthly. Circ.: 138,000. Loren Feldman, Editor. **Description:** Covers events and topics in Philadelphia. **Nonfiction:** Articles for a sophisticated audience on the Philadelphia area; 1,000-5,000 words. **Queries:** Preferred. **Payment:** On acceptance. **Contact:** Duane Swierczynski, Senior Editor.

PHOENIX
4041 N Central Ave., Suite 530, Phoenix, AZ 85012. 602-234-0840.
E-mail: phxmag@citieswestpub.com. Monthly. $3.95. Circ.: 60,000. Kathy Khoury, Managing Editor. **Description:** Covers Phoenix metro area. **Nonfiction:** Issues relating to Phoenix and surrounding metro area. Service pieces (where to go, what to do) in the city; 50-2,000 words; pay varies. **Tips:** Think small; short, timely pieces and profiles are always needed. No personal essays please. Travel stories are staff written. **Queries:** Required. **E-Queries:** Yes. **Unsolicited mss:** Does not accept. **Response:** Queries 6 weeks, submissions 2 weeks, SASE. **Freelance Content:** 80%. **Rights:** 1st NA. **Payment:** On publication. **Contact:** Kathy Khoury.

PITTSBURGH MAGAZINE
WQED Pittsburgh
4802 Fifth Ave., Pittsburgh, PA 15213-2957.
E-mail: editor@wqed.org. Web site: www.wqed.org. Monthly. $3.50/issue, $17.95/yr. Circ.: 75,000. Chris Fletcher, Publisher. **Description:** Covers Pittsburgh and surrounding region. Examines issues and strives to encourage a better understanding of

the community. **Nonfiction:** News, features, service pieces, local celebrity profiles, regional lifestyles; must have a Pittsburgh region focus. 500-4,000 words. Pay negotiable. **Art:** Yes. **Tips:** News, business, service pieces needed. **Queries:** Required. **E-Queries:** No. **Unsolicited mss:** Does not accept. **Response:** 2 months, SASE. **Freelance Content:** 60%. **Rights:** FNASR. **Payment:** On publication. **Contact:** Michelle Pilecki, Executive Editor.

PITTSBURGH SENIOR NEWS
See page 561 for full listing.
Description: Topics of interest to older adults in the Pittsburgh area.

PORTLAND
578 Congress St., Portland, ME 04101. 207-775-4339.
E-mail: staff@portlandmagazine.com. Web site: www.portlandmagazine.com. Monthly. Circ.: 100,000. Colin Sargent, Editor. **Description:** Celebrates the Portland, Maine, region by providing profiles of businesses and people, columns about life on the waterfront, and features on arts, getaways, maritime history, geography, and cuisine. **Fiction:** Fiction, to 750 words. **Nonfiction:** Articles on local people, legends, culture, trends, etc. **Queries:** Required. **E-Queries:** Yes. **Unsolicited mss:** Accepts.

PRIME TIMES
See page 562 for full listing.
Description: For older adults on Long Island, N.Y.

PROVINCETOWN ARTS
650 Commercial St., Provincetown, MA 02657. 508-487-3167.
E-mail: cbusa@mediaone.net. Annual. Circ.: 8,000. Christopher Busa, Editor. **Description:** Focuses on Cape Cod's artists, performers, and writers; covers the cultural life of the nation's oldest continuous art colony. **Fiction:** 500-5,000 words; $50-$150. **Nonfiction:** Essays, interviews, journals, performance pieces, profiles, reviews, and visual features; 500-5,000 words; $50-$150. **Poetry:** Up to 3 poems; $25-$100. **Art:** Photographs, illustrations. **Queries:** Not necessary. **E-Queries:** No. **Unsolicited mss:** Accepts. **Response:** Queries 3 weeks, submissions 4 months, SASE. **Freelance Content:** 90%. **Payment:** On publication.

RANCH & COVE
P.O. Box 676130, Rancho Santa Fe, CA 92067-6130. 760-942-2330.
E-mail: edit@ranchcove.com. Web site: www.ranchcove.com. Monthly. $25/yr. Circ.: 20,000. Collette Stefanko, Editor. **Description:** For affluent residents of Rancho Santa Fe, La Jolla, and San Diego's coastal North country, on regional lifestyle. **Nonfiction:** Upscale fashion, travel, golf, shopping, wine and dining, autos, antiques, entertainment, spas, gala events, etc; 500-1,500 words; $.10/word. **Columns, Departments:** 300-500 words. **Art:** Digital (Mac); EPS or TIF; $25-$75. **Queries:** Preferred. **E-Queries:** Yes. **Response:** 2-4 weeks, SASE. **Freelance Content:** 75%. **Rights:** one-time. **Payment:** On publication.

RANGE
See page 360 for full listing.
Description: Devoted to issues that threaten the West, its people, lifestyles, rangelands, and wildlife.

RECREATION NEWS
7339 D Hanover Parkway, Greenbelt, MD 20770. 301-474-4600.
E-mail: editor@recreationnews.com. Web site: www.recreationnews.com. Monthly. $12/yr. Circ.: 100,000. Francis X. Orphe, Editor. **Description:** Official publication of ESM Association of the Capital Region. Covers regional recreational activities, historical sites, fishing, parks, video reviews, food column, weekend getaways, day-off trips, etc. **Nonfiction:** On recreation and travel around the mid-Atlantic region for government and private sector workers in the Washington, DC, area. Conversational tone, lean and brisk; 900-2,200 words; $50 reprints, $300 cover features. **Queries:** Preferred. **Unsolicited mss:** Accepts. **Freelance Content:** 85%. **Payment:** On publication.

RHODE ISLAND MONTHLY
280 Kinsley Ave., Providence, RI 02903. 401-277-8200.
E-mail: rimonthly.com. Web site: www.rimonthly.com. Monthly. Circ.: 41,000. Paula M. Bodah, Editor. **Description:** Features on Rhode Island and southeastern Massachusetts—places, customs, people, and events. **Nonfiction:** Features, from investigative reporting and in-depth profiles to service pieces and visual stories, seasonal material; 1,000-2,000 words; $250-$1,000. **Fillers:** On Rhode Island places, customs, people, events, products and services, restaurants and food; 150-500 words; $50-$150. **Queries:** Required. **Payment:** On acceptance.

RUNNER TRIATHLETE NEWS
See page 582 for full listing.
Description: Covers running, cycling, triathlons, and duathlons in a 5-state area: Texas, Louisiana, Arkansas, Oklahoma, New Mexico.

RV JOURNAL
See page 619 for full listing.
Description: Features travel destinations for RV travelers in California, Nevada, Arizona, Oregon, Utah, and Washington.

SACRAMENTO MAGAZINE
706 56th St., Suite 210, Sacramento, CA 95819. 916-452-6200.
E-mail: krista@sacmag.com. Web site: www.sacmag.com. Monthly. Circ.: 29,000. Krista Minard, Editor. **Description:** Interesting and unusual people, places, and behind-the-scenes news items. **Nonfiction:** Articles, 1,000-1,500 words, on destinations within a 6-hour drive of Sacramento. Features, 2,500 words, on broad range of topics related to the region; pay varies. **Columns, Departments:** City Lights, 400 words; $50-$300. **Queries:** Required. **Payment:** On publication.

SAN FRANCISCO MAGAZINE

San Francisco Focus L.L.P.

243 Vallejo St., San Francisco, CA 94111-1511. 415-398-2800.

E-mail: letters@sanfran.com. Web site: www.sanfran.com. Monthly. $19. Circ.: 135,000. Bruce Kelley, Editor-in-Chief. **Description:** Exploring and celebrating San Francisco and bay area. Insightful analysis, investigative reporting, and eye-catching coverage of local food, culture, design, travel, and politics. **Nonfiction:** Service features, profiles, investigative pieces, 2,500-3,000 words. News items, 250-800 words, from business to arts to politics. Pay varies. **Queries:** Preferred. **Unsolicited mss:** Accepts. **Payment:** On acceptance. **Contact:** Lisa Trottier.

SAVANNAH

P.O. Box 1088, Savannah, GA 31402. 912-652-0293.

E-mail: lindaw@savannahnow.com. Web site: www.savannahmagazine.com. Bimonthly. $3.95/$15.95. Circ.: 11,000. Linda Wittish, Editor. **Description:** On lifestyles of residents from coastal Georgia and South Carolina low country. **Nonfiction:** On local people, travel destinations (in a day's drive), local history, restaurants, business; 500-2,500 words; $100-$350. **Columns, Departments:** Travel Business; 1,000-1,500 words; $200-$300. **Queries:** Preferred. **E-Queries:** Yes. **Unsolicited mss:** Accepts. **Response:** Queries 2-3 weeks, submissions 3-4 weeks, SASE. **Freelance Content:** 100%. **Rights:** 1st NA. **Payment:** On acceptance.

SEATTLE

423 Third Ave. West, Seattle, WA 98119. 206-284-1750.

E-mail: editor@seattlemag.com. Web site: www.seattlemag.com. 10x/year. $3.95/issue. Circ.: 40,000. Rachel Hart, Editor. **Description:** To help people live better in Seattle. **Nonfiction:** City, local issues, home, lifestyle articles on greater Seattle area; 50-2,500 words; $50-$1,200. **Art:** Film, slides; $50-$1,200. **Queries:** Required. **E-Queries:** Yes. **Unsolicited mss:** Accepts. **Response:** 3 months, SASE. **Freelance Content:** 70%. **Rights:** Exclusive 60 days. **Payment:** 30 days after publication.

SEATTLE WEEKLY

Village Voice Media, Inc.

1008 Western, Suite 300, Seattle, WA 98104. 206-623-0500.

E-mail: info@seattleweekly.com. Web site: www.seattleweekly.com. Audrey Van Buskirk, Editor. **Description:** Newsmagazine offering investigative journalism, political commentary, arts/culture, and other articles and features on the community life and news of the Seattle metro region. **Nonfiction:** Articles, 600-4,000 words. **Queries:** Preferred. **Response:** 2-6 weeks, SASE. **Payment:** On publication. **Contact:** Editorial Assistant.

SEATTLE'S CHILD

See page 384 for full listing.

Description: Investigative reports and consumer tips on issues affecting families in the Puget Sound region.

SENIOR CONNECTION

See page 563 for full listing.
Description: Publication for senior citizens in west central Florida and Tampa.

SENIOR CONNECTION

See page 563 for full listing.
Description: For Catholic seniors with connections to northern Illinois parishes.

SENIOR TIMES

See page 563 for full listing.
Description: For older adults, in Ohio.

SENIOR TIMES

See page 563 for full listing.
Description: For senior citizens in Washington State.

SILENT SPORTS

See page 585 for full listing.
Description: On bicycling, cross country skiing, running, canoeing, hiking, backpacking, and other "silent" sports. Must have regional (upper Midwest) focus.

SOUTH CAROLINA HISTORICAL MAGAZINE

See page 430 for full listing.
Description: Scholarly articles on South Carolina history.

SOUTH CAROLINA WILDLIFE

See page 587 for full listing.
Description: Published by DNR for readers interested in the outdoors.

SOUTHERN EXPOSURE

Institute for Southern Studies
P.O. Box 531, Durham, NC 27702-0531. 919-419-8311.
E-mail: info@i4south.org. Web site: www.southernstudies.org. Quarterly. $24. Circ.: 5,000. Chris Kromm, Editor. **Description:** Forum on "Southern politics and culture." **Nonfiction:** Essays, investigative journalism, oral histories, and personal narratives; 500-3,600 words; $25-$250. **Queries:** Preferred. **Payment:** On publication.

SOUTHERN OREGON HERITAGE TODAY

See page 430 for full listing.
Description: On the history of the southern Oregon region.

SPIRIT PLUS

See page 563 for full listing.
Description: For active adults aged 45-65, in New Jersey.

SPRINGFIELD
P.O. Box 4749, Springfield, MO 65808. 417-831-1600.
E-mail: springfieldmagazine@gabrielmail.com. Monthly. $16.99/yr. **Description:** About local people, places, events, and issues. **Nonfiction:** Articles must have a clear link to Springfield, Missouri. Historical/nostalgic pieces and book reviews. **Queries:** Preferred. **E-Queries:** Yes. **Unsolicited mss:** Accepts. **Response:** 2-3 weeks. **Freelance Content:** 85%. **Rights:** 1st serial. **Payment:** On publication.

SWEAT
See page 393 for full listing.
Description: Covers amateur sports and outdoor activities with an Arizona angle.

TALLAHASSEE
Rowland Publishing, Inc.
1932 Miccosokee Rd., P.O. Box 1837, Tallahassee, FL 32302-1837. 850-878-0554.
E-mail: jbettinger@rowlandinc.com. Web site: www.rowlandinc.com. Bimonthly. $2.95/$16.95. Circ.: 17,300. Julie Strauss Bettinger, Editor. **Description:** Lifestyle magazine celebrating life in Florida's Capital Region. **Nonfiction:** Feature stories on local personalities and current events. Creative nonfiction style of writing preferred; 1,500-3,000 words; pay varies. **Columns, Departments:** Work Day, The Sporting Life, Humor; 850 words; pay varies. **Queries:** Not necessary. **E-Queries:** Yes. **Unsolicited mss:** Accepts. **Response:** 4-6 weeks, SASE. **Freelance Content:** 15%. **Payment:** On publication.

TEXAS GOLFER
See page 589 for full listing.
Description: Provides golf information for Texas golfers.

TEXAS HIGHWAYS
P.O. Box 141009, Austin, TX 78714-1009. 512-486-5858.
E-mail: editors@texashighways,com. Web site: www.texashighways.com. Monthly. Circ.: 300,000. Jack Lowry, Editor. **Description:** Articles and features on Texas history, travel, and scenery. **Nonfiction:** Travel, historical, cultural, scenic features on Texas; 200-1,800 words; $.35-$.50/word. **Art:** Photos, $60-$550. **Queries:** Required.

TEXAS JOURNEY
3333 S Fairview Rd., Costa Mesa, CA 92626. 714-885-2380.
Bimonthly. Circ.: 580,000. Annette Winter, Editor. **Description:** Publication for AAA Texas members. Features travel, people, and auto news in Texas and surrounding states. **Nonfiction:** Cultural travel, consumer travel, the outdoors, personality profiles; 1,000-2,000 words; $1/word. **Columns, Departments:** Travel News, Auto News; 75-200 words. **Art:** 35mm. **Tips:** Prefers published writers. Seeks stories about off-beat and established destinations. **Queries:** Required. **E-Queries:** No. **Unsolicited mss:** Does not accept. **Response:** 6 weeks; SASE required. **Freelance Content:** 80%. **Rights:** FNASR. **Payment:** On acceptance. **Contact:** Nina Elder.

TEXAS MONTHLY

P.O. Box 1569, Austin, TX 78767-1569. 512-320-6900.
Web site: www.texasmonthly.com. Evan Smith, Editor. **Description:** Covers issues of public concern in Texas. **Nonfiction:** Features on art, architecture, food, education, business, politics, etc. Articles must appeal to an educated Texas audience and have well-researched reporting on issues (offbeat and previously unreported topics, or with novel approach to familiar topics); 2,500-5,000 words; pay varies. **Queries:** Preferred. **E-Queries:** No. **Unsolicited mss:** Accepts. **Response:** 6 to 8 weeks. **Payment:** On acceptance.

TEXAS PARKS & WILDLIFE

See page 361 for full listing.
Description: Promotes conservation and enjoyment of Texas wildlife and outdoors.

TOLEDO AREA PARENT NEWS

See page 385 for full listing.
Description: For parents in Northwest Ohio and Southern Michigan.

TORONTO LIFE

Key Media, Ltd.
59 Front St. E, Fl. 3, Toronto, Ontario M5E 1B3 Canada. 416-364-3333.
E-mail: editorial@torontolife.com. Web site: www.torontolife.com. Monthly. $34.
Circ.: 94,000. John Macfarlane, Editor. **Description:** Covers the urban scene.
Nonfiction: Articles on Toronto; 1,500-4,500 words. **Queries:** Required. **Payment:** On acceptance.

TUCSON LIFESTYLE

Old Pueblo Press
7000 E Tanque Verde, Tucson, AZ 85715. 520-721-2929.
E-mail: tucsonlife@aol.com. Monthly. $2.95. Circ.: 33,000. Sue Giles, Editor-In-Chief. **Description:** Covers subjects on Southern Arizona. **Nonfiction:** On businesses, lifestyles, the arts, homes, fashion, and travel; 1,000-4,000 words; $125-$500.
Tips: Base your article on interviews and research. No travel pieces or anecdotes as articles. **Queries:** Required. **E-Queries:** Yes. **Unsolicited mss:** Accepts.
Response: 2 weeks, SASE. **Freelance Content:** 80%. **Rights:** 1st NA. **Payment:** On acceptance. **Contact:** Scott Barker, Executive Editor.

VANCOUVER

555 W 12th Ave., Suite 300, East Tower, Vancouver,
British Columbia V5Z 4L4 Canada. 604-877-7732.
E-mail: mail@vancouvermagazine.com. Web site: vancouvermagazine.com. 10x/year.
$3.50. Circ.: 65,000. Nick Rockel, Editor. **Description:** City magazine with a focus on urban life (restaurants, fashion, shopping, and nightlife). **Nonfiction:** Seeking articles, varying lengths, including front-of-book pieces; 400-4,000 words; $.50/word.
Columns, Departments: Sports, civics, social affairs, business, politics, media;

1,500-2,000 words; $.50/word. **Art:** Slides, prints; negotiable. **Queries:** Preferred.
E-Queries: Yes. **Unsolicited mss:** Accepts. **Response:** 2 weeks minimum.
Freelance Content: 70%. **Rights:** FNASR. **Payment:** On acceptance.

VERMONT LIFE
6 Baldwin St., Montpelier, VT 05602. 802-828-3241.
Web site: www.vtlife.com. Quarterly. $3.95/$14.95. Circ.: 85,000. Tom Slayton,
Editor. **Description:** Explores and celebrates Vermont today by providing quality
photographs and articles. **Nonfiction:** Articles about people, places, history, and
issues; 200-2,000 words; $100-$700. **Art:** Slides, transparencies; no prints; $75-$500.
Tips: No "my recent trip to Vermont" or old jokes, rural homilies. Submit articles that
shed light on and accurately reflect Vermont experience today. **Queries:** Preferred.
E-Queries: Yes. **Unsolicited mss:** Accepts. **Response:** 2-4 weeks, SASE.
Freelance Content: 90%. **Rights:** 1st NA. **Payment:** On acceptance.

VERMONT MAGAZINE
North Country Publishing, L.R.
31 John Graham Ct., Suite A, P.O. Box 800, Middlebury, VT 05753. 802-388-8480.
E-mail: vtmag@sover.net. Web site: www.vermontmagazine.com. Bimonthly. Sally
West Johnson, Editor. **Description:** On all aspects of contemporary Vermont (its
people, culture, politics, and special places). **Nonfiction:** Articles; pays $150-$600.
Queries: Preferred. **Payment:** On publication.

VIRGINIA BUSINESS
Media General Operations, Inc.
P.O. Box 85333, Richmond, VA 23293-0001. 804-649-6999.
E-mail: jbacon@va-business.com. Web site: www.virginiabusiness.com. James Bacon,
Publisher/Editor-in-Chief. **Description:** Covers the business scene in Virginia.
Nonfiction: Articles, 1,000-2,500 words; pay varies. **Queries:** Required. **Payment:**
On publication.

VIRGINIA WILDLIFE
See page 361 for full listing.
Description: On fishing, hunting, outdoors and wildlife in Virginia.

WASHINGTON FLYER
Metropolitan Washington Airports Authority
1707 L Street NW, Suite 800, Washington, DC 20036. 202-331-9393.
E-mail: readers@themagazinegroup.com. Web site: www.fly2dc.com. Bimonthly.
Michael McCarthy, Editor-in-Chief. **Description:** For upscale Washington residents
and visitors. Dining, entertainment, events in the D.C. area. **Nonfiction:** Briefs and
features, 350-1,500 words; pays $150-$800. **Art:** Color photos. **Tips:** Prefers queries
via e-mail. **Queries:** Preferred. **E-Queries:** Yes. **Payment:** On publication.

THE WASHINGTONIAN
1828 L St. NW, Suite 200, Washington, DC 20036. 202-296-3600.
E-mail: editorial@washingtonian.com. Web site: www.washingtonian.com. Monthly.
$2.95/$24. Circ.: 160,000. John Limpert, Editor. **Description:** Covers Washington,
D.C., topics. **Queries:** Preferred. **E-Queries:** Yes. **Unsolicited mss:** Accepts.
Response: 2-8 weeks, SASE. **Freelance Content:** 50%. **Rights:** FNASR.
Payment: On publication.

THE WESTERN HISTORICAL QUARTERLY
See page 431 for full listing.
Description: Covers the American West—the United States, Canada, and Mexico.

WESTERN SPORTSMAN
See page 293 for full listing.
Description: On hunting and fishing in western Canada.

WINDY CITY SPORTS
See page 591 for full listing.
Description: Covers amateur sports in Chicago and the surrounding area.

WISCONSIN TRAILS
Trails Media Group, Inc.
P.O. Box 317, 1131 Mills St., Black Earth, WI 53515. 608-767-8000.
E-mail: kbast@wistrails.com. Web site: www.wistrails.com. Bimonthly. $4.95/$24.95.
Circ.: 50,000. Kate Bast, Editor. **Description:** On Wisconsin people, history, nature,
adventure, lifestyle, arts, theater, sports, recreation, and business. **Fiction:** $.25/word.
Nonfiction: 200-3,000 words, $.25/word. About the joys and experiences of living in
the Badger state (history, wildlife, natural history, environment, travel, profiles, culture). **Fillers:** Tasteful Wisconsin-oriented humor, crossword puzzles, cartoons, 50-
300 words, $.25/word. **Columns, Departments:** My WI (essays); Discover (events);
State Talk (short, quirky news); Profile (noteworthy people); Gone for the Weekend
(travel destination), 50-1,000 words, $.25/word. **Art:** Color transparencies, slides,
illustrations (8 x 11 inches largest); pay varies. **Tips:** Readers mostly in their 40s and
50s, active, love history and travel, well educated, with children and grandchildren.
Authors new to the magazine must submit resume, letter of introduction, and 3 relevant published clips; nonreturnable. Writers guidelines available, send SASE.
Queries: Required. **E-Queries:** Yes. **Unsolicited mss:** Accepts. **Response:** 3-5
months, SASE. **Freelance Content:** 40%. **Rights:** 1st NA, one-time. **Payment:** On
publication.

WISCONSIN WEST
2905 Seymour Rd., Eau Claire, WI 54703. 715-835-3800.
E-mail: mci@charter.net. Bimonthly. $2.50. Circ.: 5,000. **Description:** Covers
Western Wisconsin. **Nonfiction:** Restaurants, weekend leisure activities and getaways, famous people of western Wisconsin, history, short humor; up to 3,000 words;

$75-$150. **Art:** Slides, photos; $100-$150. **Queries:** Preferred. **E-Queries:** Yes. **Unsolicited mss:** Accepts. **Freelance Content:** 100%. **Rights:** 1st, 2nd. **Payment:** On publication.

YANKEE
Yankee Publishing, Inc.
P.O. Box 520, Dublin, NH 03444. 603-563-8111.
E-mail: queries@yankeepub.com. Web site: www.newengland.com. 10x/year. $2.99/$18.99. Circ.: 600,000. Judson D. Hale, Sr., Editor-in-Chief. **Description:** On travel and life in New England. **Nonfiction:** Narrative journalism, home and garden, travel, food, etc; 150-5,000 words; $50-$5,000. **Queries:** Preferred. **E-Queries:** Yes. **Unsolicited mss:** Accepts. **Response:** 8 weeks, SASE. **Freelance Content:** 80%. **Rights:** FNASR. **Payment:** On acceptance.

YANKEE MAGAZINE'S TRAVEL GUIDE TO NEW ENGLAND
See page 621 for full listing.
Description: Provides travel information for residents and tourists of New England.

YESTERYEAR
See page 447 for full listing.
Description: Publishes articles on antiques and collectibles for readers in Wisconsin, Illinois, Iowa, Minnesota, and surrounding states.

RELIGION

AMERICA
106 W 56th St., New York, NY 10019-3803. 212-581-4640.
E-mail: articles@americamagazine.org. Web site: www.americapress.org. Weekly. $2.75/issue. Circ.: 40,000. Thomas J. Reese, Editor. **Description:** For thinking Catholics and those interested in what Catholics are thinking. Emphasis on social justice and religious/ethical perspectives on current issues facing the church and the world. **Nonfiction:** Features on contemporary issues from a religious and ethical perspective; 1,500-2,000 words. **Poetry:** Serious poetry in contemporary prose idiom, free or formal verse, 20-35 lines. Submit 2-3 poems with SASE. Pays $2-$3/line. **Art:** Send portfolio. **Tips:** No sermons or speeches. Address educated audience who are not experts in your topic. **Queries:** Not necessary. **Unsolicited mss:** Accepts. **Response:** Queries 1 week, submission 3 weeks, SASE required. **Freelance Content:** 50%. **Rights:** All. **Payment:** On acceptance.

AMIT
Americans for Israel and Torah
817 Broadway, New York, NY 10003-4761. 212-477-4720.
E-mail: amitmag@aol.com. Web site: www.amitchildren.org. Quarterly. $35/year (with membership). Circ.: 39,000. Debra Stahl, Managing Editor. **Description:**

Published by a nonprofit, Modern Orthodox Jewish organization which sponsors a network of schools helping 15,000 underprivileged Israeli youths. **Nonfiction:** Articles of interest to Jewish women. Topics include education, the Middle East, Israel, history, holidays, travel, and culture; 2,500 words; $250-$500. **Columns, Departments:** Subject matter includes Israel, Zionism, terrorism, parenting, and the Torah. Also, interviews with AMIT students in Israel, book reviews, and features on innovators in education, art, and music; 700 words; $100. **Tips:** Avoid politics and religion. Focus on innovations in education, and on Amit students in Israel. **Queries:** Preferred. **E-Queries:** Yes. **Unsolicited mss:** Accepts. **Response:** 2 weeks, SASE required. **Freelance Content:** 50%. **Payment:** On acceptance.

ANGLICAN JOURNAL

600 Jarvis St., Toronto, Ontario M4Y 2J6 Canada. 416-924-9192.
E-mail: editor@national.anglican.ca. Web site: www.anglicanjournal.com. 10x/year. $10/year. Circ.: 245,000. Vianney (Sam) Carriere, Editor. **Description:** Newspaper of the Anglican Church of Canada. Provides news and features of the Anglican Church, articles on social and ethical issues, and human-interest pieces. **Nonfiction:** up to 1,000 words; $.23/word. **Queries:** Required. **E-Queries:** Yes. **Unsolicited mss:** Does not accept. **Response:** Varies. **Freelance Content:** 15%. **Rights:** 1st. **Payment:** On publication.

ANNALS OF ST. ANNE DE BEAUPRÉ

Redemptorist Fathers
P.O. Box 1000, St. Anne de Beaupré, Quebec G0A 3C0 Canada. 418-827-4538. Monthly. Circ.: 45,000. Father Bernard Mercier, CSs.R., Editor. **Description:** Articles, 500-1,500 words, that promote devotion to St. Anne and Christian family values. Pays $.03-$.04/word. **Tips:** Prefers work that is inspirational, educational, objective, and uplifting. No poetry. **Response:** 1 month to queries. **Freelance Content:** 80%. **Rights:** 1st NA. **Payment:** On acceptance. **Contact:** Father Roch Achard, Managing Editor.

THE B'NAI B'RITH IJM

B'nai B'rith International
1640 Rhode Island Ave. NW, Washington, DC 20036. 202-857-6646.
E-mail: ijm@bnaibrith.org. Web site: www.bnaibrith.org. 4x/year. Circ.: 160,000. Eric Rozenman, Executive Editor. **Description:** Published by B'nai B'rith, with general-interest stories. **Nonfiction:** Profiles, stories of interest to Jewish communities in U.S. and abroad, politics, arts, Middle East; 1,500-2,000 words; $450-$700. **Queries:** Preferred.

THE BANNER

CRC Publications
2850 Kalamazoo Ave. SE, Grand Rapids, MI 49560-0001. 616-224-0732.
E-mail: editorial@thebanner.org. Web site: www.thebanner.org. Biweekly. Circ.: 32,000. John D. Suk, Editor. **Description:** For members of Christian Reformed

Church in North America. **Fiction:** to 2,500 words. **Nonfiction:** to 1,800 words; pays $125-$200. **Poetry:** to 50 lines; $40. **Queries:** Preferred. **Payment:** On acceptance.

BIBLE ADVOCATE
P.O. Box 33677, Denver, CO 80233. 303-452-7973.
E-mail: bibleadvocate@cog7.org. Web site: www.cog7.org/BA. 10 issues/year. Circ.: 13,500. Calvin Burrell, editor. **Description:** Helps Christians understand and obey the Bible. **Nonfiction:** On Bible doctrine, current social and religious issues, every-day-living Bible topics, textual or Biblical book studies, prophecy and personal experience; 1500 words; $25-$55. **Poetry:** Free verse, blank verse, and traditional; 5-20 lines; $20. **Fillers:** Facts, inspirational pieces, anecdotes; 100-400 words; $20. **Columns, Departments:** Viewpoint, opinion pieces; 650 words. **Art:** Mac-compatible TIF or JPG files, 300 dpi; $10-$35/inside use, $25-$50/cover. **Tips:** No articles on Christmas or Easter. Theme list available. **Queries:** Not necessary. **E-Queries:** Yes. **Unsolicited mss:** Accepts. **Response:** 4-8 weeks; SASE required. **Freelance Content:** 10-20%. **Rights:** First, reprint, electronic. **Payment:** On publication.

BOOK & CULTURE: A CHRISTIAN REVIEW
See page 633 for full listing.
Description: Looks at Christian books, culture, and religion.

BREAD FOR GOD'S CHILDREN
P.O. Box 1017, Arcadia, FL 34265-1017.
8x/yr. Circ.: 10,000. Judith M. Gibbs, Editor. **Description:** Christian family magazine with Bible study, stories, teen pages, parent news, ideas, and more. **Nonfiction:** Articles or craft ideas based on Christian principles or activities; how to implement Christian ways into daily living; 600-800 words; $20-$30. **Tips:** Stories must be from a child's point of view, with story itself getting message across; no preaching or moralizing, no tag endings. No stories with speaking animals, occult, fantasy, or romance. **Queries:** Not necessary. **Unsolicited mss:** Accepts. **Response:** Submissions 1-6 months, SASE. **Freelance Content:** 20%. **Rights:** 1st. **Payment:** On publication.

BRIGADE LEADER
CSB Ministries,
Box 150, Wheaton, IL 60189. 630-582-0630.
E-mail: dchristensen@csbministries.org. Web site: www.csbministries.org. Quarterly. $10. Circ.: 6,000. Deborah Christensen, Managing Editor. **Description:** An evangelical Christian publication, for adult youth leaders in Christian Service Brigade Ministries (Christian Service Brigade, Girls Alive, and Brigade Air). **Nonfiction:** Leadership and inspirational articles for program leaders; 500-1,000 words; $.05-$.10/word. **Tips:** Most articles assigned; limited freelance content. Query with clips. **Queries:** Required. **E-Queries:** No. **Unsolicited mss:** Does not accept. **Response:** SASE required. **Payment:** On publication.

CAMPUS LIFE

See page 593 for full listing.
Description: Advice on teen issues and stories about teens changed by God.

CATECHIST

330 Progress Rd., Dayton, OH 45449. 937-847-5900.
Web site: www.catechist.com. Patricia Fischer, Editor. **Description:** For Catholic teachers, coordinators, and administrators in religious education programs. **Nonfiction:** Informational and how-to articles; 1,200-1,500 words; $25-$100. **Payment:** On publication.

CATHOLIC DIGEST

185 Willow St., P.O. Box 6001, Mystic, CT 06355. 651-962-6739.
E-mail: rreece@bayardpubs.com. Web site: www.catholicdigest.org. Monthly. $2.25/issue, $19.95/year. Circ.: 400,000. Richard J. Reece, Editor. **Description:** For adult Roman Catholic readers, with general-interest topics on family life, religion, science, health, good works, and relationships. **Nonfiction:** Humor, profiles, how-to, personal experiences; 1,000-3,000 words; $100-$400. **Fillers:** Up to 500 words; $2/line. **Columns, Departments:** True incidents about good works, parish life, conversion to Catholicism; 100-500 words; $2/line. **Tips:** Interested in articles about the family and career concerns of baby boomers who have a stake in being Catholic. Illustrate topic with a series of true-life, interconnected vignettes. **E-Queries:** No. **Response:** 6-8 weeks; SASE required. **Freelance Content:** 30%. **Rights:** One-time. **Payment:** On acceptance.

CATHOLIC NEAR EAST

See page 364 for full description.
Description: Profiles of cultures, histories, religions, and social issues of the peoples of Eastern Europe, India, the Middle East, and Northeast Africa.

CATHOLIC PARENT

See page 375 for full description.
Description: Parenting issues for Catholics; emphasis on values and family life.

THE CHRISTIAN CENTURY

104 S Michigan Ave., Suite 700, Chicago, IL 60603. 312-263-7510.
E-mail: main@christiancentury.org. Web site: www.christiancentury.org. Biweekly. Circ.: 30,000. John M. Buchanan, Editor. **Description:** Shows how Christian faith calls people to a profound engagement with the world and how people of faith address issues of poverty, international relations, and popular culture. **Nonfiction:** Religious angle on political/social issues, international affairs, culture, the arts, and challenges in everyday lives; 1,500-3,000 words; $75-200. **Poetry:** Free verse, traditional, haiku. No sentimental or didactic poems; 20 lines; $50. **Art:** Photos, $25-$100. **Tips:** Many readers are ministers or teachers of religion. **Queries:** Preferred.

E-Queries: Yes. **Response:** Queries 1 week, submissions 2 months, SASE required. **Freelance Content:** 90%. **Rights:** one-time. **Payment:** On publication.

CHRISTIAN EDUCATION COUNSELOR

General Council of the Assemblies of God
1445 Boonville Ave., Springfield, MO 65802-1894. 417-862-2781.
E-mail: cecounselor@ag.org. Web site: www.ag.org/cecounselor. Bimonthly. Sylvia Lee, Editor. **Description:** On teaching and administrating Christian education in the local church, for local Sunday school and Christian school personnel. **Nonfiction:** Articles, 600-800 words; pays $.05-$.10/word. **Payment:** On acceptance.

CHRISTIAN HOME & SCHOOL

3350 E Paris Ave. SE, Grand Rapids, MI 49512. 616-957-1070 x239.
E-mail: rogers@csionline.org. Web site: www.csionline.org/chs. Bimonthly. Circ.: 69,000. Gordon L. Bordewyk, Executive Editor. **Description:** For parents in Canada and U.S. who send their children to Christian schools and are concerned about challenges facing families today. Articles pay from $125-$200. **Queries:** Preferred. **Payment:** On publication.

CHRISTIAN PARENTING TODAY

See page 376 for full listing.
Description: Serves the needs of today's families in a positive and practical format.

CHRISTIAN SINGLE

See page 477 for full listing.
Description: For single adults on leisure activities, single parenting, and life from a Christian perspective.

CHRISTIAN SOCIAL ACTION

100 Maryland Ave. NE, Washington, DC 20002. 202-488-5600.
E-mail: ealsgaard@umc-gbcs.org. Web site: www.umc-gbcs.org. Bimonthly. Circ.: 50,000. Gretchen Hakola, Editor. **Description:** For United Methodist clergy and lay people interested in the role and involvement of the church in social issues. **Nonfiction:** Stories that educate, analyze, and motivate people to Christian social action on justice and advocacy issues; 1,500-2,000 words; $125-$175. **Art:** Hard copy, electronic. **Queries:** Preferred. **E-Queries:** Yes. **Unsolicited mss:** Does not accept. **Response:** Queries 4-6 weeks, SASE required. **Freelance Content:** 30%. **Rights:** 1st. **Payment:** On publication.

CHRISTIANITY TODAY

465 Gundersen Dr., Carol Stream, IL 60188. 630-260-6200.
E-mail: cteditor@christianitytoday.com. Web site: www.christianitytoday.com. 14x/year. $3.95/issue. Circ.: 150,000. David Neff, Editor. **Description:** Evangelical Christian publication covering Christian doctrines, current events, news, trends, and issues. **Nonfiction:** Doctrinal social issues and interpretive essays, 1,500-3,000

words, from evangelical Protestant perspective. Pays $200-$500. **Tips:** Seeking Internet-related stories with human interest. **Queries:** Preferred. **E-Queries:** Yes. **Unsolicited mss:** Accepts. **Response:** 3 months, SASE required. **Freelance Content:** 80%. **Rights:** One-time. **Payment:** On acceptance. **Contact:** Mark Galli.

CHURCH EDUCATOR
See page 343 for full listing.
Description: Resource for mainline Protestant Christian educators.

CLUB CONNECTION
See page 463 for full listing.
Description: Full-color publication for Missionettes ages 6-12.

CLUBHOUSE
See page 463 for full listing.
Description: Offers Christian stories, poems, puzzles, and cartoons for ages 9-12.

CLUBHOUSE JR.
See page 463 for full listing.
Description: Inspires, entertains, and teaches Christian values to kids ages 4-8.

COLUMBIA
Knights of Columbus
1 Columbus Plaza, New Haven, CT 06510. 203-772-2130.
E-mail: tim.hickey@kofc-supreme.com. Web site: www.kofc.org. Monthly. $6/year. Circ.: 1,600,000. Tim S. Hickey, Editor. **Description:** Published by the Knights of Columbus, the world's largest Catholic family fraternal service organization. Articles on current events, societal trends, parenting and family life, finances, and Catholic practice and teachings. **Nonfiction:** Articles on topics of interest to members, their families, and the Catholic layman. Topics include current events, religion, education, art, etc; 500-1,500 words; to $600. **Tips:** Free sample copy with guidelines available. Send request to address above. **Queries:** Required. **E-Queries:** Yes. **Response:** Queries 2 weeks, submissions 2 weeks, SASE required. **Freelance Content:** 80%. **Payment:** On acceptance.

COMMENTARY
165 E 56th St., New York, NY 10022. 212-751-4000.
E-mail: mail@commentarymagazine.com.
Web site: www.commentarymagazine.com. Neal Kozodoy, Editor. **Description:** Fiction, of literary quality, on contemporary social or Jewish issues, from 5,000-7,000 words. Articles, 5,000-7,000 words, on contemporary issues, Jewish affairs, social sciences, religious thought, and culture. Serious fiction; book reviews. **Payment:** On publication.

COMMONWEAL

475 Riverside Dr., Room 405, New York, NY 10115. 212-662-4200.
E-mail: commonweal@msn.com. Web site: commonwealmagazine.org. 22x/year. $3.
Circ.: 20,000. Margaret O'Brien Steinfels, Editor. **Description:** Review of public affairs, religion, literature, and the arts, published by Catholic lay people. **Nonfiction:** On political, religious, social, and literary subjects; 1,000-3,000 words; $100. **Poetry:** Submit 5 poems max. (Oct.-May), serious, witty; $.75/line. **Columns, Departments:** Brief newsy facts, behind the headlines, reflective pieces; 750-1,000 words; $75. **Tips:** Focus on religion, politics, culture; how they intertwine. No simultaneous submissions. **Queries:** Not necessary. **E-Queries:** Yes. **Unsolicited mss:** Accepts. **Response:** Queries 1 month, submissions 6 weeks, SASE required. **Freelance Content:** 20%. **Rights:** All. **Payment:** On publication.

THE COVENANT COMPANION

5101 N Francisco Ave., Chicago, IL 60625-3611. 773-784-3000.
E-mail: communication@covoffice.org. Web site: www.covchurch.org. Monthly. $19.95. Circ.: 18,000. Donald L. Meyer, Editor. **Description:** Publication of Evangelical Covenant Church. Discusses issues of faith, spirituality, social justice, local ministry, and the life of the church. **Nonfiction:** Biographical profiles, local church ministries, and interviews with authors; 1,200-1,800 words; $35-$100. **Tips:** No "rants" about the culture or political agendas. Prefers human-interest or articles on practical spirituality. **Queries:** Not necessary. **E-Queries:** Yes. **Unsolicited mss:** Accepts. **Response:** Queries 4 weeks, submissions 6 weeks, SASE required. **Freelance Content:** 40%. **Rights:** 1st NA. **Payment:** On publication.

CRUSADER

See page 644 for full listing.
Description: Christian-oriented magazine for boys, ages 9-14, especially to members of Calvinist Cadet Corps.

DAILY MEDITATION

P.O. Box 2710, San Antonio, TX 78299. 210-735-5247.
Semi-annual. $16/year. Circ.: 761. Emilia Devno, Editor. **Description:** Offers inspirational, nonsectarian religious articles that show the way to self-improvement and greater spiritual growth. **Nonfiction:** 300-1,600 words; pays $.02/word. **Poetry:** Up to 350 words; $.14/line. **Tips:** No fiction, handwritten material, meditations, photographs, or dated material. **Queries:** Not necessary. **E-Queries:** No. **Unsolicited mss:** Accepts. **Response:** SASE required. **Rights:** FNASR. **Payment:** On acceptance.

DECISION

Billy Graham Evangelistic Association
1300 Harmon Pl., P.O. Box 779, Minneapolis, MN 55440-0779.
E-mail: submissions@bgea.org. Web site: www.decisionmag.org. 12x/year. $12/yr. Circ.: 1,300,000. Kersten Beckstrom, Editor. **Description:** Offers religious inspirational,

personal experience, and how-to articles. **Nonfiction:** Personal conversion testimonies, personal experience articles on how God has intervened in a person's daily life; how Scripture was applied to solve a problem; 400-1,500 words; $30-$260. **Poetry:** Free verse and rhymed; 4-16 lines; $.60/word. **Fillers:** Anecdotes; 300-500 words; $25-$75. **Columns, Departments:** Where are they now? (Stories of people who have become Christians through Billy Graham ministries); 500-600 words; $85. **Tips:** Submit articles that have some connection with a Billy Graham or Franklin Graham ministry. **Queries:** Not necessary. **E-Queries:** Yes. **Unsolicited mss:** Accepts. **Response:** Queries 3 months, submissions 10 months, SASE required. **Freelance Content:** 10%. **Rights:** 1st. **Payment:** On publication. **Contact:** Bob Paulson.

DISCIPLESHIP JOURNAL
Box 35004, Colorado Springs, CO 80935. 719-531-3514. E-mail: sue.kline@navpress.com. Web site: www.disciplejournal.com. Bimonthly. $4.95/$23.97. Circ.: 130,000. Sue Kline, Editor. **Description:** Articles on Christian growth and practical application of scripture. **Nonfiction:** Teaching based on Scripture (e.g., what Bible says on forgiveness); how-tos (to deepen devotional life; to reach out in community); 1,000-3,000 words; $.25/word. **Columns, Departments:** On the Home Front (Q&A on family issues); Getting into God's word (devotional or Bible study); DJ+ (up to 500 words, on practical ministry, leading small groups, evangelism, etc.); 750-950 words; $.25/word. **Tips:** First-time writers encouraged to write non-theme articles, on any aspect of living as a disciple of Christ. Seeking articles encouraging involvement in world missions, personal evangelism, and Christian leadership. No testimonies, devotionals, book reviews, or news. **Queries:** Required. **E-Queries:** Yes. **Unsolicited mss:** Does not accept. **Response:** 6 weeks, SASE. **Freelance Content:** 80%. **Rights:** 1st, electronic, anthology. **Payment:** On acceptance.

DISCOVERIES
See page 464 for full listing.
Description: Full-color story paper for 3rd and 4th graders connecting Evangelical Sunday School learning with daily growth.

DISCOVERY TRAILS
See page 465 for full listing.
Description: Christian stories, activities, poems, and puzzles for kids ages 10-11.

DOVETAIL
See page 377 for full listing.
Description: Non-denominational resource for dual-faith couples and families.

ENRICHMENT
1445 N Boonville Ave., Springfield, MO 65802-1894. 417-862-2781. E-mail: enrichment@ag.org. Quarterly. $22/yr. Circ.: 33,000. Gary Allen, Editor.

Description: Resources to assist Pentecostal ministers in effective ministry. **Nonfiction:** Articles and features on wide range of ministry-related topics; 1,200-2,100 words; to $.10/word. **Queries:** Not necessary. **E-Queries:** Yes. **Unsolicited mss:** Accepts. **Response:** 1 week, SASE required. **Freelance Content:** less than 10%. **Rights:** 1st NA. **Payment:** On publication. **Contact:** Rich Knoth.

EVANGEL
Light and Life Communications
P.O. Box 535002, Indianapolis, IN 46253-5002. 317-244-3660.
Quarterly. $1.99/issue. Circ.: 12,000. Julie Innes, Editor. **Description:** Devotional in nature, seeks to increase reader's understanding of the nature and character of God and life lived under lordship of Christ. **Fiction:** Solving problems through faith; max. 1,200 words; $.04/word. **Nonfiction:** Free Methodist. Personal experience articles; short devotional items, 300-500 words (1,200 max.); $.04/word. **Poetry:** Devotional or nature; 8-16 lines. **Fillers:** Crypto puzzles, cartoons; $.10-$.20. **Queries:** Not necessary. **E-Queries:** No. **Unsolicited mss:** Accepts. **Response:** Queries 2 weeks, submissions 6-8 weeks, SASE required. **Freelance Content:** 100%. **Rights:** One-time. **Payment:** On publication.

EVANGELICAL BEACON
901 E 78th St., Minneapolis, MN 55420. 952-854-1300.
Web site: www.efc.org/beacon.html. Diane McDougall, Editor. **Description:** Published by Evangelical Free Church. **Nonfiction:** Articles that fit editorial themes; 500-2,000 words; $.20/word. **Payment:** On publication.

FAITH & FAMILY
See page 378 for full listing.
Description: How-to articles and interviews of interest to Catholic families.

FAITH TODAY
Evangelical Fellowship of Canada
P.O. Box 3745 Markham Industrial Station
Markham, Ontario L3R OY4 Canada. 905-479-5885.
E-mail: ft@efc-canada.com. Web site: www.faithtoday.ca. Bimonthly. $18. Circ.: 18,000. Gail Reid, Managing Editor. **Description:** Thoughts, trends, issues, and events from a Canadian evangelical Christian perspective. **Nonfiction:** News stories and features on social trends and church trends in Canada. Also, short, quirky items, with photo, on Christianity in Canada; 400-3,000 words; $.20-$.30/word. **Tips:** No devotionals or generic Christian-living material. **Queries:** Required. **E-Queries:** Yes. **Unsolicited mss:** Does not accept. **Response:** 3 weeks, SASE required. **Freelance Content:** 75%. **Rights:** FNASR. **Payment:** On publication.

THE FAMILY DIGEST
P.O. Box 40137, Fort Wayne, IN 46804.
Bimonthly. Circ.: 150,000. Corine B. Erlandson, Manuscript Editor. **Description:**

Dedicated to the joy and fulfillment of Catholic family and parish life. Especially looking for upbeat articles which affirm the simple ways in which the Catholic faith is expressed in daily life. **Nonfiction:** Seeking articles on family life, parish life, spiritual life, Saint's lives, prayer, how-to, and seasonal (seasonal articles should be submitted 7 months prior to issue date); 650-1,250 words; $40-$60. **Fillers:** Funny and unusual stories drawn from personal, real-life experience; 10-100 words; $25. **Tips:** Writing must have a Catholic theme. Prefers original articles, but will consider reprints of pieces that have appeared in non-competing markets. **Queries:** Not necessary. **E-Queries:** No. **Unsolicited mss:** Accepts. **Response:** 4-8 wks, SASE required. **Freelance Content:** 90%. **Rights:** 1st NA. **Payment:** On acceptance.

FELLOWSHIP
P.O. Box 271, Nyack, NY 10960-0271. 845-358-4601.
E-mail: fellowship@forusa.org. Web site: www.forusa.org. Bimonthly. $4.50/issue. Circ.: 9,000. Richard Deats, Editor. **Description:** Magazine of peace, justice, and nonviolence. Published by the Fellowship of Reconciliation, an interfaith, pacifist organization. **Nonfiction:** Articles for a just and peaceful world community; 750-2500 words. **Art:** B&W photo-essays on active nonviolence, peace and justice, opposition to war. **Queries:** Not necessary. **Unsolicited mss:** Accepts. **Freelance Content:** 25%. **Payment:** In copies.

FIRST THINGS
Institute on Religion & Public Life
156 Fifth Ave., #400, New York, NY 10010-7002. 212-627-1985.
E-mail: ft@firstthings.com. Web site: www.firstthings.com. 10x/year. Circ.: 32,000. James Nuechterlein, Editor. **Description:** General social commentary for academics, clergy, and general-educated readership on the role of religion in public life. **Nonfiction:** Essays and features; 1,500-6,000 words; $300-$800. **Poetry:** 4-40 lines. **Queries:** Required. **Payment:** On publication.

FOURSQUARE WORLD ADVANCE
1910 W Sunset Blvd., Suite 200, P.O. Box 26902, Los Angeles, CA 90026.
E-mail: comm@foursquare.org. Web site: www.foursquare.org. Ronald D. Williams, Editor. **Description:** Published by the International Church of the Foursquare Gospel. Religious fiction and nonfiction, 1,000-1,200 words, and religious poetry. Pays $75. Guidelines available. **Payment:** On publication.

THE FRIEND
See page 645 for full listing.
Description: Nonfiction literary journal for children up to 12 years of age.

FRIENDS JOURNAL
1216 Arch St., 2A, Philadelphia, PA 19107. 215-563-5629.
E-mail: info@friendsjournal.org. Web site: www.friendsjournal.org. Monthly. $29/yr. Circ.: 8,000. Susan Corson-Finnerty, Publisher/Executive Editor. **Description:**

Reflects Quaker life today by offering commentary on social issues, spiritual reflection, experiential articles, Quaker history, and world affairs. **Nonfiction:** With awareness of Friend's concerns and ways; fresh, nonacademic style; use language that clearly includes both sexes; up to 2,500 words. **Poetry:** Up to 25 lines. **Fillers:** Quaker-related humor, games, puzzles. **Tips:** Articles with positive approach to problems and spiritual seeking preferred. **Queries:** Not necessary. **E-Queries:** Yes. **Unsolicited mss:** Accepts. **Response:** Queries 3 week, submissions 4 months, SASE. **Freelance Content:** 70%. **Payment:** None.

THE GEM

P.O. Box 926, Findlay, OH 45839-0926.
Rachel Foreman, Editor. **Description:** Magazine offering true experiences of God's help, healed relationships, and maturing in faith; for adolescents to senior citizens. **Fiction:** 1,000-1,600 words; $15. **Nonfiction:** 300-1,600 words, $15. **Fillers:** $5-$10.

GOSPEL TODAY

Horizon Concepts, Inc.
761 Old Hickory Blvd., Suite 205, Brentwood, TN 37027-4519. 615-376-5656.
E-mail: gospeltodaymag@aol.com. Web site: www.gospeltoday.com. 8x/year. $3/$20. Circ.: 50,000. Teresa Hairston, Publisher/Editor. **Description:** "America's leading gospel lifestyle magazine," aimed at African-American Christians. **Nonfiction:** Human-interest stories on Christian personalities, events, and testimonials. Book reviews welcome; 1,500-2,000 words; $150-$250. **Columns, Departments:** $50-$75. **Tips:** No opinions, testimonials, or poetry. **Queries:** Required. **E-Queries:** Yes. **Unsolicited mss:** Does not accept. **Response:** Queries 6 weeks, SASE required. **Freelance Content:** 60%. **Rights:** All. **Payment:** On publication.

GROUP

Group Publishing, Inc.
P.O. Box 481, Loveland, CO 80539. 970-669-3836.
E-mail: greditor@grouppublishing.com.
Web site: www.groupmag.com www.youthministry.com. $29.95. Circ.: 55,000. Rick Lawrence, Editor. **Description:** Interdenominational Youth Ministry magazine for leaders of Christian youth. Provides ideas, practical help, inspiration, and training. **Nonfiction:** 500-2,000 words, $125-$225. **Columns, Departments:** Try this One (short ideas for groups: games, fundraisers, Bible study); Hands on Help (tips for leaders). **Tips:** Use real-life examples, personal experience. Include practical tips, self-quizzes, checklists. Use Scripture. For guidelines and copy of magazine, send $2 with 9 x 12 SASE. **Queries:** Not necessary. **Unsolicited mss:** Accepts. **Response:** 6-8 weeks, SASE required. **Freelance Content:** 70%. **Rights:** All. **Payment:** On publication.

GUIDE

Review & Herald Publishing Association
55 W Oak Ridge Dr., Hagerstown, MD 21740. 301-393-4038.

E-mail: guide@rpha.org. Web site: www.guidemagazine.org. Weekly (52/year). $42.95/year. Circ.: 33,000. Randy Fishell, Editor. **Description:** Christian publication for young people, ages 10-14. **Nonfiction:** Adventure, personal growth, Christian humor, inspiration, biography, nature; with spiritual emphasis; 800-1,200 words. **Tips:** Set forth a clearly evident Christian principle without being preachy. **Queries:** Not necessary. **Unsolicited mss:** Accepts. **Response:** 4-6 weeks, SASE required. **Freelance Content:** 95%. **Rights:** 1st, or one-time reprint. **Payment:** On acceptance.

GUIDEPOSTS
16 E 34th St., New York, NY 10016. 212-251-8100.
Web site: www.gp4k.com. Monthly. $12.97/year. Circ.: 3,200,000. Edward Grinnan, Editor. **Description:** First-person inspirational magazine about people overcoming challenges through faith. **Nonfiction:** First-person true stories of people who face challenges, fears, illnesses through faith; 500 words and up; $100-$400. **Fillers:** Spiritual quotes; $25. **Columns, Departments:** What Prayer Can Do (power of prayer); Pass it on (people helping people); His Mysterious Ways (more than coincidence); 50-500 words; $25-$100. **Tips:** Don't tell an entire life story; pick your specific "take-away" message. **E-Queries:** No. **Unsolicited mss:** Accepts. **Response:** Queries and submissions 3 months; SASE required. **Freelance Content:** 75%. **Rights:** All. **Payment:** On publication.

GUIDEPOSTS FOR TEENS
See page 595 for full listing.
Description: Interfaith publication for teens offering inspirational true stories.

HADASSAH
Women's Zionist Organization of America
50 W 58th St., New York, NY 10019-2505. 212-355-7900.
E-mail: zshluker@aol.com. Web site: www.hadassah.org. Monthly. $25/yr. Circ.: 309,000. Zelda Shluker, Senior Editor. **Description:** For Jewish Americans. **Queries:** Preferred.

JEWISH CURRENTS
22 E 17th St., #601, New York, NY 10003. 212-924-5740.
6x/year. $30. Circ.: 2,100. **Description:** Articles, reviews, fiction, and poetry on Jewish subjects. Seeks to present the Jewish point of view on an issue. **Fiction:** Jewish angle, humor sought; 2,500. **Nonfiction:** Jewish history, politics, culture, Yiddish language and literature (in English); 2,500. **Poetry:** Jewish focus. **Tips:** Reader are secular, politically liberal. **Queries:** Not necessary. **E-Queries:** No. **Unsolicited mss:** Accepts. **Response:** Queries/submissions 1 month, SASE. **Payment:** In copies.

THE JEWISH HOMEMAKER
391 Troy Ave., Brooklyn, NY 11213-5322. 718-771-0100.
E-mail: homemaker@homemaker.org. Web site: www.homemaker.org. Quarterly.

$11.97. Circ.: 11,000. Avraham M. Goldstein, Editor. **Description:** For a traditional/Orthodox Jewish audience. **Nonfiction:** Articles, 1,200-2,000 words; pay varies. **Queries:** Preferred. **Payment:** On publication.

JOURNAL OF CHRISTIAN NURSING
Nurses Christian Fellowship
P.O. Box 7895, Madison, WI 53707-7895. 608-274-4823.
E-mail: jcn.me@ivcf.org. Web site: www.ncf-jcn.org. Quarterly. $22.95. Circ.: 9,000.
Judy Shelly, Editor. **Description:** Practical, biblically-based articles to help nurses grow spiritually, meet patient's spiritual needs, and face ethical dilemmas. **Nonfiction:** Articles should help readers view nursing practice through the eyes of faith: spiritual care, ethics, values, healing and wholeness, psychology and religion, personal and professional growth, etc. Priority to nurse authors; work by others considered; 8-12 pages; $25-$80. **Poetry:** 1 page or less; $25. **Tips:** Avoid academic style. **Queries:** Not necessary. **E-Queries:** Yes. **Unsolicited mss:** Accepts. **Response:** Queries 2-3 weeks, submissions 1-2 month, SASE. **Rights:** 1st time, some reprint. **Payment:** On acceptance.

JOYFUL WOMAN
See page 626 for full listing.
Description: Encourages Christian women, of all ages, in every aspect of their lives.

LEADERSHIP
Christianity Today
465 Gundersen Dr., Carol Stream, IL 60188. 630-260-6200.
E-mail: ljeditor@leadershipjournal.net. Web site: www.leadershipjournal.net.
Quarterly. $24.95/year. Circ.: 65,000. Marshall Shelley, Editor. **Description:** Provides first-person accounts of real-life experiences in the ministry for church leaders. **Nonfiction:** First-person stories of life in ministry; situation faced, solutions found. Articles must offer practical help (how-to format) for problems church leaders face; 2,000 words; $.15/word. **Tips:** Avoid essays expounding, editorials arguing, or homilies explaining. **Queries:** Preferred. **E-Queries:** Yes. **Unsolicited mss:** Accepts. **Response:** Queries 3 weeks, submissions 6 weeks, SASE. **Freelance Content:** 30%. **Payment:** On acceptance.

LIBERTY
12501 Old Columbia Pike, Silver Spring, MD 20904-1608. 301-680-6690.
E-mail: steeli@nad.adventist.org. Web site: www.liberty magazine.org. Bimonthly. $6.95/issue. Circ.: 200,000. Lincoln Steed, Editor. **Description:** Focuses on religious freedom and church-state relations. Readers are legislators at every level, judges, lawyers, and other leaders. **Nonfiction:** Articles on religious freedom and 1st amendment rights; 1,000-2,500 words; $250 and up. **Tips:** Submit resume and clips. **Queries:** Preferred. **E-Queries:** Yes. **Unsolicited mss:** Does not accept. **Response:** Queries 1-3 months, submissions 30 days, SASE. **Freelance Content:** 95%. **Rights:** 1st NA. **Payment:** On acceptance.

LIFEWISE
See page 560 for full listing.
Description: Christian publication for older adults.

LIGHT AND LIFE
P.O. Box 535002, Indianapolis, IN 46253-5002. 317-2443660.
E-mail: llmauthors@fmcna.org. Bimonthly. $16/year. Circ.: 18,000. Doug Newton, Editor. **Description:** Social and cultural analysis from evangelical perspective. **Fiction:** 800-2,000 words. **Nonfiction:** Thoughtful articles about practical Christian living; 800-2,000 words. **Queries:** Not necessary. **E-Queries:** Yes. **Unsolicited mss:** Accepts. **Response:** Queries/submissions 6-8 weeks, SASE. **Rights:** 1st NA. **Payment:** On publication.

LIGUORIAN
One Liguori Dr, Liguori, MO 63057. 636-464-2500.
E-mail: aweinert@liguori.org. Web site: www.liguori.org. 10x/year. Circ.: 230,000. Fr. Allan Weinert, Editor. **Description:** Faithful to the charisma of St. Alphonsus, seeks to help readers develop a personal call to holiness. **Fiction:** Short stories with Catholic content; 1700-1900 words; $.12/word. **Nonfiction:** On Catholic Christian values in modern life; 1700-1900 words; $.12/word. **Queries:** Preferred. **E-Queries:** Yes. **Unsolicited mss:** Accepts. **Response:** Queries 1 week, submissions 8 weeks, SASE. **Freelance Content:** 20-30%. **Payment:** On acceptance.

LILITH
See page 369 for full listing.
Description: Showcases Jewish women writers, educators, and artists.

THE LIVING LIGHT
U.S. Catholic Conference of Bishops
Dept. of Ed., Caldwell 345, Catholic University of America
Washington, DC 20064. 202-319-6660.
E-mail: bridoyle@aol.com. Quarterly. $39.95. Circ.: 5,000. Berard Marthaler, Editor. **Description:** Catechetical educational journal sponsored by the U.S. Catholic Conference of Bishops. **Nonfiction:** Theoretical and practical articles, 1,500-4,000 words, on religious education, catechesis, and pastoral ministry. **Queries:** Preferred. **E-Queries:** No. **Unsolicited mss:** Does not accept. **Payment:** On publication.

LIVING WITH TEENAGERS
See page 380 for full listing.
Description: Educates Christian parents on how to best deal with typical issues faced by teens.

THE LOOKOUT
Standard Publishing
8121 Hamilton Ave., Cincinnati, OH 45231. 513-931-4050.

E-mail: lookout@standardpub.com. Web site: www.standardpub.com. Weekly. $23.50/year. Circ.: 100,000. Shawn McMullen, Editor. **Description:** Focuses on spiritual growth, family issues, people overcoming problems, and applying Christian faith to current issues. **Nonfiction:** 500-1,800 words; $.05-$.12/word. **Queries:** Preferred. **E-Queries:** Yes. **Unsolicited mss:** Accepts. **Response:** 6 weeks for queries, 10 weeks for submissions; SASE required. **Rights:** First or reprint. **Payment:** On acceptance.

THE LUTHERAN

8765 W Higgins Rd., Chicago, IL 60631-4183. 773-380-2540. E-mail: lutheran@elca.org. Web site: www.thelutheran.org. Monthly. Circ.: 600,000. David L. Miller, Editor. **Description:** Christian ideology, personal religious experiences, social and ethical issues, family life, church, and community of Evangelical Lutheran Church in America. **Nonfiction:** Articles on spirituality and Christian living; describing the unique life, service, challenges and problems of ELCA congregations; describing the life and work of the ELCA and of its institutions, colleges, and seminaries; 400-1,400 words; $75-$600. **Columns, Departments:** My View; opinions on a current societal event or issue in the life of this church; up to 400 words. **Art:** To accompany articles. **Queries:** Required. **E-Queries:** Yes. **Response:** 1 month. **Rights:** One-time. **Payment:** On acceptance.

MARRIAGE PARTNERSHIP

Christianity Today
465 Gundersen Dr., Carol Stream, IL 60188. 630-260-6200. E-mail: mp@marriagepartnership.com. Web site: www.marriagepartnership.com. Quarterly. $19.95/year. Circ.: 50,000. Caryn Rivadeneira, Managing Editor. **Description:** Offers realistic guidance and ideas for Christian married couples. **Nonfiction:** Related to marriage for men and women who wish to fortify their relationships; 1,000-2,000; $.15/word. **Fillers:** humor welcomed; 1200 words. **Queries:** Required. **E-Queries:** Yes. **Unsolicited mss:** Does not accept. **Response:** Queries 8 weeks, SASE. **Freelance Content:** 25%. **Rights:** 1st. **Payment:** On acceptance.

MARYKNOLL MAGAZINE

Catholic Foreign Mission Society of America
P.O. Box 311, Maryknoll, NY 10545-0311. 914-941-7590. E-mail: mkweb@maryknoll.org. Web site: www.maryknoll.org. 11x/year. $10/year. Circ.: 600,000. Frank Maurovich, Editor. **Description:** Published by the Maryknoll Fathers and Brothers. Christian-oriented publication focusing on articles concerning the work of missioners overseas. **Nonfiction:** Articles relating to missions or missioners overseas; 1,500-2,000 words; $150. **Art:** Prints or slides; $50. **Queries:** Not necessary. **E-Queries:** Yes. **Unsolicited mss:** Accepts. **Response:** SASE. **Freelance Content:** 25%. **Payment:** On publication.

MATURE LIVING

See page 560 for full listing.

Description: Focuses on the personal and spiritual needs of senior adults.

MATURE YEARS

See page 561 for full listing.

Description: Provides seniors with Christian resources to assist them with the specific problems and opportunities of aging.

THE MENNONITE

1700 S Main St., Goshen, IN 46526-4794. 574-535-6051. E-mail: editor@themennonite.org. Web site: www.themennonite.org. Twice monthly. $1.50. Circ.: 15,000. Everett Thomas, Editor. **Description:** For members of the Mennonite Church USA. **Nonfiction:** Stories, faith perspectives emphasizing Christian theme; 1,400 words; $.07/word. **Poetry:** 2 pages or less; $50-$75/poem. **Art:** Electronic preferred; $35-$50. **Queries:** Not necessary. **E-Queries:** Yes. **Unsolicited mss:** Accepts. **Response:** 2 weeks, SASE. **Freelance Content:** 20%. **Rights:** One-time and web. **Payment:** On publication. **Contact:** Everett Thomas.

MESSENGER OF THE SACRED HEART

661 Greenwood Ave., Toronto, Ontario M4J 4B3 Canada. 416-466-1195. Monthly. Circ.: 15,000. F. J. Power, S. J., Editor. **Description:** For American and Canadian Catholics. **Fiction:** Short stories; about 1,500 words; $.06/word and up. **Nonfiction:** Articles; about 1,500 words; $.06/word and up. **Payment:** On acceptance.

MIDSTREAM

See page 338 for full listing.

Description: Zionist publication with content on political U.S. and Israel culture, literature, book reviews, religion, and poetry.

MINISTRY & LITURGY

160 E Virginia St., #290, San Jose, CA 95112. 408-286-8505. Web site: www.rpinet.com/ml. Nick Wagner, Editor. **Description:** Practical, imaginative how-to help for Roman Catholic liturgy planners. **Queries:** Required.

THE MIRACULOUS MEDAL

See page 683 for full listing.

Description: Religious literary journal focusing on the Catholic Church.

MOMENT

See page 370 for full listing.

Description: On Jewish culture, politics, and religion.

MOODY
Moody Bible Institute
820 N LaSalle Blvd., Chicago, IL 60610. 312-329-2164.
E-mail: moodyedit@moody.edu. Web site: www.moody.edu. Bimonthly. Circ.: 100,000. Andrew Scheer, Managing Editor. **Description:** Articles on the Evangelical Christian experience in the home, community, and workplace. **Nonfiction:** Anecdotal articles; 1,200-2,000 word; $.15-$.20/word. **Queries:** Required. **Unsolicited mss:** Does not accept. **Payment:** On acceptance.

MY FRIEND
See page 469 for full listing.
Description: Provides families with information on aspects of the Catholic Faith.

NEW WORLD OUTLOOK
The United Methodist Church
475 Riverside Dr., Rm. 1476, New York, NY 10115-0122. 212-870-3765.
E-mail: nwo@gbgm-umc.org. Web site: http://gbgm-umc.org/nwo. Christie R. House, Editor. **Description:** On United Methodist missions and Methodist-related programs and ministries. Focus on national, global, and women's and children's issues, and on men and youth in missions. **Nonfiction:** Articles, 500-2,000 words, illustrated with color photos. **Queries:** Preferred. **Payment:** On publication.

OBLATES
9480 N De Mazenod Dr., Belleville, IL 62223-1160. 618-398-4848.
Web site: www.snows.org. Bimonthly. Membership in Missionary Association. Circ.: 450,000. Christine Portell, Editor. **Description:** Published by the Missionary Association of Mary Immaculate. **Nonfiction:** Articles, to 500 words, that inspire, uplift, and motivate through positive Christian values in everyday life; $150. **Poetry:** Perceptive, inspirational verse. Avoid obscure imagery, allusions, irreverent humor. Make rhyme and rhythm flow; 12 lines max.; $50. **Tips:** Try first-person approach. No preachy, psychological, theological, or spiritual journey pieces. Christian slant or Gospel message should be apparent, but subtle. **Queries:** Not necessary. **E-Queries:** No. **Unsolicited mss:** Accepts. **Response:** 4-6 weeks, SASE required. **Freelance Content:** 15%. **Rights:** FNASR. **Payment:** On acceptance. **Contact:** Mary Mohrman.

ON THE LINE
See page 470 for full listing.
Description: Magazine for youth, ages 9-14, that reinforces Christian values.

OTHER SIDE
2221 NE 164th St. Suite 1112, North Miami Beach, FL 33160. 215-849-2178.
E-mail: questions@theotherside.com. Web site: www.theotherside.com. Bimonthly. Circ.: 14,000. Dee Dee Risher, Doug Davidson, Coeditors. **Description:** Independent, ecumenical, progressive Christian magazine devoted to issues of social

justice, Christian spirituality, and the creative arts. **Fiction:** That deepens readers' encounter with mystery of God and the mystery of ourselves; 500-5,000 words; $75-$250. **Nonfiction:** On contemporary social, political, economic, or racial issues in the U.S. or abroad; 500-4,000 words (most under 2,000 words); $20-$350. **Poetry:** Submit up to 3 poems; to 50 lines; $15. **Payment:** On acceptance.

OUR SUNDAY VISITOR
200 Noll Plaza, Huntington, IN 46750.
E-mail: oursunvis@osv.com. Web site: www.osv.com. Weekly. $2/$61. Circ.: 66,000. Gerald Korson, Editor. **Description:** Reports on national and international news for Catholics, from a sound Catholic perspective. **Tips:** Query by mail or e-mail. No phone calls. **Queries:** Preferred. **E-Queries:** Yes. **Unsolicited mss:** Accepts. **Response:** 6 weeks, SASE. **Freelance Content:** 10%. **Rights:** 1st. **Payment:** On acceptance.

PASSPORT
See page 471 for full listing.
Description: Newspaper for preteens with resources for spiritual living.

PASTORAL LIFE
Society of St. Paul
P.O. Box 595, Canfield, OH 44406-0595. 330-533-5503.
E-mail: plmagazine@hotmail.com. Web site: www.albahouse.org. Monthly. $17/yr. Circ.: 1,200. Rev. Matthew Roehrig. SSP, Editor. **Description:** Articles, 2,000-2,500 words, addressing the issues of Catholic pastoral ministry. Pays $.04/word. **Nonfiction:** On religious, pastoral ministry; 1,000-2,500 words; $.04/word. **Tips:** Recommends query by e-mail. Writer's guidelines available. **Queries:** Preferred. **E-Queries:** Yes. **Unsolicited mss:** Accepts. **Payment:** On publication.

PENTECOSTAL EVANGEL
1445 N Boonville Ave., Springfield, MO 65802. 417-862-2781.
E-mail: pe@ag.org. Web site: www.pe.ag.org. Weekly. $24.99/year. Circ.: 260,000. Hal Donaldson, Editor. **Description:** For Assembly of God members and potential members. Provides biblical and practical articles to inspire believers. **Nonfiction:** Religious, personal experience, devotional; 800-1000 words; $.08/word. **Queries:** Preferred. **E-Queries:** Yes. **Unsolicited mss:** Accepts. **Response:** Queries 2 weeks, submissions 6 weeks, SASE. **Freelance Content:** 5%. **Rights:** 1st and electronic. **Payment:** On acceptance.

THE PENTECOSTAL MESSENGER
P.O. Box 850, Joplin, MO 64802. 417-624-7050.
Web site: www.pcg.org. John Mallinak, Editor. **Description:** Covers issues of Christian commitment. Topics include social and religious issues and the Bible. Provides articles, human interest features, inspirational stories, and seasonal material.

Edited for those in leadership. **Nonfiction:** Articles, 500-2,000 words; pays $.015/word. **Payment:** On publication.

POCKETS
See page 471 for full listing.
Description: Religious publication for kids from many different backgrounds.

PREACHING MAGAZINE
PO Box 369, Jackson, TN 38302-0369. 901-668-9948.
E-mail: preaching@compuserve.com. Web site: www.preaching.com. Bimonthly. Jonathan Kever, Editor. **Description:** For professional ministers. Each issue contains model sermons which reflect the best of preaching today. Interdenominational, rooted in evangelical convictions. **Nonfiction:** Features (guidance on preaching and worship leadership), 1,750-2,000 words, $50. Sermons, 1,250-1500 words, $35. **Fillers:** Abridged sermons, 600 words, $20. Children's sermons, 250-300, $10. **Tips:** Virtually all material written by active/retired pastors or seminary faculty; articles by non-ministers rarely accepted. **Queries:** Preferred. **E-Queries:** Yes. **Payment:** On publication.

PRESBYTERIAN RECORD
50 Wynford Dr., Toronto, Ontario M3C 1J7 Canada. 416-441-1111.
E-mail: pcrecord@presbyterian.ca. Web site: www.presbyterian.ca/record. 11x/year. $20/yr. (U.S. & Foreign). Circ.: 50,000. John Congram, Editor. **Description:** Published by The Presbyterian Church in Canada. **Fiction:** Stories of faith in action that are contemporary and often controversial in nature; 1,500 words; $50. **Nonfiction:** On children and youth ministries, lay ministries, etc; 1,500 words; $50. **Columns, Departments:** Opinion, Church in Action, Meditation; pay varies. **Art:** Prints preferred. **Queries:** Preferred. **E-Queries:** Yes. **Unsolicited mss:** Accepts. **Response:** 1-2 weeks, SASE. **Freelance Content:** 30%. **Rights:** One-time. **Payment:** On publication.

PRESBYTERIANS TODAY
100 Witherspoon, Louisville, KY 40202-1396. 502-569-5637.
E-mail: today@pcusa.org. Web site: www.pcusa.org/today. 10x/year. $15.95. Circ.: 60,000. Eva Stimson, Editor. **Description:** General-interest magazine for members of the Presbyterian church (U.S.). **Nonfiction:** About Presbyterian people and churches; guidance for daily living; current issues; 1,200-1,500 words; $300. **Fillers:** Humorous anecdotes; 100 words or less; no payment. **Queries:** Preferred. **E-Queries:** Yes. **Unsolicited mss:** Accepts. **Response:** Queries 2-4 weeks, submissions 4-6 weeks, SASE. **Freelance Content:** 30%. **Rights:** 1st. **Payment:** On acceptance.

THE PRIEST
200 Noll Plaza, Huntington, IN 46750-4304. 260-356-8400.
E-mail: tpriest@osv.com. Web site: www.osv.com. Monthly. $5/$39.95. Circ.: 6,500.

Msgr. Owen F. Campion, Editor. **Description:** Assists priests, deacons, and seminarians in day-to-day ministry. Items on spirituality, counseling, administration, theology, personalities, the saints, etc. **Nonfiction:** Historical/nostalgic, humor, inspirational, interview/profile, opinion, personal experience, religious; relating to priests and church; 1,500-5,000 words; $175-$250. **Columns, Departments:** Viewpoints; 1,000 words or less; $75. **Tips:** Freelancers most often published in "Viewpoints." **Queries:** Preferred. **E-Queries:** Yes. **Unsolicited mss:** Accepts. **Response:** Queries 5 weeks, submissions 3 months, SASE. **Freelance Content:** 25%. **Rights:** FNASR. **Payment:** On acceptance. **Contact:** Murray Hubley, Associate Editor.

PURPOSE

616 Walnut Ave., Scottdale, PA 15683-1999. 724-887-8500.
E-mail: horsch@mph.org. Web site: www.mph.org. $19.95/yr. Circ.: 11,000. James E. Horsch, Editor. **Description:** Publication for committed Christians who want to apply their faith in daily life. Suggests ways to resolve life's issues consistent with biblical principles. **Fiction:** Christian themes to nurture the desire for world peace and provide tools for peaceful living. Stories introducing children to many cultures; 750 words; up to $.05/word. **Nonfiction:** Articles to help others grow toward commitment to Christ and the church; 750 words; up to $.05/word. **Poetry:** Positive expression of love and caring; up to 16 lines; up to $20. **Queries:** Not necessary. **E-Queries:** Yes. **Unsolicited mss:** Accepts. **Response:** Up to 3 months, SASE. **Freelance Content:** 90%. **Rights:** One-time. **Payment:** On acceptance.

QUAKER LIFE

Friends United Meeting
101 Quaker Hill Dr., Richmond, IN 47374-1980. 765-962-7573.
E-mail: quakerlife@fum.org. Web site: www.fum.org/ql. 10x/year. $24/yr. Circ.: 7,000. Trish Edwards-Konic, Editor. **Description:** For members of Friends United Meeting, other Friends (Quakers), evangelical Christians, religious pacifists, and those who aspire to live a simple lifestyle. **Nonfiction:** Inspirational, first-person, articles on the Bible applied to daily living, news and analysis, devotional and study articles, and personal testimonies; 750-1,500 words. **Poetry:** Evangelical in nature. **Tips:** Sample copy $2. **Queries:** Not necessary. **E-Queries:** Yes. **Unsolicited mss:** Accepts. **Response:** Queries 2 weeks, submissions 2 months, SASE. **Freelance Content:** 80%. **Rights:** 1st and multimedia. **Payment:** in 3 copies.

QUEEN OF ALL HEARTS

26 S Saxon Ave., Bay Shore, NY 11706-8993. 631-665-0726.
Bimonthly. Father Roger Charest, S.S.M., Managing Editor. **Description:** Publication that covers Marian doctrine and devotion. Particular focus is on St. Louis de Montfort's Trinitarian and Christocentric approach to Mary in spiritual lives. **Fiction:** 1,500-2,000 words; $40-$60. **Nonfiction:** Essays, inspirational, personal experience; 750-2,000 words; $40-$60. **Poetry:** Free verse; 2 poems max. **Queries:** Preferred. **Unsolicited mss:** Accepts. **Rights:** One-time. **Payment:** On publication.

THE QUIET HOUR
Cook Communication Ministries
4050 Lee Vance View, Colorado Springs, CO 80919. 719-536-0100.
E-mail: gwilde@mac.com. Quarterly. Doug Schmidt, Managing Editor.
Description: Short devotionals. **Nonfiction:** Pays $15. **Tips:** By assignment only.
Queries: Preferred. **Freelance Content:** 100%. **Payment:** On acceptance.
Contact: Gary Wilde, Editor.

RECONSTRUCTIONISM TODAY
30 Old Whitfield Rd., Accord, NY 12404. 845-626-2427.
E-mail: Babush@ulster.net. Web site: www.jrf.org. Quarterly. $20/year. Circ.: 14,000.
Lawrence Bush, Editor. **Description:** For the Reconstructionist synagogue movement, with emphasis on creative Jewish living. **Nonfiction:** Personal Jewish journey,
with a Reconstructionist connection; 1,000-2,500 words. **Art:** Photographs, illustrations; TIF, EPS, prints. **Queries:** Preferred. **E-Queries:** Yes. **Unsolicited mss:**
Accepts. **Response:** 1 month for queries, 2 months for submissions; SASE required.
Freelance Content: 25%. **Rights:** FNAR.

REFORM JUDAISM
Union of American Hebrew Congregations
633 Third Ave., Fl. 6, New York, NY 10017. 212-650-4240.
Web site: http://uahc.org/rjmag. Quarterly. $3.50/issue. Circ.: 310,000. Aron Hirt-
Manheimer. **Description:** Published by Union of American Hebrew Congregations
to convey creativity, diversity, and dynamism of Reform Judaism. **Fiction:** Thought-
provoking, contemporary Jewish fiction; 1,200-2,000 words; $0.30/word. **Nonfiction:**
1,200-3,500 words; $0.30/word. **Columns, Departments:** 1,200-2,000 words; e.g.,
"Travel to Jewish India"; $0.30/word. **Art:** Slides, prints; pay varies. **Queries:** Not
necessary. **E-Queries:** No. **Unsolicited mss:** Accepts. **Response:** 6-8 weeks; SASE
or postage-paid postcard. **Freelance Content:** 25%. **Rights:** FNASR. **Payment:**
On publication. **Contact:** Joy Weinberg, Managing Editor.

REVIEW FOR RELIGIOUS
3601 Lindell Blvd., St. Louis, MO 63108. 314-977-7363.
E-mail: foppema@slu.edu. Bimonthly. David L. Fleming, S.J., Editor. **Description:**
Catholic spirituality tradition stemming from Catholic religious communities.
Nonfiction: Informative, practical, or inspirational articles; 1,500-5,000 words;
$6/page. **Queries:** Preferred. **Payment:** On publication.

SACRED JOURNEY
291 Witherspoon St., Princeton, NJ 08542. 609-924-6863.
E-mail: editorial@sacredjourney.org. Web site: www.sacredjourney.org. Bimonthly.
$18. Circ.: 5,000. Rebecca Laird, Editor. **Description:** Journal of Fellowship in
prayer. Focuses on spiritual practice, prayer, meditation, and service issues.
Nonfiction: Articles about spiritual life practiced by men and women of all faith traditions; to 1,500 words. **Art:** B&W prints; $40. **Tips:** Use inclusive language where

possible. **Queries:** Not necessary. **E-Queries:** Yes. **Unsolicited mss:** Accepts. **Response:** Submissions 2 months, SASE. **Freelance Content:** 75%. **Rights:** One-time. **Payment:** In copies.

ST. ANTHONY MESSENGER

28 W Liberty St., Cincinnati, OH 45210-1298. 513-241-5615.
E-mail: stanthony@americancatholic.org. Web site: www.americancatholic.org. Jack Wintz, O.F.M. Editor. **Description:** A Catholic family magazine which aims to help readers lead more fully human and Christian lives by: reporting and putting into context the major events and movements in a changing Church and world; commenting on matters of significance from the perspective of Christian faith and values; expanding awareness, tolerance, and understanding by presenting the views and achievements of others through interviews, personality profiles, and opinion articles; enriching, entertaining, and informing with fiction, columns, and features. **Tips:** Readers are people living in families or the family-like situations of Church and community. **Contact:** Amy Luken or Sharon Cross, Editorial Assistants.

SEEK

Standard Publishing
8121 Hamilton Ave., Cincinnati, OH 45220. 513-931-4050.
E-mail: ewilmoth@standardpub.com. Web site: www.standardpub.com. Weekly. Circ.: 34,000. Eileen H. Wilmoth, Editor. **Description:** Relates faith in action or Christian living, through inspirational or controversial topics, timely religious issues, testimonials. **Fiction:** 400-1,200 words; pays $.05/word. **Nonfiction:** Articles, 400-1,200 words; pays $.05/word. **Queries:** Not necessary. **E-Queries:** No. **Unsolicited mss:** Accepts. **Response:** Queries 3 months, submission 3-6 months, SASE. **Freelance Content:** 95%. **Rights:** 1st. **Payment:** On acceptance.

SENIOR CONNECTION

See page 563 for full listing.
Description: For Catholic seniors with connections to northern Illinois parishes.

SHARING THE VICTORY

See page 584 for full listing.
Description: Offers spiritual advice to coaches and athletes.

SIGNS OF THE TIMES

Pacific Press
P. O. Box 5353, Nampa, ID 83653-5353. 208-465-2577.
E-mail: signs@pacificpress.com. Web site: www.pacificpress.com/signs. Monthly. $18.95. Circ.: 200,000. Marvin Moore, Editor. **Description:** For the public, showing the way to Jesus, based on the beliefs of the Seventh-day Adventist church. **Nonfiction:** Articles, 600-1,500 words, on Christians who have performed community services; first-person experiences, to 1,000 words; health, home, marriage, human-interest pieces; inspirational articles; $.10-$.20/word. **Queries:** Not neces-

sary. **E-Queries:** Yes. **Unsolicited mss:** Accepts. **Response:** Queries 2 weeks, submission 6 weeks, SASE required. **Freelance Content:** 20%. **Rights:** First. **Payment:** On acceptance.

SPIRITUAL LIFE

2131 Lincoln Rd. NE, Washington, DC 20002-1151. 202-832-8489.
E-mail: editor@spiritual-life.org. Web site: www.spiritual-life.org. Quarterly. $4.50/$16 yr. Circ.: 11,000. Edward O'Donnell, O.C.D., Editor. **Description:** A professional religious journal, with essays on Christian spirituality with a pastoral application to everyday life. **Nonfiction:** 5,000-8,000 words; $50/page. **Art:** B&W cover; $100-$200. **Queries:** Not necessary. **E-Queries:** Yes. **Unsolicited mss:** Accepts. **Response:** Submissions 8-10 weeks, SASE. **Freelance Content:** 90%. **Rights:** FNASR. **Payment:** On acceptance.

STANDARD

6401 The Paseo, Kansas City, MO 64131. 816-333-7000.
E-mail: evlead@nazarene.org. Web site: www.nazarene.org. Weekly. $9.95. Circ.: 150,000. Everett Leadingham, Editor. **Description:** Denominational Sunday School take-home paper with leisure reading for adults (generally older adults with conservative Holiness church background). **Fiction:** Inspirational stories, Christianity in action; 1200 words; $.035/word (1st); $.02/ word (reprint). **Nonfiction:** Helpful articles; 1200 words. **Poetry:** Christian themes; 25 lines; $.25/line (min. $5). **Fillers:** Inspirational; 300-500 words. **Art:** B&W preferred; pay varies. **Tips:** New writers welcome. Prefers short fiction; avoid fictionalized Bible stories. **Queries:** Not necessary. **E-Queries:** Yes. **Unsolicited mss:** Accepts. **Response:** 3 months. **Freelance Content:** 100%. **Rights:** One-time. **Payment:** On acceptance.

STORY FRIENDS

See page 473 for full listing.
Description: General interest magazine for kids ages 4-9 that promotes and reinforces traditional values taught by Christian families.

TEACHERS INTERACTION

3558 S Jefferson Ave., St. Louis, MO 63118. 314-268-1083.
E-mail: tom@nummela@cph.org. Quarterly. $3.95/$12.95. Circ.: 14,000. Tom Nummela, Editor. **Description:** Builds up volunteer teachers of the faith, and church professionals who support them, in the ministry of sharing ideas, inspirational stories, and education. **Nonfiction:** Practical assistance for volunteer Christian teachers, especially Sunday school. Each issue on a central theme; inquire about upcoming themes; 1,000-1,200 words; $110. **Fillers:** Teachers Interchange (short activities, ideas for Sunday school classes, creative and practical); 150-200 words; $20-$40. **Columns, Departments:** 9 regular columns; 400-500 words; $55. **Art:** Color photos of children, all ages, in Christian educational settings other than day school; seeks to include children with disabilities and children of various ethnic backgrounds; $50-$100. **Queries:** Preferred. **E-Queries:** Yes. **Unsolicited mss:**

Accepts. **Response:** 10-30 days, SASE. **Freelance Content:** 30%. **Rights:** All. **Payment:** On acceptance.

TEAM NYI
NYI Ministries
6401 The Paseo, Kansas City, MO 64131. 816-333-7000.
E-mail: teamnyi@nazarene.com. Quarterly. Circ.: 10,000. Jeff Edmondson, Editor. **Description:** Focuses on the business and philosophy of youth ministry. **Nonfiction:** On youth ministry for both professional and volunteers. Must have solid Christian, biblical foundation and conform to Nazarene theology; 500-1,000 words; $50-$100. **Tips:** Avoid ideas from the '70s and '80s; 21st-century teens are different. Need a good handle on postmodern mindset and millennial generation. Send e-mail query, or cover letter with attached article. **Queries:** Preferred. **E-Queries:** Yes. **Unsolicited mss:** Accepts. **Response:** 4 weeks, SASE. **Freelance Content:** 60%. **Rights:** 1st NA, reprints, some work-for-hire assignments. **Payment:** On acceptance.

TIKKUN
See page 341 for full listing.
Description: Progressive Jewish commentary on politics, culture, and society.

TODAY'S CATHOLIC TEACHER
See page 352 for full listing.
Description: For K-12 teachers on Catholic education.

TODAY'S CHRISTIAN WOMAN
See page 629 for full listing.
Description: For Christian women, ages 20-40, on issues that impact their lives.

TRICYCLE
92 Vandam St., New York, NY 10013. 212-645-1143.
E-mail: editorial@tricycle.com. Web site: www.tricycle.com. Quarterly. **Description:** Non-profit publication devoted to exploring the nature of Buddhism in America. Examines how Buddhism changes when exposed to American traditions, its expression in literature and the arts, and how its insights can illuminate the possibilities facing people today. **Nonfiction:** All submissions must relate to Buddhism. Prefers shorter pieces (3,000 words or less). Manuscript must be typed and include word count and address on each page. **Tips:** Prefers to review query before reading manuscript. Send query letter outlining idea, biographical information (stating familiarity with subject matter), clips/writing samples, and SASE. **Queries:** Preferred. **E-Queries:** Yes. **Unsolicited mss:** Accepts.

TURNING WHEEL
P.O. Box 4650, Berkeley, CA 94704. 510-655-6169.
E-mail: turningwheel@bpf.org. Web site: www.bpf.org/bpf. Quarterly. $5/$35. Circ.: 8,000. Susan Moon, Editor. **Description:** Journal of socially-engaged Buddhism.

Covers issues of social justice and environment from a Buddhist perspective. **Nonfiction:** On social-justice work from a Buddhist perspective, experimental and theoretical; themes for each issue (e.g., aging; death penalty; class divide); 1,800-3,500 words. **Poetry:** Related to theme. **Columns, Departments:** Reviews of books and films on social/spiritual issues; 450-850 words. **Art:** Prints, TIF or EPS files. **Tips:** Avoid academic prose and new-age mushiness. Submit compelling personal experience, with analytical commentary. Contact for upcoming themes. **Queries:** Preferred. **E-Queries:** Yes. **Unsolicited mss:** Accepts. **Response:** Queries 1 month, submissions 2 months, SASE. **Freelance Content:** 40%. **Rights:** One-time. **Payment:** In copies.

U.S. CATHOLIC
Claretian Publications
205 W Monroe St., Chicago, IL 60606. 312-236-7782.
E-mail: editors@uscatholic.org. Monthly. $22/yr. Circ.: 50,000. Rev. Mark J. Brummel, C.M.F., Editor. **Description:** Celebrates vibrancy and diversity of contemporary Catholicism. Promotes a positive vision of the Catholic faith today. Combines tradition with sense of humor and firm beliefs. **Fiction:** With strong characters that cause readers to stop and consider their relationships with others, the world, and/or God. Overtly religious themes not required; 2,000 words; $300. **Poetry:** All forms and themes; no light verse; submit 3-5 original poems; up to 50 lines; $75/poem. **Queries:** Not necessary. **E-Queries:** Yes. **Unsolicited mss:** Accepts. **Response:** 8-10 weeks, SASE not required. **Freelance Content:** 10%. **Rights:** First North American. **Payment:** On acceptance. **Contact:** Maureen Abood.

THE UNITED CHURCH OBSERVER
478 Huron St., Toronto, Ontario M5R 2R3 Canada. 416-960-8500.
Web site: www.ucobserver.org. 11x/yr. **Description:** On religious trends, human problems, and social issues. **Nonfiction:** Factual articles, 1,500-2,500 words. **Tips:** No poetry. **Queries:** Preferred. **Payment:** On publication.

UNITED SYNAGOGUE REVIEW
155 Fifth Ave., New York, NY 10010. 212-533-7800.
E-mail: info@uscj.org. Web site: www.uscj.org. 2x/year. Circ.: 250,000. Ms. Lois Goldrich, Editor. **Description:** Publication of the Conservative Movement, with features related to synagogues, Jewish law, and that organization. **Nonfiction:** Stories about congregational programs or developments in Conservative Judaism; 1500 words. **Art:** Photographic prints; $200 (cover photo). **Tips:** No payment, but wide exposure to 1 million readers. Writing should be crisp but not edgy or overly familiar. **Queries:** Not necessary. **E-Queries:** Yes. **Unsolicited mss:** Accepts. **Response:** Queries immediate, submissions 1-3 months. **Freelance Content:** 25%.

THE WAR CRY

The Salvation Army

615 Slaters Lane, Alexandria, VA 22314. 703-684-5500 x518.

Web site: www.christianity.com/salvationarmyusa. Bi-weekly. Lt. Col. Marlene Chase, Editor-in-Chief. **Description:** Evangelist periodical used to spread the Word of God. **Nonfiction:** Must relate to modern life, and offer inspiration, information, or evangelization; essays with insightful perspective on living the Christian life; 800-1,500 words; $.10-$.20/word. **Art:** 5x7 or 8x10 color prints, transparencies; $50, $250 (cover). **Queries:** Not necessary. **Response:** Queries 2 weeks, SASE. **Freelance Content:** 10%. **Payment:** On acceptance.

WITH

See page 599 for full listing.

Description: Magazine for teens who are radically committed to Jesus Christ, peace, justice, and sharing God's good news through words and action.

WOMAN'S TOUCH

See page 631 for full listing.

Description: Non-profit ministry magazine for Christian women.

WONDER TIME

See page 646 for full listing.

Description: For children, ages 5-7, with emphasis on the religious instruction of children and parents.

YOU!

See page 599 for full listing.

Description: For teens, especially on moral issues, faith, and contemporary pop culture, viewed from the Catholic/Christian perspective.

YOUNG SALVATIONIST

See page 600 for full listing.

Description: Seeks to teach Christian view of everyday living, for teens.

YOUR CHURCH

Christianity Today

465 Gundersen Dr., Carol Stream, IL 60188. 630-260-6200.

E-mail: yceditor@yourchurch.net. Web site: www.yourchurch.net. Bimonthly. Circ.: 150,000. Harold B. Smith, Executive Editor. **Description:** Trade publication to help church leaders with the business side of ministry. **Nonfiction:** Articles on hiring from within a church, how to avoid affinity fraud schemes, etc; 1,250-1,500 words. **Queries:** Preferred. **Unsolicited mss:** Accepts. **Response:** Queries 1-2 months. **Freelance Content:** 10%. **Rights:** 1st. **Payment:** On acceptance.

YOUTH AND CHRISTIAN EDUCATION LEADERSHIP
See page 353 for full listing.
Description: For Christian educators who teach God's word to children and adults.

YOUTHWALK
6401 The Paseo, Kansas City, MO 64131. 816-333-7000.
E-mail: youthwalk@wordaction.com. Web site: www.waction.com. Bimonthly. $1.95.
Circ.: 24,000. Matt Price, Editor. **Description:** About theology, devotional classics,
spiritual disciplines, and the Christian calendar, in language that speaks to today's students. **Nonfiction:** Articles about teens demonstrating Christian principles in real-
life situations; 300-600 words; $30. **Columns, Departments:** Christian themes; 300-
600 words; $30. **Tips:** Articles should come from working with teenagers. **Queries:**
Required. **E-Queries:** Yes. **Unsolicited mss:** Does not accept. **Response:** Queries
30 days, submissions 2 months, SASE. **Freelance Content:** 20%. **Rights:** All.
Payment: On publication.

SCIENCE

AD ASTRA
600 Pennsylvania Ave. S.E., Suite 201, Washington, DC 20003-4316. 202-543-1900.
E-mail: adastraed@aol.com. Web site: www.nss.org/adastra. Bimonthly. Circ.: 25,000.
Frank Sietzen, Jr., Editor-in-Chief. **Description:** Lively, semi-technical features, on
all aspects of international space exploration. **Nonfiction:** Interested in "Living in
Space" articles; commercial and human space flight technology; 1,500-3,000 words;
$350-$450. **Queries:** Preferred. **Freelance Content:** 80%. **Payment:** On
publication.

AIR & SPACE/SMITHSONIAN
750 Ninth St. NW, Fl. 7, Washington, DC 20001. 202-275-1230.
E-mail: editors@airspacemag.com. Web site: www.airspacemag.com. Bimonthly.
$3.95. Circ.: 250,000. George C. Larson, Editor. **Description:** Original articles on
aerospace topics for a lay audience. **Nonfiction:** Feature stories with original reporting, research, and quotes. General-interest articles on aerospace experience, past,
present, and future; 2,000-5,000 words; $2,000-$3,500. **Columns, Departments:**
Book reviews, soft news pieces, first-person recollections, and essays; 500-1,500
words; $350-$1,500. **Art:** Yes. **Tips:** Avoid sentimentalities (the majesty of flight, etc.).
Don't rehash; original research only. Send 1-2 page proposal detailing sources and
interview list with published clips. Emphasize fresh angle. **Queries:** Required.
E-Queries: Yes. **Unsolicited mss:** Accepts. **Response:** 4-8 weeks, SASE required.
Freelance Content: 90%. **Rights:** FNASR. **Payment:** On acceptance.

AMERICAN HERITAGE OF INVENTION & TECHNOLOGY
See page 422 for full listing.
Description: Articles and illustrations on the history of technology in America.

ANNALS OF IMPROBABLE RESEARCH
P.O. Box 380853, Cambridge, MA 02238. 617-491-4437.
E-mail: air@improbable.com. Web site: www.improbable.com. Bimonthly. $24.95/year. Marc Abrahams, Editor. **Description:** Presents the mischievous, funny, and iconoclastic side of science. **Nonfiction:** Science reports and analysis; humor; 1-4 pages. **Poetry:** Brief science-related poetry. **Art:** B&W. **Queries:** Preferred. **E-Queries:** Yes. **Unsolicited mss:** Accepts. **Response:** SASE required.

ARCHAEOLOGY
3636 33rd St., Long Isand City, NY 11106. 718-472-3050.
E-mail: peter@archaeology.org. Web site: www.archaeology.org. Bimonthly. $4.95/$20. Circ.: 210,000. Peter A. Young, Editor-in-Chief. **Description:** News magazine about archaeology worldwide. Written for lay people by professionals or writers with a solid knowledge of this field. **Nonfiction:** Profiles, excavation reports, discoveries, photo essays; 500-2,500 words; $500-$1,500. **Columns, Departments:** Multimedia, museum news, book reviews; 500 words; $250-$500. **Art:** Electronic or slides; pay varies. **Queries:** Required. **E-Queries:** Yes. **Unsolicited mss:** Accepts. **Response:** 1 month, SASE required. **Freelance Content:** 5%. **Payment:** On acceptance.

ASTRONOMY
Kalmbach Publishing Co.
21027 Crossroads Circle, P.O. Box 1612, Waukesha, WI 53187. 262-796-8776.
Web site: www.astronomy.com. Monthly. $4.95/issue, $39.95/year. Circ.: 175,000. Bonnie Gordon, Editor. **Description:** Astronomical science and hobby activities, covering our solar system, Milky Way galaxy, black holes, deep-space observing, personality profiles, astronomical travel, etc. **Nonfiction:** Science stories on astronomy, astrophysics, space programs, recent discoveries. Hobby stories on equipment and celestial events; short news items; 2,000 words; $200-$1,000. **Art:** Photos of astronomical phenomena and other affiliated subjects relating to stories; digital, slides, prints; $25/use. **Queries:** Preferred. **E-Queries:** Yes. **Unsolicited mss:** Accepts. **Rights:** 1st serial, all. **Payment:** On acceptance.

ENVIRONMENT
See page 356 for full listing.
Description: Solid analysis of environmental science and policy issues.

NATURAL HISTORY
American Museum of Natural History
Central Park W at 79th St., New York, NY 10024. 212-769-5500.
E-mail: nhmag@amnh.org. Web site: www.naturalhistory.com. 10x/year. $30/year. Circ.: 225,000. Ellen Goldensohn, Editor. **Description:** Published by American Museum of National History. Articles mostly by scientists, on biological sciences, cultural and physical anthropology, archaeology, earth sciences, astronomy, vertebrates and invertebrates. **Nonfiction:** Informative articles; 800-2,500 words; $500-$2,500.

Art: $350 (full page), $500 (Natural Moment section photo). **Tips:** Read magazine first, and research recent articles before sending query. **Queries:** Preferred. **E-Queries:** No. **Unsolicited mss:** Accepts. **Response:** Queries 4-6 months. **Freelance Content:** 30%. **Rights:** 1st. **Payment:** On publication.

ODYSSEY

See page 596 for full listing.
Description: Features on science and technology for readers ages 10-16.

POPULAR SCIENCE

Time 4 Media Co.
2 Park Ave., New York, NY 10016. 212-779-5000.
E-mail: jenny.everett@time4.com. Web site: www.popsci.com. Jenny Everett, Editor.
Description: On developments in science and technology. **Nonfiction:** Short illustrated articles on new inventions and products; photo-essays, book excerpt; with photos and/or illustrations; pay varies. **Payment:** On acceptance.

SCIENCE & CHILDREN

See page 350 for full listing.
Description: Articles and classroom activities, based on current approaches to instruction and issues in science education.

SCIENCE WORLD

Scholastic, Inc.
555 Broadway, Fl. 3, New York, NY 10012-3919. 212-343-6100.
E-mail: scienceworld@scholastic.com. Web site: www.scholastic.com. Biweekly. $7.50. Circ.: 404,600. Mark Bregman, Editor. **Description:** On life science, earth science, physical science, environmental science, or health science, for 7th-10th graders, ages 12-15. **Nonfiction:** Science articles, 750 words; $200-$650. **Columns, Departments:** Science news, 200 words; pays $100-$125. **Tips:** Submit well-researched proposal, with anticipated sources, 2-3 clips of your work, and SASE. Writing should be lively, with an understanding of teens' perspectives and interests.

SCIENTIFIC AMERICAN

415 Madison Ave., New York, NY 10017. 212-754-0550.
E-mail: editors@sciam.com. Web site: www.sciam.com. Philip Yam, News Editor.
Description: Addresses all aspects of American scientific endeavor. **Queries:** Preferred.

SKY & TELESCOPE

Sky Publishing Corp.
49 Bay State Rd., Cambridge, MA 02138-1203. 617-864-7360.
E-mail: editors@skyandtelescope.com. Web site: www.skyandtelescope.com. Monthly. $37.95. Circ.: 130,000. Bud Sadler, Managing Editor. **Description:** For amateur and professional astronomers worldwide. **Nonfiction:** Articles, mention

availability of diagrams and other illustrations; $.25/word. **Columns, Departments:** Amateur Astronomers, Computers in Astronomy, Telescope Techniques, Astro Imaging, Observer's Log, Gallery. Also, 800-word opinion pieces, for Focal Point. **Queries:** Required. **Payment:** On publication.

SPACE ILLUSTRATED
120 W 45th St., New York, NY, 10036. 212-703-5800.
E-mail: thoughts@space.com. Web site: www.space.com. **Description:** The companion in-print magazine to Space.com Web site. Articles on space. **Tips:** Also publishes *Space News,* an industry publication.

TECHNOLOGY REVIEW
See page 330 for full listing.
Description: General-interest articles on technology and innovation.

TIMELINE
See page 430 for full listing.
Description: Covers fields of history, prehistory, and natural sciences.

21ST CENTURY: SCIENCE AND TECHNOLOGY
P.O. Box 16285, Washington, DC 20041. 703-777-7473.
E-mail: tcs@mediasoft.net. Web site: www.21stcenturysciencetech.com. Quarterly. $3.50/issue. Circ.: 23,000. Laurence Hecht, Editor. **Description:** Dedicated to the promotion of unending scientific progress, all directed to serve the proper common aims of mankind. **Tips:** Very low budget. **Queries:** Required. **E-Queries:** No. **Unsolicited mss:** Does not accept. **Response:** Varies, SASE. **Rights:** One-time. **Payment:** On publication. **Contact:** Marjorie Mazel Hecht, Managing Editor.

UPDATE
2 East 63rd St., New York, NY 10021. 212-838-0230.
E-mail: update@nyas.org. Web site: www.nyas.org. Dan Van Atta, Editor. **Description:** Magazine for members of the New York Academy of Sciences. On all scientific disciplines. **Nonfiction:** Essays and features (1,000-2,000 words). **Columns, Departments:** Book reviews. **Queries:** Preferred. **Payment:** honorarium, on publication.

WEATHERWISE
Heldref Publications
1319 18th St. NW, Washington, DC 20036. 202-296-6267.
E-mail: ww@heldref.org. Web site: www.weatherwise.org. 6x/yr. Circ.: 11,000. Doyle Rice, Managing Editor. **Description:** All about weather. **Nonfiction:** 1,500-2,000 words; pays $200-$500. **Columns, Departments:** 300-1,000 words; pays to $200. **Queries:** Required. **E-Queries:** Yes. **Unsolicited mss:** Accepts. **Response:** 2 months. **Freelance Content:** 50%. **Rights:** All.

YES MAG
See page 474 for full listing.
Description: Canadian children's science magazine.

SENIORS

AARP BULLETIN
601 E Street NW, Washington, DC 20049-0001. 202-434-2277.
E-mail: bulletin@aarp.org. Web site: www.aarp.org. Monthly. $10. Circ.: 21,068,000.
Elliot Carlson, Editor. **Description:** Publication of American Association of Retired
Persons. **Nonfiction:** Pay varies. **Queries:** Required. **Payment:** On acceptance.

AARP MODERN MATURITY
The American Association of Retired Persons
601 E St. NW, Washington, D.C. 20049. 202-434-6880.
E-mail: mmletters@aarp.org. Web site: www.modernmaturity.org. Bimonthly. Circ.:
22,000,000. Amelia Jones. **Description:** General-interest membership magazine for
members of AARP. **Nonfiction:** Articles of interest for people 55 and older. Health,
money, travel, consumer topics most needed; 1,500-5,000; $1/word and up.
Columns, Departments: See nonfiction topics; 300-1,500 words; $1/word and up.
Tips: No queries by phone. Call only to ask which editor handles the subject matter
you are proposing, then send material to that editor only. Welcomes new writers.
Queries: Required. **E-Queries:** Yes. **Unsolicited mss:** Does not accept.
Response: 6-8 weeks. **Freelance Content:** 80%. **Rights:** 1st worldwide.
Payment: On acceptance.

FOREVER YOUNG
Metroland Printing & Distributing
467 Speers Rd., Oakville, Ontario L6K 3S4 Canada. 905-815-0017.
E-mail: don.wall@metroland.com. Web site: www.haltonsearch.com. Monthly. $20.
Circ.: 482,500. Don Wall, Editor. **Description:** Multi-province Canadian publica-
tion, for senior citizens. **Queries:** Preferred.

GOOD TIMES
Senior Publications
25 Sheppard Ave., Suite 100, Toronto, Ontario M2N 6S7. 416-733-7600.
E-mail: goodtimes@transcontinental.ca. 11x/year. $21.95/yr. Judy Brandow, Editor.
Description: Canadian magazine for successful retirement, lifestyles for mature
market. **Nonfiction:** Celebrity profiles, also practical articles on health, beauty, cuisine, hobbies, fashion, leisure activities, travel, taxes, legal rights, consumer protection; 1,300-1,500 words; $.40/word. **Poetry:** Yes; no payment. **Columns,
Departments:** Health, relationship, travel stories for mature market; 1,500-2,000
words; $.40/word. **Art:** To accompany articles. **Tips:** Canadian content only.

Queries: Required. **E-Queries:** Yes. **Freelance Content:** 100%. **Rights:** 1st Canadian. **Payment:** On acceptance.

LIFE LINES
129 N 10th St., Rm. 408, Lincoln, NE 68508-3627. 402-441-7022.
Dena Rust Zimmer. **Description:** Magazine for seniors. **Fiction:** Short stories; to 450 words. **Poetry:** To 50 lines. **Fillers:** Short humor. **Columns, Departments:** Sports and Hobbies, Remember When . . . , Travels With . . . , Perspectives on Aging. **Payment:** No payment.

LIFEWISE
Focus on the Family
8605 Explorer Dr., Colorado Springs, CO 80920-1049. 719-531-3400.
Web site: www.family.org. Monthly. Circ.: 45,000. **Description:** Christian publication for older adults.

MATURE LIFESTYLES
P.O. Box 44327, Madison, WI 53744. 608-274-5200.
E-mail: anitaj@execpc.com. Anita J. Martin. **Description:** Newspaper for the active, 50-plus population who reside in south central Wisconsin. **Tips:** Fax 1-page inquiries to 608-274-5492. Do not send materials through the mail or electronically. **E-Queries:** No.

MATURE LIFESTYLES
News Connection USA., Inc.
220 W Brandon Blvd., Suite 203, Brandon, FL 33511.
E-mail: srconnect@aol.com. Web site: www.srconnect.com. **Description:** For readers over 50, in Florida. **Nonfiction:** Articles, 500-700 words. **Tips:** No fiction or poetry. Florida angle required. **Payment:** On publication.

MATURE LIVING
One LifeWay Plaza, Nashville, TN 37234. 615-251-2485.
E-mail: matureliving@lifeway.com. Web site: www.lifewayonline.com/mags. Monthly. $19.95/yr. Circ.: 330,000. David T. Seay, Editor-in-Chief. **Description:** A leisure reading magazine focusing on the personal and spiritual needs of senior adults to encourage growth, hope, and fulfillment in Christian living. **Queries:** Not necessary. **Unsolicited mss:** Accepts.

MATURE LIVING
Senior Publishers Media Group
255 N El Cielo Rd., #452, Palm Springs, CA 92262-6974. 760-320-2221.
E-mail: desertbiz1@aol.com. Web site: www.desertbusinessjournal.org. Monthly. $18. Circ.: 30,000. Carson Parlan, Editor. **Description:** For older adults in and around Palm Springs, Calif.

MATURE YEARS

United Methodist Publishing House

201 Eighth Ave. S, Nashville, TN 37202. 615-749-6292.

E-mail: matureyears@umpublishing.org. Quarterly. $18. Circ.: 50,000. Marvin W. Cropsey, Editor. **Description:** Seeks to help individuals in and near retirement years to understand the appropriate resources of the Christian faith that can assist them with the specific problems and opportunities of aging. **Fiction:** Stories with older adult characters in older adult situations; to 2,000 words. **Nonfiction:** Religious and inspirational articles; also, older adults in active lifestyles; 2,000 words; $.05/word. **Fillers:** Bible puzzles. **Columns, Departments:** Health and fitness, personal finance, travel, poetry, fiction. **Art:** Photos. **Tips:** Welcomes new writers. **Queries:** Preferred. **E-Queries:** Yes. **Unsolicited mss:** Accepts. **Response:** 4-8 weeks, SASE required. **Rights:** One-time NA. **Payment:** On acceptance.

MILESTONES

Philadelphia Corporation for Aging

642 N Broad St., Philadelphia, PA 19103-3424. 215-765-9000.

Web site: www.pcaphl.org. Monthly. Circ.: 60,000. Marsha Braverman, Editor. **Description:** For seniors in the greater Philadelphia area.

NETWORK

Gray Panthers Organization

733 15th St. NW, #437, Washington, DC 20005-2112. 202-737-6637.

E-mail: info@graypanthers.org. Web site: www.graypanthers.org. 6x/yr. Circ.: 30,000. George Neighbors, Editor. **Description:** National advocacy magazine for older adults.

NOT BORN YESTERDAY

Osmon Publications, Inc.

4805 Alta Canyada Rd., La Canada Flintridge, CA 91011. 818-790-0651.

Monthly. Circ.: 104,000. **Description:** For Southern California seniors. **Tips:** Buys very little freelance material.

THE OLDER AMERICAN

Massachusetts Association of Older Americans

108 Arlington St., Boston, MA 02116-5302. 617-426-0804.

E-mail: bostonsrs1@aol.com. Web site: www.maoa-inc.org. Quarterly. $50. Circ.: 10,000. Phyllis Galante, Editor. **Description:** Local, state, and national advocacy and current affairs magazine for older adults.

PITTSBURGH SENIOR NEWS

Pittsburgh Senior News, Inc.

3345 Evergreen Rd., Pittsburgh, PA 15237-2650. 412-367-2522.

Monthly. Circ.: 40,000. Teresa K. Flatley, Editor. **Description:** Topics of interest to older adults in the Pittsburgh area.

PLUS

3565 S Higuera St., San Luis Obispo, CA 93401. 805-544-8711.
E-mail: plusmag@fix.net. Web site: www.seniormagazine.com. Monthly. Circ.: 60,000. George Brand, Editor. **Description:** Features entertainment and informative articles for readers ages 50 and up. **Nonfiction:** Book reviews, profiles, travel, business, sports, movies, television, and health; 600-1,200 words. **Queries:** Preferred. **E-Queries:** No. **Unsolicited mss:** Accepts. **Response:** Queries 1 week, submission 2 weeks, SASE. **Freelance Content:** 60%. **Rights:** 1st. **Payment:** On publication.

PRIME TIMES

P.O. Box 391, Madison, WI 53701. 608-231-7272.
E-mail: tom.burton@cunamutual.com. **Description:** For credit union members 50 years and older. **Queries:** Preferred. **Contact:** Tom Burton, Managing Editor.

PRIME TIMES

Times-Beacon-Record Newspapers
P.O. Box 707, East Setauket, NY 11733-0769. 631-751-0356.
Monthly. Circ.: 50,000. Ann Fossan, Editor. **Description:** For older adults on Long Island, N.Y.

RETIRED OFFICER

201 N Washington St., Alexandria, VA 22314-2539. 703-838-8115.
E-mail: editor@troa.org. Web site: www.troa.org/magazine. Monthly. $20/yr. Circ.: 386,000. Warren S. Lacy, Editor. **Description:** For retired and soon-to-be-retired members. Readers (commissioned/warrant officers, families, and surviving spouses) represent one of the youngest, most active groups in the senior market. **Nonfiction:** Current military/political affairs, recent history (especially Vietnam and Korea), retirement topics, and general interest. Original only, no reprints; 1,400-2,500 words; $1,200-$1,800. **Columns, Departments:** Travel; financial planning; health and fitness; military family; retirement lifestyles; and general interest; 750 words; $500. **Art:** Color transparencies preferred. **Tips:** Active voice, nontechnical, with direct quotes. Optimistic, upbeat themes. **Queries:** Required. **E-Queries:** Yes. **Unsolicited mss:** Does not accept. **Response:** 90 days. **Rights:** 1st, also Internet and reprint. **Payment:** On acceptance. **Contact:** Molly Wyman.

RETIREMENT LIFE

National Association of Retired Federal Employees
606 N Washington St., Alexandria, VA 22314. 703-838-7760.
Web site: www.narfe.org. Monthly. Circ.: 400,000. Martha M. Lostrom, Director of Communications/Editor. **Description:** Focuses on issues of interest to retired federal employees. **Tips:** Does not accept freelance work.

SECURE RETIREMENT

National Committee to Preserve Social Security and Medicare
10 G St. NE, Suite 600, Washington, DC 20002-4215. 202-216-0420.

E-mail: jbouley@imaginpub.com. Web site: www.ncpssm.org. Bimonthly. Circ.: 1.000,000. Jeffrey Bouley, Editor. **Description:** Advocates health and retirement issues for members of NCPSSM. **Nonfiction:** Policy and lifestyle features on age-related and retirement issues; 500-1,500 words; payment varies. **Queries:** Preferred. **E-Queries:** Yes. **Unsolicited mss:** Accepts. **Response:** 2-6 weeks; SASE required. **Freelance Content:** 70%. **Payment:** On publication. **Contact:** Jeffrey Bouley.

SENIOR CONNECTION
Churchhill Publications
P.O. Box 38, Dundee, IL 60118. 847-428-0205.
Description: For Catholics, ages 50-plus, with connections to northern Illinois parishes.

SENIOR CONNECTION
News Connection USA, Inc.
220 W Brandon Blvd., Suite 203, Brandon, FL 33511.
E-mail: srconnect@aol.com. Web site: www.srconnect.com. Monthly. Circ.: 130,000.
Description: General-interest articles, for senior citizens in the west central and Tampa areas of Florida.

THE SENIOR TIMES
435 King St., Littleton, MA 01460. 978-742-9171.
E-mail: theseniortimes@aol.com. Monthly. Free newsstand/$18 subscription. Circ.: 28,000. Jane Jackson, Editor. **Description:** Features art and entertainment news for the active, over age 50 reader. **Nonfiction:** Articles on travel, entertainment, health, finance, senior advocacy issues, opinions, and local interviews. **Art:** Photos; 8x10 B&W; subjects from the greater Boston area (people, places, art); pay negotiable. **Queries:** Not necessary. **E-Queries:** Yes. **Unsolicited mss:** Does not accept. **Response:** SASE. **Payment:** On publication.

SENIOR TIMES
Senior Publishing Co., Inc.
P.O. Box 30965, Columbus, OH 43230-0965. 614-337-2055.
E-mail: seniortimes@iwaynet.net. Monthly. Circ.: 60,000. Roberta Keck, Editor.
Description: For older adults, in Ohio.

SENIOR TIMES
Journal News Publishing
P.O. Box 142020, Spokane, WA 99214-2020. 509-924-2440.
E-mail: vnh@iea.com. Monthly. Circ.: 60,000. Mike Huffman, Editor. **Description:** For senior citizens in Washington State.

SPIRIT PLUS
1830 Rt. 9, Toms River, NJ 08755. 732-505-9700.
E-mail: spiritmag50@aol.com. Monthly. Circ.: 250,000. Pat Jasin, editor.

Description: For active adults aged 45-65, in New Jersey. Upbeat articles on travel, sex, computers, dating, health and fitness. **Queries:** Required. **E-Queries:** Yes. **Unsolicited mss:** Does not accept. **Response:** 2 months. **Freelance Content:** 10%. **Rights:** 1st NA. **Payment:** In copies.

TODAY'S GRANDPARENT
Today's Parent Group
269 Richmond St. W, Toronto, Ontario M5V 1X1 Canada. 416-596-8680.
Web site: www.todaysparent.com. Quarterly. Circ.: 200,000. Laura Bickle, Editor.
Description: For grandparents of all ages.

WHERE TO RETIRE
Vacation Publications, Inc.
1502 Augusta Dr., Suite 415, Houston, TX 77057. 713-974-6903.
Web site: www.wheretoretire.com. 5x/yr. $11.95. Circ.: 20,000. R. Alan Fox, Publisher/Editor. **Description:** For anyone seeking retirement locale advice.

SPORTS, RECREATION, OUTDOORS

ADVENTURE CYCLIST
Adventure Cycling Association
P.O. Box 8308, Missoula, MT 59807. 406-721-1776.
E-mail: ddambrosio@adventurecycling.org. Web site: www.adventurecycling.org.
9x/year. Circ.: 25,000. Daniel D'Ambrosio, Editor. **Description:** Covers the bicycling world. **Nonfiction:** Bike travel; 1,500-3,000 words; $450-$1,200. **Columns, Departments:** Wayside (news shorts). **Queries:** Not necessary. **E-Queries:** Yes. **Unsolicited mss:** Accepts. **Response:** 3 weeks, SASE required. **Freelance Content:** 80%. **Rights:** 1st. **Payment:** On publication.

ALL-STATER SPORTS
950 Winter St., Waltham, MA 02451-1424. 614-487-1280.
Stephanie Strong, Managing Editor. **Description:** Sports magazine for high-school athletes. **Queries:** Preferred.

AMERICAN FIELD
See page 287 for full listing.
Description: Short pieces on hunting dogs and field trials for bird dogs.

AMERICAN HANDGUNNER
591 Camino de la Reina, Suite 200, San Diego, CA 92108. 619-819-4535.
E-mail: ed@americanhandgunner.com. Web site: www.americanhandgunner.com.
Roy Huntington, Editor. **Description:** Semi-technical articles on shooting sports, custom handguns, gun repair and alteration, handgun matches and tournaments, for lay readers. **Nonfiction:** Pays $100-$500. **Queries:** Required. **Payment:** On publication.

AMERICAN HUNTER

NRA Publications

11250 Waples Mill Rd., Fairfax, VA 22030-9400. 703-267-1300.

E-mail: publications@nrahq.org. Web site: nra.org. Monthly. Membership. Circ.: 1,070,000. John Zent, Editor. **Description:** On all aspects of hunting and related activities. Includes techniques, equipment, top places to hunt, legislation and current issues, and role of hunting in wildlife management. Safety and sportsmanship emphasized. **Nonfiction:** Features on deer, upland birds, waterfowl, big game, and varmints/small game. Varied styles, including expository how-to, where-to; general-interest pieces; humor; personal narratives and semi-technical articles on firearms, wildlife management, or hunting; 1,800-2,000 words; up to $800. **Columns, Departments:** Hunting Guns, Public Hunting Grounds; 1,000-1,200 words; $300-$450. **Art:** Color slides; pays on publication; pay varies, $450-$600 (cover). **Tips:** Submissions judged on 3 criteria: story angle, quality of writing, quality and quantity of photos. **Queries:** Preferred. **E-Queries:** Yes. **Unsolicited mss:** Accepts. **Response:** 2 months or more, SASE required. **Freelance Content:** 50%. **Rights:** FNASR, reprint in NRA publication. **Payment:** On acceptance.

AMERICAN RIFLEMAN

11250 Waples Mill Rd., Fairfax, VA 22030. 703-267-1336.

Web site: www.publications.nrhq.org. Mark Keefe, Editor. **Description:** Articles on use and enjoyment of sporting firearms. **Payment:** On acceptance.

AQUA-FIELD

P.O. Box 575, Navesink, NJ 07752.

17x/year. **Description:** Recreation,outdoors, and fashion publications interested in new approaches to activities or improvements on tried-and-true methods. **Nonfiction:** How-to features on hunting, fishing, fly-fishing, gardening, and outdoor adventure; 1,500-3,000 words. **Art:** Fashion photos; Color slides or B&W prints. **Queries:** Preferred.

BACKPACKER

Rodale Press

33 E Minor St., Emmaus, PA 18098. 610-967-8296.

E-mail: editor@backpacker.com. Web site: www.backpacker.com. Jonathan Dorn, Executive Editor. **Description:** On self-propelled backcountry travel (backpacking, kayaking/canoeing, mountaineering; technique, nordic skiing, health, natural science). **Nonfiction:** Articles; 250-3,000 words; pay varies. **Art:** Photos. **Tips:** Send queries to Jonathan Dorn. **Queries:** Preferred.

BACKWOODSMAN

P.O. Box 627, Westcliffe, CO 81252. 719-783-9028.

E-mail: bwmmag@ris.net. Web site: www.backwoodsmanmag.com. Bimonthly. $3.95. Circ.: 35,000. Charlie Richie, Editor. **Description:** On muzzleloaders, 19th-century woods lore, early cartridge guns, primitive survival, craft items, American history, gardening, leather crafting, homesteading, log cabin construction, mountain men, Indians, building primitive weapons. **Nonfiction:** Historical and how-to articles for the 20th-century frontiersman; No payment. **Queries:** Preferred. **E-Queries:** Yes. **Unsolicited mss:** Accepts. **Response:** 3 days, SASE. **Freelance Content:** 50%.

BASSIN'
NatCom, Inc.
15115 S 76th E Ave., Bixby, OK 74008-4114. 918-366-6191.
E-mail: ltaylor@natcom-publications.com. Web site: www.ebassin.com. 7x/yr. Circ.: 165,000. Lawrence Taylor, Editor. **Description:** How and where to bass fish, for the amateur fisherman. **Nonfiction:** Articles; 1,200-1,400 words; pays $350-$500. **Queries:** Preferred. **Payment:** On acceptance.

BASSMASTER
B.A.S.S. Publications
5845 Carmichael Rd., Montgomery, AL 36117. 334-272-9530.
E-mail: editorial@bassmaster.com. Web site: www.bassmaster.com. Monthly. $3.95. Circ.: 600,000. Dave Precht, Editor. **Description:** For members of the Bass Anglers Sportsman Society (B.A.S.S.), on fishing for freshwater bass: largemouth, small-mouth, spotted, redeye, and shoal. (White, striped, and hybrid bass covered on a limited basis.) **Nonfiction:** Features (1,200-1,800 words); shorts (250-750 words); include photos; $.30/word. **Art:** 35mm slides; pays $700 for cover. **Tips:** Promote catch-and-release, conservation, where-to-go stories about good bass fishing in North America and abroad. No first-person accounts ("How I caught my bass"). **Queries:** Preferred. **E-Queries:** Yes. **Unsolicited mss:** Accepts. **Response:** Queries 1-2 weeks, submissions 2-4 weeks, SASE required. **Freelance Content:** 80%. **Rights:** 1st, electronic. **Payment:** On acceptance.

BAY & DELTA YACHTSMAN
Recreation Publications
4090 S McCarran Blvd., Suite E, Reno, NV 89502-7529. 775-353-5100.
E-mail: don.abbott@yachtsforsale.com. Web site: www.yachtsforsale.com. Monthly. $17.60/yr. Circ.: 30,000. Don Abbott, Publisher. **Description:** Cruising stories and features, how-tos, with northern California focus. **Nonfiction:** Boating experiences, anecdotes, around San Francisco Bay and Delta; 2,000 words; pay varies. **Columns, Departments:** Boating stories, boat maintenance; 4,000 words. **Art:** TIF or JPG (300 dpi). **Queries:** Preferred. **E-Queries:** Yes. **Unsolicited mss:** Accepts. **Response:** 1 week, SASE required. **Freelance Content:** 0%. **Payment:** On publication.

BICYCLING
Rodale Press, Inc.
135 N Sixth St., Emmaus, PA 18098. 610-967-5171.
E-mail: bicycling@rodale.com. Web site: www.bicycling.com. Doug Donaldson, Associate Editor. **Description:** For cyclists, on recreational riding, fitness training,

nutrition, bike maintenance, equipment, and racing. Covers all aspects of sport (road, mountain biking, leisure, etc.). **Nonfiction:** Articles; 500-2,500 words; pays $50-$2,000. **Art:** Photos, illustrations. **Tips:** Queries preferred instead of manuscripts. Currently looking for interesting cycling personalities and adventure stories. **Queries:** Preferred. **Payment:** On acceptance.

BIRD WATCHER'S DIGEST

Parsdon Corp.
P.O. Box 110, Marietta, OH 45750-0110. 740-373-5285.
E-mail: editor@birdwatchersdigest.com. Web site: www.birdwatchersdigest.com.
Bimonthly. Circ.: 90,000. William H. Thompson III, Editor. **Description:** Bird-watching experiences and expeditions; interesting backyard topics and how-tos. **Nonfiction:** Articles for bird watchers: first-person accounts; profiles of bird species; 600-2,500 words; from $100. **Queries:** Preferred. **Response:** 8 weeks, SASE required. **Payment:** On publication.

BIRDER'S WORLD

Kalmbach Publishing Co.
21027 Crossroads Circle, P.O. Box 1612, Waukesha, WI 53187-1612. 262-796-8776.
Web site: www.birdersworld.com. Bimonthly. $4.50/$22.50. Circ.: 70,000. Charles J. Hagner, Editor. **Description:** On all aspects of birds and birding. Offers tips on birding, attracting and feeding birds, gardening, and travel. **Nonfiction:** Feature articles, 2,200-2,400 words; pays $350-$450. **Columns, Departments:** Book reviews (to 500 words); personal essays (500-1,500 words). **Queries:** Preferred. **E-Queries:** No. **Unsolicited mss:** Accepts. **Response:** 3 months, SASE (if visuals are sent). **Freelance Content:** 75%. **Rights:** 1st NA. **Payment:** On publication.

BLACK BELT

P.O. Box 918, Santa Clarita, CA 91380-9018. 661-257-4066.
Web site: www.blackbeltmag.com. Quarterly. Circ.: 85,000. Robert Young, Editor. **Description:** Articles related to self-defense (how-tos on fitness and technique; historical, travel, philosophy). **Nonfiction:** Pays $100-$300. **Payment:** On publication.

THE BOUNDARY WATERS JOURNAL

9396 Rocky Ledge Rd., Ely, MN 55731. 218-365-6184.
E-mail: bwjournal@boundarywatersjournal.com.
Web site: www.boundarywatersjournal.com. Quarterly. $4.95/issue, $18/year. Circ.: 32,000. Stuart Osthoff, Editor. **Description:** In-depth outdoor guide covering Boundary Waters Canoe Area Wilderness, Quetico Provincial Park, and surrounding Superior National Forest. **Fiction:** Must relate to coverage area; $100-$400. **Nonfiction:** Canoe routes, camping, fishing, resort vacations, hiking, hunting, photography, wildlife, ecology, outdoor cooking, area history, regional personalities; must relate to coverage area; 1-5 pages; $100-$400. **Poetry:** Up to 1 page; must relate to coverage area; $50-$100. **Art:** Color slides; B&W photos and artwork; $50/half page, $100/full page, $150/cover. **Tips:** Often needs winter stories. **Queries:** Not necessary.

E-Queries: Yes. **Unsolicited mss:** Accepts. **Response:** 1-2 weeks for queries, 1-3 months for submissions; SASE required. **Freelance Content:** 50%. **Rights:** FNAR. **Payment:** On publication.

BOW & ARROW HUNTING
Y-Visionary Publishing
LP, 265 S Anita Dr., Suite 120, Orange, CA 92868. 714-939-9991.
E-mail: editorial@bowandarrowhunting.com.
Web site: www.bowandarrowhunting.com. Joe Bell, Editor. **Description:** On bowhunting (profiles and technical pieces), primarily on deer hunting. **Nonfiction:** Articles; 1,200-2,500 words; with color slides, B&W or color photos; pays $250-$500. **Payment:** On publication.

BOWHUNTER
PRIMEDIA Enthusiast Group
6405 Flank Dr., Harrisburg, PA 17112. 717-657-9555.
E-mail: bowhunter_magazine@primediamags.com. Web site: www.bowhunter.com. 9x/year. $3.50/issue, $23.94/year. Circ.: 180,250. Dwight Schuh, Editor-in-Chief. **Description:** Information for bowhunters, on all aspects of the sport, to entertain and inform readers, making them better bowhunters. **Nonfiction:** General interest, how-to, interview/profile, opinion, personal experience, photo features; 250-2,000 words; $100-$400. **Art:** 35mm slides, 5x7 or 8x10 prints; $75-$250. **Tips:** Anticipate all questions, then answer them in article or sidebar. Must know bowhunting. **Queries:** Preferred. **E-Queries:** Yes. **Unsolicited mss:** Accepts. **Response:** Queries 1 month, submissions 5 weeks, SASE required. **Freelance Content:** 100%. **Rights:** FNASR, one-time. **Payment:** On acceptance.

BOWHUNTING WORLD
Ehlert Publishing Group
6420 Sycamore Lane N #100, Maple Grove, MN 55305. 612-476-2200.
E-mail: mstrandlund@affinitygroup.com. Bimonthly. Circ.: 130,000. Mike Strandlund, Editor. **Description:** Covers all aspects of bowhunting and competitive archery equipment, with photos. **Nonfiction:** Seeking how-to articles on bowhunting techniques, feature articles on hunting and the mechanics of archery gear (traditional to high-tech); 1,800-3,000 words. **Columns, Departments:** Mini-features; 1,000-1,600 words. **Tips:** Outline no more than 6 article ideas per query. **Queries:** Preferred. **E-Queries:** Yes. **Unsolicited mss:** Accepts. **Response:** Queries 3 week, submission 6 weeks, SASE required. **Freelance Content:** 50%. **Rights:** 1st. **Payment:** On acceptance.

BOWLERS JOURNAL INTERNATIONAL
122 S Michigan Ave., #1506, Chicago, IL 60603-6107. 312-341-1110.
Web site: www.bowlersjournal.com. Jim Dressel, Editor. **Description:** On bowling. **Nonfiction:** Trade and consumer articles; 1,200-2,200 words, with photos; pays $75-$250. **Payment:** On acceptance.

BOWLING
8410 W Cleveland Ave., Suite 205, West Allis, WI 53227. 414-321-8310.
Bimonthly. $3.50/issue. Circ.: 60,000. Bill Vint, Editor. **Description:** Covers the world of ten-pin bowling. **Nonfiction:** Seeking unique, unusual stories about bowling people and places. Human-interest features, with quality photos; 500-1,500 words; $100-$250. **Poetry:** $25-$50. **Art:** Photographs to accompany stories; prints or raw film. **Queries:** Preferred. **E-Queries:** No. **Response:** Queries 1-2 weeks, submissions 1-2 weeks, SASE required. **Freelance Content:** 20-30%. **Rights:** All. **Payment:** On acceptance.

BOYS' LIFE
See page 460 for full listing.
Description: For boys ages 8-14 covering sports, hobbies, crafts, and scouting.

BUCKMASTERS WHITETAIL
Buckmasters, Ltd.
P.O. Box 244022, Montgomery, AL 36124-4022. 334-215-3337.
E-mail: rthornberry@buckmasters.com. Web site: www.buckmasters.com. Circ.: 330,000. Russell Thornberry, Executive Editor. **Description:** For serious sportsmen. **Nonfiction:** Articles, to 2,500 words. "Big Buck Adventures" capture details and adventure of the hunt of a newly discovered trophy. Fresh, new whitetail hunting how-tos; new useful biological information about whitetail deer. Pays $250-$400. **Columns, Departments:** Entertaining deer stories. **Art:** Photos helpful. **Queries:** Preferred.

CANOE & KAYAK, INC
PRIMEDIA Enthusiast Group
P.O. Box 3146, Kirkland, WA 98083-3146. 425-827-6363.
E-mail: editor@canoekayak.com. Web site: www.canoekayak.com. Tim Jackson, Editor. **Description:** Articles and features on canoeing and kayaking adventures, destinations, boat and equipment reviews, techniques and how-tos, short essays, camping, environment, safety, humor, health, and history. **Nonfiction:** Features (1,500-2,000 words); department pieces (500-1,200 words); $.15/word. **Queries:** Preferred. **Payment:** On publication.

CASCADES EAST
Sun Publishing
716 NE Fourth St., P.O. Box 5784, Bend, OR 97708-5784. 541-382-0127.
E-mail: sunpub@sun-pub.com. Web site: www.sun-pub.com. Quarterly. Circ.: 10,000. Geoff Hill, Publisher/Editor. **Description:** Outdoor activities (fishing, hunting, golfing, backpacking, rafting, skiing, snowmobiling, etc.), history, special events, and scenic tours in central Oregon Cascades. **Nonfiction:** 1,000-2,000 words; $.05-$.15/word. **Fillers:** Travel, history, and recreation in central Oregon; $.05-.$15/word. **Art:** Photos; pays extra. **Queries:** Preferred. **Payment:** On publication.

CHESAPEAKE BAY MAGAZINE

See page 505 for full listing.

Description: For recreational boaters on the Chesapeake Bay.

CROSS COUNTRY SKIER

P.O. Box 550, Cable, WI 54821. 715-798-5500.

Web site: www.crosscountryskier.com. Lou Dzierzak, Editor. **Description:** Publishes articles on all aspects of cross-country skiing. **Nonfiction:** Features destination articles; to 2,000 words; $200-$400. **Columns, Departments:** Pieces on ski maintenance, ski techniques, health and fitness, etc; 1,000-1,500 words; $100-250. **Tips:** Published October through January. **Queries:** Preferred. **Payment:** On publication.

DAKOTA OUTDOORS

Hipple Publishing Co.

P.O. Box 669, 333 W Dakota Ave., Pierre, SD 57501. 605-224-7301.

Web site: www.capjournal.com\dakotaoutdoors. Monthly. $2.25/$10. Circ.: 8,000. Kevin Hipple, Editor. **Description:** Articles on hunting and fishing for outdoorsman in the Dakotas. **Fiction:** 1,000-1,500 words; $5-$50. **Nonfiction:** 1,000-1,500 words; $5-$50. **Art:** B&W, color. **Queries:** Not necessary. **E-Queries:** No. **Unsolicited mss:** Accepts. **Response:** Queries 2 weeks, SASE. **Freelance Content:** 75%. **Rights:** One-time. **Payment:** On publication.

THE DIVER

Seagraphics Publications Ltd.

P.O. Box 1312, Delta, British Columbia V4M 3Y8 Canada. 604-948-9937.

E-mail: divermag@axion.net. Web site: www.divermag.com. 9x/yr. Circ.: 7,000. Peter Vassilopoulos, Editor. **Description:** On scuba diving, ocean science and technology for well-educated, outdoor enthusiasts. **Nonfiction:** Illustrated articles on Canadian and North American dive destinations, interviews, personal experiences; 500-1,000 words; $2.50/column inch. **Art:** To accompany articles; original slides, color prints, maps, drawings; C$15 and up. **Tips:** Travel articles not paid. **Queries:** Not necessary. **E-Queries:** Yes. **Unsolicited mss:** Accepts. **Response:** SASE required. **Freelance Content:** 30%. **Rights:** FNAR. **Payment:** On publication. **Contact:** Barb Roy, Assistant Editor.

ELYSIAN FIELDS QUARTERLY

See page 665 for full listing.

Description: Literary review for baseball, with essays, poetry, commentary, drama, book reviews, and humor.

EXPLORE

54 St. Patrick St., Toronto, Ontario M5T 1V1 Canada. 416-599-2000.

E-mail: explore@explore-mag.com. Web site: www.explore-mag.com. James Little, Editor. **Description:** For Canada's active outdoor enthusiasts. Covers adventure travel, hiking, mountain biking, climbing, canoeing, winter sports, and more.

Nonfiction: Features (profiles, adventure stories, destinations). **Columns, Departments:** Explorata (people and outdoor events in the news); The Lowdown (outdoor gear); Techniques; Places to Go; Backcountry (humor). **Tips:** Content mostly Canadian, coast to coast to coast. **Queries:** Required. **E-Queries:** Yes.

FIELD & STREAM

2 Park Ave., New York, NY 10016. 212-779-5286.
E-mail: fsmagazine@aol.com. Web site: www.fieldandstream.com. Monthly. $3.99/$15.97. Circ.: 1,500,000. Slaton White, Editor. **Description:** The nation's largest hunting and fishing magazine. **Fiction:** On aspects of hunting and fishing. **Nonfiction:** On aspects of hunting and fishing: tactics/techniques, nostalgia, conversation essays, profiles, humor; pay, length vary. **Fillers:** Cartoons, small fillers (how-to); $100-$250. **Art:** Pay varies. **Queries:** Preferred. **E-Queries:** Yes. **Unsolicited mss:** Accepts. **Response:** 2-4 weeks, SASE required. **Freelance Content:** 85%. **Rights:** 1st NA. **Payment:** On acceptance.

FISHING FACTS

111 Shore Dr., Burr Ridge, IL 60521. 630-887-7722.
E-mail: info@midwestoutdoors.com. Web site: www.fishingfacts.com. Bimonthly. $23.95. Gene Laulunen, Publisher/Editor. **Description:** For the angler who wants to improve skills and maximize success. In-depth articles on fish behavior, techniques for taking fish from all kinds of structure, the latest in fishing products and technology, and simple tips from experts. **Nonfiction:** Seeking cutting-edge information on latest fishing techniques and tips; 750-1,500 words; $30 fee. **Art:** Submit quality, full-color prints with each article. **Tips:** No elementary fishing techniques or everyday fishing stories. **Queries:** Required. **E-Queries:** Yes. **Unsolicited mss:** Accepts. **Response:** 10 days, SASE required. **Rights:** 1st. **Payment:** On publication. **Contact:** Dena Kollman, Assistant Editor.

FLIGHT JOURNAL

Air Age Publishing
100 E Ridge, Ridgefield, CT 06877-4606. 203-431-9000.
E-mail: flightjournal@airage.com. Web site: www.flightjournal.com. Tom Atwood, Editorial Director. **Description:** Covers "the history, the hardware, and the human heart of aviation." **Nonfiction:** Articles, 2,500-3,000 words; pays $600. **Tips:** Submit 1-page outline. **Contact:** Roger Post, Editor.

FLY ROD & REEL

P.O. Box 370, Camden, ME 04843. 207-594-9544.
E-mail: pguernsey@flyrodreel.com. Web site: www.flyrodreel.com. Paul Guernsey, Editor. **Description:** Publishes articles and features on fly-fishing. **Fiction:** Occasionally. **Nonfiction:** Articles on fly-fishing, on culture and history of areas being fished, 2,000-2,500 words; pay varies. **Queries:** Preferred. **Payment:** On acceptance.

FLYER

N.W. Flyer, Inc.,
P.O. Box 39099, Lakewood, WA 98439-0099. 253-471-9888.
E-mail: kirk.gormley@flyer-online.com. Web site: www.flyer-online.com. Biweekly.
Circ.: 35,000. Kirk Gormley, Editor. **Description:** Of interest to "general aviation"
pilots. **Nonfiction:** 500-2,500 words; to $3/column inch (about 40 words). **Art:** $10
for B&W photos; $50 for color photos. **Freelance Content:** 30%. **Payment:** Within
one month of publication.

FOOTBALL DIGEST

Century Publishing Co.
990 Grove St., Evanston, IL 60201-6510. 847-491-6440.
E-mail: fb@centurysports.net. Web site: www.centurysports.net. Monthly. $23.94/yr.
Circ.: 180,000. Jim O'Connor, Editor-in-Chief. **Description:** For the hard-core foot-
ball fan. Profiles of pro and college stars, nostalgia, trends in the sport. **Nonfiction:**
Articles, 1,500-2,500 words. **Queries:** Preferred. **Payment:** On publication.

FUR-FISH-GAME

2878 E Main St., Columbus, OH 43209. 614-231-9585.
Monthly. $3.99/issue. Circ.: 107,000. Mitch Cox, Editor. **Description:** For serious
outdoorsmen of all ages. Covers hunting, trapping, freshwater fishing, predator call-
ing, camping, boating, woodcrafting, conservation, and related topics. **Nonfiction:**
Seeking short how-to, humor, and human-interest articles; 2,000-3,000 words; $100-
$250. **Art:** Varied photos (close-ups, overall scenes); Color slides, B&W, color prints;
$25. **Queries:** Required. **E-Queries:** Yes. **Unsolicited mss:** Accepts. **Freelance
Content:** 75%. **Rights:** 1st NA. **Payment:** On acceptance.

GAME AND FISH PUBLICATIONS

P.O. Box 741, Marietta, GA 30061. 770-953-9222.
Ken Dunwoody, Editorial Department. **Description:** Publishes 30 monthly outdoor
magazines for 48 states. **Nonfiction:** Articles, 1,500-2,500 words, on hunting and
fishing (how-tos, where-tos, and adventure). Profiles of successful hunters and fishermen. No hiking, canoeing, camping, or backpacking pieces. Pays $125-$175 for
state-specific articles, $200-$250 for multi-state articles. **Art:** Photos; pays $25-$75
(interior), $250 (covers). **Payment:** On acceptance.

GOLF

Time4Media
2 Park Ave., New York, NY 10016-5675. 212-779-5000.
E-mail: golfletters@golfonline.com. Web site: www.golfonline.com. Monthly. $19.94.
Circ.: 1,403,000. James Frank, Editor. **Description:** Articles, 1,000 words with photos, on golf history and travel (places to play around the world); profiles of professional tour players. Shorts, to 500 words. Pays $.75 a word, on acceptance. Queries
preferred.

GOLF COURSE NEWS

United Publications, Inc.
106 Lafayette St., P.O. Box 997, Yarmouth, ME 04096. 207-846-0600.
E-mail: aoverbeck@golfcoursenews.com. Web site: www.golfcoursenews.com.
Andrew Overbeck, Editor. **Description:** Features and news analyses, 500-1,000 words, on all aspects of golf course maintenance, design, building, and management. Pays $200, on publication.

GOLF DIGEST

5520 Park Ave., Trumbull, CT 06611. 203-373-7000.
E-mail: editor@golfdigest.com. Web site: www.golfdigest.com. Monthly. $3.99. Circ.: 1,550,000. Jerry Tarde, Editor. **Description:** Covers golf instruction, equipment, and travel. Freelance content limited. **Queries:** Required.

GOLF FOR WOMEN

4 Times Square, New York, NY 10036. 212-286-3906.
E-mail: editors@golfforwomen.com. Susan K. Reed, Editor-in-Chief. **Description:** Golf lifestyle magazine for avid women golfers. Includes travel, instruction, fashion, equipment, news. Query with clips.

GOLF JOURNAL

Golf House, 77 Liberty Corner Road, Far Hills, NJ 07931-0708. 908-234-2300.
E-mail: golfjournal@usga.org. Web site: www.golfjournal.org. 9x/year. Membership publication. Circ.: 800,000. Brett Avery, Editor. **Description:** Published by United States Golf Assn., general interest, on contemporary issues and history as seen in the game, people, and values. **Fiction:** On humor, values; 500 words and up; $1/word. **Nonfiction:** On golf history, lore, rules, equipment, general information. Focus is on amateur golf. No jokes, instruction, or travel pieces. Accepts poignant, humorous stories and essays; 500 words and up; $1/word. **Queries:** Not necessary. **E-Queries:** Yes. **Unsolicited mss:** Accepts. **Response:** Queries and submissions, 4 weeks, SASE required. **Freelance Content:** 35-40%. **Payment:** On publication.

GOLF TIPS

Werner Publishing Corp.
12121 Wilshire Blvd., #1200, Los Angeles, CA 90025-1123. 310-820-1500.
E-mail: editors@golftipsmag.com. Web site: www.golftipsmag.com. 9x/yr. $17.94. Circ.: 292,500. Dave DeNunzio, Editor. **Description:** For serious golfers. **Nonfiction:** Articles, 500-1,500 words, unique golf instruction, golf products, interviews with pro players; pays $200-$600. **Fillers:** Short "shotmaking" instruction tips. **Queries:** Preferred. **Payment:** On publication.

GOLF TODAY

204 Industrial Rd., San Carlos, CA 94070. 650-802-8165.
E-mail: golf2day@sirius.com. Web site: www.golftodaymagazine.com. Monthly. $22/yr. Circ.: 151,000. Bob Koczor, Editor. **Description:** Golf magazine for players

in California, Nevada, Arizona, and Utah. **Nonfiction:** Travel stories, golf tips, product reviews, and guest columns; $5-$15/page. **Tips:** Works with new writers. **Queries:** Not necessary. **E-Queries:** Yes. **Unsolicited mss:** Accepts. **Response:** 1 day. **Freelance Content:** 25%. **Rights:** 1st NA. **Payment:** On acceptance.

GUN DIGEST
Krause Publications, Inc.
700 E State St., Iola, WI 54990. 888-457-2873.
E-mail: ramagek@krause.com. Web site: www.krause.com. Ken Ramage, Editor.
Description: On guns and shooting, equipment, etc. **Nonfiction:** Well-researched articles, to 5,000 words; pays to $.10 a word. **Art:** Photos. **Queries:** Preferred. **Payment:** On acceptance.

GUN DOG
See page 290 for full listing.
Description: Covers all aspects of bird hunting.

GUNGAMES MAGAZINE
421 Coeur d'Alene Ave., Coeur d'Alene, ID 83814. 800-771-3020.
Web site: www.gungames.com. Bimonthly. Jocelyn Stott. **Description:** Articles and fiction, 1,200-1,500 words, about "the fun side of guns and shooting." No self-defense articles. Pays $150-$250. **Payment:** On publication.

GUNS & AMMO
PRIMEDIA Enthusiast Group
6420 Wilshire Blvd., Fl. 14, Los Angeles, CA 90048-5502. 323-782-2000.
E-mail: gunsandammo@primediacmmg.com.
Web site: www.gunsandammomag.com. Monthly. $23.94/yr. Circ.: 607,000. Lee Hoots, Editor. **Description:** On guns, ammunition, and target shooting. **Nonfiction:** Technical and general articles, 800-2,500 words; pays from $150. **Art:** Photos. **Payment:** On acceptance.

HANG GLIDING
U.S. Hang Gliding Association
31441 Santa Margarita Pkwy., A-256
Rancho Santa Margarita, CA 92688-1836. 949-888-7363.
E-mail: ushga@ushga.org. Web site: www.ushga.org. Gil Dodgen, Editor-in-Chief.
Description: On hang gliding. **Nonfiction:** Articles, 2-3 pages; pays to $50. **Queries:** Preferred. **Payment:** On publication.

HIGHWIRED SPORTS
950 Winter St., Waltham, MA 02451-1424.
E-mail: contact@highwired-inc.com. Bimonthly. $2.95/$14.95. Circ.: 100,000. Nancy Petro, Editor. **Description:** Covers high-school sports. Offers information, recognition, and inspiration for today's student-athlete. **Nonfiction:** Profiles of top teams

and athletes; articles on recruiting and scholarships, health, nutrition, training, sports camps; 300-500 words; pay varies. **Tips:** Articles on successful athlete or team needs strong distinguishing factor; what makes their story unique? **Queries:** Preferred. **E-Queries:** Accepts. **Unsolicited mss:** Accepts. **Rights:** All. **Payment:** On publication. **Contact:** Stephanie Strong.

HORSE & RIDER
PRIMEDIA Enthusiast Group
P.O. Box 4101, 741 Corporate Circle, Suite A, Golden, CO 80401. 720-836-1257.
E-mail: hrsenrider@cowles.com. Web site: www.horseandrider.com. Monthly. $3.99/issue, $19.95/year. Circ.: 165,000. René Riley, Executive Editor. **Description:** Educates, informs and entertains competitive and recreational Western riders with training articles, practical stable management techniques, hands-on health care, safe trail riding practices, and coverage of major Western events. **Nonfiction:** Personality profiles, consumer buying advice, and how-tos (training, horse care/horsekeeping); 150-2,000 words; $150-$1,000. **Fillers:** Humorous experiences; 150-1,000 words; $150-$1,000. **Columns, Departments:** Real-life horse stories, trail-riding tips, training tips; 150-1,000 words; $0-$1,000. **Art:** Send query before submitting. Include SASE and photo spec sheet outlining the details of your work; photos. **Tips:** Please be familiar with subject matter and style before sending manuscript or query. **Queries:** Preferred. **E-Queries:** No. **Unsolicited mss:** Accepts. **Response:** 3 months; SASE required. **Freelance Content:** 5%. **Rights:** 1st NA. **Payment:** On acceptance.

HOT BOAT
LFP, Inc.
8484 Wilshire Blvd., Suite 900, Beverly Hills, CA 90211-3221. 323-651-5400.
E-mail: hbmail@aol.com. Web site: www.hotboat.net. Monthly. $23.95. Circ.: 40,000. Brett Bayne, Editor. **Description:** On motorized water sport events and personalities: general-interest, how-to, and technical features. **Nonfiction:** Family-oriented articles, 600-1,000 words; pays $85-$300. **Queries:** Preferred. **Payment:** On publication.

THE IN-FISHERMAN
PRIMEDIA Enthusiast Group
Two In-Fisherman Dr., Brainerd, MN 56425-8098. 218-829-1648.
E-mail: dstange@cowles.com. Web site: www.in-fisherman.com. 8x/yr. Circ.: 300,000. Doug Stange, Editor-in-Chief. **Description:** On all aspects of freshwater fishing. **Nonfiction:** How-to articles, 1,500-4,500 words; pays $250-$1,000. **Columns, Departments:** Reflections (humorous or nostalgic looks at fishing), 1,000-1,500 words. **Payment:** On acceptance. **Contact:** Scott Lawrence.

INSIDE TEXAS RUNNING
9514 Bristlebrook Dr., Houston, TX 77083-6193. 281-498-3208.
E-mail: insidetx@aol.com. Web site: www.insidetexasrunning.com. 10x/year. $12.

Circ.: 8,000. Joanne Schmidt, Editor. **Description:** Tabloid newspaper, for runners in Texas. **Nonfiction:** Travel pieces for runners attending out-of-town races; unusual runners (not just fast runners); race write-ups; 300-1,500 words; $300-$1,500. **Columns, Departments:** Short news items for Texas Roundup (2-5 paragraphs max.). **Art:** $10-$25. **Tips:** Avoid "How I ran the marathon" articles or subject matter on other sports. Use quotes. Welcomes new writers with appropriate expertise. **Queries:** Required. **E-Queries:** Yes. **Unsolicited mss:** Accepts. **Response:** 4 weeks, SASE required. **Freelance Content:** 30%. **Rights:** One-time. **Payment:** On publication.

JOURNAL OF ASIAN MARTIAL ARTS
See page 369 for full listing.
Description: On martial arts and Asian culture.

KITPLANES
See page 440 for full listing.
Description: For designers, builders, and pilots of home-built experimental aircraft.

LAKELAND BOATING
O'Meara/Brown Publications
500 Davis St., Suite 1000, Evanston, IL 60201-4643. 847-869-5400.
E-mail: lb@omeara-brown.com. Web site: www.lakelandboating.com. Monthly. $21.95. Circ.: 38,200. Mathew Wright, Editor. **Description:** On boating in the Great Lakes and surrounding areas. **Nonfiction:** Cruising features, boating, and Great Lakes information. Also, newsy bits, maintenance tips (100 words up); 800-2,500 words; $50-$600. **Columns, Departments:** Cruising, Port O' Call, Weekender, Historical Subjects, Environment, Bosun's Locker, Antique and Classic Boats, Profiles; 800-2,500 words; $50-$600. **Tips:** Looking for freelance writers who are also skilled photographers. **Queries:** Required. **E-Queries:** Yes. **Unsolicited mss:** Accepts. **Response:** 2-4 weeks, SASE. **Rights:** FNASR and electronic. **Payment:** On publication.

MICHIGAN OUT-OF-DOORS
P.O. Box 30235, Lansing, MI 48909. 517-371-1041.
E-mail: magazine@mucc.org. Web site: www.mucc.org. Monthly. $3.50/issue, $25/year. Circ.: 100,000. Dennis Knickerbocker, Editor. **Description:** On Michigan's natural environment and outdoor recreation, with emphasis on hunting, fishing, and nature study. **Nonfiction:** Informative, entertaining features for sportsmen/women, and all who enjoy the out-of-doors; how-to, investigative, personal adventure, nature lore; 1,000-1,500 words; $90-$200. **Fillers:** Cartoons and line drawings; $30. **Columns, Departments:** By assignment; 700-800 words; $75-$100. **Art:** B&W and color photos; slides, transparencies, prints; $20-$175. **Queries:** Preferred. **E-Queries:** No. **Unsolicited mss:** Accepts. **Response:** 1 month for queries, 3-4 months for submissions; SASE required. **Freelance Content:** 75%. **Payment:** On acceptance.

MID-WEST OUTDOORS

111 Shore Dr., Hinsdale, IL 60521-5885. 638-887-7722.
E-mail: glaulenen@midwestoutdoors.com. Web site: www.midwestoutdoors.com.
Annual. $2.99/issue, $14.95/year. Circ.: 35,000. Gene Laulunen, Editor.
Description: Seeks to help people enjoy the outdoors by providing positive stories
about outdoor experiences. **Nonfiction:** Where, when, why, how-to articles about the
Midwest; 1,500 words; $30. **Tips:** Avoid first-time experience stories. **Queries:** Not
necessary. **E-Queries:** No. **Unsolicited mss:** Accepts. **Response:** varies.
Freelance Content: 95%. **Rights:** One-time and Web. **Payment:** On publication.

MOUNTAIN BIKE

Rodale Press
135 N Sixth St., Emmaus, PA 18049-2441. 610-967-5171.
E-mail: mbcrank@mountainbike.com. Web site: www.mountainbike.com. 11x/yr.
$19.97. Circ.: 150,300. Zapata Espinoza, Executive Editor. **Description:** On moun-
tain-bike touring; major off-road cycling events; political, sport, or land-access issues;
riding techniques; fitness and training tips. **Nonfiction:** Articles, 500-2,000 words;
pays $100-$650. **Columns, Departments:** Descriptions, detailing routes of off-road
rides, to 500 words; pays $75. **Queries:** Preferred. **Payment:** On publication.

MUSHING

Stellar Communications, Inc.
P.O. Box 149, Ester, AK 99725-0149. 907-479-0454.
E-mail: editor@mushing.com. Web site: www.mushing.com. Bimonthly. $24/yr. Todd
Hoener, Editor. **Description:** Dog-driving how-tos, innovations, history, profiles,
interviews, and features related to sled dogs. International audience. **Nonfiction:**
1,000-2,500 words. **Columns, Departments:** Competitive and recreational dog
drivers; weight pullers, dog packers, and skijorers; 500-1,000 words. **Art:** Photos. 50-
80% B&W; $20-$250. **Tips:** Send qualifications and clips of previous publications.
Also include a short biography. Will work new and unpublished authors. **Queries:**
Preferred. **E-Queries:** Yes. **Unsolicited mss:** Accepts. **Rights:** 1st NA. **Payment:**
On publication. **Contact:** Erica Keiko Iseri.

MUZZLE BLASTS

P.O. Box 67, Friendship, IN 47021-0067. 812-667-5131.
E-mail: mblastdop@seidata.com. Web site: www.nmlra.org. Monthly. $35/yr for
members. Circ.: 22,000. Eric A. Bye, Editor. **Description:** Published by the National
Muzzle Loading Rifle Assn. **Nonfiction:** Articles on antique muzzleloading guns,
gunmakers, events in America's past; how-tos on crafts related to muzzleloaders (gun-
building, making powder horns, engraving, etc.), safe handling, loading, etc; 1,500-
2,000 words; $150-$250. **Art:** Photos, illustrations; must reflect highest standard of
safety. **Tips:** Must know muzzleloaders (preferably traditional) and safety; generally,
avoid modern topics. **Queries:** Preferred. **E-Queries:** Yes. **Unsolicited mss:**
Accepts. **Response:** Queries 2-3 weeks, submissions 4-6 weeks. **Freelance
Content:** 70%. **Rights:** 1st NA. **Payment:** On publication.

NEW HAMPSHIRE WILDLIFE
54 Portsmouth St., Concord, NH 63301. 603-224-5953.
E-mail: nhwf@aol.com. Web site: www.nhwf.org. Bimonthly. Circ.: 7,000. Margaret Lane, Editor. **Description:** Hunting, fishing, trapping, and other active outdoor pursuits in New Hampshire. No payment offered. **Nonfiction:** First-person experiences; 400-1,500 words. **Fillers:** Wildlife, outdoors; short. **Queries:** Not necessary. **Unsolicited mss:** Accepts.

NORTHEAST OUTDOORS
Woodall Publishing Corp.
2575 Vista Del Mar, Ventura, CA 93001. 800-323-9078.
Web site: www.woodalls.com. Melinda Baccanai, Editor. **Description:** On camping and recreational vehicle (RV) touring in northeast U.S. **Nonfiction:** Prefers how-to, where-to (camp cookery, recreational vehicle hints). Articles, 1,000-2,000 words, preferably with B&W photos; pay varies.

OFFSHORE
220 Reservoir St., Suite 9, Needham, MA 02494-3133. 781-449-6204.
E-mail: editors@offshoremag.net. Web site: www.offshoremag.net. Monthly. $4.50/issue, $19.95/year. Circ.: 32,000. Betsy Frawley Haggerty, Editor. **Description:** Northeast power boaters and sailboaters (East Coast from Maine to New Jersey). **Nonfiction:** Destinations (seaports in New England, New York, New Jersey); things to do, places to see, navigation guidelines. First-hand accounts of boating adventures and mishaps. Also, fishing pieces; 1,500-3,000 words; $350-$700. **Columns, Departments:** Marina profiles (detail on Northeast marinas); Boater's Workshop (tips and techniques on boat care); 200-1500 words; $100-$350. **Art:** 35mm color slides; $45-$300/image. **Queries:** Required. **E-Queries:** Yes. **Unsolicited mss:** Accepts. **Response:** Queries 4 weeks, submissions 6 weeks, SASE. **Freelance Content:** 80%. **Rights:** 1st NA. **Payment:** On acceptance.

OUTDOOR CANADA
340 Ferrier St., Suite 210, Markham, Ontario L3R 2Z5 Canada. 905-475-8440.
E-mail: walsh@outdoorcanada.ca. 8x/year. Circ.: 80,000. Patrick Walsh, Editor-in-Chief. **Description:** Articles on fishing, hunting, and conservation. **Nonfiction:** 100-4,000 words. Payment depends on length and complexity of article; $.50/word and up. **Payment:** On acceptance.

OUTSIDE
Mariah Media, Inc.
400 Market St., Santa Fe, NM 87501-7300. 505-989-7100.
E-mail: letters@outsidemag.com. Web site: www.outsidemag.com. Monthly. $4.95/$18. Circ.: 591,000. Hal Epsen, Editor. **Description:** Active lifestyle; outdoor sports, adventure travel; environment; outdoor equipment. **Nonfiction:** On the environment, outdoor sports, how-to, personal experience, reviews of equipment, etc. 1,500-4,000 words. **Columns, Departments:** Dispatches (news events);

Destinations (places to explore). **Tips:** Departments are best areas for new writers to break in. **Queries:** Preferred. **Unsolicited mss:** Does not accept. **Response:** 2 months, SASE. **Freelance Content:** 90%. **Rights:** FNASR.

PADDLER
P.O. Box 775450, Steamboat Springs, CO 80477. 970-879-1450.
Web site: www.paddlermagazine.com. Eugene Buchanan, Editor. **Description:** On canoeing, kayaking, rafting, and sea kayaking. **Nonfiction:** Articles; pays $.15-$.25/word. **Columns, Departments:** Hotlines; Paddle People. **Tips:** Best way to break in is to target a specific department. **Queries:** Preferred. **Payment:** On publication. **Contact:** Frederick Reimers.

PARAGLIDING
United States Hang Gliding Association
31441 Santa Margarita Parkway, #A-256, Rancho Santa Margarita, CA 92668-1836. 719-632-8300.
E-mail: ushga@ushga.org. Web site: www.ushga.org. Monthly. $26/yr. Circ.: 3,500. Gil Dodgen, Editor-in-Chief. **Description:** On paragliding. **Nonfiction:** 2-3 pages; pays $50. **Queries:** Preferred. **Payment:** On publication.

PENNSYLVANIA ANGLER & BOATER
Pennsylvania Fish and Boat Commission
P.O. Box 67000, Harrisburg, PA 17106-7000. 717-657-4520.
Web site: www.fish.state.pa.us. Art Michaels, Editor. **Description:** On freshwater fishing and boating in Pennsylvania. **Nonfiction:** Articles, 500-3,000 words, with photos; pays $50-$300. **Queries:** Preferred. **Response:** SASE required. **Payment:** On acceptance.

PENNSYLVANIA GAME NEWS
Game Commission
2001 Elmerton Ave., Harrisburg, PA 17110-9797. 717-787-3745.
Monthly. $1.50/issue. Circ.: 120,000. Bob Mitchell, Editor. **Description:** Published by the state Game Commission, for promoting wildlife programs, hunting, and trapping in the state. **Nonfiction:** On hunting or wildlife, with Pennsylvania interest; 2,000 words; $.08/word. **Tips:** No controversial issues, or technical subjects by freelancers. Avoid "first deer" stories. **Queries:** Not necessary. **E-Queries:** No. **Unsolicited mss:** Accepts. **Response:** 4-6 weeks, SASE. **Freelance Content:** 40%. **Rights:** 1st. **Payment:** On acceptance.

PETERSEN'S BOWHUNTING
6420 Wilshire Blvd., Los Angeles, CA 90048-5515. 323-782-2721.
Web site: www.bowhuntingmag.com. Monthly (9/year). $3.99/11.97. Circ.: 192,000. Jay Michael Strangis, Editor. **Description:** How-to help for bowhunter enthusiasts. Also, interesting stories about bowhunting. **Nonfiction:** Bowhunting adventure stories. How-to and technical (equipment, products) articles; 2,000 words; $150-$400.

Art: Photos must accompany all manuscripts; B&W or color prints; $100-$600. **Queries:** Preferred. **E-Queries:** Yes. **Unsolicited mss:** Accepts. **Response:** Queries 3-4 days, submissions 6-7 days, SASE. **Freelance Content:** 40%. **Rights:** All, 1st (photos). **Payment:** On acceptance.

PGA MAGAZINE
Great Golf Resorts of the World, Inc.
122 Sycamore Dr., Jupiter, FL 33485-2860. 561-776-0069.
E-mail: mmarsom@aol.com. Web site: www.pga.com. Monthly. $29.95. Circ.: 30,500. Matt Marsom, Editorial Director. **Description:** On golf-related subjects. **Nonfiction:** Articles, 1,500-2,500 words; pays $300-$500. **Queries:** Preferred. **Payment:** On acceptance.

PLANE & PILOT
Werner Publishing Corp.
12121 Wilshire Blvd., Suite 1200, Los Angeles, CA 90025-1175. 310-820-1500.
E-mail: editors@planeandpilotmag.com. Web site: www.planeandpilotmag.com. Mike McMann, Publisher. **Description:** Aviation-related articles, for pilots of single-engine, piston-powered recreational airplanes. **Nonfiction:** Training, maintenance, travel, equipment, pilot reports. Occasional features on antique, classic, and kit- or home-built aircraft; 1,500-2,500 words; pay varies. **Queries:** Preferred. **Payment:** On publication.

POWER AND MOTORYACHT
260 Madison Ave., Fl. 8, New York, NY 10016. 917-256-2267.
E-mail: rthiel@primediasi.com. Monthly. Circ.: 157,400. Richard Thiel, Editor. **Description:** For affluent, experienced owners of powerboats 30 feet and larger. Reaches almost every U.S. owner of a large powerboat, with advice on how to choose, operate, and maintain their boats. **Nonfiction:** Clear, concise, authoritative articles. Include personal experience and information from marine industry experts where appropriate; 800-1,400 words; $500-$1,200. **Tips:** No stories on powerboats smaller than 30-foot, or sailboats of any length. **Queries:** Required. **E-Queries:** Yes. **Unsolicited mss:** Does not accept. **Response:** Queries 1 month, SASE required. **Freelance Content:** 20-25%. **Rights:** All, print, electronic. **Payment:** On acceptance.

POWERBOAT
1691 Spinnaker Dr., Suite 206, Ventura, CA 93001. 805-639-2222.
E-mail: edit-dept@powerboatmag.com. Web site: www.powerboatmag.com. 11x/year. $4.50/$29 yr. Circ.: 41,000. Brett Becker, Editor. **Description:** Covers all types of powerboats, from tournament inboards to offshore boats. **Nonfiction:** For high-performance powerboat owners, on achievements, water-skiing, competitions; technical articles on hull and engine developments; how-to; 500-3,000 words; pay negotiable. **Art:** 35mm or larger formats; $50-$400. **Queries:** Required. **E-Queries:** Yes.

Unsolicited mss: Accepts. **Response:** 3 weeks, SASE. **Freelance Content:** 25%. **Payment:** On publication. **Contact:** Brett Becker.

PRACTICAL HORSEMAN

PRIMEDIA Enthusiast Group
P.O. Box 589, Unionville, PA 19375. 610-380-8977.
E-mail: Prachorse@aol.com. Mandy Lorraine, Editor. **Description:** How-to articles conveying leading experts' advice on English riding, training, and horse care. **Tips:** Send clips. **Queries:** Preferred. **Payment:** On acceptance.

PRIVATE PILOT

Y-Visionary Publishing
LP, 265 S Anita Dr., Suite 120, Orange, CA 92868-3310. 714-939-9991.
E-mail: bfedork@aol.com. Web site: www.privatepilotmag.com. Monthly. $3.99/issue $21.95/year. Circ.: 60,000. Bill Fedorko, Editorial Director. **Description:** General aviation, for pilots and owners of single and multi-engine aircraft, who want to read about places to go, aircraft, and ways to save money. **Nonfiction:** Fly-in destinations, hands-on, how-to, informative articles for pilots, aircraft owners, and aviation enthusiasts; 1,500-3,000 words; $400-$700. **Art:** $300 fee for photography assignments. **Queries:** Preferred. **E-Queries:** No. **Unsolicited mss:** Accepts. **Response:** 2-4 weeks, SASE. **Freelance Content:** 80%. **Rights:** 1st NA. **Payment:** On publication.

REAL SPORTS

P.O. Box 8204, San Jose, CA 95155-8204. 408-924-7434.
E-mail: freelance@real-sports.com. Web site: www.real-sports.com. Quarterly. $9.95/$29.99. Circ.: 150,000. Brian Styers, Editor. **Description:** Authoritative coverage of women's sports. Girls' and women's sports, team sports, professional, collegiate and amateur. Uses action-oriented photographs to show drama of competition. **Nonfiction:** Women's sports coverage; 500-2,000 words; $.50/word. **Art:** Slides; pay varies. **Tips:** Submit original, insightful, realistic portraits of women's sports. **Queries:** Required. **E-Queries:** Yes. **Unsolicited mss:** Does not accept. **Response:** 2 weeks, SASE. **Freelance Content:** 70%. **Rights:** 1st. **Payment:** On publication.

ROCK & ICE

North South Publications, LLC
5455 Spine Rd., Boulder, CO 80301-3345. 303-499-8410.
E-mail: editorial@rockandice.com. Web site: www.rockandice.com. Bimonthly. Circ.: 38,000. Dougald MacDonald, Publisher/Editor-in-Chief. **Description:** For technical rock and ice climbers (sport climbers, mountaineers, alpinists, and other adventurers). **Nonfiction:** Articles, 500-4,000 words; pays $300/published page. **Art:** Slides, B&W photos considered. **Queries:** Preferred.

RUNNER TRIATHLETE NEWS

P.O. Box 19909, 14201 Memorial Dr, Houston, TX 77224. 281-759-0555.
E-mail: rtnews@ix.netcom.com. Web site: www.runnertriathletenews.com. Monthly.
Circ.: 13,500. Lance Phegley, Editor. **Description:** Covers running, cycling,
triathlons, and duathlons in a 5-state area: Texas, Louisiana, Arkansas, Oklahoma,
New Mexico. **Nonfiction:** On running for road racing, and multi-sport enthusiasts.
Pay varies. **Queries:** Preferred. **E-Queries:** Yes. **Unsolicited mss:** Accepts.
Response: Queries 3-7 days, submissions 1-3 days. **Freelance Content:** 40%.
Payment: On publication.

RUNNER'S WORLD

Rodale Press
33 E Minor St., Emmaus, PA 18098. 610-967-5171.
E-mail: rwedit@rodale.com. Web site: www.runnersworld.com. Monthly. Circ.:
550,000. Bob Wischnia, Editor. **Description:** For recreational runners who train for
and race in long-distance events. **Nonfiction:** To 3,000 words. Payment varies. **Tips:**
No first-time marathon stories. **Queries:** Required. **E-Queries:** Yes. **Unsolicited
mss:** Accepts. **Response:** 2 weeks; SASE required. **Freelance Content:** 25%.
Rights: Worldwide. **Payment:** On acceptance.

RUNNING TIMES

213 Danbury Rd., Wilson, CT 06897-4006. 203-761-1113.
E-mail: editor@runningtimes.com. Web site: www.runningtimes.com. 10x/year.
$3.99/$24.97. Circ.: 70,000. Jonathan Beverly, Editor. **Description:** For the experienced running participant and fan. **Fiction:** Running related, any genre; 1,500-3,000
words; $100-$500. **Nonfiction:** Book excerpts, essays, historical/nostalgic, how-to,
humor, inspirational, interview/profile, new product, opinion, personal experience,
photo feature, travel, news, reports; 1,500-3,000 words; $100-$500. **Columns,
Departments:** Training (short topics on enhancing performance, 1,000 words);
Sports-Med (applying medical knowledge, 1,000 words); Nutrition, 1,000 words);
Cool Down (lighter essay on aspect of the running life), 400 words; 400-1,000 words;
$50-$200. **Tips:** Get to know runners and running culture, at participant and professional, elite level. No basic, beginner's how-to, generic fitness/nutrition or generic
first-person stories. **Queries:** Preferred. **E-Queries:** Yes. **Unsolicited mss:**
Accepts. **Response:** Queries 2-4 weeks, submissions 4-6 weeks, SASE. **Freelance
Content:** 50%. **Rights:** 1st NA, electronic. **Payment:** On publication.

SAFARI

Safari Club International
4800 W Gates Pass Rd., Tucson, AZ 85745. 520-620-1220.
E-mail: sskinner@safariclub.org. Web site: www.safariclub.org. William Quimby,
Editor. **Description:** On worldwide big game hunting and/or conservation projects
of Safari Club International's local chapters. **Nonfiction:** Articles, 2,000 words; pays
$200, extra for photos. **Payment:** On publication.

SAIL

98 N Washington St., Fl. 2, Boston, MA 02114. 617-720-8600.
Web site: www.sailingmag.com. Peter Nielson, Editor. **Description:** On sailboats, equipment, racing, and cruising. How-to articles on navigation, sail trim, etc. **Nonfiction:** Articles, 1,000-2,500 words, with photos; pays $75-$1,000. **Payment:** On publication. **Contact:** Amy Ullrich.

SAILING

125 E Main St., P.O. Box 249, Port Washington, WI 53074-1915. 262-284-3494.
E-mail: sailingmag@ameritech.net. Web site: sailingonline.com. Monthly. $3.99/issue. Circ.: 40,000. Greta Schanen, Managing Editor. **Description:** Illustrated, for the experienced sailor. Covers cruises, races, boat tests, gear and book reviews, personality profiles; also regular columns. **Nonfiction:** No cruising stories that are just logbooks. No "my first sail" stories. Writers must be familiar with sailing, provide good photos, and write for readers who are also genuine sailors; 200-4,000 words; $125-$600. **Art:** 35mm transparencies; $50-$600. **Tips:** Suggest a story not done in the past four years, include good photographs, and you're in! **Queries:** Preferred. **E-Queries:** Yes. **Unsolicited mss:** Accepts. **Response:** 2-4 weeks. **Freelance Content:** 60%. **Payment:** After publication.

SALT WATER SPORTSMAN

263 Summer St., Boston, MA 02210. 617-303-3660.
E-mail: barryg@saltwatersportsman.com. Web site: www.saltwatersportsman.com. Monthly. $4.99/issue, $22.95/year. Circ.: 161,000. Barry Gibson, editor. **Description:** Covers marine sport fishing along the coasts of the United States, Canada, the Caribbean, Central America, Bermuda, and occasionally South America and other overseas locations. **Fiction:** Fishing stories, humor, mood, and nostalgia; 1,500-2,000 words; $1,000. **Nonfiction:** How-to and where-to articles; 1,200-1,500 words; $500-$750. **Columns, Departments:** Sportsman's **Tips:** short how-to-make-it; tackle, rigs, boat equipment; 100-300 words; $150. **Art:** To accompany articles; color slides and prints; $100-$500/inside use, $1,500/covers. **Tips:** No blood and thunder, no overly romantic "remember when." **Queries:** Preferred. **E-Queries:** Yes. **Unsolicited mss:** Accepts. **Response:** 2 weeks; SASE required. **Freelance Content:** 50%. **Rights:** FNASR. **Payment:** On acceptance.

SCORE GOLF

Canadian Controlled Media Communications
5397 Eglinton Ave. W, Suite 101, Toronto, Ontario M9C 5K6 Canada. 416-928-2909.
E-mail: bobw@scoregolf.com. Web site: www.scoregolf.com. 6x/yr. $18. Circ.: 120,000. Bob Weeks, Vice President, Communications. **Description:** On travel, golf equipment, golf history, personalities, and prominent professionals. Canadian content only. **Nonfiction:** Articles, 800-2,000 words (by assignment); pays $125-$600. **Fillers:** 50-100 words, on Canadian golf scene. Rarely uses humor or poems. Pays $10-$25. **Tips:** Query with SASE (IRC); send published clips. **Queries:** Required. **Payment:** On publication.

SEA

Duncan McIntosh Co.

17782 Cowan, Irvine, CA 92614. 949-660-6150.

E-mail: editorial@goboatingamerica.com. Web site: www.goboatingamerica.com. Monthly. $3.50/issue, $16.97/yr. Circ.: 50,000. Eston Ellis, Managing Editor. **Description:** Four-color, for active West Coast boat owners. Readers are power boaters and sportfishing enthusiasts, Alaska to Mexico, across the Pacific to Hawaii. **Nonfiction:** West Coast boating destination stories, new trends in power boat design, late-season maintenance secrets, how to finance a new boat; 1,200-1,600 words; $250-$400. **Columns, Departments:** Hands-On Boater (do-it-yourself boat maintenance tips); 500-1,200 words; $100-$200. **Art:** 35mm color transparencies; $50, $250 (cover). **Tips:** No articles on sailboats, cruise ships, commercial sportfishing party boats, accidents, historic vessels, or chartering. **Queries:** Not necessary. **E-Queries:** Yes. **Unsolicited mss:** Accepts. **Response:** 6 weeks. **Freelance Content:** 60%. **Rights:** 1st NA, reprint (print and electronic). **Payment:** On publication.

SEA KAYAKER

P.O. Box 17170, Seattle, WA 17029. 206-789-9536.

E-mail: editorial@seakayakermag. Web site: www.seakayakermag.com. Bimonthly. Circ.: 25,000. Christopher Cunningham, Editor. **Description:** For serious paddlers. Guides sea kayakers through coastal and island waters and gives readers both entertainment and information. **Fiction:** Short stories on ocean kayaking; 1,000-3,000 words; pays $.12/word. **Nonfiction:** Articles, 1,500-4,000 words, on ocean kayaking (technical, personal experience, profile, new product). Pays $.12-$.15/word; $.18-$.20/word (by assignment). **Art:** Send photos with submission. **Tips:** Combine personal narrative with a sense of place. **Queries:** Preferred. **E-Queries:** Yes. **Unsolicited mss:** Accepts. **Response:** 2 months, SASE. **Freelance Content:** 95%. **Rights:** FNASR or second serial. **Payment:** On publication. **Contact:** Karin Redmond, Executive Editor.

SHARING THE VICTORY

Fellowship of Christian Athletes

8701 Leeds Rd., Kansas City, MO 64129. 816-921-0909.

E-mail: stv@fca.org. Web site: www.fca.org. 9x/year. $2.50/issue. Circ.: 90,000. Allen Palmeri, Editor. **Description:** Offers spiritual advice to coaches and athletes, and those whom they influence. **Nonfiction:** 1,200-1,500 words; $100-$250. **Poetry:** Short; $25. **Tips:** All materials (profiles on Christian athletes, poem, etc.) must present Christian inspiration. **Unsolicited mss:** Does not accept. **Freelance Content:** 50%. **Payment:** On publication.

SHOTGUN SPORTS

Shotgun Sports, Inc.

P.O. Box 6810, Auburn, CA 95604-6810. 530-889-2220.

E-mail: shotgun@shotgunsportsmagazine.com.

Web site: www.shotgunsportsmagazine.com. Monthly. Circ.: 155,000. Frank Kodl,

Publisher/Editor. **Description:** On trap and skeet shooting, sporting clays, hunting with shotguns, reloading, gun tests, and instructional shooting. **Nonfiction:** Articles with photos; $25-$200. **Freelance Content:** 100%. **Rights:** 1st NA. **Payment:** On publication.

SILENT SPORTS

717 Tenth St., P.O. Box 152, Waupaca, WI 54981-9990. 715-258-5546.
E-mail: info@silentsports.net. Web site: www.silentsports.net. **Description:** On bicycling, cross country skiing, running, canoeing, hiking, backpacking, and other "silent" sports. Must have regional (upper Midwest) focus. **Nonfiction:** Articles, 1,000-2,000 words; pays $50-$100 for features; $20-$50 for fillers. **Queries:** Preferred. **Payment:** On publication.

SKATING

20 First St., Colorado Springs, CO 80906. 719-635-5200.
E-mail: lfawcett@usfsa.org. Web site: www.usfsa.org. 10x/year. $25 (U.S.), $35 (Canada). Circ.: 48,000. Laura Fawcett, Director of Publications/Editor. **Description:** Official publication of the U.S. Figure Skating Association. Communicates information about the sport to USFSA members and figure-skating fans. Promotes USFSA programs, personalities, and trends that affect the sport. **Nonfiction:** Feature articles profiling interesting USFSA members: athletes, judges, etc. Looking for what makes these people unique besides their skating; 1,500 words and up; $75-$150. **Art:** Photos, discussed when story is assigned, usually must be included. Pay negotiable. **E-Queries:** Yes. **Unsolicited mss:** Accepts. **Response:** 1-3 months, SASE required. **Freelance Content:** 75%. **Rights:** 1st serial. **Payment:** On publication.

SKI

Time4Media
929 Pearl St., Suite 200, Boulder, Co 80302-5108. 303-448-7600.
Web site: www.skinet.com. 8x/yr. $13.94. Circ.: 428,179. Andrew Bigford, Editor-in-Chief. **Description:** For experienced skiers: profiles, and destination articles. **Nonfiction:** Articles, 1,300-2,500 words; pays from $50. **Columns, Departments:** Ski Life (news items, 100-300 words). **Tips:** Send clips. **Queries:** Preferred. **Payment:** On acceptance.

SKI RACING INTERNATIONAL

Ski Racing International, Inc.
6971 Main St., Suite No. 1, Waitsfield, VT 05673-6023. 802-496-7700.
E-mail: sracing@skiracing.com. Web site: www.skiracing.com. Weekly. $29.95. Circ.: 30,000. Tim Etchells, Editor. **Description:** On race techniques and conditioning secrets. Coverage of World Cup, pro, collegiate, and junior ski and snowboard competition. **Nonfiction:** Articles by experts, with photos; pay varies.

SKIING

Time4Media
929 Pearl St., Boulder, CO 80302-5108. 303-448-7600.
E-mail: backtalk@skiingmag.com. Web site: www.skiingmag.com. 7x/year. $13.94.
Circ.: 404,361. Rick Kahl, Editor-in-Chief. **Description:** For the active skier, with
destination ideas and instructional tips. Departments include health, fitness, latest
trends in skiing industry. Also, profiles of regional runs and their users. **Nonfiction:**
Personal adventures on skis, from 2,500 words (no "first time on skis" stories); profiles
and interviews, 50-300 words. Pays $150-$300/printed page. **Fillers:** Humorous
vignettes, skiing oddities. Pays from $.15/word. **Tips:** Look for a ski adventure new,
undiscovered, close to home for a lot of people. Write in first-person. **Queries:**
Preferred. **E-Queries:** Yes. **Unsolicited mss:** Accepts. **Freelance Content:** 10%.
Contact: Helen Olsson, Executive Editor.

SKIN DIVER

PRIMEDIA Enthusiast Group
6420 Wilshire Blvd., Los Angeles, CA 90048-5502. 323-782-2960.
Web site: www.skin-diver.com. Monthly. $19.94/yr. Circ.: 230,000. Ty Sawyer, Editor.
Description: On scuba diving activities, equipment, and dive sites. **Nonfiction:**
Illustrated articles, 500-1,000 words; pays $50/published page. **Payment:** On
publication.

SKYDIVING

1725 N Lexington Ave., DeLand, FL 32724.
E-mail: sue@skydivingmagazine.com. Web site: www.skydivingmagazine.com.
Annual. $4/$20. Circ.: 14,000. Sue Clifton, Editor. **Description:** Techniques, equip-
ment, places, people, and events of sport parachuting, written by jumpers for
jumpers. **Nonfiction:** Timely news articles on sport and military parachuting; $1/per
column inch. **Tips:** Send short bio that shows skydiving experience. **Queries:**
Preferred. **E-Queries:** Yes. **Unsolicited mss:** Accepts. **Response:** 2 weeks.
Freelance Content: 40%. **Rights:** All. **Payment:** On publication.

SNOWBOARDER

PRIMEDIA Enthusiast Group
P.O. Box 1028, Dana Point, CA 92629-5028. 949-496-5922.
Web site: www.snowboardermag.com. Bimonthly. $9.99. Circ.: 137,800. Mark
Sullivan, Editor. **Description:** On snowboarding personalities, techniques, and
adventure. **Nonfiction:** Articles, with color transparencies or B&W prints; 1,000-
1,500 words; pays $150-$800. **Payment:** On publication.

SNOWEST

360 B Street, Idaho Falls, ID 83402. 208-524-7000.
E-mail: lindstrm@snowest.com. Web site: www.snowest.com. Monthly. $2.95. Circ.:
160,000. Lane Lindstrom, Editor. **Description:** SnoWest is a family-oriented, snow-
mobile publication for winter recreationists across the U.S. and parts of Canada.

Nonfiction: Manufacturer reviews, test reports, travel destinations, new product reviews, land use issues, events, technical information, anything related to winter motorized recreation. Also, fillers (500-1,500 words). Query first; 2,000 word max.; $100-$300 (with photos). **Art:** Color transparencies (Kodachrome or FujiChrome). **Tips:** Submit 10-15 photos to illustrate a feature, with people involved in every photo; show action; use dawn/dusk for dramatic lighting. **Queries:** Preferred. **Unsolicited mss:** Accepts. **Rights:** FNASR. **Payment:** On publication.

SOCCER AMERICA
P.O. Box 23704, Oakland, CA 94623. 510-528-5000.
E-mail: mike@socceramerica.com. Web site: www.socceramerica.com. Mike Woitalla, Editor. **Description:** On soccer news; profiles.

SOCCER JR.
See page 472 for full listing.
Description: Fiction and fillers about soccer for readers ages 8-14.

SOUTH CAROLINA WILDLIFE
P.O. Box 167, Columbia, SC 29202-0167. 803-734-3972.
Web site: www.scwildlife.com. Bimonthly. $10/yr. Circ.: 60,000. **Description:** Published by Dept. of Natural Resources, for readers interested in the outdoors. **Nonfiction:** South Carolina focus, on outdoor interests; 1,500 words; $.15-$.20/word. **Art:** 35mm or large transparencies; pay varies. **Tips:** Avoid first-person accounts. **Queries:** Preferred. **E-Queries:** Yes. **Unsolicited mss:** Accepts. **Response:** 3-6 weeks, SASE. **Freelance Content:** 75%. **Rights:** FNASR. **Payment:** On acceptance. **Contact:** Linda Renshaw, Managing Editor.

SPORTS ILLUSTRATED
Time, Inc.
135 W 50th St., New York, NY 10020-1201. 212-522-1212.
E-mail: letters@si.timeinc.com. Web site: www.cnnsi.com. Weekly. $80.46. Circ.: 3,205,000. Bill Colson, Managing Editor. **Description:** Sports news magazine. **Nonfiction:** 800-1,200 words; pay varies. **Queries:** Required. **E-Queries:** No. **Unsolicited mss:** Accepts. **Response:** 4 weeks, SASE required. **Freelance Content:** Less than 5%. **Rights:** All. **Payment:** On acceptance. **Contact:** Myra Gelband.

SPORTS ILLUSTRATED FOR KIDS
See page 473 for full listing.
Description: Focuses on the excitement, joy, and challenge of sports for kids 8-14.

SURFER
PRIMEDIA Enthusiast Group
P.O. Box 1028, Dana Point, CA 92629. 949-496-5922.
E-mail: surfermag@primediacmmg.com. Web site: www.surfermag.com. Monthly.

Circ.: 111,855. Sam George, Editor-in-Chief. **Description:** On surfing and surfers. **Nonfiction:** Articles, 500-5,000 words, photos; pays $.20-$.30/word, $10-$600 for photos. **Payment:** On publication.

SURFING

P.O. Box 73250, San Clemente, CA 92673. 949-492-7873.
E-mail: surfing@mcmullenargus.com. Web site: www.surfingthemag.com. Evan Slater, Editor. **Description:** Short newsy and humorous articles, 200-500 words. Pay varies. **Tips:** No first-person travel articles. **Payment:** On publication.

T'AI CHI

Wayfarer Publications
P.O. Box 39938, Los Angeles, CA 90039. 323-665-7773.
E-mail: taichi@tai-chi.com. Web site: www.tai-chi.com. Marvin Smalheiser, Editor. **Description:** For persons interested in T'ai Chi Ch'uan (Taijiquan), Qigong, and other internal martial arts, and in similar Chinese disciplines which contribute to fitness, health, and a balanced sense of well being. **Nonfiction:** Articles about different internal styles, self-defense techniques, martial arts principles and philosophy, training methods, weapons, case histories of benefits, new or unusual uses for T'ai Chi Ch'uan, interviews; 100-4,500 words; $75-500. **Art:** 4x6 or 5x7 glossy B&W prints. **Tips:** Readers' abilities range from beginners to serious students and teachers. **Queries:** Required. **E-Queries:** Yes. **Unsolicited mss:** Does not accept. **Response:** 2-3 weeks, SASE. **Freelance Content:** 85%. **Rights:** 1st NA, reprint. **Payment:** On publication.

TENNIS

Miller Publishing Group, LLC
810 Seventh Ave., Fl. 4, New York, NY 10019-5818. 212-636-2700.
E-mail: yourserve@tennis.com. Web site: www.tennis.com. Monthly. $18. Circ.: 90,700. Mark Woodruff, Editor. **Description:** Instructional articles, features, profiles of tennis stars, grassroots articles, humor. **Nonfiction:** 800-2,500 words, with photos; pay varies. **Tips:** No phone queries. **Queries:** Preferred. **Payment:** On publication.

TENNIS WEEK

5 Elm Place, Rye, NY 10580. 914-967-4890.
E-mail: tennisweek@tennisweek.com. Web site: www.tennisweek.com. 16x/year. $4/$50. Circ.: 97,000. Eugene L. Scott, Editor. **Description:** Covers the ATP and WTA (men's and women's professional tours), the tennis industry, major tournaments, new products, retail stores, schedules, scores, rankings, and earnings. **Nonfiction:** In-depth, researched articles on current issues and personalities; 1,500-2,000 words; pay varies. **Queries:** Required. **E-Queries:** No. **Unsolicited mss:** Does not accept. **Response:** SASE. **Rights:** 1st NA. **Payment:** On publication.

TEXAS GOLFER

Golfer Magazines, Inc.

10301 Northwest Freeway, Suite 418, Houston, TX 77092-8228. 713-680-1680. E-mail: info@golfermagazines.com. Web site: www.texasgolfermagazine.com. Monthly. $22. Circ.: 55,000. Bob Gray, Editor. **Description:** For Texas golfers, with golf-course and tournament information, golf tips, and news. **Nonfiction:** Articles, 800-1,500 words, for north Texas golfers. **Tips:** Most freelance by assignment. **Queries:** Required. **E-Queries:** Yes. **Unsolicited mss:** Accepts. **Response:** 2-4 Weeks, SASE. **Freelance Content:** 20%. **Rights:** All. **Payment:** On publication.

TRAILER BOATS

20700 Belshaw Ave., Carson, CA 90746-3510. 310-537-6322.

Web site: www.trailerboats.com. Monthly. $3.99/$16.97. Circ.: 98,000. Jim Hendricks, Editor. **Description:** Covers trailer boating: lifestyle, technical and how-to articles. **Nonfiction:** On boat, trailer, or tow-vehicle maintenance and operation; skiing, fishing, and cruising. Also, fillers, humor. 500-2,000 words, pays $100-$700. **Art:** Photos, slides, transparencies. **Queries:** Preferred. **Unsolicited mss:** Accepts. **Response:** Queries 6 weeks, SASE. **Freelance Content:** 51%. **Payment:** On acceptance.

TRIATHLETE

Triathlon Group of North America

2037 San Elijo, Cardiff, CA 92007-1726. 760-634-4100.

E-mail: cgandolfo@triathletemag.com. Web site: www.triathletemag.com. Monthly. $29.95/yr. Circ.: 43,000. Christina Gandolfo, Editor. **Description:** Covers the sport of triathlon. **Nonfiction:** Articles, varying lengths, with color slides; pays $.20/word. **Tips:** No "my first triathlon" stories. **Payment:** On publication.

USA CYCLING

TPG Sports

One Olympic Plaza, Colorado Springs, CO 80909-5775. 719-578-4581.

E-mail: media@usacycling.org. Web site: www.usacycling.org. Bimonthly. $25/yr (nonmembers). Circ.: 49,500. Patrice Quintero, Communications Director. **Description:** On bicycle racing; contains U.S. cycling news, race coverage and results, features, race information, information on training and coaching. **Nonfiction:** Articles on bicycle racing and racers. **Queries:** Preferred.

USA GYMNASTICS

Pan American Plaza

201 S Capitol Ave., Suite 300, Indianapolis, IN 46225. 317-237-5050.

E-mail: publications@usa-gymnastics.org. Web site: www.usa-gymnastics.org. Bimonthly. $15. Circ.: 95,000. Luan Peszek, Editor. **Description:** Covers gymnastics, including men's artistic and women's artistic, rhythmic, trampoline, tumbling, and sports acrobatics. Coverage of national and international competitions leading up to Olympic Games. In-depth features on athletes and coaches, provides coaching tips. **Nonfiction:** Gymnastics-related articles; fee negotiable. **Tips:** Query or call first to discuss article and interest level. Welcomes new writers. **Queries:** Preferred. **E-Queries:** Yes. **Unsolicited mss:** Accepts. **Response:** 4-6 weeks, SASE required. **Freelance Content:** 10%. **Rights:** 1st. **Payment:** On publication.

VELONEWS
1830 N 55th St., Boulder, CO 80301. 303-440-0601.
E-mail: vnedit@7dogs.com. Web site: www.velonews.com. 20x/year. Circ.: 48,000. Kip Mikler, Editor. **Description:** Journal of record for North American bicycle racing, and the world's largest competitive cycling publication. **Nonfiction:** On competitive cycling, training, nutrition; profiles, interviews. No how-to or touring articles; 500-1,500 words; pay varies. **Tips:** Focus on elite, competitive aspect of the sport. **Queries:** Required. **E-Queries:** Yes. **Response:** Queries 1 month, SASE. **Freelance Content:** 20%. **Payment:** On publication.

THE WATER SKIER
1251 Holy Cow Rd., Polk City, FL 33868-8200. 863-324-4341.
E-mail: satkinson@usawaterski.org. Web site: www.usawaterski.org. 9x/year. $3.50/issue. Circ.: 35,000. Scott Atkinson, Editor. **Description:** Published by USA Water Ski, national governing body for competitive water skiing in the U.S. **Nonfiction:** On water skiing (interviews, profiles must be assigned), new products, equipment for boating and water skiing; 1,500-3,000 words; pays $100-$150 (for assigned features). **Art:** Color slides. **Tips:** Submit articles about people involved in the competitive sport. **Queries:** Preferred. **E-Queries:** No. **Unsolicited mss:** Does not accept. **Response:** Queries 24 hours, submissions 1 week, SASE. **Freelance Content:** 10%. **Rights:** All. **Payment:** On publication.

WATERSKI
World Publications, LLC
460 N Orlando Ave., Winter Park, FL 32789. 407-628-5662.
E-mail: waterski@worldzine.com. Web site: www.worldpub.net. 9x/yr. Circ.: 105,000. Todd Rosticelli, Editor. **Description:** On boating and water skiing. **Nonfiction:** Instructional features, 1,350 words, including sidebars; $125-$500. **Fillers:** Quick tips, 350 words; $35. **Tips:** Travel pieces and profiles by assignment only. **Queries:** Preferred. **Freelance Content:** 25%. **Payment:** On acceptance.

WESTERN OUTDOORS
3197-E Airport Loop, Costa Mesa, CA 92626. 714-546-4370.
E-mail: lew@wonews.com. 9x/year. $3.50/$14.95. Circ.: 100,000. Lew Carpenter, Editor. **Description:** On western saltwater and freshwater fishing techniques, tackle, and destinations. Includes the states of California, Oregon, and Washington. Also Alaska, Baja California, and British Columbia. **Nonfiction:** On saltwater or freshwater fishing in the West; facts and comments must be attributed to recognized authorities in their fields; 1,500 words; $450-$600. **Art:** Quality photos and artwork to illustrate articles; 35mm; $50-$300. **Tips:** Present seasonal materials 6 months in advance. Best time to query is June. **Queries:** Required. **E-Queries:** Yes.

Unsolicited mss: Accepts. **Response:** 4-6 weeks, SASE. **Freelance Content:** 75%. **Rights:** FNASR. **Payment:** On acceptance.

WESTERN SPORTSMAN
OP Publishing Ltd.
1080 Howe St., Suite 900, Vancouver
British Columbia V6Z 2T1 Canada. 604-606-4644.
Web site: www.oppub.com. George Gruenefeld, Editor. **Description:** On hunting and fishing in British Columbia, Alberta, Saskatchewan, and Manitoba. **Nonfiction:** Informative, how-tos, to 2,000 words. **Art:** Photos. **Payment:** On publication.

WILDFOWL
PRIMEDIA Enthusiast Group
6420 Wilshire Blvd., Fl. 14, Los Angeles, CA 90048-5502. 323-782-2173.
E-mail: sparksrog@earthlink.net. Bimonthly. $24.97/yr. Circ.: 42,000. Roger Sparks, Editor. **Description:** Occasional fiction, humor, related to duck hunters and wild-fowl. Pays $400. **Payment:** On acceptance.

WINDSURFING
World Publications, LLC
460 N Orlando Ave., Winter Park, FL 32703. 407-628-4802.
E-mail: info@worldpub.com. Web site: www.windsurfingmag.com. Jason Upwright, Editor. **Description:** For experienced boardsailors. **Nonfiction:** Features and instructional pieces ($250-$300), tips ($50-$75), extra for photos. **Art:** Fast action photos. **Response:** SASE required.

WINDY CITY SPORTS
1450 W Randolph, Chicago, IL 60607. 312-421-1551.
E-mail: jason@windycitysports.com. Web site: www.windycitysports.com. Monthly. Free. Circ.: 110,000. Jason Effmann, Editor. **Description:** Covers amateur sports in Chicago and surrounding area. **Nonfiction:** up to 1,200 words. **Art:** Hard copies, electronic (300 dpi or more). **Tips:** Need to be knowledgeable in sport covered. **Queries:** Preferred. **E-Queries:** Yes. **Unsolicited mss:** Accepts. **Response:** 2 weeks, SASE. **Freelance Content:** 25%. **Rights:** 1st. **Payment:** On publication.

WOODENBOAT
P.O. Box 78, Brooklin, ME 04616. 207-359-4651.
Web site: www.woodenboat.com. Bimonthly. $5.50/$29. Circ.: 110,000. Matthew Murphy, Editor. **Description:** For wooden boat owners, builders, and designers. Covers design, construction, and maintenance. **Nonfiction:** How-to and technical articles on construction, repair, and maintenance; design, history, and use; profiles of outstanding builders, designers; wooden boat lore; 1,000-5,000 words; $.25/word. **Queries:** Required. **Unsolicited mss:** Accepts. **Response:** 3 months, SASE. **Freelance Content:** 70%. **Rights:** 1st worldwide serial. **Payment:** On publication.

YACHTING

18 Marshall St., Suite 114, South Norwalk, CT 06854. 203-299-5900.
Web site: www.yachtingnet.com. Annual. $5/issue. Circ.: 132,000. Kenny Wooton, Editor-in-Chief. **Description:** Covers news and trends in boating (power, sail, and charter) for the seasoned, upscale boating enthusiast. **Nonfiction:** Articles on upscale, recreational boating—both power and sail; 1,500 words. **Art:** Photos; $350-$1,000. **Tips:** No "how-to" articles. **Queries:** Preferred. **Unsolicited mss:** Accepts. **Response:** 1-3 months. **Freelance Content:** 15-25%. **Rights:** All. **Payment:** On publication. **Contact:** Kim Kavin.

YOUNG BUCKS OUTDOORS

See page 475 for full listing.
Description: Encourages kids of all races, genders, and abilities to step outside and enjoy themselves.

TEENS

ALL ABOUT YOU
PRIMEDIA, Inc.
6420 Wilshire Blvd., Los Angeles, CA 90048-5502. 323-782-2950.
E-mail: allaboutyou@emapusa.com. Quarterly. $19.94. Circ.: 400,000. Jane Fort, Editor. **Description:** Teen magazine for younger teens.

BREAKAWAY
Focus on the Family, Inc.
8605 Explorer Dr., Colorado Springs, CO 80920. 719-531-3400.
Web site: www.breakawaymag.com. Michael Ross, Editor. **Description:** Readers are Christian boys, ages 12-18. **Fiction:** Fiction, to 1,800 words; must have a male slant. **Nonfiction:** Real-life adventure articles, to 1,500 words; pays $.12-$.15/word. Fillers: Humor and interesting facts; 500-800 words. **Payment:** On acceptance.

BRIO
Focus on the Family, Inc.
8605 Explorer Dr., Colorado Springs, CO 80920. 719-531-3400.
E-mail: briomag@macmail.fotf.org. Web site: www.briomag.com. Monthly. Circ.: 165,000. Susie Shellenberger, Editor. **Description:** For Christian teen girls (profiles, how-to pieces, adventures that show the fun Christian teens can have together). **Fiction:** Fiction, to 2,000 words, with realistic character development, good dialogue, and a plot that teen girls will be drawn to. May contain a spiritual slant but should not be preachy. **Nonfiction:** Articles; pays $.08-$.12/word. **Fillers:** Short humorous pieces. **Payment:** On acceptance.

CAMPUS LIFE
Christianity Today
465 Gundersen Dr., Carol Stream, IL 60188. 630-260-6200.
E-mail: clmag@campuslife.net. Web site: www.campuslife.net. 9x/year. $19.95/year. Circ.: 100,000. Chris Lutes, Editor. **Description:** Advice on love, sex, self-image, popularity, and loneliness, with dramatic stories about teens radically changed by God, plus in-depth profiles about favorites in Christian music. **Fiction:** A "life lesson" with a Christian worldview, by experienced writers; 2,000 words max.; $.15-$.20/word. **Nonfiction:** First-person stories presenting the lives of teenagers, ordinary or dramatic; 2,000 words max.; $.15-$.20/word. **Tips:** Avoid religious clichés, misuse of religious language, lack of respect or empathy for teenagers. **Queries:** Required. **E-Queries:** Accepts. **Unsolicited mss:** Does not accept. **Response:** 4-6 weeks, SASE required. **Freelance Content:** 10%. **Rights:** 1st. **Payment:** On acceptance; kill fee offered.

COLLEGE BOUND MAGAZINE
Ramholtz Publishing, Inc.
1200 South Ave., Suite 202, Staten Island, NY 10314. 718-761-4800.

E-mail: editorial@collegebound.net. Web site: www.collegeboundmag.com. $15/year. Circ.: 755,000. Gina LaGuardia, Editor-in-Chief. **Description:** Provides high school students with an insider's look at all aspects of college life. **Nonfiction:** Real-life student experiences and expert voices dealing with dorm life, choosing the right college, joining a fraternity/sorority, college dating, campus events, scholarship strategies, etc; 600-1,000 words; $75-$100. **Columns, Departments:** Straight Up Strategies, Cash Crunch, Personal Statement, Debate Team; 300-600 words; $50-$75. **Tips:** Send 2-3 clips or samples of your work (from college newspaper, journalism class, etc.) **Queries:** Preferred. **E-Queries:** Yes. **Unsolicited mss:** Accepts. **Response:** 5-6 weeks for queries, 8 weeks for manuscripts; SASE required. **Freelance Content:** 75%. **Rights:** First. **Payment:** 30 days upon publication.

COSMOGIRL!

The Hearst Corp.
224 W 57th St., Fl. 3, New York, NY 10019-3212. 212-649-3000.
E-mail: inbox@cosmogirl.com. Web site: www.cosmogirl.com. Monthly. $14.90. Circ.: 790,000. Atoosa Rubenstein, Editor-in-Chief. **Description:** Teen version of *Cosmopolitan*, for girls 12-17. Snappy, teen-friendly style. **Nonfiction:** Articles, 900 words, about outstanding young women; first-person narratives of interesting or unusual happenings in the lives of young women; pay varies. **Fillers:** Fillers, 150 words, on ways readers can get involved in social issues. **Queries:** Preferred. **Payment:** On publication.

ENCOUNTER

Standard Publishing
8121 Hamilton Ave., Cincinnati, OH 45231. 513-931-4050.
E-mail: kcarr@standardpub.com. Web site: www.standardpub.com. Quarterly. $13. Circ.: 32,000. Kelly Carr, Editor. **Description:** Weekly magazine published quarterly that is focused on encouraging teens in their relationship with Jesus. Read by teens from sixth grade through twelfth grade. Fiction, nonfiction, and daily devotion. **Fiction:** Contemporary teens, uplifting and character-building, conflicts resolved realistically, with moral message; 500-1,100 words; $.08/word (1st), $.06/word (reprint). **Nonfiction:** Current issues from Christian perspective. Also, teen profiles. Topics: school, family, recreation, friends, part-time jobs, dating, music; 500-1,100; pays same as fiction. **Poetry:** from teens only; $20/poem. **Queries:** Not necessary. **E-Queries:** Yes. **Unsolicited mss:** Accepts. **Response:** Queries 1-3 weeks, submissions 8-12 weeks, SASE. **Freelance Content:** 40%. **Rights:** 1st, one-time. **Payment:** On acceptance.

GO-GIRL.COM

Ramholtz Publishing, Inc.
1200 South Ave., Suite 202, Staten Island, NY 10314. 718-761-4800.
E-mail: editorial@collegebound.net. Web site: www.go-girl.com. Monthly. Gina LaGuardia, Editor-in-Chief. **Description:** Addresses social and academic needs of adolescent females. Provides cutting-edge information not only in beauty, fitness,

fashion, entertainment, and more, but also in scholastic savviness. **Nonfiction:** Seeking articles with real-life experiences girls will relate to; lessons to learn from others like them; on entertainment personalities they adore and admire; savvy scoops on outstanding high-GPA divas, etc; 200-600 words; $50-$125. **Columns, Departments:** Go Beauty, Go Fashion, Go Serious, Go Fitness, Go Hottie, Go Play, Go Study. **Queries:** Preferred. **E-Queries:** Accepts. **Unsolicited mss:** Does not accept. **Response:** Queries to 2 months, assigned submissions 2 weeks, SASE. **Freelance Content:** 60%. **Rights:** 1st, online. **Payment:** 30 days upon publication.

GUIDEPOSTS FOR TEENS

1050 Broadway, Suite 6, Chesterton, IN 46304. 219-929-4429.
E-mail: gp4t@guideposts.org. Web site: www.gp4teens.com. Bimonthly. Circ.: 250,000. Betsy Kohn, Editor. **Description:** Interfaith publication offering teens (ages 12-18) true stories filled with adventure and inspiration. Provides quizzes, how-tos, advice, music reviews, Q&As, and profiles of role models (celebrity and "real" teens). **Nonfiction:** True first-person dangerous, miraculous, or inspirational stories; ghostwritten for (or written by) teens. Protagonist must change in course of the story; must deliver clear inspirational takeaway. **Fillers:** Quizzes (Are you a winner or a whiner? Are you dating a dud?); how-tos (how to find a good job, how to get along with your parents); Celebrity Q&As, interviews. **Art:** Send samples. **Tips:** No preachy, overtly religious stories. **Queries:** Preferred. **E-Queries:** Yes. **Unsolicited mss:** Accepts. **Response:** Queries 4 weeks, submissions 6 weeks, SASE. **Freelance Content:** 80%. **Rights:** All. **Payment:** On acceptance. **Contact:** Allison Payne, Associate Editor.

HOT

H&S Media, Inc.
2121 Waukegan Rd., Suite 120, Bannockburn, IL 60015. 847-444-4880.
E-mail: hot@hsmedia.com. Monthly. $4.99/$47.95. Circ.: 250,000. **Description:** For "tweens"—girls between ages of 8-14 years. Offers hot news on cool guys, hip groups, and successful Hollywood girls. Covers fashion trends, beauty, female celebrities, film and television stars, and musical groups. **Nonfiction:** Stories on celebrity-related events. Features on teen celebrities. Concert reviews; 500-2,000 words; $.50/word. **Art:** Slides, photographs, electronic (300 dpi). **Tips:** Successful writers have contacts in the celebrity industry, and use a teen "voice" in their articles. **Queries:** Preferred. **E-Queries:** Yes. **Unsolicited mss:** Does not accept. **Freelance Content:** 10%-25%. **Contact:** Laurel Smoke, Assistant Editor.

KEYNOTER

3636 Woodview Trace, Indianapolis, IN 46268. 317-875-8755.
E-mail: keynoter@kiwanis.org. Web site: www.keyclub.org. 7x/year. $4/year. Circ.: 200,000. Amy L. Wiser, Executive Editor. **Description:** For teens, ages 13-18, offering informative, entertaining articles on self-help, school, and community issues. **Nonfiction:** For service-minded high-school students; well-researched, with expert references, interviews with respected sources; 1,200 words; $200-$400. **Tips:** No

first-person accounts, fiction, or articles for younger readers. **Queries:** Preferred. **E-Queries:** Yes. **Unsolicited mss:** Accepts. **Response:** Queries 1-4 months, submissions 1 week, SASE required. **Freelance Content:** 65%. **Rights:** FNASR. **Payment:** On acceptance.

LISTEN

55 W Oak Ridge Dr., Hagerstown, MD 21740. 301-393-4019. E-mail: listen@healthconnection.org. Monthly. $26.95/year. Circ.: 50,000. Anita Jacobs, Editor. **Description:** Provides teens with vigorous, positive, educational approach to problems arising from use of tobacco, alcohol, and other drugs. **Fiction:** True-to-life stories; 1,000-1,200 words; $.05-$.10/word. **Nonfiction:** For teenagers, on problems of alcohol and drug abuse; personality profiles; self-improvement; drug-free activities; 1,000-1,200 words; $.05-$.10/word. **Poetry:** From high-school students only. **Tips:** Use upbeat approach. **Queries:** Preferred. **E-Queries:** Accepts. **Unsolicited mss:** Accepts. **Response:** 2 weeks queries, 3 months submissions; SASE. **Rights:** FNASR. **Payment:** On acceptance. **Contact:** Anita Jacobs.

MERLYN'S PEN

See page 647 for full listing.
Description: Features fiction, essays, and poems by America's teens.

THE NEW YORK TIMES UPFRONT

The New York Times/Scholastic Inc.
557 Broadway, New York, NY 10012-3999. 212-343-6100.
E-mail: pyoung@scholastic.com.
Web site: www.upfrontmagazine.com, www.nytimes.com/upfront. Biweekly. Peter S. Young, Editor. **Description:** News magazine for teenagers. **Nonfiction:** News articles, 500-1,500 words; pays $150 and up. **Queries:** Preferred. **Payment:** On acceptance.

ODYSSEY

Cobblestone Publishing
30 Grove St., Suite C, Peterborough, NH 03458. 603-924-7209.
E-mail: bethlindstrom2000@hotmail.com. Web site: www.cobblestonepub.com. 9x/year. Circ.: 21,000. Elizabeth Lindstrom, Editor. **Description:** Features, 750-1,000 words, on science and technology, for readers, ages 10-16. Science-related fiction, myths, legends, and science-fiction stories. Activities. Pays $.20-$.25/word. **Fiction:** Science-related stories, poems, science fiction, retold legends, etc., relating to theme; up to 1,000 words; $.20-$.25/word. **Nonfiction:** Subjects directly and indirectly related to theme; with little-known information (but don't overlook the obvious); 720-950 words; $.20-$.25/word. **Fillers:** Critical-thinking activities, experiments, models, science fair projects, etc., for children alone, with adult supervision, or in classroom setting. **Columns, Departments:** Far Out; Places, Media, People to Discover; Fantastic Journeys; 400-650 words. **Art:** Transparencies, slides, color prints; $15-$100 (B&W); $25-$100 (color). **Tips:** Material must relate to specific

theme; contact for upcoming list. Scientific accuracy, lively approach, and inclusion of primary research are crucial to being accepted. **Payment:** On publication.

SCHOLASTIC SCOPE
See page 648 for full listing.
Description: Fiction for 15-18-year-olds, with 4th-6th grade reading ability. Short stories, 400-1,200 words, on teenage interests and relationships; family, job, and school situations.

SCIENCE WORLD
See page 557 for full listing.
Description: On life science, earth science, physical science, environmental science, or health science, for 7th-10th graders, ages 12-15.

SEVENTEEN
PRIMEDIA Consumer Media & Magazine Group
850 3rd Ave., Fl. 9, New York, NY 10022-6280. 212-407-9700.
E-mail: mail@seventeen.com. Web site: www.seventeen.com. Monthly. $2.99/issue, $11.96/10-issue subscription. Circ.: 2,400,000. Darcy Jacobs, Senior Editor.
Description: Popular beauty/fashion magazine, written for young women, ages 13-21. **Fiction:** Stories with issues important and familiar to our readers, that also challenge them and make them think. **Nonfiction:** Feature stories unique and relevant to teenage girls; 2,500-3,000 words; $1/word. **Columns, Departments:** Features, Guys, Voice, Eat, Bodyline, College, Quizzes; 350-500 words. **Tips:** Ideas should spring from teenage viewpoint and sensibility, not that of parent, teacher, other adult. **Queries:** Required. **E-Queries:** Accepts. **Unsolicited mss:** Accepts. **Response:** 1-4 weeks, SASE. **Freelance Content:** 30%. **Rights:** 1st NA. **Payment:** On publication.

SISTERS IN STYLE
Sterling/Macfadden Partnership
333 Seventh Ave., Fl. 11, New York, NY 10001-5004. 212-780-3500.
E-mail: info@sterlingmacfadden.com. Web site: www.sterlingmacfadden.com. Bimonthly. Cynthia Marie Horner, Editor. **Description:** "For Today's Young Black Woman." Beauty and fashion articles, quizzes, and advice for African-American teens. **Nonfiction:** Pay varies. **Queries:** Preferred. **Payment:** On publication.

SPANK! YOUTH CULTURE ONLINE
Ububik, #505, 300 Meredith Rd., Calgary, Alberta T2E 7A8 Canada. 403-217-0468.
E-mail: happyrandom@spankmag.com. Web site: www.spankmag.com. Stephen R. Cassady, Editor. **Description:** E-zine written by youth for youth, for ages 14 to 24. Only accepts submissions from youth.

STUDY BREAKS
Shweiki Media, Inc.
8703 Botts St., San Antonio, TX 78217-6334. 210-804-0390.
E-mail: info@studybreaks.com. Web site: www.studybreaks.com. 7x/year. Circ.: 52,500. Gal Shweiki, Publisher/Editor. **Description:** For students. **Nonfiction:** Spring-break travel, European travel. **Poetry:** Drinking/smoking poems. **Fillers:** Puzzles. **Columns, Departments:** Music, videogames. **Tips:** We look for humor. **Queries:** Not necessary. **E-Queries:** Yes. **Unsolicited mss:** Accepts. **Payment:** On publication.

TEENPRENEUR
Earl G. Graves, Ltd.
130 5th Ave., Fl. 10, New York, NY 10011. 212-242-8000.
6x/year. Circ.: 4,000. **Description:** For African-American teens interested in business.

TEEN VOICES
515 Washington St., Boston, MA 02111. 617-426-5505.
E-mail: womenexp@teenvoices.com. Web site: www.teenvoices.com. Quarterly. $2.95/$19.95. Circ.: 25,000. Alison Amoroso, Editor. **Description:** Written by, for, and about teenaged and young-adult women. Offers a place to share thoughts with others the same age. **Fiction:** Short stories, any subject and length. **Nonfiction:** About any issue that is important to you, or an important experience you've had. **Poetry:** Your feelings, thoughts, etc. **Columns, Departments:** Opinions/editorial pieces. **Art:** Digital file (TIF or EPS), or hardcopy. **Tips:** Be honest, candid and true to yourself. Appreciates material that promotes feminism, equality, self-esteem, "You're more than just a pretty face." **Queries:** Not necessary. **E-Queries:** Yes. **Unsolicited mss:** Accepts. **Response:** Submissions, a few days, SASE not required. **Rights:** 1st. **Payment:** In copies.

TIGER BEAT
PRIMEDIA Enthusiast Group
470 Park Ave. S, #8, New York, NY 10016-6868. 212-545-3600.
E-mail: louise_barile@primediamags.com. Monthly. $14.95. Circ.: 300,000. Louise Barile, Editor. **Description:** On young people in show business and the music industry. **Nonfiction:** Articles, to 4 pages; pays varying rates. **Queries:** Preferred. **Payment:** On acceptance.

TWIST
Bauer Publishing Co.
270 Sylvan Ave., Englewood Cliffs, NJ 07632-2521. 201-569-6699.
E-mail: twistmail@aol.com. Web site: www.twistmag.com. Monthly. $9.97. Circ.: 366,300. Richard Spencer, Editor-in-Chief. **Description:** On relationships, entertainment, fitness, fashion, and other topics, for today's young women. **Nonfiction:** Articles, 1,500 words. **Tips:** Mostly staff-written; queries with clips required.

WHAT

108-93 Lombard Ave., Winnipeg, Manitoba R3B 3B1 Canada. 204-985-8160. E-mail: what@whatmagnet.com. Web site: www.whatmagnet.com. Bimonthly. $14. Circ.: 250,000. Leslie Malkin, Editor. **Description:** Canadian teen pop-culture magazine (including music, movie, and TV interviews, typical issues and themes affecting readers, ages 13-19). **Nonfiction:** Charged, edgy, unconventional, from pop culture to social issues; 450 words and up; pay negotiable. **Tips:** Query with working story title, 1-sentence explanation of angle, justification, and proposed treatment, potential contacts, proposed length. Welcomes new writers. **Queries:** Required. **E-Queries:** Yes. **Unsolicited mss:** Does not accept. **Response:** 1-2 months, SASE. **Freelance Content:** 60%. **Rights:** 1st Canadian. **Payment:** On publication.

WITH

722 Main St., P.O. Box 347, Newton, KS 67114. 316-283-5100. Web site: www.withonline.org. Bimonthly. $23.50/yr. Circ.: 5,000. Carol Duerksen, Editor. **Description:** "The Magazine for Radical Christian Youth." Empowers teens to be radically committed to Jesus Christ, peace, justice, and sharing God's good news through words and action. **Fiction:** First-person stories; 1,500 words; $100. **Nonfiction:** Creative, "inside the life of a teen," first-person preferred. Avoid preaching. Themes: sex and dating, Holy Spirit, integrity, service and mission; 1,500 words; pay varies. **Poetry:** Yes. **Fillers:** Wholesome humor. **Art:** 8x10 B&W. **Queries:** Not necessary. **E-Queries:** Yes. **Unsolicited mss:** Accepts. **Response:** 1 month, SASE. **Freelance Content:** 20%. **Rights:** One-time and Web site. **Payment:** On acceptance.

YM

Gruner + Jahr USA Publishing 15 E 26th St., Fl. 14, New York, NY 10010-1505. 646-758-0555. E-mail: aiverson@ym.com. Web site: www.ym.com. Monthly. $2.99/issue. Anne Marie Iverson, Editor-in-Chief. **Description:** Sourcebook for fashion, beauty, boys, advice, and features for girls, ages 12-24. **Queries:** Required. **Unsolicited mss:** Accepts. **Response:** Queries 1-2 months. **Freelance Content:** 40%. **Payment:** On publication.

YOU!

29963 Mulholland Hwy., Agoura Hills, CA 91301. 818-991-1813. E-mail: feedback@youmagazine.com. Web site: www.youmagazine.com. **Description:** For teenagers, especially on moral issues, faith, and contemporary pop culture, viewed from the Catholic/Christian perspective. No payment. **Nonfiction:** Articles, 200-1,000 words.

YOUNG AND ALIVE

P.O. Box 6097, Lincoln, NE 68506. E-mail: info@christianrecord.org. Quarterly. Circ.: 25,000. Gaylena Gibson, Editor. **Description:** Publication for young adults who are blind or visually impaired.

Presents material from a non-denominational, Christian viewpoint and features articles on adventure, biography, camping, careers, health, history, hobbies, holidays, marriage, nature, practical Christianity, sports, and travel. **Nonfiction:** Features, 800-1,400 words; pay varies. **Art:** Slides or prints; $10/photo. **Queries:** Not necessary. **E-Queries:** No. **Unsolicited mss:** Accepts. **Response:** 12 months, SASE. **Freelance Content:** 90%. **Rights:** One-time. **Payment:** On acceptance.

YOUNG SALVATIONIST

The Salvation Army

P.O. Box 269, Alexandria, VA 22313. 703-684-5500.

E-mail: ys@usn.salvationarmy.org. 10x/yr. Tim Clark, Editor. **Description:** Seeks to teach Christian view of everyday living, for teenagers. **Nonfiction:** Articles (to 600-1,200 words); short-shorts, first-person testimonies (600-800 words). Pays $.15/word ($.10/word for reprints). **Response:** SASE required. **Payment:** On acceptance. **Contact:** Youth Editor.

YOUTH UPDATE

St. Anthony Messenger Press

28 W Liberty St., Cincinnati, OH 45210. 513-241-5615.

Web site: www.americancatholic.org. Monthly. Circ.: 20,000. Carol Ann Morrow, Editor. **Description:** Newsletter that supports the growth of Catholic teens, of high school age, in a life of faith. **Nonfiction:** Biblical books; personal growth; doctrinal truths; issues of peace and justice; 2,300 words; $.16/word. **Queries:** Required. **E-Queries:** Yes. **Unsolicited mss:** Accepts. **Response:** 6-8 weeks. **Freelance Content:** 80%. **Payment:** On acceptance.

YOUTHLINE USA WEEKLY

Bartash Printing

300 Knickerbocker Rd., Cresskill, NJ 07626-1343. 201-568-1333.

E-mail: susan@youthline-usa.com. Web site: www.youthline-usa.com. Weekly. $7. Circ.: 618,000. Susan Gertler, Editor-in-Chief. **Description:** Educational magazine for children and young teens.

TRADE & TECHNICAL

AMERICAN CITY & COUNTY

PRIMEDIA Business Magazines & Media, Inc.

6151 Powers Ferry Rd. NW, Atlanta, GA 30339. 770-618-0326.

E-mail: jward@primediabusiness.com. Web site: www.industryclick.com. Janet Ward, Associate Publisher/Editor. **Description:** On local government issues (wastewater, water, solid waste, financial management, information technology, etc.). **Nonfiction:** Articles, 600-2,500 words. **Tips:** Readers are elected and appointed local government officials.

AMERICAN COIN-OP
Crain Communications, Inc.
500 N Dearborn St., Suite 1000, Chicago, IL 60610-4964. 312-337-7700.
E-mail: ppartyka@crain.com. $35. Circ.: 17,000. Paul Partika, Editor. **Description:** Articles, on successful coin-operated laundries (management, promotion, decor, maintenance). SASE for guidelines. **Nonfiction:** To 2,500 words; pays from $.08/word. **Art:** B&W photos; pays $8/each. **Queries:** Preferred.

AMERICAN DEMOGRAPHICS
See page 332 for full listing.
Description: Information on marketing to consumers.

AMERICAN LAUNDRY NEWS
500 N Dearborn St., Suite 1000, Chicago, IL 60610. 312-337-7700.
E-mail: laundrynews@crain.com. Monthly. $39/year. Circ.: 16,000. Bruce Beggs, editor. **Description:** Institutional laundry management, including hospitals, nursing homes, hotels/motels, resorts, restaurant/clubs, schools, and government institutions. **Nonfiction:** New technology, industry news and trends, profiles; 1,000-2,000 words; up to $.22/word. **Queries:** Preferred. **E-Queries:** Yes. **Unsolicited mss:** Accepts. **Response:** 1 month for queries, 2 months for submissions; SASE required. **Freelance Content:** 10%. **Rights:** All. **Payment:** On publication.

AMUSEMENT TODAY
Amusement Today, Inc.
P.O. Box 5427, Arlington, TX 76005-5427. 817-460-7220.
E-mail: info@amusementtoday.com. Web site: www.amusementtoday.com. Monthly. $35. Circ.: 3,500. Gary Slade, Editor-in-Chief. **Description:** Amusement industry publication.

AREA DEVELOPMENT
400 Post Ave., Westbury, NY 11590-2289. 516-338-0900.
E-mail: gerri@area-development.com. Web site: www.areadevelopment.com. Monthly. Circ.: 45,500. Geraldine Gambale, Editor. **Description:** Covers site-selection and facility-planning issues for industrial companies. **Nonfiction:** Stories on site selection, real estate, taxes, labor, energy, environment, government regulations; 2,000 words; $.30/word. **Queries:** Preferred. **E-Queries:** Yes. **Unsolicited mss:** Accepts. **Freelance Content:** 90%. **Payment:** On publication.

AUTOMATED BUILDER
1445 Donlon St., Suite 16, Ventura, CA 93003. 805-642-9735.
E-mail: info@automatedbuilder.com. Web site: www.automatedbuilder.com. Annual. Circ.: 25,000. Don Carlson, Editor. **Description:** For home manufacturers and dealers. **Nonfiction:** Articles on methods, materials and technologies for in-plant building industry; 750-1,000 words; $300. **Queries:** Required. **Response:** Queries 10 days, SASE required. **Freelance Content:** 10%. **Payment:** On acceptance.

BEBIDAS
P.O. Box 16116, Cleveland, OH 44116-0116. 440-331-9100.
E-mail: bebidas@aol.com. Bimonthly. Circ.: 11,000. **Description:** Trade magazine for the Latin American beverage industry. Published entirely in Spanish.

BUILDER
Hanley-Wood, LLC
One Thomas Cir. NW, Suite 600, Washington, DC 20005-5802. 202-452-0800.
E-mail: bthompso@hanley-wood.com. Web site: www.builderonline.com. 16x/yr. Circ.: 138,000. Boyce Thompson, Editor-in-Chief. **Description:** On trends and news in home building (design, marketing, new products, etc.). **Nonfiction:** Articles; to 1,500 words; pay negotiable. **Queries:** Preferred. **Payment:** On acceptance.

BUSINESS AND COMMERCIAL AVIATION
McGraw-Hill, Inc.
4 International Dr. Suite 260, Rye Brook, NY 10573-1065. 914-933-7600.
E-mail: feedback@aviationnow.com. Web site: www.aviationnow.com/bca. Monthly. Circ.: 47,000. William Garvey, Editor-in-Chief. **Description:** For pilots, on use of private aircraft for business transportation. **Nonfiction:** Articles; 2,500 words, with photos; pays $100-$500. **Queries:** Preferred. **Payment:** On acceptance.

CALIFORNIA LAWYER
1145 Market St., Fl. 8, San Francisco, CA 94103. 415-252-0500.
E-mail: tema_goodwin@dailyjournal.com. Web site: dailyjournal.com. Monthly. $5/issue, $45/year. Circ.: 140,000. Peter Allen, editor. **Description:** For lawyers. Combines hard-hitting legal news, case commentary, and technology coverage. **Nonfiction:** News, commentary, features, essays, technology, legal advice; 300-4,000 words; $300-$2,500. **Columns, Departments:** California, ESQ., Expert Advice, The Supremes, Technicalities, In Pro Per, Corporate Insider, Books, Discipline Report; 1,000-1,200 words; $500. **Art:** Photos; B&W, color; payment varies. **Tips:** Start with something small in news section. **Queries:** Preferred. **Unsolicited mss:** Accepts. **Response:** 1-6 weeks. **Freelance Content:** 80%. **Rights:** FNAR and electronic. **Payment:** On acceptance. **Contact:** Tema Goodwin, Managing Editor.

CLEANING & MAINTENANCE MANAGEMENT
13 Century Hill Dr., Latham, NY 12110-2197. 518-783-1281.
Web site: www.cmmonline.com. Paul Amos, Executive Editor. **Description:** Articles on managing cleaning and custodial/maintenance operations. Also technical/mechanical how-to articles. **Nonfiction:** Articles, 500-1,200 words; pays to $300 for commissioned features. **Art:** Photos. **Queries:** Preferred. **Payment:** On publication.

COLLEGE STORE EXECUTIVE
Executive Business Media, Inc.
825 Old Country Rd., Westbury, NY 11590-5501. 516-334-3030.

E-mail: ebmpubs@ix.netcom.com. Web site: www.ebmpubs.com. 10x/yr. $40. Circ.: 9,000. Janice A. Costa, Editor. **Description:** For college store industry; news, profiles. **Nonfiction:** Articles, 1,000 words; pays $4-$5/column inch (extra for photos). **Tips:** No general business or how-to articles. **Queries:** Preferred. **Payment:** On publication.

THE CONSTRUCTION SPECIFIER
Construction Specifications Institute
99 Canal Center Plaza, Suite 300, Alexandria, VA 22314-1588. 703-684-0300.
E-mail: csimail@csinet.org. Web site: www.csinet.org. Monthly. $40. Circ.: 18,000.
Katie Sears, Acting Editor. **Description:** Articles, 2,000-3,000 words, on the "nuts and bolts" of nonresidential construction, for owners/facility managers, architects, engineers, specifiers, contractors, and manufacturers.

COOKING FOR PROFIT
P.O. Box 267, Fond du Lac, WI 54936-0267. 920-923-3700.
E-mail: comments@cookingforprofit.com. Web site: www.cookingforprofit.com.
Colleen Phalen, Editor. **Description:** For foodservice professionals. **Nonfiction:** Profiles of successful restaurants, chains, and franchises, schools, hospitals, nursing homes, etc. Also, case studies on energy management in foodservice environment. Business-to-business articles. Pay varies. **Payment:** On publication.

DAIRY FOODS
Business News Publishing Company, LLC
1050 II Route 83, Suite 200, Bensenville, IL 60106-1096. 630-616-0200.
E-mail: phillipsd@bnp.com. Web site: www.dairyfoods.com. Monthly. Circ.: 18,000.
David Phillips, Managing Editor. **Description:** On innovative dairies, processing operations, marketing, new products for milk handlers and makers of dairy products. **Nonfiction:** Articles, to 2,500 words; pay varies.

DEALERSCOPE
North American Publishing Co.
401 N Broad St., Philadelphia, PA 19108-1080. 215-238-5300.
E-mail: jpinkerton@napco.com. Web site: www.dealerscope.com. Monthly. Circ.: 22,000. Janet Pinkerton, Editor. **Description:** On new consumer electronics, computer and electronics products, and new technologies. **Nonfiction:** Articles, to 1,000 words; pay varies. **Tips:** Query with clips and resume. **Payment:** On publication.

DENTAL ECONOMICS
Penwell, P.O. Box 3408, Tulsa, OK 74101-3408. 918-835-3161.
E-mail: joeb@pennwell.com. Web site: www.dentaleconomics.com. Monthly. $78.
Circ.: 102,000. Joseph A. Blaes, DDS, Editor. **Description:** On business side of dental practice, patient and staff communication, personal investments. **Nonfiction:** Articles, 1,200-3,500 words; pays $100-$400. **Payment:** On acceptance.

DRUG TOPICS

5 Paragon Dr., Montvale, NJ 07645. 201-358-7258.
E-mail: drug.topics@medec.com. Web site: www.drugtopics.com. Harold E. Cohen, Editor. **Description:** Covers pharmacy news, issues, trends, products marketing for pharmacists, buyers, wholesalers, academia, and others. **Nonfiction:** News stories, trends in pharmacy, editorials; 750-2,000 words. **Tips:** Payment is offered for commissioned articles only. **Queries:** Required. **Rights:** First. **Payment:** On acceptance.

ELECTRONIC INFORMATION REPORT

Simba Information
P.O. Box 4234, Stamford, CT 06907-0234. 203-358-4100.
E-mail: eir@simbanet.com. Web site: www.simbanet.com. Weekly. Linda Kopp, Executive Editor. **Description:** Covers all aspects of the marketing of electronic information.

ELECTRONIC MUSICIAN

PRIMEDIA Business Magazines & Media
P.O. Box 1929, Marion, OH 43306. 510-653-3307.
E-mail: emeditorial@primediabusiness.com.
Web site: www.emusician.com. Monthly. Steve Oppenheimer, Bio Editor. **Description:** On audio recording, live sound engineering, technical applications, and product reviews. **Nonfiction:** Articles, 1,500-3,500 words; pays $350-$750. **Payment:** On acceptance.

ENGINEERED SYSTEMS

Business News Publishing Co., LLC
P.O. Box 4270, Troy, MI 48099-4270. 248-362-3700.
E-mail: beverlyr@bnp.com. Web site: www.esmagazine.com. Monthly. Circ.: 57,000. Robert L. Beverly, Editor. **Description:** Articles, case histories, and product information related to engineered HVAC systems in commercial, industrial, or institutional buildings. **Nonfiction:** Pays $4.75/column inch, $12/illustration. **Queries:** Preferred. **Payment:** On publication.

THE ENGRAVERS JOURNAL

P.O. Box 318, Brighton, MI 48116. 810-229-5725.
E-mail: info@engraversjournal.com. Web site: www.engraversjournal.com. Monthly. Rosemary Farrell, Editor. **Description:** Trade magazine for engravers. **Nonfiction:** Articles on small business operations. Pays $75-$300. **Queries:** Preferred. **E-Queries:** No. **Unsolicited mss:** Accepts. **Rights:** Varies. **Payment:** On acceptance.

ENTERTAINMENT DESIGN

PRIMEDIA Business Magazines & Media
32 W 18th St., New York, NY 10011. 212-229-2965.
E-mail: jtien@primediabusiness.com. Web site: www.entertainmentdesignmag.com.

Jacqueline Tien, Publisher. **Description:** Trade publication that centers on the art and technology of entertainment. Articles cover design, technical, and management aspects of theater, opera, dance, television, and film for those in performing arts and the entertainment trade. **Nonfiction:** Articles, 500-2,500 words. **Queries:** Preferred. **Payment:** On acceptance.

FIRE CHIEF
29 N Wacker Dr., Fl. 9, Chicago, IL 60601. 312-609-4242.
E-mail: jwilmoth@primediabusiness.com. Web site: www.firechief.com. Monthly. Janet Wilmoth, editor. **Description:** For fire officers. **Nonfiction:** Training, safety and health, communications, fire investigation, finance and budgeting, professional development, incident command, hazmat response, vehicle maintenance; 1,000-5,000 words; up to $.30/word. **Columns, Departments:** Training Perspectives, EMS Viewpoint, Sound Off; 1,000-1,800 words. **Queries:** Preferred. **Response:** SASE. **Payment:** On publication.

FIREHOUSE
Cygnus Publishing, Inc.
445 Broad Hollow Rd., Ste. 21, Melville, NY 11747. 516-845-2700.
Web site: www.firehouse.com. Monthly. $29/year. Circ.: 1.5 million. Harvey Eisner, Editor-in-Chief. **Description:** For firefighters and fire buffs; seeks to educate, inform, and entertain. **Nonfiction:** Coverage of major fires and disasters, apparatus and equipment, communications, training, law, safety, EMS, etc; 500-2,000 words. **Art:** To accompany manuscript; photos, illustrations, charts, diagrams; color preferred. **Queries:** Required. **Response:** SASE required. **Rights:** First. **Payment:** On publication.

FOOD MANAGEMENT
Penton Media
1300 E Ninth St., Cleveland, OH 44114-1503. 216-696-7000.
E-mail: fmeditor@aol.com. Web site: www.penton.com. Monthly. Circ.: 47,895. John Lawn, Editor-in-Chief. **Description:** On food service in hospitals, nursing homes, schools, colleges, prisons, businesses, and industrial sites. **Nonfiction:** Trends, legislative issues, how-tos, management, and retail-oriented food service pieces. **Queries:** Required.

FOUNDATION NEWS & COMMENTARY
1828 L Street NW, Washington, DC 20036. 202-467-0467.
E-mail: curtj@cof.org. Web site: www.foundationnews.org. Bimonthly. $48/year. Circ.: 10,000. Jody Curtis, Editor. **Description:** Covers the world of grant making, for professional grant makers, volunteer trustees, and grant seekers. **Nonfiction:** 1,200-3,000 words; pay varies. **Tips:** Avoid fundraising topics. **Queries:** Required. **E-Queries:** Yes. **Unsolicited mss:** Accepts. **Response:** Varies. **Freelance Content:** 25%. **Rights:** All. **Payment:** On acceptance.

GLASS DIGEST

Ashlee Publishing Company, Inc.

18 E 41st St., New York, NY 10017-6222. 212-376-7722.

E-mail: glass@ashlee.com. Web site: www.ashlee.com. Monthly. $40/yr. Circ.: 11,730. Cynthia Nodson, Editorial Director. **Description:** On building projects and glass/metal dealers, distributors, storefront and glazing contractors. **Nonfiction:** Articles, 1,200-1,500 words. **Payment:** On publication.

GOVERNMENT EXECUTIVE

National Journal Group, Inc.

1501 M St. NW, Suite 300, Washington, DC 20005-1700. 202-739-8500.

E-mail: govexec@govexec.com. Web site: www.govexec.com. Monthly. $48/yr. Circ.: 60,000. Timothy Clark, President/Editor. **Description:** Articles, 1,500-3,000 words, for civilian and military government workers at the management level.

HEATING/PIPING/AIR CONDITIONING/ENGINEERING

1300 E Ninth St., Cleveland, OH 44114-1501. 216-696-7000.

E-mail: hpac@penton.com. Web site: www.hpac.com. Monthly. $65. Circ.: 31,000. Michael G. Ivanovich, Editor. **Description:** On heating, piping, and air conditioning systems and related issues (indoor air quality, energy efficiency), for industrial plants and large buildings only. **Nonfiction:** Articles, to 3,500 words; pays $70/printed page. **Queries:** Preferred. **Payment:** On publication.

HOME SHOP MACHINIST

2779 Aero Park Dr., Traverse City, MI 49686. 231-946-3712.

E-mail: nknopf@villagepress.com. Web site: www.homeshopmachinist.com. Bimonthly. $5.95. Circ.: 36,000. Neil A. Knopf, Editor. **Description:** Publishes how-to articles for serious machinists and hobbyists. **Nonfiction:** Machine how-to projects. Photos, drawings and text required. No people profiles; $40/page. **Art:** $9/photo. **Tips:** Write in first-person only; accuracy and detail essential. **Queries:** Preferred. **E-Queries:** Yes. **Unsolicited mss:** Accepts. **Response:** Queries 1 week, submissions 1 month, SASE required. **Freelance Content:** 95%. **Rights:** FNASR. **Payment:** On publication.

HOSPITALS & HEALTH NETWORKS

One N Franklin St., Fl. 29, Chicago, IL 60606. 312-893-6800.

E-mail: bsantamour@healthforum.com. Web site: www.hhnmag.com. Bill Santamour, Managing Editor. **Description:** Publication for health-care executives and hospital administrators on financing, staffing, coordinating, and providing facilities for health-care services. **Nonfiction:** Articles, 250-1,800 words; pay varies. **Unsolicited mss:** Does not accept. **Payment:** On publication.

INDUSTRIA ALIMENTICIA

Stagnito Communications, Inc.

155 Pfingsten Rd., Suite 205, Deerfield, IL 60015. 847-205-5660.

Web site: www.stagnito.com. Monthly. Circ.: 45,000. **Description:** Spanish-language publication. Covers the food-processing industry in Latin America.

INK MAKER
Cygnus Business Media
445 Broad Hollow Rd., Melville, NY 11747.
E-mail: info@inkmakeronline.com. Web site: www.inkmakeronline.com. Monthly. $66. Circ.: 6,000. Linda M. Casatelli, Editor. **Description:** Covers trends, technology, and news in the printing ink industry. Features both technical and non-technical pieces for ink manufacturers and printers. Includes interviews with printers from across the country. **Nonfiction:** Pieces on ink manufacturing and recent technical developments; 2000 words; $450-$550. **Queries:** Required. **Unsolicited mss:** Accepts. **Response:** 2-3 weeks. **Freelance Content:** 30%. **Rights:** 1st NA.

INTERCOM
Society for Technical Information
901 N Stuart St., Suite 904, Arlington, VA 22203. 703-522-4114.
E-mail: intercom@stc.org. Web site: www.stc.org. 10x/yr. Circ.: 25,000. Maurice Martin, Editor. **Description:** Industry information for technical writers, publishers, and editors.

INTERNAL MEDICINE WORLD REPORT
Medical World Communications
241 Forsgate Dr., Jamesburg, NJ 08831-1385. 732-656-1140.
E-mail: jcharnow@mwc.com. Web site: www.imwronline.com. Monthly. $180/yr. Circ.: 99,000. Jody A Charnow, Editor. **Description:** Relevant clinical news for practicing internists. **Nonfiction:** Articles based on scientific presentations at medical conferences or reports in major medical journals; 150-250 words; $.50/word. **Tips:** No articles on animal or test-tube studies. No promotional articles, reporting on talks given at events sponsored by drug companies, etc. Welcomes new writers. **Queries:** Preferred. **E-Queries:** Yes. **Unsolicited mss:** Accepts. **Response:** 1 week, SASE required. **Freelance Content:** 90%. **Rights:** All. **Payment:** On publication.

JD JUNGLE
Jungle Interactive Media
632 Broadway, Fl. 7, New York, NY 10012-2614. 212-352-0840.
E-mail: editors@jdjungle.com. Web site: www.jdjungle.com. Monthly. $12. Circ.: 132,000. Jon Gluck, Editor-in-Chief. **Description:** For law students. Seeks to provide professionals with the tools they need to be successful. Online and print versions. **Queries:** Preferred. **Unsolicited mss:** Accepts. **Response:** SASE required.

JOURNAL OF EMERGENCY MEDICAL SERVICES (JEMS)
P.O. Box 2789, Carlsbad, CA 92018. 800-266-5367.
Web site: www.jems.com. Monthly. $27.97. Circ.: 40,000. A. J. Heightman, Editor-in-Chief. **Description:** A leading voice in emergency medicine and prehospital

care, for EMTs, paramedics, nurses, physicians, EMS managers, administrators, and educators. **Nonfiction:** On provider health and professional development; innovative applications of EMS; interviews/profiles, new equipment and technology; industry news and commentary; $200-$400. **Columns, Departments:** $150-$200/departments, $25/news items. **Art:** Only real-life EMS action shots; completed model release form must accompany photos when appropriate; $150-$400 (cover). **Queries:** Preferred. **E-Queries:** Yes. **Unsolicited mss:** Accepts. **Response:** Submissions 3 months. **Freelance Content:** 70%. **Payment:** On publication.

LANDSCAPE TRADES

Horticulture Trades Association
7856 Fifth Line S., RR4, Milton, Ontario L9T 2X8 Canada. 905-875-1805.
E-mail: linerskine@landscapeontario.com. Web site: www.landscapetrades.com. 9x/yr. $45. Circ.: 8,000. Linda Erskine, Editor. **Description:** Articles on landscape design, construction, and maintenance. Features targeting retail and wholesale nursery industries. **Queries:** Required. **Unsolicited mss:** Accepts. **Response:** 2-3 weeks. **Freelance Content:** 25%. **Rights:** 1st NA. **Payment:** On publication.

LP-GAS

7500 Old Oak Blvd., Cleveland, OH 44130. 440-891-2616.
E-mail: phyland@advanstar.com. Web site: www.lpgasmagazine.com. Patrick Hyland, Editor. **Description:** On LP-gas dealer operations: marketing, management, etc. **Nonfiction:** Articles, 1,500-2,500 words, with photos; pays flat fee schedule. **Queries:** Preferred. **Payment:** On acceptance.

MACHINE DESIGN

1300 E Ninth St., Cleveland, OH 44114-1503. 216-696-7000.
E-mail: mdeditor@penton.com. Web site: www.machinedesign.com. Ronald Kohl, Editor. **Description:** On mechanical and electromechanical design topics for engineers. **Nonfiction:** Articles, to 10 typed pages; pay varies. **Queries:** Preferred. **Payment:** On publication.

MAINTENANCE TECHNOLOGY

1300 S Grove Ave., Suite 105, Barrington, IL 60010-5246. 847-382-8100.
E-mail: editors@mt-online.com. Web site: www.mt-online.com. Monthly. Circ.: 54,000. Robert C. Baldwin, Editor. **Description:** Technical articles with how-to information to increase reliability and maintainability of electrical and mechanical systems and equipment. Readers are managers, supervisors, and engineers in all industries and facilities. **Nonfiction:** Pay varies. **Queries:** Preferred. **Payment:** On acceptance.

NATIONAL FISHERMAN

121 Free St., Portland, ME 04101-3919. 207-842-5606.
E-mail: jfraser@divcom.com. Web site: www.nationalfisherman.com. Jerry Fraser,

Editor-in-Chief. **Description:** For commercial fishermen and boat builders. **Nonfiction:** Articles, 200-2,000 words; pays $4-$6/inch, extra for photos. **Queries:** Preferred. **Payment:** On publication.

THE NORTHERN LOGGER AND TIMBER PROCESSOR

P.O. Box 69, Old Forge, NY 13420-0069. 315-369-3078.

E-mail: nela@telnet.net. Monthly. Circ.: 13,200. Eric A. Johnson, Editor. **Description:** Covers the forest-product industry. **Nonfiction:** Features, 1,000-2,000 words; pays $.15/word. **Art:** Photos. **Queries:** Preferred. **Payment:** On publication.

P.I. MAGAZINE

755 Bronx Ave., Toledo, OH 43609-1723. 419-382-0967.

E-mail: pimag1@aol.com. Web site: www.pimall.com. 6x/yr. Circ.: 5,200. Bob Mackowiak, Publisher/Editor. **Description:** "America's Private Investigation Journal." Profiles of professional investigators, with true accounts of their most difficult cases. **Nonfiction:** Pays $75-$100. **Tips:** No fiction. **Payment:** On publication.

PIZZA TODAY

P.O. Box 1347, New Albany, IN 47151. 812-949-0909.

E-mail: jwhite@pizzatoday.com. Web site: www.pizzatoday.com. Jeremy White, Executive Editor. **Description:** On business management for pizza entrepreneurs. **Nonfiction:** Articles on food preparation, marketing strategies, management, hiring and training, etc; 500-1,500 words; $.50/word. **Tips:** Send query by e-mail, fax, or mail. **Queries:** Preferred. **Payment:** On acceptance.

POLICE AND SECURITY NEWS

1208 Juniper St., Quakertown, PA 18951. 215-538-1240.

E-mail: jdevery@policeandsecuritynews.com.

Web site: www.policeandsecuritynews.com. Bimonthly. $15/yr. Circ.: 22,000. James Devery, Editor. **Description:** For the law enforcement industry. Targets middle and upper management professionals within public and private law enforcement and security industries. **Nonfiction:** Law enforcement and security related articles. Written for experts in a manner which non-experts can comprehend; 500-3,000 words; $.10/word. **Tips:** Submit query, cover letter, complete ms., and bio with SASE. **Queries:** Preferred. **E-Queries:** Yes. **Unsolicited mss:** Accepts. **Response:** 1-2 weeks. **Freelance Content:** 50%. **Rights:** 1st NA. **Payment:** On publication.

POOL & BILLIARD

See page 399 for full listing.

Description: Consumer and trade magazine for the pool industry.

PRACTICE STRATEGIES

American Optometric Association

243 N Lindbergh Blvd., St. Louis, MO 63141. 314-991-4100 ext. 267.

E-mail: rfpieper@theaoa.org. Web site: www.aoanet.org. Monthly. Members. Circ.: 33,000. Bob Pieper, Editor. **Description:** Published by a section of the Journal of American Optometric Assn., on practice management issues. **Nonfiction:** On business aspects (insurance issues, motivating staff, government health programs). **Queries:** Preferred. **E-Queries:** Yes. **Unsolicited mss:** Accepts. **Response:** 1 month. **Freelance Content:** 25%. **Rights:** All. **Payment:** On publication.

PRECISION
3131 Fernbrook Lane, Suite 111, Plymouth, MN 55447.
8x/year. Circ.: 7,000. Beth Kuhlman, Editor-in-Chief. **Description:** For manufacturing job shops in Minnesota and neighboring counties. Covers trends, personalities, and successes in the manufacturing industry. **Nonfiction:** Seeking writers for profile pieces; length varies; to $100/page. **Art:** Uses some freelance photographers. Send samples of work. **Tips:** Welcomes new writers. **Queries:** Required. **E-Queries:** Yes. **Unsolicited mss:** Accepts. **Response:** 2-4 weeks, SASE required. **Freelance Content:** 50%. **Rights:** One-time and reprint. **Payment:** On publication.

PUBLISH
462 Boston St., Topsfield, MA 01983-1200. 978-887-7900.
E-mail: edit@publish.com. Web site: www.publish.com. Bimonthly. Circ.: 96,000. Melissa Reyen, Executive Editor. **Description:** On all aspects of enterprise communication and publishing technology. **Nonfiction:** Features (1,500-2,000 words); reviews (400-800 words); Pay varies. **Payment:** On acceptance.

REMODELING
One Thomas Cir. NW, Suite 600, Washington, DC 20005. 202-452-0390.
E-mail: pdeffenb@hanley-wood.com;salfano@hanley-wood.com.
Web site: www.remodelingmagazine.com. Monthly. Free. Circ.: 80,000. Paul Deffenbaugh, Sal Alfano, Editors. **Description:** For remodeling contractors. **Nonfiction:** By assignment only, 250-1,700 words, on industry news for residential and light commercial remodelers. **Queries:** Required. **E-Queries:** Yes. **Unsolicited mss:** Does not accept. **Response:** Queries 1 month. **Freelance Content:** 10%. **Rights:** All NA. **Payment:** On acceptance.

REVISTA AEREA
310 E 44th St., Suite 1601, New York, NY 10017-4420. 212-370-1740.
E-mail: revistaaerea@revistaaerea.com. Web site: www.revistaaerea.com. 8x/yr. Circ.: 12,000. **Description:** Covers both military and commercial aviation industries in Latin America, and other countries where Spanish is the primary language.

RV BUSINESS
2575 Vista Del Mar Dr., Ventura, CA 93001. 800-765-1912.
E-mail: rub@tl.com. Web site: www.rvbusiness.com. Monthly. Circ.: 21,000. John Sullaway, Editor. **Description:** Publication for the RV industry offering news and

product-related features. Also covers legislative matters affecting the industry. **Nonfiction:** Articles, to 1,500 words; pay varies. **Tips:** No generic business features.

SOFTWARE

P.O. Box 135, E Walpole, MA 02032. 508-668-9928. E-mail: jdesmond@softwaremag.com. Web site: www.softwaremag.com. Monthly. Circ.: 110,000. John P. Desmond, Publisher/Editorial Director. **Description:** For corporate systems managers and MIS personnel. **Nonfiction:** Features and information on latest software. **Tips:** E-mail abstract and brief bio to e-mail address given above. **E-Queries:** Yes. **Unsolicited mss:** Accepts. **Contact:** John P. Desmond, Editorial Director.

SOUTHERN LUMBERMAN

P.O. Box 681629, Franklin, TN 37068-1629. 615-791-1961. E-mail: ngregg@southernlumberman.com. Web site: www.southernlumberman.com. Monthly. $23/yr. Circ.: 15,500. Nanci P. Gregg, Editor. **Description:** For owners and operators of small- to medium-sized sawmills. **Nonfiction:** Ideal: a feature on a sawmill with description of equipment and tips from owner/manager on how to work efficiently, save and make money; 500-2,500 words; $100-$300. **Queries:** Preferred. **E-Queries:** No. **Unsolicited mss:** Accepts. **Response:** 4-6 weeks, SASE. **Freelance Content:** 45%. **Rights:** FNASR. **Payment:** On publication.

STITCHES

16787 Warden Ave., RR #3, Newmarket, Ontario L3Y 4W1 Canada. 905-853-1884. E-mail: stitches@attglobal.com. Monthly. $40/yr (Canada), $45 (U.S.). Circ.: 39,000. Simon Hally, Editor. **Description:** "The Journal of Medical Humor." Specializes in humor and lifestyle pieces, 250-2,000 words, for physicians. **Fiction:** Up to 2,000 words; $.35/word (Canada), $.25/word (U.S.). **Nonfiction:** Up to 2,000 words. **Poetry:** Shorter; $.50/word (Canada), $.40/word (U.S.). **Columns, Departments:** Humor. **Art:** Cartoons only. $50 (Canada), $40 (U.S.). **Queries:** Not necessary. **E-Queries:** Yes. **Unsolicited mss:** Accepts. **Freelance Content:** 95%. **Rights:** FNASR. **Payment:** On publication.

STONE WORLD

Business News Publishing
210 Route 4 E, Suite 311, Paramus, NJ 07652. 201-291-9001. E-mail: michael@stoneworld.com. Web site: www.stoneworld.com. Michael Reis, Editor/Associate Publisher. **Description:** On new trends in installing and designing with stone. For architects, interior designers, design professionals, and stone fabricators and dealers. **Nonfiction:** Articles, 750-1,500 words; pays $6/column inch. **Queries:** Preferred. **Payment:** On publication.

TECHNICAL COMMUNICATION

See page 639 for full listing.
Description: Industry information for technical writers, publishers, and editors.

TODAY'S FACILITY MANAGER
121 Monmouth St., Red Bank, NJ 07701. 732-842-7433.
Web site: www.groupc.com. Annually. $30 (nonprofessionals) Free to trade professionals. Circ.: 45,000. Jill Aronson, New Products Editor. **Description:** News and new-product information for in-house, on-site facility professionals. **Nonfiction:** 1,000-2,500 words; pays flat fee. **Tips:** Welcomes new writers. Requires solid research and reporting skills. **Queries:** Preferred. **E-Queries:** Yes. **Unsolicited mss:** Accepts. **Response:** Varies, SASE required. **Freelance Content:** 10%. **Rights:** Flexible. **Payment:** 30 days after publication.

WASTE AGE
6151 Powers Ferry Rd. NW, Atlanta, GA 30339-2941. 770-618-0112.
E-mail: bwolpin@primediabusiness.com. Web site: www.wasteage.com. Monthly. Circ.: 43,000. Bill Wolpin, Editorial Director. **Description:** Covers collection, transfer, processing, and disposal of waste. Analysis of relevant news, trends, products, people, and events. **Nonfiction:** Case studies, market analysis, how-to articles, 2,000-3,000 words, with solutions to problems in the field. **Queries:** Required. **E-Queries:** Yes. **Unsolicited mss:** Accepts. **Response:** 2 months, SASE. **Rights:** Worldwide. **Payment:** On publication.

WOODSHOP NEWS
35 Pratt St., Essex, CT 06426. 860-767-8227.
E-mail: editorial@woodshopnews.com. Web site: www.woodshopnews.com. Monthly. $3.95/$21.95. A. J. Hamler, Editor. **Description:** Business stories, profiles, and news for people who work with wood. **Nonfiction:** Business advice for professional woodworkers; profiles of shops with unique businesses, furniture lines, or stories; marketing techniques applicable to small and medium size woodworking shops; trends in equipment, new technology, and construction techniques; to 1,400 words; $150-$500. **Columns, Departments:** Pro Shop, Profiles, Jigs & Tips. **Tips:** Need profiles of woodworkers outside the Northeast region. **Queries:** Preferred. **Unsolicited mss:** Accepts. **Payment:** On publication.

WORKBOAT
347 Gerard St., Mandeville, LA 70448. 985-626-0298.
Web site: www.workboat.com. David Krapf, Editor. **Description:** Current, lively information for workboat owners, operators, crew, suppliers, and regulators. **Nonfiction:** Features, to 2,000 words, and shorts, 500-1,000 words. Topics: construction and conversion; diesel engines and electronics; politics and industry; unusual vessels; new products; profiles. Pay varies. **Queries:** Preferred. **Payment:** On publication.

TRAVEL

AAA GOING PLACES
1515 N Westshore Blvd., Tampa, FL 33607. 813-289-1391.
E-mail: sklim@aaasouth.com. Web site: aaagoingplaces.com. Bimonthly. Circ.: 4,000,000. Sandy Klim, Editor. **Description:** On domestic travel and lifestyle, for AAA Members. **Nonfiction:** Well-researched domestic and international travel, automotive, lifestyle. Third-person preferred; 800-1,200 words; $200-$400. **Art:** Color photos. **Tips:** Prefers general, rather than niche, travel stories to a destination, with an angle; e.g., Washington D.C., "The Monuments," not the annual art exhibit at Lincoln Memorial. Weekend or weeklong vacation ideas for seniors and families. Fun vacation stops, a little unusual but with lots to offer ("Hershey, Pa.: something for everyone"). **Queries:** Not necessary. **E-Queries:** Yes. **Unsolicited mss:** Accepts. **Response:** Queries 6 months, submissions 3 months, SASE. **Freelance Content:** 50%. **Rights:** 1st, Web and reprint rights, some reprints from local markets. **Payment:** On acceptance.

ARIZONA HIGHWAYS
See page 499 for full listing.
Description: Covers travel, adventure, and lifestyle in Arizona.

BIG WORLD
P.O. Box 7656, Lancaster, PA 17604-7656. 717-569-0217.
E-mail: karen@bigworld.com. Web site: www.bigworld.com. Quarterly. $3.50/$15. Circ.: 15,000. Karen Stone, Managing Editor. **Description:** For budget and independent travelers. Most readers are younger, world travelers. **Nonfiction:** Useful how-to stories or thoughtful retellings of travels. Advice on work and study abroad, humorous anecdotes, first-person experiences, other travel information. For readers who wish to responsibly discover, explore, and learn, in touch with locals and traditions, in harmony with environment; 500-2,500 words; up to $50. **Tips:** Stories should reflect earthy, on-the-cheap travel. **Queries:** Not necessary. **E-Queries:** Yes. **Unsolicited mss:** Accepts. **Response:** Queries 2 months, submissions 2 months, SASE. **Freelance Content:** 80%. **Rights:** 1st. **Payment:** On publication.

BRITISH HERITAGE
6405 Flank Dr., Harrisburg, PA 17112-2750. 717-657-9555.
Web site: www.britishheritage.com. Bimonthly. Circ.: 100,000. Bruce Heydt, Managing Editor. **Description:** Travel articles on places to visit in the British Isles. **Nonfiction:** Articles; 800-1,500 words; include detailed historical information in a "For the Visitor" sidebar. Pays $100-$200. **Payment:** On acceptance.

CARIBBEAN TRAVEL AND LIFE
460 N Orlando Ave., Winter Park, FL 32789. 407-628-4802.
E-mail: editor@caribbeantravelmag.com. Web site: www.caribbeantravelmag.com. Circ.: 135,000. Jessica Chapman, Managing Editor. **Description:** For the upscale

traveler, on travel, recreation, leisure, and culture in the Caribbean, the Bahamas, and Bermuda. **Nonfiction:** Topics include shopping, dining, arts and entertainment, and sightseeing suggestions, 500-3,000 words; pays $75-$750. **Tips:** Send published clips. **Queries:** Preferred. **Payment:** On publication.

COAST TO COAST
2575 Vista del Mar Dr., Ventura, CA 93001. 805-667-4100.
Web site: www.rv.net. 8/year. $4/$28. Circ.: 200,000. Valerie Law, Editor. **Description:** Membership magazine for a network of upscale RV resorts across North America. Focuses on travel and outdoor recreation. **Nonfiction:** Essays on travel, recreation, and good times. Destination features on a North American city or region, going beyond typical tourist stops. Activity/recreation features introduce a sport, hobby, or other diversion. Also, features on RV lifestyle; 1,200-3,500 words; $300-$600. **Art:** Slides, digital images, prints; $75-$600. **Queries:** Not necessary. **E-Queries:** Yes. **Unsolicited mss:** Accepts. **Response:** SASE. **Freelance Content:** 75%. **Rights:** 1st NA, rarely electronic. **Payment:** On acceptance.

CRUISE TRAVEL
990 Grove St., Evanston, IL 60201. 847-491-6440.
Web site: www.cruisetravelmag.com. Robert Meyers, Editor. **Description:** Ship-, port-, and cruise-of-the-month features, 800-2,000 words; cruise guides; cruise roundups; cruise company profiles; travel suggestions for one-day port stops. **Nonfiction:** Photo-features strongly recommended; pay varies. **Tips:** Query by mail only, with sample color photos. **Queries:** Preferred. **Payment:** On acceptance.

ENDLESS VACATION
9998 N Michigan Rd., Carmel, IN 46032-9640. 317-805-8120.
E-mail: julie.woodard@rci.com. Web site: www.rci.com. Bimonthly. $84/yr. Circ.: 1,200,000. Geri Bain, Editor. **Description:** Describes where to go and what to do on vacation, and why. **Nonfiction:** Focus on domestic vacation travel, with some mainstream international vacation articles. Features on new and interesting vacation options, with a solid angle; 1,000-2,000 words; $500-$1,200. **Columns, Departments:** Weekend travel destinations, health and safety on the road, short travel news-oriented and service pieces, hot news tips and travel trends; 800-1,200 words; $300-$800. **Art:** Travel-oriented photos (landscapes, scenics, people, activities, etc.); slides, originals. **Tips:** Write for doers, not dreamers. Describe activities in which readers can participate. **Queries:** Preferred. **E-Queries:** No. **Response:** 4-8 weeks. **Freelance Content:** 90%. **Rights:** 1st NA. **Payment:** On acceptance.

EPICUREAN TRAVELER
740 Stetson St., Moss Beach, CA 94038. 650-728-5389.
E-mail: mossbeach@attbi.com. Web site: www.epicurean-traveler.com. 8x/yr. $32. Circ.: 115,000. Scott Clemens, Publisher. **Description:** E-zine featuring articles on luxury travel with a special emphasis on food and wine. **Tips:** Editorial calendar is currently full, but will consider queries. All articles must have a connection to the

local food/wine of a particular region or area. **Queries:** Required. **E-Queries:** Yes. **Response:** 6 weeks. **Freelance Content:** 75%. **Rights:** 1st electronic. **Payment:** On publication.

FAMILY MOTOR COACHING

8291 Clough Pike, Cincinnati, OH 45244-2796. 513-474-3622.
E-mail: magazine@fmca.com. Web site: www.fmca.com. Monthly. $3.99/$27. Circ.: 126,000. Robbin Gould, Editor. **Description:** Published by Family Motor Coach Assn., for motorhome owners. **Nonfiction:** Travel articles, keyed to noteworthy national events. Describe scenic amenities, accommodations, geography or history; 1,500-2,000 words; pays $50-$500. **Art:** Articles with photos preferred. Transparencies preferred; digital if 400 dpi or higher. Drawings, sketches, or photos should accompany technical articles. **Tips:** Orient articles to Family Assn. members. **Queries:** Preferred. **E-Queries:** Yes. **Unsolicited mss:** Accepts. **Response:** 4-6 weeks, SASE. **Rights:** FNASR and electronic. **Payment:** On acceptance.

HIGHWAYS

2575 Vista Del Mar Dr., P.O. Box 8545, Ventura, CA 93001. 805-667-4100.
E-mail: kwinters@affinitygroup.com. Web site: www.goodsamclub.com. 11x/year. $25 yr (includes membership). Circ.: 1,000,000. Kimberley Winters, Managing Editor. **Description:** Published for Good Sam Club, recreation vehicle owner's organization. Industry news, also travel and technical features. **Fillers:** Humorous vignettes on an aspect of RV lifestyle; 800-1,400 words; $200 and up. **Columns, Departments:** Highway (columns assigned; submit ideas for consideration). **Art:** Travel features should include at least 15 color transparencies (originals). **Tips:** Do not send unsolicited manuscripts via e-mail. **Queries:** Required. **E-Queries:** Yes. **Unsolicited mss:** Does not accept. **Response:** Queries 4 weeks, submissions 8 weeks; SASE. **Freelance Content:** 40%. **Rights:** 1st NA, electronic. **Payment:** On acceptance.

HOME & AWAY INDIANA

AAA Hoosier Motor Club
3750 Guion Rd., Indianapolis, IN 46222-7602. 317-923-1500.
E-mail: editorial@homeandawaymagazine.com.
Web site: www.homeandawaymagazine.com. Bimonthly. $6. Circ.: 225,000. Kathy Neff, Editor. **Description:** On travel topics. **Nonfiction:** Articles, of varying lengths. **Art:** Photos, slides.

INTERLINE ADVENTURES

Grand Adventures Tour & Travel Publishing Corp.
211 E 7th St., Suite 1100, Austin, TX 78701-3334. 512-391-2000.
E-mail: editor@perx.com. Web site: www.perx.com. Bimonthly. $15. Circ.: 135,000. In Churl Yo, Editor. **Description:** Airline-employee news and travel information. **Nonfiction:** Articles on worldwide destinations, to 2,500 words; $300-$700. **Columns, Departments:** Golf, resorts, cruise ships, traveling with grandchildren; 800-1,000 words; $200-$400. **Queries:** Not necessary. **E-Queries:** Yes. **Unsolicited**

mss: Accepts. **Response:** 2-6 months, SASE. **Freelance Content:** 70%. **Rights:** One-time. **Payment:** On publication.

THE INTERNATIONAL RAILWAY TRAVELER

Editorial Office, P.O. Box 3747, San Diego, CA 92163. 619-260-1332. E-mail: irteditor@aol.com. Web site: www.irtsociety.com. Monthly. $65/U.S. $70/Canada. Circ.: 5,000. Gena Holle, Editor. **Description:** Train-travel stories from around the world, written with verve and wit, that show writer's love of train travel as environmentally friendly, adventurous, and exciting mode of travel. **Nonfiction:** Anything involving trains, from luxury to seat-of-the-pants trips. Hotels with a rail history, sightseeing by tram or metro. Articles must be factually sound, with ample logistical detail so readers can replicate the author's trip; 300-1,400 words; $.03/word. **Art:** Good photos of trains to go with stories; B&W glossies, transparencies, or color prints; $10 inside stories, $20 for cover. **Tips:** Your travel stories need not be written chronologically. Try building your story around a few key points or impressions from your trip. **Queries:** Preferred. **E-Queries:** Yes. **Unsolicited mss:** Accepts. **Response:** 2 months, SASE required. **Freelance Content:** 80%. **Rights:** FNASR, electronic. **Payment:** On publication.

INTERVAL WORLD

6262 Sunset Dr., Miami, FL 33143-4843. 305-666-1861. E-mail: intervaleditors@interval-intl.com. Web site: www.intervalworld.com. Quarterly. Circ.: 700,000. Lisa Willard, Editor-in-Chief. **Description:** For time-share vacationers.

ISLANDS

6309 Carpinteria Ave., Carpinteria, CA 93013. 805-745-7100. E-mail: islands@islands.com. Web site: www.islands.com. 8x/year. $4.95/issue, $24.95/year. Circ.: 280,000. Joan Tapper, Editor-in-Chief. **Description:** About islands around the world— the crossroads of romance and adventure. Photos and narratives take readers to Bora-Bora, Bali, and remote island outposts. **Nonfiction:** Illuminate what makes a place tick through strong narrative-based writing. Profiles of unforgettable people; 1,500-4,000 words; $.50/word and up. **Columns, Departments:** Horizons (short, quicky island-related items); 50-500 words. **Art:** 35mm. **Queries:** Preferred. **E-Queries:** Yes. **Unsolicited mss:** Accepts. **Response:** 3 months, SASE required. **Freelance Content:** 90%. **Rights:** All. **Payment:** On acceptance.

MICHIGAN LIVING

See page 513 for full listing.
Description: Michigan topics, also area and Canadian tourist/ recreation ideas.

THE MIDWEST TRAVELER

12901 N Forty Dr., St. Louis, MO 63141. 314-523-7350. E-mail: mright@aaamissouri.com. Web site: www.aaatravelermags.com. Bimonthly.

$3/year. Circ.: 435,000. Michael J. Right, Editor. **Description:** For AAA members in Missouri and parts of Illinois, Indiana, and Kansas. **Nonfiction:** Lively writing to encourage readers to take the trip they've just read about. Include useful travel tips. AAA properties preferred; 1,200-1,500 words; $150-$350. **Art:** Slides (color), prints, or digital; $75-$150. **Tips:** Request editorial calendar. **Queries:** Preferred. **E-Queries:** No. **Unsolicited mss:** Accepts. **Response:** 4-6 weeks, SASE. **Freelance Content:** 80%. **Rights:** 1st NA, reprint, electronic. **Payment:** On acceptance.

MOTORHOME

2575 Vista Del Mar, Ventura, CA 93001. 805-667-4100.
Web site: www.motorhomemagazine.com. Sherry McBride, Senior Managing Editor. **Description:** Covers destinations for RV travelers. Also, activities, hobbies, and how-tos. **Nonfiction:** Travel destinations and other articles; 150-2,000 words; $100-$600. **Columns, Departments:** Crossroads (varied topics: unique motorhomes to great cafes, museums to festivals; with 1-2 good color transparencies); Quick Tips (do-it-yourself ideas for motorhomes; no photo, just a sketch if necessary; 150 words; $100). **Art:** 35mm slides; $25-500. **Tips:** Departments are easiest way to break in. Readers are active travelers; most retirees, but more baby boomers entering the RV lifestyle, so some articles directed to novices, families. No diaries or product tests. **Queries:** Preferred. **E-Queries:** No. **Unsolicited mss:** Accepts. **Response:** 3-4 weeks, SASE. **Freelance Content:** 65%. **Payment:** On acceptance.

NATIONAL GEOGRAPHIC ADVENTURE

104 W 40th St., Fl. 19, New York, NY 10018. 212-790-9020.
E-mail: adventure@ngs.org.
Web site: www.nationalgeographic.com/adventure. 10x/yr. Mark Jannot. **Description:** Covers adventure and general travel (adventure as travel designed to push the envelope on experience and, to some degree, comfort). Destinations are divided evenly between U.S. and international. **Nonfiction:** Features, 4,000-8,000 words, on well-known adventures, expeditions, and scientific exploration; unknown historical tales. E.g., diving near Australia's Ningaloo Reef; paddling on New England's Merrimack River. **Columns, Departments:** Profiles, opinions, commentaries (2,000-3,000 words); Trips (500-2,000 words, how readers can bring adventure into their own lives). **Tips:** Helps to have written for other travel magazines. Carefully target query and make it compelling. Readers aged 20-55. **Queries:** Preferred. **Unsolicited mss:** Accepts. **Freelance Content:** 90%.

NATIONAL GEOGRAPHIC TRAVELER

1145 17th St. NW, Washington, DC 20036. 202-857-7000.
E-mail: traveler@nationalgeographic.com. Web site: nationalgeographic.com/traveler. Keith Bellows, Editor. **Description:** Most articles by assignment only; query first with 1-2-page proposal, resume, and published clips required. **Nonfiction:** Articles 1,500-4,000 words; pays $1/word. **Payment:** On acceptance.

NATIONAL MOTORIST
National Automobile Club
1151 E Hillsdale Blvd., Foster City, CA 94404. 650-294-7000.
Web site: www.nationalautoclub.com/html/national_motorist.html. Quarterly. Jane Offers, Editor. **Description:** Publishes articles for California travelers on motoring in the West, domestic and international travel, car care, roads, news, transportation, personalities, places, etc. **Nonfiction:** Illustrated articles, 500-1,100 words; pays from $.20/word, extra for photos. **Art:** Color slides or digital images. **Queries:** Preferred. **Response:** SASE required. **Payment:** On acceptance.

NAVIGATOR
Pace Communications, Inc.
1301 Carolina St., Greensboro, NC 27401-1090. 336-378-6065.
E-mail: navedit@paceco.com. Bimonthly. Circ.: 400,000. Brian Cook, Editor-in-Chief. **Description:** General-interest magazine distributed at Holiday Inn Express Hotels. Articles on sports, entertainment, and food. Photo essays, news on traveling trends, gear, and information. **Tips:** SASE for guidelines.

NORTHWEST TRAVEL
4969 Highway 101, #2, Florence, OR 97439. 800-348-8401.
E-mail: judy@ohwy.com. Web site: www.ohwy.com. Bimonthly. Circ.: 50,000. Stefani Blair, Stefanie Griesi, and Judy Fleagle, Editors. **Description:** Where to go and what to see in Oregon, Washington, Idaho, British Columbia, Western Montana, sometimes Alaska. Every article has a travel connection; each issue has detailed drive guide to one area. **Nonfiction:** First-person experience. Put details in sidebars; 500-1,500 words; $65-$350/features. **Fillers:** Worth a Stop; $50. **Art:** Seeking terrific slides of wildlife, artsy or dramatic scenery shots. Also does 2 annual calendars; slides, transparencies; $25-75 ($325 cover). **Queries:** Preferred. **Unsolicited mss:** Accepts. **Response:** Queries 3 months, submissions 2-3 months, SASE. **Freelance Content:** 60%. **Rights:** One-time, 1st NA (photos). **Payment:** On publication.

OUTPOST
474 Adelaide St. E, Toronto, Ontario M5A 1N6 Canada. 416-972-6635.
E-mail: editor@outpostmagazine.com. Web site: www.outpostmagazine.com. Bimonthly. Kisha Ferguson, Editor. **Description:** Adventurous and realistic look at the world and how people travel through it. **Nonfiction:** Features, 2,800-4,200 words. **Columns, Departments:** Tripping (100-1,200 words), useful travel info, serious and funny short news bits from around the world, human interest, environmental, dispatches. Health (1,800-2,000 words). Culture (300-1,500 words), reviews of books, movies, food, and profiles. Global Citizens (must include snapshot of person), see magazine for desired format. **Art:** Photos, do not submit originals unless requested. **Tips:** Seeks stories in an honest, sometimes irreverent voice. **Queries:** Required. **E-Queries:** Yes. **Unsolicited mss:** Does not accept.

RIDER
See page 304 for full listing.
Description: Covers travel, touring, commuting, and camping motorcyclists.

ROUTE 66
401 W Railroad Ave., Williams, AZ 86046. 928-635-4322.
E-mail: info@route66magazine.com. Web site: www.route66magazine.com. Paul Taylor, Publisher/Executive Editor. **Description:** Features articles on travel and life along Route 66 between Chicago and Los Angeles. **Nonfiction:** Articles, 1,500-2,000 words; pays $20/column. **Art:** Accepts B&W and color photos. **Queries:** Preferred. **Payment:** On publication.

RV JOURNAL
P.O. Box 7675, Laguna Niguel, CA 92607. 949-489-7729.
E-mail: editor@rvjournal.com. Web site: www.rvjournal.com. Quarterly. **Description:** Features travel destinations for RV travelers in California, Nevada, Arizona, Oregon, Utah, and Washington. **Nonfiction:** Travel and destination articles, 800-1,000 words. **Art:** Priority is given to articles that accompany high-quality color photographs. **Tips:** Submit query with bio and samples of previously published work. **Queries:** Required. **Unsolicited mss:** Accepts. **Rights:** 1st NA.

SOUTH AMERICAN EXPLORERS
See page 372 for full listing.
Description: Publishes feature articles on scientific studies, travel, historical personalities, archeology, exploration, social sciences, peoples and culture, etc.

SPECIALTY TRAVEL INDEX
305 San Anselmo Ave., #313, San Anselmo, CA 94960. 800-442-4922.
E-mail: info@specialtytravel.com. Web site: www.specialtytravel.com. Biannual. $6/issue. Circ.: 45,000. Risa Weinreb, Editor. **Description:** Travel directory listing 500 worldwide operators. Also provides travel articles for consumers and travel agents. **Nonfiction:** Stories on special interest, adventure-type travel, from soft adventures (e.g., cycling through French wine country) to daring exploits (an exploratory river-rafting run in Pakistan). Varied styles okay (first-person, descriptive); in general, not written in the present tense, but with a lively immediacy; 1,250 words; $300. **Art:** Slides, EPS digital, pay varies. **Tips:** Seeking off-the-beaten-path perspectives. Send published clips. **Queries:** Preferred. **E-Queries:** Yes. **Unsolicited mss:** Accepts. **Response:** 3-6 months, SASE. **Freelance Content:** 80%. **Payment:** On acceptance. **Contact:** Susan Kostrzewa, Managing Editor.

TRAILER LIFE
See page 482 for full listing.
Description: How-to articles and information on travel and lifestyle for RVers.

TRANSITIONS ABROAD

P.O. Box 1300, Amherst, MA 01004-1300. 413-256-3414.
Web site: www.transitionsabroad.com. Bimonthly. $4.95/$28. Circ.: 15,000. Max Hartshorne, Editor. **Description:** International travel and life magazine for overseas travelers of all ages who seek enriching, in-depth experiences of different cultures. Offers work, study, travel, and budget tips. **Nonfiction:** Practical how-to travel articles; 800-1,000 words; $2/word. **Columns, Departments:** Info exchange (200-300 words, free subscription); Itineraries (up to 500 words, $25-$50). **Art:** B&W, JPG; $25-$50, $150 (cover). **Tips:** Eager for new writers with information not usually found in guidebooks. Also seeking special expertise on cultural travel opportunities for specific groups: seniors, students, families, etc. No journal writing; no U.S. travel. **Queries:** Required. **E-Queries:** Yes. **Unsolicited mss:** Accepts. **Response:** SASE. **Freelance Content:** 95%. **Rights:** 1st NA. **Payment:** On publication.

TRAVEL AMERICA

990 Grove St., Evanston, IL 60201-4370. 847-491-6440.
E-mail: rmink@centurysports.net. Web site: www.travelamerica.com. Bimonthly. $5.99/$23.94. Circ.: 241,000. Robert Meyers, Editor-in-Chief. **Description:** Consumer travel magazine, exclusively U.S. destinations. **Nonfiction:** General destination stories; 1,000 words; $300. **Columns, Departments:** If You Only Have a Day (in any city); 500-600 words; $150-$175. **Art:** Slides, usually with text package; individual photos $25-$35. Uses p.r. photos most often. **Tips:** Submit short 1-page stories on narrow topics. **Queries:** Not necessary. **E-Queries:** No. **Unsolicited mss:** Accepts. **Response:** 2-6 weeks, SASE. **Freelance Content:** 80%. **Rights:** 1st. **Payment:** On publication. **Contact:** Randy Mink, Managing Editor.

TRAVEL & LEISURE

1120 Avenue of the Americas, New York, NY 10036. 212-382-5600.
E-mail: tlquery@amexpub.com. Web site: www.travelandleisure.com. Monthly. $4.50/$39. Circ.: 1,000,000. Nancy Novogrod, Editor. **Description:** Provides practical advice for leisure travelers and information on international travel destinations, luxury lodgings, and travel-related fashion and products. **Nonfiction:** Travel-related stories on shopping, trends, new hotels, products, nightlife, art, architecture; 1,000-4,000 words; $1,000-$5,000. **Columns, Departments:** T&L Reports; Smart Going. **Tips:** Departments are best chances for new writers. Writers should have same sophistication and travel experience as readers. **Queries:** Required. **E-Queries:** Yes. **Unsolicited mss:** Does not accept. **Response:** Queries 4 weeks, submissions 2 weeks, SASE. **Freelance Content:** 80%. **Rights:** 1st. **Payment:** On acceptance.

TRAVEL SMART

40 Beechdale Rd., Dobbs Ferry, NY 10522-3098. 800-327-3633.
E-mail: contactus@travelsmartnews.com. Web site: www.travelsmartnews.com. **Description:** Covers interesting, unusual, or economical destinations. Offers useful travel-related tips and practical information for vacation or business travel. **Nonfiction:** Short pieces, 250-1,000 words; $50-$150. **Tips:** Give specific details on

hotels, restaurants, transportation, e.g., costs, telephone numbers, and Web sites. Query for longer pieces. **Payment:** On publication.

TRAVEL TRADE PUBLICATIONS
15 W 44th St., Fl. 16, New York, NY 10036. 212-730-6600. E-mail: joel@traveltrade.com. Web site: www.traveltrade.com. Joel M. Abels, Editor/Publisher. **Description:** Informative, lively features, 1,400-3,000 words, on foreign and domestic travel. Query with clips.

TRAVELOCITY
15100 Trinity Blvd., Fort Worth, TX 76155. 817-785-8000. Web site: www.travelocitymagazine.com. Bimonthly. Circ.: 250,000. Adam McGill, Executive Editor. **Description:** Ranges from business travel to adventure, for readers who rely on the Web. Offers listings of Web sites, stories on booking online, ways to help people travel more effectively. **Nonfiction:** Wide-ranging travel-adventure themes (e.g., pros and cons of animal attractions—swimming with dolphins, looking for bears, etc.). **Columns, Departments:** "Loaded" (front-section pieces, 50-500 words, tips on destinations, cool restaurants, personalities, funny observations, etc.). **Tips:** All queries must include writing samples. **Queries:** Preferred. **E-Queries:** No. **Unsolicited mss:** Accepts. **Response:** SASE required.

WESTWAYS
Automobile Club of Southern California
P.O. Box 25222, Santa Ana, CA 92799-5222. 714-885-2376. E-mail: westways@aaa-calif.com. Web site: www.aaa-calif.com. Bimonthly. Circ.: 3,000,000. John Lehrer, Editor-in-Chief. **Description:** Travel articles, on southern California, the West, greater U.S., and foreign destinations. **Nonfiction:** 1,000-2,500 words; pays $1/word. **Queries:** Preferred. **Payment:** On acceptance.

YANKEE MAGAZINE'S TRAVEL GUIDE TO NEW ENGLAND
P.O. Box 520, Dublin, NH 03444. 603-563-8111. E-mail: travel@yankeepub.com. Web site: www.newengland.com. Annual. $4.99. Circ.: 100,000. Judson D. Hale, Sr., Editor-in-Chief. **Description:** Provides features and travel information for residents and tourists of New England. **Nonfiction:** 500-1,500 words; $1/word. **Art:** Photos. **Tips:** Looking for fresh ideas. **Queries:** Required. **E-Queries:** Yes. **Freelance Content:** 70%. **Payment:** On acceptance.

WOMEN

ALL THAT WOMEN WANT
E-mail: editor@allthatwomenwant.com. Web site: www.allthatwomenwant.com. Monthly. Colleen Moulding, Editor. **Description:** E-zine of general topics of interest to women.

BBW: BIG BEAUTIFUL WOMAN
Aeon Publishing Group
P.O. Box 1297, Elk Grove, CA 95759. 916-684-7904.
E-mail: sesmith@bbwmagazine.com. Web site: www.bbwmagazine.com. Bimonthly.
Circ.: 100,000. Sally E. Smith, Editor-in-Chief. **Description:** For women ages 25-45,
especially plus-size women, including interviews with successful plus-size women.
Nonfiction: Articles; 800-3,000 words; pay varies. **Queries:** Preferred. **Payment:**
On publication.

BRAIN CHILD
See page 375 for full listing.
Description: Explores the personal transformation that motherhood brings.

BRIDAL GUIDE
3 E 54th St., Fl. 15, New York, NY 10022. 800-472-7744.
Web site: www.bridalguidemag.com. Bimonthly. $4.99/issue, $7.97/year. Circ.:
250,000. Diane Forden, Editor-in-Chief. **Description:** Covers fashion, home design,
travel, and relationships. **Nonfiction:** Relationships, marriage, sexuality, fitness, psychology, finance, travel; 1,000-2,000 words; $.50/word. **Columns, Departments:**
Wedding planning, marriage, relationships, sexuality, travel; interactive and full of
humor; 1,000 words; $.50/word. **Tips:** No straight how-to planning pieces; articles
should rely on real brides' stories. Use expert sources. **Queries:** Preferred.
E-Queries: Yes. **Unsolicited mss:** Accepts. **Response:** 3 months; SASE required.
Freelance Content: 50%. **Payment:** On acceptance. **Contact:** Denise Schipani,
Executive Editor.

BRIDE AGAIN
1240 N Jefferson Ave., Suite G, Anaheim, CA 92807. 714-632-7000.
E-mail: beth@brideagain.com. Web site: www.brideagain.com. Quarterly.
$3.99/issue. Circ.: 145,000. Beth Reed Ramirez, Editor. **Description:** For "encore"
brides (women who are planning to remarry). **Nonfiction:** Helpful, positive, upbeat
articles; no first-person. Topics: remarriage, blending families/religions, etiquette,
finances, legal issues, honeymoon locations, book reviews; 1,000 words; $.35/word.
Tips: Articles specific to second-time brides. **Queries:** Not necessary. **E-Queries:**
No. **Unsolicited mss:** Does not accept. **Response:** Submissions 2 months, SASE.
Freelance Content: 70%. **Rights:** 1st NA. **Payment:** On publication.

BRIDE & GROOM
382 Boston Turnpike, Ste. 201, Shrewsbury, MA 01545.
E-mail: bgeditor@townisp.com. Web site: www.originalweddingexpo.com. 3
issues/year. Circ.: 50,000. Lisa Dayne, Editor. **Description:** Provides comprehensive
planning information to Central Massachusetts' engaged couples. **Nonfiction:**
Articles that focus on the various aspects of wedding planning; 500-1,000 words;
$100-$200. **Queries:** Preferred. **E-Queries:** Yes. **Unsolicited mss:** Accepts.

Response: 2-4 weeks; SASE required. **Freelance Content:** 40%. **Rights:** First and reprint. **Payment:** On publication.

BRIDE'S

Condé Nast Publications, Inc.
4 Times Square, New York, NY 10036. 212-286-7528.
Sally Kilbridge, Managing Editor. **Description:** For engaged couples or newlyweds on wedding planning, relationships, communication, sex, decorating, finances, careers, health, birth control, religion, and in-laws. **Nonfiction:** Articles, 800-3,000 words, for newlyweds; pays $.50/word. **Queries:** Preferred. **Unsolicited mss:** Accepts. **Payment:** On acceptance.

CHATELAINE

777 Bay St., Toronto, Ontario M5W 1A7 Canada. 416-596-5425.
E-mail: editors@chatelaine.com. Web site: www.chatelaine.com. Monthly.
$3.50/issue (Canadian). Circ.: 800,000. Rona Maynard, Editor. **Description:** Empowers Canada's busiest women to create the lives they want. Speaks to the strength of the inner woman—her passion, purpose, and sense of possibility. **Nonfiction:** Articles of interest to Canadian women, on all aspects of Canadian life. A written proposal is essential; 500-3,000 words; $500 and up. **Columns, Departments:** Upfront (relationships, health, balance). **Queries:** Required. **E-Queries:** No. **Unsolicited mss:** Accepts. **Response:** 6 weeks, SASE required. **Freelance Content:** 75%. **Rights:** 1st. **Payment:** On acceptance.

COMPLETE WOMAN

875 N Michigan Ave., Suite 3434, Chicago, IL 60611. 312-266-8680.
Bimonthly. $3.50/issue. Circ.: 350,000. Bonnie L. Krueger, Editor. **Description:** Practical advice for women on love, sex, careers, health, and personal relationships. **Nonfiction:** Article with how-to sidebars, with practical advice for women; 1,000-2,000 words. **Art:** Single-frame comics. **Tips:** Send query with clips of previous work published. **Queries:** Required. **E-Queries:** No. **Unsolicited mss:** Accepts. **Response:** 90 days. **Freelance Content:** 90%. **Rights:** One-time, all rights. **Payment:** On acceptance. **Contact:** Lora Wintz, Executive Editor.

COSMOPOLITAN

The Hearst Corp.
224 W 57th St., New York, NY 10018. 212-649-3570.
E-mail: cosmo_letters@hearst.com. Web site: www.cosmopolitan.com. Monthly.
Circ.: 2,592,887. Kate White, Editor-in-Chief. **Description:** On issues affecting young career women, with emphasis on relationships, jobs, and personal life. **Fiction:** On male-female relationships (only publishes fiction excerpted from a forthcoming novel). **Nonfiction:** Articles, to 3,000 words; features, 500-2,000 words. **Tips:** Submissions must be sent by a publisher or agent.

COUNTRY WOMAN

Reiman Publications

5400 S 60th St., Greendale, WI 53129. 414-423-8463.

E-mail: editors@countrywomanmagazine.com.

Web site: www.countrywomanmagazine.com. Bimonthly. $3.99/issue. Circ.: 1,700,000. Kathy Pohl, Executive Editor. **Description:** For women living in the country or interested in country life. Recipes, craft projects, decorating, profiles of country woman, and poetry. **Fiction:** Wholesome fiction with country perspective or rural theme; 1,000 words; $90-$125. **Nonfiction:** Nostalgia pieces, essays on farm/country life, humorous stories, decorating features, inspirational articles; 750-1,000 words; $50-$75. **Poetry:** Good rhythm and rhyme, seasonal; 12-24 lines; $10-$25. **Art:** Good candid color photos. **Queries:** Not necessary. **Unsolicited mss:** Accepts. **Response:** 2-3 months, SASE required. **Freelance Content:** 90%. **Payment:** On acceptance. **Contact:** Kathleen Anderson, Managing Editor.

ESSENCE

1500 Broadway, Fl. 6, New York, NY 10036. 212-642-0600.

E-mail: info@essence.com. Web site: www.essence.com. Monthly. Circ.: 1,200,000. Diane Weathers, Editor-in-Chief. **Description:** The first national magazine for African-American women. **Nonfiction:** Provocative articles on personal development, relationships, wealth building, work-related issues, parenting, health, political and social issues, travel, art. Cover stories on African-American celebrities. Departments: 400 words and up. Features: 1,200 words and up. Pay varies ($1/word minimum). **Queries:** Required.

FAMILY CIRCLE

Gruner + Jahr USA Publishing

375 Lexington Ave., New York, NY 10017-5514. 212-499-2000.

Web site: www.familycircle.com. 17x/year. $1.69/issue. Circ.: 5,000,000. Susan Ungaro, Editor-in-Chief. **Description:** Covers women who have made a difference. Also marriage, family, and childcare/eldercare issues; consumer affairs; psychology; humor. **Nonfiction:** Useful articles for all phases of a woman's life; true life, dramatic narratives; 1,000-2,000 words; pays $1/word. **Fillers:** Humor about family life; 70 words. **Columns, Departments:** Full Circle (current issues affecting families); 750 words. **Tips:** Often uses new writers in "Women Who Make a Difference" column. **Queries:** Required. **E-Queries:** No. **Unsolicited mss:** Accepts. **Response:** 4 weeks, SASE not required. **Freelance Content:** 80%. **Rights:** One-time, electronic. **Payment:** On acceptance.

FIRST FOR WOMEN

270 Sylvan Ave., Englewood Cliffs, NJ 07632-2521. 201-569-6699.

E-mail: firstfw@aol.com. Web site: www.ffwmarket.com. 17x/yr. $34/yr. Circ.: 1,542,000. Dena Vane, Editor-in-Chief. **Description:** Reflecting concerns of contemporary women. **Nonfiction:** Articles,1,500-2,500 words; pay varies. **Queries:** Preferred. **Response:** 2 months. **Payment:** On acceptance.

FIT PREGNANCY
See page 416 for full listing.
Description: Expert advice for the pregnant/postpartum woman and her newborn.

GLAMOUR
Condé Nast Publications, Inc.
4 Times Sq., New York, NY 10036. 212-286-2860.
E-mail: letters@glamour.com. Web site: www.glamour.com. Cindi Leive, Editor-in-Chief. **Description:** On careers, health, psychology, politics, current events, interpersonal relationships, for women, ages 18-35. **Nonfiction:** Articles, from 1,000 words; pays from $500. **Columns, Departments:** Hear Me Out (opinion page), 1,000 words. **Tips:** Fashion, entertainment, travel, food, and beauty pieces are staff-written. **Queries:** Required. **Payment:** On acceptance.

GOLF FOR WOMEN
See page 573 for full listing.
Description: Golf lifestyle magazine for avid women golfers.

GOOD HOUSEKEEPING
The Hearst Corp.
959 Eighth Ave., New York, NY 10019. 212-649-2200.
E-mail: ghkletters@hearst.com. Web site: www.goodhousekeeping.com. Monthly. $2.50/issue. Circ.: 2,400,000. Ellen Levine, Editor-in-Chief. **Description:** Expert advice on marriage and family, finances, health issues, and more. **Nonfiction:** Better Way (consumer pieces), 300-500 words. Profiles (on people involved in inspiring, heroic, fascinating pursuits), 400-600 words. My Story (first-person or as-told-to, in which a woman (using her real name) tells how she overcame a difficult problem. **Queries:** Required. **E-Queries:** No. **Unsolicited mss:** Accepts. **Response:** 2-3 months, SASE required.

HARPER'S BAZAAR
The Hearst Corp.
1700 Broadway, Fl. 37, New York, NY 10019-5905. 212-903-5000.
E-mail: bazaar@hearst.com. Web site: www.harpersbazaar.com. Monthly. Circ.: 721,000. Glenda Bailey, Editor-in-Chief. **Description:** For active, sophisticated women. **Nonfiction:** Arts, world affairs, travel, families, education, careers, health, sexuality; 1,500-2,500 words; pay varies. **Tips:** Send query with proposal of 1-2 paragraphs; include clips. **Queries:** Required. **Unsolicited mss:** Does not accept. **Response:** SASE required. **Payment:** On acceptance.

THE JEWISH HOMEMAKER
See page 540 for full listing.
Description: For a traditional Jewish audience.

JOYFUL WOMAN

P.O. Box 90028, Chattanooga, TN 37412. 423-892-6753.
E-mail: info@joyfulwoman.org. Web site: www.joyfulwoman.org. Bimonthly.
$4/$19.95. Circ.: 6,000. Carol Parks, Editor. **Description:** Encourages Christian
women, of all ages, in every aspect of their lives. **Fiction:** Thoughtful stories about
Christian women; 500-1,000 words; $20-$25. **Nonfiction:** Profiles of Christian
women, first-person inspirational true stories, practical and Bible-oriented how-to
articles; 500-1,000 words; $20-$25. **Poetry:** Occasional. **Fillers:** Occasional.
Queries: Preferred. **E-Queries:** Yes. **Unsolicited mss:** Does not accept.
Response: 4-6 weeks, SASE. **Freelance Content:** 45%. **Payment:** On publication.

LADIES' HOME JOURNAL

Meredith Corp.
125 Park Ave., Fl. 20, New York, NY 10017-5516. 212-557-6600.
E-mail: lhj@mdp.com. Web site: www.lhj.com. Monthly. $2.49/issue. Circ.: 4,100,000.
Sarah Mahoney, Editor. **Description:** Information on topics of interest to today's
woman. Most readers are in their 30s, married, and working at least part-time.
Fiction: Fiction, only through agents. **Nonfiction:** Articles on health, psychology,
human-interest stories, etc; 1,000-3,000 words; Pay varies. **Columns,
Departments:** Parenting, health, and first-person drama; 150-1,500 words. **Tips:**
Seeking human-interest pieces, shorter items, and new twists on established themes.
Queries: Preferred. **E-Queries:** Yes. **Unsolicited mss:** Accepts. **Response:**
Queries 8 weeks, submissions 4 weeks, SASE required. **Freelance Content:** 70%.
Rights: All. **Payment:** On acceptance.

LATINA

Latina Media Ventures, LLC
1500 Broadway, Suite 600, New York, NY 10036-4015. 212-642-0200.
E-mail: editor@latina.com. Web site: www.latina.com. Monthly. $20. Circ.: 200,000.
Sylvia Martinez, Editor-in-Chief. **Description:** For Hispanic women living in the U.S.

MAMM

See page 418 for full listing.
Description: On cancer prevention, treatment, and survival, for women.

MODERN BRIDE

249 W 17th St., New York, NY 10011. 212-462-3400.
Web site: www.modernbride.com. Alyssa Bellaby, Assistant Editor. **Description:** For
bride and groom, on wedding planning, financial planning, juggling career and home,
etc. **Nonfiction:** Articles, 1,500-2,000 words; pays $600-$1,200. **Fillers:** Humorous
pieces, 500-1,000 words, for brides. **Payment:** On acceptance.

MORE

Meredith Corp.
125 Park Ave., New York, NY 10017. 212-455-1190.

E-mail: more@mdp.com. Web site: www.moremag.com. 10x/year. Circ.: 700,000. Susan Crandell, Editor. **Description:** For women of baby-boomer generation; sophisticated and upscale; little service/how-to pieces. **Nonfiction:** Essays, interviews, etc. **Queries:** Preferred. **E-Queries:** No. **Unsolicited mss:** Accepts. **Response:** To 3 months, SASE. **Rights:** 1st NA, all. **Payment:** On acceptance.

MOTHERING
P.O. Box 1690, Santa Fe, NM 87504-1690. 505-984-8116.
E-mail: ashisha@mothering.com. Web site: www.mothering.com. Bimonthly. Circ.: 70,000. Ashisha, Senior Editor. **Description:** On natural family living, covering topics such as pregnancy, birthing, parenting, etc. **Nonfiction:** Articles, to 2,000 words; pays $200-$500. **Poetry:** 3-20 lines. **Queries:** Preferred. **Payment:** On publication.

MOXIE
1230 Glen Ave., Berkeley, CA 94708. 510-540-5510.
E-mail: emily@moxiemag.com. Web site: www.moxiemag.com. Emily Hancock, Editor. **Description:** Online publication for confident, assertive women. Accepts first-person accounts, fiction, nonfiction, essays, and poems. **Nonfiction:** Stories or articles about daring, bold woman who take risks and live life to the fullest. Seeks stories of women who portray strength and courage while achieving real-world accomplishments; 500-2,000 words; $10. **Tips:** Accepts submissions by e-mail only. Paste text into body of e-mail, include word count, and put title in subject line. Send complete manuscript; do not query. **E-Queries:** No. **Unsolicited mss:** Accepts.

MS.
See page 339 for full listing.
Description: Articles relating to feminism, women's roles, and social change.

NA'AMAT WOMAN
See page 370 for full listing.
Description: Covers aspects of life in Israel, Jewish women's issues, and social issues.

NATURAL LIVING TODAY
Tyler Publishing, LLC
175 Varick St., New York, NY 10014-4604. 212-924-1762.
E-mail: naturalliv@aol.com. Web site: www.naturallivingmag.com. Bimonthly. $23.70/yr. Circ.: 150,000. Alexis Tannenbaum, Editor-in-Chief. **Description:** On all aspects of a natural lifestyle for women. **Nonfiction:** Articles, 1,000-2,000 words; pays $75-$200. **Queries:** Preferred. **Payment:** On publication.

PLAYGIRL
801 Second Ave., Fl. 9, New York, NY 10017. 212-661-7878.
Monthly. $4.99. Circ.: 500,000. Michele Zipp, Editor-in-Chief. **Description:** Women's magazine focusing on sex, relationships, and women's health. **Fiction:** Erotic first-person fiction. Female perspective for Fantasy Forum section; 1,700-

2,100 words. **Nonfiction:** Articles, 750-3,000 words, on women's issues, sexuality, relationships, and celebrities, for women, ages 18 and up. Erotic fantasies, 1,300-2,000 words. **Fillers:** Quizzes. **Tips:** Easiest way to break in is to write for Fantasy Forum. **Queries:** Preferred. **E-Queries:** No. **Unsolicited mss:** Accepts. **Response:** 1 month. **Freelance Content:** 20%. **Payment:** On publication.

PRIMAVERA
See page 696 for full listing.
Description: Original fiction and poetry that reflects the experience of women of different ages, races, sexual orientations, and social classes.

REDBOOK
The Hearst Corp.
224 W 57th St., Fl. 6, New York, NY 10019-3212. 212-649-3450.
E-mail: redbook@hearst.com. Web site: www.redbookmag.com. Monthly. $15.97/yr. Circ.: 2,269,000. Ellen Kunes, Editor-in-Chief. **Description:** On relationships, marriage, sex, current social issues, crime, human interest, health, psychology, and parenting. **Fiction:** Fresh, distinctive short stories, of interest to women. No unsolicited poetry, novellas, or novels; query first. Pays from $1,500 for short stories (to 25 pages). **Nonfiction:** Articles, 1,000-2,500 words; dramatic inspirational narratives, 1,000-2,000 words; pay varies. **Tips:** Send published clips, writing samples. **Queries:** Preferred. **Response:** Allow 12 weeks, SASE required. **Payment:** On acceptance.

ROOM OF ONE'S OWN
See page 700 for full listing.
Description: Canadian literary magazine featuring short stories, poems, art, and reviews by, for, and about women.

ROSIE
Gruner + Jahr USA Publishing
375 Lexington Ave., New York, NY 10017. 212-499-1720.
Web site: www.rosiemagazine.com. Monthly. Circ.: 4,000,000. **Description:** Formerly McCall's, this magazine from talk show host Rosie O'Donnell features stories and articles on parenting, children, cooking, health and lifestyle, crafts, and fashion. Also, humor pieces and profiles of celebrities.

SAGEWOMAN
See page 491 for full listing.
Description: Articles that help women explore their spiritual and emotional nature.

SELF
Condé Nast Publications, Inc.
4 Times Square, New York, NY 10036-6522. 212-286-2860.
E-mail: comments@self.com. Web site: www.self.com. Monthly. $2.99/issue, $12/yr. Circ.: 1,300,000. Cynthia Leive, Editor-in-Chief. **Description:** Covers all aspects of

healthy lifestyle, with latest information on health, fitness, nutrition, mental wellness, beauty, and style. **Nonfiction:** Reports, features, stories, personal essays; on topics related to women's health and well-being; Up to 4,000 words. **Columns, Departments:** health, nutrition, fitness, beauty, style, psychology. **Tips:** Pitch stories with a news hook. **Queries:** Preferred. **E-Queries:** Yes. **Unsolicited mss:** Accepts. **Response:** 1 month, SASE. **Freelance Content:** 75%. **Rights:** 1st NA. **Payment:** On acceptance. **Contact:** Dana Points, Executive Editor.

SELF HELP FOR HER.COM

P.O. Box 61605, Santa Barbara, CA 93111. 413-771-7747.
E-mail: editor@selfhelpforher.com. Web site: www.selfhelpforher.com. Monthly. Edel Jarboe, Editor. **Description:** Online publication, focused on women who want to improve their lives. Articles with practical information about work, money, health and nutrition, fitness, parenting, relationships, cooking, time management. **Nonfiction:** 750-2,000 words; $30 for feature articles, $10 for first-person pieces or reprints. **Tips:** Looking for self-help articles based on interviews or research. Query with subject of article, title, word count, and 50-word description. **Queries:** Required. **E-Queries:** Yes. **Response:** 2-3 days. **Rights:** 1st online (for 1 month).

SO TO SPEAK

See page 703 for full listing.
Description: Feminist journal of language and arts, concerned with the history of women, of feminists, and looking to see the future through art.

TODAY'S CHRISTIAN WOMAN

Christianity Today
465 Gundersen Dr., Carol Stream, IL 60188. 630-260-6200.
E-mail: tcwedit@christianitytoday.com. Bimonthly. Circ.: 250,000. Jane Johnson Struck, Editor. **Description:** For women, ages 20-40, on contemporary issues and hot topics that impact their lives. Articles provide depth, balance, and biblical perspective to women's daily relationships. **Nonfiction:** Articles to help women grow in their relationship to God, and to provide practical help on family/parenting, friendship, marriage, health, single life, finances, and work; 1,000-1,800 words. **Tips:** No poetry, fiction, or Bible studies. Looking for humor, issues/hot topics, and "My Story" articles. **Queries:** Required. **E-Queries:** Yes. **Unsolicited mss:** Accepts. **Response:** 8 weeks, SASE. **Rights:** 1st. **Payment:** On acceptance.

TRUE CONFESSIONS

Sterling/Macfadden Partnership
333 Seventh Ave., Fl. 11, New York, NY 10001-5004. 212-979-4800.
E-mail: trueconfessions@sterlingmacfadden.com. Web site: www.truestorymail.com. Monthly. Pat Byrdsong, Editor. **Description:** First person told true to life stories that reflect the lives of working class families. Romance, mystery, modern social problems, etc. Stories 1,000-7,000 words. Confessions: Emotionally charged stories with a strong emphasis on characterization and well-defined plots are preferred. Stories

should be intriguing, suspenseful, humorous, romantic, or tragic. Pays $.03/word.
Tips: Seeks 3,000-4,000 word stories and stories about African-, Latina-, and Asian-Americans. **Unsolicited mss:** Accepts. **Freelance Content:** 95%. **Rights:** All.
Payment: One month after publication.

TRUE LOVE
Sterling/Macfadden Partnership
333 Seventh Ave., Fl. 11, New York, NY 10001-5004. 212-979-4800.
E-mail: away@sterlingmacfadden.com. Web site: www.truestorymail.com. Monthly.
$10.97. Circ.: 225,000. Alison Way, Editor. **Description:** Fresh, young, true-to-life
stories, on love and topics of current interest. **Nonfiction:** Pays $.03/word. **Tips:**
Must use past tense and first-person style. **Payment:** On publication.

VOGUE
Condé Nast Publications, Inc.
4 Times Square, New York, NY 10036-6518. 212-286-2860.
E-mail: voguemail@aol.com. Web site: www.vogue.com. Monthly. $28/yr. Circ.:
1,174,000. Anna Wintour, Editor-in-Chief. **Description:** General features for the
contemporary woman. **Nonfiction:** Articles, to 1,500 words, on women, entertainment and arts, travel, medicine, and health. **Queries:** Preferred.

WAHM.COM
Maricle Media, Inc.
P.O. Box 366, Folsom, CA 95763. 916-985-2078.
E-mail: cheryl@wahm.com. Web site: www.wahm.com. Weekly. Cheryl Demas,
Editor. **Description:** E-zine for work-at-home moms.

WEDDINGBELLS
34 King St. E, Suite 800, Toronto, Ontario M5C 2X8 Canada. 416-363-1574.
E-mail: info@weddingbells.com. Web site: www.weddingbells.com. Semiannual.
Circ.: 325,000. Crys Stewart, Editor. **Description:** Offers pre- and post-wedding
lifestyle and service journalism to bridal couples. **Nonfiction:** By assignment. **Tips:**
Send resume and copies of published work. **Queries:** Not necessary. **Unsolicited
mss:** Does not accept. **Contact:** Michael Killingsworth, Managing Editor.

WISCONSIN WOMAN
P.O. Box 230, Hartland, WI 53029. 262-367-5303.
E-mail: 50plus@pitnet.net. Michele Hein, Editor-in-Chief. **Description:**
Publication featuring news about women in the four county Metro Milwaukee area.

WOMAN'S DAY
Hachette Filipacchi Magazines
1633 Broadway, New York, NY 10019. 212-767-6418.
E-mail: womansday@hfmus.com. Web site: www.womansday.com. Stephanie
Abarbanel, Editor. **Description:** Covers marriage, child-rearing, health, careers,

relationships, money management. **Nonfiction:** Human-interest or service-oriented articles, 750-1,200 words. Dramatic first-person narratives of medical miracles, rescues, women's experiences, etc. Pays standard rates.

WOMAN'S OWN
Harris Publications, Inc.
1115 Broadway, Fl. 8, New York, NY 10010-2803. 212-807-7100.
E-mail: editor@womansown.com. Web site: www.womansown.com. Bimonthly. $11.97. Circ.: 253,000. Lynn Varacalli, varacalli@harris-pub.com. **Description:** Inspirational, practical advice on relationships, career, and lifestyle choices for women, ages 25-35. Topics: staying together, second marriages, working women, asserting yourself, meeting new men, sex, etc. **Nonfiction:** Articles, 1,500-2,000 words; pays $50-$500. **Fillers:** Woman in the News (profiles, 250-500 words, women who have overcome great odds); fun, in-depth quizzes; Let's Put Our Heads Together (short pieces on trends and breakthroughs). **Columns, Departments:** Suddenly Single, Moving Up, Round-Up, Mindpower, Dieter's Notes, Fashion Advisor, Financial Advisor; 800 words. **Queries:** Preferred. **Payment:** On acceptance.

WOMAN'S TOUCH
1445 Boonville, Springfield, MO 65802-1894.
E-mail: womanstouch@ag.org. Web site: www.ag.org/womanstouch. 6x/year. $9.95/issue. Circ.: 18,000. Darla Knoth, Managing Editor. **Description:** Non-profit ministry magazine for Christian women. **Nonfiction:** About triumph in times of trouble, celebrity interviews with women leaders, cooking, reaching the unchurched, testimonies, unique activities for women's groups or mature singles; 800 words; $20-$40. **Fillers:** Humor only; 500-800 words; $20-$40. **Columns, Departments:** Parenting, singlehood; 500-600 words; $20-$40. **Tips:** Seeking humor pieces, articles with fresh themes; send 3 suggested headlines with article. Publishes some book excerpts. Most readers over 35. Query or submit via e-mail. **Queries:** Required. **E-Queries:** Yes. **Unsolicited mss:** Accepts. **Response:** 12 weeks. **Freelance Content:** 20%. **Rights:** One-time. **Payment:** On publication.

WOMAN'S WORLD
Bauer Publishing Co.
270 Sylvan Ave., Englewood Cliffs, NJ 07632-2521. 201-569-6699.
E-mail: dearww@aol.com. Weekly. Circ.: 1,604,000. Stephanie Saible, Editor-in-Chief. **Description:** For middle-income women, ages 18-60, on love, romance, careers, medicine, health, psychology, family life, travel; dramatic stories of adventure or crisis, investigative reports. **Fiction:** Fast-moving short stories, 1,000 words, with light romantic theme; prefers dialogue-driven to propel the story. (Specify "short story" on outside of envelope.) Mini-mysteries, 1,200 words, with "whodunit" or "howdunit" theme. No science fiction, fantasy, horror, ghost stories, or gratuitous violence. Pays $1,000 for short stories; $500 for mini-mysteries. **Nonfiction:** Articles (query first), 600-1,800 words; pays $300-$900. **Payment:** On acceptance.

WOMEN IN BUSINESS
See page 323 for full listing.
Description: Offers information to women in business to help them grow personally and professionally.

WOMEN TODAY
Box 300, Stn. A, Vancouver, British Columbia V6C 2X3 Canada. 604-514-2000, x283. E-mail: editor@womentodaymagazine.com.
Web site: www.womentodaymagazine.com. Monthly. Claire Colvin, Editor.
Description: E-zine for women on health, relationships, career, self-esteem, family, fashion, cooking. Features journalistic, nonfiction articles for a global audience. **Tips:** Submit e-query with brief synopsis, length, and contact information. **Queries:** Required. **E-Queries:** Yes. **Response:** 4 weeks. **Rights:** One-time.

WORKING MOTHER
Working Mother Media
260 Madison Ave., Fl. 3, New York, NY 10016. 212-351-6400.
E-mail: editors@workingmother.com. Web site: www.workingmother.com. Monthly. Circ.: 750,000. **Description:** Features articles that help working women balance their professional life, family life, and inner life. Offers solutions to the stress that comes with juggling both family and career. **Nonfiction:** Articles focus on time management, money management, family relationships, and other job-related issues; 700-1,500 words. **Tips:** Send queries first. Enclose clips of previously published work. **Queries:** Required. **E-Queries:** No. **Response:** 3 months. **Rights:** All.

WORKING WOMAN
See page 323 for full listing.
Description: For women, on business, finance, and technology.

WRITING & PUBLISHING

AMERICAN JOURNALISM REVIEW
University of Maryland
1117 Journalism Bldg., Suite 2116, College Park, MD 20742-0001. 301-405-8803.
E-mail: editor@ajr.umd.edu. Web site: www.ajr.org. Monthly. $24. Circ.: 25,000. Rem Rieder, Editor. **Description:** Covers print, broadcast, and online journalism. Articles, 500-5,000 words, on trends, political issues, ethics, and coverage that falls short. Pay varies. **Queries:** Required. **E-Queries:** Yes. **Unsolicited mss:** Accepts. **Freelance Content:** 70%. **Rights:** Print and electronic. **Payment:** On publication.

BLOOMSBURY REVIEW
1553 Platte St., Suite 206, Denver, CO 80202. 303-455-3123.
E-mail: bloomsb@aol.com. Bimonthly. $3. Circ.: 50,000. Tom Auer, Editor.
Description: Book reviews, literary features, interviews, essays, and poetry.

Nonfiction: Essays, features, and interviews; 600 words or more; $10-$40. **Poetry:** Yes; $5-$15/poem. **Queries:** Preferred. **E-Queries:** Yes. **Unsolicited mss:** Accepts. **Response:** Queries 2 weeks, submissions 2 months, SASE required. **Freelance Content:** 25%. **Rights:** 1st. **Payment:** On publication.

BOOK & CULTURE: A CHRISTIAN REVIEW
Christianity Today
465 Gundersen Dr., Carol Stream, IL 60188-2415. 630-260-6200.
E-mail: bcedit@aol.com. Web site: www.christianity.net. Bimonthly. $17.95. Circ.: 20,000. Christianity Today International. **Description:** Looks at Christian books, culture, and religion.

BOOKPAGE
ProMotion, Inc.
2143 Belcourt Ave., Nashville, TN 37212. 615-292-8926.
E-mail: lynn@bookpage.com. Web site: www.bookpage.com. Monthly. Circ.: 500,000. Lynn Green, Editor. **Description:** Consumer-oriented tabloid used by booksellers and libraries to promote new titles and authors. Provides book reviews, 400 words. **Tips:** Query with writing samples and areas of interest; Editor will make assignments for reviews. **Queries:** Required.

BYLINE
P.O. Box 130596, Edmond, OK 73013. 405-348-5591.
E-mail: mpreston@bylinemag.com. Web site: www.ByLineMag.com. Monthly. $22/year. Marcia Preston, Editor. **Description:** Publication for writers. **Fiction:** Genre, mainstream or literary. No graphic sex or violence; no sci-fi; 2,000-4,000 words; $100. **Nonfiction:** On the craft and business of writing; 1,500-1,800 words; $75. **Poetry:** About writing or the creative process; 30 lines max.; $10. **Fillers:** Humor; 100-500 words; $15-$25. **Columns, Departments:** End Piece (700 words, $35); First Sale (250-300 words, $20); Great American Bookstores (500-600 words, $35-$40). **Tips:** Queries preferred for feature articles only. Include practical information that can help writers succeed. **Queries:** Preferred. **E-Queries:** Accepts. **Unsolicited mss:** Accepts. **Response:** Queries 1-6 weeks, 1 month for submissions, SASE required. **Freelance Content:** 80%. **Rights:** FNASR. **Payment:** On acceptance.

C/OASIS
491 Moraga Way, Orinda, CA 94563.
E-mail: eide491@earthlink.net. Web site: www.sunoasis.com/oasis.html. Monthly. David Eide, Editor; Vicki Colker, Poetry Editor. **Description:** Original stories, poetry, essays, as well as insightful articles about electronic publishing, legal aspects to writing, and job markets for writers. **Nonfiction:** 700-3,000 words, pays $10-20. **Tips:** Query by e-mail. Send poetry submissions to poetmuse@swbell.net c/o Vicki Colker. **Queries:** Preferred. **E-Queries:** Yes. **Unsolicited mss:** Accepts.

CANADIAN WRITER'S JOURNAL

White Mountain Publications

Box 5180, New Liskeard, Ontario P0J 1P0. 705-647-5424.

E-mail: cwj@cwj.ca. Web site: www.cwj.ca. Bimonthly. Circ.: 350. Deborah Ranchuk, Managing Editor. **Description:** Short "how-to" articles with easily understood information useful to both apprentice and professional writers. 90% Canadian content. **Fiction:** Semi-annual short fiction contests (deadlines: Sept. 30th and March 31st). **Nonfiction:** Any subject related to writing, from generating ideas to marketing and publishing. Verify sources or quotes. Book reviews, 250-500 words, on books about writing or books published in Canada; 400-2,000 words; $7.50/page (450 words). **Poetry:** Original, unpublished only; pays $2-$5/poem. **Fillers:** Humorous or seasonal items related to inspiration or the writing experience. **Columns, Departments:** Opinion pieces on issues affecting writers/publishers. **Tips:** Prefers electronic submissions. Be specific, concise. Use your personal experience and achievements. Avoid overworked subjects (overcoming writer's block, handling rejection, finding time to write, etc.). **Queries:** Preferred. **E-Queries:** Yes. **Unsolicited mss:** Accepts. **Response:** 2 months, SASE required (use IRCs). **Freelance Content:** 75%. **Payment:** On publication.

CATHOLIC LIBRARY WORLD

Catholic Library Association

100 North St., Suite 224, Pittsfield, MA 01201-5109. 413-443-2CLA.

E-mail: cla@vgernet.net. Web site: www.cathla.org. Quarterly. $60/yr. Mary E. Gallagher, SSJ, General Editor. **Description:** Articles, reviews, and association news for librarians. No payment offered. **Nonfiction:** For school, academic, and institutional archivists. **Queries:** Not necessary. **E-Queries:** Yes. **Unsolicited mss:** Accepts. **Contact:** Jean R. Bostley, SSJ.

CHILDREN'S BOOK INSIDER

901 Columbia Rd., Ft. Collins, CO 80525-1838. 800-807-1916.

E-mail: mail@write4kids.com. Web site: www.write4kids.com. Monthly. **Description:** Provides the "inside scoop" on publishing books for children.

CHILDREN'S WRITER

93 Long Ridge Rd., West Redding, CT 06896-1124. 800-443-6078.

Web site: www.childrenswriter.com. Monthly. $24.95/year. **Description:** A newsletter reporting on the marketplace for children's writing. **Nonfiction:** Pays $150-$250 for very tightly written articles; 850-2,000 words. **Queries:** Preferred. **Response:** within one month, SASE. **Rights:** First time rights.

EDITOR & PUBLISHER

770 Broadway, Fl. 7, New York, NY 10003. 646-654-5270.
Web site: www.editorandpublisher.com. Weekly. **Description:** Articles on the newspaper industry. Newspaper Web sites, features, how-tos, opinion pieces, etc. **Nonfiction:** News articles, 900 words; pay varies. **Tips:** Send complete manuscripts. **Payment:** On publication.

THE EDITORIAL EYE

66 Canal Center Plz, Suite 200, Alexandria, VA 22314-5507. 703-683-0683.
E-mail: eye@eeicommunications.com. Web site: www.eeicommunications.com/eye.
Linda Jorgensen, Editor. **Description:** Resource for editors, writers, managers, journalists, and educators. All about the written word. Focuses on clear writing, best editorial and project management practices, and changing usage and grammar.

FOLIO

1230 Avenue of the Americas, Fl. 16, New York, NY 10020-1513. 212-332-6300.
E-mail: folioedit@inside.com. Web site: www.foliomag.com. 16x/year. $96/yr. Teresa Palagano, Editor. **Description:** For the magazine publishing executive.

FOREWORD

129½ Front St., Traverse City, MI 49684-2508. 231-933-3699.
E-mail: mlink@forewordmagazine.com. Web site: www.forewordmagazine.com.
8x/year. $10/issue, $30/yr. Circ.: 15,000. Mardi Link, Editor-in-Chief. **Description:** Trade journal that reviews new titles from independent publishers and booksellers. **Columns, Departments:** "Afterword" essay, 700 words; pays $100. **Tips:** Sample copy, $5. **Queries:** Required. **E-Queries:** Yes. **Unsolicited mss:** Accepts. **Freelance Content:** 10%.

THE HORN BOOK MAGAZINE

56 Roland St., Suite 200, Boston, MA 02129. 617-628-0225.
E-mail: info@hbook.com. Web site: www.hbook.com. Bimonthly. $9.50/$47. Circ.: 18,500. Roger Sutton, Editor-in-Chief. **Description:** A critical review of introductory children's and young adult books. Also, editorials, columns, and articles about children's literature. **Nonfiction:** Critical essays on children's literature and related subjects for librarians, teachers, parents; up to 280 words. **Queries:** Not necessary. **E-Queries:** Yes. **Unsolicited mss:** Accepts. **Response:** 4-6 months, SASE required. **Payment:** On publication. **Contact:** Roger Sutton.

INTERCOM

Society for Technical Information
901 N Stuart St., Suite 904, Arlington, VA 22203. 703-522-4114.
E-mail: intercom@stc.org. Web site: www.stc.org. 10x/yr. Circ.: 25,000. Maurice Martin, Editor. **Description:** Industry information for technical writers, publishers, and editors.

THE INTERNET WRITING JOURNAL

Writers Write, Inc.

E-mail: journal@writerswrite.com. Web site: www.writerswrite.com. Claire E. White, Editor-in-Chief. **Description:** Articles on all aspects of writing, in all genres. No payment, offers byline and link to author's Web site. **Nonfiction:** 1,500+ words. **Tips:** E-query only, in body of e-mail or as text file.

IPI GLOBAL JOURNALIST

132 A Neff Annex, Columbia, MO 65211. 573-884-1599.

E-mail: globaljournalist@missouri.edu. Web site: www.globaljournalist.org. Quarterly. $19.95/yr. Circ.: 4,500. Prof. Stuart H. Loory, Editor. **Description:** International journalism publication for students, working journalists, and the general public. Encourages submissions from journalism students. **Nonfiction:** Articles on current events in international news; interviews with journalists in the field; survey articles on international press freedom concerns; 300-1,200 words; $350 fee. **Queries:** Required. **E-Queries:** Yes. **Unsolicited mss:** Does not accept. **Response:** 1-2 weeks. **Freelance Content:** 70%. **Rights:** 1st. **Payment:** On publication. **Contact:** Mary Lou LeClaire.

LAMBDA BOOK REPORT

Lambda Literary Foundation

P.O. Box 73910, Washington, DC 20056-3910. 202-462-7924.

E-mail: lbreditor@lamdalit.com. Monthly. Circ.: 8,000. Shelley Bindon, Senior Editor. **Description:** Reviews and features on gay and lesbian books. **Nonfiction:** 250-1,500 words; pays $10-$75. **Queries:** Preferred. **Payment:** On publication.

LITERARY TRAVELER

P.O. Box 400272, North Cambridge, MA 02140-0003. 617-628-3504.

E-mail: francis@literarytraveler.com. Web site: www.literarytraveler.com. Linda McGovern, Editor. **Description:** E-zine, for articles about writers or places that have literary significance. Please see Web site. **Nonfiction:** Pays $5-25. **Queries:** Preferred. **E-Queries:** Yes. **Unsolicited mss:** Accepts.

LOCUS

Locus Publications

P.O. Box 13305, Oakland, CA 94661. 510-339-9196.

E-mail: locus@locusmag.com. Web site: www.locusmag.com. Monthly. Circ.: 7,500. Charles N. Brown, editor-in-chief. **Description:** Publication covering industry news for professional writers and publishers of science fiction and fantasy.

NEWSLETTER ON NEWSLETTERS

P.O. Box 348, Rhinebeck, NY 12572. 845-876-5222.

Semi-monthly. **Description:** For professionals involved in publishing newsletters and specialized information, both in print and online.

OHIO WRITER

P.O. Box 91801, Cleveland, OH 44101. 216-421-0403.
E-mail: pwlgc@msn.com. 6x/year. Circ.: 1,000. Gail and Stephen Bellamy, Editors. **Description:** Features, interviews, how-tos, and articles relevant to writing in Ohio. Annual contest for fiction, poetry, and literary nonfiction categories. **Tips:** Sample copy, $3. **Queries:** Required. **Response:** 3 months. **Freelance Content:** 5%. **Rights:** Revert to author after publication. **Payment:** On publication.

ONCE UPON A TIME

553 Winston Ct., St. Paul, MN 55118. 651-457-6223.
E-mail: audreyouat@aol.com. Web site: http://www.members.aol.com/ouatmag. Quarterly. $25. Circ.: 1,000. Audrey B. Baird, Editor. **Description:** Support magazine that provides wisdom and advice for those who write and illustrate for children. **Nonfiction:** Writing and/or illustrating how-tos (plotting, character development, revising, dialogue, illustrating techniques and materials, etc.), how you work, handle rejections, the story behind your book, etc; 100-900 words. **Poetry:** On related topics; 30 lines. **Art:** Illustrations, black ink on white paper only. **Tips:** Use friendly style, with tips and information that really work. **E-Queries:** No. **Unsolicited mss:** Accepts. **Response:** Submissions 1 month, SASE. **Freelance Content:** 50%. **Rights:** One-time. **Payment:** In copies.

PAPYRUS

P.O. Box 270797, West Hartford, CT 06127-0797.
E-mail: ple.papyrus@eudoramail.com. Ginger Whitaker, Editor. **Description:** "The writer's craftletter featuring the black experience." **Tips:** All writers welcome to submit material with a black audience in mind.

PRESSTIME

1921 Gallows Rd., Suite 600, Vienna, VA 22182. 703-902-1600.
Web site: www.naa.org/ptime. Monthly. Circ.: 17,846. **Description:** Published by the Newspaper Association of America.

PUBLISHERS WEEKLY

Cahners Business Information
245 W 17th St., New York, NY 10011-5383. 212-463-6758.
E-mail: dmaryles@cahners.com. Web site: www.publishersweekly.com. Weekly. $139. Circ.: 34,400. Daisy Maryles, Executive Editor. **Description:** Seeking essays, 900 words, on current issue or problem facing publishing and bookselling for "My Say" column. Articles for "Booksellers' Forum" may be somewhat longer. Pay varies.

QUILL & QUIRE

Key Media, Ltd.,
70 The Esplanade #210, Toronto, Ontario M5E 1R2 Canada. 416-360-0044.
E-mail: info@quillandquire.com. Web site: www.quillandquire.com. Quarterly.

$59.95. Circ.: 7,000. Scott Anderson, Editor. **Description:** Trade publication for the Canadian publishing industry. Offers books news, author interviews, and reviews of Canadian books. Written for writers, publishers, editors, librarians, and booksellers. **Queries:** Required. **E-Queries:** Yes. **Unsolicited mss:** Does not accept. **Payment:** On acceptance.

RAINY DAY CORNER
6022 N 29th St., Arlington, VA 22207.
E-mail: Ldupie@rainydaycorner.com. Web site: www.rainydaycorner.com. Monthly. **Description:** On-line publication and print magazine with information and tips for the writing family. **Nonfiction:** Seeking short articles on how to get children and parents interested in all aspects of writing. Suggested topics: journaling, online and print newsletters, letter writing, and family history; 1,000 words max.; $10/article. **Tips:** Write at the comprehension level of children 8-18 years without talking down to them. Keep articles conversational, but factual. Open to new and unpublished writers. Updated guidelines available at Web site. **Queries:** Preferred. **E-Queries:** Yes. **Unsolicited mss:** Accepts. **Response:** 2-4 weeks, SASE required. **Rights:** Nonexclusive, electronic. **Payment:** On publication.

READERS AND WRITERS MAGAZINE
Artichoke Publishing
P.O. Box 231023, Encinitas, CA 92024. 760-632-9268.
E-mail: chas@artichokepublishing.com. Monthly. Circ.: 20,000. Charles McStravick, Managing Editor. **Description:** For writers. Offers author interviews and profiles, book reviews, and creative nonfiction articles about the writing and publishing world, about literary arts culture. **Nonfiction:** Feature-length articles (1,200-3,300 words), $20-$75; smaller articles and reviews (600-800 words), $20. **Freelance Content:** 80%.

ROMANTIC TIMES MAGAZINE
55 Bergen St., Brooklyn, NY 11201. 718-237-1097.
E-mail: kfalk@romantictimes.com. Web site: www.romantictimes.com. Kathryn Falk, Founder/CEO. **Description:** Topics on the romance-fiction publishing industry.

SCAVENGER'S NEWSLETTER
833 Main, Osage City, KS 66523-1241. 785-528-3538.
E-mail: foxscav@home.com. Web site: www.argentmoon.net/scavengers/index.htm. Monthly. $2/issue,$3/issue (Canadian). Circ.: 600. Janet Fox, Editor. **Description:** Market newsletter for science fiction, fantasy, horror, and mystery writers and artists, focusing on small presses. **Fiction:** Flash genre fiction; up to 1,200 words; $5. **Nonfiction:** Articles for genre writers/artists; up to 1,500 words; $5. **Art:** Black-and-white illustrations, 7 x 8½ inches. **Tips:** Do not ignore word-length guidelines; space

is limited. **Queries:** Not necessary. **E-Queries:** Accepts. **Unsolicited mss:** Accepts. **Response:** Queries 2-7 days, submissions 1-4 weeks. **Freelance Content:** 10%. **Payment:** On acceptance.

SMALL PRESS REVIEW

Dustbooks
P.O. Box 100, Paradise, CA 95967. 530-877-6110.
E-mail: dustbooks@dcsi.net. Web site: www.dustbooks.com. Bimonthly. $25/yr. Circ.: 2,500. Len Fulton, Editor. **Description:** Features reviews and news about small presses and magazines. **Nonfiction:** Reviews and essays on small-press literary books, publishers, and small-circulation magazines; 200 words. **Queries:** Preferred.

SOCIETY OF CHILDREN'S BOOK WRITERS & ILLUSTRATORS

8271 Beverly Blvd., Los Angeles, CA 90048. 323-782-1010.
E-mail: scbwi@scbwi.org. Web site: scbwi.org. Monthly. **Description:** Articles pertinent to writers and/or illustrators of children's books. **Nonfiction:** Pays $50 for articles. **Art:** Pays $10 for line drawings; $25 for B&W cover photo. **Queries:** Required. **Rights:** 1st time.

TECHNICAL COMMUNICATION

Society for Technical Communication
194 Aberdeen Dr., Aiken, SC 29803. 803-642-2156.
E-mail: george@ghayhoe.com. Web site: www.stc.org. Quarterly. Membership publication. Circ.: 25,000. George Hayhoe, Editor. **Description:** Industry information for technical writers, publishers, and editors. **Nonfiction:** Research results, technical communication theory, case studies, tutorials related to new laws, standards, requirements, techniques, or technologies, reviews of research, bibliographies, and bibliographic essays on technical communication. **Queries:** Not necessary. **E-Queries:** Yes. **Unsolicited mss:** Accepts.

THE WRITER

Kalmbach Publishing Co.
21027 Crossroads Circle, P.O. Box 1612, Waukesha, WI 53187-1612. 262-796-8776.
E-mail: queries@writermag.com. Web site: www.writermag.com. Monthly. Circ.: 38,000. Elfrieda Abbe, Editor. **Description:** Founded in 1887, the magazine uses articles and interviews that focus on the process of writing. **Nonfiction:** Articles, to 2,500 words. How-to, marketing ideas, publishing trends, profiles and book reviews. Payment depends on length and complexity of the articles. $50-$75 for reviews, $150-$600 for features and columsn. **Tips:** Prefers submissions through the mail, but include your e-mail address and be sure your name is on every page; list your experience, but do not send clips. If you query electronically, include your e-mail address in the body of the message. Sample copies $4.95, plus tax, S/H.

WRITER'S BLOCK MAGAZINE
500-1145 Hunt Club Rd., Ottawa, Ontario K1V 0Y3 Canada.
E-mail: dgoldberger@niva.com. Web site: www.writersblock.ca. Quarterly. Circ.: 5,000. Dalya Goldberger, Managing Editor. **Description:** Online magazine featuring articles, essays, editorials, and book reviews on the art and business of writing. Aimed at established and aspiring Canadian writers. Also publishes high-quality creative literary fiction and poetry; 2,500 words max.; offers byline.

THE WRITER'S CHRONICLE
Associated Writing Programs
MSN 1E3, George Mason University, Fairfax, VA 22030.
E-mail: awpchron@mason.gmu.edu. Web site: www.awp.org/magazine. 6x/yr. Circ.: 20,000. **Description:** Publication featuring essays, articles, and news on writing. Designed to inform and entertain student writers and teachers. **Nonfiction:** Information on grants, awards, fellowships, articles, news, and reviews. Pays $7 per 100 words, or as negotiated. **Tips:** E-mail query preferred.

WRITERS' JOURNAL
P.O. Box 394, Perham, MN 56573-0394. 218-346-7921.
E-mail: writersjournal@lakesplus.com. Web site: www.writersjournal.com. Bimonthly. Circ.: 26,000. **Description:** For writers, including professional communicators, independent/self-publishers, part- or full-time freelancers, screenwriters, desktop publishers, authors, editors, teachers, and poets. **Nonfiction:** Practical advice on business side of writing (tips, techniques, record keeping, how to increase production, taxes, financial aspects); 1,000-1,500 words. **Poetry:** Light verse, preferably about writing. Also buys a few serious pieces, any subject, any style, with strong imagery and impact; 25 lines max.; $5. **Tips:** Submit articles with positive, practical advice. *Writers' Journal* also offers eleven fiction contests and three poetry contests. Send SASE for contest guidelines or visit Web site. **Queries:** Preferred. **E-Queries:** Yes. **Unsolicited mss:** Accepts. **Response:** Queries 6 weeks, submissions 6 months, SASE required. **Rights:** One-time. **Payment:** On publication.

FICTION & POETRY

MAGAZINES

FICTION & POETRY MAGAZINES

The following section presents a list of magazines whose primary focus in most cases is publishing fiction and poetry. The fiction usually appears in the form of short stories; however, some magazines also publish excerpts from novels and longer works.

The list is divided into markets for specific genres of fiction. These include: Fiction for Children, Fiction for Teens, Literary Magazines, Mystery & Detective, Romance & Confession, and Science Fiction & Fantasy.

The largest number of magazines are found in the Literary Magazine portion. These independent and college journals often publish not only fiction and poetry but also a potent range of creative nonfiction essays on varied cultural topics, as well as book reviews and interviews with authors and artists.

Although payment from these relatively small magazines, which range in circulation from 300 to 10,000, is modest (often in copies only), publication can begin to establish a writer's serious literary credentials and often will help bring the work of a beginning writer to the attention of editors at larger magazines. Notably, some of America's leading authors still contribute work to the smaller literary magazines. Together with emerging new voices, they form a community of writers whose only criteria are excellence and the elevation of stimulating thought in literary discourse.

These literary journals, little magazines, and college quarterlies welcome work from novices and pros alike; editors are always interested in seeing traditional and experimental fiction, poetry, essays, reviews, short articles, criticism, and satire. As long as the material is well-written, the fact that a writer has not yet been widely publisher doesn't adversely affect his or her chances for acceptance.

Most of these literary publications have small budgets and staffs, so they may be slow in their reporting time; several months is not unusual. In addition, some (particularly the college-based magazines) do not read manuscripts during the summer.

Publication may also lead to having one's work chosen for reprinting in one of the prestigious annual collections of work from the little magazines.

For a complete list of the thousands of literary publications and little magazines in existence, writers may wish to consult such comprehensive reference works as *The International Directory of Little Magazines and Small Presses*, published annually by Dustbooks (P.O. Box 100, Paradise, CA 95967) and available at many public libraries.

FICTION FOR CHILDREN

AMERICAN GIRL
Pleasant Company Publications
8400 Fairway Pl., Middleton, WI 53562. 608-836-4848.
E-mail: im_agmag_editor@pleasantco.com. Web site: www.americangirl.com.
Bimonthly. $3.95/$19.95. Circ.: 650,000. Kristi Thom, Editor. **Description:** For girls ages 8 and up. **Fiction:** Protagonist should be a girl between 8 and 12. No science

fiction, fantasy, or first romance stories. Good children's literature, with thoughtful plots and characters; 2,500 words; payment varies. **Nonfiction:** By assignment only; 150-1,000 words; $1/word. **Fillers:** Visual puzzles, mazes, math puzzles, word games, simple crosswords, cartoons; $50/puzzle. **Columns, Departments:** Girls Express; short profiles of girls doing great, interesting things; 150 words; $1/word. **Tips:** The girl must be the story's "star," told from her point of view. "Girls Express" offers best chance to break in. **Queries:** Preferred. **E-Queries:** No. **Unsolicited mss:** Accepts. **Response:** 3 months; SASE required. **Freelance Content:** 5%. **Payment:** On acceptance.

BABYBUG
See page 460 for full listing.
Description: Offers simple rhymes and stories that parents will delight in reading to their babies.

BOYS' LIFE
See page 460 for full listing.
Description: For boys ages 8-14 covering sports, hobbies, crafts, and scouting.

CHIRP
Bayard Canada, The Owl Group
49 Front St. E, Fl. 2, Toronto, Ontario M5E 1B3 Canada. 416-340-2700.
E-mail: bayard@owl.on.ca. Web site: www.owlkids.com. 9x/year. **Description:** Offers puzzles, games, rhymes, stories, and songs for children, ages 2-6. Goal is to introduce preschool children to the relationship between words and pictures. **Fiction:** 300-400 words; pay varies. **Nonfiction:** 300-400 words; pay varies. **Queries:** Preferred. **E-Queries:** Yes. **Unsolicited mss:** Accepts. **Payment:** On publication.

CRICKET
Carus Publishing Co.
315 Fifth St., P.O. Box 300, Peru, IL 61354-0300. 815-224-6656.
Web site: www.cricketmag.com. $5/issue, $35.97/year. Circ.: 71,000. Marianne Carus, Editor-in-Chief. **Description:** Folk tales, fantasy, science fiction, history, poems, science, sports, and crafts, for young readers. **Fiction:** Any topic of interest to children; up to 2,000 words; $.25/word. **Nonfiction:** Science, biography, history, nature; up to 1,500 words; $.25/word. **Poetry:** Brief lyric poems; up to 25 lines; $3/line. **Fillers:** Word or math puzzles, recipes, crafts, experiments; 150-200 words; $100. **Tips:** Include bibliography with nonfiction. **Queries:** Not necessary. **E-Queries:** No. **Unsolicited mss:** Accepts. **Response:** Submissions 8-12 weeks. **Freelance Content:** 90%. **Rights:** All. **Payment:** On publication.

CRUSADER
P.O. Box 7259, Grand Rapids, MI 49510. 616-241-5616.
Web site: www.calvinistcadets.org. 7x/year. Circ.: 10,000. G. Richard Broene, Editor.
Description: Christian-oriented magazine for boys, ages 9-14, especially to mem-

bers of Calvinist Cadet Corps. Purpose is to show how God is at work in the lives of boys and in the world around them. **Fiction:** Fast-moving stories that appeal to a boy's sense of adventure and humor; 900-1,500 words; pay varies. **Tips:** Send 9 x 12 SASE for free sample copy and/or upcoming themes. Themes also available on Web site. **Queries:** Not necessary. **Unsolicited mss:** Accepts. **Payment:** On acceptance.

DISCOVERIES
See page 464 for full listing.
Description: Full-color story paper for 3rd and 4th graders connecting Evangelical Sunday School learning with daily growth.

DISCOVERY TRAILS
See page 465 for full listing.
Description: Christian stories, activities, poems, and puzzles for kids ages 10-11.

THE FRIEND
The Church of Jesus Christ of Latter-day Saints
50 E North Temple, Fl. 24, Salt Lake City, UT 84150-3226. 801-240-2210.
Monthly. $8/year. Circ.: 275,000. Vivian Paulsen, Managing Editor. **Description:** Nonfiction literary journal for children up to 12 years of age. **Nonfiction:** Articles and stories should be true and should focus on character-building qualities and wholesome values without moralizing or preaching. Stories should have universal settings, conflicts, and characters. Biographies of living people are not accepted; 1,000 words; $.11/word. **Poetry:** Poems should be uplifting and of substance. Picturable poems suitable for preschoolers are of high interest. Does not accept nature poems or those with a clever play on words; $25 and up. **Fillers:** How-to pieces on handicraft or homemaking projects. Also, cartoons, games, puzzles, and recipes. **Tips:** Does not accept fiction. Send $1.50 and 9 x 12 SASE for sample copy. **Queries:** Not necessary. **E-Queries:** No. **Unsolicited mss:** Does not accept. **Response:** Submissions 8-12 weeks. **Rights:** All. **Payment:** On acceptance.

HIGHLIGHTS FOR CHILDREN
See page 467 for full listing.
Description: Features stories, pictures, jokes, and activities for kids ages 2-12.

HOPSCOTCH
See page 467 for full listing.
Description: Magazine for girls with focus on educational activities and stories.

LADYBUG
Carus Publishing Co.
315 Fifth St., P.O. Box 300, Peru, IL 61354-0300. 815-224-6656.
Web site: www.ladybugmag.com. Monthly. $5/issue, $35.97/year. Circ.: 130,000. Paula Morrow, Editor. **Description:** Stories, poems, songs, games, and adventures for young children, ages 1-2. Each page illustrated to delight parents and children alike.

Fiction: Picture, read-aloud, and early reader stories with lively characters. Genres: adventure, humor, mild suspense, fairy tales, folktales, contemporary fiction; up to 850 words; $.25/word, $25 min. **Nonfiction:** How-to, informational, and humorous pieces, on age-appropriate topics; up to 300 words; $.25/word, $25 min. **Poetry:** Rhythmic, rhyming, serious, humorous, active; up to 20 lines; up to $3/line, $25 min. **Fillers:** Rebus, learning activities, games, crafts, songs, finger games. **Art:** see guidelines. **Tips:** Always looking for more activities. Does not accept query letters. **Queries:** Not necessary. **E-Queries:** No. **Unsolicited mss:** Accepts. **Response:** 12 weeks, SASE required. **Freelance Content:** 70%. **Rights:** 1st serial. **Payment:** On publication.

NICK, JR.
See page 470 for full listing.
Description: Fun activities, games, and stories for kids ages 2-7 and their parents.

SPELLBOUND
Eggplant Productions
P.O. Box 2248, Schiller Park, IL 60176.
E-mail: spellbound@eggplant-productions.com.
Web site: www.eggplant-productions.com. Quarterly. Raechel Henderson Moon, Editor. **Description:** Features fantasy short stories and poems for ages 9 to 13. **Fiction:** Stories with the elements of magic, myth, adventure, legend, etc. **Fillers:** Poetry, games, puzzles, recipes, and riddles. **Tips:** No stories with gore or adult content. Accepts submissions by e-mail only. **Rights:** 1st. **Payment:** $5 plus 2 copies.

STONE SOUP
P.O. Box 83, Santa Cruz, CA 95063-0083. 831-426-5557.
E-mail: editor@stonesoup.com. Web site: www.stonesoup.com. Bimonthly. $5.50/$33. Circ.: 20,000. Gerry Mandel, Editor. **Description:** Stories, poems, book reviews, and art by young writers and artists, ages 8-13. **Fiction:** Personal narratives, arrival stories, family histories, sport stories, science fiction; 2,500 words; $35. **Nonfiction:** Book reviews by children under 14. Prefers writing based on real-life experiences. **Poetry:** Free-verse only; $35. **Art:** For ages 8-13 only; please send 2-3 samples of your work. **Tips:** No adults! **Queries:** Not necessary. **E-Queries:** No. **Unsolicited mss:** Accepts. **Response:** Queries 2 weeks, submissions 4 weeks, SASE. **Freelance Content:** 100%. **Rights:** All. **Payment:** On publication.

WONDER TIME
6401 The Paseo, Kansas City, MO 64131. 816-333-7000 ext. 2244.
Weekly. None. Circ.: 14,000. Pamela Smits, Editor. **Description:** For children, ages 5-7. Emphasis on the religious instruction of children and parents. Issues are thematic. **Fiction:** A Christian emphasis to correlate with Sunday School curriculum. **Poetry:** Free verse or rhyming; 6-12 lines; $.25/word. **Columns, Departments:** Parent or family fun; 25-50 words; $15/activity. **Queries:** Preferred. **E-Queries:** No. **Unsolicited mss:** Does not accept. **Response:** 1-2 months, SASE. **Freelance Content:** 50%. **Rights:** All. **Payment:** On publication.

FICTION FOR TEENS

BREAKAWAY
See page 593 for full listing.
Description: For Christian boys, ages 12-18.

BRIO
See page 593 for full listing.
Description: For Christian teen girls (profiles, how-to pieces, adventures that show the fun Christian teens can have together).

CICADA
Carus Publishing Co.
315 Fifth St., P.O. Box 300, Peru, IL 61354-0300. 812-224-6656.
Bimonthly. $8.50/$35.97. Circ.: 15,000. Tracy Schoenle, Editor. **Description:** For teens, fiction and poetry that is thought-provoking, yet entertaining, often humorous. Also publishes stories by teens reflecting their own unique perspective. **Fiction:** Literary and genre fiction (realistic, humorous, science fiction, and fantasy); up to 10,000 words; $.25/word. **Nonfiction:** Essays on personal experience, especially from teen authors; up to 2,000; $.25/word. **Poetry:** up to 25 lines; $3/line. **Tips:** Does not accept query letters. **Queries:** Not necessary. **E-Queries:** No. **Unsolicited mss:** Accepts. **Response:** Submission 8-12 weeks, SASE. **Freelance Content:** 90%. **Rights:** All. **Payment:** On publication. **Contact:** Debbie Vetter.

CLAREMONT REVIEW
4980 Wesley Rd., Victoria, BC, Canada V84 1Y9. 250-658-5221.
E-mail: editor@theclaremontreview.com. Web site: www.theclaremontreview.com.
Semi-annual. $8/$15. Circ.: 500. Susan Field, Business Editor. **Description:** Fiction and poetry by young writers in the English-speaking world, ages 13-19. **Fiction:** Fiction, with strong voice, 500-3,000 words. **Poetry:** Poetry that stirs the heart; 1 page. **Tips:** Fantasy, science fiction not accepted. **Queries:** Not necessary. **Unsolicited mss:** Accepts. **Response:** 6 weeks, SASE. **Freelance Content:** 100%.

MERLYN'S PEN
P.O. Box 910, East Greenwich, RI 02818. 401-885-5175.
E-mail: merlynspen@aol.com. Web site: www.merlynspen.com. Annual. $29.95. Circ.: 5,000. R. James Stahl, Editor. **Description:** Fiction, essays, and poems by America's teens. All work written by students. Looking for new voices, teen writers who have something to say and say it with eloquence, honesty, and distinctiveness. **Fiction:** Realistic fiction about contemporary teen life; also science fiction, fantasy, adventure, historical fiction; to 8,500 words; $20-$200. **Nonfiction:** Personal essays, memoirs, autobiographies, humorous or descriptive essays; 500-5,000 words. **Poetry:** Free verse, metric verse; $20-$50. **Art:** B&W illustrations; by assignment, submit samples. **Tips:** No adult authors. **Queries:** Required. **E-Queries:** No. **Unsolicited mss:** Accepts. **Response:** 10-12 weeks, SASE. **Freelance Content:** 100%.

NEW MOON

P.O. Box 3620, Duluth, MN 55803-3620. 218-728-5507.
E-mail: girl@newmoon.org. Web site: www.newmoon.org. Bimonthly. $5.50/$29.
Circ.: 30,000. Deb Mylin, Managing Editor. **Description:** Celebrates girls—their accomplishments and efforts to hold onto their voices, strengths, and dreams as they move from being girls to becoming women. **Fiction:** Stories by female authors, with girls as main characters. Fiction should fit theme (contact for upcoming list), for girls ages 8-14; 900 words; $.06-$.10/word. **Nonfiction:** Women's work (profiles a woman and her job, relates to theme); Herstory (profiles a woman from history); Body Language (about puberty, body image, depression, menstruation, etc.); Girls on the Go (by girl or woman adventurers); 600 words; $.06-$.10/word. **Art:** By assignment; send samples; pay varies. **Queries:** Not necessary. **E-Queries:** Accepts. **Unsolicited mss:** Accepts. **Response:** 2 months, SASE. **Freelance Content:** 10%. **Rights:** All. **Payment:** On publication.

SCHOLASTIC SCOPE

Scholastic, Inc.
555 Broadway, New York, NY 10012-3999. 212-343-6100.
E-mail: scopemag@scholastic.com. Web site: www.scholastic.com. 18x/yr. Circ.: 750,000. Diane Webber, Editor. **Description:** Fiction for 15-18-year-olds, with 4th-6th grade reading ability. Short stories, 400-1,200 words, on teenage interests and relationships; family, job, and school situations. Plays to 5,000 words. Pays good rates. **Payment:** On acceptance.

TEEN VOICES

See page 598 for full listing
Description: Written by, for, and about teenaged and young-adult women.

LITERARY MAGAZINES

AFRICAN VOICES

270 W 96th St., New York, NY 10025. 212-865-2982.
E-mail: africanvoices@aol.com. Web site: www.africanvoices.com. Quarterly. $3/$12.
Circ.: 20,000. Carolyn A. Butts, Editor. **Description:** Literary magazine of fiction, nonfiction, poetry, and visual arts created by people of color. **Fiction:** Humorous, erotic, and dramatic fiction by ethnic writers. All themes, subjects, and styles with emphasis on style and technique; 500-2,000 words. **Nonfiction:** Investigative articles, artist profiles, essays, book reviews, and first-person narratives; 500-2,500 words. **Poetry:** All styles; avant-garde, free verse, haiku, light verse, traditional. Submit up to 5 poems; max. 3 pages. **Columns, Departments:** Book reviews; 500-1,200 words. **Art:** B&W photos. **Queries:** Preferred. **E-Queries:** Accepts. **Unsolicited mss:** Accepts. **Response:** Queries 6 weeks, submissions 6-12 weeks, SASE. **Freelance Content:** 80%. **Rights:** 1st American. **Payment:** In copies. **Contact:** Kim Horne, fiction; Layding Kalbia, poetry; Debbie Officer, book reviews.

AGNI

Boston University, Creative Writing Program
236 Bay State Rd., Boston, MA 02215. 617-353-7135.
E-mail: agni@bu.edu. Web site: www.bu.edu/agni. Semi-annual. $9.95/$17. Circ.: 1,800. Askold Melnyczuk, Editor. **Description:** Contemporary literature by established and new writers, on literary and political subjects, to engage readers in a broad cultural conversation. Length varies. Pays $20-150 ($10/page). **Fiction:** Criterion is excellence. **Nonfiction:** Thoughtful pieces on a group of books (not reviews of single books) or broader cultural or literary issues. **Poetry:** Yes. **Art:** Paintings, photos. **Tips:** Reviews submissions in the fall. **Queries:** Not necessary. **E-Queries:** No. **Unsolicited mss:** Accepts. **Response:** 2-4 months, SASE required. **Freelance Content:** 15%. **Rights:** 1st serial. **Payment:** On publication.

AGNIESZKA'S DOWRY

A Small Garlic Press, 5455 Sheridan, #3003, Chicago, IL 60640.
E-mail: marek@enteract.com, ketzle@ketzle.net.
Web site: www.enteract.com/~asgp/agnieszka.html. Marek Lugowski, Katrina Grace Craig, Editors. **Description:** On-line and in-print; a literary (primarily poetry) community. **Tips:** Policies and guidelines at Web site. Submit per guidelines by email. **E-Queries:** Yes.

ALASKA QUARTERLY REVIEW

University of Alaska-Anchorage
3211 Providence Dr., Anchorage, AK 99508. 907-786-6916.
E-mail: ayaqr@uaa.alaska.edu. Web site: www.uaa.alaska.edu/aqr. Quarterly. $6.95/$10. Circ.: 2,200. Ronald Spatz, Editorial Department. **Description:** "One of the nation's best literary magazines" (*Washington Post Book World*). **Fiction:** Experimental and traditional literary forms. No romance, children's, or inspirational/religious; up to 20,000 words. **Nonfiction:** Literary nonfiction, essays, and memoirs; 20,000 words. **Poetry:** Avant-garde, free verse, traditional. No light verse; 10 poems max. **Queries:** Not necessary. **E-Queries:** No. **Unsolicited mss:** Accepts. **Response:** SASE required. **Freelance Content:** 95%. **Rights:** 1st NA. **Payment:** In copies.

AMERICAN BOOK REVIEW

Illinois State University
Unit for Contemporary Literature, Campus Box 4241, Normal, IL 61790-4241.
Web site: www.litline.org/abr. Bimonthly. $4/issue. Circ.: 5,000. Ron Sukenick, Editor. **Description:** Literary book reviews and essays on literature; 750-1,250 words; $50. **Columns, Departments:** Reviews of literary books; 750-1,250 words; $50. **Queries:** Preferred. **E-Queries:** Yes. **Response:** Queries 1 week to 1 month, submissions 1 month, SASE required. **Freelance Content:** 20%. **Payment:** On publication. **Contact:** Rebecca Kaiser.

AMERICAN LITERARY REVIEW

University of North Texas

P.O. Box 311307, English Dept., Denton, TX 76203-1307. 940-565-2755.

E-mail: americanliteraryreview@yahoo.com. Web site: www.engl.univ.edu/alr. Bi-annual. $5.00 newsstand/$10/year. Circ.: 500. Corey Marks, Editor. **Description:** Literary journal with fiction, creative nonfiction, and poetry. Both in print and online. **Fiction:** Character-driven literary short stories. **Nonfiction:** Creative nonfiction. **Poetry:** Length varies. **Queries:** Not necessary. **E-Queries:** No. **Unsolicited mss:** Accepts. **Response:** Submissions 3 months, SASE. **Freelance Content:** 90%. **Rights:** 1st American serial. **Payment:** In copies.

AMERICAN POETRY REVIEW

1721 Walnut St., Philadelphia, PA 19103. 215-496-0439.

E-mail: dbonanno@aprweb.org. Web site: www.aprweb.org. Bimonthly. $3.95. Circ.: 20,000. Stephen Berg, David Bonanno, Editors. **Description:** Premier forum for contemporary poetry, since 1912. **Poetry:** Submit up to 4 poems, any length; $2/line. **Tips:** Do not send manuscript by fax or e-mail. **Queries:** Not necessary. **E-Queries:** No. **Unsolicited mss:** Accepts. **Response:** Submissions 6-8 weeks, SASE required. **Rights:** FNASR. **Payment:** On publication.

AMERICAN SCHOLAR

See page 332 for full listing.

Description: For intelligent people who love the English language.

AMERICAN WRITING

4343 Manayunk Ave., Philadelphia, PA 19128.

Semiannual. $6/$10. Circ.: 2,500. Alexandra Grilikhes, Editor. **Description:** Offers bold experiments in poetry and prose, especially "the voice of the loner, states of being, and initiation." **Fiction:** The voice of the loner, in whatever situation it finds itself; up to 3,500 words. **Nonfiction:** Personal essays on art, memoir, anything the writer is obsessed by; 3,500 words. **Poetry:** Nonacademic, serious material, nothing that rhymes; up to 10 pages. **Tips:** Do not query. No pieces about sports. **Queries:** Not necessary. **E-Queries:** No. **Unsolicited mss:** Accepts. **Response:** 2 weeks to 6 months, SASE. **Freelance Content:** 98%. **Rights:** 1st serial. **Payment:** In copies.

ANCIENT PATHS

PMB 223, 2000 Benson Rd. S. #115, Renton, WA 98055.

E-mail: skylar.burris@gte.net. Web site: www.literatureclassics.com/ancientpaths/magazine/table.html. Semi-annual. $6/yr. Circ.: 150. Skylar Hamilton Burris, editor. **Description:** Poetry, stories, art, and reviews. **Fiction:** Short stories, novel excerpts; prefers third-person; to 2,500 words. **Nonfiction:** Personal narratives and book reviews; to 2,500 words. **Poetry:** Free verse or formal (ballads, sonnets, quatrains, etc.); to 60 lines. **Art:** B&W art. **Tips:** Open to subtle Judeo-Christian themes; no preaching, but say something meaningful. **Queries:** Not necessary. **E-Queries:** Yes.

Unsolicited mss: Accepts. **Response:** Submissions 3-4 weeks, SASE. **Freelance Content:** 99%. **Rights:** One-time. **Payment:** One copy and $1.

ANOTHER CHICAGO MAGAZINE

3709 N Kenmore, Chicago, IL 60613-2905.
E-mail: editors@anotherchicagomag.com. Web site: www.anotherchicagomag.com.
Semiannual. $14.95. Circ.: 2,000. Barry Silesky, Editor. **Description:** Literary publication with fresh poetry, fiction, and commentary. Also, each issue features an interview with a noted writer, translations, reviews of current literature, and an 8-page center art folio. **Fiction:** Quality literary **Fiction:** Urgent, new, worldly; 30 pages or less. **Columns, Departments:** Reviews of current fiction and poetry; 500 words. **Art:** Interesting B&W photography; 8 photos (from a single artist) in each issue. **Tips:** Seeks unusual, engaged work of highest quality only. Reviews work from February 1-August 31. **Queries:** Not necessary. **E-Queries:** No. **Unsolicited mss:** Accepts. **Response:** Submissions 10 weeks or longer, SASE required. **Freelance Content:** 10%. **Rights:** FNASR. **Payment:** On publication. **Contact:** Barry Silesky.

ANTHOLOGY, INC.

P.O. Box 4411, Mesa, AZ 85211-4411. 480-461-8200.
E-mail: info@anthology.org. Web site: www.anthology.org. 6x/yr. $3.95/$20. Circ.: 1,500. Sharon Skinner, Executive Editor. **Description:** Poetry, prose, and art from new and upcoming writers and artists from around the world. E-zine and print. **Fiction:** Any genre. Also accepts stories based in the fictional city of Haven, where people make their own heroes; 5,000 words. **Nonfiction:** Any genre; 5,000 words. **Poetry:** Any style, to 100 lines. **Art:** B&W only; pays in ad space offered. **Tips:** No graphic horror or pornography. Avoid cliché and trick endings. Awards cash prizes in a variety of contests. **Queries:** Not necessary. **E-Queries:** No. **Unsolicited mss:** Accepts. **Response:** Queries to 60 days, submissions to 90 days, SASE. **Freelance Content:** 90%. **Rights:** 1st NA. **Payment:** In copies.

ANTIETAM REVIEW

Washington County Arts Council
41 S Potomac St., Hagerstown, MD 21740. 301-791-3132.
Annual. $6.30/issue. Winnie Wagaman, Managing Editor. **Description:** Publishes quality short fiction, poetry, and black and white photographs that have not been previously published. Considers material from September 1-February 1 each year. **Fiction:** Well-crafted, any subject. Prefers short stories, but will consider a novel if it works as an independent piece; to 5,000 words; $100 per story plus 2 copies. **Nonfiction:** Accepts creative nonfiction. **Poetry:** Submit up to three poems to Paul Grant, Poetry Editor; to 30 lines; $25 per poem plus 2 copies. **Art:** B&W photos. **Queries:** Not necessary. **E-Queries:** No. **Unsolicited mss:** Accepts. **Response:** 3-6 months, SASE required. **Freelance Content:** 90%. **Rights:** 1st. **Payment:** On publication.

ANTIGONISH REVIEW

St. Francis Xavier University

P.O. Box 5000, Antigonish, NS B2G 2W5 Canada. 902-867-3962, fax: 902-867-5563. E-mail: tar@stfx.ca. Web site: www.antigonishreview.com. Quarterly. $24/year. Circ.: 800. B. Allen Quigley, Editor. **Description:** Poetry, short stories, essays, book reviews. **Fiction:** 2,000-5,000 words; $50. **Nonfiction:** 2,000-5,000 words; $50-$150. **Poetry:** Any subject, any point of view. **Tips:** Considers stories from anywhere, original or translations, but encourages Atlantic Canadians and Canadian writers, and new and young writers. No submissions accepted by e-mail. **Queries:** Preferred. **E-Queries:** No. **Unsolicited mss:** Accepts. **Response:** Queries 4-6 months, SASE required. **Freelance Content:** 100%. **Payment:** On publication.

ANTIOCH REVIEW

P.O. Box 148, Yellow Springs, OH 45387. 937-769-1365.

Web site: www.antioch.edu/review. Quarterly. $35/year. Circ.: 5,100. Robert S. Fogarty, Editor. **Description:** Fiction, essays, and poetry from emerging and established authors. **Fiction:** Intelligent, compelling stories written with distinction; up to 8,000 words; $10/published page. **Nonfiction:** Social sciences, humanities, literary journalism; up to 8,000 words; $10/published page. **Poetry:** 3-6 poems; $10/published page. **Tips:** Read an issue of magazine to obtain a good idea of subjects, treatment, and lengths. **Queries:** Not necessary. **E-Queries:** No. **Unsolicited mss:** Accepts. **Response:** 12-14 weeks, SASE required. **Freelance Content:** 100%. **Payment:** On publication.

APALACHEE REVIEW

P.O. Box 10469, Tallahassee, FL 32302.

2x/year. **Description:** Literary journal for poetry. **Tips:** Simultaneous submissions encouraged. **Unsolicited mss:** Accepts. **Response:** SASE required.

ARACHNE

2363 Page Rd., Kennedy, NY 14747-9717.

E-mail: litteacher199@yahoo.com. Semiannual. $10/year. Circ.: 500. Susan L. Leach, Editor. **Description:** Magazine with rural themes. Focus is on America's grassroots authors. **Fiction:** 1,500 words. **Poetry:** Submit up to 7 poems. **Tips:** No simultaneous submissions. **Queries:** Preferred. **E-Queries:** No. **Unsolicited mss:** Accepts. **Response:** Queries 1-2 weeks, submissions up to 5 months, SASE required. **Freelance Content:** 100%. **Rights:** 1st. **Payment:** In copies.

ART TIMES

P.O. Box 730, Mt. Marion, NY 12456. 845-246-6944.

E-mail: info@arttimesjournal.com. Web site: www.arttimesjournal.com. 11x/year. Circ.: 24,000. Raymond J. Steiner, Editor. **Description:** Commentary resource on fine and performing arts. **Fiction:** No excessive sex, violence, racist themes; 1,500 words; $25 and subscription. **Nonfiction:** Feature essays are staff-written. **Poetry:** All forms; 20 lines; pays in copies. **Queries:** Not necessary. **E-Queries:** No.

Unsolicited mss: Accepts. **Response:** Submission 6 months, SASE. **Freelance Content:** 100%. **Rights:** 1st NA. **Payment:** On publication.

ASCENT

Concordia College

901 Eighth St. S, English Dept., Moorhead, MN 56562. 218-299-4000.

Web site: www.cord.edu/dept/english/ascent. 3x/year. W. Scott Olsen, Editor. **Description:** Literary magazine with fiction, essays, and poetry. No reviews or editorial articles. Submit complete manuscripts with SASE. **Tips:** Review copy of magazine before submitting. **E-Queries:** No. **Payment:** In copies.

ASIAN PACIFIC AMERICAN JOURNAL

Asian American Writers' Workshop

16 W 32nd St., Suite 10A, New York, NY 10001. 212-494-0061.

E-mail: apaj@aaww.org. Web site: www.aaww.org. Hanya Yanagihara, Editor. **Description:** Short stories, also excerpts from longer fiction works by emerging or established Asian American writers. **Poetry:** Submit up to 10 poems. **Tips:** Send 4 copies of each piece submitted, in all genres. **Queries:** Preferred. **Payment:** In copies.

THE ATLANTIC MONTHLY

See page 401 for full listing.

Description: Articles on contemporary issues and the best in fiction, travel, food, and humor.

AURA LITERARY ARTS REVIEW

University of Alabama-Birmingham

1400 University Blvd., Suite 135, Birmingham, AL 35294-1150. 205-934-3216.

Semi-annual (Spring and Fall issues). $6/issue; $25 annual subscription/patronage. Christopher Giganti, Editor-in-Chief. **Description:** Student-produced magazine for written and visual art. Accepts original, unpublished fiction and nonfiction prose, art, and poetry. Prose: up to 10,000 words; **Poetry:** Up to 10 pages. **Art:** Slides or electronic format preferred; photographs accepted. **Queries:** Not necessary. **Unsolicited mss:** Accepts. **Response:** SASE required.

BEACON STREET REVIEW

120 Boylston, Boston, MA 02116. 617-824-8750.

E-mail: beaconstreetreview@hotmail.com. Semiannual. $6/issue. Circ.: 1,000. Lori Jeanette Placek, Editor-in-Chief. **Description:** New fiction, nonfiction and poetry. **Poetry:** 5 poems. Prose: up to 25 pages total. **Tips:** Seeks more postmodern work in coming months. Blind reading policy; writer should send 4 copies of each manuscript. Annual awards of $50. **Queries:** Not necessary. **E-Queries:** No. **Unsolicited mss:** Accepts. **Response:** Queries 1-2 weeks, submissions (responds in March and November), SASE. **Rights:** 1st. **Payment:** On publication.

THE BEAR DELUXE

P.O. Box 10342, Portland, OR 97296. 503-242-1047.
E-mail: bear@teleport.com. Web site: www.orlo.org. Triannual. $16/4 issues. Circ.: 19,000. Tom Webb, Editor. **Description:** Explores environmental issues through the creative arts. **Fiction:** Environmental themes; 750-4,000 words; $.05/word. **Nonfiction:** News, reporting, interviews; seeks cultural connections to environmental issues; 200-4,000 words; $.05/word. **Poetry:** 3-5 poems; up to 50 lines; $10. **Fillers:** First-person opinion pieces, short news pieces, cartoons; 100-750 words; $.05/word, $10/cartoon. **Columns, Departments:** Portrait of an Artist, Hands-on, Reviews; 100-1,500 words; $.05/word. **Art:** B&W photos, illustrations, cartoons, paintings, etc.; $30. **Queries:** Preferred. **E-Queries:** Yes. **Unsolicited mss:** Accepts. **Response:** 1-2 months for queries, 3-6 months for submissions, SASE required. **Freelance Content:** 50%. **Rights:** First. **Payment:** On publication.

BELLINGHAM REVIEW

Western Washington University, Signpost Press
MS-9053, Bellingham, WA 98225. 360-650-4863.
E-mail: bhreview@cc.wwu.edu. Web site: www.wwu.edu/~bhreview. Semiannual. Brenda Miller, Editor-in-Chief. **Description:** Journal for fiction, poetry, and essays "of palpable quality." Up to 9,000 words, pays $15/printed page as funds allow. **Tips:** Annual contests for creative nonfiction, fiction, and poetry; $1,000 prizes; see Web site for guidelines. **Queries:** Not necessary. **E-Queries:** No. **Unsolicited mss:** Accepts. **Response:** No queries, submission 3 months, SASE required. **Freelance Content:** 100%. **Rights:** One-time. **Payment:** On publication.

BELLOWING ARK

P.O. Box 55564, Shoreline, WA 98155. 206-440-0791.
Bimonthly. $3/issue, $15/year. Circ.: 700. Robert R. Ward, Editor. **Description:** Literary magazine following the Romantic tradition. **Fiction:** Short fiction, portraying life as positive and meaningful; length varies. **Poetry:** Any style or length. **Queries:** Not necessary. **E-Queries:** No. **Unsolicited mss:** Accepts. **Response:** 2-4 months; SASE required. **Freelance Content:** 95%. **Rights:** First, reprint. **Payment:** In copies.

BELOIT FICTION JOURNAL

Beloit College, Box 11, 700 College St, Beloit, WI 53511. 608-363-2577.
E-mail: mccownc@beloit.edu. Web site: www.beloit.edu/~english/bfjournal.htm. Annual. $14.00. Clint McCown, Editor. **Description:** Literary fiction. Interested in new and established writers. **Fiction:** Literary fiction, any theme (no genre fiction). Stories from 1-40 pages long, average 15 pages. **Tips:** Submit with a great opening line, original language, strong forward movement. No pornography, political propaganda, religious dogma. Reading period: August 1-December 1. **Queries:** Not necessary. **E-Queries:** No. **Unsolicited mss:** Accepts. **Response:** 2-4 weeks, SASE required. **Payment:** In copies. **Contact:** Heather Skyler, Managing Editor.

BELOIT POETRY JOURNAL

24 Berry Cove Rd., Lamoine, ME 04605. 207-667-5598.
Web site: www.bpj.org. Quarterly. $5/$18. Circ.: 1,300. Marion Stocking, Editor.
Description: Publishes the best poems received, without bias for length, form, subject, or tradition. Looking to discover new voices. Also offers the annual Walsh Poetry Award which awards the author of the best poem or series of poems $3,000. **Poetry:** Contemporary poetry, any length or mode. Submissions must be single-spaced and only one poem per page. Put name/address on every sheet submitted. **Tips:** Avoid lineated journal entries, clichés, self-absorbed "how I feel" verse. A strong poem needs fresh insight and a distinctive music. Books reviews are written by the editor. **Queries:** Not necessary. **E-Queries:** No. **Unsolicited mss:** Accepts. **Response:** Submissions up to 4 months, SASE required. **Payment:** In copies.

BIBLIOPHILOS

Bibliophile Publishing
200 Security Bldg., Fairmont, WV 26554. 304-366-8107.
Quarterly. $5/$18. Circ.: 225. Dr. Gerald J. Bobango, Editor. **Description:** Scholastically oriented. Seeks to promote worldview of the pre-1960s, to show importance of books and scholarly endeavor (and to encourage people to relegate their PCs and laptops to the dustbin). **Fiction:** Stories about growing up in rural West Virginia in the 1930s and WWII; people with nontraditional values; stories of love and kindness; 3,000 word max.; $5-$25. **Nonfiction:** Reviews of history, literature, and literary criticism needed (e.g., Mona-Lisa's Landscape: a study of the painting's background; Cruising With the Cruisers: on Caribbean cruises, sociology of passenger and crew); 3,000 words; $5-$25. **Fillers:** "Hemingway and Faulkner Reminisce About the Prom," in their respective style; 25-300 words; $5-$10. **Columns, Departments:** Book reviews. **Art:** B&W photos; $5-$25. **Queries:** Required. **E-Queries:** No. **Unsolicited mss:** Does not accept. **Response:** Queries 2 weeks, submissions 2 weeks, SASE. **Freelance Content:** 50%. **Rights:** FNASR. **Payment:** On publication.

BITTER OLEANDER

4983 Tall Oaks Dr., Fayetteville, NY 13066-9776. 315-637-3047.
E-mail: info@bitteroleander.com. Web site: www.bitteroleander.com. Bi-annual. $8/$15. Circ.: 1,200. Paul B. Roth, Editor. **Description:** Imaginative poetry, fiction, interviews with known and new writers whose work is featured. 128 pages. **Fiction:** Original, imaginative, aware of language as possibility instead of slave; 2,500 words. **Poetry:** Imaginative, concentration on "deep image," the concrete particular. **Tips:** Seeking more contemporary poetry in translation. No confessional storytelling, overly abstract poetry. **Queries:** Not necessary. **E-Queries:** Yes. **Unsolicited mss:** Accepts. **Response:** Queries 1 week, submissions 1 month, SASE. **Freelance Content:** 80%. **Rights:** All, revert back to author. **Payment:** In copies.

BLACK BEAR REVIEW

Black Bear Publications
1916 Lincoln St., Croydon, PA 19021-8026.

E-mail: bbreview@earthlink.net. Web site: www.blackbearreview.com. Biannual. $12.00. Circ.: 750. Ave Jeanne, Editor. **Description:** International literary magazine for the concerned poet and artist. **Tips:** Prefers poems on social and environmental concerns. Avoid traditional forms. Submissions by e-mail only. **Queries:** Not necessary. **E-Queries:** Yes. **Unsolicited mss:** Does not accept. **Response:** Queries 1 week, submissions 1 week, SASE not required. **Freelance Content:** 100%. **Rights:** FNASR. **Payment:** In copies.

BLACK WARRIOR REVIEW
P.O. Box 862936, Tuscaloosa, AL 35486-0027. 205-348-4518.
E-mail: bwr@ua.edu (queries only). Web site: http://webdelsol.com/bwr. Bi-annual. $14/yr. Circ.: 2,000. Ander Monson, Editor. **Description:** The best in contemporary fiction, poetry, nonfiction, art, interviews, reviews, and photography. **Tips:** Seeking emerging writers and experimental work; writing that is fresh, that sings. Include SASE; check Web site for detailed guidelines. Does not accept e-mail submissions. **Queries:** Not necessary. **E-Queries:** Yes. **Unsolicited mss:** Accepts. **Response:** 2-5 months.

BLOOMSBURY REVIEW
See page 632 for full listing.
Description: Book reviews, literary features, interviews, essays, and poetry.

BLUE UNICORN
22 Avon Rd., Kensington, CA 94707. 510-526-8439.
3x/year. $5/$14. Circ.: 500. Ruth G. Iodice, Editor. **Description:** Has published many of the nation's best poets over the past 25 years. **Poetry:** Well-crafted poems, in form or free verse, also expert translations. Shorter is better. **Tips:** Study great poets, but develop your own voice; avoid copying whatever is popular. The sound of a poem helps make it memorable. **Queries:** Preferred. **E-Queries:** No. **Unsolicited mss:** Accepts. **Response:** Queries as possible, submissions 4-6 months, SASE required. **Freelance Content:** 100%. **Rights:** 1st. **Payment:** In copies.

BLUELINE
English Dept., SUNY, Potsdam, NY 13676. 315-267-2043.
E-mail: blueline@potsdam.edu. Web site: www.potsdam.edu/engl/blueline. Annual. $10/yr. Circ.: 600. Rick Henry, Editor. **Description:** Poems, stories, and essays on the Adirondack and regions similar in geography and spirit, or on the shaping influence of nature. **Fiction:** Yes; to 3,500 words. **Nonfiction:** On Adirondack region or similar areas; to 3,500 words. **Poetry:** Submit up to 5 poems; to 75 lines. **Queries:** Not necessary. **E-Queries:** Yes. **Unsolicited mss:** Accepts. **Response:** Queries, 1 week. **Rights:** FNASR. **Payment:** In copies.

BOSTON REVIEW
MIT, 30 Wadsworth St., E53, Room 407, Cambridge, MA 02139. 617-253-3642.
E-mail: review@mit.edu. Web site: http://bostonreview.mit.edu. Bimonthly. Circ.:

20,000. Josh Cohen, Editor. **Description:** Features on politics, literature, art, music, film, photography, and poetry. **Fiction:** 1,000-5,000 words; $40-$100. **Queries:** Preferred. **Contact:** Ian Lague, Managing Editor.

BOULEVARD
6614 Clayton Rd. #325, St. Louis, MO 63117. 314-361-2986.
Web site: www.richardburgin.com. 3x/year. $8/issue, $15/year. Circ.: 3,500. Richard Burgin, Editor. **Description:** A literary review magazine publishing fine, established writers and new writers with exceptional promise. Recent authors: Joyce Carol Oates, Stephen Dixon, Ha Jin, Alice Hoffman, and Alice Adams. **Fiction:** Well-constructed, moving stories, in an original voice; up to 30 typed pages; $150-$300. **Nonfiction:** Literary, film, music, criticism, travel pieces, memoirs, philosophical or social issues. **Poetry:** No light verse. Submit up to 5 poems of up to 200 lines; $25-$300/poem. **Tips:** No science fiction, erotica, westerns, horror, romance, or children's stories. **Queries:** Not necessary. **E-Queries:** No. **Unsolicited mss:** Accepts. **Response:** Queries 1 week, submissions 1-2 months, SASE required. **Freelance Content:** 85%. **Rights:** 1st. **Payment:** On publication.

BRIAR CLIFF REVIEW
Briar Cliff University, 3303 Rebecca St., Sioux City, IA 51104.
E-mail: currans@briarcliff.edu. Web site: www.briarcliff.edu/bcreview. Tricia Currans-Sheehan, Editor. **Description:** An eclectic literary and cultural magazine focusing on Siouxland writers and subjects. **Fiction:** Yes. **Nonfiction:** To 5,000 words; humor/satire, Siouxland history, thoughtful essays. **Poetry:** Yes. **Columns, Departments:** Book reviews. **Tips:** Manuscripts read August-October. **Payment:** In copies.

BRIDGE/STORIES & IDEAS
1357 N Ashland Ave., #3A, Chicago, IL 60622.
E-mail: submissions@bridgemagazine.org. Web site: www.bridgemagazine.org. **Description:** A magazine based on "the simple belief that separate fields of inquiry can and should be thought of as having shared horizons." **Fiction:** Realistic fiction; 2,000-5,000 words. **Nonfiction:** Critical nonfiction; 2,000-5,000 words. **Queries:** Preferred. **Response:** SASE required.

BYLINE
See page 633 for full listing.
Description: Publication for writers.

CALIFORNIA QUARTERLY
California State Poetry Society, P.O. Box 7126, Orange, CA 92863. 949-854-8024.
E-mail: jipalley@aol.com. Web site: www.Chapman.edu/comm/english/csps. Quarterly. $5/$20. Circ.: 250. Julian Palley, Editorial Board. **Description:** "California State Poetry Quarterly." **Poetry:** Brief, any subject or style. Submit up to 6 poems; up to 40 lines. **Queries:** Not necessary. **E-Queries:** Yes. **Unsolicited mss:** Accepts.

Response: 5-6 months, SASE. **Freelance Content:** 100%. **Rights:** Revert to poet. **Payment:** 1 copy/poem.

CALLALOO

Texas A&M University, Dept. of English
4227 TAMU, College Station, TX 77843-4227. 979-458-3108.
E-mail: callaloo@tamu.edu. Web site: http://callaloo.tamu.edu. Quarterly. $10/$37. Circ.: 2,000. Charles H. Rowell, Editor. **Description:** African Diaspora literary journal, with original work by and critical studies of Black writers worldwide. **Fiction:** Fiction, drama; up to 10,000 words. **Nonfiction:** Academic and cultural criticism; up to 10,000 words. **Poetry:** Up to 10 poems. **Art:** Glossy prints or slides. **Tips:** Writers should submit cover letter listing the titles of submitted works including detailed contact information of the author, with e-mail address if available. Three copies should be submitted for each manuscript, and should not bear the author's name or any other identifying information. **Queries:** Not necessary. **E-Queries:** No. **Unsolicited mss:** Accepts. **Response:** 6-8 months, SASE or e-mail required. **Freelance Content:** 100%. **Payment:** In copies.

CALYX

P.O. Box B, Corvallis, OR 97339. 541-753-9384.
E-mail: calyx@proaxis.com. Web site: www.proaxis.com/~calyx. Biannual. $9.50/issue. Circ.: 5,000. Beverly McFarland, Managing Editor. **Description:** Journal of art and literature by women, with poetry, prose, art, and book reviews. Presents wide spectrum of women's experience, especially work by unheard voices (new writers, women of color, working-class, older women). **Fiction:** 5,000 words. **Nonfiction:** 5,000 words. **Poetry:** 6 poems max. **Art:** Color cover, plus 16 pages of B&W art. See guidelines. **Tips:** Submit prose and poetry only from October 1 to December 31 (postmark date). Art submissions accepted anytime. Query regarding book reviews. **Queries:** Not necessary. **E-Queries:** No. **Unsolicited mss:** Accepts. **Response:** Submissions 6-8 months, SASE required. **Payment:** In copies and 1 volume subscription.

THE CAPE ROCK

Southeast Missouri State University, Dept. of English
Cape Girardeau, MO 63701. 573-651-2500.
E-mail: hhecht@sermovn.semo.edu. Bi-annual. $5/issue, $7 year. Circ.: 500. Harvey E. Hecht, Editor. **Description:** Poetry journal, with photography. **Poetry:** to 70 lines; pays $200 for "Best in issue." **Art:** A series of 12-15 B&W photos, featuring a sense of place; $100. **Tips:** Manuscripts read August-April. **Queries:** Not necessary. **E-Queries:** Yes. **Unsolicited mss:** Accepts. **Response:** Queries 1-2 weeks, submissions 2-4 months, SASE required. **Rights:** All; will release. **Payment:** In copies.

THE CAPILANO REVIEW

2055 Purcell Way, N Vancouver, British Columbia V7J 3H5 Canada. 604-984-1712.
E-mail: tcr@capcollege.bc.ca. Web site: www.capcollege.bc.ca/dept/tcr. 3x/year. $25/year. Circ.: 900. Sharon Theson, Editor. **Description:** Innovative poetry, fiction,

drama, and word in the visual media, in a cross-disciplinary format. **Fiction:** To 6,000 words (drama, to 10,000 words); $50-$200 (Canadian). **Poetry:** 5-6 poems; $50-$200 (Canadian). **Tips:** Does not accept simultaneous submissions. Looks for work pushing beyond the boundaries of traditional art and writing. **Queries:** Not necessary. **E-Queries:** No. **Unsolicited mss:** Accepts. **Response:** 4 months, SASE with Canadian postage or IRCs required. **Rights:** FNASR. **Payment:** On publication. **Contact:** Carol L. Hamshaw, Managing Editor.

CAPPER'S
See page 476 for full listing.
Description: Focuses on home and family, for readers in the rural Midwest.

THE CARIBBEAN WRITER
University of the Virgin Islands
RR02, Box 10,000, Kingshill St. Croix, Virgin Islands 00850. 340-692-4152.
E-mail: qmars@uvi.edu. Web site: www.thecaribbeanwriter.com. Annual. $12/issue; $20/ 2 yr. individual subscription; $40/ 2 yr. institutional subscription. Circ.: 1,200. Dr. Erika J. Waters, Editor. **Description:** Literary anthology with Caribbean focus. **Fiction:** Personal essays, also one-act plays (max. 3,500 words or 10 pages), or up to 2 short stories (15 pages or less); Caribbean experience or heritage central. **Poetry:** Caribbean focus; submit up to 5 poems. **Tips:** Original, unpublished work only (if self-published, give details). Blind submissions policy: print only the title on your manuscript; give your name, address, and title on a separate sheet. **Queries:** Not necessary. **E-Queries:** Yes. **Unsolicited mss:** Accepts. **Response:** SASE required. **Freelance Content:** 80%. **Rights:** One-time. **Payment:** In copies. **Contact:** Ms. Quilin Mars.

CAROLINA QUARTERLY
University of North Carolina, Greenlaw Hall CB#3520, Chapel Hill, NC 27599-3520.
E-mail: cquarter@unc.edu. Web site: www.unc.edu/depts/cqonline. Tara Powell, Editor. **Description:** Features poetry, fiction, nonfiction, and graphic art by new and established writers. **Tips:** Manuscripts not read May-July.

CHARITON REVIEW
Truman State University, Kirksville, MO 63501-9915. 660-785-4499.
Semiannual. Circ.: 1,800. Jim Barnes, Editor. **Description:** Quality poetry and fiction; modern and contemporary translations. **Fiction:** To 6,000 words; $5/printed page. **Poetry:** to 6,000 words; $5/printed page. **Tips:** "The only guideline is excellence."

THE CHATTAHOOCHEE REVIEW
Georgia Perimeter College
2101 Womack Rd., Dunwoody, GA 30338-4497.
Quarterly. $6/$16. Lawrence Hetrick, Editor. **Description:** Promotes fresh writing by emerging and established voices. **Fiction:** up to 5,000 words; $20/page. **Nonfiction:** $15/page; reviews $50. **Poetry:** $50/poem. **Tips:** No simultaneous submissions. Annual Lamar York Prize for Nonfiction. **Queries:** Not necessary.

E-Queries: No. **Response:** Queries 1 week, submissions 3-4 months, SASE. **Freelance Content:** 80%. **Rights:** 1st. **Payment:** On publication.

CHELSEA

P.O. Box 773, Cooper Station, New York, NY 10276.
Semiannual. $8/$13. Circ.: 1,800. Alfredo de Palchi, Editor. **Description:** New and established voices in literature. Eclectic, lively, sophisticated, with accent on translations, art, and cross-cultural exchange. Pays $15/page, plus copies. **Fiction:** Mainstream, literary; up to 25 pages. **Nonfiction:** Essays; up to 25 pages. **Poetry:** Traditional, avant-garde; 3-6 poems. **Columns, Departments:** Book reviews, by assignment. **Art:** Submit slides; color (cover), B&W inside. **Tips:** Interested in avant-garde: original ideas and use of language. **Queries:** Not necessary. **E-Queries:** No. **Unsolicited mss:** Accepts. **Response:** 3-6 months, SASE. **Rights:** 1st. **Payment:** On publication.

CHIRON REVIEW

702 N Prairie, St. John, KS 67576-1516. 620-786-4955.
E-mail: chironreview@hotmail.com. Web site: www.geocities.com/soho/nook/1748/.
Quarterly. $5/$14. Circ.: 2,000. Michael Hathaway, Publisher/Editor. **Description:** Publication featuring a wide range of contemporary creative writing (fiction and non-fiction, traditional and off-beat) including artwork and photography of featured writers. Also provides news and literary reviews. **Fiction:** Contemporary fiction; 700-3,000 words. **Nonfiction:** Essays, interviews, and reviews of literary books and magazines; 500-1,000 words. **Poetry:** Send 5 poems. **Tips:** All submissions welcome. Does not accept e-mail, simultaneous or previously published submissions. **Queries:** Not necessary. **E-Queries:** No. **Unsolicited mss:** Accepts. **Response:** Queries 2-4 weeks, Submissions 2-6 weeks, SASE required. **Freelance Content:** 100%. **Rights:** One-time. **Payment:** 1 copy.

CIA-CITIZEN IN AMERICA, INC

30 Ford St., Glen Cove, NY 11542. 516-759-8718.
E-mail: ciamc@webtv.net. 9x/year. John J. Maddox, Magazine Coordinator. **Description:** Fiction and nonfiction, to 2,000 words. Poetry to 100 words. Prefers self photos to be published with articles. Fillers accepted. Query first. Pays $40-$100.

CIMARRON REVIEW

Oklahoma State University, 205 Morrill Hall, Stillwater, OK 74078-0135.
E-mail: cimarronreview@hotmail.com. Web site: http://cimarronreview.okstate.edu.
Quarterly. Circ.: 800. E. P. Walkiewicz, Editor. **Description:** Poetry, fiction, and essays. Seeks work with individual, innovative style and contemporary themes. **Fiction:** 300-800 words, pays $50 and copies. **Tips:** Anything fresh, exciting, savvy. **Queries:** Not necessary. **E-Queries:** No. **Unsolicited mss:** Accepts. **Response:** 1-2 months, SASE required. **Rights:** FNASR. **Payment:** On acceptance.

COLORADO REVIEW

Colorado State University, English Dept., Fort Collins, CO 80523. 970-491-5449. E-mail: creview@colostate.edu. Web site: www.coloradoreview.com. Tri-annual. $9.50/issue, $24/year. Circ.: 1,300. David Milofsky, Editor. **Description:** Fiction, poetry, and personal essays by new and established writers. Seeking work that is vital, imaginative, highly realized, and avoids mere mannerism to embody human concern. Pays $5/page. **Fiction:** Short fiction, contemporary themes; up to 20 pages. **Nonfiction:** Up to 20 pages. **Poetry:** Length varies. **Art:** Slides, $100 (cover). **Tips:** No simultaneous submissions. Reading period, September-April only; submissions sent outside this period are returned unread. **Queries:** Not necessary. **E-Queries:** No. **Unsolicited mss:** Accepts. **Response:** Queries 2-4 weeks, submissions 4-6 weeks, SASE required. **Rights:** 1st NA. **Payment:** On publication. **Contact:** David Milofsky.

THE COLUMBIA REVIEW

Columbia University, 415 Dodge Hall, New York, NY 10027. 212-854-4216. E-mail: arts-litjournal@columbia.edu. Web site: www.columbia.edu/cu/arts/writing/columbiajournal/index.html. Annual. $15. Circ.: 2,200. Anindita Sinha and Erin Thompson, Editors. **Description:** Literary journal, with contemporary poetry, fiction, and creative nonfiction from established and emerging voices. **Fiction:** No restrictions (avoid children's stories or genre pieces). Open to experimental writing, mainstream narratives, work that takes risk; 25 pages or less. **Nonfiction:** Same as fiction (no reviews or academic criticism); 25 pages or less. **Poetry:** Wide range of forms and styles; 7 poems max. **Art:** Slides. **Queries:** Not necessary. **E-Queries:** No. **Unsolicited mss:** Accepts. **Response:** Queries 2 weeks, 3 months submissions, SASE required. **Freelance Content:** 65%. **Rights:** 1st U.S. **Payment:** In copies.

CONCHO RIVER REVIEW

Angelo State University, English Dept., San Angelo, TX 76909. Web site: www.angelo.edu/dept/eng. Bi-annual. $8/$14. Circ.: 300. James A. Moore, Editor. **Description:** Literary journal with fiction, essays, poetry, and book reviews. **Fiction:** Primarily Texas and Southwest topics. Traditional stories with strong sense of conflict, finely-drawn characters, and crisp dialogue; 1,500-5,000 words. **Nonfiction:** Critical papers, personal essays, and reviews. Topics on Texas and/or the Southwest; 1,500-5,000 words. **Poetry:** Send 3-5 poems at a time; 1 page or less. **Queries:** Not necessary. **E-Queries:** Yes. **Unsolicited mss:** Accepts. **Response:** Queries 2-4 weeks, submissions 3-6 months, SASE. **Freelance Content:** 100%. **Rights:** 1st. **Payment:** In copies.

CONFLUENCE

P.O. Box 336, Belpre, OH 45714-0336. E-mail: wilmaacree@charter.net. Annual. $5. Circ.: 1,000. Wilma Acree, Editor. **Description:** Presents the work of emerging and established authors. **Fiction:** Literary fiction; to 5,000 words. **Nonfiction:** Interviews, essays; to 5,000 words.

Poetry: Lyric, narrative poetry with fresh images. No rhymed poetry unless of exceptional quality; up to 60 lines. **Tips:** No previously published work, simultaneous submission. Cover letter with short bio required. **Queries:** Not necessary. **E-Queries:** Yes. **Unsolicited mss:** Accepts. **Response:** Queries 1 month, submissions 1-5 months, SASE. **Freelance Content:** 80%. **Rights:** 1st. **Payment:** On publication.

CONFRONTATION

Long Island University
C.W. Post of L.I.U., Dept. of English, Brookville, NY 11548. 516-299-2720.
E-mail: mtucker@liu.edu. Semiannual. $10. Circ.: 2,000. Martin Tucker, Editor.
Description: Literary magazine with poetry, fiction, essays, and memoir material. Also, original work by famous and emerging writers. **Fiction:** Up to 30 pages; $25-$150. **Nonfiction:** Mostly memoirs. Other nonfiction, including reviews, are assigned; $25-$150. **Poetry:** Pays $15-$100. **Tips:** Send query for nonfiction material only. Manuscripts read September through May only. **Queries:** Preferred. **E-Queries:** No. **Unsolicited mss:** Accepts. **Response:** Queries 2-4 weeks, submissions 6-8 weeks, SASE required. **Freelance Content:** 75%. **Rights:** FNASR. **Payment:** On publication.

THE CONNECTICUT POETRY REVIEW

P.O. Box 818, Stonington, CT 06378.
J. Claire White, Harley More, Editors. **Description:** Poetry, 5-20 lines; pays $5/poem. Reviews, 700 words; pays $10. **Tips:** Manuscripts read September to January, and April to June. **Payment:** On acceptance.

CONNECTICUT RIVER REVIEW

P.O. Box 4053, Waterbury, CT 06704-0053. 203-753-7815.
E-mail: editorcrr@yahoo.com for queries only.
Web site: www.hometown.aol.com/ctpoetrysociety/. Biannual. Circ.: 500. Peggy Sapphire, Editor. **Description:** Published by the Connecticut Poetry Society, $7/issue, $14/subscription, $25/membership in CPS includes CRR subscription. Fine poetry from accomplished poets, as well as emerging voices. We welcome submissions of unpublished poems (limit 3), typed, complete contact information in upper right corner, SASE required. We accept simultaneous submissions but ask for notice of acceptance elsewhere. **Payment:** one copy. Poet retains copyright. Also offers annual Connecticut River Review Poetry Contest, deadline April 30, up to 3 poems, $10 entry fee. **Poetry:** Any subject, form, length. **Queries:** Preferred. **E-Queries:** No. **Unsolicited mss:** Accepts. **Response:** Queries 6-8 weeks, submission 8-12 weeks, SASE required. **Rights:** 1st NA and reprint. **Payment:** In copies.

COTTONWOOD

University of Kansas, Box J, 400 Kansas Union, Lawrence, KS 66045.
2x/year. **Description:** Publishes new and well-known writers. No rhymed poetry. Kansas and midwestern focus. Photos, graphics, and book reviews from midwest presses also accepted. **Fiction:** Work from experience; no contrived or slick fiction.

Submit only 1 story at a time; 1,500-8,000 words. **Poetry:** Submit up to 5 poems; 10-80 lines. **Art:** Photos, other graphic arts. **Tips:** Published work eligible for annual awards. **E-Queries:** No. **Response:** 3-6 months, SASE required. **Rights:** 1st NA. **Payment:** In copies.

CRAB CREEK REVIEW
P.O. Box 840, Vashon, WA 98070.
Semiannual. Linda Clifton, Editor. **Description:** Poetry, fiction, and creative nonfiction. **Fiction:** Clear, dynamic fiction, to 4,000 words. **Nonfiction:** to 4,000 words. **Poetry:** To 80 lines. **Queries:** Preferred. **Payment:** In copies.

THE CREAM CITY REVIEW
University of WI-Milwaukee, English Dept.
P.O. Box 413, Milwaukee, WI 53201. 414-229-4708.
E-mail: creamcity@uwm.edu. Web site: www.uwm.edu/dept/english/creamcity.html.
Semi-annual. $8/$15. Circ.: 700. Karen Auvinen, Editor. **Description:** Literary journal with fiction, nonfiction, poetry, and drama. **Queries:** Not necessary. **E-Queries:** No. **Unsolicited mss:** Accepts. **Response:** Queries 2 weeks, 3 months for submissions, SASE required. **Freelance Content:** 100%. **Rights:** 1st NA. **Payment:** 1-year subscription.

CREATIVE NONFICTION
5501 Walnut, Suite 202, Pittsburgh, PA 15232. 412-688-0304.
E-mail: info@creativenonfiction.org. Web site: www.creativenonfiction.org. 3x/year.
$10/$29.95 (4 issues). Circ.: 4,000. Lee Gutkind, Editor-In-Chief. **Description:** Literary journal, devoted exclusively to nonfiction. Personal essays, memoirs literary journalism, profiles of creative nonfiction authors, book reviews. **Nonfiction:** Prose, rich with detail and distinctive voice on any subject; seeking essays based on research; $10/page. **Tips:** Can be personal but must reach out universally in some way. **Queries:** Not necessary. **E-Queries:** Yes. **Unsolicited mss:** Accepts. **Response:** Submissions 3 months, SASE. **Freelance Content:** 95%. **Rights:** 1st serial and reprint. **Payment:** On publication.

CUMBERLAND POETRY REVIEW
Acklen Station, P.O. Box 120128, Nashville, TN 37212.
2x/yr. $18/issue. Circ.: 300. Eva Touster, Editors. **Description:** Devoted to poetry and poetry criticism. No restrictions on form, style, or subject matter. **Queries:** Not necessary. **E-Queries:** No. **Unsolicited mss:** Accepts. **Response:** 6 months, SASE. **Payment:** In copies.

CUTBANK
University of Montana, English Dept., Missoula, MT 59812. 406-243-6156.
E-mail: cutbank@selway.umt.edu. Web site: www.umt.edu/cutbank. Biannual.
$6.95/$12. Circ.: 500. **Description:** Fiction and poetry, also reviews, interviews, and artwork. **Fiction:** Yes. **Poetry:** Yes. **Tips:** All work considered for Richard Hugo

Poetry Award and A.B. Guthrie, Jr. Short Fiction Award. **Queries:** Not necessary. **E-Queries:** No. **Unsolicited mss:** Accepts. **Response:** 3-4 months, SASE. **Freelance Content:** 90%. **Payment:** In copies.

DESCANT
T.C.U. Box 297270, Fort Worth, TX 76129. 817-257-6537.
E-mail: d.kuhne@tcu.edu. Web site: www.eng.tcu.edu/usefulsites/descant.htm. $12. Circ.: 750. Dave Kuhne, Editor. **Description:** Seeks quality work in traditional or innovative form. **Fiction:** No restrictions; 5,000 words. **Poetry:** 60 lines. **Tips:** Annual O'Connor Award ($500) for best short story; Colquitt Award ($500) for best poetry. Submit September through May only. **Queries:** Not necessary. **E-Queries:** No. **Unsolicited mss:** Accepts. **Response:** 6 weeks, SASE required. **Freelance Content:** 100%. **Rights:** 1st. **Payment:** In copies.

THE DISTILLERY
Motlow State Community College
P.O. Box 8500, Lynchburg, TN 37352-8500. 931-393-1700.
Web site: www.mscc.cc.tn.vs/distillery/. Semiannual. $9/$15. Circ.: 750. Dawn Copeland, Editor. **Description:** Literary journal of poetry, fiction, nonfiction, art, and photography. **Fiction:** Literary, emphasis on style, character, voice; 4,000 words. **Nonfiction:** Creative nonfiction, with a sense of style. Critical and personal essays; 4,000 words. **Poetry:** Voice, style, and image; any length. **Art:** Slides. **Tips:** Avoid warmed-over exercises in K-mart realism. **Queries:** Not necessary. **E-Queries:** No. **Unsolicited mss:** Accepts. **Response:** Submissions 2-4 months, SASE. **Rights:** 1st NA. **Payment:** In copies.

DOUBLE DEALER REDUX
The Pirate's Alley Faulkner Society
Faulkner House, 624 Pirate's Alley, New Orleans, LA 70116. 504-586-1612.
E-mail: faulkhouse@aol.com. Web site: www.wordsandmusic.org. Annual. $10. Circ.: 7,500. Rosemary James, Editor. **Description:** Poems, short stories, and essays, also portions of novels and novellas. **Tips:** Has published entire novellas with author's permission. **Queries:** Preferred. **Unsolicited mss:** Accepts. **Payment:** In copies.

DOUBLETAKE
See page 296 for full listing.
Description: Fiction, poetry, and photography devoted to revealing "extraordinary events and qualities found in everyday lives of Americans and others."

DREAMS & VISIONS
Skysong Press
35 Peter St. S, Orillia, Ontario L3V 5A8 Canada.
E-mail: skysong@bconnex.net. Web site: www.bconnex.net/~skysong. Annual. $4.95./issue. Circ.: 200. Steve Stanton, Editor. **Description:** Short literary fiction from a Christian perspective (science fiction, humor, fantasy, magic realism, contem-

porary, inspirational). No genre excluded. **Fiction:** Based on Biblical norms or traditions, but portraying spiritual truths in new, innovative ways; 2,000-6,000 words; $.005/word. **Queries:** Not necessary. **Unsolicited mss:** Accepts. **Response:** SASE w/Canadian postage. **Freelance Content:** 100%.

EARTH'S DAUGHTERS

Central Park Station, P.O. Box 41, Buffalo, NY 14215.
Web site: www.earthsdaughter.org. 3x/year. $18/year. Circ.: 2,000. Pat Colvard, Joyce Kessel, Editors. **Description:** Small, feminist literary press publishing mostly poetry. **Fiction:** Finely crafted work, feminist theme; 1,000-1,200 words. **Poetry:** Yes. **Tips:** Reader's fees for non-subscribers, $5. **Queries:** Preferred. **E-Queries:** Yes. **Unsolicited mss:** Does not accept. **Response:** Queries 2 weeks, submissions 2 months plus, SASE required. **Freelance Content:** 85%. **Rights:** 1st. **Payment:** In copies.

ELYSIAN FIELDS QUARTERLY

P.O. Box 14385, St. Paul, MN 55114-0385. 651-644-8558.
E-mail: info@efqreview.com. Web site: www.efqreview.com. Quarterly. $5.95/$22.50. Circ.: 2,000-2,500. Tom Goldstein, Editor. **Description:** The literary review for baseball, with essays, poetry, commentary, drama, book reviews, and humor. Length: 400-4,000 words. **Tips:** Must have a passion and appreciation for baseball, and be able to write well. This is not a hero-worship, nostalgia journal. Sentimental, ill-conceived, formulaic writing from would-be writers or those looking to publish a "baseball" story get tossed quickly. **Queries:** Not necessary. **E-Queries:** Yes. **Unsolicited mss:** Accepts. **Response:** 6 months (fiction/poetry), 3 months (other), SASE. **Freelance Content:** 75%. **Rights:** One-time, anthology. **Payment:** In copies.

EPOCH

Cornell University, 251 Goldwin Smith Hall, Ithaca, NY 14853-3201. 607-255-3385. Tri-annual. $5/issue, $11/year. Circ.: 1,000. Michael Koch, Editor. **Description:** Literary magazine of serious fiction and poetry. Pays $5/page and up. **Fiction:** Literary fiction. **Nonfiction:** Personal essays. **Poetry:** All types. **Queries:** Not necessary. **E-Queries:** No. **Unsolicited mss:** Accepts. **Response:** Submissions 4-6 weeks, SASE required. **Freelance Content:** 100%. **Rights:** 1st NA. **Payment:** On publication.

EUREKA LITERARY MAGAZINE

Eureka College, 300 E College Ave., Eureka, IL 61530. 309-467-6336.
E-mail: llogsdon@eureka.com. Biannual. $7.50/issue. Circ.: 500. Loren Logsdon, Editor. **Description:** Publishes stories and poems. **Fiction:** Well-written, thought-provoking stories; 2-28 pages. **Poetry:** Any length. **Queries:** Not necessary. **E-Queries:** Yes. **Unsolicited mss:** Accepts. **Response:** 2-3 weeks for queries, 4-5 months for submissions; SASE required. **Freelance Content:** 100%. **Rights:** One-time. **Payment:** In copies.

EVENT

Douglas College, P.O. Box 2503, New Westminster

British Columbia V3L 5B2 Canada. 604-527-5293.

E-mail: event@douglas.bc.ca. Web site: http://event/douglas.bc.ca. 3x/year. $8/issue, $22/year. Circ.: 1,250. Cathy Stonehouse, Editor. **Description:** Mostly fiction, poetry, and creative nonfiction. **Fiction:** Readable, stylish, with well-handled characters and strong point of view; submit up to 2 short stories; 5,000 words max.; $22/page ($500 max.). **Nonfiction:** Reviews, essays; 5,000 words max.; $22/page ($500 max.). **Poetry:** Appreciate strong narrative, sometimes confessional modes. Eclectic, always open to content that invites involvement; submit 3-8 poems. **Art:** For cover only; $150. **Tips:** Accepts e-mail queries, but does not accept e-mail submissions. **Queries:** Not necessary. **E-Queries:** Yes. **Unsolicited mss:** Accepts. **Response:** 1-6 months. **Freelance Content:** 85%. **Rights:** FNASR. **Payment:** On publication.

FICTION

The City College of New York, English Dept.

Convent Ave. at 138th St., New York, NY 10031. 212-650-6319.

E-mail: fictionmagazine@yahoo.com. Web site: www.fictioninc.com. 2-3x/year. $10/issue, $36/4 issues. Circ.: 1,700. Mark Jay Mirsky, Editor. **Description:** Journal featuring the best short fiction from new and published authors. Seeks material that is new and experimental. **Queries:** Not necessary. **E-Queries:** No. **Unsolicited mss:** Accepts. **Response:** Queries to 1 month, submissions 4-6 months, SASE. **Freelance Content:** 100%. **Rights:** All, revert to author.

FIELD: CONTEMPORARY POETRY AND POETICS

Oberlin College Press

10 N Professor St., Oberlin, OH 44074. 440-775-8124.

E-mail: oc.press@oberlin.edu. Web site: www.oberlin.edu/~ocpress. Bi-annual. $14/year. Circ.: 1,250. David Walker, Martha Collins, and Pamela Alexander, Editors. **Description:** Contemporary poetry and poetics. Seeks to be at forefront of what is happening in poetry. Fall issue features symposium on a famous writer. **Poetry:** Varied formats, length. Pays $15/page, plus copies and subscription. **Tips:** Submit 3-5 poems at one time. **E-Queries:** Yes. **Unsolicited mss:** Does not accept. **Response:** Queries 1 week, submissions 6 weeks, SASE required. **Payment:** On publication. **Contact:** Linda Slocum, Managing Editor.

FINE MADNESS

P.O. Box 31138, Seattle, WA 98103-1138.

E-mail: beastly@oz.net. Web site: www.finemadness.org. Annual. $5/$9. Circ.: 1,000. Bentley, Malek, Pitkin, Skillman, Editors. **Description:** International poetry by writers, well-known and new, highly original in language and content. **Poetry:** Form open, strong sense of language, original imagery. **Tips:** Avoid concrete poetry, light verse, topical poetry, over-dependence on form. Prefers lyrical poems that use language in thoughtful and thought-provoking way. **Queries:** Preferred. **E-Queries:**

Yes. **Unsolicited mss:** Accepts. **Response:** Queries 1-2 months, submissions 3-4 months, SASE required. **Freelance Content:** 100%.

FIRST INTENSITY
P.O. Box 665, Lawrence, KS 66044-0665. 785-479-1501.
E-mail: leechapman@aol.com. Ms. Lee Chapman, Editor. **Description:** Literary journal with poetry, short fiction, prose poetry, book reviews, interviews. Essays on poetics, writing, writers, visual artists. **Fiction:** 10 pages max. **Poetry:** 10 pages max. **Tips:** Seeking serious, experimental work, nothing "mainstream." **Queries:** Not necessary. **E-Queries:** Yes. **Unsolicited mss:** Accepts. **Response:** Queries 2 weeks, submissions 8-10 weeks, SASE required. **Freelance Content:** 50%. **Payment:** In copies.

THE FIRST LINE
K Street Ink, P.O. Box 0382, Plano, TX 75025.
E-mail: submission@thefirstline.com. Web site: www.thefirstline.com. Quarterly. $3/$10. Circ.: 200. David LaBounty, Jeff Adams, Editors. **Description:** Celebrates the first line. Provides a forum for discussing favorite lines and different short stories stemming from a common first line. **Fiction:** All stories must stem from the same first line. Line for Fall 2002, "Jimmy Hanson was a sallow man who enjoyed little in life save for his_." Writer fills in blank; 300-1,500 words. **Nonfiction:** Essays about a first line from book or story; 300-600 words. **Tips:** Also sponsors several contests with cash prizes. **Queries:** Not necessary. **E-Queries:** Yes. **Unsolicited mss:** Accepts. **Response:** 2-6 weeks; SASE required. **Freelance Content:** 90%. **Rights:** FNAR, first electronic, first anthology. **Payment:** $5/story and 1 copy. **Contact:** Robin LaBounty.

FIVE POINTS
Georgia State University, University Plaza, Atlanta, GA 30303-3083.
Web site: www.webdelsol.com/five_points. 3x/year. $7/$20. Circ.: 2,000. David Bottoms, Editor. **Description:** Publisher of quality fiction, poetry, essays, and interviews. Writing must have original voice, substance and significance. **Fiction:** 7,500 words; $15/page, $250 max. **Nonfiction:** Personal essays, literary essays, and creative nonfiction; 7,500 words; $15/page, $250 max. **Poetry:** 100 lines max. per poem; $50/poem. **Art:** Photography only. Paintings and illustrations sometimes considered; slides, prints; pay varies. **Queries:** Not necessary. **E-Queries:** No. **Unsolicited mss:** Accepts. **Response:** Queries 2 months, submission 3 months, SASE. **Freelance Content:** 10%. **Rights:** 1st NA. **Payment:** On publication.

FLINT HILLS REVIEW
Bluestem Press, Emporia State University
Dept. of English, Box 4019, Emporia, KS 66801-5087. 316-341-5216.
E-mail: webbamy@emporia.edu. Web site: www.emporia.edu/fhr. Annual. $5.50/issue. Circ.: 500. Amy Sage Webb, Philip Heldrich, Editors. **Description:** Writing, from and about Kansas and the Great Plains region, conveying a strong sense

of place. **Fiction:** Place-focused writing about or set in the region. **Nonfiction:** Interviews, essays; offers annual prize of $200. **Poetry:** Strong imagery, fidelity to place. **Art:** Place-based B&W photos, ideally which redefine the region. **Tips:** Do not send genre fiction, religious writing, or unsolicited critical essays or interviews (query first for these). **Queries:** Not necessary. **E-Queries:** Yes. **Unsolicited mss:** Accepts. **Response:** 2 months queries, 6 months submissions, SASE. **Freelance Content:** 5%. **Rights:** 1st. **Payment:** In copies.

THE FLORIDA REVIEW
University of Central Florida, English Dept.
P.O. Box 161348, Orlando, FL 32816. 407-823-2038.
Web site: http://pegasus.cc.ucf.edu/~english/floridareview/home.htm. Bi-annual. $6/$10. Circ.: 1,000. Pat Rushin, Editor. **Description:** Mainstream and experimental fiction, nonfiction, and poetry, to 10,000 words. **Queries:** Not necessary. **E-Queries:** Yes. **Unsolicited mss:** Accepts. **Response:** 2 weeks (queries), 1-2 months (submissions), SASE required. **Rights:** 1st. **Payment:** In copies. **Contact:** Terry Hess.

FLYWAY LITERARY REVIEW
206 Ross Hall, Iowa State University, Ames, IA 50011.
E-mail: flyway@iastate.edu.
Web site: www.engl.iastate.edu/publications/flyway/homepage.html. Tri-annual. $18/year. Circ.: 500. Stephen Pett, Editor. **Description:** Quality poetry, nonfiction, and fiction by new and established writers. **Fiction:** Literary fiction; up to 20 pages. **Nonfiction:** Personal essays; up to 20 pages. **Poetry:** Ambitious; "open to all poetry that takes its experience seriously, including humorous poems." **Art:** "We are always looking for cover art. Send slides or photos of work." **Queries:** Not necessary. **E-Queries:** No. **Unsolicited mss:** Accepts. **Response:** 2 weeks, SASE. **Freelance Content:** 90%. **Rights:** One-time. **Payment:** In copies.

THE FOLIATE OAK
University of Arkansas, Arts and Humanities, Monticello, AR 71656. 870-460-1247. E-mail: foliateoak@uamont.edu. Web site: www.uamont.edu/foliateoak/index.html. Monthly. Diane Payne, Faculty Advisor. **Description:** Literary journal for new and established writers. Accepts submissions electronically September-May. **Fiction:** No genre, racist, homophobic, maudlin writing. Please keep under 3,500 words. **Nonfiction:** Creative nonfiction under 3,500 words. **Poetry:** Submit up to 5 poems. **E-queries:** Yes. **Response:** 1 month. **Payment:** In copies.

FOLIO
American University, Dept. of Literature, Washington, DC 20016.
Bi-annual. $12/year. Circ.: 500. Rotating Editors. **Description:** Quality fiction and poetry. **Fiction:** Up to 10 pages. **Nonfiction:** Creative nonfiction and memoirs; up to 10 pages. **Poetry:** Up to 5 poems. **Art:** B&W photos, slides. **Tips:** Submissions read September-March 15. **Queries:** Not necessary. **E-Queries:** No. **Unsolicited**

mss: Accepts. **Response:** Submissions 2-6 months, SASE required. **Freelance Content:** 90%. **Payment:** In copies.

THE FORMALIST
320 Hunter Dr., Evansville, IN 47711.
$14 (2 issues). William Baer, Editor. **Description:** Publishes metrical poetry in contemporary idiom, using meter and traditional poetic conventions in vigorous and interesting ways. Especially interested in sonnets, couplets, tercets, ballads, the French forms etc. Does not accept haiku, sestinas, or syllabic verse of any kind. Does not have interest in any kind of erotica, blasphemy, vulgarity, or racism. Does not consider simultaneous submissions or previously published work. Submit 3-5 poems at one time. **Tips:** Offers Howard Nemerov Sonnet Award, $1,000. **Queries:** Not necessary. **Response:** 8 weeks, SASE. **Payment:** In copies.

FOURTEEN HILLS
San Francisco State University, Creative Writing Dept.
1600 Holloway Ave., San Francisco, CA 94132-1722. 415-338-3083.
E-mail: hills@sfsu.edu. Biannual. $7/issue, $12/yr. Circ.: 600. Julian Kudritzki, Editor-in-Chief. **Description:** Innovative fiction, poetry, drama, and interviews. Seeking matter or styles overlooked by traditional journals. **Fiction:** Up to 5,000 words. **Poetry:** Submit up to 5 poems. **Queries:** Not necessary. **E-Queries:** No. **Unsolicited mss:** Accepts. **Response:** Queries 2 weeks, submissions up to 10 months. **Rights:** 1st NA. **Payment:** On publication, paid in copies.

FROGPOND
P.O. Box 2461, Winchester, VA 22604-1661. 540-722-2156.
E-mail: redmoon@shentel.net. Web site: www.octet.com. 3x/year. $28/yr (US). Circ.: 1,000. Jim Kacian, Editor. **Description:** Published by Haiku Society of America. **Nonfiction:** Articles, essays, and reviews. **Poetry:** The finest haiku and related forms; $1/poem. **Tips:** Know what is current in contemporary haiku. **E-Queries:** Yes. **Unsolicited mss:** Accepts. **Response:** 2-3 weeks, SASE. **Freelance Content:** 95%. **Rights:** 1st NA. **Payment:** On acceptance.

FUGUE
University of Idaho, English Dept., Brink Hall, Room 200, Moscow, ID 83844-1102.
E-mail: ronmcf@uidaho.edu. Web site: www.uidaho.edu/ls/eng/fugue. Semiannual. $6/$10. Circ.: 300. Scott McEachern, Managing Editor. **Description:** Dedicated to new voices and quality writing. **Fiction:** Well written, traditional as well as experimental; up to 6,000 words; $20. **Nonfiction:** Seeking creative nonfiction; up to 6,000 words; $20. **Poetry:** Any length and topic; submit up to 4 poems at a time; $10. **Art:** Seeking cover art; $50. **Tips:** Don't send more than one genre together. Avoid cliché or worn-out language. Looking for new, innovative, edgy pieces. **Queries:** Not necessary. **E-Queries:** No. **Unsolicited mss:** Accepts. **Response:** Queries 2 weeks, submissions 2-4 months, SASE required. **Freelance Content:** 20%. **Rights:** One-time, reverts with credit. **Payment:** On publication.

FUTURES MYSTERIOUS ANTHOLOGY

3039 38th Ave. S, Minneapolis, MN 55406-2140. 612-724-4023.
E-mail: babs@suspenseunlimited.net. Web site: www.futuresforstorylovers.com.
Quarterly. Circ.: 2,000. Barbara (Babs) Lakey, Owner/Publisher. **Description:** "Short Tales for Story Lovers" (short fiction, primarily mystery and its subgenres). Seeking writers with verve and imagination from the seasoned to the new for Starting Line. **Fiction:** No query needed; short fiction, 500-8,000 words. **Art:** Illustrators and cartoons always needed. **Tips:** Check guidelines on Web site before submitting. **Queries:** Preferred. **Freelance Content:** 99%.

THE GEORGIA REVIEW

University of Georgia, Athens, GA 30602-9009. 706-542-3481.
E-mail: garev@uga.edu. Web site: www.uga.edu/garev. Quarterly. $9/issue. Circ.: 5,500. T. R. Hummer, Editor. **Description:** An eclectic blend of essays, fiction, poetry, graphics, and book reviews. **Fiction:** Short stories, no novel excerpts. Pays $40/printed page. **Nonfiction:** Essays, no book chapters; $40/page. **Poetry:** $3/line. **Art:** Cover plus 8-page interior portfolio, each issue; $450 for the 9 images. **Tips:** Does not accept unsolicited manuscripts during June, July, and August. See Web site for submission guidelines and published excerpts. Review past content before submitting manuscript. **Queries:** Preferred. **E-Queries:** No. **Unsolicited mss:** Does not accept. **Response:** Queries 1-2 weeks, submissions 1-3 months, SASE required. **Freelance Content:** 80%. **Payment:** On publication.

GETTYSBURG REVIEW

Gettysburg College, Gettysburg, PA 17325. 717-337-6770.
Web site: www.gettysburgreview.com. Quarterly. $6/$24. Circ.: 3,500. Peter Stitt, Editor. **Description:** Quality poetry, fiction, essays, essay reviews, and graphics by beginning and established writers and artists. **Fiction:** Literary fiction, fresh and surprising, including novel excerpts; 1,000-20,000 words; $25/printed page. **Nonfiction:** Varied (memoir, literary criticism, creative nonfiction, other); 3,000-7,000 words; $25/printed page. **Poetry:** All styles and forms; $2/line. **Queries:** Not necessary. **E-Queries:** No. **Unsolicited mss:** Accepts. **Response:** Queries 2-3 weeks, submissions 3-6 months, SASE required. **Freelance Content:** 100%. **Rights:** First North American serial. **Payment:** On publication. **Contact:** Mark Drew, Assistant Editor.

GLIMMER TRAIN STORIES

710 SW Madison St., Suite 504, Portland, OR 97205. 503-221-0836.
Quarterly. $9.95/$32. Circ.: 18,000. Linda Burmeister Davies, Editor. **Description:** Short stories by established and emerging writers—a feast of fiction. **Fiction:** Literary short stories; 1,200-8,000 words; $500/story. **Tips:** All stories to be submitted online at www.glimmertrain.com. **Queries:** Not necessary. **E-Queries:** No. **Unsolicited mss:** Accepts. **Response:** 3 months, SASE required. **Freelance Content:** 100%. **Rights:** First publication. **Payment:** On acceptance.

GLOBAL CITY REVIEW

Simon H. Rifkind Center for the Humanities, The City College of New York
138th St. & Convent Ave., New York, NY 10031. 212-650-7382.
E-mail: globalcityreview@aol.com. Web site: http://webdelsol.com/globalcityreview.
Biannual. Linsey Abrams, Editor. **Description:** Intellectual literary forum for
women, lesbian, and gay, and other culturally diverse writers; writers of color, international writers, activist writers. Thematic issues. Fiction, nonfiction, and poetry on
issues of race, gender, and women's experience. **Tips:** No queries; see Web site for
guidelines. **Payment:** In copies.

GRAIN

Saskatchewan Writers Guild
P.O. Box 67, Saskatoon, Saskatchewan S7K 3K1 Canada. 306-244-2828.
E-mail: grain@sasktel.net. Web site: www.skwriter.com. Quarterly. $7.95/$26.95.
Circ.: 1,500. Elizabeth Philips, Editor. **Description:** Canadian literary magazine;
fresh, startling, imaginative, and accessible. Often publishes new emerging writers,
and established writers from Canada and around the world. Pays $40-$175. **Fiction:**
Literary fiction in any style, well-crafted stories. No mainstream romance or histori-
cal fiction; up to 30 pages. **Nonfiction:** Creative nonfiction; up to 30 pages. **Poetry:**
Up to 8 poems. Avoid avant garde, but does publish work that pushes boundaries.
Favors thoughtful work that takes risks. **Tips:** Pay attention to a story's subtext.
Prefers imaginative fiction, even quirky. Original work only, no reprints. **Queries:**
Not necessary. **E-Queries:** No. **Unsolicited mss:** Accepts. **Response:** 1-3 months,
SASE (or give e-mail address). **Freelance Content:** 100%. **Rights:** 1st Canadian
serial. **Payment:** On publication, two copies.

GRAND STREET

214 Sullivan St., 6C, New York, NY 10012. 212-533-2944.
E-mail: info@grandstreet.com. Web site: www.grandstreet.com. Quarterly. Jean
Stein, Editor. **Description:** Art, fiction, nonfiction, and poetry. **Poetry:** Any length;
$3/line. **Queries:** Not necessary. **E-Queries:** No. **Unsolicited mss:** Does not
accept. **Response:** Queries 7 days, submissions 12-16 weeks, SASE. **Payment:** On
publication.

GRASSLANDS REVIEW

P.O. Box 626, Berea, OH 44017.
E-mail: grasslandsreview@aol.com.
Web site: www.hometown.aol.com/g/review/prof/index.htm. Semiannual. $12/yr.
Laura Kennelly, Editor. **Description:** Encourages new writers. Seeks "imagination
without sloppiness, ideas without lectures, and delight in language." Accepts manu-
scripts postmarked March or October only. **Fiction:** Short stories; 1,000-3,500 words.
Poetry: Any length. **Queries:** Not necessary. **Response:** SASE. **Payment:** In
copies.

GREEN MOUNTAINS REVIEW

Johnson State College, Johnson, VT 05656. 802-635-1350.
E-mail: gmr@badger.jsc.vsc.edu. Biannual. $7/$14. Circ.: 1,700. Neil Shepard/Tony Whedon, General Editor/Poetry Editor. **Description:** Poems, stories, and creative nonfiction by well-known and promising new authors. Also, interviews, literary criticism, and book reviews. **Fiction:** Wide range of styles and subjects; up to 30 pages. **Nonfiction:** Interviews with writers and literary essays; up to 30 pages. **Poetry:** Any type. **Art:** B&W photos. **Tips:** Publishes only 2% of submissions. Occasionally features special-theme issues. **Queries:** Not necessary. **E-Queries:** No. **Unsolicited mss:** Accepts. **Response:** 1 week-1 month, SASE. **Freelance Content:** 80%. **Rights:** FNASR. **Payment:** In copies.

THE GREENSBORO REVIEW

MFA Writing Program, Dept. of English
134 McIver Bldg., UNCG, P.O. Box 26170, Greensboro, NC 27402-6170.
E-mail: jlclark@uncg.edu. Web site: www.uncg.edu/eng/mfa/review/review.htm.
Semi-annual. $5/$10. Circ.: 800. Jim Clark, Editor. **Description:** Quality poetry and fiction. **Fiction:** Any theme, subject, or style; up to 7,500 words. **Poetry:** Varied. **Tips:** Original work only, no multiple submissions. **Queries:** Not necessary. **E-Queries:** No. **Unsolicited mss:** Accepts. **Rights:** FNASR. **Payment:** In copies.

GULF COAST

University of Houston, English Dept., Houston, TX 77204. 713-743-3223.
E-mail: gulfcoast@www.gulfcoast.uh.edu. Web site: www.gulfcoast.uh.edu.
Semiannual. $7. Circ.: 1,000. Pablo Peschiera, Editor. **Description:** A journal of literary fiction, nonfiction, poetry, and fine art. **Queries:** Not necessary. **E-Queries:** Yes. **Unsolicited mss:** Accepts. **Response:** 3-6 months, SASE.

HARP-STRINGS

P.O. Box 640387, Beverly Hills, FL 34464.
E-mail: verdure@digitalusa.net.
Web site: http://people.we.mediaone.net/dhalstead005/verdurepubs. Quarterly. $3.50/$12. Circ.: 105. Madelyn Eastlund, Editor. **Description:** Seeks poetry: narrative, lyrics, ballads, sestinas, rondeau redoubles, blank verse, villanelles, sonnets, prose poems, haiku sequences, etc. **Poetry:** Memorable, haunting, to be read again and again; 14-80 lines. **Tips:** No trite, broken prose masquerading as poetry; no confessions or raw-guts poems. No simultaneous submissions. Accepts e-mail submissions. Reads only in February, May, July, and November. **Queries:** Not necessary. **E-Queries:** Yes. **Unsolicited mss:** Accepts. **Response:** Within 1 week. **Freelance Content:** 100%. **Rights:** One-time and electronic. **Payment:** In copies.

HAWAI'I REVIEW

University of Hawaii, Dept. of English
1733 Donaggho Rd., Honolulu, HI 96822. 808-956-3030.
E-mail: hi-review@hawaii.edu. Web site: www.hawaii.edu/bop/hr.html. Bi-annual.

$10/issue. Circ.: 1,000. Michael Pulelua, Editor. **Description:** Literary poetry, fiction, nonfiction, and reviews. **Fiction:** Up to 20 pages. **Nonfiction:** Up to 20 pages. **Tips:** Submissions accepted year-round. **Queries:** Not necessary. **E-Queries:** Yes. **Unsolicited mss:** Accepts. **Response:** Queries 2-3 weeks submissions 3-6 months, SASE required. **Rights:** 1st NA.

HAYDEN'S FERRY REVIEW

Arizona State University, P.O. Box 871502, Tempe, AZ 85287-1502. 480-965-1243. E-mail: hfr@asu.edu. Web site: www.haydensferryreview.com. Biannual. $5/issue, $10/year. Circ.: 1,300. **Description:** Literary and art magazine featuring quality art, poetry, fiction, and creative nonfiction by new and established artists and writers. Pays $25/page ($100 max.) **Fiction:** Yes. **Nonfiction:** Yes. **Poetry:** Up to 6 poems. **Queries:** Not necessary. **Unsolicited mss:** Accepts. **Response:** Queries 1 week, submissions 8-12 weeks, SASE required. **Freelance Content:** 80%. **Rights:** NA serial. **Payment:** On publication. **Contact:** Poetry or Fiction Editor.

HEAVEN BONE

P.O. Box 486, Chester, NY 10918.
E-mail: heavenbone@aol.com. Annual. $10/issue. Circ.: 2,500. Steve Hirsch, Editor. **Description:** Publication featuring poetry, fiction, reviews, and artwork with emphasis on surreal, beat, experimental, and Buddhist concerns. **Fiction:** 2,500-10,000 words. **Nonfiction:** Essays on creativity, philosophy, and consciousness studies, relating to writing; 7,500 words. **Poetry:** Surreal, experimental, visual, neo-beat, and Buddhist imagery and themes. **Art:** Any digital or traditional format. **Tips:** Despite "Heaven" in title, this is not a religious publication. **Queries:** Preferred. **E-Queries:** Yes. **Unsolicited mss:** Accepts. **Response:** 3 weeks for queries, up to 1 year for submissions; SASE required. **Rights:** FNASR. **Payment:** In copies.

HIGH PLAINS LITERARY REVIEW

180 Adams St., Suite 250, Denver, CO 80206. 303-320-6828.
Tri-annual. $7.00. Circ.: 2,500. Robert O. Greer, Editor. **Description:** Publishes fiction, poetry, essays, reviews, and interviews. Seeks to bridge the gap between academic quarterlies and commercial reviews. **Fiction:** Yes; 3,000-6,500 word; $5/printed page. **Nonfiction:** Yes; $5/page. **Poetry:** Yes; $10/page. **Queries:** Preferred. **E-Queries:** No. **Unsolicited mss:** Accepts. **Response:** Submissions 6-12 weeks, SASE required. **Payment:** On publication. **Contact:** Kathy Hoernig, Editorial Assistant.

THE HOLLINS CRITIC

Hollins University, P.O. Box 9538, Roanoke, VA 24020. 540-362-6275.
E-mail: acockrell@hollins.edu. Web site: www.hollins.edu. 5x/year. $6/issue. Circ.: 500. R. H. W. Dillard, Editor. **Description:** Features an essay on a contemporary fiction writer, poet, or dramatist (cover sketch, brief biography, and book list). **Nonfiction:** Book reviews and poetry. Review poetry submissions from September-May only. Does accept unsolicited reviews; $25/poem, does not pay for book reviews.

Queries: Not necessary. **E-Queries:** No. **Unsolicited mss:** Accepts. **Response:** Submission 2 months, SASE required. **Freelance Content:** 100%. **Rights:** 1st, reverts following publication. **Payment:** On publication.

HUDSON REVIEW

684 Park Ave., New York, NY 10021. 212-650-0020.
Web site: www.hudsonreview.com. Quarterly. $8/$28. Circ.: 5,000. Paula Deitz, Editor. **Description:** Fiction, poetry, essays, book reviews; criticism of literature, art, theatre, dance, film, and music; and articles on contemporary culture. **Fiction:** Yes. **Nonfiction:** Yes. **Poetry:** Yes. **Queries:** Preferred. **E-Queries:** No. **Unsolicited mss:** Accepts. **Response:** 3 months, SASE. **Payment:** On publication.

HURRICANE ALICE

See page 366 for full listing.
Description: Articles that explore feminist issues on all aspects of culture.

THE ICONOCLAST

1675 Amazon Rd., Mohegan Lake, NY 10547.
Bimonthly. Circ.: 700. Phil Wagner, Editor. **Description:** For readers and writers of original work bypassed by corporate and institutional publications. **Fiction:** Literary stories, plots, and ideas with active characters engaged with the world; 100-3,500 words; $.01/word. **Nonfiction:** Nothing topical, fashionable, political, or academic; 100-3,500 words; $.01/word. **Poetry:** Well-crafted, with something to say; send 2-5 poems; up to 2 pages; $2-$5/poem. **Fillers:** Humor (nothing silly, self-consciously zany); 20-2,000 words; $.01/word. **Art:** Line drawings; pay varies. **Queries:** Not necessary. **Unsolicited mss:** Accepts. **Response:** Queries 1 week, submissions 1 month, SASE. **Freelance Content:** 90%. **Rights:** 1st, some one-time. **Payment:** On acceptance.

ILLYA'S HONEY

Dallas Poets Community
P.O. Box 700865, Dallas, TX 75370.
E-mail: dpcmail@dallaspoets.org. Web site: www.dallaspoets.org. Quarterly. $6/$18. Circ.: 150. Ann Howells, Wesley Hartman, Editors. **Description:** Mostly poetry, some micro-fiction. **Fiction:** Flash fiction, sharp, well-crafted; 200 words. **Poetry:** Any form, any subject; prefers free verse. **Queries:** Not necessary. **E-Queries:** No. **Unsolicited mss:** Accepts. **Response:** Submissions 4-6 months, SASE. **Freelance Content:** 98%. **Rights:** 1st NA. **Payment:** In copies.

INDIANA REVIEW

Indiana University
Ballantine Hall 465, 1020 E. Kirkwood Ave., Bloomington, IN 47405. 812-855-3439.
Web site: www.indiana.edu/~interview/ir.html. Semi-annual. $8/sample copy, $14/year. Circ.: 2,000. Shannon Gibney, Editor. **Description:** Publication for both emerging and established writers. Features quality writing within a wide aesthetic.

Fiction: Daring stories which integrate theme, language, character, and form, with consequence beyond the world of its narrator; up to 40 pages. **Nonfiction:** Lively essays on engaging topics. Interviews with established writers and book reviews; up to 30 pages; $5/page and copies. **Poetry:** Intelligent form and language, with risk, ambition, and scope. **Queries:** Not necessary. **E-Queries:** Yes. **Unsolicited mss:** Accepts. **Response:** 1 week to queries, submissions 2-3 months, SASE required. **Freelance Content:** 90%. **Rights:** FNASR. **Payment:** On publication. **Contact:** Poetry or Fiction Editor.

INTERIM
University of Nevada, Dept. of English, Las Vegas, NV 89154-5034.
Annual. Claudia Keelan, Editor. **Description:** Poetry, fiction, essays, and book reviews. **Fiction:** to 7,500 words. **Poetry:** Any form or length. **Response:** 3 weeks. **Payment:** In copies.

INTERNATIONAL POETRY REVIEW
University of North Carolina, Dept. of Romance Languages
P.O. Box 26170, Greensboro, NC 27402-6170.
Biannually. $12/$20$30. Circ.: 200. Kathleen Koestler, Editor. **Description:** Features work that crosses language barriers to present the voices of poets in different countries. **Nonfiction:** Book reviews, interviews, and short essays; to 1,500 words. **Poetry:** Original English poems and contemporary translations from other languages. **Tips:** Prefers material with cross-cultural or international dimension. **Queries:** Preferred. **Unsolicited mss:** Accepts. **Payment:** In copies.

IOWA REVIEW
University of Iowa, 308 EPB, Iowa City, IA 52242. 319-335-0462.
E-mail: iowa-review@uiowa.edu. Web site: www.uiowa.edu/~iareview. Tri-annual. $7.95/issue, $20/year. Circ.: 3,000. David Hamilton, Editor. **Description:** Essays, poems, stories, reviews. Strives to discover new writers; to be local but not provincial; experimental at times, but not without a respect for tradition. **Fiction:** Short stories; any length; $10/printed page. **Nonfiction:** Essays, reviews; any length; $10/printed page. **Poetry:** any length; $20/printed page. **Queries:** Not necessary. **E-Queries:** Accepts. **Unsolicited mss:** Accepts. **Response:** 1-3 months, SASE required. **Freelance Content:** 98%. **Rights:** FNASR. **Payment:** On publication.

THE IRISH EDITION
See page 368 for full listing.
Description: Short fiction, nonfiction, fillers, humor, and puzzles, for Irish-American and Irish-born readers.

JAMES WHITE REVIEW
See page 400 for full listing.
Description: Gay men's literary magazine, with fiction, poetry, photography, art, essays, and reviews.

JOURNAL OF NEW JERSEY POETS
The Center for Teaching Excellence, County College of Morris
214 Center Grove Rd., Randolph, NJ 07869-2086. 973-328-5471.
E-mail: szulauf@ccm.edu.
Web site: www.ccm.edu/humanities/humanities/journal/html. Irregular. $5/issue, $10/2 issues, $16/4 issues. Circ.: 900. Sander Zulauf, Editor. **Description:** Regional poetry magazine dedicated to the works of poets and artists who live or have lived in New Jersey. **Nonfiction:** Essays on poetry and book reviews on new work by New Jersey poets; up to 1,500 words. **Poetry:** Send up to 3 poems at a time (no epics). **Tips:** New Jersey not required as subject matter; seeks work universal in scope. **Queries:** Not necessary. **E-Queries:** No. **Unsolicited mss:** Accepts. **Response:** Queries 2 weeks, submissions 6 months-1 year, SASE. **Freelance Content:** 100%. **Rights:** FNASR. **Payment:** In copies.

KALEIDOSCOPE
United Disability Services
701 S Main St., Akron, OH 44311-1019. 330-762-9755.
E-mail: mshiplett@udsakron.org. Web site: www.udsakron.org. Semi-annual. Circ.: 1,000. Darshan Perusek, Ph.D., Editor-in-Chief. **Description:** Explores the experience of disability through literature and fine arts, from the perspective of individuals, families, health-care professionals, and society. Seeks to challenge and overcome stereotypical, patronizing, sentimental attitudes about disability. Pay $25 and 2 copies. **Fiction:** Character-centered stories, not action pieces. No romance; 5,000 words max. **Nonfiction:** Narratives and articles on experiences and issues of disability; 5,000 words max. **Poetry:** Free verse on disability or written by someone with a disability. Also, short nature poems and light humor; 1-5 poems. **Art:** 35mm color, B&W 8x10 glossy; up to $100. **Tips:** Photos a plus. **Queries:** Not necessary. **E-Queries:** Yes. **Unsolicited mss:** Accepts. **Response:** Queries 2 weeks, submissions 6 months, SASE required. **Freelance Content:** 60%. **Rights:** 1st serial rights. **Payment:** On publication.

KALLIOPE
Florida Community College at Jacksonville
3939 Roosevelt Blvd., Jacksonville, FL 32205. 904-381-3511.
Web site: www.fccj.org/kalliope. Semiannual. $16/yr. Circ.: 1,600. Mary Sue Koeppel, Editor. **Description:** Journal of women's literature and art with poetry, short fiction, interviews, reviews, and visual art by women. **Fiction:** Well-constructed literary work; 2,000 words. **Nonfiction:** Interviews with writers and/or artists; 200-2,000 words. **Poetry:** 3-4 pages. **Art:** Fine art, slides, or glossies. **Queries:** Not necessary. **E-Queries:** No. **Unsolicited mss:** Accepts. **Response:** Queries 1-3 weeks, submissions 3-6 months, SASE. **Freelance Content:** 100%. **Rights:** 1st. **Payment:** In copies.

KARAMU
Eastern Illinois University, English Dept., Charleston, IL 61920. 217-581-6297.
Annual. $7.50. Circ.: 500. Olga Abella, Editor. **Description:** Publishes poetry, fiction,

and essays. **Fiction:** Stories that capture something essential about life, beyond the superficial, and develop genuine voices; 3,500 words. **Nonfiction:** Any subject with the exception of religion and politics; 3,500 words. **Poetry:** Yes. **Tips:** Avoid rhyming poetry or didactic prose. **Queries:** Preferred. **E-Queries:** No. **Unsolicited mss:** Accepts. **Response:** Queries 2-3 days, submissions 4-6 months, SASE required. **Freelance Content:** 100%. **Rights:** One-time. **Payment:** In copies.

KARITOS REVIEW

N4714 Skinner Hollow Rd., Monroe, WI 53566.
E-mail: editor@karitos.com. Web site: www.karitos.com. Annual. $3. Circ.: 250. Chris Wave, Managing Editor. **Description:** Literary magazine with fiction, essays, and poetry. Send 3 submissions only. **Queries:** Not necessary. **E-Queries:** Yes. **Unsolicited mss:** Accepts.

KELSEY REVIEW

Mercer County Community College
P.O. Box B, Trenton, NJ 08690. 609-586-4800 x3326.
E-mail: kelsey.review@mccc.edu. Web site: www.mccc.edu. Annual. Free. Circ.: 1,750. Robin Schore, Editor. **Description:** Literary journal exclusively for writers living or working in Mercer Country, N.J. Fiction, essays, poetry, and line art. **Fiction:** 2,000 words. **Nonfiction:** 2,000 words. **Poetry:** Up to 6 poems. **Art:** B&W line art. **Queries:** Not necessary. **Unsolicited mss:** Accepts. **Response:** Deadline May 1. Responds by June 30. **Freelance Content:** 100%. **Rights:** None. **Payment:** In copies.

THE KENYON REVIEW

102 College Dr., Gambier, OH 43022-9623. 740-427-5208.
E-mail: kenyonreview@kenyon.edu. Web site: www.kenyonreview.org. 3 issues/year. $8/issue. $12 for double summer/fall issue. Circ.: 5,000. Tom Bigalow, Managing Editor. **Description:** Features new writing from emerging and established writers. **Fiction:** Up to 7,500 words; $10/page. **Nonfiction:** Creative nonfiction, interviews, reviews; up to 7,500 words; $10/page. **Poetry:** Up to 10 pages; $15/page. **Art:** Photos; B&W; $100. **Queries:** Not necessary. **E-Queries:** No. **Unsolicited mss:** Accepts. **Response:** 1-2 months for queries, 3-4 months for submissions; SASE required. **Freelance Content:** 90%. **Rights:** First. **Payment:** On publication. **Contact:** David H. Lynn, Editor.

KIMERA

N 1316 Hollis St., Spokane, WA 99201. 509-326-6641.
E-mail: editor@js.spokane.wa.us. Web site: http://js.spokane.wa.us/kimera. Annual. $10/yr. Circ.: 300. Jan Strever, Editor. **Description:** For fine writing, in print and online. Uses John Locke's premise,"Where is the head with no chimeras?" **Fiction:** That plays with language, has a strong sense of itself; no erotica. **Poetry:** No "message" poems. **Queries:** Not necessary. **E-Queries:** Accepts. **Unsolicited mss:** Accepts. **Response:** 3 months, SASE. **Freelance Content:** 100%. **Rights:** 1st, electronic. **Payment:** In copies.

THE KIT-CAT REVIEW

244 Halstead Ave., Harrison, NY 10528. 914-835-4833.
Quarterly. $7/$25. Circ.: 500. Claudia Fletcher. **Description:** Seeks excellence and originality. **Fiction:** E.g., "The Heisenberg Approach," a fictional excerpt from Werner Heisenberg's diary; up to 5,000 words, prefers shorter. **Nonfiction:** "Wishing for Miracles: Tijuana Interviews," a piece about life in modern-day Tijuana; up to 6,000 words, prefer shorter. **Poetry:** All types and lengths, except greeting card or deliberately obscure. **Tips:** Avoid O. Henry-type endings. No excessive vulgarity or profanity. Send $7 for sample copy, payable to Claudia Fletcher. **Queries:** Not necessary. **E-Queries:** No. **Unsolicited mss:** Accepts. **Response:** Queries 2 weeks, submissions 1 month, SASE. **Freelance Content:** 100%. **Rights:** 1st, one-time. **Payment:** On acceptance.

THE LARCOM REVIEW

P.O. Box 161, Prides Crossing, MA 01965. 978-927-8707.
E-mail: amp@larcompress.com. Web site: www.larcompress.com. Semi-annual. $12/$20. Circ.: 300. Susan Oleksiw, Editor. **Description:** Contemporary short fiction, poetry, and essays about New England life written by residents of this region and those who live outside. **Fiction:** Stories range from pieces on family life to suspense mystery fiction, from short-shorts to longer tales to be savored over an evening; 3,000 words; $25. **Nonfiction:** Entertaining, accessible essays and articles. Interviews and book reviews assigned. Pay negotiable; 3,000 words; $25. **Art:** Prints, slides, illustrations, and B&W art; $25. **Tips:** Seeking stories on all aspects of life in 6 states, including stories by New Englanders living elsewhere. Don't submit fiction and nonfiction together. **Queries:** Not necessary. **E-Queries:** No. **Unsolicited mss:** Accepts. **Response:** Submission 3-4 months, SASE. **Rights:** 1st NA. **Payment:** On publication.

THE LEDGE

78-44 80th St., Glendale, NY 11385.
Annual. $7/issue. Circ.: 1,000. Timothy Monaghan, Editor. **Description:** Seeks exceptional contemporary poetry. No restrictions on style or form. **Poetry:** up to 80 lines; pay in copies. **Queries:** Not necessary. **E-Queries:** No. **Unsolicited mss:** Accepts. **Response:** Queries 2-3 weeks, submissions 3 months, SASE. **Freelance Content:** 100%. **Rights:** FNASR. **Payment:** On publication.

LIGHT

Box 7500, Chicago, IL 60680. 847-853-1028.
Web site: www.lightquarterly.com. Quarterly. $5/$18. Circ.: 1,000. John Mella, Editor. **Description:** Devoted exclusively to light verse. **Nonfiction:** Reviews, essays. **Poetry:** Yes. **Tips:** Think James Thurber, E. B.White, Ogden Nash, etc. If it has wit, point, edge, or barb, it has a home here. **Queries:** Preferred. **E-Queries:** No. **Unsolicited mss:** Accepts. **Response:** Queries 1-4 months. **Payment:** 2 copies of issue work appeared in.

LIMESTONE CIRCLE
P.O. Box 453, Ashburn, VA 20146.
E-mail: renjef@earthlink.net. Biannual. $8/year. Circ.: 100. Renee Carter Hall, Editor. **Description:** Poetry and artwork journal. **Poetry:** Well-crafted, accessible poetry; prefers free verse, traditional, and oriental forms; 1-2 pages. **Art:** B&W artwork, photography; all styles/subjects considered. **Tips:** Seeking poems using ordinary experiences to subtly reflect extraordinary concepts; poems that use vivid images, not abstract generalizations; accessible works, subtle and deep without being obscure and difficult. **Queries:** Not necessary. **E-Queries:** Yes. **Unsolicited mss:** Accepts. **Response:** 2-8 weeks; SASE required. **Freelance Content:** 100%. **Rights:** First. **Payment:** In copies.

LITERAL LATTE
61 E Eighth St., Suite 240, New York, NY 10003.
E-mail: litlatte@aol.com. Web site: www.literal-latte.com. Bimonthly. $3/$11. Circ.: 25,000. Jenine Gordon Bockman, Editor. **Description:** Mind-stimulating literary journal brimming with stories, poetry, essays, and art. **Fiction:** Varied styles; the word is as important as the tale; 6,000 words. **Nonfiction:** Personal essays, all topics; thematic book reviews done as personal essays; 6,000 words. **Poetry:** All styles; 2,000 word max. **Fillers:** Intelligent literary cartoons. **Art:** Photocopies or slides (of photos, drawings, paintings, B&W or color). Open to styles, abstraction to photorealism. **Tips:** Looking for new talent. Annual Fiction and Poetry Awards ($1,500 in prizes for each). **Queries:** Not necessary. **E-Queries:** Accepts. **Unsolicited mss:** Accepts. **Rights:** FNASR. **Payment:** On publication.

LITERARY MAGAZINE REVIEW
University of Northern Iowa, Dept. of English Language and Literature
117 Baker Hall, Cedar Falls, IA 50614-0502. 319-273-2821.
E-mail: grant.tracey@uni.edu. Quarterly. Circ.: 500. Grant Tracey, Editor. **Description:** For writers and readers of contemporary literature. **Nonfiction:** Reviews and articles concerning literary magazines; 1,000-1,500 words. **Queries:** Required. **Payment:** In copies.

THE LITERARY REVIEW
Fairleigh Dickinson University
Mail Code M-GH2-02, 285 Madison Ave., Madison, NJ 07940. 973-443-8564.
E-mail: tlr@fdu.edu. Web site: www.theliteraryreview.org. Quarterly. $5/issue. Circ.: 2,000. Rene Steinke, editor. **Description:** International journal of poetry, fiction, essays, and contemporary review essays. **Fiction:** Any length. **Nonfiction:** Essays on contemporary literature, short reviews; any length. **Poetry:** Up to five poems; any length. **Tips:** Submissions are read only between September 1 and June 1. **Queries:** Not necessary. **E-Queries:** Yes. **Unsolicited mss:** Accepts. **Response:** 1 week for queries, 8-12 weeks for submissions; SASE required. **Rights:** FNAR. **Payment:** In copies.

LOLLIPOP
See page 333 for full listing.
Description: Fiction, essays, and "edgy" commentary on music and youth culture.

LONG SHOT
P.O. Box 6238, Hoboken, NJ 07030.
Web site: www.longshot.org. Semiannual. $8/issue, $24/2 yr. (4 issues). Circ.: 1,500. Editorial Board. **Description:** Features raw, graphic, exuberant poetry devoid of pretense. **Fiction:** To 10 pages. **Nonfiction:** To 10 pages. **Poetry:** To 8 pages. **Art:** B&W photos, drawings. **Queries:** Not necessary. **E-Queries:** No. **Unsolicited mss:** Accepts. **Response:** 8-12 weeks, SASE. **Freelance Content:** 20%. **Payment:** In copies.

THE LONG STORY
18 Eaton St., Lawrence, MA 01843. 978-686-7638.
E-mail: rpbtls@aol. Web site: www.longstorymagazine.com. $6/issue. Circ.: 1,000. R. P. Burnham, Editor. **Description:** Stories about common folk. **Fiction:** Stories with a moral/thematic core, particularly about poor and working-class people. 8,000-12,000 words (occasionally to 20,000). **Queries:** Not necessary. **E-Queries:** No. **Unsolicited mss:** Accepts. **Response:** 2 months, SASE. **Freelance Content:** 95%. **Rights:** 1st NA. **Payment:** In copies.

LONZIE'S FRIED CHICKEN LITERARY
P.O. Box 189, Lynn, NC 28750.
E-mail: lonziesfriedchicken@teleplex.net. Web site: www.lonziesfriedchicken.com. Semi-annual. $9.95/$17.95. E. H. Goree, Editor. **Description:** Accessible southern fiction and poetry. **Fiction:** Accessible, with a feel for the South; 10 pages or less. **Poetry:** Accessible, with southern themes; 40 lines. **Tips:** Contributors include "those who have always lived in the south, those trying to come home to the south, and those who have just driven through it." **Queries:** Not necessary. **E-Queries:** No. **Unsolicited mss:** Accepts. **Response:** Queries 1 week, submissions 3-6 months, SASE. **Freelance Content:** 100%. **Rights:** 1st, one-time anthology. **Payment:** In copies.

LSR
P.O. Box 440195, Miami, FL 33144. 305-447-3780.
E-mail: ejc@lspress.net. 2x/yr. $6. Circ.: 3,000. Nilda Cepero, Editor/Publisher. **Description:** Publishes poetry, book reviews, interviews, and line artwork. **Nonfiction:** Book reviews or interviews, to 750 words. **Poetry:** Submit up to 4 poems, 5-45 lines each. Style, subject matter, and content open, but prefers contemporary with meaning and message. No pornographic, religious, or surreal poetry. **Art:** Line artwork; submit up to 5 illustrations on 3.5-inch disk (to be printed 6 x 6 inches on cover, 8 x 10 on full-page inside). **Tips:** Cover letter required, include SASE and bio. "Read as many current poetry magazines as you can." **Queries:** Not necessary. **E-Queries:** No. **Unsolicited mss:** Accepts. **Response:** 9 months, SASE required. **Freelance Content:** 100%. **Rights:** 1st. **Payment:** 2 copies.

THE LUCID STONE

P.O. Box 940, Scottsdale, AZ 85252-0940.

Quarterly. $6/$16. Circ.: 200. Pauline Mounsey, Editor. **Description:** Literary journal that seeks to place quality poetry in every nook and cranny of sentient life. **Poetry:** Any length. **Art:** B&W or color photos; photos of paintings; pen-and-ink drawings. **Tips:** Appreciates a good sonnet as much as a free-verse poem. **Queries:** Not necessary. **Unsolicited mss:** Accepts. **Response:** 3-4 months, SASE. **Freelance Content:** 100%. **Rights:** 1st. **Payment:** In copies.

LYNX EYE

Scribblefest Literary Group

542 Mitchell Dr., Los Osos, CA 93402. 805-528-8146.

E-mail: pamccully@aol.com. Quarterly. $7.95/$25. Circ.: 500. Pam McCully, Editor. **Description:** Features stories, poetry, essays, and B&W artwork in both familiar and experimental formats. **Fiction:** Short stories, vignettes, novel excerpts, one-act plays, belle letters, and satires; 500-5,000 words; $10/piece and copies. **Nonfiction:** Essays only; 500-5,000 words. **Poetry:** 30 lines. **Art:** B&W drawings only. **Tips:** Avoid memoirs and autobiographical pieces. **Queries:** Not necessary. **E-Queries:** No. **Unsolicited mss:** Accepts. **Response:** 12 weeks, SASE. **Freelance Content:** 100%. **Rights:** FNASR. **Payment:** On acceptance.

MALAHAT REVIEW

University of Victoria

P.O. Box 1700, Stn CSC, Victoria, British Columbia V8W 2Y2 Canada. 250-721-8524. E-mail: malahat@uvic.ca. Web site: www.web.uvic.ca/malahat. Quarterly. $10/$30, Canadian. Circ.: 1,000. Marlene Cookshaw, Editor. **Description:** Short fiction, nonfiction, poetry, and reviews of Canadian fiction or books of poetry. Seeks balance of views and styles by established and new writers. Pays $30/page. **Queries:** Not necessary. **E-Queries:** Yes. **Unsolicited mss:** Accepts. **Response:** Up to 3 months, SASE. **Freelance Content:** 100%. **Rights:** 1st worldwide. **Payment:** On acceptance.

MANOA

University of Hawaii Press, English Dept.

1733 Donaghho Rd, Honolulu, HI 96822. 808-956-3070.

E-mail: fstewart@hawaii.edu. Web site: www.hawaii.edu/mjournal. Semiannual. Circ.: 2,500. Frank Stewart, Editor. **Description:** A Pacific journal of international fiction and poetry. **Fiction:** To 30 pages; $20-$25/page. **Nonfiction:** Essays, to 25 pages; book reviews (4-5 pages, pays $50). **Poetry:** Submit 4-6 poems; $50. **Tips:** Does not accept submissions by e-mail or in any other electronic forms. **Queries:** Preferred. **E-Queries:** No. **Payment:** On publication.

MANY MOUNTAINS MOVING

420 22nd St., Boulder, CO 80302. 303-545-9942.

E-mail: mmm@mmminc.org. Web site: www.mmminc.org. 6x/year. $4/$18. Circ.:

1,500. Naomi Horii, Editor. **Description:** Literary journal of diverse contemporary voices, from diverse cultural backgrounds. No payment. **Fiction:** to 20,000 words. **Nonfiction:** To 20,000 words. **Poetry:** Submit 3-10 poems at a time; any length. **Art:** Hard copies. **Tips:** Only interested in excellent quality work. Accepts unsolicited material May-August only. Contact for upcoming themes. **Queries:** Not necessary. **E-Queries:** No. **Unsolicited mss:** Accepts. **Response:** Submissions 4 months, SASE. **Freelance Content:** 100%. **Rights:** 1st NA.

THE MARLBORO REVIEW

P.O. Box 243, Marlboro, VT 05344.
Web site: www.marlbororeview.com. Biannual. Ellen Dudley, Editor. **Description:** Literary journal of poetry, fiction, essays, translations, reviews, and interviews. **Fiction:** up to 30 pages. **Nonfiction:** Literary/personal essays only; up to 30 pages. **Poetry:** Any length. **Art:** For cover; film or camera-ready. **Tips:** Interested in cultural, philosophical, and scientific issues as seen from the writer's perspective. **Queries:** Not necessary. **E-Queries:** Yes. **Unsolicited mss:** Accepts. **Response:** Queries 1 month, submissions to 3 months, SASE. **Freelance Content:** 80%. **Rights:** 1st. **Payment:** On publication, in copies only.

THE MASSACHUSETTS REVIEW

University of Massachusetts, South College
Amherst, MA 01003-9934. 413-545-2689.
E-mail: massrev@external.umass.edu. Web site: www.massreview.org. Quarterly. Editorial Board. **Description:** Literary publication for writers of fiction, nonfiction, and poetry. **Fiction:** Short fiction; 15-25 pages; $50. **Nonfiction:** Essays, translations, interviews; $50. **Poetry:** $.35/line ($10 min.). **Art:** Photos. **Tips:** Reviews material October 1-June 1. **Response:** SASE. **Payment:** On publication.

MICHIGAN QUARTERLY REVIEW

University of Michigan, 3032 Rackham Bldg., Ann Arbor, MI 48109-1070.
Web site: www.umich.edu/~mqr. Laurence Goldstein, Editor. **Description:** Scholarly essays and creative nonfiction on all subjects. Also publishes fiction and poetry. Pays $8 a page. Send $3.50 and two first-class stamps for sample copy. **Tips:** Annual contest for authors published in the journal. **Payment:** On publication.

MID-AMERICA POETRY REVIEW

P.O. Box 575, Warrensburg, MO 64093-0575. 660-747-4602.
3x/year. $6/$15. Robert C. Jones, Editor. **Description:** Poetry to 36 lines. **Tips:** First-time accepted poets receive complimentary one year subscription. **Queries:** Not necessary. **E-Queries:** Yes. **Unsolicited mss:** Accepts. **Response:** 2-4 weeks, SASE required. **Freelance Content:** 100%. **Rights:** 1st NA (reverts to author after 6 months). **Payment:** 2 copies plus $5 per accepted poem.

MIDSTREAM
See page 338 for full listing.
Description: Zionist publication with content on political U.S. and Israel culture, literature, book reviews, religion, and poetry.

MINDPRINTS
Allan Hancock College, Learning Assistance Program
800 South College Dr., Santa Maria, CA 93454-6399. 805-922-6966 ext. 3274.
E-mail: pafahey@hancock.cc.ca.us. Annual. $6. Circ.: 500. Paul Fahey, Editor.
Description: Literary journal of short fiction, memoirs, poetry, and art for writers and artists with disabilities and those with an interest in this field. Showcases a variety of talent from this diverse population. **Fiction:** Short-short fiction, flash fiction; 250-750 words. **Nonfiction:** Short memoir, creative nonfiction (often disability-related); 250-750 words. **Poetry:** Rhymed and prose; up to 35 lines. **Art:** B&W photos and artwork. **Tips:** Submit SASE for reply and/or for return of artwork or manuscript. Accept simultaneous submissions and reprints. All entries must include cover letter stating the author's reason for submitting to *Mindprints*, a one paragraph biography, and a list of previous publications (if applicable). **Queries:** Not necessary. **E-Queries:** Yes. **Unsolicited mss:** Accepts. **Response:** Queries 1 week, submissions 3 months, SASE. **Rights:** one-time rights. **Payment:** In copies.

THE MINNESOTA REVIEW
University of Missouri, Dept. of English
110 Tate Hall, Columbia, MO 65211. 573-882-3059.
E-mail: williamsjeff@missouri.edu. Semiannual. $12.50/yr. Circ.: 1,300. Jeffrey Williams, Editor. **Description:** A journal of committed writing, progressive in nature, committed to socialist and feminist writing. (Note: does not have a Minnesota focus; was founded there, but later moved and kept name.) **Fiction:** Political, experimental; up to 5,000 words. **Nonfiction:** Essays, reviews. **Poetry:** Political; 1-10 pages. **Tips:** Many issues organized around a special topic. **Queries:** Not necessary. **E-Queries:** No. **Unsolicited mss:** Accepts. **Response:** Queries 2-4 weeks, submissions 4-6 weeks, SASE required. **Freelance Content:** 100%. **Rights:** FNASR. **Payment:** In copies.

THE MIRACULOUS MEDAL
475 E Chelten Ave., Philadelphia, PA 19144-5785. 215-848-1010.
Quarterly. William J. O'Brien, C.M., Editor. **Description:** Religious literary journal focusing on the Catholic Church. **Fiction:** Any subject matter which does not not contradict teachings of Roman Catholic Church; 1,000-2,400; $.02/word. **Poetry:** Religious, preferably about Blessed Virgin Mary; 20 lines; $.50/line. **Tips:** Original material only. **Queries:** Preferred. **E-Queries:** No. **Response:** 6 months, SASE. **Freelance Content:** 25%. **Rights:** 1st NA. **Payment:** On acceptance.

MISSISSIPPI REVIEW

University of Southern Mississippi, Center for Writers
Southern Sta., Box 5144, Hattiesburg, MS 39406-5144. 601-266-4321.
E-mail: rief@netdoor.com. Web site: www.mississippireview.com. Frederick
Barthelme, Editor. **Description:** Literary journal, poetry and fiction. **Tips:** Annual
fiction/poetry competition; deadline, May 31. Pays $1,000 for each winning story
and poem.

THE MISSOURI REVIEW

University of Missouri-Columbia
1507 Hillcrest Hall, Columbia, MO 65211. 573-882-4474.
Tri-annual. $7.95/$22. Circ.: 6,000. Speer Morgan, Editor. **Description:** Literary
magazine with contemporary fiction, poetry, interviews, and personal essays. **Fiction:**
Yes. **Nonfiction:** Essays, book reviews, and interviews. **Poetry:** 6-14 pages of poetry
by 3-5 poets each issue; pays $125-$500. **Queries:** Not necessary. **E-Queries:** No.
Response: Submissions 6-8 weeks, SASE. **Freelance Content:** 90%. **Rights:** All;
revert to author. **Payment:** On publication.

MODERN HAIKU

P.O. Box 1752, Madison, WI 53701. 608-233-2738.
3 issues/year. $20/year. Circ.: 780. Robert Spiess, Editor. **Description:** International
journal of English-language haiku and translations, book reviews, articles, and essays.
Nonfiction: Articles and essays related to haiku; $5/page. **Poetry:** Haiku and senryu;
$1/poem. **Tips:** No sentimental, pretty-pretty, or pseudo-Japanese work. Write about
what you actually experience, not about an exotic, imaginary place. Juxtaposition of
disparate perceptions that form a harmony is desirable. **Queries:** Not necessary.
E-Queries: No. **Unsolicited mss:** Accepts. **Response:** 2 days for queries, 2 weeks
for submissions; SASE required. **Freelance Content:** 90%. **Rights:** FNASR.

NATURAL BRIDGE

University of Missouri-St. Louis, Dept. of English
8001 Natural Bridge Rd., St. Louis, MO 63121-4499. 314-516-5517.
E-mail: natural@jinx.umsl.edu. Web site: www.umsl.edu/~natural. Biannual. David
Carkeet, Editor. **Description:** Literary short fiction, personal essays, poetry, and
poetry translations. **Tips:** Submission periods are July 1 to August 31, and November
1 to December 31. Simultaneous submissions accepted. **Payment:** In copies.

NEBO

Arkansas Tech University, Dept. of English, Russellville, AR 72801-2222.
E-mail: michael.ritchie@mail.atu.edu. Biannual. $10/annual. Circ.: 100. Michael
Ritchie, Editor. **Description:** Publishes fiction and poetry. Prefers new writers.
Fiction: Experimental short fiction, realistic fiction; up to 2,000 words. **Poetry:**
Formal, metered verse; experimental free verse. **Queries:** Not necessary.
E-Queries: No. **Unsolicited mss:** Accepts. **Response:** Up to 3 months, SASE.
Rights: 1st. **Payment:** In copies.

NEBRASKA REVIEW

University of Nebraska-Omaha
Writer's Workshop, FAB 212, Omaha, NE 68182-0324. 402-554-3159.
E-mail: jreed@unomaha.edu. Bi-annual. $8/$15. Circ.: 1,000. James Reed, Editor.
Description: Contemporary fiction, poetry, and creative nonfiction. **Fiction:** Literary mainstream; 7,500 words. **Nonfiction:** Creative nonfiction and personal essays; 7,500 words. **Poetry:** Contemporary, literary; 5-6 pages max. **Tips:** Eclectic tastes, professional, non-dogmatic; in fiction, seeking strong voices. **Queries:** Not necessary. **E-Queries:** No. **Unsolicited mss:** Accepts. **Response:** Submissions 3-6 months, SASE. **Freelance Content:** 100%. **Rights:** 1st NA. **Payment:** In copies.

NEW AUTHOR'S JOURNAL

1542 Tibbits Ave., Troy, NY 12180. 518-274-2648.
Quarterly. $3.75/issue. Mario V. Farina, Editor. **Description:** Literary journal of short stories and poetry for new authors previously unpublished. **Fiction:** Short stories, up to 2,000 words. **Nonfiction:** Topical nonfiction, up to 2,000 words. **Tips:** Manuscripts read year-round. **Queries:** Not necessary. **Unsolicited mss:** Accepts. **Response:** SASE. **Rights:** Author retains all rights. **Payment:** In copies.

NEW DELTA REVIEW

Louisiana State University
15 Allen Hall, Dept. of English, Baton Rouge, LA 70803. 225-578-4079.
Web site: http://english.lsu.edu/journals/ndr. Semiannual. $7/$12. Circ.: 500. Nat Hardy and Joe Scallorns, Editors. **Description:** Literary journal, focusing especially on work of new and established writers. **Fiction:** Quality stories that compel readers to continue reading; 6,000. **Nonfiction:** Creative nonfiction, interviews, reviews, no academic essays; 5,000. **Poetry:** Submit up to 4 poems, any length; translations. **Art:** Cover art and 8 color slides of artwork (mostly paintings, but will consider all visual media); Slides. **Queries:** Not necessary. **E-Queries:** No. **Unsolicited mss:** Accepts. **Response:** Queries 1 week, submissions 3 months, SASE required. **Freelance Content:** 95%. **Rights:** 1st NA and Internet. **Payment:** In copies.

NEW ENGLAND REVIEW

Middlebury College, Middlebury, VT 05753. 802-443-5075.
E-mail: nereview@middlebury.edu. Web site: www.middlebury.edu/~nereview.
Quarterly. $7.00. Circ.: 2,000. Stephen Donadio, Editor. **Description:** Short stories, short-shorts, novellas, and excerpts from novels. Also, long and short poems, interpretive and personal essays, book reviews, critical reassessments, and letters from abroad. **Fiction:** 10,000 words; $10/page. **Nonfiction:** Exploration of all forms of contemporary cultural expression; 10,000 words; $10/page. **Poetry:** submit up to 6 poems; any length; $10/page, $20 min. **Queries:** Not necessary. **E-Queries:** No. **Unsolicited mss:** Accepts. **Response:** Queries 2 weeks, submissions 12 weeks, SASE. **Payment:** On publication.

NEW ENGLAND WRITERS NETWORK

P.O. Box 483, Hudson, MA 01749-0483.

E-mail: newnmag@aol.com. Web site: www.newnmag.net. $20/yr. Glenda Baker, Editor-in-Chief. **Description:** Literary journal with fiction, nonfiction, and poetry. **Fiction:** Short stories, novel excerpts, to 2,000 words. All genres; no pornography or excessive violence; pays $10. **Nonfiction:** Personal, humorous essays, to 1,000 words; pays $5. **Poetry:** Upbeat, positive, to 32 lines. Pays $3. **Tips:** June-August reading period. **Queries:** Not necessary. **E-Queries:** No. **Unsolicited mss:** Accepts. **Payment:** On publication.

NEW LAUREL REVIEW

828 Lesseps St., New Orleans, LA 70117. 504-947-6001.

Annual. $10. Lee Meitzen Grue, Fiction Editor. **Description:** Literary journal of poetry, essays, short fiction, poetry translations. **Fiction:** 10 pages or less. **Poetry:** Yes. **Tips:** No clichés, slick fiction, or inspirational verse. **Queries:** Not necessary. **E-Queries:** No. **Unsolicited mss:** Accepts. **Response:** Submissions 1-3 months, SASE. **Freelance Content:** 98%. **Rights:** 1st. **Payment:** In copies. **Contact:** Andy Young, Poetry Editor.

NEW LETTERS

University of Missouri-Kansas City, University House

5101 Rockhill Rd., Kansas City, MO 64110-2499. 816-235-1168.

E-mail: newletters@umkc.edu. Web site: www.iml.umkc.edu/newletters. Quarterly. $5/$17. Circ.: 6,000. James McKinley, Editor-in-Chief. **Description:** Poetry, fiction, art, and essays with fresh, sophisticated writing created by people who have read widely and who have lived interesting lives. **Fiction:** Any style, subject, or genre; 5,000 words max. **Nonfiction:** Essays, profiles; 5,000 words max. **Poetry:** Submit 3-6 poems. **Art:** Prints. **Tips:** Also offers annual literary contest for writers of poetry, fiction, and nonfiction. Deadline Mid-May. Entry fee $10. **Queries:** Not necessary. **E-Queries:** No. **Unsolicited mss:** Accepts. **Response:** 3 months, SASE. **Freelance Content:** 50%. **Rights:** 1st. **Payment:** On publication. **Contact:** Aleatha Ezra, Assistant Managing Editor.

THE NEW YORKER

The New Yorker, Inc.

4 Times Square, New York, NY 10036. 212-286-5900.

E-mail: themail@newyorker.com. Web site: www.newyorker.com. Weekly. $3.50/issue. Circ.: 851,000. **Description:** Covers the vital stories of our time with intelligence, wit, stylish prose, and a keen eye. **Fiction:** Short stories, humor, and satire. **Nonfiction:** Amusing mistakes in newspapers, books, magazines, etc. Factual and biographical articles for Profiles, Reporter at Large, etc. Political/social essays, 1,000 words. **Poetry:** Quality poetry. **Queries:** Not necessary. **E-Queries:** No. **Unsolicited mss:** Accepts. **Payment:** On publication. **Contact:** Perri Dorset.

NEXUS

Wright State University, W016A Student Union, Dayton, OH 45435. 937-775-5533. E-mail: nexus_magazine@hotmail.com. 3x/year. $7/year. Mindy Cooper, Editor. **Description:** Journal of poetry, fiction, and artwork for Wright State community, also poetry, artwork, and photography from around the world. **Fiction:** Strong, innovative fiction on human condition (short, flash fiction). **Poetry:** Essays, interviews; 1-2 pages. **Art:** B&W, compatible. **Tips:** Include brief cover letter with submissions, describing submission, previous publication, and a brief bio. **Queries:** Preferred. **E-Queries:** Yes. **Unsolicited mss:** Accepts. **Response:** 2 weeks, SASE. **Freelance Content:** 50%. **Payment:** In copies.

NIMROD INTERNATIONAL JOURNAL

University of Tulsa, 600 S College Ave., Tulsa, OK 74104-3189. 918-631-3080. E-mail: nimrod@utulsa.edu. Web site: www.utulsa.edu/nimrod. Semi-annual. $17.50/yr. Circ.: 3,000. Dr. Francine Ringold, Editor. **Description:** Quality prose and fiction by emerging writers of contemporary literature. **Fiction:** Quality fiction (no genre fiction), vigorous writing with believable characters and dialogue; 7,500 words max. **Nonfiction:** Vivid essays related to annual theme; 7,500 words max. **Poetry:** 1,900 words max. **Queries:** Not necessary. **E-Queries:** Yes. **Unsolicited mss:** Accepts. **Response:** Submissions 6-8 weeks, SASE. **Freelance Content:** 100%. **Rights:** 1st. **Payment:** In copies.

96 INC.

P.O. Box 15559, Boston, MA 02215. 617-267-0543. E-mail: to96inc@ici.net. Annual. $5/issue $15/membership to receive all mailings. Circ.: 3,000. Gold, Anderson, Mehegan, Editors. **Description:** Dedicated to publishing new voices and integrating established and novice writers. **Fiction:** All types. No restrictions on style or subject; up to 3,000 words. **Nonfiction:** Stories with useful information for other writers (new publishers, etc.); 2,500 words. **Queries:** Preferred. **E-Queries:** No. **Unsolicited mss:** Accepts. **Response:** 6 months-1 year, SASE. **Rights:** One-time. **Payment:** In copies. **Contact:** Vera Gold.

NO EXPERIENCE REQUIRED

P.O. Box 131032, The Woodlands, TX 77393-1032. E-mail: nerzine@yahoo.com. 3x/year. $5/$15. Circ.: 300. **Description:** Small literary magazine for new and undiscovered writers. **Fiction:** All genres; 2,500 words. **Poetry:** All forms; 60 lines. **Art:** Publishes in B&W. Art must be no smaller than 5x7, and no larger than 9 x 12. **Tips:** Make sure submissions are free of major spelling/grammar errors. No pornography. **Queries:** Not necessary. **E-Queries:** No. **Response:** 6 months, SASE. **Freelance Content:** 100%. **Rights:** 1st, one-time. **Payment:** In copies.

THE NORTH AMERICAN REVIEW

University of Northern Iowa
1222 W 27th St., Cedar Falls, IA 50614-0516. 319-273-6455.

E-mail: nar@uni.edu. Web site: webdelsol.com/NorthAmReview/NAR/. Bimonthly. $22/yr. Vince Gotera, Editor. **Description:** Poetry, fiction, nonfiction, and art on contemporary North American concerns and issues, especially environment, gender, race, ethnicity, and class. **Fiction:** Literary realism, multicultural, or experimental; up to 12,000 words; $20-$100. **Nonfiction:** Creative nonfiction, journals and diaries, letters, memoirs, profiles; nature, travel, and science writing; also literary journalism and essays; up to 12,000 words; $20-$100. **Poetry:** Traditional or experimental, formal or free verse (closed or open form); length varies; $20-$100. **Tips:** Likes stories with strong narrative arc and sense of humor, where characters act on the world, are responsible for their decisions, make mistakes. **Queries:** Not necessary. **E-Queries:** Yes. **Unsolicited mss:** Accepts. **Response:** 3 months submissions, SASE. **Freelance Content:** 80%. **Rights:** FNASR. **Payment:** On publication.

NORTH CAROLINA LITERARY REVIEW

East Carolina University, English Dept.
The Bate Building, Greenville, NC 27858-4353. 252-328-1537.
E-mail: bauerm@mail.edu.edu. Web site: www.ecu.edu/nclr. Annual. Circ.: 750.
Description: By and about North Carolina writers. Covers North Carolina history, culture, and literature. Mostly nonfiction, accepts some poetry and fiction by North Carolina writers. Pays $50/story or illustration. **Tips:** Sample copies $15. **Queries:** Not necessary. **Response:** 3 months. **Rights:** 1st NA. **Payment:** On publication.

NORTH DAKOTA QUARTERLY

University of North Dakota, Grand Forks, ND 58202-7209. 701-777-3322.
E-mail: ndq@sage.und.nodak.edu. Web site: www.und.nodak.edu/org/ndq/. Quarterly. $8/sample, $12/special issue. Circ.: 500-700. Robert W. Lewis, Editor. **Description:** Publishes fiction, nonfiction, poetry, and criticism, often from unique perspective of the Northern Plains. **Fiction:** Yes. **Nonfiction:** Yes. **Poetry:** Yes. **Tips:** Send $8 for sample. **Queries:** Not necessary. **E-Queries:** Yes. **Unsolicited mss:** Accepts. **Response:** Queries 2-4 weeks, submissions 2-4 months, SASE. **Freelance Content:** 90%. **Rights:** 1st serial. **Payment:** In copies.

NORTHWEST REVIEW

University of Oregon, 369 PLC, Eugene, OR 97403. 541-346-3957.
E-mail: jwitte@oregon.uoregon.edu. Web site: www.darkwing.uoregon.edu. 3x/year. $7/$20. Circ.: 1,000. John Witte, Editor. **Description:** The oldest literary journal west of the Mississippi, this publication offers a forum for talented emerging young writers. **Fiction:** All lengths. **Nonfiction:** Eclectic commentary and essays. **Poetry:** All lengths. **Queries:** Not necessary. **E-Queries:** No. **Unsolicited mss:** Accepts. **Response:** Queries immediately, submissions 8-10 weeks, SASE. **Freelance Content:** 100%. **Rights:** 1st NA serial. **Payment:** In copies.

NOTRE DAME REVIEW

University of Notre Dame, English Dept.
Creative Writing Program, Notre Dame, IN 46556.

Web site: www.nd.edu/nndr/review.htm. Bi-annual. $8/$15. Circ.: 2,000. Steve Tomasula, Senior Editor. **Description:** Literary magazine. **Fiction:** Any length. **Nonfiction:** Long and short reviews by assignment; query first. **Poetry:** Any length. **Queries:** Not necessary. **E-Queries:** No. **Unsolicited mss:** Accepts. **Response:** Queries 1 month, submissions 3-5 months, SASE. **Freelance Content:** 60%. **Rights:** 1st serial. **Payment:** On publication.

OASIS

P.O. Box 626, Largo, FL 33779-0626. 727-345-8505.
E-mail: oasislit@aol.com. Quarterly. $25/yr. Circ.: 300. Neal Storrs, Editor. **Description:** Stories and poetry, some nonfiction. **Fiction:** Style paramount, powerfully original; the style should seem to be the subject; any length. **Poetry:** Free verse with a distinct, subtle music. No old-fashioned rhymes or rhythms. **Queries:** Not necessary. **E-Queries:** Yes. **Unsolicited mss:** Accepts. **Response:** Submissions same day, SASE required. **Freelance Content:** 95%. **Rights:** 1st.

OFFERINGS

P.O. Box 1667, Lebanon, MO 65536.
Quarterly. $5/$16. Circ.: 75. Velvet Fackeldey, Editor. **Description:** Quality poetry, all forms. 30 lines max. **Tips:** Overstocked with nature poetry. **Queries:** Not necessary. **E-Queries:** No. **Unsolicited mss:** Accepts. **Response:** 4-6 weeks, SASE. **Freelance Content:** 100%. **Rights:** 1st. **Payment:** No payment.

THE OLD RED KIMONO

Floyd College, Humanities Division, P.O. Box 1864, Rome, GA 30162.
E-mail: napplega@mail.fc.peachnet.edu. Annual. $3. Circ.: 1,400. Erskine Thompson, Charles Swearinger, Editors. **Description:** Poems and short stories of all types. Fiction should be 1,500 words or less. **Tips:** Local writers constitute 50% of journal. Sponsors annual Paris Lake Poetry Contest. **Queries:** Not necessary. **E-Queries:** Yes. **Unsolicited mss:** Accepts. **Response:** 8 weeks, SASE. **Freelance Content:** 100%. **Rights:** 1st. **Payment:** On publication. Pays 2 copies.

OSIRIS

P.O. Box 297, Deerfield, MA 01342. 413-774-4027.
Semiannual. $7.50/issue. Circ.: 1,000. Andrea Moorhead, Editor. **Description:** A multilingual, international poetry journal. Features contemporary, foreign poetry in original language (English and French are the principle languages of this journal). Other works appear in original language with facing-page translation in English. **Poetry:** Length varies. **Tips:** Seeking poetry that is well-crafted, non-narrative, and lyrical. Translators need to secure permission of both poet and publisher. **Queries:** Not necessary. **E-Queries:** No. **Unsolicited mss:** Accepts. **Response:** Submissions 4-8 weeks, SASE required. **Freelance Content:** 30%. **Payment:** In copies.

OTHER VOICES

University of Illinois-Chicago, Dept. of English (M/C 162)
601 S Morgan St., Chicago, IL 60607. 312-413-2209.
E-mail: othervoices@listserv.uic.edu. Web site: www.othervoicesmagazine.org.
Semiannual. $7/issue. Circ.: 1,500. Editorial Board. **Description:** Literary journal.
Fiction: Literary short stories, novel excerpts, one-act plays; traditional or experimental; no genre fiction; up to 7,500 words. **Nonfiction:** Book reviews, interviews with esteemed fiction writers. **Tips:** Accepts manuscripts only between October 1 and April 1. **Queries:** Not necessary. **E-Queries:** No. **Unsolicited mss:** Accepts. **Response:** 3 months; SASE required. **Freelance Content:** 100%. **Rights:** First serial. **Payment:** In copies.

THE OXFORD AMERICAN

P.O. Box 1156, Oxford, MS 38655. 662-236-1836.
Web site: www.oxfordamericanmag.com. $24.95. Circ.: 45,000. Marc Smirnoff, Editor. **Description:** "The Southern Magazine of Good Writing." General-interest magazine with literary bent that explores the American South. **Fiction:** Length, pay varies. **Nonfiction:** Varies. **Poetry:** $125/poem. **Fillers:** Cartoons. **Tips:** "Writers should always learn a little bit about the homes where their writing ends up." "Writers should only send their beloved work to magazines to which they feel a special kinship." **Queries:** Not necessary. **E-Queries:** No. **Unsolicited mss:** Accepts. **Response:** Queries varies, submissions up to 3 months, SASE. **Freelance Content:** 50%. **Rights:** FNASR. **Payment:** On publication.

OYSTER BOY REVIEW

P.O.Box 77842, San Francisco, CA 94107-0842.
E-mail: editors@oysterboyreview.com. Web site: www.oysterboyreview.com.
Quarterly. Damon Sauve, Publisher. **Description:** Literary magazine, in print and online, features the underrated, ignored, misunderstood, and varietal. Authors may submit works of fiction or poetry; 2 submissions per year only. No simultaneous submissions or previously published work, include SASE. **Queries:** Not necessary. **E-Queries:** Yes. **Unsolicited mss:** Accepts. **Response:** 1-2 months. **Rights:** 1st serial. **Payment:** In copies.

PAINTBRUSH

Truman State University, Language & Literature Division
Kirksville, MO 63501. 660-785-4185.
Web site: www.paintbrush.org. Annual. $15/year. Circ.: 500. Ben Bennani, Editor.
Description: International journal of poetry and translation. **Poetry:** Serious, original, highly imaginative work; include a cover letter; 3-5 poems. **Tips:** Sponsors $2,000 Ezra Pound Poetry Award. **Queries:** Preferred. **E-Queries:** Yes. **Unsolicited mss:** Accepts. **Response:** Up to 10 weeks; SASE required. **Freelance Content:** 60%. **Rights:** FNAR. **Payment:** In copies.

PAINTED BRIDE QUARTERLY

Rutgers University, English Dept., ATG Hall, Camden, NJ 08102. 856-225-6129. E-mail: pbq.camden.rutgers.edu.

Web site: www.webdelsol.com/pbq or www.pbq.rutgers.edu. Annual anthology. $15/yr. Circ.: 1,500. Marion Wrenn, Editor. **Description:** Literary journal of fiction and poetry, in print and online. **Fiction:** Yes. **Nonfiction:** Yes. **Poetry:** Length varies. **Queries:** Not necessary. **Unsolicited mss:** Accepts. **Response:** Submissions to 3 months, SASE. **Freelance Content:** 100%. **Rights:** 1st. **Payment:** On publication.

PALO ALTO REVIEW

Palo Alto College, 1400 W Villaret, San Antonio, TX 78224-2499. 210-921-5017. E-mail: emshull@aol.com. Semi-annual. $5.00. Circ.: 500. Ellen Shull, Editor. **Description:** Fiction and articles, 5,000 words, on varied historical, geographical, scientific, mathematical, artistic, political, and social topics. **Fiction:** No experimental or excessively avant-garde fiction. **Nonfiction:** Original,unpublished articles and interviews. **Poetry:** Submit 3-5 poems; to 50 lines. **Columns, Departments:** Food for Thought (200-word think pieces); reviews, to 500 words, of books, films, videos, or software. **Art:** Photo essays welcome. **Tips:** A "journal of ideas." Send SASE for upcoming themes **Payment:** In copies.

PANGOLIN PAPERS

P.O. Box 241, Nordland, WA 98358. 360-385-3626. E-mail: trtlbluf@olympus.net. Tri-annual. $7.95/$20. Circ.: 400. Pat Britt, Editor. **Description:** Literary short stories. **Fiction:** Up to 8,000 words. **Tips:** No poetry, genre fiction, or essays. **Queries:** Not necessary. **E-Queries:** No. **Unsolicited mss:** Accepts. **Response:** Submissions 3 months, SASE required. **Rights:** 1st NA. **Payment:** In copies.

THE PARIS REVIEW

541 E 72nd St., New York, NY 10021. 212-861-0016. E-mail: queries@theparisreview.com. Web site: www.parisreview.com. Quarterly. $12/$40. Circ.: 12,000. George Plimpton, Editor. **Description:** International literary quarterly, with fiction, poetry, interviews, essays, and features from established and emerging writers and artists. **Fiction:** High literary quality. **Poetry:** Varied formats. **Fillers:** Humor. **Art:** Slides, drawings, copies. **Tips:** Annual prizes, in several categories, up to $1,000. **Queries:** Not necessary. **E-Queries:** Yes. **Unsolicited mss:** Accepts. **Response:** Queries 2-3 weeks, submissions 3-4 months, SASE. **Freelance Content:** 75%. **Rights:** 1st NA. **Payment:** On publication.

PARNASSUS

205 W 89th St., Apt. 8F, New York, NY 10024-1835. 212-362-3492. E-mail: parnew@aol.com. Web site: www.parnassuspoetry.com. Semi-annual. $12-$15. Circ.: 2,500. Herbert Leibowitz, Editor. **Description:** For in-depth analysis of contemporary books of poetry. **Nonfiction:** Critical essays and reviews on contemporary poetry. No academic or theoretical work, looks for criticism that is colorful,

idiosyncratic, well-written; 20 pages; $150. **Poetry:** Mostly by request; $25/page. **Queries:** Not necessary. **E-Queries:** Yes. **Unsolicited mss:** Accepts. **Response:** Submissions, usually in 2 months, SASE. **Freelance Content:** 100%. **Rights:** All, reverts to author. **Payment:** On publication.

PARTING GIFTS

3413 Wilshire, Greensboro, NC 27408.

Web site: http://users.aol.com/marchst. Semi-annual. $9. Robert Bixby, Editor. **Description:** Literary journal. **Fiction:** 500-1,000 words. **Poetry:** Up to 50 lines. **Tips:** Manuscripts read January-June. **Queries:** Not necessary. **E-Queries:** Yes. **Unsolicited mss:** Accepts. **Response:** Queries same day, submissions in 1 week, SASE. **Freelance Content:** 100%. **Rights:** 1st NA. **Payment:** In copies.

PARTISAN REVIEW

Boston University, 236 Bay State Rd., Boston, MA 02215. 617-353-4260.

E-mail: partisan@bu.edu. Web site: www.partisanreview.org. Quarterly. $7/$25. Circ.: 8,000. William Phillips, Editor-in-Chief. **Description:** Influential American literary and cultural journal, home to many fine writers. **Fiction:** Yes. **Poetry:** Yes. **Queries:** Preferred. **E-Queries:** No. **Unsolicited mss:** Accepts. **Response:** 4-8 weeks, SASE. **Payment:** On publication.

PASSAGES NORTH

Northern Michigan University, Dept. of English

Gries Hall, 1401 Presque Isle Ave., Marquette, MI 49855. 906-227-1203.

E-mail: passages@nmu.edu. Web site: http://vm.nmu.edu/passages. Annual. $13. Circ.: 1,000. Kate Hanson, Editor. **Description:** Literary fiction, poetry, and nonfiction, for established and emerging writers. **Fiction:** Short stories; no genre fiction; up to 5,000 words. **Nonfiction:** Interviews, essays, literary nonfiction; up to 5,000 words. **Poetry:** Up to 6 poems; up to 100 lines. **Tips:** Submissions read only from September 1 to May 1. **Queries:** Not necessary. **E-Queries:** No. **Unsolicited mss:** Accepts. **Response:** 6-8 weeks; SASE required. **Freelance Content:** 95%. **Rights:** FNAR. **Payment:** In copies.

PATERSON LITERARY REVIEW

Poetry Center at Passaic County Community College

1 College Blvd., Paterson, NJ 07505-1179. 973-684-6555.

E-mail: mgillan@pccc.cc.nj.us. Web site: www.pccc.cc.nj.us/poetry. Annual. $10. Circ.: 1,000. Maria Mazziotti Gillan, Editor. **Description:** Literary publication of poetry, fiction, book reviews, articles, and artwork. **Fiction:** 1,500 words. **Nonfiction:** 1,000 words. **Poetry:** 100-line limit. **Queries:** Not necessary. **E-Queries:** No. **Unsolicited mss:** Accepts. **Response:** Submissions 6 months, SASE required. **Freelance Content:** 100%. **Rights:** 1st.

PEARL

3030 E Second St., Long Beach, CA 90803. 562-434-4523.
E-mail: mjohn5150@aol.com. Web site: www.pearlmag.com. Bi-annual. $8/$18.
Circ.: 700. Marilyn Johnson, Joan Jobe Smith, Editors. **Description:** Contemporary
poetry and short fiction. **Fiction:** Accessible humanistic fiction, related to real life.
Ironic, serious, and intense, humor and wit welcome; 1,200 words. **Poetry:**
Humanistic; 40 lines or less. **Art:** Camera-ready B&W. **Queries:** Not necessary.
E-Queries: Yes. **Unsolicited mss:** Accepts. **Response:** Queries 1 week, submis-
sions 6-8 weeks,SASE. **Freelance Content:** 100%. **Rights:** 1st NA. **Payment:** In
copies.

PEREGRINE

P.O. Box 1076, Amherst, MA 01004. 413-253-3307.
E-mail: awapress@aol.com. Web site: www.amherstwriters.com. Annual. $12. Circ.:
1,000. Pat Schneider, Editor. **Description:** Features poetry, fiction, and personal
essays. **Fiction:** All styles, forms, and subjects; 3,000 words. **Nonfiction:** Short per-
sonal essays; to 1,500 words. **Poetry:** No greeting-card verse; 70 lines (3-5 poems).
Queries: Not necessary. **E-Queries:** No. **Unsolicited mss:** Accepts. **Response:**
Submissions 2-3 months, SASE. **Payment:** On publication. **Contact:** Nancy Rose,
Managing Editor.

PERMAFROST

University of Alaska–Fairbanks, English Dept.
P.O. Box 75720, Fairbanks, AK 99775-0640. 907-474-5398.
Web site: www.uaf.edu/english/permafrost. Annual. $8/issue. **Description:**
International literary journal for the arts. Fiction, nonfiction, poetry, and artwork of
emerging and established writers and artists. **Fiction:** to 30 pages; avoid genre fiction
(horror, sci-fi, fantasy). **Nonfiction:** To 30 pages. **Poetry:** up to 5 poems. **Art:** Yes.
Tips: Alaskan themes not essential. Reading period is September-March 15.
Queries: Not necessary. **E-Queries:** No. **Unsolicited mss:** Accepts. **Response:** 3
months, SASE. **Rights:** 1st. **Payment:** In copies.

THE PIKEVILLE REVIEW

Humanities Division, Pikeville College
147 Sycamore St., Pikeville, KY 41501. 606-218-5002.
E-mail: eward@pc.edu. Web site: www.pc.edu. Annual. $4. Circ.: 500. Elgin M.
Ward, Editor. **Description:** Contemporary fiction, poetry, creative essays, and book
reviews, for Kentucky writers and others. **Nonfiction:** Creative essays, book reviews.
Poetry: Contemporary. **Tips:** Open to new and unpublished writers. **Queries:** Not
necessary. **E-Queries:** Yes. **Unsolicited mss:** Accepts. **Response:** Queries 2 weeks,
submissions 30-60 days, SASE. **Payment:** On publication.

THE PLASTIC TOWER

P.O. Box 702, Bowie, MD 20718.
E-mail: rscottk@aol.com. Quarterly. $2.50/$8. Circ.: 250. Roger Kyle-Keith, Carol

Dyer, Editors. **Description:** Fun, irreverent, but serious about bringing enjoyable poetry to the public. **Nonfiction:** Reviews of literary and poetry magazines; 100 words. **Poetry:** Eclectic, all types of poetry, from sonnets to free verse to limericks; 40 lines max. **Art:** 10-15 small B&W illustrations per issue. **Tips:** Develop a fresh and unique voice, and you will eventually prevail. **Queries:** Not necessary. **E-Queries:** No. **Unsolicited mss:** Does not accept. **Response:** Queries 1 month, submissions to 6 months, SASE. **Freelance Content:** 80%. **Rights:** 1st NA. **Payment:** In copies. **Contact:** Roger Kyle-Keith.

PLEIADES

Central Missouri State University, Dept. of English
Warrensburg, MO 64093. 660-543-8106.
E-mail: kdp8106@cmsu2.cmsu.edu.
Web site: www.cmsu.edu/englphil/pleiades.html. 2x/year. $6/$12. Circ.: 3,000. R. M. Kinder, Kevin Prufer, and Susan Steinberg, Editors. **Description:** Traditional and experimental poetry, fiction, criticism, translations, and reviews. Cross-genre especially welcome. **Fiction:** Up to 10,000 words. **Nonfiction:** Up to 10,000 words; $10 and subscription. **Poetry:** Any length; pays $3 or copies. **Tips:** Considers simultaneous submissions. **E-Queries:** No. **Unsolicited mss:** Accepts. **Response:** Queries 1 month, submissions 2 months, SASE. **Freelance Content:** 85%. **Rights:** 1st serial, reprint online and in anthology. **Payment:** On publication.

PLOUGHSHARES

Emerson College, 120 Boylston St., Boston, MA 02116-4624. 617-824-8753.
E-mail: pshares@emerson.edu. Web site: www.pshares.org. 3x/year. $9.95/issue. Circ.: 6,000. Don Lee, Editor. **Description:** Publishes compelling fiction and poetry. Each issue is guest-edited by a prominent writer. **Fiction:** Pays $25/printed page ($50 min., $250 max.); to 30 pages. **Poetry:** Send 1-3 poems; $25/printed page. **Tips:** No genre work, or unsolicited book reviews, or criticism. Reviews submissions postmarked August 1-March 31 during these months. All other submissions received April-July are returned unread. **Queries:** Not necessary. **E-Queries:** No. **Unsolicited mss:** Accepts. **Response:** 3-5 months, SASE required. **Rights:** 1st serial. **Payment:** On publication.

POEM

Univerity of Alabama-Huntsville, English Dept.
Huntsville, AL 35899. 256-824-2379.
Semi-annual. $20. Circ.: 400. Nancy Frey Dillard, Editor. **Description:** Publishes serious lyric poetry. **Poetry:** Well-crafted, free verse. No light verse; "prose" poems; shaped, "visual" or "conceptual" poetry; or other avant-garde verse; 3-5 poems. **Tips:** Submit brief lyric poems only, with verbal and dramatic tension, that transpire from the particular to the universal. **Queries:** Preferred. **E-Queries:** No. **Unsolicited mss:** Accepts. **Response:** Queries 1 week, submissions 1 month, SASE. **Rights:** 1st. **Payment:** In copies.

POETRY

60 W Walton St., Chicago, IL 60610. 303-255-3703.
E-mail: poetry@poetrymagazine.org. Web site: www.poetrymagazine.org. Monthly.
$3.75/issue. Circ.: 10,000. Joseph Parisi, Editor. **Description:** Literary journal for
poetry, by poets famous and new. **Poetry:** Any length; $2/line. **Queries:** Not neces-
sary. **E-Queries:** No. **Unsolicited mss:** Accepts. **Response:** 4 months, SASE.
Freelance Content: 100%. **Payment:** On publication.

PORTLAND REVIEW

Portland State University
P.O. Box 751, Portland, OR 97207.
Web site: www.portlandreview.org. Tri-annual. $7/issue. Haley Hach, Editor.
Description: Short fiction, poetry, and art by both celebrated and unknown contrib-
utors. **Fiction:** Short fiction and essays. **Nonfiction:** Reviews. **Poetry:** Yes.
Queries: Not necessary.

POTOMAC REVIEW

Montgomery College, Paul Peck Humanities Institute
51 Mannakee St., Rockville, MD 20850. 301-251-7417.
Web site: www.meral.com/potomac. Semi-annual. $10/$15. Circ.: 1,500. Eli Flam,
Editor. **Description:** Regionally rooted, with a conscience, a lurking sense of humor,
and a strong environmental/nature bent. **Fiction:** Vivid, with ethical depth and in
Flannery O'Connor's words "the vision to go with it"; 3,000 words. **Nonfiction:** 3,000
words. **Poetry:** That educates, challenges, or diverts in fresh ways; up to 3 poems, 5
pages. **Art:** B&W photos, drawings, and prints. Query first. **Tips:** Contact for upcoming themes. **Queries:** Not necessary. **E-Queries:** No. **Unsolicited mss:** Accepts.
Response: Submissions 2-3 months, SASE. **Freelance Content:** 75%. **Rights:** 1st
NA. **Payment:** In copies.

POTPOURRI

P.O. Box 8278, Prairie Village, KS 66208. 913-642-1503.
E-mail: editor@potpourri.org. Web site: www.potpourri.org. Quarterly. $6.95/$16.
Circ.: 3,000. Polly W. Swafford, Editor. **Description:** A modern literary journal, falls
between serious academic journals and glitzy commercial publications. **Fiction:**
Broad genres; no racist, sexist material; 3,500 words. **Nonfiction:** Essays with literary theme. Travel with a cultural theme; 2,500 words. **Poetry:** 75 lines. **Fillers:** Light,
humorous stories with fully developed plots. **Art:** B&W line drawings. **Tips:** Seeks to
promote work reflecting a culturally diverse society. **Queries:** Not necessary.
E-Queries: Yes. **Unsolicited mss:** Accepts. **Response:** Queries 3 weeks, submissions 3 months, SASE. **Freelance Content:** 80%. **Rights:** 1st NA. **Payment:** In
copies.

THE PRAIRIE JOURNAL OF CANADIAN LITERATURE

P.O. Box 61203, Brentwood Post Office, Calgary, AB T2L 2K6 Canada.
E-mail: prairiejournal@yahoo.com. Web site: www.geocities.com/prairiejournal/.

Semiannual. $4/issue. Circ.: 600. A. Burke, Editor. **Description:** Devoted to new, previously unpublished writing. **Fiction:** Literary; any length, pay varies. **Nonfiction:** Essays, reviews, and interviews on Canadian subjects. **Poetry:** Any length. **Art:** B&W photos. **Tips:** No simultaneous submissions. **Queries:** Not necessary. **E-Queries:** No. **Unsolicited mss:** Accepts. **Response:** 2-3 months, SASE (no U.S. stamps). **Freelance Content:** 100%. **Payment:** On publication.

PRAIRIE SCHOONER
University of Nebraska
P.O. Box 880334, 201 Andrews Hall, Lincoln, NE 68588-0334. 402-472-0911.
E-mail: eflanagan2@unl.edu. Web site: www.unl.edu/schooner/psmain.htm. Quarterly. $9/$26. Circ.: 3,000. Hilda Raz, Editor. **Description:** Contemporary poetry, fiction, essay, and reviews. **Fiction:** Short stories; 18-25 pages. **Nonfiction:** Essays, book reviews, translations; 15-25 pages. **Poetry:** Submit 5-7 poems at a time. **Tips:** Annual prizes for work in the magazine, $200-$1,000. **Queries:** Not necessary. **E-Queries:** No. **Unsolicited mss:** Accepts. **Response:** Queries 3 weeks, submissions 3-4 months, SASE. **Rights:** All, electronic, can revert to author. **Payment:** In copies.

PRIMAVERA
Box 37-7547, Chicago, IL 60637.
Annual. $10. Circ.: 1,000. **Description:** Original fiction and poetry, that reflects the experience of women of different ages, races, sexual orientations, social classes. **Fiction:** 25 page max. **Poetry:** On the experiences of women. **Tips:** Encourages new writers. No confessional, formulaic, scholarly. **Queries:** Not necessary. **E-Queries:** No. **Unsolicited mss:** Accepts. **Response:** Queries 2 weeks, submissions 1-6 months, SASE required. **Freelance Content:** 100%. **Rights:** 1st. **Payment:** In copies.

PRISM INTERNATIONAL
University of British Columbia, Dept. of Creative Writing, Buch E462-1866 Main Mall, Vancouver, British Columbia V6T 1Z1 Canada. 604-822-2514.
E-mail: prism@interchange.ubc.ca. Web site: http://prism.arts.ubc.ca. Quarterly. Circ.: 1,200. **Description:** Quality fiction, poetry, drama, creative nonfiction, and literature in translation, from Canada and around the world. **Fiction:** Annual short fiction contest, $3,000 in prizes. **Nonfiction:** Annual nonfiction contest, $1,500 in prizes. Pays $40 per published page of poetry, $20 per page of prose, $10 per page Web rights. **Response:** 2-4 months. **Payment:** On publication.

PUCKERBRUSH REVIEW
76 Main St., Orono, ME 04473-1430. 207-866-4868.
Semiannual. $4. Circ.: 300. Constance Hunting, Editor. **Description:** Literary poetry, fiction, interviews, reviews, and translations; also, work from Europe. **Fiction:** Yes. **Nonfiction:** Essays, personal or literary. Literary news from specific regions and countries. **Poetry:** Yes. **Queries:** Preferred. **E-Queries:** No. **Unsolicited mss:** Accepts. **Response:** 1 month, SASE. **Freelance Content:** 90%. **Payment:** In copies.

PUDDING MAGAZINE

Pudding House Publications

60 N. Main St., Johnstown, OH 43031. 740-967-6060.

E-mail: pudding@johnstown.net. Web site: www.puddinghouse.com. Irregular. $7.95 or 3/$18.95. Circ.: 2,000. Jennifer Bosveld, Editor. **Description:** International journal of applied poetry, with poetry, short-short stories, and essays, writing exercises, reviews, and more. **Fiction:** Short-short stories. **Nonfiction:** Articles/essays on poetry in the schools and in human services; 500-2,500 words. **Poetry:** On popular culture, social concerns, personal struggle, and wide open. **Columns, Departments:** Reviews of poetry books. **Unsolicited mss:** Accepts. **Response:** Submissions, 1 day, SASE. **Freelance Content:** 98%. **Payment:** In copies.

PUERTO DEL SOL

New Mexico State University, Dept. of English

MSC 3E, P.O. Box 30001, Las Cruces, NM 88003-8001.

Web site: www.nmsu.edu/~english/puerto/puerto.html. K. West, Kevin McIlvoy, Editors. **Description:** Short stories and personal essays, to 30 pages; novel excerpts, to 65 pages; articles, to 45 pages, and reviews, to 15 pages. Poetry, photos. **Tips:** Manuscripts read September through February. **Payment:** In copies.

QUARRY

P.O. Box 1061, Kingston, Ontario K7L 4Y5 Canada. 613-548-8429. 3x/yr.. Circ.: 1,200. Suzanne Garret, Editor. **Description:** Literary magazine publishing innovative fiction, poetry, and essays by Canadain writers. **Tips:** Seeking talented new writers.

QUARTER AFTER EIGHT

Ohio University, 102 Ellis Hall, Athens, OH 45701. 740-593-2827.

E-mail: quarteraftereight@hotmail.com. Web site: www.quarteraftereight.com. Annual. $10. Circ.: 1,000. Tony Viola, Editor-in-Chief. **Description:** Literary publication. **Fiction:** Experimental fiction, sudden fiction; 10,000 words max. **Nonfiction:** Commentary, but not scholarly work; novel excerpts, essays, criticism, investigations, interviews; 10,000 words max. **Poetry:** Submit 3-5 pieces; no traditional lined poetry. **Art:** B&W photos only. **Queries:** Not necessary. **E-Queries:** No. **Unsolicited mss:** Accepts. **Response:** Submissions 12-16 weeks, SASE. **Rights:** 1st NA. **Payment:** On publication.

QUARTERLY WEST

University of Utah

200 S Central Campus Dr., Rm. 317, Salt Lake City, UT 84112-9109. 801-581-3938. E-mail: lynnkilpatrick@m.cc.utah.edu. Web site: www.utah.edu/quarterlywest. Semi-annual. $7.50/issue, $12/yr. Circ.: 1,600. David Hawkins, Editor. **Description:** Literary journal, for new writers and established authors. **Fiction:** Shorts and longer fiction, that play with form and language, not bound by convention; 500-6,000 words; pay varies. **Nonfiction:** Memoir, books reviews, essays; 500-6,000 words. **Poetry:** Up to 5 pages, 3 poems. **Tips:** No "Western" themes or religious verse. **Queries:** Not

necessary. **E-Queries:** No. **Unsolicited mss:** Accepts. **Response:** 6-8 months, SASE. **Freelance Content:** 75%. **Payment:** On publication.

QUEEN'S QUARTERLY

Queens University

144 Barrie St., Kingston, Ontario K7L 3N6 Canada. 613-533-2667.

E-mail: qquarter@post.queensu.ca. Web site: http://info.queensu.ca/quarterly. Boris Castel, Editor. **Description:** Covers a wide range of topics and fiction. **Fiction:** In English and French; to 5,000 words; to $300. **Nonfiction:** To 5,000 words; to $400. **Poetry:** Send up to 6 poems; to $400. **Art:** B&W art; to $400. **Payment:** On publication.

RAIN CROW

Rain Crow Publishing

P.O. Box 11013, Chicago, IL 60611-0013. 773-562-5786.

E-mail: rcp@rain-crow.com. Web site: www.rain-crow.com. 3x/year. Circ.: 300. Michael S. Manley, Editor. **Description:** Short fiction in many styles and genres. **Fiction:** 250-8,000 words; $5/page plus copies, discounts, and other perks. **Queries:** Not necessary. **Unsolicited mss:** Accepts. **Freelance Content:** 100%. **Rights:** One-time, non-exclusive electronic. **Payment:** On publication.

RAMBUNCTIOUS REVIEW

1221 W Pratt Blvd., Chicago, IL 60626. 773-338-2439.

3x/yr. $4/issue. Circ.: 500. Editorial Board. **Description:** New and established writers of poetry and fiction. **Queries:** Not necessary. **E-Queries:** No. **Unsolicited mss:** Accepts. **Freelance Content:** 100%. **Rights:** FNASR. **Payment:** In copies.

REAL

Stephen F. Austin State University

P.O. Box 13007, SFA Sta., Nacogdoches, TX 75962. 936-468-2059.

E-mail: real@sfasu.edu. Semi-annual. $15. Circ.: 400. W. Dale Hearell, Editor. **Description:** Short fiction, poetry, and criticism. **Fiction:** Realistic portrayal of human situations; to 5,000 words. **Nonfiction:** Well-written, scholarly articles; to 5,000 words. **Poetry:** Imagistic verse, not just reformatted prose; to 100 lines. **Art:** B&W line drawings. **Queries:** Not necessary. **E-Queries:** No. **Unsolicited mss:** Accepts. **Response:** Queries 1 week, submissions 3-6 weeks, SASE. **Freelance Content:** 100%. **Payment:** In copies.

RED CEDAR REVIEW

Michigan State University, Dept. of English

17-C Morrill Hall, E. Lansing, MI 48824-1036. 517-355-1707.

E-mail: rcreview@msu.edu. Web site: www.msu.edu/~rcreview. Biannual. $5/$6. Meg Sparling, Editor. **Description:** Publishes poetry, fiction, and creative nonfiction of all genres by both published and unpublished authors. **Fiction:** 5,000 words max. **Nonfiction:** Creative nonfiction; 5,000 words max. **Poetry:** Submit up to 5 poems.

Queries: Preferred. **E-Queries:** Yes. **Unsolicited mss:** Accepts. **Response:** Queries 3 weeks, submissions 3 months, SASE. **Payment:** In copies.

RED ROCK REVIEW
Community College of Southern Nevada, English Dept. 12A
3200 E Cheyenne Ave., North Las Vegas, NV 89030. 702-651-4094.
E-mail: richard_logsdm@ccsn.nevada.edu. Semiannual. $5.50/$10. Circ.: 1,000. Dr. Richard Logsdon, Editor. **Description:** Featuring work by new and well-established writers. **Fiction:** Mainstream fiction; 5,000 words. **Nonfiction:** Book reviews, recent poetry and fiction; interviews with literary artists; 2,000 words. **Poetry:** up to 60 lines. **Tips:** Does not accept e-mail submissions. **Queries:** Not necessary. **E-Queries:** Yes. **Unsolicited mss:** Accepts. **Response:** Queries 2 weeks, (e-mail responses sooner), submissions 3 months, SASE. **Freelance Content:** 60%. **Rights:** 1st NA. **Payment:** In copies.

RED WHEELBARROW
De Anza College, 21250 Stevens Creek Blvd., Cupertino, CA 95014. 408-864-8600.
E-mail: splitterrandolph@fhda.edu. Annual. $5/year. Circ.: 500. Randolph Splitter, Editor. **Description:** Fiction, poetry, creative nonfiction, photography, comics, and drawings. **Fiction:** Short stories; to 4,000 words. **Nonfiction:** Creative nonfiction; to 4,000 words. **Poetry:** 5 poems max. **Art:** B&W, drawings, comics, and other visual art forms. **Tips:** Accepts work in September-December only. Diverse voices welcome. Note: This publication is not affiliated with Red Wheelbarrow Press or any other similarly named publication. **Queries:** Not necessary. **E-Queries:** No. **Unsolicited mss:** Accepts. **Response:** Submissions 2-6 months, SASE required for reply. **Freelance Content:** 95%.

RIVER CITY
University of Memphis, Dept. of English
Memphis, TN 38152. 901-678-4591.
E-mail: rivercity@memphis.edu. Web site: www.people.memphis.edu/~rivercity. Semiannual. $7/issue, $12/year. Circ.: 1,200. Thomas Russell, editor. **Description:** Literary journal of the University of Memphis. **Fiction:** Original short stories. **Nonfiction:** Accepts. **Poetry:** Accepts. **Art:** Photos, B&W or color; illustrations, B&W. **Tips:** Avoid sentimental, singsong verse. See Web site for upcoming themes. **Queries:** Not necessary. **E-Queries:** Yes. **Unsolicited mss:** Accepts. **Response:** 1-3 months; SASE required. **Freelance Content:** 50%. **Rights:** One-time.

RIVER OAK REVIEW
P.O. Box 3127, Oak Park, IL 60303.
Web site: www.riveroakarts.org. Semiannual. Marylee MacDonald, Editor. **Description:** Fiction, poetry, and creative nonfiction. Limit prose to 20 pages; poetry to batches of no more than 4. **Tips:** No criticism, reviews, or translations. **Payment:** In copies.

RIVER STYX

634 N Grand Blvd., Fl. 12, St. Louis, MO 63103. 314-533-4541.
Web site: www.riverstyx.org. Tri-annual. $7/$20. Circ.: 1,500. Richard Newman, Editor. **Description:** International, multicultural literary journal. Fiction, poetry, essays, and art by emerging and established writers and artists. **Fiction:** Less than 30 pages. **Nonfiction:** Personal essays, literary interviews, etc; less than 30 pages. **Poetry:** Format open. **Art:** By request only. **Queries:** Not necessary. **E-Queries:** No. **Unsolicited mss:** Accepts. **Response:** Submissions 3-5 weeks, SASE. **Rights:** 1st NA. **Payment:** On publication.

ROANOKE REVIEW

221 College Ln., Salem, VA 24153. 504-334-1458.
Semi-annual. $5. Circ.: 300. Paul Hanstedt, Editor. **Description:** Literary magazine featuring fiction and poetry. **Fiction:** to 7,500 words. **Poetry:** to 100 lines. **Queries:** Not necessary. **Unsolicited mss:** Accepts. **Payment:** In copies.

ROCKFORD REVIEW

7721 Venus St., Loves Park, IL 61111.
Web site: www.writersguild1.tripod.com. 3x/year. $6/$20. Circ.: 250-300. Cindy Guentherman, Managing Editor. **Description:** Poetry and prose published by Rockford Writer's Guild. Send SASE for guidelines. **Fiction:** 1,300 words. **Nonfiction:** Essays, short plays; 1,300 words. **Poetry:** Experimental or traditional, to 50 lines (shorter preferred); submit up to 3. **Queries:** Not necessary. **E-Queries:** No. **Unsolicited mss:** Accepts. **Response:** Queries 2 weeks, submissions 2 months, SASE. **Rights:** 1st NA. **Payment:** In copies. **Contact:** Max Dodson (prose), Cindy Guentherman (poetry).

ROOM OF ONE'S OWN

P.O. Box 46160, Sta. D, Vancouver, British Columbia V6J 5G5 Canada.
E-mail: contactroom@hotmail.com. Web site: www.islandnet.com/Room/enter/. Quarterly. $22/yr (Can.), $25 (U.S.). **Description:** Features short stories, poems, art, and reviews by, for, and about women. **Fiction:** To 5,000 words. **Nonfiction:** Creative nonfiction and essays; to 5,000 words. **Poetry:** Prefers groups of poems, rather than single poems. **Columns, Departments:** Book reviews; to 700 words. **Art:** Seeking original art and photography (by female artists) on the female experience; slides, photos, photocopies. **Tips: Payment:** $35 CDN, 1-year subscription, and two copies; or payment all in copies, plus 1-year subscription. **E-Queries:** No. **Unsolicited mss:** Accepts. **Response:** SASE (Canadian postage or IRC). **Rights:** FNASR. **Contact:** Editorial Collective.

ROSEBUD

P.O. Box 459, Cambridge, WI 53523. 608-423-4750.
E-mail: letters@rsbd.net. Web site: www.rsbd.net. 3x/year. $6.59/$20. Circ.: 6,000. Roderick Clark, Publisher/Managing Editor. **Description:** Independent publication featuring traditional and non-traditional stories, essays, art, and poems. Literary, but

not stiff. Fiction and creative nonfiction under 3,200 words; $25. **Poetry:** Accepts many styles, but no heroic couplets; 1 page. **Tips:** Avoid pieces too generic, nostalgic, or sentimental. Does not accept straight crime, romance, or purely plot-driven pieces. **Queries:** Not necessary. **E-Queries:** No. **Unsolicited mss:** Accepts. **Response:** 40 days (with $1/fee and RFI written on envelope). **Freelance Content:** 60%. **Rights:** One-time or 1st serial.

SANSKRIT LITERARY-ARTS
University of North Carolina-Charlotte
Cone University Center, Charlotte, NC 28223. 704-687-2326.
E-mail: sanskrit@email.uncc.edu. Web site: www.uncc.edu/life/sanskrit. Annual. $10.
Circ.: 3,500. Nicole Schulz, Literary Editor. **Description:** Literary-Arts magazine.
Fiction: Short fiction and short-shorts; 3,500 words max. **Poetry:** All forms, prefers free form, modern, concrete imagery. **Art:** Slides. **Tips:** Annual deadline, first Friday in November. **Queries:** Not necessary. **E-Queries:** Yes. **Unsolicited mss:** Accepts. **Response:** SASE. **Freelance Content:** 100%. **Rights:** 1st NA, electronic.

THE SEATTLE REVIEW
University of Washington, Padelford Hall, Box 354330, Seattle, WA 98195.
E-mail: seaview@english.washington.edu.
Web site: http://depts.washington.edu/engl/seaview1.html. Colleen J. McElroy, Editor. **Description:** Stories, to 20 pages; poetry; essays on the craft of writing; art; and interviews with Northwest writers. **Tips:** Manuscripts read October 1 through May 31. **Payment:** In copies.

SENECA REVIEW
Hobart & William Smith Colleges, Geneva, NY 14456. 315-781-3392.
E-mail: senecareview@hws.edu. Web site: www.hws/senecareview. Bi-annual. $7/$11.
Circ.: 1,000. Deborah Tall, Editor. **Description:** A journal of poetry and lyric essays. Special interest in translations. **Nonfiction:** Format open. **Poetry:** Format open. **Queries:** Not necessary. **E-Queries:** No. **Unsolicited mss:** Accepts. **Response:** Submissions 2-3 months, SASE. **Freelance Content:** 100%. **Rights:** 1st NA. **Payment:** In copies and 2-year subscription.

THE SEWANEE REVIEW
University of the South, 735 University Ave., Sewanee, TN 37383-1000.
Quarterly. **Description:** Literary publication. Only unpublished work considered. Query for essays (7,500 words or less) and reviews; submit fiction (3,500-7,500 words) and poetry (6 poems, 40 lines or less) without query. **Tips:** Do not submit between June 1 and August 31. No simultaneous submissions.

SHENANDOAH
The Washington and Lee University Review, Troubadour Theater, Fl. 2, Lexington, VA 24450-0303. 540-463-8765.
Web site: http://shenandoah.wlu.edu. Quarterly. $22/yr. Circ.: 1,800. R. T. Smith,

Editor. **Description:** A literary journal that publishes poems, essays, and reviews which display passionate understanding, formal accomplishment, and serious mischief. **Fiction:** $25/page. **Nonfiction:** criticism, essays, interviews; $25/page. **Poetry:** $2.50/line. **Tips:** No simultaneous submissions. **Queries:** Not necessary. **E-Queries:** No. **Unsolicited mss:** Accepts. **Response:** Submissions 8 weeks, SASE. **Freelance Content:** 80%. **Rights:** FNASR. **Payment:** On publication.

SKYLARK
2200 169th St., Hammond, IN 46323. 219-989-2273.
E-mail: poetpam49@yahoo.com. Annual. $8. Circ.: 1,000. Pamela Hunter, Editor. **Description:** Publishes work (literary and visual) by children and mature adult artists, side-by-side. Interested in new and emerging artists and writers (of any age). **Fiction:** Well-plotted, well-characterized stories, realistic dialogue and action. Central character must be three-dimensional; 4,000 words. **Nonfiction:** Essays that reflect life in Northwest Indiana; interviews with artists, writers, poets; 3,000 words. **Poetry:** Concise wording, rich imagery, honest emotional impact; up to 30 lines. **Art:** Accepts work by either adults or children; original in design, unpublished, and original artwork (for four-color processing); B&W, color. **Queries:** Not necessary. **E-Queries:** Yes. **Unsolicited mss:** Accepts. **Response:** 3 months. **Freelance Content:** 90%. **Rights:** 1st. **Payment:** In copies.

SLIPSTREAM
P.O. Box 2071, Niagara Falls, NY 14301. 716-282-2616.
E-mail: Editors@slipstreampress.org. Web site: www.slipstreampress.org. Annual. $20. Circ.: 750-1,000. Robert Borgatti, Dan Sicoli, and Livio Farallo, Editors. **Description:** Poetry, short fiction, and graphics not normally found in mainstream publications. Seeking contemporary urban themes and poetry with a strong voice. **Fiction:** Contemporary urban themes encouraged; up to 15 pages. **Poetry:** Contemporary poetry; 1-6 pages. **Art:** Send photocopies first; B&W photos and graphics. **Tips:** No rhyming, religious, or trite verse. **Queries:** Not necessary. **E-Queries:** Yes. **Unsolicited mss:** Accepts. **Response:** Queries 1 week, submissions 2-6 weeks, SASE. **Freelance Content:** 100%. **Rights:** 1st NA. **Payment:** In copies. **Contact:** Dan Sicoli.

THE SMALL POND
P.O. Box 664, Stratford, CT 06615. 203-378-4066.
3x/year. $4/$10. Circ.: 300. Napoleon St. Cyr, Editor. **Description:** Literary journal with interesting, quirky fiction and poetry. **Fiction:** 2,500 words max. **Nonfiction:** Anything interesting; 2,500 words. **Poetry:** Any style, subject; 100 lines. **Tips:** Avoid bleeding hearts. **Queries:** Not necessary. **E-Queries:** No. **Unsolicited mss:** Accepts. **Response:** Queries 2-5 days, submissions 2-5 weeks, SASE. **Freelance Content:** 100%. **Rights:** All. **Payment:** In copies.

SNAKE NATION REVIEW

Snake Nation Press
110 West Force St., Valdosta, GA 31601. 229-244-0752.
E-mail: jeana@snakenationpress.org. Web site: www.snakenationpress.org. 3x/year.
$6/$20. Circ.: 2,000. Jean Arambula, Editor. **Description:** General-interest literary magazine featuring unpublished/underpublished writers. Open to new and experimental writing. Submissions accepted year round. Send SASE for guidelines. Editor's choice for each category (poetry, fiction, art, or photos) receives $100, all others are paid in copies. **Queries:** Not necessary. **E-Queries:** Yes. **Unsolicited mss:** Accepts. **Response:** 3-6 months. **Freelance Content:** 100%. **Rights:** One-time.

SNOWY EGRET

P.O. Box 9, Bowling Green, IN 47833. 812-829-1910.
Bi-annual. $12/20 (sample copy $8). Circ.: 400. Philip Repp, Editor. **Description:** Oldest independent journal of nature writing. Emphasis on natural history and human beings in relation to nature from literary, artistic, philosophical, and historical perspectives. Pays $2/printed page. **Fiction:** Characters who relate strongly to nature and grow in understanding of themselves and the world; 500-10,000 words. **Nonfiction:** Essays on the natural world and humans' relationship to it with detailed observations from author's own experience; 500-10,000 words. **Poetry:** Nature-oriented poems. **Columns, Departments:** First-hand experiences with landscape or wildlife encounters; 250-2,000 words. **Tips:** Submit freshly observed material, with plenty of description and/or dialogue. **Queries:** Not necessary. **E-Queries:** No. **Response:** Queries 2 weeks, submissions 2 months, SASE. **Freelance Content:** 95%. **Rights:** 1st NA, one-time. **Payment:** On publication.

SO TO SPEAK

George Mason University
4400 University Dr., MS2D6, Fairfax, VA 22030-4444. 703-993-3625.
E-mail: sts@gmu.edu. Web site: www.gmu.edu/org/sts. Bi-annual. $6/$11. Circ.: 1,300. Renee Angle, Editor. **Description:** Feminist journal of language and arts, concerned with the history of women, of feminists, and looking to see the future through art. Includes fiction, poetry, nonfiction, reviews, visual arts (B&W). **Fiction:** Literary, feminist; to 5,000 words. **Nonfiction:** Literary, lyrical, critical; reviews (feminist books and hypertext); to 4,000 words. **Poetry:** Literary, feminist; experimental, lyrical, narrative. **Art:** B&W art, seeking color cover art. **Queries:** Not necessary. **E-Queries:** No. **Unsolicited mss:** Accepts. **Response:** Submissions 3-4 months, SASE. **Payment:** In copies.

SONORA REVIEW

University of Arizona, Dept. of English, Tucson, AZ 85721. 520-321-7759.
E-mail: sonora@u.arizona.edu. Web site: www.coh.arizona.edu/sonora. **Description:** Literary journal featuring stories, poems, memoirs, personal essays, and creative nonfiction. Does not usually consider genre work (mystery, romance, etc.). Send complete manuscript. Fiction and nonfiction, 8,000 words max.; poetry, 12 pages max.

Accepts simultaneous submissions. **Tips:** Annual contests; send for guidelines. Manuscripts read year-round. **Queries:** Not necessary. **Unsolicited mss:** Accepts. **Response:** 2-3 months, SASE. **Rights:** 1st NA. **Payment:** 2 copies.

SOU'WESTER
Southern Illinois University at Edwardsville
Edwardsville, IL 62026-1438. 618-650-3190.
Bi-annual. Circ.: 300. Allison Funk and Ruth Ellen Kocher, Editors. **Description:** Small literary magazine that publishes fiction and poetry. **Queries:** Not necessary. **E-Queries:** Yes. **Response:** Submissions 3 months. **Rights:** All. **Payment:** In copies.

SOUTH CAROLINA REVIEW
Clemson University, Dept. of English, Clemson, SC 29634-0523. 864-656-5399.
E-mail: cwayne@clemson.edu.
Web site: www.hubcap.clemson.edu/aah/engl/screview.htm. Semiannual. Circ.: 450. Wayne Chapman, Editor. **Description:** Fiction, essays, reviews, interviews, and poems. **Fiction:** 1,000-6,000 words. **Queries:** Preferred. **E-Queries:** No. **Response:** Queries 1-2 weeks, 1-2 months, SASE required. **Freelance Content:** 90%. **Rights:** World. **Payment:** In copies.

SOUTHERN HUMANITIES REVIEW
9088 Haley Center, Auburn University, AL 36849.
E-mail: shrengl@auburn.edu. Quarterly. $5/$15. Circ.: 700. Dan R. Latimer, Virginia M. Kouidis, Co-editors. **Description:** Scholarly, literary magazine. **Fiction:** Short stories; 3,500-15,000 words. **Nonfiction:** Essays, criticism; 3,500-15,000 words. **Poetry:** 2 pages. **Queries:** Not necessary. **E-Queries:** Yes. **Unsolicited mss:** Accepts. **Response:** Queries 1-2 weeks, submissions 1-3 months, SASE. **Freelance Content:** 70%. **Rights:** 1st, reverts to author. **Payment:** In copies.

SOUTHERN POETRY REVIEW
Central Piedmont Community College, Advancement Studies
Charlotte, NC 28235. 704-330-6275.
Semi-annual. $10. Circ.: 1,000. Ken McLaurin, Editor. **Description:** Literary journal featuring poetry. **Poetry:** Any style, length, content. **Tips:** Use strong, clear imagery. Avoid sentimental or "proselytizing" content. **Queries:** Not necessary. **E-Queries:** Yes. **Unsolicited mss:** Accepts. **Freelance Content:** 100%. **Rights:** 1st, reverts to writer. **Payment:** On publication.

THE SOUTHERN REVIEW
Louisiana State University, 43 Allen Hall, Baton Rouge, LA 70803. 225-578-5108.
Web site: www.lsu.edu/thesouthernreview. Quarterly. Circ.: 3,100. Michael Griffith, Associate Editor. **Description:** Literary publication of contemporary literature, with special interest in Southern culture and history. **Fiction:** 4,000-8,000 words; $12/page. **Nonfiction:** essays; 4,000-10,000 words; $12/page. **Poetry:** up to 4 pages;

$20/page. **Tips:** Seeking craftsmanship, technique, and seriousness of subject matter. **Queries:** Preferred. **Response:** 2 months, SASE required. **Rights:** 1st serial. **Payment:** On publication.

SOUTHWEST REVIEW
See page 334 for full listing.
Description: Varied, wide-ranging content of adult interest: contemporary affairs, history, folklore, fiction, poetry, literary criticism, art, music, and theater.

SOW'S EAR POETRY REVIEW
19535 Pleasant View Dr., Abingdon, VA 24211-6827. 276-628-2651.
E-mail: richman@preferred.com. Quarterly. $5/issue, $10/year. Circ.: 600. Larry K. Richman, Managing Editor. **Description:** Poetry, artwork, and nonfiction. **Nonfiction:** Essays, reviews. **Poetry:** Contemporary, any style or length; up to 5 poems. **Art:** To complement poetry; B&W prints, drawings. **Tips:** Seeking poems that make the strange familiar or the familiar strange, that connect the little story of the text and the big story of the human situation. **Queries:** Not necessary. **E-Queries:** Yes. **Unsolicited mss:** Accepts. **Response:** 1 week for queries, 3-6 months for submissions; SASE required. **Freelance Content:** 100%. **Rights:** FNASR. **Payment:** In copies. **Contact:** James Owens, Editor, owens017@bama.au.edu.

SPECTACLE
Pachanga Press
101 Middlesex Turnpike, Suite 6, PMB 155, Burlington, MA 01803-4914.
E-mail: spectaclejournal@hotmail.com. Semi-annual. $7. Circ.: 1,500. Richard Aguilar, Editor. **Description:** Essays, articles, reportage, and fiction on broad spectrum of lively, unconventional themes. **Fiction:** Relevant to issue's theme; up to 5,000 words; $30 and 2 copies. **Nonfiction:** Essays, memoirs, articles, reportage, interviews, and satire; 2,000-5,000 words; $30 and 2 copies. **Tips:** Contact for coming themes. **Queries:** Not necessary. **E-Queries:** Yes. **Unsolicited mss:** Accepts. **Response:** Queries 2 weeks, submissions 6-8 weeks, SASE. **Freelance Content:** 90%. **Rights:** FNASR. **Payment:** On publication.

STAND
Virginia Commonwealth University, Dept. of English
Box 2005, Richmond, VA 23284-2005. 804-828-1331.
Web site: www.saturn.vcu.edu/~dlatane/stand.html. Quarterly. $12/$49.50. Circ.: 7,500. Jon Glover, Acting Editor. **Description:** Literary magazine. Pays "modest" amount. **Fiction:** 10,000 words. **Poetry:** Up to 250 lines. **Tips:** Probably not the right market for new writers. **Queries:** Not necessary. **E-Queries:** Yes. **Unsolicited mss:** Accepts. **Response:** Submissions 1-3 months, SASE. **Freelance Content:** 60%. **Payment:** On publication.

STORYQUARTERLY
431 Sheridan Rd., Kenilworth, IL 60043. 847-256-6998.
E-mail: storyquarterly@hotmail.com. Web site: www.storyquarterly.com. Annual. Circ.: 4,500. M. M. M. Hayes, Editor. **Description:** Contemporary American and foreign literature, full range of styles and forms. **Fiction:** Short stories, novel excerpts; 100-10,000 words. **Nonfiction:** Interviews, essays, memoir; 100-10,000 words. **Art:** B&W photographs, illustrations. **Tips:** Reads submissions October through March. **Queries:** Not necessary. **E-Queries:** Yes. **Unsolicited mss:** Accepts. **Response:** 2-6 months; SASE required. **Rights:** One-time. **Payment:** In copies.

STORYWORKS
Scholastic, Inc.
555 Broadway, New York, NY 10012. 212-343-6100.
Bimonthly. Circ.: 270,000. Lauren Tarshis, Editor. **Description:** Literature magazine for 8-12 year olds. **Queries:** Required. **Unsolicited mss:** Does not accept.

SUB-TERRAIN
204-A, 175 E Broadway, Vancouver
British Columbia, V5T 1W2 Canada. 604-876-8710.
E-mail: subter@portal.ca. Web site: www.anvilpress.com. 3x/year. $3.95 (U.S.) $4.95 (Canada). Circ.: 5,000. Brian Kaufman, Editor. **Description:** A stimulating fusion of fiction, poetry, photography and graphics from uprising Canadian, U.S., and international writers and artists. **Fiction:** 3,000 words max. **Poetry:** 3-4 pages max. **Art:** 5x7 B&W. **Tips:** Seeking work with a point of view and some passion, on issues of pressing importance (especially with urban slant). No bland, flowery, universal poetry that says nothing in style or content. **Queries:** Preferred. **E-Queries:** Yes. **Unsolicited mss:** Accepts. **Response:** Queries 1-2 weeks, submissions 2-4 months, SASE. Include IRC if outside of Canada. **Freelance Content:** 85%. **Rights:** 1st NA. **Payment:** On publication. **Contact:** Brian Kaufman.

THE SUN
Sun Publishing Co.
107 N Roberson St., Chapel Hill, NC 27516. 919-942-5282.
E-mail: sy@thesunmagazine.org. Web site: www.thesunmagazine.org. Monthly. $3.95/issue, $34 yr. Circ.: 50,000. Sy Safransky, Editor. **Description:** Essays, stories, interviews, and poetry in which people write of their struggles to understand their lives, often with surprising intimacy. Looking for writers willing to take risks and describe life honestly. **Fiction:** Fiction that feels like a lived experience; to 7,000 words; $300-$500. **Nonfiction:** Personal essays and interviews; to 7,000 words; $300-$1,000. **Poetry:** 1-2 pages; $50-$200. **Art:** B&W photographs only; $50-$200. **Tips:** No journalistic, academic, opinion pieces. **Queries:** Not necessary. **E-Queries:** No. **Unsolicited mss:** Accepts. **Response:** 3 months, SASE. **Freelance Content:** 80%. **Rights:** One-time. **Payment:** On publication.

SYCAMORE REVIEW
Pudue University, Dept. of English
Heavilon Hall, West Lafayette, IN 47907. 765-494-3783.
E-mail: sycamore@expert.cc.purdue.edu. Web site: www.sla.purdue.edu/sycamore.
Bi-annual. $7.00/$12.00. Circ.: 700. Paul D. Reich, Editor. **Description:** Literary journal. **Fiction:** yes. **Nonfiction:** Essays, interviews, translations. **Poetry:** yes. **Queries:** Not necessary. **Unsolicited mss:** Accepts. **Response:** Queries 1-2 weeks, submissions 3-4 months, SASE.

TALKING RIVER REVIEW
Lewis-Clark State College, 500 Eighth Ave., Lewiston, ID 83501. 208-799-2307.
Biannual. $7/$14. Circ.: 500. **Description:** Publishes the best work from established and first-time writers. **Fiction:** Short stories; up to 25 pages. **Nonfiction:** Literary essays; up to 25 pages. **Poetry:** Any style; 1-5 pages. **Tips:** Send only your best work. Reads manuscripts September 1-March 1. **Queries:** Not necessary. **E-Queries:** No. **Unsolicited mss:** Accepts. **Response:** No queries, submissions 3-4 months, SASE. **Freelance Content:** 100%. **Rights:** 1st. **Payment:** In copies.

TAR RIVER POETRY
East Carolina University, Dept. of English
Greenville, NC 27858-4353. 252-328-6046.
Bi-annual. $10/yr.,$18/2 years. Circ.: 650. Peter Makuck, Editor. **Description:** Formal and open form poetry, reviews, and interviews. **Poetry:** Strong imagery, figurative language; 6 pages max. **Tips:** No sentimental, flat poetry. Emphasize the visual. **Queries:** Not necessary. **E-Queries:** No. **Unsolicited mss:** Accepts. **Response:** Queries 1 week, submissions 4-6 weeks, SASE. **Freelance Content:** 100%. **Payment:** In copies.

THE TEXAS REVIEW
Sam Houston State University, English Dept.
P.O. Box 2146, Huntsville, TX 77341-2146. 936-294-1992.
E-mail: eng_pdr@shsu.edu. Web site: www.shsu.edu/~www_trp. Semi-annual. $12/yr. Circ.: 800. Paul Ruffin, Editor. **Description:** Showcases poetry, fiction, and nonfiction. **Fiction:** Yes. **Nonfiction:** Yes. **Poetry:** Yes. **Queries:** Not necessary. **E-Queries:** Yes. **Unsolicited mss:** Does not accept. **Response:** Queries 1 week, submissions 6-8 weeks, SASE. **Rights:** 1st.

THEMA
P.O. Box 8747, Metairie, LA 70011-8747. 504-887-1263.
E-mail: thema@cox.net. 3x/year. $8/$16. Circ.: 300. Virginia Howard, Editor. **Description:** Each issue is a stand-alone, thematic anthology. Provides a forum for writers, and source material for teachers of creative writing. **Fiction:** Less than 6,000 words (20 pages); $10-$25. **Nonfiction:** Less than 6,000 words. **Poetry:** 3-page max.; $10. **Tips:** Request upcoming themes. **Queries:** Not necessary. **E-Queries:** Yes. **Unsolicited mss:** Accepts. **Response:** Queries 2 weeks, submissions

4 months after deadline, SASE. **Freelance Content:** 99%. **Rights:** One-time. **Payment:** On acceptance.

THIRD COAST
Western Michigan University, Dept. of English, Kalamazoo, MI 49008-5092. Biannually. $6/$11. Circ.: 500. Shanda Hansma Blue, Editor. **Description:** Literary review for contemporary writers and readers. **Fiction:** Yes. **Nonfiction:** Creative nonfiction. **Poetry:** Yes. **Queries:** Not necessary. **E-Queries:** No. **Unsolicited mss:** Accepts. **Response:** SASE. **Freelance Content:** 80%. **Rights:** FNASR. **Payment:** On publication.

13TH MOON
University of Albany, SUNY,
Dept. of English, Albany, NY 12222. 518-442-4181.
Web site: www.albany.edu/13thmoon/main.htm. Annual. $10/issue. Circ.: 500. Judith Emlyn Johnson, Editor. **Description:** Feminist literary magazine, with literature and graphic arts by contemporary women. Seeks to draw attention to neglected categories of women artists. **Fiction:** Feminist short fiction, emphasis on work of minority women and lesbians; any length. **Nonfiction:** Feminist nonfiction, women's issues; any length. **Poetry:** Feminist; 3-5 poems. **Art:** Accepts. **Tips:** Themed issues; accepts submissions September through May. **Queries:** Preferred. **E-Queries:** No. **Unsolicited mss:** Accepts. **Response:** SASE required. **Freelance Content:** 100%. **Rights:** One-time. **Payment:** In copies.

THOUGHTS FOR ALL SEASONS
478 NE 56th St., Miami, FL 33137.
$6. Circ.: 1,000. Prof. Michel P. Richard, Editor. **Description:** Irregular serial publication that celebrates the epigram, of 2-4 lines, as a literary form. Includes humor and satire. **Poetry:** Rhyming, quatrains, limericks, nonsense verse with good imagery; up to 1 page. **Columns, Departments:** Thematic by issue; up to 10 pages. **Queries:** Not necessary. **E-Queries:** No. **Response:** Submissions 21 days, SASE. **Freelance Content:** 60%. **Payment:** In copies.

THE THREEPENNY REVIEW
P.O. Box 9131, Berkeley, CA 94709. 510-849-4545.
Web site: www.threepennyreview.com. Quarterly. Circ.: 9,000. Wendy Lesser, Editor. **Description:** "Literary and immensely readable" (Publishers Weekly). **Fiction:** To 5,000 words; to $200. **Nonfiction:** Essays on books, theater, film, dance, music, art, television, and politics; 1,500-3,000 words; to $200. **Poetry:** to 100 lines; $100/poem. **Tips:** Manuscripts read September through May. **Queries:** Preferred. **Response:** 2 months, SASE. **Payment:** On publication.

TIGHTROPE
Swamp Press
15 Warwick Ave., Northfield, MA 01360.

Annual. $6/issue. Circ.: 300. Ed Rayher, Editor. **Description:** Letterpress magazine, poetry with original graphics. **Poetry:** Any length. **Queries:** Preferred. **E-Queries:** No. **Unsolicited mss:** Does not accept. **Response:** 1-2 months, SASE. **Rights:** 1st. **Payment:** In copies.

TIMBER CREEK REVIEW

8969 UNCG Station, Greensboro, NC 27413. 336-334-2952.
E-mail: timber_creek_review@hoopsmail.com. Quarterly. $4.50/$16. Circ.: 150-180. J. M. Freiermuth, Editor. **Description:** Publishes well-written, readable short stories, poetry, and occasional literary nonfiction. **Fiction:** 2,500-7,500 words; $10-$35. **Nonfiction:** 2,500-5,000 words; $10-$35. **Poetry:** 3-30 lines; $3-$10. **Tips:** Does not accept reprints. Cover letter required. **Queries:** Not necessary. **E-Queries:** Yes. **Unsolicited mss:** Accepts. **Response:** 3-6 months, SASE. **Freelance Content:** 100%. **Rights:** 1st NA.

TRIQUARTERLY

Northwestern University, 2020 Ridge Ave., Evanston, IL 60208-4302. 847-491-3490. Web site: triquarterly.nwu.edu. 3x/year. $11.95. Circ.: 4,000. Susan Firestone Hahn, Editor. **Description:** Fiction, poetry, and critical commentary, from authors of diverse heritage, backgrounds, and styles. **Fiction:** Literary fiction (not genre); $5/page. **Nonfiction:** Query first; $5/page. **Poetry:** Serious, aesthetically informed, inventive; $.50/line. **Queries:** Not necessary. **E-Queries:** No. **Unsolicited mss:** Accepts. **Response:** Queries 2 months, submissions 3 months, SASE. **Freelance Content:** 70%. **Rights:** FNASR. **Payment:** On publication.

TWO RIVERS REVIEW

P.O. Box 158, Clinton, NY 13323.
E-mail: tworiversreview@juno.com.
Web site: http://trrpoetry.tripod.com/tworiversreview/index.html. Bi-annual. $6/$12. Circ.: 400. Philip Memmer, Editor. **Description:** Poetry that displays strong craft and clear language. **Poetry:** Original work only; all varieties with a keen sense of craft. Submit up to 4 poems at a time (no more than 3 times/calendar year). **Queries:** Not necessary. **E-Queries:** Yes. **Unsolicited mss:** Accepts. **Response:** Queries 2 weeks, submissions 3-8 weeks, SASE. **Freelance Content:** 80%. **Rights:** 1st, author may republish with credit given. **Payment:** In copies.

VERMONT INK

P.O. Box 3297, Burlington, VT 05401-3297.
E-mail: vermontink@aol.com. Web site: www.vermontink.com. Donna Leach, Editor. **Description:** Quarterly publication featuring short stories and poetry. **Fiction:** Uses well-written, entertaining, and basically G-rated stories. Accepts adventure, historical, humor, mainstream, mystery and suspense, regional interest, romance, science fiction, and westerns; 2,000-3,000 words; ¼ to ½ cent/word. **Poetry:** Upbeat and humorous; 4-20 lines; $5. **Tips:** Send complete manuscript, cover letter with short bio and SASE. Sample copy available for $4. **Queries:** Preferred.

VERSE
University of Georgia, English Dept., Athens, GA 30602.
3x/year. $8/$18. Circ.: 1,000. Brian Henry, Andrew Zawacki, Editors. **Description:** Poetry, criticism, and interviews with poets. Focus is international and eclectic, and favors the innovative over the staid. **Nonfiction:** Essays on poetry, interviews, reviews. **Poetry:** Up to 5 poems. **Queries:** Not necessary. **Unsolicited mss:** Accepts. **Response:** Queries 2 months, submissions 1-4 months, SASE. **Freelance Content:** 75%. **Rights:** 1st NA. **Payment:** 2 copies and a one-year subscription.

VESTAL REVIEW
2609 Dartmouth Dr., Vestal, NY 13850.
E-mail: editor@stny.rr.com. Web site: www.vestalreview.net. Quarterly. Free. Circ.: 2,000. Mark Budman, Sue O'Neill, Editors. **Description:** Features flash fiction. **Fiction:** Flash fiction, any genre; under 500 words; $.03-$.10/word. **Tips:** Seeking literary stories; no children's stories or syrupy romance. **Queries:** Not necessary. **E-Queries:** No. **Unsolicited mss:** Accepts. **Response:** 2 months. **Freelance Content:** 100%. **Rights:** 1st electronic. **Payment:** Within 30 days after publication.

VIRGINIA QUARTERLY REVIEW
One W Range, P.O. Box 400223, Charlottesville, VA 22904-4223. 434-924-3124.
E-mail: jco7e@virginia@edu. Web site: www.virginia.edu. Quarterly. $5/$18. Circ.: 4,000. Staige D. Blackford, Editor. **Description:** A journal of literature and discussion. **Fiction:** Quality fiction; $10/page. **Nonfiction:** Serious essays, articles, 3,000-6,000 words, on literature, science, politics, economics, etc.; $10/page. **Poetry:** $1/line. **Queries:** Preferred. **Unsolicited mss:** Accepts. **Payment:** On publication.

VISIONS-INTERNATIONAL
Black Buzzard Press
1007 Ficklen Rd., Fredericksburg, VA 22405. 540-310-0730.
2x/yr. $5.95/$12. Circ.: 750. Bradley R. Strahan, Editor. **Description:** Promotes world poetry and the arts, offering wide variety of original work and modern translations. **Poetry:** All styles and subjects, well-crafted, no amateur work; up to 3 pages. **Art:** B&W illustrations; send samples only. **Tips:** No racism, sexism, "greeting card"-ism. **Queries:** Not necessary. **E-Queries:** No. **Unsolicited mss:** Accepts. **Response:** SASE. **Freelance Content:** 95%. **Payment:** In copies.

WASCANA REVIEW
University of Regina, Dept. of English, Regina, SK, S4S 0A2 Canada. 306-585-4302.
E-mail: kathleen.wall@uregina.ca. Web site: www.uregina.ca./english/wrhome.htm. Biannual. $5/issue. Circ.: 250. Kathleen Wall, Editor. **Description:** Poetry and short fiction that combines craft with risk, pressure with grace. Wide variety of themes. **Fiction:** Fiction that displays an honest, meaningful grasp of human experience and of individuals' struggles to relate to themselves and the world around them; 5,000 words; $3/page. **Nonfiction:** Cutting-edge literary criticism; articles on contemporary short fiction and poetry; 7,500 words; $3/page. **Poetry:** Poetry of high artistic

merit; up to 6 poems; up to 2 pages; $10/page. **Queries:** Not necessary. **E-Queries:** Yes. **Unsolicited mss:** Accepts. **Response:** 1 week for queries, 2 months for submissions; SASE required. **Freelance Content:** 100%. **Rights:** FNASR. **Payment:** On publication.

WASHINGTON REVIEW

Friends of the Washington Review of Arts
P.O. Box 50132, Washington, DC 20091-0132. 202-638-0515.
Web site: www.washingtonreview.com. Bimonthly. $15. Circ.: 1,500. Clarissa Wittenberg, Editor. **Description:** Poetry; articles on literary, performing and fine arts in the Washington, D.C., area. Fiction, 1,000-2,500 words. **Tips:** Prefers regional writers. **Response:** 3 months. **Payment:** In copies.

WEBER STUDIES

Weber State University, 1214 University Cir., Ogden, UT 84408-1214. 626-6616.
E-mail: weberstudies@weber.edu. Web site: www.weberstudies.edu. Quarterly. Circ.: 1,000. Brad L. Roghaar, Editor. **Description:** Features narratives, critical commentary/opinion, fiction and poetry. Subjects deal with the environment and culture of the contemporary American west. **Fiction:** 5,000 words; $100-$150. **Nonfiction:** 5,000 words; $100-$150. **Poetry:** Submit multiple poems, up to 6 poems or 200 lines; $25-$50. **Queries:** Not necessary. **Unsolicited mss:** Accepts. **Response:** Queries 1 week, submissions 3-4 months, SASE. **Freelance Content:** 80%. **Rights:** 1st and Web archive. **Payment:** On publication.

WEST BRANCH

Bucknell University, Bucknell Hall, Lewisburg, PA 17837-2029. 570-577-1853.
E-mail: westbranch@bucknell.edu.
Web site: www.departments.bucknell.edu/stadler_center/westbranch. Semi-annual. $6/$10. Circ.: 700. Paula Closson Buck, Editor. **Description:** Literary magazine accepting original, unpublished poetry, fiction, literary nonfiction, and book reviews. **Fiction:** Realistic and avant-garde. **Nonfiction:** Format open. **Poetry:** No confessional verse. **Queries:** Not necessary. **E-Queries:** Yes. **Response:** 1 month, SASE. **Freelance Content:** 90%. **Rights:** 1st NA. **Payment:** In copies.

WESTERN HUMANITIES REVIEW

University of Utah
255 S Central Campus Dr., Room 3500, Salt Lake City, UT 84112. 801-581-6070.
E-mail: whr@mail.hum.utah.edu. Web site: www.hum.utah.edu/whr. Biannually. $14/yr. Barry Weller, Editor. **Description:** For educated readers. Pays $5/page. **Fiction:** Literary fiction, exciting and original (no genre fiction). **Nonfiction:** On humanities issues. **Poetry:** Yes. **Tips:** Reviews submissions September-May; all other submissions returned unread. **Queries:** Not necessary. **E-Queries:** No. **Unsolicited mss:** Accepts. **Response:** Queries 2 weeks, submissions 8-10 weeks, SASE. **Freelance Content:** 0%. **Rights:** 1st NA. **Payment:** On publication.

WHETSTONE

P.O. Box 1266, Barrington, IL 60011. 847-382-5626.
E-mail: baacouncil@aol.com. Annual. $7. Circ.: 850. Dale Griffith, Editor.
Description: Poetry, short fiction, novel excerpts, and creative fiction, from established and emerging artists across the country. **Fiction:** Character-driven prose that tells truth in detail; 6,500 words; pay varies. **Poetry:** Concrete rather than abstract; submit up to 7 poems. **E-Queries:** Yes. **Unsolicited mss:** Accepts. **Response:** Queries 1-3 days, submissions, 3-5 months, SASE. **Freelance Content:** 100%.

WILLOW SPRINGS

MS-1, Eastern Washington University,
705 W First, Spokane, WA 99204. 509-623-4349.
Biannual. $6/$11.50. Circ.: 1,200. Christopher Howell, Editor. **Description:** Poetry, short fiction, and nonfiction, of literary merit. **Tips:** No multiple submissions. Submit prose and poetry in separate envelopes. Manuscripts read September 15-May 15. **Queries:** Not necessary. **E-Queries:** No. **Unsolicited mss:** Accepts. **Response:** 4-8 weeks, SASE. **Freelance Content:** 100%. **Rights:** 1st. **Payment:** In copies.

WINDSOR REVIEW

University of Windsor, Dept. of English
Windsor, Ontario N9B 3P4 Canada. 519-253-3000.
E-mail: uwrevu@uwindsor.ca. Web site: www.windsorreview.com. Biannual. $15 issue. Circ.: 500. Marty Gervais, Editor. **Description:** Literary fiction and poetry. **Fiction:** Literary fiction; under 5,000 words; $50/story. **Nonfiction:** Interviews with well-known writers; 3,000-7,000 words; $50. **Poetry:** All types; experimental, concrete or traditional; $15/poem. **Art:** Prefer B&W. $100-$200. **Tips:** Does not accept e-mail submissions. **Queries:** Not necessary. **E-Queries:** Yes. **Unsolicited mss:** Accepts. **Response:** Submissions 1-3 months, SASE. **Freelance Content:** 90%. **Rights:** 1st. **Payment:** On publication.

WITNESS

Oakland Community College
27055 Orchard Lake Rd., Farmington Hills, MI 48334. 734-996-5732.
E-mail: stinepj@umich.edu. Web site: www.webdelsol.com/witness. Semi-annual. Peter Stine, Editor. **Description:** Literary journal featuring fiction, poetry, essays, memoirs, and artwork. **Fiction:** Fiction, 5-20 pages; pays $6/page. **Nonfiction:** Essays, 5-20 pages; pays $6/page. **Poetry:** Submit up to 3 at a time; pays $10/page. **Tips:** Accepts simultaneous submissions. Do not submit material electronically. **Payment:** On publication.

THE WORCESTER REVIEW

6 Chatham St., Worcester, MA 01609.
Web site: www.geocities.com/paris/leftbank. Annual. $10/$20. Rodger Martin, Editor. **Description:** Literary journal. **Fiction:** 4,000 words. **Nonfiction:** Critical articles about poetry with New England connection. **Poetry:** Submit up to 5 poems at a time.

Tips: Send $6 for sample copy. **Queries:** Not necessary. **E-Queries:** No. **Unsolicited mss:** Accepts. **Response:** Submissions 6 months, SASE. **Rights:** 1st. **Payment:** In copies.

YALE REVIEW

Yale University, P.O. Box 208243, New Haven, CT 06520-8243. 203-432-0499. Quarterly. $28/yr. Circ.: 6,000. J. D. McClatchy, Editor. **Description:** Literary magazine with fiction, nonfiction, and poetry. **Fiction:** $400/story. **Nonfiction:** $500. **Poetry:** Serious poetry; pay varies. **Queries:** Not necessary. **E-Queries:** No. **Unsolicited mss:** Accepts. **Response:** Queries 1 month, submissions 2 months, SASE. **Freelance Content:** 30%. **Rights:** 1st serial. **Payment:** On publication.

YEMASSEE

University of South Carolina, Dept. of English, Columbia, SC 29208. 803-777-2085. Web site: www.cla.sc.edu/engl/index.html. Biannual. $15 ($7 student). Circ.: 500. Corinna McLeod, Editor. **Description:** Literary journal of poetry, short fiction, one-act plays, brief essays, and interviews. **Fiction:** Short, smart, accessible, character-driven; to 5,000 words. **Nonfiction:** Literary reviews, interviews with literary figures; to 3,000 words. **Poetry:** No fixed length; prefers poems under 3 pages. **Tips:** Offers $200 award for fiction and poetry in each issue. **Queries:** Not necessary. **E-Queries:** No. **Unsolicited mss:** Accepts. **Response:** 2 months after each deadline, SASE required. **Freelance Content:** 100%. **Rights:** 1st.

ZOETROPE: ALL STORY

916 Kearny St., San Francisco, CA 94133. 415-788-7500. E-mail: info@all-story.com. Web site: www.all-story.com. Quarterly. Circ.: 20,000. Francis Ford Coppola, Publisher. **Description:** Literary publication of stories and one-act plays. **Fiction:** Stories and one-act plays; under 7,000 words. **Tips:** No submissions accepted from June 1 through August 31. **Queries:** Preferred. **Response:** 4 months, SASE. **Payment:** On acceptance.

ZYZZYVA

P.O. Box 590069, San Francisco, CA 94159-0069. 415-752-4393. E-mail: editor@zyzzyva.org. Web site: www.zyzzyva.org. 3x/year. $11/$24. Circ.: 4,000. Howard Junker, Editor. **Description:** A journal of West coast writers and artists. Pays $50/piece. **Fiction:** Freestanding (i.e., no book excerpts). **Nonfiction:** Essays. **Poetry:** Yes. **Tips:** Accepts material only from current West Coast (California, Oregon, Washington, Hawaii, Alaska) residents. **Queries:** Not necessary. **E-Queries:** No. **Unsolicited mss:** Accepts. **Response:** Submissions 1 month, SASE. **Freelance Content:** 85%. **Rights:** 1st serial. **Payment:** On publication.

MYSTERY & DETECTIVE

ALFRED HITCHCOCK'S MYSTERY MAGAZINE

Dell Magazines, 475 Park Ave. S, Fl. 11, New York, NY 10016. 212-686-7188. Web site: www.themysteryplace.com. 11x/year. $3.50/issue. **Description:** Original mystery short stories. **Fiction:** Well-plotted, plausible mystery, suspense, detection, and crime stories. Ghost stories, humor, futuristic, or atmospheric tales considered if they include a crime (or the suggestion of one); up to 14,000 words; $.08/word. **Tips:** Submissions by new writers strongly encouraged. No reprints. **Queries:** Not necessary. **E-Queries:** No. **Unsolicited mss:** Accepts. **Response:** Submissions to 3 months, SASE required. **Freelance Content:** 100%. **Rights:** Anthology, foreign serial. **Payment:** On acceptance.

COZY DETECTIVE MYSTERY

Ink Publications
686 Jake Ct., McMinnville, OR 97128-2546.
E-mail: detectivemag@onlinemac.com. 3-5x/year. $4.95/issue. Tom Youngblood, Editor. **Description:** Mystery fiction by new authors breaking into the genre. Stories must be heavy on character and mystery content. **Tips:** No stories over 6,000 words. **Queries:** Preferred. **E-Queries:** Yes. **Unsolicited mss:** Accepts. **Response:** 6 weeks, SASE. **Rights:** FNASR. **Payment:** In copies.

ELLERY QUEEN'S MYSTERY MAGAZINE

Dell Magazines, 475 Park Ave. S, Fl. 11, New York, NY 10016. 212-686-7188. Web site: www.themysteryplace.com. 11x/year. $3.50/$39.97. Circ.: 300,000. Janet Hutchings, Editor. **Description:** A leading mystery magazine. Features quality writing, original plots, and professional craftsmanship. **Fiction:** Mystery and crime **Fiction:** Police procedurals, private-eye stories, tales of suspense, traditional whodunits, cozies; 250-20,000 words (usually 2,500-8,000 words); $.05-$.08/word. **Tips:** Interested in new authors. Seeking private-eye stories (avoid sex, sadism, sensationalism for its own sake). "We are always in the market for the best detective, crime, and mystery stories being written today." **Queries:** Not necessary. **E-Queries:** No. **Unsolicited mss:** Accepts. **Response:** 3 months; SASE required. **Freelance Content:** 95%. **Rights:** 1st serial. **Payment:** On acceptance.

HARDBOILED

Gryphon Publications
P.O. Box 209, Brooklyn, NY 11228-0209.
Web site: www.gryphonbooks.com. Gary Lovisi, Editor. **Description:** Hard-hitting fiction by new masters. Mind-blasting nonfiction and riveting private eye and crime stories. **Fiction:** Cutting-edge crime fiction, with impact; under 3,000 words. **Tips:** Sample copy $8. New double issue: 200+ pages, $20. **Queries:** Preferred. **E-Queries:** No. **Unsolicited mss:** Accepts. **Response:** Queries 2 weeks, submissions 6 weeks, SASE. **Freelance Content:** 35%. **Rights:** 1st NA.

THE MYSTERY REVIEW

P.O. Box 233, Colborne, Ontario, Canada K0K 1S0. 613-475-4440.
E-mail: mystrev@reach.net. Web site: www.TheMysteryReview.com. Quarterly.
Barbara Davey, Editor. **Description:** Reviews, interviews, word games, and puzzles
related to mystery titles and authors. No fiction. Pays honorarium. **Nonfiction:** True
crime, interviews with authors or others related to the mystery genre; 2,000-5,000
words. **Fillers:** Short filler articles, puzzles, and word games related to the mys-
tery/suspense genre. **Columns, Departments:** Book Reviews, Book Shop Beat;
500-700 words. **Art:** To accompany stories; B&W photos, illustrations. **Queries:**
Preferred. **E-Queries:** Yes. **Unsolicited mss:** Accepts. **Freelance Content:** 90%.
Rights: 1st. **Payment:** On publication.

MYSTERY TIME

P.O. Box 2907, Decatur, IL 62524.
Semiannual. $10/yr. Circ.: 100. Linda Hutton, Editor. **Description:** Encourages
beginning writers who can produce a clever plot. Female characters preferred.
Fiction: Suspense; a touch of humor is always welcome; 1,500 words. **Poetry:** Must
relate to mysteries or famous authors; 20 lines; $5/poem. **Tips:** Rely on plot twists,
rather than blood 'n' gore. Short stories only, do not submit novels. **Queries:** Not necessary. **E-Queries:** No. **Unsolicited mss:** Accepts. **Response:** Submission 1 month,
SASE. **Freelance Content:** 90%. **Rights:** One-time. **Payment:** On acceptance.

NEW MYSTERY MAGAZINE

101 W 23rd St., New York, NY 10011. 212-353-1582.
Quarterly. Charles Raisch, Editor. **Description:** Mystery, crime, detection, and suspense short stories. **Fiction:** Prefers sympathetic characters in trouble, visual scenes;
2,000-6,000 words; pays to $500. **Columns, Departments:** Book reviews, 250-2,000
words, of upcoming or recent novels. **Tips:** No true-crime stories accepted.
Payment: On publication.

OVER MY DEAD BODY!

P.O. Box 1778, Auburn, WA 98071-1778.
E-mail: omdb@Worldnet.att.net. Web site: www.overmydeadbody.com. Quarterly.
$5.95/$20. Circ.: 1,000. Cherie Jung, Editor. **Description:** Mystery, suspense, and
crime fiction and nonfiction. **Fiction:** Mystery or crime-related fiction, from cozy to
hardboiled, including suspense, and cross-over mysteries; 750-4,000 words;
$.01/word. **Nonfiction:** Author profiles/interviews, mystery-related travel articles;
500 words and up; $10-$25. **Art:** Photographs to accompany mss. **Queries:**
Required. **E-Queries:** Yes. **Unsolicited mss:** Accepts. **Response:** 4-6 weeks,
SASE. **Freelance Content:** 100%. **Rights:** FNASR. **Payment:** On acceptance.
Contact: Bill Wemple.

THE STRAND

P.O. Box 1418, Birmingham, MI 48012-1418. 248-788-5948.
E-mail: strandmag@worldnet.att.net. Web site: www.strandmag.com. Quarterly.

Andrew Gulli, Managing Editor. **Description:** Featured pieces are modeled after the writing styles of Sir Arthur Conan Doyle, Daphne de Maurier, and Robert Louis Stevenson. **Fiction:** 3,000-5,000 words; $50-$150. **Payment:** On publication.

ROMANCE & CONFESSION

BLACK ROMANCE/BRONZE THRILLS
Sterling/Macfadden Partnership
333 Seventh Ave., Fl. 11, New York, NY 10001-5004. 212-979-4800.
E-mail: tpowell@sterlingmacfadden.com. Bimonthly. $19/yr. Circ.: 70,000. Takesha Powell, Editor. **Description:** Short romantic fiction for African-American women. **Fiction:** Romance fiction, first-person, featuring African-American women; 19-21 pages; pay varies. **Nonfiction:** On relationships. **Columns, Departments:** On spicing up romance/sex lives for couples; tips on dating, beauty; 3 pages; $125. **Tips:** Avoid cultural stereotypes. Stories should be juicy (mild sex scenes), romantic, but not offensive. **Queries:** Not necessary. **E-Queries:** Yes. **Unsolicited mss:** Accepts. **Response:** 3-4 weeks, SASE. **Freelance Content:** 100%. **Rights:** All. **Payment:** On publication.

BLACK SECRETS
Sterling/MacFadden Partnership
333 Seventh Ave., Fl. 11, New York, NY 10001-5004. 212-780-4800.
E-mail: tpowell@sterlingmacfadden.com. Web site: www.sterlingmacfadden.com. Monthly. $11/yr. Circ.: 70,000. Takesha Powell, Editor. **Description:** For African-American women. **Fiction:** Erotic, short, romantic fiction; $100. **Columns, Departments:** $125. **Queries:** Required. **E-Queries:** Yes. **Unsolicited mss:** Accepts. **Response:** SASE required. **Freelance Content:** 100%. **Rights:** All. **Payment:** On publication.

INTIMACY
Sterling/Macfadden Partnership
333 Seventh Ave., Fl. 11, New York, NY 10001. 212-780-3500.
E-mail: takpow@aol.com. Web site: www.sterlingmacfadden.com. Bimonthly. $2.99/issue. Circ.: 50,000. Takesha D Powell, Editor. **Description:** Short, first-person romantic fiction for African-American women. **Fiction:** For black women, ages 18-45. Must have contemporary plot with two romantic/intimate love scenes; 19-21 pages. **Tips:** Avoid clichés, profanity, stereotypes. **Queries:** Not necessary. **E-Queries:** Yes. **Unsolicited mss:** Accepts. **Response:** 3-4 weeks, SASE required. **Freelance Content:** 100%. **Rights:** All. **Payment:** On publication.

JIVE
Sterling/MacFadden Partnership
333 Seventh Ave., Fl. 11, New York, NY 10001-5004. 212-780-3500.
E-mail: tpowell@sterlingmacfadden.com. Web site: www.sterlingmacfadden.com.

Monthly. $19/yr. Circ.: 65,000. Takesha Powell, Editor. **Description:** Romantic fiction for African-American women. **Fiction:** Focus on emotions of main character; pays $100-$125. **Queries:** Required. **E-Queries:** Yes. **Unsolicited mss:** Accepts. **Freelance Content:** 100%. **Rights:** All. **Payment:** On publication.

ROMANCE AND BEYOND

3527 Ambassador Caffery Pkwy., PMB 9, Lafayette, LA 70503-5130. 337-991-9095. E-mail: rbeyond@aol.com. Web site: www.romanceandbeyond.com. Annual. Softcover Anthology $9.99. Mary Tarver, Editor. **Description:** Speculative romantic short stories and poetry, combining elements of romance with science fiction, fantasy, and the paranormal. **Fiction:** Up to 10,000 words; $.005/word. **Poetry:** Length varies; pays in copies. **Tips:** Internal conflict created by attraction between hero and heroine. Tone can be dark to humorous, but story must be a romance with happy ending. Sources of external conflict left to your imagination, the more original the better. Reading period February-May. Annual contest: October-January. **Queries:** Not necessary. **E-Queries:** No. **Unsolicited mss:** Accepts. **Response:** Submission 4 months, SASE. **Freelance Content:** 100%. **Rights:** One-time. **Payment:** On acceptance.

ROMANTIC TIMES MAGAZINE

See page 638 for full listing.
Description: Topics on the romance-fiction publishing industry.

TRUE ROMANCE

Sterling/McFadden Partnership
333 Seventh Ave., Fl. 11, New York, NY 10001. 212-979-4800.
E-mail: pvitucci@sterlingmacfadden.com. Monthly. $2.99/issue. Circ.: 225,000. Pat Vitucci, Editor. **Description:** Dramatic stories of personal redemption, romance, family relationships, humor, women's issues. **Fiction:** Topical stories based on news events; intriguing subjects; 5,000-10,000 words; $.03/word. **Poetry:** Up to 24 lines; $10-$30. **Columns, Departments:** Cupid's Corner (photo and 1,000 words), $50; Passages (up to 2,000 words), $50-$100. **Tips:** Readers must sympathize with the narrator. Stories are to be written in first person narrative. Please read an issue or two before submitting. **Queries:** Preferred. **E-Queries:** Yes. **Unsolicited mss:** Accepts. **Response:** 8-12 months, SASE. **Freelance Content:** 100%. **Payment:** On publication.

WOMAN'S WORLD

See page 631 for full listing.
Description: For women, ages 18-60, on a variety of nonfiction topics; includes dramatic stories of adventure, crisis, or romance.

SCIENCE FICTION & FANTASY

ABSOLUTE MAGNITUDE
P.O. Box 2988, Radford, VA 24143.
Web site: www.sfsite/dnaweb/home.htm. Quarterly. Warren Lapine. **Description:** Character-driven, technical science fiction. **Fiction:** No fantasy, horror, satire, or funny science fiction; 1,000-25,000 words; $.03-$.07/word. **Payment:** On publication.

ANALOG SCIENCE FICTION AND FACT
475 Park Ave. S, New York, NY 10016. 212-686-7188.
E-mail: analog@dellmagazines.com. Web site: www.analogsf.com. 11x/year. $3.50/issue, $39.97/year. Circ.: 50,000. Stanley Schmidt, Editor. **Description:** Science fiction, with strong characters in believable future or alien settings. Home to many of science fiction's foremost writers, with long tradition of discovering and cultivating new talent. **Fiction:** Short stories, 2,000-7,500 words; novelettes, 10,000-20,000 words; serials, to 80,000 words; $.04-$.08/word. **Nonfiction:** Future-related articles; 4,000 words; $.06/word. **Poetry:** Yes; $1/line. **Tips:** Queries required for serials and nonfiction only. **Queries:** Preferred. **E-Queries:** No. **Unsolicited mss:** Accepts. **Response:** 1 month, SASE required. **Freelance Content:** 100%. **Rights:** FNASR, nonexclusive foreign serial. **Payment:** On acceptance.

ASIMOV'S SCIENCE FICTION MAGAZINE
475 Park Ave. S, Fl. 11, New York, NY 10016. 212-686-7188.
E-mail: asimovs@dellmagazines.com. Web site: www.asimovs.com. 11x/year. Circ.: 40,000. Gardner Dozois, Editor. **Description:** Short, character-oriented science fiction and fantasy. **Fiction:** Stories in which characters, rather than science, provide main focus for reader's interest. Mostly serious, thoughtful fiction, some humorous; Up to 30,000 words; $.06-$.08/word. **Poetry:** Up to 40 lines; $1/line. **Tips:** Borderline fantasy fine, but no Sword & Sorcery. No explicit sex or violence. **Queries:** Not necessary. **E-Queries:** No. **Unsolicited mss:** Accepts. **Response:** No queries please, submission 2-3 months, SASE required. **Freelance Content:** 90%. **Rights:** First English Rights, nonexclusive reprint rights. **Payment:** On acceptance.

CENTURY MAGAZINE
Century Publishing, Inc.
P.O. Box 336, Hastings-on-Hudson, NY 10706.
Web site: www.centurymag.com. Robert K. J. Killheffer. **Description:** Literary science fiction, fantasy, and magic realism. **Fiction:** 1,000-20,000 words; pays $.04-$.06/word. **Payment:** On acceptance.

DRAGON
Wizards of the Coast, Inc.
1801 Lind Ave. SW, Renton, WA 98055-4068. 425-226-6500.
E-mail: dragon@wizards.com. Web site: www.wizards.com. Monthly. $34.95. Circ.: 45,000. Dave Gross, Editor. **Description:** On fantasy and science fiction role-playing

games. **Fiction:** Fantasy, 1,500-8,000 words; pays $.05-$.08/word. **Nonfiction:** Articles, 1,500-7,500 words; pays $.04/word. **Tips:** All submissions must include a disclosure form. **Payment:** On publication.

FLESH AND BLOOD

121 Joseph St., Bayville, NJ 08721.
E-mail: horrorjack@aol.com. Web site: www.horrorseek.com/horror/fleshblood. 3x/year. Circ.: 500. Jack Fisher, Editor. **Description:** Features dark fantasy, bizarre, and supernatural stories. Despite name, prefers work that is subtle, magic realism, bizarre eccentric, avant-garde, or any mix thereof. **Fiction:** Currently seeking horror/dark fantasy work. Should have one or more of the following elements: darkly fantastic, surreal, supernatural, bizarre, offbeat; 4,000 words max; $.01-$.02/word. **Tips:** Do not exceed maximum word count. Stories should be unique, entertaining, and imaginative. The more descriptive and dark, the better. Avoid stories with insane main characters; about obese people who eat others or who are evil; stories not set in the modern day; over-used vampire, werewolf stories; tales about evil gods and their followers; based solely on monsters; excessive gore, blood, sex, etc. Be sure to include SASE and brief letter listing previous publication credits. **Queries:** Not necessary. **E-Queries:** Yes. **Unsolicited mss:** Accepts. **Response:** 1-2 months, SASE required. **Rights:** FNASR, reprints. **Payment:** On publication.

HADROSAUR TALES

Hadrosaur Productions
P.O. Box 8468, Las Cruces, NM 88006.
E-mail: hadrosaur@zianet.com. Web site: www.hadrosaur.com. Semi-annual. $6.95/$11. Circ.: 150. David Summers, Editor. **Description:** Short stories and poetry. **Fiction:** Literary science fiction and fantasy. Contemporary or historical fiction welcome if it includes a mythic or science-fictional element. Psychological or character-oriented horror considered if it does not present any graphic violence; 6,000 words max; $6/story. **Poetry:** Poems with science fiction/fantasy imagery and themes; 50 lines max; $2. **Art:** Pen-and-ink line drawings (cover); pay negotiable. **Tips:** Avoid cliche-fantasy (e.g., lone knight goes off to slay the evil dragon). **Queries:** Not necessary. **E-Queries:** Yes. **Unsolicited mss:** Accepts. **Response:** Queries 1 week, submissions 1-6 weeks, SASE. **Freelance Content:** 100%. **Rights:** One-time. **Payment:** On acceptance.

THE LEADING EDGE

3163 JKHB, Provo, UT 84604.
E-mail: tle@byu.edu. Web site: http://leadingedge.byu.edu. Semiannual. $11.85 (3 issues). Circ.: 500. Ben Olsen, Editor. **Description:** Science fiction and fantasy. Publishes many new writers. **Fiction:** 18,000 words max; $.01/word ($10-$100 max.). **Nonfiction:** On science fiction, fantasy, or author interviews; 10,000 words max; pays in copies. **Poetry:** Length varies; $10/poem. **Columns, Departments:** Book reviews; pays in copies. **Tips:** Avoid rehashed plots, poor mechanics, poor plot resolution. No sex, graphic violence, or strong language. **Queries:** Not necessary.

E-Queries: No. **Unsolicited mss:** Accepts. **Response:** Submissions 4-6 months, SASE. **Freelance Content:** 100%. **Rights:** FNASR. **Payment:** On publication.

LOCUS

Locus Publications
P.O. Box 13305, Oakland, CA 94661. 510-339-9196.
E-mail: locus@locusmag.com. Web site: www.locusmag.com. Monthly. Circ.: 7,500. Charles N. Brown, Editor-in-Chief. **Description:** Publication covering industry news for professional writers and publishers of science fiction and fantasy.

MAGAZINE OF FANTASY & SCIENCE FICTION

P.O. Box 3447, Hoboken, NJ 07030.
E-mail: fandsf@aol.com. Web site: www.fsfmag.com. Monthly. $3.50/issue (U.S.), $3.95 (Canada). Circ.: 40,000. Gordon Van Gelder, Editor. **Description:** Digest-sized, devoted to speculative fiction. **Fiction:** Prefers character-oriented stories. Science fiction element may be slight, but present; up to 25,000 words; $.05-$.08/word. **Tips:** Receives much fantasy, needs science fiction or humor. **Queries:** Preferred. **E-Queries:** No. **Unsolicited mss:** Accepts. **Response:** 8 weeks, SASE. **Rights:** worldwide serial, and option on anthology. **Payment:** On acceptance.

NIGHT TERRORS

1202 W Market St., Orrville, OH 44667-1710. 330-683-0338.
E-mail: dedavidson@night-terrors-publications.com.
Web site: www.night-terrors-publications.com. Annual. $6/issue. Circ.: 1,000. Mr. D. E. Davidson, Editor. **Description:** Short stories of psychological horror, the supernatural, or occult. Emphasis on "continuing terror"; stories should have beginning, middle, and end, but in the end, the terror/threat should not be resolved. **Fiction:** 2,000-5,000 words; pay in copies or by arrangement. **Tips:** Prefers stories which make the reader think and grow edgy, not those which make them flinch or grow nauseous. No horror in which women or children are abused; no stories with child as point-of-view character. **Queries:** Not necessary. **E-Queries:** Yes. **Unsolicited mss:** Accepts. **Response:** Queries 1 week, submissions 12 weeks, SASE. **Freelance Content:** 95%. **Rights:** FNASR. **Payment:** On publication.

OF UNICORNS AND SPACE STATIONS

P.O. Box 200, Bountiful, UT 84011-0200.
E-mail: mailroom@genedavis.com. Web site: www.genedavis.com. Semiannual. $4/$16 (4 issues). Circ.: 500. Gene Davis, Editor. **Description:** Science fiction and fantasy magazine for adults with a family-oriented writing style. **Fiction:** Science fiction or fantasy, sometimes a little horror; 250-5,000 words; $.05/word. **Poetry:** Prefers fixed form poetry; any reasonable length; $.05/word, $5 max. **Art:** B&W line art. **Queries:** Not necessary. **E-Queries:** Yes. **Unsolicited mss:** Accepts. **Response:** 3 months, SASE. **Freelance Content:** 100%. **Payment:** On publication.

ON SPEC

P.O. Box 4727, Edmonton, AB T6E 5G6 Canada. 780-413-0215.
E-mail: onspec@canada.com. Web site: www.icomm.ca/onspec/. Quarterly. $22/year.
Circ.: 1,500. Diane Walton, Editor. **Description:** Publishes science fiction, horror,
fantasy, and speculative fiction. **Fiction:** Science fiction, fantasy, horror, ghost stories,
fairy stories, magic realism, speculative fiction; up to 6,000 words; C$50-C$180.
Nonfiction: By assignment. **Poetry:** Science fiction, fantasy themes; blank, free
verse, discursive prose; up to 100 lines; C$20. **Fillers:** Science fiction, fantasy, horror,
ghost stories, fairy stories, magic realism, speculative fiction; up to 1,000 words; C$50.
Art: Illustrations by assignment; B&W; $50/inside use, $200/cover. **Queries:** Not
necessary. **E-Queries:** Yes. **Unsolicited mss:** Accepts. **Response:** 1-2 weeks; SASE
required. **Rights:** FNASR. **Payment:** On acceptance.

OUTER DARKNESS

1312 N Delaware Pl., Tulsa, OK 74110. 918-832-1246.
Quarterly. $2.95 (by mail, $3.95). Circ.: 500. Dennis Kirk. **Description:** "Where
Nightmares Roam Unleashed," horror and science fiction. Illustrated, also poetry,
cartoons, and interviews. **Fiction:** Traditional horror and science fiction; to 5,000
words. **Nonfiction:** Interviews with authors, artists, editors; up to 1,500 words.
Poetry: Some free verse, prefers traditional rhyming; up to 30 lines. **Fillers:**
Cartoons. **Art:** All stories illustrated; submit sample work. **Tips:** If no word within
normal response time, send a follow-up letter to inquire. **Queries:** Not necessary.
E-Queries: No. **Response:** Queries 2 weeks, submissions 6-8 weeks, SASE.
Freelance Content: 25%. **Rights:** 1st. **Payment:** In copies.

PEGASUS ONLINE

E-mail: editors@pegasusonline.com. Web site: www.pegasusonline.com. Quarterly.
Scott Marlowe, Editor. **Description:** E-zine for fantasy and science-fiction writers
and readers. Fiction up to 7,500 words in either genre. No payment.

REALMS OF FANTASY

Sovereign Media Co.
11305 Sunset Hills Rd., Reston, VA 20190. 703-471-1556.
Bimonthly. Circ.: 110,000. **Description:** Topics and reviews of interest to readers of
science fiction.

SCAVENGER'S NEWSLETTER

See page 638 for full listing.
Description: Market newsletter for science fiction, fantasy, horror, and mystery writers and/or artists with focus on small presses.

THE SILVER WEB

Buzzcity Press
P.O. Box 38190, Tallahassee, FL 32315. 850-385-8948.
E-mail: buzzcity@yourvillage.com. Ann Kennedy, Editor. **Description:** Fantastical

fiction, including science fiction, dark fantasy, etc. **Tips:** Currently not accepting unsolicited submissions. **Queries:** Preferred.

SPACE AND TIME

138 W 70 St. 4B, New York, NY 10023-4468.
Web site: www.cith.org/space&time.html. Biannual. $5/issue. Circ.: 2,000. Gordon Linzner, Editor. **Description:** Science fiction, fantasy, horror, and things that fall between the cracks. Also, a healthy selection of poetry (same genre), along with the occasion short feature. **Fiction:** Science-fiction, fantasy, horror; 10,000 words max.; $.01/word. **Poetry:** All styles and forms (rhymed, unrhymed, etc.). **Art:** B&W artwork assigned, to illustrate specific stories. Send photocopied samples; $10. **Tips:** Avoid clichés. No media fiction. Appreciates material that deserves to be in print, but which other magazines don't quite know what to do with. **Queries:** Not necessary. **E-Queries:** No. **Unsolicited mss:** Accepts. **Response:** Submissions 1-4 months. **Freelance Content:** 99%. **Rights:** FNASR. **Payment:** On publication.

STRANGE HORIZONS

P.O. Box 1693, Dubuque, IA 52004-1693.
E-mail: editor@strangehorizons.com. Web site: www.strangehorizons.com.
Mary Anne Mohanraj, Editor-in-Chief. **Description:** E-zine of speculative and science fiction. Features art, articles, fiction, poetry, and reviews. **Fiction:** To 5,000 words; pays $.04/word. **Nonfiction:** Articles, 1,000-5,000 words; pay varies. **Poetry:** To 100 lines. **Columns, Departments:** Art and book reviews, 750-1,000 words. **Tips:** Submit all material via email: fiction@strangehorizons.com; poetry@strangehorizons.com; gallery@strangehorizons.com; articles@strangehorizons.com. No simultaneous submissions. **Queries:** Required. **E-Queries:** Yes. **Rights:** 1st, worldwide (exclusive for 2 months, then reverts to author).

TALEBONES

Fairwood Press
5203 Quincy Ave. SE, Auburn, WA 98092.
E-mail: talebones@nventure.com. Web site: www.fairwoodpress.com. Quarterly. $5/issue, $18/year. Circ.: 650. Patrick and Honna Swenson, Editors. **Description:** Science fiction and dark fantasy. **Fiction:** Sci-fi and dark fantasy stories with a punch, often slanted toward darker fiction; 6,000 words; $.01-$.02/word. **Poetry:** All suitable forms and themes; $10. **Fillers:** Cartoons; $10. **Art:** Most formats; $15-50. **Tips:** Send cover letter, but keep it to the point. **Queries:** Not necessary. **E-Queries:** Yes. **Unsolicited mss:** Accepts. **Response:** 1-8 weeks, SASE. **Rights:** FNASR. **Payment:** On acceptance.

THE URBANITE

Urban Legend Press
P.O. Box 4737, Davenport, IA 52808.
Web site: http://theurbanite.tripod.com. 3x/year. Circ.: 1,000. Mark McLaughlin, Editor. **Description:** Dark fantasy, horror (no gore), surrealism, reviews, and social

commentary. **Fiction:** To 3,000 words; pays $.02-$.03/word. **Poetry:** Free-verse, to 2 pages, $10. **Tips:** Query for coming themes. **Payment:** On acceptance.

WEIRD TALES

123 Crooked Ln., King of Prussia, PA 19406. 610-275-4463. E-mail: owlswick@netaxs.com. Web site: www.weird-tales.com. Quarterly. $4.95/issue, $16/year. Circ.: 10,000. George Scithers and Darrel Schweitzer, Editors. **Description:** Horror and fantasy fiction. **Fiction:** Short stories with supernatural content; fantasy and horror; up to 10,000 words; $.02-$.06/word. **Tips:** Send hard copy of manuscript. **Queries:** Not necessary. **E-Queries:** Yes. **Unsolicited mss:** Accepts. **Response:** 1 week for queries, 1-3 months for submissions; SASE required. **Freelance Content:** 90%. **Rights:** FNASR. **Payment:** On publication.

BOOK PUBLISHERS

GENERAL ADULT BOOKS

This and the two following sections feature publishers, in turn, of general adult books, juvenile books, and religious books. These lists include a wide range of options, from some of the largest trade publishers to a selected list of many smaller presses and university presses.

Many publishers are willing to consider either unsolicited queries or manuscripts, but an increasing number have a policy of only reading submissions sent to them via literary agents. Since finding an agent willing to take on a new writer's work is not always an easy task, many writers still choose to present their manuscripts directly to publishers on their own.

Before even considering submitting a complete manuscript to an editor, it is always advisable to send a brief query letter describing the proposed book, and an SASE. The letter should also include information about the author's special qualifications for dealing with the particular topic covered, as well as any previous publication credits. An outline of the book (or a synopsis for fiction) and a sample chapter may also be included.

While it is common courtesy to submit a book manuscript to only one publisher at a time, it is often acceptable to submit the same query or proposal in advance to more than one editor simultaneously, as it takes an editor less time to review a query and respond with some indication of further interest. When sending multiple queries, however, always state clearly in your letter that you are doing this.

With any submission of manuscript materials to a publisher, be sure to enclose sufficient postage for the manuscript's return.

Royalty rates for hardcover books usually start at 10% of the retail price of the book and increase after a certain number of copies have been sold. Paperbacks generally have a somewhat lower rate, about 5% to 8%. Smaller presses and university presses sometimes base their royalty on net receipts (i.e., what they get after discounts), rather than the retail price (the "list price" printed on the book). It is customary for the publishing company to pay the author a cash advance against royalties when the book contract is signed or when the finished manuscript is received. Some publishers pay on a flat-fee basis.

Writers seeking publication of book-length poetry manuscripts are encouraged to consider contests that offer publication as the prize (see Prizes, in Other Markets & Resources).

A CAPPELLA BOOKS

Chicago Review Press
814 N Franklin St., Chicago, IL 60610. 312-337-0747.
Web site: www.ipgbook.com.
Description: Publisher of books on music, performing arts, and film. **Number of Books/Yr.:** 3-4 titles/yr. 30-40% of books from first-time authors; 50% unagented.
Proposal Process: Submit query, 2 sample chapters, and SASE. Responds in 1 month to queries. **Payment:** Royalty.

A.R.E. PRESS
Edgar Cayce's Association for Research and Enlightenment
215 67th St., Virginia Beach, VA 23451. 757-428-3588.
Web site: www.edgarcayce.org.
Description: Publishes materials that center on spirituality and self-help.

AAA PUBLISHING
1000 AAA Dr., MS66, Heathrow, FL 32746. 407-444-7915.
E-mail: lspence@national.aaa.com.
Lisa Spence, Editor.
Description: Publishes atlases and travel guides.

ABINGDON PRESS
United Methodist Publishing House
201 Eighth Ave. S, P.O. Box 801, Nashville, TN 37203. 615-749-6301.
Web site: www.abingdon.org.
Joseph A. Crowe, Editor.
Description: General-interest books: mainline, social issues, marriage/family, self-help, exceptional people, etc. **Proposal Process:** Query with outline and 1-2 sample chapters. Guidelines available.

HENRY N. ABRAMS, INC.
La Martiniere Groupe
100 Fifth Ave., New York, NY 10011. 212-206-7715.
E-mail: submissions@abramsbooks.com. Web site: www.abramsbooks.com.
Mark McGowan, Publisher.
Description: Publisher of illustrated art books. **Number of Books/Yr.:** 150 titles/yr.
Proposal Process: Submit outline, sample chapters, and illustrations. **Payment:** Royalty. **Contact:** Eric Himmel, Editor-in-Chief.

ACADEMIC PRESS
A Harcourt Science and Technology Company
525 B St., Suite 1900, San Diego, CA 92101. 619-231-0926.
E-mail: ap@acad.com. Web site: www.academicpress.com.
Description: Scientific and technical books and journals for research scientists, students, and professionals; upper-level undergraduate and graduate science texts.
Contact: Editorial Department.

ACADEMY CHICAGO PUBLISHERS
363 W Erie St., Chicago, IL 60610. 312-751-7300.
E-mail: academy363@aol.com. Web site: www.academychicago.com.
Anita Miller, Editor.
Description: General-adult quality fiction and nonfiction. Classic mysteries; history; biographies; travel; books by and about women. No how-to, explicit sex, grotesque

violence, sci-fi, horror. **Proposal Process:** Query with 4 sample chapters. SASE required. **Contact:** Jordan Miller.

ACTIVITY RESOURCES
20655 Hathaway Ave., Hayward, CA 94541. 510-782-1300.
E-mail: info@activity_resources.com. Web site: www.activityresources.com.
Mary Laycock, Editor.
Description: Math educational material only. Main focus is grades K-8. **Proposal Process:** Submit complete manuscript. **Payment:** Royalty.

ADAMS MEDIA CORPORATION
57 Littlefield St., Avon, MA 02322. 508-427-7100.
E-mail: editors@adamsmedia.com. Web site: www.adamsmedia.com.
Gary Krebs, Director of Publishing.
Description: Nonfiction trade paperbacks with strong backlist potential. Subject categories include: self-help, how-to, lifestyles, relationships, parenting, inspiration, popular reference, business, small business, careers, and personal finance, among others. **Number of Books/Yr.:** 100 titles/year. **Proposal Process:** Query with outline and sample chapters, and SASE. Response time: 1 month. Multiple queries accepted. No electronic queries. Hard copy. **Payment:** Royalty.

ADAMS-BLAKE PUBLISHING
8041 Sierra St., Fair Oaks, CA 95628. 916-962-9296.
E-mail: media@adams-blake.com. Web site: www.adams-blake.com.
Monica Blane, Senior Editor.
Description: Technical subjects for the corporate market. Books on business, careers, and technology. **Number of Books/Yr.:** 5 titles/year (100 submissions), 90% first-time authors, 100% unagented. **Proposal Process:** Query with outline. Response time: 4 weeks. Considers multiple queries. No electronic queries. Hard-copy format preferred. **Payment:** Royalty, 10-15% net.

ADAMS-HALL PUBLISHING
P.O. Box 491002, Los Angeles, CA 90049. 800-888-4452.
Sue Ann Bacon.
Description: Business and personal finance books with wide market appeal. **Proposal Process:** Query with proposed book idea, a listing of current competitive books, author qualifications, why the book is unique, and SASE. **Payment:** Royalty. **Tips:** Do not send complete manuscript. Submit query first.

ADDAX PUBLISHING GROUP INC.
8643 Hauser Dr., Suite 235, Lenexa, KS 66215. 913-438-5333.
E-mail: addax1@addaxpublishing.com. Web site: www.addaxpublishing.com.
Description: Sports, entertainment and children's books. **Number of Books/Yr.:** 20 titles/yr. 50% of books from first-time authors; 75% unagented. **Payment:** Royalty.

ADDICUS BOOKS

P.O. Box 45327, Omaha, NE 68145. 402-330-7493.
E-mail: info@addicusbooks.com. Web site: www.addicusbooks.com.
Rod Colvin, President.
Description: Independent press publishing nonfiction titles on economics, investing, business, self-help, health, how-to, and regional. **Number of Books/Yr.:** Publishes 5-10 titles/yr. 70% of books from first-time authors; 60% from unagented writers. Responds in 1 month. **Payment:** Royalty.

ADDISON-WESLEY

Pearson Inc.
75 Arlington St., Suite 300, Boston, MA 02116. 617-848-6000.
Web site: www.aw.com.
Description: Several separate publishing groups. Educational nonfiction on current topics including computer science, economics, finance, mathematics, and statistics.
Contact: Editorial Department.

ADVENTURES UNLIMITED

P.O. Box 74, Kempton, IL 60946. 815-253-6390.
Web site: www.adventuresunlimitedpress.com.
Description: Publishes books on Atlantis, ancient civilizations, science, alternative science and health, conspiracy, UFOs, etc.

AEGIS PUBLISHING GROUP LTD.

796 Aquidneck Ave., Newport, RI 02842-7246. 401-849-4200.
E-mail: aegis@aegisbooks.com. Web site: www.aegisbooks.com.
Robert Mastin, Publisher.
Description: Publisher of books on telecommunications and data networking. Materials target both industry professionals and general consumers. **Sample Titles:** *Telecom Made Easy,* by June Langhoff; *The Cell Phone Buyer's Guide,* by Penelope Stetz.

AFRICAN AMERICAN IMAGES

1909 W 95th St., Chicago, IL 60643. 773-445-0322.
E-mail: aaf@africanamericanimages.com. Web site: africanamericanimages.com.
Description: Publishes adult and children's nonfiction Afrocentric books. **Number of Books/Yr.:** 6 titles/year (100 submissions), 50% first-time authors, 80% unagented. Writers subsidize 10% of the cost of book production. **Proposal Process:** Query with complete manuscript. Considers multiple queries. Hard-copy format. **Payment:** Royalty (10% net). **Tips:** Write to promote self-esteem, collective values, liberation, and skill development. See guidelines. **Contact:** Editorial Department.

THE AFRICAN WORLD PRESS, INC.

11 Princess Rd., Trenton, NJ 08648. 609-844-9583.
E-mail: awprsp@africanworld.com. Web site: www.africanworld.com.

Kassahun Checole, Publisher.
Description: Publisher of nonfiction and poetry. Material focuses on African, African-American, Caribbean, and Latin-American issues. **Proposal Process:** Query. **Payment:** Royalty.

AHSAHTA PRESS
MFA Program, Boise State University, Dept. of English
1910 University Dr., Boise, ID 83725-1525. 208-426-2195.
E-mail: ahsahta@boisestate.edu. Web site: ahsahtapress.boisestate.edu.
Janet Holmes, Director.
Description: Trade paperback books specializing in poetry. **Number of Books/Yr.:** 3 books/year; 50% first-time authors; 100% unagented. 300 submissions per yr. **Proposal Process:** Send complete manuscript. Response time: 3 months. No electronic queries. Hard copy only. **Payment:** Annual royalty.

AIRLIFE BOOKS
Airlife Publishing, Ltd.,
101 Longden Rd., Shrewsbury, Shropshire SY3 9EB England.
E-mail: info@airlifebooks.com. Web site: www.airlifebooks.com.
Description: Publishes books covering civil and military aviation, pilot training, military and naval history, and modeling.

ALASKA NORTHWEST BOOKS
Graphic Arts Center Publishing Co.
P.O. Box 10306, Portland, OR 97296-0306. 503-226-2402.
E-mail: tricia@gacpc.com. Web site: www.gacpc.com.
Tricia Brown, Acquisitions Editor.
Description: Alaska Northwest Books and WestWinds Press imprints are regional and publish books on Alaskan and Western subjects: history, natural history, memoir, cookbooks, reference guides, children's books, humor, and travel. **Number of Books/Yr.:** 6-8 titles/year (250 Alaskan Northwest submissions and 100 Westwinds Press submissions), 10% by first-time authors, 90% unagented. **Proposal Process:** For nonfiction, query with outline and sample chapters. For children's books, send complete manuscript. Considers electronic queries. Prefers hard-copy format. **Payment:** Pays royalty (10-12% net). **Sample Titles:** Alaska Northwest Books: *Through Yup'ik Eyes* (memoir); *Alone Across the Arctic* (nonfiction adventure); *Quilt of Dreams* (ages 5+). Westwinds Press Books: *San Francisco's Golden Gate Park* (travel); *Heaven on the Half Shell* (history/cooking); *A Child's California* (ages 7+). **Tips:** Avoid poetry, adult fiction, and native "legend" written by non-Native Americans. Children's book authors should avoid partnering with an illustrator before submission has been accepted.

ALBION PRESS
4532 W Kennedy Blvd., Suite 233, Tampa, FL 33609. 813-805-2665.
E-mail: mcgregpub@aol.com.
Dave Rosenbaum, Acquisitions.

Description: Publishes only nonfiction, with an emphasis on sports and true crime. **Number of Books/Yr.:** 12 titles/year (300 submissions), 50% first-time authors, 50% unagented. **Proposal Process:** Query with outline and sample chapters, and SASE. Prefer hard copy but multiple and electronic queries accepted. Response time: 2 months. **Payment:** Royalty.

ALGONQUIN BOOKS OF CHAPEL HILL
Workman Publishing
P.O. Box 2225, Chapel Hill, NC 27515-2225. 919-967-0108.
Web site: www.algonquin.com.
Dana Stamey, Managing Editor.
Description: Trade books, literary fiction and nonfiction, for adults.

ALLWORTH PRESS
10 E 23rd St., Suite 510, New York, NY 10010-4402. 212-777-8395.
Web site: www.allworth.com.
Nicole Potter, Editor.
Description: Business and self-help books for artists; designers; photographers; writers; film, television, and performing artists; as well as books about business, money, and law for the general public. **Proposal Process:** Query with outline and sample chapters. **Payment:** Royalty.

ALPINE PUBLICATIONS
225 S Madison Ave., Loveland, CO 80537. 970-667-9317.
Web site: www.alpinepub.com.
B. J. McKinney, Publisher.
Description: Books about dogs and horses; breed books, care, training, health, management, etc. No stories, true or fiction. **Number of Books/Yr.:** 4 titles/year (50 submissions), 50% by first-time authors, 100% unagented. **Proposal Process:** Submit outline and sample chapters or complete ms, and SASE. Response time: 8-10 weeks. Electronic and multiple queries accepted. Hard copy preferred. **Payment:** Royalty.

ALYSON PUBLICATIONS
6922 Hollywood Blvd., Suite 1000, P.O. Box 4371
Los Angeles, CA 90078. 323-860-6074.
Web site: www.alyson.com.
Description: Gay, lesbian, bisexual, and transgender fiction and nonfiction books, from 65,000 words. Alyson Wonderland imprint: Also publishes children and young adult titles with gay/lesbian themes. **Proposal Process:** Query with outline only. **Payment:** Royalty. **Tips:** See Web site for guidelines.

AMACOM BOOKS
1601 Broadway, Suite 6, New York, NY 10019. 800-262-9699.
Web site: www.amacombooks.org.
Description: Solution-oriented books, business concerns.

AMADEUS PRESS

Timber Press, Inc.

133 SW Second Avenue, Suite 450, Portland, OR 97204. 503-227-2878.

Web site: www.amadeuspress.com.

Description: Publishes trade books and textbooks on classical music.

AMBER BOOKS

1334 E Chandler Blvd., Suite 5-D67, Phoenix, AZ 85048. 480-460-1660.

E-mail: amberbk@aol.com. Web site: www.amberbooks.com.

Tony Rose, Publisher.

Description: Publishes African-American self-help books, career-guide books, and biographies on successful entertainment personalities. Aims to publish materials that help African-Americans earn an income, obtain education, and find the empowerment to succeed. **Sample Titles:** *Wake Up and Smell the Dollars! Whose Inner City is This Anyway?,* by Dorothy Pitman Hughes; *Beautiful Black Hair,* by Shamboosie; *The African-American Teenager's Guide to Personal Growth, Health, Safety, Sex, & Survival,* by Debrah Harris-Johnson; *Yes, Yes, Yes: The Unauthorized Biography of Destiny's Child,* by Kelly Kenyatta. **Contact:** Tony Rose.

AMERICAN INSTITUTE OF
AERONAUTICS AND ASTRONAUTICS, INC.

1801 Alexander Bell Dr., Suite 500, Reston, VA 20191-4344. 703-264-7505.

Web site: www.aiaa.org.

Description: Publisher of materials on aerospace technology. Publications include the AIAA Educational series, *Progress in Astronautics and Aeronautics,* several general-interest aerospace publications, and technical journals.

AMERICAN PARADISE PUBLISHING

P.O. Box 781, St. John, USVI 00831.

E-mail: info@americanparadisepublishing.com.

Web site: www.americanparadisepublishing.com.

Pamela Gaffin, Editor.

Description: Local books, 80-300 pages. Useful, practical books that help our Virgin Island readers lead better and more enjoyable lives. Guidebooks, cookbooks, how-to books, books on sailing, yacht cruising, hiking, snorkeling, sportfishing, local history, and West Indian culture, specifically aimed at Caribbean readers/tourists. Query with outline and sample chapters. Royalty.

ANDREWS MCMEEL PUBLISHING

Andrews McMeel Universal

4520 Main St., Kansas City, MO 64111. 816-932-6700.

E-mail: publicity@amuniversal.com. Web site: www.amuniversal.com/amp.

Description: Publisher of best-sellers, humor collections, general nonfiction trade, gift books, children's books, and calendars.

ANDROS BOOK PUBLISHING

P.O. Box 12080, Prescott, AZ 86304. 520-778-4491.
E-mail: androsbks@aol.com. Web site: www.hometown.aol.com/androsbks.
Susanne Bain, Publisher.
Description: Small publishing house specializing in home schooling, school choice, and parental involvement in education. **Proposal Process:** Send proposal letter, two sample chapters and table of contents, and SASE. **Tips:** Currently seeks uplifting material about home school and positive parental involvement in children's education or school choice issues. Looking less for feel-good works than for "how-to or how we do it." Looking for personal experience.

ANHINGA PRESS

P.O. Box 10595, Tallahassee, FL 32302-0595. 850-521-9920.
E-mail: info@anhinga.org. Web site: www.anhinga.org.
Rick Campbell, Editorial Director.
Description: Publishes books of contemporary poetry. **Number of Books/Yr.:** 4 titles/year (average 750 submissions), 50% by first-time authors, 99% unagented. **Proposal Process:** Query or send complete manuscripts with SASE. Response time: 6 weeks. Multiple queries accepted. No electronic queries. **Payment:** Royalty or flat fee.

ANTHROPOSOPHIC PRESS INC.

P.O. Box 799, Great Barrington, MA 10230. 413-528-8233.
E-mail: service@anthropress.org. Web site: www.anthropress.org.
Description: Publisher of Rudolf Steiner's works on anthroposophy. Also publishes materials on spirituality, religion, philosophy, and psychology.

ANVIL PRESS

204A-175 East Broadway St.
Vancouver, British Columbia V5T IW2 Canada. 604-876-8710.
Web site: www.anvilpress.com.
Brian Kaufman, Editorial Director.
Description: Home of the 3-day novel-writing contest. Fiction, poetry, creative non-fiction, some nonfiction contemporary, and progressive literature. **Number of Books/Yr.:** 6 titles/year, (200 submissions), 80% first-time authors, 100% unagented. **Proposal Process:** Query with outline and sample chapters. Considers multiple queries. Electronic queries accepted (letter only). Response time: 4-6 months. Hardcopy format preferred. **Payment:** Royalty 10-15% net. Flat fee advance $200-$500. **Sample Titles:** Adult nonfiction anthology: *Exact Fare Only, Good Bad Ugly Tales of Urban Transit.* Poetry: *Full Magpie Dodge.* **Tips:** Canadian authors only. Avoid sending formulaic writing. Looking for originality in style and voice, contemporary modern.

APA BOOKS

American Psychological Association
750 First St. NE, Washington, DC 20002-4242. 202-336-5500.

Web site: www.apa.org.

Description: Publisher of books and journals reflecting current research and discovery in the field of psychology. Materials have scholarly, professional focus. Also publishes children's books and online information services and databases. **Proposal Process:** Submit prospectus with curricular vita. Prospectus should include the table of contents, purpose, audience, market analysis, anticipated length, proposed schedule, and the theories or ideas that will be explored in the book. **Sample Titles:** *Antisocial Behavior in Children and Adolescents*, by John B. Reid, Ph.D.; *Child Art in Context: A Cultural and Comparative Perspective*, by Claire Golamb, Ph.D.

APERTURE

20 East 23rd St., New York, NY 10010. 212-505-5555.

E-mail: editorial@aperture.org. Web site: www.aperture.org.

Ray K. Metzker.

Description: Photography books. **Proposal Process:** Submit 1 page synopsis; hard copy only. Include delivery memo that describes work, format, and the number of images, SASE. Allow 6-8 weeks for response.

APPALACHIAN MOUNTAIN CLUB BOOKS

5 Joy St., Boston, MA 02108. 617-523-0655.

Web site: www.outdoors.org.

Beth Krusi, Publisher/Editor.

Description: Regional (New England) and national nonfiction titles, 175-350 pages, for adults, juveniles, and young adults. Topics include guidebooks on non-motorized backcountry recreation, nature, outdoor recreation skills (how-to books), mountain history/biography, search and rescue, conservation, and environmental management. **Number of Books/Yr.:** 12 titles/year (40 submissions). 75% first-time authors. **Proposal Process:** Query with outline and sample chapters. Multiple queries considered. Response time: 3 months. Hard-copy format. **Payment:** Royalty. **Tips:** Check the Web site for more information and complete submissions guidelines. **Contact:** Editorial Department.

APPLEWOOD BOOKS

128 The Great Road, P.O. Box 365, Bedford, MA 01730. 781-271-0055.

Web site: www.awb.com.

Description: Publishes books on culture, nostalgia, history, literature, cookbooks, etc.

AQUAQUEST PUBLICATIONS, INC.

18 Garvies Point Rd., Glen Cove, NY 11542. 516-759-0475.

E-mail: editorial@aquaquest.com. Web site: www.aquaquest.com.

Description: Publisher of books on underwater adventures and scuba diving. Books cover a range of underwater and marine topics such as travel, diving, shipwrecks, marine life, historical, technical, photography, and fiction. **Sample Titles:** *Diving Micronesia*, by Eric Hanauer; *Solo Diving, 2nd Ed: The Art of Underwater Self-sufficiency*, by Robert Von Maier.

ARCADE PUBLISHING
141 Fifth Ave., New York, NY 10010. 212-475-2633.
E-mail: arcadeinfo@arcadepub.com.
Richard Seaver, President.
Description: Adult fiction and nonfiction. No unsolicited submissions. **Contact:** Greg Comer and Darcy Falkenhagen, Editors.

ARCADIA PUBLISHING
2A Cumberland St., Charleston, SC 29401. 843-853-2070.
Web site: www.arcadiapublishing.com.
Description: Regional & local history.

ARCHER BOOKS
P.O. Box 1254, Santa Maria, CA 93456. 805-934-9977.
Web site: www.archer-books.com.
Description: Publisher of fiction, nonfiction, and poetry.

ARENA EDITIONS
425 Sandoval St., Santa Fe, NM 87501-2632. 505-986-9132.
Description: Publishes high-quality photography books.

ARSENAL PULP PRESS
103-1014 Homer St., Vancouver, British Columbia V6B 2W9 Canada. 604-687-4233.
Web site: www.arsenalpulp.com.
Description: Publisher of fiction, gay and lesbian literature, pop culture, etc.

ART MEDIA RESOURCES LTD.
1507 S Michigan Ave., Chicago, IL 60605. 312-663-5351.
Web site: www.artmediaresources.com.
Description: Publishes titles on Asian art.

ARTE PUBLICO PRESS
University of Houston, 4800 Calhoun, Houston, TX 77204-2174. 713-743-2601.
E-mail: gbventura@uh.edu. Web site: www.arte.uh.edu.
Nicolas Kanellos, Editorial Director.
Description: Contemporary and historical literature by U.S. Hispanics, in both Spanish and English, with a focus on women's literature. Pinata Books. Novels, short stories, poetry, drama, and autobiographies. **Number of Books/Yr.:** 30 titles/year (200 submissions), 80% first-time authors, 20% unagented. **Proposal Process:** Query with outline and sample chapters, and SASE. Accept multiple and electronic queries. Response time: 1 month. Hard-copy format preferred. **Payment:** Royalty. **Sample Titles:** Adult fiction: *Home Killings*. Adult nonfiction: *Conflicts of Interest: The Collected Letters of Maria Amparo Ruiz de Burton*. Children's: (3-8) *Pepita Takes Time*. (8-13) *Trino's Time/Ankiza*. **Tips:** Looking for work by and about Hispanics in the U.S.

ARTECH HOUSE PUBLISHERS
685 Canton St., Norwood, MA 02062. 781-769-9750.
Web site: www.artechhouse.com.
Description: Professional-level books on telecommunications, wireless, microwave, radar, computer security, software engineering.

ARTISAN
708 Broadway, New York, NY 10003-9508. 212-614-7528.
Description: Illustrated cookbooks, gift books, and calendars.

ASM PRESS
American Society for Microbiology
1752 N St. NW, Washington, DC 20036-2904. 202-737-3600.
E-mail: books@asmusa.org. Web site: www.asmpress.org.
Description: Publishes reference manuals, scholarly monographs, and textbooks for the molecular biology and microbiological sciences. **Proposal Process:** Submit proposal with clear explanation of how book will be beneficial to the microbiology community. Also include market analysis, table of contents, and current curriculum vitae. **Tips:** See Web site for detailed submission guidelines. **Contact:** Jennifer Adelman, Editorial Assistant.

ASSOULINE PUBLISHING, INC.
601 W 26th St., New York, NY 10001. 212-989-6810.
E-mail: contact@assouline.com. Web site: www.assouline.com.
Description: Publisher of illustrated books specializing in photography, design, fashion, history, religion, food, sports, and travel.

AUDIO LITERATURE
370 W San Bruno Ave., Suite F, San Bruno, CA 94066. 650-583-9700.
Web site: www.audiouniverse.com.
Description: Publisher of audio materials on a wide range of subjects including religion, philosophy, business, biography, self-help, and literature.

THE AUDIO PARTNERS PUBLISHING CORPORATION
1133 High St., Auburn, CA 95603. 530-888-7803.
Web site: www.audiopartners.com.
Description: Audiobooks.

AUGSBURG FORTRESS, PUBLISHERS
100 S Fifth St., Suite 700, P.O. Box 1209
Minneapolis, MN 55440-1209. 612-330-3300 or 800-426-0115.
E-mail: booksub@augsburgfortress.org.
Web site: www.augsburgfortress.org,www.fortresspress.com.
Description: Publishes books that focus on biblical studies, history of Christianity, theology, ethics, religious studies, etc.

AVALANCHE PUBLISHING
15262 Pipeline Ln., Huntington Beach, CA 92649. 714-898-2400.
Web site: www.avalanchepub.com.
Description: Calendars and gift books.

AVALON BOOKS
Thomas Bouregy & Co., Inc.
160 Madison Ave., New York, NY 10016. 212-598-0222.
E-mail: avalon@avalonbooks.com. Web site: www.avalonbooks.com.
Erin Cartwright, Editor.
Description: Hardcover secular romances, mysteries, and westerns for the library market. Our books are wholesome, adult fiction, suitable for family reading. **Number of Books/Yr.:** 60 titles/year. Receives 2,000 queries and 1,200 mss/year. 65% of books from first-time authors; 80% from unagented writers. **Proposal Process:** Query with first 3 chapters and outline. SASE for guidelines. Response time: 1 month to queries; 4 months to mss. **Payment:** Royalty 5-15%. **Tips:** No old-fashioned, predictable, formulaic books. Avoid graphic or premarital sex or sexual tension in your writing.

AVALON TRAVEL PUBLISHING
5855 Beaudry St., Emeryville, CA 94608. 510-595-3664.
Web site: www.travelmatters.com.
Aimee Larsen, Publishing Associate.
Description: Travel guides, 200-1,000 pages. **Proposal Process:** Will consider multiple submissions. Query. **Payment:** Royalty.

AVERY
A Member of Penguin Putnam Inc.
375 Hudson St., Fl. 4, New York, NY 10014. 212-366-2744.
Web site: www.penguinputnam.com.
Dara Stewart, Editor.
Description: Publisher of trade books in alternative health, health, fitness, nutrition, and self-help. **Proposal Process:** Query with outline or sample chapters.

BAEN BOOKS
Baen Publishing Enterprises
P.O. Box 1403, Riverdale, NY 10471-0671. 718-548-3100.
Web site: baen.com.
Jim Baen, Editor-in-Chief.
Description: Strongly plotted science-fiction; innovative fantasy. **Proposal Process:** Query with synopsis and manuscript. **Payment:** Advance and royalty. **Tips:** Send SASE or check Web site for guidelines.

BALLANTINE BOOKS
The Ballantine Publishing Group/Random House, Inc.
1540 Broadway, New York, NY 10036. 212-782-9000.

Web site: www.randomhouse.com/bb.

Leona Nevler, Editor.

Description: General fiction and nonfiction. **Proposal Process:** Accepts material only through agents. **Tips:** Accepts agented submissions only.

BALSAM PRESS

36 E 22nd St., New York, NY 10010. 212-475-6895.

Barbara Krohn, Executive Editor.

Description: General and illustrated adult nonfiction. **Proposal Process:** Query first. **Payment:** Royalty.

BANTAM BOOKS

Description: An imprint of Bantam Dell Publishing Group. See below.

BANTAM DELL PUBLISHING GROUP

Random House, Inc.

1540 Broadway, New York, NY 10036. 212-782-9000.

Web site: www.bantamdell.com.

Description: Executive Vice President and Deputy Publisher: Nita Taublib. Acquisitions: Toni Burbank (nonfiction: self-help, health/medicine, nature, spirituality, philosophy); Jackie Cantor (fiction: general commercial, literary, women's fiction, memoir); Tracy Devine (fiction and nonfiction: narrative nonfiction, history, adventure, military, science, general upscale commercial fiction, women's fiction, suspense); Anne Groell (fiction: fantasy, science fiction); Ann Harris (fiction and nonfiction: general commercial, literary, science, medicine, politics); Susan Kamil (The Dial Press, literary fiction and nonfiction); Robin Michaelson (nonfiction: health, women's health, child care/parenting, psychology, self-help); Bill Massey (fiction and nonfiction: thrillers, suspense, historical, military, nature/outdoors, adventure, popular science); Kate Miciak (fiction: mystery, suspense, historical fiction); Wendy McCurdy (fiction: romance, women's fiction); Danielle Perez (fiction and nonfiction: suspense/thrillers, women's fiction, inspiration/spirituality, self-help, personal development, health, animals); Beth Rashbaum (nonfiction: health, psychology, self-help, women's issues, Judaica, history, memoir. Imprints: Bantam, Dell, Delacorte Press, Delta, The Dial Press. The Dial Press publishes 6-12 titles per year of quality literary fiction and nonfiction, on subjects that include biography, Americana, contemporary culture, government/politics, history, memoirs, psychology, women's issues/studies. 75% of their books are from first-time authors. **Sample Titles:** *The Cottage,* by Danielle Steel (Delacorte, fiction); *A Painted House,* by John Grisham (Dell, fiction); *Body of Lies,* by Iris Johansen (Bantam, fiction); *Love, Greg and Lauren,* by Greg Manning (Bantam, nonfiction); *Safe Harbor,* by Luanne Rice (Bantam, fiction); *The Wisdom of Menopause,* by Christiane Northrup, M.D. (Bantam, nonfiction); *Inside Delta Force,* by Eric Haney (Delacorte, nonfiction); *American Chica,* by Marie Arana (The Dial Press, fiction).

BARBOUR PUBLISHING: HEARTSONG PRESENTS

Barbour Publishing, Inc.

P.O. Box 719, Uhrichsville, OH 44683. 740-922-6045.

E-mail: info@heartsongpresents.com.

Web site: www.barbourbooks.com or www.heartsongpresents.com.

Rebecca Germany, Acquisitions Editor.

Description: Adult mass-market inspirational romance (contemporary and historical). **Number of Books/Yr.:** 52 titles/year (300 submissions), 15% first-time authors, 90% unagented. **Proposal Process:** Query with outline (1-2 pages), 2-3 sample chapters. No electronic queries. Multiple queries okay. Response time: 3-4 months. Prefer hard-copy format. **Payment:** Royalty (8% net). **Tips:** SASE for guidelines.

BARD PRESS

LongStreet Press

2140 Newmarket Pkwy., Suite 122, Marietta, GA 30067. 800-927-1488.

E-mail: ray@bardpress.com. Web site: www.bardpress.com.

Description: High-quality business and self-help books. **Number of Books/Yr.:** 3-4 titles/year. **Proposal Process:** Submit short query with title, subject, and market. **Sample Titles:** *Owners Manual for the Personality at Work*, by Pierce J. Howard, Ph.D., and Jane Mitchell Howard, M.A.; *Masters of Networking*, by Ivan R. Misner, Ph.D., and Don Morgan, M.A.

BARRON'S EDUCATIONAL SERIES, INC.

250 Wireless Blvd., Hauppauge, NY 11788. 631-434-3311.

E-mail: info@barronseduc.com. Web site: www.barronseduc.com.

Wayne Barr, Director of Acquisitions.

Description: Publishes juvenile nonfiction (science, nature, history, hobbies, and how-to), fiction for middle-grade students and teens, and picture books for ages 3-6. Also publishes adult nonfiction (test preparation, business, pet care, childcare, cookbooks, foreign languages). **Proposal Process:** Query with SASE. See guidelines.

WILLIAM L. BAUHAN, PUBLISHER

P.O.Box 443, Dublin, NH 03444. 877-832-3738.

E-mail: info@bauhanpublishing.com. Web site: www.bauhanpublishing.com.

William L. Bauhan, Editor.

Description: Publishes biographies, fine arts, gardening, architecture, and history books, with an emphasis on New England. **Proposal Process:** Submit query with outline and sample chapter.

BAY BOOKS

Soma Publishing

555 De Haro St., Suite 220, San Francisco, CA 94107. 415-252-4350.

E-mail: info@baybooks.com. Web site: www.baybooks.com.

Floyd Yearout, Editor.

Description: Publishes hardcover, trade paperback, coffee table, and full-color illustrated gift books. Topics include gardening, interior design, and cookbooks. Also publishes companion books to television shows and other media programming. **Number of Books/Yr.:** 10. Receives 30 queries/year. 20% of books from first-time authors. **Payment:** Royalties vary substantially. Offers $0-$25,000 in advance. **Sample Titles:** *Gusto Italiano, Avventura, Urban Ore, Low-Carb Meals in Minutes, Modern Essentials, Fresh Paint.* **Tips:** Authors should submit ideas or outlines with biographical information and a rationale as to why the book will sell.

BAYLOR UNIVERSITY PRESS
P.O. Box 97363, Waco, TX 76798-7363. 254-710-3164.
E-mail: David_Holcomb@baylor.edu. Web site: www.baylor.edu/~BUPress.
J. David Holcomb, Editor.
Description: Scholarly nonfiction, especially religion, history, and church-state issues. **Proposal Process:** Query with outline. **Payment:** Royalty.

BEACON PRESS
25 Beacon St., Boston, MA 02108-2892. 617-742-2110.
Web site: www.beacon.org/Beacon.
Deborah Chasman, Editorial Director.
Description: Publisher of general nonfiction. Subject matter includes world affairs, women's studies, anthropology, history, philosophy, religion, gay and lesbian studies, nature writing, African-American studies, Latino studies, Asian-American studies, and Native-American studies. **Proposal Process:** Agented manuscripts only. **Sample Titles:** Series: *Concord Library* (nature writing); *Barnard New Women Poets.*

BECKETT PUBLICATIONS, INC.
15850 Dallas Pkwy., Dallas, TX 75248. 972-991-6657.
Web site: www.beckett.com.
Description: Collectibles, sports, etc.

BEHRMAN HOUSE INC.
11 Edison Place, Springfield, NJ 07081. 973-379-7200.
Web site: www.behrmanhouse.com.
David Behrman, Acquisitions.
Description: Hebrew language and Judaica textbooks for children. Adult Jewish nonfiction. **Number of Books/Yr.:** 20 titles/year. Receives 200 submissions/year. 20% of books from first-time authors; 95% unagented. **Proposal Process:** Query with outline and sample chapters. **Payment:** Flat fee or royalty.

BELLWETHER-CROSS PUBLISHING
18319 Highway 20 W, East Dubuque, IL 61025. 815-747-6255.
E-mail: jwhite@shepherd-inc.com.
Janet White, Senior Developmental Editor.
Description: Publisher of college textbooks and lab manuals related to environmental science, biology, botany, astronomy, oceanography, etc. Also computer

software related to the publishing industry. **Number of Books/Yr.:** 55 titles/year (600 submissions), 100% by first-time authors, 100% unagented. **Proposal Process:** For educational materials, query with proposed book idea, list of current competitive books, and bio. For trade nonfiction, query with outline and sample chapters. SASE. Prefers electronic format. Multiple queries accepted. Response time: 2 weeks. **Payment:** Royalty.

BENJAMIN CUMMINGS

Pearson Inc.
1301 Sansome St., San Francisco, CA 94111. 415-402-2500.
Web site: www.aw.com/bc.
Description: Educational nonfiction. Publishes work on chemistry, health/kinesiology, life science, physics, and astronomy.

THE BERKLEY PUBLISHING GROUP

Penguin Putnam, Inc.
375 Hudson St., New York, NY 10014. 726-282-5074.
E-mail: online@penguinputnam.com. Web site: www.penguinputnam.com.
Denise Silvestro, Senior Editor.
Description: General-interest fiction and nonfiction; science fiction, suspense, mystery, and romance. Publishes both reprints and originals. Paperback books, except for some hardcover mysteries and science fiction. Imprints include Ace Books, Diamond, Jam, Jove, Perige, and Riverhead Books. **Number of Books/Yr.:** 800 titles/year. **Proposal Process:** Submit through agent only. **Payment:** Royalty.

BERKSHIRE HOUSE PUBLISHERS

480 Pleasant St., Suite 5, Lee, MA 02138. 413-243-0303.
E-mail: info@berkshirehouse.com. Web site: www.berkshirehouse.com.
Philip Rich, Editorial Director.
Description: Publishes a series of regional travel guides and books on specific destinations of unusual charm and cultural importance, e.g., the Berkshires in western Massachusetts. Occasionally publishes New England cookbooks or books on country inns and country living. **Number of Books/Yr.:** 8-10 titles/year (average 300 submissions), 10% by first-time authors, 97% unagented. **Proposal Process:** Query letter, outline, prospectus, sample chapter if desired. Considers multiple and electronic queries. Response time: 4 weeks; varies. We do not consider children's manuscripts. **Payment:** Pays royalty. **Sample Titles:** *The Finger Lakes Book* (in *Great Destinations* series); *The New Red Lion Inn Cookbook; The Hamptons Book,* 4th edition; *The Nantucket Book,* 2nd edition; *The Napa and Sonoma Book,* 6th edition (spring 2002). Children's: We publish no children's books with the exception of *Willie Was Different,* a story by Norman Rockwell. **Tips:** Avoid submitting general cookbooks (i.e. those not related to inns, etc.), memoirs, autobiographies, and biographies and history titles that are unrelated to New England. No how-to books, or titles on self-help, health, religion, etc. No poetry or fiction (with the possible exception of a novel related to this region).

BERLITZ PUBLISHING CO.

Berlitz International, Inc.
400 Alexander Park, Princeton, NJ 08540-6306. 609-514-9650.
E-mail: publishing@berlitz.com. Web site: www.berlitz.com.
Description: Publisher of language instruction materials.

BERRETT-KOEHLER PUBLISHERS, INC.

235 Montgomery St., Suite 650, San Francisco, CA 94104. 415-288-0260.
Web site: www.bkconnection.com.
Description: Books on work, business, and organizations. Seeks to publish work that inspires a more humane, ethical, and globally conscious world. **Proposal Process:** Send proposal, outline, and 2-4 sample chapters.

THE BESS PRESS

3565 Harding Ave., Honolulu, HI 96816. (808) 734-7159.
E-mail: editor@besspress.com. Web site: www.besspress.com.
Revé Shapard, Editor.
Description: Nonfiction books about Hawaii and the Pacific for adults, children, and young adults. **Proposal Process:** Query with outline. Hard copy. **Payment:** Royalty.

BEYOND WORDS PUBLISHING

20827 NW Cornell Rd., Suite 500, Hillsboro, OR 97124. 503-531-8700.
E-mail: info@beyondword.com. Web site: www.beyondword.com.
Jenefer Angel, Adult Acquisitions Editor.
Description: Publisher of photography, children's books, and books on personal growth, women, and spirituality. **Number of Books/Yr.:** 25 titles/year (4,000 submissions), 90% first-time authors, 75% unagented. **Proposal Process:** Submit outline and sample chapters for adult titles; complete manuscript for juvenile titles. SASE. Multiple queries accepted. No electronic queries. Prefers hard-copy format. Response time: 3 months. **Payment:** Royalty. **Tips:** No adult fiction, poetry, or fiction stories by children. Looking for original and creative children's stories. **Contact:** Barbara Mann, Children's Managing Editor.

BICK PUBLISHING HOUSE

307 Neck Rd., Madison, CT 06443. 203-245-0073.
E-mail: bickpubhse@aol.com. Web site: www.bickpubhouse.com.
Dale Carlson, President.
Description: Books, 64-250 pages, for teens and adults on wildlife rehabilitation, special needs/disabilities, and psychology. **Proposal Process:** Submit outline and sample chapters. **Payment:** Royalty.

BILINGUAL BOOKS INC.

1719 W Nickerson St., Seattle, WA 98119. 206-284-4211.
Web site: www.bbks.com.
Description: Publisher of trade and educational books for learning foreign languages.

BILINGUAL/REVIEW PRESS

Arizona State University, Hispanic Research Center
P.O. Box 872702, Tempe, AZ 85287-2702. 480-965-3867.
E-mail: brp@asu.edu. Web site: www.asu.edu/brp.
Description: Publishes high-quality fiction, nonfiction, and poetry. Titles are by or about U.S. Hispanics. Publishes both established and emerging writers. **Number of Books/Yr.:** 8-10 titles/year. **Sample Titles:** *The Pearl of the Antilles,* by Andrea O'Reilly Herrera; *The Hot Empire of Chile,* by Kent Paterson.

BINFORD & MORT PUBLISHING

5245 NE Elam Young Pkwy., Suite C, Hillsboro, OR 97124. 503-844-4960.
E-mail: polly@binfordandmort.com. Web site: www.binfordandmort.com.
Pam Henningsen, Publisher.
Description: Nonfiction books about the Pacific Northwest. **Number of Books/Yr.:** 10 titles/year (average 200 submissions), 5% by first-time authors, 90% unagented. **Proposal Process:** Submit query. Accepts multiple queries. No electronic queries. Responds in 3 months. Prefers electronic or hard-copy format. **Payment:** Pays royalty, typically 5-10% range. **Tips:** Does not accept children's stories or poetry.

BLACK BUZZARD PRESS

Vias, Visions-International
1007 Ficklen Rd., Fredericksburg, VA 22405. 540-310-0730.
Bradley R. Strahan, Acquisitions Editor.
Description: Publishes serious, carefully-crafted poetry. No light verse, religious, or polemic poetry. **Number of Books/Yr.:** 2 titles/year (average 100 submissions), 50% by first-time authors, 100% unagented. **Proposal Process:** Query with SASE. Hard copy. No electronic or multiple queries. **Payment:** Royalty. **Tips:** Read a sample to see what kind of work is published. Send $5 for chapbooks or $11 for full-length book.

BLACKBIRCH PRESS, INC.

260 Amity Rd., P.O. Box 3573, Woodbridge, CT 06525. 203-387-7525.
E-mail: staff@blackbirch.com. Web site: www.blackbirch.com.
Beverly Larson, Editorial Director.
Description: Publishes books in a series, for 6- to 16-year-olds. Series include *The Library of Famous Women* and *Building America.* **Number of Books/Yr.:** 70-90 titles/year. Receives 400 queries and 75 mss/year. 100% unagented. **Proposal Process:** E-mail queries acceptable. **Payment:** Royalty

JOHN F. BLAIR, PUBLISHER

1406 Plaza Dr., Winston-Salem, NC 27103-1470. 336-768-1374.
E-mail: blairpub@blairpub.com. Web site: www.blairpub.com.
Carolyn Sakowski, Editor.
Description: Books, 70,000-100,000 words: biography, history, folklore, and guidebooks, with southeastern tie-in. **Proposal Process:** Query. No electronic submissions. **Payment:** Royalty.

BLOOMBERG PRESS

Bloomberg LP

100 Business Park Dr., P.O. Box 888, Princeton, NJ 08542-0888. 609-279-4670.

Web site: www.bloomberg.com/books.

Kathleen Peterson, Senior Acquisitions Editor.

Description: Nonfiction, varying lengths, on topics such as investing, finance, and personal finance. **Proposal Process:** Query with outline and sample chapter or send complete manuscript. SASE. **Payment:** Royalty.

BLOOMSBURY

175 Fifth Ave., Suite 300, New York, NY 10010. 212-674-5151.

Web site: www.bloomsbury.com.

Description: High-quality publisher of fiction and nonfiction.

BLUE HERON PUBLISHING

1234 SW Stark St., Portland, OR 97205. 503-221-6841.

E-mail: publisher@blueheronpublishing.com.

Web site: www.blueheronpublishing.com.

Daniel Urban, Acquisitions Editor.

Description: Books on writing and teaching writing for adults and young adults. Northwestern and Western fiction for adults, universities, and high schools (especially multicultural themes), political mysteries. Original cookbooks, guides, and how-to books that address such issues as health, wellness, finance, travel, career, and lifestyle. **Number of Books/Yr.:** 10-12 titles/year (400-500 submissions). **Proposal Process:** Query with outline and SASE. Hard copy. Multiple queries and electronic queries OK. Response time: 2-4 months. **Payment:** Royalty. **Tips:** Publishes for general readers, writers, teachers, and young readers. No short fiction or nonfiction. Guidelines, including current needs, are posted on Web site. **Contact:** Dennis Stovall, Publisher.

BLUEFISH RIVER PRESS

P.O. Box 1398, Duxbury, MA 02332. 781-934-5564.

E-mail: info@bluefishriverpress.com. Web site: www.bluefishriverpress.com.

Description: Publisher of serious fiction and books on sports with particular emphasis on baseball. **Number of Books/Yr.:** 5 titles/year. Receives 100 submissions/year. 50% by first-time authors; 50% unagented. **Proposal Process:** Send outline with sample chapter. Multiple queries accepted. Response time: 1 week. **Payment:** Royalty 7-15%. **Tips:** Submit query by e-mail. **Contact:** David Pallai.

BLUSHING ROSE PUBLISHING

123 Bolinas, Fairfax, CA 94930. 415-458-2090.

Web site: www.blushingrose.com.

Description: Wedding, baby albums, giftbooks, etc.

BONUS BOOKS

160 E Illinois St., Chicago, IL 60611. 312-467-0580.

E-mail: bb@bonus-books.com. Web site: www.bonus-books.com.

Erin Kahl, Acquisitions Editor.

Description: Publishes primarily nonfiction trade books, both paperback and hardcover. **Number of Books/Yr.:** 20-30 titles/year (average 600-800 submissions), 20% by first-time authors, 97% unagented. **Proposal Process:** Query with complete manuscript, include SASE. Multiple and electronic queries accepted. Prefers hardcopy format. **Payment:** Royalty. **Sample Titles:** *Get the Edge at Blackjack* (games & gambling), *Stock Car Champions* (sports), *The Coin Collector's Survival Manual* (collectibles), *The Continuing Journey: Pinpointing Affluence in the 21st Century* (fundraising). **Tips:** No fiction or poetry.

BOOK PUBLISHING COMPANY

415 Farm Rd., P.O. Box 99, Summertown, TN 38483. 931-964-3571.

Web site: www.bookpubco.com.

Description: Books on vegetarian nutrition and cooking, alternative health, and Native American culture.

BOTTOM DOG PRESS, INC.

c/o Firelands College of BGSU, Huron, OH 44839. 419-433-5560.

E-mail: lsmithdog@aol.com.

Larry Smith, Director.

Description: Publishes collections of personal essays, fiction (90-160 pages), and poetry (50 poems). Subject matter should have a midwestern or working class angle. **Proposal Process:** Query first. Do not send manuscripts. **Payment:** Royalty.

BOWTIE PRESS

Fancy Publications, Inc.

P.O. Box 6050, Mission Veijo, CA 92690. 949-855-8822.

Web site: www.bowtiepress.com.

Description: Publishes books on pets, motorcycles, and horses. **Tips:** Do not submit material electronically. **Contact:** Acquisition.

BOYDELL & BREWER LTD.

668 Mt. Hope Ave., Rochester, NY 14620. 585-275-0419.

Web site: www.boydell.co.uk.

Description: Books on Medieval studies, German literature, music, and Early English texts.

BRANDEN PUBLISHING COMPANY

P.O. Box 812094, Wellesley, MA 02482. 781-235-3634.

E-mail: branden@branden.com. Web site: www.branden.com.

Adolfo Caso, Editorial Department.

Description: General trade, mostly nonfiction, 250-300 pages. Subject matter includes African-American, military, and Italian-American studies. Also, health-related themes and biographies with emphasis on women. **Sample Titles:** *Affirmative Action, Boston Freedom Trail, Exposing Feminism, Fighting Men—Civil War.*

BRASSEY'S, INC.
22841 Quicksilver Dr., Dulles, VA 20166. 703-661-1548.
E-mail: don@booksintl.com. Web site: www.brasseysinc.com.
Don McKeon, Publisher.
Description: Established publisher of generally military-related nonfiction that has recently expanded to include sports titles. Nonfiction books, 75,000-130,000 words. National and international affairs, history, foreign policy, defense, military biography, sports, and transportation. **Number of Books/Yr.:** 60 titles/year (900 submissions), 10% first-time authors, 60% unagented. **Proposal Process:** Send query with synopsis, author bio, outline, sample chapters, and SASE. Response time: 1-2 months. Accepts electronic queries. Prefers hard-copy format. **Payment:** Royalty.

GEORGE BRAZILLER PUBLISHERS
171 Madison Ave., New York, NY 10016. 212-889-0909.
George Braziller, Publisher.
Description: Fiction and nonfiction. Art history, collections of essays and short stories, anthologies. **Proposal Process:** Send art history manuscripts to Art Editor; others to Fiction Editor. Send outline with sample chapters.

BREAKAWAY BOOKS
P.O. Box 24, Halcottsville, NY 12438. 212-898-0408.
E-mail: garth@breakawaybooks.com. Web site: www.breakawaybooks.com.
Garth Battista, Publisher.
Description: Fiction and essays on sports, specifically on the experience of being an athlete. **Number of Books/Yr.:** 8 titles/year (hundreds of submissions), 80% first-time authors, 80% unagented. **Proposal Process:** Query with outline, sample chapters and SASE. Response time is slow. Accepts multiple queries. Prefers electronic queries. **Payment:** Royalty. **Tips:** Literary writing of the highest quality. No genre stories, how-tos, or celebrity bios.

BRICK TOWER PRESS
1230 Park Ave., New York, NY 10128. 212-427-7139.
Web site: www.bricktowerpress.com.
Description: Cookery, gardening, autobiography, military and maritime history.

BRIDGE WORKS
P.O. Box 1798, Bridgehampton, NY 11932. 631-537-3418.
E-mail: bap@hamptons.com.
Barbara Phillips, Editorial Director.
Description: Small press specializing in quality fiction and nonfiction. No family memoirs, cookbooks, sci-fi, supernatural, or romances. Biography, public policy, and

essays on a single subject are welcome. **Number of Books/Yr.:** 6-10 titles/year and receives 2,000 submissions and inquiries. 50% first-time authors, 50% unagented. **Proposal Process:** Query with outline and sample chapters, include SASE. Prefers hard copy, but electronic queries accepted. No multiple queries. Response time: 1 month. **Payment:** Royalty. **Tips:** Receives many admissions from agents; any unagented mss must be fresh and original in content, characters, and setting.

BRISTOL PUBLISHING ENTERPRISES
P.O. Box 1737, San Leandro, CA 94577. 510-895-4461.
Web site: www.bristolcookbooks.com.
Patricia Hall, Editor.
Description: Cookbooks, craftbooks, health, and pet care. **Number of Books/Yr.:** 12-20 titles/year (300 submissions), 18% first-time authors, 100% unagented. **Proposal Process:** Query with outline and sample chapters. Multiple queries accepted, no electronic queries. Prefers hard-copy format. SASE required. **Payment:** Royalty. **Tips:** See Web site.

BROADWAY BOOKS
Doubleday Broadway Publishing Group/Random House, Inc.
1540 Broadway, New York, NY 10036. 212-782-9000.
Web site: www.randomhouse/broadway.
Description: Adult nonfiction; small and very selective fiction list. **Proposal Process:** No unsolicited submissions. Query first.

BROWNTROUT PUBLISHERS, INC.
P.O. Box 280070, San Francisco, CA 94128-0070. 650-340-9800.
E-mail: production@browntrout.com. Web site: www.browntrout.com.
Description: Publishes fine art and photography in the format of calendars, books, and postcard books. **Proposal Process:** Accepts submissions from professional photographers only. Photographers should send query letter with tear sheets or samples if available. Material cannot be returned.

BUCKNELL UNIVERSITY PRESS
Bucknell University, Lewisburg, PA 17837. 570-577-3674.
Web site: www.departments.bucknell.edu/univ_press.
Greg Clingham, Editorial Director.
Description: Scholarship and criticism in English, American and comparative literature, cultural studies, history, philosophy, modern languages (especially Hispanic and Latin American studies), anthropology, political science, classics, cultural geography, or any combination of the above. **Number of Books/Yr.:** 38 titles/year (500 submissions,) 50% by first-time authors, 100% unagented. **Proposal Process:** Query with outline and sample chapters. No multiple or electronic queries. Response time: Proposals 1 month, manuscripts 3-4 months. Hard-copy format preferred. **Payment:** Royalty, 10% net. **Tips:** Excellent scholarship in the humanities and related social sciences; no "popular" material.

BULFINCH PRESS

3 Center Plaza, Boston, MA 02108. 617-263-2797.

Web site: www.bulfinchpress.com.

Michael L. Sand, Executive Managing Editor.

Description: Publisher of illustrated fine art and photography books, coffeetable books, and books on photojournalism, painting, and design (interior, exterior, and architecture). **Number of Books/Yr.:** 50 titles/year. **Proposal Process:** Query with outline or proposal, sample artwork and text (no originals), author/artist bio, and SASE. Accepts multiple queries. No electronic queries. Response time: 1 week- 1 month. Hard-copy format preferred. **Tips:** Visual material is crucial. **Contact:** Emily Martin, Department Assistant.

BULL PUBLISHING

P.O.Box 1377, Boulder, CO 94025-2865. 800-676-2855.

Web site: www.bullpub.com.

Description: Books on health, nutrition, self-help, etc.

BURFORD BOOKS

32 Morris Ave., Springfield, NJ 07081. 973-258-0960.

Web site: www.burfordbooks.com.

Peter Burford, Acquisitions Editor.

Description: Publishes books on sports, the outdoors, military history, food, and wine. **Number of Books/Yr.:** 25 titles/year (250 submissions), 50% first-time authors, 50% unagented. **Proposal Process:** Query with outline. Considers multiple and electronic queries. Prefers hard-copy format. Response time: 3 weeks. **Payment:** Royalty. **Tips:** Seeking well-written books on practically anything that can be done outside, from golf to gardening.

BUSCA, INC.

P.O. Box 854, Ithaca, NY 14851-0854. 607-546-4247.

Web site: www.buscainc.com.

Description: Topics related to shamanism and consciousness with some popular appeal as well as academic interest.

BUTTE PUBLICATIONS

P.O. Box 1328, Hillsboro, OR 97123-1328. 503-648-9791.

Web site: www.buttepublications.com.

Description: Publishes material related to deafness and education, especially for teachers of Pre-K-12 students. Also publishes college textbooks and resources for parents and professionals. Concentration is on the reading and writing aspects of teaching children who are deaf.

C&T PUBLISHING

1651 Challenge Dr., Concord, CA 94520.

E-mail: ctinfo@ctpub.com. Web site: www.ctpub.com.

Darra Williamson, Editor-in-Chief.
Description: Quilting books, 48-200 finished pages. Focus is how-to, although will consider picture, inspirational, or history books on quilting. **Proposal Process:** Send query, outline, or sample chapters. Multiple queries considered. **Payment:** Royalty.

CAMBRIDGE UNIVERSITY PRESS
40 W 20th St., New York, NY 10011-4211. 212-924-3900.
Web site: www.cup.org.
Richard Ziemacki, Director.
Description: Publisher of scholarly books and college textbooks. Subjects include the behavioral, biological, physical, and social sciences. Content also includes computer science and technology, as well as the humanities such as literature, music, and religion.

CARDINAL PUBLISHERS GROUP
7301 Georgetown Road, Suite 118, Indianapolis, IN 46268. 317-879-0871.
Web site: www.cardinalpub.com.
Description: Specializing in distribution for small and mid-sized trade nonfiction book, video, and DVD publishers.

CAREER PRESS/NEW PAGE BOOKS
3 Tice Rd., Franklin Lakes, NJ 07417. 201-848-0310.
E-mail: mlewis@nisusa.net. Web site: www.careerpress.com.
Michael Lewis, Acquisitions Editor.
Description: Publisher of adult nonfiction books on business, career, education, personal finance, and reference. Seeks to publish high-quality work that will help improve the lives of their readers. **Proposal Process:** Prefers complete manuscript, but will consider proposals. Include table of contents, estimated book length, two complete sample chapters, author bio, market analysis, and previously published clips. Responds within 30 days.

CAROUSEL PRESS
P.O. Box 6038, Berkeley, CA 94706-0038. 510-527-5849.
E-mail: carol@carousel-press.com. Web site: www.carousel-press.com.
Carole T. Meyers, Publisher.
Description: U.S. and Europe round-up travel guides. **Number of Books/Yr.:** 1 title/year (25 submissions), 50% by first-time authors, 75% unagented. **Proposal Process:** Send letter, table of contents, and sample chapter with SASE. Multiple and electronic queries accepted. Hard copy. **Payment:** Modest advance and royalty. **Tips:** We publish 1 or 2 new books each year and will consider out-of-print books that the author wants to update.

CARROLL AND GRAF PUBLISHERS, INC.
Avalon Publishing Group
161 William St., New York, NY 10038. 646-375-2570.

Web site: www.avalonpub.com.
Tina Pholman, Senior Editor.
Description: General fiction and nonfiction. **Number of Books/Yr.:** 120 titles/year, 10% of books from first-time authors. **Proposal Process:** No unagented submissions.

CARSON-DELLOSA PUBLISHING COMPANY
4321 Piedmont Pkwy., Greensboro, NC 27410. 336-632-0084.
Web site: www.carsondellosa.com.
Description: Publisher of educational materials and resources for teachers.

CASSANDRA PRESS
P.O. Box 150868, San Rafael, CA 94915. 415-382-8507.
Description: New age, holistic health, metaphysical, and psychological books. **Number of Books/Yr.:** 2 titles/year. **Proposal Process:** Query with outline and sample chapters, or complete manuscript. Include SASE. Accepts multiple queries, no electronic queries. Prefers hard-copy format. **Payment:** Royalty. **Contact:** Editorial Department.

CATBIRD PRESS
16 Windsor Rd., North Haven, CT 06473-3015. 202-230-2391.
E-mail: catbird@pipeline.com. Web site: www.catbirdpress.com.
Robert Wechsler, Acquisitions Editor.
Description: Publishes fiction, translations, and creative nonfiction. **Number of Books/Yr.:** 4 titles/year, 10% first-time authors, 75% unagented. **Proposal Process:** Send outline with sample chapters and SASE. Response time: 1 month. Accepts multiple queries, but please notify. No electronic queries. Prefers hard-copy format. **Payment:** Royalty, typically 7½%-12½%. **Sample Titles:** Fiction: *All His Sons*, by Frederic Raphael. **Tips:** Interested in high-quality writing, fiction that is not realistic, but instead takes one of the many alternative approaches to reality, with an interest in form and structure—more than plot and character.

CCLS PUBLISHING HOUSE
Cultural Center for Language Studies
3181 Coral Way, Miami, FL 33145. 305-529-8563.
E-mail: info@cclscorp.com. Web site: www.cclscorp.com.
Luiz Goncalves, President.
Description: Language school and publishing house whose focus is to teach and create both multimedia and print language-instruction materials for students learning English or Spanish.

CEDCO PUBLISHING COMPANY
100 Pelican Way, San Rafael, CA 94901. 800-227-6162.
Web site: www.cedco.com.
Description: High-quality calendars, books, stationary, and CD-ROMs.

CHARLES RIVER MEDIA
20 Downer Ave., Suite 3, Hingham, MA 02043. 781-740-0400.
Web site: www.charlesriver.com.
Description: Publisher of books on computers, programming, networking, game development, and graphics.

CHECKMARK BOOKS
Facts On File, Inc.
132 W 31st St., New York, NY 10001-2006. 212-967-8800.
E-mail: llikoff@factsonfile.com. Web site: www.factsonfile.com.
Laurie Likoff, Editor.
Description: Focuses on careers, education, health, popular history and culture, fashion, and fitness. Looking for materials that fit a particular market niche that are high-quality, with a strong reference component. No memoirs, autobiographies, or fiction. **Proposal Process:** Query, with sample chapters or outline. **Payment:** Advance against royalty.

CHELSEA GREEN PUBLISHING CO.
P.O. Box 428, White River Junction, VT 05001. 802-295-6300.
E-mail: aberolz@chelseagreen.com. Web site: www.chelseagreen.com.
Alan Berolzheimer, Acquisitions Editor.
Description: Environmental publisher that encourages human consumption to harmonize with the natural world. Books have a strong practical orientation and cover whole food and organic agricultural, shelter, renewable energy, and livelihood.

CHICAGO REVIEW PRESS
814 N Franklin St., Chicago, IL 60610. 312-337-0747.
E-mail: publish@ipgbook.com. Web site: www.ipgbook.com.
Cynthia Sherry, Editor.
Description: Nonfiction: activity books for children, general nonfiction, parenting, how-to, and regional gardening and other regional topics. **Proposal Process:** Query with outline and sample chapters.

CHINA BOOKS
2929 24th St., San Francisco, CA 94110. 415-282-2994.
E-mail: info@chinabooks.com. Web site: www.chinabooks.com.
Greg Jones, Senior Editor.
Description: Publishes books on all subjects relating to China, Chinese culture, and Chinese-American history. Adult nonfiction of varying lengths, also juvenile picture books, fiction, nonfiction, and young adult books. **Tips:** No novels or poetry. No "My trip to China" proposals.

CHRONICLE BOOKS
85 Second St., Fl. 6, San Francisco, CA 94105. 415-537-3730.
E-mail: frontdesk@chroniclebooks.com. Web site: www.chroniclebooks.com.

Description: Publisher of fiction, children's books, giftbooks, and nonfiction titles on art, photography, architecture, design, travel, nature, and food. **Number of Books/Yr.:** 175. **Proposal Process:** Send proposal (complete manuscript for fiction) with SASE. Proposal could include a cover letter with brief description of project, outline, introduction, sample text/chapters, sample illustrations/photographs (duplicates, not originals), market analysis, and brief bio. **Tips:** Does not publish romances, science fiction, fantasy, westerns, or other genre fiction. **Contact:** Editorial Department.

CITY LIGHTS BOOKS

261 Columbus Ave., San Francisco, CA 94133. 415-362-8193.
E-mail: staff@citylights.com. Web site: www.citylights.com.
Description: Publisher of literature and books on political and social issues.

CLARKSON POTTER PUBLISHERS

The Crown Publishing Group/Random House, Inc.
201 E 50th St., New York, NY 10022. 212-751-2600.
Web site: www.randomhouse.com.
Lauren Shakely, Editorial Director.
Description: Illustrated trade books about such topics as cooking, gardening, and decorating. **Proposal Process:** Submissions accepted through agents only.

CLEAR LIGHT PUBLISHERS

823 Don Diego, Santa Fe, NM 87501-4224. 800-253-2747.
E-mail: clpublish@aol.com. Web site: www.clearlightbooks.com.
Harmon Houghton, Publisher.
Description: Focuses on Southwestern themes, especially Native American cultures. Publishes nonfiction, fiction, picture books, and young adult books. Fiction includes: multicultural, historical, inspirational, and regional. Seeking nonfiction mss on history, multicultural, ethnic issues, nature, religion, biographies of Native Americans. **Proposal Process:** Query with SASE.

CLEIS PRESS

P.O. Box 14684, San Francisco, CA 94114-0684. 415-575-4700.
Web site: www.cleispress.com.
Frédérique Delacoste, Acquisitions Editor.
Description: Lesbian and gay studies, literature by women, human rights, sexuality, and travel. Fiction and nonfiction, 200 pages. No poetry. **Proposal Process:** Send SASE with 2 first-class stamps for catalog before querying. **Payment:** Royalty.

CLOVER PARK PRESS

P.O. Box 5067-T, Santa Monica, CA 90409-5067. 310-452-7657.
E-mail: cloverparkpr@loop.com. Web site: http://members.loop.com/~cloverparkpr/.
Martha Grant, Acquisitions Editor.
Description: Nonfiction adult books on California (history, natural history, travel, culture, or the arts), biography of extraordinary women, nature, travel, exploration,

scientific/medical discovery, travel, adventure. **Proposal Process:** Query with out-line, sample chapter, author bio, and SASE.

COFFEE HOUSE PRESS

27 N Fourth St., Suite 400, Minneapolis, MN 55401. 612-338-0125.
Web site: www.coffeehousepress.org.
Allan Kornblum, Publisher.
Description: Publishes literary novels, full-length short story collections, poetry, essays, memoir, and anthologies. **Number of Books/Yr.:** 14 titles/year (5,000 sub-missions), 15% by first-time authors, 10% unagented. **Proposal Process:** Query with sample chapters. Considers multiple queries. No electronic queries. Response time: Sample 4-6 weeks, manuscript 2-6 months. Hard-copy format preferred. **Payment:** Royalty. **Sample Titles:** *Ex Utero,* by Laurie Foos (fiction); *Our Sometime Sister,* by Norah Labiner (fiction); *Glory Goes and Gets Some,* by Emily Carter (fiction). **Tips:** No genre fiction (mysteries, gothic romances, westerns, science fiction, or books for children).

COLLECTOR'S GUIDE PUBLISHING, INC.

Box 62034, Burlington, Ontario L7R 4K2 Canada. 905-637-5737.
E-mail: cgp2@globalserve.net. Web site: www.cgpublishing.com.
Description: Publishes materials on music, biographies, reference, etc.

COLLECTORS PRESS, INC.

P.O. Box 230986, Portland, OR 97281. 503-684-3030.
Web site: www.collectorspress.com.
Description: Publisher of popular culture art books.

CONARI PRESS

2550 Ninth St., Suite 101, Berkeley, CA 94710. 510-649-7192.
Web site: www.conari.com.
Leslie Berriman, Editorial Director.
Description: Publishes books on health, personal growth, spirituality, women's issues, and relationships. **Number of Books/Yr.:** 35 titles/year (600 submissions). **Proposal Process:** Submit outline, sample chapters, and 6½ x 9½-inch SASE. Hard copy. Multiple queries OK. No electronic queries. Response time: 3-6 months. **Payment:** Royalty. **Contact:** Heather McArthur, Julie Kessler.

CONFLUENCE PRESS

Lewis-Clark State College
500 Eighth Ave., Lewiston, ID 83501-2698. 208-792-2336.
E-mail: conpress@lcsc.edu. Web site: www.confluencepress.com.
James R. Hepworth, Editor.
Description: Trade poetry, fiction, novels, essays, literary criticism, photography, art, science, and folklore. Special interest in the literature of the contemporary and American west. **Number of Books/Yr.:** 2 titles/year (1,000 submissions), 50% first-

time authors, 75% unagented. **Proposal Process:** SASE. Include a formal cover letter. Multiple queries accepted. Hard copy. Response time: 6 weeks. **Payment:** Royalty. **Sample Titles:** Adult nonfiction: *Tony and the Cows: A True Story from the Range Wars*, by Will Baker. Adult poetry: *Out of the Ruins*, by William Johnson. **Tips:** Seeks writing about the contemporary American Northwest.

CONTEMPORARY BOOKS
A Division of McGraw-Hill Trade
Two Penn Plaza, Fl. 11, New York, NY 10121. 212-904-2000.
Description: General reference, sports, health, fitness, parenting, self-help, foreign language.

CONTINUUM INTERNATIONAL
370 Lexington Ave., Suite 1700, New York, NY 10017. 212-953-5858.
Web site: www.continuumbooks.com.
Description: Publisher of scholarly books.

COPPER CANYON PRESS
P.O. Box 271, Port Townsend, WA 98368. 360-385-4925.
E-mail: poetry@coppercanyonpress.org. Web site: www.coppercanyonpress.org.
Sam Hamill, Editor.
Description: Poetry publisher. **Number of Books/Yr.:** 18 titles per year; (out of 1,000 submissions) 10% first-time authors; 95% unagented. **Proposal Process:** No unsolicited manuscripts. **Payment:** Royalty. **Sample Titles:** *Cool, Calm & Collected*, by Carolyn Kizer; *Spring Essence: The Poetry of Ho Xuan Huong*, translated by John Balaban. **Tips:** Currently not accepting unsolicited manuscripts. Check Web site for updates.

CORNELL UNIVERSITY PRESS
Box 250, Sage House, 512 E State St., Ithaca, NY 14850. 607-277-2338.
Web site: www.cornellpress.cornell.edu.
Frances Benson, Editor-in-Chief.
Description: Scholarly nonfiction with particular strengths in anthropology, Asian studies, biological sciences, classics, history, industrial and labor relations, literary criticism and theory, natural history, philosophy, politics and international relations, psychology, Slavic studies, veterinary science, music, religion, and women's studies. **Number of Books/Yr.:** 150 titles/year, 30% first-time authors, 90% unagented. **Proposal Process:** Query with outline, sample chapters, and SASE. Response time: 6-8 weeks. Hard-copy format preferred but electronic query accepted. No multiple queries. **Payment:** Royalty. **Sample Titles:** *Breaking the Watch: The Meanings of Retirement in America*, by Joel Savishinsky; *Field Guide to the Birds of Cuba*, by Orlanda Garrido and Arturo Kirkconnel; *The Evidence of Things Not Said*, by James Baldwin; and *The Promise of American Democracy*, by Lawrie Balfour. **Tips:** Looking for academically sound books that contribute to scholarship and appeal to the educated general reader.

COUNCIL OAK BOOKS

1290 Chestnut St., Suite 2, San Francisco, CA 94109.
E-mail: kevincob@pacbell.net. Web site: www.counciloakbooks.net.
Kevin Bentley, Editor.
Description: Publisher of distinguished nonfiction books based in personal, intimate history (letters, diaries, memoir, and first-person adventure/travel); Native American history and spiritual teachings; small inspirational gift books; unique vintage photo books and Americana. **Number of Books/Yr.:** 10 titles/year (300 submissions), 25% by first-time authors, 75% unagented. **Proposal Process:** Send query and outline with SASE. Do not send complete manuscript. Multiple and electronic queries accepted. Hard-copy format preferred. **Payment:** Royalty. **Tips:** Looking for unique, elegant voices whose history, teachings, and experiences illuminate our lives. No fiction, poetry, or children's books.

COUNTERPOINT PRESS

717 D Street NW, Suite 203, Washington, DC 20004. 202-393-8088.
Web site: www.counterpointpress.com.
Description: History, philosophy, art, nature, poetry, fiction. **Contact:** Acquisitions Editor.

THE COUNTRYMAN PRESS, INC.

W. W. Norton & Co.
P.O. Box 748, Woodstock, VT 05091. 802-457-4826.
Web site: www.countrymanpress.com.
Description: Publishes nonfiction material on New England history and culture. Topics include country living, gardening, nature and the environment, and travel. Also publishes regional guidebooks on hiking, walking, canoeing, kayaking, bicycling, mountain biking, cross-country skiing, and flyfishing for all parts of the U.S. **Proposal Process:** Submit query or outline and 3 sample chapters, along with SASE. **Payment:** Royalty.

COZY HOMESTEAD PUBLISHING

5425 S Fulton-Lucas Rd., Swanton, OH 43558. 419-826-2665.
E-mail: dawnhallcookbook@aol.com.
Dawn Hall, Editor.
Description: Low-fat cookbooks.

CRAFTSMAN BOOK COMPANY

6058 Corte del Cedro, P.O. Box 6500, Carlsbad, CA 92018. 760-438-7828.
E-mail: jacobs@costbook.com. Web site: www.craftsman-book.com
Laurence D. Jacobs, Editor.
Description: Construction manuals for the professional builder and contractor. **Number of Books/Yr.:** 12 titles/year (30 submissions), 90% by first-time authors, 100% unagented. **Proposal Process:** Query with outline and SASE. Multiple and electronic queries accepted. Prefers hardy copy format. **Payment:** Royalty. **Tips:**

Looking for simple, practical hands-on text written in the second person. Only material for the professional builder. No handyman or do-it-yourself material.

CRANE HILL PUBLISHERS

3608 Clairmont Ave., Birmingham, AL 35222. 205-714-3007.
E-mail: cranemail@cranehill.com. Web site: www.cranehill.com.
Shelley Duluca, Managing Editor.
Description: History, biography, memoirs, folklore, cookbooks, art, photography, and humor. Quality books that reflect the history, perceptions, experience, and customs of people in regional locales around the U.S. **Payment:** Royalty. **Sample Titles:** *A Tribe of Warrior Women: Breast Cancer Survivors*, by Melissa Springer; *Just As I Am: Americans with Disabilities*, by Carolyn Sherer and Ellen Dossett.

CREATIVE HOMEOWNER

24 Park Way, P.O. Box 38, Upper Saddle River, NJ 07458-0038. 201-934-7100.
E-mail: info@creativehomeowner.com. Web site: www.creativehomeowner.com.
Timothy O. Bakke, Editorial Director.
Description: Books on lifestyle for the home and garden. Topics include interior design/decorating, gardening/landscaping, and home improvement/repair. **Number of Books/Yr.:** 12-16 titles/year (20-30 submissions), 70% by first-time authors, 98% unagented. **Proposal Process:** Query. Accepts multiple and electronic queries. Response time: 2-4 months. Hard-copy format preferred. **Payment:** Flat fee, typical range is $20,000-$40,000. **Sample Titles:** *Wiring: Basic & Advanced Projects* (home improvement); *Lyn Peterson's Real-Life Decorating* (home decorating); *Advanced Home Gardening* (gardening). **Tips:** Avoid passive voice. Prefers straightforward, expository, instructional text in clear language.

CREATIVE PUBLISHING INTERNATIONAL

5900 Green Oak Drive, Minnetonka, MN 55343. 952-936-4700.
Web site: www.creativepublishinginternational.com.
Description: Publisher of how-to books and books on nature, wildlife, and photography. Also has NorthWord Press imprint and partners with Black & Decker and Singer to create quality how-to books.

CROSS CULTURAL PUBLICATIONS, INC.

P.O. Box 506, Notre Dame, IN 46556. 219-273-6526.
E-mail: crosscult@aol.com. Web site: crossculturalpub.com.
Cyriac K. Pullapilly, General Editor.
Description: All academic disciplines, also general-interest books. Special interest in intercultural and interfaith issues. Prefers books that push the boundaries of knowledge and existing systems of religion, philosophy, politics, economics, ethics, justice and arts (whether through fiction, nonfiction, or poetry). **Number of Books/Yr.:** 30 titles/year (5,000 submissions), 30% by first-time authors, 90% unagented. **Proposal Process:** Send proposal with table of contents, resume, and SASE. Multiple and electronic queries considered. Hard-copy format preferred. **Payment:** Royalty. **Tips:**

Primary concern is subject matter, then organization, clarity of argument, literary style. No superficially argued books.

THE CROSSING PRESS
1201 Shaffer Rd., Suite B, Santa Cruz, CA 95060. 408-722-0711.
Web site: www.crossingpress.com.
Elaine Goldman Gill, Publisher.
Description: Publisher of books, videos, and audios on natural and alternative health, spirituality, personal growth, self-help, empowerment, and cookbooks. **Proposal Process:** Submit proposal with outline, market analysis, sample chapters, and author bio. Allow 8 weeks for response. **Payment:** Royalty. **Tips:** No longer accepts fiction, poetry, or calendars. **Contact:** Acquisitions Editor.

THE CROSSROAD PUBLISHING COMPANY
481 Eighth Avenue, Suite 1550, New York, NY 10001. 212-868-1801.
Web site: www.crossroadpublishing.com.
Description: Spiritual, religious.

CUMBERLAND HOUSE PUBLISHING
431 Harding Industrial Dr., Nashville, TN 37211. 615-832-1171.
E-mail: info@cumberlandhouse.com. Web site: www.cumberlandhouse.com.
Tilly Katz, Editorial Director.
Description: Publishes historical nonfiction books, cooking, mystery, and Christian titles. **Number of Books/Yr.:** 60 titles/year (1,300 submissions), 50% by first-time authors, 75% unagented. **Proposal Process:** Query with outline. No multiple or electronic queries accepted. Prefers hard-copy format. Response time: 3-6 months. **Payment:** Royalty. **Sample Titles:** Adult: *I Remember Joe DiMaggio* (sports), *At Home in the Kitchen* (cooking), *The Journey of Prayer* (Christian), and *Return Again to the Scene of the Crime* (history). **Tips:** No poetry or westerns. Accepts fiction, but more interested in nonfiction works.

CURBSTONE PRESS
321 Jackson St., Willimantic, CT 06226. 860-423-5110.
E-mail: info@curbstone.org. Web site: www.curbstone.org.
Judith Doyle and Alexander Taylor, Co-Directors.
Description: Fiction, creative nonfiction, poetry books, and picture books that reflect a commitment to social change, with an emphasis on contemporary writing from Latin America and Latino communities in the U.S. **Proposal Process:** Submit query describing manuscript. Enclose 10-20 sample pages. Does not accept unsolicited complete manuscripts. **Payment:** Royalty. **Sample Titles:** *My Mother's Island,* by Marnie Mueller; *Maroon,* by Danielle Legros Georges. **Tips:** Do not submit manuscript or sample pages via e-mail. **Contact:** Alexander Taylor, Co-Director.

DA CAPO PRESS
Perseus Books Group
10 East 53rd St., New York, NY 10022. 212-207-7528.
Web site: www.dacapopress.com.
Andrea Schulz, Editorial Director/Acquisitions.
Description: Publisher of general nonfiction papers. Topics include film, dance, theatre, history, literature, art, sports, and African-American studies. **Number of Books/Yr.:** 60 titles/year (250 submissions). **Proposal Process:** Query with outline and sample chapters. Multiple queries accepted. No electronic queries. Prefers hardcopy format. Response time: 3-6 months. **Payment:** Royalty. **Tips:** We do fairly serious nonfiction with backlist potential; we're not right for very commercial frontlist-only titles.

DALKEY ARCHIVE PRESS
ISU Campus Box 4241, Normal, IL 61790-4241. 309-874-2274.
E-mail: cwpost@dalkeyarchive.com. Web site: www.dalkeyarchive.com.
John O'Brien, Founder/Publisher.
Description: Avant-garde, experimental fiction, publishes only reprints of the highest literary quality. **Proposal Process:** No unsolicited manuscripts. **Contact:** Chad Post, Submissions Editor.

THE DANA PRESS
The Dana Foundation
900 15th St., NW, Washington, DC 20005. 202-737-9200.
E-mail: lbarnes@dana.org. Web site: www.dana.org/books/press.
Description: Publishes health and popular science books about the brain for the general reader.

JOHN DANIEL AND COMPANY
P.O. Box 21922, Santa Barbara, CA 93121. 805-962-1780.
E-mail: dandd@danielpublishing.com. Web site: www.danielpublishing.com.
John Daniel, Publisher.
Description: Publishes books, to 200 pages, in the field of belles lettres and literary memoirs; stylish and elegant writing; essays and short fiction dealing with social issues; one poetry title per year. Fiction and nonfiction under 70,000 words. **Number of Books/Yr.:** 4 titles/year (3,000 submissions), 25% by first-time authors, 100% unagented. **Proposal Process:** Send synopsis or outline with no more than 50 sample pages and SASE. Allow 4 weeks for response. Hard-copy format preferred. Accepts multiple queries, no electronic queries. **Payment:** Royalty. **Sample Titles:** Adult Fiction: *The Yellow Ribbon Snake*, by J. R. Dailey. Adult nonfiction: *Hollywood's Revolutionary Decade*, by Charles Champlin. Poetry: *The Privacy of Wind*, by Perie Longo. **Tips:** Looking for good writing that works, poetry that sings, memoirs and essays that make us think.

JONATHAN DAVID PUBLISHERS, INC.

68-22 Eliot Ave., Middle Village, NY 11379. 718-456-8611.

E-mail: info@jdbooks.com. Web site: www.jdbooks.com.

Alfred J. Kolatch, Editor-in-Chief.

Description: Publishes hardcover and trade paperback originals and reprints. Nonfiction only. Subject areas include sports, reference, and biography. Area of specialization is popular Judaica. **Number of Books/Yr.:** 25 titles/year (hundreds of submissions), 25% by first-time authors, 90% unagented. **Proposal Process:** Query with outline, sample chapter, resume, and SASE. No multiple queries. Accepts electronic queries, but prefers hard-copy format. **Payment:** Royalty or outright purchase. **Sample Titles:** *Drawing a Crowd, Bill Gallo's Greatest Sport Moments* (Gallo/Cornell). *The President of the United States and the Jews* (Dalin/Kolatch). The *Baseball Catalog: Millennium Edition* (Schlossberg). *From Central Park to Sinai* (Newberger). *Reel Jewish* (Samberg).

DAVIES-BLACK PUBLISHING

Division of Consulting Psychologists Press, Inc.

3803 E Bayshore Rd., Palo Alto, CA 94303. 650-969-8901.

E-mail: www.cpp-db.com. Web site: www.cpp-db.com.

Connie Kallback, Acquisitions Editor.

Description: Books, 250-400 manuscript pages. Professional and trade titles in business and careers focusing on behavioral aspects. Send manuscript queries to clk@starband.net.

DAVIS PUBLICATIONS, INC.

50 Portland St., Worcester, MA 01608. 508-754-7201.

Web site: www.davis-art.com.

Helen Ronan, Editor-in-Chief.

Description: Books, 100-300 manuscript pages, for the art education market; mainly for teachers of art, grades K-12. Must have an educational component. **Proposal Process:** Grades K-8, address Claire M. Golding; grades 9-12, address Helen Ronan. Query with outline and sample chapters. **Tips:** Royalty.

DAW BOOKS, INC.

The Penguin Group/Penguin Putnam Inc.

375 Hudson St., Fl. 3, New York, NY 10014-3658. 212-366-2096.

E-mail: daw@penguinputnam.com. Web site: www.dawbooks.com.

Elizabeth R. Wollheim, Publisher.

Description: Specializes in science fiction and fantasy. Mostly for adults (but some are appropriate for young adults). **Contact:** Submissions Editor.

DAYBREAK BOOKS

Imprint of Rodale Books, Inc.
400 S Tenth St., Emmaus, PA 18098. 610-967-5171.
Web site: www.rodalepress.com.
Neil Wertheimer.
Description: Four main categories: motivation, inspiration, self-help, and spiritual. Thematic interests include grief/loss, loneliness, and relationships. **Proposal Process:** Send proposal, bio, table of contents, and 2-3 sample chapters. **Payment:** Flat fee.

DEARBORN TRADE PUBLISHING, INC.

A Kaplan Professional Company
155 N Wacker Dr., Chicago, IL 60606-1719. 312-836-4400.
E-mail: hull@dearborn.com. Web site: www.dearborntrade.com.
Don Hull, Editorial Director.
Description: Professional and consumer books on investing, real estate, sales and marketing, general management, and business. **Proposal Process:** Query with outline and sample chapters. **Payment:** Royalty and flat fee.

IVAN R. DEE PUBLISHER, INC.

1332 N. Halsted St., Chicago, IL 60622-2637. 312-787-6262.
E-mail: editorial@ivanrdee.com. Web site: www.ivandee.com.
Ivan R. Dee, Editor.
Description: Serious nonfiction for general readers, in hardcover and paperback. Topics include history, biography, politics, literature, and theatre. **Number of Books/Yr.:** 50 titles/year (1,000 submissions). **Proposal Process:** Query with outline and sample chapters, and SASE. Multiple and electronic queries accepted. Hard copy. **Payment:** Royalty.

DEL REY BOOKS

The Ballantine Publishing Group/Random House, Inc.
1540 Broadway, Fl. 11, New York, NY 10036. 212-782-8393.
E-mail: delrey@randomhouse.com. Web site: www.randomhouse.com/delrey/.
Betsy Mitchell, Editor-in-Chief.
Description: Science fiction and fantasy, 60,000-120,000 words, average; agented submissions only. **Proposal Process:** No unsolicited submissions. **Payment:** Royalty. **Contact:** Editors: Steve Saffell, Chris Schluep, Kathleen David.

DELACORTE PRESS

Description: An imprint of Bantam Dell Publishing Group. See page 739.

DELL BOOKS

Description: An imprint of Bantam Dell Publishing Group. See page 739.

DELMAR LEARNING

Thompson Learning, P.O. Box 15015, Albany, NY 12212. 800-998-7498.
E-mail: info@delmar.com. Web site: www.delmar.com.
Description: Technical nonfiction textbooks for post-secondary learning institutions. Topics include agriscience, electronics, graphic design, nursing, allied health, cosmetology, travel/tourism, etc. **Tips:** Author guidelines available in PDF format on Web site.

DELTA BOOKS

Description: An imprint of Bantam Dell Publishing Group. See page 739.

THE DERRYDALE PRESS

4720 Boston Way, Lanham, MD 20706. 301-459-3366.
Web site: www.derrydalepress.com.
Description: Books on the outdoors, including hunting, fishing, and nature writing.

DEVIN-ADAIR PUBLISHERS, INC.

P.O. Box A, Old Greenwich, CT 06870. 203-531-7755.
J. Andrassi, Editor.
Description: Publisher of books on conservative affairs, Irish topics, photography, Americana, self-help, health, gardening, cooking, and ecology. **Proposal Process:** Send outline, sample chapters, and SASE. **Payment:** Royalty.

THE DIAL PRESS

Description: An imprint of Bantam Dell Publishing Group. See page 739.

DIMI PRESS

3820 Oak Hollow Ln. SE, Salem, OR 97302-4774. 503-364-7698.
E-mail: dickbook@earthlink.net. Web site: www.home.earthlink.net/~dickbook.
Dick Lutz, President.
Description: Assists self-publishers in producing their books. Also publishes nonfiction on unusual things in nature, e.g., unique animals, different cultures, astonishing natural events or disasters. Also, books on travel (no travel guides). **Proposal Process:** Query. **Payment:** Royalty. **Tips:** Queries without SASE will not be answered. Guidelines available on Web site.

THE DONNING COMPANY

184 Business Park, Suite 206, Virginia Beach, VA 23462. 757-497-1789.
E-mail: info@donning.com. Web site: www.donning.com.
Scott Rule, Marketing Director.
Description: Publishes coffee-table pictorial histories of local communities, colleges, businesses, and regional heritage. Contracts with authors for photo and text research and writing. Send samples of work for consideration. **Proposal Process:** Query with outline and sample chapters. **Payment:** Royalty.

DORLING KINDERSLEY
Pearson Inc.

375 Hudson St., New York, NY 10014. 212-213-4800.

Web site: www.dk.com.

Description: Picture books and fiction for middle-grade and older readers. Also, illustrated reference books for both adults and children. **Proposal Process:** Send outline and sample chapter. **Payment:** Royalty or flat fee.

DOUBLEDAY
Doubleday Broadway Publishing Group/Random House, Inc.

1540 Broadway, New York, NY 10036. 212-782-8911.

Web site: www.randomhouse.com.

William Thomas, V.P./Editor-in-Chief.

Description: Publishes high-quality fiction and nonfiction. Publishes hardcover and trade paperback originals and reprints. **Tips:** Does not respond to unsolicited submissions or queries.

DOWN THERE PRESS
938 Howard Street, Suite 101, San Francisco, CA 94103. 415-974-8985.

Web site: www.goodvibes.com/dtp/dtp.

Description: Addresses self-awareness and sexual health issues.

DUMONT MONTE
70 Sherwood Place, Greenwich, CT 92121. 203-622-8488.

Web site: www.dumontverlag.de.

Description: Publisher of illustrated books and calendars on lifestyle, cooking, decoration, art, etc.

THOMAS DUNNE BOOKS
St. Martin's Press, 175 Fifth Ave., New York, NY 10010. 212-674-5151.

Thomas L. Dunne, Publisher.

Description: Adult fiction (mysteries, trade, etc.) and nonfiction (history, biographies, science, politics, humor, etc.). **Proposal Process:** Agented queries only. Submit query with outline, sample chapters, and SASE. **Payment:** Royalty. **Tips:** No unsolicited manuscripts.

DUQUESNE UNIVERSITY PRESS
600 Forbes Ave., Pittsburgh, PA 15282-0101. 412-396-6610.

Web site: www.dupress.duq.edu.

Susan Wadsworth-Booth, Director.

Description: Scholarly publications in the humanities and social sciences; creative nonfiction (book-length only) by emerging writers.

DURBAN HOUSE PUBLISHING

7502 Greenville Ave., Suite 500, Dallas, TX 75231. 214-890-4050.
Web site: www.durbanhouse.com.
Description: Publisher of mystery and thriller novels. **Sample Titles:** *Deadly Illumination,* by Serena Stier; *What Goes Around,* by Don Goldman.

EAGER MINDS PRESS

Hambleton-Hill Publishing
1501 County Hospital Rd., Nashville, TN 37218. 615-254-2451.
Description: Seeks submissions from members of the Society of Children's Book Writers and Illustrators, agented authors, and previously published writers who can submit a list of writing credits. **Contact:** Dayne Kellon, Assistant Publisher.

EAKIN PRESS

P.O. Drawer 90159, Austin, TX 78709-0159. 512-288-1771.
Web site: eakinpress.com.
Melissa Roberts, Editor.
Description: Regional trade books for children and adults. Nonfiction length: 50,000-150,000 words; fiction 20,000-30,000 words. **Number of Books/Yr.:** 65 titles/year (average 1,200 submissions), 40% by first-time authors, 1% unagented. **Proposal Process:** Query with outline. Subsidizes. Multiple queries accepted. No electronic queries. Prefers hard-copy format. **Payment:** Pays royalty. **Tips:** Focuses on history, culture, geography, etc., of Texas and the Southwest. Remember: an active and enthusiastic author can sell more books than an expensive advertising campaign bought by a publisher.

EASTERN WASHINGTON UNIVERSITY PRESS

Eastern Washington University, Mail Stop 1
705 W First Ave., Spokane, WA 99201. 509-623-4286.
Scott Poole, Editor.
Description: Poetry, poetry translations, fiction, and nonfiction. **Number of Books/Yr.:** 6 titles/year (75 submissions). **Proposal Process:** Send complete manuscript, query with outline, or Mac-compatible diskette. Response time: 3-6 months. Prefers hard-copy format. Accepts multiple queries. **Payment:** Royalty. **Contact:** Chris Howell.

ECLIPSE PRESS

1736 Alexandria Dr., Lexington, KY 40504. 859-276-2361.
Web site: www.eclipsepress.com.
Description: Publisher of books on horses and other horse-related topics.

ECW PRESS

2120 Queen St. E, Suite 200, Toronto, Ontario M4E 1E2 Canada. 416-694-3348.
Web site: www.ecwpress.com.

Tips: Unsolicited manuscripts accepted. Include SASE or IRC (outside of Canada) if materials should be returned.

EMC/PARADIGM PUBLISHING INC.

875 Montreal Way, St. Paul, MN 55102. 651-290-2800.
E-mail: educate@empc.com. Web site: www.emcp.com.
George Provol, Publisher.
Description: Information technology and allied health texts and digital media for the post-secondary career education market. **Proposal Process:** No unsolicited manuscripts. **Payment:** Royalty.

ENTREPRENEUR BOOKS

2445 McCabe Way, Irvine, CA 92614. 949-261-2325.
E-mail: jcalmes@entrepreneur.com. Web site: www.entrepreneur.com.
Mike Drew, Marketing Director.
Description: Nonfiction general and small business trade books. Areas include: business skills, motivational as well as how-to and general business including leadership, marketing, accounting, finance, new economy, and business growth and start-ups, customer relations, innovation, stock market and online trading. **Number of Books/Yr.:** 15-20 titles/year (600 submissions), 30% first-time authors. **Proposal Process:** Query with outline, sample chapters, and SASE. Response time: 2 weeks. Multiple and electronic queries accepted. Prefers electronic or hard-copy format. **Payment:** Royalty, range is 5-15%. **Sample Titles:** Nonfiction business: *At Work with Thomas Edison: 10 Business Lessons from America's Greatest Innovator.* **Contact:** Jere L. Calmes, Editorial Director.

EPIC PUBLISHING COMPANY

2101 S Pioneer Way, Las Vegas, NV 89117. 702-871-7263.
Web site: www.epicpublishing.com.
Description: Publishes general books.

EPICENTER PRESS, INC.

P.O. Box 82368, Kenmore, WA 98028. 425-485-6822.
E-mail: info@epicenterpress.com. Web site: www.epicenterpress.com.
Kent Sturgis, Publisher.
Description: Quality nonfiction trade books emphasizing Alaska. Regional press whose interests include but are not limited to the arts, history, environment, and diverse cultures and lifestyles of the North Pacific and high latitudes.

PAUL S. ERIKSSON, PUBLISHER

P.O. Box 125, Forest Dale, VT 05745. 802-247-4210.
Description: Publishes general nonfiction and some fiction. **Proposal Process:** Send outline and cover letter and 3 chapters, SASE required. **Payment:** Royalty. **Contact:** Editorial Department.

M. EVANS & CO., INC.

216 E. 49th St., New York, NY 10017. 212-688-2810.

E-mail: gdek@mevans.com. Web site: www.mevans.com.

George C. de Kay, Editorial Department.

Description: Small commercial publisher of books of all sorts. No poetry or belles lettres. General nonfiction with an emphasis on health, cooking, history, relationships, current affairs, how-to, crime; small list of adult commercial fiction. **Number of Books/Yr.:** 30 titles/year, (500 submissions), 10-20% by first-time authors, 10% unagented. **Proposal Process:** Query with outline, sample chapters, and SASE. Multiple and electronic queries okay. Hard-copy format preferred. **Payment:** Royalty. **Sample Titles:** *The Third Consequence,* by Chris Stewart; *Bragging Rights,* by Richard Ernsberger. **Tips:** Open to adult books for which we can identify a market. **Contact:** P. J. Dempsey, Marc Baller.

EXCALIBUR PUBLICATIONS

P.O. Box 35369, Tucson, AZ 85740-5369. 520-575-9057.

E-mail: excalibureditor@earthlink.net.

Alan M. Petrillo, Editor.

Description: Publishes work on military history, strategy, and tactics, history of battles, military and historical personalities, firearms, arms and armor. **Number of Books/Yr.:** 10 titles/year, 75% first-time authors, 95% unagented. **Proposal Process:** Query with an outline or synopsis of the work, along with the first three chapters, and SASE. If artwork is part of work, include samples. Multiple queries accepted, no e-queries. Response: 4-6 weeks. **Payment:** Royalty/flat fee. **Tips:** Seeking well researched and documented work. The writer should have a mastery of the subject matter. Unpublished writers are welcome and strongly encouraged.

FACTS ON FILE, INC.

132 W 31st St., New York, NY 10001. 212-967-8800.

E-mail: llikoff@factsonfile.com. Web site: www.factsonfile.com.

Laurie Likoff, Editor.

Description: Reference books on science, health, literature, language, history, the performing arts, ethnic studies, popular culture, and sports, etc. **Number of Books/Yr.:** 100-150 titles/year (200-250 submissions), 10% by first-time authors, 30% unagented. **Proposal Process:** Query with outline, sample chapter, and SASE. Unsolicited synopses welcome. Multiple queries okay. No electronic queries. Response time: 4-6 weeks. Prefers hard-copy format. **Payment:** Royalty. **Tips:** Strictly a reference and information publisher. (No fiction, poetry, computer books, technical books, or cookbooks.)

FAIR WINDS PRESS

33 Commercial St., Gloucester, MA 01930-5089. 978-282-9590.
Web site: www.fairwindspress.com.
Description: Publishes material on New Age, spirituality, and health.

FAIRVIEW PRESS

2450 Riverside Ave. S., Minneapolis, MN 55454. 800-544-8207.
E-mail: press@fairview.org. Web site: www.fairviewpress.org.
Lane Stiles, Director.
Description: Grief and bereavement, aging and seniors; caregiving; palliative and end of life care; health and medicine (including complementary medicine). Also topics of interest to families, including childcare and parenting; psychology and self-help; inspiration and spirituality. **Number of Books/Yr.:** 6-12 titles/year (2,500 submissions), 50% by first-time authors, 70% unagented. **Proposal Process:** Send query with sample chapters and complete manuscript, include SASE. Multiple queries accepted. No electronic queries. Hard copy. **Payment:** Varies. **Tips:** No fiction; no longer acquiring children's picture books or adult memoirs.

FAITH LIBRARY PUBLICATIONS

P.O. Box 50126, Tulsa, OK 74150-0126. 918-258-1588.
E-mail: flp@rhema.org. Web site: www.rhema.org.
Description: Publisher of books and materials that offer information to church ministries. Aim is to help young ministries grow.

FALCON PUBLISHING

The Globe Pequot Press
246 Goose Ln., P.O. Box 480, Guilford, CT 06437. 203-458-4500.
Web site: www.falcon.com.
Description: Publishes books on nature, outdoor recreation, travel, cooking, and regional history.

FARRAR, STRAUS & GIROUX, INC.

19 Union Sq. W, New York, NY 10003. 212-741-6900.
Description: Adult and juvenile literary fiction and nonfiction.

FAWCETT/IVY BOOKS

The Ballantine Publishing Group/Random House, Inc.
201 E 50th St., Fl. 9, New York, NY 10022.
Description: Adult mysteries, regencies, and historical romances, 75,000-120,000 words. **Proposal Process:** Acquisitions through agents. Query with outline and sample chapters. Average response time is 3-6 months. **Payment:** Royalty. **Contact:** Editorial Department.

FREDERICK FELL PUBLISHERS, INC.

2131 Hollywood Blvd., Suite 305, Hollywood, FL 33020. 954-925-5242.
E-mail: info@fellpub.com. Web site: www.fellpub.com.
Barbara Newman, Acquisitions Editor.
Description: New Age, self-help, how-to, business, hobbies, and inspirational.
Number of Books/Yr.: 30 titles/year (2,000 submissions), 50% by first-time authors,
90% unagented. **Proposal Process:** Query with sample chapters and SASE.
Response time: 2 months. Multiple queries okay. No electronic queries. Hard-copy
format preferred. **Payment:** Royalty. **Sample Titles:** Since 1942, we have been pub-
lishing titles such as *The Greatest Salesman In the World,* by best-selling author Og
Mandino. Recent launch, *Fell's Official Know-It-All Guides.* **Tips:** Seeking experts in
all genres to help to make *Fell's Official Know-It-All Guides* series grow. **Contact:**
Lori Horton, Assistant Editor.

W.H. FREEMAN & COMPANY

Henry Holt & Co., Inc.
41 Madison Ave., Fl. 37, New York, NY 10010. 212-576-9400.
Web site: www.whfreeman.com.
Description: Publisher of textbooks and educational materials. Also publishes serious nonfiction for the general reader.

THE FEMINIST PRESS AT THE CITY UNIVERSITY OF NEW YORK

The Graduate Center, 365 Fifth Ave, New York, NY 10016. 212-817-7915.
Web site: www.feministpress.org.
Jean Casella, Publisher.
Description: Educational press publishing books by and about multicultural
women. Strives to resurrect the voices of women that have been repressed and silent.
Publishes reprints of significant "lost" fiction, original memoirs, autobiographies,
biographies, multicultural anthologies, nonfiction, and educational resources. **Tips:**
Particular interest in international literature. Accepts no original fiction by U.S.
authors; reprints and imports only. Accepts only e-mail queries of 200 words. See
Web site for submission guidelines. **Contact:** Jean Casella.

FERGUSON PUBLISHING COMPANY

200 W Jackson Blvd., Fl. 7, Chicago, IL 60606. 312-692-1000.
Web site: www.fergpubco.com.
Andrew Morkes, Managing Editor.
Description: Nonfiction for the juvenile, young adult, and college markets relating
to career preparation and reference.

FINDHORN PRESS LTD.

The Press Building, The Park, Forres, IV36, 3TZ Scotland. 0144-1309-690582.
Description: Publishes books on spirit, healing, and self-help.

FIREBRAND BOOKS

LPC Group
22 Broad St., Suite 34, Milford, CT 06460. 203-878-6417.
Web site: www.firebrandbooks.com.
Nancy K. Bereano, Publisher.
Description: Feminist and lesbian fiction and nonfiction. Paperback and library edition cloth. **Payment:** Royalty. **Tips:** Not accepting new material at this time.

FIRESIDE CATHOLIC PUBLISHING

9020 E 35th St. N, P.O. Box 780189, Wichita, KS 67278-0189. 888-676-2040.
Description: Publishes Bibles.

FISHER BOOKS

A Member of the Perseus Books Group
11 Cambridge Center, Cambridge, MA 02142. 617-252-5200.
Web site: www.fisherbooks.com.
Description: Books on pregnancy, parenting, and health.

FITZROY DEARBORN PUBLISHERS

919 N Michigan Ave., Suite 760, Chicago, IL 60611-1427. 312-587-0131.
Web site: www.fitzroydearborn.com.
Description: Academic reference.

FODOR'S TRAVEL PUBLICATIONS

Random House Information Group/Random House, Inc.
280 Park Ave., New York, NY 10171-0002. 212-572-8702.
E-mail: kcure@fodors.com. Web site: www.fodors.com.
Karen Cure, Editorial Director.
Description: Publishes fact-packed travel guidebook series, covering destinations around the world. Every book is highly detailed. Both foreign and US destinations. **Number of Books/Yr.:** 40/titles/year (100 submissions), 100% unagented. **Proposal Process:** Query first, then send an outline and sample. Response time: 2-10 weeks. Multiple queries accepted. No electronic queries. Hard-copy format preferred. **Payment:** Flat fee, depending on the work performed. **Sample Titles:** *Escape to Morocco, Cuba, Brazil, Escape to Ireland, Pocket Aspen.* All travel guides. **Tips:** Avoid pitching general-interest guidebooks to destinations we already cover. Avoid travel literature and other personal narratives.

FOOTSTEPS PRESS

P.O. Box 75, Round Top, NY 12473.
E-mail: krause5@francomm.com. Web site: www.brasseyinc.com.
Bill Munster, Editor.
Description: Saddle-stitched chapbooks, done on quality paper, with photographs to accent the poems. Usually 300-500 copies printed. **Number of Books/Yr.:** 2 or more titles/year (200+ submissions), 100% by first-time authors, 100% unagented. **Proposal**

Process: Query with complete manuscript and SASE. Hard copy. Accepts multiple queries, no electronic queries. **Payment:** Flat fee. **Tips:** Material submitted may be on any topic. Also looking for anything related to poems about movies or prose poems.

FORDHAM UNIVERSITY PRESS
University Box L, Bronx, NY 10458-5172. 718-817-4780.
Saverio Procario, Director.
Description: Scholarly books and journals, computer diskettes, videos.

FORGE BOOKS
Tom Doherty Associates, LLC
175 Fifth Ave., New York, NY 10010. 212-388-0100.
E-mail: inquiries@tor.com. Web site: www.tor.com.
Patrick Nielsen Hayden, Senior Editor.
Description: General fiction; limited nonfiction, from 80,000 words. **Proposal Process:** Query with complete synopsis and first 3 chapters. **Payment:** Advance and royalty.

FORUM
Prima Publishing
3000 Lava Ridge Ct., Roseville, CA 95661. 916-787-7000.
Web site: www.primapublishing.com.
David Richardsom, Editor.
Description: Serious nonfiction books on current affairs, business, public policy, libertarian/conservative thought, high-level management, individual empowerment, and historical biography. **Proposal Process:** Submit outline and sample chapters/market research, include SASE. Multiple queries accepted. Hard-copy format preferred. **Payment:** Royalty and flat fee, standard range.

FOTOFOLIO/ARTPOST
Fotofolio, Inc.
561 Broadway, New York, NY 10012. 212-226-0923.
E-mail: submissions@fotofolio.com. Web site: www.fotofolio.com.
Description: Publishes fine art and photography in the format of books, postcards, posters, boxed cards, calendars, T-shirts, and gifts. **Proposal Process:** Photographers may submit color or B&W photocopies, laser copies, or promotional pieces. Do not send work via e-mail or disk. Accepts material by mail only. Material will not be returned.

FOUQUE PUBLISHERS
244 Fifth Ave., New York, NY 10011. 646-486-1061.
Description: Publisher of fiction and nonfiction.

FOUR WALLS EIGHT WINDOWS
39 W. 14th, #503, New York, NY 10011. 212-206-8965.
E-mail: edit@4w8w.com. Web site: www.4w8w.com.
John Oakes, Acquisitions Editor.

Description: Popular science, history, biography, politics. **Number of Books/Yr.:** 30 titles/year (5,000 submissions), 15% first-time authors, 10% unagented. **Proposal Process:** Query with outline, include SASE. Response time: 2 months. Multiple and electronic queries accepted. Hard-copy format preferred. E-mail queries are accepted; e-mail submissions are not. Unsolicited manuscripts not accepted. **Payment:** Royalty. **Tips:** Write for free catalog or visit our Web site; send e-mail for a complete set of submission guidelines. Note: No poetry, commercial fiction (i.e., conventional romances, mysteries, thrillers, etc.).

OLIN FREDERICK, INC.

P.O. Box 547, Dunkirk, NY 14048. 716-672-6176.
E-mail: magwynne@olinfrederick.com. Web site: www.olinfrederick.com.
Description: Political nonfiction including works of critique, assessment, and debate of current issues, as well as biography, history, economics, health and medicine, business, and other subjects; political fiction; and poetry, all focused on "revealing the truth about issues in the government." **Proposal Process:** Query with outline, synopsis, author bio, and SASE. Please, no sample chapters. **Payment:** Royalty.

MICHAEL FRIEDMAN PUBLISHING GROUP

230 Fifth Ave., New York, NY 10010. 212-685-6610.
E-mail: editorial@metrobooks.com. Web site: www.metrobooks.com.
Nathaniel Marunas, Editorial Director.
Description: Publisher of nonfiction books that are informative and entertaining. Subject matter includes music, gardening, food, history, sports, art/architecture, African-American studies, etc. Imprints: MetroBooks and Friedman/Fairfax. **Tips:** Does not accept unsolicited manuscripts.

FULCRUM PUBLISHING

16100 Table Mountain Pkwy., Suite 300
Golden, CO 80403. 303-277-1623/800-992-2908.
Web site: www.fulcrum-books.com.
Daniel Forrest-Bank, Managing Editor.
Description: Adult trade nonfiction: gardening, travel, nature, history, education, and Native American culture; focus on western regional topics. **Proposal Process:** Send cover letter, sample chapters, table of contents, author credentials, and market analysis. **Payment:** Royalty.

GALLOPADE INTERNATIONAL

665 Highway 74 S, Suite 600, Peachtree City, GA 30269. 770-631-4222.
E-mail: info@gallopade.com. Web site: www.gallopade.com.
Description: Full-color pocket guide, activity books, maps, stickers, etc.

GEMSTONE PRESS

A Division of LongHill Partners, Inc.
Sunset Farm Offices, P.O. Box 237, Woodstock, VT 05091-0237. 802-457-4000.

Web site: www.gemstonepress.com.

Description: Publishes books on identifying, buying, selling and enjoying jewelry/gems.

GLENBRIDGE PUBLISHING LTD.

19923 E Long Ave., Aurora, CO 80016. 720-870-8381.

E-mail: glenbr@eazy.net.

James A. Keene, Editor.

Description: Publisher of nonfiction titles on self-help, business, education, cooking. etc. **Number of Books/Yr.:** 4-6 titles/year, (15,000 submissions), 85% first-time authors, 98% unagented. **Proposal Process:** Query with sample chapter and SASE. Multiple queries okay. No electronic queries. Hard-copy format. Response time: 1 month. **Payment:** Royalty. **Sample Titles:** Adult nonfiction: (3 Book Club Selections) *Three Minute Therapy; Change Your Thinking, Change Your Life,* by Michael Edelstein with David R. Steele; *Living Thin: An Attitude, Not a Diet* and *Living Young: An Attitude, Not an Age,* by Sylvia Goldman. **Tips:** Please send double-spaced material. **Contact:** Mary B. Keene, President.

THE GLOBE PEQUOT PRESS

246 Goose Ln., Guilford, CT 06437. 203-458-4500.

Web site: www.globe-pequot.com.

Shelley Wolf, Submissions Editor.

Description: Publishes nonfiction with national and regional focus. Topics include travel, outdoor recreation, home-based businesses, etc. **Proposal Process:** Query with sample chapter, contents, and one-page synopsis. SASE required. **Payment:** Royalty or flat fee.

DAVID R. GODINE PUBLISHER

9 Hamilton Place, Boston, MA 02108. 617-451-9600.

E-mail: info@godine.com. Web site: www.godine.com.

Description: Publisher of fiction, nonfiction, poetry, photography, children's books, cookbooks, and translations. **Number of Books/Yr.:** 20 titles/year (800-1,000 submissions). **Proposal Process:** Query with SASE. Response time: 2-4 weeks. No multiple queries. Does not accept multiple manuscripts and prefers agented authors. **Tips:** Does not accept unsolicited submissions. Agent queries only.

GOLDEN WEST PUBLISHERS

4113 N Longview, Phoenix, AZ 85014. 602-265-4392.

E-mail: goldwest1@mindspring.com. Web site: www.goldenwestpublishers.com.

Hal Mitchell, Editor.

Description: Publisher of cookbooks, nonfiction Western history titles, and travel books. Currently seeking writers for state and regional cookbooks. **Proposal Process:** Query. **Payment:** Royalty or flat fee.

GOOD BOOKS
P.O. Box 419, Intercourse, PA 17534-0419. 717-768-7171.
Web site: www.goodbks.com.
Description: Cookbooks, family and parenting, etc.

GOOSEBERRY PATCH
600 London Rd., P.O. Box 190, Delaware, OH 43015. 740-369-1554.
Web site: www.gooseberrypatch.com.
Lisa Watkins, Production Manager.
Description: Publisher of cookbooks, calendars, etc.

GOSPEL LIGHT PUBLICATIONS
Gospel Light Publications/Regal Books
2300 Knoll Drive, Ventura, CA 93003-7383. 805-644-9721.
Web site: www.gospellight.com.
Description: Publishes books on adult guidance and aging. Not accepting unsolicited manuscripts.

GRAPHIC ARTS CENTER PUBLISHING CO.
3019 Northwest Yeon Ave., P.O. Box 10306, Portland, OR 97296-0306. 503-226-2402.
Web site: www.gacpc.com.
Description: Publishes photo-essays, gift books, travel guides, calendars, etc.

GRAYWOLF PRESS
2402 University Ave., Suite 203, St. Paul, MN 55114. 651-641-0077.
Web site: www.graywolfpress.org.
Fiona McCrae, Executive Editor.
Description: Literary fiction (short story collections and novels), poetry, and essays.
Number of Books/Yr.: Publishes 16 titles/year. Receives 2,500 queries/year. 20% of books from first-time authors; 50% unagented. **Proposal Process:** Send SASE for guidelines. Response: 3 months to queries. **Payment:** Royalty; offers advance.

GREAT QUOTATIONS
8102 Lemont Rd., #300, Woodridge, IL 60517. 630-390-3586.
Ringo Suek, Editor.
Description: Gift book with humorous, inspiration, and business categories. 100-150 pages with short sentences. **Number of Books/Yr.:** 50 titles/year (250 manuscripts), 50% by first-time authors, 70% unagented. **Proposal Process:** Query with outline and sample chapters or send complete manuscript, and SASE. Multiple and electronic queries preferred. **Payment:** Royalty and flat fee. **Sample Titles:** (Humorous) e.g., *Secret Language of Women*, short sayings about relationship of men vs. women.

GREENLINE PUBLICATIONS
P.O. Box 590780, San Francisco, CA 94159-0780. 415-386-8646.
E-mail: funrises@aol.com. Web site: www.funrises.com.

Description: Publisher of The FunGuides travel guides. **Sample Titles:** *The Fun Also Rises Travel Guide North America,* by Alan Davis; *The Fun Also Rises International Travel Guide,* by Alan Davis.

GREENWOOD PUBLISHING GROUP
88 Post Rd W, Westport, CT 06881. 203-226-3571 x 3390.
Web site: www.greenwood.com.
Description: Publisher of professional and scholarly nonfiction reference titles and textbooks. Subject matter includes business, economics, natural science, law, the humanities, and the social sciences. **Tips:** See Web site for specific submission guidelines. Submit book proposal to one editor only.

GREYSTONE BOOKS
Greystone Books/Douglas & McIntyre, 2323 Quebec St., Suite 201, Vancouver, British Columbia V5T 4S7 Canada. 604-254-7191.
Description: Publishes titles on natural history, sports, environmental issues, popular culture, and health.

GRIFFIN PUBLISHING GROUP
2908 Oregon Court, Suite I-5, Torrance, CA 90503. 310-381-0485.
E-mail: griffinbooks@earthlink.net. Web site: www.griffinpublishing.com.
Robin Howland.
Description: Books on business, education, general trade, language, sports/fitness, and the Olympics.

GROVE/ATLANTIC, INC.
841 Broadway, New York, NY 10003. 212-353-7960.
Joan Bingham, Executive Editor.
Description: Distinguished fiction and nonfiction. **Number of Books/Yr.:** 60 titles/year. 10-15% of books from first-time authors. **Proposal Process:** Query. No unsolicited manuscripts. **Payment:** Royalty.

GRYPHON HOUSE, INC.
P.O. Box 207, Beltsville, MD 20704. 301-595-9500.
E-mail: kathyc@ghbooks.com. Web site: www.gryphonhouse.com.
Kathy Charner, Editor-in-Chief.
Description: Publisher of early childhood learning and activity books for teachers and parents.

HANCOCK HOUSE PUBLISHERS
1431 Harrison Ave., Blaine, WA 98230-5005. 604-538-1114.
E-mail: david@hancockwildlife.org. Web site: www.hancockwildlife.org.
Ingrid Luters, Production Director.
Description: Adult nonfiction: guidebooks, biographies, natural history, popular science, conservation, animal husbandry, and falconry. Some juvenile nonfiction.

Proposal Process: Query with outline and sample chapters or send complete manuscript. Multiple queries considered. **Payment:** Royalty.

HARBOR PRESS, INC.
P.O. Box 1656, Gig Harbor, WA 98335. 253-851-5190.
Web site: www.harborpress.com.
Description: Books on health, diet, psychology, parenting, self-improvement, etc.

HARCOURT BRACE PROFESSIONAL PUBLISHING
525 B St., Suite 1900, San Diego, CA 92101-4495. 619-699-6716.
E-mail: sbernstein@harcourt.com. Web site: www.harcourt.com.
Sidney Bernstein, Publisher.
Description: Professional books for practitioners in accounting, auditing, tax and financial planning, law, business management. **Proposal Process:** Query. **Payment:** Royalty and work-for-hire.

HARCOURT, INC.
525 B St., Suite 1900, San Diego, CA 92101. 619-699-6560.
Web site: www.harcourt.com.
Louise Pelan, Publisher.
Description: Publisher of general trade adult and children's books. **Number of Books/Yr.:** 120 titles/year, 5% of books from first-time authors. **Proposal Process:** No unsolicited manuscripts, queries, or illustrations. Accepts agented work only. **Payment:** Royalty.

HARLEQUIN BOOKS/U.S.
300 E 42nd St., Fl. 6, New York, NY 10017. 212-682-6080.
Denise O'Sullivan, Associate Senior Editor.
Description: Contemporary romances, 70,000-75,000 words. Harlequin American Romances (bold, exciting romantic adventures, "where anything is possible and dreams come true"). Harlequin Intrigue (set against a backdrop of mystery and suspense, worldwide locales). Paperback. **Proposal Process:** Query. **Tips:** Send for tip sheets, SASE.

HARLEQUIN ENTERPRISES, LTD.
225 Duncan Mill Rd., Don Mills, Ontario, Canada M3B 3K9. 416-445-5860.
Web site: www.eharlequin.com.
Randall Toye, Editorial Director.
Description: Mira Books (contemporary women's fiction, to 100,000 words). Harlequin Superromance (contemporary romance, to 85,000 words, with a mainstream edge). Harlequin Temptation (sensuous, humorous contemporary romances, to 60,000 words). Duets (the lighter side of love, to 55,000 words). Red Dress Ink (the trials and tribulations of singlehood, to 110,000 words). **Proposal Process:** Query.

HARPERCOLLINS PUBLISHERS

10 E 53rd St., New York, NY 10022-5299. 212-207-7000.
Web site: www.harpercollins.com.
Description: High-quality book publisher with many imprints. **Proposal Process:** Adult trade books, send to Managing Editor for Fiction, Nonfiction (biography, history, etc.). For reference books: submissions from agents only. For college texts: address queries to College Department (no unsolicited manuscripts; query first).

HARPERPRISM

HarperCollins Publishers
10 E 53rd St., New York, NY 10022-5299. 212-207-7000.
John Douglas, Executive Editor.
Description: Science fiction/fantasy. **Proposal Process:** No unsolicited manuscripts. **Payment:** Query.

HARVARD BUSINESS SCHOOL PRESS

60 Harvard Way, Boston, MA 02163. 617-783-7500.
Web site: www.hbsp.harvard.edu.
Description: Professional nonfiction titles on business and management.

HARVARD COMMON PRESS

535 Albany St., Boston, MA 02118-2500. 617-423-5803.
E-mail: bshaw@harvardcommonpress.com.
Web site: www.harvardcommonpress.com.
Bruce Shaw, Publisher.
Description: Adult nonfiction: cookbooks, travel guides, books on childcare and parenting, health, small business, etc. **Proposal Process:** Send outline, analysis of competing books, and sample chapters or complete manuscript. SASE. **Payment:** Royalty.

HARVARD UNIVERSITY PRESS

79 Garden St., Cambridge, MA 02138-1499. 617-495-2600.
Web site: www.hup.harvard.edu.
Mary Ann Lane, Managing Editor.
Description: Scholarly books and serious works of general interest in the humanities, the social and behavioral sciences, the natural sciences, and medicine. Does not normally publish poetry, fiction, festschriften, memoirs, symposia, or unrevised doctoral dissertations.

HATHERLEIGH PRESS

5-22 46 Ave., Suite 200, Long Island, NY 11101. 212-832-1584.
E-mail: margaret@hatherleighpress.com. Web site: www.hatherleighpress.com.
Margaret Miller, Editor.
Description: Publisher of nonfiction titles on the topics of health, fitness, and self-help. Publishes *Living With* series of chronic illness books. Also publishes material on

losing weight and keeping fit, usually with a unique angle or target audience. **Number of Books/Yr.:** 25 titles/year (100 submissions), 20% first-time authors, 90% unagented. **Proposal Process:** Query with sample chapter and SASE. Multiple and electronic queries considered. Response time: 3-6 months. Hard-copy format preferred. 160-300 pages. **Payment:** Royalty or flat fee. **Sample Titles:** *Our Complete Guide to Navy Seal Fitness, Helping Your Children Cope with Your Cancer, Exercises for Chemotherapy Patients, Living With Hepatitis B: A Survivor's Guide.* **Tips:** No first-person accounts, e.g., "How I survived this illness." It helps if you can bring a celebrity draw to the project. Experts in the fields of health and fitness who can write are very desirable.

HAWORTH PRESS, INC.
10 Alice St., Binghamton, NY 13904-1580. 607-722-5857.
Web site: www.haworthpressinc.com.
Bill Palmer, Managing Editor.
Description: Scholarly press interested in research-based adult nonfiction. Topics include psychology, social work, gay and lesbian studies, women's studies, and family/marital relations. Also covers some subject matter related to recreation and entertainment. **Proposal Process:** Send outline with sample chapters or complete manuscript. **Payment:** Royalty.

HAY HOUSE
P.O. Box 5100, Carlsbad, CA 92018-5100. 760-431-7695.
E-mail: jkramer@hayhouse.com. Web site: www.hayhouse.com.
Jill Kramer, Editor.
Description: Publishes books that center on the topics of self-help, New Age, transformational, and alternative health. **Number of Books/Yr.:** 45 titles/year (2,000 submissions), 2% first-time authors, 10% unagented. **Proposal Process:** Query with outline, a few sample chapters, and SASE. Multiple queries accepted. No electronic queries. Hard copy. Response time: 3 weeks. **Payment:** Royalty. **Tips:** Audience is concerned with the planet, the healing properties of love, and self-help principles. Readers are interested in taking more control of their lives. Research the market thoroughly to make sure that there aren't too many books already on the subject that you're interested in writing about. Make sure to have a unique slant on ideas. No poetry, children's books, or books of quotations.

HAZELDEN PUBLISHING
The Hazelden Foundation
15245 Pleasant Valley Rd., P.O. Box 176
Center City, MN 55012-0176. 651-213-4000.
E-mail: info@hazelden.org. Web site: www.hazelden.org.
Description: Self-help books, curricula, videos, audios, and pamphlets relating to addiction, recovery, spirituality, mental health, chronic illness, and family issues. **Proposal Process:** Query with outline and sample chapters. Multiple queries considered. **Payment:** Royalty.

HEALTH COMMUNICATIONS, INC.

3201 SW 15th St., Deerfield Beach, FL 33442. 954-360-0909.
E-mail: editorial@hcibooks.com. Web site: www.hci-online.com.
Christine Belleris, Editorial Director.
Description: Books, 250 pages, on self-help, recovery, inspiration, and personal growth for adults. **Proposal Process:** Query with outline and 2 sample chapters and SASE. **Payment:** Royalty.

HEALTH INFORMATION PRESS

4727 Wilshire Blvd., #300, Los Angeles, CA 90010. 323-954-0224.
Web site: medicalbookstore.com.
Kathryn Swanson, Acquisitions Editor.
Description: Simplify complicated health and medical issues so that consumers can make informed decisions about their health and medical care. Books average 250 pages. **Proposal Process:** Query with outline, sample chapters. **Payment:** Royalty.

HEALTH PRESS

P.O. Box 37470, Albuquerque, NM 87176-7470. 505-888-1394.
E-mail: goodbooks@healthpress.com. Web site: www.healthpress.com.
K. Frazier, Editor.
Description: Health-related adult and children's books, 100-300 pages. "We're seeking cutting-edge, original manuscripts that will excite, educate, and help readers." Author must have credentials, or preface/intro must be written by M.D., Ph.D., etc. Controversial topics are desired; must be well researched and documented. **Proposal Process:** Submit outline, table of contents, and first chapter with SASE. **Payment:** Royalty.

HEALTHY HEALING PUBLICATIONS

P.O. Box 436, Carmel Valley, CA 93924. 831-659-8324.
Web site: www.healthyhealing.com.
Description: Books on health, wellness, and nutrition.

HEARST BOOKS

The Hearst Corp.
959 Eighth Ave., New York, NY 10019. 212-649-2000.
E-mail: hearstbooks@hearst.com. Web site: www.hearstbooks.com.
Jacqueline Deval, Vice President/Publisher.
Description: Publishes general trade nonfiction titles in conjunction with Hearst magazines. Subject matter includes how-to, cooking, decorating/interior design, crafts, gardening, lifestyle, etc. **Number of Books/Yr.:** 30 titles/year.

HEAVEN & EARTH PUBLISHING

P.O. Box 249, East Montpelier, VT 05651. 802-476-4775.
E-mail: hevnerth@bypass.com. Web site: www.heavenandearth.ws.
Description: Publisher of metaphysical/New Age books.

HEBREW UNION COLLEGE PRESS

3101 Clifton Ave., Cincinnati, OH 45220. 513-221-1875 ext. 293.

E-mail: hucpressphuc.edu.

Barbara Selya, Acquisitions Editor.

Description: Scholarly Jewish Publisher on very specific topics in Judaic studies. Target audience is mainly rabbis and professors. **Number of Books/Yr.:** 4 titles/year (15 submissions), 100% unagented authors. **Proposal Process:** Query with outline and sample chapters, hard copy preferred. Response time: 1 week. **Tips:** No Holocaust memoirs or fiction.

HEIMBURGER HOUSE PUBLISHING COMPANY

7236 Madison St., Forest Park, IL 60130-1765. 708-366-1973.

Web site: www.heimburgerhouse.com.

Description: Publishes model and prototype railroad books and magazines.

HEINEMANN

361 Hanover St., Portsmouth, NH 03801. 603-431-7894.

Web site: www.heinemann.com.

Description: Practical theater, drama education, professional education, K-12, and literacy education. **Proposal Process:** Query.

HEMINGWAY WESTERN STUDIES SERIES

Boise State University, 1910 University Dr., Boise, ID 83725. 208-426-1999.

Web site: www.boisestate.edu/hemingway/series.htm.

Tom Trusky, Editor.

Description: Publishes artists and writers of eccentric format books (multiple editions) relating to Rocky Mountain environment, race, religion, gender, and other public issues.

HENRY HOLT AND COMPANY

115 W 18th St., New York, NY 10011-4113. 212-886-9200.

E-mail: info@hholt.com. Web site: www.henryholt.com.

Sara Bershtel, Acquisitions.

Description: Distinguished works of biography, history, fiction, current events, and natural history. **Proposal Process:** Prefers submissions from literary agents.

HERITAGE HOUSE PUBLISHING CO.

The Heritage Group

#301-3555 Outrigger Rd., Nanoose Bay

British Columbia V9P 9K1 Canada. 250-468-5328.

E-mail: editorial@heritagehouse.ca. Web site: www.heritagehouse.ca.

Vivian Sinclair, Managing Editor.

Description: Publisher of recreation guides, nature books, and special-interest titles. Dedicated to publishing nonfiction by Canadian authors. **Proposal Process:** Submit introduction, table of contents, 2-3 sample chapters, and SASE. **Tips:** See Web site for specific submission guidelines. **Contact:** Audrey McClennan, Editor.

HEYDAY BOOKS

P.O. Box 9145, Berkeley, CA 94709. 510-549-3564.
Web site: www.heydaybooks.com.
Description: Publisher of literature, history, etc.

HIGGINSON BOOK COMPANY

148 Washington St., Salem, MA 01970. 978-745-7170.
E-mail: acquisitions@higginsonbooks.com. Web site: www.higginsson.books.
Laura Bjorklund, Editor.
Description: Nonfiction genealogy and local history only, 20-1,000 pages. Specializes in reprints. **Number of Books/Yr.:** 500 submissions/year, 99% unagented.
Proposal Process: Query with outline and sample chapters, and SASE. Multiple queries accepted. Electronic queries preferred. Response time: 1 month. **Payment:** Royalty. **Tips:** Specialty press-genealogies and local history only.

HIPPOCRENE BOOKS

171 Madison Ave., New York, NY 10016. 212-685-4371.
E-mail: hippocrene.books@verizone.net. Web site: www.hippocrenebooks.com.
George Blagowidow, Editorial Director.
Description: Foreign language dictionaries and learning guides; trade nonfiction, including bilingual anthologies of classic poetry, proverbs and short stories; international cookbooks; history, military history, WWII and Holocaust studies; Polish-interest titles, and Judaic interest titles. **Number of Books/Yr.:** 50 titles/year (200-300 submissions), 80% by first-time authors, 90% unagented. **Proposal Process:** Send query letter describing project and its marketability, with projected table of contents. Multiple queries accepted. Response time: 1-2 months. Hard-copy format preferred. **Payment:** Royalty, typically 6-10%. Flat fee $500-$1,500. **Sample Titles:** *Imperial Mongolian Cooking* (cookbook); *Swahili Practical Dictionary* (foreign language reference); *Spain—An Illustrated History, Children's Illustrated Chinese Dictionary* (nonfiction, ages 5-10). **Contact:** Anne E. McBride(cooking, travel, biography, history); Caroline Gates (foreign language/dictionaries); Anne Kemper (illustrated histories).

HOHM PRESS

P.O. Box 2501, Prescott, AZ 86302. 928-778-9189.
Web site: www.hohmpress.com.
Regina Sara Ryan, Senior Editor.
Description: Publishes books on nutrition, natural health, transpersonal psychology, religious studies, enneagrams, parenting, children, women's studies, poetry, and music. **Proposal Process:** Submit cover letter with summary of manuscript. Send outline with sample chapter; SASE.

HOLLOWAY HOUSE PUBLISHING COMPANY
8060 Melrose Ave., Los Angeles, CA 90046-7082. 323-653-8060.
Web site: www.hollowayhousebooks.com.
Description: Publishes titles on Black Americans and the Black experience.

HOME BUILDER PRESS
National Association of Home Builders
1201 15th St. NW, Washington, DC 20005-2800. 800-223-2665.
E-mail: dtennyson@nahb.com. Web site: www.builderbooks.com.
Doris M. Tennyson, Senior Editor.
Description: How-to and business management books, 150-200 pages, for the building industry professional and consumers. Writers must be experts. **Number of Books/Yr.:** 15 titles (60% unagented authors). **Proposal Process:** Query with outline and sample chapter. Response time 1-2 months. **Payment:** Royalty.

HOME PLANNERS
3275 West Ina Rd., Suite 110, Tucson, AZ 85741. 520-297-8200.
E-mail: pdague@homeplanners.com. Web site: www.homeplanners.com.
Paulette Dague, Acquisitions Editor.
Description: Publisher of how-to reference materials on planning and design for homes, landscapes, and outdoor projects. **Number of Books/Yr.:** 12-15 titles/year. **Proposal Process:** Query with SASE or submit a proposal with outline, sample chapters, and photocopies of artwork.

HOMESTEAD PUBLISHING
4030 W Lake Creek Dr., Jackson, WY 83001. 307-733-6248 .
Carl Schreier, Publisher.
Description: Fiction, guidebooks, art, history, natural history, and biography. **Payment:** Royalty.

HONOR BOOKS
2448 E 81st St., Suite 4800, P.O. Box 55388, Tulsa, OK 74155. 918-523-5623.
E-mail: info@honorbooks.com. Web site: www.honorbooks.com.
Jeff Dunn, Editor.
Description: Publisher of inspirational, devotional, and motivational books and materials.

HORSDAL & SCHUBART/TOUCHWOOD EDITIONS
The Heritage Group
#6-356 Simcoe St., Victoria, British Columbia V8V 1L1. 250-360-2031.
E-mail: touchwoodeditions@shaw.ca. Web site: www.touchwoodeditions.com.
Vivian Sinclair, Managing Editor.
Description: Publishes nonfiction titles on the outdoors and travel in Western and Northern Canada. Also publishes biography, fiction, history, and creative nonfiction. **Number of Books/Yr.:** 8-10 titles/year, 50% of books from first-time authors, 100%

unagented. **Proposal Process:** Does not accept unsolicited manuscripts. Submit query with outline and 2-3 sample chapters. Do not e-mail query; send hard copy. **Payment:** Royalty.

HOUGHTON MIFFLIN COMPANY

222 Berkeley St., Boston, MA 02116-3764. 617-351-5000.
Web site: www.hmco.com.
Janet Silver, Editor-in-Chief.
Description: Trade literary fiction, nonfiction, biography, history, gardening, nature books, cookbooks. Adult fiction/nonfiction to 100,000 words. **Number of Books/Yr.:** 120 titles/year. **Proposal Process:** Query with outline and SASE. Hard-copy format preferred. Response time: 6 months. Multiple or electronic queries not accepted. **Tips:** Unsolicited manuscripts are generally rejected.

HOWARD UNIVERSITY PRESS

2225 Georgia Ave. NW, Suite 720, Washington, DC 20059. 202-238-2570.
E-mail: howardupress@howard.edu.
D. Kamili Anderson, Director.
Description: Discerning nonfiction scholarly research addressing the contributions, conditions, and concerns of African-Americans, other people of African descent, and people of color globally in a broad range of disciplines. **Number of Books/Yr.:** 3-6 titles/year (100+ submissions), 20% first-time authors, 90% unagented. **Proposal Process:** Query with outline and sample chapters. Response time: 3-6 months. No multiple or electronic queries. Hard copy. **Payment:** Royalty, 7.5% range. Advance flat fee, range $1,500-$2,500. **Tips:** No fiction, poetry, or autobiography. Writers are sometimes asked to subsidize the cost of book production.

HOWELL PRESS

1713-2D Allied Ln., Charlottesville, VA 22903. 434-977-4006.
E-mail: rhowell@howellpress.com. Web site: www.howellpress.com.
Ross A. Howell, Jr., Editorial Director.
Description: Publishes and distributes illustrated and gift books on history, transportation, aviation, cooking, wine appreciation, quilts and crafts, and topics of regional interest. **Number of Books/Yr.:** 10-12 titles/year (300 submissions), 60% first-time authors, 95% unagented. **Proposal Process:** Query with outline and sample chapters; multiple queries and electronic queries considered. Hard-copy format preferred. **Payment:** Royalty. **Tips:** We seek "novelty" cooking and gift books. **Contact:** Ross A. Howell.

HP BOOKS

The Putnam Berkley Group/Penguin Putnam, Inc.
375 Hudson St., New York, NY 10014.
E-mail: online@penguinputnam.com. Web site: www.penguinputnam.com.
Description: How-tos on cooking, automotive topics. **Proposal Process:** Query with SASE.

HUDSON HILLS PRESS

1133 Broadway, Suite 1301, New York, NY 10010-8001. 212-929-499.
Description: Publishes books on fine art and photography.

HUMAN KINETICS PUBLISHERS, INC.

P.O. Box 5076, Champaign, IL 61825-5076. 217-351-5076.
E-mail: hk@hkusa.com. Web site: www.humankinetics.com.
Rainer Martens, Publisher.
Description: Publisher of nonfiction reference, self-help, and textbooks on health, medicine, recreation, and sports. **Number of Books/Yr.:** 120 titles/year. 30% of books from first-time authors; 90% unagented. **Proposal Process:** Submit outline with sample chapters and artwork.

HUNTER HOUSE PUBLISHERS

P.O. Box 2914, 1515½ Park St., Alameda, CA 94501-0914. 510-865-5282.
E-mail: acquisitions@hunterhouse.com. Web site: www.hunterhouse.com.
Jeanne Brondino, Acquisitions Editor.
Description: Nonfiction materials for families and communities. Topics include health, women's health, personal growth, sexuality and relationships, violence intervention and prevention, and counseling resources. **Number of Books/Yr.:** 21 titles/year (300 submissions), 5% first-time authors, 80% unagented. **Proposal Process:** Query for guidelines, then submit complete proposal. Response time: 2 months for query, 3 months for proposal. Hard-copy format preferred. Multiple and electronic queries accepted. **Payment:** Royalty, 12% of net. **Sample Titles:** *Chinese Herbal Medicine Made Easy,* by Thomas Richard Joiner; *Men's Cancers,* by Pamela J. Haylock, R.N. **Tips:** No autobiographies, memoirs, or personal stories. No fiction. Emphasis on self-help.

HUNTER PUBLISHING, INC.

239 S Beach Route, Hobe Sound, FL 33455. 561-546-7986.
E-mail: hunterp@bellsouth.net. Web site: www.hunterpublishing.com.
Michael Hunter, Acquisitions Department.
Description: Travel guides to the U.S., South America, and the Caribbean. **Number of Books/Yr.:** 70 titles/year (300 submissions), 40% by first-time authors, 90% unagented. **Proposal Process:** Send query and outline and SASE. Response time: 2 weeks. Accepts electronic and multiple queries. **Payment:** Royalty. **Tips:** No travelogs; just practical guide books to various destinations, average 300 pages.

HYSTERIA

Sourcebooks, Inc.
955 Connecticut Ave., #5310, Bridgeport, CT 06607.
E-mail: laugh@hysteriabooks.com. Web site: www.sourcebooks.com.
Deborah Werksman, Editor.
Description: Publishes humor books. **Proposal Process:** Query with sample chapters or complete manuscript. SASE for guidelines. **Payment:** Royalty.

IDEA GROUP PUBLISHING

Idea Group, Inc.

1331 East Chocolate Ave., Hershey, PA 17033-1117. 717-533-8845.

Web site: www.idea-group.com.

Description: Publisher of journals, cases, and books on information science, education, technology, and management. **Proposal Process:** Submit 2-4 page proposal with suggested titles (3-5), introduction, list of objectives, target audience, current competitors, table of contents, and timetable. **Contact:** Senior Academic Editor.

IMPACT PUBLISHERS, INC.

P.O. Box 6016, Atascadero, CA 93423-6016. 805-466-5917.

E-mail: editor@impactpublishers.com. Web site: www.impactpublishers.com.

Melissa Froehner, Publisher.

Description: Popular and professional psychology books, from 200 pages. Titles on personal growth, relationships, families, communities, and health for adults. Nonfiction children's books for *Little Imp* series on issues of self-esteem. **Proposal Process:** Query with outline and sample chapters. **Payment:** Royalty. **Tips:** "Writers must have advanced degrees and professional experience in human-service fields."

INDIANA UNIVERSITY PRESS

601 N Morton St., Bloomington, IN 47404-3797. 812-855-4203.

Web site: www.indiana.edu~iupress.

Jane Lyle, Managing Editor.

Description: Scholarly nonfiction, especially cultural studies, literary criticism, music, history, women's studies, African-American studies, science, philosophy, African studies, Middle East studies, Russian studies, anthropology, regional, etc. **Proposal Process:** Query with outline and sample chapters. **Payment:** Royalty.

INDO US BOOKS

37-46 74th St., Jackson Heights, NY 11372. 718-899-5590.

Web site: www.indousbooks.com.

Description: Publisher of books and journals on philosophy, health, herbals, music, beauty care, and religion. Seeks to bring the culture of India closer to those living in the United States.

INNER OCEAN PUBLISHING INC.

1037 Makawao, P.O. Box 1239, Makawao, HI 96768. 808-573-8000.

Web site: www.innerocean.com.

John Elder, Publisher.

Description: Publishes titles on self-help, personal growth, new science, consciousness, business, and inspirational nonfiction.

INNER TRADITIONS INTERNATIONAL / BEAR AND COMPANY

One Park St., P.O. Box 388, Rochester, VT 05767. 802-767-3174.

E-mail: info@innertraditions.com. Web site: www.innertraditions.com.
Jon Graham, Acquisitions Editor.
Description: Publisher of nonfiction titles on indigenous cultures, perennial philosophy, visionary art, spiritual traditions of the East and West, holistic health/healing, sexuality, and self-development. Seeks to "help transform our culture philosophically, environmentally, and spiritually." **Number of Books/Yr.:** 60 titles/year (1,000 submissions), 30% first-time authors, 65% unagented. **Proposal Process:** Query with outline and sample chapters, and SASE. Multiple and electronic queries accepted, but hard copy preferred. Response time: 6-12 weeks. **Payment:** Royalty. **Sample Titles:** Adult nonfiction: *Star Ancestors; Yoga for the Three Stages of Life; Asthma: The Complete Guide to Integrative Therapies.* Picture books: *Birth of the Ganga; Ancient Celtic Festivals and How We Celebrate Them Today.* **Contact:** Jeanie Levitan.

INNISFREE PRESS, INC.
136 Roumfort Rd., Philadelphia, PA 19119-1632. 215-247-4085.
E-mail: innisfreep@aol.com. Web site: www.innisfreepress.com.
Marcia Broucek, Publisher.
Description: Adult nonfiction, 40,000-60,000 words, on spiritual issues. No fiction, poetry, or disease "survival" stories. **Proposal Process:** Accepts multiple queries. Query with outline and sample chapters. **Payment:** Royalty.

INSIGHT GUIDES
Langenscheidt Publishing Group
46-35 54th Rd., Maspeth, NY 11378. 718-784-0055.
E-mail: feedback@langenscheidt.com. Web site: www.langenscheidt.com.
Description: Publishes travel guides, phrasebooks, foreign language dictionaries, and travel reference titles.

INTERLINK PUBLISHING
46 Crosby St., Northampton, MA 01060. 413-582-7054.
E-mail: info@interlinkbooks.com. Web site: www.interlinkbooks.com.
Michel Moushabeck, Acquisitions Editor.
Description: Independent publisher specializing in world travel, literature, history, translated fiction, and illustrated children's books from around the world. Uses 3 imprints: Crocodile Books, Interlink Books, Olive Branch Press. **Number of Books/Yr.:** 50 titles/year (500 submissions), 25% first-time authors, 50% unagented. **Proposal Process:** Submit query with outline and 2 sample chapters, include SASE. Response time: 4-6 weeks. Considers multiple queries. No electronic queries. Hard copy. **Payment:** Royalty, range is 5%-10%. **Sample Titles:** Adult: *A Traveler's History of China,* by Stephen G. Haw; *Pancho Villa & The Mexican Revolution,* by Manuel Plana. Children's: *The Fish Prince & Other Stories,* by Jane Yolen and Shulamith Oppenheim; *How Much Land Does a Man Need?* by Leo Tolstoy, illustrated by Elana Abesinona. **Tips:** Study their list carefully before sending your submission.

INTERNATIONAL MARINE

The McGraw-Hill Companies

P.O. Box 220, Camden, ME 04843-0220. 207-236-4838.

Jonathan Eaton, Editorial Director.

Description: Books on boating (sailing and power). Imprint: Ragged Mountain Press, books on sports and outdoor recreation.

IRON CROWN ENTERPRISES

P.O. Box 1605, Charlottesville, VA 22902. 434-295-4280.

John Curtis III.

Description: Supplemental texts, 80,000-230,000 words, to accompany fantasy role-playing games. **Proposal Process:** Extremely specific market. Study one of our existing products before querying. **Tips:** Royalty or flat fee.

IRONWEED PRESS

P.O. Box 754208, Parkside Station, Forest Hills, NY 11375.

Description: Publisher of American literature and history. One original fiction title is selected each year for the Ironweed Press Fiction Prize competition. **Proposal Process:** Query with outline, sample chapters, or complete manuscript for American literature and history titles. Accepts multiple queries. Send SASE for guidelines for Ironweed Press Fiction Prize. **Payment:** Royalty.

ISI BOOKS

Intercollegiate Studies Institute

3901 Centerville Rd., P.O. Box 4431, Wilmington, DE 19807-0431. 302-652-4600.

E-mail: isi@isi.org. Web site: www.isibooks.org.

Description: Publisher of interdisciplinary nonfiction titles in the humanities and social sciences. Books explore current political, economic, and social issues.

JAI PRESS, INC.

Elsevier Science, Ltd.

655 Avenue of the Americas, New York, NY 10010-5107. 203-323-9606.

E-mail: jai@jaipress.com. Web site: www.jaipress.com.

Roger A. Dunn, Managing Director.

Description: Research and technical reference books on subjects like business, economics, management, sociology, political science, computer science, life sciences, and chemistry. **Proposal Process:** Query or send complete manuscript. **Payment:** Royalty.

JALMAR PRESS

B. L. Winch & Associates

24426 S Main St., Suite702, Carson, CA 90745. 310-816-3085.

E-mail: jalmarpress@att.net. Web site: www.jalmarpress.com.

Susanna Palomones, Editor.

Description: Activity-driven books that help kids develop their social, emotional, ethical, and moral skills that lead to academic achievement and lifelong learning.

Number of Books/Yr.: 10 titles/year (200 submissions), 1-2% first-time authors, 100% unagented. **Proposal Process:** Query with complete manuscript, include SASE. Multiple and electronic queries accepted. Hard copy. Response time: 4-6 weeks. **Payment:** Royalty. **Tips:** Does not publish children's story books. Market is teachers and school counselors.

ALICE JAMES BOOKS

University of Maine at Farmington, 238 Main St., Farmington, ME 04938.
E-mail: ajb@umf.maine.edu. Web site: www.umf.maine.edu/~ajb.
April Ossmann, Director.
Description: Adult poetry, no light verse. **Number of Books/Yr.:** 5 titles/year (1,000 submissions), 60% first-time authors, 90% unagented. **Proposal Process:** Query with complete manuscript and SASE. Multiple and electronic queries accepted. Prefers hard-copy format. Response time: 4 months. **Payment:** Flat fee. **Tips:** Serious poetry. See our Web site for requirements on poetry competitions.

JENKINS GROUP INC.

Jenkins Group, Inc.
400 W. Front St., Suite 4A, Traverse City, MI 49684. 213-933-0445.
E-mail: info@bookpublishing.com. Web site: www.bookpublishing.com.
Jim Barnes, Director of Marketing.
Description: Production, consulting, and marketing services for independent authors and publishers. Free monthly newsletter.

JEWISH LIGHTS PUBLISHING

A Division of LongHill Partners, Inc.
Sunset Farm Offices, P.O. Box 237, Woodstock, VT 05091-4544. 802-457-4000.
Web site: www.jewishlights.com.
Description: Publishes books on spirituality, life cycle, philosophy, theology, etc.

JIST PUBLISHING

8902 Otis Ave., Indianapolis, IN 46216-1033. 317-613-4200.
E-mail: editorial@jist,com. Web site: www.jist.com.
Description: Job search and career development. **Number of Books/Yr.:** 35 (60+ submissions). **Proposal Process:** Query with outline and sample chapters. Response time: 2 weeks. Hard-copy format preferred. No electronic or multiple queries. **Payment:** Royalty or flat fee basis. **Tips:** Varies greatly—see our Web site, because we have four imprints; submission guidelines also on our Web site. **Contact:** Lori Cates Hand, Trade Editor, or Susan Pines, Institutional and Reference Books Editor.

THE JOHNS HOPKINS UNIVERSITY PRESS

2715 N Charles St., Baltimore, MD 21218. 410-516-6900.
Trevor Lipscombe, Editor-in-Chief.
Description: Subject areas include ancient studies; history of science, medicine, and technology; history; literary criticism; political science; religious studies; and science.

Proposal Process: Unsolicited queries and proposals are accepted, but no unsolicited poetry or fiction. No e-mail submissions. Hard copy only. Include resume, description of the project, sample text, and descriptive table of contents.

JOHNSON BOOKS

Johnson Publishing Co.
1880 S 57th Ct., Boulder, CO 80301. 303-443-9766.
E-mail: books@jpcolorado.com.
Steve Topping, Editorial Director.
Description: Nonfiction titles on environmental subjects, archaeology, geology, natural history, astronomy, travel guides, outdoor guidebooks, fly fishing, and regional topics. **Proposal Process:** Send proposal. **Payment:** Royalty.

JONA BOOKS

P.O. Box 336, Bedford, IN 47421. 812-278-8370.
E-mail: jonabook@kiva.net. Web site: www.kiva.net/~jonabook.
Marina Guba, Editor.
Description: Humor, true crime, law enforcement, old west and military history. 50,000 word minimum. **Number of Books/Yr.:** 5 titles/year (200 submissions), 50% first-time authors, 80% unagented. **Proposal Process:** Query with outline and sample chapters, and SASE. Multiple and electronic queries accepted. Hard-copy format preferred. **Payment:** Royalty. **Tips:** Looking for more true crime, stories of individual soldiers, and true stories from the old West. Fiction should be based on historical events.

THE JOSEPH HENRY PRESS

National Academy Press
2101 Constitution Ave. NW, Washington, DC 20418. 202-334-3320.
E-mail: smautner@nas.edu. Web site: www.nap.edu.
Stephen Mautner, Executive Editor.
Description: Publishes general trade nonfiction titles that address topics in science, technology, and health. **Number of Books/Yr.:** 12-15 titles/year. **Tips:** Extremely selective in choosing authors. Most acquisitions are either commissioned or come through agents. **Contact:** Stephen Mautner.

JOVE BOOKS

The Putnam Berkley Group/Penguin Putnam, Inc.
375 Hudson St., New York, NY 10014.
E-mail: online@penguinputnam.com. Web site: www.penguinputnam.com.
Description: Fiction and nonfiction. **Proposal Process:** No unsolicited manuscripts. Query first.

KALMBACH PUBLISHING CO.

21027 Crossroads Circle, P.O. Box 1612, Waukesha, WI 53187-1612. 262-796-8776.
E-mail: books@kalmbach.com. Web site: www.kalmbachbooks.com.

Dick Christianson, Editor-in-Chief.
Description: Reference materials and how-to books for serious hobbyists in the rail fan, model railroading, plastic modeling, toy train collecting/operating hobbies; how-to books for writers. **Number of Books/Yr.:** 20 titles/year (100 submissions), 50% by first-time authors, 80% unagented. **Proposal Process:** Query first. Upon approval, follow with detailed outline and complete a sample chapter with photos, drawings, and how-to text. Include SASE. Accepts multiple and electronic queries. Prefers hard-copy format. Response time: 2 months to queries. **Payment:** Royalty, 10% on net price. **Sample Titles:** *The Writer's Handbook 2002, The Basics of Ship Modeling,* Mike Ashey. **Tips:** The hobby books are about half text and half illustrations. Authors must be able to furnish good photographs and rough drawings. Telephone inquiries welcomed to save time, misconceptions, and wasted work. **Contact:** Kent Johnson, Senior Acquisitions Editor (hobbies); Philip Martin, Acquisitions Editor (*Writer's Handbook,* writing books).

KAR-BEN COPIES

6800 Tildenwood Ln., Rockville, MD 20852. 800-452-7236.
E-mail: karben@aol.com. Web site: www.karben.com.
Judyth Groner, Executive Editor.
Description: Books on Jewish themes for preschool and elementary children (to age 9): picture books, fiction, and nonfiction. **Number of Books/Yr.:** 8-10 titles/year. Receives 50-100 queries and 300-400 mss/year. 5% of books from first-time authors, 100% from unagented writers. **Proposal Process:** Complete manuscript preferred. SASE. **Payment:** Royalty.

KENSINGTON PUBLISHING CORP.

850 Third Ave., New York, NY 10022-6222. 212-407-1500.
Web site: www.kensingtonbooks.com.
Michaela Hamilton, Editor-in-Chief.
Description: Publisher of historical romance, Regency romance, Brava erotic romance, women's contemporary fiction, gay fiction and nonfiction, Asian fiction and nonfiction, mysteries, thrillers, suspense, horror, westerns, mainstream novels, African-American fiction and nonfiction, health, alternative health, pets, New Age, self-help, true crime, popular culture, entertainment, film, television, wicca, gambling, current events, politics, military, business, Judaica, sports, women's issues, cookbooks, biography, and spirituality. Publishes hardcover originals, trade paperback, and mass-market paperback originals and reprints. **Number of Books/Yr.:** 600 titles/year. **Proposal Process:** Contact editors for guidelines. Unsolicited submissions only for the following lines: Arabesque, Encanto, Zebra Ballad Romance (serial fiction). All other kinds of submissions, agented only. **Payment:** On a book-by-book basis. **Sample Titles:** Fiction authors: Fern Michaels, Stella Caneson, Shanon Drake, Janelle Taylor. Alternative health authors: Gary Nulli. Mystery authors: Jonie Jacobs, Troy Soos, Mary Roberts Rinehart

KENT STATE UNIVERSITY PRESS
P.O. Box 5190, 307 Lowry Hall, Terrace Dr., Kent, OH 44242-0001. 330-672-7913.
Web site: www.kentstateuniversitypress.com.
Joanna Hildebrand Craig, Editor-in-Chief.
Description: Interested in high-quality, scholarly works in history and literary criticism, American studies, regional topics for Ohio, biographies, the arts, and general nonfiction.

KEY PORTER BOOKS
70 The Esplanade, Toronto, Ontario M5E 1R2 Canada. 416-862-7777.
E-mail: cmclieon@keyporter.com. Web site: www.keyporter.com.
Description: Publisher of books on natural history, self-help, health, environment, food and wine, gardening, business, sports, and children's books. Does not accept unsolicited materials.

KIPLINGER BOOKS
1729 H St. NW, Washington, DC 20006. 202-887-6680.
E-mail: dharrison@kiplinger.com. Web site: www.kiplinger.com/books.
Description: Publishes material on personal finance and business management.

KIVAKI PRESS
376 Rosscraggon Rd., Arden, NC 28704-2514. 828-684-1988.
Greg Cumberford.
Description: Nonfiction books for the academic, holistic health, and environmental markets covering such topics as person/place narratives, ecological restoration, deep ecology, and indigenous epistemologies. **Proposal Process:** Complete manuscript may be submitted on disk with hard copy of synopsis. If not submitting on disk, send synopsis only for manuscripts over 200 pages. Reports in 6-8 weeks. **Payment:** Royalty.

KLUWER ACADEMIC PUBLISHERS
233 Spring St., Fl. 7, New York, NY 10013-1570. 212-620-8000.
E-mail: info@plenum.com. Web site: www.wkap.nl.
Description: Trade nonfiction, approximately 300 pages, on popular science, criminology, psychology, social science, anthropology, health, the humanities, engineering, and law. Imprints include Kluwer Academic, Plenum Publishing, and Kluwer Law International. **Proposal Process:** Query with outline, SASE. Hard-copy format. **Payment:** Royalty.

ALFRED A. KNOPF, INC.
The Knopf Publishing Group/Random House, Inc.
299 Park Ave., New York, NY 10171. 212-572-2104.
Web site: www.randomhouse.com/knopf.
Description: Distinguished adult fiction and general nonfiction. **Proposal Process:** Query for nonfiction. **Contact:** Editorial Board.

KRAUSE PUBLICATIONS, INC.

700 E State St., Iola, WI 54990-0001. 715-445-2214.

Web site: www.krause.com.

Description: Publisher of general nonfiction on a wide variety of topics. Subject matter includes antiques and collectibles, sewing and crafts, automotive, numismatics, sports, philatelics, outdoors, guns and knives, toys, records, and comics.

KRISHNAMURTI PUBLICATIONS OF AMERICA

P.O. Box 1560, Ojai, CA 93024. 805-646-2726.

E-mail: kfa@kfa.org. Web site: www.kfa.org.

Description: Educational, critical, and scholarly essays.

LANGENSCHEIDT PUBLISHERS, INC.

Langenscheidt Publishing Group

46-35 54th Rd., Maspeth, NY 11378. 718-784-0055.

E-mail: feedback@langenscheidt.com. Web site: www.langenscheidt.com.

Description: Publishes travel guides, phrasebooks, foreign language dictionaries, and travel reference titles.

LANTERN BOOKS

1 Union Square W, Suite 201, New York, NY 10003. 212-414-2275.

E-mail: info@booklightinc.com. Web site: www.lanternbooks.com.

Description: Books on spirituality, health and healing, animal advocacy, religion, social thought, and vegetarianism.

LARK BOOKS

Sterling Publishing

67 Broadway, Asheville, NC 28801. 828-253-0467.

E-mail: nicole@larkbooks.com. Web site: www.larkbooks.com.

Nicole Tuggle, Acquisitions Editor.

Description: Distinctive books for creative people in crafts, how-to, leisure activities, and gardening. **Proposal Process:** Query with outline. **Payment:** Royalty.

THE LAST GASP OF SAN FRANCISCO

777 Florida St., San Francisco, CA 94110. 415-824-6636.

E-mail: lastgasp@hooked.net. Web site: www.lastgasp.com.

Description: Publisher of books, comics, and magazines that reflect an eclectic mix of topics. Subject matter includes pop culture, fashion, horticulture, occultism, literature, erotica, art, and humor.

LAUREL GLEN PUBLISHING

Advantage Publishers Group

5880 Oberlin Dr., San Diego, CA 92121. 858-457-2500.

E-mail: manam@advmkt.com. Web site: www.advantagebooksonline.com.

Description: Books on gardening, cooking, decorating, lifestyle, self-improvement.

LAWRENCE HILL BOOKS
814 N Franklin, Chicago, IL 60610. 312-337-0747.
E-mail: frontdesk@ipgbook.com. Web site: www.ipgbook.com.
Description: Publishes titles on Black and African-American topics and interests.

LECTORUM PUBLICATIONS, INC.
Scholastic, Inc.
524 Broadway, New York, NY 10012-3999. 212-965-7466.
E-mail: crivera@scholastic.com. Web site: www.lectorum.com.
Description: Publisher and distributor of children's books written or translated in Spanish. **Sample Titles:** *La Historia de Johnny Appleseed,* translated by Teresa Mlawer; *Calor: A Story of Warmth for All Ages,* by Amado Pena.

HAL LEONARD BOOKS
151 W 46th St., Fl. 8, New York, NY 10036. 646-562-5892.
E-mail: bschaefer@halleonard.com. Web site: www.halleonard.com.
Ben Schafer, Editor.
Description: Publishes music books: nonfiction, biographies, history, reference, and technical. **Proposal Process:** Query with sample chapters and outline. **Payment:** Royalty or flat fee. **Tips:** Will only accept material that has a theme or topic connected to music.

LIBRA PUBLISHERS, INC.
3089 C Clairemont Dr., Suite 383, San Diego, CA 92117. 858-571-1414.
William Kroll, Editorial Director.
Description: Publisher of titles on behavioral and social sciences, medical and general nonfiction, some fiction and poetry, and professional journals.

LINCOLN-HERNDON PRESS, INC.
400 S Grand Ave., Springfield, IL 62703. 217-535-1010.
E-mail: lhp@cityscape.net. Web site: www.lincolnherndon.com.
James E. Myers, Editor.
Description: Humor—jokes and stories on various fields. **Number of Books/Yr.:** 3 titles/year, 1% first-time authors, 3% unagented. **Proposal Process:** Send query with complete manuscript, and SASE. No multiple or electronic queries. Hard copy. **Payment:** Royalty. **Contact:** Jean Saul, Assistant Publisher.

LINDEN PUBLISHERS
1750 N Sycamore, Suite 305, Hollywood, CA 90028-8662.
Description: Publishes poetry and plays. **Proposal Process:** Query. **Payment:** Royalty and flat fees.

LINTEL
24 Blake Lane, Middletown, NY 10940. 914-344-1690.
Description: Poetry and experimental fiction. **Tips:** Does not accept unsolicited mss.

LION BOOKS

Sayre Ross Co., 210 Nelson Road, Scarsdale, NY 10583. 914-725-2280.
Harriet Ross, Editor.
Description: Nonfiction; young adult, sports instruction, craft activity books, politics, black studies. **Number of Books/Yr.:** 14 titles/year. Receives 60-150 queries and 100 mss/year. 60% of books from first-time authors. **Payment:** Royalty.

LITTLE, BROWN & CO., CHILDREN'S BOOKS

Time Warner, Inc.
3 Center Plaza, Boston, MA 02108-2084. 617-227-0730.
Web site: www.twbookmark.com.
Maria Modugno, Editor-in-Chief.
Description: Fiction, biography, history, travel, drama, art and photography, juvenile, health and fitness, paperback, cookbooks, mysteries, reference, science, sports, poetry, inspirational. **Proposal Process:** No unsolicited manuscripts.

LLEWELLYN PUBLICATIONS

P.O. Box 64383, St. Paul, MN 55164-0383. 612-291-1970.
Web site: www.llewellyn.com.
Nancy J. Mostad, Acquisitions Manager.
Description: New Age, occult metaphysical of how-to, self-help nature for adult/young adult audience. **Number of Books/Yr.:** 100 titles/year (2,500 submissions), 100% by first-time authors, 99% unagented. **Proposal Process:** Query. Multiple and electronic queries accepted. Response time: 2 weeks. Hard-copy format. **Payment:** Royalty. **Sample Titles:** *True Mystic Experiences, A Witch's Book of Dreams, Wild Girls,* (all New Age trade paperback). **Tips:** Interested in any story as long as the theme is authentic occultism, and the work is entertaining and educational.

LONE PINE PUBLISHING

1901 Raymond Ave. SW, Suite C, Renton, WA 98055. 425-204-5965.
E-mail: heleni1@mindspring.com. Web site: www.lonepinepublishing.com.
Description: Publishes books on nature, gardens, and outdoor recreation.

LONELY PLANET PUBLICATIONS

150 Linden St., Oakland, CA 94607. 510-893-8555.
E-mail: info@lonelyplanet.com. Web site: www.lonelyplanet.com.
Description: Travel books and guidebooks.

LONG WIND PUBLISHING

108 N Depot Dr., Fort Pierce, FL 34950. 561-595-0268.
E-mail: publisher@longwindpub.com. Web site: www.longwindpub.com.
Description: Publisher of fine art photography and illustrated books. **Tips:** No children's books.

LONGSTREET PRESS, INC.

2140 Newmarket Pkwy., Suite 122, Marietta, GA 30067. 770-980-1488.
E-mail: info@longstreetpress.com. Web site: www.longstreetpress.com.
Scott Bard, President/Editor.
Description: Nonfiction, varying lengths, appealing to a general audience. **Proposal Process:** Query with outline and sample chapters. Accepts very little fiction, and only through an agent. SASE. Allow 5 months for response. **Payment:** Royalty. **Sample Titles:** *The Millionaire Next Door,* by Thomas Stanley; *Fuqua: A Memoir,* by J. B. Fuqua

LOTUS PRESS INNER WORLDS MUSIC

P.O. Box 325, Twin Lakes, WI 53181. 262-889-8561.
E-mail: lotuspress@lotuspress.com. Web site: www.lotuspress.com.
Description: Publishes titles on alternative health, aromatherapy, and herbalism.

LOUISIANA STATE UNIVERSITY PRESS

P.O. Box 25053, Baton Rouge, LA 70894-5053. 225-578-6295.
E-mail: lsupress@lsu.edu. Web site: www.lsupress.edu.
L.E. Phillabaum, Director.
Description: Scholarly adult nonfiction, dealing mainly with the U.S. South, its history and its culture. **Proposal Process:** Query with outline and sample chapters. **Payment:** Royalty.

LYONS PRESS

246 Goose Ln., Guilford, CT 06437. 800-962-0973.
E-mail: jcassell@lyonspress.com. Web site: www.lyonspress.com.
Jay Cassell, Senior Editor.
Description: Literary nonfiction, travel, fishing, hunting, outdoor sports, science, cookbooks, horses, gardening, and history. **Number of Books/Yr.:** 50 titles/year (200 submissions), 10% by first-time writers, 30% unagented. **Proposal Process:** Send query with outline, sample chapters, or complete manuscript. Multiple queries okay. No electronic queries. Response time: 6 weeks. Query with outline. **Payment:** Royalty.

MACADAM/CAGE PUBLISHING

155 Sansome St., #620, San Francisco, CA 94104. 415-986-7502.
E-mail: info@macadamcage.com. Web site: www.macadamcage.com.
Pat Walsh, Editor.
Description: Historical, mainstream, contemporary fiction and narrative nonfiction such as memoirs. **Number of Books/Yr.:** Publishes 10-20 titles per year, 75% first-time authors. **Proposal Process:** Query with author's bio, cover letter with estimated word count, and 3 sample chapters. Responds in 3-4 months. **Payment:** Royalty. **Sample Titles:** *Snow Island,* by Katherine Towler; *Letters to Montgomery Clift,* by Noel Alumit; *Walking Through Shadows,* by Bev Marshall **Tips:** Does not accept electronic submissions.

MACMILLAN REFERENCE USA

The Gale Group
300 Park Ave. S, Fl. 9, New York, NY 10010. 917-534-2100.
E-mail: frank.menchaca@gale.com.
Frank Menchaca, Vice President.
Description: Multi- and single-volume titles for junior high, high school, college, and public libraries, primarily in science and social studies areas.

MADISON BOOKS

4720 Boston Way, Lanham, MD 20706. 301-459-3366.
Michael Dorr, Editorial Director/Acquisitions.
Description: Adult trade nonfiction on music, art, biography, history, and literature.
Number of Books/Yr.: 20 titles/year (200 submissions), 5% by first-time authors, 50% unagented. **Proposal Process:** Query with outline and sample chapters, SASE. Response time: 2-4 months. Hard-copy format preferred. Accepts multiple queries. No electronic queries. **Payment:** Royalty. **Tips:** Submit work with a journalistic style.
Contact: Christine Joaquim, Assistant Editor.

MANDALA PUBLISHING

2240-B Fourth St., San Rafael, CA 94901. 415-460-6112.
E-mail: mandala@mandala.org. Web site: www.mandala.org.
N. D. Koster, Acquisitions Editor.
Description: Books on Indian art, culture, religion, and philosophy. **Proposal Process:** Submit summary, table of contents, and sample chapter, c/o N. D. Koster.

MARVEL ENTERPRISES, INC.

10 E 40th St., New York, NY 10016. 212-696-0808.
E-mail: jcollado@marvel.com. Web site: www.marvel.com.
Description: Publisher of comic books. **Proposal Process:** Accepts artwork from letterers, pencilers, and inkers. Does not accept unsolicited written material or character ideas. Artists should submit story ideas with photocopies of work. Do not send originals. **Tips:** See Web site for specific submission guidelines.

MCFARLAND & COMPANY, INC.

P.O. Box 611, Jefferson, NC 28640. 336-246-4460.
E-mail: info@mcfarlandpub.com. Web site: www.mcfarlandpub.com.
Robert Franklin, President.
Description: Nonfiction, primarily scholarly and reference. Very strong lists in general reference, performing arts, baseball, history (U.S., world, Civil War), women's studies. **Tips:** Seeking thorough, authoritative coverage of subjects not already exhausted by existing books. Sells mostly to libraries and individuals interested in specialized topics. See Book Proposals section on Web site for submission guidelines.

MCGREGOR PUBLISHING

4532 W Kennedy Blvd., Suite 233, Tampa, FL 33609. 813-805-2665.

E-mail: mcgregpub@aol.com.

Dave Rosenbaum, Acquisitions.

Description: Publishes only nonfiction, with an emphasis on sports and true crime. **Number of Books/Yr.:** 12 titles/year (300 submissions), 50% first-time authors, 50% unagented. **Proposal Process:** Query with outline and sample chapters, and SASE. Prefers hard copy but multiple and electronic queries accepted. Response time: 2 months. **Payment:** Royalty.

MEL BAY PUBLICATIONS, INC.

4 Industrial Drive, Pacific, MO 63069. 636-257-3970.

E-mail: email@melbay.com. Web site: www.melbay.com.

Description: Publishes music books, videos, CDs, DVDs, and material on instruments.

MENASHA RIDGE PRESS

2000 First Ave. N, Suite 1400, Birmingham, AL 35203. 205-322-0439.

E-mail: info@menasharidge.com. Web site: www.menasharidge.com.

Bud Zehmer, Acquisitions Editor.

Description: How-to and where-to guidebooks to all outdoor, high adventure sports and activities; limited nonfiction about adventure sports; general travel books. **Number of Books/Yr.:** 20 titles/year (60 submissions), 15% first-time authors, 90% unagented. **Proposal Process:** Query with outline. Considers multiple and electronic queries. Response time: 1-3 months. **Payment:** Royalty, 10% range. **Sample Titles:** *60 Hikes Within 60 Miles: Raleigh* (sports); *Ethnic Food Lover's Companion* (dining); *Inn-to-Inn Walking Guide: Virginia & West Virginia* (sports). **Tips:** Examine market to truly evaluate whether your book is unique.

MENTOR BOOKS

The Penguin Group/Penguin Putnam, Inc.

375 Hudson St., New York, NY 10014. 212-366-2000.

Web site: www.penguinputnam.com.

Description: Nonfiction for the college and high-school market. **Proposal Process:** Query required. **Payment:** Royalty.

MEREDITH CORP. BOOK PUBLISHING

1716 Locust St., Des Moines, IA 50309-3023. 515-284-3000.

Web site: www.meredith.com.

James D. Blume, Editor-in-Chief.

Description: Books on gardening, crafts, decorating, do-it-yourself, cooking, health; mostly staff-written. "Interested in freelance writers with expertise in these areas." **Proposal Process:** Query with SASE.

MERIWETHER PUBLISHING LTD.

Contemporary Drama Service

885 Elkton Dr., Colorado Springs, CO 80907. 719-594-4422.

E-mail: merpcds@aol.com. Web site: www.meriwetherpublishing.com.

Renee Congdon, Editorial Assistant/Publicist.

Description: Publisher of theater, performing arts, and educational books.

MICHIGAN STATE UNIVERSITY PRESS

1405 S Harrison Rd., Suite 25, East Lansing, MI 48823-5202. 517-355-9543.

E-mail: msupress@msu.edu. Web site: www.msupress.msu.edu.

Martha Bates, Acquisitions Editor.

Description: Scholarly nonfiction, with concentrations in history, regional history, women's studies, African-American history, contemporary culture. Also, series about Native Americans, rhetoric, and poetry. **Number of Books/Yr.:** 35 titles/year (average 2,400 submissions) 75% by first-time authors, 100% unagented. **Proposal Process:** Query with complete manuscript. Multiple queries accepted. Response time: 2 months. Hard-copy format preferred. **Payment:** Pays royalty, range is negotiable. **Sample Titles:** *This is the World* (fiction), *Sixties Sandstorm* (environmental), *Flow of Life in the Atmosphere* (science), *Sorrow's Kitchen* (poetry), and *Peninsula* (creative nonfiction.) **Tips:** Lucid writing, original perspective, original scholarship.

MID-LIST PRESS

4324 12th Ave. S, Minneapolis, MN 55407-3218.

Web site: www.midlist.org.

Description: Literary fiction (novels and short fiction collections), poetry, and creative nonfiction. Does not publish anthologies, so do not send individual short stories or poems. **Number of Books/Yr.:** 5 titles/year (3,000 submissions), 90% first-time authors, 99% unagented. **Proposal Process:** Query letter with SASE. Response time: varies. Will accept multiple and electronic queries. **Payment:** Royalty. **Sample Titles:** Adult Fiction: Recent titles/novels—*The Hand Before the Eye*, by Donald Friedman; *Quick Bright Things*, by Ron Wallace. Adult nonfiction: *One Degree West*, by Julene Bair. Adult poetry: *Jonah's Promise*, by Adam Sol. **Tips:** Interested in submissions of the highest literary quality. Read some of the books we've published in the past to get a sense of our standards. Guidelines available online or with SASE.

MIDDLE PASSAGE PRESS, INC.

5517 Secrest Dr., Los Angeles, CA 9001. 323-298-0266.

E-mail: bramwell@usc.edu.

Barbara Bramwell, Editor.

Description: Small press. Nonfiction that focuses on African-American experience in the historical, social, and political context of American life. **Proposal Process:** Query with sample chapters. **Payment:** Royalty.

THE MIT PRESS
5 Cambridge Center, Cambridge, MA 02142. 617-253-5646.
Web site: http://mitpress.mit.edu.
Larry Cohen, Editor-in-Chief.
Description: Books on computer science/artificial intelligence, cognitive sciences, economics, finance, architecture, aesthetic and social theory, linguistics, technology studies, environmental studies, and neuroscience.

MODERN LANGUAGE ASSOCIATION
The Modern Language Association of America, 26 Broadway, Fl. 3, New York, NY 10004-1789. 646-576-5000.
Web site: www.mla.org.
Description: Publishes books and style guides for students and teachers focusing on language, literature, grammar, and composition.

THE MONACELLI PRESS
10 E 92nd St., New York, NY 10128. 212-831-0248.
E-mail: info@monacellipress.com. Web site: www.monacellipress.com.
Andrea Monfried, Editor.
Description: Publisher of illustrated books on art, architecture, design, and photography. **Number of Books/Yr.:** 25 titles/year. Receives 100 submissions/year. 10% of books from first-time authors.

MONTANA HISTORICAL SOCIETY
P.O. Box 201201, Helena, MT 59620.
E-mail: mkohl@state.mt.us. Web site: www.montanahistoricalsociety.org.
Martha Kohl, Editor.
Description: Publishes books on Montana history. **Number of Books/Yr.:** 5 titles/year, (20 submissions), 20% first-time authors, 100% unagented. **Proposal Process:** Query with outline and sample chapters, and SASE. Prefer hard-copy format. Electronic query OK. No multiple queries. **Payment:** Royalty. **Sample Titles:** *Journeys to the Land of Gold: Emigrant Diaries from the Bozeman Trail, 1863-1866*, a two-volume, edited compendium of all known firsthand accounts of Bozeman Trails travels; *Anaconda Copper, Montana Air Pollution, and the Courts, 1890-1920*, a landmark environmental history; and *A Guide to Historical Hamilton, Montana*, an architectural and history guidebook to this Montana town. **Tips:** Looking for well-researched, well-written regional history. Writers should avoid overexposed topics like western gunfighting.

MONTEREY BAY AQUARIUM PRESS
886 Cannery Row, Monterey, CA 93940. 831-648-4847.
E-mail: mgelizondo@mbayaq.org. Web site: www.montereybayaquarium.org.
Description: Publishes titles on natural history and conservation of the oceans for both adults and children.

WILLIAM MORROW AND CO., INC.

HarperCollins Publishers

10 E 53rd St., New York, NY 10022. 212-207-7000.

Web site: www.harpercollins.com.

Michael Morrison, Editorial Director.

Description: Adult fiction and nonfiction. **Proposal Process:** Query.

MOTORBOOKS INTERNATIONAL

Motorbooks International/MBI Publishing Co.

Galtier Plaza, Suite 200, 380 Jackson St., St. Paul, MN 55101-3885.

E-mail: trade@motorbooks.com. Web site: www.motorbooks.com.

Description: Publisher of books on automotive, motorcycles, tractors, railroading, trucks, boating, aviation, and military.

MOUNTAIN PRESS PUBLISHING

1301 S Third W, P.O. Box 2399, Missoula, MT 59806. 406-728-1900.

E-mail: info@mtnpress.com. Web site: www.mountian-press.com.

Kathleen Ort, Science Editor; Gwen McKenna, History Editor;

Jennifer Carey, Geology Editor.

Description: Nonfiction trade books for general audiences, primarily adults. Considers proposals for projects in natural history (including field guides for plants, wildlife, etc.), western history, or frontier history. No technical earth science or ecology. **Number of Books/Yr.:** 12 titles/year (150 submissions), 20% first-time authors, 90% unagented. **Proposal Process:** Query with outline and sample chapters, SASE. Multiple and electronic queries accepted. Response time: 1 week-3 months. **Payment:** Royalty. **Sample Titles:** Mountain Press is best known for Western history and natural history, and for its state-by-state series *Roadside Geology* and *Roadside History*. Recent titles include: *Wild Berries of the West; Sacagawea's Son: The Life of Jean Baptiste Charbonneau; Dinosaurs Under the Big Sky*.

THE MOUNTAINEERS BOOKS

1001 SW Klickitat Way, Suite 201, Seattle, WA 98134. 206-223-6303.

E-mail: acquisitions@mountaineers.org. Web site: www.mountaineerbooks.org.

David Emblidge, Editor-in-Chief.

Description: Nonfiction only on the outdoors involving noncompetitive, nonmotorized, self-propelled activities such as mountain climbing, hiking, walking, skiing, canoeing, kayaking, snow shoeing, and adventure travel. Also publishes environmental and conservation subjects, narratives of expeditions, and adventure travel. **Number of Books/Yr.:** 50-60 titles/year (400-500 submissions), 50% by first-time authors, 90% unagented. **Proposal Process:** Query with outline and sample chapters, include SASE. Response time: 2-4 months. Accepts multiple and electronic queries. Hard-copy format preferred. **Payment:** Royalty, typical range is $2,400-$4,500. **Sample Titles:** Adult: Outdoor recreation: *Florida State Parks, Best Hikes w/Children Utah, 75 Year-Round Hikes in Northern California*. Adventure narrative:

The Wildest Dream, Stone Palaces. **Contact:** Cassandra Conyers, Acquisitions Editor, Christine Hosler, Assistant Acquisitions Editor.

MOYER BELL
54 Phillips St., Wickford, RI 02852-5126. 401-294-0106.
Web site: www.moyerbell.com.
Britt Bell, Publisher.
Description: Adult fiction, nonfiction, and poetry. Please call for submission guidelines.

MUSEUM OF NEW MEXICO PRESS
228 E Palace Ave., Santa Fe, NM 87501. 505-827-6455.
E-mail: mwachs@oca.state.nm.us. Web site: www.mnmpress.org.
Mary Wachs, Editorial Director.
Description: Publisher of art and photography on Native America and the Hispanic Southwest. **Proposal Process:** Submit proposal with resume or curriculum vitae. Include table of contents, a sample chapter, and samples of artwork if material is illustrated.

MUSTANG PUBLISHING CO., INC.
P.O. Box 770426, Memphis, TN 38177. 901-684-1200.
E-mail: mustangpub@aol.com. Web site: www.mustangpublishing.com.
Rollin A. Riggs, Acquisitions Editor.
Description: General nonfiction for an 18-50 year-old readership. **Number of Books/Yr.:** 4 titles/year (1,000 submissions), 75% by first-time authors, 100% unagented. **Proposal Process:** Query with outline and sample chapters and SASE. No electronic queries. Multiple queries okay. Response time: 1 month, prefers hard-copy format. No e-queries. **Payment:** Royalty (6-8%net). **Sample Titles:** *The Complete Book of Golf Games, 101 Classic Jewish Jokes, Medical School Admissions: The Insider's Guide.* **Tips:** No travel, memoirs. No phone calls.

THE MYSTERIOUS PRESS
Warner Books
1271 Avenue of the Americas, New York, NY 10020. 212-522-7200.
Web site: www.twbookmark.
Sara Ann Freed, Editor-in-Chief.
Description: Publishes mystery, suspense, and crime novels. **Number of Books/Yr.:** 45 titles/year. **Proposal Process:** Agented manuscripts only. **Payment:** Royalty.

THE NAIAD PRESS, INC.
P.O. Box 10543, Tallahassee, FL 32302. 850-539-5965.
Web site: www.naiadpress.com.
Barbara Grier, Editorial Director.
Description: Adult fiction, 48,000-50,000 words, with lesbian themes and charac-

ters: mysteries, romances, gothics, ghost stories, westerns, regencies, spy novels, etc. **Proposal Process:** Query with letter and one-page précis only. **Payment:** Royalty.

NATUREGRAPH PUBLISHERS
P.O. Box 1047, Happy Camp, CA 96039. 530-493-5353.
E-mail: nature@sisqtel.net. Web site: www.naturegraph.com.
Barbara Brown, Editor.
Description: Publishes adult nonfiction books under two main categories: natural history and nature; and Native American culture, outdoor living, land, and Indian lore. **Number of Books/Yr.:** 2-3 titles/year (400 submissions), almost 100% by first-time authors, 100% unagented. **Proposal Process:** Query with outline and SASE. Response time: 1 month. Hard-copy format preferred. Multiple queries okay. No electronic queries. **Payment:** Royalty. **Tips:** No children's books.

THE NAVAL INSTITUTE PRESS
U.S. Naval Institute, 291 Wood Rd., Annapolis, MD 21402-5035. 410-268-6110.
E-mail: esecunda@usni.org. Web site: www.usni.org.
Paul Wilderson, Executive Editor.
Description: Nonfiction, 60,000-100,000 words: military histories, biographies, ship guides. Occasional military fiction, 75,000-110,000 words. **Proposal Process:** Query with outline and sample chapters. **Payment:** Royalty.

NEW AMSTERDAM BOOKS
Ivan R. Dee, Publisher, 1332 N Halsted St., Chicago, IL 60622-2694. 312-787-6262.
E-mail: editorial@ivanrdee.com. Web site: www.ivanrdee.com.
Description: Publishes titles on art history, biography, cooking, politics, theater/drama, and international fiction.

NEW DIRECTIONS
80 Eighth Ave., New York, NY 10011. 212-255-0230.
Web site: www.ndpublishing.com.
Barbara Epler, Editor-in-Chief.
Description: Stylistically experimental fiction and poetry. **Proposal Process:** Submit sample chapters or complete manuscript. **Payment:** Royalty.

NEW HARBINGER PUBLICATIONS
5674 Shattuck Ave., Oakland, CA 94609-1662. 510-652-0215.
E-mail: tesilya@newharbinger.com. Web site: www.newharbinger.com.
Catharine Sutker, Acquisitions Manager.
Description: Self-help psychology books, workbooks on life issues, women's topics and balanced living. Read by lay people and used by mental health professionals. **Number of Books/Yr.:** 45 titles (600+ submissions), 75% first-time authors, 90% unagented. **Proposal Process:** Query with an outline and sample chapters. Response time 1 month. Accept electronic, hard copy submissions. Electronic queries OK. **Payment:** Royalty 10% of net cash receipts. **Sample Titles:** *The*

Anxiety & Phobia Workbook and *The Woman's Guide to Total Self-Esteem.* **Contact:** Tesilya Hanauer.

NEW HORIZON PRESS

P.O. Box 669, Far Hills, NJ 07931. 908-604-6311.

E-mail: nhp@newhorizonpressbooks.com.

Web site: www.newhorizonpressbooks.com.

Dr. Joan Dunphy, Editor-in-Chief.

Description: Nonfiction stories of courageous individuals. Incredible tales of real people with an intense human interest appeal. Also publishes investigative journalism that probes important public issues. **Number of Books/Yr.:** 12 titles/year, 90% first-time authors, 50% unagented. **Proposal Process:** Send query with outline and sample chapters. Include SASE. Multiple and electronic queries okay. Response time: 4 weeks. Hard-copy format preferred. **Payment:** Royalty. **Sample Titles:** Hardcover: *The Other Side, Deadly Deception.* Trade paper: *Older Women, Younger Men.* Children's: *I Am So Angry I Could Scream, A Special Raccoon.* **Tips:** First-time authors welcome. For adult nonfiction, seeking the unsung hero; someone who has taken it upon themselves to correct a social injustice. Also, adult true crimes. **Contact:** Lynda Hatch.

THE NEW PRESS

450 W 41st St., Fl. 6, New York, NY 10036. 212-629-8802.

Web site: www.thenewpress.com.

Andre Schiffrin, Director.

Description: Serious nonfiction in the fields of history, politics, African-American studies, economics, labor, multicultural education, media, and Latin-American studies, among others. Does not publish U.S. fiction or poetry, but has a program in international fiction. **Number of Books/Yr.:** 50 titles/year (from several hundred submissions), 20% by first-time authors, 50% unagented. **Proposal Process:** Query. Response time: 2 months. Multiple queries considered. No electronic queries. Hard-copy format preferred. **Payment:** Royalty.

NEW VICTORIA PUBLISHERS

P.O. Box 27, Norwich, VT 05055. 802-649-5297.

E-mail: newvic@aol.com. Web site: www.newvictoria.com.

Rebecca Béguin, Acquisitions Editor.

Description: Publishes mostly mysteries and lesbian novels. **Number of Books/Yr.:** 6 titles/year (150-200 submissions), 2-3% first-time authors, 100% unagented. **Proposal Process:** Query with outline and sample chapters; SASE. No electronic queries. Multiple queries okay. Prefer hard-copy format. Response time: 2-3 weeks. **Payment:** Royalty, 10%. **Sample Titles:** *Day Stripper,* mystery; *Mommy Deadest,* mystery; *Circles of Power,* feminist history.

NEW WORLD LIBRARY

14 Pamaron Way, Novato, CA 94949. 415-884-2100.

Web site: www.nwlib.com.

Georgia Hughes, Editorial Director.

Description: New World Library is dedicated to publishing books that inspire and challenge us to improve the quality of our lives and our world. **Number of Books/Yr.:** 30 titles/year (2,000 submissions), 10% by first-time authors, 50% un-agented. **Proposal Process:** Send query with sample chapters or complete manu-script. Multiple queries okay. No electronic queries. Response time: 90 days. Hard-copy format preferred. **Payment:** Royalty. **Tips:** Seeks books that inspire and instruct and have a spiritual approach. No personal memoirs or fiction. Books must combine clear writing with a strong voice and unique message.

NEW YORK UNIVERSITY PRESS

838 Broadway, Fl. 3, New York, NY 10003. 212-998-2575.

E-mail: nyupress.info@nyu.edu. Web site: www.nyupress.nyu.edu.

Description: Scholarly nonfiction in history, law, religion, media studies, cultural studies, sociology, politics, anthropology, and psychology. No fiction or poetry. **Proposal Process:** Submit proposal with sample chapters and curriculum vitae.

NEWCASTLE PUBLISHING

19450 Greenbriar Dr., Tarzana, CA 91356-5524. 818-787-4378.

Daryl Jacoby, Editor.

Description: Nonfiction manuscripts, 200-250 pages, for older adults on personal health, health care issues, psychology, and relationships. No fads or trends. We want books with a long shelf life. **Proposal Process:** Multiple queries considered. **Payment:** Royalty.

NEWMARKET PRESS

18 E 48th St., New York, NY 10017.

Keith Hollaman.

Description: Nonfiction on health, psychology, self-help, child care, parenting, music, film, and personal finance. **Proposal Process:** Query. **Payment:** Royalty.

NICHOLS PUBLISHING

1025 Andrew Dr., Suite 100, West Chester, PA 19380. 610-918-3900.

E-mail: pnalle@aol.com. Web site: www.chiltonsonline.com.

Description: Publisher of Chilton (R) Automotive Repair and SELOC (R) marine maintenance and repair manuals. Manuals are intended for professional mechanics, do-it-yourself car and boat enthusiasts, instructors, and students.

NICOLAS-HAYS INC.

P.O. Box 2039, York Beach, ME 03910-2039. 207-363-1558.

E-mail: nhi@ici.net. Web site: www.nicolashays.com.

Description: Books on Jungian psychology, Eastern philosophy, and women's psycho-spirituality.

NO STARCH PRESS

555 De Haro St., Suite 250, San Francisco, CA 94107. 415-863-9900.
E-mail: info@nostarch.com. Web site: www.nostarch.com.
Description: Publisher of computer books. **Number of Books/Yr.:** 10 titles/yr.

NOLO

950 Parker St., Berkeley, CA 94710. 510-549-1976.
E-mail: order@nolo.com. Web site: www.nolo.com/manuscripts.cfm.
Sandy Coury, Editor.
Description: Publisher of do-it-yourself legal information. **Contact:** Acquisitions
Editor.

NORTH COUNTRY PRESS

P.O. Box 546, Unity, ME 04988-0546. 207-948-2208.
E-mail: ncp@unisets.net.
Patricia Newell / Mary Kenney, Publishers.
Description: Nonfiction with a Maine and/or New England tie-in with emphasis on
the outdoors; also limited fiction (Maine-based mysteries). **Proposal Process:** Query
with SASE, outline, and sample chapters. No unsolicited manuscripts. **Payment:**
Royalty. **Tips:** Publish high-quality books for people who love New England.

NORTHEASTERN UNIVERSITY PRESS

360 Huntington Ave., 416 CP, Boston, MA 02115. 617-373-5480.
E-mail: nupress@neu.edu. Web site: www.nupress.neu.edu.
William Frohlich, Elizabeth Swayze, John Weingartner.
Description: Nonfiction, 50,000-200,000 words: trade and scholarly titles in music,
criminal justice, women's studies, ethnic studies, law, society, and American history.
Proposal Process: Submit query with outline and sample chapter. **Payment:**
Royalty.

NORTHERN ILLINOIS UNIVERSITY PRESS

310 N Fifth St., DeKalb, IL 60115. 815-753-1826.
Web site: www.niu.edu/univ_press.
Mary L. Lincoln, Editorial Director.
Description: Publishes nonfiction titles on history, politics, anthropology, archaeology, and literary and cultural studies. **Number of Books/Yr.:** 18 titles/year (500 submissions), 50% first-time authors, 1% unagented. **Proposal Process:** Query with outline and sample chapters. Multiple and electronic queries accepted. Response time
varies. Prefers hard-copy format. **Payment:** Varies. **Sample Titles:** Adult: *Possessed:
Women, Witches, and Demons in Imperial Russia,* by Christine D. Worobec.

NORTHWESTERN UNIVERSITY PRESS

625 Colfax St., Evanston, IL 60208-4210. 847-491-5313.
E-mail: nupress@northwestern.edu. Web site: www.nupress.northwestern.edu.
Description: Trade and scholarly books.

NORTHWORD PRESS

5900 Green Oak Dr., Minnetonka, MN 55343.

E-mail: bharold@creativepub.com. Web site: www.howtobookstore.com.

Description: Adult and children's nature and wildlife topics. **Number of Books/Yr.:** 15-20 titles/year. (250 submissions), 25% by first-time authors, 50% unagented. **Proposal Process:** Send query, outline, sample chapters, and complete manuscript (for children's only). Accepts multiple queries. Response time: 90 days. **Payment:** Royalty on half of projects. Typical royalty range is 10-12% net. Flat fee on half of projects. Typical fee range $3,000-$10,000. **Sample Titles:** Adult: *America From 500 Feet!; Chased by the Light.* Children ages 7-11: *Big Cats!; Penguins; Ferocious Fangs; Lions.* Children ages 5-8: *Friendships in Nature; We Are Dolphins.* **Tips:** No poetry or personal memoirs/essays on nature. Also, no "green" or animal rehabilitation stories. **Contact:** Barbara Harold (adult titles) and Aimee Jackson (children's titles).

W.W. NORTON AND CO., INC.

500 Fifth Ave., New York, NY 10110.

Web site: www.wwnorton.com.

Starling Lawrence, Editor-in-Chief.

Description: High-quality literary fiction and nonfiction. **Proposal Process:** Send outline, 3 sample chapters, and SASE to Editorial Department. **Tips:** No occult, paranormal, religious, genre fiction (formula romance, science fiction, westerns), arts and crafts, young adult, or children's books.

NTC/CONTEMPORARY PUBLISHING GROUP

3250 S Western Ave., Chicago, IL 60608. 773-247-4092.

John T. Nolan, Vice President and Publisher.

Description: Nonfiction trade books with a strong focus on sports and fitness, parenting, self-help, general reference, health, careers, business, foreign language, and dictionaries. **Number of Books/Yr.:** 400 titles/year (600 submissions), 10% first-time authors, 20% unagented. **Proposal Process:** Send query, outline. Considers electronic and multiple queries. Response time: 3 weeks. Hard-copy format preferred. **Payment:** Royalty (7.5% list paper, 10-15% list cloth) or flat fee—typical range is $1,000-$4,000. **Sample Titles:** Sport: *Mindgames: The Autobiography of Phil Jackson* and *Grand Slam!* Self-help: *Finding Our Fathers.* Foreign language: *Instant Recall French Vocabulary.* Business: *Successful Direct Marketing Methods* (7th edition). Careers: *Guide to Internet Job Searching.*

O'REILLY & ASSOCIATES INC.

1005 Graverstein Hwy. N, Sebastopol, CA 95472. 707-829-0515.

E-mail: proposals@oreilly.com. Web site: www.oreilly.com.

Description: Publishes materials on computer technology and consumer health.

OHIO UNIVERSITY PRESS/SWALLOW PRESS

Scott Quadrangle, Athens, OH 45701. 740-593-1155.

Web site: www.ohiou.edu/oupress/.

David Sanders, Director.

Description: Scholarly nonfiction, 300-400 manuscript pages. Especially interested in Victorian studies, contemporary history, regional studies, and African studies. Swallow Press: general interest and frontier Americana. **Proposal Process:** Query with outline and sample chapters. **Payment:** Royalty. **Tips:** Annual Hollis Summers Poetry Award Competition. Contest guidelines available at Web site.

ONJINJINKTA PUBLISHING

The Betty J. Eadie Press

909 SE Everett Mall Way, Suite A120, Everett, WA 98208. 425-290-7809.

E-mail: peter@onjinjinkta.com. Web site: www.onjinjinkta.com.

Peter Orullian, Senior Editor.

Description: Publishes nonfiction books with inspiration or spiritual content, must contain redeeming themes. Publishes nonfiction aimed at strengthening virtues, also books whose topics extol family values. **Number of Books/Yr.:** 8 titles/year (2,000 submissions), 80% first-time authors, 70% unagented. **Proposal Process:** Accepts multiple queries. Query with outline and sample chapters. Hard-copy format preferred. Multiple queries accepted. No electronic queries. **Payment:** Advance and royalty. **Sample Titles:** Adult fiction: *Until Forever*, grief and redemption. Adult nonfiction: *Ripple Effect*, how choice affects many people. Children's fiction: *Caterpillar Jones* (7-14), teaches kids to be courageous. **Tips:** No New Age books or category fiction. Seeking books with clearly defined subject matter, authoritative writing, and original approaches to classic themes of spirituality. **Contact:** Tom Eadie, Submissions.

OPEN COURT PUBLISHING CO.

332 S Michigan Ave., Suite 1100, Chicago, IL 60604. 312-939-1500.

Web site: www.opencourtbooks.com.

David Ramsay Steele, Editor.

Description: Scholarly books on philosophy, eastern thought, and related areas. Trade books of a thoughtful nature on social issues, Jungian thought, psychology, public policy, education, social issues, and contemporary culture. **Number of Books/Yr.:** 13 titles/year (1,200 submissions), 20% by first-time authors, 70% unagented. **Proposal Process:** Send sample chapters with outline, SASE, and resume. Response time: varies. Hard-copy format preferred. No multiple or electronic queries. **Payment:** Royalty.

OPEN HAND PUBLISHING

P.O. Box 20207, Greensboro, NC 27420. 336-292-8585.

E-mail: openhndl@bellsouth.net.

Description: Books that reflect the diverse cultures within the United States, with emphasis on the African-American. Publish books which promote positive social change as well as better understanding between all people. **Proposal Process:** Query. **Payment:** Royalty.

ORCHISES PRESS

George Mason University

P.O. Box 20602, Alexandria, VA 22320-1602. 703-683-1243.

E-mail: lathbury@gmu.edu. Web site: http://mason.gmu.edu/~rlathbur.

Roger Lathbury, Editor.

Description: Original poetry, essays, some humor, textbooks, reprints. No fiction, children's books, or cookbooks. **Number of Books/Yr.:** 5-8 titles/year (500 submissions), 20-40% first-time authors, 90% unagented. **Proposal Process:** Query with sample chapters and complete manuscript, include SASE. Multiple queries accepted. No electronic queries. Hard-copy format preferred. **Payment:** Royalty. **Tips:** For poetry, Orchises is a hard market—unless some work has appeared in serious magazines of national stature (*The Atlantic Monthly, Poetry, The New Yorker*) chances are slim. Poetry must be technically adroit, intellectually precise, and sophisticated.

OREGON STATE UNIVERSITY PRESS

101 Waldo Hall, Corvallis, OR 97331-6407. 541-737-3166.

E-mail: mary.braun@orst.edu. Web site: http://osu.orst.edu/dept/press.

Mary Elizabeth Braun, Acquiring Editor.

Description: Publishes scholarly books in a limited range of disciplines and books of importance to the Pacific Northwest, especially those dealing with the history, natural history, culture, and literature of the region; or with natural resource issues. **Proposal Process:** Query with summary of manuscript.

OSBORNE/MCGRAW HILL

2600 Tenth St., Berkeley, CA 94710. 510-549-6600.

Web site: www.osborne.com.

Roger Stewart, Editorial Director.

Description: General computer books, from beginner to technical levels. Subject areas: networking, programming, databases, certification, applications, internet, e-business, robotics. **Number of Books/Yr.:** 200 titles/year (1,000 submissions), 15% by first-time authors, 30% unagented. **Proposal Process:** Query. Multiple queries okay. Response time: 1-2 weeks. Electronic format preferred. **Payment:** Royalty (10-15% of net). **Tips:** Avoid topics that are already over-published. Knowledge of audience and technical proficiency are crucial. First-time authors should be prepared to submit sample chapters. **Contact:** Roger Stewart (Consumer), Wendy Rinaldi (programming), Tracy Dunkelberger (networking), Gareth Hancock (certification).

OTTENHEIMER PUBLISHERS INC.

5 Park Center Court, Suite 300, McDonough Crossroads

Owings Mills, MD 21117-4200. 410-902-9100.

E-mail: ahirshiii@ottenheimerpub.com.

Description: Mass market, trade, and novelty books.

THE OVERLOOK PRESS

Distributed by Penguin Putnam Inc.
141 Wooster St., Fl. 4, New York, NY 10012. 212-673-2210.
Tracy Carns, Editor.
Description: Literary fiction, fantasy/science fiction, foreign literature in translation. General nonfiction, including art, architecture, design, film, history, biography, crafts/lifestyle, martial arts, Hudson Valley regional interest, and children's books. **Proposal Process:** Query with outline, sample chapters, and SASE. **Payment:** Royalty.

OXFORD UNIVERSITY PRESS

198 Madison Ave., New York, NY 10016. 212-726-6000.
Web site: www.oup-usa.org.
Description: Serious nonfiction, trade, and academic books in the humanities and social sciences; college textbooks, medical, scientific, technical, and reference books. **Number of Books/Yr.:** 1,500 titles/year. 40% of books from first-time authors, 80% unagented. **Proposal Process:** Query. **Payment:** Royalty.

PACHYDERM PRESS

P.O. Box 661016, Birmingham, AL 35266-1016. 205-822-4139.
Web site: www.pachydermpress.com.
Description: Coffeetable books, magazines, calendars, and posters.

PANTHEON BOOKS

The Knopf Publishing Group/Random House, Inc.
201 E 50th St., Fl. 25, New York, NY 10022. 212-751-2600.
Daniel Frank, Editorial Director.
Description: Quality fiction and nonfiction. **Proposal Process:** Query. **Payment:** Royalty.

PARA PUBLISHING

P.O. Box 8206-238, Santa Barbara, CA 93118-8206. 805-968-7277.
E-mail: info@parapublishing.com. Web site: www.parapublishing.com.
Dan Poynter, Publisher.
Description: Adult nonfiction books on parachutes and skydiving only. Author must present evidence of having made at least 1,000 jumps. **Proposal Process:** Query. **Payment:** Royalty.

PARAGON HOUSE

2700 University Ave. W, Suite 200, St. Paul, MN 55114-1016. 651-644-3087.
E-mail: paragon@paragonhouse.com. Web site: www.paragonhouse.com.
Laureen Enright, Editorial Director.
Description: Publishes reference and scholarly titles in the areas of biography, history, philosophy, psychology, religion, spiritual health, political science, and international relations. **Number of Books/Yr.:** 12-15 titles/year (4,500-5,000 submissions),

80% by first-time authors, 90% unagented. **Proposal Process:** Query with an abstract of your project, must include a summary of your premise, main arguments, and conclusion (see guidelines). Electronic or hard-copy format preferred. Response time: 3 months. Electronic queries accepted. **Payment:** Royalty, typically 10% net. **Sample Titles:** *Philosophy of Human Rights, Doing Right By Children.* **Tips:** No fiction, poetry, or New Age materials. Seeking scholarly, nonfiction books of cultural and intellectual appeal with international and interdisciplinary character.

PARENTING PRESS

P.O. Box 75267, Seattle, WA 98125. 206-364-290.
E-mail: office@parentingpress.com. Web site: www.parentingpress.com.
Carolyn J. Threadgill, Editor.
Description: Publishes books offering practical life (social) skills to children, parents, and care-givers. Books offer concrete skills modeling and problem-solving processes and acknowledge the importance of feelings and teaching responsibility. **Number of Books/Yr.:** 6 titles/year (500+ submissions), 80% by first-time authors, 100% unagented. **Proposal Process:** Query with outline, sample chapters, and SASE. Multiple queries and electronic queries accepted. Hard-copy format. Response time: 6 weeks. **Payment:** Royalty. **Tips:** Niche is building social skills, dealing with feelings, and preventing abuse. Seeking authors with expertise derived from working with children.

PASSPORT BOOKS

4255 W Touhy Ave., Lincolnwood, IL 60712. 847-679-5500.
E-mail: ntcpubz@aol.com.
John Nolan, Editorial Director.
Description: Adult nonfiction, 200-400 pages, picture books up to 120 pages, and juvenile nonfiction. **Proposal Process:** Send outline and sample chapters for books on foreign language to Christofer Brown; for travel and culture to Adam Miller. Multiple queries considered. **Payment:** Royalty and flat fee.

PAUL DRY BOOKS

117 S 17th St., Suite 1102, Philadelphia, PA 19103. 215-732-9939.
E-mail: editor@pauldrybooks.com. Web site: www.pauldrybooks.com.
Description: Publishes literary fiction and nonfiction.

PEACHPIT PRESS

Pearson Inc.
1249 Eighth St., Berkeley, CA 94710. 510-524-2178.
Web site: www.peachpit.com.
Marjorie Baer, Executive Acquisitions Editor.
Description: Books on computer and graphic-design topics. **Proposal Process:** Query with outline and sample chapters for manuscripts, 100-1,100 words, or see proposal template on Web site.

PEARSON EDUCATION INC.
Pearson Inc.
201 W 103rd St., Indianapolis, IN 46290. 317-581-3500.
Web site: www.pearsoneducation.com.
Description: Publisher of integrated educational textbooks, assessment tools, and educational services.

PELICAN PUBLISHING CO., INC.
P.O. Box 3110, Gretna, LA 70054. 504-368-1175.
Web site: www.pelicanpub.com.
Nina Kooij, Acquisitions Editor.
Description: General trade. Travel guides (destination specific, no travelogues); children's (holiday, ethnic or regional); popular history (not scholarly); cookbooks (cuisine specific). **Number of Books/Yr.:** 90 titles/year (5,000 submissions) 10% by first-time authors, 90% unagented. **Proposal Process:** Query with outline and sample chapters. SASE required. No multiple or electronic queries. Hard-copy format required. **Payment:** Royalty. **Tips:** No autobiographical material. See complete guidelines at Web site.

PENGUIN PUTNAM, INC.
Pearson Inc.
375 Hudson St., New York, NY 10014. 212-366-2000.
Web site: www.penguinputnam.com.
Phyllis Gran, President.
Description: General interest fiction and nonfiction paperbacks. Owns several imprints including The Penguin Group, The Putnam Berkley Group, and Penguin Putnam Books for Young Readers. **Payment:** Royalty.

THE PENNSYLVANIA STATE UNIVERSITY PRESS
University Support Bldg. 1, Suite C, 820 N University Dr.
University Park, PA 16802. 814-865-1327.
Web site: www.psupress.org.
Peter Potter, Editor-in-Chief.
Description: Scholarly nonfiction, including anthropology, art history, classical thought, East European studies, economics, environmental studies, gender studies, history, Latin American studies, law, literary criticism, philosophy, photography, political science, religion, and sociology. **Proposal Process:** Query with outline and SASE. Multiple queries considered. **Payment:** Royalty.

THE PERMANENT PRESS
4170 Noyac Rd., Sag Harbor, NY 11963. 631-725-1101.
Web site: www.thepermanentpress.com.
Judith Shepard, Editor.
Description: Literary fiction. Original and arresting adult novels. **Number of Books/Yr.:** 12 titles/year (6,000-7,000 submissions), 30-40% by first-time authors, 70%

unagented. **Proposal Process:** Send query with outline and sample chapters. SASE. Multiple queries OK. No electronic queries. Hard-copy format preferred. **Payment:** Royalty. **Tips:** Seeks distinctive writing style and original voice in adult fiction.

PERSEUS PUBLISHING
11 Cambridge Center, Cambridge, MA 02142.
Web site: www.perseuspublishing.com.
Chris Coffin, Managing Editor.
Description: Publishes books in business, science, health, parenting, psychology, and general nonfiction. **Number of Books/Yr.:** 130 titles/year (800-1,000 submissions), 40% first-time authors, 40% unagented. **Proposal Process:** Query with outline and sample chapters. Response time: 2 months. Multiple and electronic queries accepted. Hard-copy format preferred. **Payment:** Royalty. **Tips:** Looking for serious professionals, with in-depth knowledge of the subject matter they are tackling.

PERSPECTIVES PRESS
P.O. Box 90318, Indianapolis, IN 46290-0318. 317-872-3055.
E-mail: ppress@iquest.net. Web site: www.perspectivespress.com.
Pat Johnston, Publisher.
Description: Publisher of nonfiction books on infertility, adoption, and closely related reproductive health and child welfare issues (foster care, etc.). **Proposal Process:** Query. **Payment:** Royalty. **Tips:** "Writers must read our guidelines before submitting."

PETER PAUPER PRESS, INC.
202 Mamaroneck Ave., Suite 400, White Plains, NY 10601-5376. 914-681-0144.
E-mail: orders@peterpauper.com. Web site: www.peterpauper.com.
Description: Fine gift books.

PETERSON'S
Thompson Learning
2000 Lenox Dr., Fl. 3, Princeton Pike Corporate Center
Lawrenceville, NJ 08648. 609-896-1800.
Web site: www.peterson.com.
Description: Publisher of books and online products that offer information on colleges, universities, test preparation, study abroad, summer opportunities, graduate programs, and career exploration. **Number of Books/Yr.:** 200 titles/year. Receives 250-300 submissions/year. **Payment:** Royalty. **Contact:** Denise Rance, Acquisitions.

PHANES PRESS
P.O. Box 6114, Grand Rapids, MI 49516. 510-632-4700.
Web site: www.phanes.com.
Description: Spiritual, philosophical, and cosmological traditions of the Western World. **Sample Titles:** *The Voice of the Earth: An Exploration of Ecopsychology,* by Theodore Roszak; *Paths of Freedom,* by Neal McMann and Ron Oliver.

PHILOMEL BOOKS

Penguin Putnam Books for Young Readers/Penguin Putnam, Inc.
345 Hudson St., New York, NY 10014. 212-414-3610.
Web site: www.penguinputnam.com.
Patricia Lee Gauch, Editorial Director.
Description: Juvenile picture books and young adult fiction, particularly fantasy and historical. Fresh, original work with compelling characters and sense of the dramatic. **Proposal Process:** Query. **Contact:** Michael Green, Senior Editor.

PINEAPPLE PRESS

P.O. Box 3889, Sarasota, FL 34230. 941-359-0886.
E-mail: info@pineapplepress.com. Web site: www.pineapplepress.com.
June Cussen, Editor.
Description: Trade fiction and nonfiction about Florida. **Number of Books/Yr.:** 20 titles/year (1,500 submissions), 95% by first-time authors, 99% unagented. **Proposal Process:** Query with outline, sample chapters, and SASE. Hard-copy format. Multiple queries OK. No electronic queries. **Payment:** Royalty. **Tips:** Looking for excellent books on Florida.

PLATYPUS MEDIA

627 A Street NE, Washington, DC 20002. 202-546-1674.
E-mail: info@platypusmedia.com. Web site: www.platypusmedia.com.
Description: Publishes books for children, parents, and teachers.

PLAYERS PRESS, INC.

P.O. Box 1132, Studio City, CA 91614. 818-789-4980.
Robert Gordon, Editor.
Description: Publishes plays and musical books on the performing arts, theatre, film, television, costumes, makeup, technical theatre, technical film, etc. **Number of Books/Yr.:** 30 titles/year (1,000 submissions), 60% first-time authors, 80% unagented. **Proposal Process:** Query with manuscript-size SASE and 2 #10 SASEs for correspondence. Include resume and/or biography. Responds in 3-12 months. No multiple or electronic queries. Hard copy. **Payment:** Royalty.

POCKET BOOKS

Simon & Schuster, Inc.
1230 Avenue of the Americas, New York, NY 10020. 212-698-7000.
Maggie Crawford, V.P./Editorial Director.
Description: Adult and young adult fiction and nonfiction. **Payment:** Royalty.

POISONED PEN PRESS

6962 E First Ave., Suite 103, Scottsdale, AZ 85251.
E-mail: editor@poisonedpenpress.com. Web site: www.poisonedpenpress.com.
Monty Montee, Editor.

Description: Adult mysteries on crime and detection. **Number of Books/Yr.:** 3-5 **Proposal Process:** Query with outline, sample chapters, and SASE. **Payment:** Royalty.

POLESTAR BOOK PUBLISHERS
P.O. Box 5238, Station B, Victoria, British Columbia V8R 6N4 Canada. 250-361-9718.
E-mail: pstarvic@direct.ca.
Lynn Henry, Managing Editor.
Description: Publishes poetry, fiction, sports, juvenile and teen nonfiction, and general trade nonfiction. **Proposal Process:** Submit outline and sample chapters. Accepts unsolicited manuscripts.

POMEGRANATE
Pomegranate Communications, Inc.
210 Classic Court, P.O. Box 6099, Rohnert Park, CA 94927-6099. 707-586-5500.
E-mail: info@pomegranate.com. Web site: www.pomegranate.com.
Description: Publisher of nonfiction titles on a variety of subjects including history, multicultural studies, women's studies, photography, music, and humor. Special emphasis on art.

PONCHA PRESS
P.O. Box 280, Morrison, CO 80465. 303-697-2384.
E-mail: bosgood@ponchapress.com. Web site: www.ponchapress.com.
Barbara Osgood-Hartness, Editor-in-Chief.
Description: Publisher of fiction and nonfiction.

POPULAR PRESS
Bowling Green State University, Bowling Green, OH 43402. 419-372-7865.
Ms. Pat Browne, Editor.
Description: Publisher of books of criticism on pop culture subjects such as film, television, literature, and women's studies (200-450 pages). **Number of Books/Yr.:** 15 titles/year (350 submissions), 50% by first-time authors, 100% unagented. **Proposal Process:** Query with outline. SASE. Response time: 3-6 months. No multiple or electronic queries. Send hard copy. **Payment:** Flat fee or royalty.

POSSIBILITY PRESS
One Oakglade Cir., Hummelstown, PA 17036. 717-566-0468.
E-mail: posspress@aol.com. Web site: www.possibilitypress.com.
Marjorie L. Markowski, Editor/Publisher.
Description: Trade paperback originals. How-to, self-help. Subjects include business, current significant events, pop psychology, success/motivation, inspirational, entrepreneurship, sales and marketing, home-based business topics, and human interest success stories. "Our mission is to help the people of the world grow and become the best they can be, through the written and spoken word." **Proposal Process:** SASE for guidelines. Query with outline and 3 sample chapters. **Tips:**

Focuses on creating and publishing bestsellers by authors who speak and consult. Seeking authors serious about making a difference in the world.

POWERHOUSE BOOKS
180 Varick St., Suite 1302, New York, NY 10014. 212-604-9074.
E-mail: info@powerhousebooks.com. Web site: www.powerhousebooks.com.
Description: Publisher of photography, innovative art, and pop culture nonfiction titles.

PRAEGER PUBLISHERS
Greenwood Publishing Group, Inc.
88 Post Rd. W, Westport, CT 06881-5007. 203-226-3571.
Web site: www.praeger.com.
Description: General nonfiction; scholarly and textbooks in the social sciences.
Proposal Process: Query with outline. **Payment:** Royalty.

BYRON PREISS VISUAL PUBLICATIONS
24 W 25th St., Fl. 11, New York, NY 10010. 212-645-9870.
E-mail: bpreiss@bpvp.com. Web site: www.ibooksinc.com.
Byron Preiss, Publisher.
Description: Book packager. Seeks samples from established authors who work to meet specifications on firm deadlines. Genres: science fiction, fantasy, horror, juvenile, young adult, nonfiction. **Payment:** Pays advance against royalties for commissioned work. **Contact:** Clarice Levin, Managing Editor.

PRESIDIO PRESS
505-B San Marin Dr., Suite 300, Novato, CA 94945-1340. 415-898-1081.
E-mail: mail@presidiopress.com. Web site: www.presidiopress.com.
Mr. E. J. McCarthy, Executive Editor.
Description: Publish nonfiction and nonfiction military-related books. Specializes in military memoirs, biographies, unit histories, and battle and campaign books. **Number of Books/Yr.:** 42 titles/year (1,500 submissions), 75% by first-time authors, 80% unagented. **Proposal Process:** Send query, outline. SASE. Multiple and electronic queries accepted. Hard copy. **Payment:** Royalty. **Sample Titles:** *The Greatest War— Americans in Combat—1941-1945; Black Sheep One—The Life of Gregory "Pappy" Boyington; America's Secret Air War Against the Soviet Union—A Cold War History.* **Tips:** Look for well-written American military history that will make a contribution to the historiography of the subject.

PRESTEL PUBLISHING
175 Fifth Avenue, Suite 402, New York, NY 10010. 212-955-2720.
E-mail: sales@prestel-usa.com. Web site: www.prestel.com.
Description: Publishes books on art, architecture, and photography.

PRICE STERN SLOAN, INC.

The Putnam Berkley Group/Penguin Putnam, Inc.
345 Hudson St., New York, NY 10014. 212-414-3610.
Web site: www.penguinputnam.com.
Jon Anderson, Publisher.
Description: Witty and quirky novelty juvenile titles. Imprints include Troubadour Press, Wee Sing, and MadLibs. **Proposal Process:** No unsolicited manuscripts accepted. Query first. **Payment:** Royalty. **Tips:** No novels or picture books.

PRIMA PUBLISHING

3000 Lava Ridge Ct., Roseville, CA 95661. 916-787-7000.
Web site: www.primapublishing.com.
Alice Feinstein, Editorial Director.
Description: Nonfiction books in diverse areas including health, parenting and education, business, and current affairs. **Proposal Process:** Query with outline and 1 sample chapter and market research. Response time: 6-8 weeks. Hard-copy format preferred. **Payment:** Royalty and flat fee, standard range. **Sample Titles:** Adult: *Helping Your ADD Child* (parenting); *How to Plan an Elegant Wedding in 6 Months or Less* (home); *Internal Cleansing* (health). **Contact:** David Richardson, Denise Sternad, Jamie Miller, Jennifer Base Sander.

PRIMER PUBLISHERS

5738 N Central Ave., Phoenix, AZ 85012. 602-234-1574.
E-mail: info@primerpublishers.com; info@renaissancehousepublishers.com.
Bill Fessler, Acquisitions.
Description: Travel and regional subjects, especially about the Southwest U.S. Also publishes history (20th century, World War II, and Middle East conflicts), and "Living the Simple Life" philosophical writings. No fiction. General adult audience. **Number of Books/Yr.:** 5-10 titles/year (20 submissions), 50% by first-time authors, 99% unagented. **Proposal Process:** Send query, outline, and sample chapters if available. Prefer hard-copy format. No multiple queries. Response time: 1 month. **Payment:** Royalty (8% net) or flat fee. **Sample Titles:** *Railroads of Colorado, Gems & Minerals of California, Arizona Cactus, The Denver Mint.*

PRINCETON ARCHITECTURAL PRESS

37 E Seventh Street, New York, NY 10003-8027. 212-995-9620.
Web site: www.papress.com.
Description: Publisher of architecture and graphic design books including architectural monographs, cities and landscapes, guidebooks, history, theory, and professional practice.

PRINCETON UNIVERSITY PRESS

41 William St., Princeton, NJ 08540. 609-258-4900.
Web site: www.pup.princeton.edu.
Terry D. Vaughn, Editor-in-Chief.

Description: Scholarly and scientific books on all subjects. **Proposal Process:** Submit brief proposal with curriculum vitae. **Tips:** No American history proposals or history of science.

PROJECT MANAGEMENT INSTITUTE PUBLISHING DIVISION

Four Campus Blvd., Newton Square, PA 19073-3299. 610-356-4600.
E-mail: pmihq@pmi.org. Web site: www.pmi.org.
Description: Publisher of books and resources on project management and general business/management.

PROMETHEUS BOOKS

59 John Glenn Drive, Amherst, NY 14228. 800-421-0351.
Web site: www.prometheusbooks.com.
Description: Popular science, social sciences, New Age, religion, psychology, current events, humanism, health, biographies, politics, education, and children's titles.

PRUETT PUBLISHING COMPANY

7464 Arapahoe Rd., Suite A-9, Boulder, CO 80303. 303-449-4919.
E-mail: pruettbks@aol.com. Web site: www.pruettpublishing.com.
Jim Pruett, Acquisitions Editor.
Description: Publishes books dealing with outdoor recreation travel and history. **Number of Books/Yr.:** 10 titles/year (300 submissions), 50% first-time authors, 90% unagented. **Proposal Process:** Send outline and sample chapters. Multiple queries considered. Accepts electronic queries. Preferred format: electronic and hard copy. **Payment:** Royalty (net 10-12%). **Sample Titles:** *Fly Fishing the Coast of Texas.*

PUCKERBRUSH PRESS

76 Main St., Orono, ME 04473-1430. 207-581-3832.
Constance Hunting, Editorial Director.
Description: Publishes poetry, fiction, and belles lettres. **Number of Books/Yr.:** 3 titles/year (500 submissions), 60% first-time authors, 100% unagented. **Proposal Process:** Send query with complete manuscript, SASE. Response time: 3 months. Multiple queries accepted. No electronic queries. **Payment:** Royalty, range 10% net. **Sample Titles:** Poetry: *Settling,* by Patricia Ranzoni; *A Night-Sea Journey,* by Michael Alpert. Novel: *The Crow on the Spruce,* by Chenoweth Hall. **Tips:** Literary only. Avoid crime, incest, prison, detective, police, mystery, and religious themes.

PURDUE UNIVERSITY PRESS

1207 SCC-E, West Lafayette, IN 47907-1207. 765-494-2038.
E-mail: libpup@omni.cc.purdue.edu. Web site: www.thepress.purdue.edu.
Description: Books that are worthy in their scholarship and vital in their content.

QED PRESS

155 Cypress St., Fort Bragg, CA 95437. 707-964-9520.
E-mail: publishing@cypresshouse.com. Web site: www.cypresshouse.com.

Joe Shaw, Editor.
Description: Publisher of books on health and healing, self-help, and how to fold paper airplanes. **Proposal Process:** Query with outline and sample chapters. **Payment:** Royalty.

QUIXOTE PRESS
1854 345th Ave., Wever, IA 52658. 319-372-7480.
E-mail: maddmack@interl.com.
Bruce Carlson, President.
Description: Adult fiction and nonfiction including humor, folklore, and regional cookbooks. **Proposal Process:** Query with sample chapters and outline. **Payment:** Royalty.

RAINBOW BOOKS, INC.
P.O. Box 430, Highland City, FL 33846-0430. 941-648-4420.
E-mail: naip@aol.com.
Betsy Lampe, Editor.
Description: Publishes nonfiction books. Also, a very small list of mystery fiction. **Number of Books/Yr.:** 15-20 titles/year (600 submissions), 85% first-time authors, 99% unagented. **Proposal Process:** Query with outline and sample chapters, include SASE. Multiple queries accepted. No electronic queries. Hard-copy format preferred. **Payment:** Royalty. **Tips:** Looking for a broad range of nonfiction books. In mystery fiction, primarily seeking "cozies" of no more than 70,000 words. Write for guidelines, SASE. **Contact:** Betty Wright.

RAINCOAST BOOKS
9050 Shaughnessy St., Vancouver, British Columbia V6P 6E5 Canada. 604-323-7100.
E-mail: wave@raincoast.com. Web site: www.raincoast.com.
Brian Scrivener, Editorial Director.
Description: Regional, national, and international titles on the environment, sports, travel, and cooking. Also, children's books, adult fiction, and nonfiction. **Proposal Process:** Submit query with outline and sample chapters. Include color photographs or slides or artwork for illustrated material. **Sample Titles:** *Mount Appetite*, by Bill Gaston; *A Reckless Moon*, by Dianne Warren.

RAM PUBLICATIONS & DISTRIBUTION
2525 Michigan Avenue, Building A2, Santa Monica, CA 90404. 310-453-0043.
E-mail: rampub@gte.net.
Description: Publisher of books on architecture, furniture design, graphics, contemporary art and theory, popular culture, poetry, literature, etc.

REALLY GREAT BOOKS
P.O. Box 861302, Los Angeles, CA 90086. 213-624-8555.
E-mail: info@reallygreatbooks.com. Web site: www.reallygreatbooks.com.
Description: Publishes fiction, guidebooks, and titles on popular culture and film.

RED CRANE BOOKS

P.O. Box 33950, Santa Fe, NM 87594. 505-988-7070.
E-mail: marianne@redcrane.com. Web site: www.redcrane.com.
Marianne O'Shaughnessy, Acquisitions Editor.
Description: Art and folk art, bilingual material with Spanish and English, cookbooks, gardening, herbal guides, natural history, novels, social and political issues, and social history. No children's books. **Proposal Process:** Send a short synopsis, 2 sample chapters, resume, and SASE. **Tips:** Topics vary year to year. Write for guidelines.

RED MOON PRESS

P.O. Box 2461, Winchester, VA 22604-1661. 540-722-2156.
E-mail: redmoon@shentel.net.
Description: Publishes books, anthologies, and individual volumes of contemporary haiku.

RED SAGE PUBLISHING, INC.

P.O. Box 4844, Seminole, FL 33775. 727-391-3847.
E-mail: alekendall@aol.com. Web site: www.redsagepub.com.
Alexandria Kendall, Editor.
Description: Romance-historical, vampire, contemporary, fantasy, all genres. Novellas. 25,000 to 35,000 words. **Number of Books/Yr.:** 1 title/year (300 submissions), ¼% first-time authors, ½% unagented. **Proposal Process:** Query with outline and sample chapters, and SASE. Hard-copy format preferred. Response time: 3 months. No multiple or electronic queries. **Tips:** Story should focus on main character's relationship with great character development. Plot should support main character's relationship. Fast pacing and high-interest characters and plot. High-sensuality romance, hot, hot, hot!

THE RED SEA PRESS

11 Princess Rd., Trenton, NJ 08648. 609-844-9583.
E-mail: awprsp@africanworld.com. Web site: www.africanworld.com.
Kassahun Checole, Publisher.
Description: Adult nonfiction, 360 double-spaced manuscript pages. Focus on nonfiction material with a specialty on the Horn of Africa. **Proposal Process:** Query.
Payment: Royalty.

RED WHEEL/WEISER LLC

Publishers of Red Wheel and Weiser Books
368 Congress St., Fl. 4, Boston, MA 02210. 800-423-7087.
E-mail: orders@redwheelweiser.com. Web site: www.redwheelweiser.com.
Description: Red Wheel: Publisher of spirituality, inspirational, and self-help books. Weiser Books: "One of America's oldest and most distinguished publishers of metaphysical books."

REDMOND TECHNOLOGY PRESS
8581 154th Ave. NE, Redmond, WA 98052. 425-861-9628.
E-mail: editor@redtechpress.com. Web site: www.redtechpress.com.
Description: Publishes computer books aimed at the mainstream business user.

SAMUEL WEISER
368 Congress St., Boston, MA 02210. 617-547-1324.
E-mail: email@redwheelweiser.com. Web site: www.redwheelweiser.com.
Ms. Pat Bryce, Editor.
Description: Nonfiction titles on self-help, spirituality, esoteric studies, astrology, Eastern philosophy, and alternative health. **Proposal Process:** Query with sample chapters or complete manuscript. Multiple queries accepted. **Payment:** Royalty.

REGNERY PUBLISHING, INC.
One Massachusetts Ave., NW, Washington, DC 20001. 202-216-0600.
Web site: www.regnery.com.
Harry Crocker, Executive Editor.
Description: Nonfiction titles on current affairs, politics, history, biography and other subjects. The Lifeline Press imprint publishes health titles, and the Capital Press imprint publishes business titles. **Number of Books/Yr.:** 35 titles/year. **Proposal Process:** Send query with outline and SASE. Hard copy. No multiple or electronic queries. **Payment:** Royalty.

RIO NUEVO PUBLISHERS
451 N Bonita Ave., Tucson, AZ 85745. 520-623-9558.
E-mail: info@rionuevo.com.
Description: Publisher of books on Southwest and Northern Mexico.

RISING TIDE PRESS
P.O. Box 30457, Tucson, AZ 85751. 520-888-1140.
E-mail: books@risingtidepress.com. Web site: www.risingtidepress.com.
Brenda Kazen, Editorial Director.
Description: Lesbian/feminist fiction and nonfiction. Books for, by, and about women. Fiction, romance, mystery, and young adult and adventure, science fiction/fantasy. **Number of Books/Yr.:** 6-10 titles/year (3,000 submissions), 75% first-time authors, 95% unagented. **Proposal Process:** Query with sample chapters, include SASE. Response time: 2-3 months. Hard copy. Accepts multiple queries. **Payment:** Royalty.

RIVER CITY PUBLISHING
1719 Mulberry St., Montgomery, AL 36106. 877-408-7078.
E-mail: jdavis@rivercitypublishing.com. Web site: www.rivercitypublishing.com.
Jim Davis, Editor.
Description: Publishes fiction, nonfiction, poetry, art, and children's books about life in America today and yesterday (most books tend to be about the South).

Transforming from a regional press to a national literary press. **Sample Titles:** *These People Are Us*, short stories by one of America's hottest new authors; and *Vanishing Florida*, a guide to vacation spots most tourists never see. **Tips:** Generally publishes authors with extensive track records; no romances, science fiction, textbooks, young adult novels, extremely religious books, or books about the Civil War.

RIVERHEAD BOOKS
The Putnam Berkeley Group/Penguin Putnam, Inc.
375 Hudson St., New York, NY 10014.
Web site: www.penguinputnam.com.
Mary South, Editor.
Description: Fiction and nonfiction. **Proposal Process:** Unagented queries preferred. **Payment:** Royalty.

RIVEROAK PUBLISHING
Eagle Communication International
2448 E 81st St., Suite 4800, Tulsa, OK 74137. 918-523-5838.
E-mail: jeffd@riveroakpublishing.com. Web site: www.riveroakpublishing.com.
Description: Christian living, self-help, fiction, motivational, gift books. **Number of Books/Yr.:** 40-50 titles/year. Receives 1,000 queries and 500 mss/year. 5% of books from first-time authors, 80% from unagented writers. **Proposal Process:** Query with outline/summary, table of contents, 3 sample chapters, brief author bio, contact info, and SASE. Responds in 2-3 months. **Payment:** Royalty.

RIVERWOOD BOOKS
P.O. Box 3400, Ashland, OR 97520. 541-488-6415.
E-mail: sscholl@jeffnet.org.
Steven Scholl, Publisher.
Description: General trade publisher: nonfiction (health, family, relationships, travel, memoirs, history), fiction, children's, young adult, and poetry.

RIZZOLI INTERNATIONAL PUBLICATIONS, INC.
300 Park Ave. S, New York, NY 10010. 212-387-3620.
Marta Hallett, Publisher.
Description: Publisher of illustrated books on art, architecture, and lifestyle. **Proposal Process:** Query with SASE or response card. Response time: varies. Hard copy preferred, electronic queries accepted. Considers multiple queries. **Tips:** Does not publish fiction or children's books. Books are highly illustrated in the categories of art, architecture, and lifestyle. **Contact:** David Morton, Sr. Editor, Architecture; Liz Sullivan, Senior Editor, Lifestyle; Isabel Venero, Editor, Art.

ROBERTS RINEHART PUBLISHERS
5360 Manhattan Circle #101, Boulder, CO 80303.
E-mail: rrinehart@rowman.com.
Description: Book publisher of Ireland, Irish life, natural history, museum catalogs.

ROBINS LANE PRESS

P.O. Box 207, Beltsville, MD 20705. 301-595-9500.

E-mail: info@robinslane.com. Web site: http://www.robinslane.com.

Description: Timely, unique books on subjects of interest to today's parents. **Number of Books/Yr.:** 8 titles/year (100 submissions), 75% first-time authors, 90% unagented. **Proposal Process:** Query with outline and sample chapters if available. Multiple queries considered. Response time: 6-8 weeks. Prefers hard-copy format. Electronic queries accepted. **Contact:** Acquisitions Editor.

ROC

The Penguin Group/Penguin Putnam Inc.

375 Hudson St., New York, NY 10014. 212-366-2000.

Web site: www.penguinputnam.com.

Laura Anne Gilman.

Description: Publisher of science fiction and fantasy. Strongly discourages unsolicited submissions.

RODALE BOOKS

400 S Tenth St., Emmaus, PA 18098-0099. 610-967-5171.

E-mail: tami.booth@rodale.com. Web site: www.rodale.com.

Tami Booth, Vice President/Editor-in-Chief.

Description: Publisher of books on consumer science, memoir, health, fitness, gardening, environment, cooking, quilting, pet care, spirituality, and general nonfiction. **Contact:** Tami Booth (health and lifestyle), Stephanie Trade (general books), and Stephen Madden (sports and fitness).

RODMELL PRESS

2147 Blake St., Berkeley, CA 94704-2715. 510-841-3123.

E-mail: rodmellprs@aol.com. Web site: www.rodmellpress.com.

Donald Moyer, Editor.

Description: Books on yoga, Buddhism, and aikido.

ROUGH GUIDES

345 Hudson St., Fl. 4, New York, NY 10014. 212-414-3635.

E-mail: mail@roughguides.com. Web site: www.roughguides.com.

Description: Reference titles across a wide range of subjects including music, the web, movies, and computers. Guides and phrase-books for independent travel.

ROUTLEDGE

Taylor & Francis Group

29 W 35th St., New York, NY 10001. 212-216-7800.

E-mail: doconnor@routledge-ny.com. Web site: www.routledge-ny.com.

Description: Trade, academic, professional books in the humanities and social sciences.

ROWMAN & LITTLEFIELD PUBLISHERS INC.

4720 Boston Way, Lanham, MD 20706. 301-459-3366.

E-mail: nrothschild@rowman.com. Web site: www.rowmanlittlefield.com.

Description: Innovative and thought-provoking books for an educated audience. **Number of Books/Yr.:** 1,000 titles/year. **Payment:** Offers advance.

ROYAL FIREWORKS PRESS

First Ave., Unionville, NY 10988. 845-726-3333.

Charles Morgan, Editor.

Description: Publishes books for gifted children, their parents and teachers. Also publishes novels for all children and young adults. **Number of Books/Yr.:** 100 titles/year (2,000 submissions), 40% first-time authors, 95% unagented. **Proposal Process:** Submit complete manuscripts with a brief plot overview. No multiple or electronic queries. Allow a 3-week response time. Hard copy. **Payment:** Royalty. **Tips:** Looking for historical fiction; books on growing up; books about kids solving problems, science fiction, mystery-adventure.

RUMINATOR BOOKS

1648 Grand Ave., St. Paul, MN 55105. 651-699-7038.

E-mail: books@ruminator.com. Web site: www.ruminator.com.

Pearl Kilbride, Editor.

Description: Publishes fiction, memoirs, articles on contemporary affairs, cultural criticism, travel essays, nonfiction, and international literature. No genre fiction, self-help, children's books, or poetry. Prefers books that examine the human experience or comment on social and cultural mores. **Proposal Process:** Query with outline and sample chapters. **Payment:** Royalty.

RUNNING PRESS

125 S 22nd St., Philadelphia, PA 19103-4399. 800-810-4145.

E-mail: comments@runningpress.com. Web site: www.runningpress.com.

Description: Specializes in publishing illustrated nonfiction titles for adults and children. Publishes educational, inspirational, pop-culture-oriented, historical non-fiction, self-help, Miniature Editions (TM), and creative how-to kits for children and adults. **Proposal Process:** Query with outline or table of contents and 2-3 page writing sample. Multiple queries accepted. No electronic queries. Hard copy. Response time: 4 weeks. **Payment:** Royalty for some projects; flat fee for others. **Sample Titles:** *The Counselors: Conversations with 18 Women Who Have Changed the World; Danny Boy; How to Live 365 Days a Year; The Keeper of Lime Rock; Mr.*

Potato Head: Celebrating 50 Years of One Sweet Potato. **Tips:** No fiction or poetry. **Contact:** Susan Phillips.

RUTGERS UNIVERSITY PRESS

100 Joyce Kilmer Ave., Piscataway, NJ 08854-8099. 732-445-7762.
Web site: www.rutgerspress.edu.
Melanie Halkias, Editor-in-Chief.
Description: Scholarly publisher of religion, history of medicine, biological sciences, media studies, art, literature, history, gender studies, and multicultural studies. Also interested in general studies that have a strong scholarly basis. **Number of Books/Yr.:** 20 titles/year (1,200 submissions), 35% by first-time authors, 85% un-agented. **Proposal Process:** Query with outline and sample chapters. Send humanities proposals to Theresa Liu; science and social sciences proposals to Suzanne Kellam. Hard-copy format preferred. No electronic queries. Multiple queries okay. **Payment:** Royalty. **Sample Titles:** Titles: *Hard Road to Freedom, The Story of African America, Biological Theories of Race at the Millennium, Bohemians, The Glamorous Outcasts.* **Tips:** Avoid anything too jargon-laden. Most interested in projects with a strong scholarly foundation. **Contact:** Theresa Liu, Editorial Assistant.

RUTLEDGE HILL PRESS

P.O. Box 141000, Nashville, TN 37214-1000. 615-902-2333.
E-mail: tmenges@rutledgehillpress.com. Web site: www.rutledgehillpress.com.
Lawrence M. Stone, Publisher.
Description: General nonfiction, self-help, gift books, cookbooks, regional history and topics such as regional humor. **Number of Books/Yr.:** 40 titles/year (1,000 submissions), 35% first-time authors, 70% unagented. **Proposal Process:** Query with outline and sample chapters. SASE required. Multiple and electronic queries accepted. Hard-copy format preferred. **Payment:** Flat fee. **Tips:** Interested in adult nonfiction.

RYLAND PETERS & SMALL INC.

519 Broadway, Fl. 5, New York, NY 10012. 646-613-8682.
E-mail: info@rylandpeters.com. Web site: www.rylandpeters.com.
Description: Publisher of stationery and illustrated gift books on cookery, gardening, lifestyle, and interior design.

SAGE PUBLICATIONS INC.

2455 Teller Rd., Thousand Oaks, CA 91320. 805-499-0721.
Web site: www.sagepub.com.
Description: Publishes books and materials for researchers, professionals, scholars, policymakers, and students.

ST. MARTIN'S PRESS

175 Fifth Ave., New York, NY 10010. 212-674-5151.
Web site: www.stmartins.com.

Description: General adult fiction and nonfiction. **Payment:** Royalty. **Tips:** Does not accept unagented submissions.

J.S. SANDERS & CO.

Ivan R. Dee, Publisher
1332 N Halsted St., Chicago, IL 60622-2694. 312-787-6262.
E-mail: editorial@ivanrdee.com. Web site: www.ivanrdee.com.
Description: General trade nonfiction, biographies, histories, and classics. Titles focus on the history, literature, and culture of the South.

SANDLAPPER PUBLISHING CO, INC.

P.O. Box 730, Orangeburg, SC 29116-0730. 803-531-1658.
E-mail: agallmanl@mindspring.com.
Amanda Gallman, Managing Editor.
Description: Nonfiction books on South Carolina history, culture, and cuisine.
Proposal Process: Query with outline, sample chapters, and SASE.

SANTA MONICA PRESS

P.O. Box 1076, Santa Monica, CA 90406. 310-230-7759.
E-mail: books@santamonicapress.com. Web site: www.santamonicapress.com.
Description: Publisher of lively and modern how-to books, fiction, poetry, and books on popular culture, arts, and entertainment. **Proposal Process:** Send cover letter and outline indicating the nature and scope of each chapter. Include two sample chapters and photocopies of any photographs or illustrations. Be sure to state in cover letter the intended audience, explanation as to why book is unique, summary of competitive or similar books, anticipated length, brief bio, and complete contact info. Also include SASE if work should be returned. **Sample Titles:** *Offbeat Museums; Offbeat Food; Letter Writing Made Easy!; Cafe Nation; Collecting Sins; Blues for Bird.* **Tips:** No phone calls. **Contact:** Acquisitions Editor.

SARABANDE BOOKS INC.

2234 Dundee Rd., Suite 200, Louisville, KY 40205. 502-458-4028.
E-mail: sarabandeb@aol.com. Web site: www.sarabandebooks.org.
Description: Nonprofit literary press publishing poetry and short fiction.

SASQUATCH BOOKS

615 Second Ave., Suite 260, Seattle, WA 98104. 206-467-4300.
E-mail: books@sasquatchbooks.com. Web site: www.sasquatchbooks.com.
Gary Luke, Editor.
Description: Regional books covering the west coast of the U.S. only. Food, travel, gardening, pop culture, and literary nonfiction. **Number of Books/Yr.:** 40 titles/year, 30% by first-time authors, 30% unagented. **Proposal Process:** Query with SASE. Response time: 3 months. No multiple or electronic queries. Hard copy. **Payment:** Royalty. **Tips:** Regional only (Pacific Northwest, Alaska, and California).

SCARECROW PRESS

4720 Boston Way, Lanham, MD 20706. 301-459-3366.

Web site: www.scarecrowpress.com.

Shirley Lambert, Editorial Director.

Description: Single volume reference titles; historical dictionaries (of countries, religious organizations, wars, movements, cities, and ancient civilizations); scholarly, professional, and textbooks in selected disciplines. Bruce Phillips (music); Rebecca Massa (film); Kim Taboy (young adult literary criticism reference titles, historical dictionaries); Sue Easun (information studies, military history, children's literary criticism); Elizabeth Crow (all other inquiries). **Number of Books/Yr.:** 175 titles/year, 20% by first-time authors, 95% unagented. **Proposal Process:** Query with subject matter, scope, and intended purpose of your mss. E-queries accepted. **Response time:** 2-4 months. **Payment:** Royalty, 5% and up—negotiated. **Tips:** See guidelines.

SCHIFFER PUBLISHING LTD.

4880 Lower Valley Rd., Atglen, PA 19310. 610-593-1777.

E-mail: schifferbk@aol.com.

Description: Publisher of books on collectibles, antiques, military history, arts and crafts, art and design, and New Age topics.

SCOTT FORESMAN

1900 E Lake Ave., Glenview, IL 60025.

Web site: www.scottforesman.com.

Susanne Singleton, Publisher.

Description: Elementary textbooks. **Proposal Process:** Must have proper educational credentials in order to submit. **Payment:** Royalty or flat fee.

SEA HILL PRESS

6101 200th St. SW, Suite 205, Lynwood, WA 98036. 425-697-3606.

E-mail: byron@seahillpress.com.

Description: Publisher of coffee table books and cookbooks.

SEAL PRESS

300 Queen Anne Ave. N, #375, Seattle, WA 98109. 206-722-1838.

E-mail: leslie.miller@avalonpub.com. Web site: www.sealpress.com.

Leslie Miller, Senior Editor.

Description: Publishes titles ranging from literary fiction to health, popular culture, women's studies, parenting, and travel/outdoor adventure. Currently focusing acquisitions in two popular series: *Adventura* (focuses on women's travel/adventure writing) and *Live Girls* (showcases the voices of modern feminism). **Number of Books/Yr.:** 15 titles/year (1,500 submissions), 20% first-time authors, 20% unagented. **Proposal Process:** Query. No electronic or multiple queries. Hard-copy format preferred. Response time: 2-4 months. **Payment:** Royalty, 7% net. **Tips:** No unsolicited or unagented manuscripts considered.

SELF-REALIZATION FELLOWSHIP PUBLISHERS

3208 Humboldt St., Los Angeles, CA 90031. 323-276-6002.
E-mail: sales@srfpublishers.org. Web site: www.srfpublishers.org.
Description: Publisher of Paramahansa Yogananda's books.

SEVEN LOCKS PRESS

3100 W Warner Ave., Suite 8, Santa Ana, CA 92704. 714-545-2526.
E-mail: sevenlocks@aol.com. Web site: www.sevenlockspress.com.
Description: Publishes nonfiction material on contemporary topics, self-help issues, public affairs, and critical issues of our time.

SEVEN STORIES PRESS

140 Watts St., New York, NY 10013. 212-226-8760.
E-mail: info@sevenstories.com. Web site: www.sevenstories.com.
Daniel Simon, Acquistions.
Description: Small press. Fiction and nonfiction. **Proposal Process:** Query with SASE. **Payment:** Royalty. **Contact:** Editor.

SHAMBHALA PUBLICATIONS, INC.

Horticultural Hall
300 Massachusetts Ave., Boston, MA 02115. 617-424-0030.
E-mail: editors@shambhala.com. Web site: www.shambhala.com.
Peter Turner, Executive Editor.
Description: Publishes titles on Eastern religion, especially Buddhism and Taoism, as well as psychology, self-help, arts, literature, health/healing, and philosophy. **Proposal Process:** Query Laura Stone with outline and sample chapters. **Payment:** Flat fee and royalty.

SHERMAN ASHER PUBLISHING

P.O. Box 2853, Santa Fe, NM 87504. 505-984-2686.
E-mail: sapublish@att.net. Web site: www.shermanasher.com.
Description: Publishes memoirs, poetry, fiction and how-to-write books. **Tips:** Absolutely no unsolicited manuscripts. Queries only.

SIERRA CLUB BOOKS

85 Second St., San Francisco, CA 94105. 415-977-5733.
E-mail: danny.moses@sierraclub.org. Web site: www.sierraclub.org/books.
Danny Moses, Editor-in-Chief.
Description: Publishes books about nature, ecology, and environmental issues. **Number of Books/Yr.:** 20 titles/year (1,000 submissions), 10-20% by first-time authors, 40-50% unagented. **Proposal Process:** Query with outline. Considers multiple and electronic queries. Response time: 1 month. Prefers electronic format. **Payment:** Royalty, typical range is 10% net. **Sample Titles:** *Seasons of the Arctic*, *The Mountain World*, and *The Spirit of the Valley*.

SIGNATURE BOOKS PUBLISHING, LLC
564 W 400 N, Salt Lake City, UT 84116-3411. 801-531-1483.
E-mail: people@signaturebooks.com. Web site: www.signaturebooksinc.com.
George Smith, President.
Description: Publisher of fiction, nonfiction, essays, and humor on Western and Mormon Americana. Seeks to present history and culture in a scholarly, professional manner. **Proposal Process:** Submit query letter outlining thesis or plot with resume or curriculum vitae. Does not accept unsolicited manuscripts. **Payment:** Royalty. **Sample Titles:** *Mormon Mavericks,* by John Sillito; *Being Different,* by Stanford J. Layton. **Contact:** Gary James Bergera, Editor.

SILHOUETTE BOOKS
300 E 42nd St., New York, NY 10017. 212-682-6080.
Web site: www.eharlequin.com.
Tara Gavin, Editorial Director.
Description: Contemporary and historical romance. Other imprints: Mills & Boon, Harlequin, MIRA, Red Dress Ink, and Steeple Hills books. **Number of Books/Yr.:** 300-350 titles/year. **Proposal Process:** Query with outline and sample chapters. SASE required. Prefers hard-copy format. No multiple or electronic queries. **Payment:** Royalty. **Tips:** We encourage you to read many books from each series. The series that emerges as your favorite is probably where you should submit your manuscript.

SILK LABEL BOOKS
1 First Ave., P.O. Box 700, Unionville, NY 10988-0700. 845-726-3434.
William F. V. Neumann, Editorial Director.
Description: Adult fiction, mystery, humor, science fiction, historical fiction. **Number of Books/Yr.:** 50 titles/year (500 submissions), 50% first-time authors, 80% unagented. **Proposal Process:** Query with complete manuscript, and SASE. Hard-copy format preferred. Subsidizes. **Payment:** Royalty.

SILMAN-JAMES PRESS
3624 Shannon Rd., Los Angeles, CA 90027. 323-661-9922.
E-mail: silmanjamespress@earthlink.net.
Gwen Feldman, Jim Fox, Editors.
Description: Publisher of books on film, filmmaking, the motion picture industry, music, and the performing arts. Also includes Siles Press imprint, which publishes books on chess and other general nonfiction subjects. **Number of Books/Yr.:** 6 titles/year. 40% of books from first-time authors; 90% from unagented writers. **Proposal Process:** Query with outline and sample chapters. Accepts phone queries. Responds in 2 weeks-3 months. **Payment:** Royalty. **Sample Titles:** Book on acting: *Improvising Acting While Speaking Scripted Lines,* by Stephen Book; *In the Blink of an Eye: A Perspective on Film Editing,* 2nd edition, by Walter Murch; *Comic Insights: The Art of Stand-Up Comedy,* by Franklyn Ajaye.

SILVER LAKE PUBLISHING
2025 Hyperion Ave., Los Angeles, CA 90027. 323-663-3082.
Web site: www.silverlakepub.com.
Description: Personal finance, small business management, consumer reference, popular economics.

SILVERBACK BOOKS INC.
55 New Montgomery St., Suite 516, San Francisco, CA 94105-3431. 415-348-8595.
E-mail: info@silverbackbooks.com. Web site: www.silverbackbooks.com.
Description: Publisher of cookbooks.

SMITH AND KRAUS, INC.
P.O. Box 127, Lyme, NH 03768. 603-643-6431.
E-mail: sandk@sovernet. Web site: www.smithkraus.com.
Marisa Smith, Publisher.
Description: Publishes monologue and scene anthologies, biographies of playwrights, translations, books on career development (in theater) and the art of theater, and teaching texts for young actors (K-12). **Number of Books/Yr.:** 30 titles/year (500+ submissions), 20% by first-time authors, 50% unagented. **Proposal Process:** Query with SASE. Response time is 1-2 months. No multiple queries. Electronic queries accepted as well as hard copy. **Payment:** Royalty and flat fee. **Tips:** Material of interest to the theater community.

GIBBS SMITH, PUBLISHER
P.O. Box 667, Layton, UT 84041. 801-544-9800.
E-mail: info@gibbs-smith.com. Web site: www.gibbs-smith.com.
Madge Baird, Editor.
Description: Publisher of cookbooks, gift books, architecture guides, monographs, children's picture and activity books, and other materials related to home and hearth and western culture/lifestyle. **Tips:** We're looking for fresh insights into home decorating and inspirational stories that can be illustrated and sold as adult gift books, suitable for any occasion. **Contact:** Suzanne Taylor.

SMITHSONIAN INSTITUTION PRESS
750 Ninth Street NW, Suite 4300, Washington, DC 20560-0950. 202-275-2300.
E-mail: inquiries@sipress.si.edu.
Description: general trade and illustrated books in American studies, natural sciences, photography, aviation and spaceflight history, and anthropology.

SNOW LION PUBLICATIONS

P.O. Box 6483, Ithaca, NY 14851. 607-273-8519.

E-mail: tibet@snowlionpub.com. Web site: www.snowlionpub.com.

Description: Publishes titles exclusively on Tibetan Buddhism.

SOHO PRESS

853 Broadway, New York, NY 10003. 212-260-1900.

Web site: www.sohopress.com.

Juris Jurjevics, Acquisitions Editor.

Description: Publishes adult literary fiction, mysteries, nonfiction memoirs, travel books, and materials on social and cultural history. **Number of Books/Yr.:** 40 titles/year (2,000 submissions), 10% by first-time authors, 10% unagented. **Proposal Process:** Query with the first three sample chapters. Response time: 2 months. Considers multiple queries. No electronic queries. Hard copy. **Payment:** Royalty (net 10%, 12.5%, 15%). **Sample Titles:** Adult: *Gloria,* by Keith Maillard; *Death of a Red Heroine,* Qui Xaolung; *The Gravity of Sunlight,* by Rosa Shand. **Tips:** No mass-market how-to, cooking, or religious books.

SOUNDPRINTS

353 Main Ave., Norwalk, CT 06851. 203-840-2274.

E-mail: chelsea.shriver@soundprints.com. Web site: www.soundprints.com.

Chelsea Shriver, Assistant Editor.

Description: Publishes books on wildlife and history to educate and entertain. Manuscript must have an exciting storyline while at the same time be based on fact and supported by careful research. **Number of Books/Yr.:** 12 titles/year (100 submissions), 100% unagented. **Proposal Process:** Does not accept unsolicited manuscripts due to the specific guidelines for each series. Submit published writing samples for review. **Payment:** Flat fee. **Sample Titles:** Currently publishes 6 series: *Smithsonian Oceanic Collection, Smithsonian's Backyard, Smithsonian Odyssey Collection, Smithsonian Let's Go to the Zoo!, Soundprints Multicultural/Make Friends Around the World, Soundprints Read-and-Discover, Early Reading Chapter Books,* and *Soundprints Wild Habitats.* **Tips:** Catalog available upon request. **Contact:** Chelsea Shriver, Assistant Editor.

SOURCEBOOKS CASABLANCA

Sourcebooks, Inc.

P.O. Box 4410, Naperville, IL 60567-4410. 603-961-3900.

E-mail: todd.stocke@sourcebooks.com. Web site: www.sourcebooks.com.

Todd Stocke, Editorial Director.

Description: The nonfiction, relationships/love imprint of Sourcebooks, Inc. **Proposal Process:** Query with outline and sample chapters. **Payment:** Royalty. **Sample Titles:** *1001 Ways to Be Romantic,* by Gregory Godek; *Seduction,* by Snow Raven Starborn; and *365 Kisses,* by Kathy Wagoner.

SOURCEBOOKS, INC.

P.O. Box 4410, Naperville, IL 60567-4410. 630-961-3900.

E-mail: todd.stocke@sourcebooks.com. Web site: www.sourcebooks.com.

Todd Stocke, Editorial Director.

Description: Publishes general interest nonfiction titles in a wide rage of categories: entertainment, history, sports, general self-help/psychology, personal finance, small business, marketing and management, parenting, health and beauty, reference, biography, gift books and women's issues. Launched a fiction imprint, Sourcebooks Landmark, in 2001. **Number of Books/Yr.:** 100 titles/year (3,000+ submissions), 10% first-time authors, 20% unagented. **Proposal Process:** Query with outline and sample chapters, include SASE. Multiple queries OK. No electronic queries. Prefer hard-copy format. **Payment:** Royalty. **Sample Titles:** Adult fiction: *Man and Boy,* by Tony Parsons; *The Other Adonis,* by Frank Deford. Adult nonfiction: *What Flavor Is Your Personality,* by Alan Hirsch, M.D.; *Bathroom Stuff,* by Holman Wang; and *Seduced by Hitler,* by Adam LeBor and Roger Boyes. **Tips:** Know your competition, make your book stand apart.

SOUTH END PRESS

7 Brookline St., Cambridge, MA 02139-4146. 617-547-4002.

Web site: www.southendpress.org.

Jill Petty, Editor.

Description: Nonprofit, collectively run book publisher with more than 200 titles in print. Committed to the politics of radical social change. Encourage critical thinking and consecutive action on the key political, cultural, social, economic, and ecological issues shaping life in the United States and in the world. **Number of Books/Yr.:** 10 titles/year (1,000 submissions), 5% first-time authors, 95% unagented. **Proposal Process:** Query with sample chapters; multiple queries are accepted. Response time: 6-8 weeks. Hard-copy format preferred. **Payment:** Royalty.

SOUTHERN ILLINOIS UNIVERSITY PRESS

P.O. Box 3697, Carbondale, IL 62902-3697. 618-453-2281.

E-mail: jewil@siu.edu. Web site: www.siu.edu/~siupress.

Description: Nonfiction on the humanities, 200-300 pages. **Proposal Process:** Query with outline and sample chapters. **Payment:** Royalty.

SOUTHERN METHODIST UNIVERSITY PRESS

Box 415, Dallas, TX 75275-0415. 214-768-1433.

E-mail: klang@mail.smu.edu.

Kathryn Lang, Acquisitions Editor.

Description: Publishes literary fiction, books on life in the Southwest (both fiction and nonfiction), and books on film, theater, and the performing arts. Also publishes nonfiction titles on medical humanity issues, ethics, and death/dying. **Number of Books/Yr.:** 12 titles/year (2,500 submissions), 80% by first-time authors, 90% unagented. **Proposal Process:** Query with outline and sample chapters. Response time: 1 month. Prefers hard-copy format. Accepts multiple queries. No electronic queries. **Payment:** Royalty (net 10%). **Sample Titles:** *The Price You Pay,* fiction; *Biography of Wright Payman; La Scala West* (history of Dallas Opera).

SPECTACLE LANE PRESS

Box 1237, 2165 Country Manor Drive, Mt. Pleasant, SC 29465-1237. 843-971-9165.
E-mail: jaskar44@aol.com.
James A. Skardon, Editor.
Description: Humor, text, and cartoons. Lifestyle texts. Subject matter varies, including satire, self-help, business, sports, and television topics. Mostly trade paperback and occasional cloth. **Number of Books/Yr.:** 1-3 titles/year (300 submissions), 90% by first-time writers, 90% unagented. **Proposal Process:** Query with outline and sample chapters, and SASE. No multiple queries, electronic queries accepted. Response time: 2-4 weeks. **Payment:** Advance against royalty. **Sample Titles:** *The Difference Between Cats and Dogs,* by Bob Zahn (cartoons). **Tips:** Humor should be current and sophisticated, nothing scatological. Writing should be clear, straightforward, well-organized, with base of solid expertise on nonhumor subjects.

SPHINX PRESS

Sourcebooks, Inc.
P.O. Box 4410, Naperville, IL 60567-4410. 630-961-3900.
E-mail: info@sourcebooks.com.
Mark Warda, Editor.
Description: Nonfiction books on legal self-help. **Proposal Process:** Query with outline and sample chapters. **Payment:** Royalty.

SPINSTERS INK

P.O. Box 22005, Denver, CO 80222. 303-761-5552.
E-mail: spinster@spinstersink.com. Web site: www.spinsters-ink.com.
Sharon Silvas, Editor.
Description: Adult fiction and nonfiction books, 200-plus pages, that deal with social justice and/or significant issues in women's lives from a feminist perspective and encourage change and growth. **Number of Books/Yr.:** 6/year. 50% first-time authors; 80% unagented. **Proposal Process:** Query with outline; multiple queries considered. Response time 90 days. E-query OK. SASE. **Payment:** Royalty.

SPRINGHOUSE PUBLISHING

1111 Bethlehem Pike, P.O. Box 908, Springhouse, PA 19477. 215-646-8700.
E-mail: jrobinso@lww.com. Web site: www.springnet.com.
Description: Information for nursing students and other healthcare professionals.

SQUARE ONE PUBLISHERS, INC.

16 First Street, Garden City Park, NY 11040. 516-535-2010.
E-mail: sq1info@aol.com. Web site: www.squareonepublishers.com.
Description: Publisher of nonfiction on vintage poster art, collectibles, cooking, general interest, history, how-to, parenting, self-help, travel, etc.

STA-KRIS, INC.

P.O. Box 714, Grantsburg, WI 54840. 715-463-2907.
E-mail: stakris@grantsburgtelcom.net. Web site: www.stakris.com.
Kathy Wagoner, President.
Description: Nonfiction adult-level gift books that portray universal feelings, truths, and values; or have a special-occasion theme. **Proposal Process:** Query with bio, list of credits, complete manuscript, and SASE.

STACKPOLE BOOKS

5067 Ritter Rd., Mechanicsburg, PA 17055. 717-796-0412.
E-mail: jschnell@stackpolebooks.com. Web site: www.stackpolebooks.com.
Judith Schnell, Editorial Director.
Description: Looking for good, well-researched work on interesting topics such as the outdoors, nature, fishing, fly fishing, climbing, paddling, sports, sporting literature, history, and military reference. **Number of Books/Yr.:** 80 titles/year (150 submissions), 20% first-time authors, 70% unagented. **Proposal Process:** Submit queries with sample chapters to acquisitions editor for the line: Marl Allison (nature), Judith Schnell (fishing/sports), Leigh Ann Berry (history), Kyle Weaver (Pennsylvania). No electronic or multiple queries. Hard copy. **Payment:** Royalty; advance or flat fee. **Tips:** No poetry, cookbooks, fiction, or books on crafts. History books must have some original research involved. **Contact:** Acquisitions Editor.

C.D. STAMPLEY ENTERPRISES

P.O. Box 33172, Charlotte, NC 28233. 704-333-6631.
E-mail: info@stampley.com. Web site: www.stampley.com.
Crews Walden, President.
Description: Publisher of family Bibles, study Bibles, religious reference materials, and children's educational materials.

STANFORD UNIVERSITY PRESS

Stanford University, Stanford, CA 94305-2235. 650-723-9434.
Web site: www.sup.org.
Norris Pope, Editor.
Description: Furthers the University's research and teaching mission primarily through books of significant scholarship. Also publishes some professional books, advanced textbooks, and intellectually serious popular works. **Number of Books/Yr.:** 120 titles/year (2,000 submissions), 35% by first-time authors, 95% unagented. **Proposal Process:** Query with outline and sample chapters. Response time: varies. Multiple queries accepted. No electronic queries. Hard copy. **Payment:** Royalty. **Tips:** No original fiction or poetry.

STARBURST PUBLISHERS

P.O. Box 4123, Lancaster, PA 17604. 717-293-0939.
E-mail: editorial@starburstpublishers.com. Web site: www.starburstpublishers.com.
Description: Publishes titles on self-help, health, and inspiration. Sells to both the

American Booksellers Association and the Christian Booksellers Association markets. **Number of Books/Yr.:** 15-20 titles per year (1,000 submissions). **Proposal Process:** Query with outline for nonfiction book, synopsis for fiction book, and 3 sample chapters. Considers multiple queries. Hard copy. **Payment:** Royalty, range 6-16% net. **Sample Titles:** *What's in the Bible for . . . Teens?* (religion); *Cheap Talk with the Frugal Friends* (self-help/finance). **Tips:** No poetry, young adult, or children. Books that will work in both the ABA and CBA (evangelical Christian) markets. **Contact:** Acquisitions: Editorial Department.

STARRHILL PRESS

River City Publishing
1719 Mulberry St., Montgomery, AL 36106. 877-408-7078.
E-mail: jdavis@rivercitypublishing.com. Web site: www.rivercitypublishing.com.
Jim Davis, Editor.
Description: Publishes smart softcover volumes on a variety of topics including art, gardening, health, history, literature, music, and travel. Books are topical, intriguing, and make great gifts. **Sample Titles:** *Kind Hearts: Self-Esteem and the Challenges of Aging*, uplifting advice for those lucky enough to live into old age, and those lucky enough to care for them. **Tips:** Generally publishes authors with extensive track records.

STATE UNIVERSITY OF NEW YORK PRESS

State University Plaza, Albany, NY 12246-0001. 518-472-5000.
Web site: www.sunypress.edu.
James H. Peltz, Editor-in-Chief.
Description: Publishes scholarly and trade books in the humanities and social sciences. **Number of Books/Yr.:** 200 titles/year (1,200 submissions), 99% unagented authors. **Proposal Process:** Query with outline and sample chapters. No electronic queries. Multiple queries accepted. Response time: 4-6 weeks. Hard-copy format preferred. **Payment:** Royalty (typically 5-10%).

STEERFORTH PRESS

P.O. Box 70, South Royalton, VT 05068. 802-763-2808.
Web site: www.steerforth.com.
Michael Moore, Editor.
Description: Adult nonfiction and some literary fiction. Novels, serious works of history, biography, politics, current affairs. **Proposal Process:** Does not accept unsolicited proposals or manuscripts.

STEMMER HOUSE PUBLISHERS, INC.

2627 Caves Rd., Owings Mills, MD 21117. 410-363-3690.
E-mail: stemmerhouse@home.com. Web site: www.stemmer.com.
Barbara Holdridge, Editorial Director.
Description: Nonfiction for adults, including the International Design Library, and nonfiction books and audiocassettes for children. **Number of Books/Yr.:** 4 titles/year

(2,000 submissions), 50% by first-time authors, 95% unagented. **Proposal Process:** Query with sample chapters, SASE. Considers multiple and electronic queries. Response time: 2 weeks. Prefer hard-copy format. **Payment:** Royalty, 5%-10% net. **Sample Titles:** Adult: *Japanese Garden Journey* (garden appreciation). Children's: *North Atlantic on the Great Ship Normandie,* by Peter Mandel (ages 8-12).

STEMMLE PUBLISHERS INC.

799 Broadway, Suite 414, New York, NY 10003. 212-253-0138.
E-mail: info@stemmleusa.com.
Description: Photography titles. **Sample Titles:** *West Point,* by Marcia Lippman; *Photographs,* by William Ropp; *The Faces of Photography,* by Tina Ruisinger.

STERLING PUBLISHING

387 Park Ave. S, New York, NY 10016. 212-532-7160.
Web site: www.sterlingpub.com.
Sheila Anne Barry, Acquistions Manager.
Description: Publishes books on a wide variety of topics. Subject matter includes how-to, hobby, woodworking, alternative health and healing, fiber arts, crafts, dolls and puppets, ghosts, wine, nature, oddities, new consciousness, puzzles, juvenile humor and activities, juvenile nature and science, medieval history, Celtic topics, gardening, alternative lifestyle, business, pets, recreation, sports and games books, reference, and home decorating. **Proposal Process:** Query with outline, sample chapter, and sample illustrations. **Payment:** Royalty. **Tips:** Unsolicited manuscripts accepted, please accompany with a SASE. **Contact:** Steve Magnuson, Vice-President, Editorial.

STEWART HOUSE PUBLISHING, INC.

1180 Medical Court, Suite A, Carmel, IN 46032. 317-574-8910.
E-mail: kproctor@stewarthousepub.com.
Description: Time Passages Commemorative Yearbooks.

STODDART PUBLISHING CO. LIMITED

895 Don Mills Rd., 400-2 Park Centre
Toronto, Ontario, M3C 1W3 Canada. 416-445-3333.
Web site: www.stoddartpub.com.
Donald Bastian, Managing Editor.
Description: Nonfiction with particular emphasis on business and finance, autobiography, military history, humor, and sports. Committed to publishing Canadian authors and Canadian subjects. **Proposal Process:** Query with an outline, 2-3 sample chapters, and SASE; multiple queries are accepted. Responds in 12 weeks. **Payment:** Royalty. **Tips:** No submissions via e-mail or disk; hard copies only.

STONEYDALE PRESS PUBLISHING CO.

523 Main St., Box 188, Stevensville, MT 59870-2839. 406-777-2729.
E-mail: info@stoneydale.com.
Dale A. Burk, Publisher.

Description: Adult nonfiction, primarily how-to, on outdoor recreation with emphasis on big game hunting; some regional history of Northern Rockies. Specialized market. **Proposal Process:** Query with outline and sample chapters essential. **Payment:** Royalty.

STOREY PUBLISHING
210 Mass Moca Way, Adams, MA 01247. 413-346-2100.
Web site: www.storeybooks.com.
Deborah Balmuth, Editorial Director.
Description: Publisher of nonfiction how-to books in the areas of gardening, crafts, natural health, building, pets/animals, and nature. Also gift books and juvenile nature books. **Number of Books/Yr.:** 40 titles/year, 50% first-time authors, 80% unagented. **Proposal Process:** Send query with outline and sample chapters, and SASE. Multiple queries accepted. No electronic queries. Hard copy. Response time: 2-3 months. **Payment:** Royalty or flat fee. **Tips:** Well-researched competitive analysis and clearly defined "hook" to make proposed book stand out from competition. Clear, hard-working content, with imaginative presentation.

STORMLINE PRESS
P.O. Box 593, Urbana, IL 61801.
E-mail: rbial@alexia.lis.uiuc.edu.
Raymond Bial, Editor.
Description: Distinctive works of literary and artistic value, with emphasis on rural and small town. **Number of Books/Yr.:** 1 title/year, 10% first-time authors, 10% unagented. **Proposal Process:** Query with outline and sample chapters, SASE. Multiple queries accepted. No electronic queries. Hard copy. **Payment:** Flat fee. **Sample Titles:** Nonfiction: *Living with Lincoln* and *When the Waters Recede*, by Dan Guillory. Fiction: *Silent Friends*, by Margaret Lacey. **Tips:** Please review the kinds of books published by our press to gain a sense of the types of books we publish. We are a very small publisher and do not have the staff to respond to inquiries or submissions. We do not accept unsolicited manuscripts.

STRAWBERRY HILL PRESS
Strictly Book Promotions, Inc.
21 Isis St., Suite 102, San Francisco, CA 94103. 415-626-2665.
E-mail: strictly@bookpromo.com.
Daniel F. Vojir, Editor.
Description: Nonfiction: biography, autobiography, history, cooking, health, how-to, philosophy, performance arts, and the Third World. **Proposal Process:** Query with sample chapters, outline, and SASE. **Payment:** Royalty.

STRING LETTER PUBLISHING
255 West End Avenue, San Rafael, CA 94901. 415-485-6946.
E-mail: books@stringletters.com. Web site: www.stringletter.com.
Description: Publisher of contemporary adult music.

SUCCESS SHOWCASE PUBLISHING

131 W Sunburst Lane, Suite 220, Tempe, AZ 85284 . 480-831-8334.
E-mail: info@confessionsofshamelessselfpromoters.com.
Web site: www.confessionsofshamelessselfpromoters.com.
Description: Publishes books on successful marketing strategies.

SUMMIT BOOKS

Simon & Schuster Trade/Simon & Schuster, Inc.
1230 Avenue of the Americas, New York, NY 10020. 212-698-7000.
Web site: www.simonsays.com.
Description: General-interest fiction and nonfiction of high literary quality. No category books. **Proposal Process:** Query through agents only. **Payment:** Royalty.

SUMMIT UNIVERSITY PRESS

P.O. Box 5000, Corwin Springs, MT 59030-5000. 406-848-9295.
E-mail: info@summituniversitypress.com.
Web site: www.summituniversitypress.com.
Description: Books on spirituality and personal growth. **Sample Titles:** *Dreams: Exploring the Secrets of Your Soul*, by Dr. Marilyn C. Barrick.

SUNDANCE PUBLISHING

P.O. Box 1326, Littleton, MA 01460. 800-343-8204.
Web site: www.sundancepub.com.
M. Elizabeth Strauss, Director Publishing.
Description: Curriculum materials to accompany quality children's, young adult, and adult literature. **Payment:** Flat fee only.

SYBEX INC.

1151 Marina Village Pkwy., Alameda, CA 94501. 510-523-8233.
E-mail: proposals@sybex.com. Web site: www.sybex.com.
Jordan Gold, VP/Publisher.
Description: Publisher of books on computers and software. **Number of Books/Yr.:** 180 titles/year.

SYRACUSE UNIVERSITY PRESS

621 Skytop Rd., Suite 110, Syracuse, NY 13244-5290. 315-443-5534.
E-mail: twalsh01@syr.edu. Web site: http://sumweb.syr.edu/su_press/.
Description: Scholarly general and regional nonfiction.

THE TAUNTON PRESS INC.

63 S Main St., Newtown, CT 06470. 203-426-8171.
E-mail: tt@taunton.com. Web site: www.taunton.com.
Description: Publishes books on home design, fiber arts, woodworking and gardening.

TAYLOR TRADE PUBLISHING

Rowman & Littlefield Publishing Group

4720 Boston Way, Lanham, MD 20706. 301-459-3366.

Web site: www.rlpgbooks.com.

Michael Dorr, Editorial Director/Acquisitions.

Description: Adult trade nonfiction on sports, gardening, history, entertainment, health, sports, nature, regional interest. **Number of Books/Yr.:** 20 titles/year. **Proposal Process:** Send outline of manuscript with sample chapters. **Contact:** Michael Dorr, Rick Rinehart, Jill Langford.

TE NEUES PUBLISHING COMPANY

16 W 22nd St., New York, NY 10010-5803. 212-627-9090.

E-mail: tnp@teneues-usa.com. Web site: www.teneues.com.

Description: Art, photography, architecture, design, travel.

TEACHERS COLLEGE PRESS

1234 Amsterdam Ave., New York, NY 10027. 212-678-3929.

E-mail: tcpress@tc.columbia.edu. Web site: www.teacherscollegepress.com.

Brian Ellerbeck, Executive Acquisitions Editor.

Description: Publisher of books and materials that focus on all areas of education including curriculum, leadership, teacher education, early childhood, child development, language, literacy, etc. Also publishes materials on psychology, sociology/culture, history, philosophy, and women's studies.

TEHABI BOOKS

4920 Carroll Canyon Road, San Diego, CA 92121-3735. 858-450-9100.

E-mail: nancy.cash@tehabi.com. Web site: www.tehabi.com.

Description: Books on history, travel, sports, personalities, nature, and wildlife.

TEMPLE UNIVERSITY PRESS

USB 306, 1601 N Broad St., Philadelphia, PA 19122-6099. 215-204-8787.

E-mail: tempress@temple.edu. Web site: www.temple.edu/tempress/.

Janet Francendese, Editor-in-Chief.

Description: Adult nonfiction. **Proposal Process:** Query with outline and sample chapters. **Payment:** Royalty.

TEN SPEED PRESS

P.O. Box 7123, Berkeley, CA 94707. 510-559-1600.

Web site: www.tenspeed.com.

Kirsty Melville, Editorial Department.

Description: Publisher of career and business books, cookbooks, and general nonfiction. **Number of Books/Yr.:** 150 titles/year (5,000 submissions), 30% first-time authors, 30% unagented. **Proposal Process:** Query with outline and sample chapters, include SASE. Electronic queries okay. Hard copy. No electronic queries. Response time: 6 weeks. **Payment:** Royalty. **Sample Titles:** *What Color Is Your*

Parachute?, Damn Good Resume, and *Hiring Smart.* **Tips:** Familiarize yourself with our house and our list before submitting mss. Provide a rational for why we are the best publishing house for your work.

TEXAS A&M UNIVERSITY PRESS
John H. Lindsey Building, Lewis St., 4354 TAMU
College Station, TX 77843. 979-845-1436.
E-mail: dlv@tampress.tamu.edu. Web site: www.tamu.edu/upress.
Mary Lenn Dixon, Editor-in-Chief.
Description: American and military history, Eastern European studies, presidential studies, anthropology, natural history, literary fiction, Southwestern and Western studies. **Contact:** Diana L. Vance, Editorial Assistant.

THAMES & HUDSON INC.
500 Fifth Ave., New York, NY 10110. 212-354-3763.
E-mail: info@thames.wwnorton.com. Web site: www.thamesandhudsonusa.com.
Description: Publishes illustrated books on art, architecture, decorative arts, design, fashion, photography, travel, history, archaeology, spirituality, and natural history.

THIRD WORLD PRESS
P.O. Box 19730, Chicago, IL 60619. 773-651-0700.
E-mail: twpress3@aol.com. Web site: www.thirdworldpress.com.
Haki R. Madhubuti, Publisher.
Description: Progressive Black Publishing. Adult fiction, nonfiction, and poetry, as well juvenile fiction and young adult books. **Proposal Process:** Query with outline. Send SASE or e-mail for guidelines. **Payment:** Royalty.

THORSONS
4720 Boston Way, Lanham, MD 20706. 301-731-9526.
E-mail: karen.kreiger@harpercollins.uk. Web site: www.thorsons.com.
Description: Publishes material on health, personal development, alternative health, inspiration, sex, parenting, psychology, religion, self-help, and spirituality.

THUNDER BAY PRESS
Advantage Publishers Group
5880 Oberlin Dr., San Diego, CA 92121. 858-457-2500.
E-mail: beckyj@advmkt.com. Web site: www.advantagebooksonline.com.
Description: Highly illustrated, well-written, creatively designed promotional books.

THUNDER'S MOUTH PRESS
Avalon Publishing Group
161 William St., Fl. 16, New York, NY 10038. 212-614-7880.
Web site: www.avalonpub.com.
Description: Publishes adult trade books in a variety of subject areas. Concentrates heavily on pop culture, current events, contemporary culture, fantasy and role-playing

games, and biography. **Number of Books/Yr.:** 50 titles/year (thousands of submissions), 10% by first-time authors, 0% unagented. **Proposal Process:** Send query with complete manuscript. Response time: varies. No multiple or electronic queries.

THURMAN HOUSE
5 Park Center Court, Suite 300, Owings Mills, MD 21117. 410-902-9100.
E-mail: sales@thurmanhouse.com.
Description: Children's books, cookbooks, reference books.

TIARE PUBLICATIONS
213 Forest St., Lake Geneva, WI 53147. 414-248-4845.
E-mail: info@tiare.com. Web site: www.tiare.com.
Gerry L. Dexter, Editor.
Description: Adult nonfiction. Practical how-to guides. **Number of Books/Yr.:** 6 titles/year (40 submissions), 90% unagented. **Proposal Process:** Query with outline and sample chapters, and SASE. Electronic queries accepted. No multiple queries. Hard copy. Response time: 2 weeks. **Payment:** Royalty.

TILBURY HOUSE
2 Mechanic St., #3, Gardiner, ME 04345. 207-582-1899.
Web site: www.tilburyhouse.com.
Jennifer Elliott, Publisher.
Description: Small, independent publisher of children's books that deal with cultural diversity or the environment, appeal to children and parents as well as the educational market, and offer possibilities for developing a separate teacher's guide. Adult books: nonfiction books about Maine or the Northeast. **Proposal Process:** Query with outline and sample chapters. Prefers electronic or hard-copy format. Accepts unsolicited manuscripts. **Payment:** Pays on publication. **Sample Titles:** Children's: *Talking Walls,* by first-time author Margy Burns Knight.

TIMBER PRESS, INC
133 SW Second Ave., Suite 450, Portland, OR 97204. 503-227-2878.
Web site: www.timberpress.com.
Description: Publishes high-quality books on plants and flowers for gardeners, horticulturists, and botanists.

TOKYOPOP
Mixx Entertainment, Inc.
5900 Wilshire Blvd., Suite 2000, Los Angeles, CA 90036-5020. 323-692-6700.
E-mail: info@tokyopop.com. Web site: www.tokyopop.com.
Description: Japanese Manga, graphic novels, and comic books.

TOR BOOKS
Tom Doherty Associates, LLC
175 Fifth Ave., New York, NY 10010. 212-388-0100.

E-mail: inquiries@tor.com. Web site: www.tor.com.
Patrick Nielsen Hayden, Senior Editor.
Description: Science fiction and fantasy, from 80,000 words. **Proposal Process:** Query with complete synopsis and first 3 chapters. **Payment:** Advance and royalty.

TORCHLIGHT PUBLISHING INC.
P.O. Box 52, Badger, CA 93603. 559-337-2200.
E-mail: torchlight@spiralcomm.net. Web site: www.torchlight.com.
Description: Features articles on health and vegetarianism, leadership, motivation and self-improvement, spirituality and religion, etc. **Contact:** Susanne Bolte.

TORMONT/BRIMAR PUBLICATIONS
338 Saint Antoine St. East, Montreal, Quebec H2Y 1A3 Canada. 514-954-1441.
E-mail: dianem@tormont.ca. Web site: www.tormont.com.
Diane Mineau, Editorial Director.
Description: Children's books, cookbooks, dictionaries, encyclopedias, and general interest books.

TOWLEHOUSE PUBLISHING
1312 Bell Grimes Ln., Nashville, TN 37207. 615-366-9120.
E-mail: vermonte@aol.com. Web site: www.towlehouse.com.
Description: Nonfiction publisher specializing in "Potent Quotables" and *Good Golf!* series. Always looking for riveting books about American pop culture, American history, and Christianity.

TRAFALGAR SQUARE PUBLISHING
Howe Hill Rd., P.O. Box 257, North Pomfret, VT 05053. 802-457-1911.
E-mail: tsquare@sover.net.
Web site: www.trafalgarsquarebooks.com or horseandriderbooks.com.
Description: Originates fine equestrian books.

TRANSACTION PUBLISHERS
Rutgers State University, 35 Berrue Circle, Piscataway, NJ 08854. 732-445-2280.
E-mail: trans@transactionpub.com. Web site: www.transactionpub.com.
Description: Publisher of social science books—economics, political science, history, sociology, anthropology, psychology, etc.

TRAVEL PUBLISHERS ASSOCIATION
P.O. Box 5346, Madison, WI 53705-0346. 608-233-5488.
E-mail: travpubs@ginkgopress.com. Web site: www.travelpubs.com.
Description: Publisher of travel books.

TRAVELERS' TALES, INC.
330 Townsend St., Suite 208, San Francisco, CA 94107.
E-mail: submit@travelerstales.com. Web site: www.travelerstales.com.

Description: Travel writing by world-famous authors and new voices. **Sample Titles:** *Travelers' Tales Greece, Travelers Tales' Ireland, A Women's Path: Women's Best Spiritual Travel Writing,* and *Not So Funny When It Happened.* **Tips:** Publishes travel books that inspire, educate, and better prepare travelers with tips and wisdom. Titles have original essays and are not typical journalistic travel books.

TRIUMPH BOOKS
601 South LaSalle St., Suite 500, Chicago, IL 60605. 312-939-3330.
Web site: www.triumphbooks.com.
Thomas Bast, Editorial Director.
Description: Publisher of books on sports, recreation, and popular culture. **Proposal Process:** Query with SASE or submit proposal with outline, 1-2 sample chapters, and art/illustrations. **Sample Titles:** *Few and Chosen,* by Whitey Ford

TURTLE POINT PRESS
103 Hog Hill Rd., Chappaqua, NY 10514. 914-244-3840.
Web site: www.turtlepoint.com.
Jonathan D. Rabinowitz, President.
Description: Forgotten literary fiction, historical and biographical; some contemporary fiction, poetry, 200-400 typed pages. Also publishes imprint Books & Co. **Proposal Process:** Query with sample chapters. Multiple queries considered. **Payment:** Royalty.

TURTLE PRESS
S.K. Productions
P.O. Box 290206, Wethersfield, CT 06129-0206. 860-529-7770.
E-mail: editorial@turtlepress.com. Web site: www.turtlepress.com.
Cynthia Kim, Editor.
Description: Publishes books on mind-body, Eastern philosophy, holistic fitness, and martial arts. **Number of Books/Yr.:** 4-8 titles/year (350 submissions), 40% first-time authors, 90% unagented. **Proposal Process:** Query with outline and sample chapters, and SASE. Response time: 2-4 weeks. Multiple and electronic queries accepted but prefers hard-copy format. **Payment:** Royalty.

TUTTLE PUBLISHING
153 Milk St., Fl. 5, Boston, MA 02109-4809. 617-951-4080.
E-mail: info@tuttlepublishing.com. Web site: www.tuttlepublishing.com.
Description: Publishes titles on various aspects of Asian culture such as cooking, martial arts, spirituality, design, philosophy, travel, and language. **Contact:** Editorial Acquisitions.

TWO-CAN PUBLISHING
Zenith Entertainment, Ltd.
234 Nassau St., Princeton, NJ 08542. 609-921-6700.
E-mail: tomhaworth@two-canpublishing.com.

Web site: www.two-canpublishing.com.
Description: Books that absorb, entertain, inform and explain for children, teachers and parents around the world.

ULYSSES TRAVEL GUIDES

4176 St.-Denis St., Montreal, Quebec H2W 2M5 Canada. 514-843-9882.
E-mail: info@ulysses.ca. Web site: www.ulyssesguides.com.
Description: Travel guidebooks that offer cultural and tourist information for various regions.

UNIVERSITY OF AKRON PRESS

374-B Bierce Library, Akron, OH 44325-1703. 877-UAPRESS.
E-mail: uapress@uakron.edu. Web site: www.uakron.edu/uapress.
Michael J. Carley, Editor.
Description: Publishes 5 series: *Poetry; Ohio History and Culture; Technology and the Environment; Law, Politics, and Society; International, Political, and Economic History.* **Number of Books/Yr.:** 12 titles/year (100 submissions), 40% first-time authors, 100% unagented. **Proposal Process:** Query with outline and chapters. Multiple and electronic queries accepted. Prefer hard-copy format. Response time: 1-2 months. **Payment:** Royalty. **Tips:** See Web site for submission guidelines.

UNIVERSITY OF ALABAMA PRESS

20 Research Dr., Tuscaloosa, AL 35487-0380. 205-348-1561.
Web site: www.uapress.ua.edu.
Curtis Clark, Editor-in-Chief.
Description: Scholarly and general regional nonfiction. Submit to appropriate editor: Daniel J. J. Ross (history, military history, Latin American history, and Jewish studies); Curtis Clark (African-American, Native American and women's studies, public administration, theater, English, rhetoric, and communication); Judith Knight (archaeology and anthropology). **Number of Books/Yr.:** 55 titles; 90% unagented and 50% first-time authors. **Proposal Process:** Send cover letter, curriculum vitae, outline, sample chapter(s), and a prospectus outlining the proposed length, illustrations, etc. **Payment:** Royalty, 5-10%.

UNIVERSITY OF ARIZONA PRESS

355 S Euclid Ave., Suite 103, Tucson, AZ 85719. 520-621-1441.
E-mail: szuter@uapress.arizona.edu. Web site: www.uapress.arizona.edu.
Christine Szuter, Director.
Description: Scholarly and popular nonfiction: Arizona, American West, anthropology, archaeology, environmental science, geography, Latin America, Native Americans, natural history, space sciences, western and environmental history. **Proposal Process:** Query with outline, sample chapters, and current curriculum vitae or resume. **Payment:** Royalty. **Contact:** Patti Hartmann and Yvonne Reineke, Acquiring Editors.

UNIVERSITY OF ARKANSAS PRESS
The University of Arkansas
201 Ozark Ave., Fayetteville, AR 72701-1201. 501-575-3246.
E-mail: uaprinfo@cavern.uark.edu. Web site: www.uuapress.com.
Lawrence J. Malley, Director/Editor-in-Chief.
Description: Scholarly nonfiction and poetry. Query. Royalty.

UNIVERSITY OF CALIFORNIA PRESS
2120 Berkeley Way, Berkeley, CA 94720. 510-642-4247.
Web site: www.ucpress.edu.
Lynn Withey, Acting Director.
Description: Scholarly nonfiction. **Proposal Process:** Query with cover letter, out-line, sample chapters, curriculum vitae, and SASE.

UNIVERSITY OF CHICAGO PRESS
1427 E 60th St., Chicago, IL 60637-2954. 773-702-7700.
Web site: www.press.uchicago.edu.
Description: Scholarly, nonfiction, advanced texts, monographs, clothbound and paperback, reference books.

UNIVERSITY OF GEORGIA PRESS
330 Research Dr., Athens, GA 30602-4901. 706-369-6130.
E-mail: emontjoy@ugapress.uga.edu. Web site: www.uga.edu/ugapress.
Nicole Mitchell, Director.
Description: Short story and poetry collections, scholarly and creative nonfiction, Southern and American history, regional studies, biography and autobiography. For nonfiction, query with outline and sample chapters. Poetry collections considered in September and January only; short fiction in April and May only. A $20 fee is required for all poetry and fiction submissions. Royalty. SASE for competition guidelines.

UNIVERSITY OF HAWAII PRESS
2840 Kolowalu St., Honolulu, HI 96822. 808-956-8694.
Web site: www.hawaii.edu/uhpress.
Patricia Crosby, Pam Kelly, Keith Leber, and Masako Ikeda, Editors.
Description: Scholarly books on Asian, Southeast Asian, Asian-American, Hawaiian and Pacific studies from disciplines as diverse as the arts, history, language, literature, natural science, philosophy, religion, and the social sciences. **Proposal Process:** Query with outline and sample chapters. **Payment:** Royalty.

UNIVERSITY OF ILLINOIS PRESS
1325 S Oak St., Champaign, IL 61820-6903. 217-333-0950.
E-mail: uipress@uiuc.edu. Web site: www.press.uillinois.edu.
Willis Regier, Director/Editor-in-Chief.
Description: Scholarly and regional nonfiction. **Proposal Process:** Rarely considers multiple submissions. Query. **Payment:** Royalty.

UNIVERSITY OF IOWA PRESS

119 W Park Rd., Iowa City, IA 52242-1000. 319-335-2000.
E-mail: holly-carver@uiowa.edu. Web site: www.uiowa.edu/~uipress.
Holly Carver, Director.
Description: Nonfiction. Short fiction and poetry published only through annual competitions. **Proposal Process:** Query with SASE. **Payment:** Pay varies.

UNIVERSITY OF MASSACHUSETTS PRESS

P.O. Box 429, Amherst, MA 01004-0429. 413-545-2217.
E-mail: wilcox@umpress.umass.edu. Web site: www.umass.edu/umpress.
Bruce Wilcox, Director.
Description: Publisher of scholarly and general-interest books. Also publishes material in African-American studies, American studies, architecture, and environmental design. **Proposal Process:** Query with SASE.

UNIVERSITY OF MINNESOTA PRESS

111 Third Ave. S, Suite 290, Minneapolis, MN 55401-2520. 612-627-1970.
Web site: www.upress.umn.edu.
Doug Armato, Editorial Director.
Description: Nonprofit publisher of selected general-interest books and academic books for scholars. No original fiction or poetry. Areas of emphasis include: American studies, anthropology, art and aesthetics, cultural theory, film and media studies, gay and lesbian studies, geography, literary theory, political and social theory, race and ethnic studies, sociology and urban studies. **Number of Books/Yr.:** 110 titles/year, 50% by first-time authors, 99% unagented. **Proposal Process:** Query with outline, detailed prospectus or introduction, table of contents, sample chapter, and resume. Multiple queries considered. No electronic queries. Response time: 4-6 weeks. Hard copy. **Payment:** Royalty, 6-10% net. **Sample Titles:** *Postmodern Fables,* by Jean-Francois Lyotard; *The Capture of Speech and Other Writings,* by Michel de Certeau.

UNIVERSITY OF MISSOURI PRESS

2910 LeMone Blvd., Columbia, MO 65201-8227. 573-882-7641.
E-mail: upress@umsystem.edu. Web site: www.system.missouri.edu/upress.
Beverly Jarrett and Clair Willcox, Acquisitions.
Description: Scholarly books on American and European history; American, British, and Latin American literary criticism; political philosophy; intellectual history; regional studies; and short fiction.

UNIVERSITY OF NEBRASKA PRESS

233 N Eighth St., Lincoln, NE 68588. 402-472-3581.
E-mail: pressmail@unl.edu. Web site: www.nebraskapress.unl.edu.
Gary Dunham, Editor-in-Chief.
Description: Scholarly and trade books; Bison Books imprint; selected series in literary nonfiction, history, literature, and culture of the American West. **Number of Books/Yr.:** 90 titles/year, 20% first-time authors, 75% unagented authors. **Proposal

Process: Query with outline and sample chapters; SASE required. Accepts electronic queries. No unsolicited mss; no multiple queries. **Payment:** Royalty **Sample Titles:** *Cold Snap as Yearning*, by Robert Vivian; *Standing Up to the Rock*, by T. Louise Freeman Toole. **Contact:** Ladette Randolph, literary nonfiction.

UNIVERSITY OF NEVADA PRESS

MS 166, Reno, NV 89557. 775-784-6573.
E-mail: dalrympl@scs.unr.edu.
Joanne O'Hare, Editor-in-Chief.
Description: Publishes fiction, nonfiction, and poetry. Nonfiction topics include environmental studies, geography, anthropology, history, biography, natural history, regional (Nevada and the West), mining, gaming, and Basque studies. **Proposal Process:** Query first, with outline or table of contents, synopsis, estimated length, completion date of manuscript, and resume. **Payment:** Royalty. **Contact:** Joanne O'Hare.

UNIVERSITY OF NEW MEXICO PRESS

University of New Mexico
1720 Lomas Blvd. NE, Albuquerque, NM 87131. 505-277-2346.
E-mail: unmpress@unm.edu. Web site: www.unmpress.com.
Luther Wilson, Director.
Description: Scholarly nonfiction on social and cultural anthropology, archaeology, Western history, art, and photography. **Proposal Process:** Query. **Payment:** Royalty.

UNIVERSITY OF NORTH CAROLINA PRESS

P.O. Box 2288, Chapel Hill, NC 27515-2288. 919-966-3561.
E-mail: uncpress@unc.edu. Web site: www.uncpress.unc.edu.
David Perry, Editor-in-Chief.
Description: General-interest books (75,000-125,000 words) on the lore, crafts, cooking, gardening, travel, and natural history of the Southeast. No fiction or poetry, or memoirs of living persons. **Proposal Process:** Query. **Payment:** Royalty.

UNIVERSITY OF NORTH TEXAS PRESS

P.O. Box 311336, Denton, TX 76203-1336. 940-565-2142.
Web site: www.unt.edu/untpress.
Ronald Chrisman, Director.
Description: Publishes titles on military history, Texas history, multicultural topics, and women's history. **Number of Books/Yr.:** 16 titles/year (250 submissions), 95% unagented. **Proposal Process:** Send manuscript or query with sample chapters; no multiple queries. Electronic queries accepted. Hard copy preferred. Response time: Queries 2 weeks, submissions 3 months. **Payment:** Royalty. **Sample Titles:** Series include: *War and the Southwest* (perspectives, histories, and memories of war from authors living in the Southwest); *Western Life* series; and *Texas Writers* (critical biographies of Texas writers). **Tips:** Prefers writing with scholarly rigor while still

appealing to general audience. Avoid personal narrative, unless needed to make an analytical point. No memoirs. Prefers subjects of regional (Southwest) interest. **Contact:** Ronald Chrisman.

UNIVERSITY OF NOTRE DAME PRESS

University of Notre Dame
310 Flanner Hall, Notre Dame, IN 46556. 219-631-6346.
Web site: www.undpress.nd.edu.
Rebecca DeBoer, Executive Editor.
Description: Academic books, hardcover and paperback; philosophy, Irish studies, literature, theology, international relations, sociology, and general interest.

UNIVERSITY OF OKLAHOMA PRESS

1005 Asp Ave., Norman, OK 73019-0445. 405-325-5111/877-894-3798.
E-mail: cerankin@ou.edu. Web site: www.ou.edu/oupress.
Charles E. Rankin, Assistant Director/Editor-in-Chief.
Description: Books, to 350 pages, on the history of the American West, Indians of the Americas, classical studies, literary criticism, natural history, women's studies, and Native American and Chicano literature. **Proposal Process:** Query. **Payment:** Royalty.

UNIVERSITY OF PENNSYLVANIA PRESS

4200 Pine St., Philadelphia, PA 19104-4011. 215-898-6261.
E-mail: custserv@pobox.upenn.edu. Web site: www.upenn.edu/pennpress.
Eric Halpern, Editor.
Description: Scholarly nonfiction. **Proposal Process:** Query.

UNIVERSITY OF PITTSBURGH PRESS

3400 Forbes Ave., Pittsburgh, PA 15260. 412-383-2456.
Web site: www.pitt.edu/~press.
Cynthia Miller, Director.
Description: Scholarly nonfiction (philosophy of science, Latin American studies, political science, urban environmental history, culture, composition, and literacy). For poetry send SASE for rules and reading periods.

UNIVERSITY OF PUERTO RICO PRESS

Cond Vick Center, Avenida Munoz Rivera 867, Oficina 300-Edificio D
Hato-Rey, Puerto Rico 00925. 787-250-0550.
Juan Abascal, Editor-in-Chief.
Description: General nonfiction.

UNIVERSITY OF TENNESSEE PRESS

Conference Center Bldg., Suite 110, Knoxville, TN 37996-4108. 865-974-3321.
E-mail: harrison@utpress.org. Web site: www.utpress.org.
Joyce Harrison, Acquisitions Editor.

Description: Publishes scholarly and general-interest titles in the following subject areas: American studies, African-American studies, Appalachian studies, archaeology, architecture, Civil War studies, folklore, history, literary studies, material culture, and religion. **Number of Books/Yr.:** 30-35 titles/year, 99% unagented. **Proposal Process:** Query and include SASE. Multiple and electronic queries accepted. Hard copy. **Payment:** Royalty. **Tips:** Scholarly treatment, unique contributions to scholarship. Readable style. Authors should avoid formatting their manuscripts (making them look like books). Sample material should be double spaced on 8½ x 11 paper.

UNIVERSITY OF TEXAS PRESS

University of Texas, P.O. Box 7819, Austin, TX 78713-7819. 512-232-7600.
E-mail: utpress@uts.cc.utexas.edu. Web site: www.utexas.edu/utpress.
Theresa May, Editor-in-Chief.
Description: Scholarly works: Latin American/Latino studies, Native American studies, anthropology, Texana, natural science and history, environmental studies, Classics, Middle Eastern studies, film and media studies, gender studies, Texas architecture, photography/art. **Number of Books/Yr.:** 90-100 titles/year (800 submissions), 5% first-time authors, 98% unagented. **Proposal Process:** Query with proposal only and SASE. Multiple and electronic queries accepted. Response time: up to 3 months. **Payment:** Royalty. **Sample Titles:** Recent publications: *How Cities Work, Galveston and the 1900 Storm, Intercultural Communication, Class Struggle in Hollywood, Guide to Offshore Wildlife,* and *Cuba and the Politics of Passion.* **Tips:** No fiction, except occasional translation of literature (Latin American or Middle Eastern). No poetry. Please, no phone calls. **Contact:** Allison Faust, Associate Editor.

UNIVERSITY OF TORONTO PRESS

10 St. Mary St., Suite 700, Toronto, Ontario M4Y 2W8 Canada. 416-978-2239.
E-mail: utpbooks@utpress.utoronto. Web site: www.utpress.utoronto.ca.
Bill Harnum, Senior Vice-President .
Description: Scholarly and general trade titles, and academic journals. Subjects include philosophy, social sciences, classical and Medieval studies, language, literature and literary theory, religion, music, education, history, etc. **Proposal Process:** Submit query with outline and sample chapters. Accepts unsolicited manuscripts.

UNIVERSITY OF UTAH PRESS

1795 E South Campus Dr., Rm. 101, Salt Lake City, UT 84112. 801-581-6771.
Web site: www.upress.utah.edu.
Dawn Marano, Acquisitions Editor.
Description: Literary nonfiction of nature, place, and community from 250 pages.
Proposal Process: Query. **Payment:** Royalty.

UNIVERSITY OF VIRGINIA PRESS

P.O. Box 400318, Charlottesville, VA 22904-4318. 434-924-1373.
E-mail: bz2v@virginia.edu. Web site: www.upress.virginia.edu.
Boyd Zenner, Acquiring Editor.

Description: Generally scholarly nonfiction and regional general interest books with emphasis on history, literature, and environmental studies.

UNIVERSITY OF WISCONSIN PRESS
University of Wisconsin
1930 Monroe St., Fl. 3, Madison, WI 53711-2059. 608-263-1110.
E-mail: uniscpress@uwpress.wisc.edu. Web site: www.wisc.edu/wisconsinpress/.
Raphael Kadushin, Acquisitions Editor.
Description: Trade nonfiction, scholarly books and regional titles on the Midwest. Offers Brittingham Prize in Poetry and Pollak Prize in Poetry; query for details.

UNIVERSITY PRESS OF COLORADO
5589 Arapahoe Avenue, 206C, Boulder, CO 80303. 720-406-8849.
E-mail: archer@spot.colorado.edu. Web site: www.upcolorado.com.
Darrin Pratt, Editorial Director.
Description: Scholarly nonfiction in archaeology, environmental studies, local interest titles, history of the American West, and mining history. **Number of Books/Yr.:** 16 titles/year. **Proposal Process:** Query with outline and sample chapters. Hard copy. Multiple and electronic queries accepted. Response time: quick turnaround. **Sample Titles:** *In the Realm of Nachan Kan* (archaeology), *Environmental Conflict in Alaska* (environmental studies), *Cutthroat & Campfire Tales* (American West). **Tips:** Currently not taking submissions for fiction, biographies and memoirs. **Contact:** David Archer, Editor.

UNIVERSITY PRESS OF FLORIDA
15 NW 15th St., Gainesville, FL 32611-2079. 352-392-1351.
Web site: www.upf.com.
Deidre Bryan, Managing Editor.
Description: Scholarly and general audience books in archaeology, anthropology, history, women's studies, and Floridians. No fiction. **Number of Books/Yr.:** 80 titles/year (800 submissions), 15% first-time authors, 95% unagented. **Proposal Process:** Query with outline and sample chapters, SASE. Multiple and electronic queries accepted. Hard copy. **Payment:** Royalty. **Tips:** Nonfiction only.

UNIVERSITY PRESS OF KANSAS
University of Kansas
2501 West 15th Street, Lawrence, KS 66049-3905. 785-864-4154.
E-mail: upress@ku.edu. Web site: www.kansaspress.ku.edu.
Description: General interest trade and academic books specializing in American history/culture, military history, legal studies, Western Americana, politics/presidential studies, and the Great Plains and Midwest regions.

UNIVERSITY PRESS OF KENTUCKY
663 S Limestone St., Lexington, KY 40508-4008. 606-257-8150.
E-mail: agals1@uky.edu. Web site: www.kentuckypress.com.

Stephen Wrinn, Managing Editor.
Description: Scholarly books in the major fields. Serious nonfiction of general interest. Books related to Kentucky and the Ohio Valley, the Appalachians, and the South. No fiction, drama, or poetry. **Proposal Process:** Query.

UNIVERSITY PRESS OF MISSISSIPPI
3825 Ridgewood Rd., Jackson, MS 39211-6492. 601-432-6205.
E-mail: press@ihl.state.ms.us. Web site: www.upress.state.ms.us.
Seetha Srinivasan, Editor.
Description: Scholarly and trade titles in American literature, history, and culture; southern studies; African-American, women's and American studies; popular culture; folklife; art and architecture; natural sciences; health; and other liberal arts.

UNIVERSITY PRESS OF NEW ENGLAND
23 S Main St., Hanover, NH 03755-2048. 603-643-7100.
E-mail: university.press@dartmouth.edu. Web site: www.upne.com.
Phyllis Deutsch, Editor.
Description: Publisher of titles on nature and the environment, fiction of New England, Jewish studies, women's studies, American studies, and maritime studies. **Number of Books/Yr.:** 80 titles/year (3,000 submissions), 30% by first-time authors, 80% unagented. **Proposal Process:** Query. Prefer not to receive multiple queries. No electronic queries. Prefers hard-copy format. Response time: 3-6 months **Payment:** Royalty, 0-10% net. **Sample Titles:** Adult: Hardscrabble fiction of New England, *Erasure*, by Percival Everett. Environment: *Body and Earth*, by Andrea Olsen. Decorative arts: *American Furniture*, by Luke Beckerdite. Women's & Jewish studies: *Jews of Brooklyn*, edited by Ilana Abramovitch and Sean Galvin. **Contact:** Ellen Wicklum, Editor; John Landrigan, Editor.

UPSTART BOOKS
P.O. Box 800, W5527 Hwy.. 106, Fort Atkinson, WI 53538-0800. 920-563-9571.
Web site: www.highsmith.com.
Matt Mulder, Editor.
Description: Publishes activity and curriculum resource books, 48-240 pages, for librarians and teachers of pre-K-12. Focuses on reading activities, Internet skills, library skills, and storytelling activity books. **Number of Books/Yr.:** 15 titles/year (250 submissions), 30% by first-time authors, 100% unagented. **Proposal Process:** Query with outline and sample chapters. Multiple and electronic queries accepted. Hard copy. Response time: 1 month. **Payment:** Royalty. **Tips:** No books for children.

VAN DER PLAS PUBLICATIONS
1282 Seventh Ave., San Francisco, CA 94122. 415-665-8214.
E-mail: rob@vanderplas.net. Web site: www.vanderplas.net.
Description: Publisher of general and sports-related material.

VANDAMERE PRESS

P.O. Box 17446, Clearwater, FL 33762. 727-556-0950.

Jerry Frank, Editor.

Description: History, biography, disability studies, health care issues, military, the nation's capital for a national audience. **Number of Books/Yr.:** 10 titles/year (2,500 submissions), 10% first-time authors, 75% unagented. **Proposal Process:** Query with outline, sample chapters and manuscript, SASE. Multiple queries accepted. No electronic queries. Response time: 1-6 months. **Payment:** Royalty. **Contact:** Art Browa.

VELOPRESS

1830 N 55th St., Boulder, CO 80301. 303-440-0601.

E-mail: velopress@7dogs.com. Web site: www.velopress.com.

Description: Publisher of books for cyclists and multi-sport athletes.

VERSO

180 Varick St., Fl. 10, New York, NY 10014. 212-807-9680.

E-mail: versoinc@aol.com. Web site: www.versobooks.com.

Description: Books with a radical perspective on topics in the social sciences, humanities, and politics. **Proposal Process:** Submit proposal with short overview of book's main themes, table of contents, brief bio of author/contributors, target markets, potential competitors, and intended timetable. Limit proposal to 10 pages; do not send complete manuscript.

VIKING

The Penguin Group/Penguin Putnam Inc.

375 Hudson St., New York, NY 10014. 212-366-2000.

Web site: www.penguinputnam.com.

Description: Publisher of fiction and nonfiction, including psychology, sociology, child-rearing and development, cookbooks, sports, and popular culture. **Proposal Process:** Query. **Payment:** Royalty.

VINTAGE ANCHOR PUBLISHING

The Knopf Publishing Group/Random House, Inc.

299 Park Ave., New York, NY 10171. 212-751-2600.

Web site: www.randomhouse.com.

Martin Asher, Editor-in-Chief.

Description: Adult trade paperbacks and reprints. Quality fiction, serious nonfiction, multicultural, sociology, psychology, philosophy, women's interest, etc. Includes Anchor Books and Vintage Books imprints. **Number of Books/Yr.:** 200 titles/year. Receives 700 queries/year. 5% of books from first-time authors. **Proposal Process:** Accepts agented submissions only.

VITAL HEALTH PUBLISHING

P.O. Box 152, Ridgefield, CT 06877. 914-763-0708.

E-mail: vitalhealth@compuserve.com. Web site: www.vitalhealth.net.

David Richard, Publisher.
Description: Promotes health and wellness through books, videos, and other products that focus on the integration of mind, body, and spirit.

VIZ COMMUNICATIONS, INC.

Shogakukan, 689 Bryant St., San Francisco, CA 94107. 415-546-7073.
E-mail: dallas@viz.com. Web site: www.viz.com.
Description: U.S. publisher of Japanese animation and comics for English-speaking audiences.

VOYAGEUR PRESS

123 N Second St., Stillwater, MN 55082. 651-430-2210.
E-mail: mdregni@voyageurpress.com. Web site: www.voyageurpress.com.
Michael Dregni, Editorial Director.
Description: Books, 15,000-100,000 words, on nature and the environment, country living and farm heritage, travel and photography, and regional history. "Photography—contemporary and/or historical—is very important for most of our books." **Proposal Process:** See guidelines. Query with outline and sample chapters. **Payment:** Royalty.

WALDMAN HOUSE PRESS INC.

525 N Third St., Minneapolis, MN 55401-1201. 612-341-4044.
E-mail: nedw@waldmanhouse.com.
Ned Waldman, Publisher.
Description: Gift books and children's books.

WALKER AND COMPANY

435 Hudson St., New York, NY 10014. 212-727-8300.
Description: Adult nonfiction, focusing on history, science, math, technology, health. Crime fiction. Books for young readers, including picture books, young adult novels. **Number of Books/Yr.:** 60 titles/year, 5% by first-time authors. **Proposal Process:** Query with synopsis and SASE. Multiple queries accepted. No electronic queries. Hard copy. **Payment:** Royalty. **Sample Titles:** Adult Nonfiction: *Galileo's Daughter*, by David Sobel; *E=mc²*, by David Bodanis; *Brunelleshi's Dome*, by Ross King. **Tips:** No adult fiction, poetry, travel, biography, photo books, New Age, or memoirs. **Contact:** Michael Seidman (mysteries), Emily Easton (juvenile), George Gibson (adult nonfiction).

WALTER FOSTER PUBLISHING INC.

23062 La Cadena Dr., Laguna Hills, CA 92653. 949-380-7510.
E-mail: info@walterfoster.com. Web site: www.walterfoster.com.
Barbara Kimmel, Managing Editor.
Description: Titles for artists of all ages and skill levels.

WARNER BOOKS

Time and Life Bldg., 1271 Avenue of the Americas
New York, NY 10020. 212-522-7200.
Web site: www.twbookmark.com.
Maureen Egen, President.
Description: Hardcover, trade paperback and mass market paperback, reprint and original, fiction and nonfiction, audio books and gift books. **Number of Books/Yr.:** 250 titles/year. Publishes book 2 years after acceptance. **Payment:** Royalty. **Sample Titles:** *Up Country*, by Nelson DeMille; *Jack*, by John F. Welch; *A Bend in the Road*, by Nicholas Sparks; *Cane River*, by Lalita Tademy; *Rich Dad, Poor Dad*, by Robert Kiyosaki **Tips:** Does not accept unsolicited manuscripts or proposals.

WARWICK PUBLISHING

Warwick Communications, Inc.
161 Frederick St., Suite 200, Toronto, Ontario M5A 4P3 Canada. 416-596-1555.
E-mail: lisa@warwickgp.com. Web site: www.warwickgp.com.
Description: General-interest nonfiction with a focus on sports, cooking, and personal finance. **Proposal Process:** Send query with brief outline or table of contents, SASE. Responds within 3 months. **Sample Titles:** *Icewine: The Complete Story*, by John Schreiner. **Tips:** Does not accept proposals for fiction, poetry, drama, or children's picture books. **Contact:** Editor.

WASHINGTON STATE UNIVERSITY PRESS

P.O. Box 645910, Pullman, WA 99164-5910. 800-354-7360.
E-mail: wsupress@wsu.edu. Web site: www.wsu.edu/wsupress.
Glen Lindeman, Editor.
Description: Books on Northwest history, prehistory, natural history, culture and politics. 200-500 pages. Focus is on the greater Pacific Northwest region— Washington, Idaho, Oregon, western Montana, British Columbia, and Alaska. **Proposal Process:** Query. **Payment:** Royalty.

WASHINGTON WRITERS PUBLISHING HOUSE

P.O. Box 15271, Washington, DC 20003.
Description: Poetry and fiction by writers in the greater Washington, D.C., and Baltimore area only. SASE for guidelines.

WATSON-GUPTILL PUBLICATIONS

770 Broadway, New York, NY 10003. 646-654-5000.
E-mail: info@watsonguptill.com. Web site: www.watsonguptill.com.
Description: Publisher of illustrated, nonfiction, instructional books on art, photography, graphic design, home decor, crafts, music, film, entertainment, performing arts, popular culture, architecture, interior design. **Proposal Process:** Query to Editorial Department with proposal, detailed outline, author bio, sample text and artwork (no originals). No telephone or e-mail submissions or queries. **Payment:** Royalty. **Tips:** Demonstrate the need in the marketplace for your book. **Contact:** Harriet Pierce.

WAYNE STATE UNIVERSITY PRESS

4809 Woodward Ave., Detroit, MI 48201. 313-577-6131.
Web site: www.wsupress.wayne.edu.
Arthur B. Evans, Director/Acquistions.
Description: Scholarly books only, with rare exceptions in the *Great Lakes Books* series. **Number of Books/Yr.:** 50 titles/year (150 submissions). **Proposal Process:** Send query with complete manuscript, include SASE. Hard copy. No multiple queries. Electronic queries accepted. **Sample Titles:** Series: *African-American Life, American Jewish Civilization, Contemporary Film & Television, Humor in Life and Letters, Kritik: Germany Literary Theory and Culture, Raphael Patai Series in Jewish Folklore and Anthropology,* and the *William Beaumont Series. Urban Studies and Labor* is a developing series. **Tips:** No works of fiction. View Web site for details. **Contact:** Jane Hoehner, Acquisitions Editor.

WELDON OWEN PUBLISHING

814 Montgomery St., San Francisco, CA 94133-5111. 415-291-0100.
E-mail: info@weldonowen.com. Web site: www.weldonowen.com.
Description: High-quality illustrated reference books.

WESLEYAN UNIVERSITY PRESS

110 Mt. Vernon St., Middletown, CT 06459-0433. 860-685-2420.
E-mail: tradko@wesleyan.edu. Web site: www.wesleyan.edu/wespress.
Tom Radko, Director.
Description: Scholarly press focusing on poetry, music, dance, performance arts, and science fiction. Also covers gay/lesbian, gender, cultural, regional, and American studies. **Number of Books/Yr.:** 30 titles/year (1,500 submissions), 1% first-time authors, 97% unagented. **Proposal Process:** Query with outline and sample chapters, SASE. Multiple and electronic queries accepted. Hard copy. Response time: 2-4 weeks. **Payment:** Royalty. **Sample Titles:** *Wesleyan Poetry* series: 64-136 pages. **Tips:** Write for a complete catalog and submission guidelines. **Contact:** Suzanna Tamminen, Editor-in-Chief.

WESTCLIFFE PUBLISHERS

P.O. Box 1261, Englewood, CO 80150-1261. 303-935-0900.
E-mail: editor@westcliffepublishers.com. Web site: www.westcliffepublishers.com.
Description: Publisher of high-quality nature and landscape photography books, trail and travel guides, and books with regional focus. **Proposal Process:** Submit proposal with brief description of concept of book, table of contents, sample chapter(s), bio/resume, and target market. **Contact:** Managing Editor.

WESTVIEW PRESS

Perseus Book Group
5500 Central Ave., Boulder, CO 80301. 303-444-3541.
E-mail: wvproposal@perseusbooks.com. Web site: www.westviewpress.com.

Description: Academic, professional and reference books. **Proposal Process:** Send query via e-mail.

WHITE CLOUD PRESS
P.O. Box 3400, Ashland, OR 97520. 541-488-6415.
E-mail: sscholl@jeffnet.org. Web site: www.whitecloudpress.com.
Steven Scholl, Publisher.
Description: Nonfiction on religion, current events, travel, memoirs, and mythology.
Sample Titles: *The Unlimited Mercifier,* by S. Hirtenstein; *The Garden of Life,* by Stephen Mason

WHITECAP BOOKS
351 Lynn Ave., North Vancouver, British Columbia V7J 2C4 Canada. 604-980-9852.
E-mail: whitecap@whitecap.ca. Web site: www.whitecap.ca.
Robert McCullough.
Description: Juvenile books, 32-84 pages, and adult books, varying lengths, on such topics as natural history, gardening, cookery, and regional subjects. **Proposal Process:** Query with table of contents, synopsis, and 1 sample chapter. **Payment:** Royalty and flat fee.

WHITSTON PUBLISHING COMPANY
1717 Central Ave., Suite 201, Albany, NY 12205. 518-452-1900.
E-mail: whitston@capital.net. Web site: www.whitston.com.
Michael Laddin, Editor.
Description: Publishes nonfiction, scholarly, reference, literary criticism, and anthologies. **Number of Books/Yr.:** 6-12 titles/year (65 submissions), 100% un-agented. **Proposal Process:** Send queries, outlines, sample chapters or manuscripts, and SASE. Multiple or electronic queries accepted. Response time: 2-6 months. Hard-copy format preferred. **Payment:** Royalty. **Sample Titles:** Adult nonfiction: *The Major Essays of Henry David Thoreau; Hugh Kenner: A Bibliography; The Collected Plays of Theodore Dreiser.*

W. WHORTON & COMPANY
1900 E 87th St., Chicago, IL 60617. 773-721-7500.
E-mail: will.horton@gte.net. Web site: www.wwhorton.com.
Description: Publisher of educational books and materials.

WILDCAT CANYON PRESS
2716 Ninth St., Berkeley, CA 94710. 510-848-3600.
E-mail: info@wildcatcanyon.com. Web site: www.wildcatcanyon.com.
Description: Publisher of books on relationships, fashion, self-care, and parenting.

WILDERNESS PRESS
1200 Fifth St., Berkeley, CA 94710. 510-558-1666.
E-mail: mail@wildernesspress.com. Web site: www.wildernesspress.com.

Jannie Dresser, Managing Editor.
Description: Nonfiction books about outdoor activities and travel. **Number of Books/Yr.:** 12 titles/year (250 submissions), 25% by first-time authors, 90% unagented. **Proposal Process:** Query with outline and SASE. Considers multiple or electronic queries. Prefers either electronic, hard-copy format. **Payment:** Royalty, typical is 10-12% of net. No flat fee.

JOHN WILEY & SONS, INC.
605 Third Ave., New York, NY 10158-0012. 212-850-6000.
Web site: www.wiley.com.
Gerard Helferich, Publisher, General Interest Books.
Description: History, biography, memoir, popular science, health, self-improvement, reference, African-American, narrative nonfiction, business, computers, cooking, architecture/graphic design, and children's nonfiction. **Number of Books/Yr.:** 1,500 titles/year. **Proposal Process:** Query with outline. Response time: 2 weeks-1 month. Multiple queries accepted. Prefer electronic format. **Payment:** Royalty, range varies. **Sample Titles:** Adult: *The Inextinguishable Symphony: A True Story of Love and Music in Nazi Germany,* by Martin Goldsmith. *The Power of Gold: The History of an Obsession,* by Peter L. Bernstein. *Splendid Soups,* by James Peterson. *The Scientific American Science Desk Reference.* Children's: *New York Public Library Amazing Explorers,* by Brendon January. *Revolutionary War Days,* by David C. King.

WILEY/HALSTED
John Wiley & Sons
605 Third Ave., New York, NY 10158-6000. 212-850-6000.
Description: Publishes textbooks, educational materials, and reference books. **Proposal Process:** Query. **Payment:** Royalty.

WILLOW CREEK PRESS
P.O. Box 147, Minocqua, WI 54548. 715-358-7010.
E-mail: books@willowcreekpress.com. Web site: www.willowcreekpress.com.
Andrea Donner, Editor.
Description: Nonfiction publisher whose books are most generally related to the outdoors, wildlife, pets, hunting, fishing and cooking. Books, 25,000-50,000 words. **Number of Books/Yr.:** 20 titles/year, 30% first-time authors, 80% unagented. **Proposal Process:** Send an outline and sample of the actual work—not just a query letter, and SASE. Multiple queries accepted. No electronic queries. Hard copy. Response time: 4-6 weeks. **Payment:** Royalty. **Sample Titles:** Gift books: *What Dogs Teach Us, 101 Uses for a Lab.* Outdoor books: *Fishing the National Parks, Bear vs. Man.* Pets: *The 10-Minute Retriever, Urban Dog.* **Tips:** Avoid long letters explaining your work and what will be written; let the writing speak for itself.

WILSHIRE BOOK COMPANY
12015 Sherman Rd., N. Hollywood, CA 91605-3781. 818-765-8579.
E-mail: mpowers@mpowers.com. Web site: www.mpowers.com.

Marcia Grad, Editorial Director.

Description: Publishes materials on self-help, motivation, psychology, recovery, adult fables, how-to, etc. Looking for adult fables that teach principles of psychological and/or spiritual growth, 30,000-60,000 words. **Number of Books/Yr.:** 25 titles/year (2,500 submissions), 80% by first-time authors, 90% unagented. **Proposal Process:** Query with complete manuscript. Multiple and electronic queries accepted. Hard copy. Response time: 2 months. **Payment:** Royalty. **Sample Titles:** Two bestsellers: *The Knight in Rusty Armor,* by Robert Fisher; and *The Princess Who Believed in Fairy Tales,* by Marcia Grad. **Tips:** Welcomes phone calls to discuss a manuscript.

WINDHAM BAY PRESS

P.O. Box 1198, Occidental, CA 95465-1198. 707-823-7150.

E-mail: ellnsearby@aol.com.

Description: Publishes travel guidebooks. **Tips:** Does not solicit manuscripts.

WINDSWEPT HOUSE PUBLISHERS

P.O. Box 159, Mount Desert, ME 04660. 207-244-5027.

E-mail: windswt@acadia.net. Web site: www.booknotes.com/windswept.

Mavis Weinberger, Acquisitions Editor.

Description: Adult and children's books (all ages), mostly relating to the Maine/New England region: novels, poetry, nature, history. **Number of Books/Yr.:** 4 titles/year. **Proposal Process:** No unsolicited manuscripts. Send SASE for guidelines. **Payment:** Royalty, to 10%. No flat fee. **Tips:** Children's books needing pictures should come complete with illustrations.

WINE APPRECIATION GUILD

360 Swift Ave., South San Francisco, CA 94080. 415-866-3020.

E-mail: info@wineappreciation.com. Web site: www.wineappreciation.com.

Description: Publishes books on wine.

WOODBINE HOUSE

6510 Bells Mill Rd., Bethesda, MD 20817. 301-897-3570.

E-mail: info@woodbinehouse.com. Web site: www.woodbinehouse.com.

Nancy Gray Paul, Acquisitions Editor.

Description: Publishes books for or about children with disabilities only. Current needs include parenting, reference, special education, and chapter books for young readers. **Proposal Process:** Query or submit complete manuscript with SASE. Guidelines. **Payment:** Royalty.

WORDWARE PUBLISHING

2320 Los Rio Blvd., Suite 200, Plano, TX 75074. 972-423-0090 .

E-mail: gbivona@wordware.com. Web site: www.republicoftexaspress.com.

Ginnie Bivona, Acquisitions Editor.

Description: Publishes books related to Texas, history, ghost stories, humor, travel guides, and general interest topics. No fiction or poetry. **Number of Books/Yr.:** 30 titles/year (100+ submissions), 50% by first-time authors, 90% unagented. **Proposal Process:** Query with outline and include SASE. Multiple and electronic queries accepted. Hard-copy format preferred. **Payment:** Royalty. **Sample Titles:** Wordware Computer Books **Tips:** Looking for interesting, entertaining books for the mainstream reader. We do not publish family memoirs unless they are famous, or better yet, infamous.

WORKMAN PUBLISHING CO., INC.

708 Broadway, New York, NY 10003-9555. 212-254-5900.
Web site: www.workman.com.
Susan Bolotin, Editorial Director.
Description: Publisher of nonfiction and calendars for adult and juvenile markets. **Number of Books/Yr.:** 40 titles/year. **Proposal Process:** Query with outline and sample chapters, include SASE. Considers multiple queries. No electronic queries. Response time: varies. Prefers hard-copy format. **Payment:** Royalty or flat fee, range varies. **Tips:** See Web site for details.

WORLD ALMANAC BOOKS

World Almanac Education Group
512 Seventh Ave., New York, NY 10018. 646-312-6000.
E-mail: walmanac@aol.com.
Description: Reference books.

WORLD LEISURE CORPORATION

177 Paris St., Boston, MA 02128. 617-569-1966.
E-mail: editor@worldleisure.com. Web site: www.worldleisure.com.
Description: Articles on skiing, family travel, vacations, etc.

WORLDWIDE LIBRARY

225 Duncan Mill Rd., Don Mills, Ontario M3B 3K9 Canada. 416-445-5860.
E-mail: feroze_mohammed@harlequin.ca.
Randall Toye, Editorial Director.
Description: Action adventure, paramilitary adventure, science fiction, and post-nuclear holocaust fiction. **Number of Books/Yr.:** 36 titles/year, 1% by first-time authors, 99% unagented. **Proposal Process:** Query with outline and sample chapters. Response time: 3 months. Multiple queries accepted. No electronic queries. Hard copy. **Payment:** Flat fee. Typical range: $3,000-$6,000. **Sample Titles:** Adult: *The Executioner, Deathlands, Outlanders, Stonyman, The Destroyer, SuperBolan.*

YALE UNIVERSITY PRESS

302 Temple St., New Haven, CT 06520-9040. 203-432-0960.
Web site: www.yale.edu/yup/.
Jonathon Brent, Editorial Director.

Description: Adult nonfiction; 400 manuscript pages. **Proposal Process:** Query. **Payment:** Royalty. **Contact:** Gretchen Ring, Assistant.

YANKEE PUBLISHING, INC.

P.O. Box 520, Dublin, NH 03444. 603-563-8111.
E-mail: queries@yankeepub.com. Web site: www.almanac.com.
Judson D. Hale, Sr., Editor-in-Chief.
Description: Publishes *The Old Farmer's Almanac.*

YMAA

4354 Washington St., Roslindale, MA 02131. 617-323-7215.
E-mail: ymaa@aol.com. Web site: www.ymaa.com.
Description: Publishes titles on Asian healing, health, spirituality, and martial art disciplines.

ZOO PRESS

P.O. Box 22990, Lincoln, NE 68542. 402-770-8104.
E-mail: editors@zoopress.org.
Description: Small book publisher that strives to expose the best emerging writers. Promotes work that displays originality, integrity, authenticity, and aesthetic beauty. **Number of Books/Yr.:** 10 titles/yr. **Proposal Process:** Send cover letter and one copy of each manuscript. Also include title page with contact info and table of contents. SASE. **Tips:** Also offers two contests: The Paris Review Prize in Poetry and The Kenyon Review Prize in Poetry for a First Book.

JUVENILE BOOKS

Children's book publishing is big business, and getting bigger. With the blockbuster sales of the *Harry Potter* series by author J. K. Rowling, writing children's books has once again been shown to be a legitimate avenue to literary fame and, on occasion, fortune. In fact, curiously, some studies suggest that many children's books are sold to adults who intend to keep the books for themselves, making the question of what makes a children's book hit the bestseller lists an interesting one. For instance, the Dr. Seuss book, *Oh, The Places You'll Go!*, is a perennial favorite as a college graduation gift, although the sales show up in the children's book category.

The market for juvenile books is very diverse. Children's books range from colorful board books for toddlers to social-realism novels for young adults on subjects that just a few decades ago were taboo. Many books are issued in series, while others are released as stand-alone titles.

However, as in all areas of publishing, while there is tremendous diversity across the field, there is also increasing specialization by individual publishers. Each seeks to find its own profitable niche within that broad expanse of interest.

Before sending off materials, it is important to study each publisher under consideration very carefully. Start by getting a copy of their guidelines for author queries and submissions; often these can be found on their Web site. Also, request a catalog.

The publisher's catalog is one of the best vehicles to understand precisely the kind of books a publisher is acquiring. A marketing tool, a publisher's catalog reveals the special appeal that each book holds for the publisher and—it hopes—for bookstore buyers, librarians, and many eventual readers. A publisher's catalog tells how each book is different from (or similar to) others in the field. Reading a catalog carefully can help you understand clearly the kind of books a publisher is seeking.

As always, before you send a query letter or other materials, you may wish to get the name of the current editor at the publishing house who is in charge of the particular line or type of book that you are proposing. If this information is not available on the Web site, make a very brief phone call. Explain your project in just one or two sentences, ask whom to send the query (or manuscript) to, confirm the address, and then thank the receptionist and hang up. Do not try to harangue an editor or pitch your proposal on the phone; a busy editor seldom has time to listen to your idea, and you will not be as convincing as you can be by presenting a professional, well-written query that can be studied in leisure. Trying to pitch an idea on the phone is usually just the best way to annoy an editor.

Be polite, be professional, and remember to target your writing, making sure the language, style, and content are appropriate to your target readers.

ABBEVILLE PUBLISHING GROUP
116 W 23rd St., Suite 500, New York, NY 10011. 646-375-2039.
Web site: www.abbeville.com.
Description: Publisher of fine art and illustrated books. Books cover a wide variety of subjects including art/architecture, children's, decorative arts, design, music/media,

animals, sports, gardening, travel, etc. **Proposal Process:** Does not accept unsolicited submissions or proposals.

ABDO PUBLISHING
4940 Viking Drive., Suite 622, Edina, MN 55435. 612-831-1317.
Web site: www.abdopub.com.
Description: Children's nonfiction books from ages 0-12.

ACCORD PUBLISHING LTD.
1732 Wazee St., Suite 202, Denver, CO 80202-1284. 303-298-1300.
Web site: www.accordpublishing.com.
Ken Fleck, Editor.
Description: Publisher of children's books, calendars, and educational materials.

ADVANCE PUBLISHING
6950 Fulton St., Houston, TX 77022. 713-695-0600.
E-mail: info@advancepublishing.com. Web site: www.advancepublishing.com.
Description: Publisher of children's picture books, junior biographies, and educational texts and materials.

ALL 50 STATES
P.O. Box 10130, Golden Valley, AZ 86413-2130. 520-565-2336.
Description: Educational materials.

ALL ABOUT KIDS PUBLISHING
6280 San Ignacio Ave., Suite C, San Jose, CA 95119. 408-578-4026.
Web site: www.aakp.com.
Description: Publishes picture books, board books, chapter books, educational books, and how-to books.

ATHENEUM BOOKS FOR YOUNG READERS
Simon & Schuster Children's Publishing/Simon & Schuster, Inc.
1230 Avenue of the Americas, New York, NY 10020. 212-698-7200.
Web site: www.simonsays.com.
Description: Picture books, juvenile fiction, and nonfiction as well as illustrated collections. Query. No unsolicited manuscripts.

AVISSON PRESS, INC.
3007 Taliaferro Rd., Greensboro, NC 27408. 336-288-6989.
Martin L. Hester, Editor.
Description: Young adult biography only. Some literary topics and books by assignment only. **Number of Books/Yr.:** 6-8 titles/year (750 submissions), 25% first-time authors, 80% unagented. **Proposal Process:** Query with outline or sample chapter, bio and SASE. Hard-copy format preferred. Multiple queries accepted. No electronic queries. Response time: 2 weeks. **Payment:** Royalty. **Sample Titles:** *The*

Experimenters: Twelve Great Chemists; *Eight Who Made a Difference: Pioneer Women in the Arts*; *Prince of the Fairway: The Tiger Woods Story*. **Tips:** Young adult biography, collective biography. Women/minorities especially, but any good subject matter.

BENCHMARK BOOKS

Marshall Cavendish
99 White Plains Rd., P.O. Box 2001, Tarrytown, NY 1059. 914-332-8888.
Web site: www.marshallcavendish.com.
Kate Nunn, Editorial Director.
Description: Nonfiction school and library books for children K-8. **Number of Books/Yr.:** 120 titles/year, 5% first-time authors, 75% unagented. **Proposal Process:** Send query, outline, and sample chapters. Multiple queries okay. No electronic queries. Hard-copy format preferred. SASE required. **Payment:** Royalty. **Tips:** Quality treatment of curriculum-related topics. Series only; no single titles. **Contact:** Joyce Stanton, Angela Cabalano, Doug Sanders.

BIG GUY BOOKS, INC.

523 Encinitas Blvd., Suite 107, Encinitas, CA 92024. 760-944-0133.
E-mail: info@bigguybooks.com. Web site: www.timesoldiers.com.
Description: Picture/adventure books.

BLACK BUTTERFLY CHILDREN'S BOOKS

Writers and Readers Publishing, Inc.
62 E Starrs Plain Rd., Danbury, CT 06810. 203-744-6010.
Deborah Dyson, Editor.
Description: Titles featuring black children and other children of color, ages 9-13, for *Young Beginners* series. Picture books for children to age 11; board books for toddlers. Query. Royalty.

BLOOMSBURY CHILDREN'S BOOKS

Bloomsbury Publishing PLC, 175 Fifth Ave., Fl. 3, New York, NY 10010.
Victoria Wells Arms, Editorial Director.
Description: Publisher of picture books, literary nonfiction, and middle-grade/young adult fiction, such as mysteries and historical fiction.

THE BLUE SKY PRESS

Scholastic Inc.
555 Broadway, New York, NY 10012. 212-343-6100.
Web site: www.scholastic.com.
Bonnie Verburg, Editorial Director.
Description: Fantasy, fairy tales, folklore, adventure.

BOOKS FOR YOUNG READERS

Henry Holt and Company
115 W 18th St., New York, NY 10011.

E-mail: info@henryholt.com. Web site: www.henryholt.com/byr.
Description: Publishes a wide variety of books for children of all ages including picture books, fiction, and nonfiction. **Tips:** Manuscript should be typed and double-spaced. Complete manuscripts preferred. Do not submit textbooks or manuscripts written by children. Query letter and SASE required. Do not send original art.

BOYDS MILLS PRESS
815 Church St., Honesdale, PA 18431. 570-253-1164.
Web site: www.boydsmillspress.com.
Kathryn Yerkes, Manuscript Coordinator.
Description: Children's books of literary merit, from picture books to novels. **Number of Books/Yr.:** 50 titles/year (8,500 submissions), 40% first-time authors, 60% unagented. **Proposal Process:** Send outline and sample chapters for young adult novels and nonfiction, complete manuscripts for all other categories. Response time: 30 days. Hard copy preferred, electronic format okay. No multiple queries. **Payment:** Varies. **Tips:** Varied literary fiction. Avoid well-worn themes; no series or romances.

CANDLEWICK PRESS
2067 Massachusetts Ave., Cambridge, MA 02140. 617-661-3330.
E-mail: bigbear@candlewick.com. Web site: www.candlewick.com.
Karen Lotz, Publisher; Elizabeth Bicknell, Editorial Director.
Description: Publisher of high-quality children's books and young adult fiction. Also publishes picture books for ages birth through 8. **Tips:** Humorous and/or non-rhyming picture-book texts about universal childhood experiences. High-quality literary fiction for older readers. Currently not accepting unsolicited manuscripts.

CAPSTONE PRESS, INC.
P.O. Box 669, Mankato, MN 56001. 952-352-0024.
E-mail: freelance.writing@capstone-press.com. Web site: www.capstone-press.com.
Helen Moore, Acquisitions Editor.
Description: Nonfiction children's books for schools and libraries. Content includes curriculum-oriented topics, sports, and pleasure-reading materials. **Number of Books/Yr.:** 250 titles/year, 5-10% first-time authors, 99% unagented. **Proposal Process:** Query only, does not accept submissions or proposals. No multiple queries. Response time: 4-6 weeks. Electronic queries okay for potential assignments. Either electronic or hard-copy format. **Payment:** Flat fee. **Sample Titles:** Grades 3-9, *Stealth Bombers: The B-2 Spirits*, by Bill Sweetman; grades 2-6, *The Boyhood Diary of Charles Lindbergh*, by Megan O'Hara; grades 1-5, *Greece*, by Janet Rienecky; grades K-3, *Frogs: Leaping Amphibians*, by Adele Richardson. **Tips:** No fiction or poetry. We do hire freelance authors to write titles on assignment.

CAROLRHODA BOOKS, INC.
A Division of Lerner Publishing Group
241 First Ave. N, Minneapolis, MN 55401. 612-332-3344.

Web site: www.lernerbooks.com.

Rebecca Poole, Submissions Editor.

Description: Complete manuscripts for ages 4-12: biography, science, nature, history, photo-essays, and historical fiction. Guidelines available. Hardcover. **Proposal Process:** Submissions are accepted in the months of March and October only. Work received in any other month will be returned unopened. SASE required for authors who wish to have their material returned. Please allow 2 to 6 months for response. No phone calls.

CARTWHEEL BOOKS

Scholastic, Inc.

557 Broadway, New York, NY 10012. 212-343-6100.

Web site: www.scholastic.com.

Ken Geist, Editorial Director.

Description: Picture, novelty, and easy-to-read books, to about 1,000 words, for children, preschool to third grade. No novels or chapter books. Royalty or flat fee.

CHARLESBRIDGE PUBLISHING

85 Main St., Watertown, MA 02472. 617-926-0329.

E-mail: tradeeditorial@charlesbridge.com. Web site: www.charlesbridge.com.

Description: Nonfiction and fiction children's picture books. Children's nonfiction picture books under Charlesbridge imprint, fiction picture books under Talewinds or Whispering Coyote imprints. **Number of Books/Yr.:** 25 titles/year (2,500-3,000 submissions), 10% first-time authors, 20% unagented. **Proposal Process:** Send complete manuscript. Exclusive submissions only: must indicate on envelope and cover letter. Include SASE. Hard copy. **Payment:** Royalty or flat fee. **Tips:** Not acquiring board books, folk tales, alphabet books, or nursery rhymes at this time.

CHELSEA HOUSE PUBLISHERS

1974 Sproul Rd., Suite 400, Broomall, PA 19008. 610-353-5166.

E-mail: sue_naab@chelseahouse.com. Web site: www.chelseahouse.com.

Sally Cheney, Editorial Director.

Description: Leading publisher of quality nonfiction books for children and young adults. Features biographies, sports, multicultural studies, science, and high school/college-level literary criticism. Age range is 8-15 years for most materials with the exception of literary criticism, which is geared for readers of high school level and up. **Number of Books/Yr.:** 350 titles/year (500+ submissions), 25% first-time authors, 98% unagented. **Proposal Process:** No unsolicited manuscripts. Query with outline and 2 sample chapters. Only send complete manuscript if asked to. Include SASE. Accepts multiple and electronic queries. Electronic format preferred. **Payment:** Pays flat fee ($1,500-$3,500). **Sample Titles:** Award-winning series include: *Your Government: How It Works*; *21st Century Health & Wellness*; *Crime, Justice & Punishment*; *Galaxy of Superstars*; *Black Americans of Achievement*. **Tips:** No autobiographical or fictionalized biography. Writing should be clear and direct, but lively. **Contact:** Sue Naab.

CHILD AND FAMILY PRESS

Child Welfare League of America
440 First St. NW, Fl. 3, Washington, DC 20001-2085. 202-942-0263.
E-mail: ptierney@cwla.org. Web site: www.cwla.org.
Peggy Porter Tierney, Assistant Director.
Description: Positive, upbeat picture books for children. **Number of Books/Yr.:** 20 titles/year (100 submissions), 50% first-time authors, 100% unagented. **Proposal Process:** Send complete manuscript. Multiple and electronic queries are considered. Response time: 3 months. Hard-copy format preferred. **Payment:** Royalty. **Tips:** "Avoid anything too cutesy, moralistic, or patronizing."

CHILDREN'S BOOK PRESS

2211 Mission St., San Francisco, CA 94110. 415-821-3080.
E-mail: cbookpress@cbookpress.org. Web site: www.cbookpress.org.
Ina Cumpiano, Senior Editor.
Description: Bilingual and multicultural picture books, 750-1,500 words, for children in grades K-6. Publishes contemporary stories reflecting the traditions and culture of minorities and new immigrants in the U.S. Seeks to help encourage a more international, multicultural perspective on the part of all young people. Query. **Payment:** Advance on royalty. **Tips:** See Web site for specific guidelines.

CHILDREN'S PRESS

Scholastic, Inc.
90 Sherman Turnpike, Danbury, CT 06816. 203-797-3500.
Web site: www.grolier.com.
John Sefridge, Publisher.
Description: Science, social studies, and biography, to 25,000 words, for supplementary use in libraries and classrooms. Royalty or outright purchase. Currently overstocked; not accepting unsolicited manuscripts. No phone inquiries.

CHOUETTE PUBLISHING

4710 Rue Saint-Ambroise, Montreal, Quebec H4C 2C7 Canada. 514-925-3325.
E-mail: lucie.rochette@editions-chouette.com.
Lucie Rochette, Editor.
Description: Picture and activity books for children.

CLARION BOOKS

A Division of Houghton Mifflin Co.
215 Park Ave. S, New York, NY 10003. 212-420-5889.
Web site: www.hmco.com.
Dinah Stevenson, Editorial Director and Associate Publisher/Vice President.
Description: Publishes picture books, nonfiction, and fiction for infants-grade12. **Number of Books/Yr.:** 50-60 titles/year (1,000+ submissions), 5% first-time authors, 50-75% unagented. **Proposal Process:** Send query with complete manuscript. No unsolicited material. Multiple queries okay. No electronic queries. Hard-copy format

preferred. **Payment:** Royalty. **Contact:** Michele Coppola, Editor; Jennifer Greene, Editor; Julie Strauss-Gabel, Associate Editor.

COUNCIL FOR INDIAN EDUCATION

2032 Woody Dr., Billings, MT 59102. 406-652-7398.
E-mail: hapcie@aol.com. Web site: www.cie-mt.org.
Hap Gilliland, Editor.
Description: Books dealing with Native American life and culture for children ages 5-18. Fiction, nonfiction, and young adult books, 100-300 pages. **Number of Books/Yr.:** 6 titles/year (100 submissions), 75% by first-time authors, 100% unagented. **Proposal Process:** Query with complete manuscript. Hard-copy format preferred. Response time: 3 months. Multiple queries okay. No electronic queries. **Payment:** Flat fee for short stories in anthologies; royalty for books. **Tips:** Authentic Native American life (past or present) with good plot. No profanity, no condescending material for any culture. Books evaluated for authentic lifestyle by 20-member Intertribal Indian board.

CRABTREE PUBLISHING COMPANY

PMB 16A, 350 Fifth Ave., Suite 3308, New York, NY 10118. 800-387-7650.
Web site: www.crabtreebooks.com.
Description: Colorful nonfiction children's books featuring sports, science, social studies, art, and biographies.

CREATIVE TEACHING PRESS

15342 Graham St., Huntington Beach, CA 92649-1111. 714-895-5047.
E-mail: webmaster@creativeteaching.com. Web site: www.creativeteaching.com.
Description: Publisher of educational books and materials.

CRICKET BOOKS

Carus Publishing Co.
332 S Michigan Ave., Suite 1100, Chicago, IL 60604. 312-939-1500.
Web site: www.cricketbooks.net.
Description: Publishes picture books, chapter books, and middle-grade novels for children ages 7-14. Marc Aronson, Acquisitions Editor, will be handling fiction and nonfiction for teenagers. **Number of Books/Yr.:** 25 titles/year (1,500 submissions), some first-time and unagented authors. **Proposal Process:** Nonfiction: send query with outline and sample chapters, include SASE. Fiction: send query with outline and complete manuscript, include SASE. Response time: 2 months for proposals/ 3 months for manuscripts. Considers multiple queries. No electronic queries. Prefers hard-copy format. **Payment:** Royalty, typical range 10%. **Sample Titles:** *John Riley's Daughter*; *Scorpio's Child*, by Kezi Mathews; *Seek*, by Paul Fleischman. **Tips:** Check recent titles for guidance. Avoid talking animals who are learning to accept that they are "different." No religious messages. **Contact:** Carol Saller, Editor.

CROWN BOOKS FOR YOUNG READERS

Random House Children's Media Group/Random House, Inc.
1540 Broadway, Fl. 19, New York, NY 10036. 212-782-9000.
Web site: www.randomhouse.com.
Description: Children's nonfiction (science, sports, nature, music, and history) and picture books for ages 3 and up. Send complete manuscript and SASE for picture books. **Contact:** Editorial Department.

DAWN PUBLICATIONS

P.O. Box 2010, Nevada City, CA 95959. 800-545-7475.
Web site: www.dawnpub.com.
Glenn J. Hovemann, Editor.
Description: Nature-awareness/natural science illustrated picture books for children. No talking animals, fantasies, or legends. No e-mail submissions. Writer's guidelines available on Web site. **Number of Books/Yr.:** 6 (60% first-time authors). **Proposal Process:** Submit complete manuscript. Response 2-3 months. Hard copy only. **Payment:** Royalty. **Sample Titles:** *Salmon Stream*; *Earth and You*.

DIAL BOOKS FOR YOUNG READERS

Penguin Putnam Books for Young Readers/Penguin Putnam Inc.
345 Hudson St., New York, NY 10014.
Web site: www.penguinputnam.com.
Lauri Hornik, Editorial Director.
Description: Lively, unique picture books for children ages 2-8, and middle grade and young adult novels. Send complete manuscript for picture books; outline and two sample chapters for novels.

DOVER PUBLICATIONS

31 E Second St., Mineola, NY 11501. 516-294-7000.
Description: Publisher of books on art, crafts, music, etc.

DUTTON CHILDREN'S BOOKS

Penguin Putnam Books for Young Readers/Penguin Putnam Inc.
345 Hudson St., New York, NY 10014. 212-414-3700.
Web site: www.penguinputnam.com.
Stephanie Owens Lurie, Publisher.
Description: Publishes trade children's books for ages 0-18. Publisher's list includes board books, picture books, early readers, chapter books, novels, and nonfiction. Titles are sold to bookstores, schools, and libraries. **Tips:** Seeking clever wordsmiths who can tell a compelling story, with distinctive style and memorable characters that learn or change in the course of the story. **Contact:** Stephanie Owens Lurie.

EARLY CHILDHOOD PUBLICATIONS

337 Country Rd. 965, Green Forest, AR 72638. 870-553-2575.
Description: Publisher of learning materials.

EDC PUBLISHING
10302 E 55th Pl., Tulsa, OK 74146.
Web site: www.edcpub.com.
Description: Publisher of educational materials.

EDUPRESS
208 Avenida Fabricante, Suite 200, San Clemente, CA 92672. 949-366-9499.
Web site: www.edupressinc.com.
Description: Publishes hands-on, educational activities and materials. **Contact:** Amanda Meinke.

EERDMANS BOOKS FOR YOUNG READERS
William B. Eerdmans Publishing Co.
255 Jefferson Ave. SE, Grand Rapids, MI 99503. 616-459-4591.
Web site: www.eerdmans.com/youngreaders.
Judy Zylstra, Editor-in-Chief.
Description: High-quality picture books, novels, and biographies for all ages (preschool though young adult). Some titles have spiritual themes; others deal with historical events or social concerns. Seeking stories with depth, "tales worth telling," works that delight in life's joys, but also works that offer honest hope and comfort in the face of life's challenges. **Number of Books/Yr.:** 12-15/year; 3,000 submissions. **Proposal Process:** Typed, double-spaced. Send complete mss for picture books and those under 200 pages. For longer books, send query letter and 3-4 sample chapters. Responds in 2-3 months.

ENSLOW PUBLISHERS, INC.
40 Industrial Rd., P.O. Box 398, Berkeley Heights, NJ 07922-0398. 908-771-9400.
Web site: www.enslow.com.
Description: Focuses on books for young adults for schools and public libraries. Nonfiction books: primarily biography, social issue or science-related, and back-to-school curriculum. No fiction or picture books. **Number of Books/Yr.:** 175 titles/year, 50% first-time writers, 99% unagented. **Proposal Process:** Send query with outline and sample chapters. No electronic or multiple queries. Prefers hardcopy format. **Payment:** Royalty or flat fee. **Tips:** Always seeking new or established authors who can write nonfiction in interesting and exciting manner. Propose a new title for an existing series, or possibly a new series idea.

EVAN-MOOR EDUCATIONAL PUBLISHERS
18 Lower Ragsdale Dr., Monterey, CA 93940. 831-649-5901.
Web site: www.evan-moor.com.
Description: Instructional materials for grades Pre-K-6.

FIREFLY BOOKS LTD.
3680 Victoria Park Ave., Willowdale, Ontario M2H 3K1 Canada. 416-499-8412.
E-mail: valerie@fireflybooks.com. Web site: www.fireflybooks.com.

Valerie Hatton, Publicity Manager.
Description: Publishes books on a variety of topics including cooking, gardening, astronomy, health, natural history, reference, and sports. Also publishes children's books and calendars.

FITZHENRY & WHITESIDE
195 Allstate Pkwy., Markham, Ontario L3R 4T8 Canada. 905-477-9700.
Web site: www.fitzhenry.ca.
Description: Publisher of reference, natural science, and children's books.

FRANKLIN WATTS
Scholastic, Inc.
90 Sherman Turnpike, Danbury, CT 06813. 203-797-3500.
Web site: www.publishing.grolier.com.
Description: Curriculum-oriented nonfiction for grades K-12, including science, history, social studies, and biography. No unsolicited submissions.

FREE SPIRIT PUBLISHING
217 Fifth Ave. N, Suite 200, Minneapolis, MN 55401-1724. 612-338-2068.
E-mail: help4kids@freespirit.com. Web site: www.freespirit.com.
Description: Award-winning publisher of books for parents, teens, educators, counselors and everyone else who cares about kids.

FRONT STREET, INC.
20 Battery Park Ave., Suite 403, Asheville, NC 28801. 828-236-3097.
E-mail: contactus@frontstreetbooks.com. Web site: www.frontstreetbooks.com.
Joy Neaves, Editor.
Description: An independent publisher of books for children and young adults.
Number of Books/Yr.: 10-15 titles/year, 30% by first-time authors, 90% unagented.
Proposal Process: Check Web site for submission guidelines. **Payment:** Royalty.
Tips: Currently not accepting picture book manuscripts that are not accompanied by illustrations.

GARETH STEVENS PUBLISHING
330 West Olive St., Suite 100, Milwaukee, WI 53212. 414-332-3520.
E-mail: info@gspub.com. Web site: www.garethstevens.com.
Mark Sachner, Creative Director.
Description: Publisher of quality educational children's books.

GIRL PRESS
P.O. Box 480389, Los Angeles, CA 90048. 323-822-0044.
Web site: www.girlpress.com.
Description: Dedicated to making strong books for teenage girls. Nonfiction, biography, instructional titles. **Tips:** Seeking new ideas and new writers, in fiction.

GREENE BARK PRESS INC.

P.O. Box 1108, Bridgeport, CT 06601-1108. 203-372-4861.
Web site: www.greenebarkpress.com.
Thomas J. Greene, Publisher.
Description: Publisher of children's picture books for ages 3-9. **Number of Books/Yr.:** 1-6. **Proposal Process:** Send cover letter with brief synopsis including the authors' background, name, address, etc. Send colorful copies of artwork (do not send originals) if available. Include SASE for response. **Payment:** Does not give royalty advances. Authors are given 10% royalty; illustrators are either paid flat fee or royalty between 3%-5%. **Tips:** Prefers artwork to accompany manuscript, but will not disqualify submissions without art. Do not send queries by telephone, fax, or e-mail. Rarely publishes juvenile novels.

GREENWILLOW BOOKS

HarperCollins Publishers
1350 Avenue of the Americas, New York, NY 10019. 212-261-6627.
Web site: www.harperchildrens.com.
Description: Children's books and picture books for all ages. Fiction and nonfiction. Currently not accepting unsolicited manuscripts or queries. Please call after April 1, 2002, for an update. **Number of Books/Yr.:** 50 titles per year, with 90% unagented authors; 2% first-time authors. **Proposal Process:** For novels: query with a synopsis and sample chapters. Submit complete manuscript for picture books. Submit in hard copy only. **Payment:** Royalty.

GROSSET & DUNLAP PUBLISHERS

Penguin Putnam Books for Young Readers/Penguin Putnam Inc.
345 Hudson St., New York, NY 10014.
Web site: www.penguinputnam.com.
Debra Dorfman, President.
Description: Mass-market children's books. Not accepting unsolicited manuscripts. Royalty.

HARCOURT INC./CHILDREN'S BOOK DIVISION

525 B St., Suite 1900, San Diego, CA 92101-4495. 619-261-6616.
Web site: www.harcourtbooks.com/childrens/childrn.html.
Description: Juvenile fiction and nonfiction for beginning readers through young adults. Imprints include Gulliver Books, Red Wagon Books, Odyssey Classics, Silver Whistle, Magic Carpet Books, Harcourt Children's Books, Harcourt Young Classics, Green Light Readers, Harcourt Paperbacks, Voyager Books/Libros Viajeros. No unsolicited submissions or queries.

HARPERCOLLINS CHILDREN'S BOOKS

HarperCollins Publishers
1350 Avenue of the Americas, New York, NY 10019. 212-261-6500.
Web site: www.harpercollins.com.

Kate Morgan Jackson, Editor-in-Chief.
Description: Picture books, chapter books, and fiction and nonfiction for middle-grade and young adult readers. Imprints (Avon, HarperFestival, HarperTempest, HarperTrophy, Joanna Cotler Books, Laura Geringer Books, and Greenwillow Books) are committed to producing imaginative and responsible children's books. From preschool to young adult titles. Royalty.

HOLIDAY HOUSE, INC.
425 Madison Ave., New York, NY 10017. 212-688-0085.
Suzanne Reinoehl, Acquisitions.
Description: General juvenile fiction and nonfiction. Query with SASE. Royalty. Hardcover only. **Number of Books/Yr.:** 60 titles/year. Receives 3,000 submissions/year. 2-5% of books from first-time authors; 50% unagented. **Payment:** Royalty.

HOUGHTON MIFFLIN CO./TRADE & REFERENCE DIVISION
222 Berkeley St., Boston, MA 02116-3764. 617-351-5000.
Web site: www.hmco.com.
Description: Quality adult and children's fiction, nonfiction, and reference materials. Imprints include Houghton Mifflin, Mariner, Clarion, American Heritage, Chambers, Larousse, and Kingfisher.

HUMANICS PUBLISHING GROUP
P.O. Box 7400, Atlanta, GA 30357. 404-874-1930.
E-mail: humanics@mindspring.com. Web site: www.humanicspub.com.
W. Arthur Bligh, Editor.
Description: Self-help, philosophy, spirituality. Teacher resource (pre-K to 3). **Number of Books/Yr.:** 20 titles/year (600 submissions), 70% first-time authors, 90% unagented. **Proposal Process:** Query with outline, sample chapters and SASE. Electronic queries accepted. No multiple queries. Hard copy. **Payment:** Royalty. **Tips:** Interested in books that provide help, guidance, and inspiration.

HYPERION
77 W 66th St., New York, NY 10023. 212-456-0114.
Will Schwalbe, Editor-in-Chief.
Description: Material accepted from agents only. No unsolicited manuscripts or queries considered.

ILLUMINATION ARTS PUBLISHING
13256 Northup Way, Suite 9, P.O. Box 1865, Bellevue, WA 98009. 425-644-7185.
Web site: www.illumin.com.
Description: Publishes uplifting/spiritual children's picture books.

SARA JORDAN PUBLISHING

P.O. Box 490, Niagara Falls, NY 14302-0490. 905-938-5050.
Web site: www.songsthatteach.com.
Description: Publisher of educational materials with particular emphasis on music and songs that teach. Does not accept unsolicited manuscripts or illustrations.

JUST US BOOKS

356 Glenwood Ave., East Orange, NJ 07017. 973-672-7701.
E-mail: justusbook@aol.com. Web site: www.justusbooks.com.
Cheryl Willis Hudson, Editorial Director.
Description: Specializes in children's books and learning materials that focus on the Black experience. No unsolicited material.

KANE/MILLER BOOK PUBLISHERS INC.

P.O. Box 8515, La Jolla, CA 92038. 858-456-0540.
Web site: www.kanemiller.com.
Description: Publishes picture books from all over the world. **Tips:** Does not publish brand new work—only American editions of books previously published in foreign countries.

KIDS CAN PRESS LTD.

2250 Military Rd., Tonawanda, NY 14150. 416-925-5437.
E-mail: info@kidscan.com.
Valerie Hussey, Publisher.
Description: Picture books, 24 pages; juvenile nonfiction, 24-144 pages; and young adult novels, to 256 pages. Not accepting mss.

ALFRED A. KNOPF BOOKS FOR YOUNG READERS

Random House Children's Media Group/Random House, Inc.
201 E 50th St., New York, NY 10022. 212-752-2600.
Web site: www.randomhouse.com/kids.
Description: Distinguished juvenile fiction and nonfiction. Query; no unsolicited manuscripts. Royalty. Guidelines. Imprint of Random House Children's Media Group.

LEARNING HORIZONS

One American Rd., Cleveland, OH 44144. 216-252-7300.
Web site: www.learninghorizons.com.
Description: Publisher of hands-on learning materials for kids in preschool through grade 6. Content covers language, math, science, and social studies.

LEE & LOW BOOKS

95 Madison Ave., New York, NY 10016. 212-779-4400 x24.
E-mail: lmay@leeandlow.com. Web site: www.leeandlow.com.
Louise May, Executive Editor.
Description: Quality children's book publisher specializing in multicultural themes.
Number of Books/Yr.: 12-15 titles/year (1,500 submissions), 35% first-time authors,
80% unagented. **Proposal Process:** We consider manuscripts from writers at all levels of experience. Prefers hard copy. Include SASE. **Payment:** Advance/royalty.
Tips: No folk tales or animal stories. Seeking character-driven realistic fiction about
children of color, with special interest in stories set in contemporary U.S. Visit Web
site for details.

LERNER PUBLISHING CO.

A Division of Lerner Publishing Group
241 First Ave. N, Minneapolis, MN 55401. 612-332-3344.
Web site: www.lernerbooks.com.
Jennifer Zimian, Submissions Editor.
Description: Publishes primarily nonfiction for readers of all grade levels. List
includes titles encompassing nature, geography, natural and physical science, current
events, ancient and modern history, world art, special interest, sports, world cultures,
and numerous biography series. Some young adult and middle grade fiction. No
alphabet, puzzle, song or text books, religious subject matter or plays. **Proposal
Process:** Submissions are accepted in the months of March and October only. Work
received in any other month will be returned unopened. SASE required for authors
who wish to have their material returned. Please allow 2 to 6 months for response. No
phone calls.

ARTHUR A. LEVINE BOOKS

Scholastic, Inc.
557 Broadway, New York, NY 10012. 212-343-4436.
Web site: www.scholastic.com.
Arthur A. Levine, Publisher.
Description: Beautiful picture books and literary fiction for children of all ages.
Proposal Process: Query before sending submission. First-time authors welcome.

LITTLE MAI PRESS

102 River Dr., Lake Hiawatha, NJ 07034. 973-331-9648.
E-mail: lmaipress@aol.com.
Description: Publisher of children's books.

LITTLE SIMON

Simon & Schuster Children's Publishing/Simon & Schuster, Inc.
1230 Avenue of the Americas, New York, NY 10020.
Web site: www.simonsayskids.com.
Cindy Eng Alvarez, Vice President/Editorial Director.

Description: Novelty books, board books, pop-up books, lift-the-flap, and touch-and-feel books. No picture or chapter books. Audience is children 6 months to 8 years.

LITTLE TIGER PRESS
12221 W Feerick St., Wauwatosa, WI 53222-2117. 414-466-6900.
Amy Mascillino, Director.
Description: Publishes illustrated children's books with endearing story lines. Query. No unsolicited manuscripts.

LOBSTER PRESS
1620 Sherbrooke St. W, Suite C, Montreal, Quebec H3H 1C9 Canada. 514-904-1100.
E-mail: editorial@lobsterpress.com. Web site: www.lobsterpress.com.
Description: Publisher of high-quality children's books. Titles include picture books, travel guides for kids, *Millennium Generation* series, and *Pet-Sitters' Club* series. Also publishes travel guides, adult nonfiction, self-help, and illustrated titles. **Number of Books/Yr.:** 25 titles/year. Receives 200 queries and 1,500 mss/year. 90% of books from first-time authors; 75% from unagented writers. **Payment:** Royalty.

LUCENT BOOKS
The Gale Group
10911 Technology Place, San Diego, CA 92127. 858-485-7424.
Web site: www.lucentbooks.com.
Chendra Howard, Acquisitions Editor.
Description: Books for junior high/middle school students, 18,000-25,000 words. *Overview* series: current issues (political, social, historical, environmental topics). Other series include: *World History*; *The Way People Live* (exploring daily life and culture of communities worldwide, past and present); *Modern Nations*. No unsolicited material; work is by assignment only. Flat fee. Query for guidelines and catalog.

MAGINATION PRESS
750 First St. NE, Washington, DC 20002. 202-218-3982.
Web site: www.maginationpress.com.
Darcie Conner Johnston, Managing Editor.
Description: Publishes illustrated story books and nonfiction of a clearly psychological nature for children. Picture books for children 4-11; fiction for children 8-12; nonfiction for children 8-18. **Number of Books/Yr.:** 8-12 titles/year, (500 submissions), 50% first-time authors, 80% unagented. **Proposal Process:** Submit query with complete mss, and SASE. No electronic submissions. Multiple queries accepted. Hard copy. Response time: 3-5 months. **Payment:** Royalty. **Sample Titles:** Children's Nonfiction: Ages 4-8; 8-13; teens to college age. *I Don't Want to Talk About It* (about divorce, for ages 4-8). *Putting on the Brakes: Young People's Guide to Understanding Attention Deficit Hyperactivity Disorder.* **Tips:** See submission guidelines. Looking for strong self-help and psychological content in stories that focus on an issue that affects children, plus engaged writing. No young adult fiction or chapter books. Many of these books are written by medical or mental-health professionals.

MARGARET K. MCELDERRY BOOKS

1230 Sixth Ave., New York, NY 10020. 212-698-2761.

Web site: www.simonsayskids.com.

Emma D. Dryden, Vice President/Editorial Director.

Description: Books for all ages: infant through young adult; literary hardcover trade; fiction; some poetry and nonfiction. Guidelines available. **Number of Books/Yr.:** 25-30 titles/year (4,000 submissions), 35% by first-time authors, 50% unagented. **Proposal Process:** Query with outline and sample chapters. Response time: 3 months. Accepts both multiple and electronic queries. Prefers hard-copy format. **Payment:** Royalty. **Tips:** Looking for unique perspectives on unique topics of interest to children. No science fiction, does publish some fantasy. **Contact:** Sarah Nielsen, Assistant Editor.

MEADOWBROOK PRESS

5451 Smetana Dr., Minnetonka, MN 55343. 952-930-1100.

Web site: www.meadowbrookpress.com.

Bruce Lansky, Editorial Director.

Description: Features articles on parenting, pregnancy and childbirth, party planning, and relationships. Guidelines available. **Number of Books/Yr.:** 20 titles/year (600 submissions), 80% first-time authors, 90% unagented. **Proposal Process:** Send query with SASE. Hard-copy format preferred. Multiple queries accepted. **Payment:** Royalty or flat fee. **Sample Titles:** *Pregnancy, Childbirth, and the Newborn*; *The Toddler's Busy Book*.

MILKWEED EDITIONS

1011 Washington Ave. S., Suite 300, Minneapolis, MN 55415. 612-332-3192.

Web site: www.milkweed.org.

Emilie Buchwald, Editorial Director.

Description: Literary fiction; literary nonfiction about the natural world; poetry; literary novels for middle graders (ages 8-13). Guidelines available. **Number of Books/Yr.:** 15 titles/year (3,000 submissions), 60% by first-time authors, 75% unagented. **Proposal Process:** Query with SASE. Hard-copy format. Response time: 2-6 months. Multiple queries okay. No electronic queries. **Payment:** Royalty. **Sample Titles:** *Ecology of a Cracker Childhood,* by Janisse Ray; *Turning Over the Earth,* by Ralph Black; *The $66 Summer,* by John Armistead. **Tips:** Looking for a fresh, distinctive voice. No genre fiction, picture books, etc. Seeks to give new writers a forum; publishing history isn't as important as excellence and originality. **Contact:** Elisabeth Fitz, First Reader.

THE MILLBROOK PRESS

P.O. Box 335, 2 Old New Milford Rd., Brookfield, CT 06804. 203-740-2220.

Web site: www.millbrookpress.com.

Kristin Vibbert, Manuscript Coordinator.

Description: Children's book publisher, with 3 imprints: Copper Beech, Twenty-First Century, and Roaring Brook. Quality nonfiction for the school and library market for grades Pre-K-6. Main market is elementary schools, but titles range from infant picture books to YA historical fiction. **Number of Books/Yr.:** 150 titles/year (5,000 submissions), 50% by first-time authors, 75% unagented. **Proposal Process:** Query with outline and sample chapters, include SASE. Response time: 1 month. Hard copy. Multiple queries okay. No electronic queries. **Payment:** Royalty or flat fee. **Tips:** Send SASE for guidelines or catalog, or check Web site.

MODERN PUBLISHING

Unisystems, Inc.

155 E 55th St., New York, NY 10022. 212-826-0850.

Web site: www.modernpublishing.com.

Description: Publisher of licensed and non-licensed books for children ages 2-10. Books feature favorite characters and come in a variety of formats, including coloring/activity books, educational workbooks, hardcover, paperback, seasonal, and novelty.

MONDO PUBLISHING

980 Avenue of the Americas, Fl. 2, New York, NY 10018. 212-268-3560.

Don L. Curry, Executive Editor.

Description: Children's trade and educational. Picture books, nonfiction, and early chapter books for readers ages 4-10. Beautiful books that children can read on their own and enjoy over and over. **Number of Books/Yr.:** 50 titles/year (1,000 submissions), 30% by first-time authors. **Proposal Process:** Query with complete manuscript. No multiple or electronic queries. Hard copy. **Payment:** Varies.

NATIONAL GEOGRAPHIC SOCIETY

1145 17th St. NW, Washington, DC 20036-4688. 202-828-5492.

E-mail: jtunstal@ngs.org.

Nancy Feresten, Editorial Director.

Description: Mainly nonfiction books in the areas of history, adventure, biography, multicultural themes, science, nature, and reference for children ages 4-14. **Number of Books/Yr.:** 25 titles/year (1,000 submissions), 5% first-time authors, 50% unagented. **Proposal Process:** Query with complete manuscript, and SASE. Response time: several months. Multiple queries accepted. Hard-copy format preferred. **Payment:** Royalty or flat fee. **Tips:** We like a strong writer's voice telling an interesting story on a subject of interest to young people.

THE OLIVER PRESS

Charlotte Square, 5707 W. 36th St., Minneapolis, MN 55416. 952-926-8981.

E-mail: queries@oliverpress.com. Web site: www.oliverpress.com.

Denise Sterling, Editor.

Description: Publishes collective biographies for middle and senior high school students. Currently offering six different curriculum-based series such as *Profiles, Business Builders,* and *Innovators* (history of technology). Ages 10-young adult. **Proposal Process:** Submit proposals for books, 20,000-25,000 words, on people who have made an impact in such areas as history, politics, crime, science, and business. SASE. Multiple and electronic queries accepted. Hard copy. **Payment:** Royalty or flat fee. **Tips:** Book proposals should fit one of our existing series; provide brief summaries of 8-12 people who could be included. Looking for authors who thoroughly research their subject and are accurate and good storytellers. No fiction, picture books, or single-person biographies. **Contact:** Jenna Anderson, Editor.

ORCA BOOK PUBLISHERS

P.O. Box 468, Custer, WA 98240-0468. 250-380-1229.

E-mail: orca@orcabook.com. Web site: www.orcabook.com.

Description: Publishes children's picture books, young readers, and juvenile fiction, and young adult fiction. **Proposal Process:** Submit query with 1-page cover letter and SASE. Do fax or e-mail query. Does not accept multiple queries. **Tips:** Manuscripts can also be sent to Canadian office:

P.O. Box 5626, Victoria, British Columbia V8R 6S4 Canada.

RICHARD C. OWEN PUBLISHERS, INC.

Children's Book Dept., P.O. Box 585, Katonah, NY 10536. 914-232-3903.

Web site: www.rcowen.com.

Janice Boland, Editor.

Description: Brief, original, well-structured children's books that youngsters (in K-2 grades) can read by themselves. Also short, snappy bright articles, stories for children, ages 7-8. **Number of Books/Yr.:** 15 titles/year (1,000 submissions), 95% first-time authors, 100% unagented. **Proposal Process:** Send SASE for guidelines. Query with complete manuscript. Multiple queries okay. No electronic queries. Prefers hard-copy format. **Payment:** R yalty for writers. Flat fee for illustrators. **Sample Titles:** Fiction and nonfiction: *Young Learners* collection; *Fluent Readers* collection. **Tips:** Fresh, bright, energetic, crisp, clear style. Subjects that appeal to today's children.

PACIFIC VIEW PRESS

P.O. Box 2657, Berkley, CA 94702.

Pam Zumwalt, Acquisitions Editor.

Description: Small publishing house specializing in nonfiction for 8- to 12-year-olds. Focus on the culture and history of countries of the Pacific Rim. Also, for middle-grade readers: Asian and Chinese cooking books and books on innovative aspects of Chinese history.

PEACHTREE PUBLISHERS, LTD.

1700 Chattahoochee Ave., Atlanta, GA 30318-2112. 404-876-8761.

E-mail: hello@peachtree-online.com. Web site: www.peachtree-online.com.

Description: Fiction and nonfiction, children's, middle readers, young adults, adult nonfiction: regional, health, regional travel (Southeast only) **Proposal Process:** Send full manuscript or three sample chapters plus table of contents, with SASE for response or return of materials. Send all submissions via U.S. mail. No e-mail or fax queries or submissions. 4-6 months for response. **Tips:** Strong writing with unique subject matter or approach. No adult fiction, fantasy, sci-fi, romance, anthologies, poetry, or short stories. **Contact:** Helen Harriss.

PHIDAL PUBLISHING INC.
5740 Ferrier St., Montreal, Quebec H4P 1M7 Canada. 514-738-0202.
E-mail: info@phidal.com. Web site: www.phidal.com.
Description: Children's books.

PINATA BOOKS
Arte Publico Press
University of Houston, 4800 Calhoun, Houston, TX 77204-2174. 713-743-2841.
Web site: www.arte.uh.edu.
Nicolas Kanellos, President.
Description: Picture books, fiction, and autobiographies for children and young adults. Query with outline and sample chapters, or send complete manuscript.
Payment: Royalty.

PIPPIN PRESS
229 E. 85th St., Gracie Sta., Box 1347, New York, NY 10028. 212-288-4920.
Barbara Francis, Editor-in-Chief.
Description: Publishes early chapter books, middle group fiction, and unusual non-fiction for children ages 7-12. Also publishes humor for all ages. **Number of Books/Yr.:** 6 titles/year (3,000 submissions), 10% by first-time authors, 90% unagented. **Proposal Process:** Query with SASE. No unsolicited manuscripts. Hardcopy format. No multiple or electronic queries. **Payment:** Royalty. **Tips:** Looking for childhood memoirs and small chapter books (64 pages) on historical events in which young people are the heroes. **Contact:** Joyce Segal, Senior Editor.

PLAYHOUSE PUBLISHING
1566 Akron-Peninsula Rd., Akron, OH 44313. 330-926-1313.
E-mail: webmaster@playhousepublishing.com.
Web site: www.playhousepublishing.com.
Description: Novelty, fiction, and picture books. **Tips:** Writers should submit queries and book proposals electronically. All copy must be contained in the body of e-mail. Attachments will not be opened.

PLAYMORE INC. PUBLISHERS
230 Fifth Avenue, Suite 711, New York, NY 10001. 212-251-0600.
E-mail: johnb@playmorebooks.com. Web site: www.playmorebooks.com.
Description: Publisher of children's books.

PLEASANT COMPANY PUBLICATIONS
8400 Fairway Pl., Middleton, WI 58562-0998. 608-836-4848.
Web site: www.americangirl.com.
Description: Books, 40,000-60,000 words, for 7-13 year old girls: historical fiction,

contemporary fiction, and contemporary advice and activity. Query with outline and sample chapters or send complete manuscript. Royalty or flat fee. **Tips:** Small "concept-driven" list. No picture books.

POLYCHROME PUBLISHING CORPORATION
4509 N Francisco, Chicago, IL 60625. 773-478-4455.
E-mail: polypub@earthlink.net.
Description: Books that promote racial, ethnic, cultural, religious tolerance, respect and understanding.

PUFFIN BOOKS
Penguin Putnam Books for Young Readers/Penguin Putnam Inc.
345 Hudson St., New York, NY 10014-3647. 212-414-2000.
Web site: www.penguinputnam.com/childrens.
Tracy Tang, President/Publisher.
Description: Children's fiction and nonfiction for all ages.

G.P. PUTNAM'S SONS BOOKS FOR YOUNG READERS
Penguin Putnam Books for Young Readers/Penguin Putnam Inc.
345 Hudson St., Fl. 14, New York, NY 10014. 212-366-2000.
Web site: www.penguinputnam.com.
Nancy Paulsen, President/Publisher.
Description: Publishes general trade nonfiction and fiction for ages 2-18. Mostly picture books and middle-grade novels. **Number of Books/Yr.:** 45 titles/year (average 12,000 submissions), 5% by first-time authors, 50% unagented. **Proposal Process:** Children's novels: query with 3 sample chapters. Picture books: send complete manuscript (if less than 10 pages). Considers multiple queries. No electronic queries. Hard-copy format preferred. Response time: 1-3 months. **Payment:** Pays royalty. **Sample Titles:** *Saving Sweetness*, by Diane Stanley, illustrated by Brian Karas (ages 4-8); and *Amber Brown Sees Red*, by Paula Danziger (ages 7-10). **Tips:** Multicultural books should reflect different cultures accurately, but unobtrusively. Stories about children who are physically or cognitively disabled should portray them accurately, without condescension. Avoid series, romances. Very little fantasy.

RAINBOW BRIDGE PUBLISHING
323 W Martin Ln., P.O. Box 571470
Salt Lake City, UT 84157-1470. 800-598-1441.
E-mail: rainbow@xmission.com. Web site: www.rbpbooks.com.
Description: Parent and teacher resource materials for students between preschool and eighth grade. Topics include math, reading, writing, science, geography and language arts.

RAINTREE
15 E 26th St., New York, NY 10010. 646-935-3702.
Web site: www.raintreesteckvaughn.com.

Eileen Robinson, Editorial Director.
Description: Children's nonfiction in series only. No single titles. All published books are curriculum-oriented. **Number of Books/Yr.:** 200 titles/year (500 submissions), a few first-time authors, almost all are unagented. **Proposal Process:** Query with outline and sample chapters, include SASE. Response time: 2-4 months. Multiple queries accepted with advance notice. No electronic queries. **Payment:** Flat fee (varies). **Sample Titles:** *America into a New Millennium* (ages 11-14); *Phosphorus* (ages 11-14); *The Secret World of Snakes* (ages 8-10); *Pollution and Conservation* (ages 8-10).

RANDOM HOUSE BOOKS FOR YOUNG READERS
Random House Children's Media Group/Random House, Inc.
201 E 50th St., New York, NY 10022. 212-751-2600.
Web site: www.randomhouse.com/kids.
Kate Klimo, Vice President/Publishing Director.
Description: Fiction and nonfiction for beginning readers; paperback fiction line for 7- to 9-year-olds. No unsolicited manuscripts. Agented material only.

THE READER'S DIGEST ASSOCIATION, INC.
Readers Digest Rd., Pleasantville, NY 10570-7000. 914-238-1000.
Web site: www.rd.com.
Description: Publisher of the magazine *Reader's Digest* as well as do-it-yourself books on home improvement, gardening, cooking, etc; children's books; Select Editions; reading series; Young Families products; music collections, home videos, and other special interest magazines.

RED WAGON BOOKS
Harcourt, Inc./Children's Book Division
525 B St., Suite 1900, San Diego, CA 92101-4495. 619-231-6616.
Description: Fiction and nonfiction for children. Query with SASE.

MORGAN REYNOLDS, INC.
620 S Elm St., Suite 223, Greensboro, NC 27406. 336-275-1311.
E-mail: editors@morganreynolds.com. Web site: www.morganreynolds.com.
John Riley, Publisher.
Description: Lively, well written biographies and histories for young adults. Suitable subjects include important historical events and important historical and contemporary figures. **Number of Books/Yr.:** 20 titles/year (300 submissions), 50% first-time authors, 90% unagented. **Proposal Process:** Send query with outline and sample chapters, SASE. Multiple queries considered. Multiple and electronic queries considered. Prefers hard-copy format. Response time: 1 month. **Payment:** Royalty. **Sample Titles:** Children's Nonfiction: *Edgar Rice Burroughs: Creator of Tarzan*; *The Firing on Fort Sumter: A Splintered Nation Goes to War*. **Tips:** Only nonfiction, for young adults. Avoid eccentric topics, autobiographies, and "cute" writing styles. Market includes middle- and high-school libraries and public libraries. **Contact:** Laura Shoemaker.

RISING MOON
Northland Publishing
P.O. Box 1389, Flagstaff, AZ 86002-1389. 928-774-5251.
E-mail: info@northlandpub.com. Web site: www.northlandpub.com.
Rebecca Gomez, Children's Editor.
Description: Picture books for children ages 5-8. Fiction and nonfiction, ages 8-12; no longer accepts unsolicited manuscripts. Interested in material on contemporary subjects. **Number of Books/Yr.:** 10-12 titles/year (3,000 submissions), 25% unagented. **Proposal Process:** No unsolicited manuscripts. Considers multiple queries. Electronic queries not accepted. Prefers hard-copy format. Response time: 3 months. **Payment:** Royalty or flat fee. **Sample Titles:** *When Kangaroo Goes to School; The Old Man and the Flea; My Best Friend Bear.* **Tips:** Please submit through your agent, and review guidelines carefully first. **Contact:** Tammy Gales, Editor.

THE ROSEN PUBLISHING GROUP
29 E 21st St., New York, NY 10010. 212-777-3017.
Kathy Kuhtz Campbell, Managing Editor.
Description: Publishes nonfiction children and young adult titles for the school and library market. Rosen books encompass a wide variety of topics and issues that affect young people's lives in the areas of careers, guidance, science, health, history, social studies, art, culture, and sports. Also publisher of *PowerPlus Books,* a 12-book series of nonfiction titles correlated to the curriculum for students in grades 4-8. **Number of Books/Yr.:** 200 titles/year. **Proposal Process:** Query. Hard copy. No electronic queries. **Payment:** Royalty and/or flat fee. **Tips:** Nonfiction work-for-hire series format (6 books to a series).

SANDCASTLE PUBLISHING
1723 Hill Dr., P.O. Box 3070, South Pasadena, CA 91031-6070.
Description: A 12-year-old company specializing in books that introduce children to the performing arts. Fiction and nonfiction titles range from easy reading to young adult.

SCHOLASTIC PROFESSIONAL BOOKS
Scholastic, Inc.
524 Broadway, New York, NY 10012-3999. 212-965-7287.
Web site: www.scholastic.com.
Adriane Rozier, Editorial/Production Coordinator.
Description: Books by and for teachers of kindergarten through eighth grade. Instructor Books: practical, activity/resource books on teaching reading and writing, science, math, etc. Teaching Strategies Books: 64-96 pages on new ideas, practices, and approaches to teaching. Query with outline, sample chapters or activities,

contents page, and resume. Flat fee or royalty. Multiple queries considered. 8½ x 11 SASE for guidelines.

SEASTAR BOOKS
11 E 26th St., Fl. 17, New York, NY 10010.
Andrea Spooner, Editor-in-Chief.
Description: Publisher of literary children's hardcover books. Picture books and middle-grade fiction and nonfiction. Only accepts submissions from SCBWI members.

SHOE STRING PRESS
2 Linsley St., P.O. Box 657, North Haven, CT 06473-2517. 203-239-2702.
E-mail: books@shoestringpress.com. Web site: www.shoestringpress.com.
Diantha C. Thorpe, Editor.
Description: Books for children and teenagers, including juvenile nonfiction for ages 10 and older. Resources that share high standards of scholarship and practical experience for teachers and librarians. Imprints include Linnet Books, Archon Books, and Linnet Professional Publications. Submit outline and sample chapters.
Payment: Royalty.

SILVER MOON PRESS
160 Fifth Ave., Suite 622, New York, NY 10010. 212-242-6499.
E-mail: mail@silvermoonpress.com. Web site: www.silvermoonpress.com.
Hope Killcoyne, Editor.
Description: American historical fiction for children, ages 8-12. Educational test prep material/English language arts, and social studies. **Number of Books/Yr.:** 5 titles/year (75-100 submissions), 80% first-time authors, 80% unagented. **Proposal Process:** Query with outline and sample chapters. Multiple and electronic queries accepted. Response time: 1-3 months. Hard copy. **Payment:** Royalty. **Tips:** American historical fiction. Young protagonists. Biographical fiction. **Contact:** Karin Lillebo.

SIMON & SCHUSTER BOOKS FOR YOUNG READERS
Simon & Schuster Children's Publishing/Simon & Schuster, Inc.,
1230 Avenue of the Americas, New York, NY 10020. 212-698-2851.
Web site: www.simonsays.com.
Steve Geck, V.P. Associate Publisher.
Description: Books for ages preschool through high school: picture books to young adult; nonfiction for all age levels. Hardcover only. Request guidelines before querying. SASE required for reply.

SPORTS PUBLISHING INC.
804 N Neil, Champaign, IL 61820. 217-359-5940.
E-mail: mpearson@sagamorepub.com. Web site: www.sportspublishing.com.
Mike Pearson, Editor.

Description: Leading publisher of regional sports covering a wide range of sports. A series for readers in grades 3-5 is entitled *Kids Superstars.*

STODDART KIDS BOOKS
895 Don Mills Rd., 400-2 Park Centre, Toronto
Ontario M3C 1W3 Canada. 416-445-3333.
Web site: www.stoddartpub.com.
Kathryn Cole, Publisher.
Description: Books for children of all ages, this Canadian publisher has traditionally focused on fiction. In 1999, however, it introduced its first nonfiction series, the *Discovery* series. Stoddart plans to continue to expand its nonfiction list. It is looking for titles with hands-on activities using a fresh approach, for ages 8-11 years.

STORY LINE PRESS
Three Oaks Farm, P.O. Box 1240, Ashland, OR 97520-0055. 541-512-8792.
Web site: www.storylinepress.com.
Robert McDowell, Editorial Director.
Description: Fiction, nonfiction, and poetry of varying lengths. **Number of Books/Yr.:** 12 titles/year (8,000 submissions), 10% by first-time authors, 80% unagented. **Proposal Process:** Query with outline, sample chapters and SASE. Multiple and electronic queries accepted. Hard-copy format preferred. **Payment:** Royalty.

TEACHER CREATED MATERIALS
6421 Industry Way, Westminster, CA 92683.
Web site: www.teachercreated.com.
Description: Quality resource books covering all areas of the educational curriculum. Books are created by teachers for teachers and parents. **Tips:** Send 10 to 12 sample pages, tentative table of contents, summary of audience, content, and objectives, and SASE. Mail materials to P.O. Box 1040, Huntington Beach, CA, 92647. Does not accept electronic submissions.

TIME-LIFE FOR CHILDREN
Time-Life, Inc.
2000 Duke St., Alexandria, VA 22314. 703-838-7000.
Web site: www.timelife.com.
Mary J. Wright, Managing Editor.
Description: Juvenile books. Publishes series of 12-36 volumes (no single titles). Author must have a series concept. Publisher has discontinued accepting unsolicited work.

MEGAN TINGLEY BOOKS
Little, Brown & Co.
3 Center Plaza, Boston, MA 02108. 617-227-0730.
Web site: www.twbookmark.com.
Megan Tingley, Editorial Director.

Description: Fiction and nonfiction for preschoolers through young adults. Mainly picture books. No mystery, romance, or science fiction. Agented submissions only.

TOY BOX PRODUCTIONS

7532 Hickory Hills Court, Whites Creek, TN 37189. 615-299-0822.
E-mail: lori@crttoybox.com. Web site: www.crttoybox.com.
Description: Publishes audio books for children. Fully illustrated, perfect-bound books with cassette or CD packaged in vinyl pouch series. **Sample Titles:** *The Time Travelers Adventures* and *Bible Stories for Kids.*

TRICYCLE PRESS

Ten Speed Press
P.O. Box 7123, Berkeley, CA 94707. 510-559-1600.
Web site: www.tenspeed.com.
Nicole Geiger, Publisher.
Description: Publisher of books for children. Titles are picture books, board books, "tween" books, and photographic nonfiction. Also, "real life" books that help children cope with issues. Submit complete manuscripts. Activity books: submit about 20 pages and complete outline. **Number of Books/Yr.:** 20 titles/year (8,000-10,000 submissions), 15-20% by first-time authors, 50% unagented. **Proposal Process:** No queries. Send outline and sample chapters for novels and activity books, complete mss for picture books. No electronic queries or faxed submissions. Prefers hard-copy format. **Payment:** Royalty; typical range is 15-20% net. **Sample Titles:** Children's: *G is for Googol,* by David Schwartz, illustrations by Marissa Moss (8 and up); *Storm Boy,* by Paul Owen Lewis; *Ancient Fire,* by Mark London Williams.

TROLL COMMUNICATIONS

100 Corporate Dr., Mahwah, NJ 07430. 201-529-4512.
Web site: www.troll.com.
M. Francis, Editor.
Description: Juvenile fiction and nonfiction. Query preferred. Royalty or flat fee.

TUNDRA BOOKS

McClelland & Stewart
481 University Ave., Suite 900, Toronto, Ontario M5G 2E9 Canada. 416-598-4786.
E-mail: mail@mcclelland.com. Web site: www.tundrabooks.com.
Kathy Lowinger, Publisher.
Description: Fiction, nonfiction, books for young adults, myths and legends, history, and picture books.

TURTLE BOOKS

866 United Nations Plaza, Suite 525, New York, NY 10017. 212-644-2020.
Web site: www.turtlebooks.com.
John Whitman, Publisher.

Description: Children's picture books only. Submit complete manuscript with SASE. **Payment:** Royalty.

TWENTY-FIRST CENTURY BOOKS
The Millbrook Press
P.O. Box 335, 2 Old New Milford Rd., Brookfield, CT 06804. 203-740-2220.
Web site: www.millbrookpress.com.
Kristen Vibbert, Manuscript Coordinator.
Description: Curriculum-oriented publisher for the school and library market, focusing on current issues, U.S. history, science, biography and social studies, etc. **Number of Books/Yr.:** 135 titles/year (2,000 submissions). **Proposal Process:** Query with outline. Considers multiple queries. Response 2-3 months. Hard copy. No electronic queries. **Payment:** Royalty. **Sample Titles:** *Breast Cancer* (ages 12-up); *Heroes of the Holocaust* (ages 12-up); *Steve Jobs: Think Different* (ages 10-up). **Tips:** Accepts submissions through agents only. Requires proposals with strong tie to curriculum for grades 5 and up. Picture books, activity books, parent's guides, etc., will not be considered. Send SASE for guidelines or catalog.

VIKING CHILDREN'S BOOKS
Penguin Putnam Books for Young Readers/Penguin Putnam Inc.
345 Hudson St., New York, NY 10014. 212-366-2000.
Web site: www.penguinputnam.com.
Elizabeth Law, Editor-in-Chief.
Description: Fiction and nonfiction, including biography, history, and sports, for ages 7-14. Humor and picture books for ages 3-8. Query Children's Book Dept. with outline and sample chapter. For picture books, please send entire manuscript. SASE. Advance and royalty.

ALBERT WHITMAN & CO.
6340 Oakton St., Morton Grove, IL 60053. 847-581-0033.
Web site: www.albertwhitman.com.
Kathleen Tucker, Editor-in-Chief.
Description: Children's books. Picture books for ages 2-8; novels, biographies, mysteries, and nonfiction for middle-grade readers. Send SASE for guidelines. Send complete manuscript for picture books, 3 chapters and outline for longer fiction; query for nonfiction. Royalty. Do not e-mail or fax.

WILEY CHILDREN'S BOOKS
605 Third Ave., New York, NY 10158-0012. 212-850-6000.
Web site: www.wiley.com.
Description: Publisher of nonfiction books, 96-128 pages, for children 8-12. Query. Royalty.

WILLIAMSON PUBLISHING CO.

P.O. Box 185, Charlotte, VT 05445. 802-425-2102.

Web site: www.williamsonbooks.com.

Susan Williamson, Editorial Director.

Description: How-to-do-it learning books based on a philosophy that says "learning is exciting, mistakes are fine, and involvement and curiosity are wonderful." **Number of Books/Yr.:** 15 titles/year (800-1,000 submissions), 50% by first-time authors, 90% unagented. **Proposal Process:** Send query with outline and sample chapters. Response time: 2-3 months. No multiple or electronic queries. Hard copy. **Payment:** Royalty or flat fee. **Sample Titles:** *Bridges; Little Hands Art Book; Hands on Math for Real World Fun; The Kids Book of Natural History.* **Tips:** Looking for knowledgeable writers who know their subject and love kids. Writing should be filled with information and how-to activities that make learning a positive and memorable experience. All of our books are written directly to kids, although they are also often used by teachers and parents. Also looking for illustrators who work in B&W and can combine how-to illustrations along with a sense of "kid humor."

WIZARDS OF THE COAST

1801 Lind Ave. SW, P.O. Box 707, Renton, WA 98055. 425-226-6500.

Web site: www.wizards.com.

Description: Publisher of fantasy and science fiction series for juvenile and young-adult markets.

WORLD BOOK, INC.

233 N Michigan Ave., Suite 2000, Chicago, IL 60601. 312-729-5800.

Web site: www.worldbook.com.

Description: World-renowned and award-winning children's nonfiction books. Publishes encyclopedias, reference materials, and multimedia products.

YEARLING BOOKS

Random House Children's Media Group/Random House, Inc.,
1540 Broadway, New York, NY 10036.

Description: Children's titles. Not accepting unsolicited material. Imprints include Skylark Books.

ZINO PRESS CHILDREN'S BOOKS

Knowledge Unlimited, Inc.,
P.O. Box 52, Madison, WI 53701. 608-836-6660.

Web site: www.zinopress.com.

Dave Schreiner, Editor-in-Chief.

Description: Multicultural and rhyming books for children.

RELIGIOUS BOOKS

Religious book publishing is growing in leaps and bounds. In the 21st century, it ranges from books on Jewish traditions to Christian devotionals, from picture books for children to religious romances, from scholarly works on theology to the popular prophesy of the fictional *Left Behind* series (published by Tyndale House), found high on *The New York Times* bestseller lists.

Clearly, each publisher of religious books has a distinctive mission, often with a specialized sense of ideal approach and language to be used. Publishers expect their authors to be knowledgeable about readers' needs, to be familiar with the appropriate methods and concerns required for any book in this field to succeed.

Perhaps even more so than for other markets, before sending off materials, research each publisher under consideration carefully. Request a catalog, and get a copy of their guidelines for queries and submissions (often found on publisher Web sites). Be sure to send an SASE with your query, as well as sufficient return postage for any subsequent materials or illustrations sent.

ACCENT PUBLICATIONS
Cook Communications Ministries
4050 Lee Vance View, P.O. Box 36640, Colorado Springs, CO 80936. 719-536-0100.
Web site: www.cookministries.com.
Dr. James T. Dyet, Managing Editor.
Description: Nonfiction church resources for Christian education curriculum programs for the local church; evangelical Christian perspective; no trade books. Guidelines available. Royalty. Paperback only.

JASON ARONSON, INC.
230 Livingston St., Northvale, NJ 07647-1726. 201-767-4093.
Web site: www.aronson.com.
Dana Salzman, Associate Publisher.
Description: Nonfiction on all aspects of Jewish life, including such topics as anti-semitism, the Bible, Hasidic thought, genealogy, medicine, folklore and storytelling, interfaith relations, the Holocaust, the Talmud, women's studies, and travel.
Proposal Process: Send complete manuscript or query with outline and sample chapters. **Payment:** Royalty.

BAKER BOOK HOUSE
P.O. Box 6287, Grand Rapids, MI 49516-6287. 616-676-9185.
Web site: www.bakerbooks.com.
Description: Evangelical publisher offering more than 200 releases per year in its five separate divisions. Publishes hardcover and trade paperbacks in both fiction and nonfiction categories: trade books for the general public, professional books for church and parachurch leaders; texts for college and seminary classrooms. Topics include contemporary issues, women's concerns, parenting, singleness, children's books, Bible study, Christian doctrine, reference books, books for pastors and church

leaders, textbooks for Christian colleges and seminaries, and literary novels focusing on women's concerns. **Tips:** Does not accept unsolicited proposals. See Web site for guidelines.

BETHANY HOUSE PUBLISHERS

11400 Hampshire Ave. S., Minneapolis, MN 55438. 952-829-2500.
Web site: www.bethanyhouse.com.
Description: Religious fiction and nonfiction. Adults: personal growth books, divorce, euthanasia, women's issues, spirituality, abortion, and cults. Adult manuscripts should be 75,000 words or longer. Typical novels range up to 125,000 words. Children and teens: first chapter books, 6,000-7,500 words, of biblical lessons and Christian faith for ages 7-10; imaginative stories and believable characters, 20,000-40,000 words, for middle grade readers; and at least 40,000-word stories with strong plots and realistic characters for teens of ages 12-17. **Proposal Process:** Does not accept unsolicited manuscripts or book proposals. Does accept 1 page only facsimile proposals directed to Adult Nonfiction, Adult Fiction, or YA/Children editors. See Web site for current fax number. Continues to accept queries, proposals, and manuscripts through established literary agents, recognized manuscript services, and writer's conferences attended by editorial staff.

BLUE DOLPHIN PUBLISHING, INC.

P.O. Box 8, Nevada City, CA 95959-0008. 530-265-6925.
E-mail: bdolphin@nutshel.net. Web site: www.bluedolphinpublishing.com.
Paul M. Clemens, President.
Description: Books, 200-300 pages, on comparative spiritual traditions, lay and transpersonal psychology, self-help, health, healing, and whatever helps people grow in their social awareness and conscious evolution. **Proposal Process:** Query with outline, sample chapters, and SASE. **Payment:** Royalty.

BROADMAN AND HOLMAN PUBLISHERS

127 Ninth Ave. N, Nashville, TN 37234-0115.
Bucky Rosenbaum, V.P. Trade.
Description: Trade, academic, religious, and inspirational nonfiction. Query with SASE. Royalty. Guidelines available with SASE.

THE CATHOLIC UNIVERSITY OF AMERICA PRESS

240 Leahy Hall, 620 Michigan Ave. NE, Washington, DC 20064. 202-319-5052.
E-mail: cua-press@cua.edu. Web site: http://cuapress.cua.edu.
David J. McGonagle, Director.
Description: Scholarly books (humanities, social studies, theology). Query first.

CHRISTIAN PUBLICATIONS

3825 Hartzdale Dr., Camp Hill, PA 17011. 717-761-7044.
E-mail: editors@cp-horizon.com. Web site: www.christianpublications.com.
David Fessenden, Managing Editor.

Description: Adult nonfiction from an evangelical Christian viewpoint, centering on personal spiritual growth, often with a "deeper life" theme. **Number of Books/Yr.:** 30-35 titles/year (1,000 submissions), 20% first-time authors, 90% unagented. **Proposal Process:** Query with outline, proposal, and sample chapters; include SASE. Multiple and electronic queries accepted. Response time: 2-3 months. Hard-copy format preferred. **Payment:** Royalty, 10% net. Flat fee paid on booklets only, range is $100-$200. **Sample Titles:** *Thirsting After God* (devotional). *As You Walk Along the Way* (parenting). **Tips:** Seeking writing that grows out of author's personal relationship with Christ and experience in Christian service, whether lay or ordained. Especially interested in books on spiritual growth, Christian living, family, marriage, home schooling, leadership, inspirational, devotional. Not interested in "new believer" material or "everything about the Bible in 150 pages." May consider theological and Bible study books, but no Bible commentaries.

CONCORDIA PUBLISHING HOUSE
3558 S Jefferson Ave., St. Louis, MO 63118-3968. 314-268-1187.
E-mail: boverton@cphnet.org. Web site: www.cph.org.
Jane Wilke, Editor.
Description: Practical family books and devotionals. Must have explicit Christian content. No poetry. E-mail queries only. Royalty.

COOK COMMUNICATIONS MINISTRIES
4050 Lee Vance View, Colorado Springs, CO 80918. 719-536-3271.
Web site: www.cookministries.com.
Description: Faith Kids Books: fiction that "helps children better understand themselves and their relationship with God"; nonfiction that illuminates the Bible; picture books for ages 1-7; fiction for ages 8-10, 10-12, and 12-14. Life Journey General Titles: fiction with underlying spiritual theme; books on parenting from a Christian perspective. Lengths and payment vary. Query required. Guidelines available.

CROSSWAY BOOKS
1300 Crescent St., Wheaton, IL 60187. 630-682-4300.
Web site: www.crosswaybooks.org.
Description: Evangelical Christian book publisher. See guidelines on Web site before submitting.

CRYSTAL CLARITY PUBLISHERS
14618 Tyler Foote Rd., Nevada City, CA 95959. 530-478-7600.
E-mail: clarity@crystalclarity.com. Web site: www.crystalclarity.com.
Description: Publishes inspirational nonfiction titles on meditation, yoga, health/well-being, family issues, money, nature, spirituality and Eastern and Western thought.

DEVORSS & COMPANY

1046 Princeton Dr., Marina del Ray, CA 90292. 310-822-8940.

Web site: www.devorss.com.

Description: Publisher of nonfiction titles on body, mind, and spirit. Write for guidelines. Send SASE for reply and return of materials.

DIVINE POWER INC.

139 Glen St., Glen Cove, NY 11542. 516-676-7000.

Web site: www.divinepower.org.

Description: Publisher of spiritual titles.

WILLIAM B. EERDMANS PUBLISHING CO., INC.

255 Jefferson Ave. SE, Grand Rapids, MI 49503. 616-459-4591.

Web site: www.eerdmans.com.

Jon Pott, Editor.

Description: Publishes nonfiction books that focus on Christian theology, religious history and biography, ethics, philosophy, literary studies, and spiritual growth.

FORTRESS PRESS

Augsburg Fortress

Publishers, P.O. Box 1209, Minneapolis, MN 55440. 612-330-3300.

E-mail: roy.harrisville@augsburgfortress.org. Web site: www.fortresspress.com.

Roy Harrisville, General Manager.

Description: Publishing house of Evangelical Lutheran Church in America. Books of biblical studies, theology, ethics, professional ministry, and church history for academic and professional markets, including libraries. Query.

GENESIS PUBLISHING CO., INC.

1547 Great Pond Rd., North Andover, MA 01845-1216. 978-688-6688.

Web site: www.genesisbook.com,www.genesispc.com.

Gerard M. Verschuuren, President.

Description: Adult fiction and nonfiction, especially religion and philosophy books. Query. **Payment:** Royalty.

HACHAI PUBLISHING

156 Chester Ave., Brooklyn, NY 11218. 718-633-0100.

E-mail: info@hachai.com. Web site: www.hachai.com.

D. L. Rosenfeld, Editor.

Description: Publishes Judaica children's picture books for readers ages 2-8. Interested in stories that convey traditional Jewish experience in modern times, traditional Jewish observance such as holidays and year-round mitzvahs, and positive character traits. **Number of Books/Yr.:** 4 titles/year (300 submission), 60% first-time authors, 90% unagented. **Proposal Process:** Query or send complete manuscript, and SASE. Multiple queries accepted. No electronic queries. Hard copy. Response time: 6 weeks. **Payment:** Flat fee.

HARPER SAN FRANCISCO

HarperCollins Publishers

353 Sacramento St., Suite 500, San Francisco, CA 94111-3653. 415-477-4400.

Web site: www.harpercollins.com.

Description: Books on spirituality and religion. No unsolicited manuscripts; query required. **Contact:** Acquisitions Editor.

HARVEST HOUSE PUBLISHERS

990 Owen Loop N, Eugene, OR 97402. 541-343-0123.

Carolyn McCready, Editorial Director.

Description: Providing high-quality books and products that glorify God, affirm biblical values, help people grow spiritually strong, and proclaim Jesus Christ as the answer to every human need. Query. **Sample Titles:** Adult fiction: *City Girl*, by Lori Wick (Yellow Rose Trilogy). Picture books: *My Very First Book of Manners* (10 pages). Children's fiction: *Amazing Mazes for Kids*, by Steve & Becky Miller. Adult nonfiction: *Awesome God*, by Neil T. Anderson and Rich Miller. **Tips:** Harvest House no longer accepts unsolicited submissions. However, this publisher is serviced by The Writer's Edge and First Edition. **Contact:** Pat Mathis.

JOURNEY FORTH BOOKS

Bob Jones University Press

1700 Wade Hampton Blvd., Greenville, SC 29614. 370-1800 ext 4350.

E-mail: jb@bjup.com. Web site: www.bjup.com/books.

Nancy Lohr (Youth Manuscript Editor), Suzette Jordan (Adult Manuscript Editor).

Description: Books for young readers, ages 6-teen, that reflect "the highest Christian standards of thought, feeling, and action." **Number of Books/Yr.:** 10 titles/year (500 submissions). **Proposal Process:** Query with outline and sample chapters or complete manuscript. Accepts multiple queries. **Payment:** Royalty or flat fee—negotiable. **Sample Titles:** Adults: *Proverbs Commentary*; *God's Prophetic Blueprint*; Children: *Little Bear and the Cruncheroo Cookies* (ages 2-6); *Arby Jenkins Meets His Match* (ages 9-12); *The Way of Escape* (YA). **Tips:** Secular conflicts are considered, but only within a Christian worldview. Avoid modern humanistics philosophy in stories; instead, emphasize a biblically conservative lifestyle that best serves the individual and society. The writing must be excellent and the story engaging. For our adult nonfiction line, we prefer KJV and adherence to our statement of faith. **Contact:** Nancy Lohr or Suzette Jordan.

JUDSON PRESS

American Baptist Churches

P.O. Box 851, Valley Forge, PA 19482-0851. 610-768-2109.

E-mail: randy.frame@abc-usa.org. Web site: www.judsonpress.com.

Randy Frame, Editor.

Description: Publishes resources to enhance individual Christian living and the life of the church. **Number of Books/Yr.:** 30 titles/year (700 submissions), 20% first-time authors, 90% unagented. **Proposal Process:** Query with proposal, table of contents, estimated length of book, sample chapters, target audience, expected completion date, and bio. Multiple queries accepted. Electronic queries okay, but not for proposals. Hard-copy format preferred. **Payment:** Royalty. **Tips:** Avoid life stories or poetry. Looking for unusually good writing and original ideas.

KREGEL PUBLICATIONS

P.O. Box 2607, Grand Rapids, MI 49501-2607. 616-451-4775.
E-mail: kregelbooks@kregel.com. Web site: www.kregel.com.
Dennis Hillman, Publisher.
Description: Evangelical Christian publisher interested in pastoral ministry, Christian education, family and marriage, devotional books, and biblical studies. Also publishes adult and juvenile fiction (with solid Christian message), children's literature, and academic titles. No poetry, general fiction, or cartoons. **Proposal Process:** Query with summary, target audience, brief bio, an outline or table of contents, 2 sample chapters, and an SASE. Allow 6-8 weeks for a response. **Payment:** Royalty.

LOYOLA PRESS

3441 N Ashland Ave., Chicago, IL 60657-1397. 773-281-1818.
E-mail: editorial@loyolapress.com. Web site: www.loyolapress.org.
Jim Manney, Editorial Director.
Description: Religious and ethics-related material for college-educated, Christian readers. Offers practical spirituality from a Catholic perspective. Books cover prayer, relationships, and applying Christian insights to everyday concerns. **Number of Books/Yr.:** 30 titles/year (200 submissions) 25% by first-time authors, 75% unagented. **Proposal Process:** Send query with outline. Multiple and electronic queries accepted. Hard-copy format preferred. Response time: 4-6 weeks. **Payment:** Royalty, typically 15% net. **Sample Titles:** *Spirituality at Work*; *Book of Catholic Prayer*; *Raising Faith-Filled Kids*. **Tips:** Does not accept academic or children's material, poetry, or fiction.

MOODY PRESS

820 N LaSalle Blvd., Chicago, IL 60610-3284. 312-329-8047.
E-mail: acquisitions@moody.edu. Web site: www.moodypress.org.
Description: Evangelical Christian books in categories such as Christian living, women, marriage/family, finances, and fiction. No phone queries. Only agented proposals will be considered. **Contact:** Acquisitions Coordinator.

MOREHOUSE PUBLISHING

4775 Linglestown Rd., Harrisburg, PA 17112. 717-541-8130 .
E-mail: dfarring@morehousegroup.com. Web site: www.morehousepublishing.com.
Debra Farrington, Publisher and Editorial Director.
Description: An Episcopal publisher specializing in theology, pastoral care, church administration, spirituality, Anglican studies, and books for children ages 1-6. **Number of Books/Yr.:** 30-35 titles/year (500-750 submissions), 60% by first-time authors, 90% unagented. **Proposal Process:** Query with cover letter, brief proposal,

resume, short book description, outline, market analysis, sample chapters (20 pages). Multiple queries okay. No electronic queries. Response time: 4-6 weeks. Hard-copy format preferred. **Tips:** Children's books should contain rich theological concepts framed in terms children can understand. Must be clearly Christian, or Judeo-Christian; should approach subject matter in fresh, exciting ways. No fiction, poetry.

MULTNOMAH PUBLISHERS, INC.

P.O. Box 1720, Sisters, OR 97759. 541-549-1144.
Web site: www.multnomahbooks.com.
David Webb, Managing Editor.
Description: Evangelical, Christian publishing house. Multnomah Books are message-driven, clean, moral, uplifting fiction and nonfiction. Does not accept unsolicited manuscripts. **Proposal Process:** Submit 2-3 sample chapters with outline, cover letter, and SASE. **Payment:** Royalty.

THOMAS NELSON PUBLISHERS

P.O. Box 141000, Nashville, TN 37214-1000. .
Description: Publishes nonfiction adult inspirational, motivational, devotional, self-help, Christian living, prayer, and evangelism titles. Also, fiction from a Christian perspective. **Tips:** Does not accept unsolicited manuscripts.

NEW CANAAN PUBLISHING COMPANY

P.O. Box 752, New Canaan, CT 06840. .
E-mail: djm@newcanaanpublishing.com. Web site: www.newcanaanpublishing.com.
Kathy Mittelstadt, Editor.
Description: Publisher of children's books for readers ages 5-16. Also publishes young adult fiction/nonfiction and Christian titles. **Number of Books/Yr.:** 3-4 titles/year, (120 submissions), 50% first-time authors, 100% unagented. **Proposal Process:** Submit complete manuscript, and SASE. Accepts multiple queries, no electronic queries. Response time: 6 months. Hard copy. **Payment:** Royalty. **Tips:** Seeking strong educational and moral content.

NEW LEAF PRESS, INC.

P.O. Box 726, Green Forest, AR 72638. 870-438-5288.
E-mail: nlp@newleafpress.net. Web site: www.newleafpress.net.
Roger Howerton, Acquisitions Editor.
Description: Nonfiction, 100-400 pages, for Christian readers: how to live the Christian life, devotionals, gift books. No poetry. fiction, or personal stories. Master Books is looking for projects related to creationism, including children's books, scholarly works and books for the layman. **Number of Books/Yr.:** 15-20 titles/year (500-600 submissions), 15% first-time authors. **Proposal Process:** Query with outline and sample chapters. Multiple queries accepted. Response time: 3 months. **Payment:** Royalty, 10% of net. **Sample Titles:** Adult nonfiction, Master Books: *The Answers Book*; *Special Wonders of the Wild Kingdom*; *Buried Alive*; *When He Appears*; *The Wonder of It All*. Adult nonfiction, New Leaf Press: *365 Fascinating Facts about*

Jesus; *The Silent War*; *Living For Christ in the Endtimes*. Young adult: *The Children's Illustrated Bible*. **Tips:** Tell us why this book is marketable and to which market(s) it is directed. How will it fulfill the needs of Christians?

NORTH STAR PUBLICATIONS INC.

P.O. Box 227, East Sandwich, MA 02537-0227. 508-420-6188.
E-mail: norbook@aol.com. Web site: www.northstarpublications.com.
Description: Publisher of books on psychology, health, spirituality, inspirational, and some biography.

OUR SUNDAY VISITOR PUBLISHING

200 Noll Plaza, Huntington, IN 46750. 219-356-8400.
E-mail: booksed@osv.com. Web site: www.osv.com.
Jacquelyn M. Lindsey, Mike Dubruiel, and Beth McNamara, Acquisitions Editors.
Description: Nonfiction Catholic-oriented books of various lengths. **Number of Books/Yr.:** 20-30 titles/year (500+ submissions), 10% first-time authors, 90% unagented. **Proposal Process:** Query with proposal with outline/define market. Include SASE. Response time: 3 months. **Payment:** Royalty. **Sample Titles:** *Our Sunday Visitor's Treasury of Catholic Stories* by Gerald Costello.

PARACLETE PRESS

P.O. Box 1568, Orleans, MA 02653. 508-255-4685.
E-mail: mail@paracletepress.com. Web site: www.paracletepress.com.
Editorial Review Committee.
Description: An ecumenical publisher. Specializes in full-length, nonfiction works for the adult Christian market. **Number of Books/Yr.:** 16 titles/year, (150-250 submissions). **Proposal Process:** Query with summary of proposed book and its target audience, estimated length of book, table of contents, and 1-2 sample chapters. Multiple queries accepted. Response time: 8 weeks. **Payment:** Royalty.

PAULINE BOOKS & MEDIA

Daughters of St. Paul
50 Saint Paul's Ave., Jamaica Plain, MA 02130-3491. 617-522-8911.
Web site: www.pauline.org.
Description: Roman Catholic publications for both adults and children.

PAULIST PRESS

997 Macarthur Blvd., Mahwah, NJ 07430. 201-825-7300.
Web site: www.paulistpress.com.
Lawrence Boadt, Publisher.
Description: Adult nonfiction, 120-250 pages, on ecumenical theology, Roman Catholic studies, liturgy, spirituality, church history, ethics, religious education, and Christian philosophy. Also publishes a limited number of story books for children. **Proposal Process:** For adult books, query with SASE. For juvenile books, submit

complete manuscript, with one sample illustration. No multiple submissions. **Payment:** Flat fee or royalty. **Contact:** Paul McMahon, Editorial Director.

QUEST BOOKS

Theosophical Publishing House
306 W Geneva Rd., P.O. Box 270, Wheaton, IL 60189-0270. 630-665-0130.
E-mail: questbooks@aol.com. Web site: www.theosophical.org.
Brenda Rosen, Acquisitions Editor.
Description: Nonfiction books on Eastern and Western religion and philosophy, holistic health, healing, transpersonal psychology, men's and women's spirituality, creativity, meditation, yoga, ancient wisdom. Query with outline and sample chapters. Royalty or flat fee. **Contact:** Vija Bremanis.

ST. ANTHONY MESSENGER PRESS

28 W Liberty St., Cincinnati, OH 45210-1298. 513-241-5615.
E-mail: stanthony@americancatholic.org. Web site: www.americancatholic.org.
Lisa Biedenbach, Managing Editor.
Description: Publisher of inspirational nonfiction for Catholics. Supports a Christian lifestyle in our culture by providing material on scripture, church history, education, practical spirituality, parish ministries, and family-based religious education programs. Also publishes liturgy resources, Franciscan resources, prayer aids, and children's books. **Proposal Process:** Query with 500-word summary. **Payment:** Royalty.

SAINT MARY'S PRESS

702 Terrace Heights, Winona, MN 55987-1320. 800-533-8095.
Web site: www.smp.org.
Lorraine Kilmartin, Editor-in-Chief.
Description: Progressive Catholic publisher. Nonfiction stories about and by Catholic teens. Prayer guides and scriptural titles for teens written from an explicitly Catholic perspective.

SCHOCKEN BOOKS

The Knopf Publishing Group/Random House, Inc.,
299 Park Ave., New York, NY 10171. 212-572-2838.
Web site: www.schocken.com.
Altie Karper, Editorial Director.
Description: Fiction and nonfiction books of Jewish interest. **Number of Books/Yr.:** 9 titles/yr. **Proposal Process:** Query with outline and sample chapters. No electronic queries. Multiple queries okay. Response time: 1 month. Hard copy. **Payment:** Royalty. **Tips:** Looking for well-written fiction, history, biography, current affairs of Jewish interest for general readers.

SHAW BOOKS

2375 Telstar Dr., Suite 160, Colorado Springs, CO 80920-3669. 719-590-4999.
Description: Publisher of nonfiction books, 120-320 pages, with an evangelical Christian perspective. Some fiction and literary books. Query. Flat fee or royalty.

STANDARD PUBLISHING

8121 Hamilton Ave., Cincinnati, OH 45231. 513-931-4050.
Web site: www.standardpub.com.
Diane Stortz, Ruth Frederick, Editorial Directors.
Description: Christian children's books—board books, picture books, coloring books, Christian church curriculum/teacher resources. **Number of Books/Yr.:** 100 titles/year (2,000 submissions), 15% by first-time authors, 80% unagented. **Proposal Process:** Query with outline. Multiple queries accepted. No electronic queries. Hardcopy format. Response time: 3 months. **Payment:** Royalty (typically 5-10%) and flat fee (varies). **Sample Titles:** *My Good Night Devotions* (children's devotions, ages 3-6); *Noah, Noah!* (board book, ages 3-6). **Tips:** Currently seeking picture books, early readers, and board books. Call or write for up-to-date guidelines before submitting.

STEEPLE HILL

300 E 42nd St., Fl. 6, New York, NY 10017. 212-682-6080.
Web site: www.eharlequin.com.
Tara Gavin, Editorial Director.
Description: Romance titles with an element of Christian faith, 70,000-75,000 words, that promote strong family values and high moral standards. **Number of Books/Yr.:** 36 titles/year. **Proposal Process:** Query with two- to five-page double-spaced synopsis of the story and SASE with sufficient postage. No multiple or electronic queries. Prefers hard-copy format. Response time: 3 months. **Payment:** Royalty. **Tips:** Write from the heart. Physical interaction should emphasize emotional tenderness rather than sexual desire. Avoid situations with sexual intercourse between characters unless they are married. **Contact:** Tracy Farell (Senior Editor) or Editorial Coordinator.

TRINITY PRESS INTERNATIONAL

4795 Lingles Town Rd., Harrisburg, PA 17105. 717-541-8130.
Web site: www.trinitypressintl.com.
Henry L. Carrigan, Jr., Editorial Director.
Description: Serious studies and research in Bible and theology/religion, interfaith studies, African-American religious life and thought, biblical interpretation, and methodology. **Number of Books/Yr.:** 30 titles/year. **Proposal Process:** Query the editor with outline and sample chapters or send complete manuscript. Multiple and electronic queries are considered. Response time: 4-6 weeks. Hard-copy format preferred. **Payment:** Royalty.

TYNDALE HOUSE

351 Executive Dr., Carol Stream, IL 60188. 630-668-8300.
Web site: www.tyndale.com.

Description: Adult suspense fiction and nonfiction on subjects of concern to Christians. **Number of Books/Yr.:** 200+ titles/year. **Proposal Process:** No unsolicited mss. Agented only. Response time: 3-4 months. Hard copy. No electronic queries. **Payment:** Royalty. **Sample Titles:** Fiction: *The Mark*; *The Indwelling*. Nonfiction: *How Now Shall We Live?*; *The Control Freak*. Children's: *Mars Diaries*; *Little Blessings* series. **Tips:** No unsolicited manuscripts. Send SASE for guidelines and proposals.

UAHC PRESS

633 Third Ave., New York, NY 10017. 212-650-4120.
E-mail: uahcpress@uahc.org. Web site: www.uahcpress.com.
Rabbi Hara Person, Editorial Director.
Description: Publishes trade books and textbooks of Jewish interest for preschool through adult readers. **Number of Books/Yr.:** 18 titles/year (300 submissions), 17% by first-time authors, 100% unagented. **Proposal Process:** Query with outline and sample chapters. Response time: 4-8 weeks. Multiple queries considered. Hard-copy format preferred. **Payment:** Royalty. **Sample Titles:** Adult: *The Reform Judaism Reader: North American Documents*, by Michael A. Meyer and W. Gunther Plaut (reference); *Jewish Living: A Guide to Contemporary Reform Practice*, by Mark Washofsky (Jewish sourcebook). Children's: *The God Around Us, Volume II, The Valley of Blessings*, by Mira Pollak Brichto (ages 2-5); *Solomon and the Trees*, by Matt Biers-Ariel (ages 5-8). **Tips:** Seeking books dealing with Jewish topics in areas of textbooks for religious school classrooms, children's trade books, and adult nonfiction.

THE UPPER ROOM MINISTRIES

1908 Grand Ave., Nashville, TN 37202. 615-340-7000.
Web site: www.upperroom.org.
JoAnn Miller, Acquisitions Editor.
Description: Focuses on Christian spiritual formation (families, churches, small groups, congregational leaders, and individuals). **Number of Books/Yr.:** 25 titles/year (300 submissions), 2% by first-time authors, 100% unagented. **Proposal Process:** Query with outline, sample chapters, and SASE. Multiple queries considered. Hard-copy format preferred. **Payment:** Royalty. **Tips:** Keep these categories in mind: Opening Our Hearts and Minds to God, Walking Together with Christ, Preparing the Spiritual Way for Emerging Generations, Maturing as Spiritual Leaders, and Realizing Our Oneness in Christ. No fiction or poetry.

W PUBLISHING

545 Marriott Dr., Suite 750, P.O. Box 141000, Nashville, TN 37214. 615-902-3602.
David Moberg, Editor.
Description: Christian fiction and nonfiction, 65,000-95,000 words, dealing with the relationship and/or applications of biblical principles to everyday life. Royalty. No unsolicited manuscripts.

WESTMINSTER JOHN KNOX PRESS

Presbyterian Publishing Corporation

100 Witherspoon St., Louisville, KY 40202-1396. 502-569-5342.

E-mail: cnewman@ctr.pcusa.or. Web site: www.wjk.org.

Stephanie Egnotovich, Executive Editor.

Description: Books that inform, interpret, challenge, and encourage religious faith and living. Query Karen Kaye, Assistant Editor; do not send complete manuscript. Royalty. SASE for guidelines.

ZONDERKIDZ

Zondervan Publishing

5300 Patterson Ave. SE, Grand Rapids, MI 49530. 616-698-6900.

Web site: www.zondervan.com.

Julie Marchese, Editorial Assistant.

Description: Publishes children's books based on Christian values. **Tips:** Prospective writers must follow guidelines closely, or submissions will go unread.

ZONDERVAN PUBLISHING HOUSE

HarperCollins Publishers

5300 Patterson Ave. SE, Grand Rapids, MI 49530. 616-698-6900.

E-mail: zpub@zph.com. Web site: www.zondervan.com.

Diane Bloem, Manuscript Editor.

Description: Publisher of Christian titles. General fiction and nonfiction for children and adults. Send SASE for guidelines. Do not send manuscripts or queries via e-mail. No poetry, drama, sermons, cookbooks, or dissertations. Payment varies. **Number of Books/Yr.:** 150 titles per year. **Proposal Process:** Query with outline and sample chapters. Will consider multiple queries. **Payment:** Varies. **Sample Titles:** *When Bad Things Happen to Good Marriages*; *Hustling God*; *The Life Promises Bible*. **Tips:** Does not accept unsolicited manuscripts and proposals sent by air or surface mail. Authors may submit their work by faxing their proposals to 616-698-3454, c/o Book Proposal Review Editor; or they may submit work electronically to First Edition, The ECPA Manuscript Service at www.ecpa.org.

OTHER MARKETS
& RESOURCES

AGENTS

As the number of book publishers that will consider only agented submissions grows, more writers are turning to agents to sell their manuscripts. The agents in the following list handle both literary and dramatic material. Included in each listing are such important details as type of material represented, submission procedure, and commission. Since agents derive their income from the sales of their clients' work, they must represent writers who are selling fairly regularly to good markets. Nonetheless, many of the agents listed here note they will consider unpublished writers. Always query an agent first, and enclose a self-addressed, stamped envelope; most agents will not respond without it. Do not send any manuscripts until the agent has asked you to do so; and be wary of agents who charge fees for reading manuscripts. All of the following agents have indicated they do not charge reading fees; however, some charge for copyright fees, manuscript retyping, photocopies, copies of books for use in the sale of other rights, and long distance calls.

To learn more about agents and their role in publishing, the Association of Authors' Representatives, Inc., publishes a canon of ethics as well as an up-to-date list of AAR members. Write to: Association of Authors' Representatives, P.O. Box 237201, Ansonia Station, New York, NY 10023, or visit their Web site: www.aar-online.org.

Another good source which lists agents and their policies is Literary Market Place, a directory found in most libraries.

ABRAMS ARTISTS AGENCY
275 Seventh Ave., Fl. 26, New York, NY 10001. 646-486-4600.
Description: Plays and screenplays. Averages 1,000 queries/submissions per year. Unpublished writers considered. Query with synopsis, up to 10 sample pages, bio/resume, SASE required. No electronic queries. Multiple queries okay. Commission: 10% scripts. Fees: None. **Contact:** Charmaine Ferenczi.

BRET ADAMS LTD.
448 W 44th St., New York, NY 10036.
Description: Screenplays, teleplays, stage plays, and musicals. Unproduced writers considered. Query with synopsis, bio, resume, and SASE. Commission: 10%. Fees: None. **Contact:** Bruce Ostler, Bret Adams.

MICHAEL AMATO AGENCY
1650 Broadway, Suite 307, New York, NY 10019-6833.
Description: Screenplays. Send query or complete manuscript. Commission: 10%. Fees: None.

MARCIA AMSTERDAM AGENCY
41 W 82 St., #9A, New York, NY 10024.
Description: Adult and young adult fiction; mainstream nonfiction. Screenplays and teleplays: comedy, romance, psychological suspense. Query with resume, SASE; mul-

tiple queries okay; 2-week exclusive for requested submissions, 2 days to 2 weeks to respond to queries. 14,000 submissions per year; 5-6% unsolicited material accepted. Accepts unsolicited queries, but not manuscripts. Considers unpublished writers. No electronic queries. Commission: 15% books; 10% screen or TV, 20% foreign. Fees: photocopying and shipping. **Contact:** Marcia Amsterdam.

AXELROD AGENCY
49 Main St., P.O. Box 357, Chatham, NY 12037. 413-637-2000.
E-mail: steve@axelrodagency.com.
Description: Fiction and nonfiction, film and TV rights, software. No unsolicited mss; query first. No reading fee. Commissions: 15% domestic, 20% foreign. **Contact:** Steven Axelrod.

MALAGA BALDI LITERARY AGENCY
204 W 84th St., Suite 3 C, New York, NY 10024. 212-579-5075.
E-mail: mbaldi@aol.com. **Description:** Quality literary adult fiction and nonfiction. Averages thousands of queries/submissions per year; 2% of unsolicited material accepted. Considers unsolicited queries/manuscripts. Unpublished writers considered. Query first; if interested, will ask for proposal, outline, and sample pages for nonfiction, complete manuscript for fiction. SASE required. Response time: to 10 weeks. No electronic queries. Multiple queries okay. Commission: 15%. Fees: None. **Contact:** Malaga Baldi.

THE BALKIN AGENCY
P.O. Box 222, Amherst, MA 01004. 413-548-9835.
E-mail: balkin@crocker.com.
Description: Specializes in adult nonfiction, professional books, and college textbooks. No fiction. No unsolicited mss; query first; submit outline and 1 sample chapter. No reading fee. 15% agency commission, 20% foreign rights. **Contact:** Rick Balkin.

LORETTA BARRETT BOOKS
101 Fifth Ave., New York, NY 10003. 212-242-3420.
Description: Specializes in fiction and nonfiction. Handles film and TV rights. No unsolicited mss; query first with SASE. Submit outlines, sample chapters (nonfiction); synopsis, (fiction). No reading fee. Representatives on West Coast and in all major foreign countries. **Contact:** Loretta Barrett, Nick Mullendore.

BERMAN, BOALS, & FLYNN
208 W 30th St., Suite 401, New York, NY 10001. 212-868-1068.
Description: Full-length stage plays, musicals. Considers unsolicited queries, but not manuscripts. Unpublished, unproduced writers considered only rarely, unless recommended by industry colleagues. Query with SASE, bio, and resume. Commission: 10%. **Contact:** Judy Boals.

BIG SCORE PRODUCTIONS

P.O. Box 4575, Lancaster, PA 17604. 717-293-0247.
E-mail: bigscore@bigscoreproductions.com.
Web site: www.bigscoreproductions.com.
David Robie, Agent.
Description: Nonfiction and fiction. Specializes in inspiration and self-help non-fiction, and commercial fiction. No children's books or poetry. Represents 10-20 clients. 25% of clients are new or previously unpublished writers. Send query or proposal with outline and table of contents. Welcomes new writers. See Web site for guidelines.

REID BOATES LITERARY AGENCY

Box 328, 69 Cooks Crossroad, Pittstown, NJ 08867-0328. 908-730-8523.
Description: Adult mainstream nonfiction only. Agents in film and in all major foreign markets. Query first with SASE. Unpublished writers considered. No multiple queries or unsolicited manuscripts. Commission: 15%. Fees: None. **Contact:** Reid Boates.

BOOK DEALS, INC.

417 N Sangamon St., Chicago, IL 60606. 312-491-0300.
E-mail: bookdeals@aol.com. Web site: www.bookdealsinc.com.
Description: General-interest adult fiction and nonfiction. Ave. 6,000 queries/submissions per year; less than 1% unsolicited material accepted. Considers unsolicited queries, but not manuscripts. Considers unpublished writers with professional credentials, quality work. Query with SASE. Responds: 2-3 weeks for queries, 4-6 weeks for submissions. Accepts electronic and multiple queries. Commission: 15% domestic, 20% foreign. Fees: copying, shipping. See Web site for details. **Contact:** Caroline Carney.

BOOKSTOP LITERARY AGENCY

67 Meadow View Rd., Orinda, CA 94563. 925-254-2664.
Description: Juvenile and young adult fiction and nonfiction, also illustration for children's books. Unpublished writers considered. Mss evaluation services available. No queries; send complete manuscript (fiction), sample chapters and outline (nonfiction). No reading fee. Commission: 15%. Fees: photocopying, shipping. **Contact:** Kendra Marcus.

GEORGES BORCHARDT, INC.

136 E. 57th St., New York, NY 10022. 212-753-5785.
Description: Fiction and nonfiction. No unsolicited mss. Handles film and TV rights, software. Commission: 15%.

BRANDT & HOCHMAN LITERARY AGENTS

1501 Broadway, New York, NY 10036. 212-840-5760.
Description: Fiction and nonfiction. No unsolicited mss; query first. No reading fee.

Agents in most foreign countries. Foreign rep: AM Heath & Co. Ltd. (UK). No submissions by fax; include SASE with query. **Contact:** Carl D. Brandt, Gail Hochman, Marianne Merola, Charles Schlessiger, Meg Giles.

ANDREA BROWN LITERARY AGENCY, INC

P.O. Box 1027, Montara, CA 94037. 650-728-1783.
Description: Children's and young adult fiction and nonfiction only. Film and TV rights. Query with outline, sample pages, bio, and resume, and SASE; no faxes. Commission: 15% domestic; 20% foreign. Fees: None. **Contact:** Andrea Brown.

CURTIS BROWN LTD.

10 Astor Pl., New York, NY 10003. 212-473-5400.
Peter L. Ginsberg, President. **Description:** Handles general trade fiction and nonfiction, juvenile. No unsolicited mss; query first with SASE. Submit outline or sample chapters. No reading fee. Other fees: photocopies, express mail, etc. Handles software, film and TV rights, multimedia. Reps in all major foreign countries.

KNOX BURGER ASSOCIATES

425 Madison Avenue, New York, NY 10017. 212-759-8600.
E-mail: kburger@haroldober.com. **Description:** Adult fiction and nonfiction. No science fiction, fantasy, or romance. Highly selective. Unsolicited queries accepted, but not unsolicited manuscripts. Query with SASE. No multiple or electronic queries. Commission: 15%. Fees: Photocopying. **Contact:** Knox Burger.

SHEREE BYKOFSKY ASSOCIATES, INC.

16 W 36th St., New York, NY 10018.
Description: Adult nonfiction and fiction. Unpublished writers considered. Query with outline, up to 3 sample pages or proposal, and SASE. Multiple queries okay if noted as such. Commission: 15%. Fees: None.

MARTHA CASSELMAN

P.O. Box 342, Calistoga, CA 94515-0342. 707-942-4341.
Martha Casselman. **Description:** Trade nonfiction, food and cookbooks. No fiction, poetry, short stories, children's or YA books. No unsolicited mss; query first (not by fax). Submit brief sample and synopsis (no simultaneous submissions) with SASE, query letter with SASE. No reading fee. Some expenses (copying, overnight mail).

JULIE CASTIGLIA LITERARY AGENCY

1155 Camino del Mar, Suite 510, Del Mar, CA 92014. 858-755-8761.
Julie Castiglia, PEN and AAR. **Description:** Specializes in ethnic, commercial, and literary fiction, science, biography, psychology, women's issues, business/finance, popular culture, health, and niche books. Submit query letter. No phone queries. Handles TV and film rights. Major postal, mss copying, and other unusual expenses. No reading fee.

HY COHEN LITERARY AGENCY

66 Brookfield Rd., Upper Montclair, NJ 07043-1327. 973-783-9494.
E-mail: cogency@comcast.net.
Hy Cohen, Director.
Description: Quality adult and young adult fiction and nonfiction. Averages several hundred queries/submissions per year; few unsolicited material accepted. Considers unsolicited queries and manuscripts. Unpublished writers considered. Query with SASE. Multiple submissions encouraged. Accepts electronic queries. Responds: Several days to queries, 2 weeks to submissions. Commission: 10% domestic; 20% foreign. Fees: Phone, photocopying, postage.

DON CONGDON ASSOCIATES

156 Fifth Ave., Suite 625, New York, NY 10010. 212-645-1229.
E-mail: dca@doncongdon.com
Don Congdon, Susan Ramer, Michael Congdon, Cristina Concepcion, AAR.
Description: Handles any and all trade books, for professional writers. Handles film and TV rights for regular clients. No unsolicited mss; query first with SASE. No reading fee.

DOE COOVER AGENCY

P.O. Box 668, Winchester, MA 01890. 781-721-6000.
Description: Handles a broad range of nonfiction, including memoirs, biographies, business, social science, cooking, and gardening. Also handles literary fiction, software, TV and film rights (only on agency projects). Averages 500 queries/submissions per year; 2% unsolicited material accepted. Considers unsolicited queries, but not manuscripts. Unpublished writers considered. Query with outline, sample pages, bio/resume, SASE. Responds: 2 weeks. Multiple queries okay. No electronic queries. Commission: 15%. Fees: None. **Contact:** Frances Kennedy.

RICHARD CURTIS ASSOCIATES

171 E 74th St., New York, NY 10021. 212-772-7363.
Web site: www.curtisagency.com.
Description: Commercial adult nonfiction and commercial fiction by published authors. Averages 3,000 submissions/queries per year; less than 1% unsolicited material accepted. No unsolicited manuscripts. Considers unpublished writers in nonfiction only. Query with bio/resume and SASE. Responds: 4 weeks to queries. No electronic or multiple queries. Commission: 15% domestic; 20% foreign. Fees: some expenses for copying and shipping, for accepted work. **Contact:** Pamela Valvera.

DARHANSOFF, VERRILL, FELDMAN LITERARY AGENTS

236 W 26th St., Suite 802, New York, NY 10001. 917-305-1300.
Description: Fiction and nonfiction, literary fiction, history, science, biography, pop culture, and current affairs. No unsolicited mss; query first. Film and TV rights handled by Los Angeles associates, Lynn Pleshette, Richard Green, and UTA. Agents in many foreign countries. **Contact:** Liz Darhansoff, Leigh Feldman, Charles Verrill.

SANDRA DIJKSTRA LITERARY AGENCY, PMB

515, 1155 Camino del Mar, Del Mar, CA 92014. 858-755-3115.
E-mail: sdla@dijkstraagency.com.
Description: Adult literary and commercial fiction. Historical and inspirational non-fiction and mysteries. Unsolicited queries and manuscripts not considered. Unpublished writers considered. Query with outline and bio/resume. Submit first 50 pages and synopsis (fiction); proposal (nonfiction). SASE required. Responds in 4 weeks to queries, 6-8 weeks to submissions. No electronic queries. Multiple queries accepted. Commission: 15% domestic, 20% foreign. Fees: Clients billed for mailing and copy costs. Some editorial services for clients. **Contact:** Stacy Carlock.

JONATHAN DOLGER AGENCY

49 E 96th St., 9B, New York, NY 10128. 212-427-1853.
Description: Adult fiction and nonfiction; illustrated books. No unsolicited mss; query first with SASE. Film and TV rights handled by Los Angeles associate. Agents in all principal foreign countries. **Contact:** Jonathan Dolger, Dee Ratterree.

DWYER & O'GRADY, INC.

P.O. Box 239, East Lempster, NH 03605. 603-863-9347.
Description: Specializes in children's fiction with emphasis on picture books and middle grade/young adult readers. Not accepting new clients. No unsolicited mss; query by letter first. No telephone queries. Handles film and TV rights. No reading fee. Member: ABA, SCBWI, Society of Illustrators. **Contact:** Elizabeth O'Grady.

JANE DYSTEL LITERARY MANAGEMENT

One Union Square W., Suite 904, New York, NY 10003. 212-627-9100.
Web site: www.dystel.com.
Description: Adult fiction and nonfiction. Averages 15,000 queries/submission per year; 10% unsolicited material accepted. Considers unsolicited queries, but not manuscripts. Unpublished writers considered. Query with bio/resume. Responds: 3-5 weeks to queries, 2 months to submissions. Accepts electronic queries. No multiple queries. Commission: 15% domestic, 19% foreign. Fees: None. Editorial feedback on projects chosen to represent.

EDUCATIONAL DESIGN SERVICES

P.O. Box 253, Wantaugh, NY 11793.
Description: Educational texts (K-12 only). Averages 300 queries/submissions per year; 3% unsolicited material accepted. Considers unsolicited queries and manuscripts. Unpublished writers considered. Query with outline, sample pages or complete manuscript, bio/resume, and SASE. No electronic queries. Considers multiple queries. Responds: 4-6 weeks for queries and submissions. Commission: 15% domestic, 25% foreign. Fees: None. **Contact:** Bertram L. Linder.

ETHAN ELLENBERG LITERARY AGENCY

548 Broadway, Suite #5E, New York, NY 10012. 212-431-4554.
E-mail: agent@ethanellenberg.com.
Web site: www.ethanellenberg.com.
Description: Seeking established and new writers in wide range of genres. All commercial fiction: thrillers, mysteries, children's romance, women's fiction, ethnic, science fiction, fantasy, general fiction. Also, literary fiction with strong narrative. No poetry or short stories. Nonfiction: current affairs, health, science, psychology, cookbooks, new age, spirituality, pop-science, pop-culture, adventure, true crime, biography, and memoir. For fiction, query with first 3 chapters, synopsis, SASE. For nonfiction, a proposal with sample material, if possible, and SASE. Averages 10,000 queries/submission per year; 5% unsolicited material accepted. Accepts unsolicited queries and manuscripts. Responds 1-2 weeks for queries, 4-6 weeks for submissions. No phone calls. Accepts electronic and multiple queries. Commission: 15% domestic; 20% foreign. No reading fees, some fees for copying, shipping. **Contact:** Ethan Ellenberg, Michael Psaltis.

ANN ELMO AGENCY

60 E. 42nd St., New York, NY 10165. 212-661-2880.
Description: Handles books, plays, movie and TV rights, and teenage books. No unsolicited mss; query letters only. No reading fee. Agents in all European countries.
Contact: Lettie Lee, Andree Abecassis, Mari Cronin.

FELICIA ETH

555 Bryant St., Suite 350, Palo Alto, CA 94301. 650-375-1276.
Felicia Eth, AAR.
Description: Selective mainstream literary fiction; diverse nonfiction including psychology, health, popular science, women's issues, investigative journalism, and biography. No unsolicited mss; query first for fiction, proposal for nonfiction. Handles film and TV rights for clients' books only, through subagents in L.A. No reading fee. Foreign rights agents and reps in all major territories.

FARBER LITERARY AGENCY

14 E 75th St., New York, NY 10021. 212-861-7075.
E-mail: farberlit@aol.com. Web site: www.donaldfarber.com.
Description: All original fiction and nonfiction, adult, young adult and children, plays. Considers unpublished writers and unsolicited queries. Query with outline, 3 chapter, SASE. Averages 4,000 queries/submissions per year. Accepts unsolicited manuscripts. Responds: queries 3-5 days, submissions 3-10 weeks. No electronic queries. Considers multiple queries. Commission: 15%, includes legal services of Donald C. Farber, entertainment attorney. No fees. Editorial services in exceptional cases, for a fee. **Contact:** Ann Farber.

FLANNERY LITERARY

1140 Wickfield Ct., Naperville, IL 60563-3300. 630-428-2682.
E-mail: flanlit@aol.com.
Description: Fiction and nonfiction for children and young adults, all genres, infant to college age. Accepts unsolicited queries/manuscripts. Unpublished writers considered. Query by letter only (no phone or fax queries); multiple queries okay, SASE required. Responds: 2 weeks for queries, 3-4 weeks for submissions. No electronic queries. Commission: 15% domestic, 20% foreign. Fees: None. **Contact:** Jennifer Flannery.

FOGELMAN LITERARY AGENCY

7515 Greenville Ave., Suite 712, Dallas, TX 75231. 214-361-9956.
E-mail: info@fogelman.com. Web site: www.fogelman.com.
Description: Women's fiction, romance, mystery, suspense, and thrillers. Nonfiction that targets a female audience, or has commercial/pop-culture appeal. Published authors may call, unpublished authors are invited to submit a query (1-2 pages) with SASE. Handles TV and film rights. Commission: 15% domestic; 10% foreign. Fees: None. **Contact:** Evan M. Fogelman or Linda Kruger.

ROBERT A. FREEDMAN DRAMATIC AGENCY

1501 Broadway, Suite 2310, New York, NY 10036. 212-840-5760.
Description: Screenplays, teleplays, and stage plays. No unsolicited mss; send query first. Multiple queries okay. Commission: Standard. No reading fees. Fees: Photocopying. **Contact:** Robert A. Freedman or Selma Luttinger for stage plays; Robin Kaver for screenplays or teleplays..

GELFMAN SCHNEIDER

250 W 57th St., Suite 2515, New York, NY 10107. 212-245-1993.
E-mail: gsla@msn.com.
Description: Contemporary women's commercial fiction; literary and commercial fiction; mystery and suspense; some nonfiction. Ave. 2,000 queries/submissions per year. Considers unsolicited queries/not manuscripts. Unpublished writers considered. Query with outline, sample pages, and bio; SASE required. No electronic queries, by mail only. Responds in 4-6 weeks to queries. Responds to multiple queries. Commission: 15% domestic; 20% foreign; 15% film and dramatic. Fees: None. **Contact:** Cathy Gleason.

GEM LITERARY SERVICES

4717 Poe Rd., Medina, OH 44256.
Description: Fiction, all genres (no erotica), and nonfiction. Submit complete manuscript with SASE, short bio, and 2-5 page synopsis for fiction; chapter outline for nonfiction. Mark envelope: "Submission." Commission: 15% domestic; 20% foreign and film rights. Fees: None. **Contact:** Darla L. Pfenninger.

GOODMAN ASSOCIATES

500 West End Ave., New York, NY 10024. 212-873-4806.
Description: Adult book-length fiction and nonfiction. No plays, screenplays, poetry, textbooks, science fiction, or children's books. Accepting new clients on a highly selective and limited basis. No unsolicited mss; query first with SASE. No reading fee. Handles film and TV rights for clients' materials. Reps in Hollywood and major foreign markets. **Contact:** Elise Simon Goodman.

GRAYBILL & ENGLISH, LLC

1920 N St. NW, Suite 620, Washington, DC 20036. 202-861-0106.
Web site: www.graybillandenglish.com.
Description: 20% adult fiction, 80% adult nonfiction. Nina Graybill: nonfiction, literary/commercial fiction. Elaine English: women's fiction, including romance (single titles). Kristen Auclair: nonfiction, women's issues, literary fiction. Jeff Kleinman: nonfiction, especially historical, literary/commercial fiction. Lynn Whitakker: nonfiction, literary fiction, women's fiction, mystery. Send query letter with bio, proposal or up to 3 sample chapters, and SASE. No unsolicited manuscripts. Averages 3,000 queries/submissions per year; accepts less than 10% unsolicited material. Considers unpublished writers. Responds: 2-3 weeks to queries, up to 8 weeks for requested submissions. Multiple queries okay. Commission: 15% domestic, 20% foreign and dramatic. Fees: Photocopying, shipping, etc. Members of AAR.

SANFORD J. GREENBURGER ASSOCIATES

55 Fifth Ave., Fl. 15, New York, NY 10003. 212-206-5600.
Web site: www.greenburger.com. **Description:** All types of fiction and nonfiction, including sports books, health, business, psychology, parenting, science, biography, gay; juvenile books. Unpublished writers with strong credentials considered. Query with proposal, including sample pages, bio, and SASE. Multiple queries okay. Considers unsolicited queries and manuscripts. Responds: Queries and submissions, 4-6 weeks. Commission: 15% domestic; 20% foreign. Fees: Photocopying. **Contact:** Heide Lange.

CHARLOTTE GUSAY LITERARY AGENCY

10532 Blythe, Los Angeles, CA 90064. 310-559-0831.
E-mail: gusay1@aol.com. Web site: www.mediastudio.com/gusay. **Description:** Adult/juvenile fiction, nonfiction, screenplays, books to film, young adult material suitable for film. Averages 2,000 queries/submissions per year. Accepts unsolicited queries, but not manuscripts. Considers unpublished writers. Submit 1-page query only, with bio/resume and SASE. Multiple queries discouraged. Responds: 3-6 weeks for queries, 6-8 weeks for submissions. Commission: 15%. No reading fees. If accepted, we share out-of-pocket expenses. Occasional nonfiction book proposal consultation. **Contact:** Charlotte Gusay.

HARDEN CURTIS ASSOCIATES
850 Seventh Ave., Suite 405, New York, NY 10019.
Description: Stage plays. Query with bio and resume, SASE; no multiple queries.
Commission: 10%. Fees: None. Not accepting new clients at this time.

JOY HARRIS LITERARY AGENCY
156 Fifth Ave., Suite 617, New York, NY 10010. 212-924-6269.
Joy Harris, AAR.
Description: Adult fiction and nonfiction. Submit outline or sample chapters. No
unsolicited mss; query first with return postage. Film and TV rights. Agents in all
major territories. No fees.

JOHN L. HOCHMANN BOOKS
320 E 58th St., New York, NY 10022-2220. 212-319-0505.
Description: Adult nonfiction, biography, history, textbooks for college courses with
heavy enrollment, gay/lesbian, popular medical. **Contact:** Theodora Eagle.

THE BARBARA HOGENSON AGENCY, INC.
165 West End Ave., Suite 19-C, New York, NY 10023.
Description: Adult fiction, nonfiction, stage plays. Query with bio and synopsis,
SASE. Multiple queries okay. Commission: 10% plays; 15% books. Fees: None.
Contact: Barbara Hogenson.

IMG BACH LITERARY AGENCY
22 E 71st St., New York, NY 10021. 212-489-5400.
E-mail: ckrupp@imgworld com.
Description: Specializes in fiction and nonfiction. No unsolicited mss; query first
with SASE. Handles film and TV rights. No reading fee. Foreign rep: Sophia Seidner.
Contact: Julian Bach, Carolyn Krupp.

JCA LITERARY AGENCY
27 W 20th St., Suite 1103, New York, NY 10011. 212-807-0888.
Jeff Gerecke, Tony Outhwaite, Peter Steinberg, AAR.
Description: Adult fiction and nonfiction. Unpublished writers considered. Query
with sample pages; multiple queries okay. Commission: 15% domestic; 20% foreign.
Fees: Photocopying, shipping. "Be straightforward, to-the-point. Don't try to hype us
or bury us in detail." No unsolicited manuscripts. No children's books, no screenplays.

NATASHA KERN LITERARY AGENCY
P.O. Box 2908, Portland, OR 97208-2908. 503-297-6190.
Web site: www.natashakern.com.
Description: Full-service agency, commercial adult fiction and nonfiction books,
represents bestselling authors, as well as beginners. Co-agents in Hollywood and all
foreign markets. Nonfiction: health, natural science, investigative journalism, inspiration, new age, psychology, self-help, parenting, gardening, business, also current, con-

troversial and women's issues. Fiction: specializes in thrillers, mysteries, mainstream women's fiction, historicals, romances. No horror, true crime, children's or young adult, short stories, poetry, scripts, software, sports, photography, cookbooks, gift books, scholarly works. Averages 10,000 queries/submissions per year; 1% unsolicited material accepted. Considers unsolicited queries, but not manuscripts. Considers unpublished writers. Responds: 3-4 weeks for queries, 8 weeks for submissions. Considers multiple queries. Commission: 15% domestic; 10% foreign. Fees: None. **Contact:** Natasha Kern.

KIDDE, HOYT & PICARD

335 E 51st St., New York, NY 10022. 212-755-9465.
E-mail: khp@worldnet.att.net. Web site: http://khp.home.att.net. **Description:** Mainstream fiction, literary fiction, romance, mysteries, and general nonfiction. Averages 5,000 queries/submission per year. Will consider authors who have published short stories, articles, essays, or other short works. Consideration is also given to participants of writing workshops and related degree programs. Unsolicited queries considered, but not unsolicited manuscripts. Query letter should include short synopsis of work, past writing experience, and SASE. Multiple queries okay. Responds: 2 weeks to queries, 1 month to submissions. Do not fax queries. Commission: 15% domestic, 20% foreign. Fees: Photocopying. "Looking for exciting, witty, compelling characters, in psychologically suspenseful plot (fiction)—and the counterpart of that in nonfiction." **Contact:** Katharine Kidde, Zarinah Jones.

KIRCHOFF/WOHLBERG, INC.

866 United Nations Plaza, Suite 525, New York, NY 10017. 212-644-2020.
Description: Children and young adult fiction and nonfiction tradebooks only. No adult titles. No unsolicied mss. Query first with outline, sample chapter, SASE. No fees. **Contact:** Lisa Pulitzer-Voges.

HARVEY KLINGER, INC.

301 W 53rd St., New York, NY 10019. 212-581-7068.
Description: Mainstream adult fiction and nonfiction, literary and commercial. Unpublished writers considered. Query with outline, sample pages, and bio/resume. No multiple queries; no phone calls or faxes. Averages 5,000 queries per year; 1% unsolicited material accepted. No unsolicited manuscripts. Responds 4-6 weeks for queries and 2-3 months for submissions. SASE required. Commission: 15% domestic, 25% foreign. Fees: Photocopying, shipping. "We critique clients' work carefully to get manuscript in best possible form before submitting to publishers." **Contact:** Harvey Klinger.

BARBARA S. KOUTS

P.O. Box 560, Bellport, NY 11713. 631-286-1278.
Description: Adult/children's fiction and nonfiction. Unpublished writers considered. Query with bio/resume. Multiple queries okay. Averages 1,500 queries per year; 10% unsolicited material accepted. Accepts unsolicited material, but not manuscripts.

Considers unpublished writers. Responds: 1 week for queries, 6-8 weeks for submissions, SASE required. No electronic queries. Multiple queries okay. Commission: 10%, 20% foreign. **Contact:** Barbara Kouts.

OTTO R. KOZAK LITERARY AGENCY

P.O. Box 152, Long Beach, NY 11561.
Web site: www.internationalliteraryagent.com.
Description: Scripts only. Represents writers of family-oriented movie and TV movie scripts and docudramas based on true stories. Averages 400 queries/submission per year; 5% unsolicited material accepted. Considers unsolicited queries, but not manuscripts. Unproduced script writers considered. Query with outline, SASE required. Do not send full manuscript. Responds: 2 weeks to queries, 4 weeks to submissions. No electronic queries. Accepts multiple queries. Commission: 10%. Fees: None. Editorial services on occasion. See Web site for details. **Contact:** Yitka Kozak.

EDITE KROLL LITERARY AGENCY, INC

12 Grayhurst Pk., Portland, ME 04102. 207-773-4922.
Description: Feminist and issue-oriented nonfiction, humor, children's fiction, and picture books written and illustrated by artists. No genre. Unpublished writers considered. Query with outline and sample chapter (dummy for picture books), a brief note about the author, and SASE; multiple queries okay. Keep queries brief; no phone or e-queries.Commission: 15% U.S.; 20% foreign. Fees: Photocopying, legal. **Contact:** Edite Kroll.

THE LA LITERARY AGENCY

P.O. Box 888, Pacific Palis: des, CA 90272. 310-459-8415.
E-mail: laliteraryag@aol.com. **Description:** Adult fiction and nonfiction books; handles film and TV rights. No unsolicited mss., query first with outline, sample pages (approx. 50), bio/resume, SASE. No reading fee. **Contact:** Ann Cashman.

PETER LAMPACK AGENCY

551 Fifth Ave., Suite 1613, New York, NY 10014. 212-687-9106.
E-mail: renboPLA@aol.com. **Description:** Commercial and literary fiction; nonfiction by experts in a given field (especially autobiography, biography, law, finance, politics, history). No horror, sci-fi, westerns, romance. Handles motion picture/TV rights from book properties only. No original screenplays. Averages 3,000 queries/submissions per year; less than 1% unsolicited material accepted. Considers unsolicited queries, but not manuscripts. Unpublished writers considered. Query should include the nature of the submission, plus author's credentials. Sample chapter, synopsis, SASE required, e-mail address if applicable. Responds: 3 weeks to queries and submissions. No electronic queries accepted. Multiple queries okay. Commission: 15% domestic; 20% foreign. Fees: None. **Contact:** Loren Soeiro.

THE LANTZ OFFICE

200 W 57th St., Suite 503, New York, NY 10019. 212-586-0200.
Description: Adult fiction and nonfiction. Stage plays. Query with bio and resume; no multiple queries. Fees: None. **Contact:** Robert Lantz.

MICHAEL LARSEN/ELIZABETH POMADA

1029 Jones St., San Francisco, CA 94109. 415-673-0939.
E-mail: larsenpoma@aol.com. Web site: www.larsen-pomada.com.
Description: New voices and fresh ideas in literary/commercial fiction and nonfiction for adults. Averages 5,000 queries/submission per year; 1% of unsolicited material accepted. Considers unsolicited queries. Unpublished writers welcome. Query (fiction) with first 10 pages, synopsis of finished work, and phone number. SASE required. For nonfiction, read and follow Michael's book *How to Write a Book Proposal,* then send by mail or e-mail the title or promotion plan. Responds in 6-8 weeks to queries, 4-6 weeks to submissions. No electronic queries. Multiple queries okay with notice. Commission: 15% domestic, 20% foreign. Fees: None. **Contact:** Elizabeth Pomada (fiction), Michael Larsen (nonfiction).

ELLEN LEVINE LITERARY AGENCY

15 E 26th St., Suite 1801, New York, NY 10010. 212-889-0620.
Ellen Levine, Diana Finch, Elizabeth Kaplan, and Louise Quayle, AAR.
Description: General fiction and nonfiction. Handles film and TV rights for clients only. No unsolicited mss; query with SASE, then submit outline and sample chapters. No reading fees. Representatives in Hollywood.

NANCY LOVE LITERARY AGENCY

250 E 65th St., Suite 4A, New York, NY 10021. 212-980-3499.
Description: Adult nonfiction: health, self-help, parenting, medical, psychology, women's issues, memoirs (literary), current affairs, pop science. Popular reference if by an authority, with a fresh slant. Adult fiction: mysteries and thrillers only. Averages 2,000 queries/submissions per year; 1% unsolicited material accepted. Considers unsolicited queries, but not manuscripts. Query with SASE. Responds: 4 weeks to queries. No electronic queries. Multiple submissions accepted. Commission: 15% domestic, 20% foreign. Fees: Photocopying, overseas shipping. Editorial services: Light editing, not in-depth rewrite or collaboration. "Looking for brands, authorities with a track record." **Contact:** Jane McCarthy.

DONALD MAASS LITERARY AGENCY

160 W 95th St., Suite 1B, New York, NY 10025. 212-757-7755.
Description: Fiction only. No unsolicited mss. Query first with SASE. Handles film and TV rights. No reading fee. **Contact:** Donald Maass.

GINA MACCOBY LITERARY AGENCY

P.O. Box 60, Chappaqua, NY 10514. 914-238-5630.
Description: Fiction and nonfiction for adults and children. Handles film and TV

rights. No unsolicited mss; query first with SASE. No reading fee. Agents in Hollywood and many foreign countries. Foreign rep: A. M. Heath & Co.

CAROL MANN LITERARY AGENCY
55 Fifth Ave., New York, NY 10003. 212-206-5635.
E-mail: kim@carolmannagency.com.
Carol Mann; Jim Fitzgerald; Ms. Leylha Ahuile.
Description: General nonfiction and literary fiction. Specializes in current affairs, self-help, popular culture, psychology, parenting, history. Does not accept genre fiction (mystery, romance, etc). Member AAR. Represents 100 clients; 25% of clients are new/unpublished writers. 70% nonfiction; 30% novels. **Contact:** Kim Goldstein.

MANUS & ASSOCIATES LITERARY AGENCY
445 Park Ave., Fl. 10, New York, NY 10022. 212-644-8020.
Web site: www.manuslit.com.
Description: General fiction and dramatic nonfiction books, TV and motion picture rights. No unsolicited mss; query first with synopsis and first 30 pages. No reading fee. Representatives on West Coast and all major foreign countries; handles software only in connection with our books. **Contact:** Janet Wilkens Manus.

ELISABETH MARTON AGENCY
One Union Square W., Rm. 612, New York, NY 10003-3303.
Description: Plays only. Not considering new work at this time. Commission: 10%. Fees: None. **Contact:** Tonda Marton.

JED MATTES, INC.
2095 Broadway, #302, New York, NY 10023-2895. 212-595-5228.
E-mail: general@jedmattes.com.
Description: Fiction and nonfiction. Handles film and TV rights. No unsolicited mss; query first. No reading fee. Agents in many foreign countries. Foreign reps: Greene & Heaton Ltd. (UK); the Marsh Agency. **Contact:** Jed Mattes, Fred Morris.

HENRY MORRISON, INC.
P.O. Box 235, Bedford Hills, NY 10507. 914-666-3500.
Henry Morrison.
Description: Fiction and nonfiction, screenplays. Handles film and TV rights. Send query and outline first with SASE. No reading fee; fee for mss copies, galleys, and bound books for foreign and domestic submissions.

JEAN V. NAGGAR LITERARY AGENCY
216 E 75th St., New York, NY 10021. 212-794-1082.
Description: Strong adult mainstream fiction and nonfiction, from literary to commercial, with a good story told in a distinctive voice. Solid nonfiction; little self-help, no sports or politics. Averages 6,000 queries/submission per year. Considers unsolicited queries, but not unsolicited manuscripts. Considers some unpublished writers.

Query with outline, SASE, bio, and resume. No electronic or multiple queries. Responds: 48 hours to queries, several weeks for requested manuscript submissions. Commission: 15% domestic, 20% foreign. Fees: None. **Contact:** Jean Naggar, Alice Tasman.

RUTH NATHAN AGENCY

141 E 33 St., New York, NY 10016. 212-481-1185.

Description: Few illustrated books, fine art and decorative arts, biography in those areas, true crime, show business, medieval historical fiction (no fantasy). No unsolicited mss; query first. Send 1-page outline and sample chapters. Fees: Copying, Fed Ex, phone calls. Represented in Los Angeles by Renaissance Agency, and in most major foreign countries. No reading fee.

NEW ENGLAND PUBLISHING ASSOCIATES

P.O. Box 5, Chester, CT 06412. 860-345-7323.

Description: Provides editorial guidance, representation, and mss development for book projects. Handles general interest nonfiction for adult market, particularly reference, true crime, biography, women's issues, current events, history and politics. Query first; submit outline, table of contents with one paragraph description, bio, and sample chapters. No reading fee; commissions only. Handles film and TV rights through AMG-Renaissance Agency. **Contact:** Elizabeth Frost-Knappman, Edward W. Knappman, Kris Sciari, Vicki Harlow, Ron Formica.

BETSY NOLAN LITERARY AGENCY

224 W 29th St., Fl. 15, New York, NY 10001. 212-967-8200.

E-mail: 74731.2172@compuserve.com.

Description: Adult nonfiction, especially popular psychology, child care, cookbooks, gardening, music books, African-American and Jewish issues. Some literary fiction. No unsolicited mss; query first. Submit outline, no more than 3 sample chapters, author background. No reading fee. Commission: 15%. **Contact:** Betsy Nolan.

RICHARD PARKS AGENCY

138 E 16th St., Fl. 5, New York, NY 10003-3561. 212-254-9067.

Description: General trade adult nonfiction; fiction by referral only. Unpublished writers considered. Query with SASE; multiple queries okay if noted as such. No phone calls or faxed queries. Accepts unsolicited queries. Does not accept unsolicited manuscripts. Responds to queries: 2-4 weeks, 4-6 weeks for submissions. No electronic queries. Commission: 15% domestic; 20% foreign. Fees: Photocopying. **Contact:** Richard Parks.

JAMES PETER ASSOCIATES

P.O. Box 358, New Canaan, CT 06840. 203-972-1070.

E-mail: gene_brissie@msn.com.

Description: Any adult nonfiction subject. Considers unsolicited queries, but not manuscripts. Unpublished writers considered. Query with outline, sample pages, and bio/resume, SASE required. Responds: 2-3 weeks to queries. No electronic queries. Accepts multiple queries. Commission: 15% domestic, 20% foreign. Fees: None. **Contact:** Gene Brissie.

ALISON PICARD, LITERARY AGENT
P.O. Box 2000, Cotuit, MA 02635. 508-477-7192.
E-mail: ajpicard@aol.com.
Description: Adult fiction, nonfiction, and juvenile/young adult, screenplays. No poetry, short stories or plays. Averages 500 queries/submissions per year; 5% accepted. Considers unsolicited queries, but not manuscripts. Unpublished writers considered. Multiple queries okay. Responds: 1 weeks for queries, 2 months for submissions, SASE required. Commission: 15%. Fees: None. E-queries: No. **Contact:** Alison Picard.

PINDER LANE & GARON-BROOKE ASSOCIATES
159 W 53rd St., #14-E, New York, NY 10019. 212-489-0880.
Description: Fiction and nonfiction, film and TV rights. No unsolicited mss; query first. No reading fee. Submit short synopsis. Representatives in Hollywood and all foreign markets. **Contact:** Dick Duane, Robert Thixton, Roger Hayes.

SUSAN ANN PROTTER
110 W 40th St., Suite 1408, New York, NY 10018. 212-840-0480.
Susan Ann Protter, AAR. **Description:** Fiction and nonfiction, health/medicine, how-to, mysteries, thrillers, science, science fiction, psychology, biography, reference, self-help. No juveniles. No unsolicited mss; query first with letter and SASE. Do not query by phone, e-mail, or fax please. No reading fee. Agents in Hollywood and all major foreign countries.

JODY REIN BOOKS, INC.
7741 S Ash Ct., Littleton, CO 80122. 303-694-4430.
Description: Commercial and narrative nonfiction, by writers with media contacts, experience and expertise in their field. Also, outstanding works of literary fiction by award-winning short-story writers and commercially viable screenplays. Averages 2,000 queries/submissions per year; less than 1% unsolicited material accepted. Considers unsolicited queries, but not manuscripts. Unpublished writers considered. Query with SASE. Responds: 2-4 weeks to queries, 4-6 weeks to submissions. No electronic queries. Considers multiple queries. Commission: 15% domestic, 25% foreign. Fees: Copying, shipping. E-queries: No. **Contact:** Alexandre Philippe for listings and Kristin Nelson for all other queries..

GAIL ROSS LITERARY AGENCY
1666 Connecticut Ave. NW, Suite 500, Washington, DC 20009.
Description: Adult nonfiction. Unpublished writers considered. Query with outline, sample pages, resume, and SASE. Multiple queries okay. Commission: 15%. Fees: None. **Contact:** Gail Ross, Jennifer Manguera.

JANE ROTROSEN AGENCY

318 E 51st St., New York, NY 10022. 212-593-4330.

Jane Rotrosen, AAR.

Description: Fiction and nonfiction. No unsolicited mss; query first by referral only. Submit brief description. Handles film and TV rights. No reading fee. 15% commission in USA and Canada. Represented abroad and on the West Coast. Member: Authors Guild. **Contact:** Donald Cleary, Business Affairs.

PETER RUBIE LITERARY AGENCY

240 W 35 St., Suite 500, New York, NY 10001. 212-279-1776.

E-mail: peterrubie@prlit.com. Web site: www.prlit.com.

Peter Rubie.

Description: Literate fiction and nonfiction, all types, for adults. See Web site for details. Seeks authors with strong writing backgrounds or recognized experts in their fields. No romance or children's books. Averages 1,000 queries/submission per year; 5% unsolicited material accepted. Considers unsolicited queries, but not manuscripts. Unpublished writers considered. Query with outline, sample pages, bio, and resume, SASE required. Responds: 6-8 weeks to queries, 12-14 weeks to submissions. Considers electronic and multiple queries. Commission: 15% domestic; 20% foreign. Fees: Copying, shipping. **Contact:** Peter Rubie or June Clark.

RUSSELL & VOLKENING, INC.

50 W 29th St., Suite 7E, New York, NY 10001. 212-684-6050.

Description: General fiction and nonfiction, film and TV rights. No screenplays, romance, science fiction, children's or juvenile submissions. Submit outline and 2 sample chapters. No reading fee.

SANDUM & ASSOCIATES

144 E 84th St., New York, NY 10028. 212-737-2011.

Howard E. Sandum, Director.

Description: Primarily nonfiction and literary fiction. Query with sample pages and bio/resume. Multiple queries okay. Commission: 15% domestic; 10% when foreign or TV/film subagents are used. New clients by referral only.

SHUKAT COMPANY, LTD.

340 W 55th St., Suite 1A, New York, NY 10019-3744. 212-582-7614.

E-mail: staff@shukat.com. **Description:** Represents writers for theatre, film, and TV. Personal management of composers, lyricists and directors. No unsolicited mss. Query first. Submit outline and sample chapters. No reading fee. Member AAR. **Contact:** Scott Shukat, Pat McLaughlin, Maribel Rivas.

BOBBE SIEGEL, LITERARY AGENT

41 W 83rd St., New York, NY 10024. 212-877-4985.

Description: Adult fiction and nonfiction. No plays (dramatic or screen), romances, juvenile, humor, or short stories. Considers unsolicited queries/not manuscripts.

Unpublished writers considered. Query; multiple queries okay. SASE required. Responds: 2-3 weeks for queries, 2-3 months for submissions. No electronic queries. Commission: 15%, foreign 10%. Fees: None. Editorial services suggested if needed. **Contact:** Bobbe Siegel or Pete Siegel, Associate.

JACQUELINE SIMENAUER LITERARY AGENCY
P.O. Box AG, Mantoloking, NJ 08738. 914-597-9964.
Description: Nonfiction: medical, popular psychology, how-to/self-help, women's issues, health, alternative health concepts, spirituality, New Age, fitness, diet, nutrition, current issues, true crime, business, celebrities, reference, social issues. Fiction: literary and mainstream commercial. Prefers query with three chapters and synopsis. Multiple queries okay. Commission: 15% domestic, 20% foreign. **Tips:** Unpublished writers considered. Queries: Required. E-queries: Yes. Unsolicited mss: Accepts. **Contact:** Jacqueline Simenauer (nonfiction), Fran Pardi (fiction).

THE SPIELER AGENCY
154 W 57th St., Rm. 135, New York, NY 10019. 212-757-4439.
Description: Nonfiction, literary fiction (no romance novels or thrillers). Averages 1,000 queries/submissions per year; less than 1% unsolicited material accepted. Considers unsolicited queries, but not manuscripts. Unpublished writers considered. Query with outline, SASE (or material will not be returned); no multiple queries or electronic queries. Responds: 2 weeks to queries, 6-8 weeks to submissions. Commission: 15% domestic, 20% foreign. Fees: Third-party charges (e.g., messengers, photocopying). **Contact:** Ada Muellner.

PHILIP G. SPITZER LITERARY AGENCY
50 Talmage Farm Ln., East Hampton, NY 11937. 631-329-3650.
E-mail: spitzer516@aol.com. Philip Spitzer, AAR. **Description:** Adult fiction and nonfiction. Query. Literary fiction, suspense/mystery. Film and TV rights. No unsolicited mss; query first with outline and sample chapters. No reading fee, copying fee. Foreign rights agents in all major markets.

WALES LITERARY AGENCY
P.O. Box 9428, Seattle, WA 98109-0428. 206-284-7114.
E-mail: waleslit@aol.com.
Description: Mainstream and literary fiction and nonfiction. No unsolicited mss. Query first with SASE. Submit outline and sample chapter. No reading fee. Handles film and TV rights. **Contact:** Elizabeth Wales, Meg Lemke, and Adrienne Reed.

JOHN A. WARE LITERARY AGENCY
392 Central Park W, New York, NY 10025. 212-866-4733.
Description: Adult fiction and nonfiction. Literate, accessible, noncategory fiction, plus thrillers and mysteries. Nonfiction: biography, history, current affairs, investigative journalism, social criticism, nature, Americana and folklore, "bird's eye view" of phenomena, science, medicine, sports. Unpublished writers considered. Query letter

only, with SASE; multiple queries okay. Averages 2,000 queries per year; 1-2% unsolicited material accepted. Accepts unsolicited queries, but not manuscripts. No telephone or fax queries. Responds in 2 weeks to queries; as arranged to submissions. Commission: 15% domestic, 20% foreign. Fees: Photocopying. **Contact:** John Ware.

WATKINS/LOOMIS AGENCY
133 E 35th St., Suite 1, New York, NY 10016. 212-532-0080.
Description: Adult literary fiction and nonfiction: biographies, memoirs, and others; cookbooks. No romance, self-help, or novelty books. Averages 500 queries/submissions per year; 5% unsolicited material accepted. Considers unsolicited queries and manuscripts. Unpublished writers considered. Query letter with first 3 chapters for fiction, and a query letter plus synopsis for nonfiction, SASE required. We only accept submissions sent via regular mail (hard copy). Responds: 2 weeks for queries and 6 weeks for submissions. No electronic or multiple queries. Fees: None. **Contact:** Katherine Fausset.

SANDRA WATT & ASSOCIATES
1750 N Sierra Bonita, Los Angeles, CA 90046. 323-874-0791.
Description: Looking for well-written adult fiction and nonfiction. Averages 200 queries/submissions per year; 2% of unsolicited material accepted. Accepts unsolicited manuscripts/not queries. Unpublished writers sometimes considered. Query with bio/resume, SASE required. Responds: 1 weeks to queries, 3 weeks to submissions. No electronic queries. Accepts multiple queries. Commission: 15% domestic and foreign. Fees: None. **Contact:** Sandra Watt.

WIESER & WIESER
25 E 21st St., New York, NY 10010. 212-260-0860.
Description: Specializes in trade and mass market adult fiction and nonfiction books. Unpublished writers considered. Query with outline and bio/resume. Submit outline, 25 opening pages, SASE; no reading fee. Commission: 15%. Fees: photocopying, shipping. **Contact:** Olga Wieser, Jake Elwell.

WITHERSPOON ASSOCIATES
235 E 31st St., New York, NY 10016. 212-889-8626.
Description: Adult fiction and nonfiction. Unpublished writers considered. Query with sample pages; no multiple queries. Handles film and TV. Commission: 15%. Fees: None. **Contact:** Kimberly Witherspoon.

ANN WRIGHT REPRESENTATIVES
165 W 46th St., Suite 1105, New York, NY 10036-2501. 212-764-6770.
E-mail: danwrightlit@aol.com. **Description:** Fiction and screenplays with strong film potential, varied subjects. Considers only queries or referrals, with SASE. Averages 6,000 queries/submissions per year; ½% unsolicited material accepted. Considers unsolicited queries, but not manuscripts. Unpublished writers considered, specializes in encouraging new writers. Responds: 1-2 weeks to queries, 4-8 weeks for

submissions. No electronic queries. Accepts multiple queries (agency only). Commission: 10% Film/TV, 10%-20% literary. Fees: Photocopying, shipping. "Always open to new writers of screen material and to new authors of fiction with strong film potential." **Contact:** Dan Wright.

WRITERS HOUSE
21 W 26th St., New York, NY 10010. 212-685-2400.
Description: Represents trade books of all types, fiction and nonfiction, including all rights; handles film and TV rights. No plays, screenplays, teleplays, or software. Must send query first. No reading fee. **Contact:** Submissions.

WRITERS' PRODUCTIONS
P.O. Box 630, Westport, CT 06881. 203-227-8199.
Description: Literary quality fiction and nonfiction. Averages 1,500 queries/submissions per year; not accepting new clients or queries at this time. Commission: 15% domestic; 25% foreign, dramatic, multimedia, software sales, licensing, and merchandising. **Contact:** David L. Meth.

ZACHARY SHUSTER HARMSWORTH LITERARY AGENCY
1776 Broadway, Suite 1405, New York, NY 10019. 617-262-2400.
Description: Commercial and literary adult fiction and nonfiction, biography, memoirs, business, psychology, and medicine. Averages 2,000 queries/submissions per year; accepts less than 1% unsolicited material. Considers unpublished/unproduced writers. Query with sample pages (no more than 30 pages), SASE required. Do not fax queries. Responds: 1-2 months for queries, 2-4 months for submissions. No electronic queries. Multiple queries accepted. Commission: 15% domestic; 20% foreign. Fees: None.

SUSAN ZECKENDORF ASSOCIATES
171 W 57th St., New York, NY 10019. 212-245-2928.
Description: Commercial fiction and nonfiction. Mysteries, thrillers, literary fiction, science, biography, health, parenting, social history, classical music. Averages 3,000 queries/submissions per year; 2% of unsolicited material accepted. Considers unsolicited queries, but not manuscripts. Unpublished writers considered. Query with outline and bio/resume, SASE required. Responds: 1 week to queries, 2 weeks to submissions. No electronic queries. Multiple queries accepted. Commission: 15% domestic; 20% foreign. Fees: Photocopying. Offers some editorial suggestions. "We're a small agency providing individual attention." **Contact:** Susan Zeck.

ARTS COUNCILS

State arts councils are a resource frequently overlooked by writers, but they offer useful services that can boost a writer's career. First of all, many offer cash awards of various sorts. One type of award is a "project" grant; that is, a specific award to complete a specified piece of work. These are awarded based on details of a proposal the individual author or a sponsoring arts group submits. The criteria for project grants are the quality of writing (based on sample poems or pages of fiction or nonfiction submitted), the clarity of the project, and some indication of community support, such as a letter of support from a community group. For instance, a project to publish an anthology of multicultural writers from your state might qualify for a grant. Other projects can be as diverse and creative as printing poems on placards to place in public transit vehicles, or on billboards or in other nontraditional venues.

The other type of cash support is a fellowship award. Many states offer awards for writers based on the general quality of their work. There is no "project" requirement; the money awarded is simply to further the author's career and is "unrestricted"; that is, it may be used for any purpose at all.

Arts councils have printed or online guidelines that give all the application information for grants and fellowships.

The review process often involves peer groups of writers, creative artists, and arts administrators from around the state. The important thing to know is that these panels constantly rotate their membership. Review is somewhat subjective; a panel that hated your work one year may love it the next. Don't give up applying for fellowships, in particular—which are the easiest to apply for—just because you did not win in the first year you applied. Keep sending in your 1-page form and 10 best poems (or whatever is requested) each year. You may be pleasantly surprised one year to be selected for a writing fellowship award.

For project grants, after you get a rough idea of your desired project, you may wish to call the arts council to talk briefly with a grants officer. This person may be able to help you think through some key elements of your project that will need to be covered in a proposal. Many arts councils also offer regional grants-writing workshops and sometimes fund local agencies that in turn offer awards to authors.

Finally, arts councils have a variety of other services, such as newsletters which publish information on regional and national prize competitions, requests for submissions for regional collections of writing, and so on.

All writers should contact their state agencies and get on their mailing list, to keep abreast of these valuable services.

ALABAMA STATE COUNCIL ON THE ARTS

201 Monroe St., Suite 110, Montgomery, AL 36130-1800. 334-242-4076.
E-mail: randy@arts.state.al.us. Web site: www.arts.state.al.us.
Description: Newsletter, workshops, conferences, and grants.
Contact: Randy Shoults, L.T. Program Manager.

ALASKA STATE COUNCIL ON THE ARTS

411 W Fourth Ave., Suite 1E, Anchorage, AK 99501-2343. 907-267-6610.
E-mail: aksca_info@eed.state.ak.us. Web site: www.aksca.org.
Charlotte Fox, Director.
Description: Workshops, conferences, grants, roster, and newsletter.
Contact: Pat Oldenburg.

ALBERTA FOUNDATION FOR THE ARTS

901 Standard Life Centre, 10405 Jasper Ave. NW
Edmonton, Alberta T5J 4R7 Canada. 780-427-2921.
Web site: www.affta.ab.ca.
Description: Grant programs and competitions.
Contact: W. J. Byrne.

ARIZONA COMMISSION ON THE ARTS

417 W Roosevelt, Phoenix, AZ 85003-1226. 602-255-5882.
E-mail: general@ArizonaArts.org. Web site: www.arizonaarts.org.
Description: Newsletter, workshops, conference, grants, and
fellowships for Arizona writers.
Contact: Paul Morris, Public Information/Literature Director.

ARKANSAS ARTS COUNCIL

1500 Tower Bldg., 323 Center St., Little Rock, AR 72201. 501-324-9766.
E-mail: info@arkansasarts.com. Web site: www.arkansasarts.com.
Contact: James E. Mitchell, Executive Director.

BRITISH COLUMBIA ARTS COUNCIL

800 Johnson St., Fl. 5, Victoria, British Columbia V8W 1N3 Canada. 250-356-1718.
E-mail: walter.quan@gems9.gov.bc.ca. Web site: www.bcartscouncil.gov.bc.ca.

CALIFORNIA ARTS COUNCIL

1300 I St., Suite 930, Sacramento, CA 95814. 916-322-6555.
E-mail: cac@cwo.com. Web site: www.cac.ca.gov.
Barry Hessenius, Executive Director.
Description: Supports small presses and writers with fellowships. Currently inaugu-
rating a Poet Laureate Program.
Tips: Does not give grants to writers to finish or publish books.

COLORADO COUNCIL ON THE ARTS

750 Pennsylvania St., Denver, CO 80203-3699. 303-894-2617.
E-mail: coloarts@state.co.us. Web site: www.coloarts.state.co.us.
Description: Newsletter and grants.
Contact: Fran Holden, Executive Director.

COMPAS: WRITERS & ARTISTS IN THE SCHOOLS

304 Landmark Center, 75 W Fifth St., St. Paul, MN 55102. 651-292-3249.
E-mail: dei@compas.org. Web site: www.compas.org.
Description: Nonprofit organization that collaborates with a wide of variety of arts, education, government, business, and philanthropic partners to employ professional artists, provide technical assistance, and offer grants to artists and agencies.
Contact: Daniel Gabriel, Director.

CONNECTICUT COMMISSION ON THE ARTS

1 Financial Plaza, Hartford, CT 06103. 860-566-4770.
Web site: www.ctarts.org. Linda Dente, Artist Fellowships Manager.
Contact: Douglas C. Evans, Executive Director.

DELAWARE DIVISION OF THE ARTS

Carvel State Bldg., 820 N French St., Wilmington, DE 19801. 302-577-8278.
Web site: www.artsdel.org.
Description: Offers fellowships and grants to individual artists from Delaware.
Contact: Kristin Pleasanton, Art and Artist Services Coordinator.

FLORIDA ARTS COUNCIL

The Capitol, Tallahassee, FL 32399-0250.
Web site: www.dos.state.fl.us.
Contact: Judee L. Pehijohn, Director.

GEORGIA COUNCIL FOR THE ARTS

260 14th St. NW, Suite 401, Atlanta, GA 30318. 404-685-2787.
Betsy Baker, Executive Director.
Contact: Ann Davis, Grants Manager, Literature.

HAWAII STATE FOUNDATION ON CULTURE AND THE ARTS

250 S Hotel St., Fl. 2, Honolulu, HI 96813. 808-586-0307.
E-mail: sfca@sfca.state.hi.us. Web site: www.state.hi.us/sfca.
David C. Farmer, Executive Director.
Description: Programs include Art in Public Places, Arts in Education, Community Outreach, Foundation Grants, Folk Arts, Individual Artists Fellowships, and History and Humanities.
Contact: Ronald Yamakawa, Interim Executive Director.

IDAHO COMMISSION ON THE ARTS

P.O. Box 83720, Boise, ID 83720-0008. 208-334-2119.
E-mail: cconley@ica.state.id.us.
Description: The state's principal cultural agency supports Idaho writers through annual grants and awards, readings, and workshops. No grants are given for publication.
Contact: Cort Conley, Director.

ILLINOIS ARTS COUNCIL
James R. Thompson Center, 100 W Randolph, Suite 10-500
Chicago, IL 60601. 312-814-6750.
E-mail: Susan@arts.state,il.us or info@arts.state.il.us.
Web site: www.state.il.us/agency/iac.
Sue Eleuterio, Director of Literature Programs.
Description: Annual Fellowships in Poetry and Prose (Deadline, December 1).
Literary Arts Award for authors published in nonprofit Illinois literary publications
(Deadline, March 1). Newsletter, workshops, grants, and prizes.

INDIANA ARTS COMMISSION
402 W Washington St., Rm. 072, Indianapolis, IN 46204-2741. 317-232-1268.
Web site: www.in.gov/iac.
Contact: Dorothy Ilgen, Executive Director.

INSTITUTO DE CULTURA PUERTORRIQUENA
P.O. Box 9024184, San Juan, PR 00902-4184. 787-724-3210.
E-mail: apoyo@icp.prstar.net.
Web site: www.icp.prstar.net.
Description: Newsletter, workshops, conferences, grants, and prizes.

IOWA ARTS COUNCIL
Iowa Dept. of Cultural Affairs
State Historical Building, 600 E Locust, Des Moines, IA 50319-0290. 515-281-4011.
E-mail: sarah.oltrogge@dca.state.ia.us.
Sarah Oltrogge, Public Relations Specialist.
Description: Seeks to make the arts available to individuals living in Iowa. Offers
numerous grant opportunities for artists in art education, technical assistance and
professional development, folklife, community development, and operational support
for mid-size and major arts organizations.

KANSAS ARTS COMMISSION
700 SW Jackson, Suite 1004, Topeka, KS 66603-3761. 785-296-3335.
E-mail: kac@arts.state.ks.us. Web site: http://arts.state.ks.us.
Contact: Robert T. Burtch, Editor.

KENTUCKY ARTS COUNCIL
Old Capitol Annex, 300 W Broadway, Frankfort, KY 40601-1980. 502-564-3757.
E-mail: kyarts@mail.state.ky.us. Web site: www.kyarts.org.
Description: Offers programs, grants, virtual exhibits, and arts education.
Contact: Gerri Combs, Executive Director.

LOUISIANA DIVISION OF THE ARTS
Box 44247, Baton Rouge, LA 70804. 225-342-8180.
E-mail: arts@crt.state.la.us. Web site: www.crt.state.la.us/arts.
Description: Workshops, conference, grants, and newsletter.
Contact: James Borders, Executive Director.

MAINE ARTS COMMISSION
25 State House Station, 193 State St., Augusta, ME 04333-0025. 207-287-2724.
E-mail: kathy.shaw@state.me.us. Web site: www.mainearts.com.
Description: Newsletter, workshops, and grants.
Contact: Alden C. Wilson, Director.

MANITOBA ARTS COUNCIL
93 Lombard Ave., Suite 525, Winnipeg, Manitoba R3B 3B1 Canada. 204-945-2237.
E-mail: mmorton@artscouncil.ca.
Web site: www.net-mark.mb.ca/netmark/mac.

MARYLAND STATE ARTS COUNCIL
Literature Program
175 W Ostend St., Suite E, Baltimore, MD 21230. 410-767-6555.
E-mail: pdunne@mdbusiness.state.md.us. Web site: www.msac.org.
Theresa M. Colvin, Executive Director.
Description: Grants, awards, newsletter.
Contact: Pamela Dunne, Literature Program Director.

MASSACHUSETTS CULTURAL COUNCIL
10 St. James Avenue, Fl. 3, Boston, MA 02116. 617-727-3668.
E-mail: mcc@art.state.ma.us. Web site: www.massculturalcouncil.org.
Mary Kelley, Director.
Description: Newsletter and grants.
Contact: Charles Coe, Literature Coordinator.

MICHIGAN COUNCIL FOR ARTS AND CULTURAL AFFAIRS
525 W Ottawa, P.O. Box 30705, Lansing, MI 48909-8205. 517-241-4011.
Web site: www.cis.state.mi.us/arts.
Contact: Betty Boone, Executive Director.

MINNESOTA STATE ARTS BOARD
Park Square Court, 400 Sibley St., Suite 200
St. Paul, MN 55101-1928. 651-215-1600, 800- 8MN-ARTS.
E-mail: msab@arts.state.mn.us. Web site: www.arts.state.mn.us.
Robert Booker, Executive Director.
Description: Offers newsletter, workshops, and grants.
Contact: Amy Frimpong, Artist Assistance Program Associate.

MISSISSIPPI ARTS COMMISSION

239 N Lamar St., Suite 207, Jackson, MS 39201. 601-359-6030.
Web site: www.arts.state.ms.us.
Contact: Beth Batton, Arts-Based Community Development Center.

MISSOURI ARTS COUNCIL

Wainwright Office Complex, 111 N Seventh St., Suite 105
St. Louis, MO 63101-2188. 314-340-6845.
E-mail: nboyd@mail.state.mo.us. Web site: www.missouriartscouncil.org.
Norree Boyd, Executive Director.
Description: Newsletter, conferences, grants.
Contact: Beverly Strohmeyer, Assistant Director for Programs.

MONTANA ARTS COUNCIL

P.O. Box 202201, Helena, MT 59620-2201. 406-444-6430.
Web site: www.art.state.mt.us. E-Mail: mac@state.mt.us.
Contact: Arlynn Fishbaugh, Executive Director.

NEBRASKA ARTS COUNCIL

Joslyn Carriage House, 3838 Davenport St., Omaha, NE 68131-2329. 402-595-2122.
Web site: www.nebraskaartscouncil.org.
Contact: Jennifer Severin, Executive Director.

NEVADA ARTS COUNCIL

716 N Carson St., Suite A, Carson City, NV 89701. 775-687-6680.
E-mail: fkmorrow@clan.lib.nv.us. Web site: www.nevadaculture.org.
Fran Morrow, Artist's Services Coordinator.
Description: Workshops, conferences, newletter, and grants.

NEW BRUNSWICK ARTS BOARD

P.O. Box 6000, Fredericton, New Brunswick E3B 5H1 Canada. 506-453-4307.
E-mail: artsnb@gov.nb.ca.

NEW HAMPSHIRE STATE COUNCIL ON THE ARTS

Phenix Hall, 40 N Main St., Concord, NH 03301-4974. 603-271-2789.
E-mail: jmento@nharts.state.nh.us. Web site: www.state.nh.us/nharts.
Rebecca Lawrence, Director.
Description: Newsletter, workshops, conference, grants, and prizes.
Contact: Julie Mento, Artist Services Coordinator.

NEW JERSEY STATE COUNCIL ON THE ARTS

Artist Services, P.O. Box 306, Trenton, NJ 08625. 609-292-6130.
E-mail: Beth@arts.sos.state.nj.us. Web site: www.njartscouncil.org.
Description: Workshops, newletter, conferences, grants.
Contact: Beth Vogel, Program Officer.

NEW MEXICO ARTS

P.O. Box 1450, Santa Fe, NM 87504-1450. 505-827-6490.
E-mail: aweisman@oca.state.nm.us.
Ann Weisman, AIE/Locals Coordinator.

NEW YORK STATE COUNCIL ON THE ARTS

175 Varick St., New York, NY 10014. 212-387-7000.
E-mail: kmasterson@nysca.org. Web site: www.nyslittree.org.
Description: Offers support to a wide range of literary and multi-disciplinary writing or literary organizations in the state of New York through the Literature Program (LIT). Program's objective is to develop and support literary activity around the state. New applicants are encouraged to apply. Applicants must provide completed NYSCA application forms and specific additional narrative for the category in which they are applying. Application deadline: March 1.
Tips: Does not offer a separate writer-in-residence category to individual writers. Does offer translation grants and guest editorships.
Contact: Kathleen Masterson, Director, Literature Program.

NEWFOUNDLAND & LABRADOR ARTS COUNCIL

P.O. Box 98, St. John's, Newfoundland A1C 5H5 Canada. 709-726-2212.
E-mail: nlacmail@newcomm.net. Web site: www.nlac.nf.ca.

NORTH CAROLINA ARTS COUNCIL

Dept. of Cultural Resources, Raleigh, NC 27699-4632. 919-733-2111.
E-mail: debbie.mcgill@ncmail.net. Web site: www.ncarts.org.
Description: On-line newsletter, grants.
Contact: Deborah McGill, Literature Director.

NORTH DAKOTA COUNCIL ON THE ARTS

418 E Broadway, Suite 70, Bismarck, ND 58501-4086. 701-328-3954.
E-mail: comserv@state.nd.us. Web site: www.discovernd.com/arts.
Description: Newsletter and grants.
Contact: Janine Webb, Director.

NORTHWEST TERRITORIES ARTS COUNCIL

Dept. of Education, Culture, and Employment
P.O. Box 1320, Yellowknife, Northwest Territory X1A 2L9 Canada. 867-920-3103.

NOVA SCOTIA ARTS COUNCIL

1660 Hollis St., Suite 302, P.O. Box 1559, Halifax
Nova Scotia B3J 1V8 Canada. 902-422-1123.
E-mail: nsartscouncil@ns.sympatico.ca.
Web site: www.novascotiaartscouncil.ns.ca/contact.html.
Description: Grants to individuals, organizations, and small groups.

OHIO ARTS COUNCIL
727 E Main St., Columbus, OH 43205-1796. 614-466-2613.
Web site: www.oac.state.oh.us.
Contact: Bob Fox, Literature Program Coordinator.

OKLAHOMA ARTS COUNCIL
P.O. Box 52001-2001, Oklahoma City, OK 73152-2001. 405-521-2931.
E-mail: jennifer@arts.state.ok.us. Web site: www.state.ok.us/~arts.
Betty Price, Executive Director.
Description: Workshops, conferences, newsletters, grants.
Contact: Jennifer James.

ONTARIO ARTS COUNCIL
151 Bloor St. W, Fl. 5, Toronto, Ontario M5S 1T6 Canada. 416-969-7413.
E-mail: jstubbs@arts.on.ca.
Description: Awards, grants, and scholarships
Contact: Janet Stubbs.

OREGON ARTS COMMISSION
775 Summer St. NE, Salem, OR 97301-1284. 503-986-0086.
E-mail: oregon.artscomm@state.or.us . Web site: http://art.econ.state.or.us.
Contact: Assistant Director.

PENNSYLVANIA COUNCIL ON THE ARTS
Room 216, Finance Bldg., Harrisburg, PA 17120. 717-787-6883.
E-mail: www.artsnet.org/pca/.
Contact: James Woland, Literature Program.

PRINCE EDWARD ISLAND COUNCIL OF THE ARTS
115 Richmond St., Charlottetown
Prince Edward Island C1A 1A7 Canada. 902-368-4410.
Description: Contests and grants.
Contact: Ferne Taylor.

RHODE ISLAND STATE COUNCIL ON THE ARTS
83 Park St., Fl. 6, Providence, RI 02903-1037. 401-222-3880.
E-mail: randy@risca.state.ri.us. Web site: www.risca.state.ri.us.
Randall Rosenbaum, Executive Director.
Description: Offers workshops and grants.
Contact: Karolye Cunha.

SASKATCHEWAN ARTS BOARD
2135 Broad St., Regina, Saskatchewan S4P 3V7 Canada. 306-787-4056.
E-mail: sab@artsboard.sk.ca. Web site: www.artsboard.sk.ca/.

SOUTH CAROLINA FICTION PROJECT

South Carolina Arts Commission

1800 Gervais St., Columbia, SC 29201. 803-734-8696.

E-mail: goldstsa@arts.state.sc.us. Web site: www.state.sc.us/arts.

Description: Offers short story competition for South Carolina residents only.

Contact: Sara June Goldstein, Director, Program Director for Literary Arts.

SOUTH DAKOTA ARTS COUNCIL

800 Governors Dr., Pierre, SD 57501-2294. 605-773-3131.

E-mail: sdac@stlib.state.sd.us. Web site: www.sdarts.org.

Description: Offers grants, workshops, conferences, and a newsletter.

Contact: Dennis Holub, Executive Director.

TEXAS COMMISSION ON THE ARTS

P.O. Box 13406, Austin, TX 78711-3406. 512-475-3327.

E-mail: front.desk@arts.state.tx.us. Web site: www.arts.state.tx.us.

Description: Newsletter, workshops, conferences, grants.

Contact: Gaye Greever McElwain, Director of Marketing.

UTAH ARTS COUNCIL

617 E South Temple, Salt Lake, UT 84102-1177. 801-236-7555.

Web site: www.dced.state.ut.us/arts.

Contact: Guy Lebeda, Literary Coordinator.

VERMONT ARTS COUNCIL

136 State St., Drawer 33, Montpelier, VT 05633-6001. 802-828-3294.

E-mail: mbailey@vermontartscouncil.org. Web site: www.vermontartscouncil.org.

Description: Workshops, newsletter, conferences, grants.

Contact: Michele Bailey, Director of Artist Programs.

VIRGINIA COMMISSION FOR THE ARTS

223 Governor St., Lewis House, Fl. 2, Richmond, VA 23219-2010. 804-225-3132.

E-mail: pbaggett.arts@state.va.us . Web site: www.arts.state.va.us.

Donna Champ Banks, Program Coordinator.

Description: Workshops, conferences, and grants.

Contact: Peggy J. Baggett, Executive Director.

WASHINGTON STATE ARTS COMMISSION

234 E Eighth Ave., P.O. Box 42675, Olympia, WA 98504-2675. 360-586-2421.

E-mail: bitsyb@wsac.wa.gov. Web site: www.arts.wa.gov.

Kris Tucker, Director.

Description: Newsletter, workshops, grants (for nonprofit organizations only, no individuals).

Contact: Bitsy Bidwell, Community Arts Development Manager.

WEST VIRGINIA DIVISION OF CULTURE & HISTORY

West Virginia Division of Culture & History, The Cultural Center
1900 Kanawha Blvd. E, Charleston, WV 25305. 304-558-0220.
E-mail: gordon.simmons@wvculture.org. Web site: www.wvculture.org.
Gordon Simmons, Individual Artist Services.

WISCONSIN ARTS BOARD

101 E Wilson St., Fl. 1, Madison, WI 53702. 608-266-0190.
E-mail: artsboard@arts.state.wi.us. Web site: www.arts.state.wi.us.
George Tzougros, Executive Director.
Description: Newsletter, workshops, conferences, and grants.
Contact: Mark Fraire.

WYOMING ARTS COUNCIL

2320 Capitol Ave., Cheyenne, WY 82002. 307-777-7742.
E-mail: mshay@state.wy.us. Web site: www.wyoarts.state.wy.us.
John G. Coe, Executive Director.
Description: Offers three literary contests to writers from Wyoming. The
Blanchan/Doubleday Memorial Award (Deadline: May 1) offers two awards of $1000
given in the category of Writing by Women and Nature. The Warren Adler Fiction
Award (Deadline: June 1) offers $1,000 for the best short story. The Literature
Fellowship Award (Deadline: July 15) offers four awards of $2,500 for work in any cat-
egory. Note: Also offers awards for the performing and visual arts.
Contact: Michael Shay, Literature Program Manager.

COLONIES

Writers' colonies offer solitude and freedom from everyday distractions so that writers can concentrate on their work. Though some colonies are quite small, with space for just three or four writers at a time, others can provide accommodations for as many as 30 or 40. The length of a residency may vary, too, from a couple of weeks to five or six months. These programs have strict admissions policies, and writers must submit a formal application or letter of intent, a resume, writing samples, and letters of recommendation. As an alternative to the traditional writers' colony, a few of the organizations listed offer writing rooms for writers who live nearby. Write for application information first, enclosing a stamped, self-addressed envelope. Residency fees are subject to change.

EDWARD F. ALBEE FOUNDATION

14 Harrison St., New York, NY 10013. 212-266-2020.
Jacob Holder, Secretary.
Description: On Long Island, "The Barn" (William Flanagan Memorial Creative Persons Center), offers 1-month residences to 12 writers each season, from June 1 to October 1. Criteria: Talent and need. Applications (writing samples, project description, and resume) are accepted January 1-April 1. No fees, but residents are responsible for their own food and travel expenses.

MARY ANDERSON CENTER: AN ARTIST COLONY

101 St. Francis Dr., Mount St. Francis, IN 47146. 812-923-8602.
E-mail: maca@iglou.com. Web site: www.maryandersoncenter.org.
Debra Carmody, Executive Director.
Description: Residencies and retreats on the grounds of a Franciscan friary with 400 acres of rolling hills and woods. Private rooms for up to seven writers, musicians, and visual artists. Also includes working space and a visual artist's studio; meals are provided. Residencies of 1 week to 3 months, granted based on project proposal and artist's body of work; apply year-round (with $15 application fee). Daily fee: $30/day, can be reduced in some cases.

ATLANTIC CENTER FOR THE ARTS

1414 Art Center Ave., New Smyrna Beach, FL 32168. 386-427-6975, 800-393-6975.
E-mail: program@atlanticcenterforthe arts.org.
Web site: www.atlanticcenterforthearts.org.
Nicholas Conroy, Program and Residency Manager.
Description: The center is on central Florida's east coast, with 67 acres of pristine land on tidal estuary. All buildings, connected by wooden walkways, are handicapped-accessible and air-conditioned. Offers unique environment for sharing ideas, learning, and collaborating on interdisciplinary projects. Master artists meet with talented artists for readings and critiques, with time for individual work. Residencies: 2-3 weeks. Fees: None, meals provided M-F. Residents are selected by Master Artist in-Residence. Application deadlines vary. Please see Web site.

BYRDCLIFFE ARTS COLONY

Artists' Residency Program
Woodstock Guild, 34 Tinker St., Woodstock, NY 12498. 845-679-2079.
E-mail: wguild@ulster.net. Web site: www.woodstockguild.org.
Carla T. Smith, Director.
Description: The Villetta Inn, at 400-acre arts colony, offers private studios and separate bedrooms, a communal kitchen, and a peaceful environment for fiction writers, poets, playwrights, and visual artists. One-month residencies offered June to September. Fee: $600 per month, $5 application fee. Submit application, resume, writing sample, and 2 letters of recommendation. Deadline: April 1. Send SASE for application.

CAMARGO FOUNDATION

125 Park Square Ct., 400 Sibley St., St. Paul, MN 55101-1982. 651-290-2237.
E-mail: camargo@jeromefdn.org.
Michael Pritina, Director.
Description: Maintains a center of studies in France for 9 scholars and graduate students each semester to pursue projects in humanities and social sciences on France and Francophone culture. Also, one artist, one composer, and one writer accepted each semester. Offers furnished apartments and a reference library in city of Cassis. Research should be at advanced stage and not require resources unavailable in Marseilles-Aix-Cassis region. Send application form, curriculum vitae, 3 letters of recommendation, and project description. Writers, artists, and composers must send work samples. Deadline: February 1. **Contact:** Ellen Guettler.

CENTRUM

P.O. Box 1158, Port Townsend, WA 98368. 360-385-3102.
E-mail: sally@centrum.org. Web site: www.centrum.org.
Sally Rodgers, Coordinator.
Description: For writers and other creative artists, 1-week to 1-month residencies, September to May. Applicants selected by a peer jury receive free housing. Some stipends ($300 or less) available for Seattle area artists. Previous residents may return on a space-available basis for a rental fee. Deadline: August 1. Application fee, $10.

DJERASSI RESIDENT ARTISTS PROGRAM

2325 Bear Gulch Rd., Woodside, CA 94062. 650-747-1250.
E-mail: drap@djerassi.org. Web site: www.djerassi.org.
Description: Offers 4-week residencies, at no cost, to artists in literature (prose, poetry, drama, playwrights/screenwriters), choreography, music composition, visual arts, and media arts/new genres. Application fee: $25. Located in spectacular rural setting in Santa Cruz Mountains, 1 hour south of San Francisco. Postmark deadline for applications: February 15, for residency the following year. For application, send SASE, or visit Web site.

DORLAND MOUNTAIN ARTS COLONY

P.O. Box 6, Temecula, CA 92593. 909-302-3837.
E-mail: dorland@ez2.net. Web site: www.ez2.net/dorland/.
Karen Parrott, Director.
Description: Dorland is a nature preserve and "retreat for creative people" in the Palomar Mountains of Southern California. "Without electricity, residents find a new, natural rhythm for their work." Novelists, playwrights, poets, nonfiction writers, composers, and visual artists are welcomed for residencies of 1-2 months. Fee: $300/month includes cottage, fuel, and firewood. Send SASE for application. Deadlines: March 1 and September 1.

DORSET COLONY HOUSE

P.O. Box 510, Dorset, VT 05251. 802-867-2223.
E-mail: theatre@sover.net. Web site: www.theatredirectories.com.
John Nassivera, Director.
Description: Writers and playwrights (up to 8 at a time) are offered low-cost rooms with kitchen facilities at historic Colony House, for residencies of 2-3 weeks in the fall and spring. Applications accepted year-round. Fee: $120/week; financial aid is limited. For details, send SASE. **Contact:** Barbara Ax.

FINE ARTS WORK CENTER IN PROVINCETOWN

24 Pearl St., Provincetown, MA 02657. 508-487-9960.
E-mail: fawc@capecod.net. Web site: www.fawc.org.
Hunter O'Hanian, Executive Director.
Description: Fellowships (living and studio space, monthly stipends) offered at Fine Arts Work Center on Cape Cod, for fiction writers and poets to work independently. Residency are for 7 months (October 1 to May 1) for 10 writers and 10 visual artists; no fees. Deadline: December 1 for writers, February 1 for visual artists. Send SASE for details. **Contact:** Melanie Braverman.

GLENESSENCE WRITERS COLONY

1447 W Ward Ave., Ridgecrest, CA 93555. 760-446-5894.
Description: Glenessence is a luxury villa in the Upper Mojave Desert (private rooms with bath, pool, spa, courtyard, shared kitchen, fitness center, and library). Children, pets, and smoking prohibited. Residencies for $565/month; meals not provided. Reservations on a first-come basis. Seasonal (January through May). **Contact:** Allison Swift, Director.

TYRONE GUTHRIE CENTRE

Annaghmakerrig, Newbliss, County Monaghan, Ireland. 353-47-54003.
E-mail: thetgc@indigo.ie. Web site: www.tyroneguthrie.ie.
Sheila Pratschke, Director.
Description: On a 450-acre forested estate, the center offers peace and seclusion to writers and other artists. All art forms represented. Residencies of 1-3 months throughout the year. Fee: £2,550/month; financial assistance available to Irish residents

only. Some longer-term self-catering houses in old farmyard are available at £380/week. Writers chosen based on curriculum vitae, samples of published work, and outline of intended project. Applications accepted year-round. **Contact:** Sheila Pratschke.

THE HAMBIDGE CENTER
P.O. Box 339, Rabun Gap, GA 30568. 706-746-5718.
E-mail: center@hambidge.org. Web site: www.hambidge.org.
Description: The center is on 600 pristine acres of quiet woods in the north Georgia mountains. Eight private cottages available. All fellowships partially underwritten, residents contribute $125/week. Residencies of 2-8 weeks, year-round, for serious artists in all disciplines. Download application from Web site or send SASE. Deadlines: November 1 for May to October; May 1 for November to April.

HEADLANDS CENTER FOR THE ARTS
944 Fort Barry, Sausalito, CA 94965. 415-331-2787.
E-mail: arasin@headlands.org.
Description: On 13,000 acres of open coastal space, residencies are available to current residents of Ohio, New Jersey, North Carolina, and California. Application requirements vary by state. Deadline: June. Decisions announced October for residencies beginning March. No residency or application fees. Send SASE for details. **Contact:** Allison Rasin, Public Relations Manager.

HEDGEBROOK
2197 Millman Rd., Langley, WA 98260. 360-321-4786.
E-mail: hedgebrk@whidbey.com. Web site: www.hedgebrook.org.
Linda Bowers, Executive Director.
Description: Provides women writers, published or not, of all ages and from all cultural backgrounds, with a natural place to work. The retreat is on 48 acres of farmland and woods on Whidbey Island in Washington State. Each writer has her own cottage (6 available), with electricity and woodstove. A bathhouse serves all 6 cottages. Lunch brought to cottage in a basket; communal dinner; emphasis on organic and whole foods. Limited travel scholarships available. Residencies: 1 week to 2 months, no charge for residency. Stipend program available for low income, either without college degree, or aged 55 and over. Application deadlines: March 15 and October 1. Visit Web site for more information or to download application.

KALANI OCEANSIDE RETREAT CENTER
Artist-in-Residence Program
RR2, Box 4500 Beach Road, Pahoa, HI 96778. 808-965-7828, 800-800-6886.
E-mail: kalani@kalani.com. Web site: www.kalani.com.
Richard Koob, Program Coordinator.
Description: In a rural coastal setting of 113 botanical acres, Kalani Oceanside Retreat hosts and sponsors educational programs to bring together creative people from around the world in culturally and artistically stimulating environment. Housing

with bathrooms, B&W darkroom, various studio spaces for performing and visual artists and writers. Residencies: 2 weeks to 2 months, available year-round. Fees: $50 to $105/day, meals available at extra fee. Applications accepted year-round. **Contact:** Rachel Gonzalez, G.M.

THE MACDOWELL COLONY

100 High St., Peterborough, NH 03458. 603-924-3886.
E-mail: info@macdowellcolony.org. Web site: www.macdowellcolony.org.
Description: Studios, room, and board for writers to work in a woodland setting. Stipend available, up to $1,000 depending on financial need. Selection is competitive. Apply by January 15 for May through August; by April 15 for September through December; by September 15 for January through April. Residencies: Up to 8 weeks; 80-90 writers accepted each year. Send SASE for application or e-mail for more information. **Contact:** Courtney Bethel, Admissions Coordinator.

THE MILLAY COLONY FOR THE ARTS

454 E Hill Rd., P.O. Box 3, Austerlitz, NY 12017-0003. 518-392-3103.
E-mail: leslie@millaycolony.org. Web site: www.millaycolony.org.
Description: At Steepletop (former home of Edna St. Vincent Millay), writers are provided studios, universally accessible living quarters, and meals at no cost. Residencies: 1 month and run from April through November. Deadline for yearly submissions is November 1 for the coming season. Applications reviewed by independent jurors, selection based on talent. For applications send SASE or e-mail application@millaycolony.org. **Contact:** Martha Hopewell, Executive Director, or Leslie Magson, Executive Assistant.

MILLETT FARM: AN ART COLONY FOR WOMEN

295 Bowery, New York, NY 10003.
Description: Summer residencies for women writers and visual artists at picturesque tree farm in rural New York. For housing, all residents contribute 5 hours of work each weekday morning and $300/month for meals. Preference to writers who can stay all summer or at least 6 weeks. Also, 1-week master class ($500) available with Kate Millett. For details, send SASE. **Contact:** Kate Millett, Director.

MOLASSES POND WRITERS' RETREAT AND WORKSHOP

15 Granite Shore, Milbridge, ME 04658. 207-546-2506.
Description: Led by published authors who teach writing at University of New Hampshire, this 1-week workshop is held in June; with time for writing, as well as manuscript critique and writing classes. Up to 10 writers stay in a colonial farmhouse with private bed/work rooms for each, common areas for meals and classes. Fee: $450 (lodging, meals, and tuition). Applicants must be serious about their work. No children's literature or poetry. Submit statement of purpose and 15-20 pages of fiction or nonfiction between February 1 and March 1. **Contact:** Martha Barron Barrett and Sue Wheeler, Coordinators.

MONTANA ARTISTS REFUGE

P.O. Box 8, Basin, MT 59631. 406-225-3500.
E-mail: mar@mt.net. Web site: www.montanarefuge.org.
Jennifer Pryor, Coordinator.
Description: In a rural environment, this artist nonresidency program offers living and studio space to self-directed artists in all disciplines. Writers can work with other artists or in solitude. Residencies, with kitchen facilities and private phone, from 3 months to 1 year; with rents $395-$550/month. One soundproof apartment available for writer or musician/composer. Financial aid available. Send SASE for details.
Contact: Joan Van Doynttoven, Residency Coordinator.

NEW YORK MILLS ARTS RETREAT
AND REGIONAL CULTURAL CENTER

24 N Main Ave., New York Mills, MN 56567. 218-385-3339.
E-mail: nymills@uslink.net. Web site: www.kulcher.org.
Heather Humbert Price, Arts Retreat Coordinator.
Description: A small house and studio are provided to 6-8 selected professional, emerging artist in all disciplines. Applicants from Minnesota and New York City may be eligible for Jerome Foundation Fellowships which provide stipends of $750-1500. Special emphasis is given to providing opportunities for artists of color. Each fellowship artist returns a minimum of 8 hours of community service, usually teaching in area schools. Deadlines: April 1 and October 1. **Contact:** Kayleen Roberts.

NORTHWOOD UNIVERSITY

Alden B. Dow Creativity Center, 4000 Whiting Dr.
Midland, MI 48640-2398. 989-837-4478.
E-mail: creativity@northwood.edu. Web site: www.northwood.edu/abd.
Liz Drake, Assistant Director.
Description: Fellowships for individuals to pursue project ideas without interruption. A project idea should be innovative, creative, and have potential for impact in its field. Four 10-week residencies (early-June to mid-August) awarded yearly. Application fee: $10. A $750 stipend plus room and board are provided. No spouses or families. Deadline: December 31.

OX-BOW

37 S Wabash Ave., Chicago, IL 60603. 800-318-3019.
E-mail: ox-bow@artic.edu. Web site: www.ox-bow.org.
Description: One- and two-week residencies (mid-June to mid-August) for writers to reside and work in secluded, natural environment in Michigan. Fee: $410/week. Primarily for the visual arts, Ox-Bow nurtures the creative process through instruction, example, and community. Resident writers encouraged to present a reading of their work and to participate in the community life at Ox-Bow. For application, write or call. Deadline: Mid-February.

RAGDALE FOUNDATION

1260 N Green Bay Rd., Lake Forest, IL 60045. 847-234-1063.
E-mail: ragdalel@aol.com. Web site: www.ragdale.org.
Melissa Mosher, Admissions.
Description: This Lake Forest estate, 30 miles north of Chicago on 55 acres of prairie, is now an artists' retreat for 3 visual artists, 1 composer, and 8 writers at a time. Allows time and peaceful space for writers to finish works in progress, to begin new works, to solve creative problems, and to experiment in new genres. Residencies: 2 weeks to 2 months. Fee: $15/day; some fee waivers available, based on financial need. Send SASE for details. Application fee: $20. **Contact:** Melissa Mosher.

SASKATCHEWAN WRITERS/ARTISTS
COLONIES AND INDIVIDUAL RETREATS

P.O. Box 3986, Regina, Saskatchewan S4P 3R9, Canada. 306-565-8785.
E-mail: skcolony@attglobal.net. Web site: www.skwriter.com/colonies.html.
Description: Rural St. Peter's Abbey, near Humboldt, offers a 6-week summer colony (July-August) and a 2-week winter colony in February; also, individual retreats (for Canadian residents only) offered year-round, for up to 3 residents at a time. Christopher Lake, near Prince Albert in Northern Saskatchewan, is the site of a 2-week colony in late summer. Fees: $150/week ($200 for non-members). December 1 deadline for winter colony; May 1 deadline for summer. **Contact:** Shelley Sopher, Colony Coordinator.

JOHN STEINBECK ROOM

Long Island University, Southampton College Library
Southampton, NY 11968. 631-287-8382.
E-mail: library@southampton.liu.edu.
Description: At Long Island University, the John Steinbeck Room provides a basic research facility to writers with either a current book contract or a confirmed magazine assignment. The room is available for a period of 6 months with one 6-month renewal permissible. Send SASE for application. **Contact:** Robert Gerbereux, Library Director.

THURBER HOUSE RESIDENCIES

c/o Thurber House, 77 Jefferson Ave., Columbus, OH 43215. 614-464-1032.
E-mail: thurberhouse@thurberhouse.org. Web site: www.thurberhouse.org.
Description: Residencies in the restored home of James Thurber are awarded to creative fiction and nonfiction journalists, poets, and playwrights. Residents work on their own writing projects, and in addition to other duties, teach a class at the Ohio State University. A stipend of $6,000 per quarter is provided. Deadline: December 15, for letter of interest and curriculum vitae (for the following academic year). If invited to apply, material deadline is December 31. **Contact:** Trish Houston, Residencies Director.

TWO WHITE WOLVES RETREAT

P.O. Box 16727, Encino, CA 91416. 818-464-3779.

E-mail: twowhitewolvesretreat@yahoo.com.

Description: Offers residency at the beautiful and peaceful Maine retreat comprised of 15.7 acres. One hour away from Bangor and 3 miles to get supplies in Dover-Foxcraft. Property is being made into a fauna sanctuary. Writers welcome to apply for residency for short or long-term stay. One-time fee of $25 for guest application with no fee for entire stay. No hunting is allowed and residents must be self-contained during their stay. A full portfolio is available upon request. **Contact:** Kate Alexander, Director.

UCROSS FOUNDATION

Residency Program, 30 Big Red Ln., Clearmont, WY 82835. 307-737-2291.

E-mail: ucross@wyoming.com. Web site: ucrossfoundation.org.

Description: Residencies of 2-8 weeks, in the foothills of Big Horn Mountains of Wyoming, allow writers, artists, and scholars to concentrate on their work. Two residency sessions annually: February-June and August-December. No charge for room, board, or studio space. $20 application fee. Deadlines: March 1 for the fall session; October 1 for the spring session. Send SASE for details. **Contact:** Sharon Dynak, Executive Director.

VIRGINIA CENTER FOR THE CREATIVE ARTS

Box VCCA, Sweet Briar, VA 24595. 434-946-7236.

E-mail: vcca@vcca.com. Web site: www.vcca.com.

Description: A working retreat for writers, composers, and visual artists in Virginia's Blue Ridge Mountains. Residencies from 2 weeks to 2 months available year-round. Deadlines: 15th of January, May, and September; about 300 residents accepted each year, 22 at any one time. Limited financial aid is available. Send SASE for details or visit Web site. **Contact:** Suny Monk, Executive Director.

THE WRITERS ROOM

10 Astor Pl., Fl. 6, New York, NY 10003. 212-254-6995.

E-mail: writersroom@writersroom.org. Web site: www.writersroom.org.

Donna Brodie, Executive Director.

Description: In the East Village, the Writers Room offers a quiet work space for all types of writers, at all stages of their careers. The Room holds 29 desks separated by partitions, a typing room with 5 desks, a kitchen, and a library. Open 24 hours/day, 365 days/year. There is a one-time $50 application fee (also, send 3 references); fees for a 3-month period include $225 for a "floater" desk. Part-time memberships at reduced rates available. Call, fax, or write for application (no visits without appointment), or visit Web site. Currently a 2-year wait for full-time membership. **Contact:** Angela Patrinos.

THE WRITERS STUDIO
The Mercantile Library Association
17 E 47th St., New York, NY 10017. 212-755-6710.
E-mail: mercantile_library@msn.com.
Harold Augenbraum, Director.
Description: A quiet place for writers to rent space to allow them to produce good work. A carrel, locker ($15 fee), small reference collection, electrical outlets, and membership in the Mercantile Library are available for $200 for 3 months. Submit application, resume, and writing samples; applications considered year-round. Must have proof of previously published work and current contract with a publisher.
Contact: Ann Keisman.

HELENE WURLITZER FOUNDATION OF NEW MEXICO
Box 1891, Taos, NM 87571. 505-758-2413.
E-mail: hwf@taosnet.com.
Michael A. Knight, Director.
Description: Rent-free, fully furnished houses, with free utilities, in Taos on 18-acre campus, offered to writers and artists in creative (not performing) media. Residency is usually 3 months, April 1 to September 30, and on a limited basis October through March. Send SASE for application and guidelines. Deadline: January 18 for following year. **Contact:** Michael A. Knight, Director.

YADDO
Box 395, Saratoga Springs, NY 12866-0395. 518-584-0746.
E-mail: chwait@yaddo.org. Web site: www.yaddo.org.
Candace Wait, Program Coordinator.
Description: A 400-acre estate, with private bedrooms and studios for each visiting artist. All meals provided. Visual artists, writers, choreographers, film/video artists, performance artists, composers, and collaborators, working at a professional level, are invited for stays from 2 weeks to 2 months. No residency fee. Deadlines: January 15 and August 1. Application fee: $20. Send SASE for form. **Contact:** Candace Wait.

WRITERS' CONFERENCES

Each year, hundreds of writers' conferences are held across the country. The following list, arranged by state, represents a sampling of conferences; each listing includes the location of the conference, the month during which it is usually held, and the name and address of the person from whom specific information may be received. Writers are advised to write or e-mail directly to conference directors for full details, or check the Web sites. Always enclose an SASE. Additional conferences are listed annually in the April issue of *The Writer* magazine (Kalmbach Publishing Co., 21027 Crossroads Circle, P.O. Box 1612, Waukesha, WI 53187-1612).

Writers' conferences are a great opportunity not only to develop writing skills in specific areas but also to meet and develop lasting friendships with other writers, as well as with agents and editors.

ARIZONA

AMERICAN CHRISTIAN WRITERS CONFERENCE
Phoenix, Ariz., November 1-2, 2002; October 31-November 1, 2003.
Description: Locates, educates, and motivates Christian writers and speakers.
Contact: Reg A. Forder, P.O. Box 110390, Nashville, TN 37222. 800-219-7483.
E-mail: acwriters@aol.com. Web site: www.acwriters.com.

ARIZONA STATE POETRY SOCIETY
ANNUAL FALL CONFERENCE
Tempe, Ariz., November 9 2002 (2003 dates TBA).
Description: Location varies each year. Usually in early November. Registration fee varies, depending on meals included, etc. Winners of ASPS Annual National/Poetry Contests are read (prizes awarded); may include workshops, speaker, and/or reader, panel of poets, open readings, etc. **Contact:** Genevieve Sargent, 1707 N Sunset Dr., Tempe, AZ 85281-1551. 480-990-7300.

SPRING POETRY FESTIVAL
Location varies each year; held annually on a Saturday in April.
Description: Free, may include workshop, guest speaker/reader, advance contest, and open readings. Hosted by branches of the Arizona State Poetry Society located in various cities in Arizona. **Contact:** Genevieve Sargent, 1707 N Sunset Dr., Tempe, AZ 85281-1551. 480-990-7300.

WRITERS' ROUNDUP
Phoenix, Ariz., October 19, 2002 (2003 dates TBA).
Description: One full day of workshops, networking, and book signings.
Contact: Sandra L. Lagesse, Valley of the Sun Romance Writers, Inc., P.O. Box 1201, Glendale, AZ 85318-2012.
E-mail: vos@azauthors.com8. Web site: www.azauthors.com/vos.html.

ARKANSAS

AMERICAN CHRISTIAN WRITERS CONFERENCE
Little Rock, AR, February 7-8, 2003.
Description: Locates, educates, and motivates Christian writers and speakers.
Contact: Reg A. Forder, P.O. Box 110390, Nashville, TN 37222. 800-219-7483.
E-mail: acwriters@aol.com. Web site: www.acwriters.com.

ARKANSAS WRITERS' CONFERENCE
Little Rock, Ark., June 7-8, 2002 (2003 dates TBA).
32 contests offered; deadline for contest entries is April 30.
Description: Sponsored by the National League of American Penwomen, Arkansas Pioneer Branch; principal speaker is Leonard Bishop, novelist and author of *Dare to Be a Great Writer.* Send SASE for more information. **Contact:** Barbara Longstreth Mulkey, 17 Red Maple Ct., Little Rock, AR 72211.

OZARK CREATIVE WRITERS CONFERENCE
Eureka Springs, Ark., October 9-11, 2003.
Contest entries must be in by August 25.
Description: For writers who seriously want to become published; includes well-known authors, agents, and editors in several fields. **Contact:** Marcia Camp, Business Manager, 75 Robinwood Dr., Little Rock, AR 72227. 501-225-8619. Web site: www.ozarkcreativewriters.org.

CALIFORNIA

AMERICAN CHRISTIAN WRITERS CONFERENCE
Sacramento, Calif., October 11-12, 2002; October 10-11, 2003.
Anaheim, Calif., October 18-19, 2002; October 17-18, 2003.
San Diego, Calif., October 24-25, 2003.
Description: Locates, educates, and motivates Christian writers and speakers.
Contact: Reg A. Forder, P.O. Box 110390, Nashville, TN 37222. 800-219-7483.
E-mail: acwriters@aol.com. Web site: www.acwriters.com.

CONFERENCE ON WRITING AND ILLUSTRATING FOR CHILDREN (31st ANNUAL)
Los Angeles, Calif., August 2-5, 2003.
Description: Workshops, panels, manuscript and portfolio critiques, with top children's book writers, illustrators, editors, and agents. **Contact:** SCBWI, 8271 Beverly Blvd., Los Angeles, CA 90048. 323-782-1010.
E-mail: conference@scbwi.org. Web site: www.scbwi.org.

MENDOCINO COAST WRITERS CONFERENCE

Fort Bragg, Calif., June 6-8, 2002 (2003 dates TBA).
Early bird discount if reserved by April 20.
Description: Small, friendly, seaside setting. Top presenters are all dedicated teachers as well. Limited to 100. **Contact:** Jan Boyd, College of the Redwoods, 1211 Del Mar, Fort Bragg, CA 95437. 707-961-6248.
E-mail: mcwc@jps.net. Web site: www.mcwcwritewhale.com.

POETRY WORKSHOP

Olympic Valley, Calif., July 20-27, 2002 (2003 dates TBA).
Apply by May 10.
Description: Explores the art, craft, and business of writing through morning workshops, craft lectures, seminars, panel discussions of editing and publishing, and staff readings, as well as brief individual conferences or optional afternoon sessions. **Contact:** Brett Hall Jones, Squaw Valley Community of Writers, P.O. Box 1416, Nevada City, CA 95959. 530-274-8551. E-mail: svcw@oro.net.
Web site: www.squawvalleywriters.org.

ROUND TABLE COMEDY WRITERS CONVENTION

Agoura Hills, Calif., July 18-20, 2002 (2003 dates TBA).
Contact: Linda Perret, 818-865-7833. E-mail: rtcomedy@aol.com.

SANTA BARBARA WRITER'S CONFERENCE

Santa Barbara, Calif., June 21-28, 2002 (2003 dates TBA).
Description: Covers all genres of writing, for a maximum of 350 students. **Contact:** Mary or Barnaby Conrad, P.O. Box 304, Carpinteria, CA 93014.

SCREENWRITING WORKSHOP

Olympic Valley, Calif., August 3-10, 2002 (2003 dates TBA).
Apply by May 10.
Description: Explores the art, craft, and business of writing through morning workshops, craft lectures, seminars, panel discussions of editing and publishing, and staff readings, as well as brief individual conferences or optional afternoon sessions. **Contact:** Brett Hall Jones, Squaw Valley Community of Writers, P.O. Box 1416, Nevada City, CA 95959. 530-274-8551.
E-mail: svcw@oro.net. Web site: www.squawvalleywriters.org.

SOUTHERN CALIFORNIA WRITERS' CONFERENCE

Los Angeles, Calif., October 4-6, 2002 (2003 dates TBA).
San Diego, Calif., February 14-17, 2003.
Description: Devoted to the art, craft, and business of writing professionally; emphasis on interactive troubleshooting and critiquing. **Contact:** Michael Steven Gregory, 4406 Park Blvd., Suite E, San Diego, CA 92116. 619-233-4651.
E-mail: msg@writersconference.com. Web site: www.writersconference.com.

WRITERS WORKSHOP

Olympic Valley, Calif., August 3-10, 2002 (2003 dates TBA).
Apply by May 10. Description:
Covers fiction, narrative, nonfiction, and memoir. Explores the art, craft, and business of writing through morning workshops, craft lectures, seminars, panel discussions of editing and publishing, and staff readings, as well as brief individual conferences or optional afternoon sessions. **Contact:** Brett Hall Jones, Squaw Valley Community of Writers, P.O. Box 1416, Nevada City, CA 95959. 530-274-8551.
E-mail: svcw@oro.net. Web site: www.squawvalleywriters.org.

COLORADO

AMERICAN CHRISTIAN WRITERS CONFERENCE

Colorado Springs, Colo., September 5-6, 2003.
Description: Locates, educates, and motivates Christian writers and speakers.
Contact: Reg A. Forder, P.O. Box 110390, Nashville, TN 37222. 800-219-7483.
E-mail: acwriters@aol.com. Web site: www.acwriters.com.

ASPEN SUMMER WORDS

Aspen, Colo., June 22-26, 2002 (2003 dates TBA).
Description: A writing retreat and literary festival in the heart of the Colorado Rockies. **Contact:** Aspen Writers' Foundation, 110 East Hallam St., Suite 116 Aspen, CO, 81611. 970-925-3122.
E-mail: info@aspenwriters.org. Web site: www.aspenwriters.org.

CANYONLANDS WRITERS RIVER TRIP

Grand Junction, Colo., July.
Description: Limited to 16 participants. Includes several days of peaceful floating through the Colorado Canyons National Conservation Area, followed by whitewater excitement of Westwater Canyon. Allows time for instructional sessions, critiques, writings, hiking, and relaxing. See Web site for current faculty, dates, and fees.
Contact: Canyonlands Field Institute, P.O. Box 68, Moab, UT 84532. 435-259-7750.
E-mail: cfiinfo@canyonlandsfieldinst.org. Web site: www.canyonlandsfieldinst.org.

COLORADO CHRISTIAN WRITERS CONFERENCE

Estes Park, Colo., May 15-17, 2003.
Description: Six continuing sessions, 36 workshops, and more to encourage and equip Christian writers. **Contact:** Marlene Bagnull, 316 Blanchard Rd., Drexel Hill, PA 19026. 610-626-6833.
E-mail: mbagnull@aol.com. Web site: www.writehisanswer.com.

NATIONAL WRITERS ASSOCIATION
FOUNDATION CONFERENCE

Denver, Colo., June 13-15, 2003.

Reserve by June 1.

Description: Features major film producers, authors, editors, agents, publishers, and marketing specialists. **Contact:** Sandra J. Whelchel, 3140 S Peoria St., #295, Aurora, CO 80014. 303-841-0246.

E-mail: sandywrter@aol.com. Web site: www.nationalwriters.com.

PUBLISHING INSTITUTE

Denver, Colo., July 14-August 8, 2003.

Applications due by Apr. 1.

Description: An intensive, full-time, four-week graduate level course that devotes itself to all aspects of book publishing. **Contact:** Pearlanne Zelarney, 2075 S University Blvd., Denver, CO 80210. 303-871-2570.

E-mail: pi-info@du.edu. Web site: www.du.edu/pi.

RWA NATIONAL CONFERENCE

Denver, Colo., July 17-20, 2002 (2003 dates TBA).

Description: 2002 theme: Writing in the Rockies. **Contact:** 3707 FM 1960 W, Suite 555, Houston, TX 77068. 281-440-6885.

E-mail: info@rwanational.org. Web site: www.rwanational.org.

STEAMBOAT SPRINGS WRITERS CONFERENCE

Steamboat Springs, Colo., July 19, 2003.

Contact: Harriet Freiberger, P.O. Box 775063, Steamboat Springs, CO 80477. 970-879-8079. E-mail: mshfreiberger@cs.com.

THE SAN JUAN WORKSHOPS

Ouray, Colo., May-July (2003 dates TBA).

Reserve by May 1.

Description: Workshops for Christian writers, advanced writers, and writers of the landscape. **Contact:** Jill Patterson, 1617 27th St., Park Tower, #706, Lubbock, TX 79405. 806-765-7885. E-mail: inkwellliterary@mac.com.

Web site: http://homepage.mac.com/inkwellliterary.

CONNECTICUT

WESLEYAN WRITERS CONFERENCE

Middletown, Conn.; Held annually the third week in June.

Description: One of the nation's oldest conferences, Wesleyan welcomes both established and new writers of fiction, poetry, short and long nonfiction, and journalism. The program includes seminars, lectures, readings, manuscript consultations, and publishing advice. Scholarships and teaching fellowships are available.

Contact: Anne Greene, Wesleyan Writers Conference, Middletown, CT 06459. 860-685-3604. E-mail: agreene@wesleyan.edu.

Web site: www.wesleyan.edu/writing/conferen.html.

FLORIDA

AMERICAN CHRISTIAN WRITERS CONFERENCE
Orlando, Fla., November 23, 2002; July 11-12, 2003.
Fort Lauderdale, Fla., November 30, 2002; November 29, 2003.
Description: Locates, educates, and motivates Christian writers and speakers.
Contact: Reg A. Forder, P.O. Box 110390, Nashville, TN 37222. 800-219-7483.
E-mail: acwriters@aol.com. Web site: www.acwriters.com.

FIRSTNOVELFEST
2003 Orlando, Fla., October.
Description: Reserve by June 30. Over 40 workshops, 4 agents, keynote speaker, banquet, and networking opportunities. **Contact:** Gardenia Press, P.O. Box 18601, Milwaukee, WI 53218-0601. 866-861-9443.
E-mail: books@gardeniapress.com. Web site: www.gardeniapress.com.

WRITING THE REGION:
MARJORIE KINNAN RAWLINGS WRITERS WORKSHOP
Gainesville, Fla., July 23-27, 2003.
Description: Five-day workshop in historic setting; features fiction, nonfiction, poetry, travel writing, children's writing, screen and play writing, and workshop on characters, setting, dialogue etc. **Contact:** Norma M. Homan, P.O. Box 12246, Gainesville, FL 32604. 888-917-7001.
E-mail: shakes@ufl.edu. Web site: www.writingtheregion.com.

GEORGIA

AMERICAN CHRISTIAN WRITERS CONFERENCE
Atlanta, Ga., May 16-17, 2003.
Description: Locates, educates, and motivates Christian writers and speakers.
Contact: Reg A. Forder, P.O. Box 110390, Nashville, TN 37222. 800-219-7483.
E-mail: acwriters@aol.com. Web site: www.acwriters.com.

SOUTHEASTERN WRITERS WORKSHOP
EPWORTH-BY-THE-SEA (28TH)
St. Simon's Island, Ga., June 15-21, 2003.
Description: A week-long workshop of intensive study in all areas of writing, including fiction, nonfiction, poetry, and the business of writing. Agents-in-residence to meet with students; free manuscript critiques; contests. **Contact:** Amy Munnell.
E-mail: purple@southeasternwriters.com. Web site: www.southeasternwriters.com.

HAWAII

MAUI WRITERS CONFERENCE

Maui, Hawaii, August 29-September 2, 2002 (2003 dates TBA). **Description:** Covers fiction, nonfiction, and screenwriting, with smaller sessions available on poetry, journalism, and children's writing. Offers agent and editor consultations. **Contact:** Shannon Tullius, P.O. Box 1118, Kihei, HI 96753. 888-974-8373. E-mail: writers@maui.net. Web site: www.mauiwriters.com.

IDAHO

AMERICAN CHRISTIAN WRITERS CONFERENCE

Boise, Idaho, Sept. 12-13, 2003. **Description:** Locates, educates, and motivates Christian writers and speakers. **Contact:** Reg A. Forder, P.O. Box 110390, Nashville, TN 37222. 800-219-7483. E-mail: acwriters@aol.com. Web site: www.acwriters.com.

ILLINOIS

AMERICAN CHRISTIAN WRITERS CONFERENCE

Quad Cities, Ia./Ill., August 8-9, 2003. **Description:** Locates, educates, and motivates Christian writers and speakers. **Contact:** Reg A. Forder, P.O. Box 110390, Nashville, TN 37222. 800-219-7483. E-mail: acwriters@aol.com. Web site: www.acwriters.com.

MISSISSIPPI VALLEY WRITERS CONFERENCE (30th ANNUAL)

Rock Island, Ill., June 8-13, 2003. Reserve by May 15. **Description:** Offers nine one-hour workshops daily and individual conferences with instructors. Classes include Basics for Beginners, Juvenile Workshop, Nonfiction, Short Fiction, Basics of the Novel, Marketing to Magazines, Screenwriting, Romance, and Poetry. **Contact:** B. J. Elsner, P.O. Box 4971, Rock Island, IL 61201. 309-786-3406. E-mail: beej@qconline.com. Web site: www.midwestwritingcenter.org.

MISSISSIPPI VALLEY YOUNG AUTHORS CONFERENCE

Rock Island, Ill., June 11, 2003. **Description:** One-day conference for young authors grades 8-12. **Contact:** B. J. Elsner, P.O. Box 4971, Rock Island, IL 61201. 309-786-3406. E-mail: beej@qconline.com. Web site: www.midwestwritingcenter.org.

INDIANA

AMERICAN CHRISTIAN WRITERS CONFERENCE
Fort Wayne, Ind., March 28-29, 2003.
Description: Locates, educates, and motivates Christian writers and speakers.
Contact: Reg A. Forder, P.O. Box 110390, Nashville, TN 37222. 800-219-7483.
E-mail: acwriters@aol.com. Web site: www.acwriters.com.

AMERICAN CHRISTIAN WRITERS CONFERENCE
Indianapolis, Ind., August 2, 2003.
Description: Locates, educates, and motivates Christian writers and speakers.
Contact: Reg A. Forder, P.O. Box 110390, Nashville, TN 37222. 800-219-7483.
E-mail: acwritersr@aol.com. Web site: www.acwriters.com.

ROPEWALK WRITERS RETREAT
New Harmony, Ind., June 9-15, 2002 (2003 dates TBA).
Reserve by May 1.
Description: Gives participants an opportunity to attend workshops and to confer privately with one of five prominent writers; encourages writers to write, not simply listen to others talk about writing. In addition, several writers will present papers or give lectures, open to all participants, on aspects of the craft of writing.
Contact: Linda Cleek, USI Extended Services, 8600 University Blvd., Evansville, IN 47712. 812-464-1863. E-mail: ropewalk@usi.edu. Web site: www.ropewalk.org.

IOWA

IOWA SUMMER WRITING FESTIVAL
Iowa City, Iowa, June-July.
Description: 125 week-long and weekend workshops across the genres. **Contact:** Amy Margolis, 100 Oakdale Campus, W310, University of Iowa, Iowa City, IA 52242. 319-335-4160. E-mail: iswfestival@uiowa.edu. Web site: www.uiowa.edu/~iswfest.

KANSAS

WRITERS WORKSHOP IN SCIENCE FICTION
Lawrence, Kan., June 30-July 12, 2003.
Reserve by May 31.
Description: Intensive workshop involving critiquing of four stories each, aimed at preparing writers to publish regularly. **Contact:** James Gunn, English Dept. University of Kansas, Lawrence, KS 66045. 785-864-3380.
E-mail: jgunn@ku.edu. Web site: http://falcon.cc.ukans.edu/~sfcenter.

KENTUCKY

AMERICAN CHRISTIAN WRITERS CONFERENCE
Louisville, KY, January 18, 2003.
Description: Locates, educates, and motivates Christian writers and speakers.
Contact: Reg A. Forder, P.O. Box 110390, Nashville, TN 37222. 800-219-7483.
E-mail: acwriters@aol.com. Web site: www.acwriters.com.

APPALACHIAN WRITERS WORKSHOP (26th ANNUAL)
Hindman, Ky.
Submit manuscript by June 1.
Description: Well-known authors who are from and/or write about Appalachia teach workshops in several genres. Includes nightly readings and book signings, readings by participants, sharing and learning. **Contact:** Sam L. Linkous or Mike Mullins, Hindman Settlement School, P.O. Box 844, Hindman, KY 41822. 606-785-5475.
E-mail: sam-linkous@hindmansettlement.org or mike-mlm@tgtel.com.
Web site: www.hindmansettlement.org.

GREEN RIVER WRITERS SUMMER RETREAT
Louisville, Ky., July 19-27, 2002 (2003 dates TBA).
Description: Writers' retreat with activities generated by participants: sharing, critiquing, free-writing. **Contact:** Mary O'Dell, 703 Eastbridge Ct., Louisville, KY 40223. 502-245-4902.
E-mail: mary_odell@ntr.net. Web site: www.greenriverwriters.com.

LOUISIANA

TENNESSEE WILLIAMS / NEW ORLEANS LITERARY FESTIVAL
New Orleans, La., March 26-30, 2003.
Description: Annual five-day celebration showcasing national and regional scholars, writers, and performing artists. Programs include panels, classes, theatrical performances, walking tours, and more. **Contact:** Festival Office, 938 Lafayette St., #328, New Orleans, LA 70113. 504-581-1144.
E-mail: info@tennesseewilliams.net. Web site: www.tennesseewilliams.net.

MAINE

STONECOAST WRITERS' CONFERENCE
Freeport, Maine, July 19-28, 2002 (2003 dates TBA).
Description: College-accredited workshops in novel, short story, poetry, nonfiction, and popular fiction. **Contact:** USM Summer Session, P.O. Box 9300, Portland, ME 04104. 207-780-5617.
E-mail: summer@usm.maine.edu. Web site: www.usm.maine.edu/summersession.

MARYLAND

YOUR STATE OF HEALTH / YOUR STATE OF MIND: HOW WRITING IMPACTS ON HEALTH

Arnold, Md., April 12, 2003.
Description: Panel discussions and workshops with authors who have published books on all aspects of health-related issues. **Contact:** Hannelore Hahn, International Women's Writing Guild, P.O. Box 810, Gracie Station, New York, NY 10028. 212-737-7536. E-mail: dirhahn@aol.com. Web site: www.iwwg.com.

MASSACHUSETTS

AMHERST WRITERS & ARTISTS RETREATS, WORKSHOPS, AND INTENSIVE TRAININGS IN WORKSHOP LEADERSHIP

Mass.; various dates and locations.
Description: See Web site for more details. **Contact:** Pat Schneider, P.O. Box 1076, Amherst, MA 01004. 413-253-3307.
E-mail: pat@amherstwriters.com. Web site: www.amherstwriters.com.

CREATIVE WRITING WITH PATRICIA LEE LEWIS

Westhampton, Mass.
(2003 dates TBA).
Description: Guided writing sessions with constructive responses.
Contact: Patricia Lee Lewis, 292 Chesterfield Rd., Westhampton, MA 01027. 413-527-5819. E-mail: patricia@writingretreats.org.
Web site: www.writingretreats.org.

HARVARD SUMMER SCHOOL WRITING PROGRAM

Cambridge, Mass., June 24-August 16, 2002 (2003 dates TBA).
Description: Offers small classes, college credit, a reading series, a student magazine, and workshops on special topics. **Contact:** Harvard Summer School Writing Program, 51 Brattle St., Cambridge, MA 02138. 617-496-5000.
E-mail: summer@hudce.harvard.edu. Web site: www.summer.harvard.edu.

MICHIGAN

AMERICAN CHRISTIAN WRITERS CONFERENCE
Grand Rapids, Mich., June 6-7, 2003.
Description: Locates, educates, and motivates Christian writers and speakers.
Contact: Reg A. Forder, P.O. Box 110390, Nashville, TN 37222. 800-219-7483.
E-mail: acwriters@aol.com. Web site: www.acwriters.com.

RETREAT FROM HARSH REALITY
Hickory Corners, Mich., May 2-4, 2003.
Description: Sponsored by the Mid-Michigan chapter of Romance Writers of America. **Contact:** Pam Trombley, 6845 Forest Way, Harbor Springs, MI 49740. (231) 526-2153.
E-mail: ptrombley@voyager.net. Web site: www.midmichiganrwa.com.

WALLOON WRITERS' RETREAT
Boyne City, Mich., September 25-28, 2003.
Description: Writers and poets, new and established, attend workshops, readings, and provocative panel discussions. **Contact:** John D. Lamb, Springfed Arts, P.O. Box 304, Royal Oak, MI 48068. 248-589-3913.
E-mail: johndlamb@ameritech.net. Web site: www.springfed.org.

WRITERS' CONFERENCE (41st ANNUAL)
Rochester, Mich., October 18-19, 2002 (2003 TBA).
Description: Features private and group manuscript evaluations, writing laboratories, and a choice of 36 presentations conducted by published authors, agents, and editors. Reserve for luncheon by October 11. **Contact:** Gloria J. Boddy, 221 Varner Hall, Oakland University, Rochester, MI 48309. 248-370-4386.
E-mail: gjboddy@oakland.edu. Web site: www.oakland.edu/contin-ed/writersconf.

MINNESOTA

AMERICAN CHRISTIAN WRITERS CONFERENCE
Minneapolis, Minn., August 15-16, 2003.
Description: Locates, educates, and motivates Christian writers and speakers.
Contact: Reg A. Forder, P.O. Box 110390, Nashville, TN 37222. 800-219-7483.
E-mail: acwriters@aol.com. Web site: www.acwriters.com.

SPLIT ROCK ARTS PROGRAM
Duluth, Minn., July 6-August 9, 2003.
Description: Series of week-long residential workshops in creative writing, visual arts, design, and creativity enhancement. Held on the University of Minnesota's Duluth campus and at the Cloquet Forestry Center, the program is a popular destination for an eclectic audience of lifelong learners because of its promise of intensive

study with outstanding writers and artists from around the world. Registration opens in March. **Contact:** Sherry Lee, University of Minnesota, 360 Coffey Hall, 1420 Eckles Ave., St. Paul, MN 55108-6084. 612-625-8100.
E-mail: srap@cce.umn.edu. Web site: www.cce.umn.edu/splitrockarts.

TO MARKET, TO MARKET
Jefferson City, Mo., April 19-20, 2002 (2003 dates TBA).
Description: Sponsored by the Missouri Writers Guild. Includes seminars on both fiction and nonfiction; both published and aspiring writers are welcome.
Contact: Vicki Cox, Missouri Writers Guild, P.O. Box 1895, Lebanon, MO 65536.
E-mail: vcox01@yahoo.com.

NEVADA

AUTHOR'S VENUE JOURNEY CONFERENCE
Lake Tahoe, NV, April 24-27, 2003.
Description: In a different location each year, the Journey Conference offers workshops with top authors, editor and agent appointments, banquets, and more. Attend this premier conference and take a journey to publication. **Contact:** Stephanie Dooley, Author's Venue, LLC, 600 Central Ave. SE, Suite 235, Albuquerque, NM 87102. 505-244-9337.
E-mail: info@authorsvenue.com. Web site: www.authorsvenue.com.

NEW HAMPSHIRE

NEW ENGLAND WRITERS CONFERENCE (15th ANNUAL)
Hanover, N.H., July 20, 2002 (2003 dates TBA).
Description: Includes a distinguished panel, seminars in all genres, poetry and fiction awards, book sales, and open readings. **Contact:** Dr. Frank and Susan C. Anthony, directors, P.O. Box 483, Windsor, VT 05089. 802-674-2315.
E-mail: newvtpoet@aol.com.
Web site: http://hometown.aol.com/newvtpoet/myhomepage/index.html.

ODYSSEY FANTASY WRITING WORKSHOP
Manchester, N.H., June 16-July 25, 2003.
Reserve by April 15.
Description: Intensive six-week workshop for writers of fantasy, science fiction, and horror, run by Jeanne Cavelos, former senior editor at Bantam Doubleday Dell and winner of the World Fantasy Award. **Contact:** Jeanne Cavelos, 20 Levesque Ln., Mont Vernon, NH 03057. 603-673-6234. E-mail: jcavelos@sff.net. Web site: www.sff.net/odyssey.

NEW MEXICO

THE GLEN WORKSHOP
Santa Fe, N.M., August 11-14, 2002 (2003 dates TBA).
Description: Sponsored by *Image: A Journal of the Arts and Religion*; includes morning workshops in writing and visual arts, and evening readings, lectures, and concerts. **Contact:** Mary Kenagy, Image, 3307 3rd Ave. W., Seattle, WA 98119. 206-281-2988. E-mail: glenworkshop@imagejournal.org.
Web site: www.imagejournal.org.

SOUTHWEST WRITERS CONFERENCE (21st ANNUAL)
Albuquerque, N.M., September 5-8, 2002 (2003 dates TBA).
Early bird registration by July 15.
Description: Provides opportunities to meet with some of the top editors, agents, and authors in the literary profession. **Contact:** Southwest Writers, 8200 Mountain Rd. NE, Suite 106, Albuquerque, NM, 87110. 505-265-9485.
E-mail: swriters@aol.com. Web site: www.southwestwriters.org.

TAOS SUMMER WRITERS' CONFERENCE (5th ANNUAL)
Taos, N.M., July 12-18, 2003.
Description: Features writing workshops, readings, craft panels, and special events.
Contact: Sharon Oard Warner, director, University of New Mexico, Taos Summer Writers Conference, Humanities Bldg., Albuquerque, NM 87131. 505-277-6248.
E-mail: taosconf@unm.edu. Web site: www.unm.edu/~taosconf.

NEW YORK

AMERICAN CHRISTIAN WRITERS CONFERENCE
Syracuse, N.Y., June 20-21, 2003.
Description: Locates, educates, and motivates Christian writers and speakers.
Contact: Reg A. Forder, P.O. Box 110390, Nashville, TN 37222. 800-219-7483.
E-mail: acwriters@aol.com. Web site: www.acwriters.com.

ASJA WRITERS CONFERENCE (2003)
New York, N.Y.
Description: For freelance nonfiction writers; includes panels and workshops featuring top editors, publishers, agents, and writers. **Contact:** Brett Harvey, ASJA, 1501 Broadway, Suite 302, New York, NY 10036. 212-997-0947.
E-mail: staff@asja.org. Web site: www.asja.org.

BIG APPLE WORKSHOPS
New York, N.Y., October 12-13, 2002.
New York, N.Y., April 20-21, 2003.
Description: Includes a writing workshop, speakers, and an open house with authors

and agents. **Contact:** Hannelore Hahn, International Women's Writing Guild, P.O. Box 810, Gracie Station, New York, NY 10028. 212-737-7536. E-mail: dirhahn@aol.com. Web site: www.iwwg.com.

CHENANGO VALLEY WRITERS' CONFERENCE

Hamilton, N.Y., June 16-22, 2002 (2003 dates TBA).
Description: Offers daily workshops of 10 or fewer participants, personal consultations, craft talks, panel discussions, readings, and informal conversations. **Contact:** Matt Leone, Colgate University, Hamilton, NY 13346. 315-228-7770. E-mail: mleone@mail.colgate.edu.

GOTHAM WRITERS' WORKSHOP

New York, N.Y, April, June/July, September/October, January.
Description: Offers 10-week, one-day intensive, and on-line workshops in fiction, screenwriting, nonfiction, memoir, poetry, songwriting, playwriting, science fiction, business writing, romance writing, mystery, TV and comedy writing; taught by professional teachers who are also accomplished, working writers. **Contact:** Dana Miller, 1841 Broadway, #809, New York, NY 10023. 212-974-8377. E-mail: office@write.org. Web site: www.writingclasses.com.

"REMEMBER THE MAGIC" 25th ANNIVERSARY SUMMER CONFERENCE

Saratoga Springs, N.Y., August 9-16, 2003.
Reserve by July 15.
Description: A joyous gathering of 550 women from all over the world; over 70 workshops offered each day. **Contact:** Hannelore Hahn, International Women's Writing Guild, P.O. Box 810, Gracie Station, New York, NY 10028. 212-737-7536. E-mail: dirhahn@aol.com. Web site: www.iwwg.com.

WRITING FOR CHILDREN

Chautauqua, N.Y., July 12-19, 2003.
Description: Intensive workshop for individuals interested in writing and illustration children's literature; includes individual and group sessions. **Contact:** Kent L. Brown, Jr., Highlights Foundation, 814 Court St., Honesdale, PA 18431. 570-251-1192. E-mail: klbrown@highlightsfoundation.org. Web site: www.highlightsfoundation.org.

NORTH CAROLINA

AMERICAN CHRISTIAN WRITERS CONFERENCE

Charlotte, N.C., April 11-12, 2003.
Description: Locates, educates, and motivates Christian writers and speakers.
Contact: Reg A. Forder, P.O. Box 110390, Nashville, TN 37222. 800-219-7483.
E-mail: acwriters@aol.com. Web site: www.acwriters.com.

BLUE RIDGE MOUNTAIN CHRISTIAN WRITERS CONFERENCE
Ridgecrest, N.C., April 6-10, 2003.
Description: Designed to train, motivate, encourage, equip, and inspire you to develop your God-given gift to the fullest, in the panoramic mountains of Western North Carolina. **Contact:** Yvonne Lehman, P.O. Box 128, Ridgecrest, NC 28770. 828-669-3596. E-mail: rhawkin@lifeway.com.
Web site: www.ridgecrestconferencecenter.com.

OHIO

AMERICAN CHRISTIAN WRITERS CONFERENCE
Columbus, Ohio, May 30-31, 2003.
Description: Locates, educates, and motivates Christian writers and speakers. **Contact:** Reg A. Forder, P.O. Box 110390, Nashville, TN 37222. 800-219-7483. E-mail: acwriters@aol.com. Web site: www.acwriters.com.

THE KENYON REVIEW'S WRITERS WORKSHOP
Gambier, Ohio, June 21-29, 2003.
Description: Daily workshop meetings in poetry, fiction, and creative nonfiction; includes time for individual work, meetings with instructors, and public readings. **Contact:** Ellen Sheffield, *The Kenyon Review,* Walton House, Gambier, OH 43022. 740-427-5207. E-mail: kenyonreview@kenyon.edu. Web site: www.kenyonreview.org.

OKLAHOMA

AMERICAN CHRISTIAN WRITERS CONFERENCE
Oklahoma City, OK, March 7-8, 2003.
Description: Locates, educates, and motivates Christian writers and speakers. **Contact:** Reg A. Forder, P.O. Box 110390, Nashville, TN 37222. 800-219-7483. E-mail: acwriters@aol.com. Web site: www.acwriters.com.

OKLAHOMA FALL ARTS INSTITUTES
Lone Wolf, Okla., September-October.
Description: A series of four-day workshop retreats for amateur and professional artists, public school teachers and college and university instructors. **Contact:** Jessica Buzzard or Gayla Foster, 105 N Hudson, Suite 101, Oklahoma City, OK 73102. 405-319-9019. E-mail: okarts@okartinst.org. Web site: www.okartinst.org.

OREGON

PORTLAND STATE UNIVERSITY
HAYSTACK SUMMER PROGRAM IN THE ARTS
Cannon Beach, Ore., July 12- August 9, 2002 (2003 dates TBA).
Description: Weekend and week long workshops for writers and artists on the Oregon coast. **Contact:** Elizabeth Snyder, P.O. Box 1491, Portland State University, Portland, OR 97207-1491. 503-725-4186.
E-mail: snydere@ses.pdx.edu. Web site: www.haystack.pdx.edu.

PENNSYLVANIA

GREATER PHILADELPHIA CHRISTIAN WRITERS CONFERENCE
Langhorne, Pa., May 15-17, 2002 (2003 dates TBA).
Description: Six continuing sessions, 36 workshops, and more to encourage and equip Christian writers. **Contact:** Marlene Bagnull, 316 Blanchard Rd., Drexel Hill, PA 19026. 610-626-6833.
E-mail: mbagnull@aol.com. Web site: www.writehisanswer.com.

LIFE IN THE SPOTLIGHT: POLISHING
YOUR PRESENTATIONS AND PROMOTING YOUR BOOKS
Honesdale, Pa., Spring/Fall.
Description: Offers many useful tips and strategies for making polished presentations and promoting yourself to schools, libraries, bookstores, and the media. **Contact:** Maggie Ewain, Highlights Foundation, 814, Court St., Honesdale, PA 18431. 570-251-4552. E-mail: maewain@highlightsfoundation.org.

MONTROSE CHRISTIAN WRITERS CONFERENCE
Montrose, Pa., July 20-25, 2003.
Description: Workshops and classes for all writers, beginners through experienced, published writers. Manuscript review and editorial appointments available. **Contact:** Donna Kosik, Montrose Bible Conference, 5 Locust St., Montrose, PA 18801. 570-278-1001. E-mail: donna@montrosebible.org. Web site: www.montrosebible.org.

NONFICTION—IT'S MORE THAN JUST THE FACTS!
Honesdale, Pa., Spring/Fall.
Description: The key to good nonfiction writing is solid research—research that offers the author juicy anecdotes and insightful quotations that can enliven any subject, no matter how dry. **Contact:** Maggie Ewain, Highlights Foundation, 814 Court St., Honesdale, PA 18431. 570-251-4552.
E-mail: maewain@highlightsfoundation.org.

PHILADELPHIA WRITERS' CONFERENCE

Philadelphia, Pa., Held annually the first or second weekend of June.

Description: Walk-in registration permitted. Beginners welcome. Contest and workshop critique submissions deadline is April 30 (with paid registration). Must be 18 years or older. Registrants choose one workshop each from three groups of four for a total of three workshops. Appointments with agents and editors available. Rap sessions Friday night. Scholarships available. First-place winners receive free tuition for the following year. Contest winners will be published in anthology. **Contact:** Millie Murden, 107 Newington Dr., Hatboro, PA 19040-4508. 215-674-1639. E-mail: pwc@pwcgold.com. Web site: www.pwcgold.com.

ROOM TO CREATE: RETREAT FOR WRITERS AND ILLUSTRATORS OF CHILDREN'S LITERATURE

Honesdale, Pa., Spring/Fall.

Description: We all know it takes hard work to create high-quality writing and illustrations for children. But it also takes time, a carefully chosen space, and encouragement. This retreat combines all three. **Contact:** Maggie Ewain, Highlights Foundation, 814, Court St., Honesdale, PA 18431. 570-251-4552. E-mail: maewain@highlightsfoundation.org.

THE HEART OF THE NOVEL: DEVELOPING CHARACTERS THAT READERS CARE ABOUT

Honesdale, Pa., Spring/Fall.

Description: In this workshop, writers will create that unforgettable character and make it grow throughout several chapters of a book. **Contact:** Maggie Ewain, Highlights Foundation, 814, Court St., Honesdale, PA 18431. 570-251-4552. E-mail: maewain@highlightsfoundation.org.

THE INSIDER'S GUIDE TO CHILDREN'S PUBLISHING

Honesdale, Pa., Spring/Fall.

Description: Intensive workshop focusing on the business side of publishing; answers questions about contracts, agents, advances, and more. **Contact:** Maggie Ewain, Highlights Foundation, 814, Court St., Honesdale, PA 18431. 570-251-4552. E-mail: maewain@highlightsfoundation.org.

WRITING FOR CHILDREN FOUNDERS WORKSHOPS

Boyds Mills, PA, Spring/Fall.

Description: Offers a variety of workshops to help writers grow. Provides unprecedented access to faculty and offers opportunities for writers at all levels to share their knowledge. Workshops focus on the craft of writing, finding the time/space in which to work, and the successful marketing of writers and their books. **Contact:** Maggie Ewain, Highlights Foundation, 814 Court St., Honesdale, PA, 18431. 570-251-1192. E-mail: maewain@highlightsfoundation.org. Web site: www.highlightsfoundation.org.

WRITING FROM THE HEART: TELLING YOUR STORIES ON PAPER

Honesdale, Pa., Spring/Fall.

Description: Helps you utilize the powerful resources within you, to make your writing strong and original and give it "voice;" designed for writers of serious intent who have been writing and trying for publication for more than a year. **Contact:** Maggie Ewain, Highlights Foundation, 814 Court St., Honesdale, PA 18431. 570-251-4552. E-mail: maewain@highlightsfoundation.org.

YOU REALLY OUGHT TO PUBLISH THAT

Stroudsburg, Pa., June 24-27, 2002 (2003 dates TBA).

Description: Led by Rev. Dr. Donna Schaper; located at Kirkridge Retreat and Study Center. Writing workshop for the clergy that teach the formula for turning sermons into op-eds, prayers into poems, and stories into radio/print features or memoirs. Fee: $295. **Contact:** 2495 Fox Gap Rd., Bangor, PA 18013. 610-588-1793. E-mail: kirkridge@fast.net. Web site: www.kirkridge.org.

SOUTH CAROLINA

SOUTH CAROLINA WRITERS WORKSHOP CONFERENCE (12th ANNUAL)

Myrtle Beach, S.C., October 18-20, 2002.

Discount if reserved by September 20.

Description: Writers' conference featuring agents, editors, and bestselling authors. Workshop sessions will focus on practical information on how to become established in the literary industry. **Contact:** Steve Vassey, SCWW, P.O. Box 7104, Columbia, SC 29202. 803-794-0832.

E-mail: vasseyws@hotmail.com. Web site: www.4bnc.com/scww.

TENNESSEE

AMERICAN CHRISTIAN WRITERS CONFERENCE

Chattanooga, TN, January 25, 2003.

Description: Locates, educates, and motivates Christian writers and speakers. **Contact:** Reg A. Forder, P.O. Box 110390, Nashville, TN 37222. 800-219-7483. E-mail: acwriters@aol.com. Web site: www.acwriters.com.

AMERICAN CHRISTIAN WRITERS: MENTORING RETREAT EAST

Nashville, Tenn., July 25-26, 2003.

Description: Locates, educates, and motivates Christian writers and speakers. **Contact:** Reg A. Forder, P.O. Box 110390, Nashville, TN 37222. 800-219-7483. E-mail: acwriters@aol.com. Web site: www.acwriters.com.

TENNESSEE MOUNTAIN WRITERS CONFERENCE

Garden Plaza Hotel, Oak Ridge, Tenn., April 4-5, 2003.

Description: Two full days of writing workshops. Presenters to be announced.
Contact: Joy Margrave, P.O. Box 5435, Oak Ridge, TN 37831-4895.
E-mail: tnmtnwrite@aol.com. Web site: www.tnmtnwrite@aol.com.

TEXAS

AMERICAN CHRISTIAN WRITERS CONFERENCE

Houston, TX, February 15, 2003.

Austin, TX, February 21-22, 2003.

Dallas, TX, February 28-March 1, 2003.

Description: Locates, educates, and motivates Christian writers and speakers.
Contact: Reg A. Forder, P.O. Box 110390, Nashville, TN 37222. 800-219-7483.
E-mail: acwriters@aol.com. Web site: www.acwriters.com.

CAT WRITERS' ASSOCIATION ANNUAL CONFERENCE

Houston, Texas, November 22-24, 2002 (2003 dates TBA).

Reserve by Nov. 9.

Description: Seminar topics are of interest to all writers and include contract advice, media training, creating and selling a nonfiction project, manuscript critiques, and more. **Contact:** Kim Thornton, 22841 Orchid Creek Ln., Lake Forest, CA 92630. 949-454-1368. E-mail: kthornton@cox.net. Web site: www.catwriters.org.

TEXAS CHRISTIAN WRITERS CONFERENCE

Houston, Texas, August 3, 2002 (2003 dates TBA).

Reserve by July 15.

Description: 3-4 workshops on the craft of writing. One-on-one sessions with faculty members. Faculty: Dennis Hensley, Cecil Murphey, DiAnn Mills, and Denella Kimura.
Contact: Martha Rogers, 6038 Greenmont, Houston, TX 77092. 713-686-7209.
E-mail: rrogersll@houston.rr.com.

UTAH

DESERT WRITERS WORKSHOP

Moab, Utah, October.

Description: A retreat-style 5-day workshop focusing on relationships to the natural world and Western themes. See Web site for current faculty, dates, and fees.
Contact: Canyonlands Field Institute, P.O. Box 68, Moab, UT 84532. 435-259-7750.
E-mail: cfiinfo@canyonlandsfieldinst.org. Web site: www.canyonlandsfieldinst.org.

SOUTHERN UTAH UNIVERSITY WRITERS CONFERENCE

Cedar City, Utah, July 15-19, 2002 (2003 dates TBA).
Reserve by June 15.
Description: Workshop for beginning and advanced writers, English teachers, and college students to learn the techniques of writing and understanding fiction, poetry, etc. 3 credits (semester hours). Fee: $210, includes lunch and university credit. **Contact:** David Nyman, Southern Utah University, Cedar City, UT 84720. 435-586-1995. E-mail: nyman@suu.edu.

VERMONT

WILDBRANCH WORKSHOP IN OUTDOOR, NATURAL HISTORY AND ENVIRONMENTAL WRITING

Craftsbury Common, Vt., Held annually the 2nd or 3rd week of June.
Reserve by May 1.
Description: A week-long workshop of classes, lectures, discussion groups, and readings in the craft and techniques of fine writing about the world outdoors. **Contact:** David Brown, Sterling College, Craftsbury Common, VT 05827. 800-648-3591.
E-mail: wldbrnch@sterlingcollege.edu.
Web site: www.sterlingcollege.edu/wildbranch.htm.

VIRGINIA

AMERICAN CHRISTIAN WRITERS CONFERENCE

Richmond, Va., April 4-5, 2003.
Description: Locates, educates, and motivates Christian writers and speakers. **Contact:** Reg A. Forder, P.O. Box 110390, Nashville, TN 37222. 800-219-7483.
E-mail: acwriters@aol.com. Web site: www.acwriters.com.

MID-ATLANTIC WRITERS CONFERENCE

Fredericksburg, Va., May 3-5, 2002 (2003 dates TBA).
Description: Features 20 speakers, workshops, panel discussions, children's writing program, writing contest, and agent/editor consultations by appointment. **Contact:** Roberta Gold, 1239 Harbor View Cir., Oak Grove, VA 22443. 804-224-7723.
E-mail: tymeout96@aol.com.
Web site: www.virginiawritersclub.org/conference2002.html.

WASHINGTON

AMERICAN CHRISTIAN WRITERS CONFERENCE

Seattle, Wash., September 19-20, 2003.
Description: Locates, educates, and motivates Christian writers and speakers.

Contact: Reg A. Forder, P.O. Box 110390, Nashville, TN 37222. 800-219-7483. E-mail: acwriters@aol.com. Web site: www.acwriters.com.

CENTRUM'S PORT TOWNSEND WRITERS' CONFERENCE

Port Townsend, Wash., July 10-20, 2003.
Writing sample for critiqued workshop due by June 1; full payment due by June 14.
Description: Explore widely diverse opinions, styles and genres with many of the nation's leading poets, novelists, and other writers. Select a critiqued workshop limited to 16 participants led by the faculty member of your choice or open enrollment workshops with no critique session. **Contact:** Carla Vander Ven, Centrum, P.O. Box 1158, Port Townsend, WA 98368. 360-385-3102. E-mail: carla@centrum.org. Web site: www.centrum.org.

PACIFIC NORTHWEST WRITERS ASSOCIATION
SUMMER CONFERENCE

Seattle, Wash., July 11-14, 2002 (2003 dates TBA).
Description: Writers from around the country attend this conference, which offers almost 60 workshops, seminars, and master classes that are geared for every experience level, genre, and style. Writers may also schedule appointments with agents and editors. **Contact:** Dennis Globus, PNWA, P.O. Box 2016, Edmonds, WA 98020. 866-217-7692. E-mail: pnwa@melbycameronhull.com. Web site: www.pnwa.org.

WYOMING

JACKSON HOLE WRITERS CONFERENCE (12th ANNUAL)

Jackson, Wyo., June 27-30, 2002 (2003 dates TBA).
Description: Directed toward fiction, screen writing, and creative nonfiction, offering programs relevant to all three disciplines: story structure, narrative thrust, character development, work habits, and business techniques. **Contact:** Keith Guille, P.O. Box 3972, Laramie, WY 82071. 307-766-2938. E-mail: kguille@uwyo.edu. Web site: http://outreach.uwyo.edu/conferences/jacksonwriters.

INTERNATIONAL

AMERICAN CHRISTIAN WRITERS: WRITERS CRUISE

Caribbean, December 1-8, 2002; November 30-March 7, 2003.
Description: Locates, educates, and motivates Christian writers and speakers. **Contact:** Reg A. Forder, P.O. Box 110390, Nashville, TN 37222. 800-219-7483. E-mail: acwriters@aol.com. Web site: www.acwriters.com.

ART WORKSHOP INTERNATIONAL

Assisi, Italy, June 25-July 22, 2002 (2003 dates TBA).
Reserve by May 10.

Description: Live and work in a 12th-century hill town. Instructional courses include fiction, poetry, memoir, visual arts, and art history. **Contact:** Bea Kreloff, 463 West St., 1028H, New York, NY 10014. 866-341-2922. E-mail: bk@artworkshopintl.com. Web site: www.artworkshopintl.com.

BLOODY WORDS MYSTERY CONFERENCE
Ottawa, Ont., June 13-15, 2003.
Description: A gathering of lovers of the mystery genre for panels, discussions, readings, workshops, and a banquet. **Contact:** Linda Wiken, Prime Crime Books, 891 Bank St., Ottawa, ON K1S 3W4, Canada. 613-238-2583. E-mail: prime.crime@rogers.com. Web site: www.bloodywords.com.

CREATIVE WRITING & YOGA
Yelapa, Mexico, February-March (2003 dates TBA). Reserve by January.
Isle of Skye, Scotland, May-June (2003 dates TBA).
Pura Vida, Costa Rica, July (2003 dates TBA). Reserve by May.
Contact: Patricia Lee Lewis, 292 Chesterfield Rd., Westhampton, MA 01027. 413-527-5819. E-mail: patricia@writingretreats.org.
Web site: www.writingretreats.org.

CREATIVE WRITING / VOICE OF THE SOUL
Antigua, Guatemala, February 27-March 8, 2003.
Description: 10-day workshop with Sharon Doubiago. **Contact:** Liza Fourre, Art Workshops in Guatemala, 4758 Lyndale Ave. S., Minneapolis, MN 55409. 612-825-0747. E-mail: info@artguat.org. Web site: www.artguat.org.

DOLCE VITA WRITERS' HOLIDAY
Tuscany, Italy, March, October.
Description: Seven-day holiday in Italy; includes five sessions of writing and marketing instruction, three cooking classes with an Italian chef, and sightseeing. **Contact:** Michael Sedge, The Sedge Group, Via Venezia 14/b, 80021 Afragola (NA) Italy. 1-800-340-7711 (authorization code: SEDGE).
E-mail: msedge@thesedgegroup.com. Web site: www.absolutewrite.com/dolcevita.

FICTION WRITING / SHAPING AND STRUCTURING YOUR STORY
Antigua, Guatemala, March 13-22, 2003.
Description: 10-day workshop with Gladys Swan. **Contact:** Liza Fourre, Art Workshops in Guatemala, 4758 Lyndale Ave. S., Minneapolis, MN 55409. 612-825-0747. E-mail: info@artguat.org. Web site: www.artguat.org.

NEW DIRECTIONS IN TRAVEL WRITING
Antigua, Guatemala, March 29-April 7, 2003.
Description: 10-day workshop with Richard Harris. **Contact:** Liza Fourre, Art

Workshops in Guatemala, 4758 Lyndale Ave. S, Minneapolis, MN 55409. 612-825-0747. E-mail: info@artguat.org. Web site: www.artguat.org.

POETRY / SNAPSHOTS IN WORDS
Antigua, Guatemala, February 14-23, 2003.
Description: 10-day workshop with Roseann Lloyd. **Contact:** Liza Fourre, Art Workshops in Guatemala, 4758 Lyndale Ave. S, Minneapolis, MN 55409. 612-825-0747. E-mail: info@artguat.org. Web site: www.artguat.org.

SPOLETO WRITERS' WORKSHOP
Spoleto, Italy, July 20-August 2, 2002 (2003 dates TBA).
Apply by June 1.
Description: Workshop for serious writers in poetry, fiction and creative nonfiction. Includes writing exercises and focuses on new directions and fresh approaches to revision. **Contact:** With applications: Rosellen Brown, Spoleto Writers' Workshop, 5421 S. Cornell Ave., Apt. 16, Chicago, IL 60615. For more information: Spoleto Arts Symposia, 760 West End Ave., Suite 3-A, New York, NY 10025. 212-663-4440. E-mail: clintoneve@aol.com. Web site: www.spoletoarts.com.

WIRED WRITING STUDIO
Banff, Alberta, Canada, October 5-19, 2003.
Description: Two-week on-site residency at the Banff Centre, followed by 20 weeks of online editing, discussions, and readings with faculty. **Contact:** Writing and Publishing Program Coordinator, 107 Tunnel Mountain Dr., Box 1020, Banff, AB T1L 1H5, Canada. 403-762-6278.
E-mail: writing_publishing@banffcentre.ca. Web site: www.banffcentre.ca/arts.

WRITERS' CONFERENCE AND BOOKFAIR (23rd ANNUAL)
Winchester, Hampshire, England, June 27, 28, 29, 2003.
Reserve by June 20.
Description: Offers 60 lectures, 20 courses, and 300 one-to-one appointments with 60 leading novelists, poets, playwrights, commissioning editors and literary agents at this national festival of writing. Also offers 15 writing competitions with 62 prizes. This conference is followed by a weeklong writing workshop from June 30-July 4, 2003. **Contact:** Barbara Large, Chinook, Southdown Road, Shawford, Hampshire, SO21 2BY, England. 44 (0) 1962-712307.
E-mail: writerconf@aol.com. Web site: www.gmp.co.uk/writers/conference.

WRITERS HOLIDAY AT CAERLEON
Wales, UK, Held annually end of July. Reserve by May.
Description: Residential writers' conference with a choice of several courses, together with a host of lectures, numerous After-Tea Sessions of seminars, talks, discussion groups, and workshops on a wide variety of topics and genres. **Contact:** Anne Hobbs, School Bungalow, Church Rd., Pontnewydd, Cumbran, South Wales, NP44 1AT. 01633-489438. E-mail: writersholiday@lineone.net. Web site: www.writersholiday.net.

DRAMA & THEATER

Community, regional, and civic theaters and college dramatic groups offer the best opportunities today for playwrights to see their work produced, whether on the stage or in dramatic readings.

Indeed, aspiring playwrights will be encouraged to hear that many well-known playwrights received their first recognition in the regional theaters. Payment is generally nominal, but regional and university theaters usually buy only the right to produce a play, and all further rights revert to the author. Since most directors like to work closely with authors on any revisions necessary, theaters will often pay the playwright's expenses while in residence during rehearsals.

The thrill of seeing your play come to life on the stage is one of the pleasures of being on hand for rehearsals and performances. In addition to producing plays and giving dramatic readings, many theaters also sponsor competitions or new-play festivals. Aspiring playwrights should query college and community theaters in their region to find out which ones are interested in seeing original scripts.

Dramatic associations of interest to playwrights include the Dramatists Guild (1501 Broadway, Suite 701, New York, NY 10036), and Theatre Communications Group, Inc. (355 Lexington Ave., New York, NY 10017), which creates the annual *Dramatists Sourcebook: The Playwright's Companion*, published by Feedback Theatrebooks (305 Madison Ave., Suite 1146, New York, NY 10165), an annual directory of theaters, play publishers, and prize contests seeking scripts. See Organizations for Writers listings (in Other Markets & Resources section of this book) for details on dramatists' associations.

Some of the theaters on this list require that playwrights submit all or some of the following with scripts—cast list, synopsis, resume, recommendations, and return postcard—and with scripts and queries, SASEs must always be enclosed.

Also, writers who want to try their hand at writing screenplays for television or film may find it helpful to gain experience in playwriting and further their knowledge of dramatic structure by working in amateur, community, or professional theaters.

The following list also includes a number of publishers of full-length or one-act plays for use by juvenile and adult drama programs.

A. D. PLAYERS
2710 W Alabama, Houston, TX 77098. 713-439-0181.
E-mail: adplayer@hern.org. Web site: www.adplayers.org.
Description: Full-length comedies, dramas, musicals, or one-act children's plays and adaptations with Judeo-Christian world view. Send synopsis and/or brief writing sample to Literary Manager.

ACTORS' PLAYHOUSE AT THE MIRACLE THEATRE
280 Miracle Mile, Coral Gables, FL 33134. 305-444-9293.
E-mail: jchacin@actorsplayhouse.org. Web site: www.actorsplayhouse.org.

Javier Chacin, Literary Manager.
Description: Seeking new readings for comedy, drama, and musicals. Smaller casts preferred. Minimal set restrictions for readings/workshop productions. Looking to expand Reading Series, 6-10 readings/season. A new black box space allows workshop performances of already read material, and small performance pieces.

ACTORS THEATRE OF LOUISVILLE
316 W Main St., Louisville, KY 40202. 502-584-1265.
Web site: www.actorstheatre.org.
Tanya Palmer, Literary Manager.
Description: Literary Prize/Award offers: National Ten-Minute Play Contest: for plays to 10 pages which have not had an equity production. U.S. citizens or residents. Limit: 1 script per person. Prize: $1,000 Heideman Award, possible production. Write for guidelines, SASE. Deadline December 1. No fees.

ALABAMA SHAKESPEARE FESTIVAL
The State Theatre, 1 Festival Dr., Montgomery, AL 36117-4605. 334-271-5300.
E-mail: gorel@asf.net. Web site: www.asf.net.
Kent Thompson, Artistic Director.
Description: Southern and African-American themes/writers. Seeking new full-length plays for production. Sponsors local young playwrights' contest (new). Offers workshops/readings; 1-2 will see full production. SASE. See our list of productions on Web site. Avoid cinematic styles, gritty subject/language. No musicals. Tips: Be familiar with Southern playwriting. Avoid cliché, plays that recall the movies. **Contact:** Gwen Orel, Literary Manager.

ALLEY THEATRE
615 Texas Ave., Houston, TX 77002. 713-228-9341.
Web site: www.alleytheatre.org.
Travis Mader, Dramaturg.
Description: Full-length plays, including translations and adaptations. SASE.

ALLIANCE THEATRE COMPANY
1280 Peachtree St. NE, Atlanta, GA 30309. 404-733-4650.
E-mail: Freddie.Ashley@woodruffcenter.org. Web site: www.alliancetheatre.org.
Susan V. Booth, Artistic Director.
Description: New full-length children's plays, comedy or drama. Plays for a culturally diverse community told in stylish or adventurous ways. SASE. **Contact:** Literary Department.

AMERICAN LITERATURE THEATRE PROJECT
Fountain Theatre, 5060 Fountain Ave., Los Angeles, CA 90029.
Simon Levy.
Description: One-act and full-length stage adaptations of classic and contemporary

American literature. Sets and cast size unrestricted. Send synopsis and SAS postcard. Standard pay, set by Dramatists Guild.

AMERICAN LIVING HISTORY THEATER
P.O. Box 752, Greybull, WY 82426.
Dorene Ludwig, Artistic Director.
Description: One-act dramas, ideally, 1 or 2 characters, about American historical and literary characters and events. Nonfiction, historically accurate, primary source material. SAS postcard.

AMERICAN PLACE THEATRE
111 W 46th St., New York, NY 10036.
David Kener, Associate Artistic Director.
Description: Agented submissions only. Seek challenging, innovative works, not obviously commercial. SAS postcard.

AMERICAN REPERTORY THEATRE
64 Brattle St., Cambridge, MA 02138. 617-496-2000.
Description: No unsolicited material. **Contact:** Office of New Play Development.

AMERICAN STAGE
P.O. Box 1560, St. Petersburg, FL 33731.
Description: Full-length comedies and dramas. Send synopsis with short description of cast and production requirements. SAS postcard. Pays negotiable rates. Submit September-January.

AMERICAN STAGE COMPANY
FDU, Box 336, Teaneck, NJ 07666. 201-692-7720.
James Vagias, Executive Producer.
Description: Full-length comedies, dramas, and musicals for cast of 5-6, single set. No unsolicited scripts.

AMERICAN THEATRE OF ACTORS
314 W 54th St., New York, NY 10019.
James Jennings, Artistic Director.
Description: Full-length dramas for a cast of 2-6. Submit complete play. Responds in 1-2 months. Send SASE.

ANCHORAGE PRESS PLAYS, INC.
International Agency of Plays for Young People
P.O. Box 2901, Louisville, KY 40201. 502-583-2288.
E-mail: applays@bellsouth.net. Web site: www.applays.com.
Marilee Miller, Publisher.
Description: Publishes plays, proven in multiple production, for children in grades K-12. Varies each year. Royalty.

MAXWELL ANDERSON PLAYWRIGHTS SERIES

P.O. Box 671, W. Redding, CT 06896.

Bruce Post, Artistic Director.

Description: Produces 6 professional staged readings of new plays each year. Send complete script with SASE.

ARENA STAGE

1101 Sixth St. SW, Washington, DC 20024. 202-554-9066.

Michell T. Hall, Literary Manager.

Description: No unsolicited scripts accepted from unrepresented writers. Send synopsis, 10 pages of dialogue, bio, and reviews if available. Currently looking for American settings and themes. SASE.

ARKANSAS ARTS CENTER CHILDREN'S THEATRE

P.O. Box 2137, Little Rock, AR 72203. 501-372-4000.

Bradley Anderson, Artistic Director.

Description: Seeks solid, professional full-length or one-act scripts, especially work adapted from contemporary and classic literature. Some original work. SASE.

ARKANSAS REPERTORY THEATRE COMPANY

601 S. Main, P.O. Box 110, Little Rock, AR 72203-0110. 501-378-0445.

E-mail: therep@alltel.net. Web site: www.therep.org.

Brady Moody, Literary Manager.

Description: Full-length comedies, dramas, and musicals; prefers up to 8 characters. Send synopsis, cast list, resume, and SASE; do not send complete manuscript. Responds in 3 months.

BAKER'S PLAYS

P.O. Box 69922, Quincy, MA 02269-9222. 617-745-0805.

E-mail: editor@bakersplays.com. Web site: www.bakersplays.com.

Ray Pape, Associate Editor.

Description: Send submissions to the attention of the editor. No writing samples, complete plays only. Prefers produced plays for high school, community, and regional theatres. Publishes full-length or one-act plays for young audiences, musicals and chancel dramas. Please include cover letter, resume, and press clippings if available. CD, tape, or sheet music must accompany musical submissions. Include SASE with pre-paid priority shipping for return of scripts. Responds in 6-8 months.

BARTER THEATER

P.O. Box 867, Abingdon, VA 24212-0867.

E-mail: barter@naxs.com.

Richard Rose, Artistic Director.

Description: Full-length dramas, comedies, adaptations, and children's plays. Submit synopsis, dialogue sample and SASE. Responds in 6-8 months. Pays standard royalty.

BERKELEY REPERTORY THEATRE

2025 Addison St., Berkeley, CA 94704. 510-647-2900.

Web site: www.berkeleyrep.org.

Tony Taccone, Artistic Director.

Description: Seeking new full-length plays for production, 5 mainstage/2 parallel season productions, mid-level career and above. Some work commissioned. No restrictions on cast or set. Agent submissions only; no unsolicited scripts accepted. See Web site for guidelines. **Contact:** Luan Schooler, Literary Manager.

BERKSHIRE THEATRE FESTIVAL

P.O. Box 797, Stockbridge, MA 01262.

E-mail: info@berkshiretheatre.org. Web site: www.berkshiretheatre.org.

Kate Maguire, Executive Director.

Description: Full-length comedies, musicals, and dramas; cast to 8. Submit through agent only.

BOARSHEAD THEATER

425 S Grand Ave., Lansing, MI 48917. 517-484-7800.

E-mail: boarshead-admin@boarshead.org. Web site: www.boarshead.org.

John Peakes, Artistic Director.

Description: Seeking new full-length plays, comedy and drama, cast of 4-10. Single or unit set preferred. SASE. Send only 10 pages of representative dialogue, cast list (with descriptions), number of sets, and a one-page (only) précis.

BRISTOL RIVERSIDE THEATRE

P.O. Box 1250, Bristol, PA 19007.

Susan D. Atkinson.

Description: Full-length plays, up to 15 actors, and simple set. SASE.

CALIFORNIA UNIVERSITY THEATRE

California University of Pennsylvania, 250 University Ave., California, PA 15419.

Web site: www.cup.edu.

Dr. Richard J. Helldobler, Chairman.

Description: Unusual, avant-garde, and experimental one-act and full-length comedies and dramas, children's plays, and adaptations. Cast size varies. Submit synopsis with short, sample scene(s). SASE. Payment available.

CENTER STAGE

700 N Calvert St., Baltimore, MD 21202. 410-685-3200.

James Magruder, Resident Dramaturg.

Description: Full-length comedies, dramas, translations, adaptations. No unsolicited manuscripts. Send synopsis, a few sample pages, resume, cast list, and production history. SASE. Responds in 8-10 weeks.

CHILDSPLAY INC.

P.O. Box 517, Tempe, AZ 85280-0517. 480-350-8101.
E-mail: childsplayaz@juno.com. Web site: www.childsplayaz.org.
David Saar, Artistic Director.
Description: Seeking new full-length and one-act children's plays, multi-genera-
tional, 45-120 minutes: dramas, musicals, and adaptations for family audiences. Cast
up to 12. Set: no restrictions. Productions may need to travel. Prefer visual, theatrical
pieces rather than didactic message plays. SASE. **Contact:** Graham Whitehead.

CIRCLE IN THE SQUARE THEATRE SCHOOL

1633 Broadway, New York, NY 10019-6795.
E-mail: circleinthesquare@att.net. Web site: www.circlesquare.org.
Dr. Rhonda R. Dodd, Associate Director.
Description: Accepts scripts, tapes, and sheet music for children's theatre using 4-6
adult actors. Prefers multi-cultural or American historical themes, 35-45 minutes
long, may include music. SASE.

CITY THEATRE COMPANY

1300 Bingham St., Pittsburgh, PA 15203.
Web site: www.citytheatrecompany.org.
Carlyn Aquiline, Literary Manager/Dramaturg.
Description: Commissions, develops, and produces contemporary plays of substance and ideas that engage diverse audiences. Interests: new plays; compelling stories; unconventional form, content, and use of language; under-represented voices
(women, writers of color, writers who are disabled). Full-length dramas, comedies,
musicals, adaptations, translations, solo plays. Prefers cast limit of 8. No unsolicited or
e-mail submissions. Agent submission, or query with resume, synopsis, character
breakdown, dialogue sample (15 pages), development/production history, music
demo, SASE. No phone calls.

I. E. CLARK PUBLICATIONS

P.O. Box 246, Schulenburg, TX 78956.
E-mail: ieclark@cvtv.net. Web site: www.ieclark.com.
Donna Cozzaglio, Artistic Director.
Description: Publishes one-act and full-length plays and musicals, for children,
young adults, and adults, that have been produced. Serious drama, comedies, classics,
fairytales, melodramas, and holiday plays. Responds in 2-6 months. Royalty.

CLASSIC STAGE COMPANY

136 E 13th St., New York, NY 10003. 212-677-4210.
E-mail: info@classicstage.org. Web site: www.classicstage.org.
Barry Edelstein, Artistic Director.
Description: Not currently seeking new productions. Produces classical plays, often
in new full-length translations or adaptations. Smaller cast is better, as appropriate;
same for set. SASE.

THE CONSERVATORY THEATRE ENSEMBLE
Tamalpais High School, 700 Miller Ave., Mill Valley, CA 94941.
E-mail: sbrash@marin.k12.ca.us.
Susan Brashear, Artistic Director.
Description: Comedies, dramas, children's plays, adaptations, and scripts on high school issues, for casts of 8-20. Plays with flexible casting, adaptable to "ensemble" style. One-act, 30-minute plays are especially needed; produces 50 short plays each season using teenage actors. Send synopsis and resume.

CONTEMPORARY DRAMA SERVICE
Meriwether Publishing Co., 885 Elkton Dr., Colorado Springs, CO 80907.
E-mail: merpcds@aol.com. Web site: meriwetherpublishing.com.
Arthur Zapel, Executive Editor.
Description: Publishes plays and supplemental textbooks on theatrical subjects for middle school, high school, and college students. Accepts new full-length and one-act plays—comedy or musical. Prefers large-cast scripts with limited staging requirements. No obscene language, unsuitable subject matter, or violence. Prefers comedic material, but publishes some serious work appropriate to educational markets. Include SASE. **Contact:** Ted Zapel.

CROSSROADS THEATRE CO.
7 Livingston Ave., New Brunswick, NJ 08901. 732-729-9559.
Les Edwards, Executive Director.
Description: Full-length and one-act dramas, comedies, musicals, and adaptations; issue-oriented experimental plays with honest, imaginative, and insightful examinations of the African-American experience. Also interested in African and Caribbean plays and plays exploring cross-cultural issues. No unsolicited scripts; query first with synopsis, cast list, and resume. SASE.

DELAWARE THEATRE COMPANY
200 Water St., Wilmington, DE 19801-5030.
Web site: www.delawaretheatre.org.
Fontaine Syer, Artistic Director.
Description: Full-length comedies and dramas. Cast up to 10. Responds in 6 months. Unsolicited manuscripts from local authors only. Agent submissions considered. SASE.

DENVER CENTER THEATRE COMPANY
1050 13th St., Denver, CO 80204.
E-mail: denvercenter@dcpa.org. Web site: www.denvercenter.org.
Donovan Marley, Artistic Director.
Description: No longer accepting unsolicited scripts. **Contact:** Bruce K. Sevy, Associate Artistic Director/New Play Development.

DETROIT REPERTORY THEATRE
13103 Woodrow Wilson Ave., Detroit, MI 48238.
Barbara Busby. **Description:** Full-length comedies and dramas. Scripts accepted October-April. Pays royalty. SASE.

DORSET THEATRE FESTIVAL
P.O. Box 510, Dorset, VT 05251. 802-867-2223.
E-mail: theatre@sover.net. Web site: www.theatredirectories.com.
Description: Seeking new full-length scripts with general audience appeal, comedy and drama. Cast: Prefer less than 8. Prefer unit set. Also operates a writers' colony, Dorset Colony for Writers. SASE. Tips: Most new plays come from professional contacts or through our writers' colony.

DRAMATIC PUBLISHING COMPANY
311 Washington St., Woodstock, IL 60098. 815-338-7170.
E-mail: plays@dramaticpublishing.com. Web site: www.dramaticpublishing.com.
Linda Habjan, Editor.
Description: Publishes full-length and one-act plays and musicals for professional, stock, amateur, and children's theater market. Send SASE. Royalty. Responds in 4-6 months.

DRAMATICS
Educational Theatre Association
2343 Auburn Ave., Cincinnati, OH 45219-2815. 513-421-3900.
E-mail: dcorathers@edta.org. Web site: www.edta.org.
Don Corathers, Editor
Monthly September-May. Circ.: 37,000. **Description:** Magazine for high school theatre students: acting, directing, playwriting, technical subjects, book reviews. Publishes articles, interviews, how-tos. Also publishes one-act and full-length plays for high school production. Pays $25 to $400 honorarium for one-time, non-exclusive publication rights. Complete manuscripts preferred. **Art:** Graphics and photos accepted. **Tips:** Does not publish didactic scripts or musicals. Be aware of the script's production demands. Readers are active theatre students and teachers. Queries: Not necessary. Unsolicited mss: Accepts. Payment: On acceptance. **Contact:** Don Corathers.

EAST WEST PLAYERS
120 N Judge John Aiso St., Los Angeles, CA 90012. 213-625-7000.
E-mail: info@eastwestplayers.org. Web site: www.eastwestplayers.org.
Tim Dang, Artistic Director.
Description: Seeking new full-length plays in comedy, drama, musicals, and special material dealing with Asian/Asian Pacific/Asian-American issues. Offers periodic contests and workshops/readings. **Tips:** Avoid Asian stereotypes.

ELDRIDGE PUBLISHING CO.

P.O. Box 1595, Venice, FL 34284. 800-447-8243.

E-mail: info@histage.com. Web site: www.histage.com.

Susan Shore, Editorial Department.

Description: Publishes one-act and full-length plays and musicals for schools, churches, and community theater groups. Comedies, tragedies, dramas, children's theater, adaptations, interactive plays, and religious plays (all holidays). Submit complete manuscript with cover letter. Responds in 2 months. Flat fee for religious plays, royalty for all else.

ENSEMBLE STUDIO THEATRE

549 W 52nd St., New York, NY 10019. 212-247-4982.

Web site: www.ensemblestudiotheatre.org.

Curt Dempster, Artistic Director.

Description: Seeking new full-length and one-act plays: comedy, drama, and science/technology, plays by African-American women writers. New one-act plays, 15-45 minutes (annual spring one-act play marathon; deadline, December 1). New full-length plays by African-American women ("Going to the River Series"; deadline, January 15). New readings of plays in development. **Contact:** Tom Rowan, Literary Manager.

FLORIDA STAGE

262 S Ocean Blvd., Manalapan, FL 33462.

Desmond Gallant, Literary Manager.

Description: Full-length comedies, dramas, and musicals. Agent submissions only. Royalty. Responds in 9 months.

FLORIDA STUDIO THEATRE

1241 N Palm Ave., Sarasota, FL 34236. 941-366-9017.

E-mail: james@fst2000.org. Web site: www.fst2000.org.

Richard Hopkins, Artistic Director.

Description: Seeking new full-length plays in comedy, drama, musicals, children's and adaptations; highly theatrical, innovative plays with universal themes. Cast: Less than 10. Single set. Offers contests, workshops, readings. All submissions considered for our new play festivals. **Contact:** James Ashford, Casting and Literary Coordinator.

THE GLOBE THEATRES

P.O. Box 122171, San Diego, CA 92112-2171.

Jack O'Brien, Artistic Director.

Description: Full-length comedies, dramas, and musicals. No unsolicited manuscripts. Submit through agent, or query with synopsis.

THE GOODMAN THEATRE

170 N Dearborn St., Chicago, IL 60601. 312-443-3811.

E-mail: staff@goodman-theatre.org. Web site: www.goodman-theatre.org.

Description: No unsolicited scripts; queries from recognized literary agents or producing organizations required for full-length comedies or dramas. **Contact:** Literary Manager.

THE GUTHRIE THEATER
725 Vineland Pl., Minneapolis, MN 55403. 612-377-2224.
E-mail: joh@guthrietheater.org.
Description: Full-length dramas and adaptations of world literature, classic masterworks, oral traditions, and folktales. No unsolicited scripts; send query with synopsis, resume, and professional recommendation. Responds in 3-4 months.

HARRISBURG COMMUNITY THEATRE
513 Hurlock St., Harrisburg, PA 17110. 717-232-5501.
Thomas G. Hostetter, Artistic Director.
Description: Full-length comedies, dramas, musicals, and adaptations; cast to 20; prefers simple set. Query first, then submit script with cast list, resume, synopsis, and SAS postcard. Best time to submit: June-August. Responds in 6 months. Negotiable rates.

HARTFORD STAGE COMPANY
50 Church St., Hartford, CT 06103. 860-525-5601.
Web site: www.hartfordstage.org. Shelley Butler. **Description:** Full-length plays, all types, for cast up to 12. No unsolicited manuscripts; submit through agent or send synopsis. Pays varying rates.

HEUER PUBLISHING COMPANY
P.O. Box 248, Cedar Rapids, IA 52406. 319-364-6311.
E-mail: editor@hitplays.com. Web site: www.hitplays.com.
C. Emmett McMullen, Artistic Director/Editor.
Description: Publishes new full-length and one-act plays for comedy, drama, musicals, and adaptations. Prefers large cast, mostly female, and simple sets. Tips: No violence or derogatory, racist, or sexist language or situations.

HIPPODROME STATE THEATRE
25 SE Second Pl., Gainesville, FL 32601.
Tamerin Dygert.
Description: Full-length plays with unit sets and casts up to 6. No unsolicited manuscripts. Agent submissions and professional recommendations only. Send synopsis and scene sample only, with any reviews. May-August.

HOLLYWOOD THESPIAN COMPANY
12838 Kling St., Studio City, CA 91604-1127.
Rai Tasco, Artistic Director.
Description: Full-length comedies and dramas for integrated cast. Include cast list and SAS postcard with submission.

HONOLULU THEATRE FOR YOUTH

2846 Ualena St., Honolulu, HI 96819.

Web site: www.htyweb.org.

Mark Lutwak, Artistic Director.

Description: Plays, 60-90 minutes, for young people and family audiences. Adult casts. Contemporary issues, Pacific themes, etc. Unit sets, small cast. Query or send cover letter with synopsis, cast list, and SASE. Royalties negotiable. Tips: See Web site for more information about season.

HORIZON THEATRE COMPANY

P.O. Box 5376, Station E, Atlanta, GA 31107. 404-523-1477.

Web site: www.horizontheatre.com.

Lisa Adler, Artistic Directors.

Description: Full-length comedies, dramas, and satires. Encourages submissions by women writers. Cast up to 10. Submit synopsis with cast list, resume, and recommendations. Pays percentage. Readings. Responds in 6 months.

HUNTINGTON THEATRE COMPANY

264 Huntington Ave., Boston, MA 02115-4606. 617-266-7900.

Nicholas Martin, Artistic Director.

Description: Agent submissions only.

ILLINOIS THEATRE CENTER

371 Artists' Walk, P.O. Box 397, Park Forest, IL 60466. 708-481-3510.

Description: Full-length comedies, dramas, musicals, and adaptations, for unit/fragmentary sets, up to 8 cast members. Send summary and SAS postcard. No unsolicited manuscripts. Negotiable rates. Workshops and readings offered.

JEWISH REPERTORY THEATRE

1395 Lexington Ave., New York, NY 10128. 212-415-5550.

Web site: www.jrt.org.

Ran Avni, Artistic Director.

Description: Full-length comedies, dramas, musicals, and adaptations, with up to 10 cast members, relating to the Jewish experience. Pays varying rates. Enclose SASE.

KUMU KAHUA THEATRE

46 Merchant St., Honolulu, HI 96813. 808-536-4222.

Harry Wong III, Artistic Director.

Description: Full-length plays, especially relevant to life in Hawaii. Prefers simple sets for arena productions. Submit resume and synopsis. Pays $50 per performance. Readings. Contests.

LOS ANGELES DESIGNERS' THEATRE

P.O. Box 1883, Studio City, CA 91614-0883. 323-650-9600.

E-mail: ladesigners@juno.com.

Richard Niederberg, Artistic Director.

Description: Seeking proposals for new, full-length plays: comedy, drama, musicals, adaptations. Can incorporate religious, social, or political themes, street language, nudity, etc. No cast or set restrictions. Looking to commission scripts on work-for-hire basis. Has produced over 400 original works since 1970.

LOVE CREEK PRODUCTIONS

162 Nesbit St., Weehawken, NJ 07086.

E-mail: creekread@aol.com.

Le Wilhelm, Managing Director.

Description: Seeking new plays for production: one-act and full-length. Cast: 6 or more characters for full-lengths. For Developmental Series, minimal production values. We welcome new authors, well-crafted scripts with responsible treatment of humanistic theme. Tips: Must first send SASE for submission guidelines. Scripts that do not meet guidelines will not be considered. One-acts have better chance for production. **Contact:** Cynthia Granville-Callahan.

THE MAGIC THEATRE

Fort Mason Ctr., Bldg. D, San Francisco, CA 94123. 415-441-8001.

E-mail: magicthtre@aol.com.

Laura Hope Owen, Literary Manager.

Description: Comedies and dramas, interested in political, non-linear, and multicultural work for mainstage productions. Query with synopsis, resume, first 10-20 pages of script, and SASE; no unsolicited manuscripts. Pays varying rates. Tips: Smaller casts preferred (6 and under). E-queries: No.

MANHATTAN THEATRE CLUB

311 W 43rd St., New York, NY 10036. 212-399-3000.

E-mail: lit@mtc-nyc.org. Web site: www.manhattantheatreclub.com.

Lynne Meadow, Artistic Director.

Description: Seeking new full-length American plays: comedy, drama, musicals, adaptations. Sponsors MTC Playwriting Fellowships. Offers workshops/readings. Comprehensive play development programs. **Contact:** Elizabeth Bennett, Literary Manager.

MCCARTER THEATRE COMPANY

91 University Pl., Princeton, NJ 08540. 609-258-6500.

Web site: www.mccarter.org.

Emily Mann, Artistic Director.

Description: Seeking new full-length plays: comedies, dramas, adaptations. **Contact:** Liz Engleman, Literary Director.

METROSTAGE

1201 N Royal St., Alexandria, VA 22314. 703-548-9044.

Web site: www.metrostage.com.

Carolyn Griffin, Producing Artistic Director.

Description: Seeking new full-length plays in comedy, drama, small musicals. Cast: 2-6 preferred. Unit sets preferred. Workshops/readings offered. Interested only in plays with history of readings and development. SASE.

MILL MOUNTAIN THEATRE

One Market Sq. SE, Fl. 2, Roanoke, VA 24011. 540-342-5749.
E-mail: outreach@millmountain.org. Web site: www.millmountain.org.
Jere Lee Hodgin, Artistic Director.
Description: Seeking full-length and one-act new plays: comedy, drama, musicals, children's. Mill Mountain Theatre New Play competition. Centerpiece, one-act reading series. Tips: See guidelines at Web site. **Contact:** Literary Coordinator.

NATIONAL BLACK THEATRE

Institute of Action Arts, 2033 Fifth Ave., Harlem, NY 10035.
Theatre Arts Program. **Description:** Drama, musicals, and children's plays. Scripts should reflect African and African-American lifestyle. Historical, inspirational, and ritualistic forms appreciated. Workshops and readings.

NATIONAL DRAMA SERVICE

MSN 160 Lifeway, One Lifeway Plaza, Nashville, TN 37234.
E-mail: churchdrama@earthlink.net. **Description:** Publishes dramatic material "that communicates the message of Christ . . . scripts that help even the smallest church enhance their ministry with drama." Scripts, 2-7 minutes long: drama in worship, puppets, clowns, Christian comedy, mime, movement, readers theater, creative worship services, and monologues. Payment varies, on acceptance. Guidelines available.

NEW ENSEMBLE ACTORS THEATRE

138 S Oxford St., Suite 1D, Brooklyn, NY 11217. 718-398-4979.
E-mail: spmime@netzero.net.
Ms. Scottie Davis, Artistic Director.
Description: Currently seeking new plays by African-American writers. Project of Salt & Pepper Mime Co., surreal, mimetic, sci-fi, fantasy.

NEW YORK SHAKESPEARE FESTIVAL/JOSEPH PAPP PUBLIC THEATER

425 Lafayette St., New York, NY 10003. 212-539-8500.
Web site: www.publictheatre.org.
Rick DesRochers, Literary Manager.
Description: Full-length plays, translations, adaptations, musicals, operas, solo pieces. Submit synopsis, 10-page sample scene, letter of inquiry, and CD or cassette of 3-5 songs for musicals or operas.

NEW YORK STATE THEATRE INSTITUTE

37 First St., Troy, NY 12180.
Patricia Di Benedetto Snyder, Producing Artistic Director.

Description: Emphasis on new, full-length plays and musicals for family audiences. Query with synopsis and cast list. Payment varies.

ODYSSEY THEATRE ENSEMBLE
2055 S Sepulveda Blvd., Los Angeles, CA 90025. 310-477-2055.
Web site: www.odysseytheatre.com.
Ron Sossi, Artistic Director.
Description: Seeking new full-length comedies, dramas, musicals, and adaptations: provocative subject matter, or plays that stretch and explore the possibilities of theater. Cast: limit to 10. Offers workshops/readings. **Contact:** Sally Essex-Lopresti, Literary Manager.

OLDCASTLE THEATRE COMPANY
Bennington Center for the Arts, P.O. Box 1555, Bennington, VT 05201.
Eric Peterson, Artistic Director.
Description: Full-length comedies, dramas, and musicals for small cast (up to 10). Submit synopsis and cast list in the winter. Responds in 6 months. Offers workshops and readings. Pays expenses for playwright to attend rehearsals. Royalty.

PAPER MILL: THE STATE THEATRE OF NEW JERSEY
Papermill, Brookside Dr., Millburn, NJ 07041.
Mark S. Hoebee, Associate Director.
Description: A 1,000-seat state-of-the-art theatre presenting full-length plays and musicals. Submit completed work, including script, synopsis, resume, and tape for musicals. Responds in 6-12 months.

PENGUIN REPERTORY COMPANY
P.O. Box 91, Stony Point, Rockland County, NY 10980.
Joe Brancato, Artistic Director.
Description: Full-length comedies and dramas, cast size to 4. Submit script, resume, and SASE. Payment varies.

PEOPLE'S LIGHT AND THEATRE COMPANY
39 Conestoga Rd., Malvern, PA 19355.
Alda Cortese, Literary Manager.
Description: Full-length comedies, dramas, and adaptations. No unsolicited manuscripts; query with synopsis and 10 pages of script. Payment negotiable.

PIER ONE THEATRE
Box 894, Homer, AK 99603-0894. 907-235-2333.
E-mail: lance@xyz.net. Web site: www.pieronetheatre.org.
Lance Petersen, Artistic Director.
Description: Seeking new full-length and one-act comedies, dramas, musicals, children's plays, and adaptations. Offers workshops/readings. **Tips:** Do not start the play

with a phone call! No AIDS plays, new age plays; must have something wonderful and unique to offer.

PIONEER DRAMA SERVICE

P.O. Box 4267, Englewood, CO 80155. 303-779-4035.
E-mail: editors@pioneerdrama.com. Web site: www.pioneerdrama.com.
Steven Fendrich, Publisher.
Description: Publishes full-length and one-act plays, also musicals, melodramas, and children's theater. No unproduced plays or plays with mostly male casts. Simple sets preferred. Query first. Royalty. **Contact:** Beth Somers, Submissions Editor.

PLAYHOUSE ON THE SQUARE

51 S Cooper in Overton Sq., Memphis, TN 38104.
Jackie Nichols, Artistic Director.
Description: Full-length comedies, dramas; cast up to 15. Contest deadline: April for fall production. Pays fee.

PLAYS

Kalmbach Publishing Co., P.O. Box 600160, Newton, MA 02460. 617-332-4063.
E-mail: lpreston@playsmag.com. Web site: www.playsmag.com.
Elizabeth Preston, Editor.
Description: "The drama magazine for young people." Publishes one-act plays, for production by people ages 7-17. Comedies, dramas, farces, skits, holiday plays. Also adaptations of classics, biographies, puppet plays, creative dramatics. No religious themes. Cast: at least 8 characters. Sets, within capabilities of amateur set designers (school teachers, students, volunteers). **Tips:** Read copy of magazine to get a feel for the kinds of plays we publish. Spec sheet also available; send SASE to Kalmbach Publishing Co., P.O. Box 1612, Waukesha, WI, 53187-1612.

PLAYWRIGHTS HORIZONS

630 Ninth Ave., #708, New York, NY 10036. 212-564-1235.
Web site: www.playwrightshorizons.org.
Sonya Sobieski, Literary Manager.
Description: Full-length, original comedies, dramas, and musicals by American authors. No one-acts, adaptations, or screenplays. Synopses discouraged; send script, resume and SASE, include tape for musicals. Off-Broadway contract.

PLAYWRIGHTS' PLATFORM

164 Brayton Rd., Boston, MA 02135.
Web site: www.theatermirror.com.
George Sauer, Artistic Director.
Description: Full-length and one-act plays of all kinds. Script development workshops and public readings for Massachusetts playwrights only. Tips: Massachusetts residents only. No sexist or racist material.

POPLAR PIKE PLAYHOUSE

7653 Old Poplar Pike, Germantown, TN 38138. 901-755-7775.
E-mail: efblue@aol.com. Web site: www.ppp.org.
Frank Bluestein, Artistic Director.
Description: Full-length and one-act comedies, dramas, musicals, and children's plays. We are in a high school; most plays feature high-school students, with characters that students can realistically portray and understand.

PRINCETON REP COMPANY/
PRINCETON REP SHAKESPEARE FESTIVAL

One Palmer Square, Suite 541, Princeton, NJ 08542. 609-921-3682.
E-mail: prcreprap@aol.com. Web site: www.princetonrep.org.
Victoria Liberatori, Artistic Director.
Description: Seeks full-length plays which address contemporary issues in challenging and provocative terms, and adaptations/translations of classical plays, especially the Greeks and Shakespeare. Particular interest: plays by or about women. Considered for reading, workshop, and production. Submit 10-page dialogue sample, 2-page synopsis, cast list, set requirements, and resume. Responds within 9-12 months.

THE PUERTO RICAN TRAVELING THEATRE

141 W 94th St., New York, NY 10025. 212-354-1293.
Miriam Colon Valle, Artistic Director.
Description: Full-length and one-act comedies, dramas, and musicals; cast up to 8; simple sets. Prefer plays on contemporary Hispanic experience, with social, cultural, or psychological content. Payment negotiable.

THE REPERTORY THEATRE OF ST. LOUIS

P.O. Box 191730, St. Louis, MO 63119.
E-mail: sgregg@repstl.org.
S. Gregg, Associate Artistic Director.
Description: Query with brief synopsis, technical requirements, and cast size. Unsolicited manuscripts are returned unread.

ROUND HOUSE THEATRE

12210 Bushey Dr., Suite 101, Silver Spring, MD 20902. 301-933-9530.
E-mail: dcrosby@round-house.org. Web site: www.round-house.org.
Jerry Whiddon, Producing Artistic Director.
Description: Seeking new full-length plays, translations, adaptations, musicals, solo pieces, and plays for young audiences. Cast: 8-10 actors max. Unit set preferred. Offers workshops/reading, revisions for New Voices series (November and June, readings of local playwrights). No unsolicited scripts; will accept synopsis. Send 10-page dialogue sample, cast, tech requirements, resume and SASE for response. Address all submissions c/o Production Department. Responds in 2 months to queries, 12 months for scripts. **Contact:** Danisha Crosby, Director of Productions.

SAMUEL FRENCH, INC.

45 W. 25th St., New York, NY 10010.
E-mail: samuelfrench@earthlink.net. Web site: www.samuelfrench.com. Lawrence Harbison, Editor. **Description:** Publishes full-length plays and musicals. One-act plays, 20-45 minutes. Children's plays, 45-60 minutes. Stage plays. Unpublished writers considered. Query with complete manuscript; unsolicited and multiple queries okay. No fees.

SEATTLE REPERTORY THEATRE

155 Mercer St., Seattle, WA 98109. 206-443-2210.
Web site: www.seattlerep.org.
Sharon Ott, Artistic Director.
Description: Full-length comedies, dramas, and adaptations. No unsolicited submissions.

SINISTER WISDOM

P.O. Box 3252, Berkeley, CA 94703.
Quarterly. Alexis Alexander, Artistic Director.
Description: Publishes one-act (15 pages or less) lesbian drama that reflects diverse and multicultural experiences. Responds in 3-9 months; write for upcoming themes. SASE. Payment: in copies.

SOCIETY HILL PLAYHOUSE

507 S Eighth St., Philadelphia, PA 19147.
Web site: www.societyhillplayhouse.com.
Walter Vail.
Description: Full-length dramas, comedies, and musicals, up to 6 cast members, simple set. Submit synopsis and SASE. Responds in 6 months. Nominal payment.

SOUTH COAST REPERTORY

P.O. Box 2197, Costa Mesa, CA 92628. 714-708-5500.
Web site: www.scr.org.
Jennifer Kiger, Literary .
Description: Full-length comedies, dramas, musicals, juveniles. Query with synopsis and resume. Payment varies.

SOUTHERN APPALACHIAN REPERTORY THEATRE

P.O. Box 1720, Mars Hill, NC 28754. 828-689-1384.
E-mail: sart@mhc.edu. Web site: www.sartheatre.com. Bill Gregg, Artistic Director.
Description: Seeking new full-length plays: comedy, drama, and musicals. Ones that explore and celebrate the culture, history, or life in Southern Appalachian region are especially welcomed. Scripts received all year, but cut-off is October 31 for each year's submissions. Enclose SASE for return of script. Musicals must include the book and tape or CD of 4 songs. New plays are defined as unproduced and unpublished. Workshops are OK. Adaptations of books are not accepted. Southern Appalachian

Playwrights Conference in spring; 4 plays read and discussed; playwrights get room and board. One play may receive full production during the following SART season. First-time authors welcome. Tips: Avoid scripts that read like screenplays, and use of profanity for shock value only. **Contact:** Managing Director.

STAGE LEFT THEATRE

3408 N. Sheffield, Chicago, IL 60657. 773-883-8830.
E-mail: sltchicago@aol.com. Web site: www.stagelefttheatre.com.
Jessi D. Hill, Artistic Director.
Description: Produces and develops plays that raise the level of debate on social and political issues. Full-length comedies, dramas, and adaptations for cast of 1-12. Shows include post-show discussions. New authors welcomed. Offers workshops/ readings. New-play development program, Downstage Left, send for guidelines. **Contact:** Jessi D. Hill.

STAGE ONE: PROFESSIONAL
THEATRE FOR YOUNG AUDIENCES

501 W Main St., Louisville, KY 40202. 502-589-5946.
E-mail: stageone@stageone.org. Web site: www.stageone.org. Moses Goldberg, Artistic Director. **Description:** Seeking new children's plays, adaptations of classics and original plays for young audiences (ages 4-18). No restrictions on cast or set. **Tips:** Seeks plays relevant to young people and their families, related to school curriculum, and classic tales of childhood, ancient and modern.

STAGES REPERTORY THEATRE

3201 Allen Pkwy., #101, Houston, TX 77019. 713-527-0220.
E-mail: stagestheatre.com. Web site: www.stagestheatre.com.
Rob Bundy, Artistic Director.
Description: Southwest Festival of New Plays. Divisions: Children's Theatre, Texas Playwrights, Women Playwrights, and Hispanic Playwrights. Seeking new plays: comedy and drama (full-length). Cast: 6-8 max. Unit set with multiple locations preferable. Tips: Not interested in realistic domestic dramas, prefer theatrically told stories.

STATE THEATER COMPANY

719 Congress Ave., Austin, TX 78701. 512-472-2901.
Scott Kanoff, Artistic Director.
Description: Seeking new full-length plays, comedy and drama. Annual Harvest Festival. Submission period December 1-March 1. **Contact:** Michelle Polger, Associate Artistic Director.

STATE UNIVERSITY OF NEW YORK AT STONY BROOK

Theatre Arts Dept., Stony Brook, NY 11794.
Web site: www.sunysb.edu.
Richard Dunham, Artistic Director.

Description: One-act and full-length comedies and dramas. Submit synopsis with resume and SASE. No unsolicited manuscripts. Offers workshops and readings.

STUDIO ARENA THEATRE

710 Main St., Buffalo, NY 14202-1990.
Description: Comedies and dramas, cast up to 8. Interested in plays of theatrical/nonrealistic nature. Include synopsis, resume, cast list, and sample dialogue. Do not send full script.

MARK TAPER FORUM

135 N Grand Ave., Los Angeles, CA 90012. 213-972-8033.
E-mail: vshaskan@ctgla.org. Web site: www.taperahmanson.com.
Gordon Davidson, Artistic Director.
Description: Seeking new full-length plays. Annual New Work Festival, offering selected playwrights resources to work on their plays. Each play gets at least one open public rehearsal in a small Los Angeles theater. Deadline: March 1. **Contact:** Pier Carlo Talenti, Literary Manager.

THEATER OF THE FIRST AMENDMENT

George Mason University, Center for the Arts MSN 3E6, Fairfax, VA 22030.
Rick Davis, Artistic Director.
Description: Full-length and one-act comedies, drama, and adaptations. Cultural history made dramatic as distinct from history dramatized; large battles joined; hard question asked; word and image stretched. Send synopsis and resume with return postcard.

THEATRE BUILDING CHICAGO

1225 W Belmont Ave., Chicago, IL 60657-3205. 773-929-7367.
E-mail: jsparks@theatrebuildingchicago.org. Web site: www.theatrebuilding.org.
John Sparks, Artistic Director.
Description: New musicals only, all styles, full-length and one-act (10 min.), for children, young adults, opera and Broadway audiences, etc. Writers workshop meets monthly (fee based). No restrictions on cast. No sets or lighting in developmental programming. Sponsors contests. Write, call or e-mail for submission application. Tips: Single author projects discouraged.

THEATREWORKS

1100 Hamilton Ct., Menlo Park, CA 94025. 650-463-1950.
Web site: www.theatreworks.org.
Robert Kelley, Artistic Director.
Description: Full-length comedies, dramas, and musicals. Submit complete script or synopsis with SAS postcard and SASE, cast list, theatre resume, production history. For musicals, include cassette of up to 6 songs, with lyrics. Responds in 4-5 months. Payment negotiable.

THEATREWORKS/USA
151 W 26th St., Fl. 7, New York, NY 10001. 212-647-1100.
E-mail: info@theatreworksusa.org. Web site: www.theatreworksusa.org.
Barbara Pasternack, Artistic Director.
Description: Seeking new one-act (60-90 minute) plays and musicals for children's productions, celebrating history's heroes/heroines, or dramatizing historical event. Adaptations of fairy tales, literary classics, and contemporary children's literature. Literate, creative, entertaining, with something to say to young audience. Cast: 6 actors. Production must be tourable in 2 vans. **Contact:** Michael Alltop, Assistant Artistic Director.

WALNUT STREET THEATRE COMPANY
825 Walnut St., Philadelphia, PA 19107.
Bernard Havard, Producing Artistic Director.
Description: Mainstage: Full-length comedies, dramas, musicals, and popular, upbeat adaptations; also, plays for studio stage, cast of 1-4. Submit 10-20 sample pages with SAS postcard, character breakdown, synopsis. Musical submissions must include audio cassette or CD. Responds in 6 months with SASE. Payment varies. **Contact:** Beverly Elliott, Literary Manager.

THE WESTERN STAGE
156 Homestead Ave., Salinas, CA 93901. 831-755-6980.
Web site: www.westernstage.org.
Jeffrey Heyer, Literary Manager.
Description: Ongoing submissions. Send query. Prefers adaptations of works of literary significance and/or large cast shows.

WILL GEER THEATRICUM BOTANICUM
P.O. Box 1222, Topanga, CA 90290.
E-mail: theatricum@earthlink.net. Web site: www.theatricum.com.
Ellen Geer, Artistic Director.
Description: Seeking new full-length plays: comedy, drama, and musicals for large outdoor rustic stage. All types of scripts for outdoor theater. Playreading performances.

WOOLLY MAMMOTH THEATRE COMPANY
917 M St. NW, Washington, DC 20001.
E-mail: mary@woollymammoth.net.
Mary Resing, Literary Manager.
Description: Looking for edgy, provocative, language- and character-driven work. Accepts solicited scripts only. Payment varies.

GREETING CARD PUBLISHERS

Companies selling greeting cards and novelty items (T-shirts, coffee mugs, buttons, etc.) often have their own specific requirements for the submission of ideas, verse, and artwork. In general, however, each verse or message should be typed double-space on a 3 x 5 or 4 x 6 card. Use only one side of the card, and be sure to put your name and address in the upper left-hand corner. Keep a copy of every verse or idea you send. (It's also advisable to keep a record of what you've submitted to each publisher.) Always enclose an SASE, and do not send out more than ten verses or ideas in a group to any one publisher. Never send original artwork unless a publisher indicates a definite interest in using your work.

AMBERLEY GREETING CARD COMPANY

11510 Goldcoast Dr., Cincinnati, OH 45249-1695. 513-489-2775.
E-mail: dcronstein@amberleygreeting.com. Web site: www.amberleygreeting.com.
Dan Cronstein, Editor.
Description: Humorous ideas for cards: birthday, illness, friendship, anniversary, congratulations, "miss you," etc. Short, humorous verse OK. SASE for guidelines. Pays $150. Rights: All. **Contact:** Chuck Marshall.

BRILLIANT ENTERPRISES

117 W Valerio St., Santa Barbara, CA 93101-2927.
Web site: www.ashleighbrilliant.com.
Ashleigh Brilliant.
Description: Illustrated epigrams emphasizing truth, wit, universality, and originality. Payment is $60. This line of greeting cards is very unusual and should be studied carefully before material is submitted. Send $2 for catalog and samples. Rights: All. Payment: On acceptance.

COMSTOCK CARDS

600 S Rock, Suite 15, Reno, NV 89502-4115.
Web site: www.comstockcards.com.
Description: Adult humor, outrageous or sexual, for greeting cards, invitations, and notepads. SASE. Payment varies, on publication. Guidelines on Web site. **Contact:** Production Department.

CONTENOVA GIFTS

879 Cranberry Ct., Oakville, Ontario L6L 6J7 Canada.
Jeff Sinclair.
Description: Catchy, humorous, and sentimental one-liners for ceramic gift mugs. Submit on 3 x 5 cards; up to 15 ideas at a time. Payment varies, on acceptance. Guidelines.

DAYSPRING GREETING CARDS

P.O. Box 1010, Siloam Springs, AR 72761.

E-mail: info@dayspring.com

Description: Inspirational material for everyday occasions and most holidays. Currently only accepting freelance copy submissions from published greeting card authors. Qualified writers should send samples of their published greeting cards (up to 5 cards or copies; the words "Previously Published" must be written on lower left corner of the mailing envelope containing the submissions). Payment is $50 on acceptance. Send SASE for guidelines, or e-mail and type in the word "write" for guidelines.

DESIGN DESIGN, INC.

P.O. Box 2266, Grand Rapids, MI 49501-2266.

Tom Vituj, Creative Director.

Description: Short verses for both humorous and sentimental concepts for greeting cards. Everyday (birthday, get well, just for fun, etc.) and seasonal (Christmas, Valentine's Day, Easter, Mother's Day, Father's Day, Graduation, Halloween, Thanksgiving) material. Flat fee payment on publication. SASE.

DUCK & COVER

P.O. Box 21640, Oakland, CA 94620.

E-mail: duckcover@aol.com.

Jim Buser, Editor.

Description: Does not produce any greeting cards. However, makes buttons, magnets, and stickers with fresh, original, and outrageous slogans. Send SASE for writer's guidelines.

EPHEMERA, INC.

P.O. Box 490, Phoenix, OR 97535. 541-535-4195.

E-mail: mail@ephemera-inc.com. Web site: www.ephemera-inc.com.

Description: Provocative, irreverent, and outrageously funny slogans for novelty buttons, magnets, and stickers. Submit a typed list of slogans. SASE. Pays $40 per slogan. Pays on acceptance. Looking for satirical slogans about pop culture, free speech, work attitudes, women's and men's issues, coffee, booze, pot, drugs, food, aging boomers, teens, gays and lesbians. Surprise us!

FRAVESSI GREETINGS, INC.

215 Moody Rd., Eufield, CT 06083. 860-814-4420.

Description: Short verse, mostly humorous or sentimental; cards with witty prose. Christmas and everyday material. Pays varying rates, on acceptance.

FREEDOM GREETING CARDS

Plesh Creative Group, Inc., 75 West St., Walpole, MA 02081. 508-668-1224.

Web site: www.freedomgreetings.com.

Suzanne Comeau, Editorial Department.

Description: Traditional and humorous messages for everyday occasions and all major seasons. Pays negotiable rates, on acceptance. Query with SASE.

KATE HARPER DESIGNS

P.O. Box 2112, Berkeley, CA 94702.

E-mail: kateharp@aol.com.

Description: Contact via e-mail only. Pays $25 and gives name credit on front of card. Currently seeking quotes for new line, "Cardz with an attitude," edgy humor, and other themes such as birthday, Christmas, love, and thank you. Also looking for quotations with humor and wit about everyday life. Buys 100% freelance work.

OATMEAL STUDIOS GREETING CARD COMPANY

Box 138 TW, Rochester, VT 05767. 802-767-3171.

Web site: www.awoc.com/guidelines.

Dawn Abraham, Editor.

Description: Humorous ideas for all occasions. We pay $75 for each idea we purchase. Your ideas must be original! We look forward to seeing your work!

PARAMOUNT CARDS, INC.

P.O. Box 6546, Providence, RI 02940-6546.

Description: Light humor, traditional, and inspirational sentiments for everyday occasions, Christmas, Valentine's Day, Easter, Mother's Day, Father's Day, Graduation, and Thanksgiving. Submit each idea (5-10 per submission) on a 3 x 5 card with name and address on each. Include SASE. Payment varies on acceptance.

Contact: Editorial Freelance Coordinator.

RECYCLED PAPER GREETINGS, INC.

3636 N Broadway, Chicago, IL 60613-4488.

Gretchen Hoffman, John LeMoine.

Description: Seeks original copy that is hip, flip, and concise. Risqué material considered. Send up to 10 pieces; mock-up ideas complete with artwork required. Will not consider ideas without appropriate artwork included with submission. Allow 12 weeks for response. Payment made if design tests well and is picked up for distribution. SASE for guidelines.

REGENCY THERMOGRAPHERS

Taylor Corporation

64 N Conahan Dr., P.O. Box 2009, Hazelton, PA 18201.

Web site: www.regencythermo.com

Description: Quotations for wedding invitations; clever invitation verses for birthday parties and other special occasions. Does not accept freelance materials.

ROCKSHOTS, INC.

20 S Vandam St., Fl. 4, New York, NY 10013. 212-243-9661.

Web site: www.rockshots.com.

Bob Vesce, Editor.

Description: Humorous, soft line of greeting cards. Combination of sexy and humorous come-on type greeting and "cute" insult cards. Card gag can adopt a sentimental style, then take an ironic twist and end on an offbeat note. No sentimental or conventional material. Put gag lines on 8 x 11 paper with name, address, phone, and social security numbers in right corner, or individually on 3 x 5 cards. Submit 10 ideas/batch. Pays $50/gag line. **Tips:** Send SASE for writer's guidelines. Response: SASE required. Rights: Greeting Card. Payment: On acceptance.

SANGAMON COMPANY

Route 48 W, P.O. Box 410, Taylorville, IL 62568.

Description: SASE for guidelines to experienced free lancers only. Work on assignment. Pays competitive rates, on acceptance.

MARCEL SCHURMAN COMPANY

101 New Montgomery, Fl. 6, San Francisco, CA 94105. 415-284-0133.
Deanne Quinones.

Description: Seeking sincere, positive, and clever text ideas for traditional and humorous greeting cards. Seeking text that goes beyond the standard generic verse. Poetry and off-color humor are not appropriate for this line. Flat fee per text purchase. Send SASE for submission guidelines.

SPS STUDIOS, INC.
PUBLISHERS OF BLUE MOUNTAIN ARTS

P.O. Box 1007, Boulder, CO 80306. 303-449-0536.
E-mail: editorial@spsstudios.com.
Patti Wayant, Editorial Manager.

Description: Poem and writings about real emotions and feelings that one person would want to share with or express to another person. Also material for special occasions and holidays: birthdays, get well, Christmas, Valentine's Day, Easter, etc. Submit seasonal material 5 months in advance of holiday. No artwork. Include SASE. Pays $200 per poem for each of first two works chosen for publication on a card (payment scale escalates after that). **Tips:** "Definitely get a feel for what we publish by trying to find our cards and books in stores, but don't study them too closely, as we're looking for fresh, new ideas—not rewrites of existing cards." Rights: All rights (for work that is published on a card); one-time (for work that is published in a book). Payment: On publication. **Contact:** Editorial Dept.

VAGABOND CREATIONS, INC.

2560 Lance Dr., Dayton, OH 45409. 937-298-1124.
E-mail: vagabond@siscom.net. Web site: www.vagabondcreations.com.
George F. Stanley, Jr..

Description: Greeting cards with graphics only on cover (no copy) and short punch line inside: birthday, everyday, Valentine's Day, Christmas, and graduation. Mildly risqué humor with double entendre acceptable. Ideas for illustrated theme stationery. Pays $20, on acceptance. **Tips:** Check publishers who are looking for freelance contributors. Do not send style of material that publisher cannot use. Response: SASE required. Rights: All. Payment: On acceptance.

CAROL WILSON FINE ARTS, INC.

P.O. Box 17394, Portland, OR 97217.

Gary Spector.

Description: Publishes copy for greeting cards for all occasions. Tone can be serious, upbeat, supportive, or whimsical. Primary customers are female. Prefers short material.

ORGANIZATIONS

AMERICAN SOCIETY OF JOURNALISTS AND AUTHORS, INC.
1501 Broadway, Suite 302, New York, NY 10036. 212-997-0947.
E-mail: execdir@asja.org. Web site: www.asja.org.
Brett Harvey, Executive Director.
Description: A national organization of independent writers of nonfiction, promoting high standards of writing. ASJA offers extensive benefits: referral services, many discount services, and ways to explore professional issues and concerns with other writers; also produces a free electronic bulletin board for freelancers on contract issues in the new-media age. Members receive a monthly newsletter with confidential market information. Membership open to professional freelance writers of nonfiction; qualifications judged by the membership committee. Call or write for application details.

ARIZONA BOOK PUBLISHING ASSOCIATION
975 E Guadalupe Rd., Suite 20, Tempe, AZ 85283. 602-274-6264.
Web site: www.azbookpub.com.
Description: Serves the needs of Arizona book publishers and promotes the publishing industry in this state. Offers a newsletter and awards.

ASSITEJ/USA-INTERNATIONAL ASSOCIATION OF THEATRE FOR CHILDREN AND YOUNG PEOPLE
724 Second Ave. S, Nashville, TN 37210. 615-254-5719.
E-mail: usassitej@aol.com.
Description: Promotes development of professional theater for young audiences and international exchange. Provides a link between professional theaters, artists, directors, training institutions, and arts agencies; sponsors festivals and forums for interchange among theaters and theater artists. Annual dues: $65 (individual), $35, (retiree), $30 (student).

ASSOCIATED WRITING PROGRAMS
George Mason University, Mail Stop 1E3, Fairfax, VA 22030. 703-993-4301.
Web site: www.awpwriter.org.
Description: Nonprofit organization of teachers, writers, writing programs, and lovers of literature. Awards: for poetry, short fiction, and creative nonfiction; Thomas Dunne Books Award for novels; Prague Summer Seminars Fellowship Competition. Annual conferences. See Web site for contest guidelines. Annual dues: $59 ($37 for students), $20 for subscription to *AWP Chronicle* only.

ASSOCIATION OF AMERICAN PUBLISHERS INC.
71 Fifth Ave., New York, NY 10003-3004. 212-255-0200.
E-mail: sbrandwein@publishers.org. Web site: www.publishers.org.
Patricia Schroeder, President.

Description: National trade organization for the U.S. publishing industry. **Contact:** Sara Brandwein, Deputy Director, PSP Division.

THE AUTHORS GUILD, INC.

31 E 28th St., Fl. 10, New York, NY 10016. 212-563-5904.
E-mail: staff@authorsguild.org. Web site: www.authorsguild.org.
Paul Aiken, Executive Director.
Description: The largest organization of published writers in America. Membership offers free reviews of publishing and agency contracts, access to group health insurance, and seminars on subjects of concern. Authors Guild also lobbies on behalf of authors on issues such as copyright, taxation, freedom of expression. A writer who has published a book in the last 7 years with an established publisher, or has published 3 articles in general-circulation periodicals in the prior 18 months is eligible for active membership. An unpublished writer with a contract offer may be eligible for associate membership. First-year annual dues: $90.

THE AUTHORS LEAGUE OF AMERICA

31 E 28th St., Fl. 10, New York, NY 10016. 212-564-8350.
Description: A national organization representing 14,000 authors and dramatists on matters of joint concern, such as copyright, taxes, freedom of expression. Membership is restricted to authors and dramatists who are members of the Authors Guild and the Dramatists Guild.

CATHOLIC BOOK PUBLISHERS ASSOCIATION

8404 Jamesport Dr., Rockford, IL 61108. 815-332-3245.
Web site: www.cbpa.org.
Description: Organization for Catholic book publishers in the U.S. and abroad. Offers newsletter, member directory, and professional resources.

DRAMATISTS GUILD OF AMERICA.

1501 Broadway, Suite 701, New York, NY 10036-3909. 212-398-9366 Ext. 11.
E-mail: membership@dramatistsguild.com. Web site: www.dramatistsguild.com.
Christopher Wilson, Executive Director.
Description: National, professional association of playwrights, composers, and lyricists who work to protect author rights and to improve working conditions. Services include use of guild contracts, a toll-free number for members in need of business advice, discount tickets, access to health insurance programs and group term-life insurance plan, many seminars. Frederick Loewe room is available to members for readings and rehearsals at a nominal fee. Publishes *Dramatists Guild Resource Directory* and *The Dramatist Magazine*. All playwrights, produced or not, are eligible for membership. Annual dues: $125 (active), $75 (associate), $35 (student). **Contact:** Tom Epstein, Director of Membership Services.

INTERNATIONAL ASSOCIATION OF CRIME WRITERS/NORTH AMERICAN BRANCH

P.O. Box 8674, New York, NY 10116-8674. 212-243-8966.

E-mail: mfrisque@igc.org.

Mary A. Frisque, Executive Director.

Description: Promotes communications among crime writers worldwide, encourages translation of crime writing into other languages, and defends authors against censorship. The North American branch of IACW also sponsors conferences, publishes quarterly newsletter, *Border Patrol,* and awards annual Hammett prize for literary excellence in crime writing (fiction or nonfiction) by U.S. or Canadian author. Membership open to published authors of crime fiction, nonfiction, and screenplays. Agents, editors, critics, and booksellers are also eligible to apply. Annual dues: $50.

Contact: William Heffernan, President.

INTERNATIONAL WOMEN'S WRITING GUILD

Box 810, Gracie Station, New York, NY 10028-0082. 212-737-7536.

E-mail: iwwg@iwwg-com. Web site: www.iwwg.com.

Hannelore Hahn, Executive Director.

Description: A network for personal and professional empowerment of women through writing. Services include 6 issues of a 32-page newsletter, a list of literary agents, independent small presses, and publishing services, access to group health insurance plan, writing conferences, referral services, and events, including an annual summer conference at Skidmore College in Saratoga Springs, N.Y., regional writing clusters, and year-round supportive networking. Any woman may join regardless of portfolio. Annual dues: $45.

MYSTERY WRITERS OF AMERICA

17 E 47th St., Fl. 6, New York, NY 10017. 212-888-8171.

Mary Beth Becker, Executive Director.

Description: Works to raise the prestige of mystery and detective writing, to encourage the reading of mysteries, and to defend the rights and increase the income of all writers in mystery, detection, and fact-crime writing. Each year, presents the Edgar Allan Poe Awards for the best mystery writing in a variety of fields. Membership classes: "active" (open to any writer who has made a sale in mystery, suspense, or crime writing), "associate" (professionals in allied fields), "corresponding" (writers living outside the U.S.), and "affiliate" (general members). Annual dues: $80 ($60 for "corresponding").

NATIONAL ASSOCIATION OF SCIENCE WRITERS

P.O. Box 294, Greenlawn, NY 11740. 516-757-5664.

E-mail: diane@nasw.org. Web site: www.nasw.org.

Ms. Diane McGurgan, Executive Director.

Description: Promotes and helps to improve the flow of accurate information about science through all media. Anyone actively engaged in the dissemination of science information is eligible to apply. Members must be principally involved in reporting on science through newspapers, magazines, TV, or other media that reach the public directly. Annual dues: $60, students $15.

NATIONAL CONFERENCE OF EDITORIAL WRITERS

6223 Executive Blvd., Rockville, MD 20852.

E-mail: ncewhqs@erols.com. Web site: www.ncew.org.

Description: A nonprofit organization, NCEW works to improve the quality of editorial pages and broadcast editorials, and to promote high standards among opinion writers and editors. Offers networking opportunities, regional meetings, page exchanges, foreign tours, educational opportunities and seminars, annual convention, and a subscription to quarterly journal, *The Masthead.* Membership is open to opinion writers and editors for general-circulation newspapers, radio or television stations, and syndicated columnists; teachers and students of journalism; and others who determine editorial policy. Annual dues (based on circulation or broadcast audience), $90-$200 (journalism educators: $100; students: $50).

THE NATIONAL LEAGUE OF AMERICAN PEN WOMEN

PEN Arts Building, 1300 17th St. N.W., Washington, DC 20036-1973. 202-785-1997.

E-mail: NLAPW1@juno.com.

Web site: http://members.aol.com/penwomen/pen.htm.

Wanda A. Rider, PhD., National President.

Description: Promotes development of creative talents of professional women in the arts. Membership is through local branches, in categories of Art, Letters, and Music.

NATIONAL WRITERS ASSOCIATION

3140 S Peoria, #295, Aurora, CO 80014. 303-841-0246.

E-mail: sandywrter@aol.com. Web site: www.nationalwriters.com.

Sandy Whelchel, Executive Director.

Description: Full-service organization assisting writers, from formatting a manuscript to assistance finding agents and publishers. Awards cash prizes in 5 contests each year. Published book contest, David R. Raffelock Award for Publishing Excellence. Referral services, conferences, and financial assistance also offered. Annual dues: $65 Individual, $35 Student, $85 Professional.

NATIONAL WRITERS UNION

113 University Place, 6th Fl., New York, NY 10003. 212-254-0279.

E-mail: nwu@nwu.org. Web site: www.nwu.org.

Jonathan Tasini, President.

Description: Works for equitable payment and fair treatment for freelance writers through collective action. Membership over 6,000, includes authors, poets, cartoonists, journalists, and technical writers in 17 chapters nationwide. Offers contract and agent information, group health insurance, press credentials, grievance handling, a quarterly magazine, and sample contracts and resource materials. Sponsors workshops and seminars. Membership open to writers who have published a book, play, 3 articles, 5 poems, a short story, or an equivalent amount of newsletter, publicity, technical, commercial, government, or institutional copy, or have written unpublished material and are actively seeking publication. Annual dues: $95-$260.

NEW DRAMATISTS
424 W 44th St., New York, NY 10036.
Web site: www.newdramatists.org.
Todd London, Artistic Director.
Description: Helps gifted playwrights secure the time, space, and tools to develop their craft. Services include readings and workshops, a director-in-residence program, national script distribution for members, artist work spaces, international playwright exchange programs, script copying facilities, and a free ticket program. Membership open to residents of New York City and surrounding tri-state area. National memberships for those outside the area who spend time in NYC. Apply between July 15 and September 15. No annual dues.

NORTHWEST PLAYWRIGHTS GUILD
318 SW Palatine Hill Rd., Portland, OR 97219. 503-452-4778.
E-mail: bjscript@teleport.com. Web site: www.nwpg.org.
Barbara Callander, Director.
Description: Chapters in Portland (Oregon) and Seattle (Washington). Encourages the creation and production of new plays. Support through play development, staged readings, and networking for play competitions and production opportunities. Oregon chapter offers Page to Stage and Living Room Theater to help playwrights develop new work. Monthly and quarterly newsletters. Annual dues: $25. **Contact:** Bill Johnson, Office Manager.

OUTDOOR WRITERS ASSOCIATION OF AMERICA
121 Hickory St., Suite 1, Missoula, MT 59801. 406-728-7434.
E-mail: owaa@montana.com. Web site: www.owaa.org.
Steve Wagner, Meeting Director.
Description: A non-profit organization of outdoor communicators. Awards: Ham Brown Award, Jade of Chiefs, Excellence in Craft, Mountain of Jade Award, Jackie Pfeiffer Memorial Award. Also, referral services and conferences. Dues: $100 individual, $40 student, $300 supporting.

PEN AMERICAN CENTER
568 Broadway, New York, NY 10012. 212-334-1660.
E-mail: pen@pen.org. Web site: www.pen.org.
Michael Roberts, Executive Director.
Description: One of over 130 centers worldwide of International PEN. Members are poets, playwrights, essayists, editors, and novelists, also literary translators and agents who have made a substantial contribution to the literary community. Main office in New York City; branches in Boston, Chicago, New Orleans, Portland, Oregon, and San Francisco. Programs and services include literary events and awards,

outreach projects, assistance to writers in financial need, and international and domestic human-rights campaigns on behalf of literary figures imprisoned because of their writing. Membership open to writers who have published 2 books of literary merit, also editors, agents, playwrights, and translators who meet specific standards; apply to membership committee. Annual dues, $75. **Contact:** John Morrone.

THE PLAYWRIGHTS' CENTER
2301 Franklin Ave. E., Minneapolis, MN 55406. 612-332-7481.
E-mail: info@pwcenter.org. Web site: www.pwcenter.org.
Carlo Cuesta, Executive Director.
Description: Provides services to support playwrights and playwriting, nurtures artistic excellence and new visions, fosters initiative and leadership, practices cultural pluralism, discovers emerging artists, and connects playwrights with audiences. Annual awards: McKnight Residency and Commission, McKnight Advancement Grant, Jerome fellowships, Many Voices residencies, Many Voices Cultural Collaboration Grants. Members may apply for all programs and participate in special activities, including classes, outreach programs, and PlayLabs. Annual dues: $75 local individual, $30 student/senior, $40 low-income member, $40 member over 100 miles. **Contact:** Kristen Gandrow, Playwright Services Director.

POETRY SOCIETY OF AMERICA
15 Gramercy Park, New York, NY 10003. 212-254-9628.
Web site: www.poetrysociety.org.
Alice Quinn, Executive Director.
Description: Seeks to raise awareness of poetry, to deepen understanding of it, and to encourage more people to read, listen to, and write poetry. Presents more than 40 readings and events across the country each year, and places posters on buses and subways through "Poetry in Motion." Also offers annual contests for poetry, seminars, conferences, poetry festivals, and publishes a journal. Annual dues: from $40 ($25 for students). **Contact:** Brett Lauer.

POETS AND WRITERS
72 Spring St., New York, NY 10012. 212-226-3586.
Web site: www.pw.org. Elliot Figman, Executive Director.
Description: Fosters the professional development of poets and fiction writers and promotes communication throughout the literary community. A non-membership organization, it offers a magazine for poets and writers with information on markets for writers, and a directory of American poets and fiction writers, also support for readings and workshops at varied venues.

PUBLICATION RIGHTS CLEARINGHOUSE
National Writers Union
113 University Pl., Fl. 6, New York, NY 10003. 212-254-0279.
Web site: www.nwu.org.
Description: The collective-licensing agency of the National Writers Union created

in 1996 to help writers license and collect royalties for the reuse of their published works in electronic databases and other media. It is modeled after similar organizations in the music industry. Writers license non-exclusive secondary rights to the PRC; the PRC licenses those rights to secondary users and distributes payment to writers. Enrollment open to NWU members and to non-members.

ROMANCE WRITERS OF AMERICA
3707 FM 1960 West, Suite 555, Houston, TX 77068. 281-440-6885.
E-mail: info@rwanational.com. Web site: www.rwanational.org.
Allison Kelley, Executive Director.
Description: A nonprofit organization for published or unpublished writers interested in the field of romantic fiction. Offers conferences, and awards: RITA (for published romance novels), Golden Heart (for unpublished manuscripts). Annual dues, $75.

SCIENCE FICTION AND FANTASY WRITERS OF AMERICA
P.O. Box 877, Chestertown, MD 21620.
E-mail: execdir@sfwa.org. Web site: www.sfwa.org/org/sfwa_info.htm.
Jane Jewell, Executive Director.
Description: Promotes the professional interests of science fiction and fantasy writers. Presents annual Nebula Award for excellence in the field; publishes the *Bulletin* and *SFWA Handbook* for members (also available to non-members). Any writer who has sold a work of science fiction or fantasy is eligible. Annual dues: $50 (active), $35 ("affiliate"), plus $10 installation fee; send for application.

SISTERS IN CRIME
P.O. Box 442124, Lawrence, KS 66044-8933.
E-mail: sistersincrime@juno.com. Web site: www.sistersincrime.org.
Eve K. Sandstrom, President.
Description: Fights discrimination against women in the mystery field, educates publishers and the public about inequalities in the treatment of female authors, and increases awareness of their contribution to the field. Membership open to all: writers, readers, editors, agents, booksellers, librarians. Publishes a quarterly newsletter and Books in Print membership directory. Annual dues: $35 (U.S.), $40 (foreign).

SOCIETY OF AMERICAN TRAVEL WRITERS
1500 Sunday Dr., Suite 102, Raleigh NC 2760. 919-787-5181.
E-mail: nshore@satw.org. Web site: www.satw.org.
Cathy Kerr, Executive Director.
Description: Represents writers and other professionals who strive to provide travelers with accurate reports on destinations, facilities, and services. Active membership limited to travel writers and freelancers with a steady volume of published or distributed work about travel. Application fees: $250 (active), $500 (associate). Annual dues: $130 (active), $250 (associate).

SOCIETY OF CHILDREN'S BOOK WRITERS & ILLUSTRATORS
8271 Beverly Blvd., Los Angeles, CA 90048. 323-782-1010.
E-mail: scbwi@scbwi.org. Web site: www.scbwi.org.
Lin Oliver, Executive Director.
Description: A national organization of authors, editors, publishers, illustrators, librarians, and educators; for beginners and established professionals alike. Offers varied services: referrals, conferences, grants program. Full memberships open to anyone who has had at least 1 children's book or story published. Associate memberships open to all interested in children's literature. Annual dues: $50. Annual awards: Golden Kite Book Award, Magazine Merit Award.

SOCIETY OF ENVIRONMENTAL JOURNALISTS
P.O. Box 2492, Jenkintown, PA 19027. 215-884-8174.
E-mail: sej@sej.org. Web site: www.sej.org.
Beth Parke, Executive Director.
Description: Dedicated to improving the quality, accuracy, and visibility of environmental reporting. Serves 1,200 members and the journalism community with quarterly newsletter, annual and regional conferences, EJToday news digest service, TipSheet, comprehensive Web site, awards, mentor programs, and membership directory. Annual dues: $40, $30 (student).

SOCIETY OF PROFESSIONAL JOURNALISTS
3909 N Meridian St., Indianapolis, IN 46208. 317-927-8000.
E-mail: spj@spj.org. Web site: www.spj.org.
Terrence Harper, Executive Director.
Description: Serves the interests of print, broadcast, and wire journalists (9,000 members and 300 chapters). Services: Journalists' legal defense fund, freedom of information resources, professional development seminars, and awards. Members receive *Quill*, a monthly magazine on current issues in the field. Also promotes ethical reporting. Annual dues: $70 (professional), $35 (student).

THEATRE COMMUNICATIONS GROUP
355 Lexington Ave., New York, NY 10017. 212-697-5230.
Web site: www.tcg.org. Terence Nemeth, Vice President.
Description: National organization offers a wide array of services to strengthen, nurture, and promote the not-for-profit American theatre (artistic and management programs, advocacy activities, International programs and publications). Seeks to increase organizational efficiency of member theatres, encourages artistic talent and achievement, and promotes greater public appreciation for the theatre field. Individual members receive *American Theatre* magazine. Annual dues: $35 (individual).

WESTERN WRITERS OF AMERICA
1012 Fair St., Franklin, TN 37064. 615-791-1444.
E-mail: Tncrutch@aol.com. Web site: www.westernwriters.org.
James A. Crutchfield, Secretary/Treasurer/Managing Editor.

Description: Open to professional writers of fiction and nonfiction on the history and literature of the American West. Promotes distribution, readership, and appreciation of the West and its literature. Annual convention last week of June. Sponsors annual Spur Awards, Owen Wister Award, and Medicine Pipe Bearer's Award for published work and produced screenplays. Annual dues: $75.

WRITERS GUILD OF AMERICA, EAST

555 W 57th St., Suite 1230, New York, NY 10019-2967. 212-767-7806.
Web site: www.wgaeast.org.
Mona Mangan, Executive Director.
Description: See Writers Guild of America, West.

WRITERS GUILD OF AMERICA, WEST

7000 W Third St., Los Angeles, CA 90048. 323-951-4000.
Web site: www.wga.org.
Victoria Riskin, President.
Description: Writers Guild of America represents writers in motion pictures, broadcast, cable, and new media industries, including news and entertainment. To qualify for membership, a writer must meet requirements for employment or sale of material. Basic dues: $25/quarter plus 1.5% of earnings. Also, quarterly dues based on percentage of the member's earnings in any of the fields over which the guild has jurisdiction. Initiation fee: $1,500 for WGAE (writers living east of the Mississippi), $2,500 for WGAW (for those west of the Mississippi). **Tips:** Also publishes *Written By,* an official publication for screen and television writers.

WRITERS INFORMATION NETWORK

The Professional Association for Christian Writers
P.O. Box 11337, Bainbridge Island, WA 98110. 206-842-9103.
E-mail: writersinfonetwork@juno.com. Web site: www.bluejaypub.com/win.
Elaine Wright Colvin, Founder/Director.
Description: Provides a link between Christian writers and the religious publishing industry. Publishes the *WIN-Informer,* a magazine of industry news and trends, market reports, professional advice on marketing, ethics, contracts, editor relations, writing problems and concerns, author/speaker referral services, etc. Annual dues: $35.

PRIZES & AWARDS

Writers seeking the thrill of competition should review this list of literary prize offers, many designed to promote the as-yet-unpublished author. Most of the competitions listed here are for unpublished manuscripts and usually offer publication in addition to a cash prize. The prestige that comes with winning one of the more established awards can do much to further a writer's career, as editors, publishers, and agents are likely to consider the future work of the prize winner more closely.

There are hundreds of literary contests open to writers in all genres, and the following list covers a representative number of them. The summaries given below are intended merely as guides; since submission requirements are more detailed than space allows, writers should send an SASE for complete guidelines before entering any contest. Writers are also advised to check the monthly "Prize Offerings" column of *The Writer* magazine (Kalmbach Publishing Co., 21027 Crossroads Circle, P.O. Box 1612, Waukesha, WI 53187-1612) for additional contest listings and up-to-date contest requirements. Deadlines are annual unless otherwise noted.

ACADEMY OF AMERICAN POETS
Walt Whitman Award
588 Broadway, Suite 1203, New York, NY 10012-3250. 212-274-0343.
E-mail: academy@poets.org. Web site: www.poets.org.
Description: Award of $5,000 plus publication, and a 1-month residency at Vermont Studio Center, for a book-length poetry manuscript by a poet who has not yet published a volume of poetry. Deadline: November 15. $20 entry fee.

AKRON POETRY PRIZE
University of Akron Press
374 B Bierce Library, Akron, OH 44325-1703. 877-UAPRESS.
E-mail: uapress@uakron.edu. Web site: www.akron.edu/uapress/poetry.html.
Description: Unbound manuscripts, 60-100 pages. Include list of previously published poems. Entries must be postmarked between May 15-June 30. SASE. Entry fee: $25. Prize: $1,000 and publication.

AMERICAN ACADEMY OF ARTS AND LETTERS
Richard Awards, 633 W 155th St., New York, NY 10032.
Description: Offers subsidized productions or staged readings in New York City by a nonprofit theater for a musical, play with music, thematic review, or any comparable work. Deadline: November 1.

AMERICAN ANTIQUARIAN SOCIETY
Fellowships for Historical Research, 185 Salisbury St., Worcester, MA 01609.
James David Moran, Director of Outreach.
Description: At least 3 fellowships, for creative and performing artists, writers, filmmakers, and journalists, for research on pre-20th century American history.

Residencies 4-8 weeks; travel expenses and stipends of $1,200 per month. Write for guidelines. Deadline: October.

AMERICAN MARKETS NEWSLETTER COMPETITION

American Markets Newsletters 1974 46th Ave., San Francisco, CA 94116.
Description: Fiction and nonfiction to 2,000 words, both published and unpublished. All entries will be considered for worldwide syndication whether they win or not. Deadlines: July 31 and December 31. Entry fee: AMN subscribers, $6 for 1 entry, $9 for 2 entries, $12 for 3 entries; non-subscribers, $7.50/entry. Prizes: $250, $50, $30.

ANHINGA PRIZE FOR POETRY

Anhinga Press, P.O. Box 10595, Tallahassee, FL 32302-0595. 850-521-9920.
E-mail: info@anhinga.org. Web site: www.anhinga.org.
Description: A $2,000 prize for an unpublished full-length collection of poetry, 48-72 pages, by a poet who has published no more than one full-length collection. Deadline: May 1. Entry fee: $20.

ASF TRANSLATION PRIZE

American-Scandinavian Foundation
58 Park Ave., New York, NY 10016. 212-879-9779.
E-mail: ahenkin@amscan.org. Web site: www.amscan.org.
Andrey Henkin.
Description: Translations of literary prose (50+ pages) or poetry (25+ pages) originally written in Danish, Finnish, Icelandic, Norwegian, or Swedish. Send SASE or e-mail for guidelines. Deadline: June 1. Prizes: $2,000, $500 plus publication of excerpt and medallion. **Contact:** Andrey Henkin. No entry fee.

ASSOCIATION OF JEWISH LIBRARIES

315 Maitland Ave., Teaneck, NJ 07666. 201-862-0312.
E-mail: rkglasser@aol.com. Web site: www.jewishlibraries.org.
Rachel Glasser, Coordinator.
Description: Sydney Taylor Manuscript Competition. Stories must have a positive Jewish focus, universal appeal, and be for readers aged 8-11. Required length—64-200 pages, double-spaced. Writer must have no previously published fiction works. Deadline: December 1. Prize: $1,000. No entry fee.

AWP AWARD SERIES

Associated Writing Programs, George Mason University
Mail Stop 1E3, Fairfax, VA 22030. 703-993-4301.
E-mail: awp@gmu.edu. Web site: www.awpwriter.org.
Description: Open to all authors writing in English. Only book-length manuscripts are eligible: for poetry, 48 pages minimum text; short story collections and creative nonfiction, 150-300 manuscript pages; novels at least 60,000 words. Send a business-size SASE for guidelines. $10,000 advance against earnings for novel; $2,000 hono-

rarium for poetry, short fiction, and nonfiction. Deadline: submissions must be post-marked between January 1 and February 28. $20 entry fee ($10 if AWP member).

THE BELLINGHAM REVIEW

Western Washington University, MS-9053, Bellingham, WA 98225.
Web site: www.wwu.edu/~bhreview.
Description: Tobias Wolff Award in Fiction: prizes of $500 plus publication, $250, $100, for short story or novel excerpt. Deadline: March 15. Annie Dillard Award in Nonfiction: prizes of $500 plus publication, $250, $100, for previously unpublished essays. Deadline: March 15. 49th Parallel Poetry Award: publication and prizes of $500, $250, $100. Deadline: March 15. Entry fees.

BEVERLY HILLS THEATRE GUILD

Julie Harris Playwright Award
2815 N Beachwood Dr., Los Angeles, CA 90068-1923. 323-465-2703.
Marcella Meharg, Director.
Description: Offers prize of $5,000, $2,000, and $1,000 for an unpublished full-length play. Deadline: November 1.

BIRMINGHAM-SOUTHERN COLLEGE

Hackney Literary Awards
P.O. Box 549003, Birmingham, AL 35282-9765. 205-226-4921.
E-mail: dcwilson@bsc.edu.
Web site: www.bsc.edu/eventsoncampus/specialevents/hackneyliteraryawards.
Annie Green, Director.
Description: Awards, open to writers nationwide, presented as part of Birmingham-Southern College "Writing Today" Conference. Awards $5,000 in annual prizes for poetry and short fiction (in national and state categories), plus a $5,000 prize for an unpublished novel. Write or request by e-mail for details (include mailing address for guidelines).

BOISE STATE UNIVERSITY

Rocky Mountain Artists' Book Competition
Hemingway Western Studies Center, Boise, ID 83725.
Description: A prize of $500, and publication, for up to 3 books. Manuscripts (text and/or visual material) and proposals considered for short-run printing of books on public issues concerning the Inter-Mountain West. Deadline: Year-round.

BOSTON REVIEW

Poetry Contest, MIT, E53-407, Cambridge, MA 02139. 617-253-3642.
Web site: http://bostonreview.mit.edu.
Description: Annual poetry contest for original, unpublished poems. Send 5 poems, to 10 pages. Submit 2 copies. Deadline: June 1. Entry fee: $15. Prize: $1,000 and publication.

BOX TURTLE PRESS
Mudfish Poetry Prize, 184 Franklin St., New York, NY10013 . 212-219-9278.
Jill Hoffman, Director. **Description:** Awards $1,000 and publication. Deadline: April 29. Entry fee $15 for 3 poems, $2 for each additional poem.

JOSEPH E. BRODINE/BRODINSKY POETRY CONTEST
Connecticut Poetry Society
P.O. Box 4053, Waterbury, CT 06704-0053. 203-753-7815.
E-mail: wtarzia@nvctc5comment.edu.
Web site: http://hometown.aol.com/ctpoetrysociety.
Description: Original, unpublished poetry up to 40 lines. Send 2 copies of each poem, one with no contact information and the other with complete contact information. Include SASE for notification of results. Deadline: July 31. Entry fee: $2/poem. Maximum five poems per contest. Prize: $150, $100, $50, plus publication in the *Connecticut River Review*. All entries will be considered for publication unless "For Contest Only" is marked on submission. Does not accept simultaneous submissions. **Tips:** Identify each submission as Brodine/Brodinsky Contest.

CASE WESTERN RESERVE UNIVERSITY
Marc A. Klein Playwriting Award, Dept. of Theater Arts
10900 Euclid Ave., Cleveland, OH 44106-7077. 216-368-4868.
E-mail: ksg@po.cwru.edu.
Description: A prize of $1,000, plus production, for an original, previously unproduced full-length play by a student currently enrolled at an American university or college. Deadline: March 15.

CHELSEA AWARDS
P.O. Box 773, Cooper Station, New York, NY 10276-0773.
Description: Awards for Fiction and Poetry. Prizes: $1,000 each, plus publication in Chelsea's literary magazine. Traditional and experimental fiction, previously unpublished, up to 30 typed pages or 7,500 words. Collection of 4-6 poems, not to exceed 500 lines. Focus is on quality and fresh, original use of language. Deadlines: June 15 (fiction), December 15 (poetry). Entry fee: $10, includes discounted subscription. Send SASE for guidelines.

CHICKEN SOUP FOR THE SOUL
P.O. Box 30880, Santa Barbara, CA 93130. 805-563-2945.
Web site: www.chickensoup.com.
Description: Original essays, short stories, and poems up to 1,200 words that are uplifting, inspiring, and present a positive viewpoint. Open to U.S. residents only. Authors whose stories are used will be compensated $300 per piece.

CLEVELAND STATE UNIVERSITY POETRY CENTER PRIZES
2121 Euclid Ave., Cleveland, OH 44115-2214. 216-687-3986.
E-mail: poetrycenter@csuohio.edu.

Web site: www.csuohioedu/poetrycenter.
Description: Award of $1,000 and publication for a previously unpublished book-length volume of poetry in two categories: First Book and Open Competition (for poets who have published a collection of at least 48 pages published with a press run of at least 500). Postmark deadline: February 1. Entry fee: $20.

CNW/FFWA FLORIDA STATE WRITING COMPETITION
Florida Freelance Writers Association
P.O. Box A, North Stratford, NH 03590. 603-922-8338.
Web site: www.writers-editors.com.
Description: Contest open to all writers. Categories include fiction, nonfiction, children's, and poetry. Send SASE for guidelines and entry form, or print out from Web site. Entry fee $5-$20. Deadline March 15. Prizes $50-$100. **Contact:** Dana K. Cassell.

COALITION FOR THE ADVANCEMENT OF JEWISH EDUCATION
David Dornstein Memorial Creative Writing Contest
261 W 35th St., Floor 12A, New York, NY 10001. 212-268-4210.
Description: The annual David Dornstein Memorial Creative Writing Contest for Young Adult Writers offers prizes of $700, $200, and $100, and publication, for the 3 best original, previously unpublished short stories. Submissions must be up to 5,000 words, have a Jewish theme or topic, and be authored by writers aged 18-35. Deadline: December 31. **Contact:** Judi Resnick, Communications Coordinator.

COLORADO STATE UNIVERSITY
Colorado Prize for Poetry
Colorado Review, Dept. of English, Fort Collins, CO 80523.
Web site: www.coloradoreview.com.
Description: A prize of $1,500, plus publication, for a book-length collection of original poems. Deadline: January 13. Entry fee: $25. Entry fee includes one-year subscription to *Colorado Review*. Send SASE for guidelines, or check Web site.

JANE CUNNINGHAM CROLY/
GFWC PRINT JOURNALISM CONTEST
General Foundation of Women's Clubs
1734 N St. NW, Washington, DC 20036. 202-347-3168.
E-mail: skranz@gfwc.org. Web site: www.gfwc.org.
Description: Award offered for excellence in covering issues of concern to women. Submit 3 stories published in 2001 that demonstrate a concern for the rights and advancement of women, an awareness of women's sensitivity and strength, and/or an attempt to counteract sexism. Deadline: March 3. Entry fee: $50. $1,000 Prize.
Contact: Sally Kranz.

DOROTHY DANIELS HONORARY WRITING AWARDS
National League of American Pen Women
P.O. Box 1485, Simi Valley, CA 93062. 805-493-1081.

E-mail: cdoering@adelphia.net.

Description: Original, unpublished poetry to 50 lines, fiction to 2,000 words and nonfiction to 1,500 words. SASE. Deadline: July 31. Entry fee: $5/poem; $5/fiction or nonfiction entry. Prizes: $100 in 3 categories.

MARGUERITE DE ANGELI CONTEST

Delacorte Press/Random House, Inc., 1540 Broadway, New York, NY 10036. Web site: www.randomhouse.com/kids.

Description: Contemporary or historical fiction manuscripts, 80-144 pages for readers ages 7-10. Open to U.S. and Canadian writers who have not previously published a novel for middle-grade readers. SASE for notification is required. SASE for return if requested. Deadline: June 30. No entry fee. Prize: $1,500 cash, $3,500 advance and publication.

DELACORTE PRESS CONTEST

Delacorte Press/Random House, Inc.
1540 Broadway, New York, NY 10036. 212-354-6500.
Web site: www.randomhouse.com/kids.

Description: Prize for First Young Adult Novel. A writer who has not previously published a young adult novel may submit a book-length manuscript with a contemporary setting, for readers ages 12-18. Prize is $1,500, plus $6,000 advance, and hardcover and paperback publication. Deadline: December 31.

DRURY UNIVERSITY

Playwriting Contest, 900 N Benton Ave., Springfield, MO 65802. 417-873-7430.
E-mail: sasher@drury.edu. Sandy Asher, Director.

Description: Prizes of $300 and two $150 honorable mentions, plus possible production (Open Eye Theatre), for original, previously unproduced one-act plays. Deadline: December 1 of even-numbered years.

DUBUQUE FINE ARTS PLAYERS

One-Act Playwriting Contest
1686 Lawndale Dr., Dubuque, IA 52001. 563-582-5502.
E-mail: garms@clarke.edu.
Web site: www.community.iowa.com/ic/oneactplaycontest.
Gary Arms, Contest Coordinator.

Description: Prizes of $600, $300, and $200, plus full production of all winners if possible. Seeking original one-act plays of up to 40 minutes. Deadline: Jan. 31. Entry fee: $10.

DUKE UNIVERSITY PRESS

1317 W Pettigrew St., Durham, NC 27705.
E-mail: alexad@duke.edu. Web site: http://cds.aas.duke.edu/1-t/.
Tom Rankin, Center's Director.

Description: A grant of up to $10,000, for a writer and photographer working together in the formative stages of a documentary project to ultimately result in a publishable work. Collaborative submissions on any subject are welcome. Deadline: January 31. (accepts submissions only during month of January). See Web site for details. **Contact:** Alexa Dilworth, Award Administrator.

EMPORIA STATE UNIVERSITY
Bluestem Award, Emporia State University
English Dept., Emporia, KS 66801-5087. 620-341-5216.
E-mail: bluestem@emporia.edu. Web site: www.emporia.edu/bluestem/.
Philip Heldrich, Director.
Description: Bluestem Award offers a prize of $1,000, plus publication, for a previously unpublished book of poems in English by a U.S. author. Deadline: March 1. Entry fee: $18. **Contact:** Philip Heldrich.

EVENT CREATIVE NONFICTION CONTEST
The Douglas College Review
P.O. Box 2503, New Westminister, BC V3L 5B2. 604-527-5293.
E-mail: event@douglas.bc.ca. Web site: http://event.douglas.bc.ca.
Description: Creative nonfiction up to 5,000 words, typed and double-spaced. Does not accept previously published material. Entry fee: $25 (includes a subscription to Event magazine.) Deadline: April 15. Prizes: Three $500 prizes and publication.

WILLIAM FAULKNER CREATIVE WRITING COMPETITION
Pirate's Alley Faulkner Society
624 Pirate's Alley, New Orleans, LA 70116. 504-586-1609.
E-mail: faulkhouse@aol.com. Web site: www.wordsandmusic.org.
Description: Unpublished works of fiction, nonfiction or poetry. Send SASE or see Web site for guidelines and entry form. Deadline: April 30. Entry fees: $10-$35. Prizes $250- $7,500.

THE FLORIDA REVIEW
University of Central Florida, Dept. of English, Editors' Awards
P.O. Box 6222950, Orlando, FL 32816. 407-823-2038.
Web site: http://pegasus.cc.ucf.edu/~english/floridareview/home.htm.
Description: Unpublished fiction and memoirs to 10,000 words, poetry to 40 lines. SASE. Entry fee: $12. Prizes: Three $1,000 awards.

FOUR WAY BOOKS
Poetry Prizes, P.O. Box 535, Village Station, New York, NY 10014. 212-619-1105.
E-mail: four_way_editors@yahoo.com. Web site: www.fourway.com.
Martha Rhodes, Director.
Description: Offers different prizes annually. Awards cash honorarium and book publication. Deadline: March 31. Entry fee. Check Web site for guidelines between January 1 and March 31. **Contact:** K. Clarke, Contest Coordinator.

JOHN GASSNER MEMORIAL PLAYWRITING AWARD

The New England Theatre Conference, Northeastern University
360 Huntington Ave., Boston, MA 02115.
E-mail: mail@netconline.org. Web site: www.netconline.org.
Description: New, unpublished full-length plays that have not been produced by a professional or Equity company. Open to New England residents and NETC members. SASE. Entry fee: $10. Deadline: April 15. Prizes: $1,000 and $500. Guidelines and applications available on Web site.

GEORGE WASHINGTON UNIVERSITY

Jenny McKean Moore, Writer-in-Washington
Dept. of English, Washington, D.C. 20052.
Description: A salaried teaching position for 2 semesters, for a creative writer (various mediums in alternate years) with "significant publications and a demonstrated commitment to teaching. Need not have conventional academic credentials." Deadline: Nov. 15.

ALLEN GINSBERG POETRY AWARDS

Poetry Center at Passaic County Community College
1 College Blvd., Paterson, NJ 07505. 973-684-6555.
Web site: www.pccc.cc.nj.us/poetry. **Description:** Up to 5 previously unpublished poems, up to 2 pages each. Send 4 copies of each entry. Do not submit poems that imitate Allen Ginsberg's work. SASE. Deadline: April 1. Entry fee: $13. Prizes: $1,000, $200, and $100. **Contact:** Maria Mazziotti Gillan.

GLIMMER TRAIN PRESS

Semiannual Short Story Award for New Writers
710 SW Madison St., #504, Portland, OR 97205. 503-221-0836.
Description: Prizes of $1,200 (plus publication), $500, and $300, for stories of 1,200-7,500 words by writers whose fiction has never appeared in a nationally distributed publication. Deadlines: March 31; September 30. Entry fee. Submit work on-line at www.glimmertrain.com using on-line submission procedures.

GROLIER POETRY PRIZE

6 Plympton St., Cambridge, MA 02138. 617-547-4648.
Web site: www.grolier-poetry.com.
Description: Two $150 honorariums, for poetry manuscripts of up to 10 double-spaced pages, including no more than 5 previously unpublished poems, by writers who have not yet published a book of poems. Deadline: May 1. Entry fee.

VIOLET REED HAAS POETRY CONTEST

Snake Nation Press, 110 W Force St., Valdosta, GA 31601. 229-244-0752.
E-mail: jeana@snakenationpress.org. Web site: www.snakenationpress.org.
Jean Arambula, Editor.

Description: Awards $500 plus publication for poetry mss of 50-75 pages. Entry Fee: $10. Deadline: June 15. Offered annually, independent judge.

MARILYN HALL AWARDS

Beverly Hills Theatre Guild, P.O. Box 39729, Los Angeles, CA 90039-0729.
Dick Dotterer, Competition Coordinator.
Description: Awards $200, $300, and $500 for plays for young and adolescent audiences 45-90 minutes in length. Authors must be U.S. citizen or legal resident and may submit up to 2 English-written scripts that have not been previously submitted or published. Plays must be original or adaptations or translations; no musicals. Plays may have had one non-professional or educational theatre production. Deadline: Postmarked last day of February each year. Submissions only accepted between January 15 and deadline. Authors will be notified the following June. Send SASE for guidelines. Materials will not be returned.

AURAND HARRIS MEMORIAL PLAYWRITING AWARD

The New England Theatre Conference, Northeastern University
360 Huntington Ave., Boston, MA 02115.
E-mail: mail@netconline.org. Web site: www.netconline.org.
Description: New, unpublished full-length plays for young audiences. Open to New England residents and NETC members. SASE. Entry fee: $20. Deadline: May 1. Prizes: $1,000 and $500. Guidelines and applications available on Web site.

JULIE HARRIS PLAYWRIGHT AWARDS

Beverly Hills Theatre Guild, P.O. Box 39729, Los Angeles, CA 90039-0729.
Dick Dotterer, Competition Coordinator.
Description: Annual award for original, full-length play 90 minutes or more. Authors must be U.S. citizen or legal resident and may submit 1 English-written manuscript that has not been previously submitted, published, or produced. Deadline: postmarked by November 1. Scripts only accepted between August 1 and deadline; authors will be notified the following June. Send SASE for guidelines. Materials will not be returned.

HIGHLIGHTS FOR CHILDREN FICTION CONTEST

Highlights for Children, 803 Church St., Honesdale, PA 18431. 570-253-1080.
Description: Annual contest with a different theme each year. Write for more information. Stories for beginning readers to 500 words, for others up to 900 words. No stories that glorify war, crime, or violence. SASE. Three winners receive $1000 each and publication in *Highlights*. Deadline: January 1 to February 28. No entry fee.

IOWA POETRY PRIZE

University of Iowa Press, 100 Kuhl House, Iowa City, IA 52242.
Web site: www.uiowa.edu/~uipress.
Description: Book-length collection of poems, written originally in English, 50-150

manuscript pages. Open to new as well as established poets. Name on title page only. Deadline: April 30 (postmarked during April). Entry fee: $20. Prize: Publication.

JAMES JONES FIRST NOVEL FELLOWSHIP

James Jones Literary Society, P.O. Box 111, Wilkes University, English Dept. Wilkes-Barre, PA 18766. 570-408-4530.

E-mail: english@wilkes.edu. Web site: www.wilkes.edu//humanities/jones.html.

Description: Award honors the spirit of unblinking honesty, determination, and insight into modern culture exemplified by the late James Jones, author of *From Here to Eternity*. Open to all American writers who have not published a novel. Submit 2-page (maximum) outline and first 50 pages. Put your name, address, phone number, and e-mail address on the title page only. Prize: $5,000 first prize and attendance at the society's annual conference to accept the award; $250 honorarium for runner-up. Deadline: March 1. $15 entry fee.

THE LEDGE ANNUAL POETRY AWARDS CONTEST

78-44 80th St., Glendale, NY 11385.

Timothy Monaghan, Editor. **Description:** Awards three monetary prizes ($1,000, $250, and $100) and publication in *The Ledge* for unpublished poetry. Accepts simultaneous submissions. Deadline: April 30. Entry Fee: $10. Include SASE. Winners announced in August. Queries: Not necessary. E-queries: No. Unsolicited mss: Accepts. Response: Queries 2-3 weeks, submissions 3 months, SASE. Freelance Content: 100%. Rights: FNASR. Payment: On publication.

THE LEDGE ANNUAL POETRY CHAPBOOK CONTEST

78-44 80th St., Glendale, NY 11385.

Timothy Monaghan, Editor. **Description:** Awards $1,000 to winner of annual poetry chapbook contest. Authors may submit 16-28 pages of poetry with title page, bio and acknowledgements. Accepts simultaneous submissions. No restrictions on form or content. Deadline: October 31. Entry Fee: $12. Include SASE. Queries: Not necessary. E-queries: No. Unsolicited mss: Accepts. Response: Queries 2-3 weeks, submissions 3 months, SASE. Freelance Content: 100%. Rights: FNASR. Payment: On publication.

NAOMI LONG MADGETT POETRY AWARD

Lotus Press, P.O. Box 21607, Detroit, MI 48221. 313-861-1280.

E-mail: lotuspress@aol.com.

Description: Submit book-length manuscripts, 60-80 pages. By African-American poets only. Submit 3 copies. SASE or e-mail us for guidelines. Prize: $500 plus publication. Deadline: June 1.

BARBARA MANDIGO KELLY PEACE POETRY AWARDS

Nuclear Age Peace Foundation, PMB 121, 1187 Coast Village Rd., Suite 1 Santa Barbara, CA 93108-2794. 805-965-3443.

E-mail: wagingpeace@napf.org. Web site: www.wagingpeace.org.

Description: Original, unpublished poetry. Open to all writers. All poems must be the original work of the poet, unpublished, and in English. Deadline: July 1. Entry fees: $10 for 1-3 poems, none for youth entries. Prizes: $1,000 for adults, $200 for ages 13-18; $200 for under age 12. Honorable mentions in each category. Winners are announced in October by mail and on the Nuclear Age Peace Foundation Web site.

RICHARD J. MARGOLIS AWARD
Blue Mountain Center, 294 Washington St., Suite 610, Boston, MA 02108.
Description: Awarded annually to a promising journalist or essayist whose work combines warmth, humor, wisdom, and a concern with social issues. Apply with up to 30 pages of published or unpublished work. Deadline: July 1. Prize: $5,000 grant and 1-month residency at the Blue Mountain Center in the Adirondacks. Include short bio., description of current and anticipated work, 3 writing samples. See Web site for more details.

MID-LIST PRESS FIRST SERIES AWARDS FOR POETRY AND THE NOVEL
Mid-List Press, 4324 12th Ave. S, Minneapolis, MN 55407-3218. 612-822-3733.
E-mail: guide@midlist.org. Web site: www.midlist.org.
Description: Unpublished poetry collections and novels. Poetry manuscripts must be at least 60 pages; novels must be at least 50,000 words. See Web site for detailed guidelines. SASE. Deadline: February 1. Entry fee: $20. Prize: Publication and advance against royalties. All submissions must follow guidelines exactly and include entry form.

MID-LIST PRESS FIRST SERIES AWARDS FOR SHORT FICTION AND CREATIVE NONFICTION
Mid-List Press, 4324 12th Ave. S, Minneapolis, MN 55407-3218. 612-822-3733.
E-mail: guide@midlist.org. Web site: www.midlist.org.
Description: Unpublished short fiction collections and creative nonfiction. Manuscripts must be at least 50,000 words. See Web site for detailed guidelines. SASE. Deadline: July 1. Entry fee: $20. Prize: Publication and advance against royalty. All submissions must follow guidelines exactly and include entry form.

MISSISSIPPI REVIEW PRIZE
The Center for Writers, University of Southern Mississippi
P.O. Box 5144, Hattiesburg, MS 39406. 601-266-4321.
E-mail: rief@netdoor.com. Web site: www.mississippireview.com.
Description: Prizes: $1,000 in 2 categories—short story and poem. Short stories to 4,000 words. 3 poems to 10 pages total. Place contact information on first page. Entry fee: $15. Deadline: August 31. Winners announced in January. Winners and finalists published in spring.

MISSISSIPPI VALLEY POETRY CONTEST
Midwest Writing Center, P.O. Box 3188, Rock Island, IL 61204. 319-359-1057.
Description: Up to 5 unpublished poems, to 50 lines each. Nine categories. K-12

poets encouraged. Deadline: April 1. Entry fee: $3 (students) and $5 (adults). Total prizes $1,500-$1,700. **Contact:** Max Molleston.

MOONLIGHT & MAGNOLIA FICTION WRITING CONTEST

P.O. Box 180489, Richland, MS 39218-0489. 601-825-7263.
E-mail: Hoover59@aol.com.
Description: Annual competition for writers of science fiction, fantasy, and horror stories. Open to unpublished writers or those who have not published more than two stories in a national, 5,000+ circulation magazine. Submissions must be unpublished and not under contract. Stories up to 10,000 words. SASE. Entry fee: $7.50 per story, $2.50 per each additional story (3 entries per contest maximum). Prizes: $250 first prize, $100 second prize, and $50 third prize. Deadline: December 31.

NATIONAL CHILDREN'S THEATRE FESTIVAL

Actors' Playhouse at the Miracle Theatre
280 Miracle Mile, Coral Gables, FL 33134. 305-444-9293.
E-mail: maulding@actorsplayhouse.org. Web site: www.actorsplayhouse.org.
Barbara S. Stein, Executive Producing Director.
Description: Literary prize offering $500, full production, and author's transportation and lodging to the Festival based upon availability. Deadline: August 1. Entry Fee: $10 reading fee per entry. See Web site for complete rules and guidelines.
Contact: Earl Maulding, Festival Director.

HOWARD NEMEROV SONNET AWARD

The Formalist, 320 Hunter Drive, Evansville, IN 47711.
Description: Original and unpublished sonnets. No translations. Place name, address, and phone number on the back of each entry. SASE. Deadline: June 15. Entry fee: $3/sonnet. Prize: $1,000 and publication. Entries cannot be returned. Send SASE for contest rules.

NEW ENGLAND POETRY CLUB

11 Puritan Rd., Arlington, MA 02476-7710.
Virginia Thayer, Contest Coordinator
Diana Der-Hovanessian. **Description:** Various prizes for original, unpublished poems in English. Submit poems in duplicate, name on one only. Mark with name of contest. $1,000 for Varoujan prize, $250 for Mumford, Houghton prizes. $500 for Sheila Matton prize for book published in last 2 years. Send SASE for details. No fee for students or members paying $25 in dues.

NEW LETTERS LITERARY AWARDS

New Letters, University of Missouri-Kansas, University House
5101 Rockhill Rd., Kansas City, MO 64110. 816-235-1168.
E-mail: ezraa@umkc.edu. Web site: www.umkc.edu/newsletters.
Description: Three categories: fiction (short story), poetry, and creative nonfiction.

SASE or see Web site for guidelines. Deadline: Mid-May. Entry fee: $10. Prizes: $1,000 and publication.

S.C. PLAYWRIGHTS CENTER
S.C. Playwrights Center, 1001 Bay St., Suite 101, Beaufort, SC 29902. 843-524-7773.
Description: Submit 3 copies of a play in play format with a synopsis. Reading time should be 30-90 minutes. No previous productions, musicals, or translations; must be original with a maximum of 8 characters. SASE for details. Selected playwrights will attend the Annual South Carolina Playwrights Conference. $10 reading fee. Deadline: March 31.

SLIPSTREAM ANNUAL POETRY CHAPBOOK COMPETITION
Slipstream Press, P.O. Box 2071, Niagara Falls, NY 14301.
Web site: www.slipstreampress.org.
Description: Awards $1,000 plus 50 copies to winning poetry chapbook manuscript poet. Deadline: December 1. Entry Fee: $10. Send up to 40 pages of poetry with any style, format, or theme. Simultaneous submissions accepted provided the author keeps publisher informed of status. Previously published material is also accepted. All entrants receive a copy of winning chapbook and a one-issue subscription.

SNAKE NATION PRESS AWARD FOR SHORT FICTION
Snake Nation Press, 110 W Force St., Valdosta, GA 31601. 229-244-0752.
E-mail: jeana@snakenationpress.org. Web site: www.snakenationpress.org.
Jean Arambula, Editor.
Description: Awards $1,000 plus publication for a collection of published or unpublished short stories by a new or underpublished writer. Entry fee: $20, independent judge. Deadline: June 15, entries accepted year-round.

SONORA REVIEW ANNUAL CONTEST
University of Arizona, Dept. of English, Tucson, AZ 85721. 520-321-7759.
E-mail: sonora@u.arizona.edu. Web site: www.coh.arizona.edu/sonora.
Description: Awards $250 plus publication in Spring issue of *Sonora Review*. Stories must be original and unpublished. No novel chapters or simultaneous submissions. Send SASE for return of manuscript. Deadline: December 1. Entry fee: $10. **Tips:** See Web site for detailed guidelines. Queries: Not necessary. Unsolicited mss: Accepts.

SOW'S EAR CHAPBOOK COMPETITION
Sow's Ear Poetry Review
19535 Pleasant View Dr., Abingdon, VA 24211-6827. 276-628-2651.
E-mail: richman@preferred.com.
Larry K. Richman, Managing Editor.
Description: Open to adults. Send 22-26 pages of poetry plus a title page and a table of contents, all without name. On a separate sheet list chapbook title, name, address, phone number, e-mail address (if available), and publicity credits if any. No length limit on poems, but no more than one poem per page. Send manuscripts in March or

April. Deadline: May 1. Previously published poems accepted if writer holds the publication rights. Reading fee: $10. Prizes: Publication, $1,000, 25 copies; $200; and $100. Send SASE or e-mail address for notification. **Contact:** James Owens, Editor, owens017@bama.ua.edu.

SOW'S EAR POETRY COMPETITION

Sow's Ear Poetry Review
19535 Pleasant View Dr., Abingdon, VA 24211-6827. 276-628-2651.
E-mail: richman@preferred.com.
Larry K. Richman, Managing Editor.
Description: Open to adults. Author's name should not be on poems, but on a separate sheet with poem titles, address, phone, and e-mail address if available. No length limit on poems. Simultaneous submissions acceptable. (Editors will check with finalists before sending to final judge.) Entering five poems or more entitles writer to a subscription. Poems should be sent in September or October. Deadline: November 1. Reading fee is $2/poem. Include SASE or e-mail address for notification. Entries will not be returned. Poetry: Contemporary poetry in English; any style or length; up to 5 poems. Art: To complement poetry; B&W prints, drawings. **Tips:** Seeking poems that make the strange familiar or the familiar strange, that connect the little story of the text and the big story of the human situation. Queries: Not necessary. E-queries: Yes. Unsolicited mss: Accepts. Response: 1 week for queries, 3-6 months for submissions; SASE required. Freelance Content: 100%. Rights: FNASR. Payment: In copies. **Contact:** James Owens, Editor, owens017@bama.ua.edu.

SPOON RIVER POETRY PRIZE

Dept. of English Publication Unit, Illinois State University, Normal, IL 61790.
Web site: www.litline.org/spoon/spooncontest.html.
Description: Submit 2 copies (one with name and address, the other without) of 3 unpublished poems, up to 10 pages total. SASE. Entry fee: $16. Deadline: April 15. Prize: $1,000.

ANN STANFORD POETRY PRIZE

Professional Writing Program
University of Southern California, WPH 404, Los Angeles, CA 90089. 213-740-3252.
E-mail: mpw@mizar.usc.edu.
Description: Send up to 5 unpublished poems with SASE. Entry fee: $10. Prizes: $1,000, $200, and $100 plus publication of winners. All entrants receive free issue of SCA. Deadline: April 15.

PETER TAYLOR PRIZE FOR THE NOVEL

Knoxville Writer's Guild, P.O. Box 2565, Knoxville, TN 37901.
Web site: www.knoxvillewritersguild.org.
Description: Unpublished novels of 40,000 words or more. SASE. See Web site for details. Entry fee: $20. Deadline: April 30. Prize: $1,000 plus publication by the University of Tennessee Press. **Contact:** Brian Griffin.

EDWARD DAVIN VICKERS POETRY CONTEST

Georgia Poetry Society, 3822 Clubhouse Pl., Gainesville, GA 30501. 770-531-9473.
Description: Original, unpublished poetry. 80 lines maximum. Send 2 copies of each poem with contest name in upper right-hand corner, entry name and address on 1 copy only. Deadline: July 15. Entry fee: $5 for 1 poem, $1 for each additional poem. Prizes: $250, $100, $50.

WASHINGTON PRIZE

The Word Works, P.O. Box 42164, Washington, DC 20015.
E-mail: editor@wordworksdc.com. Web site: www.wordworksdc.com.
Description: Original poetry by a living American writer. Send 48-64 page manuscript with name, address, phone number, e-mail address, and signature on title page only. Include table of contents, acknowledgments page, and a brief bio. No mss are returned. Deadline: March 1. Entry fee: $20. All entrants receive a copy of the winning book. $1,500 award for the winner and publication. See Web site for complete submission guidelines.

WALLACE W. WINCHELL POETRY CONTEST

Connecticut Poetry Society
P.O. Box 4053, Waterbury, CT 06704-0053. 203-753-7815.
E-mail: wtarzia@nvctc5comment.edu.
Web site: http://hometown.aol.com/ctpoetrysociety.
Description: Original, unpublished poetry up to 40 lines. Send 2 copies of each poem, one with no contact information and the other with complete contact information. Include SASE for notification of results. Deadline: December 31. Entry fee: $2/poem. Maximum five poems per contest. Prize: $150, $100, $50. plus publication in the *Connecticut River Review.* All entries will be considered for publication unless "For Contest Only" is marked on submission. Does not accept simultaneous submissions. **Tips:** Identify each submission as Wallace W. Winchell Poetry Contest.

YOUNG WRITERS' AWARD

Turning Wheel, Journal of the Buddhist Peace Fellowship,
P.O. Box 4650, Berkeley, CA 94704. 510-655-6169.
E-mail: sue@bpf.org. Web site: www.bpf.org.
Susan Moon, Editor.
Description: $500 offered for an essay by a writer 30 years of age or younger who has not been previously published in Turning Wheel, on the theme of an issue. Themes and guidelines available on Web site. Entry fee: None. Do not submit material by fax. **Contact:** Marianne Dresser, Associate Editor.

SYNDICATES

Syndicates buy material from writers and artists to sell to newspapers all over the country and the world. Authors are paid either a percentage of the gross proceeds or an outright fee. Of course, features by people well known in their fields have the best chance of being syndicated. In general, syndicates want columns that have been popular in a local newspaper or magazine. Since most syndicated fiction has been published previously in magazines or books, beginning fiction writers should try to sell their stories to magazines before submitting them to syndicates.

Always query syndicates before sending manuscripts, since their needs change frequently, and be sure to enclose SASEs with queries and manuscripts.

AGEVENTURE NEWS SERVICE
Demko Publishing, 21946 Pine Trace, Boca Raton, FL 33428. 561-482-6271.
E-mail: editor@demko.com. Web site: www.demko.com.
David Demko, Writer/Editor.
Description: Age Venture presents work to international audience of 3 million readers in 29 countries. Topics must address baby-boomer and retiree concerns. Submissions should be between 250-500 words; specify costs for use at time of submission. Submit manuscripts as e-mail text (no attached files).

AMPERSAND COMMUNICATIONS
2311 S Bayshore Dr., Miami, FL 33133-4728. 305-285-2200.
E-mail: amprsnd@aol.com. Web site: www.ampersandcom.com.
George Leposky, Editor.
Description: Feature material for online use, and for newspapers, magazines, and special-interest publications. Sells content to end-users directly and through marketing agreements with other online syndication services. Topics include: book reviews, humor, business, medicine and health, business travel, pets, cooking, food, and wine, senior lifestyles, environmental issues, timesharing and vacation ownership, home improvement, travel. No unsolicited mss; query first.

ARTHUR'S INTERNATIONAL
2613 High Range Dr., Las Vegas, NV 89134. 702-228-3731.
E-mail: arthurintl@aol.com.
Marvin C. Arthur, President.
Description: Short stories and fine arts. Presently overstocked with material and not considering adding more authors.

ASK THE BUILDER
3166 N Farmcrest Dr., Cincinnati, OH 45213-1112. 513-531-9229.
E-mail: tim@askthebuilder.com. Web site: www.askthebuilder.com.
Tim Carter, Editor.
Description: Features articles on residential building and remodeling. Submit electronic press-release or product information via e-mail; lead with a 100-word (max.)

summary of the press release. Color images for the Ask the Builder e-zine should be in GIF or JPG format (width: 250 pixels; height: proportional; resolution: 72 dpi; send as e-mail attachment). Note: Only submit news and information if it is relevant to home building and remodeling.

BUDDY BASCH FEATURE SYNDICATE

720 West End Avenue, No. 1216, New York, NY 10025-6299. 212-666-2300.
Buddy Basch, Publisher/Editor.
Description: Entertainment, travel, human interest, science and medical, food. Accepts little freelance, query with SASE; or send mss with SASE.

BLACK CONSCIENCE SYNDICATION

308-A Deer Park Rd., Dix Hills, NY 11746. 631-462-3933.
E-mail: cldavis@suffolklib.ny.us.
Clyde Davis, President.
Description: All types of material covering black issues is accepted: book reviews, poetry, cartoons, sports, music, and politics. Query with SASE.

COPLEY NEWS SERVICE

Box 120190, San Diego, CA 92112. 619-293-1818.
E-mail: infofax@copleynews.com. Web site: www.copleynews.com.
Glenda Winders, Editorial Director.
Description: Features columns on: music, books, cars, fashion, films, sports, gardening, photography, and other special interests. 1,500 subscribers. Accepts unsolicited mss.

HARRIS & ASSOCIATES FEATURES

15915 Caminito Aire Puro, San Diego, CA 92128. 858-485-9027.
E-mail: rhh1234@yahoo.com.
Dick Harris, Editor.
Description: Sports features; golf and golf travel; sports personalities. Maximum 2,500 words. Send one-page query first. Pay varies.

HISPANIC LINK NEWS SERVICE

1420 N St. NW, Washington, DC 20005. 202-234-0280.
E-mail: charles@hispaniclink.org.
Mr. Charles A. Ericksen, Editor.
Description: Trend articles, opinion and personal experience pieces, and general features with Hispanic focus, 650-700 words; editorial cartoons. Pays $25 for op-ed columns and cartoons, on acceptance. Send SASE for guidelines.

THE HOLLYWOOD INSIDE SYNDICATE

P.O. Box 49957, Los Angeles, CA 90049-0957. 818-509-7840.
E-mail: holywood@ez2.net. Web site: www.ez2.net/hollywood.
John Austin, Director.

Description: Anything on world-class celebrities, up to 1,500 words, or column items for internationally syndicated "Hollywood Inside" column. SASE required.

KING FEATURES SYNDICATE
888 Seventh Ave., New York, NY, 10017. 212-455-4000.
E-mail: kfscartoonist@hearst.com. Web site: www.kingfeatures.com.
Jay Kennedy, Editor-in-Chief
Description: Columns, comics. Does not buy individual articles; looking for ideas for nationally syndicated columns. Submit cover letter, 6 sample columns of 650 words each, bio sheet and any additional clips, and SASE. No simultaneous submissions. Send SASE for guidelines. **Contact:** Glenn Mott, Managing Editor.

NATIONAL NEWS BUREAU
P.O. Box 43039, Philadelphia, PA 19129. 215-849-9016.
E-mail: nnbfeature@aol.com. Web site: www.nationalnewsbureau.com.
Harry Jay Katz, Publisher.
Description: Articles, 500-1,500 words, celebrity interviews, consumer news, how-tos, travel pieces, reviews, entertainment pieces, features, etc. Pays on publication. **Contact:** Andy Edelman, Features Editor.

NEW DIMENSIONS RADIO
P.O. Box 569, Ulkiah, CA 95482. 707-468-5215.
E-mail: info@newdimensions.org. Web site: www.newdimensions.org.
Rose Holland, Associate Producer.
Description: Programming presents a diversity of views from many different traditions and cultures, and strives to provide listeners with practical knowledge and perennial wisdom. New Dimensions fosters living a more healthy life of mind, body, and spirit while deepening their connections to self, family, community, the natural world, and the planet. No unsolicited manuscripts; query first.

NEW YORK TIMES SYNDICATION SALES
122 E 42nd St., Fl. 14, New York, NY 10168. 212-499-3300/800-972-3550.
E-mail: nytsf@nytimes.com. Web site: www.nytimes.com/syndicate.
Mr. Cristian Edwards, Executive Vice President.
Description: Articles on international, seasonal, health, lifestyle, and entertainment topics, to 1,500 words (previously published or unpublished). Query with published article or tear sheet and SASE. No calls please. Pays 50% royalty on collected sales.

NEWSPAPER ENTERPRISE ASSOCIATION/
UNITED FEATURE SYNDICATE
200 Madison Ave., Fl. 4, New York, NY 10016. 212-293-8500/800-221-4816.
Rebecca Shannonhouse, Editor.
Description: National features and columns on news, politics, sports, business, entertainment, books, and lifestyles, for over 600 daily newspapers. Payment varies.

UNITED PRESS INTERNATIONAL, INC.

1510 H St. NW, Suite 700, Washington, DC 20005. 202-898-8000.

John O'Sullivan, Editor-in-Chief.

Description: Feature news, news pictures. Accepts freelance photography.

WORLDWIDE MEDIA

24226 Davida Ln., Laguna Niguel, CA 92677. 949-215-3751.

E-mail: wwm@wwmedia.net.

Helen J. Lee, Acquisitions Director.

Description: International newspaper syndicate servicing overseas publications. Seeks articles, columns, and puzzles (previously published preferred) to be sold for reprint in foreign publications. Must have global appeal. No poetry. Query with SASE or via e-mail. **Tips:** SASE required for return of sample works submitted with queries. Prefers queries by e-mail. Looking for borderless and timeless articles that will be appropriate for usage by foreign publication. Queries: Preferred. E-queries: Yes. Unsolicited mss: Accepts. Response: Queries 30 days submissions 60-90 days, SASE Freelance Content: 80%. Rights: International syndication. Payment: On publication and collection.

TELEVISION & FILM

Given the quantity of television programming on commercial, educational, and cable stations, plus the hundreds of major-studio and independent films released each year, freelance writers may feel this is a promising market. However, it is very competitive.

Several things may help a writer with good ideas and writing skills to break in. First, finding an agent who specializes in scripts is very helpful; most television or film producers will look at material submitted from recognized agents first before looking at other submissions. Another requirement is submitting the information in the correct format; writers must be prepared to learn the special techniques and conventions of scriptwriting, either by taking a workshop through a university or at a writers' conference. Also, there are a number of good books written on this subject, as well as computer programs designed to format scripts in the accepted manner.

Experience gained in playwriting for live theater is always valuable practice for producing good scripts with solid dramatic structure and appealing characters. Finally, developing industry contacts is often helpful; one place to begin is with local associations of scriptwriters. A beginning writer may sometimes be lucky enough to team up with a more experienced partner to work on a project and thereby start to develop the skills, experience, and credentials needed to improve and move to the next level.

AMERICAN FILM INSTITUTE
2021 N Western Ave., Los Angeles, CA 90027. 323-856-7600.
Web site: www.afi.com.
Description: Nonprofit film institute. **Contact:** Rachel Peller, Director of Public Relations.

ANGEL FILMS
967 Hwy. 40, New Franklin, MO 65274-9778. 573-698-3900.
E-mail: angelfilm@aol.com.
Matthew Eastman, V.P. Production.
Description: Seeking projects that can be used to produce feature films and television animation for children. Query with SASE.

ARTISAN ENTERTAINMENT, INC.
2700 Colorado Avenue, Fl. 2, Santa Monica, CA 90404. 310-449-9200.
Web site: www.artisanent.com. **Description:** Develops, produces, markets, and distributes motion pictures domestically and through distributors internationally. **Tips:** Does not accept unsolicited material; must submit through agent.

BIG EVENT PICTURES
11288 Ventura Blvd., #909, Studio City, CA 91604.
E-mail: bigevent1@hotmail.com.
Michael Cargile, President.
Description: Seeking all genres in film except for horrors and erotic thrillers.

Looking for unique stories with strong characters. Query by e-mail only. E-queries: Yes.

BKS ENTERTAINMENT
619 Palisade Ave. Fl. 1, Englewood Cliffs, NJ 07632. 201-568-4800.
Description: Develops television entertainment and distributes programming.

BLUE MAN GROUP
3900 Las Vegas Blvd. South, Las Vegas, NV 89119. 702-262-4111.
Description: National theatre company with four sit-down productions in New York, Boston, Chicago, and Las Vegas.

CINEMANOW, INC.
4553 Glencoe Ave., Suite 380, Marina del Rey, CA 90292. 310-314-2000.
Description: Works with the Internet and other technologies to develop and distribute innovative film programs. Opportunities for freelancers.

COBBLESTONE FILMS
1484 Reeves St, Suite 203, Los Angeles, CA 90035.
E-mail: cstonefilms@aol.com.
Jacqui Adler, Producer.
Description: Seeking commercial, concept, or character-driven screenplays. Completed work only. Synopsis must be provided before we will review screenplay. Synopsis and query letters will only be accepted via e-mail. Send e-mail queries and synopsis to the attention of Development Executive.

COMEDY CENTRAL
1775 Broadway, New York, NY 10019. 212-767-8600.
Description: 24-hour basic cable station with eclectic mix of original programming, including standup comedy, sketch comedy, basic television shows, and movies.

CORPORATION FOR PUBLIC BROADCASTING
401 Ninth St. NW, Washington, DC 20004. 202-879-9600.
E-mail: comments@cpb.com. Web site: www.cpb.com.
Description: Private nonprofit corporation. Promotes noncommercial public telecommunications services (television, radio, online, and digital) for the American people.

DINO DE LAURENTIS COMPANY
100 Universal City Plaza, Bldg. 5195, Universal City, CA 91608. 818-777-2111.
Description: Located on the Universal Studios lot, DDLC produces major motion pictures.

WALT DISNEY COMPANY
500 S Buena Vista St., Burbank, CA 91521-7235. 818-560-1000.
Web site: www.disney.com. **Description:** Film, animated features, television, theater. **Tips:** Must submit work through an agent.

DLT ENTERTAINMENT
31 W 56th St., New York, NY 10019. 212-245-4680.
Web site: www.dltentertainment.com.
Description: International producer of TV program for network, cable, and PBS.

E! ENTERTAINMENT TELEVISION
5750 Wilshire Blvd., Los Angeles, CA 90036. 323-954-2400.
Web site: www.eentertainment.com.
Description: TV station specializing in programming related to the entertainment scene. **Tips:** Before submitting material, send fax (323-954-2660) to the news department with a brief explanation of proposed material and a request for a contact person.

FOX LATIN AMERICA CHANNEL
11833 Mississippi Ave., Los Angeles, CA 90025. 310-447-7310.
Description: Fox channel for the growing Latin America audience.

RICHARD FRANKEL PRODUCTIONS
729 Seventh Ave., Fl. 12, New York, NY 10019. 212-302-5559.
Web site: www.rfpny.com.
Description: Independent theatrical production and general management company.

GRANADA ENTERTAINMENT
11812 San Vicente Blvd., Suite 500, Los Angeles, CA 90049.
Description: Develops and produces movies and series for the U.S. television market.

GRB ENTERTAINMENT
13400 Riverside Dr., Fl. 3, Sherman Oaks, CA 91423. 818-728-7600.
Description: Production company that produces reality and documentary programs for ABC, NBC, FOX, USA, TNT, AMC, and TLC.

HALLMARK CHANNEL
12700 Ventura Blvd., Suite 200, Studio City, CA 91604. 818-755-2400.
Description: Cable TV provider of quality family entertainment. Submit manuscript to Programming.

HBO
2049 Century Park E, Suite 4100, Los Angeles, CA 90067. 310-201-9200.
Description: Premium cable-television network; some original productions.
Contact: Story Department.

HBO
1100 Sixth Ave., New York, NY 10036-6737. 212-512-1000.
Description: New York division. **Tips:** All material must be submitted through an agent.

JIM HENSON COMPANY
1416 N La Brea, Hollywood, CA 90028. 323-802-1500.
Web site: www.henson.com.
Description: Developer of the Muppets and other animated feature movies and TV programs.

INDEPENDENT TELEVISION SERVICE (ITVS)
501 York St., San Francisco, CA 94110. 415-356-8383.
Web site: www.itvs.org.
Lois Vossen, Director of Broadcast Distribution and Communications.
Description: Unique in American public television, ITVS was established by Congress to fund and present programs that "involve creative risks and address the needs of underserved audiences, especially children and minorities," while granting artistic control to independent producers. ITVS is funded by the Corporation for Public Broadcasting, a private corporation funded by the American people.

LAKESHORE ENTERTAINMENT
5555 Melrose Ave., Hollywood, CA 90038. 323-956-4222.
Description: Major independent-film production and distribution company.
Contact: Elliott Kjose.

LIONS GATE ENTERTAINMENT
4553 Glencoe Ave., Suite 200, Marina del Rey, CA 90292. 310-314-2000.
Web site: www.lionsgate-ent.com.
Description: Develops and produces feature films, television series and movies, mini-series, reality-based and animated programming.

LOCKWOOD FILMS
12569 Boston Dr., RR #41, London, Ontario N6H 5L2 Canada. 519-657-3994.
E-mail: nancycjohnson@hotmail.com.
Nancy Johnson, President. **Description:** Seeking material for family entertainment, series, mini-series, movies of the week, specials (seasonal). Send synopsis with resume or sample scripts. Include SASE.

THE MARSHAK/ZACHARY COMPANY
8840 Wilshire Blvd. Fl. 1, Beverly Hills, CA 90211-2606. 310-358-3191.
E-mail: marshakzachary@aol.com.
Alan Mills, Associate.
Description: Seeking films for theatrical, network, and cable release. Audiences of

all ages. Submit a 1-line description and a short synopsis. SASE required for response. Topic must be focused.

MEDIACOM DEVELOPMENT CORP.

P.O. Box 73033, Las Vegas, NV 89170-3033. 702-991-9011.
E-mail: fgirard@mail.com.
Felix Girard, Director/Program Development.
Description: Looking for flexible, creative subject matter. Needs good, fresh projects from freelancers on a specific topic (special and series) for pay TV and cable. Send query by e-mail or fax (248-282-0764) before sending manuscript. No phone pitches.

MINDSTORM

1434 Sixth St., Suite 1, Santa Monica, CA 91401. 310-393-1183.
Karina Duffy, President.
Description: Seeking videotapes, script work that is unique, with good character development, for target audience in mid-20s or 30s. Looking for female-driven scripts (drama/comedy). Query with synopsis and resume.

MOVIE MAGIC TECHNOLOGIES, INC.

5700 Wilshire Blvd., Suite 600, Los Angeles, CA 90036. 323-634-3400.
Description: Leading provider of project management applications and information systems for the entertainment industry. Provides software and new technology to studios, TV networks, production companies, agencies, and independent professionals.

NASH ENTERTAINMENT

1438 N Gower St., Suite 150, Box 10, Hollywood, CA 90028. 323-468-4600.
Description: Produces reality specials and series for major networks and cable channels.

NEW CONCORDE

11600 San Vicente Blvd., Los Angeles, CA 90049. 310-820-6733.
Description: Independent film production and distribution company.

NEW REGENCY PRODUCTIONS

10201 W Pico Blvd., Bldg. 12, Los Angeles, CA 90035. 310-369-8300.
Web site: www.newregency.com. **Description:** Makes and distributes movies, television, and music.

PAX COMMUNICATIONS CORPORATION

601 Clearwater Park Rd., West Palm Beach, FL 33401. 561-659-4122.
Description: Family-entertainment TV, free of senseless violence.

PLANET GRANDE PICTURES
23440 Civic Center Way, Suite 104, Malibu, CA 90265. 310-317-1545.
Description: Full-service television/film company. **Tips:** Does not accept unsolicited manuscripts.

PORCHLIGHT ENTERTAINMENT
11777 Mississippi Ave., Los Angeles, CA 90025. 212-302-5559.
E-mail: info@porchlight.com. Web site: www.porchlight.com.
Description: Produces and distributes family-oriented programs and movies.

REEL LIFE WOMEN
10158 Hollow Glen Circle, Bel Air, CA 90077. 310-271-4722.
E-mail: feigenparrentlit@aol.com.
Joanne Parrent, Co-President.
Description: Seeking material for mass audience. Query with synopsis, resume, SASE.

SHOWTIME NETWORKS
10880 Wilshire Blvd., Suite 1600, Los Angeles, CA 90024.
Web site: www.sho.com. **Description:** Cable channel featuring movies, sports specials, and original programming.

SPIRIT DANCE ENTERTAINMENT
1023 North Orange Dr., Los Angeles, CA 90038-2317. 323-512-7988.
E-mail: spiritdancemail@netscape.net
Robert Wheaton, Editor.
Description: Seeking scripts for feature-length films with a strong emotional base, well-developed characters. Considers material of almost any genre; welcomes music-driven material. Material should show the writer's passion for screenwriting and the material. Query with short synopsis. No unsolicited screenplays.

SUNBOW ENTERTAINMENT
100 Fifth Ave., Fl. 3, New York, NY 10011. 212-893-1600.
Description: Division of Sony Wonder; develops and distributes quality children's and family animation, plus live-action television.

TELEMUNDO NETWORK GROUP
2290 W Eighth Ave., Hialeah, FL 33010. 305-884-8200.
Description: Fastest growing Spanish-language television network. Features a wide range of programming, including novellas, talk shows, original sitcoms, etc.

TIMELINE FILMS
11819 Wilshire Suite 205, Los Angeles, CA 90025. 310-268-0399.
Web site: www.timelinefilms.com.
Description: Produces documentaries for television, mainly about the film industry and the performing arts.

TURNER ENTERTAINMENT NETWORKS
1050 Techwood Dr., Atlanta, GA 30318. 404-827-1700.
Description: Involved with TBS, Cartoon Network, TNT, Turner Classic Movies, etc.

UNAPIX ENTERTAINMENT, INC.
15910 Ventura Blvd., Fl. 9, Encino, CA 91436. 818-981-8592.
Description: Global film, television, video distribution, and production company.

USA FILMS
8800 Sunset Blvd., Fl. 6, Hollywood, CA 90069. 310-385-4400.
Description: Produces motion pictures.

WINTER FILMS
415 N Camden Dr., Suite 114, Beverly Hills, CA 90210. 310-288-0150.
Description: Independent motion-picture production company. **Tips:** Prefers work to be submitted through an agent.

XENON PICTURES
1440 Ninth St., Santa Monica, CA 90401. 310-451-5510.
Web site: www.xenon.com.
Description: Specializes in urban, Hispanic, martial arts, foreign, and art-house films. **Tips:** Must submit material through an agent.

GLOSSARY

Advance—The amount a publisher pays a writer before a book is published; it is deducted from the royalties earned from sales of the finished book.

Agented material—Submissions from literary or dramatic agents to a publisher. Some publishing companies accept agented material only.

All rights—Some magazines purchase all rights to the material they publish, which means that they can use it as they wish, as many times as they wish. They cannot purchase all rights unless the writer gives them written permission to do so.

Assignment—A contract, written or oral, between an editor and writer, confirming that the writer will complete a specific project by a certain date, and for a certain fee.

B&W—Abbreviation for black-and-white photographs.

Book outline—Chapter-by-chapter summary of a book, frequently in paragraph form, allowing an editor to evaluate the book's content, tone, and pacing, and determine whether he or she wants to see the entire manuscript for possible publication.

Book packager—Company that puts together all the elements of a book, from initial concept to writing, publishing, and marketing it. Also called **book producer** or **book developer.**

Byline—Author's name as it appears on a published piece.

Clips—Copies of a writer's published work, often used by editors to evaluate the writer's talent.

Column inch—One inch of a typeset column; often serves as a basis for payment.

Contributor's copies—Copies of a publication sent to a writer whose work is included in it.

Copy editing—Line-by-line editing to correct errors in spelling, grammar, and punctuation, and inconsistencies in style. Differs from **content editing,** which evaluates flow, logic, and overall message.

Copy—Manuscript pages before they are set into type.

Copyright—Legal protection of creative works from unauthorized use. Under the law, copyright is secured automatically when the work is set down for the first time in written or recorded form.

Cover letter—A brief letter that accompanies a manuscript or book proposal. A cover letter is not a query letter (see definition).

Deadline—The date on which a written work is due at the editor's office, agreed to by author and editor.

Draft—A complete version of an article, story, or book. First drafts are often called **rough drafts.**

Electronic rights—Refers to the use of an article in electronic form, rather than hard-copy formats. The term is not very precise, and it is a good idea to pin down exactly what the publisher means by electronic rights, and consider what rights are reasonable to allow considering the fee, advance, or royalty amount being offered.

Fair use—A provision of the copyright law allowing brief passages of copyrighted material to be quoted without infringing on the owner's rights.

Feature—An article that is generally longer than a news story and whose main focus is an issue, trend, or person.

Filler—Brief item used to fill out a newspaper or magazine column; could be a news item, joke, anecdote, or puzzle.

First serial rights—The right of a magazine or newspaper to publish a work for the first time in any periodical. After that, all rights revert to the writer.

FNASR (First North American Serial Rights)—This refers to the specific right to use an author's work in a serial periodical, in North America, for its first appearance. Thereafter, rights to reprint the work remain with the author.

Ghostwriter—Author of books, articles, and speeches that are credited to someone else.

Glossy—Black-and-white photo with a shiny, rather than a matte, finish.

Hard copy—The printed copy of material written on a computer.

Honorarium—A modest, token fee paid by a publication to an author in gratitude for a submission.

International reply coupon (IRC)—Included with any correspondence or submission to a foreign publication; allows the editor to reply by mail without incurring ring cost.

Internet rights—See also electronic rights. This refers to the rights to post an author's work on a Web site, and possibly to distribute or allow the distribution of the article further via the Internet.

Kill fee—Fee paid for an article that was assigned but subsequently not published; usually a percentage of the amount that would have been paid if the work had been published.

Lead time—Time between the planning of a magazine or book and its publication date.

Libel—A false accusation or published statement that causes a person embarrassment, loss of income, or damage to reputation.

Little magazines—Publications with limited circulation whose content often deals with literature or politics.

Mass market—Books appealing to a very large segment of the reading public and often sold in such outlets as drugstores, supermarkets, etc.

Masthead—A listing of the names and titles of a publication's staff members.

Ms—Abbreviation for manuscript; mss is the plural abbreviation.

Multiple submissions—Also called **simultaneous submissions.** Complete manuscripts sent simultaneously to different publications. Once universally discouraged by editors, the practice is gaining more acceptance, though some still frown on it. **Multiple queries** are generally accepted, however, since reading them requires less of an investment in time on the editor's part.

NA (North American)—Sometimes appears as 1st NA; refers the right to publish the North American appearance of a piece of work, leaving the author free to market other appearances of the same work elsewhere.

No recent report—This indicates that we do not have sufficient recent information to verify the listing shown; the listing given being the same as that which appeared in the previous year's *Handbook*. Each such listing will be removed from the *Handbook* in the following year unless verified.

On speculation—Editor agrees to consider a work for publication "on speculation," without any guarantee that he or she will ultimately buy the work.

One-time rights—Editor buys manuscript from writer and agrees to publish it one time, after which the rights revert to the author for subsequent sales.

Op-ed—A newspaper piece, usually printed opposite the editorial page, that expresses a personal viewpoint on a timely news item.

Over-the-transom—Describes the submission of unsolicited material by a freelance writer; the term harks back to the time when mail was delivered through the open window above an office door.

Payment on acceptance—Payment to writer when manuscript is submitted.

Payment on publication—Payment to writer when manuscript is published.

Pen name—A name other than his or her legal name that an author uses on written work.

Public domain—Published material that is available for use without permission, either because it was never copyrighted or because its copyright term is expired, Works published at least 75 years ago are considered in the public domain.

Q-and-A format—One type of presentation for an interview article, in which questions are printed, followed by the interviewee's answers.

Query letter—A letter—usually no longer than one page—in which a writer proposes an article idea to an editor.

Rejection slip—A printed note in which a publication indicates that it is not interested in a submission.

Reporting time—The weeks or months it takes for an editor to evaluate a submission.

Reprint rights—The legal right of a magazine or newspaper to print an article, story, or poem after it has already appeared elsewhere.

Royalty—A percentage of the amount received from retail sales of a book, paid to the author by the publisher. For hardcovers, the royalty is generally 10% on the first 5,000 copies sold; 12 1/2% on the next 5,000 sold; 15% thereafter. Paperback royalties range from 4% to 8%, depending on whether it's a trade or mass-market book.

SASE—Self-addressed, stamped envelope, required with all submissions that the author wishes returned—either for return of material or (if you don't need material returned) for editor's reply.

Slush pile—The stack of unsolicited manuscripts in an editor's office.

Tear sheets—The pages of a magazine or newspaper on which an author's work is published.

Unsolicited submission—A manuscript that an editor did not specifically ask to see.

Vanity publisher—Also called **subsidy publisher.** A publishing company that charges an author all costs of printing his or her book. No reputable book publisher operates on this subsidy basis.

Web rights—See Internet rights.

Work for hire—When a work is written on a "for hire" basis, all rights in it become the property of the publisher. Though the work-for-hire clause applies mostly to work done by regular employees of a company, some editors offer work-for-hire agreements to freelancers. Think carefully before signing such agreements, however, since by doing so you will essentially be signing away your rights and will not be able to try to resell your work on your own.

Worldwide—Refers to the right to publish an article anywhere in the world (however, this right may be limited by other wording in a contract to publication in the English language only, or in-print only, or in electronic form only, etc.).

Writers guidelines—A formal statement of a publication's editorial needs, payment schedule, deadlines, and other essential information.

INDEX